ALBUM OF
AMERICAN HISTORY

RELATED WORKS

Atlas of American History

Dictionary of American History
(in six volumes)

Dictionary of American Biography
(in twenty-one volumes)

ALBUM OF AMERICAN HISTORY

COLONIAL PERIOD

James Truslow Adams
Editor in Chief

R. V. Coleman
Managing Editor

W. J. Burke
Associate Editor

Atkinson Dymock
Art Director

NEW YORK
CHARLES SCRIBNER'S SONS
1944

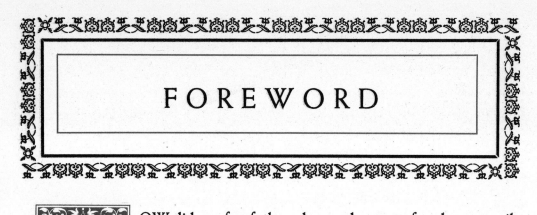

FOREWORD

OW did our forefathers dress; what sort of tools or utensils did they use, in what kinds of occupations; what did their houses look like, inside and out; in a word, if we could suddenly step into their world, what would we see?

No amount of verbal description, however accurate or vivid, can make us visualize the life of the past as can pictures of that life. But the pictures must be authentic; they must be the delineation of that life as seen by those who lived within it, not the interpretation of those who lived long afterward and could only see the earlier life through the spectacles of their own times.

The intent of the present work is to tell the history of America through pictures made at the time the history was being made. The test, in general, has been: Is the picture authentic; was it made during the period it represents; and does it illustrate some significant aspect of the life of the times?

In this work the pictures themselves *are* the history, and the text assumes the subordinate role which pictures have had in the past. The text seeks merely to identify the time, place and subject, together with the minimum requirement of explanatory narrative for the general setting, without intending to make it in any sense a complete, however brief, history of the nation. In this book we have a thread of text which explains the pictures, instead of scattered pictures which only scantily illustrate a text.

To obtain the pictorial material used in the *Album of American History*, the editors have searched far and wide in the museums, libraries and private collections of the country, and have fortunately been able to bring together a greater body of material than in the beginning seemed possible. The source of each picture has, with very few exceptions, been indicated, a procedure which we trust may be of interest to those who turn the pages merely for entertainment, and which will assuredly be of value to the scholar.

The selection and arrangement of subjects has been made with a view to presenting a panorama of the life of the times rather than with the thought of showing every house, or implement or piece of furniture that is usually considered historically important. The editors have aimed to include not only representative homes of the wealthy, but representative homes of the poor; they have aimed to show those objects so familiar to the life of the times that ordinarily no picture would be preserved; they have tried to re-create the humble occupation side by side with the more spectacular one; they have striven to reach into areas not ordinarily mentioned in our standard histories as well as into those which have, perhaps, had too much attention.

The outline followed in this volume has been that established in the founding of America. The book begins with the first vague notions of a new world; the discovery of America is made and settlements are attempted; then we see the various settlements which took permanent hold, one by one; and by the beginning of the Eighteenth Century, when the English colonies were blending into a unified group, the life up and down the coast is treated somewhat as a whole, broken, chronologically, into three chapters ending with the struggle which brought a new nation, the United States, into being.

While the present volume is a unit in itself and, from a point of view of interest and completeness, not dependent upon subsequent volumes, the intent is to continue the work, from period to period of our history, in three or four more volumes which, when complete, will provide a history of America through pictures.

It will be obvious to those familiar with the *Dictionary of American Biography*, the *Dictionary of American History* and the *Atlas of American History* that the *Album of American History* is a natural part of that great body of national history begun in 1926 and carried forward year after year in these various works published by the House of Scribner. The *Dictionary of American Biography* (in 21 volumes) records the *lives* of those men and women who took a significant part in our national development. Next came the *Dictionary of American History* (in 6 volumes) which records, alphabetically, the thousands of separate *events*, *trends* or *ideas* which made up our history; and following this came the *Atlas of American History*, which through a series of maps, especially drawn under the supervision of scholars familiar with each period and area, shows *where* our history was made. The *Album of American History* is designed to show what our history *looked like*.

In all of these works of co-operative scholarship the publishers and editors have been deeply indebted to the many scholars who have willingly contributed their help and advice. Had it not been for the courtesy and aid extended to us by those in charge of numerous museums, libraries, historical societies, and private collections, the preparation of the present work would have been an impossible task. Although many institutions and individuals are especially mentioned elsewhere, we wish here to express our great obligation not only to all those named but to many others.

As Editor in Chief it is a great pleasure to express once more my appreciation of the contribution of the Managing Editor, R. V. Coleman. We have now worked happily together for many years and, as was the case in our similar relationship in editing the *Dictionary of American History* and the *Atlas of American History*, I have found how invaluable has been not only his wide knowledge of all sections of our country but also his equally wide range of friendship among the scholars, librarians and curators throughout the land.

The Associate Editor, W. J. Burke, has contributed much by his interest and enthusiasm, and his indefatigable energy in searching out and gathering the material for the pictures. In addition, he is mainly responsible for writing the text and running commentary.

In such a work as this the assembling of the material for the printer presents difficulties not encountered by the editors of printed books, even when illustrated. The technical, historical and artistic problems are all of a complexity not generally understood. For all these aspects of our task we are deeply indebted to the Art Director, Atkinson Dymock.

Nor do works of this kind come into being without constant and careful checking of those thousand-and-one details which in the aggregate make the book what it is. For this most essential work, I wish to express my thanks to Marion G. Barnes and to Louise Rubes.

We complete the volume in the hope that it may prove useful to the scholar, as well as entertaining and stimulating to the general reader, young and old.

JAMES TRUSLOW ADAMS

Oct. 18, 1943

ACKNOWLEDGMENT

WITHOUT the advice and assistance of the museums, libraries and individuals in whose possession were the originals of the pictures and objects reproduced in this work, its preparation and publication would have been impossible. Throughout we have aimed to give proper credit in each case and will not attempt to reprint the entire list here, but wish to make particular acknowledgment of the aid given us by the following:

Albany Institute of History and Art, Albany, N. Y.
American Antiquarian Society, Worcester, Mass.
American Geographical Society, New York, N. Y.
The Museum of the American Numismatic Society, New York, N. Y.
American Scenic and Historic Preservation Society, New York, N. Y.
American Swedish Historical Museum, Philadelphia, Pa.
The American-Swedish News Exchange, Inc., New York, N. Y.
Ancient and Honourable Artillery Company, Boston, Mass.
Mrs. Imogene Anderson, New York, N. Y.
The Magazine *Antiques*, New York, N. Y.
The Atwater Kent Museum, Philadelphia, Pa.
The Baltimore Museum of Art, Baltimore, Md.
Bowdoin College Museum of Fine Arts, Brunswick, Me.
Prof. Marion J. Bradshaw, Bangor, Me.
The Brooklyn Museum, Brooklyn, N. Y.
The Bucks County Historical Society, Doylestown, Pa.
Major Charles T. Cahill, Boston, Mass.
Mrs. Louise W. Carmichael, Fredericksburg, Va.
Carolina Art Association, Gibbes Memorial Art Gallery, Charleston, S. C.
The Charleston Museum, Charleston, S. C.
The Cincinnati Art Museum, Cincinnati, Ohio
Columbia University in the City of New York, N. Y.

Cooper Union for the Advancement of Science and Art, Museum for the Arts
of Decoration, New York, N. Y.

Enoch Pratt Free Library, Baltimore, Md.

The Essex Institute, Salem, Mass.

Dr. Henry Chandlee Forman, Macon, Ga.

Frick Art Reference Library, New York, N. Y.

Harvard College Library, Cambridge, Mass.

The Hispanic Society of America, New York, N. Y.

Historic American Buildings Survey, National Park Service, U. S. Department
of the Interior, Washington, D. C.

The John Carter Brown Library, Providence, R. I.

Mr. J. Frederick Kelly, New Haven, Conn.

Mrs. Bella C. Landauer, New York, N. Y.

Landis Valley Museum, Lancaster, Pa.

Library of Congress, Washington, D. C.

Litchfield Historical Society, Litchfield, Conn.

Maine Historical Society, Portland, Me.

Maryland Historical Society, Baltimore, Md.

Mr. George Carrington Mason, Newport News, Va.

Massachusetts Historical Society, Boston, Mass.

The Metropolitan Museum of Art, New York, N. Y.

William L. Clements Library, University of Michigan, Ann Arbor, Mich.

The Moravian Historical Society, Nazareth, Pa.

Museum of the American Indian, Heye Foundation, New York, N. Y.

Museum of the City of New York, N. Y.

Museum of Fine Arts, Boston, Mass.

National Park Service, U. S. Department of the Interior, Washington, D. C.

New Castle Historical Society, New Castle, Del.

New Hampshire Antiquarian Society, Hopkinton, N. H.

New Hampshire Historical Society, Concord, N. H.

New Haven Colony Historical Society, New Haven, Conn.

New York Academy of Medicine, New York, N. Y.

The New-York Historical Society, New York, N. Y.

The New York Public Library, New York, N. Y.

New York State Library, The University of the State of New York,
Albany, N. Y.

North Carolina Department of Conservation and Development,
Raleigh, N. C.

The North Carolina Historical Commission, Raleigh, N. C.

The Archives of the University of Notre Dame, Notre Dame, Ind.
Old Quinabaug Village, Sturbridge, Mass.
Onondaga Historical Association, Syracuse, N. Y.
Pennsylvania German Society, Norristown, Pa.
Philadelphia Museum of Art, Philadelphia, Pa.
Pilgrim Society, Plymouth, Mass.
Dr. J. Hall Pleasants, Baltimore, Md.
Pocumtuck Valley Memorial Association of Deerfield, Mass.
Rhode Island Historical Society, Providence, R. I.
The Society for the Preservation of New England Antiquities, Inc.,
    Boston, Mass.
Mr. Harry Stone, New York, N. Y.
The Valentine Museum, Richmond, Va.
Vermont Historical Society, Montpelier, Vt.
Mr. Philip B. Wallace, Philadelphia, Pa.
Wells Historical Museum, Southbridge, Mass.
Colonial Williamsburg, Inc., Williamsburg, Va.
Wilmington Institute Free Library, Wilmington, Del.
Miss Alice Winchester, New York, N. Y.
Yale University Art Gallery, New Haven, Conn.
The Historical Society of York County, York, Pa.

CONTENTS

CONTENTS

ALBUM OF
AMERICAN HISTORY

1
FROM COLUMBUS TO JAMESTOWN

America Has Been a Land of Dreams

from the beginning. Viking sea-rovers and nameless fishermen may have sighted its shores before the days of Christopher Columbus, but fact and fiction are hopelessly confused. As the Fifteenth Century neared its close the search for a direct route to rich Cathay occupied the minds of men, stimulating the imagination. Whether this route lay East or West was a matter of conjecture.

Columbus Sailed West ∴ .

Woodcut. 1493. A contemporary interpretation of what Columbus found.

And in 1492 Discovered America . . .

but was deeply disappointed in not finding Cathay. Legend would have us believe that he found a region full of cannibals and monsters.

Cannibals

Woodcut made at Augsburg ca. 1505.

Monsters

Pieter Van der Aa *Voyagien.* 1706-07.

Mystery . . .

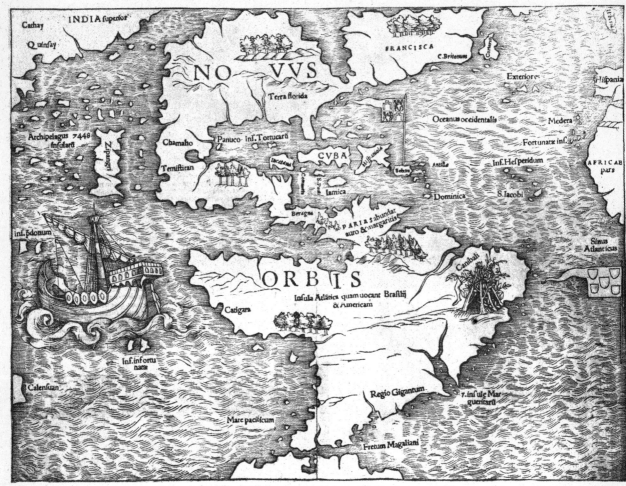

A map from Münster's edition of Ptolemy. 1540

Note the name "Americam." Here is shown a fair understanding of the New World, although Japan (Zipangri) and China (Cathay) are placed across a narrow sea from our west coast. The New World perils are shown—giants (Gigantum) and Cannibals (Canibali).

And Glory . . .

Amerigo Vespucci. Date depicted 1497. Date issued ca. 1585

Courtesy, Stokes Collection. The New York Public Library.

When rumors of gold unleashed the "Age of Discovery," among the many voyages was the somewhat vague but well publicized ones by an Italian, Amerigo Vespucci, whose name was attached to the New Continent in 1507 by a German geographer, Waldseemüller. In the early days of our Republic there was much sentiment in favor of calling it Columbia in honor of Columbus.

... and Gold

Courtesy, The Hispanic Society of America, New York.

Spanish treasure chest. 16th Century

In the New World were found strange barbaric civilizations, rich in gold. The American dream became the quest for this gold—and a new spirit was born, a spirit of boundless free energy and of dawning science. From these came "America."

With Fife and Drum ...

Bosscher *Omnium Pene Europae*. 1581.
Courtesy, The Hispanic Society of America, New York.

With Spear and Matchlock Musket

the Spanish soldiers came and conquered. With the Spanish soldiers were brave Jesuit priests ...

Introducing Christianity

following the example of Columbus.

Columbus planting the Cross and giving trinkets to the savages

Herrera *Historia General de las Indias*. 1728.
Courtesy, The Hispanic Society of America, New York.

Florida (Land of Flowers)

became a land of bloodshed. The Spanish built the fortified city of St. Augustine in 1565.

St. Augustine, Florida

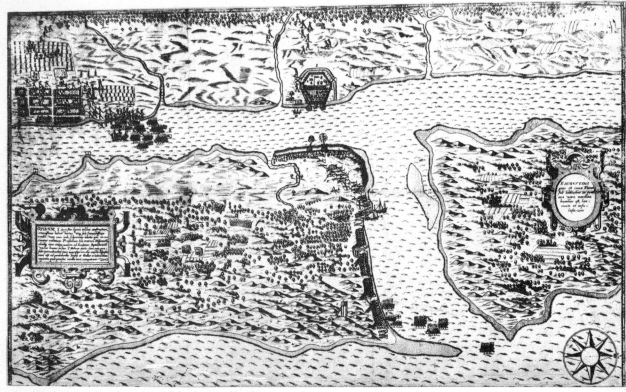

Arnoldus Montanus *De Nieuwe en Onbekende Weereld.* 1671.

Fleur de Lis

The French, a year earlier, had built Fort Caroline at the mouth of the St. Johns River. Jacques Le Moyne, an artist with the expedition, has left us these pictures of the fort, with its moat and bastions, cannon, and flag with its *Fleur de Lis*, the lilies of France.

Fort Caroline completed   The beginnings of Fort Caroline in Florida

Drawings by Jacques Le Moyne in De Bry *Grands Voyages.* 1592.

Roanoke

In 1584 a new name appeared on the maps. It was Roanoke. Sir Walter Raleigh tried to found a colony on Albemarle Sound in what is now North Carolina. When his expedition brought reports of the new region Queen Elizabeth named it Virginia in honor of herself.

Sir Walter Raleigh

Elizabethan coin, showing a ship

Ship such as the ones sent out by Sir Walter Raleigh

Hollar *Navium Variae Figurae et Formae.* 1647.

We see the Indian palisades, the fishermen, the English landing party, and the sunken ships off the barrier of Hatteras, then, as now, a graveyard of ships. We see again what Sixteenth Century ships looked like.

Map of Roanoc. Engraved by Theodore De Bry, 1590, after the original by John White.

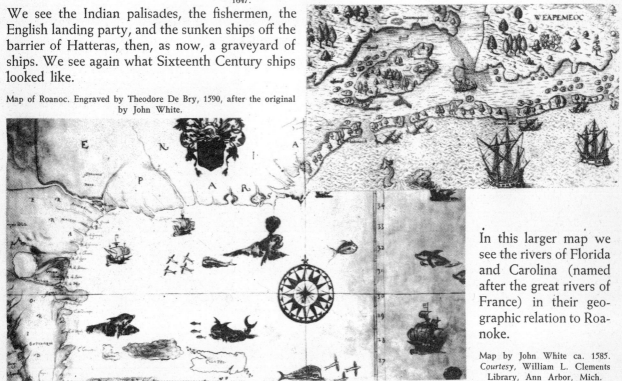

In this larger map we see the rivers of Florida and Carolina (named after the great rivers of France) in their geographic relation to Roanoke.

Map by John White ca. 1585. *Courtesy,* William L. Clements Library, Ann Arbor, Mich.

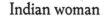

Before the White Man Was the Indian

Note the Indian repast, the ceremonial dance, the corn in various stages of growth, the houses, and the platform in the upper cornfield. A scarecrow on this platform kept the birds from eating the crop.

Close-up view of the palisade

Indian chief   Indian woman

All illustrations on this page are water colors by John White ca. 1585. *Courtesy,* The William L. Clements Library, Ann Arbor, Mich.

Indians fishing . . .

cooking food in earthen pots . . .

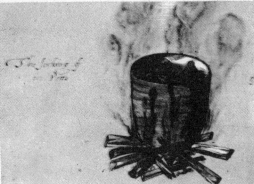

eating . . .

broiled fish.

Note the dugout

Water colors by John White ca. 1585. *Courtesy*, The William L. Clements Library, Ann Arbor, Mich.

Opposite is the Indian method of making a dugout. The trees were felled with fire, the wood was burned out, and the dugout finished by scraping with shells and stones.

As engraved by Theodore De Bry. 1590.

Homesick

The Roanoke colonists were soon hungry and homesick. They lived in constant fear of being wiped out by the Spaniards. In 1586 the discouraged settlers saw a fleet of twenty-three sail. Were the dreaded Spaniards approaching? A joyous shout went up. It was Sir Francis Drake, fresh from the sacking of Spanish-held St. Domingo, Cartegena, and St. Augustine.

Drake's fleet. Detail of an engraving from *Expeditio Francisci Draki eqvitis angli in Indias Occidentalis.* 1588.

Drake, who had visited California in 1579 and taken possession of it in the name of Queen Elizabeth, was now a greater hero than ever in the eyes of his countrymen at Roanoke Island. Most of them accepted his offer to take them back to England.

Drake in California. Note the formal act of annexation. Drake recorded that he nailed a brass plate to a "firm poste." He named California New Albion.
Van der Aa *Voyagien.* 1706-07.

The brass plate left in California by Drake in 1579. It was found in 1936 on the western shore of San Francisco Bay. It reads:

"BEE IT KNOWNE VNTO ALL MEN BY THESE PRESENTS   IVNE 17 1579 BY THE GRACE OF GOD AND IN THE NAME OF HERR MAIESTY QVEEN ELIZABETH OF ENGLAND AND HERR SVCCESSORS FOREVER I TAKE POSSESSION OF THIS KINGDOME WHOSE KING AND PEOPLE FREELY RESIGNE THEIR RIGHT AND TITLE IN THE WHOLE LAND VNTO HERR MAIESTIES KEEPEING NOW NAMED BY ME AN TO BEE KNOWNE VNTO ALL MEN AS NOVA ALBION.

FRANCIS DRAKE

An English ship
A water color by John White. 1585.

The Lost Colony

Scarcely had Drake departed when a relief expedition under Grenville arrived, and finding Roanoke deserted, left fifteen men to hold the place until more settlers could be brought. These came in 1587 under John White, he who made the pictures we have just seen. They did not find the fifteen men, nor did White's own colony, including his granddaughter, Virginia Dare, the first white child born in America, survive except in a never-dying legend built around three letters CRO engraved on a tree and the word CROATON engraved on a doorpost.

Courtesy, Department of Conservation and Development, Raleigh, N. C.

Roanoke Island as it appears today. What an unhappy site this was for a colony!
It had practically no advantages to recommend it.

The Folly of It All

To reach Roanoke all vessels had to risk the hazards of the treacherous reef off Hatteras, which, as has already been pointed out, was a graveyard of ships. It was much more dangerous to sail from Boston to Charleston throughout the whole Colonial Era than to cross the Atlantic Ocean.

Courtesy, Department of Conservation and Development, Raleigh, N. C.

Shipwreck on Hatteras beach

Time and Tide

Courtesy, Department of Conservation and Development, Raleigh, N. C.

Seascape near Roanoke Island. Aerial view of Oregon Inlet

The Vine That Forgot to Die

Courtesy, Department of Conservation and Development, Raleigh, N. C.

One of the ancient scuppernong grapevines in the Mother Vineyard at Roanoke Island. It was growing when the first white men landed at Roanoke. Surviving the storms and blights of more than three centuries it antedates the beginning of our nation and is both a witness to our youth and a promise of our strength.

Shifting Sands

Courtesy, Dept. of Conservation and Development, Raleigh, N. C.

Oregon Inlet from the air, showing the shifting dunes near the site of Roanoke Colony

Courtesy, Dept. of Conservation and Development, Raleigh, N. C.

Sand dunes on the banks near Roanoke Island

JAMESTOWN

The fate of the Roanoke settlement did not deter the English from colonizing America. In 1606 James, "by the grace of God, King of England, Scotland, France, and Ireland, Defender of the Faith, &c." issued a charter under which a group of "Adventurers," shortly to be known as the Virginia Company of London, were authorized to plant a colony in "that part of America, commonly called Virginia."

In 1607 the ships *Susan Constant*, under Captain Christopher Newport, the *Goodspeed*, under Captain Bartholomew Gosnold, and the *Discovery*, under Captain John Ratcliffe, dropped anchor at the entrance of Chesapeake Bay. Exploration disclosed a broad river which was named the James in honor of the King, and a site on its low shores was chosen for a settlement which was called Jamestown.

Courtesy, The American Scenic and Historic Preservation Society.

Jamestown, Va.

Hollar *Navium Variae Figurae et Formae*. 1647.

17th Century ship

Pieter Van der Aa *Voyagien*. 1706-07.

The English in Virginia

One of the first structures erected at Jamestown was a so-called fort, probably little more than a wooden structure enclosed in a palisade. The first houses may have resembled these.

Defense and Shelter

Fludd *Tractatus Secundus.* 1618.

Herrera *Historia General de las Indias.* 1728.

Note the method of building a ship (caravel).
Spanish houses in the West Indies. 16th Century.

Greate Gunns . . .

Fludd *Tractatus Secundus.* 1618.

Cannon, called "great gunns," defended Jamestown

They may have been as crude as these Spanish houses in the West Indies, or as large as these in Bermuda. Note here the cannon, and the stocks where law-breakers were punished.

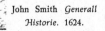

John Smith *Generall Historie.* 1624.

. . . and Drums

Fludd *Tractatus Secundus.* 1618.

The rat-a-tat-tat or the roll of the drum was frequently heard and with many meanings: the arrival of a ship, the call to arms; the opening of the assembly, or—all too often—a requiem for the dead.

Among the settlers at Jamestown was John Smith, whose importance to the colony has probably lost nothing from his own account of it. That he was the prime explorer of Virginia there can be no doubt. He left us a map of Virginia so accurate that it is still referred to in boundary disputes.

From his *Generall Historie*. 1624.

John Smith's Map of Virginia

John Smith . . .

Smith was captured by the Indians, and brought before their chief, Powhatan. (See his dwelling in Smith's map above.) Powhatan's comely daughter, legend says, saved Smith from death by pleading with her father to show clemency. In 1614 she married John Rolfe, one of the English colonists at Jamestown, who took her to England in 1616, where she was presented to the King and Queen, and had this portrait painted by Simon de Passe. The following year as she was preparing to return to Virginia she died of smallpox.

Portrait by Simon de Passe.

and Pocahontas

Adventure Story

English readers of the Seventeenth Century were thrilled by John Smith's romantic account of his adventures, and these are the very pictures they looked at as they turned the pages of his book. This, for them, was America.

Illustration from John Smith's *Generall Historie*. 1624.

In the lower right-hand corner we see Pocahontas saving John Smith's life

Here we see John Smith visiting an Indian village. He is being greeted by a friendly Indian.

Pieter Van der Aa *Voyagien*.
1706-07.

The Jamestown colonists were sent over to develop trade, and were instructed to look for new agricultural and drug products, precious minerals, and furs.

They found ginseng which had a ready market in Europe where it was used as a drug.

They found the sweet-smelling sassafras, also used widely as a drug

Mark Catesby *The Natural History of Carolina.* 1754.

Ginseng

Potatoes

They found both the Spanish potato and the Virginia potato

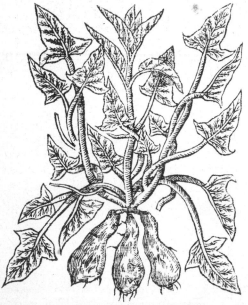

Mark Catesby *The Natural History of Carolina.* 1754.

Sassafras

John Parkinson *Paradisi in Sole.* 1629.

Spanish, or Sweet potatoes

Virginia, or Irish potatoes

John Parkinson *Paradisi in Sole.* 1629.

The persimmon tree was everywhere, its ripe fruit was eaten, and persimmon beer, recommended to the Jamestown colonists by the Indians was sometimes substituted for more palatable drinks if these were not obtainable.

John Parkinson *Paradisi in Sole*. 1629.

Persimmon

Silk

They found mulberry trees in abundance, the leaves of which were used as a food for silk worms. They had high hopes of manufacturing silk at Jamestown, but this dream was soon shattered.

John Parkinson *Paradisi in Sole*. 1629.

The Mulberry

They Found No Gold

Gold was not found, and a shipload of yellow soil, which seemed to contain gold dust, when tested in England, proved to be worthless. The mighty forests which surrounded them supplied thousands of staves, and these were cut and shipped to England.

Water wheel

Zeising *Theatri Machinarum*. 1607-10.

A water wheel and sawmill were built

Sawmill

Edward Williams *Virginia Richly and Truly Valued*. 1650.

The Venetian Art of Glassmaking

Glassmakers were among those who settled at Jamestown in 1607. Fuel, potash, and glass sands were plentiful. The art of making glass was a secret confined to a small guild, and a few Venetian families were the greatest artisans.

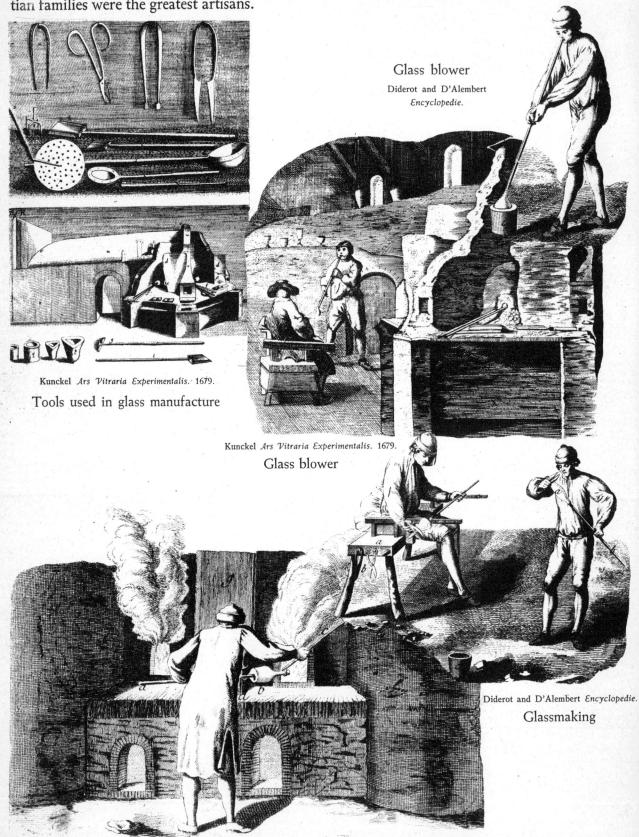

Glass blower

Diderot and D'Alembert *Encyclopedie.*

Kunckel *Ars Vitraria Experimentalis.* 1679.

Tools used in glass manufacture

Kunckel *Ars Vitraria Experimentalis.* 1679.

Glass blower

Diderot and D'Alembert *Encyclopedie.*

Glassmaking

Diderot and D'Alembert *Encyclopedie. Recueil des Planches.* 1762-72.

Glass furnace

Money

Glass beads were made at Jamestown. They were used as a medium of exchange, the Indians placing a high value upon them.

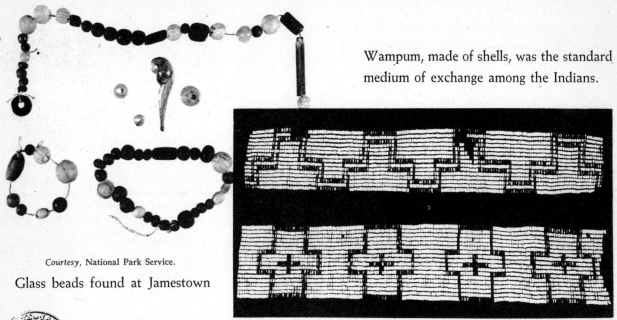

Wampum, made of shells, was the standard medium of exchange among the Indians.

Courtesy, National Park Service.

Glass beads found at Jamestown

Courtesy, Museum of the American Indian, Heye Foundation, New York.

Wampum

There were very few English coins at Jamestown. There was no need for them. Now and then a coin has been found by the excavators of Jamestown.

Double Crown
James I. Period

Until tobacco farms were planted the Jamestown colony languished. Its promoters were discouraged. They resorted to a publicity campaign in an attempt to glorify Virginia, hoping to find gullible investors and settlers. The title-page of *Nova Britannia* is an example of this advertising. Tobacco became the most important medium of exchange in Virginia. John Rolfe, the husband of Pocahontas, discovered a new method of curing tobacco in 1612 which immediately made it a profitable item of export.

The picture of the ship is interesting for it gives us an idea of the kind of craft the Jamestown settlers had come over in two years earlier.

NOVA BRITANNIA.

OFFERING MOST

Excellent fruites by Planting in
VIRGINIA.

Exciting all such as be well affected
to further the same.

LONDON
Printed for SAMVEL MACHAM, and are to be sold at
his Shop in Pauls Church-yard, at the
Signe of the Bul-head.
1609.

Tobacco . . .

Recent excavations at Jamestown have unearthed hundreds of clay pipes. Apparently every man smoked. James I. protested against the obnoxious habit in vain. Sir Walter Raleigh, who was largely responsible for the founding of Roanoke and Jamestown, was an ardent champion of tobacco and is credited with introducing it to England.

The medicinal value of tobacco rose in popular estimation, and its praises were sung in numerous books. Among them was Gilles Everard's *Panacea*. Here we see Gilles enjoying a good smoke.

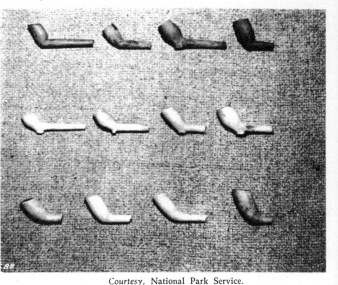

Courtesy, National Park Service.

Clay pipes found at Jamestown

Gilles Everard *Panacea*. 1659.

and Slaves

The successful cultivation of tobacco opened up possibilities for mass production, lacking only one thing—cheap labor. Slavery was the ultimate answer. As far back as 1562 John Hawkins had discovered that money was to be made by calling on the West Coast of Africa, picking up shiploads of Negroes and selling them in the slave marts of the West Indies. Queen Elizabeth in fact granted Hawkins a coat-of-arms with a captive Negro as its crest. The first cargo of Negroes arrived at Jamestown in 1619, although there is some question as to whether these first arrivals were sold as slaves for life or only for a term of years as were the white indented servants.

Negro Houses *on the Coast of* GUINEA.

A New and General Collection of Voyages. 1745-47.

Although tobacco was much the most important export from Virginia there were many other products as this price list for the year 1621 will show. Here also is a glowing account of Virginia.

(44)

this Countrey; I fhall with his pardon believe him, diftruftfull of Gods providence; or if he be fo vitioufly difpofed as to hope after a Land where he may enjoy an undifturbed plenty without the fweat of his browes, the Maps are fo extreamely deficient in the defcription of fuch a Countrey, that I muft defire him to looke for a new World and Kingdome, for fuch an eafie accommodation.

If any make an Objection why this Countrey ftored with all thefe Riches, furnifhed with all thefe Staples, hath fo long held downe her head in the lowneffe of a defperate condition? Why being capable to crowne her browes with Garlands of Rofes and plenty, fhe fate defolate amongft the Willowes of neglect and poverty? Let them but recall their Memory, how by the prevailency of *Gondamore* the Corporation was diffolved, their patent cancelled, to which if wee adde the cooperation of the Indian treachery in their firft maffacre, they will ceafe their wonder at its languifhing condition, and convert it to a full admiration, how that Colony could ever raife her endangered head out of thofe Gulfes of diftraction, in which the Gold of Spaine, the difincouragement of the Court, the difcontent of the better fort of Planters, and the defperate negligence of the more inconfiderable had in humane opinion irrecoverably involved her.

But the incomparable Virgin hath raifed her dejected head, cleared her enclouded reputation, and now like the Eldeft Daughter of Nature expreffeth a priority in her Dowry; her browes encircled with opulency to be believed by no other triall, but that of experience, her unwounded wombe full of all thofe Treafuries which indeere Provinces to refpect of glory, and may with as great Juftice as any Countrey the Sunne honours with his eye-beames, entitle her felfe to an affinity with Eden, to an abfolute perfection above all but Paradize.

And this thofe Gentlemen to whom fhe vouchfafes the honour of her Embraces, when by the bleffings of God upon their labours fited with the beauty of their Cornefield, they fhall retire into their Groves checkered with Vines, Olives, Mirtles, from thence dilate themfelves into their Walkes covered in a manner, paved with Orenges and Lemmons, whence furfeited with variety, they incline to repofe in their Gardens upon nothing leffe perfumed then Rofes and Gilly-flowers. When they fhall fee their numerous Heards wanton

Edward Williams *Virgo Triumphans*, 1650.

(45)

wanton with the luxury of their Pafture, confeffe a narrowneffe in their Barnes to receive their Corne, in bofomes to expreffe fully their thankefulneffe to the Almighty Authour of thefe bleffings, will chearefully confeffe: Whilft the Incomparable Roanoak like a Queene of the Ocean, encircled with an hundred attendant Iflands, and the moft Majeftick Carolana fhall in fuch an ample and noble gratitude by her improvement repay her Adventurers and Creditors with an Intereft fo far tranfcending the Principall.

◆◆◆◆◆◆◆◆◆◆◆◆◆◆◆◆◆◆◆◆◆◆◆◆◆◆◆◆◆◆◆◆◆◆

A valuation of the Commodities growing and to be had in Virginia: *valued in the year,*1621.

And fince thofe Times improved in all more or leffe, in fome ⅓, in others ½, in many double, and in fome treble.

Iron, ten pounds the Tun.
Silke Coddes, two fhillings fix pence the pound.
Raw filk, 1 3s 4d. the pound, now at 25s. and 28. *per* pound.
Silke graffe to be ufed for Cordage, 6d. the pound: but we hope it will ferve for many better ufes, and fo yeeld a far greater rate, wherof there can never be too much planted. Of this Q. *Elizabeth* had a filke Gowne made.
Hemp, from 10s. to 22s. the hundred,
Flax, from 22s, to 30s. the hundred.
Cordage, from 20s. to 24s. the hundred.
Cotton wooll, 8d. the pound.
Hard pitch, 5s. the hundred.
Tarre, 5s. the hundred.
Turpentine, 12s. the hundred.
Rozen, 5s. the hundred.
Madder crop, 4s. the hundred: courfe madder, 25s. the hundred.
Woad, from 12s. to 20 the hundred.
Annice feeds, 40s. the hundred.
Powder Sugar, Panels, Mufcavadoes and whites, 25s. 40. and 3l. the hundred. H 3 Sturgeon,

Pomet *A Compleat History of Druggs.* 1725.

Sumac

Sumac was used for tanning leather

(46)

Sturgeon, and Caveare, as it is in goodneffe.
Salt, 30s. the weight.
Maftick, 3s. the pound.
Salfa Perilla wild, 5l. the hundred.
Salfa Perilla domeftick, 10l. the hundred.
Red earth Allenagra, 3s. the hundred.
Red Allum, called Carthagena Alum, 10s. the hundred.
Roach Allum, called Ronnifh Allum, 10s. the hundred.
Berry graine, 2s. 6d the pound: the powder of graine, 9s. the pound: it groweth on trees like Holly berries.
Mafts for fhipping, from 12s. to 3l. a peece.
Pot-afhes, from 12s. the hundred, to 14. now 40. and 35s. the hundred.
Sope-afhes, from 6s. to 8s. the hundred.
Clapboard watered, 30s. the hundred.
Pipe ftaves, 4l. the thoufand.
Rape-feed oyle, 10l. the tun, the cakes of it feed Kine fat in the Winter.
Oyle of Walnuts, 12l. the tun.
Linfeed oyle 10l. the tun.
Saffron, 20s. the pound.
Honey, 2s. the gallon.
Waxe, 4l. the hundred.
Shomacke, 7s. the hundred, whereof great plenty in Virginia, and good quantity will be vented in England.
Fuftick yong, 8s. the hundred.
Fuftick old, 6s. the hundred, according to the fample.
Sweet Gums, Roots, Woods, Berries for Dies and Drugs, fend of all forts as much as you can, every fort by it felfe, there being great quantities of thofe things in Virginia, which after proof made, may be heere valued to their worth. And particularly, we have great hope of the Pocoon root, that it will prove better then Madder.
Sables, from 8s. the payre, to 20s. a payre.
Otter skins, from 3s. to 5s. a piece.
Luzernes, from 2s. to 10 a piece.
Martins the beft, 4s. a piece.
Wild Cats, 8d. a piece.
Fox skins, 6d. a piece.

(47)

Muske Rats skins, 2s. a dozen: the cods of them will ferve for good perfumes.
Bever skins that are full growne, in feafon, are worth 7s. a piece.
Bever skins, not in feafon, to allow two skins for one, and of the leffer, three for one.
Old Bever skins in Mantles, gloves or caps, the more worne, the better, fo they be full of fur, the pound weight is 6s.
The new Bevers skins are not to bee bought by the pound, becaufe they are thicke and heavy Leather, and not fo good for ufe as the old.
Pearles of all forts that ye can find: Ambergreece as much as you can get: Criftall Rocke: fend as much as you can, and any fort of Minerall ftones, or earth that weighs very heavy.
Preferve the Walnut trees to make oile of, & cut them not down, fo alfo preferve your Mulberry and Cheftnut trees very carefully.
In the month of June, bore holes in divers forts of Trees, wherby you fhall fee what gums they yield, and let them bee well dried in the Sun every day, and fend them home in very dry caske.

Pomet *A Compleat History of Druggs.* 1725.

Woad

A blue dye was made from woad

Iron

Even iron ore was found in Virginia, not in mines but fished out of ponds and swamps. It was called bog iron.

Diderot and D'Alembert Encyclopedie. Recueil des Planches. 1762-72.

Bog iron

Indian Massacre

In 1622 occurred a setback of a sort which was to plague Americans on their frontiers for two hundred and fifty years—an Indian massacre, in this case planned by Powhatan's brother, which all but wiped out the English settlements, outside of fortified Jamestown.

Indian massacre in Virginia

An engraving by Theodore De Bry. 1590.

Zeising Theatri Machinarum. 1607-10.

Quickly, however, the settlements were rebuilt. Trees were felled, and logs were cut.

Lifting a stone

Zeising Theatri Machinarum. 1607-10.

Bricks . . .

Wooden huts at Jamestown were gradually replaced by brick houses. The bricks were made at Jamestown as excavations made on the site by the National Park Service conclusively prove.

Courtesy, National Park Service.

Old brick kiln excavated at Jamestown. Note the partially fired bricks still in place.

The bricks were of different sizes. The average dimension would be about 9 x 3⅜ x 2⅜ inches. In color they ranged from light orange, through salmon and red, up to a dark brownish red. They were comparatively soft.

Bricklaying as practiced in Europe in 1607 is shown opposite.

Zeising *Theatri Machinarum.* 1607-10.

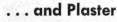

. . . and Plaster

Here we see the plaster on the walls of the excavated State House in Jamestown.

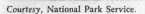

Courtesy, National Park Service.

Here are the foundations of the first State House at Jamestown. South of the ruin is the James River.

Courtesy, National Park Service.

Jamestown Lives Again

Hardly a trace of this first permanent English settlement in America remained among the ruins of Jamestown until the National Park Service began its excavations. That is why these old foundations and relics are so dramatic, so charged with historical significance. Jamestown comes to life under the spade of the archaeologist. Here we see the foundations of the "Country House," built around 1640. Upon its foundations the remains of two other houses were found, the "William Sherwood House," built some forty years later, and the "Ambler House," built between 1710 and 1721.

Courtesy, National Park Service.
Foundation of the "Country House"

Above—at right.
Ruins of the "Ambler House."
Courtesy, American Scenic and Historic Preservation Society.

Opposite
Foundation of Ambler House
Courtesy, National Park Service.

Fortunately a few Seventeenth Century houses still stand in the neighborhood of Jamestown, among them being the Adam Thoroughgood House, and Bacon's Castle.

Courtesy, National Park Service.
Bacon's Castle. Built ca. 1650

Courtesy, National Park Service.
The Adam Thoroughgood House. Built ca. 1640

The first Virginia mansion of great size was Greenspring, built three miles above Jamestown by Governor William Berkeley, around 1642. It stood until 1796 when William Ludwell Lee replaced it with a house designed by Benjamin Latrobe, who made this drawing of the older house.

The House of God

One of the first buildings erected at Jamestown was a church. It was replaced by a fine brick edifice. The ruined tower shown below was attached to the fifth Jamestown church, 1639-44.

The Old Brick Church in Isle of Wight County gives us a good idea of 17th Century church architecture in Virginia.

Courtesy, National Park Service.

Views of the old church at Jamestown

Old Brick Church, Isle of Wight County, Va. 17th Century. Also known as St. Luke's Church, or Newport Parish Church.

Interior of Old Brick Church, Isle of Wight County, showing methods of construction. This picture was taken shortly before the roof fell in during a storm in 1887. The church was restored in 1894.

Magic Casement

Let us visit a Seventeenth Century Jamestown house and get acquainted with the life of the people. Through a leaded casement window the occupant of the house sees us approach. Battered though it is, one can almost hear, across the centuries, the faint squeak of the latch as an English hand reaches through a lace cuff to open the window and wave to us.

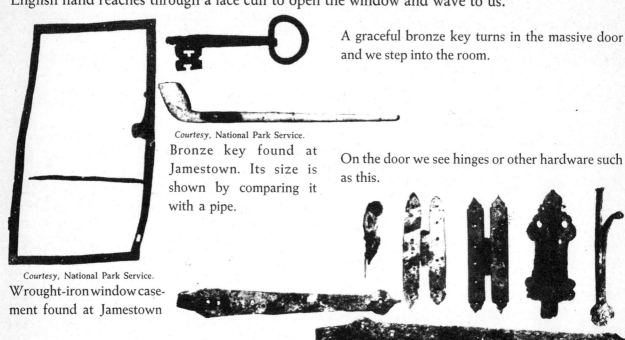

A graceful bronze key turns in the massive door and we step into the room.

Courtesy, National Park Service.

Bronze key found at Jamestown. Its size is shown by comparing it with a pipe.

On the door we see hinges or other hardware such as this.

Courtesy, National Park Service.

Wrought-iron window casement found at Jamestown

Courtesy, National Park Service.

Hinges and other hardware found at Jamestown

We are greeted by a Virginia gentleman and his wife —and it may be thus that we see them.

Cavalier

The gentleman may have looked like this

Naturally he wore spurs. Here is all that remains of one found at Jamestown.

Jaquemin Iconographie du Costume.

If our host does not have on his jack-boots and spurs he may wear low shoes with buckles like these.

Shoe buckle found at Jamestown

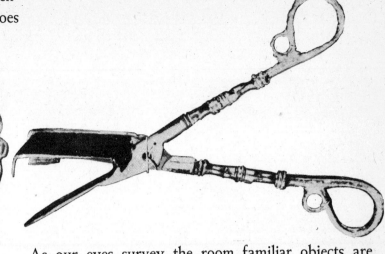

As our eyes survey the room familiar objects are noted. We see a candle snuffer. Rush-lights were commonly used, but candles were not unknown as these snuffers prove.

A spigot, dagger hilt, ring, and other objects

We see a jew's harp

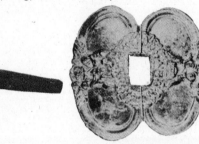

On the shelves we see flasks, jugs, bottles, plates, and other beautiful objects. The Jamestown men were heavy drinkers. Beer mugs and wine bottles were conspicuous.

Drinking
Wine bottle found at Jamestown

Bottles excavated at Jamestown

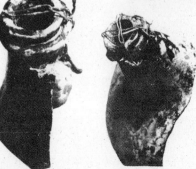

Note how the caps were held on the bottle top by wire. Screw tops were not used at Jamestown.

Bottle tops found at Jamestown

One of the features of a Jamestown dinner was a German wine imported in a glazed stoneware jug bearing a crest. One of these jugs was found at Jamestown. In the crest can be seen the date 1661.

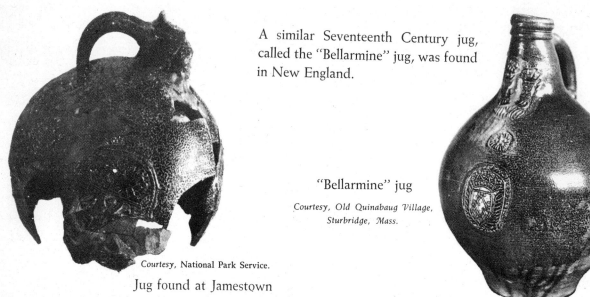

A similar Seventeenth Century jug, called the "Bellarmine" jug, was found in New England.

"Bellarmine" jug

Courtesy, Old Quinabaug Village, Sturbridge, Mass.

Courtesy, National Park Service.

Jug found at Jamestown

In the Sixteenth Century Cardinal Bellarmine was sent into the Low Countries, where he was unpopular with the Protestants. Having a short stature and a large stomach like the Longbeard bottles, and, as was said, holding like them much vinous liquor, his name was given to the jugs shown above.

Courtesy, National Park Service.

Pottery objects found at Jamestown

Eating

The knives, forks, and spoons used at Jamestown were of lovely workmanship, offering a surprising contrast to the rough-and-tumble life of this outpost of civilization, a life beset with hardships of all kinds.

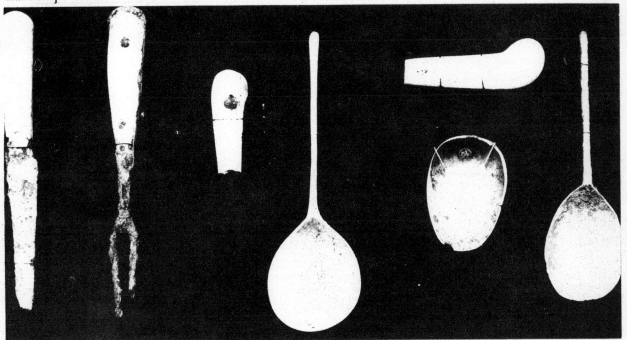

Courtesy, National Park Service.

Spoons, knives and forks unearthed at Jamestown

Courtesy, National Park Service.

"Chuckatuck" spoon

Here was found the first bit of pewter bearing the "touch" of an American maker, the so-called "Chuckatuck" spoon made by Joseph Copeland in 1675.

Somewhere on the wall hung a strange mask. Whose face did it represent?

Courtesy, National Park Service.

The fireplace was ornamented with delftware tiles like this one

Courtesy, National Park Service.

Linen Chest still used in Lower Chapel, Middlesex County, Va. 17th Century.

Courtesy, Mr. George C. Mason, Newport News, Va.

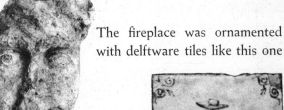

In the corner was an adz, reminder that there was work to be done

Courtesy, National Park Service.

"Ye Englyshe Nation"

The founders of little Jamestown lie buried, but their spirit lives. What they planted became not only the "Old Dominion" of history and legend, the Virginia of Washington, Jefferson and Lee, but the cradle of our nation. Had they like their predecessors failed in trying to realize Sir Walter Raleigh's dream of an "Englyshe nation" in the New World, the Pilgrims and Puritans might never have come to the wilderness which had proved so baffling. Jamestown itself, the center of the young colony, was destroyed in Bacon's Rebellion, 1675-76, but the seat of government was moved to Williamsburg, a better site, and the colonists marched on.

The Dead

Courtesy, National Park Service.

View of the Travis graveyard at Jamestown Island

The Living

At Williamsburg was founded the College of William and Mary in 1693; which still lives, a hallowed link with the past.

Courtesy, Colonial Williamsburg, Inc. Photo by Richard Garrison.

Wren Building. College of William and Mary, Williamsburg, Va. 1695. Designed by Sir Christopher Wren, the architect who built St. Paul's Cathedral in London.

II

FISHERMEN, PILGRIMS AND "DOWN-EASTERS"

Fog

In the fog-bound North Atlantic, fishermen from Western Europe, long before Columbus, discovered another part of America. That this land furnished a place on which to sort and dry their catch of fish was all that mattered to them. With the taciturnity of deep-sea fishermen, they probably did not talk about it.

Courtesy, American Geographic Society, New York.

North Atlantic Seascape

Cod

Bretons, Basques, Spaniards, Portuguese, and Englishmen, in boats such as these, fished for cod on the Grand Banks. The methods have changed but little through the centuries.

Fishing for cod on the Grand Banks

Duhamel du Monceau *Traité générale des pesches.* 1769-1777.

On the submerged tablelands called banks the prolific codfish provided an inexhaustible supply of food for the European markets. The Catholic countries, with a church calendar containing many fast days, looked forward to the arrival of the fishing fleets.

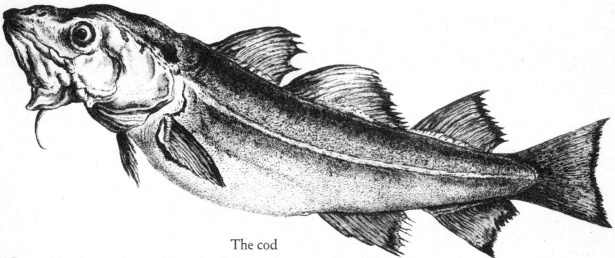

The cod

"Green" cod was dressed on the fishing vessels, salted down in barrels and taken home for immediate consumption.

Packing "green" cod

"Dried" cod was prepared on land at fishing stages. These stages were erected on the shores of those parts of North America now known as Newfoundland, Nova Scotia, and Maine.

Drying cod

Illustrations from Duhamel du Monceau *Traité générale des pesches*.
1769-77.

Cold and Desolate

Here we catch our first glimpse of that part of America bathed by the Labrador current. It was a bleak, forbidding region, but teemed with fur-bearing animals and marine life, sources of potential wealth greater than the gold of the Incas.

Fishing stage

Salting down cod

Note the piles of salt, the fish being dressed and laid out on the stages to dry, and the stumps of the trees along the shore, where a partial clearing has been made.

Here we see a close-up of the fishermen at their tasks. The boys at the salt pile are being directed to place it on the pile of fish at the left.

Fishing stages

The feel of the Maine coast is in these pictures, but it was still a convenient place to dry fish and not for permanent settlement.

Illustrations from Duhamel du Monceau *Traité générale des pesches.*
1769-77.

Northwest Passage

The lure of the East with its silks and spices was not wholly lacking even in these Northern waters. Between 1497 and 1542 attempts were made by the Cabots, acting under the King of England, and by Jacques Cartier, acting for the King of France, to seek a Northwest Passage to Japan and India. When they failed to get through, interest lapsed, but the fishermen kept on fishing.

Sebastian Cabot

Jacques Cartier

Samuel de Champlain

Champlain's astrolabe. Note the date 1603 on the spoke near the bottom.

Champlain explored the Bay of Fundy and attempted to found a settlement at St. Croix Island. Here is what it was supposed to look like according to a book published by Champlain in 1613. As the book was calculated to inspire Frenchmen to settle in America the illustrations may have been purposely exaggerated.

Champlain *Voyages*. 1613.

With the opening of the Seventeenth Century came a new era, that of settlement. Samuel de Champlain, again for the King of France, explored the St. Lawrence country, and on June 7, 1613, accidentally lost his astrolabe (an instrument used to make astronomical observations). It was found in the Province of Ontario, Canada, in 1867, and is now in the museum at Fort Ticonderoga, New York.

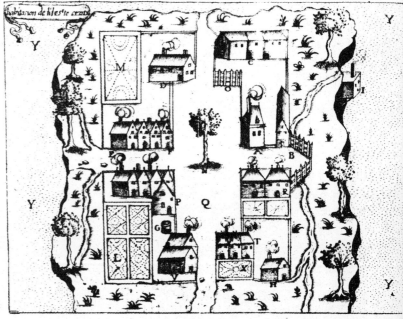

"Salvages"

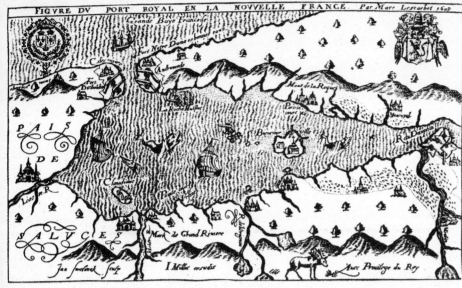

Lescarbot *Histoire de la Nouvelle France.* 1609.

Port Royal

The French soon moved across the Bay of Fundy and started a new settlement at Port Royal, shown here. Note that there were "salvages" about, not to mention moose. Note also the church and the cannon.

Prayers

Side by side with discovery and settlement went the conversion of the Indians by the Jesuit priests, and here we see Father Le Clercq attempting to teach the Indians a Christian prayer, and Father Jumeau conducting a mass for the Miramichi. Note the moose and the dance of the Miramichi.

Courtesy, The Champlain Society, and the University of Toronto Press, Toronto, Canada.

Illustration inserted in a copy of Father Le Clercq's *Nouvelle Relation de la Gaspesie*

Dreams

The urge to create settlements in this new land was not confined to the French. The merchants of Bristol, England, had long profited from fisheries in the North Atlantic. In Bristol lived Sir Ferdinando Gorges, an influential man of great wealth and vision. He dreamed of establishing a feudal domain across the sea.

The wharfs at Bristol. England

Barrett, *History and Antiquities of Bristol.* 1789.

Sagadahoc

At the same time that the Virginia Company of London was organizing, Gorges and others formed the Virginia Company of Plymouth, which sent an expedition to found a settlement at the mouth of the Sagadahoc (Kennebec) River on the coast of Maine. The settlement was made in the summer of 1607, some three months after the founding of Jamestown, in Virginia.

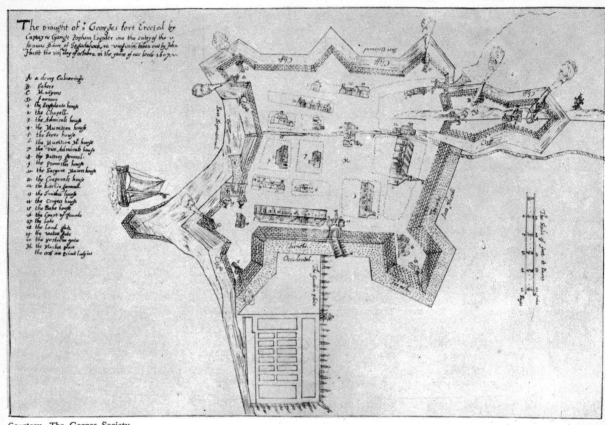

Courtesy, The Gorges Society.

Contemporary map of Sagadahoc

In this crude drawing we see houses and fortifications that most likely did not exist, but like Champlain's drawings were meant to arouse colonizing zeal at home. The truth is that Sagadahoc was abandoned the following year, its English garrison sailed back home and the settlement was forfeited to the wilderness. The birch trees marched in again.

Courtesy, Marion J. Bradshaw *The Maine Land.*
1941.

Maine Birches

Courtesy, Federal Works Agency,
Washington, D. C.

Maine Birches

The Coast of Maine

It seemed for the moment that the Maine coast was to be left to the French, who, in 1613, established a little settlement at Somes Sound, near Mount Desert. However, the English from Jamestown made short work of this settlement, Samuel Argall chasing the French out in no uncertain manner.

Somes Sound

George E. Street *Mount Desert.*

Courtesy, Federal Works Agency, Washington, D. C.

Thunder Hole. Mount Desert Island

The following year Captain John Smith made a detailed drawing of the New England coast, on which young Prince Charles, son of James I, placed English names, some of which stuck, although not in the same places. The area from the Penobscot River southward was thus established as a prospective region for English settlement.

John Smith's Map of New England 1614

Meanwhile the title from the English King to this stretch of coast underwent some changes. The Virginia Company of Plymouth expired and was superseded by a grant to another group of proprietors known as the Council for New England, prominent in which was Sir Ferdinando Gorges, still intent on establishing a feudal regime in America.

Scrooby

The English background of the first permanent settlement is interesting. On the road from London to York was the little village of Scrooby (spelled Scrubey on this map by John Ogilby). Here, as in other places all over England, was a group of nonconformists, those who refused to conform to the practices of the Church of England. The group at Scrooby, including William Brewster and John Robinson, the preacher, made plans to escape with their followers to more liberal Holland. Religious thinking in this era of bitter feelings was tinctured with the fear of persecution.

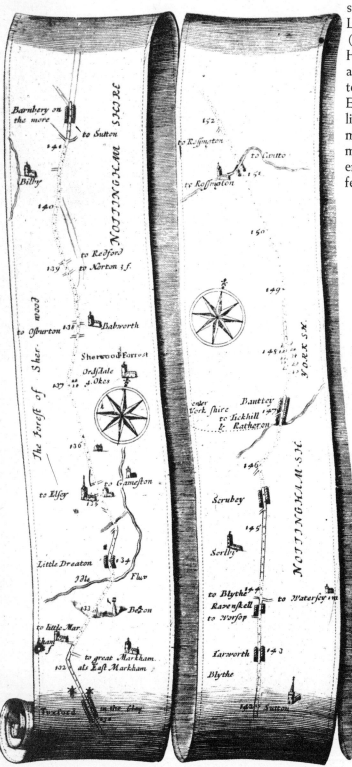

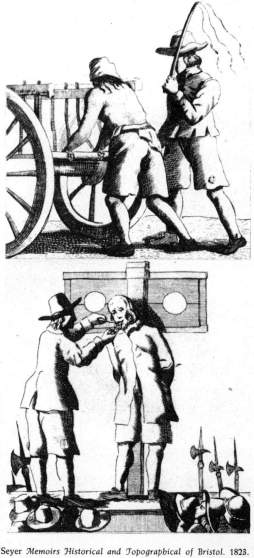

Seyer *Memoirs Historical and Topographical of Bristol.* 1823.

Two contemporary examples of the English mode of punishment

John Ogilby Britannia. 1698.

Road map showing the location of Scrooby

Leyden

Finally, in 1608, they reached Amsterdam and shortly thereafter took up residence in the city of Leyden, center of the textile industry in which many of them found employment.

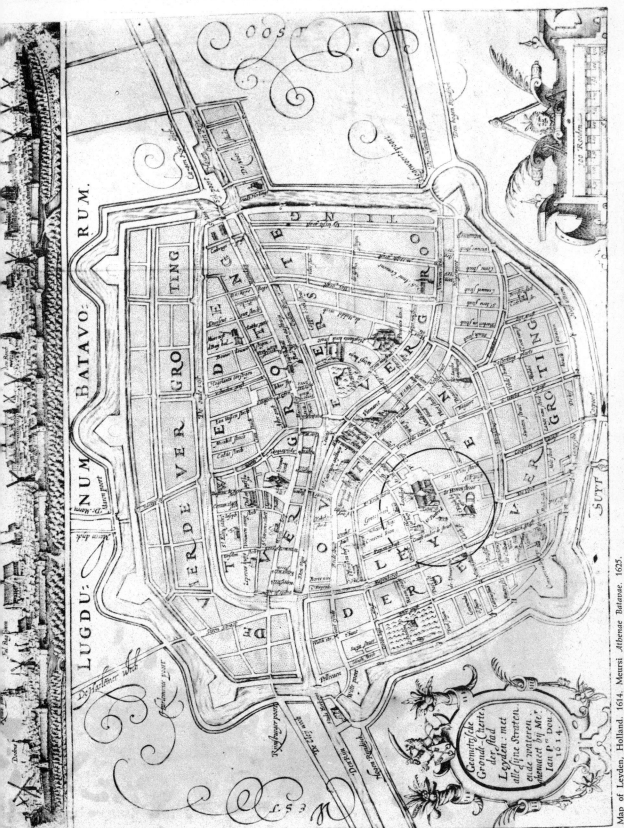

Map of Leyden, Holland. 1614. Meursi *Athenae Batavae*. 1625.
John Robinson's house was on Clock Street, near St. Peter's cathedral (shown within the circle on the map)

William Bradford, whose journal is our main source of information about Plymouth Colony, was a member of the non-conformist group at Leyden, and called himself a fustianworker, which means cloth worker. At Leyden he married Dorothy May, who was destined to fall overboard and drown when the *Mayflower* reached Cape Cod.

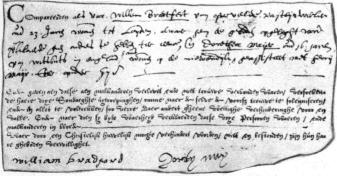

Marriage record of William Bradford
and Dorothy May

The substance of this record is that William Bradford, aged twenty-three, fustianworker, and Dorothy May, aged sixteen, were bethrothed and asked for the customary three Sunday proclamations to that effect, that they were free persons and not related to each other in blood, and in view of these facts were eligible for marriage.

But these exiled Englishmen were not happy in Holland. They yearned for a permanent sanctuary where their children could grow up in the pure faith and retain their native English language. The new land of America appealed to them and when a group of London merchants, thinking of opportunities for trade, offered to finance their removal to the new world, they accepted.

One group embarked at the Dutch town of Delftshaven, in 1620, in the *Speedwell*, which was to carry them to England, where they were to join the new colony for America.

The Pilgrims embarking at Delftshaven. This 17th Century painting has been
attributed to the Dutch painter Albert Cuyp.

Bound for America . . .

The separation of friends and relatives was a heartbreaking moment—for not all were equal to the pilgrimage—and this contemporary picture, although not identified as an actual portrayal of the Pilgrims, suggests the pathos of a similar scene.

Model of the *Mayflower*

Courtesy, The New York Historical Society, New York.

Herckmans *Der Zee-Vaert Lof*. 1634.

Bon Voyage!

. . . On the Mayflower

At Southampton the *Speedwell* was joined by a larger vessel of 180 tons, the *Mayflower*, together with a group of laborers and other colonists gathered up in London by the merchants —and the voyage was on. But, the *Speedwell* having proved unseaworthy, both vessels put back into Plymouth from whence, in the month of September, 1620, the *Mayflower*, with 87 passengers and 14 servants (including both the Leyden and the London people), together with a crew of 48, started westward across the Atlantic.

As the *Mayflower* moved out of Plymouth Harbor, its passengers may well have sighted a British warship such as this.

British Ship. 16th Century

Charnock *An History of Naval Architecture*. 1801.

Mayflower Compact

As the *Mayflower* neared the shores of America, it became evident that, unless some form of government was established, the ungodly among the colonists (meaning those from the London group) would not only wreck the dream of founding a new Kingdom of God in America, but would wreck the whole colony as well. Accordingly, the famous *Mayflower Compact* was drawn up and signed by the male passengers. Among the names on this document were those of William Bradford, William Brewster, and Myles Standish.

From Bradford's *History of Plymouth Plantation.*

The Mayflower Compact

Winsor *Narrative and Critical History of America.* v. 3. 1884.

Autographs of the *Mayflower* Pilgrims

Sand dunes
Photo by U. S. Forest Service.

The Pilgrim's First View of America

The *Mayflower* dropped anchor at Cape Cod in November 1620. The sand dunes offered little hope of sustenance.

The ungodly. Scene in a London Coffee House. 17th Century

Plymouth

The Pilgrims explored Cape Cod, under the leadership of Captain Myles Standish, had a brief skirmish with Indians, and finally chose a spot for settlement which they named Plymouth. Here on a bleak December day they set foot, as legend would have it, on the rock which has become enshrined in our history.

Plymouth Rock

On the edge of the wilderness they erected a rude shelter. They heard the howl of the timber wolf.

Hexham *Principles of the Art Military.* 1637.

Military costume of the Pilgrim Period

Deer tracks were seen

They smelled the skunk

Mark Catesby *The Natural History of Carolina.* 1754.

Engraved by Sartain after a painting by Doughty.
Cabinet of Natural History. 1830.

The First Winter

Crude wigwams and shacks were built or cellars covered over. Bark, thatch and wattles daubed with beach mud were the materials at hand. The Pioneer Village, reconstructed at Salem, Mass., attempts to re-create the first buildings of the Pilgrims and Puritans. It can be definitely stated that cabins made of horizontal logs were not used in these early English settlements.

English wigwams

Framework of an English wigwam

Framework of
a colonial house

*Courtesy, The President and
Fellows of Harvard College.*

One-room cottage with thatch roof

Later, when conditions warranted more permanent dwellings, frame houses were erected.

Courtesy, Society for the Preservation of New England Antiquities, Boston.

Interior of an English wigwam

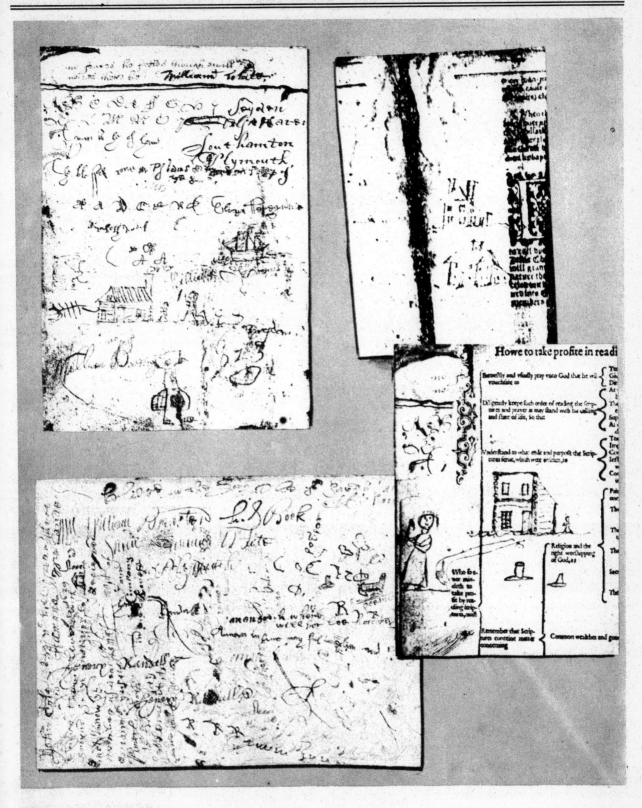

Marginal notes and drawings believed to have been made by Pilgrim hands. These crude notes and sketches were found in a *Bible* dated 1588, bound with *The Book of Common Prayer* and Sternhold and Hopkins' *Psalms and Hymns*. Note the type of houses. One is a distinct salt box house, and immediately above it is a type of 17th Century house with two chimneys, found in Virginia. The rough lean-to seems to be constructed of horizontal logs, which might cast some doubt on the authenticity of the drawings, since it is now generally believed that the Swedes on the Delaware were the first to build log cabins.

Corn and Sugar

The Pilgrims made friends with the Indians, remnants of once powerful tribes, but now weakened by war and disease, and the White Men and the Red Men exchanged tools and utensils, wearing apparel and other objects, thus instituting a system of barter. The Indians taught the Pilgrims how to plant corn, and how to make maple sugar. The first crop of corn saved the Plymouth colonists from starvation.

Indians making maple sugar

Lafitau *Moeurs Sauvages.* 1723.

Indians planting corn

DeBry *Grandes Voyages.* 1590.

Indian sugar camp. Painting by Capt. S. Eastman. This picture, though of a much later date, catches the true atmosphere of the New England woods.

Schoolcraft *Indian Tribes.* 1853.

Wampum

Dickeson. *The American Numismatical Manual.* 1859.

Wampum

The Indian medium of exchange was wampum, beads or shells strung together in definite patterns, the color and quantity of the beads and shells establishing the value of the belt of wampum.

Wampum belts

Courtesy, Museum of the American Indian. Heye Foundation, New York City.

Musket and Pike

Myles Standish was the military leader of the Pilgrims. He was probably equipped in the manner of this musketeer of the period. The heavy matchlock musket had to be rested on a forked rod in firing. Pikes were also used, and as Myles Standish put his men through their military exercises they went through the motions shown here, taken from a contemporary manual of arms for the use of the pike. Only sixteen of the thirty-three motions are reproduced below.

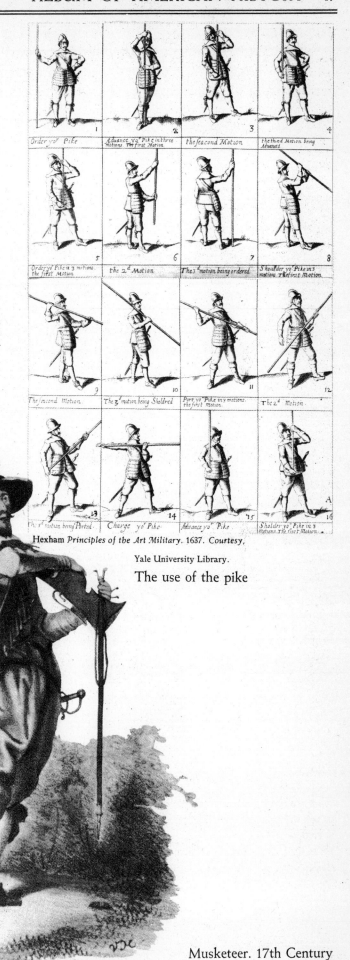

Hexham *Principles of the Art Military.* 1637. Courtesy, Yale University Library.

The use of the pike

Musketeer. 17th Century

Pioneer groups soon explored and settled Cape Cod and the region near Plymouth, establishing towns at Duxbury, Scituate, Sandwich, Bourne, Dennis, Barnstable, Yarmouth, and other localities. Their houses were built around huge chimneys, as the illustration on page 44 shows, and in the beginning many of them caught fire, the flames eating through the mud daub of the chimney and igniting the wattles. Some of the Plymouth houses, like the Allyn House, were medieval in appearance, with sharp gables, an overhang at the first story, and with leaded casement windows.

Allyn House. Plymouth, Mass.
Bartlett *The Pilgrim Fathers*. 1853.

Whitefield *The Homes of Our Forefathers*. 3 v. 1880-86.
John Alden House. Duxbury, Mass. 1653

Left
Standish House. Duxbury, Mass. Built by Alexander Standish, son of Myles Standish
Whitefield *The Homes of Our Forefathers*. 3 v. 1880-86.

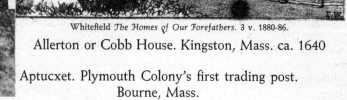

Whitefield *The Homes of Our Forefathers*. 3 v. 1880-86.
Allerton or Cobb House. Kingston, Mass. ca. 1640

Aptucxet. Plymouth Colony's first trading post.
Bourne, Mass.

Howland House. Plymouth, Mass.

The Major John Bradford House. Kingston, Mass.

Whitefield *The Homes of Our Forefathers.* 3 v. 1880-86.

Bradford House. Before restoration

Welcome Stranger

The pious Pilgrim Fathers would have opened their doors to us in true Christian hospitality had we visited Plymouth, and they would have shared their simple meal with us and given us a bed for the night. We might have entered a room like this.

Thomas Hart House. Ipswich, Mass. ca. 1640

"Give Us This Day Our Daily Bread"

Opening the Bible shown on the table in the Hart House we would have seen this title-page, so familiar to the Pilgrims. The table itself, a carved oak wainscot chair-table, could be used as a chair when the table top was lifted and swung backwards.

Courtesy, Massachusetts Historical Society, Boston.

Genevan Bible. 1599

Courtesy, Pilgrim Hall, Plymouth, Mass.

Iron pot belonging to Captain Myles Standish

In the fireplace would be found an iron pot like the above.

The court-cupboard against the wall held a variety of objects, including drinking vessels, the day's food supply, table linens, etc. Some houses had press-cupboards, with the lower part enclosed, such as we see here.

In Pilgrim Hall in Plymouth is Peregrine White's cradle. Peregrine was born on the *Mayflower*, the first Pilgrim child of the New World.

Courtesy, Pilgrim Hall, Plymouth, Mass.

Press-cupboard. 17th Century

Chairs

When little Peregrine White was old enough to sit in a high-chair it was no doubt similar to the one brought over by the Mather family to Massachusetts Bay in 1630.

John Carver, the first Governor of Plymouth Colony, brought a chair with him which is still preserved, and it has given the name Carver to this type.

The original Carver chair

Courtesy, Pilgrim Hall, Plymouth, Mass.

Courtesy, American Antiquarian
Society, Worcester, Mass.
Mather high-chair

Here we see the Brewster chair, said to have belonged to Elder William Brewster.

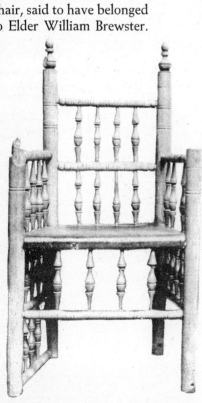

Courtesy, Pilgrim Hall, Plymouth, Mass.

Courtesy, Pilgrim Hall, Plymouth, Mass.
Carved oak wainscot chair. 17th Century

The Kitchen Was the Center of Family Life

Entering the restored kitchen of the Harlow House in Plymouth we see this scene. The musket on the massive wooden beam over the fireplace is pointed to a Betty lamp, an early type of lighting device containing a wick soaked in grease or some oily substance. The Pilgrims most likely used rush lights. Dry rushes were gathered, soaked in grease, and fastened in an iron holder. These rushes burned unevenly and made a flickering light. Note the bake oven in the chimney. The wooden bench or settle could be placed in front of the fireplace. Its high back served as a protection against cold air coming from the back of the room.

Another fireplace in the Harlow House shows a bake oven in the chimney and the long wooden shovel used for putting things in the oven. A three-legged pot is set on an iron trivet. The chair is a turned slat-back chair.

Fireplace. Harlow House, Plymouth, Mass.

Courtesy, Pilgrim Hall, Plymouth, Mass.
Kitchen. Harlow House. Plymouth, Mass.

Rush light holders

Courtesy, Mrs. J. Insley Blair Collection, Cooper Union Museum for the Arts of Decoration, New York.

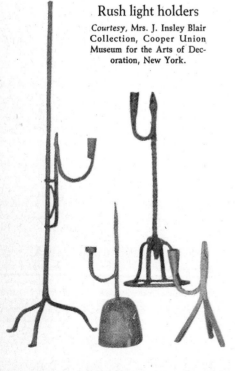

Women Plain . . .

The women of Plymouth made their own clothing from wool and linen, wool carded and spun by hand, and linen from homegrown flax.

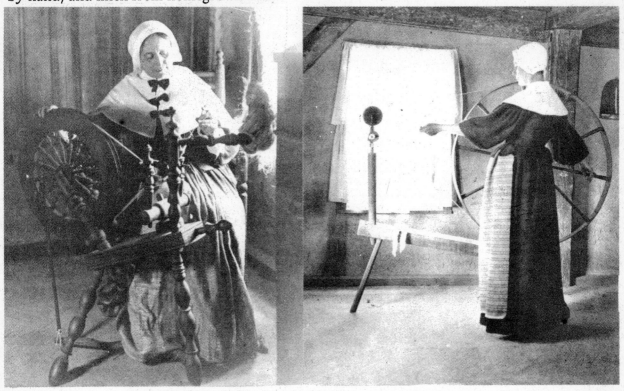

Photographs by E. P. Laughlin. *Courtesy*, Pilgrim Hall, Plymouth, Mass.

Flax wheel   Spinning wheel

The costumes shown above reveal a charming simplicity. More elaborate clothing was worn on Sundays and special occasions, as these contemporary English fashion plates will show.

. . . And Women Vain

Hollar *Ornatus Muliebris Anglicanus*. London, 1640. *Courtesy*, The New York Public Library.

"Woman's Work Is Never Done"

Courtesy, Plymouth Antiquarian Society. Photo by E. P. McLaughlin.

Harlow House. Plymouth, Mass.

Here is a Pilgrim woman at a colonial loom. Her right hand holds a wooden shuttle containing a strand of yarn, called the woof, which is thrown between the shed of lengthwise yarn, called the warp. The left hand pulls the batten towards the weaver, pushing the woof tightly against the woven edge. This is called battening. The heddles, immediately back of the batten and reed, separate the warp threads in such a manner that the shuttle, in passing through the shed, goes under one warp thread and over the next, and vice versa the next time the shuttle is thrown, thus tying the strands firmly together.

Courtesy, Plymouth Antiquarian Society.

Interior. Harlow House

Here we see Pilgrim women at the churn. The large shallow stone is a primitive drain board and shows the Dutch influence.

Close-up of stone drain board

Wooden scales

Courtesy, Pilgrim Hall, Plymouth, Mass.

Napkins, bed linen and clothing were kept in chests and trunks like these.

17th Century chest

Courtesy, Pilgrim Hall, Plymouth, Mass.

Below

Trunk. Colonial Period

Courtesy, Pocumtuck Valley Memorial Association, of Deerfield, Mass.

Below

Curious style of folding table

Courtesy, Mrs. J. Insley Blair Collection, Tuxedo Park, N. Y.

Turkey-work carpets (table cloths were then called carpets) were thrown over tables like these.

The most common table in Plymouth was the long trestle table around which the entire family sat during meals. It was usually of oak and pine and was made on the spot, there being an abundance of timber.

Courtesy, The Metropolitan Museum of Art, New York.

Wooden Trenchers . . .

Most of the tableware at Plymouth was made of wood. Two people or more ate from the same wooden plate or trencher. They ate with their fingers, there being no forks and very few spoons. Saffron-stained fingers were wiped on napkins, of which there were plenty.

Courtesy, Pocumtuck Valley Memorial Association of Deerfield, Mass.

Wooden tableware

. . . and Wooden Tankards

The Pilgrims drank huge quantities of beer and ale, and when their first orchards came to maturity, even greater quantities of cider.

Burl

From Indian corn the Pilgrims made mush, or "hasty pudding," hoe cakes, and hominy, or samp as the Indians called it. Samp was eaten from bowls made of burl, knotty growths on old trees which were carved into useful shapes by the Indians.

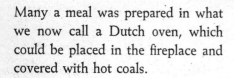

Below, Utensils made of burl

Courtesy, Old Quinabaug Village, Sturbridge, Mass.

Courtesy, The Essex Institute,
Salem, Mass.

Wooden tankards

Many a meal was prepared in what we now call a Dutch oven, which could be placed in the fireplace and covered with hot coals.

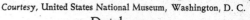

Courtesy, United States National Museum, Washington, D. C.

Dutch oven

Pounding Corn

Schoolcraft *Indian Tribes.* 1854.
Indian woman pounding corn with mortar and pestle

Peirce *Indian History.* 1878.
Zerviah G. Mitchell, direct descendant of Massasoit, Chief of the Wampanoags

Courtesy, American Museum of Natural History, New York. Painting by Arthur A. Jansson.

Old windmill at Eastham. Cape Cod, Mass.

Trees

Below Peregrine White's pear
tree. Plymouth, Mass.
Russell *Guide to Plymouth.* 1846.

Courtesy, Essex Institute, Salem, Mass.
Ancient Oak Tree. Peabody, Mass.

"Yarbs"

The women planted herb gardens, and all foods were seasoned with herbs, which were also used for medicinal purposes.

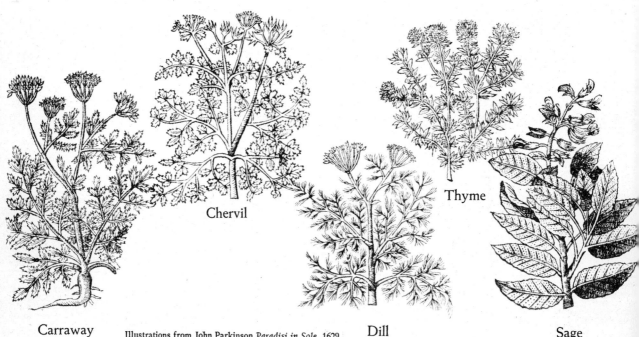

Carraway   Illustrations from John Parkinson *Paradisi in Sole.* 1629.   Chervil   Dill   Thyme   Sage

"Thy Kingdom Come..."

We will now leave the homes of the Pilgrims and accompany them to church.

Painting by Boughton. *Courtesy*, The New York Public Library.

Pilgrims going to church

This painting is enshrined in the hearts of Americans, and it seems fitting to reproduce it. The men carried their muskets to church, placing them on a gun rack. In the center of the picture is seen the preacher with his Bible. The costume is correct for the period. Here we see the garb of Governor Edward Winslow, one of the founders of Plymouth Colony.

Courtesy, Pilgrim Hall, Plymouth, Mass.

Portrait of Governor Edward Winslow

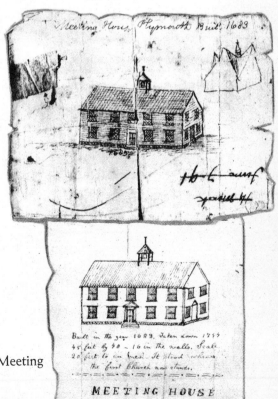

These drawings show the Second Meeting House in Plymouth, built in 1683.

Courtesy, Colonial Society of Massachusetts, Boston.

Here are the christening mitts and shirt of Governor William Bradford.

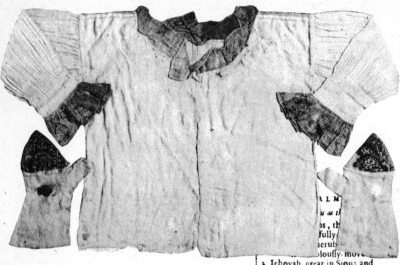

Courtesy, The Essex Institute, Salem, Mass.

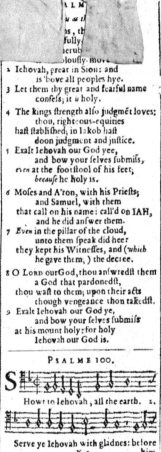

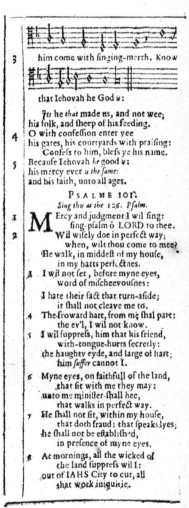

"Old Hundred"

The Pilgrims used Ainsworth's *The Book of Psalmes*. The favorite hymn tune in it was "Old Hundred." New England hills echoed with this hymn for generations.

Ainsworth *The Book of Psalmes*. 1618. Courtesy, The New York Public Library.
Psalms 99, 100, and 101

Here They Buried Their Dead

W. H. Bartlett *The Pilgrim Fathers*. 1853.
Burial hill. Plymouth, Mass.

Children

Pilgrim children had to work hard. Idle hands were sinful. The girls embroidered samplers. They were allowed to play with dolls, rag dolls for the most part, such as the one shown here, but the Indian girls taught them how to make corn-husk dolls. The features of the rag doll were drawn with charcoal, or painted with poke-berry juice. This is the real folk doll of America.

Rag doll

Courtesy, The Doll Museum, Wenham, Mass.

Corn-husk dolls

Courtesy, The Doll Museum, Wenham, Mass.

Courtesy, The Essex Institute, Salem, Mass.

Sampler made by Mary Hollingworth before 1675

High Street

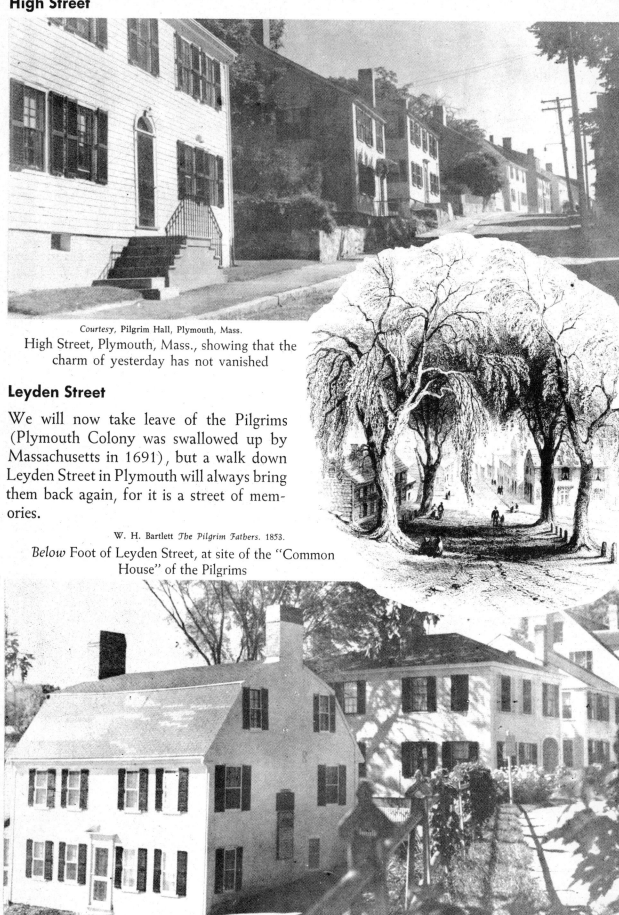

Courtesy, Pilgrim Hall, Plymouth, Mass.

High Street, Plymouth, Mass., showing that the charm of yesterday has not vanished

Leyden Street

We will now take leave of the Pilgrims (Plymouth Colony was swallowed up by Massachusetts in 1691), but a walk down Leyden Street in Plymouth will always bring them back again, for it is a street of memories.

W. H. Bartlett *The Pilgrim Fathers.* 1853.

Below Foot of Leyden Street, at site of the "Common House" of the Pilgrims

Courtesy, Pilgrim Hall, Plymouth, Mass.

"Down-Easters"

The Pilgrims were not the only early settlers on the New England coast. Various merchants and traders were developing grants which they had obtained from the Council for New England.

On the lower side of Boston Bay, Wessagusset (Weymouth) had a more or less continuous existence from 1622 onward. John Mason and others settled Strawberry Bank on the Piscataqua River, now Portsmouth, N. H.

Farther up the coast were fishing and trading colonies centering around Richmond's Island (Cape Elizabeth).

Rev. Robert Jordan's baptismal basin

Courtesy, Maine Historical Society, Portland, Maine.

Courtesy, The Maine Historical Society, Portland, Me., and the American Numismatic Society, New York.

Seventeenth Century coins (obverse and reverse) from the Castine Hoard, discovered in 1840 on the banks of the Bagaduce River, near Penobscot, Me. *Upper left.* Lima, Peru. Philip IV. 8 Reales. 1659. *Upper right.* France. Louis XIII. Ecu blanc. 1652. *Lower left.* Massachusetts. Pine Tree Shilling. 1652. *Center.* Netherlands. Leewen Daalder (Lion dollar). 1641. *Lower right.* Potosi (now Bolivia). Charles II. 8 Reales. 1678.

Courtesy, Maine Historical Society. Portland, Maine.
Coins unearthed at Richmond's Island

Monhegan

In Maine, at and off the mouth of the Kennebec (then called the Sagadahoc), were the trading and fishing posts of Pemaquid and Monhegan Island. The latter was the favorite rendezvous of British mariners. Even today its bleak rocks present a scene not vastly different from the one that met the eyes of the first white men.

Marion J. Bradshaw *The Maine Land*. 1941.

Monhegan Island

Pemaquid

At Pemaquid was once a flourishing settlement. Ancient cellars and pavements have been excavated on the site which may go back as far as the Fifteenth Century.

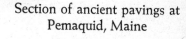

Section of ancient pavings at Pemaquid, Maine

Seventeenth Century felling axe found in Maine

Courtesy, Bucks County Historical Society, Doylestown, Pa.

Maine

In the Northeasterly part of Maine was a debatable land where the English and French were to fight it out for 140 years. Fort Pentegoet was soon to be established as a French frontier post on the Penobscot, to which place came Frenchmen from Quebec by canoe or on snowshoes, and from whence the Jesuit priests carried forward their Christianization of the Indian.

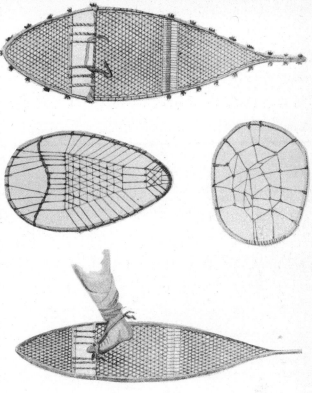

Schoolcraft *Indian Tribes.* Pt. III. 1853.
Snowshoes

Bacquerie de la Potherie *Histoire de l'Amerique Septentrionale.* 1753.
Canadian on snowshoes

Indian convert
Bacquerie de la Potherie, *Histoire de l'Amerique Septentrionale.* 1753.

Along the rivers and bays and by the wooded lakes of Maine embryo settlements began which were to become Bar Harbor, Augusta, Portland, York, and other towns of today.

Courtesy, Federal Works Agency,
Washington, D. C.

Scene on shore of Great Pond,
Acadia National Park, Mount
Desert, Me.

The Crown Collection, in the British Museum.
The fort at Saco, Maine

Fur Trade

The English and French traders fought for fur trading rights in these wilderness outposts. Beaver skins were much in demand. In Europe fur was the fashion.

Here we have a rather quaint conception of the beaver and beavers building their huts.

The World Displayed. 1759

New Hampshire

Isles of Shoals. New Hampshire. These pictures show
the bleak and rocky terrain

Harper's Magazine. Oct. 1874.

There were early settlements at the Isles of Shoals (which were divided between Mason and
Gorges), and along the banks of the Piscataqua. Besides the furs and fisheries there was the
lucrative lumbering industry to attract bold "adventurers" like John Mason. New Hampshire
timber was used in the building of British ships. Each ship from England brought supplies for
hardy settlers.

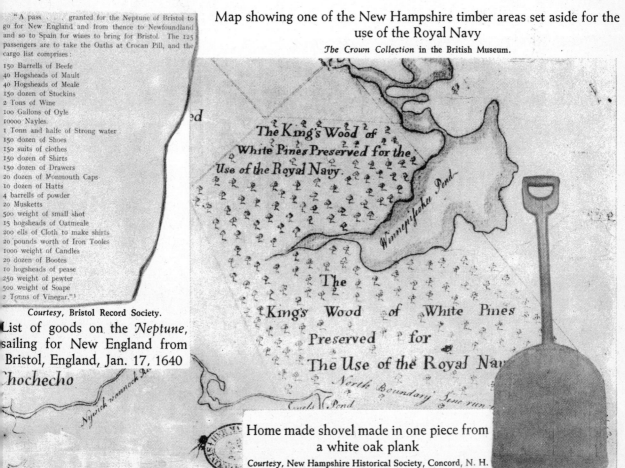

"A pass . . . . granted for the Neptune of Bristol to
go for New England and from thence to Newfoundland
and so to Spain for wines to bring for Bristol. The 125
passengers are to take the Oaths at Crocan Pill, and the
cargo list comprises:

150 Barrells of Beefe
40 Hogsheads of Mault
40 Hogsheads of Meale
150 dozen of Stockins
2 Tons of Wine
100 Gallons of Oyle
10000 Nayles.
1 Tonn and halfe of Strong water
150 dozen of Shoes
150 suits of clothes
150 dozen of Shirts
150 dozen of Drawers
20 dozen of Monmouth Caps
10 dozen of Hatts
4 barrells of powder
20 Musketts
500 weight of small shot
15 hogsheads of Oatmeale
200 ells of Cloth to make shirts
20 pounds worth of Iron Tooles
1000 weight of Candles
20 dozen of Bootes
10 hogsheads of pease
250 weight of pewter
500 weight of Soape
2 Tonns of Vinegar."[1]

Courtesy, Bristol Record Society.

List of goods on the *Neptune,*
sailing for New England from
Bristol, England, Jan. 17, 1640

Map showing one of the New Hampshire timber areas set aside for the
use of the Royal Navy

The Crown Collection in the British Museum.

The King's Wood of
White Pines Preserved for the
Use of the Royal Navy.

Winnipiseokee Pond

The
King's Wood of White Pines
Preserved for
The Use of the Royal Navy

North Boundary Line run

Home made shovel made in one piece from
a white oak plank

Courtesy, New Hampshire Historical Society, Concord, N. H.

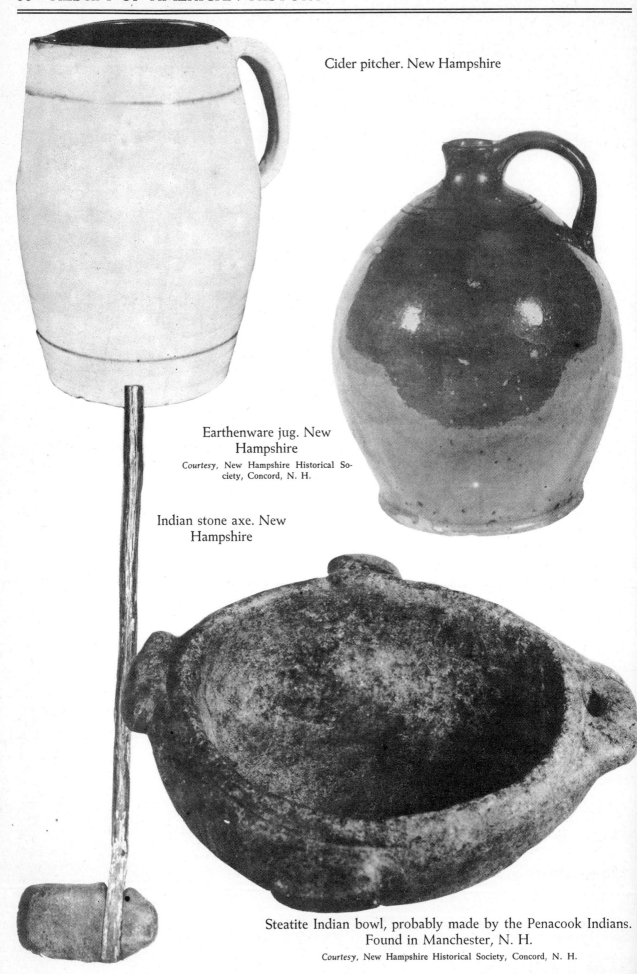

Cider pitcher. New Hampshire

Earthenware jug. New
Hampshire
Courtesy, New Hampshire Historical So-
ciety, Concord, N. H.

Indian stone axe. New
Hampshire

Steatite Indian bowl, probably made by the Penacook Indians.
Found in Manchester, N. H.
Courtesy, New Hampshire Historical Society, Concord, N. H.

Courtesy, New Hampshire Historical Society, Concord, N. H.

Early doll's cradle. New Hampshire

Cane chair. 17th Century

Courtesy, New Hampshire Historical Society, Concord, N. H.

Whitefield *The Homes of Our Forefathers*.
3 v. 1880-86.

Vaughn House. Portsmouth, N. H.
ca. 1670

Trappers and woodsmen returning from the White Mountains told of a great stone face, now known as the old man of the mountain.

The Old Man of the Mountain

Charlton *New Hampshire As It Is*. 1857.

Right

Undated map showing the location of Strawberry Bank and other New Hampshire settlements

Courtesy, The Crown Collection in The British Museum.

As Strawberry Bank grew in importance, forts were erected at the mouth of the Piscataqua River. By the end of the Seventeenth Century these forts presented a formidable appearance.

Below

Fort William and Mary, on the Piscataqua River

Courtesy, Public Archives of Canada. Ottawa, Canada.

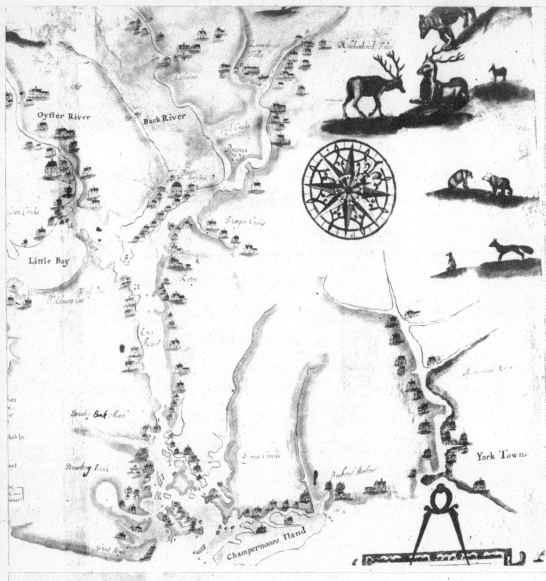

3

THE PURITANS

Stern Coasts

Along New England's shores

Among the many small fishing ventures along the New England coast, was one at Cape Anne, established by a stock company of Dorchester, England, in about 1625. Three years later the settlement was moved to Naumkeag (Salem), and under a reorganized management (the New England Company) John Endecott was sent over as Governor.

Courtesy, Essex Institute, Salem, Mass.

Gov. Endecott's sundial, the oldest time-piece in New England. It was made by William Bowyer in 1630, the year the Puritans founded the Massachusetts Bay Colony

Courtesy, The Commonwealth of Massachusetts State Library.

John Endecott, first governor of the Massachusetts Bay Company

By still another reorganization of this company the region about Massachusetts Bay was, by royal charter in 1629, granted to the Massachusetts Bay Company, and in 1630 came the Great Migration of the so-called Puritans.

Charter of the Massachusetts Bay Colony. 1629. Portrait of
John Winthrop, first governor under the Charter.

The preliminary hardships over, this new colony flourished as had no previous English colony
in the New World. From it were soon settled the new colonies of Connecticut, Rhode Island
and New Haven, including the eastern end of Long Island; while it dominated the life of
Plymouth and New Hampshire, and even annexed Maine. It was the seed pot from which
grew New England.

Stern Faces

Rev. John Cotton

Rev. Richard Mather
Wood engraving by John Foster.

William Pynchon
Courtesy, Essex Institute, Salem, Mass.

Puritans

The Puritans were those members of the Church of England who wished to hold to the gains of the Protestant Reformation. They were opposed to the retention of a ritual and an episcopacy not unlike that of the Church of Rome. The Puritans leaned towards congregationalism, which permitted each congregation the freedom of regulating its own affairs. Unlike the Pilgrims, the Puritan leaders were relatively wealthy. John Winthrop's memorandum giving his reasons for emigrating show mixed motives. Political and economic considerations as well as religious ones animated the Puritans. They glimpsed a church-state which would make the leaders important, and to effect this they would have to be as independent of England as possible.

Forsaking the Old . . .

Thompson *History and Antiquities of Boston.* 1856.
The Old Vicarage, Boston, England, where John Cotton resided

To Embrace the New

Church used by Roger Williams at Salem, Mass. (Restored)

T. Allen *The History of the County of Lincoln.* 1833-34.
St. Botolph's Church. Boston, England, where John Cotton was vicar

Place Names

The settlement at Shawmut was also called Tremontaine, or Tri-mountain, on account of its three hills, and on one of the hills was placed a beacon. From these historical associations come the names Tremont Street and Beacon Hill, in Boston.

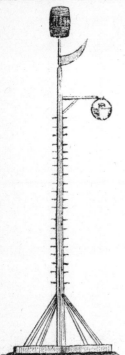

Courtesy, Essex Institute, Salem, Mass. Photo by Eric Muller.

Reconstructed Pioneer Village at Naumkeag, or Salem, Mass., showing the ship *Arbella* and houses of the Puritan period

Early beacon on Beacon Hill. The barrel of pitch was to be lighted in case of a threatened invasion

As soon as rude shelters—often mere covered cellars—were ready, the Puritans took their belongings from the ships in trunks such as this.

Trunk covered with cowhide, owned by Jonathan Corwin of Salem

Courtesy, Essex Institute, Salem, Mass.

They Felled the Trees

The sound of the axe was heard as the men felled trees to make clearings and to secure timber for houses.

Colonial axes

Courtesy, Essex Institute, Salem, Mass.

Broad axes

Courtesy, Society for the Preservation of New England Antiquities, Boston.

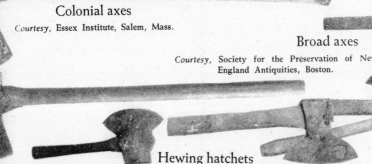

Hewing hatchets

The blacksmith set up his forge and anvil, made and mended tools, and beat out iron hinges. Later he would make shoes for oxen. Horses were not brought to America in the beginning.

They Sawed Planks

The carpenters sawed planks and made staves.

Cats *Wercken.* 1658.

Garzoni *Allegemeine Schawplatz.*
1641.

Courtesy, Essex Institute, Salem, Mass.
17th Century saw

Made Shingles

Courtesy, Society for the Preservation of New England Antiquities, Boston.
Draw knives

This shows the method of using a shaving horse.

Shaving horse, on which shingles, clapboards, and barrel staves were shaved
Courtesy, Society for the Preservation of New England Antiquities, Boston.

They Had to Be Good Carpenters . . .

Shingles were also split from blocks of wood by means of the frow and frow club, and boards were squared and planed.

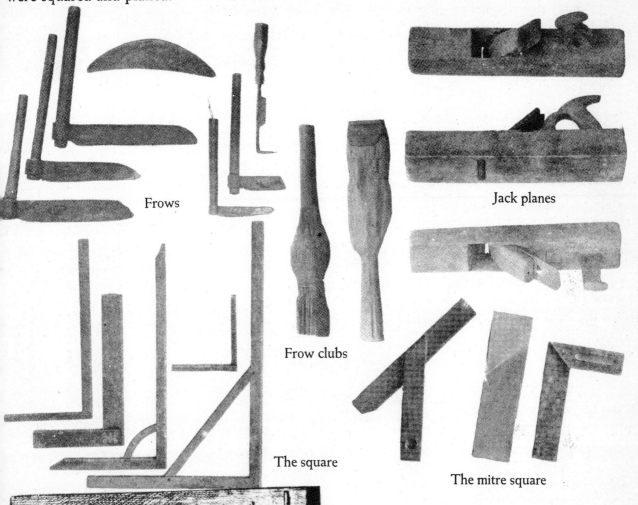

Frows

Frow clubs

The square

Jack planes

The mitre square

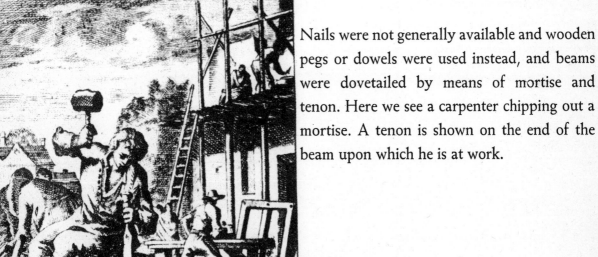

Nails were not generally available and wooden pegs or dowels were used instead, and beams were dovetailed by means of mortise and tenon. Here we see a carpenter chipping out a mortise. A tenon is shown on the end of the beam upon which he is at work.

Carpenter at work

Van der Lys and Luyken *Spiegel van het menselyk bedryf.* 1718.

... To Build Houses Like These

Note in this old house the huge chimney, the casement windows and the sturdy door.

The Old House. Cutchogue, Long Island, N. Y. 17th Century. The early houses at Salem were very similar to this Puritan house on Long Island

Courtesy, The Magazine *Antiques*, and Mr. James Van Alst.

"Scotch-Boardman House." Saugus, Mass. Built 1651

The Abraham Browne, Jr. House. Watertown, Mass. ca. 1663

Some of the Puritan houses had a medieval look with their many gables and their second-story overhang.

Courtesy, Essex Institute, Salem, Mass.

John Ward House. Salem, Mass. Built 1684

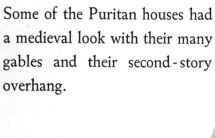

Whitefield *The Homes of Our Forefathers*. 3 v. 1880-86.

Whipple House. Ipswich, Mass. ca. 1640   Iron works house. Saugus, Mass. 1643

Whitefield *The Homes of Our Forefathers*. 3 v. 1880-86.

Lynde House. Melrose, Mass. 17th Century   Pierce-Little House. Newbury, Mass.

There were a few brick mansions such as the Pierce-Little House.

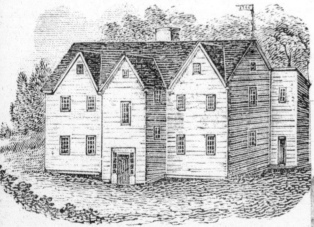

Barber *Historical Collections*. 1841.
Leonard House. Raynham, Mass. 17th Cent.

Whitefield *The Homes of Our Forefathers*. 3 v. 1880-86.
Sutton House. Ipswich, Mass. 17th Cent.

Old Boston and New

The houses in Boston, England, had some influence on the architecture of its young namesake in New England. All of these old houses were standing when the Puritans left for America.

Old house in Archer Lane, Boston, England
Pishey Thompson *History and Antiquities of Boston.* 1856.

Pishey Thompson *History and Antiquities of Boston.* 1856.
The Old Three Tuns, Boston, England

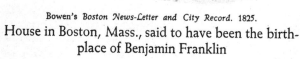

Bowen's Boston *News-Letter and City Record.* 1825.
House in Boston, Mass., said to have been the birthplace of Benjamin Franklin

Pishey Thompson *Collections for a Topographical and Historical Account of Boston.* 1820.
Old house in Boston, England, showing overhang

We will enter a Puritan house and see how its occupants lived during the course of a New England day. From a bedroom like this the mother and father awoke early and dressed by the faint gleams of rush lights or betty lamps.

Courtesy, The American Wing, The Metropolitan Museum of Art, New York.

Thomas Hart House. Ipswich, Mass. ca. 1640

By the Light of Betty Lamps

Note the "Betty lamp" on the wall, suspended on a trammel. A rush light is seen on the oak chest beside the Bible. The casement windows were kept closed at night, for the Puritans thought that fresh night air was injurious to health.

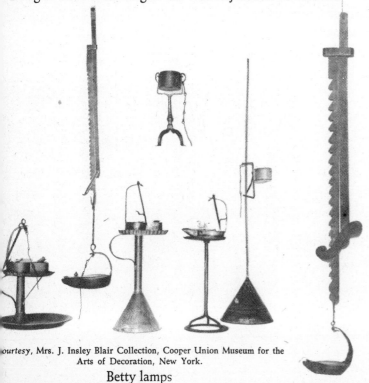

Trammel, with betty lamp

Courtesy, Old Quinabaug Village, Sturbridge, Mass.

ourtesy, Mrs. J. Insley Blair Collection, Cooper Union Museum for the Arts of Decoration, New York.

Betty lamps

Rush light

Courtesy, Mrs. J. Insley Blair Collection, Cooper Union Museum for the Arts of Decoration, New York

The wealthier Puritans arose from beds like these, in paneled rooms, and dressed by the light of candles, which were not so common in those days, and which were comparatively expensive unless made at home in a candle mould.

Room from the Shaw House, Hampton, N. H.

Courtesy, The American Wing, The Metropolitan Museum of Art, New York.

Candle mould

When the sun came up the casement windows would be swung open to let in light and sunshine if it were a summer's day. In poorer houses oiled paper was used instead of window glass, but many a Puritan house was adorned with leaded casements such as those pictured here.

They Flung Open Casement Windows

Courtesy, Society for the Preservation of New England Antiquities, Boston.
Original casement windows
Abraham Browne, Jr. House, Watertown, Mass. ca. 1663

Courtesy, The Essex Institute, Salem, Mass.
Casement window. 17th Century

Chests

Clothes were taken from carved oak chests like these, or from wooden pegs in the wall timbers.

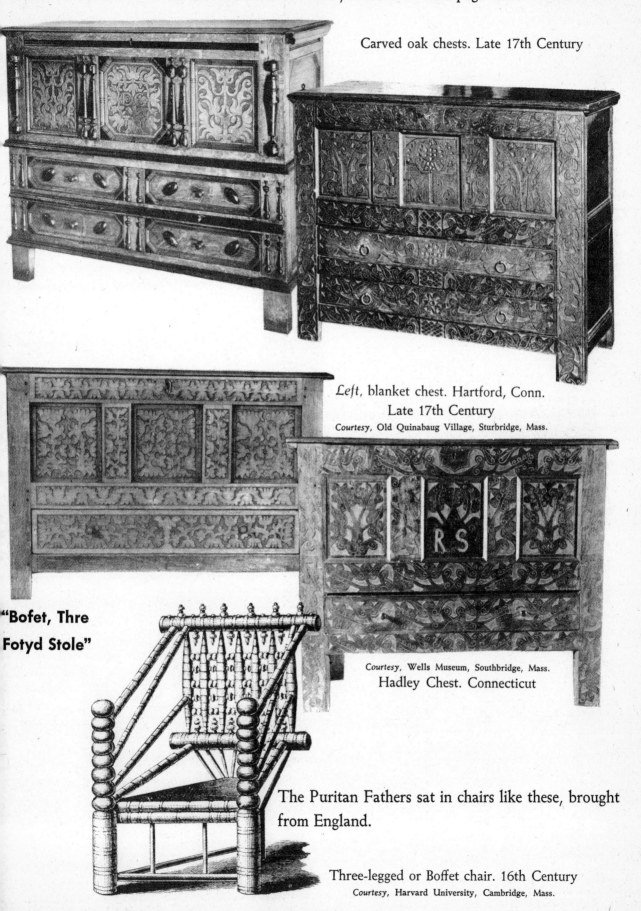

Carved oak chests. Late 17th Century

Left, blanket chest. Hartford, Conn.
Late 17th Century
Courtesy, Old Quinabaug Village, Sturbridge, Mass.

"Bofet, Thre
Fotyd Stole"

Courtesy, Wells Museum, Southbridge, Mass.
Hadley Chest. Connecticut

The Puritan Fathers sat in chairs like these, brought from England.

Three-legged or Boffet chair. 16th Century
Courtesy, Harvard University, Cambridge, Mass.

The Puritan pulled on his hose or hosen, as breeches were then called.

Doublet and Hose

Turned slat-back chair. ca. 1650

Wainscot chair. ca. 1600

Hose. ca. 1630

He sat in chairs like these while he pulled on his jackboots.

He then put on his doublet, and reached for his coat.

Doublet, hose, and cloak. ca. 1630

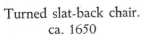

Left, Doublet. ca. 1630

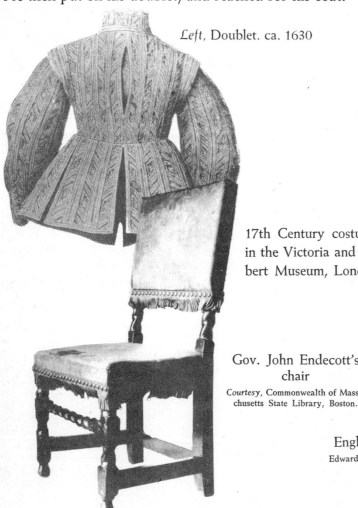

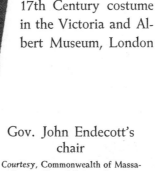

17th Century costume in the Victoria and Albert Museum, London

Gov. John Endecott's chair

Courtesy, Commonwealth of Massachusetts State Library, Boston.

English costume. 1650

Edward Pugh *London.* v. 4. 1807.

"Obed! Josiah! Come Down!"

Thus shouted the Puritan father to his sons sleeping in the attic. They bore Biblical names chosen from John Speed's *Genealogy of the Bible* which was usually appended to the Genevan version of the *Holy Bible*, the one the Puritans used in preference to the King James version.

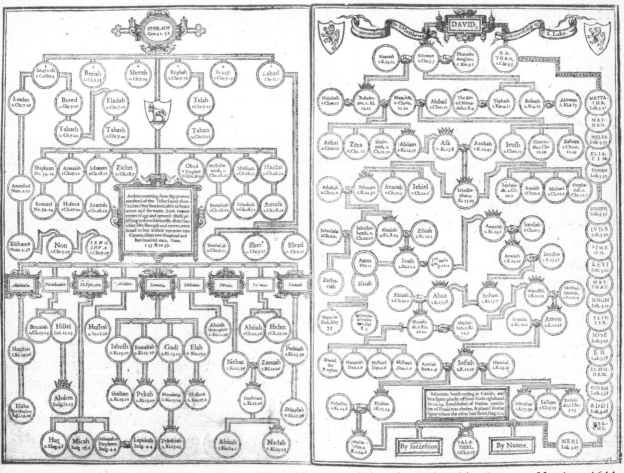

Two pages from John Speed's *Genealogy of the Bible*, appended to the *Holy Bible*. Genevan Version. 1611

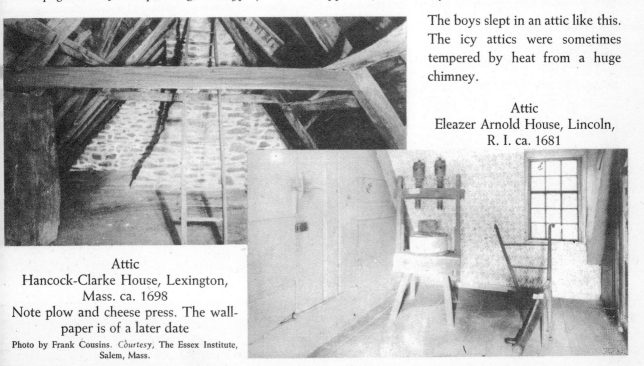

The boys slept in an attic like this. The icy attics were sometimes tempered by heat from a huge chimney.

Attic
Eleazer Arnold House, Lincoln, R. I. ca. 1681

Attic
Hancock-Clarke House, Lexington, Mass. ca. 1698
Note plow and cheese press. The wallpaper is of a later date
Photo by Frank Cousins. Courtesy, The Essex Institute, Salem, Mass.

The chimney seen in the attic of the Arnold House looked like this from the outside. It occupied the whole end of the house, a typical feature of early New England dwellings.

Obed and Josiah and their younger brothers came tumbling down stairs like these, for their father's strict command was one to be promptly obeyed. They had to listen to morning prayer.

Courtesy, Society for the Preservation of New England Antiquities, Boston.

Eleazer Arnold House, Lincoln, R. I. ca. 1681

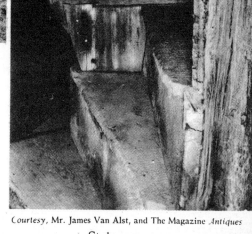

Courtesy, Mr. James Van Alst, and The Magazine *Antiques*

Stairway
The Old House, Cutchogue, Long Island, N. Y.

If the fire had gone out one of the boys would be sent to a neighbor's house to borrow some live coals in a fire scoop, for there were no matches in those days.

Stairways

Stairway
Samuel Wentworth
House, Portsmouth,
N. H. ca. 1671

Courtesy, The Metropolitan Museum of Art, New York.

Fire scoop
Courtesy, Onondaga Historical Association, Syracuse, N. Y.

The mother or grandmother, the latter often only in her thirties, was up early to start the breakfast. Life centered in the kitchen, and its warmth, cosiness, and appetizing odors made it doubly attractive on a frosty morning. Families were large, despite the fact that infant mortality was high.

Women . . .

Hollar *Ornatus Muliebris Anglicanus.* 1640.
Female attire. 17th Century

And Many Babies

Artist unknown. *Courtesy,* Mrs. William Scofield and Mr. Andrew W. Sigourney.
Mrs. Elizabeth Clarke Freake and baby Mary. 1674

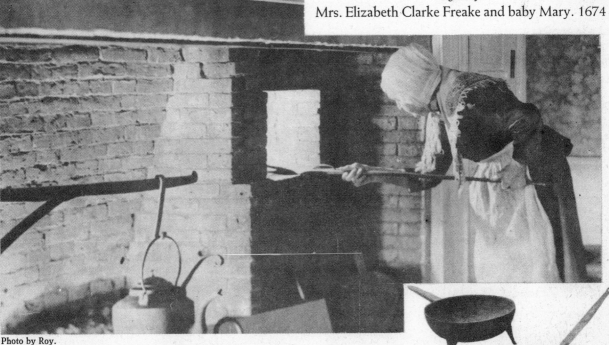

Photo by Roy.

Firing the brick oven
Ocean-Born-Mary House, Henniker, N. H.

Utensils with legs which kept them the proper distance
from the hot coals in the fireplace
Courtesy, The Metropolitan Museum of Art, New York.

Kitchens

The kitchen fireplace could not have looked like this, but almost every article in this picture is an authentic Colonial kitchen utensil. Note the trivets above the settle, and the Dutch ovens and roasting kitchen on the hearth. The roasting kitchen was open in the back and the heat from the fire roasted meats to a turn. A spit, operated by a handle, was attached to one end.

Kitchen exhibit

Courtesy, Pocumtuck Valley Memorial Association of Deerfield, Mass.

Below Kitchen Parson Capen House, Topsfield, Mass.
Courtesy, The Metropolitan Museum of Art, New York.

Another view of the Parson Capen kitchen, showing the pine settle, the chamber or lantern clock, and the press cupboard and Carver chair near it, and the slat-back chair by the fireplace.

Wood and Pewter

Meals were commonly served on wooden trenchers, but some families boasted pewter plates, brought from England.

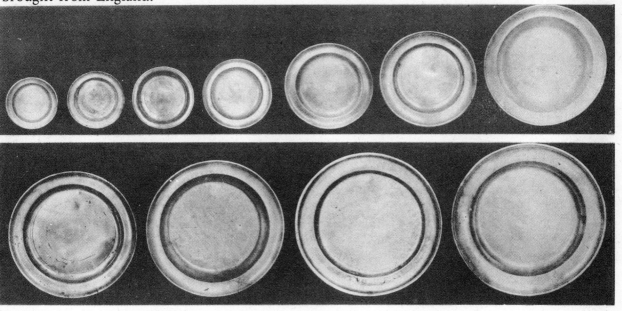

Kerfoot *American Pewter*. 1924. *Courtesy*, Crown Publishers, New York.

Pewter plates

Porringers, of wood or pewter, were used for porridge. Corn meal for mush was pounded with mortar and pestle.

Kitchen

Abraham Browne, Jr. House, Watertown, Mass. ca. 1663, showing mortar and pestle near the fireplace. To the left is a bannister-back chair

Courtesy, Society for the Preservation of New England Antiquities, Boston.

Pewter porringers

Kerfoot *American Pewter*. 1924. *Courtesy*, Crown Publishers, New York.

Courtesy, Old Quinabaug Village, Sturbridge, Mass.

Burl utensils

Other bowls were made by the Indians from burl, the knotted growths on old trees.

Courtesy, Old Quinabaug Village, Sturbridge, Mass.

Burl bowl

Division of Labor

After breakfast the whole family busied itself with the day's occupations. One of the boys yoked the ox team to the cart and went to gather hay from the meadows, if it were summer, or to the woods to gather sap from sugar maples if it were spring.

Courtesy, Old Quinabaug Village, Sturbridge, Mass.

Sap buckets

Ox team

Drawn by F. O. C. Darley. Engraved by K. Huber.

Ox team. Cape Cod. A throw back to the olden time

The women and girls worked in the herb and vegetable gardens. In wet weather the women wore pattens on their feet in lieu of rubbers.

Courtesy, Philadelphia Museum of Art, Philadelphia.

Wooden patten. Wooden sole, iron ring, leather strap

Woman with vegetable basket. Note the pattens

Hollar *Ornatus Muliebris Anglicanus*. 1640.

Snow-bound

The New England winter had its hardships, but it had its beauties.

> "All day the hoary meteor fell;
> And when the second morning shone,
> We looked upon a world unknown."
> —*Whittier*

Birches in winter

Marion J. Bradshaw *The Maine Land*. 1941.

Fish and Fowl

The housewife may have exchanged some article she had made with her own hands for a couple of chickens.

Sometimes skunks invaded the chicken pen and killed a fat hen or rooster.

Braun *Civitates Urbis Terrarum*. 1618.

Cabinet of Natural History. 1830-34.

The women cleaned the fish.

Clams were abundant along the beaches, and they kept many a family from starving, according to early colonial records.

Clam rake

Courtesy, New Haven Colony Historical Society, New Haven, Conn.

Braun *Civitates Urbis Terrarum*. 1618.

Vegetables and Herbs

Every Puritan woman knew the virtues of all the common herbs. Foods were seasoned with them, and many family remedies were concocted from herbs.

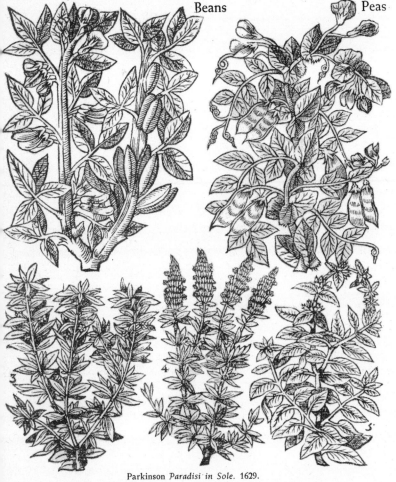

Beans   Peas

Bacqueville de la Potherie *Histoire de l'Amerique Septentrionale.* 1753.

Seneca or snakeroot

Parkinson *Paradisi in Sole.* 1629.

Savory (3) Hyssop (4) and Pennyroyal (5)

From the Indians the Puritans learned the medicinal value of snakeroot, or seneca as it was sometimes called.

There were no seed catalogues, but John Parkinson's *Paradisi in Sole* was an encyclopedia of gardening information. Then there was the almanac, dear to our forefathers. They planted everything according to the phases of the moon.

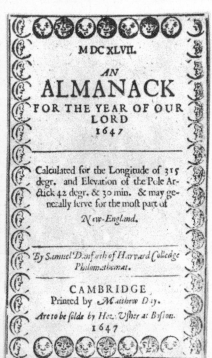

MDC XLVII.

AN

ALMANACK

FOR THE YEAR OF OUR LORD
1647

Calculated for the Longitude of 315 degr. and Elevation of the Pole Arctick 42 degr. & 30 min. & may generally serve for the most part of

New-England.

By *Samuel Danforth of Harvard Colledge Philomathemat.*

CAMBRIDGE
Printed by *Matthew Day.*

Are to be solde by Hez. Usher at Boston.
1647

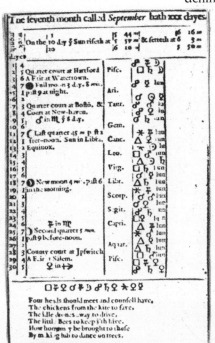

Title-page and sample pages from Samuel Danforth's *Almanack.* 1647

The Salem and Watertown fairs are mentioned

Red Men

Indians there were, and they occasionally committed mischief, but they were not a serious threat in the beginning. Some were converted to Christianity by John Eliot and other missionaries, but these "Praying Indians" were few in number and generally reverted to savagery.

Courtesy, Maryland Historical Society, Annapolis, Md.
John Eliot preaching to the Indians

The Train Band

Because of the Indian menace men and boys were compelled by law to devote a certain number of hours to militia drill. The militia was called the train band. The sound of fife and drum brought the train band post haste to the town common. Seventeenth century musical instruments, including the fife and drum, are shown here.

A man like Governor John Leverett of the Massachusetts Bay Colony made a handsome figure in his military uniform.
By an unknown artist. Courtesy, The Essex Institute, Salem, Mass.

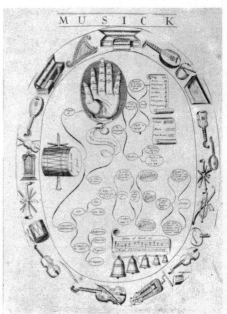

Richard Blome The Gentleman's Recreation. 1686.

Captain John Underhill, the professional soldier hired by the Massachusetts Bay Colony to train its militia, was a swashbuckling person. We can almost hear him barking the commands: "Rest your musket! Draw out your match!"

Courtesy, Yale University Library.
Hexham *Principles of the Art Military*. 1637.
Manual of arms used by Captain Underhill

Courtesy, The Commonwealth of Massachusetts State Library.
Gov. John Endecott's sword

"Give Fire!"

Hexham *Principles of the Art Military.* 1637.
Courtesy, Yale University Library.

The matchlock musket used by the Puritans was a cumbersome weapon which had to be rested on a forchette (forked stick) stuck in the ground. One wonders how the soldiers ever shot an Indian with a weapon which took so long to fire. Extra ammunition was carried in the bandoleer thrown over the left shoulder, to which a powder flask was attached on the right side.

The First Frontier

By 1635 most of the good land about Massachusetts Bay had been taken, and our first "West-ward Movement" occurred—to the Connecticut Valley.

From the new River Towns of Windsor, Hartford and Wethersfield, Roger Ludlow, writ-ing to "the Governor and brethren of the Massachusetts Bay", voiced the spirit both of Puri-tanism and of many succeeding American Frontiers.

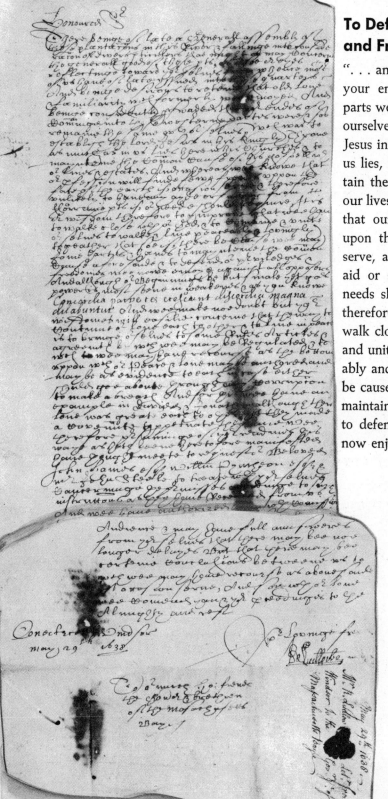

To Defend Our Privileges and Freedoms

". . . and being confidently persuaded that your ends of coming into these western parts were, and so remained, the same with ourselves, which was to establish the Lord Jesus in his Kingly Throne, as much as in us lies, here in his churches, and to main-tain the common cause of his gospel with our lives and estates; and whereas we know that our profession will find few friends upon the face of the world, if occasion serve, and therefore unlikely to have any aid or succour from foreign parts if our needs should so require, it is our wisdom therefore to improve what we have and to walk close with our God, and to combine and unite ourselves to walk and live peace-ably and lovingly together, that so, if there be cause, we may join hearts and hands to maintain the common cause aforesaid, and to defend our privileges and freedoms we now enjoy against all opposers."

Roger Ludlow's letter

Courtesy, Massachusetts Historical Society, Boston.

Connecticut Colony

Odell Shepard *Connecticut Past and Present*. 1939. *Courtesy*, Alfred A. Knopf, New York.

The Connecticut River

Windsor . . .

Hartford . . .

Whitefield *The Homes of Our Forefathers*. 3 v. 1880-86.

Old Stone Fort. Windsor,
Conn. 17th Century

Barber *Connecticut Historical Collections*. 1838.

Meeting House. Hartford, Conn. This was the
first church building erected in Connecticut

. . . and Wethersfield

Onion field. Weth-
ersfield, Conn.

S. Peters *A General History
of Connecticut*. 1829.

Barber *Connecticut Historical Collections*.
1838.

House of the Rev. Thomas
Hooker, Hartford's first religious leader

Ancient elm tree at
Wethersfield

Pendants

The Connecticut settlers built sturdy frame houses, and the second-story overhang, with pendants, was a distinctive feature.

J. Frederick Kelly *The Early Domestic Architecture of Connecticut.* 1924.
Courtesy, The Yale University Press.

Upper left, Whitman House, Farmington; upper right, the Older Cowles House, Farmington; lower left, from a demolished house, Farmington; lower right, Moore House, Windsor.

Upper left, Gleason House, Farmington; upper right, Caldwell House, Guilford; lower left, Hyland-Wildman House, Guilford; lower right, Hollister House, South Glastonbury.

Peace and Plenty

Whitefield *The Homes of Our Forefathers.* 3 v. 1880-86.

Whitman House. Farmington, Conn. ca. 1660

Hempstead House. New London, Conn. 1643

Kelly *Early Domestic Architecture of Connecticut.* Courtesy, The Yale University Press.

Stairway. Brockway House. Hamburg, Conn.

Whitefield *The Homes of Our Forefathers.* 3 v. 1880-86.

Mill at New London, Conn., built by John Winthrop, son of Gov. John Winthrop of Massachusetts. ca. 1650

Above Clark House. Stratford, Conn.

To the left Whitfield House or Old Stone House. Guilford, Conn. ca. 1640

Whitefield *The Homes of Our Forefathers.* 3 v. 1880-86.

Saybrook

At the mouth of the Connecticut River still another group had built a fort to keep out the Dutch. George Fenwick was sent from England to govern this settlement, and with him came his young wife, whose tombstone, still standing a stone's throw from the old fort, is perhaps a symbol of the rude life which a delicate lady endured far from friends at home.

Courtesy, Mrs. Gilman C. Gates.
Grave of Lady Fenwick at Saybrook. She died there in 1645

Rhode Island

Almost at the same time that Connecticut was coming into being, Roger Williams, disagreeing with his fellow ministers of Boston on matters of doctrine and law, fled into the Narragansett country and became the father of Rhode Island as well as the Baptist Church in America. To escape the Puritan wrath, many other men and women fled to the sanctuary of Rhode Island.

Picturesque America. 1872-74.
Indian Rock. Narragansett, R. I.

Williams House. Providence, R. I. Built by Joseph Williams, son of Roger Williams
Whitefield, *The Homes of Our Forefathers.* 3 v. 1880-86.

Baptist Shrine

Downing *Early Homes of Rhode Island.* 1937.
Courtesy, Garrett and Massie, Richmond, Va.

Interior of Elder Ballou meeting house

To the left Elder Ballou meeting house. Cumberland, R. I.
Built before 1749

Whitefield *The Homes of Our Forefathers.* 3 v. 1880-86.

To the left Fenner House. Johnston, R. I. 17th Century

Whitefield *The Homes of Our Forefathers.* 3 v. 1880-86.

Below left Coddington House. Newport, R. I. 1641

Below right Gorton House. Providence, R. I. 17th Century. One part of the house was built by Samuel Gorton

Whitefield *The Homes of Our Forefathers.* 3 v. 1880-86.

Ye Olde Ordinarie

Whitefield *The Homes of Our Forefathers.* 3 v. 1880-86.
Roger Mowry's "Ordinarie" Providence, R. I. 1653

Among those who found Rhode Island a haven of tolerance was William Blackstone, the first white settler (1623) on the land where Boston now stands. Being a Church of England man, he did not get along with the Puritans. He moved to Rhode Island in 1634 and died there in 1675.

Courtesy, Rhode Island Historical Society, Providence.

Sachem Ninigret. A Niantic Indian of Rhode Island. He visited Boston in 1637

Whitefield *The Homes of Our Forefathers.* 3 v. 1880-86.
The deserted grave of William Blackstone, near Lonsdale, R. I.

What Was It?

Was this old tower at Newport there when Rhode Island was settled, or was it built subsequently? Was it an old mill? Was it some pre-Columbian structure?

Schoolcraft *Indian Tribes.* 1851-57.

Pequots—on the War Path

Whether it was due to these new settlements, or simply to the perversity—white as well as red —of human nature, the year 1637 found the Pequot Indians actively engaged against the whites. The new colony of Connecticut joined with Massachusetts in a war of extermination. The first real battle took place easterly of the present Thames River in eastern Connecticut, where the colonial forces under Captains John Mason and John Underhill set fire to the Pequot forts, burning alive some 500 Indian men, women and children. Those who tried to escape were shot. From a book which Underhill wrote, we get this picture of what took place.

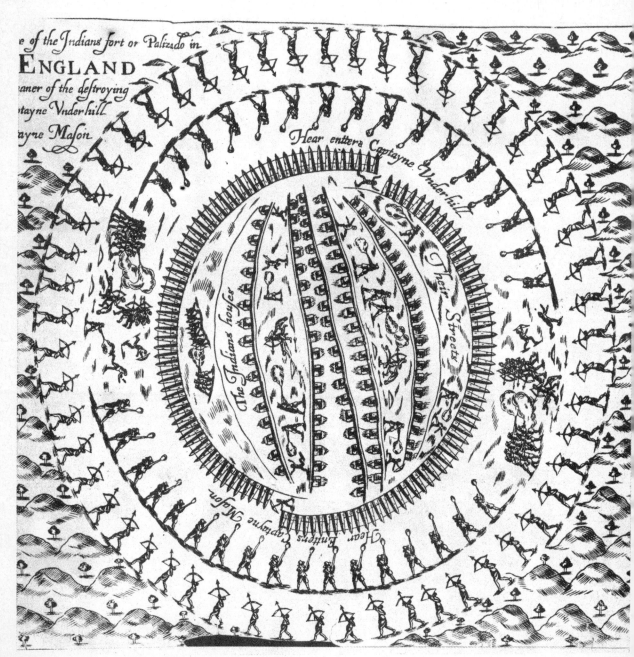

John Underhill *News from America.* 1638.

The defeat of the Pequots

And Still Another New Colony

The defeat of the Pequots was probably only one factor in the establishment, under the guidance of Theophilus Eaton, of a new colony at the mouth of the Quinnipiac River, known as New Haven Colony.

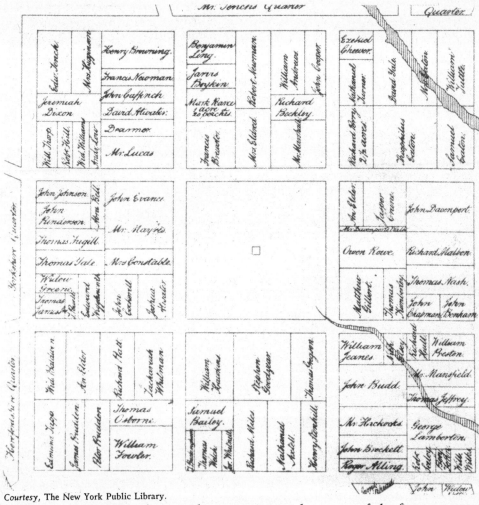

Courtesy, The New York Public Library.

Plan of New Haven, Conn. 1641, showing the nine squares, the names of the first property owners, and the church in the center of the town. This is a notable example of New England town planning, and the original nine squares still make up the heart of present day New Haven and Yale University.

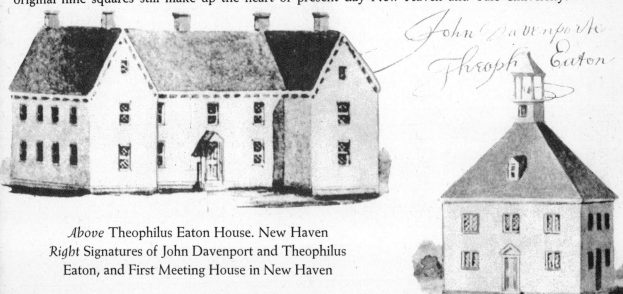

Above Theophilus Eaton House. New Haven
Right Signatures of John Davenport and Theophilus Eaton, and First Meeting House in New Haven

West Rock

A prominent feature of the landscape around New Haven was West Rock.

West Rock

Courtesy, *Connecticut Magazine.*

Whitefield, *The Homes of Our Forefathers.* 3 v. 1880-86.
An early house in Norwalk

To the Left, Interior of Ogden House. Fairfield, Conn.
Note the size of the fireplace and the wooden beams
Courtesy, Miss Mary Allis.

Settlements at Fairfield and Norwalk soon followed the one at New Haven.

Above, Ogden House. Fairfield, Conn.
Shingled salt box type
Courtesy, Miss Mary Allis.

To the Left, Taylor House. Norwalk (now Westport), Conn. ca. 1690. One of the best examples of the salt box type of house. The long slope of the rear roof, accentuated by a lean-to, characterizes the so-called salt box house.

Long Island

The men of Connecticut crossed Long Island Sound and established a settlement at Southampton in 1640. Others from Massachusetts founded Southold at about the same time. These towns in Eastern Long Island resisted the Dutch influence in the western part of the island.

Sayre House. Southampton, L. I.

J. T. Adams, *History of the Town of Southampton*. 1918.

Below, View of Southold, L. I. The house at the extreme left was built in the 17th Century

Lambert, *History of the Colony of New Haven*. 1838.

Indian. Engraved on a Powder Horn

Courtesy, Mr. Stewart Culin.

Saw Mill. Long Island

J. T. Adams, *History of the Town of Southampton*. 1918.

Above, Mill. Bridgehampton, L. I.

J. T. Adams, *History of the Town of Southampton*. 1918.

And Still the Indian

From 1637 to 1675 the Indian made little trouble, but in the latter year "King Philip" gave the colonists a real struggle.

King Philip. Engraving by Paul Revere

Defense

These block houses to the north indicate the direction from which the Indian threat was next to come.

Detail of the Gilman Garrison House, Exeter, N. H. Alleged date ca. 1650

William Damme Garrison House, Dover, N. H. ca. 1698

McIntire Garrison House
York, Maine. ca. 1640

Jenkins Garrison House
York, Maine

To the left Peter Tufts
House or "Old Fort,"
also known as the Crad-
dock House, Medford,
Mass. 1677-80. The oc-
cupants fired at Indians
through the portholes
(left)

Whitefield *The Homes of Our Forefathers.* 3 v. 1880-86.

Tavern Tales

Rumors of French and Indian forays in the northern settlements were carried from town to town, and in the taverns each stranger was questioned by eager listeners and treated to flip, a drink made by thrusting a hot poker or loggerhead into a mug of sweetened beer flavored with a dash of rum.

Right The Wayside Inn. Sud-
bury, Mass. ca. 1686
Whitefield *The Homes of Our Forefathers.*
3 v. 1880-86.

Poore's Tavern, Old New-
bury, Mass. ca. 1650
Whitefield *The Homes of Our Forefathers.*
3 v. 1880-86.

America's Oldest Military Company

To foster a military spirit John Underhill and others founded the Ancient and Honourable Artillery Company in Boston, in 1638. It is still in existence, and has its headquarters in Faneuil Hall.

Facsimile of the original charter of the Ancient and Honourable Artillery Company. This charter was signed by Gov. John Winthrop

Courtesy, Major Charles T. Cahill, Boston.

The flag of the Cross of St. George, the first flag used by the Ancient and Honourable Artillery Company

Courtesy, Major Charles T. Cahill, Boston.

Gov. John Endicott, whose sundial is shown at the head of this chapter, once cut the Cross of St. George from the British flag at Salem, because he held that it was a symbol of Popery. Such fanaticism was not uncommon in the annals of the early Puritans.

Ships

Returning from Indian skirmishes the men and older boys put down their muskets and went back to work. Some joined the cod fishing expeditions to the Maine coast. The abundance of timber made shipbuilding a profitable venture, and the shipyards of New England were soon building ships for the British fleet. The maritime importance of Massachusetts was apparent from the very beginning. As early as 1631, John Winthrop launched his "Blessing of the Bay", a thirty ton bark, at Mistick, now Medford, Mass.

Carver *History of Boston*. 1834.

A 19th Century conception of the
"Blessing of the Bay"

Van der Aa *Voyagien*. 1606-07.

Shipbuilding. 17th Century

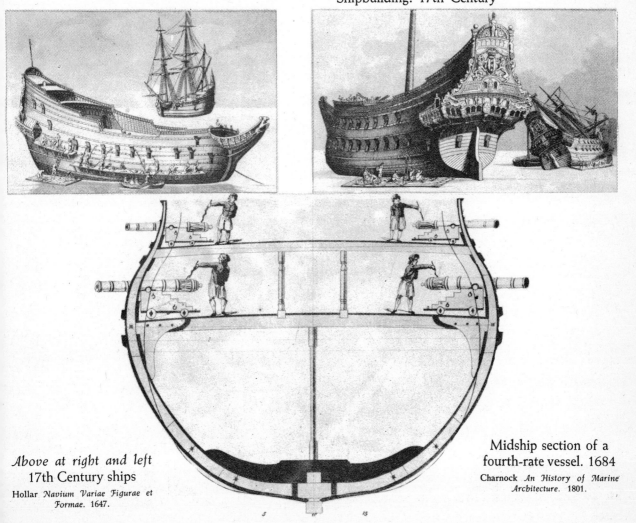

Above at right and left
17th Century ships

Hollar *Navium Variae Figurae et
Formae*. 1647.

Midship section of a
fourth-rate vessel. 1684

Charnock *An History of Marine
Architecture*. 1801.

Excitement

Sometimes a whale was washed ashore and this was an exciting episode. The men cut up the whale and rendered the blubber in large iron kettles placed over fires built on the beach, obtaining valuable whale oil.

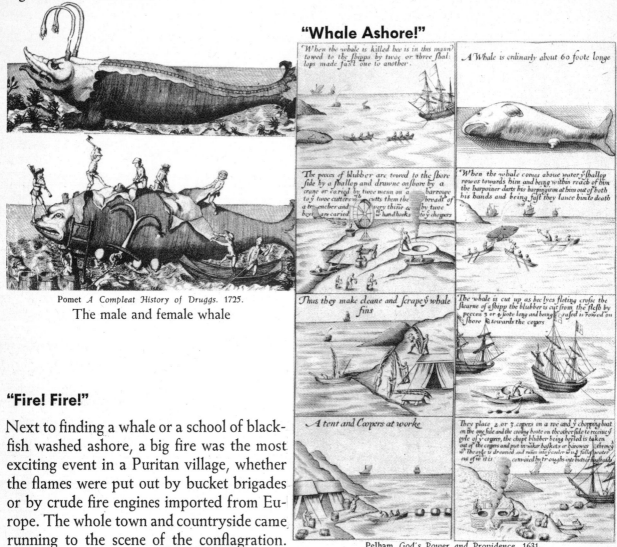

Pomet *A Compleat History of Druggs.* 1725.
The male and female whale

"Whale Ashore!"

Pelham *God's Power and Providence.* 1631.
Whaling scenes. 16th Century

"Fire! Fire!"

Next to finding a whale or a school of black-fish washed ashore, a big fire was the most exciting event in a Puritan village, whether the flames were put out by bucket brigades or by crude fire engines imported from Europe. The whole town and countryside came running to the scene of the conflagration.

Zeising *Theatri Machinarum.* 1607-10.

All Men Were Not Free and Equal

Well-to-do Puritans brought indented servants to America. These men and women were bound by contract to from five to seven years, as a rule, before they were free to own land or to start a business of their own. In the crafts one had to work as an apprentice for seven years before becoming a master craftsman.

Rev. Cotton Mather

Judge Samuel Sewall

Courtesy, Massachusetts Historical Society, Boston.

Mather was a Puritan . . .

The Reverend Cotton Mather, vain and irascible, wrote books, and is remembered.

The Puritan shoemaker, scissors grinder, farmer, furrier, fisherman, carpenter, cooper, and blacksmith are forgotten.

Right Scissors grinder

Garzoni *Allgemeine Schawplatz.* 1641.

Below Shoemakers

Engraving by A. Boose. 1635.

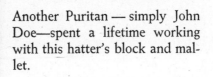

Sewall was a Puritan . . .

Judge Samuel Sewall helped to burn witches, wrote a chatty diary—is remembered.

Another Puritan — simply John Doe—spent a lifetime working with this hatter's block and mallet.

Courtesy, Pocumtuck Valley Memorial Association of Deerfield, Mass.

Spinning and Weaving

We have seen John Doe's family going forth in the morning—the son with the ox cart, the women with their vegetable baskets—the men drilling and fighting, building ships and cutting up a whale. Let us return to them and watch them at other tasks.

Most of the rugs, carpets, linens, and clothes were made by hand in the home. The women carded wool, after it had been washed and dried. The teeth of the wool-cards combed out the matted fibres. These fibres were then put on a spindle and twisted into yarn. This was done by means of the spinning wheel. The spinning was usually done in the warm kitchen. The stool on which the spinner sat was called a linset.

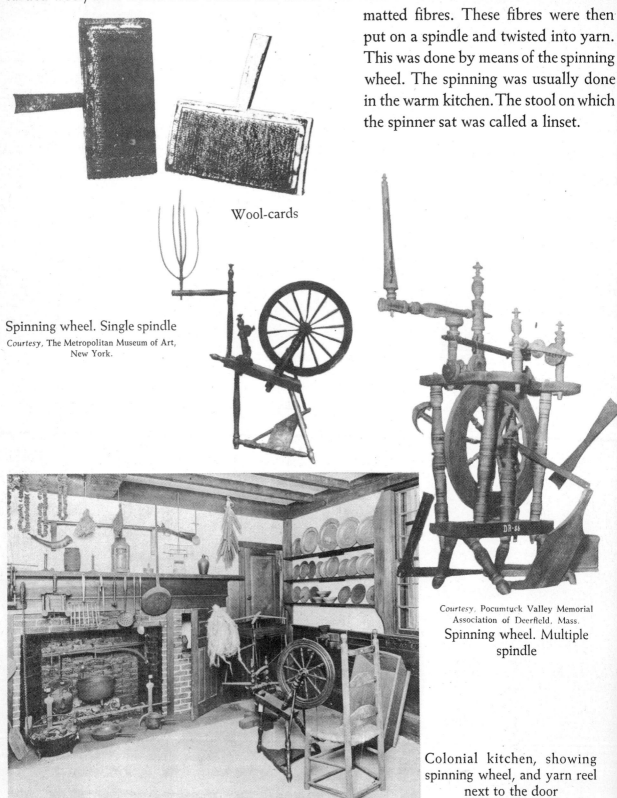

Wool-cards

Spinning wheel. Single spindle
Courtesy, The Metropolitan Museum of Art, New York.

Courtesy, Pocumtuck Valley Memorial Association of Deerfield, Mass.
Spinning wheel. Multiple spindle

Colonial kitchen, showing spinning wheel, and yarn reel next to the door
Courtesy, The Essex Institute, Salem, Mass.

The Birth of New England Industry

The spun yarn was wound into skeins on reels like these found in Connecticut.

Courtesy, The Magazine *Antiques*, New York.

Primitive reel   Turned reel   Clock reel

The skeins of yarn were then ready for the loom.

Colonial loom

Courtesy, Pocumtuck Valley Memorial Association of Deerfield, Mass.

17th Century weavers at work

Cats *Wercken*. 1658.

Flax

Linen was made from flax which was grown in New England from seed. The flax plant was from twenty to forty inches high. The round seed pod contained ten flat seed from which linseed oil was made. When its bright blue flower fell the flax was uprooted and when dry was drawn into thin fibres by the flax brakes and hatchels, the same tools used in dressing hemp.

Flax brake

Drawing hemp fibres through hatchels

Universal Magazine. 1756.

Hemp

Heckling hemp. Note the similarity between the flax brake and the hemp brake in this picture

Universal Magazine. 1756.

To the left Hemp plant

Universal Magazine. 1756.

Rope was made from hemp, and almost every New England town had a rope walk where rope was manufactured.

Twisting rope

Diderot and D'Alembert *Encyclopedie. Recueil des Planches.* 1762-72.

Domestic room, show-
ing reel, spinning
wheel, flax brake,
hatchel, and skeins of
wool and flax

Courtesy, Pocumtuck Valley
Memorial Association,
Greenfield, Mass.

Leather

Hides were tanned with tannic acid, leached
by being passed through a series of vats, the
hair was removed, the hides stretched and
shaved, etc. It took a year to prepare hide
for shoe leather.

Tan bark mill. New Hampshire

Granite Monthly. Sept. 1880

Oak bark used in tanning leather had to be ground with a stone
wheel operated by an ox or horse.

Tanners

Garzoni *Allgemeine Schawplatz.* 1641.

Diderot and D'Alembert *Encyclopedie. Recueil des Planches.* 1762-72.

Tanners at work

Bayberry Candles

The women boiled the berries of the prolific bayberry bush and obtained a wax from which sweet-smelling candles were made.

The Bayberry

Catesby *Natural History of Carolina*. 1754.

Skins and Furs

Beaver skins were not only used for money but were made into hats. Other skins and furs were used for rugs and coats. The raccoon, the bear, the deer and the opossum supplied the Puritans with warm clothing—as well as an article of trade much desired in Europe.

Furrier

Garzoni *Allgemeine Schawplatz*. 1641.

Tools

Below
Cabinet-maker

Garzoni *Allgemeine Schawplatz*. 1641.

Room from West Boxford, Mass. ca. 1675-1704.
Note the furniture

Courtesy, Museum of Fine Arts, Boston.

Furniture

The Puritan was handy with tools of all kinds. He made simple benches, tables and chairs. Sometimes the local turner or cabinet-maker was given the task of making the more elegant pieces of furniture.

Coopers and wheelwrights made barrels and wagon wheels.

Cooper's shave and wheelwright's spoke shave

Courtesy, Bucks County Historical Society, Doylestown, Pa.

At right The Turner. 17th Century

Etching by Jan Joris Van Vliet.

Windmills

There were a number of windmills in early New England. The Puritan took his corn and wheat to the grist mill and had them ground into meal and flour—if there was a good wind blowing.

Mechanism of a windmill

Natrus *Groot Volkomen Moolenboeck.* 1734.

Tide Mills

Other mills were built in inlets where the incoming and outgoing tides turned the wheels that ground the corn. There was never a lack of power. Some of these old tide mills still stand.

Tide mill. Hingham, Mass. Built 1643

Courtesy, *Old-Time New England.* Apr. 1935.

Spice . . .

Tea and coffee were unknown to the Puritans in the early days, but spices were used, and almost every family owned a spice mill. What a pleasant odor filled the kitchen where spice was being ground or bayberry wax was being boiled!

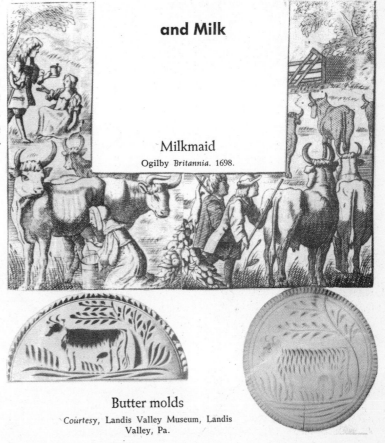

and Milk

Milkmaid

Ogilby Britannia. 1698.

Spice mill

Courtesy, Pocumtuck Valley Memorial Association, of Deerfield, Mass.

Butter molds

Courtesy, Landis Valley Museum, Landis Valley, Pa.

There Were No Professional Doctors

Many Puritans, young and old, were killed by contagious diseases, occupational injuries, and by superstitions and taboos. The minister was usually a quack doctor, and the old women prescribed herb remedies. Midwives were kept busy, and there were few ways to ease the pains of child-birth. The crude surgery of the time was performed without benefit of anesthesia. Scultetus was the advanced authority on surgery during the Puritan Era, and here we see his methods demonstrated.

 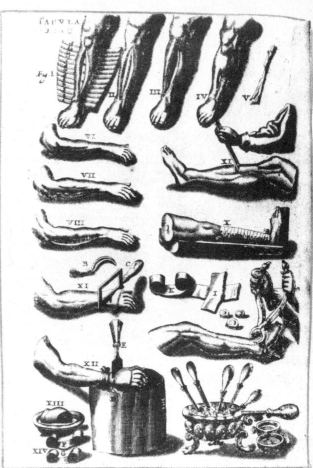

Scultetus *Chyrurgeons Store-House.* 1674.

Ear, nose and throat operations. 17th Century   Amputation. 17th Century

At the beginning of the Eighteenth Century a few barbers came to America. The itinerant barber was frequently a surgeon. In the early days some member of the family usually cut the hair of the men and boys.

To the left
Barber shop. 17th Century
Garzoni *Allgemeine Schawplatz.* 1641.

To the right
Method of cutting hair in Connecticut. A pumpkin shell was placed over the head and the hair was trimmed around the rim of the shell. From this custom came the phrase "pumpkin head"
S. Peters *A General History of Connecticut.* 1829.

The Children

Robert Gibbs

Courtesy, Museum of Fine Arts, Boston.

John Quincy

Puritan children were dressed as we see above. Like all other children they played with stick horses, toys, and dolls.

Elizabethan doll

De Bry *Grandes Voyages.* 1590.

Compare this rag doll with the Elizabethan one (*left*) given to an Indian child by the English settlers at Roanoke Colony. A doll was called a babe or baby in colonial times.

Courtesy, Doll Museum, Wenham, Mass.

The Horn-Book

Schools were few and far between in the Puritan Era. The alphabet was taught to the children by means of a horn-book, made from a piece of wood and a thin covering of horn.

Learning the ABC's

Hornbye's Horn-book. 1622.

Miss Campion, with horn-book. 1661

Tuer *History of the Horn-Book.* 1896.

"Young Obadias, David, Josias, All Were Pious"

The celebrated *New England Primer*, first printed at Boston in 1690, ran through dozens of editions. Generations of Puritan children wore out the pages.

Two pages from *The New England Primer*

Title-page of *Woe to Drunkards.* 1622

The strict teachings of the Puritan clergy were carried over into the schools, and into all walks of life, acting like a wet moral blanket on the natural animal spirits of young men and women. Puritan youth contrived to have fun at the husking bee, the village fair, and the clam bake in spite of this spirit of "Thou shalt not." Frequently they made too many trips to the hard-cider barrel.

The average Puritan was a perfectly normal human being once he was out of earshot of the sermons which consigned him to eternal punishment. Life went on despite the awful pronouncements in *The Day of Doom*, by the lugubrious poet, Michael Wigglesworth of Malden.

The Day of Doom

Pages from *The Day of Doom* (1673 edition), a best-seller of its day

Sunday Dress

Let us go to church with the Puritans. Here we see the women in their Sunday best. They wore masks to protect themselves from wind and sun, and wore chicken skin gloves in bed to keep their hands white.

Hollar *Ornatus Muliebris Anglicanus.* 1640.

Here is Anne Pollard with her Bible.

She no doubt carried a foot stove filled with hot coals, for there was no heat in the church.

Foot stove

Courtesy, Onondaga Historical Association,
Syracuse, N. Y.

Cold Feet

Beds were warmed at night by moving a warming pan, filled with hot coals, between the cold sheets.

Anne Pollard. Portrait painted in 1721 when she was 100 years old

Courtesy, Massachusetts Historical Society, Boston.

Warming pan

Courtesy, Metropolitan Museum of Art, New York.

Man of God

Courtesy, Yale University Art Gallery.

Rev. John Davenport
Portrait by an unknown artist. 1670

They sang from the "The Bay Psalm Book," the first book in English printed in America.

The Puritan minister was dressed like the Reverend John Davenport, of New Haven.

The congregation knew the poem and prayer in front of their Genevan version of the *Bible* by heart.

¶ Of the incomparable Treasure of the holy Scriptures, with a Prayer *for the true vse of the same.*

Esai.12.3 & 49 10.reue.21.16. and 22.17. Ierem.13.15. psal.119.160. reue.2.7.and 22.2.psal.119. 141,144. Iohn 6.35.

HEre is the Spring where waters flow, to quench our heat of sinne: Here is the Tree where trueth doth grow, to leade our liues therein: Here is the Iudge that stints the strife, when mens deuices faile: Here is the Bread that feeds the life, that death can not assaile.

Luke 2.10. The tidings of Saluation deere, comes to our eares from hence:

Ephes.6.16. The fortresse of our Faith is heere, and shield of our defence.

Matth.7.6. Then be not like the hogge, that hath a pearle at his desire,

2.Pet.2.22. And takes more pleasure of the trough and wallowing in the mire.

Matth.6.22. Reade not this booke, in any case, but with a single eye:

Psal.119.27, 73. Reade not, but first desire Gods grace, to vnderstand thereby.

Iude 20. Pray still in faith, with this respect, to fructifie therein,

Psal.119.11. That knowledge may bring this effect, to mortifie thy sinne.

Ioshua 1.8. Psal.1.1,2. Then happy thou, in all thy life, what so to thee befalles:

Psal.94 12,13. Yea, double happy shalt thou be, when God by death thee calles,

O Gracious God and most mercifull Father, which hast vouchsafed vs the rich and precious iewell of thy holy Word, assist vs with thy Spirit, that it may be written in our hearts to our euerlasting comfort, to reforme vs, to renew vs according to thine owne image, to build vs vp, and edifie vs into the perfect building of thy Christ sanctifying and increasing in vs all heauenly vertues. Grant this, O heauenly Father, for Iesus Christes sake. Amen.

Poem and prayer in front matter of the *Holy Bible*. Genevan version. 1606

The First Book . . .

and the Press on Which it was Printed

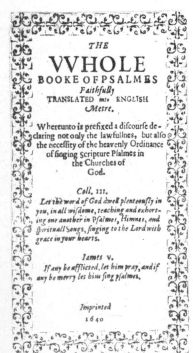

THE
WHOLE
BOOKE OF PSALMES
Faithfully
TRANSLATED into ENGLISH
Metre.

Whereunto is prefixed a discourse declaring not only the lawfulnes, but also the necessity of the heavenly Ordinance of singing scripture Psalmes in the Churches of God.

Coll. III.

Let the word of God dwell plenteously in you, in all wisdome, teaching and exhorting one another in Psalmes, Himnes, and spirituall Songs, singing to the Lord with grace in your hearts.

Iames v.

If any be afflicted, let him pray, and if any be merry let him sing psalmes.

Imprinted
1640

Title-page of "The Bay Psalm Book". Printed by Stephen Daye, Cambridge, Mass. 1640

Printing press used by Stephen Daye in printing "The Bay Psalm Book"

Courtesy, Vermont Historical Society, Montpelier, Vt.

The Meeting House

"Old Ship" Meeting House, Hingham, Mass. 1681

Some of the timbers of the "Old Ship" Meeting House, from a duplication of them in The Metropolitan Museum of Art, New York, showing the influence of the Gothic style in Puritan architecture.

There was nothing democratic in the seating of the Puritan congregation. Each church had its rented pews, and the seating committee allotted pews according to official rank, social prestige, and wealth. Feelings were injured right and left by this unpopular committee.

Building the church roof and steeple

Institut de France. Academie Royale des Sciences. Description des Arts et Metiers. 1761-80.

Art was Satan's Work

The pewter or silver communion service in the Puritan churches was invariably elegant, and this was about the only concession to art these ascetic iconoclasts were willing to make. The Puritan church banned instrumental music, as well as murals, stained glass, tapestries, and statuary. Stark simplicity, within and without the church, was the rule.

Silver communion cup. First church in Boston. Given by John Winthrop

Courtesy, The Trustees, First Church in Boston.

Coin was Scarce

Very little coin was dropped in the collection box, for there was very little in circulation. Most of the members paid their church dues in corn, fruits, furs and skins, and other commodities. The church attic was frequently used as a storehouse.

Massachusetts issued its famous "Pine Tree Shilling" in 1652. The mint was closed in 1683.

The "Pine tree shilling"

Courtesy, Massachusetts Historical Society, Boston, and The Chase National Bank, New York.

Bibles, coins, and other valuables, were often kept in a desk box.

American oak desk box. 1671. Found in Greenfield, Mass.

David Rejoiceth

The Puritans had been brought up on the resounding psalms of Sternhold and Hopkins appended to the Genevan version of the *Bible*.

In the *Book of Exodus* in this same Genevan version they found a justification for the punishment of witches.

"Thou Shalt Not Suffer a Witch to Live"

Thomas Sternhold and John Hopkins
The Whole Book of Psalmes. 1606

Page from the *Book of Exodus* in *The Holy Bible*. Genevan version, 1611, showing the moral precepts which the Puritans followed to the letter. Note paragraph eighteen.

Witch cicatrix. A scar or wound on a tree, which, in healing, took the form of a witch

Courtesy, The Essex Institute, Salem, Mass.

"For Covenanting with the Devil"

Fanatical witch hunts spread throughout New England, culminating in the infamous witchcraft trials in Salem, Massachusetts in 1692, in which eighteen innocent and harmless men and women were hanged, and one old man, Giles Corey, was pressed to death. Judge Samuel Sewall and the Reverend Cotton Mather were leaders in the effort to discover and punish persons suspected of witchcraft. They repented of their parts in this shocking episode at Salem, but repentance came too late to stay the hangman's hand.

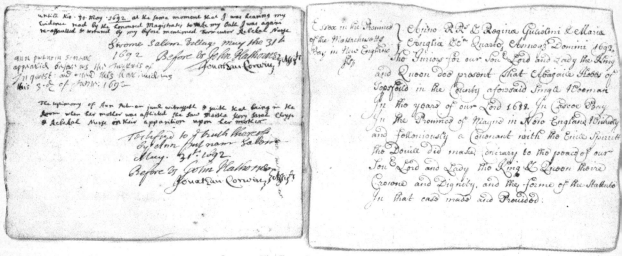

Courtesy, The Essex Institute, Salem, Mass.

Depositions of Mrs. Ann Putnam and Ann Putnam, Jr. before magistrates Hathorne and Corwin, Salem, May 31, 1692

Indictment against Abigail Hobbs of Topsfield "For Covenanting with the Devil." 1692

"I Know Not the Least Thinge of Witchcraft"

Excerpt from the petition of Mary Easty, from the court files of Essex County, Salem, Mass.

Rebecca Nurse, an aged woman of Danvers, Massachusetts was hanged for witchcraft. Her house still stands, and is called the "Witch House."

Rebecca Nurse House, Danvers, Mass. 1678

Courtesy, Society for the Preservation of New England Antiquities, Boston.

In spite of the exhortations of the Puritan divines the "Old Adam" got in his work and fit punishment was meted out by the magistrates.

Public Humiliation

Stocks

Puritans in the Stocks. A satirical drawing by Hogarth to illustrate a scene from Butler's *Hudibras*

Gaol

Old gaol. York, Maine

Courtesy, Historic American Buildings Survey, Washington, D. C.

Gossips and scolds were placed on the ducking stool and ducked in the local pond, or were forced to wear a barbaric contraption known as a brank, or scolding bridle.

Brank, or scolding bridle

Courtesy, New Haven Colony Historical Society, New Haven, Conn.

The Scarlet Letter

One harsh Puritan custom was exemplified by the so-called Scarlet Letter Law, which compelled persons convicted of adultery to wear the letter "A" sewed to their upper garments. Nathaniel Hawthorne's masterpiece *The Scarlet Letter*, was inspired by this law.

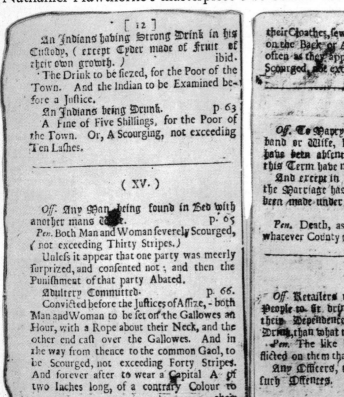
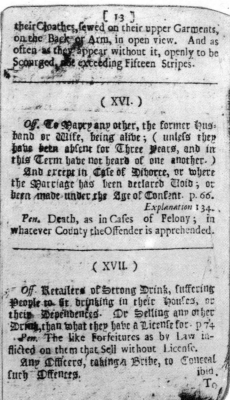

Abstract of the Lawes, showing the Scarlet Lettter clause

Courtesy, Essex Institute, Salem, Mass.

Regicides

These same Puritans were ready to defy their own King by harboring the "Regicides," who had caused Charles I. to be beheaded, and who fled to America from England after the Restoration. The Reverend John Davenport, Governor Leete, and William Jones hid two of the Regicides, William Goffe and Edward Whalley in a cave on West Rock near New Haven, Conn.

Judges Cave

Whalley, Goffe, Dixwell

Map showing Dixwell's grave. John Dixwell, one of the Regicides, lived in New Haven under the name of Mr. Davids and is buried in the town green

Stiles *A History of Three of the Judges of King Charles I.* 1794.

"Go Back to England! Leave Us Alone!"

The Puritans wanted to govern themselves without too much interference from the Royal Governors sent over from England. One of the more unpopular governors was Sir Edmond Andros. Church doors were used as bulletin boards and one day in 1689 this broadside was seen posted on church doors and other public places.

Governor Andros had infuriated the people of Connecticut in 1687 by appearing in Hartford and demanding that the Connecticut Charter of 1662 be surrendered to him. To avoid this ignominy the charter was hidden in an old oak tree, known thereafter as the "Charter Oak." It fell to the ground Aug. 21, 1856.

Warning to Gov. Andros
Apr. 18, 1689

AT THE TOWN-HOUSE in

BOSTON:

April 18th 1689

SIR,

OUr Selves as well as many others the Inhabitants of this Town and Places adjacent, being surprized with the Peoples sudden taking to Arms, in the first motion whereof we were wholly ignorant, are driven by the present Exigence and Necessity to acquaint your *Excellency*, that for the Quieting and Security of the People Inhabiting this Countrey from the imminent Dangers they many wayes lie open, and are exposed unto, and for your own Safety; We judge it necessary that you forthwith Surrender, and Deliver up the Government and Fortifications to be Preserved, to be Disposed according to Order and Direction from the Crown of *England*, which is suddenly expected may Arrive, Promising all Security from violence to your Self, or any other of your Gentlemen and Souldiers in Person or Estate: or else we are assured they will endeavour the taking of the Fortifications by Storm, if any opposition be made.

To *Sr. Edmond Andros* Knight.

William Stoughton.	Simon Bradstreet.	Wait Winthrop.
Thomas Danforth.	John Richards.	Samuel Shrimpton.
	Elisha Cook.	William Brown.
	Isaac Addington,	Barthol. Gidney.
	John Foster·	
	Peter Sergeant.	
	David Waterhouse.	
	Adam Winthrop.	
	John Nelson.	

Boston Printed by *Samuel Green.* 1639.

The Connecticut Charter. 1662

Barber *Connecticut Historical Collection.* 1838.
The Charter Oak as it appeared in 1836

Old print of the "Charter Oak" made shortly after it fell in 1856

Communications and Travel

Hartford was the midway station in the first postal route in New England in 1672. Governor Lovelace of New York (when the English took New Amsterdam from the Dutch in 1664 they changed the name to New York in honor of the Duke of York), wrote to Governor Winthrop of Connecticut explaining the new postal route from New York to Boston. Part of this route is still known as the Boston Post Road.

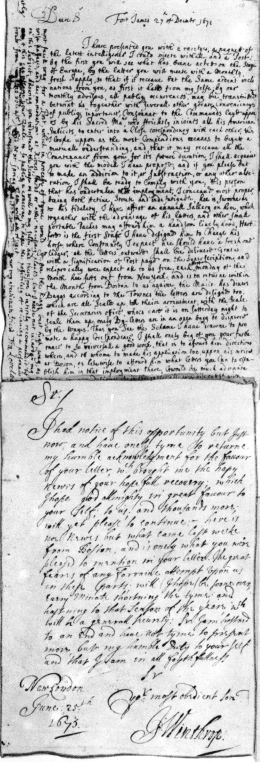

How letters were folded and sealed

Courtesy, Harvard University Library.

Left Letter dated Dec. 27, 1672, from Gov. Lovelace of New York to Gov. Winthrop of Connecticut

Stokes Iconography of Manhattan Island.

Letters like this were carried in the postman's pouch. They were written with a goose quill, and blotted with black sand, which was kept in a receptacle called a standish.

Letter by John Winthrop the Younger, Governor of Connecticut

Courtesy, Harvard University Library.

62   THE JOURNAL OF

we arrived, and Had a Dinner of Fryed Venison, very savoury. Landlady wanting some pepper in the seasoning, bid the Girl hand her the spice in the little *Gay* cupp on yᵉ shelfe. From hence we Hasted towards Rye, walking and Leading our Horses neer a mile together, up a prodigios high Hill; and so Riding till about nine at night, and there arrived and took up our Lodgings at an ordinary, wᵗʰ a French family kept. Here being very hungry, I desired a fricasee wᶜʰ the Frenchman undertakeing, managed so contrary to my notion of Cookery, that I hastned to Bed superless; And being shewd the way up a pair of stairs wᶜʰ had such a narrow passage that I had almost stopt by the Bulk of my Body, But arriving at my apartment found it to be a little Lento Chamber furnisht amongst other Rubbish with a High Bedd and a Low one, a Long Table, a Bench and a Bottomless chair,— Little Miss went to scratch up my Kennell wᶜʰ Russeled as if shee'd bin in the Barn amongst the Husks, and supose such was the contents of the tickin — nevertheles being exceeding weary, down I laid my poor Carkes (never more tired)

MADAM KNIGHT   63

and found my Covering as scanty as my Bed was hard. Annon I heard another Russelling noise in Yᵉ Room—called to know the matter —Little miss said shee was making a bed for the men; who, when they were in Bed, complained their leggs lay out of it by reason of its shortness—nay poor bones complained bitterly not being used to such Lodgings, and so did the man who was with us; and poor I made but one Grone, which was from the time I went to bed to the time I Riss, which was about three in the morning, Setting up by the Fire till Light, and having discharged our ordinary wᶜʰ was as dear as if we had had far Better fare — we took our leave of Monsier and about seven in the morn come to New Rochell a french town, where we had a good Breakfast. And in the strength

Page from the journal of Sarah Kemble Knight (1704). Madam Knight made the trip from Boston to New York in 1704, and her record of the experience is an American travel classic.

New England Charm . . .

The stern, sometimes fanatical, words and deeds of the Puritans may blind us to their integrity, sincerity, and simplicity. The old houses they lived in, now mellowed by time, have a charm that increases with the years. The men and women who built houses like these have left us a precious heritage.

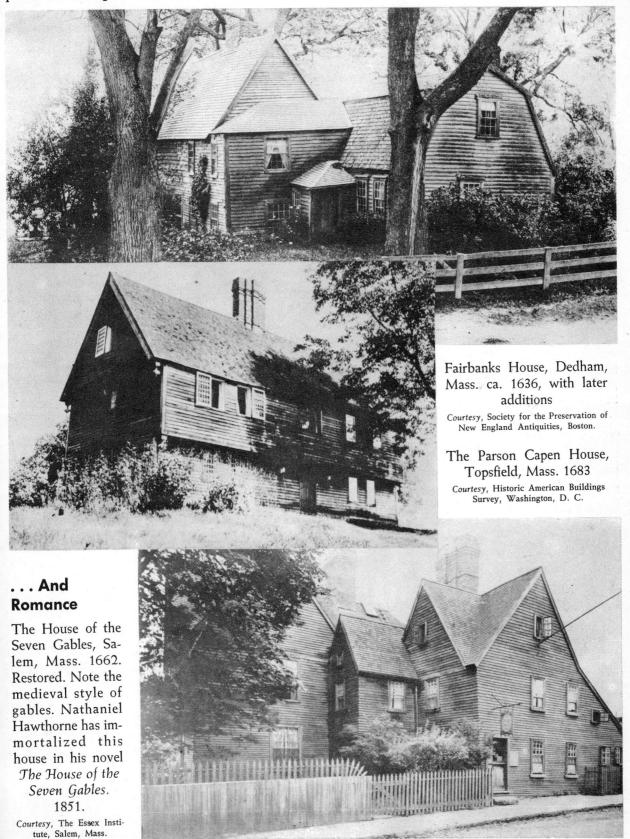

Fairbanks House, Dedham, Mass. ca. 1636, with later additions

Courtesy, Society for the Preservation of New England Antiquities, Boston.

The Parson Capen House, Topsfield, Mass. 1683

Courtesy, Historic American Buildings Survey, Washington, D. C.

. . . And Romance

The House of the Seven Gables, Salem, Mass. 1662. Restored. Note the medieval style of gables. Nathaniel Hawthorne has immortalized this house in his novel *The House of the Seven Gables.* 1851.

Courtesy, The Essex Institute, Salem, Mass.

They Were Naïve in Art . . .

Gravestone. Charter Street Burying
Ground, Salem, Mass.

Courtesy, The Essex Institute, Salem, Mass.

Province House,
Boston. ca. 1676

Drake *Old Landmarks
of Boston.* 1873.

Upper left
Shem Drowne's weathervane, ca. 1720,
which once adorned Province House in
Boston. Another of Drowne's weather-
vanes, in the form of a grasshopper, may
still be seen on Faneuil Hall, Boston

Courtesy, Massachusetts Historical Society, Boston.

But They Knew How to Lay Out a Town

Model of Old Quinabaug Village, Sturbridge,
Mass., a restoration of a typical New
England village

Courtesy, Old Quinabaug Village, Sturbridge, Mass.

They Founded at Boston and Cambridge a Center of American Culture

In 1636, at New Towne, now Cambridge, Massachusetts, they founded
Harvard College.

Right Harvard Hall, built 1672-82,
Stoughton Hall, 1698-1700, and
Massachusetts Hall, 1718-20

Engraving by William Burgis. 1726.

Puritan Poet

Anne Bradstreet, wife of Governor Simon Bradstreet, was New England's first poet. Her volume of poetry, *The Tenth Muse*, was published in 1650.

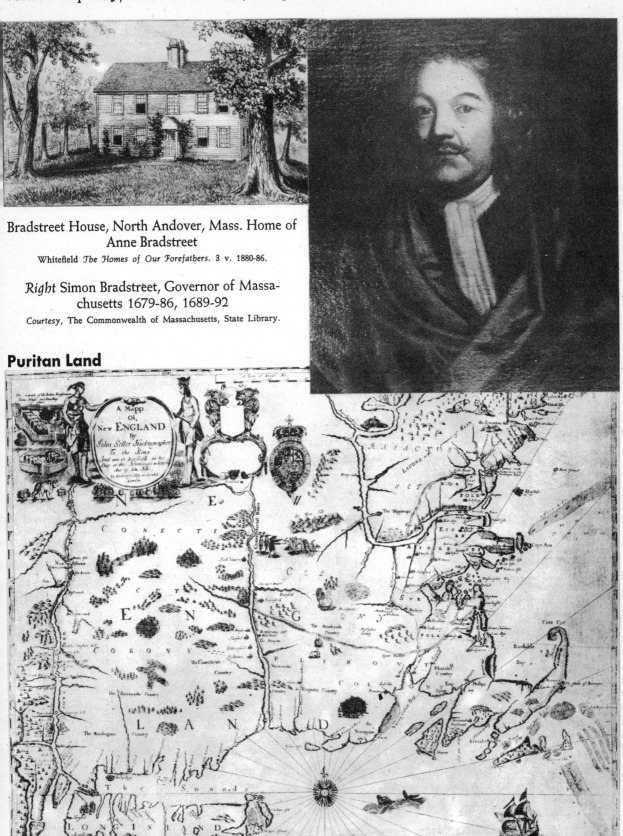

Bradstreet House, North Andover, Mass. Home of Anne Bradstreet

Whitefield *The Homes of Our Forefathers.* 3 v. 1880-86.

Right Simon Bradstreet, Governor of Massachusetts 1679-86, 1689-92

Courtesy, The Commonwealth of Massachusetts, State Library.

Puritan Land

John Seller *Atlas Maritimus.* 1675.

Map of New England

4

THE HUDSON AND THE DELAWARE

Henry Hudson . . .

In 1609 Henry Hudson, an English navigator in the employ of the Dutch, sailed between the wooded palisades of a picturesque river in America in search of the Northwest Passage to India. His yacht, or vlie-boat, a vessel of eighty tons burden called the *Half Moon*, finally dropped anchor at a spot which is now Albany, New York. Hudson's name was given to the river.

Courtesy, The New-York Historical Society, New York.

Model of the Half Moon

Pontanus *Rerum et Urbis Amstelodamensium Historia.* 1611.

Dutch ships of Henry Hudson's day

And His Beautiful River

Aquatint view of the
Hudson River. 1802

Courtesy, Stokes Collection,
The New York Public Library.

The Shot That Lost An Empire

In this same year of 1609, Champlain, the Frenchman, pushing south from the St. Lawrence country, met and massacred a body of Iroquois Indians at the present site of Fort Ticonderoga. Champlain dropped the Iroquois chief with a single shot from his arquebus. The Indians had never heard the sound of a gun before, and this unequal contest aroused their undying hatred, a fact which was to play a crucial part in the future of America. While Champlain was making implacable enemies for the French, Henry Hudson, a few miles to the southwest, was making friends for the Dutch.

Champlain *Voyages*. 1613.

The Dutch West India Company

Courtesy, Vinkhuizen Collection, The New York Public Library.

French soldier. 1608

Hudson's report on the beauties of the Hudson River scenery did not impress the merchants of Amsterdam nearly so much as the beaver skins he showed them. Furs were the fashion in Europe, and American pelts were in great demand. The Dutch West India Company was formally chartered in 1621 to exploit the New World.

Dapper *Historische Beschryvinghe van Amsterdam*. 1663.

The West India House. Amsterdam

The West India Company was backed by the wealth and power of Holland. Its Director-General in New Amsterdam, as the little Dutch settlement on the tip of Manhattan Island was called, was a person of considerable importance. Manhattan Island had been purchased from the Indians by Peter Minuit in 1626 for the equivalent of twenty-four dollars. A few Dutch settlers had lived on the island from 1613-14.

Early Views of New Amsterdam

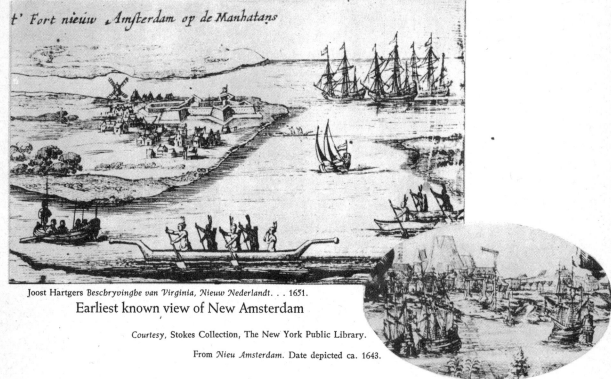

t' Fort nieuw Amsterdam op de Manhatans

Joost Hartgers *Beschryvinghe van Virginia, Nieuw Nederlandt*. . . 1651.

Earliest known view of New Amsterdam

Courtesy, Stokes Collection, The New York Public Library.

From *Nieu Amsterdam*. Date depicted ca. 1643.

Here are later views of New Amsterdam, in one of which the fur trade is symbolized.

Carolus Allard *Orbis Habitabilis*. 1700-10.

"Old Wooden Leg"

Peter Stuyvesant arrived in New Amsterdam with his famous wooden leg in 1646, and things began to hum. It was his task as Director-General to restore the prestige of the Dutch West India Company, which had been lowered by the weak administration of Wouter Van Twiller.

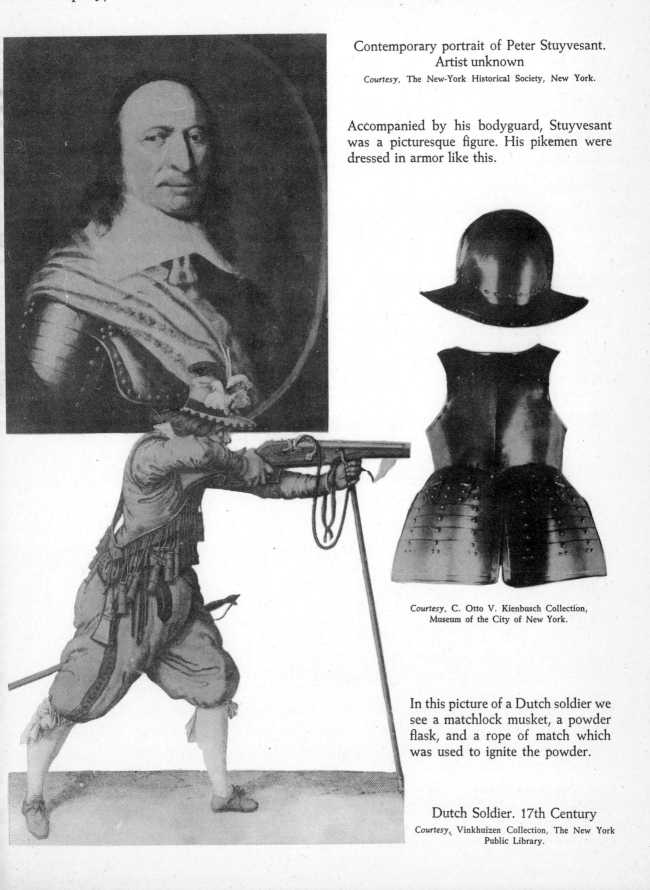

Contemporary portrait of Peter Stuyvesant. Artist unknown

Courtesy, The New-York Historical Society, New York.

Accompanied by his bodyguard, Stuyvesant was a picturesque figure. His pikemen were dressed in armor like this.

Courtesy, C. Otto V. Kienbusch Collection, Museum of the City of New York.

In this picture of a Dutch soldier we see a matchlock musket, a powder flask, and a rope of match which was used to ignite the powder.

Dutch Soldier. 17th Century

Courtesy, Vinkhuizen Collection, The New York Public Library.

When Broadway Was Young

We know what New Amsterdam looked like in 1660 thanks to the Castello Plan, and a careful topographical model based upon it. Let us stroll through its quaint streets.

Courtesy, Museum of the City of New York.

Model of New Amsterdam. Based on the Castello Plan. 1660

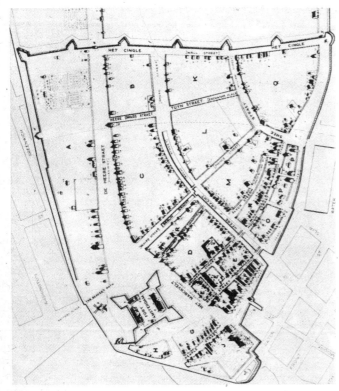

Courtesy, Museum of the City of New York.

At left Key to the above model

From the fort in the foreground we go up De Heere Straet or Breede Wegh (Broadway) until we come to the city limits at Het Cingle (Wall Street). In Section A, to our left are the gardens of the Dutch West India Company. In Section B, across from the gardens, is Peter Stuyvesant's orchard. In Section E, is the storehouse of the Company, with quarters for employees. Jacob Steendam, the poet, lived at no. 2 in Section G. Peter Stuyvesant's house is at no. 1 in Section J. The City Hall or Stadthuys is at nos. 8-9 in Section O. Other houses in this picture have been identified by I. N. Phelps Stokes in his *Iconography of Manhattan Island.*

That New Amsterdam was a small-scale imitation of Old Amsterdam in the Mother Country, this map will show.

Left A small section of a map of Amsterdam, Holland

Braun *Civitates Orbis Terrarum.* 1618.

New Amsterdam had a fine harbor, and under Peter Stuyvesant its wharfs were busy. Stuyvesant established a weigh house and market, which no longer exist, but this picture (*below*) of the weigh house in Amsterdam may suggest a parallel.

Pontanus *Rerum et Urbis Amstelodamensium Historia.* 1611.

Stadthuys

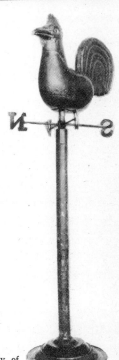

Left Stadthuys. New Amsterdam, in 1679

Valentine's Manual.

This weathervane was once on the Stadthuys. Washington Irving acquired it and placed it on his house at "Sunnyside". He gave it to the Saint Nicholas Society of New York in 1848.

Weathervane

Courtesy, The Saint Nicholas Society of New York, New York City.

Official business was transacted at the Government House, or Stadthuys.

Dutch Houses

The Dutch style of architecture was distinct from the English. Built mostly of brick and stone their houses were high and narrow, with steep, stair-step gables. The windows were protected by swinging wooden shutters or storm windows. Here are a few of the old houses in New Amsterdam.

Valentine's Manual. 1847.

Old Dutch House. Broad
Street. 1698

Valentine's Manual. 1853.

Dutch Cottage. Beaver Street. 1679

Note the Dutch door was made in two sections, the top part could be swung open independently of the lower part.

Valentine's Manual. 1847.

Old Dutch House. Pearl
Street. 1626. Rebuilt 1697

Valentine's Manual. 1858.

The Vechte-Cortelyou House at Gowanus (now in Brooklyn). 1699

At right Another view of the
Vechte-Cortelyou House.
Painting by an unknown
artist

Courtesy, The New-York Historical
Society, New York.

Farms

A few blocks from Fort Amsterdam one came to the farms or "boweries" of the Dutch squires, and beyond the clearings were the primeval woods.

Bogardus farm looking southwards towards New Amsterdam. ca. 1679

Note the windmills in the picture. Note also the similarity between the above view and this scene below, which shows the country around Amsterdam, Holland.

Van der Heide *Bescbryving . . . Slang-Brand-Spuiten . . .* 1690.
Dutch landscape

These trees in Central Park are the only remnants of a mighty forest that once covered Manhattan Island.

Windmills

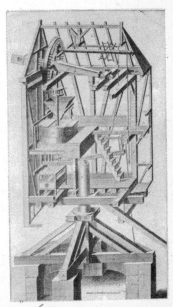

Right Mechanism of a windmill

Diderot and D'Alembert *Encyclopedie. Recueil des Planches.* 1762-72.

Where The Dutch Went . . .

Probably many of the tools, utensils, articles of dress, furniture, etc., shown in these animated scenes from a contemporary Dutch book by a popular author, could be duplicated in New Amsterdam.

Tailor   Dentist   Barber

. . . There Was Holland

Blacksmith   Farmer   The market

Domestic scene   Milady's toilet   Gentleman being undressed for bed

Illustrations from Cats *Wercken.* 1658.

Pots and Pans

Cats
Wercken. 1658.

Cats *Wercken.* 1658.

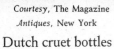

Courtesy, The Magazine
Antiques, New York

Dutch cruet bottles

Let No One Starve

Packing meat. Allegorical piece by Peter Breughel the Elder

Silver

Left Silver cordial cup by Gerrit Onkelbag

Courtesy, The Mabel Brady Garvan Collection, Yale University Art Gallery.

Right Silver caudle cup by Gerrit Onkelbag

Courtesy, Museum of the City of New York.

The Eternal Feminine

Dutch merchant's wife

Cats *Wercken*. 1658.

At right   Old print in
Musée du Costume,
Paris

Courtesy, The New-York Historical Society,
New York.
Linen press

Linen press
Courtesy, Brooklyn Museum, Brooklyn, N. Y.

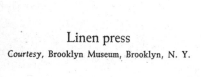

Courtesy, French & Company, Inc., New York.
Dutch cushion cover

Dutch Interiors

Let us step inside some of the old houses of New Netherland.

Courtesy, Museum of the City of New York.
New Amsterdam setting

At right Dutch cabinet in walnut with
pewter inlay. ca. 1680
Courtesy, Edward Garratt, Inc., New York.

Delftware plate. 17th Century
Courtesy, Rijks Museum, Amsterdam.

Courtesy, Brooklyn Museum, Brooklyn, N. Y.
Dining room of Schenck House,
Canarsie Park, Brooklyn

Schenck House

Dutch interiors. New Amsterdam. 17th Century.

From an exhibition in the Parish Hall of St. Mark's in-the-Bouwerie, New York City, March, 1943

The later Dutch influence is shown in this reconstructed room in the American wing of the Metropolitan Museum of Art in New York. The fireplace is from the Benjamin Hasbrouck House, High Falls, N. Y., and the Dutch door is from the Stephen Thors House, New Hackensack, N. Y.

Every house had its mouse
Cats *Wercken*. 1658.

Courtesy, New York Museum of Science and Industry.

Flemish lamp. The lower spout caught any unburned fat or oil

At right Dutch chandelier. 17th Century

Courtesy, French and Company, Inc., New York.

Courtesy, The New York Historical Society, New York.

Kas made in Holland. 17th Century. It belonged to James Beekman (1732-1807) of New York

Amusements

In the summer the men enjoyed bowling on the green. A section of lower Manhattan is still called Bowling Green.

Braun *Civitates Orbis Terrarum*. 1618.

The happiest event in New Amsterdam was the annual kermiss, or fair. No picture of the New Amsterdam kermiss exists, but contemporary Dutch paintings will give a fair idea of their joyous nature.

Kermiss of St. George. By Peter Breughel the Elder

Kermiss of Hoboken, in Holland. By Peter Breughel the Elder

Dutch Children

Children's games, the heritage of centuries of folkways, were the same in New Netherland as they were in Holland.

Children at play. By Peter Breughel the Elder

Cats *Wercken.* 1658.

Dutch toys. Probably New York
Courtesy, Metropolitan Museum of Art, New York.

Cats *Wercken.* 1658.
The game of marbles

Toyland

Courtesy, Mr. Joseph B. Brenauer, New York·
and the Museum of the City of New York.

Child's kas

At right Dutch boy. Primitive
painting by unknown artist.
New Amsterdam.

Courtesy, Mr. Harry Stone, New York.

Cats *Wercken.* 1658.

Toy shop

At right The manufacture of
wooden shoes. The children of
New Amsterdam wore wooden
shoes

Diderot and D'Alembert *Encyclopedie.*

Fire! . . .

The people of New Amsterdam ran into the streets to witness the spectacle of a fire.

Van der Heide *Beschryving . . .*
Slang-Brand-Spuiten . . . 1690.

Down at the busy wharves were ships and sailors.

. . . And Water

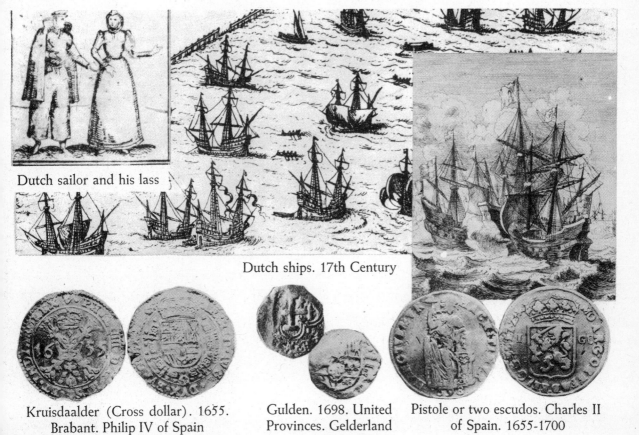

Dutch sailor and his lass

Dutch ships. 17th Century

Kruisdaalder (Cross dollar). 1655.
Brabant. Philip IV of Spain

Gulden. 1698. United
Provinces. Gelderland
and Zeeland

Pistole or two escudos. Charles II
of Spain. 1655-1700

Courtesy, The American Numismatic Society, New York.

Dutch Faces

Let us look at some typical Dutch faces as recorded by the early painters in New York.

Above Barent Rynders, merchant. Portrait by an unknown artist

Courtesy, The New-York Historical Society, New York.

To the right Peter Schuyler (1657-1724), the first mayor of Albany. He was a friend of the Iroquois Indians, who called him "Quidor". This portrait hangs in the mayor's office at Albany, N. Y.

Below Mrs. Gerret Duyckinck. Portrait by Gerret Duyckinck. The Duyckincks were married in 1683

Above Mrs. Barent Rynders. Portrait by an unknown artist. She was Hester Leisler, daughter of Jacob Leisler, who made himself Governor of New York in 1689, and was hanged for high treason in 1691, only to receive posthumous vindication

Courtesy, The New-York Historical Society, New York.

Below DePeyster Boy. One of the children of Abraham De Peyster, Jr.
Portrait by an unknown artist

Courtesy, The New-York Historical Society, New York.

Fort Orange

For many years the Dutch settlement at Fort Orange (Albany, New York) was fully as important as New Amsterdam. It was the center of the fur trade, and was near the great Mohawk Trail, gateway to the rich lands of the Five Nations. Here is a layout of Fort Orange.

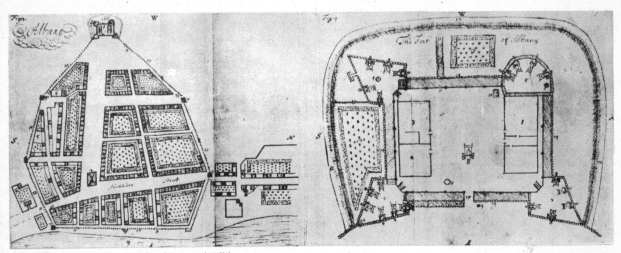

John Miller *New York Considered and Improved.* 1695.

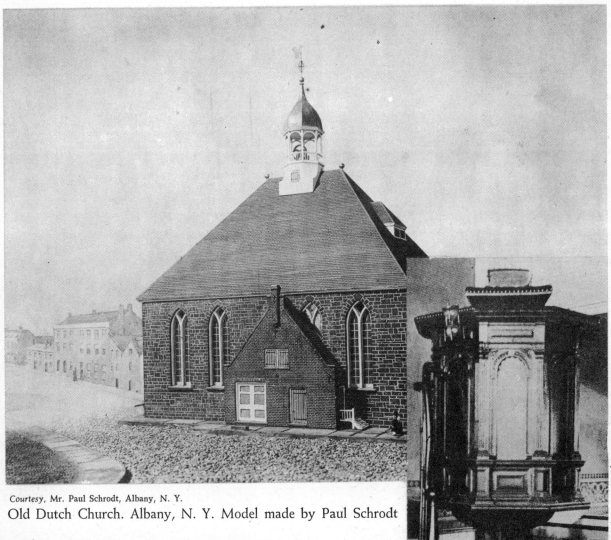

Courtesy, Mr. Paul Schrodt, Albany, N. Y.

Old Dutch Church. Albany, N. Y. Model made by Paul Schrodt

To the right Pulpit shipped from Holland, April, 1657, and placed in the Dutch Church at Fort Orange

Courtesy, Williams Press, Inc., Albany, N. Y.

Patroon

At Fort Orange lived the wealthy patroon Kiliaen Van Rensselaer. The Dutch West India Company granted large tracts of land and feudal privileges to patroons.

Left Portrait of Kiliaen Van Rensselaer

Courtesy, The New-York Historical Society, New York.

Below Manor of Rensselaerswyck. 1660

Courtesy, Holland Society, New York City.

Above Cannon of Rensselaerswyck. It was made in 1630

Courtesy, Williams Press, Inc., Albany, N. Y.

Left Title-page of the Dutch West India Company's publication setting forth the rights and privileges of patroons

Esopus

Esopus, later Kingston, N. Y., was an important settlement between Fort Orange and New Amsterdam.

Drawing by B. Eastman. Schoolcraft *Indian Tribes*. Pt. III. 1853.   Esopus Landing. Hudson River

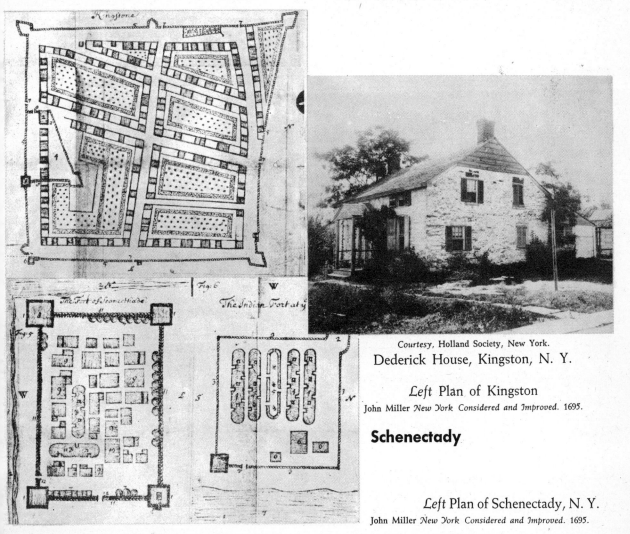

Courtesy, Holland Society, New York.

Dederick House, Kingston, N. Y.

Left Plan of Kingston

John Miller *New York Considered and Improved*. 1695.

Schenectady

Left Plan of Schenectady, N. Y.

John Miller *New York Considered and Improved*. 1695.

Shawangunk

Courtesy, The Holland Society, New York.

Old Dutch Church at Shawangunk, N. Y.

Staten Island

Billop House. Staten Island, N. Y.
Courtesy, American Scenic and Historic Preservation Society.

Tarrytown

Below Sleepy Hollow Church.
Tarrytown, N. Y.
Barber and Howe *Historical Collections in the State of New York. 1842.*

Courtesy, American Scenic and Historic Preservation Society.
Sleepy Hollow Church. Tarrytown, N. Y.
1699

Jamaica

Left Old Stone Church. Jamaica, L. I. 1699

Right First Reformed Church (Dutch), Jamaica, L. I. 1716. At the right are old-fashioned hay scales

Onderdonk *History of the First Reformed Dutch Church, Jamaica, L. I. 1884.*

Dutch Into English

In 1664 New Netherland was surrendered to the English. New Amsterdam and Fort Orange, henceforth known as New York and Albany, retained their Dutch character for many years but the political power of the Dutch was broken, a power that had opened up the Hudson River Valley, challenged the English in Connecticut and Long Island, and which had, under domineering Peter Stuyvesant, successfully supplanted the Swedes on the Delaware.

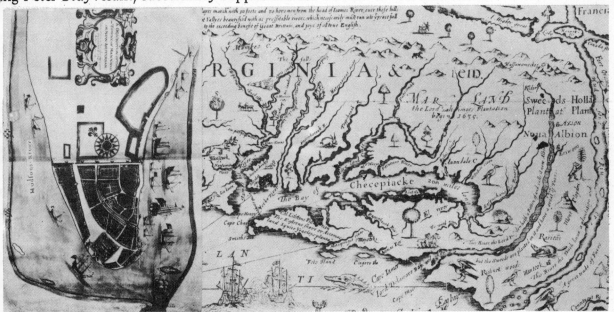

Crown Collection in the British Museum.
New Amsterdam shortly before it was taken over by the English

From Virginia Farrer's map showing the Hudson and Delaware settlements. 1651

And on the Delaware New Amstel became Newcastle.

Courtesy, Wilmington Institute Free Library.
Old Dutch House. New Amstel (Newcastle, Del.)

Courtesy, Delaware Society for the Preservation of Antiques.
Tile House. New Amstel (Newcastle, Del.)

Cosmopolis

Always of a mixed population New Amsterdam, after it became New York, took on a cosmopolitan aspect with the influx of the English, Jews, Negroes from Africa, friendly Indians, swashbuckling pirates from Madagascar, and exiled Huguenots from France, and many others. Eighteen languages could be heard in the streets. Religious tolerance and commercial activity was making New York a thriving port.

Pirates and Pirate Gold

Left John Morgan, pirate

Right Francois Lolonois, pirate

Exquemeling *Bucaniers of America.* 1684.

Pirate coins. *Left* Algiers. Muhammad IV. 1648-1687 A. D. *Right* Morroco Filali Sherifs Ismail. 1672-1727 A. D. Coin struck at Fez and dated 1092 A. H.; i. e., 1681 A. D.

Courtesy, The American Numismatic Society, New York.

Into New York came trade goods from regions as widely separated as Africa and Spanish America.

Slave Trader

Thomas Gage *Nouvelle Relation.* 1720.

The fair of Porto Bello

Dapper *Umstandliche und eigentliche beschreibung von Africa.* 1670.

Quakers

There were a number of Quakers in New York and Long Island. Some of them settled at Flushing, Long Island, and the Quaker leader George Fox visited them shortly after William Penn founded Pennsylvania.

J. Milbert *A Series of Picturesque Views in North America.* 1825.

View of Flushing, Long Island, showing the Bowne House, built in 1661

George Fox

J. Milbert *A Series of Picturesque Views in North America.* 1825.

George Fox preaching to the Quakers of Flushing, Long Island

The Swedes on the Delaware

Mention has already been made of the Swedes. Their dream of empire was short-lived, but they added a memorable chapter to American history. Gustavus Adolphus, King of Sweden, died before his plans for American colonization were carried out, but his chancellor, Axel Oxenstierna, continued them.

Courtesy, Nordiska Museet, Stockholm.

Globe engraved by William Jansson, Amsterdam, and dedicated to Gustavus Adolphus, 1617

Engravings by Thomas C. Holm.

Indians in New Sweden

Peter Minuit, the Dutch navigator, was employed by the Swedes to take the first contingent of Swedish and Finnish settlers to America in the ships *Kalmar Nyckel* and *Vogel Grip*. He sailed in 1637 and arrived at the present site of Wilmington, Del., in 1638. At this spot the Swedes built Fort Christina.

Courtesy, Wilmington Institute Free Library.

Swedish house. Wilmington, Del.

Courtesy, Colonial Society of New York.

Spot where the Swedes landed in Delaware. Etching by Robert Shaw

Johan Printz

The Colony took root, and the arrival of Governor Johan Printz in 1643 was the beginning of expansion, for Printz meant to challenge Dutch supremacy in the region of the Delaware.

Left Portrait of Johan Printz

Courtesy, American Swedish Historical Museum, Philadelphia.

Below Silver mug used by Johan Printz in America

Courtesy, American Swedish Historical Museum, Philadelphia.

Printz brought along a fully equipped bodyguard and many servants and built a palace called Printzhof on Tinicum Island, some miles above Fort Christina.

Courtesy, The American-Swedish News Exchange, Inc., New York.

Swedish helmet. 17th Century. Kungl. Livrust-kammaren, Stockholm

Left Swedish block house. Naaman's, Del. ca. 1654

Courtesy, The Wilmington Institute Free Library, Wilmington, Del.

Below Swedish muskets. 17th Century. Kungl. Livrustkammaren, Stockholm

Courtesy, The American-Swedish News Exchange, Inc., New York.

The Swedes, among whom were a number of Finns, brought their costume, their furniture, and their style of architecture to America. The Finnish log cabin was soon adapted in the region of the Delaware. There is evidence to support the claim that Brandywine Creek in Delaware and Pennsylvania was named for Andrew Brandwyn, a Finn who lived on its banks.

Acerbi Travels Through Sweden. 1802.

Finns singing. The Finns held hands while singing. They achieved a closer harmony as a result

A Collection of the Dresses of Different Nations. 1757-1772.

Swedish woman. 17th Century

Finnish Bath

The Finns poured water over heated stones, thus producing a great quantity of steam. They beat their bodies with twigs to stimulate circulation. Afterwards they rolled in the snow to close their pores. Some American Indians followed a similar practice.

Right Finnish bath
Acerbi Travels Through Sweden. 1802.

Left Three-legged stool. Blekinge, Sweden

Courtesy, The American-Swedish News Exchange, Inc., New York.

n Wooden Things

The Swedes brought their clothing and table linens in chests like these. Wood was their favorite art medium, and they were born carpenters and wood workers.

Swedish chests. 17th Century
Courtesy, Nordiska Museet, Stockholm.

They Found Delight

Photo by Philip B. Wallace.
Courtesy, American Swedish Historical Museum, Philadelphia:
Wooden milk pail

Courtesy, American Swedish Historical Museum, Philadelphia, Pa.
Swedish chest. Brought to Delaware by the Sinnickson family. 17th Century

Courtesy, Nordiska Museet, Stockholm.
Swedish clothes chest. 1670

They Drank

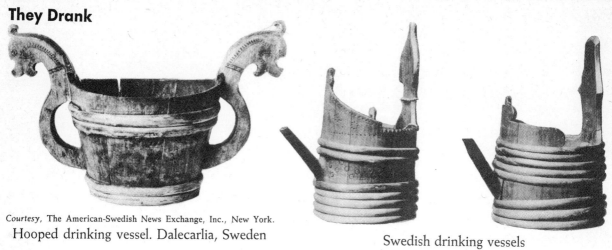

Courtesy, The American-Swedish News Exchange, Inc., New York.
Hooped drinking vessel. Dalecarlia, Sweden

Swedish drinking vessels

They Sat . . .

And Rocked the Cradle

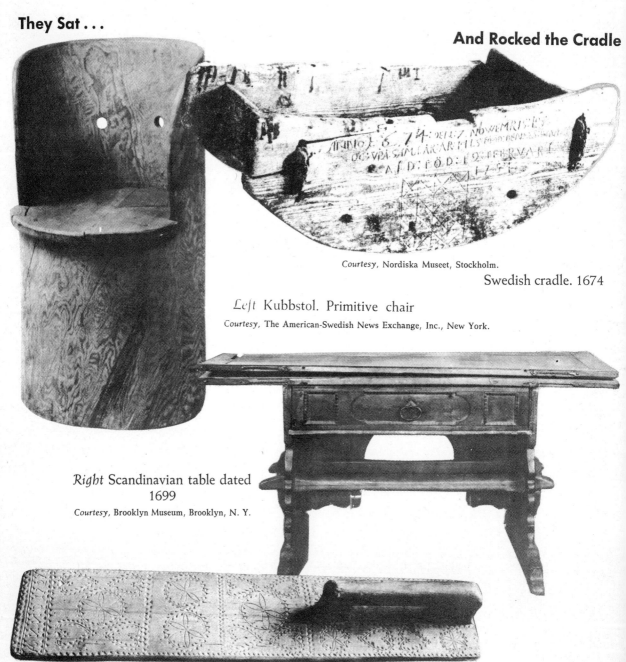

Courtesy, Nordiska Museet, Stockholm.

Swedish cradle. 1674

Left Kubbstol. Primitive chair
Courtesy, The American-Swedish News Exchange, Inc., New York.

Right Scandinavian table dated
1699
Courtesy, Brooklyn Museum, Brooklyn, N. Y.

Courtesy, American Swedish Historical Society Museum, Philadelphia.   Photo by Philip A. Wallace.
Swedish mangle. A device for smoothing cloth

They Lived in Rooms Like These

Courtesy, Nordiska Museet, Stockholm.

Room from Dalarna, Sweden

Right Built-in bed

Courtesy, Nordiska Museet, Stockholm.

Courtesy, American Swedish Historical Museum, Philadelphia.

Reconstructed interior, showing a typical bunk

Clocks

Courtesy, The American-Swedish News Exchange, Inc., New York.

Swedish room showing a typical tall clock

Swedish clock

Courtesy, American-Swedish Historical Society Museum, Philadelphia.

Log Cabins

The cabin made of horizontal logs, so familiar on the American frontier, was brought to America by the Swedes and Finns.

Below Darby Creek Log House. Pennsylvania

Courtesy, Old Time New England, 1927.

Courtesy, The American-Swedish News Exchange, Inc., New York.

This log storehouse in Sweden shows a roof-spanned opening between two log units. A log building was an indivisible structure, and to enlarge it another complete unit had to be built. This open space is called a "dog-trot" or "breeze-way" in our southern states.

Farm Life

Columbian Magazine. 1787.

Landscape near Wilmington, Del., country of the Swedes

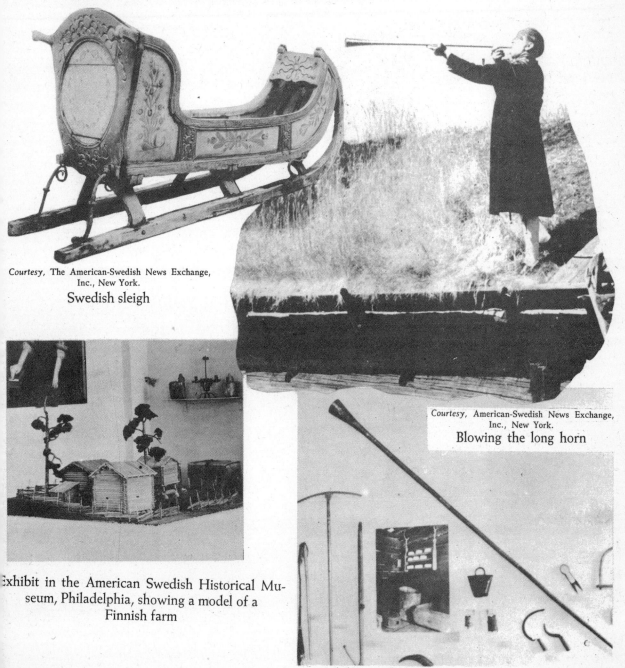

Courtesy, The American-Swedish News Exchange,
Inc., New York.

Swedish sleigh

Courtesy, American-Swedish News Exchange,
Inc., New York.

Blowing the long horn

Exhibit in the American Swedish Historical Museum, Philadelphia, showing a model of a
Finnish farm

Exhibit in the American Swedish Historical Museum, Philadelphia, showing the long horn

Swedish Artist

One of America's foremost portrait painters was Gustavus Hesselius (1682-1755), a Swede. John Hesselius, a son, was also a prolific portrait painter.

Courtesy, Historical Society of Pennsylvania, Philadelphia.

Gustavus Hesselius. Self-portrait

Courtesy, Historical Society of Pennsylvania, Philadelphia.

Mrs. Gustavus Hesselius. Portrait by Gustavus Hesselius

McKenney and Hall *History of the Indian Tribes*. 1836.

Tishcohan. Delaware chief. Painted from life by Gustavus Hesselius in 1735, at the request of John Penn. The original painting from which this print was made is owned by the Historical Society of Pennsylvania, at Philadelphia

Courtesy, Baltimore Museum of Art, Baltimore.

Portrait of Charles Calvert as a child. By Gustavus Hesselius

They Built Churches

The Swedes in America have been immortalized in two famous churches, "Gloria Dei" in Philadelphia, and "Old Swedes" in Wilmington. The models for both existed in Stockholm, as the Braun view below will prove.

Below "Old Swedes". Swedish Lutheran Church. Wilmington, Del. Dedicated 1699. Engraved by John Sartain

Elizabeth Montgomery *Reminiscences of Wilmington.* 1851.

John C. Clay *Annals of the Swedes on the Delaware.* 1835.

"Gloria Dei". Swedish Lutheran Church. Philadelphia, Pa. Dedicated 1700

STOCKHOLM

Braun *Civitates Orbis Terrarum.* 1618. *Courtesy,* The New York Public Library.

View of Stockholm

"Old Swedes" has a cupola similar to the one on the castle, and "Gloria Dei" has a steeple similar to the one on the church to the right. Note also the log cabins in the foreground.

They Planted Lutheranism in America

Photo by Philip B. Wallace.
Courtesy, Philip B. Wallace, Philadelphia.
A modern view of "Gloria Dei."
Philadelphia

John C. Clay *Annals of the Swedes on the Delaware.* 1835.
The Rev. Nicholas Collin. One of the early ministers of "Gloria Dei"

Interior of "Gloria Dei"
Photo by Philip B. Wallace.

Cantankerous old Peter Stuyvesant finally broke the power of Johan Printz in 1655, and the Swedish colony in America was taken over by the Dutch. When William Penn founded Pennsylvania in 1683 he allowed the Swedes and the Finns on the Delaware to become English citizens, and they lived in peace and harmony, contributing their peculiar gifts to the epic of America.

Delaware Architecture

Other groups besides the Swedes settled along the Delaware as these pictures reveal.

Courtesy, Wilmington Institute Free Library, Wilmington, Del.

Two views of the Stidham House, Wilmington, Del. 17th Century. Demolished 1888

Courtesy, The News-Journal Company, Wilmington, Del.

Jacquett House, Long Hook Farm, Del. ca. 1660

Courtesy, The News-Journal Company, Wilmington, Del.

Samuel Dickinson House, Kingston-Upon-Hull, Kent County, Del.

Ferris A History of the Original Settlements on the Delaware. 1846.

Episcopal Church, New Castle, Del. 1704

Ferris A History of the Original Settlements on the Delaware. 1846.

Above Friends Meeting House, Wilmington, Del.

Left Blackwater Presbyterian Church, between Frankford and Ocean View, Del.

Courtesy, Wilmington Institute Free Library.

New Jersey

After the surrender of New Netherlands to the English, the region now known as New Jersey was divided between Sir George Carteret and John Lord Berkeley, favorites of the Duke of York. East Jersey was soon settled by Puritans from Connecticut and Long Island, and West Jersey by the Quakers under William Penn. Newark, in East Jersey, became a Puritan stronghold under the leadership of the Rev. Abraham Pierson. Burlington and Salem in West Jersey felt the Quaker influence.

Section of a view of Newark, New Jersey. The New England influence is at once visible in the layout of the town

Courtesy, Friends Historical Association, *Bulletin.*

Octagonal church Burlington, N. J., erected by the Quakers. It was based on the fifteenth century structure shown *Right*, the Abbot's kitchen of Glastonbury Abbey, Somersetshire, England

Courtesy, Historic American Buildings Survey.

Alexander Grant House, Salem, N. J.

Art in Colonial New Jersey

Courtesy, American Antiquarian Society, Worcester, Mass.

Governor Lewis Morris. Portrait by John Watson
in 1715

John Watson. Self portrait. Watson was New
Jersey's most famous early painter

Architecture

Courtesy, Historic American Buildings Survey, Washington, D. C.

Hancock House. Hancock's Bridge, N. J.

Cedar Plank House, Hancock's Bridge, N. J.

Courtesy, Historic American Buildings Survey.

Revell House, Burlington, N. J. 1685

Courtesy, Historic American Buildings Survey.

Terheun House, Hackensack, N. J. ca. 1670

5

MARYLAND

"With a Gentle East Wind Blowing . . ."

Tanner *Societas Jesu Apostolorum Imitatrix.* 1694. *Courtesy*, The New York Public Library.

A Jesuit at prayer

Father White, a Jesuit priest, sailing for America wrote these words: "On the Twenty Second of the Month of November, in the year 1633, being St. Cecilia's day, we set sail from Cowes, in the Isle of Wight, with a gentle East wind blowing."

This gentle wind was carrying the *Ark* and the *Dove* to America to found Lord Baltimore's province of Maryland, chartered in 1632.

George Calvert, the first Lord Baltimore, died before the charter passed the Great Seal, but his son, Cecilius Calvert, the second Lord Baltimore, carried out his father's plans to found a Catholic settlement on Chesapeake Bay, sending his younger brother, Leonard, to act as governor.

The Calverts Founded a Dynasty

Courtesy, Maryland Historical Society, Baltimore, Md.

George Calvert, first Lord Baltimore   Cecilius Calvert, second Lord Baltimore   Leonard Calvert

Hand-Picked

Maryland's first settlers were carefully chosen by Cecilius Calvert, and as far as possible he personally interviewed the men and women who were to take passage on the *Ark* and the *Dove*. In 1633 he issued a pamphlet advertising the advantages of Maryland.

Mexico, there haue beene and are yet dayly yeare by yeare, brought thence to *Seuill*, 5. or 600. thousand Hides at a time: Goates likewise may be had from the Ilands nigh at hand; as many, as shall be desired. Besides these, there are Muske-rats, Squirrels, Beauers, Badgers, Foxes, Martins, Pole-cats, Wesels and Minkes; which yet hurt not the Poultry, nor their Egges. Among their Birds, the Eagle is the greatest deuourer. Hawkes there are of sundry sorts; which all prey commonly vpon fish: Sparrow-hawkes, Lanerets, Gosse-hawkes, Falcons, and Osperaies. Partridges not much bigger then our Quailes: but haue beene seene a hundred in a Couie. Infinite store of wild Turkeyes, nigh as big againe as our tame. There are Owsels and Black-birds with red shoulders, Thrushes, and diuers sorts of smaller Birds, some redde, some blew, scarce so bigge as Wrens. In winter, is great plenty of Swannes, Cranes, and Pigeons, Herons, Geese, Brants, Ducks, Wigeon, Dottrell, Oxeis, Parrats, and much other fowle vnknowne in our parts. Limonds thriue wonderfully there, Apricockes and Meli-Cottons, come in such abundance, as a Gentleman in Towne protested hee cast a hundred bushels to the Hogs this last yeare, he had so many more then hee could spend. It hath Chochas and Garvanzas, and is excellent for Beanes, Pease, and all manner of Pults and Rootes: whereof Pease in ten dayes rise 14. inches high. The Corne is very plentifull in each of three Harvests in the same yeare, yeelding in greatest penurie two hundred for one, in ordinary yeares fiue or sixe hundred, and in the better, fifteene or sixteene hundred for one: which increase of Corne beeing so great, it is very easie to keepe all manner of Poultrie and Fowle for the Table all the yeare long. This Corne maketh good bread and beere. It is likely all the fruites of *Italy* will agree with that Soyle, as Figs, Melons, Pomegranates, Oranges, Oliues, Berenjenas, and

and the like: which in time, will be had there; as our Apples already are, where they grow to a much better taste and season then they doe heere. Of rich dyes, and drugs, there is no want; as of Tobacco, Saxaphrase, Bole-armoniacke and the like, though not to be esteemed with the former. As for Minerals little hath beene discouered, but seeing the lower grounds, giue many faire shewes, the Mountaines may not be doubted. As for Copper, the North-west Hils haue that store, as the Natiues themselues part the sollid mettall from the same without fire; and beate it into Plates from the raw oare, for Gold, this only can be sayd, that the neighbouring nation, commonly weareth bracelets of rude gobbets of gold about their armes; and therefore, it is like there are mines of Gold not farre of. As for Pearle, they were large chaines thereof, though deformed by burning the Oisters and boaring them ill. I omit their Iron which they have already, their Glasse, Hempe, and Flaxe, which is very excellent in this land: with many other Commodities, which time, industry and Art will discouer; The fruites whereof may be easier tasted, then beleeved.

February, 10. *anno* 1633.

Any man that desireth to adventure in this Plantation, may bee informed of euery particular more at large concerning the Transportation and Provisions for their men, and also for the speedy raising of them, if hee repayre to the Lord BALTEMORE, who hath good advantage to assist him in those things, by reason of the many Provisions hee maketh both for himselfe and others in that kinde: Provided alwayes, that they assigne one to oversee their Accompts for their better satisfaction, and his Lordships discharge. And this the sayd Lord BALTEMORE will bee able to doe for them, if

Courtesy, The New York Public Library.

Two pages from *A Declaration of the Lord Baltimore's Plantation in Maryland*. 1633

After a long voyage the colonists landed at an island called St. Clement's, and recorded that "On the day of the Annunciation of the Most Holy Virgin Mary in the year 1634, we celebrated the Mass for the first time, on this island."

This, and succeeding steps in the observance of the Mass, is from *Ceremonies and Religious Customs of the Various Nations of the Known World*. 1733-34.

Left

Father White blessing the Indians

Tanner *Societas Jesu Apostolorum Imitatrix*. 1694.

Beautiful Robes

Father Marquette's
chasuble. 1618

Courtesy, The Archives of the University of Notre Dame, South Bend, Ind.

Throughout North America, from the time of Columbus, Spanish and French priests intoned the solemn words of the Mass. It was heard on Florida beaches, along the Mississippi, in Canada, in California, and in New Mexico. It was the one changeless ceremony in a world of change. In Maryland, between Anglican Virginia and Puritan New England, the Catholic Church was to gain a permanent foothold in the English colonies. Maryland Jesuits conducted Indian missions and made with their own hands the things they needed.

Tanner *Societas Jesu Apostolorum Imitatrix.* 1694.

Tanner *Societas Jesu Apostolorum Imitatrix.* 1694.

An Historic Document

In 1649 the Maryland Assembly passed a law often cited as a milestone of religious freedom, but both partisans and critics can find support for their views by a careful analysis of this document. In the fifth paragraph are sentiments that foreshadow the *Bill of Rights*.

Jesus Christ brought before Annas.

the INTROITUS.

St Peter denies Christ thrice.

the PRIEST says the KYRE ELEYSON.

J.C. looking on Peter makes him weep.

the PRIEST turning to the people says
DOMINUS VOBISCUM.

A LAW
of
MARYLAND
Concerning
RELIGION.

Forasmuch as in a well-governed and Christian Commonwealth, Matters concerning Religion and the Honour of God ought to be in the first place to be taken into serious consideration, and endeavoured to be settled. Be it therefore Ordained and Enacted by the Right Honourable CÆCILIUS Lord Baron of Baltemore, absolute Lord and Proprietary of this Province, with the Advice and Consent of the Upper and Lower House of this General Assembly, That whatsoever person or persons within this Province and the Islands thereunto belonging, shall from henceforth blaspheme GOD, that is curse him; or shall deny our Saviour JESUS CHRIST to be the Son of God; or shall deny the Holy Trinity, the Father, Son, & Holy Ghosts or the Godhead of any of the said Three Persons of the Trinity, or the Unity of the Godhead, or shall use or utter any reproachful speeches, words, or language, concerning the Holy Trinity, or the Unity of the Godhead, shall be punished with death, and confiscation or forfeiture of all his or her Lands and Goods to the Lord Proprietary and his Heirs.

And be it also enacted by the Authority, and with the advice and assent aforesaid, That whatsoever person or persons shall from henceforth use or utter any reproachful words or speeches concerning the blessed Virgin MARY, the Mother of our Saviour, or the holy Apostles or Evangelists, or any of them, shall in such case for the first Offence forfeit to the said Lord Proprietary and his Heirs, Lords and Proprietaries of this Province, the sum of Five pounds Sterling, or the value thereof to be levied on the goods and chattels of every such person so offending; but in case such offender or offenders shall not then have goods and chattels sufficient for the satisfying of such forfeiture, or that the same be not otherwise speedily satisfied, that then such offender or offenders shall be publickly whipt, and be imprisoned during the pleasure of the Lord Proprietary, or the Lieutenant or Chief Governor of this Province for the time being: And that every such offender and offenders for every second offence shall forfeit Ten Pounds Sterling, or the value thereof to be levied as aforesaid; or in case such offender or offenders shall not then have goods and chattels within this Province sufficient for that purpose, then to be publickly and severely whipt and imprisoned as before is expressed: and that every person or persons before mentioned, offending herein the third time, shall be for such third offence, forfeit all his lands and goods, and be for ever banished and expelled out of this Province.

And be it also further Enacted by the same Authority, advice, and assent, That whatsoever person or persons shall from henceforth upon any occasion of offence, or otherwise in a reproachful manner or way, declare, call, or denominate, any person or persons whatsoever, inhabiting, residing, trafficking, trading or commercing within this Province, or within any the Ports, Harbours, Creeks or Havens to the same belonging, an Heretick, Schismatick, Idolater, Puritan, Presbyterian, Independant, Popish Priest, Jesuit, Jesuited Papist, Lutheran, Calvinist, Anabaptist, Brownist, Antinomian, Roundhead, Separatist, or other name or term in a reproachful manner relating to matter of Religion, shall for every such offence forfeit and lose the sum of Ten shillings Sterling, or the value thereof, to be levied of the goods and chattels of every such offender and offenders, the one half thereof to be forfeited and paid unto the person & persons of whom such reproachful words are, or shall be spoken or uttered, and the other half thereof to the Lord Proprietary and his Heirs, Lords and Proprietaries of this Province: But if such person or persons who shall at any time utter or speak any such reproachful words or language, shall not then have goods or chattels sufficient and overt within this Province to satisfy the penalty aforesaid, or that the same be not otherwise speedily satisfied, that then the person and persons so offending shall be publickly whipt, and shall suffer imprisonment without Bail or Mainprise until he, she, or they, respectively, shall satisfie the party offended or grieved by such reproachfull Language, by asking him or her respectively forgiveness publickly, for such his offence, before the Magistrate or chief Officer or Officers of the Town or place where such offence shall be given.

And be it further likewise enacted by the authority and content aforesaid, that every person and persons within this Province, that shall at any time hereafter prophane the Sabbath, or Lords day, called Sunday, by frequent swearing, drunkenness, or by any uncivil or disorderly Recreation, or by working on that day when absolute necessity doth not require, shall for every such first offence forfeit two shillings six pence Sterling, or the value thereof, and for the second offence five shillings Sterling, or the value thereof; and for the third offence, and for every time he shall offend in like manner afterwards, Ten shillings Sterling, or the value thereof; and in case such offender or offenders shall not have sufficient goods or chattels within this Province to satisfy any of the aforesaid penalties respectively imposed for prophaning the Sabbath or Lords day called Sunday as aforesaid, then in every such case the party so offending shall for the first and second offence in that kind be imprisoned till he or she shall publickly in open Court before the chief Commander, Judge or Magistrate of that County, Town, or Precinct wherein such offence shall be committed, acknowledge the scandal and offence he hath in that respect given, against God, and the good and civil Government of this Province: and for the third offence and for every time after shall also be publickly whipt.

And whereas the inforcing of the Conscience in matter of Religion hath frequently fallen out to be of dangerous consequence in those Commonwealths where it hath been practised, and for the more quiet and peaceable Government of this Province, and the better to preserve mutual love & unity amongst the Inhabitants here, Be it therefore also by the Lord Proprietary with the advice and assent of this Assembly, ordained and enacted, except as in this present Act is before declared and set forth, that no person or persons whatsoever within this Province, or the Islands, Ports, Harbors, Creeks, or Havens thereunto belonging, professing to believe in Jesus Christ, shall from henceforth be any ways troubled, molested or discountenanced, for, or in respect of his or her Religion nor in the free exercise thereof within this Province or the Islands thereunto belonging, nor any way compell'd to the belief or exercise of any other Religion, against his or her consent, so as they be not unfaithful to the Lord Proprietary, or molest or conspire against the civil Government, established or to be established in this Province under him and his Heirs. And that all and every person and persons that shall presume contrary to this Act and the true intent & meaning thereof, directly or indirectly, either in person or estate, wilfully to wrong, disturb, or trouble, or molest any person or persons whatsoever within this Province, professing to believe in Jesus Christ, for or in respect of his or her Religion, or the free exercise thereof within this Province, otherwise then is provided for in this Act, that such person or persons so wronged, shall be compelled to pay treble damages to the party so wronged or molested, and for every such offence shall also forfeit Twenty shillings Sterling in Money, or the value thereof, half thereof for the use of the Lord Proprietary and his Heirs, Lords and Proprietaries of this Province, and the other half thereof for the use of the Party so wronged or molested as aforesaid; or if the party so offending as aforesaid, shall refuse or be unable to recompense the party so wronged, or to satisfy such fine or forfeiture, then such offender shall be severely punished by publick whipping and imprisonment during the pleasure of the Lord Proprietary or his Lieutenant or chief Governor of this Province for the time being, without Bail or Mainprise.

And be it further also enacted by the authority and consent aforesaid, that the Sheriff or other Officer or Officers from time to time to be appointed and authorized for that purpose of the County, Town, or Precinct where every particular offence in this present Act contained, shall happen at any time to be committed, and whereupon there is hereby a forfeiture, fine, or penalty imposed, shall from time to time distrain, and seize the goods and estate of every such person so offending as aforesaid against this present Act or any part thereof, and sell the same or any part thereof for the full satisfaction of such forfeiture, fine, or penalty as aforesaid, restoring to the party so offending, the remainder or overplus of the said goods or estate, after such satisfaction so made as aforesaid.

Courtesy, The New York Public
Library.

Jesus Christ accused before Pilate.

the Priest reads the Epistle.

J.C. accused before Herod makes no reply.

the Priest bowing down before the Alter says
MUNDA COR KO.

Jesus Christ sent back from Herod to Pilate.

the Priest reads the Gospel.

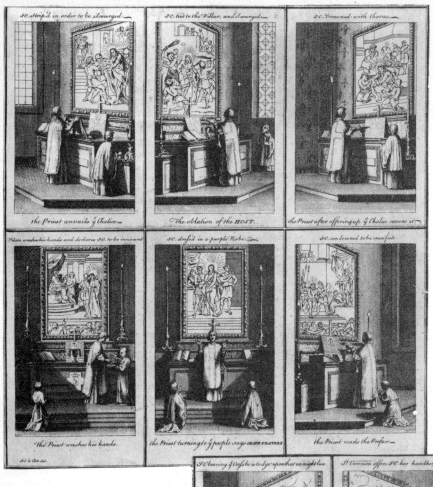

the stout of JC descends into Limbo

the Priest puts a small part of the Host into the
CHALICE.

JC being expired several people return smiting their breasts.

the Priest smites his breast repeating three times
AGNUS DEI &c.

the Body of JC enter'd in a New Sepulchre

the Priest receives the Communion

the Body of JC is imbalmed

the Priest takes the ABLUTION.

the Resurrection of Jesus Christ

the Post-communion

JC appears to his Mother and his Disciples.

the Priest turning to the people says,
DOMINUS VOBISCUM.

JC appears to, and instructs his disciples for 40 days.

the LAST COLLECTS.

Jches le Clerc del.

JC in the presence of his Disciples, ascends into Heaven.

the Priest turning to the People says
ITE MISA EST.

JC sends the H: Ghost to his Apostles.

the Priest gives Benediction to the Congregation.

C Du Bose so.

Chesapeake Bay

That these early Maryland houses were modelled after those of the homeland is evident from these pictures (*Below*) of English houses of the period

Thompson *History and Antiquities of Boston.* 1856.

The first permanent settlement in Maryland was at St. Mary's City. The original dwellings were crude, but it was not long until such homes as these were built. Already we note the influence of climate, for brick houses were the rule in Maryland as contrasted with the frame houses of New England. The chimney structure was also different.

Left Leigh House on St. Mary's Hill, Freehold, St. Mary's City

Forman *Jamestown and St. Mary's.* 1938

Courtesy, Dr. Henry C. Forman, Wesleyan College, Macon, Ga.

St. Mary's City

Below Manor of Cornwaley's Crosse. St. Mary's County, Md. Built ca. 1690. This is not the original house of 1642

Courtesy, Dr. Henry C. Forman, Wesleyan College, Macon, Ga.

Annapolis

Courtesy, A. Aubrey Bodine, The Sun, Baltimore, Maryland.

Sands House. Annapolis, Md. ca. 1680

Courtesy, Hall of Records, Annapolis.

Aunt Lucy Smith's cook shop, Annapolis

Courtesy, Hall of Records, Annapolis.

Jonas Green House. Annapolis, Md. ca. 1680

Old Treasury. ca. 1690. Annapolis, Md.

Courtesy, Dr. Henry C. Forman, Wesleyan College, Macon, Ga.

Artifacts found on the site of the Governor's Castle. St. Mary's City. Note the branding iron in the form of the letter K, a fragment of a diamond pane from a leaded window, and a piece of lead stripping called a calme.

Courtesy, Dr. Henry C. Forman, Wesleyan College, Macon, Ga.

Fireplace, "Tudor Hall", St. Mary's County, Md.

Mount Airy

Mount Airy. Prince George's County, Md. The old Calvert mansion, the earliest part of which was built ca. 1680 for a hunting lodge. Benedict Calvert, son of Charles, fifth Lord Baltimore, resided here. Originally called "His Lordship's Kindness".

Courtesy, Enoch Pratt Free Library, Baltimore, Maryland.

Cedar Park

Here we see a transitional example of Maryland's domestic architecture.

Cedar Park, Anne Arundel County, Md. Built ca. 1700 by Richard Galloway.

Courtesy, Mr. Edgar H. Pickering, Baltimore. Photo by Pickering Studio.

Regional Types

Courtesy, Dr. Henry C. Forman, Wesleyan College, Macon, Ga.

The "Folly". St. Mary's County, Md.   "Long Lane Farm". St. Mary's County, Md.

Chesapeake Bay Country

Above Breton Bay, St. Mary's County, Md., as seen from "Tudor Hall", Leonardtown

To the Right Irish Creek, Talbot County, Md.

Courtesy, Dr. Henry C. Forman, Wesleyan College, Macon, Georgia.

The Governor Lived In Style

The Governor's Castle at St. Mary's City, built in 1639, was excavated in 1940. Its foundations showed that it covered an area of 2,934 square feet, making it the largest structure ever erected in the English colonies, up to that time. It was blown up in 1694 when seventeen kegs of gunpowder exploded in its basement.

The Governor's "Castle" at St. Mary's City, 1639. It was the forerunner of the Governor's "Palace" at Williamsburg, Va. Reconstruction by Dr. Henry C. Forman, Wesleyan College, Macon, Ga.

Worldly Goods

What the colonists in Maryland wore, what tools and utensils they used, what furniture they had, etc., is strikingly revealed in the inventory of Justinian Snowe, dated 1639. The goods are valued in pounds of tobacco.

Maryland Archives. v. 4.

Gentleman Planter

Plantation life formed the basic pattern of colonial civilization in Maryland and Virginia. The hundreds of bays, inlets and rivers made construction of roads unnecessary. Transportation was chiefly by water. The tobacco growers had their private wharves in both Virginia and Maryland, and ships from England stopped at these wharves to unload manufactured articles in exchange for cargoes of tobacco, staves, American dye or drug-producing plants such as sumac, woad, sassafras and ginseng.

Courtesy, Duke University Library, Durham, N. C.

Cartouche from the Fry and Jefferson map of Virginia and Maryland. 1775

At Right is a similar scene, even to the details of the coopers hammering hogsheads, and a gentleman with a pipe, who seems to be dickering over the price of the cargo.

Detail from a map by Henry Popple. 1733

In this picture we see scantily dressed slaves, a cooper tightening the end of a tobacco hogshead, and a bookkeeper checking off the cargo. The loading crane and the ship appear in the background. Other hogsheads are seen in the warehouse.

Courtesy, Historic American Buildings Survey, Washington, D. C.

Tobacco barns, Calvert County, Md.

"Maryland, My Maryland"

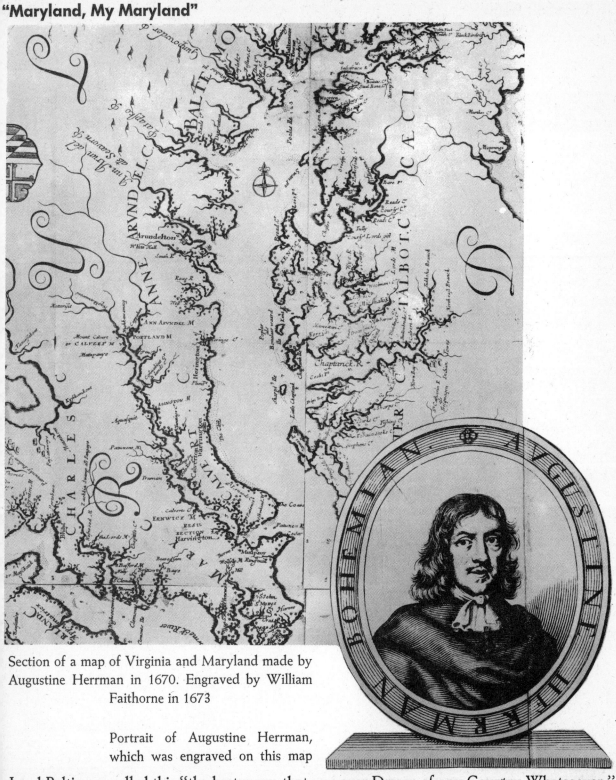

Section of a map of Virginia and Maryland made by
Augustine Herrman in 1670. Engraved by William
Faithorne in 1673

Portrait of Augustine Herrman,
which was engraved on this map

Lord Baltimore called this "the best mapp that was ever Drawn of any Country Whatsoever,"
and was so pleased that he gave Herrman 13,000 acres of land in what is now Cecil County,
Maryland, upon which Herrman built Bohemia Manor, indicated in the upper right-hand
corner of the map.

Note the plantation houses that dot the irregular shores of Chesapeake Bay and the Patux-
ent River. Note St. Mary's at the bottom of the map. In 1694 the seat of government was
moved to Anne Arundel Towne (Arundelton on the map) which later became Annapolis.
Baltemore Towne, at the top of the map was not the present city of Baltimore, which was not
founded until 1729, on the Patapsco River, farther to the South.

He Stood His Ground

William Claiborne, of Virginia, had a profitable trading post on Kent Island in the Chesapeake, and resisted the encroachments of the Calverts. His name appears frequently in the early annals of Maryland.

She Gave A "Towne" Her Name

Portrait of William Claiborne. Owned by W. C. Claiborne, New Orleans, La.

At Right Anne Arundel, wife of Cecilius Calvert, second Lord Baltimore. Annapolis (Anne Arundel Towne), and Anne Arundel County, Md., perpetuate her name and memory

This Tree Still Stands

When Herrman made his map he may have rested under this very oak. If it could talk it would relate the history of Maryland from the beginning.

Courtesy, Maryland Geological Survey.

Wye Oak, Wye Mills, Talbot County, Md.

This Barn Stood Until 1937

This venerable structure, considered to be the original barn of Mrs. Mary Troughton, friend of Lord Baltimore, stood at St. Mary's until it was destroyed in 1937.

Courtesy, Dr. Henry C. Forman, Wesleyan College, Macon, Ga.

Old barn. St. Mary's City, Md. 17th Cent. Forman *Jamestown and St. Mary's.* 1938

Plantation Life

The Maryland planters remained near the water and there built their mansions. They had little intercourse with each other or the outside world, each plantation being an independent social and economic unit made up of the planter and his family, white indented servants and Negro slaves. This accounts for the scarcity and slow growth of towns and cities in Maryland and Virginia, as compared to New England. Even today Marylanders speak of counties more often than they do of towns. A stranger always received a hospitable welcome in Maryland, for he brought news of the outside world.

[4]

Should talk to you Unmannerly;
But if you please to go with me
To yonder House, you'll welcome be.
Encountring soon the smoaky Seat,
The Planter old did thus me greet:
" Whether you come from Goal or Colledge,
" You're welcome to my certain Knowledge;
" And if you please all Night to stay,
" My Son shall put you in the way.
Which offer I most kindly took,
And for a Seat did round me look:
When presently amongst the rest,
He plac'd his unknown *English* Guest,
Who found them drinking for a whet,
A Cask of (*b*) Syder on the Fret,
Till Supper came upon the Table,
On which I fed whilst I was able.
So after hearty Entertainment,
Of Drink and Victuals without Payment;
For Planters Tables, you must know,
Are free for all that come and go.
While (*i*) Pon and Milk, with (*k*) Mush well sour'd,
In wooden Dishes grac'd the Board;
With (*l*) Homine and Syder-pap,
(Which scarce a hungry Dog wou'd lap)
Well stuff'd with Fat, from Bacon fry'd,
Or with *Molossus* dulcify'd:
Then out our Landlord pulls a Pouch,
As greasy as the Leather Couch
On which he sat, and straight begun,
To load with Weed his *Indian* Gun;
In length, scarce longer than ones Finger,
Or that for which the Ladies linger:
His Pipe smoak'd out with aweful Grace,
With aspect grave and solemn pace;
The reverend Sire walks to a Chest,
Of all his Furniture the best,
Closely confin'd within a Room,
Which seldom felt the weight of Broom;

(*b*) Syder-pap is a sort of Food made of Syder and small Homine, like our Oat-
meal. (*i*) Pon is Bread made of *Indian-Corn*. (*k*) Mush is a sort of Hasty-pudding
made with Water and *Indian* Flower. (*l*) Homine is a Dish that is made of boiled
Indian Wheat, eaten with *Molossus*, or Bacon-Fat.

[5]

From thence he lugs a Cag of Rum,
And nodding to me, thus begun:
I find, says he, you don't much care,
For this our *Indian* Country Fare;
But let me tell you, Friend of mine,
You may be glad of it in time,
Tho' now your Stomach is so fine;
And if within this Land you stay,
You'll find it true what I do say.
This said, the Rundlet up he threw,
And bending backwards strongly drew:
I pluck'd as stoutly for my part,
Altho' it made me sick at Heart,
And got so soon into my Head
I scarce cou'd find my way to Bed;
Where I was instantly convey'd
By one who pass'd for Chamber-Maid;
Tho' by her loose and sluttish Dress,
She rather seem'd a *Bedlam-Bess*:
Curious to know from whence she came,
I prest her to declare her Name.
She Blushing, seem'd to hide her Eyes,
And thus in Civil Terms replies;
In better Times, e'er to this Land,
I was unhappily Trapann'd;
Perchance as well I did appear,
As any Lord or Lady here,
Not then a Slave for twice two (*a*) Year.
My Cloaths were fashionably new,
Nor were my Shifts of Linnen Blue;
But things are changed now at the Hoe,
I daily work, and Bare-foot go,
In weeding Corn or feeding Swine,
I spend my melancholy Time.
Kidnap'd and Fool'd, I hither fled,
To shun a hated Nuptial (*b*) Bed,

(*a*) 'Tis the Custom for Servants to be obliged for four Years to very servile
Work; after which time they have their Freedom.
(*b*) These are the general Excuses made by *English* Women, which are sold, or
sell themselves to *Mary-Land*.

C   And

Two pages from Ebenezer Cook's *Sot-Weed Factor*. 1708, describing a visit to a Maryland plantation

One of the delicacies of Maryland often seen on the planter's table was the canvas-back duck.

The Cabinet of Natural History. 1830-34.

Three-Notch Roads and Ox Carts

When a land journey was undertaken it meant dangerous travel along trails through woods filled with Indians. Trees were notched to keep the wayfarer from getting lost. Some of the old three-notch roads still exist in Maryland.

Three-notch road, St. Mary's County, Md. The three notches are shown on the tree below

Courtesy, Maryland Geological Survey.

Now and then a traveler met a two-wheeled ox cart. Ox carts are still used in certain sections of Maryland

Below Two-wheeled ox carts, Port Tobacco, Charles County, Md.

Courtesy, Maryland Geological Survey.

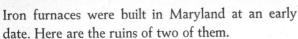

In the Maryland woods the traveler came upon charcoal-burner's huts like these, a type of structure that goes back to the dim past of England. Charcoal was used by the blacksmith and the distiller.

Iron furnaces were built in Maryland at an early date. Here are the ruins of two of them.

Courtesy, Maryland Geological Survey.

Curtis Creek Furnace, Furnace Creek, Anne Arundel County, Md.

Nassawango Furnace, near Snow Hill, Worcester County, Md.

Courtesy, Maryland Geological Survey.

Charcoal-burner's hut. Cecil County, Md.

The Church of England

The Maryland planter ordered his Sunday clothes direct from London. If he was a member of the Church of England he went to a church like this.

Left Male costume. 1700

Pugh *London.* v. 4. 1807.

Below St. Luke's church. "Old Wye."
Wye Mills, Md. ca. 1700

Courtesy, Enoch Pratt Free Library, Baltimore, Md.

He could borrow books from the parish libraries founded by the Reverend Thomas Bray, that indefatigable promoter of useful knowledge.

Courtesy, The New York Public Library.

Bookplate used in Maryland

Note in Bray's essay the suggestion that there should be a bookplate in each book designating the parish library it belonged to, to avoid loss and theft. One of these bookplates is shown here.

Two pages from Thomas Bray's *An Essay Towards Promoting All Necessary and Useful Knowledge.* 1697

Bray had the quaint notion that the size of a book, regardless of the size of the type, should determine the number of days it could be kept by the reader, as this excerpt will show.

"In My Father's House Are Many Mansions"

Catholics and Protestants lived side by side in Maryland, and the latter often boasted a majority in the Maryland Assembly, despite the fact that the Proprietors, the Calverts, were staunch Catholics. When William and Mary came to the English throne a band of Maryland Protestants took up arms against the Catholics. They captured St. Mary's City in 1689, and printed there this *Declaration*.

(3 8)

(I)

THE

DECLARATION

OF THE

REASONS and MOTIVES

For the PRESENT

Appearing in Arms

OF

THEIR MAJESTIES

Proteſtant Subjects

In the PROVINCE of

MARYLAND.

Licens'd, *November 28th 1689.* J. F.

Although the Nature and State of Affairs relating to the Government of this Province, is ſo well and notoriouſly known to all Perſons any way concerned in the ſame, as to the People and Inhabitants here, who are more immediately Intereſted, as might excuſe any *Declaration* or *Apology* for this preſent inevitable *Appearance*: Yet foraſmuch as (by the *Plots, Contrivances, Inſinuations, Remonſtrances,* and *Subſcriptions,* carried on, ſuggeſted, extorted, and obtained by the Lord *Baltemore,* his Deputies,

A   ties,

Left Facsimile reproduction of the first page of *The Declaration of the Reasons and Motives for the Present Appearing in Arms of Their Majesties Protestant Subjects in the Province of Maryland.*
1689
Courtesy, The Library of Congress.

Below Jesuit priest in America
Tanner *Societas Jesu Apostolorum Imitatrix.* 1694.

"Meeting House"

Courtesy, Dr. Henry C. Forman, Wesleyan College, Macon, Ga.
Trinity Church, Dorchester County, Md. ca. 1680.
A miller's grave near the church is marked by
a millstone

Courtesy, Dr. Henry C. Forman, Wesleyan College, Macon, Ga.
Interior of Old Gunpowder Meeting, Baltimore
County, Md., showing huge beams

A Poet Advertises Maryland

The beauties of Maryland were sung by George Alsop, an indented servant, who upon working out his term of service, was so pleased with Maryland and the opportunities it afforded that he wrote its history in verse. The burden of his song was that his friends in England should settle without delay in this sylvan paradise. In Maryland one breathed freedom's air. How else could one explain the unprecedented request of Margaret Brent before the Maryland Assembly in 1639. She asked for the right to vote! She was almost three hundred years ahead of her time.

Women's Rights

View here the Shadow whose Ingenious Hand
Hath drawne exalt the Province Mary Land
Display'd her Glory in such Scænes of Witt
That those that read must fall in Love with it
For which his Labour hee deserves the praise
As well as Poets doe the wreath of Bays.
Anno Do.ᵗ 1666. Ætatis Suæ 28.   H.W.

George Alsop

Frontispiece of his *A Character of the Province of Mary-Land.*
1666

ffriday 21ᵗʰ Jan.

The ffreemen bownd to attend the Assembly appeared except mʳ ffenwick, mʳ Thorneborough, Mʳ Brookes & George Saphyer

Summons to George Saphyer to be att the Assembly forthwᵗʰ vppon sight &c

was read certaine orders to be obserued in the howse during the Assembly

Came Mʳˢ Margarett Brent and requested to have vote in the howse for her selfe and voyce allso for that att the last Court 3ᵈ Jan: it was ordered that the said Mʳˢ Brent was to be lookd uppon and received as his Lʳ Attorney. The Gouᵗ denyed that the sᵈ Mʳˢ Brent should have any uote in the howse. And the sᵈ Mʳˢ Brent protested agst all proceedings in this pñt Assembly, unlesse shee may be pñt. and have vote as aforesᵈ

Orders &c.

Published eod.   1 That noe one of the howse shall use any reuyling speeches or name any one by name but by another signification Viz. the Gent. that spoke last or the like.

Maryland Archives.

Margaret Brent's request denied

"Of Thee I Sing"

Picturesque Views of American Scenery. Published by M. Carey & Son, Philadelphia. 1820.

Jones' Falls near Baltimore. Painted by J. Shaw. Engraved by J. Hill

6

THE CAROLINAS AND GEORGIA

Plato Refuted

Plato's ideal republic was one managed by philosophers. In planning the government of th
Carolinas the philosophical mind of John Locke evolved an elaborate *Constitution*, but it wa
doomed to failure. It was not adapted to the realities of colonial life. Locke, as secretary t
Anthony Ashley Cooper, later to become the Earl of Shaftesbury, was delegated to write thi
bizarre document, which provided for such offices as palatine, chamberlain, high steward, land
grave, cazique, and eight supreme courts, and such land divisions as signiories, baronies, an
manors.

The Earl
of Shaftesbury

John Locke

Fundamental Conſtitutions

OF

CAROLINA.

OUR Sovereign Lord the King having out of His Royal
Grace and Bounty, granted unto us the Province of *Carolina*, with all the Royalties, Proprieties, Juriſdictions
and Privileges of a *County Palatine*, as large and ample as
the County Palatine of *Durham*, with other great Privileges; for the
better Settlement of the Government of the ſaid Place, and eſta-
bliſhing the Intereſt of the Lords Proprietors with Equality, and
without Confuſion, and that the Government of this Province may
be made moſt agreeable to the Monarchy under which we live, and
of which this Province is a Part; and that we may avoid erecting
a numerous *Democracy*, we the *Lords* and *Proprietors* of the Province
aforeſaid, have agreed to this following Form of *Government*, to be
perpetually eſtabliſhed amongſt us, unto which we do oblige our ſelves,
our Heirs and Succeſſors, in the moſt binding Ways that can be deviſed.

§. 1. THE *Eldeſt* of the *Lords Proprietors* ſhall be *Palatine*, and
upon the Deceaſe of the *Palatine*, the *Eldeſt* of the Seven
ſurviving *Proprietors* ſhall always ſucceed him.

§. 2. There ſhall be *Seven* other *Chief Offices* erected, *viz.* The
*Admirals, Chamberlains, Chancellors, Conſtables, Chief-Juſtices, High-
Stewards* and *Treaſurers*; which Places ſhall be enjoy'd by none but
the *Lords Proprietors*, to be aſſign'd at firſt by Lot, and upon the
Vacancy of any one of the Seven Great Offices by Death, or otherr-
wiſe, the *Eldeſt Proprietor* ſhall have his Choice of the ſaid Place.

§. 3. The whole Province ſhall be *divided* into *Counties*; each County ſhall conſiſt of Eight *Signiories*, Eight *Baronies*, and Four *Precincts*;
each *Precinct* ſhall conſiſt of Six *Colonies*.

lina.   *37*
part thereof, ei-
or *One and Twen-
ty Ye*

§. 2
Co-heir[s] ll be *divided* amongſt
ſcena to th ſhall all entirely de-
nors than one, If there be more *Man-
ſhall have her *Choice*, the Se-
cond next, and ſo on, again at the Eldeſt, till all the *Mannors* be taken up; that ſo the *Privileges* which belong to *Mannors* being *indiviſible*, the Lands of the *Mannors* to which they are annexed,
may be *kept entire*, and the *Mannor* not loſe thoſe Privileges, which
upon parcelling out to ſeveral Owners, muſt neceſſarily ceaſe.

§. 21. Every Lord of a *Mannor*, within his *Mannor*, ſhall have al
the Powers, Juriſdictions, and Privileges, which a *Landgrave* or *Caſſique* hath in his *Baronies*.

§. 22. In every *Signiory, Barony*, and *Mannor*, all the *Leet-Men* ſhall
be under the Juriſdiction of the reſpective Lords of the ſaid *Signiory,
Barony*, or *Mannor*, without Appeal from him. Nor ſhall any *Leet-
Man* or *Leet-Woman* have Liberty to go off from the Land of their
particular Lord, and live any where elſe, without Licenſe obtained
from their ſaid Lord, under Hand and Seal.

§. 23. All the Children of *Leet-Men* ſhall be *Leet-Men*, and ſo to
all Generations.

§. 24. No Man ſhall be capable of having a *Court-Leet* or *Leet-Men*,
but a *Proprietor, Landgrave, Caſſique*, or *Lord of a Mannor*.

§. 25. Whoever ſhall voluntarily enter himſelf a *Leet-Man* in the
Regiſtry of the County Court, ſhall be a *Leet-Man*.

§. 26. Whoever is Lord of *Leet-Men*, ſhall upon the *Marriage* of a
Leet-Man or *Leet-Woman* of his, give them Ten Acres of Land for
their Lives, they paying to him therefore not more than one Eighth
part of all the Yearly Produce and Growth of the ſaid Ten Acres.

§. 27. No *Landgrave* or *Caſſique* ſhall be *try'd* for any *Criminal*
Cauſe, in any but the *Chief-Juſtice's* Court, and that by a Jury of
his *Peers*.

§. 28. There ſhall be *Eight Supreme Courts*. The Firſt called, *The Palatine's Court*, conſiſting of the *Palatine*, and the other Seven *Proprietors*. The other Seven Courts of the other Seven Great Officers,
ſhall conſiſt each of them of a *Proprietor*, and Six *Councellors* added to
him. Under each of theſe latter Seven *Courts* ſhall be a *College* of
Twelve *Aſſiſtants*. The Twelve *Aſſiſtants* of the ſeveral *Colleges* ſhall
be choſen; Two out of the *Landgraves, Caſſiques*, or eldeſt Sons of
Pro

The Lords Proprietors

John Colleton, a planter of Barbadoes, friend of King Charles II, had obtained for himself and seven other proprietors a charter for Carolina in 1664. The eight proprietors were Colleton, Lord Ashley, Sir William Berkeley, John Lord Berkeley, Lord Craven, the Duke of Albemarle, the Earl of Clarendon, and Sir George Carteret.

Ligon *A True & Exact History of the Island of Barbadoes.* 1673.

From Public Records Office, London

The Great Seal of the Lords Proprietors of the Province of Carolina, showing on the reverse the coats of arms of the eight signatories

Charles Towne

The first settlers in South Carolina, mostly from Barbadoes, founded Charles Towne on the Ashley River in 1670, naming it in honor of their sovereign. The plantation system, patterned on the prevailing system in the West Indies, was established from the very beginning. Negro labor was an important factor.

Herman Moll's map showing the names of the early settlers in South Carolina.
1715

Palmettoes

The Roberts view of Charles Town. 1739
Courtesy, Stokes Collection, The New York Public Library.

At the Edge of the Unknown

Beyond the narrow limits of the town stretched the swampy wilderness. Early waterfront towns gave the effect of a stage setting, lacking depth. The urban fringe was a narrow wedge between the mystery and immensity of the sea and the mystery and wildness of the unexplored forests and streams. The spire of St. Philip's Church, marked (E) on the Roberts view, punctuated the wilderness like an exclamation point of God.

St. Philip's Church

Designs for church clock towers taken from *A Book of Architecture* by James Gibbs. 1726

Charles Town. (Second section)

Guns and Steeples

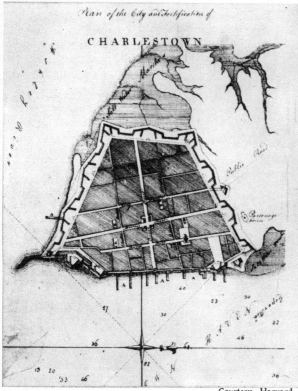

Courtesy, Harvard University Library.

Plan by William Gerard De Brahm. ca. 1760.
It shows how the town had expanded.

Plan by William Gerard De Brahm. ca. 1760.
Fort Johnson was built to protect Charlestown
from the Spanish threat from Florida

St. Michael's Church. 1752. It was copied
from St. Martin's-in-the-Fields, London

Courtesy, The Charleston Museum.

Stoney *Plantations of the South Carolina Low Country.* 1939. *Courtesy,* Carolina
Art Association, Charleston, S. C. Photo by Frances B. Johnston.

Interior of St. James' Church, Goose Creek, S. C. 1711

Huguenots and Acadians

Charleston, even today, has a certain French atmosphere. Huguenot names are sprinkled through the telephone book. The Huguenots were driven from France in 1685-86, and many found refuge in South Carolina. Another French stream poured from Nova Scotia in 1755, the ill-fated Acadians immortalized in Longfellow's *Evangeline*. The French exiles were industrious and thrifty. They built beautiful mansions among the oak and cypress trees laden with Spanish moss, and their rice and indigo plantations were sources of ever-increasing wealth.

Photo by U. S. Forest Service.

Courtesy, Carolina Art Association, Charleston, S. C.

Scene near Charleston. Water color by Charles
Fraser. 1801

Right Hampton, near Charleston. Begun by Noe
Serre in 1735. Home of the Horry family,
prosperous Huguenots

Courtesy, Mr. Archibald Rutledge, the present owner.

Under the Magnolias

The English planters vied with the Huguenots in the extent of their rice fields and in the elegance of their mansions.

Below "Brabants", near Charleston.
Water color by Charles Fraser

Courtesy, Carolina Art Association, Charleston, S. C.

Courtesy, University of North Carolina Press.

Rose Hill Plantation, home of
Charles Heyward

Left Medway. Built by Jan Van Arrsens in 1686. It shows the Dutch influence

Stoney *Plantations of the Carolina Low Country.* 1939.
Courtesy, Carolina Art Association, Charleston, S. C.
Photo by Frances B. Johnston.

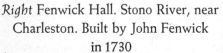

Right Fenwick Hall. Stono River, near
Charleston. Built by John Fenwick
in 1730

Courtesy, Carolina Art Association, Charleston, S. C.
Stoney *Plantations of the Carolina Low Country.*
Photo by Ben Judah Lubschez.

Middleton Place

Stoney *Plantations of the Carolina Low Country.* 1939. *Courtesy,* Carolina Art Association, Charleston, S. C. Photo by Ben Judah Lubschez.

Middleton Place. Built by John Williams in 1738, enlarged 1755. The Dutch gables are prominent.

View of the Ashley River from Middleton Place

Courtesy, Carolina Art Association, Charleston, S. C. Photo by Frances B. Johnston.

A Charleston Kitchen

Dutch oven and kitchen fireplace

Courtesy, The Charleston Museum, Charleston, S. C.

Rice Seed from Madagascar

What tobacco was to Virginia and Maryland, rice was to South Carolina. Rice seed was brought to South Carolina from Madagascar around 1694. The rice was threshed with flails and forks, and the husks were removed by pounding them with a wooden pestle in a mortar made of a hollow stump. The Negroes of South Carolina still pound rice in this primitive fashion.

Below Negro women pounding rice

Rutledge *Home by the River.* 1941.

Catesby *Natural History of Carolina.* 1754.
Rice plant

Below Hoes and rice hook
Courtesy, The Charleston Museum, Charleston, S. C.

The rice fields were flooded at intervals, weeded, and cultivated. Canals traversed the rice fields, and locks like these were built.

Mules bogged down in the soggy rice fields, and special boots had to be strapped to their feet.

Mule boots
Courtesy, The Charleston Museum, Charleston, S. C.

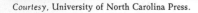

Winnowing Rice

Courtesy, The Charleston Museum, Charleston, S. C.

Rice scales

Courtesy, The Charleston Museum, Charleston, S. C.

Winnowing house. Hopsewee Plantation, South Santee River, S. C.

Courtesy, The Charleston Museum, Charleston, S. C.

Piggins. Used on a rice plantation

Water color by Alice R. Huger Smith. Sass *A Carolina Rice Plantation of the Fifties*. 1936. Courtesy, William Morrow & Co., Inc., New York.

Winnowing Rice

R.H. Latrobe Esq.' Del.

Explanations to the Machine.

Grav'd for Drayton's Hist.' of S.' Carolina by J.Akin Philad.

A. The Windlass for raising the Flood Gate.
B. Holes fore a Pin by which the Windlass & Flood Gate are secured.
C. The great driving Cog Wheel, fixed on the Water wheel shaft.
D. A large Wheel revolving on the same Axle with the small Wheel Y.
E. A Small Lanthorn Wheel impelled by the large Cog Wheel D.
F. Mill Stones.
G. Hopper.

H. Funnel thro which the rough Rice falls from the Loft.
I. Funnel from the Mill Stone discharging into the Windfan Hopper.
L. A Strap worked by a Crank, for moving a riddle within the Fan.
M. Hulls or Chaff flying thro the Door.
N. The Hulled rice discharging from the Wind-Fan into the Bin O.
Y. A Cog Wheel Moving the Axle S.
Q. The Pestles.

R. The Mortars.
TT. Two Moveable Beams, supporting the Axle S.
U. End of the Cross Beam into which the Screw K plays, and also supports the long moveable Beam VV. on which the upper Mill Stone reels, raised at pleasure by Screw K.
W. A Band which works the Pulley of the Wind-Fan.
X. A long cross beam connecting the Beating & Grinding Parts.

Drayton *A View of South-Carolina.* 1802.

Water rice machine

Hall *Forty Etchings from Sketches made with the Camera Lucida in North America.* 1829.

Rice fields in South Carolina

Supposing the Land to be purchased @ 10/ ⅌ acre v: g: 200 acres - - - - 100.. 0..0
To build a Barn and Pounding Machine purchasing boards & Timber - - 220.. 0..0
To purchase 40 working hands @ £45 - - - - - - - - - - - - - - -1800.. 0..0
To purchase working Oxen and Horses - - - - - - - - - - - - - - 60.. 0..0
To two Carts and Collars - - - - - - - - - - - - - - - - - - - 10.. 0..0
To Hoes, Axes, Spades, and other Plantations Tools - - - - - - - - 30.. 0..0
To annual Expences for Tax & Quit Rent £5.. & first year's Provision £50.. - 55.. 0..0
To Overseers Wages - 50.. 0..0
To Negroe Shoes £6..10..0 Do. cloathing £20..0..0 & 13 Blankets ⅌ annum £5..6.. 31..16.0
To Box of Medicine & Doctors fees £20.. for Deaths of Negroes ⅌ an. £100.. 120.. 6..0

£2476..16..0

The aforementioned Number of Negroes will plant 130 acres of Rice, making 350 barrels @ 40/ £700..0..0, also 70 acres of Provision, will nearly clear £28..5..5.. ⅌ Cent Interest.

The next years Provision-Article falling away the expended Capital will only be £2426..16..0, and the Interest on it will nearly be £29 ⅌ Cent. Those who plant Indigo will raise their Interest much higher. NB. the above Calculation is on Land, which is ready cleared and fenced, for if this is to be done, so full a Crop cannot be expected the first, and at times not the second year, especially if the Undertaker is not a professed Planter, and has not a very faithfull and industrious well experienced Overseer.

Around 1750 William Gerard De Brahm, a surveyor, estimated the cost of operating a 200 acre rice plantation as follows:

Slavery

To make rice growing profitable the planters of South Carolina needed cheap labor. Lacking White laborers they imported Negro slaves from the West Indies. The West Indies were clearing houses for slaves brought from Africa. The Dutch, French, Portuguese, and English traders were all interested in this traffic.

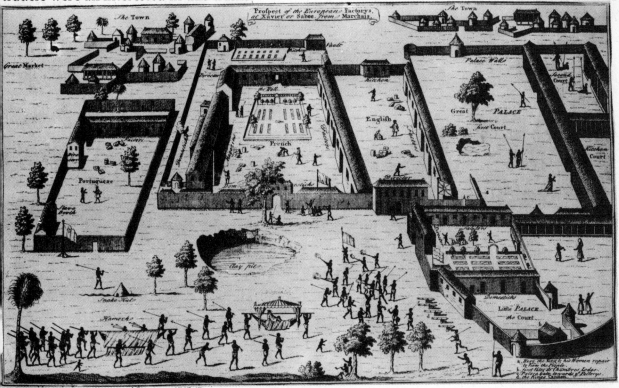

A New and General Collection of Voyages. 1745-47.

European trading center in Africa

Through the hot, still nights came the sound of the drums, and the voices of Negro songsters, voices that sang the strange music of Africa.

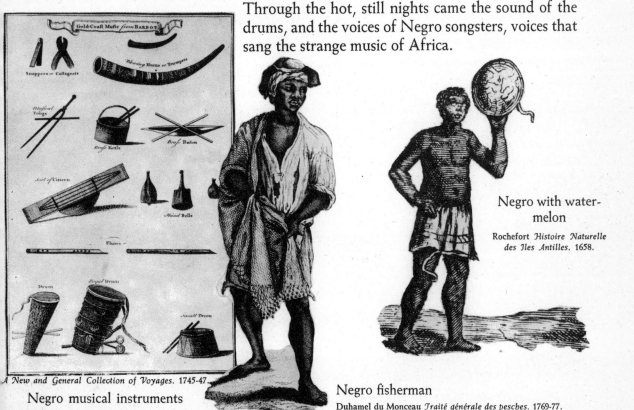

Negro with water-melon

Rochefort *Histoire Naturelle des Iles Antilles.* 1658.

A New and General Collection of Voyages. 1745-47.

Negro musical instruments

Negro fisherman

Duhamel du Monceau *Traité générale des pesches.* 1769-77.

Links With the Past

Left Water color painting discovered near Orangeburg, S.C. Early 19th century

Courtesy, Mrs. John D. Rockefeller, Jr. Collection of American Folk Art, Williamsburg, Va.

Hot and thirsty Negroes trudged along behind crude wooden plows, drank from gourd dippers, and when the day's work was done retired to slave quarters near the plantation house.

Guion G. Johnson *A Social History of the Sea Islands.* 1930. *Courtesy,* University of North Carolina Press.

Courtesy, North Carolina Historical Commission, Raleigh, N. C.

Courtesy, *Rutledge Home by the River.* 1941.

Slave quarters, "Melrose", Wedgefield Vicinity, S. C.

Courtesy, Historic American Buildings Survey, Washington, D. C.

Indigo

Next to rice, indigo was the most important crop in South Carolina. Governor West instructed that the indigo plant be brought from Barbadoes as early as 1674. Eliza Lucas in 1744 was the first to make it profitable. She hired Andrew Deveaux to perfect a new process of producing indigo, from which a blue dye, much in demand in Europe, could be obtained, and she advocated the use of slave labor. The Huguenots, particularly the Legares, Ravenels, St. Juliens, Marions, Mottes, and Peronneaus, made their fortunes in indigo.

Courtesy, Lesesne Family of Charleston, S. C.

Processing of indigo on a plantation near Charleston, S. C.

Pomet A Compleat History of Druggs. 1725.

Negroes processing indigo

Indigo plant

Institut de France. Academie des Sciences. Descriptions des Arts et Metiers. 1770.

Negroes cultivating indigo

Salt

Salt was a Carolina product of great value. Salt marshes were converted into salt yards. By a process of evaporation the saline content of sea water became crystalized, and the piles of salt were conveyed to the plantations by boat.

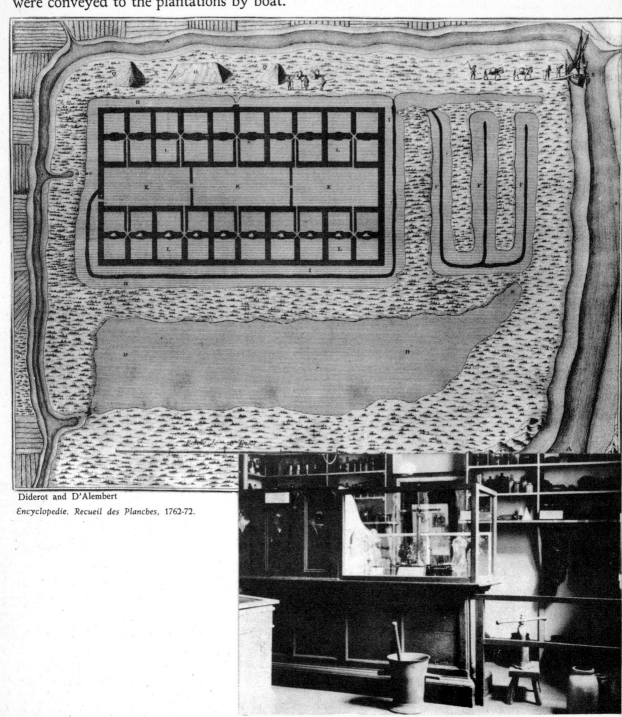

Diderot and D'Alembert
Encyclopedie. Recueil des Planches, 1762-72.

Courtesy, The Charleston Museum.
Apothecaries' Hall. Charleston

Yellow Fever

The climate of South Carolina before the development of modern medical science took a heavy toll of lives. Yellow fever, smallpox, and other diseases ran rampant. The apothecary shop was a popular place in old Charleston. The planter stopped there to lay in supplies, for he performed the duties of a doctor when his family or slaves needed medical attention.

North Carolina

North Carolina and South Carolina were under the same English governors until 1712. North Carolina became a Royal Colony in 1729 when the King bought out the proprietors. Bath was the first North Carolina settlement of any size, and was incorporated in 1705, followed shortly thereafter by New Bern, Edenton, Beaufort, and Brunswick.

St. Thomas Church. Bath. 1734

St. Paul's Church, Edenton. 1736

Courtesy, North Carolina Historical Commission, Raleigh, N. C.

North Carolina was a wild country filled with animals like these if we are to believe John Brickell.

Cabinet of Natural History. 1830-34.

The Panther

Brickell The Natural History of North Carolina. 1737.

Pioneer Life

In the back country settlers might look out from their cabin doors and see a bear and cub lumbering across the clearing, and as they walked through the underbrush they might hear the spine-chilling warning of the deadly rattlesnake.

Catesby *Natural History of Carolina.* 1754.

Mason *The Lure of the Great Smokies.* 1927.
Courtesy, Houghton, Mifflin. Boston.

Flying squirrel

Bowman *Land of High Horizons.* 1938.
Courtesy, Southern Publishers, Kingsport, Tenn.

Kalm *Reis door Noord Amerika.* 1772.

Raccoon

Indians

The Tuscarora War in 1711 almost wiped out the white settlers in North Carolina, and the Cherokee were to be feared as well as the Tuscarora. Remnants of the Cherokee still reside in the mountains of North Carolina.

Scalps

Maxwell *Valhalla in the Smokies*. 1938.
Courtesy, Mr. George A. Exline, Cleveland, O.

Cherokee

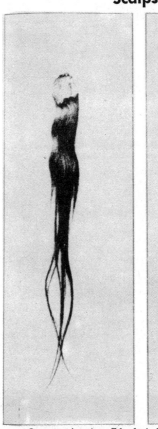

Courtesy, American Ethnological Bureau. *Bulletin*. 1918.

Engraving by F. O. C. Darley.

Sudden attack

Schoolcraft *Indian Tribes*. 1853.

Pirates

Along the seacoast bold pirates captured the planters' ships. The boldest of all, the notorious Black Beard, had a hangout on the North Carolina coast.

Black Beard carried a small arsenal on his person, and stuck lighted tapers in his hair.

Here we see Governor Spotswood's *Proclamation* concerning Black Beard.

Johnson *A General History of the Lives and Adventures of the Most Famous Highwaymen . . . (etc.). 1736.*

Captain Teach, better known as Black Beard

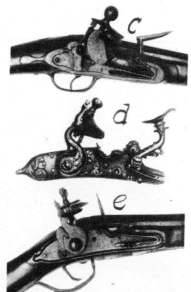

Courtesy, The Magazine *Antiques*, New York.

Details of colonial muskets (c) Miquelet (d) Snaphaunce (e) Flintlock

Right Proclamation of Governor Alexander Spotswood of Virginia. 1718. Spotswood's men brought Black Beard to bay, captured his ship, and brought his head back on a pole

Of BLACK-BEARD.   79

By his Majesty's Lieutenant Governor, and Commander in Chief, of the Colony and Dominion of *Virginia,*

A PROCLAMATION,

Publishing the Rewards given for apprehending, or killing, Pyrates.

Whereas, by an Act of Assembly, made at a Session of Assembly, begun at the Capital in Williamsburgh, the eleventh Day of November, in the fifth Year of his Majesty's Reign, entituled, An Act to encourage the apprehending and destroying of Pyrates: It is, amongst other Things enacted, that all and every Person, or Persons, who, from and after the fourteenth Day of November, in the Year of our Lord one thousand seven hundred and eighteen, and before the fourteenth Day of November, which shall be in the Year of our Lord one thousand seven hundred and nineteen, shall take any Pyrate, or Pyrates, on the Sea or Land, or in Case of Resistance, shall kill any such Pyrate, or Pyrates, between the Degrees of thirty four, and thirty nine, of Northern Latitude, and within one hundred Leagues of the Continent of Virginia, or within the Provinces of Virginia, or North-Carolina, upon the Conviction, or making due Proof of the killing of all, and every such Pyrate, and Pyrates, before the Governor and Council, shall be entitled to have, and receive out of the publick Money, in the Hands of the Treasurer of this Colony, the several Rewards following; that is to say, for Edward Teach, commonly call'd Captain Teach, or Black-Beard, one hundred Pounds, for every other Commander of a Pyrate Ship, Sloop, or Vessel, forty Pounds; for every Lieutenant, Master, or Quarter-Master, Boatswain, or Carpenter, twenty Pounds; for every other inferior Officer, fifteen Pounds, and for every private Man taken on Board such Ship, Sloop,

Tidewater and Piedmont

The Anglican gentry developed their plantations in the Tidewater region, and tobacco became the chief crop. Ships from England docked at the private wharves of the planters, bringing books, clothing, furniture, tools, utensils, and drugs from London. There was a distinct social cleavage between Tidewater and Piedmont, between landed gentry and "buckskins".

Photo by U. S. Forest Service.

Cypress swamp, Northampton County, N. C.

Left Indian dugout found in the Great Dismal Swamp, North Carolina

Courtesy, Mariners' Museum, Newport News, Va.

Photo by Barden.
Courtesy, N. C. Historical Commission.

Orton Plantation
Cape Fear, N. C. 1725

Courtesy, Metropolitan Museum of Art, New York.

Silver tea set by John Letelier and Thomas Shields, Baltimore

Buckskin suit

Courtesy, Valentine Museum, Richmond, Va.

Brick

Here are three types of early North Carolina houses.

Left Newbold-White House. Early 18th Century. Harveys Neck, Perquimans County, N. C. Note the huge chimney, the small end windows and the dormers, called "dog houses" by the Negroes. This is a 17th Century Virginia type reminiscent of Jamestown

Illustrations from Johnston & Waterman *The Early Architecture of North Carolina* 1940. *Courtesy,* University of North Carolina Press.

Log

Courtesy, Library of Congress.

Above McIntyre Log Cabin. ca. 1726. Near Charlotte, Mecklenberg County, N. C. Note the saddle-notched corners

Stone

Left Michael Braun Rock House. 1766. Near Salisbury, Rowan County, N. C. This shows the Moravian influence. The Moravians built the same type in Pennsylvania

Illustrations from Johnston & Waterman, *The Early Architecture of North Carolina* 1940. *Courtesy,* University of North Carolina Press.

Moravians

A Moravian sect settled at Salem, now Winston-Salem, North Carolina, and influenced the domestic and ecclesiastical architecture of the surrounding region. Other Moravian groups settled in Georgia and Pennsylvania, as we shall see when we come to those colonies.

Log house. Winston-Salem, N. C. 1766

Right Adam Spach House, near Winston-Salem, N. C. 1774

Courtesy, North Carolina Historical Commission,
Raleigh, N. C.

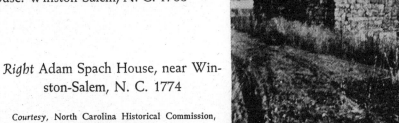

Kurze Zuverlassige Nachricht. 1757.

Moravians baptising the Indians

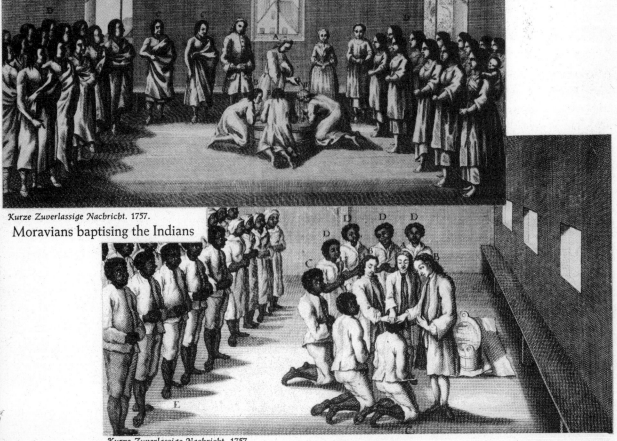

Kurze Zuverlassige Nachricht. 1757.

Moravians teaching Negroes the religious rites of Christianity

Mountain Country

The great mountain barriers in the western part of North Carolina beckoned to hardy settlers, for beyond them lay unclaimed wealth. Pioneers probed the gaps in these mountains looking for trails that would lead them to the "Promised Land". The Scotch-Irish, fiercely independent and disdaining the soft life of the Tidewater region, were among the first to flock to the mountain country.

Picturesque America. 1872-74.

The Great Smoky Mountains

Ballads

Folk ballads of England and Scotland were heard in the mountains of North Carolina. A favorite was "Barbara Allen".

Mason *The Lure of the Great Smokies.* 1927.
Courtesy, Houghton, Mifflin, Boston

Mountain grist mill

Courtesy, Columbia University Press, New York.
Dorothy Scarborough *A Song Catcher in the Southern Mountains.* 1937.

Georgia

Georgia was founded as the result of salesmanship. Months before the actual settlement, reformers, speculators, visionaries, adventurers, and persecuted religious sects printed and had circulated books, pamphlets, and magazine articles setting forth in glowing terms the advantages of Georgia. A Board of Trustees was to manage this Utopia, which was to be run along the lines of a huge philanthropic institution. Rum and slavery were prohibited, and debtors' prisons were emptied in order to find willing pioneers. One of the active promoters of the project was James Edward Oglethorpe. In 1732 he and nineteen other persons obtained a charter from King George II, in whose honor the new colony was named. With Oglethorpe at their head the first settlers landed in February, 1733.

Left The Trustees of Georgia Receiving the Indians in 1734. A painting by Verelst

James Oglethorpe. Portrait by Ravenet

Left James Oglethorpe as an old man. The sketch was made while he was attending the sale of the library of Dr. Samuel Johnson in London

Savannah

The first permanent settlement in Georgia was at Savannah, laid out along formal lines at the edge of a mighty forest of pines.

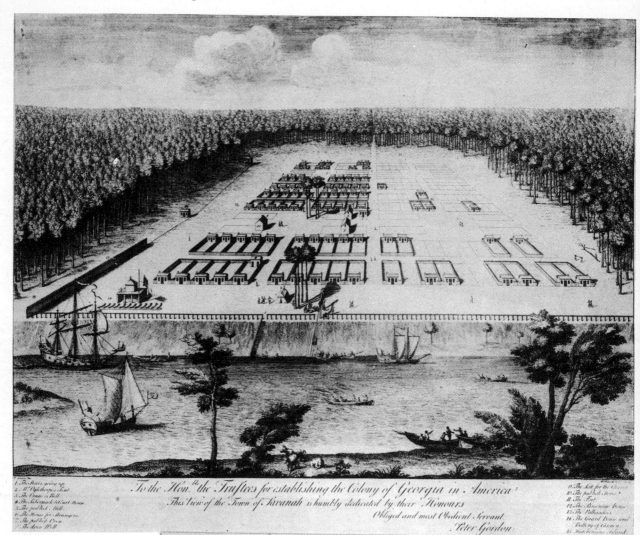

To the Hon.ble the Trustees for establishing the Colony of Georgia in America
This View of the Town of Savanah is humbly dedicated by their Honours
Obliged and most Obedient Servant
Peter Gordon

Courtesy, Stokes Collection, The New York Public Library.

Peter Gordon's view of Savannah. 1734

Urlsperger *Der Ausfuhrlichen Nachrichten.* 1747.

Map of the County of Savannah, showing the Moravian town of Ebenezer

The Salzburgers

The first religious sect to immigrate to Georgia was the Salzburger Lutherans in 1734. Protestant groups in Germany had been driven from town to town in the many religious wars. In this picture of their wanderings we see an example of the restless western push of the American pioneers, wagons and all. The great frontier trek did not begin at the Cumberland Gap and western New England, it began in Holland, and Germany, in Scotland and Ireland, and was merely continued in America—it was in the blood.

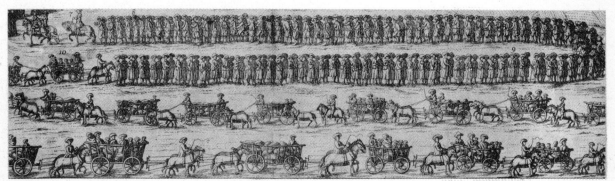

Die Krafft und Wahrheit des Gottlichen Wortes. 1732.

Humanity on the march, in search of freedom and security

The leader of these Salzburger immigrants was John Martin Bolzius.

Below Log cabin in Georgia

Hall *Forty Etchings from Sketches Made with the Camera Lucida in North America.* 1829.

JOHANN MARTIN BOLZIVS
Erster Evangel Prediger der Salzburgl. Colonistengemeine
zu Ebenezer in Georgien.
geb. A. C. 1703. den 15ten Decbr.   ordinirt 1733. den 11ten Novbr.

Urlsperger *Americanisches Ackerwerk Gottes.* 1754.

Ebenezer

Another German sect, the Moravians, came to Georgia in 1735, 1736, and 1738, under A. G. Spangenberg, David Nitzchmann, and Peter Boehler. They founded the town of Ebenezer in 1734. In 1736 they abandoned this settlement and founded New Ebenezer.

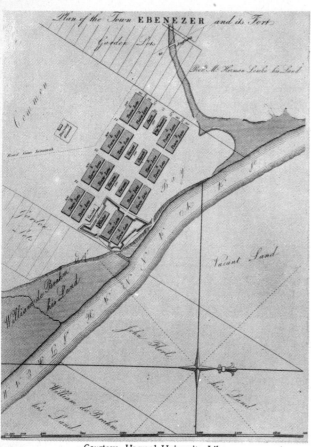

Courtesy, Harvard University Library.

Plan by William Gerard De Brahm. ca. 1770

Urlsperger *Der Ausfuhrlichen Nachrichten.* 1735.

Tomo-Chi-Chi and his nephew

Creek Indians

To the west were the Creek Indians and other tribes. They were friendly to Oglethorpe and he took some of them to London for an interview with the King. While on this trip Chief Tomo-Chi-Chi had his portrait painted.

Schoolcraft *Indian Tribes.*

Creek house

Right Creek Indian. Pencil sketch by John Trumbull.

Fur Trade

Pack trains loaded with furs, sold to the white traders by the Indians in exchange for bottles and beads and other trinkets, wended their way from the Alabama country to the fur marts of Savannah and Charleston. Augusta, Georgia, was destined to become the center of this lucrative trade which had been inaugurated as early as 1685 by Charleston merchants.

Courtesy, The Alabama Anthropological Society.

Trade bottles unearthed at Indian sites in Alabama. They date from 1685 to around 1810. The square bottles were called Dutch gins.

Silk Trade

The presence of mulberry trees in Georgia had encouraged the Trustees to believe that silk could be produced on a large scale, and the Moravians took instructions in its manufacture. Some silk was actually exported, but the industry never flourished.

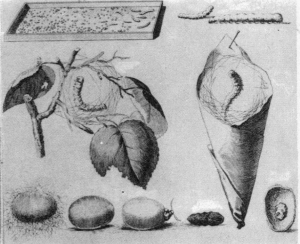

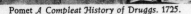
Pomet A Compleat History of Druggs. 1725.

Diderot and D'Alembert Encyclopedie. Recueil des Planches, 1762-72.

Fear of Spain

It soon became apparent that the real motive behind the colonization of Georgia was the creation of a buffer state between South Carolina and Spanish-held Florida. Strong fortifications were constructed in Georgia to repel the Spanish attack, as these plans will reveal.

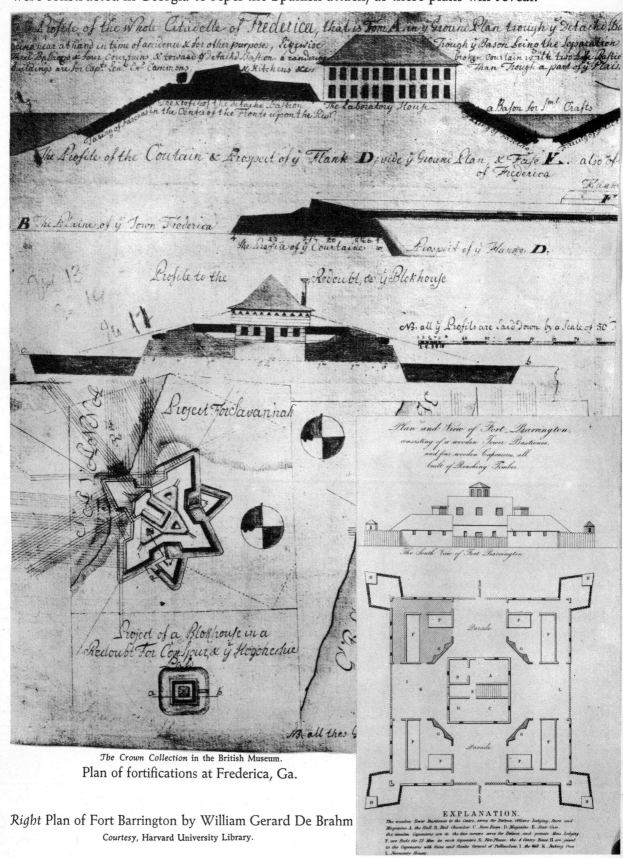

The Crown Collection in the British Museum.
Plan of fortifications at Frederica, Ga.

Right Plan of Fort Barrington by William Gerard De Brahm

Courtesy, Harvard University Library.

The War of Jenkins' Ear

In 1739-43 Great Britain and Spain fought the War of Jenkins' Ear. The Georgia settlements were threatened with extinction, but Oglethorpe thwarted Spanish plans by marching boldly into Florida. He failed in an attempt to capture St. Augustine.

The Crown Collection in the British Museum.

View of the Governor's House. St. Augustine, Fla.

Courtesy, Harvard University Library.

Plan of St. Augustine by William Gerard De Brahm

The Crown Collection in the British Museum.

View from the Governor's House. St. Augustine.

Views of Fort San Marco, St. Augustine. Begun in the 17th Century and completed in 1756.

Oglethorpe was able to isolate the Pensacola garrison on the Gulf of Mexico from the stronger force at St. Augustine. Driven back to Georgia he won the decisive battle of Bloody Marsh on St. Simon Island, thus ending the Spanish threat.

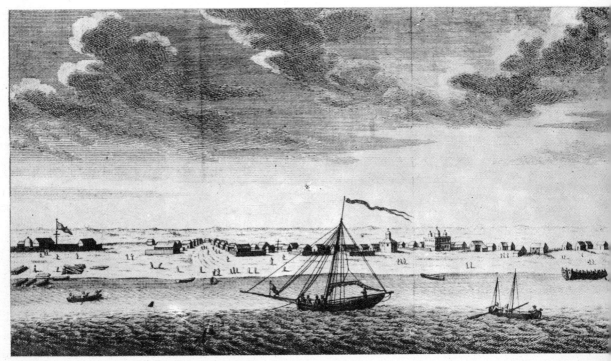

Courtesy, Stokes Collection, The New York Public Library.

View of Pensacola, Fla. 1743

Methodists

John Wesley, the founder of Methodism, accepted the charge of the Georgia mission in 1735, but did not stay long. His disciple, George Whitefield, came to Georgia in 1738 and founded an orphanage named Bethesda, near Savannah. He placed it under the management of James Habersham, who soon went to Charleston, S. C., to found the great mercantile establishment of Habersham and Harris. Whitefield visited the other English colonies in America, raised huge sums of money for charitable purposes, and set in motion a frenzy of evangelism.

John Wesley

George Whitefield

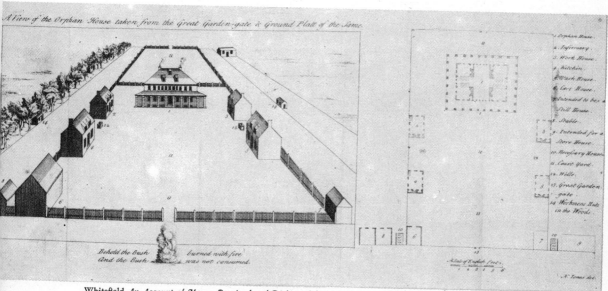

Whitefield *An Account of Money Received and Disbursed for the Orphan-House in Georgia.* 1741.

Orphanage at Bethesda

Georgia became a Royal Province in 1752, the Trustees being forced to sell out to their King. Their Utopia had collapsed. The Moravians moved to Pennsylvania. The Scotch settlers remained, prospered and survived. Rum and slavery were introduced. The stage was set for cotton.

7

PENNSYLVANIA

Engraving by John Sartain. William Penn as a young soldier in Ireland

It was fortunate that William Penn's father was a wealthy and influential admiral in His Majesty's Navy—fortunate for Pennsylvania and the Quakers. Charles II, to discharge a debt of £16,000 owed to Admiral Penn, gave Pennsylvania to his son.

The handsome and brilliant young Penn had been a disappointment to his father, forsaking court society and a government career to embrace the religion of the Quakers, a persecuted sect founded by George Fox, an unlettered preacher. William Penn publicly defended the Quakers with such eloquence that he was imprisoned in the Tower of London. Here, behind grim walls, he wrote some of the masterpieces of Quaker literature.

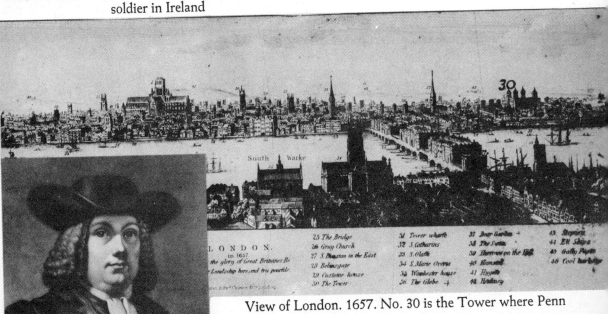

View of London. 1657. No. 30 is the Tower where Penn was imprisoned

Penn the Quaker

Towns on the Delaware

The Pennsylvania charter was granted in 1681, and William Penn made preparations to found a Quaker settlement. Thomas Holme surveyed the region between the Delaware and Schuylkill rivers, and located the site of Philadelphia.

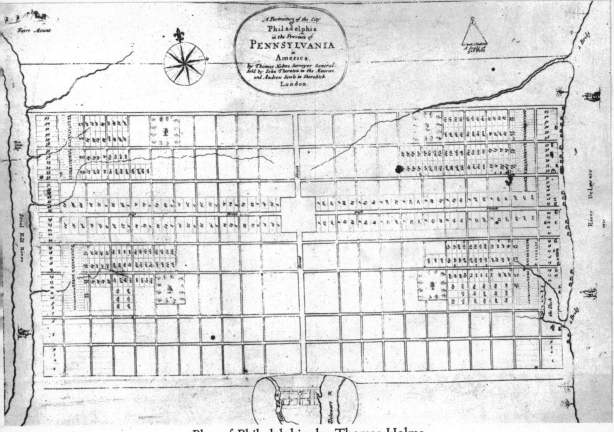

Plan of Philadelphia, by Thomas Holme

Contrast the broad, straight streets with the narrow, crooked streets and alleys of contemporary European cities. This is an early example of intelligent city planning. Note spaces provided for parks

Penn first took possession of New Castle on the Delaware, ceded to him by the Duke of York, and also of the Swedish town of Upland, which he renamed Chester. From these he proceeded up the Delaware to Philadelphia, where he arrived in October, 1682, on the ship *Welcome*.

Penn landing at Chester

John F. Watson *Annals of Philadelphia.* 1830.

Penn landing at Philadelphia

"Never Sworn to and Never Broken"

Advertising Pennsylvania on playing cards

One of the first things that Penn accomplished was a lasting treaty with the Indians. His policy, like that of the Swedes on the Delaware, was to live in peace and harmony with the Indians and to pay them for their land. Voltaire remarked that this was "the only treaty never sworn to and never broken."

Penn's treaty with the Indians, at Shackamaxon (now Kensington), in 1682. Painting by Benjamin West

Benjamin West (1728-1820), who painted the famous treaty scene, was born not far from the site depicted. This American painter was to achieve the honor of becoming the President of the Royal Academy in London in 1792, succeeding Sir Joshua Reynolds.

Birthplace of Benjamin West, near Chester, Pa.

Mason Locke Weems, later known as "Parson" Weems, who created the legend of George Washington and the cherry tree, wrote a life of Penn, and in it is a list of goods given to the Indians in exchange for land.

Excerpt from *The Life of William Penn*, by Mason Locke Weems. 1822

The Walking Purchase

In 1686 the Delaware Indians deeded to William Penn a tract in the fork of the Delaware and Lehigh rivers embracing an area in depth as far as a man could walk in a day and a half, or about forty miles. In 1737 Thomas Penn, by the ruse of hiring expert walkers increased the distance to 66½ miles, thereby arousing the ire of the Delaware Indians.

Courtesy, The New York Public Library.
Along the Lehigh River

Lappawinsoe. Delaware chief, one of the signers of the Walking Purchase. A painting by the Swedish artist, Gustavus Hesselius, 1735.

McKenney and Hall *History of the Indian Tribes.* 1836.

Below Indian Village in Pennsylvania

Below Cabin in the clearing

Right Log cabin in Pennsylvania

Shurtleff *Log Cabin Myth.* 1939.

Courtesy, Harvard University Press.

The Sawkill

The American Landscape. 1830.

Falls of the Sawkill

Day *Historical Collections of the State of Pennsylvania.* 1843.

Old Assembly House and Penn's Landing Place.
Chester, Pa.

Right Town Hall. Chester, Pa.
Built 1724

George Smith *History of Delaware County Pennsylvania.* 1862.

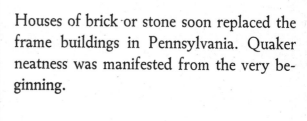

About a mile and a half northwest from Chester, on the left bank of Chester cr., and a short distance above the mill of Richard Flowers, there still exists an humble cottage, built principally of brick, of which the annexed is a correct sketch. This is the original dwelling erected by Richard Townsend, for the accommodation of his family while he was tend-

ing the first mill erected in the province. The mill stood some forty rods above the cottage. The original mill is all gone, but the rocks around bear traces of its existence, and the log platform still remains under water at the place where the original ford was, on the road to Philadelphia. The partners in this mill were William Penn, Caleb Pusey, and Samuel Carpenter, and their initials are inserted in the curious antiquated iron vane which was once erected on the roof of the mill, and is still engaged in its 144th year of duty on the top of Mr. Flowers' house. In this cottage, no doubt, Penn, Pusey, and Carpenter have often met to count their gains, and to devise plans for the future good of the province. The hipped roof of the cottage was added by Samuel Shaw, who, before the revolution, erected the second mill near this place.

Houses of brick or stone soon replaced the frame buildings in Pennsylvania. Quaker neatness was manifested from the very beginning.

Left Caleb Pusey House, near Chester, Pa.
Day *Historical Collections of the State of Pennsylvania.* 1843.

Letitia Street House

William Penn lived at the Letitia Street House in Philadelphia, built for him, 1682-83.

Watson *Annals of Philadelphia.* 1830.
Letitia House. Named for Penn's daughter

Right Letitia Street House as it appears today
Courtesy, Philadelphia Museum of Art, Philadelphia.

Penn Lived Here

Left Letitia Street House. First
floor front
Courtesy, Philadelphia Museum of Art, Philadelphia.

Right Letitia Street House. First
floor rear

Courtesy, Pennsylvania Museum of Art, Philadelphia.

The Penn Doll

"Letitia Penn", a doll brought to Pennsylvania by William Penn in 1699

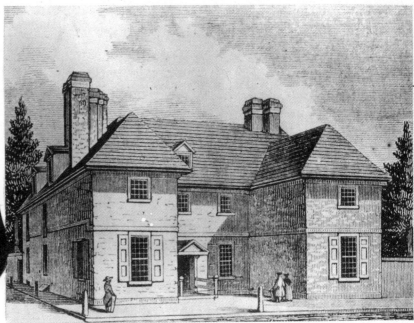

Slate Roof House. Philadelphia. Occupied by William Penn, 1699-1700

Quaker Meeting Houses

Left Quaker meeting

Ernst Von Helle *Nord-Amerika*. 1800.

Below William Penn's Meeting House. Chester, Pa.

"Many Mansions"

George Smith *History of Delaware County Pennsylvania.* 1862.

Friends Meeting House. Haverford, Pa. Built 1700.
Note the wagon shed

Views of Philadelphia. 1827-30.

Friends Meeting House. Merion, Pa. Built ca. 1700

Below Modern view of Friends
Meeting House. Merion, Pa.
Photo by Philip B. Wallace.

Smith *History of Delaware County Pennsylvania.*

St. David's Church, Radnor, Pa.

Photo by Philip B. Wallace.

Modern view of St. David's Church.
Radnor, Pa.

Right St. Paul's Church. Chester, Pa. 1703
Smith *History of Delaware County, Pennsylvania.*

Quaker Women

The Society of Friends permitted women to preach, and Rebecca Jones of Philadelphia was one of the best known. Here we see some of her relics.

Photo by Philip B. Wallace.

Miniature facsimile of the dress
worn by Rebecca Jones

Photo by Philip B. Wallace.

Linen mittens and silk reticule belonging to Rebecca Jones

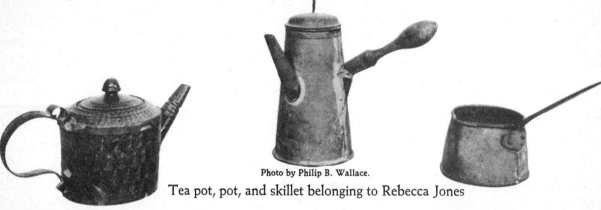

Photo by Philip B. Wallace.

Tea pot, pot, and skillet belonging to Rebecca Jones

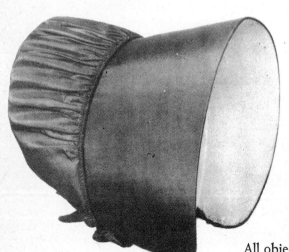

Quaker bonnet of
silk

Photo by Philip B. Wallace.

Photo by Philip B. Wallace.

Utensil holder made by a
Quakeress

All objects on this page are furnished through the courtesy of the
Atwater Kent Museum, Philadelphia

Friends

Quakeress costume

Courtesy, Philadelphia Museum of Art,
Philadelphia.

Courtesy, Bulletin, Friends Historical Society, Philadelphia.

Quakeress preaching

Courtesy, Bulletin, Friends Historical Society,
Philadelphia.

A Quaker synod

Primitive painting by Ed-
ward Hicks

Quaker farm

The Moravians Arrive

The Moravians in Georgia, refusing to bear arms under Oglethorpe, moved to Pennsylvania. They founded the towns of Bethlehem and Nazareth. Swarms of persecuted Moravians in Saxony fled to Pennsylvania to join their brethren.

Moravian colonists being married in a group ceremony before departing for America

Kurze Zuverlassige Nachricht. 1757.

Left Pottery. Sgraffito decoration. Pennsylvania

Bethlehem, Pa. Sketch by Governor Thomas Pownall, engraved by Paul Sandby. 1761.

Henry *History of the Lehigh Valley*. 1860.

Bethlehem Islands in the Lehigh River

Kurze Zuverlassige Nachricht. 1757.

Moravian christening

Kurze Zuverlassige Nachricht. 1757.

Children's love-feast

Music and . . .

The Moravians brought to America a lively appreciation for church music. Bethlehem, Pennsylvania, even today, is noted for its music festivals.

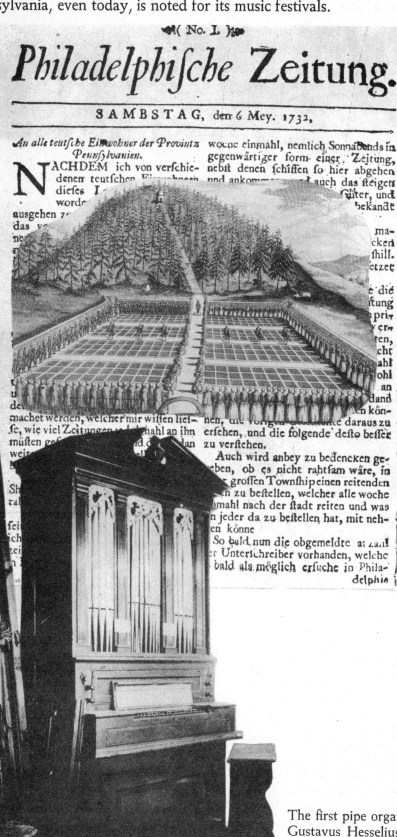

Left The Moravians brought this beautiful custom to Pennsylvania. Note the musical instruments held by the men to the left

Easter liturgy
Kurze Zuverlassige Nachricht. 1757.

Mysticism

The Germans were also inclined to mysticism. Johannes Kelpius founded the Pietist sect called The Woman of the Wilderness. He lived in a cave near Germantown, Pennsylvania.

Johannes Kelpius
Der Deutsche Pionier. 1870.

The first pipe organ built in America. It was made by Gustavus Hesselius and John G. Klemm in Philadelphia. Installed in the "Gemein-House" in Bethlehem in 1746

Courtesy, Moravian Historical Society, Nazareth, Pa.

Lutherans

The German followers of Martin Luther found in hospitable Pennsylvania a seed-plot for their faith. Their church at Trappe is a Lutheran shrine.

Day Historical Collections of the State of Pennsylvania. 1843.

Trappe

Wertenbaker *The Founding of American Civilization.* 1938.

Below Modern view of Trappe

Courtesy, The Historical Society of York County, York, Pa.

Drawings by Lewis Miller.

Good Earth

The arts of husbandry flourished in Pennsylvania, and with unerring instinct the shrewd farmers chose some of the most fertile acres in all the world.

Courtesy, Landis Valley Museum, Landis Valley, Pa.

Wooden plow

Courtesy, The New York Historical Society, New York.

Metamorphosis of an American farm

Sketch by Governor Thomas Pownall. Engraved by James Peake. 1761

Good Apples

Courtesy, Landis Valley Museum.

Cider press

Hexerei

The Germans put decorative "hex" symbols on their barns to ward off evil spirits.

Wertenbaker The Founding of American Civilization. 1938.

Barn decorations, Berks County, Pa.

American Guide Series. Pennsylvania.
Courtesy, Oxford University Press.

Logs

Following the example of the Swedes and Finns the early settlers in Pennsylvania erected log cabins and barns.

Courtesy, Old Time New England. 1927.

Slifer log house. Bucks County, Pa.

Courtesy, Pennsylvania German Society.

Landis' Store

Left Log barn
Courtesy, Landis Valley Museum.

Locks

Courtesy, Landis Valley Museum.

Barn locks

Meat and Lard

Meat barrel

Courtesy, Landis Valley Museum.

Outdoor furnace with iron kettles. In these kettles were made soap, lard, and apple butter, and on wash day they were used for boiling clothes

Butcher . . .

Courtesy, Landis Valley Museum.

Pennsylvania butchering tools and utensils

Baker . . .

Pennsylvania German Society. Proceedings. 1899.

Outdoor bake oven. Pennsylvania

Right Pennsylvania kitchen. Original
sketch by Lewis Miller

Courtesy, The Historical Society of York County,
York, Pa.

And Candle Stick Maker

Courtesy, Landis Valley Museum, Landis Valley, Pa.

Candle stick molds

Candle-dipping reel

Courtesy, Bucks County Historical Society, Doylestown, Pa.

Home Made Bread!

Courtesy, The Metropolitan Museum of Art, New York.

Pennsylvania dough trough

Right Bread basket

Courtesy, Landis Valley Museum, Landis Valley, Pa.

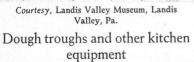

Courtesy, Landis Valley Museum, Landis Valley, Pa.

Dough troughs and other kitchen equipment

Below Rolling pins, towel rollers, etc.

Courtesy, Landis Valley Museum, Landis Valley, Pa.

Cheese

Cheese making

Diderot and D'Alembert *Encyclopedie. Recueil des planches.* 1762-72.

Marzipan

The Pennsylvania Germans loved cakes and cookies. Artistic moulds were made for the special festival cookies called "Marzipan."

Courtesy, Landis Valley Museum, Landis Valley, Pa.

Designs in marzipan moulds

The same folk-art was carried over into butter mould designs.   **Butter Moulds**

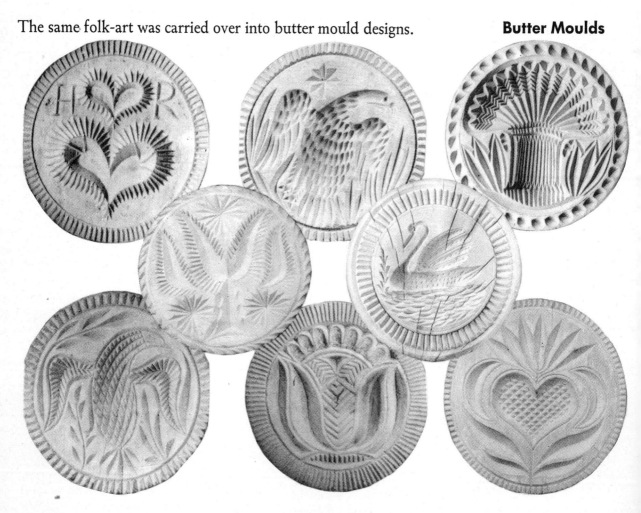

Courtesy, Landis Valley Museum, Landis Valley, Pa.

Wooden butter moulds. Pennsylvania

Tulips

The favorite decorative motif of the Pennsylvania Germans was the tulip. It appeared time and again in various forms.

Butter mould. Tulip design

Courtesy, Philadelphia Museum of Art, Philadelphia.

Pennsylvania German pottery dish. Slip decoration (Sgraffito). 1769

Left Pine wall corner cupboard. Pennsylvania German. Note the tulip design in the piece of pottery

Courtesy, Philadelphia Museum of Art, Philadelphia.

Below Dower chest made by Christian Setzer. 1785

Courtesy, The Magazine *Antiques*, New York.

They Never Dreamed of Electricity, Aluminum, or Stainless Steel

Wooden sink and drain board

Right Settle used in front of the kitchen fireplace

In every Pennsylvania kitchen were ingenious hand-made utensils and gadgets.

Knife and fork cleaner

Miscellaneous kitchen utensils

Miscellaneous objects. Note the bootjack in foreground

Dutch oven

Left Muffin irons

All objects on this page are reproduced through the courtesy of the Landis Valley Museum, Landis Valley, Pa.

They Could Make or Mend Anything

Courtesy, Landis Valley Museum, Landis Valley, Pa.

Hobby-horse. Lancaster County, Pa.

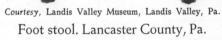

Courtesy, Bucks County Historical Society, Doylestown, Pa.

Mouse traps. Pennsylvania

Cries of London. ca. 1790.

Tinker

Courtesy, Landis Valley Museum, Landis Valley, Pa.

Foot stool. Lancaster County, Pa.

Right Chair mender

Cries of London. ca. 1790.

Mills and Ferries

Along the rivers of Pennsylvania were mills, furnaces, and ferries.

Courtesy, Pennsylvania German Society.

Ruins of an old mill on Cresheim Creek, Pennsylvania

Courtesy, Landis Valley Museum, Landis Valley, Pa.

Mill stone. Used to crush oak bark
for tannery

Birthplace of David Rittenhouse, Papermill Run,
Germantown, Pa.

The Rittenhouse family had a paper mill here as early as 1690

Mendenhall Ferry. Schuylkill River

Line engraving by William Birch.

Courtesy, Landis Valley Museum, Landis Valley, Pa.

Mill at Ephrata Cloister, Ephrata, Pa.

The Wall of the Alleghenies

The Pennsylvania settlers occupied the farm lands east of the Alleghenies. They crouched at the slopes of these mountains, for beyond them lay danger—the French and Indians. They sent a few traders, missionaries, and explorers into the mountains and built outposts on the Susquehanna River, but the great westward push awaited its appointed hour.

Below The Susquehanna
Picturesque America. 1872-74.

Courtesy, Mrs. Evan Randolph and J. B. Lippincott Co., Philadelphia.

Shoomac Park. Ridge Road. Falls of the Schuylkill

Water color by Köllner ca. 1714

Lancaster, Pa.

Carlisle, Pa.

Edouard C. V. Colbert, Comte de Maulevrier *Voyage.* ca. 1796-98.

Courtesy, Institut Francais de Washington, and the Johns Hopkins Press, Baltimore.

8

THE FIRST HALF
OF THE EIGHTEENTH CENTURY

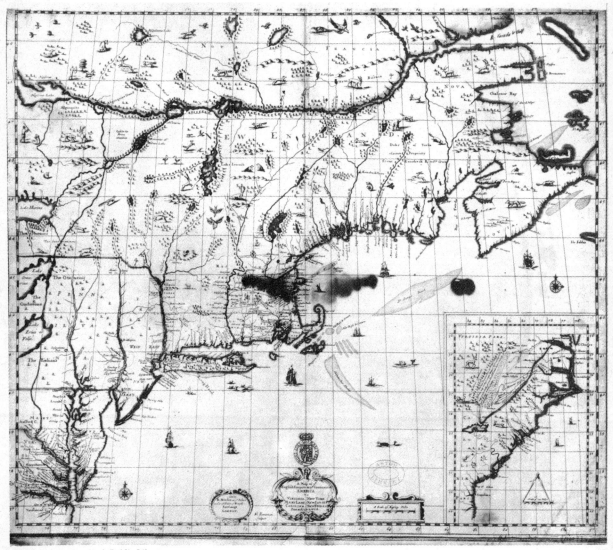

Courtesy, The New York Public Library.

Map of the English colonies in North America. ca. 1700

At the beginning of the Eighteenth Century the American colonies were firmly established, with the exception of Georgia (chartered 1732), but in spite of the common dangers and hardships of the wilderness there was as yet no general realization of a common destiny. Each colony clung tenaciously to its own form of political and economic organization—to its trade with the hinterland or its trade from the sea. Schemes for colonial union found no soil in which to take root. Each of the colonies looked first to itself, next to the Mother Country, and scarcely at all to its sister colonies up and down the Atlantic seaboard.

It is interesting to note that Jamestown, St. Mary's City, and Plymouth were declining, while Williamsburg, Charleston, Boston, New York, and Philadelphia were growing in size and importance. Commerce and population increased wherever the Royal governors held court, and where good natural harbors existed.

Where Virginia's Royal Governor Presided

Photo by Richard Garrison. *Courtesy*, Colonial Williamsburg, Inc.
The Capitol at Williamsburg, Va. Restored

Williamsburg's "Rosetta Stone"

The "Frenchman's map" of Williamsburg, Va. 1782

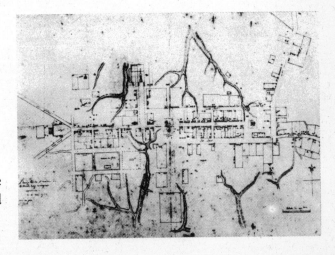

The previous discovery of this map, which gave the exact location of every building, greatly facilitated the recent restoration of this colonial capital.

Courtesy, Colonial Williamsburg, Inc.

New York

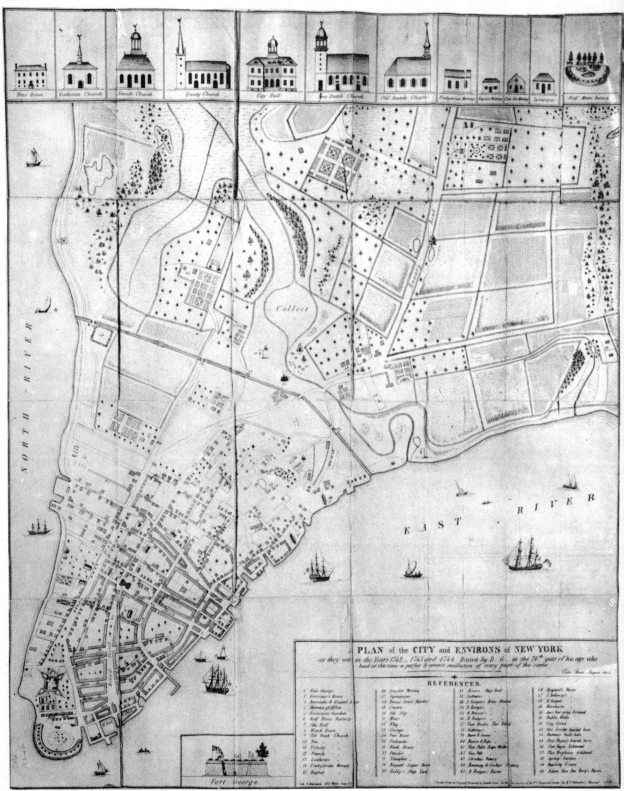

Valentine's Manual. 1854.

New York and environs. 1742-44

Dutch New Amsterdam ended at Wall Street. Note how the town has spread northward. The number of churches, including a synagogue and a Quaker meeting house, indicate that religious tolerance was at work. Almost every church had a crowing cock for a weathervane. Even at this early period New York was developing its cosmopolitan aspect, a characteristic which it has never lost.

Sky Line

London Magazine. Aug. 1761. Date depicted 1746. *Courtesy,* The New York Public Library.

View of New York

Note the busy harbor scene. In the lower right-hand corner is an old Dutch house and the Brooklyn ferry. Note the cow pen. Both horses and oxen are seen. The buildings across the water still bear the mark of Dutch architecture. By looking at the foregoing map of New York many of the churches and other buildings in this view can be identified. Through the streets at night went the watchman with his staff and lantern.

Night watchman

Courtesy, Mr. Ledyard Cogswell, Jr. Albany, N. Y.

The First St. Peter's Church. Albany, N. Y.
1714-15

I. N. Phelps Stokes Iconography of Manhattan Island. 1915-28.

New Dutch church. New York. Finished 1731

Boston

Carwitham view of Boston. Date depicted ca. 1731-36. Based on the Burgis view of 1722

Note the many churches, the long wharf, and the rural aspects of the environs. American seaport towns clustered around the waterfront. Rivers and harbors were the main highways of commerce.

Philadelphia

Peter Cooper's painting of Philadelphia. 1718-20

Detail of Bartram House. Philadelphia

Back of These Towns—Wilderness

Henry *History of the Lehigh Valley.* 1860.

Slatington, Lehigh County, Pennsylvania

Hanson *Old Towns of Norridgewock and Canaan.* 1849.

Skowhegan and Bloomfield, Maine

Left Red fox

The Cabinet of Natural History. 1830-34.

Collot *Voyage dans L'Amerique Septentrionale.* 1826.

Cabin in the clearing

Left Vignette by F. O. C. Darley

Civilization

In spite of the primitive life on the frontier fringes a high state of civilization prevailed among the wealthier inhabitants of American cities and plantations. Their houses were elegantly furnished. Their costume followed the latest London and Paris styles. The houses of the poor have not been preserved, but many of the mansions of the wealthy merchants and planters have survived intact. Let us open the doors and enter some of them.

Doorway. Stenton, Logan Park, Philadelphia.
ca. 1721

Courtesy, The Essex Institute, Salem, Mass. Photo by Frank Cousins.

Courtesy, The Essex Institute, Salem, Mass. Photo by Frank Cousins.
Doorway. Warner House, Portsmouth, N. H.

Courtesy, Pocumtuck Valley Memorial Association of Deerfield, Mass.
Connecticut Valley doorway
Sheldon House, Deerfield, Mass.

New England

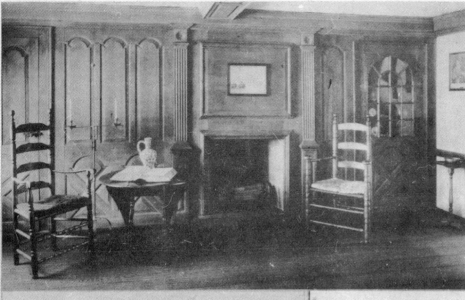

Room from Newington, Conn. 2nd quarter of 18th Century

Low ceilings prevailed in New England. The Holy Bible rests on the butterfly table. Note the built-in cupboard and the slat-back chairs. Pictures began to adorn the carefully plastered walls.

Courtesy, American Wing, The Metropolitan Museum of Art, New York.

Whitefield *The Homes of Our Forefathers.* 3 v. 1880-86.

Silliman House. Bridgeport, Conn.   King House. Newport, R. I. ca. 1710

Shumway House, Fiskdale, Mass. ca. 1740

Note the cupboard, the long hinges of the doors, the unique chest of drawers above the fireplace, and the warming pan and fireback. The chair at the gate-legged table is the Dutch style, with its cyma curves.

Courtesy, Museum of Fine Arts, Boston, Mass.

Courtesy, Museum of Fine Arts, Boston.

Room from West Boxford, Mass. ca. 1725

Whitefield *The Homes of Our Forefathers*. 1880-86.

Moll Pitcher House, Marblehead, Mass. ca. 1720.
(Not to be confused with the Moll Pitcher who was
a heroine of the American Revolution)

Details of stairways, "The Lindens",
Danvers, Mass. 1745

Courtesy, Essex Institute, Salem, Mass.

Orne House. Marblehead,
Mass. ca. 1730

Courtesy, Museum of Fine Arts,
Boston.

Pennsylvania

Rooms from Millbach,
Lebanon County,
Pa. 1752

The Pennsylvania
Germans loved deco-
rative design and color

Courtesy, Philadelphia Museum
of Art, Philadelphia.

Maryland

Living room. Henry Sewall House. Secretary, Md. 1720. Note the high ceiling, the cane chairs, and the wide door, designed for a warm climate

Courtesy, The Brooklyn Museum, Brooklyn, N. Y.

Room from Eltonhead Manor, Calvert County, Md. ca. 1720

Courtesy, Baltimore Museum of Art.

Entrance hall of Drayton Hall, Ashley River, S. C. 1740

Courtesy, Carolina Art Association, Charleston, S. C.

Old Virginia

Bed chamber of Governor's Palace, Williamsburg, Va.

In Virginia expensive carved beds were imported from England. Most New England beds were home made, and much simpler.

Courtesy, Colonial Williamsburg, Inc. Photo by Richard Garrison.

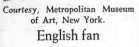
Courtesy, Metropolitan Museum of Art, New York.

English fan

Portrait of Evelyn Byrd, a Virginia belle

Kitchen. Governor's Palace, Williamsburg, Va.

The Governor's Palace in Williamsburg was built 1706-20, and was the center of fashion and social life in Virginia.

Courtesy, Colonial Williamsburg, Inc. Photo by Richard Garrison.

Exteriors

The exterior of American houses during this period show even more striking regional differences.

Whitefield *The Homes of Our Forefathers*, 1880-86.

Tillinghast Mansion, Providence, R. I. ca. 1710

Courtesy, Essex Institute, Salem, Mass.

Joseph Cabot House, Salem, Mass. 1748

Frary House, Deerfield, Mass.

Courtesy, Pocumtuck Valley Memorial Association of Deerfield, Mass.

Van Courtlandt Mansion, New York. 1748

Courtesy, Essex Institute, Salem, Mass.

Brick and Stone

Courtesy, Essex Institute, Salem, Mass. Photo by Frank Cousins.

Gov. Keith House, Graeme Park, Pennsylvania. 1721

Left Abel Nickolson House, Salem County, N. J. 1722

Maryland Mansion

Courtesy, Baltimore Museum of Art, and The Hughes Co., Baltimore.

Doughoregan Manor, Howard County, Md. The home of the Carroll family. 1727

South Carolina

Courtesy, The Charleston Museum, Charleston, S. C.

Drayton Hall, Ashley River, S. C. 1740

Mansions of the Old Dominion

"Westover." North front, Charles City County, Va.

Built by William Byrd II. 1726. One of the finest examples of Georgian architecture in America

"Stratford," Westmoreland County, Va.

Built by Thomas Lee between 1725 and 1730. Birthplace of Robert E. Lee. The huge chimneys are a feature. The kitchen and servants' quarters were separate dependencies a few yards away from the main house. These dependencies were typical of the South. The planter did not want the odors of the kitchen to permeate the dining room. Food was carried to the house in covered dishes.

Left Brass kettle used at "Eagle Point", Gloucester County, Va., and later at "Brampton", Madison County, Va.

Courtesy, Valentine Museum, Richmond, Va.

Costume

Let us look at the costume worn by the occupants of beautiful homes such as those just shown.

Wedding slipper worn by Elizabeth Wilson of Kingston, R. I. Oct. 15, 1730

Courtesy, United Shoe Machinery Corporation, Boston, Mass.

Dress worn at wedding of Mary, granddaughter of Gov. Leverett of Massachusetts. 1719

Courtesy, Essex Institute, Salem, Mass.

Costume dolls were the fashion. Here we see "Mehetable Hodges" or the Salem Doll

Courtesy, Mrs. Imogene Anderson, New York.

Button samples. 18th Century. Colonial costume required many buttons, and button salesmen called on fashionable ladies and gentlemen and allowed them to choose their buttons from sample cards.

Courtesy, Cooper Museum for the Arts of Decoration, New York.

Puritan Face

Courtesy, Essex Institute, Salem, Mass.

Abigail Gerrish and her grandmother, Abigail (Flint)
Holloway Gerrish. Painted by John Greenwood,
ca. 1750

A Gentleman from Maine

Courtesy, The Bowdoin College Museum of Fine Arts, Brunswick, Me.

William Bowdoin
Portrait by Robert Feke. 1748

Mayor of New York

Courtesy, The New-York Historical Society, New York.

Caleb Heathcote. Portrait made ca. 1710, by an unknown artist. Heathcote lived at the Manor of Scars-
dale in Westchester County, N. Y., and was mayor
of New York City, 1711-13

Patron of Yale College

Courtesy, Yale University Art Gallery.

Elihu Yale. Portrait by Zeeman. Yale gave funds to
the Collegiate School at Saybrook, Conn., which
honored him by renaming the institution Yale College in 1745, after its removal to New Haven

The Deerfield Massacre

To regard these elegant homes and this expensive costume as a true index of American life during the first half of the Eighteenth Century would be misleading. The bulk of the population were not rich or clad in fine clothes. They faced daily hardships, and on the frontier fringe were subjected to dangers of all kinds. We may cite as one example that on the early morning of February 29, 1704, a body of French soldiers and Indian allies surprised the sleeping inhabitants of Deerfield, a western outpost in Massachusetts, massacred about fifty men, women, and children, and carried over a hundred into captivity. The town was burned to the ground with the exception of a few houses.

Left Indian House, Deerfield, Mass. Restored

In this house a small group of defenders successfully resisted the Indian raid of 1704.

Courtesy, Pocumtuck Valley Memorial Association of Deerfield, Mass.

Right The attack on Indian House Woodcut by Alexander Anderson

Captives
A drawing by F. O. C. Darley

Blockhouse and Garrison

The Deerfield tragedy shocked the American colonies. Frontier defenses were strengthened. The French and Indians lurked in the woods from Maine to western Pennsylvania, and along the whole length of the Appalachian chain of mountains. No one knew where the enemy would strike next. The English blamed the French for stirring up Indian hatred. Father Rasle, a French missionary at Norridgewock, Me., was killed by the English in 1724, accused of fomenting trouble among the Abenaki Indians.

Blockhouse and sawmill
Anburey Travels Through America. 1789.

Courtesy, Maine Historical Society.
Strong box belonging to
Father Rasle

Courtesy, Maine Historical Society.
Bell belonging to Father
Rasle

July 14th. 1703.
Prices of Goods

Supplyed to the

Eastern Indians,

Truckmasters ; and of the Peltry received
by the Truckmasters of the said *Indians.*

One yard Broad Cloth, *three* Beaver skins, *in season.*
One yard & half Gingerline, *one* Beaver skin, *in season.*
One yard Red or Blew Kerfey, *two* Beaver skins, *in season.*
One yard good Duffels, *one* Beaver skin, *in season.*
One yard & half broad fine Cotton, *one* Beaver skin, *in season*
Two yards of Cotton, *one* Beaver skin, *in season.*
One yard & half of half thicks, *one* Beaver skin, *in season.*
Five Pecks Indian Corn, *one* Beaver skin, *in season.*

What *shall be accounted in Value equal*
One Beaver in season : *Viz.*

One Otter skin in season, is one Beaver
One Bear skin in season, is one Beaver,
Two Half skins in season, is one Beaver

Courtesy, The New York Public Library.

Travel

Between the cities and the frontier blockhouses, were isolated farms and plantations connected by water or narrow, foot-worn Indian trails. Roads, if they existed, were full of snow drifts in the winter, and mud holes in the spring. A few hardy souls traveled by horseback, and around New York and Philadelphia short stage coach routes were laid out. The large rivers were not bridged and the ferryman did a brisk business, particularly if he ran a tavern at the water's edge.

Diderot and D'Alembert *Encyclopedie. Recueil des planches.* 1762-72.

English saddles. 18th Century

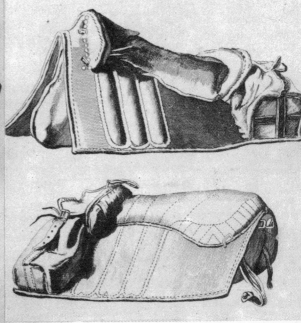

Above Postman's saddle
Below Postilion's saddle
The postilion rode one of the horses hitched to the stage coach.

Valentine's Manual. 1853.

Cato's Tavern on the Boston Post Road. ca. 1712

Below Old Spread Eagle Inn near Lancaster, Pa.

Note the worm fence made of hand-hewn rails, and the stumps in the clearing.

Courtesy, Pennsylvania German Society.

Ferry and Tavern

This Act was passed in the 6th Year of the Reign of his present Majesty King George II.

An ACT to regulate the Ferry between the City of New-York and the Island of Nassau, and to establish the Ferriage thereof.

BE it Enacted by his Excellency the Governor, the Council, and the General Assembly, and it is hereby Enacted by the Authority of the same, That from the Twelfth Day of June next ensuing, and at all Times hereafter, the Ferriage for transporting Men, Women, Horses, Cattle, Grain, and all Manner of Goods, Wares and Merchandizes, over the said Ferry, either forward or backward, shall be, and hereby are established, to be and remain after the Rates and Prices following, That is to say,

Rates to be taken for Ferriage.

For transporting every Person from the City of New-York to the Island of Nassau, or from the Island of Nassau to the City of New-York, Ten Grains of Sevil, Pillar or Mexico Plate, or Two Pence in Bills of Credit, made current in this Colony; and if after Sun-set, double that Rate; unless a Neglect or Refusal in the Ferry-Man, to transport Passengers over sooner: Always Provided, That a Sucking-Child, or some Remnants of Goods, or other small Goods (not herein-after-rated) which a Woman carries in her Apron, or a Man or a Boy under his Arm, shall be free from Ferriage.
For every Horse or Beast, One Shilling in like Money.
For every live Calf or Hog, Four Pence in like Money.
For every live Sheep or Lamb, Three Pence in like Money.
For every dead Hog, Three Pence in like Money.
For every dead Sheep, Lamb or Calf, Two Pence in like Money.
For every Barrel of Rum, Sugar, Molasses, or other full Barrel, Eight Pence in like Money.
For every empty Barrel, Three Pence in like Money.
For every empty Pipe or Hogshead, Nine Pence in like Money.
For every Beast's Hide, Three Pence in like Money.
For every undressed Calf, Sheep or Deer Skin, One Penny in like Money.
For every Pail of Butter, One Penny in like Money.
For every Firkin or Tub of Butter, Two Pence in like Money.
For every Bushel of Salt, Wheat, Grain, Seeds, or any other Thing usually measured, and sold by the Bushel, One Half-penny in like Money.
For every full Pipe or full Hogshead, Four Shillings in like Money.
For every Inch Board, One Penny in like Money.
For every Board of one Inch and an Half, One Penny Half-penny in like Money.
For every Waggon, Five Shillings in like Money.
For every Pair of Cart-Wheels, Eighteen Pence in like Money.
For every Cupboard, Press for Cloaths, or Writing-Desk, One Shilling in like Money.
For every full Trunk or Chest, One Shilling in like Money.
For every empty Trunk or Chest, Nine Pence in like Money.
For every Half Barrel of Flour, or any other Half Barrel, Four Pence in like Money.
For every Barrel of Bread, Six Pence in like Money.
For every Bag of Bread, One Penny Half-penny in like Money.
For every Gammon of Bacon, Turkey or Goose, One Half-penny in like Money.
For every Hundred of Eggs, Three Eggs, and so in like Proportion for a greater or lesser Number.
For every Dunghill Fowl, Brant, Duck, Heath-Hen or Partridge, One Farthing in like Money.

For every Dozen of Pigeons, Quails or Snipes, One Penny in like Money.
For every Dozen of smaller Birds, One Half-penny in like Money.
For every Hundred Weight of Iron, Steel, Shot, Pewter or Iron, Copper or Brass Kettles or Pots, Six Pence in like Money, and in that Proportion for a greater or lesser Quantity.
For every Hundred Weight of Gun-Powder, One Shilling in like Money.
For every Sythe or Sith, One Half-penny in like Money.
For every Firkin of Soap, Two Pence in like Money.
For every Cheese, One Half-penny in like Money.
For every Corn Fan, Three Pence in like Money.
For every Hundred of Shingles, Six Pence in like Money.
For every Cedar Bolt, One Penny in like Money.
For every common Bag of Cotton-Wool, One Penny in like Money.
For every Bale of Cotton-Wool or Hops, Eighteen Pence in like Money.
For every Coach, Six Shillings in like Money.
For every Chaise, Three Shillings in like Money.
For every single Sleigh, Eighteen Pence in like Money.
For every double Sleigh, Two Shillings in like Money.
For every Piece of Ozenbrigs, Two Pence in like Money.
For every Piece of Blankets or Duffils, Eighteen Pence in like Money.
For every Piece of Cotton, Pennistone, Flannel or Frize, Four Pence in like Money.
For every Piece of Broad-Cloth, Kersey, Strouds, Halfthicks and Druggets, Three Pence in like Money.
For every Piece of Wadding, Two Pence in like Money.
For every Piece of Duroys, Calaminoes, Shalloons, or other Stuff, and for every Piece of Garlix, Holland, or other Linnen, One Penny in like Money.
For every empty Firkin or Pail, One Half-penny in like Money.
For every Side of Sole-Leather, Two Pence in like Money.
For every Side of Upper-Leather, One Penny in like Money.
For every Hundred Weight of Bever, Raccoon-Skins, or Cat's, Nine Pence in like Money, and so in Proportion for a greater or lesser Quantity.
For every half Dozen of Hats, One Penny Half-penny in like Money.
For every Dozen of Fish, called Sheepshead, Two Pence in like Money.
For every Hundred Weight of Dying-Wood, Eight Pence in like Money, and so in Proportion for a greater or lesser Quantity.
For every Hundred Weight of Copperas, Allom or Brimstone, Six Pence in like Money, and so in Proportion for a greater or lesser Quantity.
For every Chair, One Penny in like Money.
For every half Dozen Pair of Wool-Cards, One Penny in like Money.
For every Saddle without a Horse, Two Pence in like Money.
For every Rug, One Penny in like Money.
For every Gun, One Penny in like Money.
For every Spade, One Half-penny in like Money.
For every Case with Bottles, Three Pence in like Money.
For every Looking-Glass of Two Foot high and upwards, Four Pence in like Money.
For every Looking-Glass of One Foot high, Two Pence in like Money.
For every Hundred Weight of Rice, Two Pence in like Money, and so in

Courtesy, The New York Public Library.

Ferry rates. ca. 1733

Courtesy, Pennsylvania German Society. Proceedings. 1912.

The Red Lion Inn near Holmesburg, Pa. Built 1730

Note the sign.

Philadelphia Ferry

From George Heap's View of Philadelphia.

Courtesy, The New-York Historical Society, New York

Courtesy, Bucks County Historical Society, Doylestown, Pa.

Tavern sign of the Red Lion Tavern, shown above

The Great Awakening

Around the year 1740 a wave of religious frenzy swept the American colonies. It has been called The Great Awakening. Eloquent preachers like George Whitefield and Jonathan Edwards attracted huge crowds wherever they went. This common religious excitement helped to break down the inter-colonial isolation. The evangelists and their followers carried news from one town to another, rich and poor alike were linked by a new bond of fellowship, and the spirit of democracy was emerging.

Rev. George Whitefield

After bringing Methodism to Georgia, Whitefield visited other colonies. He enjoyed a sensational success as an evangelist and raised large sums of money for charitable institutions.

Rev. Jonathan Edwards

An engraving after a painting now thought to have been the work of Joseph Badger.

George Ninde *George Whitefield*. 1924.
Courtesy, Abingdon Press, Nashville, Tenn.

Field pulpit used by George Whitefield
George Ninde *George Whitefield*. 1924

Courtesy, The Forbes Library, Northampton, Mass.

Home of Jonathan Edwards, Northampton, Mass.

Sinners In the Hands of an Angry God

Jonathan Edwards preached a sermon at Enfield, Mass., in 1741 entitled *Sinners in the Hands of An Angry God* which pictured the torments of Hell. Mass hysteria often followed the fiery sermons preached by Edwards.

SINNERS
In the Hands of an
Angry GOD.
A SERMON

Preached at *Enfield*, July 8th 1741.

At a Time of great Awakenings ; and attended with remarkable Impressions on many of the Hearers.

By *Jonathan Edwards*, A.M.
Pastor of the Church of CHRIST in Northampton.

Amos ix 2, 3. *Though they dig into Hell, thence shall mine Hand take them ; though they climb up to Heaven, thence will I bring them down. And though they hide themselves in the Top of Carmel, I will search and take them out thence ; and though they be hid from my Sight in the Bottom of the Sea, thence I will command the Serpent, and he shall bite them.*

The Second Edition.

TON : Printed and Sold by S. KNEELAND
T. GREEN in Queen-Street over against the
1742.

Courtesy, Museum of Fine Arts, Boston.

Mrs. Jonathan Edwards. Portrait by Joseph Badger. Sarah Pierpont of New Haven married Jonathan Edwards in 1727, and was described by her husband as being "always full of joy and pleasure".

Camp meeting in the woods. Drawing by F. O. C. Darley

of an angry GOD. 11

Thief ; D
quick f
ing r
of

Death, but what are contained in the
Grace, the Promises 'that are given in
om all the Promises are Yea and Amen.
y have no Interest in the Promises of the
Grace that are not the Children of the
that don't believe in any of the Promises
nt, and have no Interest in the *Mediator*
nt.

hatever some have imagined and pre-
Promises made to natural Men's earnest
knocking, 'tis plain and manifest that
s a natural Man takes in Religion, what-
he makes, till he believes in Christ, God
Manner of Obligation to keep him a *Mo-*
ernal Destruction.

So that thus it is, that natural Men are held in the Hand of God over the Pit of Hell ; they have deserved the fiery Pit, and are already sentenced to it ; and God is dreadfully provoked, his Anger is as great towards them as to those that are actually suffering the Executions of the fierceness of his Wrath in Hell, and they have done nothing in the least to appease or abate that Anger, neither is God in the least bound by any mise to hold 'em up one Moment ; the Devil is for them, Hell is gaping for them, the Flames gather

to speak with them, and could inquire of them, one by one, whether they expected when alive, and when they used to hear about Hell, ever to be the Subjects of that Misery, we doubtless should hear one & another reply, No, I never intended to come here ; I had laid out Matters otherwise in my Mind ; I thought I should contrive well for my self ; I thought my Scheme good ; I intended to take effectual Care ; but it came upon me unexpected ; I did not look for it at that Time, and in that Manner ; it came

Log College and the Presbyterians

Many sectarian schools and colleges were founded as a result of this religious stirring. Log College, established in 1726 at Neshaminy, Pennsylvania, by William Tennent, was the nucleus from which Princeton University, as well as many other Presbyterian schools and churches, sprang. Samuel Finley conducted a school for ministers at Nottingham, Pa., 1744-1761, and became president of the College of New Jersey (Princeton).

Samuel Finley. Portrait engraved by John Sartain

Ferris *History of the Original Settlements on the Delaware.* 1846.

First Presbyterian Meeting House, Wilmington, Del. 1740

Lutherans

In 1742, Heinrich Melchior Muhlenberg came to Pennsylvania to serve as a German Lutheran missionary. He founded churches and schools, and his sons, Frederick Augustus Conrad and John Peter Gabriel, became distinguished clergymen.

Courtesy, Pennsylvania German Society. Proceedings

Heinrich Melchior Muhlenberg

Courtesy, The Historical Society of York County, York, Pa.

Lutheran christening. Sketch by Lewis Miller

In 1745 Heinrich Melchior Muhlenberg married Anna Maria, daughter of Conrad Weiser of Tulpehocken.

Conrad Weiser House, near Womelsdorf, Pa. Weiser was a famous interpreter of Indian languages at treaty conferences

Right Conrad Weiser
Courtesy, Pennsylvania German Society. Proceedings. 1898.

Mennonites

The sect of Amish Mennonites around Lancaster, Pennsylvania always dressed in austere black. They were industrious farmers and lived to themselves.

Courtesy, Landis Valley Museum.
Mennonite buggy

Courtesy, Pennsylvania German Society. Proceedings. 1911.
Amish couple

Kurze Zuverlassige Nachricht. 1757.
Foot washing, a ritual practiced by the Amish and Moravian sects

Ephrata Cloister

None of the German sects in Pennsylvania were more interesting or culturally significant than that established at Ephrata near Lancaster under the leadership of Conrad Beissel in 1735. The Brethren and Sisters lived in humble simplicity in the manner of medieval monks and nuns. Ephrata had its own grist mill, paper mill, printing press, book bindery, bakery, tannery and other self-supporting adjuncts. The Brethren made furniture and other necessaries, and the Sisters illuminated manuscripts, copied musical scores, and did exquisite needlework.

Photo by Philip B. Wallace.

Saal and Sister House. Ephrata Cloister

Kimball *Domestic Architecture of the American Colonies.* 1922.

Porch of the Sister House. Ephrata Cloister

Above Title-page of a hymn book printed at Ephrata Cloister

Right Ephrata Sister. Illuminated manuscript

Jews

Synagogues in New York, Newport, Charleston, and other American cities provided places of worship for the growing Jewish population.

Ceremonies and Religious Customs of the Various Nations of the Known World. 1733-34.

Blowing the shophar on the Jewish New Year, an ancient custom. The interior of Trouro Synagogue in Newport, R. I., is strikingly similar to the one shown here.

Courtesy, Redwood Library, Newport, R. I.

Jacob Rodriguez Rivera of Newport, R. I. Portrait by Gilbert Stuart. The Rivera family improved lighting facilities in the 1740's by the introduction of spermaceti candles

Courtesy, Museum of the City of New York.

Silver tankard made for the Livingston family by the Jewish silversmith, Myer Myers

Puritans and Anglicans

The Puritans and Anglicans were the leading religious groups in America and dominated the ecclesiastical and political life of the colonies. The provincial governors, being Church of England men, were in a position to exert considerable authority, particularly in the southern colonies, whereas the Puritans of New England, by sheer force of numbers, constituted a serious threat to Anglican leadership.

Courtesy, Essex Institute, Salem, Mass.

St. Peter's Church. Salem, Mass. Water color by George Perkins 1733

Right Bruton Parish Church, Williamsburg, Va. 1710-15

Courtesy, Colonial Williamsburg, Inc.

Whitefield *The Homes of Our Forefathers.* 3 v. 1880-86.

St. Michael's Church. Marblehead, Mass. 1714

Specimen of New England church music

Walter *Grounds and Rules of Musick Explained.* 1721.

Louisburg

If the Great Awakening brought the American colonies together spiritually, the successful military and naval engagements against the French at Louisburg on Cape Breton Island in 1744-45, gave them visions of future independence. The much-publicized Louisburg campaign proved to the raw provincial troops that they could fight and win battles as well as the better-trained British regulars. The Americans began to feel cocky.

London Magazine. 1746.

British Foot Guards. Exercises from the British Manual of Arms

Sir William Pepperell of Kittery, Me., was chosen to lead the American troops at the siege of Louisburg. He knew little about the art of siege, and his troops knew even less, but in spite of recklessness, lack of discipline, and inexperience they carried the day.

Sir William Pepperell. From a painting
by John Smibert

Flag carried at the siege of Louisburg

Fear Was Routed

Fear of the French, a New England complex, was partially overcome by the victory at Louisburg. New England breathed easier. Bonfires of victory were lighted, Louisburg was celebrated in poem and sermon.

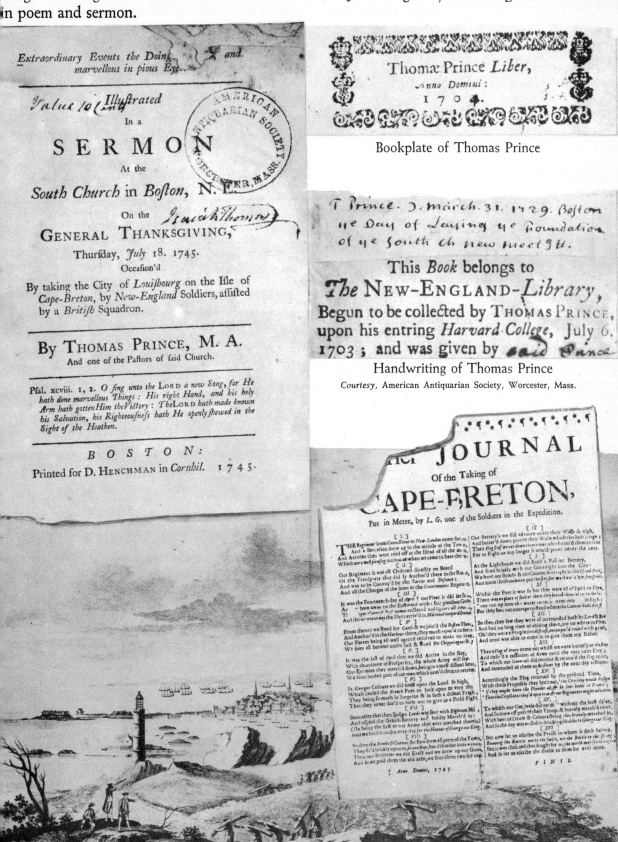

Extraordinary Events the Doing, and marvellous in pious Eyes

Value 10 Cent Illustrated

In a

SERMON

At the

South Church in Boston, N. E.

On the *Isaiah Thomas*

GENERAL THANKSGIVING,

Thursday, *July* 18. 1745.

Occasion'd

By taking the City of *Louisbourg* on the Isle of *Cape-Breton*, by *New-England* Soldiers, assisted by a *British* Squadron.

By THOMAS PRINCE, M. A.
And one of the Pastors of said Church.

Psal. xcviii. 1, 2. *O sing unto the* LORD *a new Song, for He hath done marvellous Things : His right Hand, and his holy Arm hath gotten Him the Victory :* The LORD *hath made known his Salvation, his Righteousness hath He openly shewed in the Sight of the Heathen.*

B O S T O N :

Printed for D. HENCHMAN in *Cornhil*. 1 7 4 5.

Thomæ Prince *Liber,*
Anno Domini :
1704

Bookplate of Thomas Prince

T Prince. 2. march. 31. 1729. Boston
ye Day of Laying ye foundation
of ye South ch new meet Ht.

This *Book* belongs to
The NEW-ENGLAND-*Library,*
Begun to be collected by THOMAS PRINCE,
upon his entring *Harvard-College,* July 6.
1703 ; and was given by *said Prince*

Handwriting of Thomas Prince

Courtesy, American Antiquarian Society, Worcester, Mass.

JOURNAL

Of the Taking of

CAPE-BRETON,

Put in Metre, by *L. G.* one of the Soldiers in the Expedition.

Courtesy, The Stokes Collection, The New York Public Library.

View of Louisburg

Currency Was Stabilized—Business Boomed

The expenses of the Louisburg adventure all but bankrupted the New England colonies, particularly Massachusetts. Great Britain, to keep Massachusetts solvent, shipped £183,649 to Boston. This precious cargo included 217 chests of Spanish dollars and 100 barrels of copper coin. This enabled Massachusetts to stabilize her currency and pay off her debts. Business boomed immediately. The previous currency had been called old tenor, and it had depreciated in value so much that a pound sterling was equivalent to eleven pounds old tenor. Each colony had a different rate of exchange, further complicating business transactions.

Courtesy, American Numismatic Society, New York.

Rosa Americana penny. 1723

Courtesy, Old-Time New England.

Massachusetts paper money. 1744

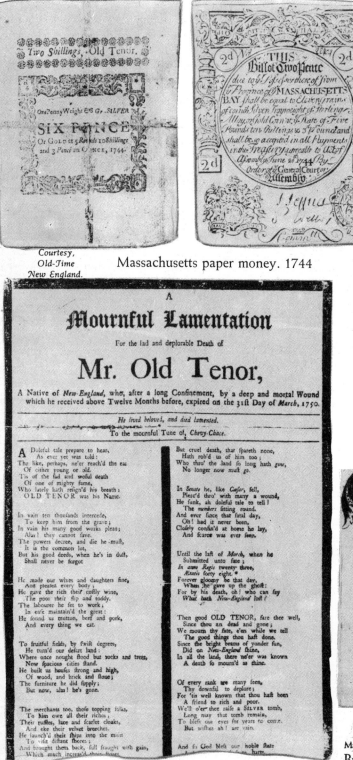

A

Mournful Lamentation

For the sad and deplorable Death of

Mr. Old Tenor,

A Native of *New-England*, who, after a long Confinement, by a deep and mortal Wound which he received above Twelve Months before, expired on the 31st Day of March, 1750.

He lived beloved, and died lamented.

To the mournful Tune of, *Chevy-Chace.*

Promissory note. New Hampshire. 1734

Courtesy, Colonial Society of Massachusetts.

Reverse of same *above*

Broadside lamenting the death of old tenor

Courtesy, The Massachusetts Historical Society, Boston.

"Old Fan'l"

Men like Peter Faneuil, Huguenot merchant prince of Boston, foresaw the glorious future of the American colonies. He built Faneuil Hall and offered it as a gift to the citizens of Boston, but the gift was accepted by the close vote of 367 to 360.

BOSTON.

POMPEY for Plays, a Theatre gave *Rome*,
GRESHAM to *London*, an Exchange for Wealth,
FANEUIL to *Boston*, gives a worthier Dome,
A Hall for LIBERTY, a Change below for *Health*.

Monday laſt being the Annual Meeting of the Town, to chuſe meet Perſons to ſerve in the ſeveral Offices the Year enſuing, the ſame was opened with Prayer, by the Rev. Dr. CHAUNCY: After which Mr. JOHN LOVELL, Maſter of the firſt Grammar-School in the Town, pronounced an Oration to the Acceptance of a great Aſſembly on the Death of PETER FANEUIL Eſq; the generous Benefactor to the Town, of the ſtately Edifice wherein they were convened. And then the Town proceeded to the Choice of Officers, & the following were choſen. Viz.

The Hon. *Thomas Cuſhing*, Eſq; Moderator.

Mr. *Ezekiel Goldthwait* Town-Clerk.

For Select-Men, the Hon. *John Jeffries* Eſq; Capt. *Alexander Forſyth*, *Jonas Clark* Eſq; *Thomas Hutchinſon* Eſq; Mr. *Thomas Hancock*, Mr. *Middlecott Cooke*, and Capt. *John Steel*.

For Town-Treaſurer, the Hon. *Joſeph Wadſworth* Eſq;

For Overſeers of the Poor, the Hon. *Jacob Wendell* Eſq; *William Tyler*, Eſq; Col. *John Hill*, *Thomas Hubbard* Eſq; *Daniel Henchman* Eſq; Mr. *Edward Bromfield*, Col. *William Downe*, *Andrew Oliver*.

For Aſſeſſors, Meſſi. *Richard Buckley*, *Joſhua Blanchard*, *Jacob Parker*, *Daniel Pecker*, *Nathaniel Barber*, *William Fairfield*, *Nathaniel Gardner*.

Clerk of *Faneuil-Hall* Market, Mr. *John Stanford*.

The Town have voted that *Faneuil-Hall* Market ſhall be opened three Days in the Week only, viz. *Tueſdays*, *Thurſdays* and *Saturdays*, and be ſhut up on thoſe Days at 12 o'Clock, till the Meeting in *May* next; and the Select-Men are deſired to conſult what is farther neceſſary to be done for the better regulating ſaid Market, and report to ſaid Meeting.

A Number of the Inhabitants having petitioned for Part of Fort-Hill to be improved for a Bowling-green, the Select Men were impowered to leaſe out to ſuch of the Petitioners as appeared for the ſame, ſo much of ſaid Hill as they tho't proper for that Purpoſe, with this Reſtriction, That the ſame ſhall be quitted by the Leſſees whenever the Town require it.

Cuſtom-Houſe, BOSTON.

Entred In, Kilder from Bonavyar, Blackador from Honduras, Gorham from N. Carolina, Elwell from Maryland.

Outward Bound, Everden for

Boston Weekly Magazine, May 16, 1743.

Note the references to Faneuil

Faneuil Hall. Designed by John Smibert. In 1805 Charles Bulfinch added a third story to Smibert's original design of 1740-42

Willis American Scenery. 1840.

More Ships

Shipbuilding boomed after Louisburg. The Royal Navy increased its orders for American-built vessels, and colonial merchants began to expand their private shipping business.

Steel *The Elements and Practice of Rigging and Seamanship*. 1794.

Diderot and D'Alembert Encyclopedie. Recueil des Planches, 1762-72.

Shipbuilding yard. 18th Century

Rope

Diderot and D'Alembert *Encyclopedie. Recueil des Planches,* 1762-72.

Twisting hemp into ropes for ships

Sail

Steel *The Elements and Practice of Rigging and Seamanship.* 1794.

A sail loft

Right Commodore Edward Tyng. ca. 1744

Courtesy, Yale University Art Gallery.

Barrels

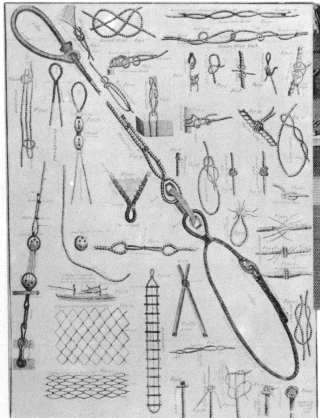

Institut de France. Academie des Sciences. Descriptions des Arts et Metiers.

Coopers at work

Steel *The Elements and Practice of Rigging and Seamanship.*

"Rule of Three"

Young apprentices were needed for all the trades. Boys entering trade were expected to know the mathematical "Rule of Three", a short-cut to calculation.

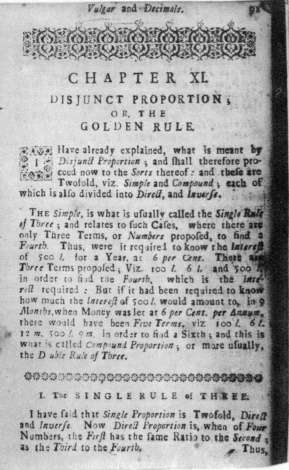

Vulgar and Decimals. 91

CHAPTER XL.
DISJUNCT PROPORTION;
OR, THE
GOLDEN RULE.

I Have already explained, what is meant by *Disjunct Proportion* ; and shall therefore proceed now to the *Sorts* thereof : and these are Twofold, viz. *Simple* and *Compound* ; each of which is also divided into *Direct*, and *Inverse*.

THE *Simple*, is what is usually called the *Single Rule of Three* ; and relates to such Cases, where there are only Three Terms, or *Numbers* proposed, to find a *Fourth*. Thus, were it required to know the *Interest* of 500 *l.* for a Year, at 6 *per Cent.* There are *Three* Terms proposed ; Viz. 100 *l.* 6 *l.* and 500 *l.* in order to find the *Fourth*, which is the *Interest* required : But if it had been required to know how much the *Interest* of 500 *l.* would amount to, in 9 *Months*, when Money was let at 6 *per Cent. per Annum*, there would have been *Five* Terms, viz 100 *l.* 6 *l.* 12 *m.* 500 *l.* 9 *m.* in order to find a *Sixth* ; and this is what is called *Compound Proportion* ; or more usually, the *Double Rule of Three*.

I. The SINGLE RULE of THREE.

I have said that *Single Proportion* is Twofold, *Direct* and *Inverse*. Now *Direct Proportion* is, when of *Four* Numbers, the *First* has the same Ratio to the *Second* ; as the *Third* to the *Fourth*.   Thus,

Courtesy, Plimpton Collection, Columbia University Library, New York.

Page from Isaac Greenwood's *Arithmetick*. 1729.
The beginning of a lengthy explanation of the
"Rule of Three"

An Indenture for placing forth an Apprentice.

THIS Indenture made, &c. Witnesseth, That *A. B.* Son of, &c. hath of his own free and voluntary Will (or by and with the Consent of his Father) placed and bound himself Apprentice unto *D. E.* of, &c. Pewterer, to be taught in the said Trade, Science or Occupation of a Pewterer, which he the said *D. E.* now useth, and with him as an Apprentice to dwell, continue and serve from the Day of the Date hereof unto the full End and Term of Seven Years from thence next ensuing, and fully to be compleat and ended ; During all which Term, the said Apprentice his said Master well and faithfully shall serve, his Secrets keep, his lawful Commands gladly do, Hurt to his said Master he shall not do, nor wilfully suffer to be done by others, but of the same to his Power shall forthwith give Notice to his said Master. The Goods of his said Master he shall not imbezle or waste, nor them lend without his Consent to any ; at Cards, Dice, or any other unlawful Games he shall not play ; Taverns or Alehouses he shall not frequent ; Fornication he shall not commit, Matrimony he shall not contract ; from the Service of his said Master he shall not at any Time depart or absent himself without his said Master's Leave ; But in all Things, as a good and faithful Apprentice, shall and will Demean and Behave himself towards his said Master and all his, during the said Term. And the said Master his said Apprentice the said Trade, Science, or Occupation of a Pewterer, with all Things thereunto belonging, shall and will teach and instruct, or cause to be well and sufficiently taught and instructed, after the best Way and Manner that he can ; And shall and will also find and allow unto his said Apprentice, Meat, Drink, Washing, Lodging, and Apparrel, both Linnen and Woollen, and all other Necessaries fit and convenient for such an Apprentice during the Term aforesaid. And at the End of the said Term shall and will give to his said Apprentice one new Suit of Apparel, &c. In Witness, &c.

Bb 2   Licence.

Form of indenture, from *The American Instructor*. 1748.

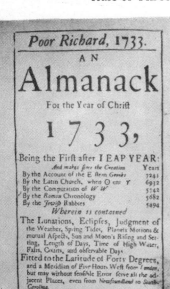

Poor Richard, 1733.
AN
Almanack
For the Year of Christ
1733,
Being the First after LEAP YEAR:

	Years
And makes since the Creation	
By the Account of the Eastern Greeks	7241
By the Latin Church, when ☉ ent ♈	6932
By the Computation of W. W.	5742
By the Roman Chronology	5682
By the Jewish Rabbies	5494

Wherein is contained

The Lunations, Eclipses, Judgment of the Weather, Spring Tides, Planets Motions & mutual Aspects, Sun and Moon's Rising and Setting, Length of Days, Time of High Water, Fairs, Courts, and observable Days

Fitted to the Latitude of Forty Degrees, and a Meridian of Five Hours West from London, but may without sensible Error serve all the adjacent Places, even from Newfoundland to South-Carolina.

By RICHARD SAUNDERS, Philom.

PHILADELPHIA:
Printed and sold by B. FRANKLIN, at the New Printing Office near the Market
The Third Impression.

Benjamin Franklin began his career as a "printer's devil", and the moral precepts of his *Poor Richard's Almanack* did much to form the character of the young tradesmen.

Whitefield *The Homes of Our Forefathers*.
Old schoolhouse, Connecticut

Printing press used by
Benjamin Franklin
Courtesy, National Museum,
Washington, D. C.

Some Went to College

Yale College. 1749
Engraved by Thomas Johnston after a drawing
by John Greenwood

Courtesy, Connecticut Magazine.
First building at Yale College

Home of George Berkeley, Middle-
town, R. I. Bishop Berkeley of Ireland was one of the benefactors of
Yale College and gave it many books

For Tender Minds

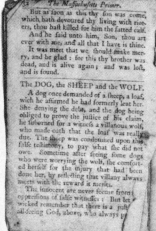

Courtesy, Plimpton Collection,
Columbia University Library,
New York.

Above Pages from the
Massachusetts Primer

Left Pages from the
New England Primer
Enlarged. 1736

Courtesy, Plimpton Collection,
Columbia University Library,
New York.

Books

Benjamin Franklin founded the Library Company of Philadelphia in 1731. Abraham Redwood founded the Redwood Library in Newport, R. I., in 1748. James Logan in Philadelphia, Thomas Prince and the Mathers in Boston, William Byrd in Virginia, and a few other patrons of letters had fairly large private libraries.

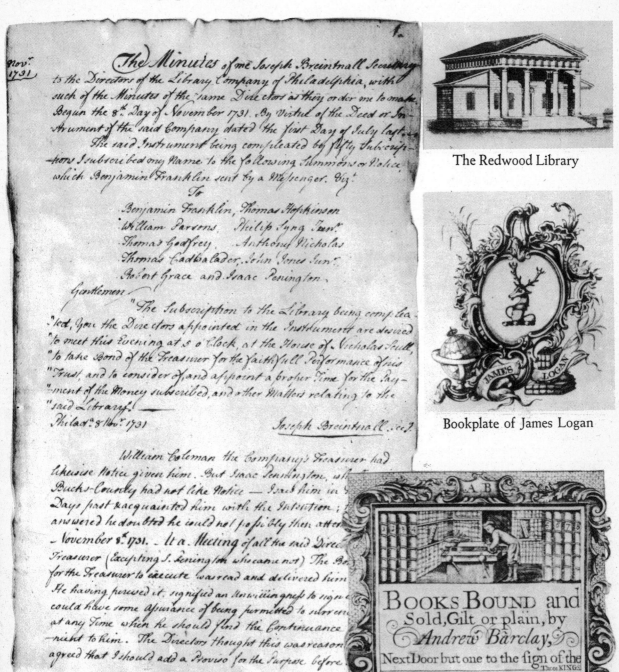

The Redwood Library

Bookplate of James Logan

Excerpt from the *Minutes* of the
Library Company, Philadelphia,
1731

Courtesy, American Antiquarian Society,
Worcester, Mass.

Trade card of Andrew Barclay,
bookbinder

Freedom of the Press

In 1733, Peter Zenger criticized the high-handed policies of Governor William Cosby in the pages of *The New-York Weekly Journal*. Cosby issued a proclamation offering a reward for the apprehension of the author of the offending articles. Zenger was arrested and brought to trial, and through the eloquent defense made by his lawyer, Andrew Hamilton of Philadelphia, was acquitted. This famous trial helped to establish the idea of the freedom of the press in America.

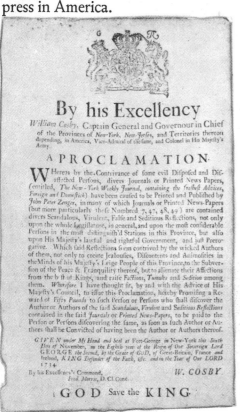

Courtesy, The New York Public Library.

Left Typical front page of an American newspaper

Courtesy, Maryland Historical Society, Baltimore, Md.

Crime and Punishment

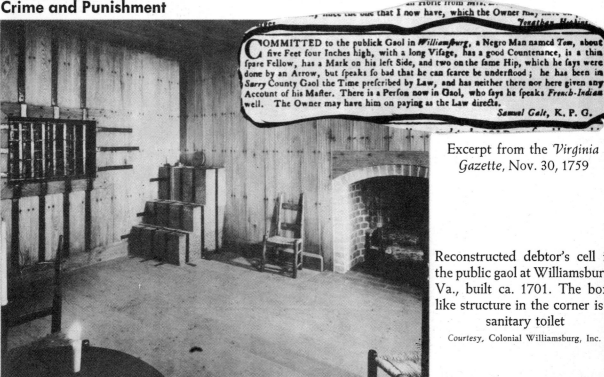

Excerpt from the *Virginia Gazette*, Nov. 30, 1759

Reconstructed debtor's cell in the public gaol at Williamsburg, Va., built ca. 1701. The box-like structure in the corner is a sanitary toilet

Courtesy, Colonial Williamsburg, Inc.

...aws Were Passed

...ouse of Burgesses. The Capitol. Williamsburg, Va.

The General Assembly of Virginia met here from the early years of the eighteenth century until 1779, when it was moved from Williamsburg to Richmond.

Williamsburg, Va.
ca. 1740

... copper plate found ... the Bodleian Library, Oxford, which ...ay have been the work of John Bartram, ...e colonial botanist. ...he upper panel ...hows William and ...ary College, (1) ...rafferton Hall. (2) ...he Wren Building, ...nd (3) the President's House. The ...iddle panel shows ...4) the Capitol. (5) ...est elevation of the ...ren building. (6) ...he Governor's Palace.

...ourtesy, Colonial Williamsburg, Inc.

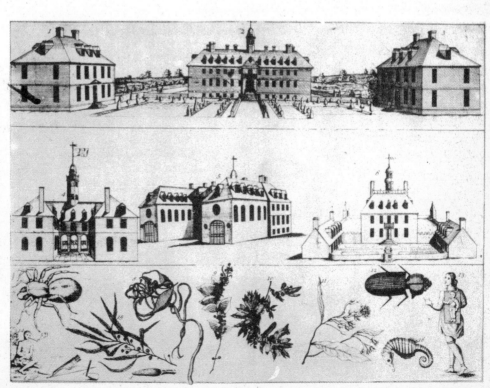

The Art of the Silversmith

The arts developed slowly in America, due to lack of schools and the absence of patrons, and to Puritan prejudice, but as merchants and planters accumulated wealth they built finer houses and furnished them with more expensive objects. Almost from the beginning the silversmiths were active, and their art developed much more rapidly than the fine arts of music and painting.

Left Silver porringer by John Burt, Boston

Courtesy, Museum of Fine Arts, Boston.

Silver cup by John Coney, Boston

Courtesy, Museum of Fine Arts, Boston.

Silver porringer by Benjamin Burt, Boston

Courtesy, Metropolitan Museum of Art, New York.

Below Left Silver tankard by Edward Winslow, Boston

Courtesy, Philadelphia Museum of Art, Philadelphia.

Below Silver brazier by Johann de Nys, Philadelphia

Courtesy, Philadelphia Museum of Art, Philadelphia.

Courtesy, Mabel Brady Garvan Collection, Yale University Art Gallery.
Silver tankard by Peter Van Dyck, New York. It has the Wendell coat of arms

Courtesy, Yale University Art Gallery.
Silver tray by Jacob Hurd

Left Silver teapot by Jacob Hurd
Courtesy, Yale University Art Gallery.

Right Silver casters by Adrian Bancker, New York
Courtesy, Collection of Herbert L. Pratt and the Museum of the City of New York.

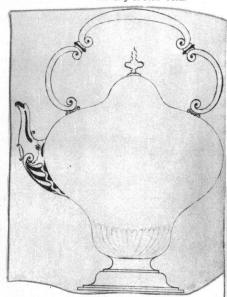

Courtesy, Pleasants and Sill *Maryland Silversmiths.* 1930.
Design for a teapot by William Faris, Baltimore

Courtesy, Mabel Brady Garvan Collection, Yale University Art Gallery.
Sugar box by Edward Winslow, Boston

Left Monteith bowl by John Coney, the earliest form of the "Monteith" in America

Below Silver dish ring by Myer Myers. Unique sample of an American dish ring

Courtesy, Mabel Brady Garvan Collection, Yale University Art Gallery.

Silver nutmeg grater by William Cross, Boston

Courtesy, Metropolitan Museum of Art, New York.

The Hunger For Beauty

Puritan austerity could not kill the human instinct for artistic expression. In spite of rigid taboos the busy fingers of many a young woman recorded the dreams of the heart in lively flights of the imagination.

American embroidered pieces. ca. 1740

Courtesy, Museum of Fine Arts, Boston.

9

THE SELF-CONSCIOUS ERA

After 1750 the American colonies grew more self-conscious; more critical of Great Britain's colonial attitude; more articulate in the cause of liberty. American harbors were filled with shipping; tremendous natural resources were being tapped; the arts and sciences were beginning to take root; newspapers were multiplying.

Philadelphia

Sections of a view of Philadelphia by George Heap. Church steeples dominated the sky line.

Newspapers

Specimens of newspaper printing in the American colonies

The Mason and Dixon Line

Photo by Philip B. Wallace.

Boundary disputes which had retarded progress were slowly being settled. Maryland had long been the chief sufferer in this respect. To reach Philadelphia by sea one had to enter Maryland territory. William Penn and his descendants carried on a fight for this vital strip. In 1763 two English surveyors, Charles Mason and Jeremiah Dixon, began their survey of the boundary between Pennsylvania and Maryland now known as the Mason and Dixon Line, completed in 1767. One of the original markers, bearing the Calvert coat of arms on one side, and the Penn coat of arms on the other, is shown here. Had the full claims of either Penn or Calvert been honored, Baltimore would now be in Pennsylvania or Philadelphia in Maryland.

Baltimore was still a village. Here we see a portrait of Mrs. John Moale (Ellin North), said to have been the first white child born in Baltimore. Her father, Robert North, helped lay out Baltimore Town in 1729.

Mrs. John Moale (1740-1825) and her granddaughter. Painting by Joshua Johnson, Negro artist. ca. 1800

Courtesy, Mr. Roswell P. Russell, Baltimore, the owner of the portrait, and Dr. J. Hall Pleasants, Baltimore.

Baltimore

View of Baltimore, Md. Aquatint based on a sketch made by John Moale in 1752. It was then a town of less than fifty houses and two hundred inhabitants. Note the sloop (26), the brig (27) and the architectural style of the buildings. The untamed wilderness lay at the backdoor of every Maryland house, even as late as 1752

Colleges Were Springing Up

View of the College of New Jersey, later to become Princeton University, Princeton, N. J. 1764. The architect was Robert Smith of Philadelphia. This view was engraved by H. Dawkins after a drawing by W. Tennent

View of Rhode Island College, Providence, R. I., later to become Brown University. Founded 1764. This view was made in 1793

Courtesy, John Carter Brown Library.

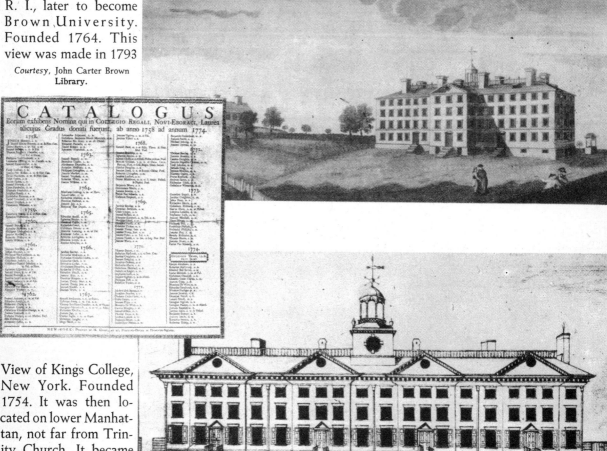

View of Kings College, New York. Founded 1754. It was then located on lower Manhattan, not far from Trinity Church. It became Columbia College in 1784

Merchant Princes Were Arising

Courtesy, Museum of Fine Arts, Boston.

John Amory of Boston. Portrait by John Singleton Copley. 1768

For LONDON,

THE Ship FRIENDSHIP, *Benson Fearon* Master, lying at *Bermuda* Hundred, on *James* River, will take in Tobacco at 12 Pounds per Ton, with Liberty of Consignment.

All Persons inclinable to ship, are desired to apply to Mess. *Atkinson* and *Newsum*, Merchants in *Petersburg*; to Colonel *Thomas Tabb* in *Amelia*, or to the Captain on board.

For MADEIRA,

THE Brigantine BETSEY, Captain *Stagg*, a Letter of Marque, well provided.

Gentlemen desirous of Wine from *Madeira*, by the Return of the Vessel, are desired to send their Orders, immediately, to Colonel *Lewis Burwell*, as she will sail in a few Days.

To be SOLD to the highest Bidders, on Monday the 17th of December *next, if fair (if not, the next fair Day)* at the late Dwelling-House of Mr. Thomas Thorpe, *deceased,* in King and Queen, ALL the Houshold-Goods, Plate and Books, with a new Chair and Harness, the Stocks of Cattle, Horses and Hogs; also 20 Negroes. Six Months Credit will be allowed, the Purchasers giving Bond and Security to

Graham Frank, Executor.

JUST imported in the *Good-Intent,* Capt. *Reddick,* and to be sold cheap, for ready Money, by the Subscriber, living at the Palace, in *Williamsburg*; where Gentlemen

For LEITH, Garden-Seeds, by

The Brig *Gordon,* George *Richan,* Master; Will sail the 7th current. For freight or passage, agree with *Andrew*

Christopher Ayscough. ...reil Peas, Spanish Mor-.. White Blossom Beans, ...h Turnip, early Dutch Cabbage, Red Cabbage, late Colliflower, Colli-...er, topped Raddish.

For LONDONDERRY,

The Snow *Prince Edward, Thomas Morrison* Master; Will sail will all convenient speed, having the greatest part of her cargoe ready. For freight or passage agree with said master, or *Garri*... *Vanhorne.*

N. B. The boat... the vessel about the 3... bring back the said b... of THREE POUN... LINGS to any per... the same. She is a cl... matting on bows and ... ask'd how they came ...ell's, opposite the M...

For LONDONDERRY

Shipping notices from the *Virginia Gazette* and *New York Mercury*

Left Bookplate of Stephen Cleveland, showing nautical influence

Courtesy, The Bella C. Landauer Collection, The New-York Historical Society, New York.

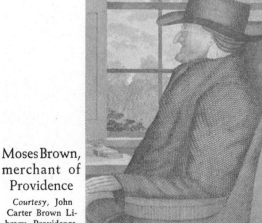

Moses Brown, merchant of Providence

Courtesy, John Carter Brown Library, Providence, R. I.

Salem Magnate

Elias Hasket Derby of Salem, Massachusetts, operated a large fleet of ships. He and other merchant princes could afford fine mansions, rare china, elegant costumes, and all the luxuries of Europe. They had their private wharfs and warehouses.

Courtesy, The Essex Institute, Salem, Mass.

School Street, Salem, Mass. Before 1774. Water color by Dr. Joseph Orne

Right Elias Hasket Derby (1734-99) Portrait by James Frothingham

Courtesy, Peabody Museum, Salem, Mass.

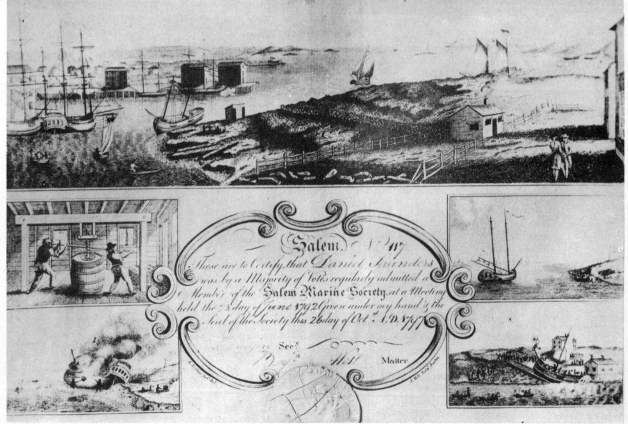

Courtesy, The Essex Institute, Salem, Mass.

View of Salem showing Derby's wharf. The view depicted is earlier than the date on the certificate.

His Plate

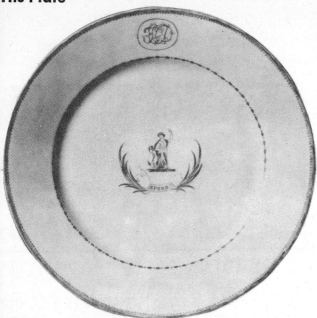

Courtesy, Museum of Fine Arts, Boston.

Chinese export porcelain plate made especially
for Elias Hasket Derby

His Tea House

Courtesy, The Essex Institute, Salem, Mass.

His Wife

Courtesy, The Essex Institute, Salem, Mass.

Silk brocade dress worn by Mrs. Elias Hasket
Derby

His Ship

Courtesy, The Essex Institute, Salem, Mass.

Ship *Grand Turk*. 1781. Built for Elias Hasket
Derby, and used in the China trade

Ship Figureheads

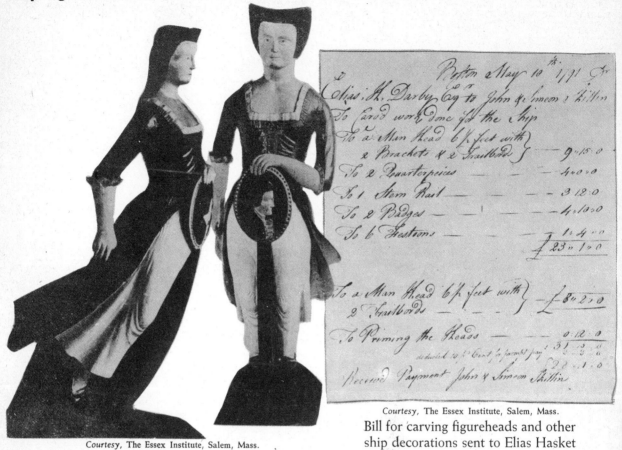

Courtesy, The Essex Institute, Salem, Mass.

Figurehead by Samuel McIntire of Salem

Courtesy, The Essex Institute, Salem, Mass.

Bill for carving figureheads and other ship decorations sent to Elias Hasket Derby by the noted wood carvers, the brothers Skillin of Boston

Left Ship's figurehead found near Nantucket, Mass.
18th Century

Courtesy, The New-York Historical Society, New York.

Below Making rope for ships

Steel *The Elements and Practice of Rigging and Seamanship*. 1794.

Rope

Counting House

Courtesy, Bella C. Landauer Collection, The New-York Historical
Society, New York.

Merchant's Counting House. Published by T.
Dolson, Philadelphia. 18th Century

18th Century ships

Shipping

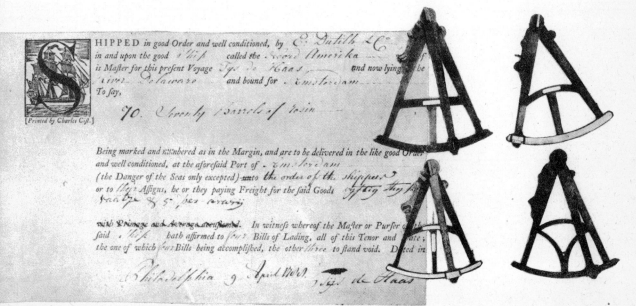

Courtesy, Bella C. Landauer Collection, The New-York Historical Society, New York.

Shipping bill. 1755

Courtesy, Peabody Museum, Salem, Mass.

Navigator's quadrants

Master and Seamen

Courtesy, The New York Public Library.

Agreement between master and seamen. 1758

The ships on this page are from Steel *Elements and Practice of Rigging and Seamanship.* 1794

Chamber of Commerce

The first Chamber of Commerce in America was founded in New York City in 1768, and is still in existence. It was the Chamber of Commerce of the State of New York. It met first in Fraunces Tavern, and the next year moved to the Royal Exchange.

Courtesy, The Emmet Collection, The New York Public Library.
Royal Exchange. New York. 1754

Great Seal of the Chamber of Commerce of the State of New York. 1770

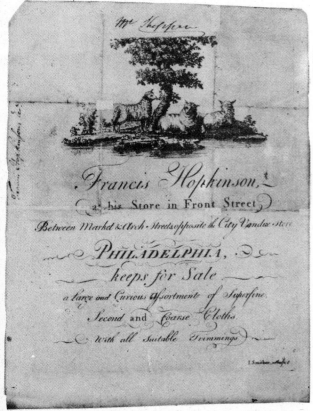

Courtesy, The Bella C. Landauer Collection. The New-York Historical Society, New York.
Trade card of Francis Hopkinson

"Pieces of Eight"

Among the coins that circulated in New York were the Spanish Eight Reales, called "Pieces of Eight".

Courtesy, American Numismatic Society, New York.
Eight Reales. 1767. The silver mines of Potosi (Bolivia) supplied the metal for these coins

Courtesy, American Numismatic Society, New York.
Shilling. George II. 1758

A La Mode

Fine cloth was imported from England, Holland, and France, and the ladies and gentlemen of the American colonies kept abreast of the London and Paris styles.

Courtesy, Litchfield Historical Society and The Metropolitan Museum of Art.

Benjamin Tallmadge and son, of Litchfield, Conn.   Mrs. Benjamin Tallmadge and children, of Litchfield, Conn.

Portraits by Ralph Earl

Courtesy, Carolina Art Association, Charleston, S. C.

Bernard Eliot of Charleston   Mrs. Bernard Eliot of Charleston

Portraits by Jeremiah Theus

Presenting . . .

Courtesy, Museum of Fine Arts, Boston.

Courtesy, Yale University Art Gallery.

Mr. and Mrs. Isaac Winslow. Portraits by John Singleton Copley

Gov. Jonathan Trumbull, Jr., of Conn., with his wife and eldest daughter. Portraits by John Trumbull

Whitefield *The Homes of Our Forefathers.* 1880-86.

They Sat For Copley Gov. Trumbull's house and war office, Lebanon, Conn.

It was fashionable to have a portrait painted by John Singleton Copley, the Boston artist.

Courtesy, Fogg Museum of Art, Harvard University.

Thomas Boylston   Mrs. Thomas Boylston

Portraits by John Singleton Copley

The Hairdresser's Art

Courtesy, Museum of Fine Arts, Boston.

Portrait of Miss Skinner by John Singleton Copley

Courtesy, Essex Institute, Salem, Mass.

Portrait of Esther (Gerrish) Carpenter by an unknown artist

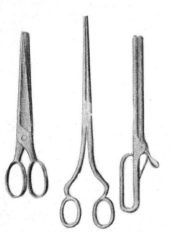

RICHARD THOMPSON, PERUKE-MAKER and HAIR-CUTTER from LONDON, GIVES this publick notice, that he intends following his business, at the house of Mr. Christopher Ring in Broughton-street. Whoever please to favour him with their custom shall be duly attended at a reasonable price.

ALEXANDER BELL, from VIRGINIA, GIVES notice to the publick, that he will erect machines for preventing houses from being struck by lightening, after the newest and best manner, at a reasonable rate. Those who chuse to employ him, may call on him at Mr. John Lyons's shop, where ... may see the machines. His ... about thre... in this place.

A Gentleman's Watch . . .

And A Lady's

Courtesy, The New-York Historical Society, New York.

Watch made by Green of London, 1763-64, and owned by Major-General Philip Schuyler of New York

Right Gold chatelaine and watch

Courtesy, Collection of Miss Julia Lawrence Wells, and the Museum of the City of New York.

They Lived in Philipse Manor

Left Mr. and Mrs. Philip Philipse of Yonkers, N. Y. Portraits by John Wollaston

Courtesy, Museum of the City of New York.

Below Philipse Manor. Yonkers, New York

Engraved by James Smillie

College President

Courtesy, The Metropolitan Museum of Art, New York.

Margaret Sylvester Chesebrough. Portrait by Joseph Blackburn, 1754

Courtesy, Yale University Art Gallery.

Ezra Stiles, president of Yale University. Portrait by Nathaniel Smibert

Flowered Silk

Courtesy, Philadelphia Museum of Art, Philadelphia.

Dress of cream-colored silk worn by Jane Galloway, who married Col. Joseph Shippen of Philadelphia in 1768. The blue quilted petticoat was made ca. 1775

Courtesy, Essex Institute, Salem, Mass.

Brocade dress, with silver lace stomacher, worn by the mother of Dr. Benjamin Lynde Oliver. 1765

Courtesy, Essex Institute, Salem, Mass.

Flowered silk brocade dress worn by Mrs. Sarah Clarke, sister of Timothy Pickering. ca. 1760

Embroidery

Courtesy, Old Quinabaug Village, Sturbridge, Mass.

Embroidered crewelwork lady's pocketbook. 1762

Right Pocketbook made by Eliza Willard in 1760

Courtesy, Essex Institute, Salem, Mass.

Left Embroidery frame. ca. 1755
Courtesy, Metropolitan Museum of Art, New York.

Below Needlepoint picture worked by Sarah Warren, Massachusetts. 1748
Courtesy, Estate of Francis Sever, and The Museum of Fine Arts, Boston.

Textiles

Early American quilt

Early American textiles, two-toned blue resist
Courtesy, Cooper Union Museum for the Arts of Decoration, New York.

The Tailor

Diderot and D'Alembert *Encyclopedie. Recueil des planches.* 1762-72.

Tailor

Tailor's advertisement

New York Mercury. 1753.

PATRICK AUDLEY, Taylor,
who for many years past, hath work'd in the best shops in *Great-Britain* and *Ireland*; has, on the encouragement of some gentlemen, settled in this city, where he will carry on his trade, and engage to finish any kind of work, in the newest and neatest manner, now used either in *London* or *Paris*. He makes gentlemen's laced and plain cloaths, hunting dresses, uniforms for horse and foot, pantine sleeve, racolues for clergymen and others, ladies josephs, riding habits: These, and all other kinds of dresses, that are wore in *London*, *Paris* or *Dublin*, shall be done in the most agreeable fashions, at reasonable prices, and finish'd without loss of time. *N. B.* As he is a stranger in this part of the world, he humbly hopes that gentlemen and ladies will be pleased to favour him with their commands, which shall be carefully executed, by their most humble, and obedient servant,   PATRICK AUDLEY.

Courtesy, Valentine Museum, Richmond, Va.

Velvet suit worn by Dr. John Peter Le Mayeur, George Washington's dentist

The Shoemaker

Diderot and D'Alembert *Encyclopedie. Recueil des planches.* 1762-72.

Shoemaker

Courtesy, The Essex Institute, Salem, Mass.

Shoes worn at wedding by the granddaughter of Gov. Simon Bradstreet, of Mass., 1760

Courtesy, Rhode Island School of Design, Providence, R. I.

Portrait of Theodore Atkinson, Jr., by Joseph Blackburn

The Hatter

Institut de France. Academie des sciences. Descriptions des arts et metiers. 1765.

Preparing wool for felt   Hatters at work

Institut de France. Academie des sciences. Descriptions des arts et metiers. 1765.

Hat shop

A PRICE CURRENT of SKINS, &c. usually imported at London, from NORTH - AMERICA.

		Season'd.	Damag'd Stage.
		l. d. s. d.	l. d. s. d.
First Sort.	Beaver Parchment, per lb.	7. 7—7 9	3 3—3 7
Second Do.	Ditto	4 0—5 3	2 0—3 6
First Sort.	Beaver Cub	5 2—0 0	2 3—2 5
Second Do.	Ditto	3 9—4 9	2 0—2 2
	Beaver Coat	5 0—5 5	2 7—4 0
	Bear per Skin	15 6—22 6	6 0—10 0
	Ditto Cub	10 6—16 0	Mix'd.
	Otter	14 0—19 0	7 6—12 0
	Fisher	4 7—6 0	Mix'd.
	Martin	4 6—7 0	3 0—4 1
	Ditto fine	8 0—13 0	4 6—5 6
	Wolf	9 6—18 6	5 6—6 6
	Wolverin	10 0—12 0	Mix'd.
	Cat cased	4 6—5 0	
	Ditto fine	12 0—15 0	6 0—7 0
	Cat open	3 6—4 6	1 6—2 0
	Mink	3 9—5 6	0 11—2 0
	Fox Silver	15 0—60 0	
	Fox Cross	10 0—12 0	
	Fox Red	4 6—7 0	2 0—2 6
	Fox Grey	2 4—3 6	1 0—1 6
	Raccoon	1 6—2 11	0 4—0 11
	Musquash	0 4—0 8	Mix'd.
	Elk	25 6—27 0	
	Deer in the Hair	3 6—7 6	2 4—3 11
	Deer half dreſt per lb.	3 0—3 1	1 5—1 10
	Caſtorum	5 8—8 2	

To Sale, February 25 and 26, 1767.

Your moſt humble Servant, SAMUEL ROBINSON.

Price list of skins. 1767

The best hats were made from beaver skins.

Hatters

Universal Magazine. London. Apr. 1750.

Colonial Life At Its Best

Door of Mt. Pleasant, Philadelphia

Let us step in the door of a fine house in Philadelphia and see the hall.

Mt. Pleasant, Fairmount Park, Philadelphia

Entrance hall, Mt. Pleasant

Front bedroom, Mt. Pleasant

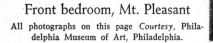

All photographs on this page *Courtesy*, Philadelphia Museum of Art, Philadelphia.

New York Elegance

Let us step into the Beekman mansion in New York.

Beekman mansion, New York
Valentine's Manual. 1854.

Blue room. Beekman mansion
Valentine's Manual. 1861.

Blue room. Beekman mansion

Green room. Beekman mansion

These rooms have been restored in the museum of The New-York Historical Society.

Two above photographs *Courtesy,* The New-York Historical Society, New York.

Portsmouth, New Hampshire

Room from the Samuel
Wentworth House,
Portsmouth, N. H.
1761

Courtesy, The Metropolitan Museum of Art, New York.

Room from the Metcalf
Bowler House, Portsmouth, N. H. Before
1765

Courtesy, The Metropolitan Museum of Art, New York.

Gov. Benning Wentworth House, Little
Harbor, N. H. 1755

Whitefield *The Homes of Our
Forefathers*. 1880-86.

Wall Decorations

Courtesy, The Metropolitan Museum of Art, New York.

Section of the great hall of the Van Rensselaer Manor House, Albany, N. Y. The wall paper was painted in London especially for this room, now restored in its 18th Century elegance in the American Wing of The Metropolitan Museum of Art, in New York

Left Jeremiah Lee Mansion, Marblehead, Mass., built 1768, showing wall paper purchased in London

Courtesy, The Essex Institute, Salem, Mass.

Below Stairway. Jeremiah Lee Mansion

Courtesy, The Essex Institute, Salem, Mass. Photo by Frank Cousins.

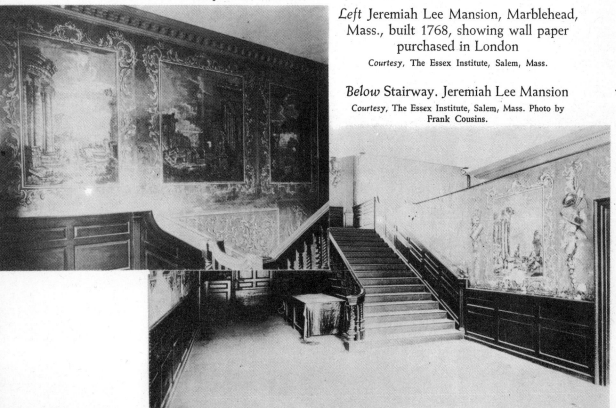

Down South

Left Daphne Room, Raleigh Tavern, Williamsburg, Va.

Courtesy, Colonial Williamsburg, Inc.
Photo by Richard Garrison.

Right Room from Almodington, Maryland. ca. 1750

Courtesy, Metropolitan Museum of Art,
New York.

Left Room from "The Abbey", Chestertown, Md.

Courtesy, Baltimore Museum of Art,
Baltimore.

Right Room from "Habre de Venture", Port Tobacco, Charles County, Md.

Courtesy, Baltimore Museum of Art,
Baltimore.

Annapolis

Left Brice House, Annapolis, Md. 1740

Below Paca House, Annapolis, Md. 1763

Courtesy, Hall of Records, Annapolis, Md.

Baltimore

Below Mount Clare, Baltimore, Md. 1754

Courtesy, Mr. Laurence Hall Fowler, Baltimore.

Charleston

Above Gibbes House, Charleston, S. C.

Left Pringle House, Charleston, S. C.

Humble Architecture

Despite the sumptuousness of many colonial mansions there was nothing approaching modern plumbing or even that of ancient Rome. The "temple" was a necessary adjunct to every home, but in spite of its architectural adornments it was still a privy.

Stoney Plantations of the Carolina Low Country. 1939.
Courtesy, Carolina Art Association, Charleston, S. C. Photo by Ben Judah Lubschez.

Kitchen. "Oakland", in South Carolina

Courtesy, Historic American Buildings Survey,
Washington, D. C.

Nathan Dean's privy. East Taunton, Mass.

Courtesy, Historic American Buildings Survey, Washington, D. C.

Meat house. "Old House of the Hinges", East New Market, Md.

Courtesy, Historic American Buildings Survey,
Washington, D. C.

Judge Samuel Horton's privy. Danvers, Mass.

Right Smokehouse. "Mordington", Frederica vicinity, Delaware

Courtesy, Historic American Buildings Survey,
Washington, D. C.

Poems In Silver

The silverware of the period was in keeping with the fine houses. It has never been surpassed.

Silver chafing dish by John Burt, Boston
Courtesy, Metropolitan Museum of Art, New York.

Silver salt cellars by Charles Le Roux, New York
Courtesy, Metropolitan Museum of Art, New York.

Courtesy, Collection of Mrs. de Lancey Walton Ward and the Museum of the City of New York. Silver marrow spoon by Thomas Hammersley

Top of silver caster by Jonathan Otis, Newport, R. I.
Courtesy, Metropolitan Museum of Art, New York.

Silver cream pitcher and sugar bowl by Paul Revere, Boston
Courtesy, Metropolitan Museum of Art, New York.

Silver tongs by William Grigg, New York
Courtesy, Metropolitan Museum of Art, New York.

Courtesy, Metropolitan Museum of Art, New York.

Silver tankard by John Le Roux,
New York

Courtesy, The New-York Historical Society, New York.

Moulds for "rat tail" spoons

Proud . . .

Courtesy, Collection of Robert R. Livingston and Mrs. Laura Livingston Davis,
and the Museum of the City of New York.

Silver soup tureen and pair of vegetable dishes belonging to the
Livingston family. By J. B. Fouache. These reflect contemporary
European taste

And Humble

Courtesy, Landis Valley Museum, Landis Valley, Pa.

Gourd dipper

Fine China

Courtesy, Essex Institute, Salem, Mass.

Monteith Lowestoft
China objects from the table service of Samuel Chase, Annapolis, Md., with Chase
coat of arms

Courtesy, Metropolitan Museum of Art, New York.

Stiegel Glass

The most beautiful glassware and ironware of America was made by William Henry Stiegel in Lancaster County, Pennsylvania. The self-styled "Baron" Stiegel operated Elizabeth Furnace and Charming Forge, the very names of which reflect the romantic spirit of this master craftsman.

Courtesy, Metropolitan Museum of Art, New York.

Glassware by Stiegel

Left Glassware by Stiegel

Courtesy, The Philadelphia Museum of Art, Philadelphia.

Glassmakers at work

Diderot and D'Alembert *Encyclopedie. Recueil des planches.* 1762-72.

Courtesy, Metropolitan Museum of Art, New York.

Fine Furniture

Courtesy, The Magazine *Antiques*.

Lowboy in style of William Savery, Philadelphia.
ca. 1750

Courtesy, The Magazine *Antiques* and Philip J. Birckhead.

Lowboy by John Goddard, Newport, R. I.
ca. 1760

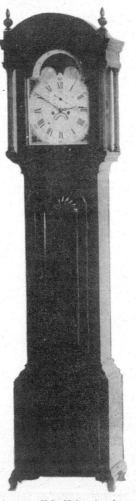

Courtesy, Yale University Art Gallery.

Secretary by John Goddard, Newport, R. I. ca. 1770

Courtesy, Yale University Art
Gallery.

Tall clock by John
Goddard, Newport,
R. I. ca. 1770

Courtesy, Estate of George Drew Egbert, and the Museum
of the City of New York.

Highboy. ca. 1760

Block-front escrutoire. 1760-70

Tall clock by William Claggett

Courtesy, The Magazine Antiques, New York.
Furniture label of William
Savery, Philadelphia

WILLIAM SAVERY.

**Tick! Tock!
Tick! Tock!**

Common House Clocks, 8 day
Spring Clocks and Time-pieces
of different constructions made by
Aaron Willard
BOSTON.

DIRECTIONS for setting the CLOCK.

First place up the case in the place where it
is to stand, and secure it; then put the Clock
in the case, and hang on the pendulum and
weights, observing that the heaviest weight
be put on the pulley marked S. Wind up
the lines on the barrels, taking care that
they run regularly in the grooves, then
put the pendulum in motion.

Courtesy, Mr. Charles W. Lyon, New York, and The Magazine Antiques.
Clock label of Aaron Willard, Boston

STRIKE
SILENT
Hyram Faris
ANNAPOLIS

Courtesy, Dr. J. Hall Pleasants,
Baltimore, Md.
Clock face design by
Hyram Faris of An-
napolis

Courtesy, Old Quinabaug Village,
Sturbridge, Mass.
Tall clock by Benjamin
Cheney of Hartford,
Conn.

The Franklin Stove

Heating was a problem in the colonial house. One either baked in front of the fireplace or froze in the far corners of the room. Benjamin Franklin, the universal genius of the period, came forward with a stove which proved a blessing to mankind.

Courtesy, Landis Valley Museum, Landis Valley, Pa.

Cannon stove of the type designed by "Baron" Stiegel

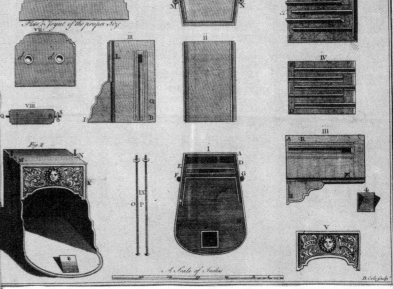

Courtesy, The Metropolitan Museum of Art, New York.

The Franklin stove

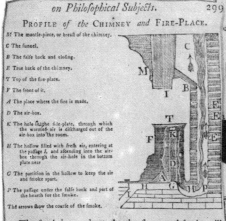

The fire being made at A, the flame and smoke will ascend and strike the top T, which will thereby receive a considerable heat. The smoke, finding no passage upwards, turns over the top of the air-box, and descends between it and the back plate to the holes at B, in the bottom plate, heating, as it passes, both plates of the air-box, ...nd the said .... front plate, b...

Benjamin Franklin *Experiments and Observations on Electricity*. 4th edition. 1769.

Illustration showing the construction of the Franklin stove

Stove Plates

Pennsylvania craftsmen designed beautiful stove plates and fire backs.

Courtesy, Bucks County Historical Society, Doylestown, Pa.

Amusements

The men and women of the American colonies enjoyed life. Those who could afford it went to the theatre, rode to hounds, played billiards, attended balls and assemblies. The poor played cards, went fishing and hunting, attended horse races, fairs, markets, husking bees, or got drunk in the local taverns. All classes consumed enormous quantities of cider, beer, and rum.

Courtesy, Dr. Wyndham B. Blanton, and The Metropolitan Museum of Art, New York.

End of the fox hunt. American school. ca. 1780

Left Fox hunting scene on the birth certificate of Caleb Lippincott. 1772

Courtesy, Philadelphia Museum of Art, Philadelphia.

TO BE RUN FOR,

At SUNBURY, on THURSDAY the first of DECEMBER next;

A GIVE-AND-TAKE-PURSE OF

TWENTY POUNDS STERLING,

The best in three heats, each heat two miles, on the following conditions, viz.

HORSES 14 hands high to carry 10 stone, all above that to carry weight for inches, and all under to be allowed the odds.

No horse to start, unless proof is made that the horse has been ten weeks in the province before the day of running.

Each person entering a horse, if a subscriber, to pay half a guinea for each horse, and every other person to pay a guinea and a half; provided the horses be entered ten days before the day of running; any horse entered after that day to pay three guineas.

No subscriber allowed to enter another man's horse to save the entrance money.

Likewise to be run the day following, a PURSE, value FIFTEEN POUNDS STERLING. The conditions as above.—No horse who run the first day to start for this purse.

The third day's sport is the INNKEEPER's PURSE, value at least SIX POUNDS STERLING, for Galloways not above 13 hands high, to carry 8 stone, all under to be allowed weight for inches.

An ASSEMBLY each night at Mr. WILLIAMS's long-room.

There will be encouragement for cudgel-playing every forenoon.

Georgia Gazette, Oct. 20, 1763.

To be SOLD, by

LEAKE & BANCKER,

Near the *Fly-Market,*

A parcel of choice *West-India &* New-York distill'd RUM, *molasses, coarse and fine salt, cordage, and a parcel of sole and upper leather, also a few cases of drinking-glasses, and decanters, &c.*

New York Mercury, 1753-54.

To be SOLD, by

Benjamin Payne,

At his House opposite the *Old-Slip-Market,* at the Sign of Admiral WARREN;

Choice Madeira *wine, rum, brandy, geneva and arrack ; bohea tea and Muscovado sugar, with sundry other liquors by wholesale or retale.*

Just published, and to be sold by the Printer hereof, and by Garrat Noel, Bookseller, in Dock-street,

Price ONE SHILLING,

THE GRAVE.

A POEM.

By ROBERT BLAIR.

New York Mercury, 1753-54.

The Cup That Cheers

Courtesy, Metropolitan Museum of Art,
New York.

Doorway. Captain Clapp's Tavern, Westfield, Mass. ca. 1750

Courtesy, Colonial Williamsburg, Inc. Photo by Richard Garrison.

Raleigh Tavern

Virginia gentlemen talked politics, horses, and intrigues in the barroom of the Raleigh Tavern in Williamsburg.

Billiards

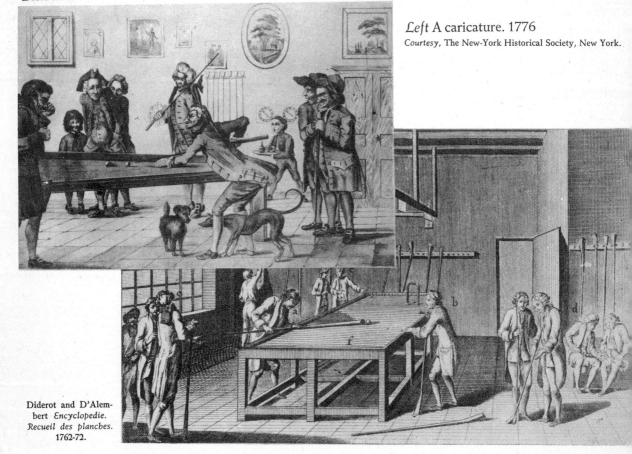

Left A caricature. 1776
Courtesy, The New-York Historical Society, New York.

Diderot and D'Alembert *Encyclopedie. Recueil des planches.* 1762-72.

The Early Theatre

Some of the gentlemen in the Raleigh Tavern bar may have just come from a performance of Shakespeare's *The Merchant of Venice*.

By Permission of the Honble ROBERT DINWIDDIE,
Esq; His Majesty's Lieutenant-Governor, and Commander in
Chief of the Colony and Dominion of *Virginia*.

By a Company of COMEDIANS, *from* LONDON,
At *the* THEATRE *in* WILLIAMSBURG,
On *Friday* next, being the 15th of *September*, will be presented,
A PLAY, Call'd,
THE
MERCHANT of VENICE.
(Written by *Shakespear*.)
The Part of *ANTONIO* (the MERCHANT) to be perform'd by
Mr. CLARKSON,
GRATIANO, by Mr. SINGLETON,
Lorenzo, (with Songs in Character) by Mr. ADCOCK.
The Part of *BASSANIO* to be perform'd by
Mr. RIGBY.
Duke, by Mr. Wynell.
Salanio, by Mr. Herbert.
The Part of *LAUNCELOT*, by Mr. HALLAM.
And the Part of *SHYLOCK*, (the JEW) to be perform'd by
Mr. MALONE.
The Part of *NERISSA*, by Mrs. ADCOCK,
Jessica, by Mrs. Rigby.
And the Part of *PORTIA*, to be perform'd by
Mrs. HALLAM.
With a new occasional PROLOGUE.
To which will be added, a FARCE, call'd,
The ANATOMIST:
OR,
SHAM DOCTOR.
The Part of *Monsieur le Medecin*, by
Mr. RIGBY.
And the Part of *BEATRICE*, by Mrs. ADCOCK.
** No Person, whatsoever, to be admitted behind the Scenes.
BOXES, 7s. 6d. PIT and BALCONIES, 5s. 9d. GALLERY, 3s. 9d.
To begin at Six o'Clock.
Vivat Rex.

THE Snow *Frances, Paul Loyall*, Master, who will be at his Moorings, at Capt.
Dansie's, in *Pamunkey*, will take in Tobacco for *London*, either from *York* or *Rap-
pahanock* River, at 7 l. per Ton, with Liberty of Consignment. Gentlemen inclined
are desired to send their Orders to Mr. *John Norton*, Mr. *Hugh M^c___*

Theatre advertisement in the *Virginia Gazette*, Williamsburg, Va. Aug. 28, 1752

They also bought lottery tickets. Lotteries were the rage. Americans have always liked to bet or take chances. Lottery tickets helped build some of the early American colleges and hospitals.

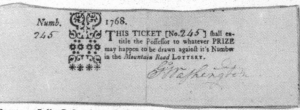

Numb. 245. 1768. THIS TICKET [No. 245] shall entitle the Possessor to whatever PRIZE may happen to be drawn against it's Number in the *Mountain Road* Lottery. *G. Washington*

Courtesy, Bella C. Landauer Collection, The New-York Historical Society, New York.

Lottery ticket of George Washington, 1768

(N° 3770.)
THIS shall entitle the Owner to such Prize as shall be drawn against it in W. BYRD's Lottery. 1767. *Byrd*

Courtesy, Bella C. Landauer Collection, The New-York Historical Society, New York.

Lottery ticket of William Byrd, 1767

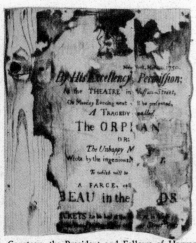

By His Excellency's Permission;
At the THEATRE in Nassau-Street,
On Monday Evening next will be presented,
A TRAGEDY called
The ORPHAN
OR,
The Unhappy M___
Wrote by the ingenious___
To which will be
A FARCE, call
BEAU in the ___DS
TICKETS ___

Courtesy, the President and Fellows of Harvard College.

Earliest American playbill extant, 1750. Nassau-Street Theatre, New York. The play was Otway's *The Orphan*, followed by a farce called *Beau in the Sudds*

By Permission.
THIS is to inform the PUBLICK, That this EVENING, being Monday the 3d Instant, Will be exhibited (*for the last Night but five*) at a new House built for that Purpose, in *Adam Van Denberg's* Garden, The usual Performances of the celebrated
Anthony Joseph Dugee,
On a *Slack Wire* scarcely perceptible, with and without a Balance. I. He raises the *Wire* to a Swing, then rises on his Feet, walking forwards and backwards in full Swing; and turns himself, and swings to Admiration on one Foot. II. He will balance a Hat on his Nose. III. He balances a *Straw* on the Edge of the Rim of his Hat. IV. He plays with four *Balls* at once, in a surprizing Manner. V. He balances a Pyramid of Glasses full of Wine, on the Edge of a drinking Glass. VI. He will stand on his Head on the Wire, in full Swing. VII. He wheels a Wheel-barrow, with his Negro Boy in it on the Wire. *Also*, Several new Exercises on the *Stiff-Rope*, by Mr. DUGEE, the *Indian*, and young *Negro Boy*. In particular, the *Indian* intends to entertain the Company, by eating his Supper standing on his Head at the same Time, on the Nob of a Chair. With several curious *Equilibres*, on a Table, three Pins and a Chair, by the young *Negro Boy*. The whole to conclude with a *Dance*, called, the *Drunken Peasant*. Doors open'd at six o'Clock, and to begin precisely at Seven. TICKETS to be Sold at the House of Mr. *James Ackland*, at the *Royal-Exchange*; and at the Printing-Office opposite the *Old-Slip-Market*, PITT, four Shillings, GALLERY, two Shillings.
N. B. Mr. Dugee intends to perform every Monday, Wednesday and Friday, in every Week during his Residence here, but there will be different Performances every Night.

Advertisement in the *New York Mercury*. 1753

Harvard Boys Played Cricket . . .

Courtesy, The Colonial Society of Massachusetts, Boston.

View of Harvard College. 1795

Or Rode Over to Charlestown
To See a Spectacle . . .

A few LINES on

Magnus Mode, Richard Hodges & J. Newington Clark.

Who are Sentenc'd to stand one Hour in the

Pillory at Charlestown;

To have one of their EARS cut off, and to be Whipped 20 Stripes at the public Whipping-Post, for making and passing Counterfeit DOLLARS, &c.

BEHOLD the villains rais'd on high !
(The Post they've got attracts the eye :)
Both Jews and Gentiles all appear
To see them stand exalted here ;
Both rich and poor, both young and old,
The dirty slut, the common scold :
What multitudes do them surround,
Many as bad as can be found.
And to encrease their sad disgrace,
Throw rotten eggs into their face,
And pelt them sore with dirt and stones,
Nay, if they could wou'd break their bones,
Their malice to such height arise,
Who knows but they'll put out their eyes :
But pray consider what you do
While thus expos'd to public view.
Justice has often done its part,
And made the guilty rebels smart ;
But they went on did still rebel,
And seem'd to storm the gates of hell.
To no good counsel would they hear ;
But now each one must loose an EAR,

And they although against their will
Are forc'd to chew this bitter pill ;
And this day brings the villains hence
To suffer for their late offence ;
They on th' Pillory stand in view :
A warning sirs to me and you !
The drunkards song, the harlots scorn,
Reproach of some as yet unborn.
But now the Post they're forc'd to hug,
But loath to take that naufeous drug
Which brings the blood from out their veins,
And marks their back with purple stains.
From their disgrace, now warning take,
And never do your ruin make
By stealing, or unlawful ways ;
(If you would live out all your days)
But keep secure from Theft and Pride ;
Strive to have virtue on your side.
Despise the harlot's flattering airs,
And hate her ways, avoid her snares ;
Keep clear from Sin of every kind,
And then you'll have true peace of Mind.

Courtesy, The New York Public Library.

Broadside. 1767

or Played At Cards

Courtesy, Cincinnati Art Museum, Cincinnati.

18th Century playing cards exported to America by Henry Hart of London

Extra! Extra!

Morbid broadsides took the place of sensational newspaper stories in the colonial era. Here is a typical one from Salem, Massachusetts, with all its gruesome details.

THE

PARTICULARS

Of the late melancholly and shocking

TRAGEDY,

Which happened at *Salem*, near *Boston*, on Thursday, the 17th Day of *June*, 1773.

Which Particulars, together with the Verses that are annexed, are printed in this Form at the Request of the Friends and Acquaintance of the Ten deceased Persons; and are recommended as very proper to be posted up in every House in NEW-ENGLAND, to keep in Remembrance the most forrowful Event, of the Kind, that has happened in AMERICA since its first Discovery. But to depicture this unhappy Catastrophe in its true Colours, must shock the tenderest Feelings of Humanity, and would serve to extenuate this Detail to the Size of a Volume, instead of a Sheet— Shocking indeed must one imagine it for their Friends on Shore at MARBLEHEAD, and at the small Distance of an Hundred Yards, to behold these distressed People just launching into Eternity, and not able to afford them the least of their wonted Assistance! Surely the Shrieks and Cries of the poor drowning Souls, which seemed to reach the Heavens (more especially the Lamentations of the Women, as the pregnant Situation of Five of them made the Scene more dreadful) must pierce the Soul of the Spectator, and melt his Heart, ever were it adamant!

SALEM, June, 1773.

THURSDAY, the Seventeenth, towards the Evening, (the proceeding Part of the Day having been very warm) the Horizon, Westward and Northward, was rendered very dark and gloomy by the extensive Appearance of many black Clouds, presaging a Thunder Storm; it however consisted chiefly of heavy Gusts of Wind. At this Time four or five Boats from the Harbour, were employed in bringing paving Stones from the Islands below; after much Concern with Regard to their Safety they all happily returned the next Day. Two or three Boats were also out, at the same Time, from this Place, on Parties of Pleasure; but all returned safe excepting one, the Fate of which was, perhaps, one of the most distressing Events that ever happened in or near this Place, an Account of which is as follows:

A large two-mast Boat, belonging to the Custom-House, of twenty-nine Feet Keel, with a Deck extending about half-way from Head to Stern, forming a considerable Cabbin, with about seven Tons of Ballast, sailed from Capt. *Derby's* Wharf between 10 and 11 o'Clock in the Forenoon, proceeded to Baker's Island, where they went ashore, staid and dined. In the Afternoon they went on board the Boat, and stood to the Eastward of the Island, for the Purpose of Fishing; then, about the Middle of the Afternoon, returned and anchored between Baker's-Island and the Milery (Island,) where they drank Tea. After they came to Sail again the Clouds were seen rising; and as the Weather appeared dark and threatening, they determined to try for Marblehead Harbour. As the Wind arose, they furl'd the Jibb, and took a double Reef in their Mainsail.— Mr. *William Ward* was the Commander of the Boat; and as the Wind increased, he was desired by the other Men, who apprehended Danger, to lower the Sails; but he declined, saying the Boat would stand it; and the others, trusting his Judgment, thought proper to submit. The 7 Women were all confined in the Cabbin. About 7 o'Clock, Ward being at Helm, a sudden, smart

Gust of Wind canted the Boat over on one Side; Mr. John Becket, who stood near the Cabbin, opened the Door, but had only Time to tell the Women they were all going to the Bottom; he heard their Shrieks, immediately jumped upon the Deck, and the Boat instantly sunk. Out of 12 Persons on board, 10 were drowned.

The Names of the Deceased are as follow, viz.

Mrs. *Sarah Becket*, Wife of Mr. John Becket, and Daughter of Mr. William Brown, deceased.
Mr. *Nathaniel Diggadon*, Tidewaiter; and Mrs. *Diggadon*, his Wife.
Mr. *William Word*, Boatman; and Mrs. *Mary Ward*, his Wife, Daughter of Mr. John Masury.
Miss *Esther Masury*, Sister to the above Mrs. Ward.
Mrs. *Desire Holman*, Wife of Mr. John Holman, Mariner, now at Sea.
Mr. *Paul Kimball*, Cooper, and Mrs. *Lydia Kimball*, his Wife, Daughter of Dr. Fairfield.
Mrs. *Rebecca Giles*, Widow of the late Mr. Eleazer Giles, and Daughter of Capt. John White.

Mr. *John Becket*, Husband to the above Mrs. Becket, and his Apprentice, named *Philip Becket*, were the only two who were saved.
Mr. Becket found that *John and* Kimball, Ward, and Diggadon, had got into a small Skiff, (which floated off the Boat as she sunk) and the Lad had hold of a Piece of Plank, about three Feet long. Mr. Becket swam for the Skiff, which before he could reach, overset, when Kimball and Diggadon sunk; Ward got hold of Mr. Becket, but in a Minute or two was disengaged and sunk also. There were now none left but Mr. Becket and the Lad, the former held to the Skiff, and the latter to the Piece of Plank.—As this Disaster happened within about one Mile of Marblehead, it was

seen by some People there, who, by their timely and vigorous Efforts, got off a small Schooner, which the Tide had left a-Ground near a Foot, and happily took up Mr. Becket and the Lad, after they had been in the Water about half an Hour.

The next Day, Friday, a great Number of People, from this Town and Marblehead, in two Sloops and a Number of Boats, went off to endeavour to weigh the funken Boat, (one of the Masts of which could just be seen at low Water) and also to recover the Bodies.— They succeeded in getting up the Boat, and after towing her up to a Wharf, which they reached between 8 and 9 o'Clock in the Evening, searched the Cabbin for the Bodies of the unfortunate Women, when those of Mrs. Giles, Mrs. Becket, Mrs. Kimball, Mrs. Ward, Mrs. Holman, and Miss Masury, were found, all of which were landed on the same Wharf from which with so much Cheerfulness and Gaiety they departed the Day before.

The Bodies of the three Men are not found: And that of Mrs. Diggadon, which was thought to be in the Cabbin, is missing. The six that were found were all buried on Saturday, Mrs. Ward and her Sister (Miss Esther Masury) in one Grave, and the others separate. The Solemnity of the several Processions drew together a vast Number of People, and the Funerals were attended by People of all Ranks.

This Event is rendered still more affecting by the Situation of the five married Women, who, it is said, were all pregnant, and 2 or 3 of them far advanced.

We are desired to mention, that it was owing to the Assistance received from Marblehead, that the Attempt to weigh the Boat so well succeeded as to get her up on Friday: Some of the most respectable Inhabitants of that Town, Captains of Vessels, and a great Number of others, exerted themselves in an extraordinary Manner for that Purpose; for which they have the sincere Thanks of the Friends of the deceased in particular, as well as the most grateful Acknowledgment of the Town in general.

The *Salem* TRAGEDY.

Being a Relation of the drowning of Ten Persons, who were taking their Pleasure on the Water, June 17th, 1773.

YOU who at Morning call your Friends
  To mingle in Delight,
Think seriously what sad Events
  May happen before Night.

2. This smiling Company were met,
  And left the Wharf all gay,
Which of them when he trod the Boat,
  Thought it was their dying Day.

3. The Pastimes of the Day were o'er,
  They sat at chearful Tea;
The Winds and Waves begin to roar,
  And Death demands his Prey.

4. How couldst thou, Pilot, hear the Cry,
  O low'r, O low'r the Sail!"
Fool-hardy thou thy Skill must try,
  Nor female Shrieks prevail.

5. See how the Picture shews all this,
  So dismally adorn'd!
Fiolicks are finish'd, Sports are past,
  And Boats to Coffins turn'd.

Salem tragedy. Broadside dated 1773

Fire! Fire!

Fires were always exciting events for young and old. Everyone came running post haste to the scene of the blaze.

Courtesy, North Carolina Historical Commission, Raleigh, N. C.

Fire engine. Salem, N. C. It was ordered from Europe in 1784

Courtesy, Old Quina-baug Village, Stur-bridge, Mass.

Leather fire buckets from Portsmouth, N. H. 1789

Courtesy, New Hampshire Antiquarian Society, Hopkinton, N. H. Kimball Studio.

Fire engine, New Hampshire

Fireman's certificate. New York. 1787

Valentine's Manual. 1851.

Public Health

Poor sanitation, the lack of doctors, cold houses, and the rigors of colonial life resulted in a high mortality rate. Quack doctors flourished, surgery was brutal, and epidemics raged uncontrolled. The apothecary's shop dispensed pills and powders.

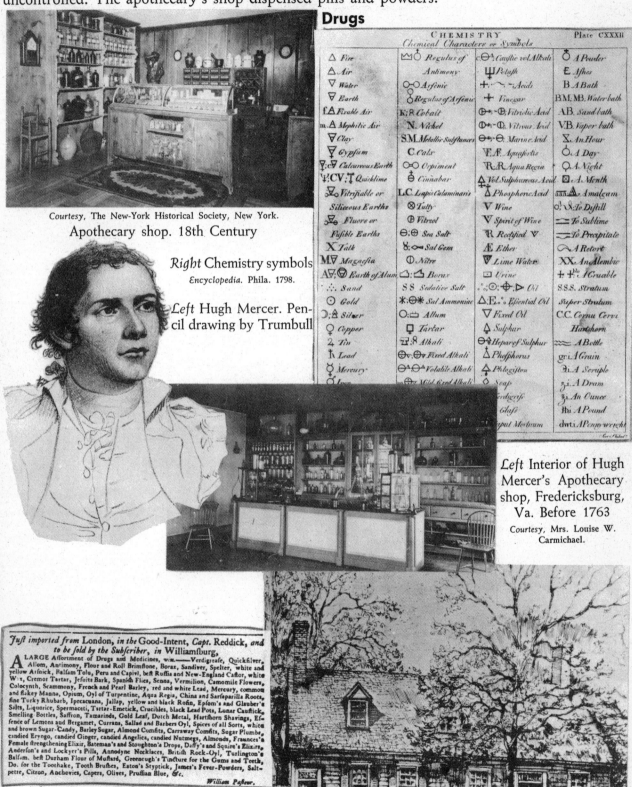

Courtesy, The New-York Historical Society, New York.

Apothecary shop. 18th Century

Right Chemistry symbols
Encyclopedia. Phila. 1798.

Left Hugh Mercer. Pencil drawing by Trumbull

Left Interior of Hugh Mercer's Apothecary shop, Fredericksburg, Va. Before 1763

Courtesy, Mrs. Louise W. Carmichael.

Advertisement in the *Virginia Gazette.*
Nov. 30, 1759
Hugh Mercer's Apothecary shop,
Fredericksburg, Va.

Courtesy, Mrs. Louise W. Carmichael.

The Poor and the Afflicted

A view of the House of Employment, Alms-House, Pennsylvania Hospital, and part of the City of Philadelphia. Engraved by J. Hulett after a drawing by Nicholas Garrison. 1767. The House of Employment was built in 1767. The hospital was first opened in 1756

Philadelphia was the medical center of America. Benjamin Rush, John Redman, William Shippen, John Morgan, Abraham Chovet, Thomas Cadwalader, and John Kearsley, Sr., were all great doctors.

Benjamin Rush, M. D. After a
portrait by Thomas Sully

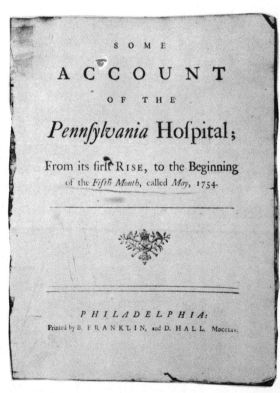

SOME

ACCOUNT

OF THE

Pennsylvania Hospital;

From its first RISE, to the Beginning
of the *Fifth Month*, called *May*, 1754.

PHILADELPHIA:
Printed by B. FRANKLIN, and D. HALL. MDCCLIV.

PHILADELPHIA, *July* 16.
Extract of a Letter from Chester, in Pennsylvania, July 13, 1752.
"On Thursday last a Person that went by the Name of Charles Hamilton came here, and offered to Sale at several Houses in Town sundry Medicines for different Disorders; pretending he was brought up to the Business of a Doctor and Surgeon, under one Doctor GREEN, a noted Mountebank in England; and that he embarked on Board a Brigantine, at Topsham, in England, last Fall, for Philadelphia, one Robinson Commander, but was cast away the latter End of January on the Coast of North-Carolina; and that he had travelled from thence through Virginia and Maryland, and has a Pass signed by some Magistrates in Virginia and Maryland, and one in Newcastle County: But it being suspected that the Doctor was a Woman in Mens Cloaths, was taken up, examined, and found to be a Woman; and confessed that she had used that Disguise for several Years. She is very bold, and can give no good Account of herself; says she is about Twenty-eight Years of Age, though she seems to be about Forty. She wears a blue Camblet Coat, with Silver Twist Buttons, too large for her. She is detained in Prison here, 'til we see whether any Body appears against her, if not she will be discharged. She says now her Name is Charlotte Hamilton."

Item from *Virginia Gazette*, Aug. 28, 1752

Runaway Slaves

After 1750 Negro slavery became more and more of an economic problem. Agriculture, particularly in the South, was based largely on this cheap labor. Many New England families owned Negro servants and apprentices. Both in the North and the South the Negro was regarded as property, and was bought and sold at public auction. Often slaves attempted to run away and the newspapers of the day were filled with advertisements offering rewards for their apprehension.

TO BE SOLD, on board the Ship *Bance-Island*, on tuesday the 6th of *May* next, at *Ashley-Ferry*; a choice cargo of about 250 fine healthy NEGROES, just arrived from the Windward & Rice Coast. —The utmost care has already been taken, and shall be continued, to keep them free from the least danger of being infected with the SMALL-POX, no boat having been on board, and all other communication with people from *Charles-Town* prevented.

Austin, Laurens, & Appleby.

N. B. Full one Half of the above Negroes have had the SMALL-POX in their own Country.

Courtesy, The Library of Congress, Washington, D. C. ca. 1763.

Slave auction

To be SOLD at publick Auction, on the 20th of December next, at Todd's *Warehouse,* in King and Queen County,
SEVERAL choice grown Negroes, Horses, Colts, &c. Credit will be given till the 20th of October next, the Purchasers giving Bond and Security to the Proprietor, who will attend on the Day of Sale. According to Custom, Five per Cent. Discount will be allowed for ready Money.

To be SOLD to the highest Bidders, for ready Money or short Credit, on Friday the 14th of December next, at the Plantation of Edward Munford, deceased, in Dinwiddie County,
TEN or 12 valuable *Virginia* born Slaves, chiefly Fellows; one of them an extraordinary good Carpenter, about 25 Years old.—Likewise some Houshold Furniture, being Part of the Estate of *Edward Munford,* deceased.
Joshua Poythress, } Administrators.
George Turnbull, }

JUST IMPORTED.

VEry handsome Setts of China, Cups and Saucers, to be sold by *William Ballantine* ... Mill-Bridge.

ANY Person that wants to put out a Child to a wet Nurse with a good Breast of Milk, may hear of one by Enquiring at the Printer's hereof.

ANY Person that has a Negro Child to give away may hear of one that will accept of it by Enquiring at the Printer's.

A Very commodious new House, with a good Yard, Garden, Well, &c. near the Seat of the Hon. Judge *Dudley* in *Roxbury*: TO BE LET, Inquire of the Printer.

TO BE SOLD, a very honest, likely, strong and hearty Negro Woman, that has had the Small Pox, about 30 Years of Age, and can do any sort of Houshold Work, an excellent Breeder, for which Reason she is to be disposed of; and a young Male Child to Enquire of the Printer.

RUN-away on the 11th of October, from *Carden Proctor,* of this city, watch-maker, an *English* servant girl, named, *Mary Wright,* about 22 years of age, thick and short, a brown complexion: Had she went away, a short strip'd cotton gown, a quilted petticoat, and took a brown and a light colour'd one with her, and may change them, the better to escape. Whoever takes up and secures the said run-away, so that her master may have her again, shall receive THIRTY SHILLINGS reward, and all reasonable charges, paid by CARDEN PROCTOR. N. B. She was brought in here by Capt. [...] from *London,* and lived for some time with [...] Dyer, in this city.

RUN-away on the 5th of October, *from* Capt. *Charles Ware,* of the city of New-York, a negro man, named, Joe, or Joseph, short and well set, about 38 or 40 years of age, pitted with the small-pox, speaks good English, lately come with his master from the Bay, and pretends to be free; he can play on the banjoe: Had on when he went away, a red waistcoat, with metal buttons, an olive colour'd [...] coat, an old blue great coat and a darkish wig, or woollen cap. Whoever apprehends him, and brings him to his master Mr. Charles Ware, or to Evert Byvanck, shall have TWENTY SHILLINGS reward, and all reasonable charges paid, by CHARLES WARE.

Just imported from London, in the brig *Maria, Thomas Miller* master, a parcel of choice goods, to be sold by JASPER FARMER, such as blankets, duffils, and sundry other sorts of dry goods, fit for the season; with a small parcel of best CHESHIRE CHEESE and CHINA.

To be SOLD, A likely Negro Man, about 25 years old, can be well recommended, inquire of the printer.

To be SOLD, A Negro Wench, this country born, has had the small-Pox, fit for town or country business, inquire of the printer.

Hermitage, the 16th Sept. 1763.

WHEREAS the subscriber's plantation, lately Chief Justice Grover's, now named Hermitage, is grievously and unsufferably annoyed and disturbed by negroes, who come there by land and water in the night-time, and not only rob, steal, and carry off hogs, poultry, sheep, corn, and his potatoes, but create very great disorders among his slaves, by debauching his slave wenches, who have husbands, the property of the subscriber; and some are so audacious as to debauch his very house wenches: These therefore are to give notice to all proprietors of slaves, that, after the 16th September 1763, the subscriber is determined to treat all negroes that shall be found within his fences, after sun-set, and before sun-rise, as thieves, robbers, and invaders of his property, by shooting them, and for that intent he has hired a white man properly armed for that purpose.
PATRICK MACKAY

[...] NEWMAN PRINTER may meet with [...]

RAN away from the Subscriber, living in *Petersburg,* on *Tuesday* the 4th Instant, Two Servant Men, viz.
Thomas Penney, an *English* Man, about 5 Feet 6 Inches high, by Trade a Taylor; he speaks broad, and had on when he went away, a coarse grey Jacket, a strip'd Holland Shirt, Oznabrig Trowsers, and a Pair of new Shoes.
James Croslon, an *English* Man, of a small Stature, pitted with the Small-pox; had on a coarse Cloth Jacket, a strip'd Holland Shirt, Oznabrig Trowsers, and new Shoes. Whoever apprehends and conveys them to me, shall have Two Pistoles Reward, paid by Robert Stobo.

August 7, 1762.

RAN away from the Ship *Alverton,* lying at *Berkeley,* in *James* River, on *Thursday* the 30th of *July* last, a Servant Man, named *John Almond,* an *English* Man, about 5 Feet 4 Inches high, with a round Face and small Mouth; had on when he went away a brown Jacket with Metal Buttons, and Leather Breeches under a Pair of Oznabrig Trowsers. Whoever secures and conveys him to me, shall have a Pistole Reward, paid by James Winster.

August 14, 1762.

RAN from the Subscriber, at *Hampton,* Two Negroe Men, one named *Boatswain,* a lusty Fellow, he has had the Small-pox, and has been mark'd on the Temple; had on a brown Linen Shirt, wide Trowsers, and blue Fearnothing Waistcoat. The other named *George,* a very black, short, well-set Fellow; had on a white Shirt, black Plush Breeches, and a blue Fearnothing Waistcoat. Whoever secures and conveys them to me, at *Sarah's* Creek, in *Glocester* County, shall have a Pistole Reward for each, besides what the Law allows, paid by John Briggs.

TAKEN up by the Subscriber, living in *York* County, a Bay Mare, about 13 Hands and a half high, branded on the near Buttock M. The Owner may have her of me, on proving his Property, and paying Charges.
Nathaniel Crawley, Jun.

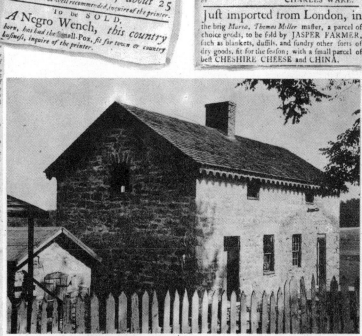

Courtesy, Historic American Buildings Survey, Washington, D. C.
Slave quarters, "Hampton", Towson vicinity, Maryland

Work All Day Long

Negroes were brought from the sugar fields and cotton plantations of the West Indies.

Edwards *The History . . . of the British Colonies in the West Indies.*
v. 2. 1794.

The Black Venus

Pomet *A Compleat History of Druggs.* 1725.

Sugar plantation

Diderot and D'Alembert *Encyclopedie.*
Recueil des planches. 1762-72.

Cotton

Courtesy, Mr. George Arents, New York.

Tobacco

Negro Poet

Some Negroes were given a liberal education. Phillis Wheatley the poet is a shining example.

Courtesy, The New York Public Library.

P O E M S

ON

VARIOUS SUBJECTS,

RELIGIOUS AND MORAL.

BY

PHILLIS WHEATLEY,

NEGRO SERVANT to Mr. JOHN WHEATLEY,
of BOSTON, in NEW ENGLAND.

LONDON:
Printed for A. BELL, Bookseller, Aldgate; and sold by
Messrs. COX and BERRY, King-Street, BOSTON.
M DCC LXXIII.

Children

The pleasures and hardships of childhood in the colonial era were largely dependent upon circumstances of birth and environment. The wealthier families gave their children expensive toys and beautiful clothing; the poorer families gave their children homemade toys and garments, and, all too often, exacted long hours of labor from them. Many became apprentices to hard taskmasters at a tender age. They matured rapidly. In conformity to the traditions of gentility which then prevailed all children were taught good manners. Disrespect to one's elders brought quick punishment.

Courtesy, Essex Institute, Salem, Mass.
Sarah (Northey) King and her daughter.
Artist unknown

Courtesy, Maryland Historical Society, and Frick Art Reference Library, New York.
Eleanor Darnall (later Mrs. Daniel Carroll).
Portrait by J. E. Kühn

Courtesy, Mr. Ledlie Irwin Laughlin, Princeton, N. J.
Pewter nursing bottles, Colonial Period

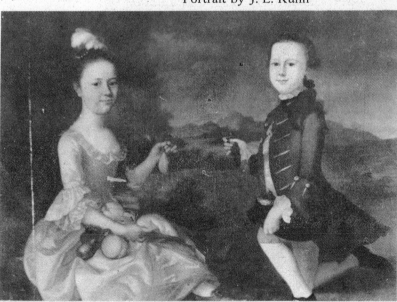

Courtesy, The Bowdoin College Museum of Fine Arts, Brunswick, Me.
James Bowdoin III and his sister Elizabeth as children. ca. 1760.
Portrait by Joseph Blackburn

Toys

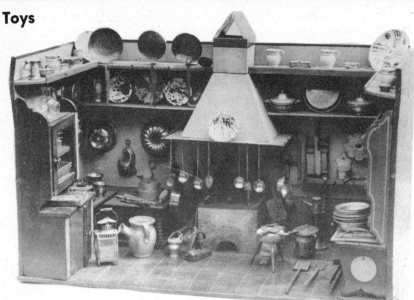

Kitchen toys. Probably New York. 18th Century

Courtesy, The Metropolitan Museum of Art, New York.

Below Jointed wooden dolls. 18th Century. The center doll is of later date. The noses of the 18th Century dolls were carved, not painted

Courtesy, Doll Museum, Wenham, Mass.

Dolls

Courtesy, Mrs. Imogene Anderson, New York, the present owner.

"Abigail Van Rensselaer." Wax doll. ca. 1760

Grave doll. 18th Century. When children died their dolls were put in a glass-covered box and placed on the grave

Courtesy, Mrs. Imogene Anderson, New York, the present owner.

Young Dreamer

Little Goody Twoshoes

Courtesy, Museum of Fine Arts, Boston.

Henry Pelham. Portrait by John Singleton Copley

Courtesy, Plimpton Collection, Columbia University Library, New York.

Pages from *The History of Little Goody Twoshoes*, 1787

Reading, Writing, And Arithmetic

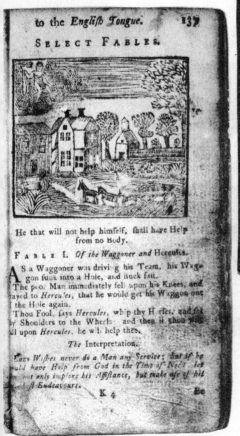

Page from Thomas Dilworth's *A New Guide to the English Tongue.* 1770

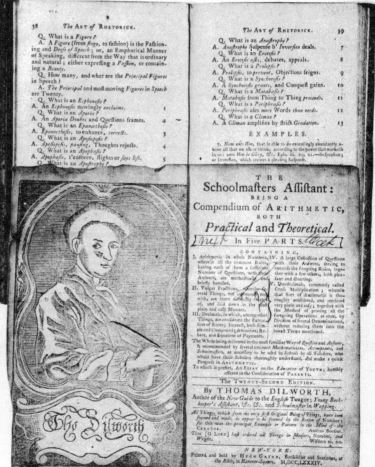

Selections from John Sterling's *A System of Rhetoric.* 1788

Courtesy, Plimpton Collection, Columbia University Library, New York.

The House That Jack Built

[6]

This is the Dog that worried the Cat, that killd the Rat, that eat the Malt that lay in the House that Jack built.

[7]

This is the Cow with the crumpled horn, that toss'd the Dog, that worried the Cat, that killed the Rat, that eat the Malt, that lay in the House that Jack built.

Courtesy, Plimpton Collection, Columbia University Library, New York.

Pages from *The House That Jack Built*. 1790

AT the House formerly *Thomas Chalkley's* in *Letitia* Court, near *Blackhorse* Alley, are Taught WRITING, ARITHMETICK, with the true Grounds of the FRENCH TONGUE, at *Twenty Shillings* per Quarter, by
THOMAS BALL.

P. S. For the more speedy Instruction of his Scholars, he has calculated the following Tables, *viz.* 1. A Table for knowing the Genders of Nouns by their Terminations. 2. A Table for the Forming of Tenses. 3. A Table of all the irregular Verbs. 4. A Table representing the Terminations of the simple Tenses of Verbs. Which Tables, together with a nice Explanation of all the *French Particles* (now in the Press) will be of great Use to those who have a Desire to learn a Language so necessary and polite.

N. B. His Wife teaches Writing and French. Likewise Singing, Playing on the Spinet, Dancing, and all sorts of Needle-Work are taught by his Sister lately arrived from *London.*

Just imported in the Captains *Shoals* and *Miller* from *London*, and in the *Grace*, Capt. *Nealson*, from *Bristol*; a choice assortment of EUROPEAN AND INDIA GOODS, suitable for the season, to be sold cheap, by *ASPINWALL* and *DOUGHTY*, at their store next door to Col. *DePeyster's*, Treasurer. Also Globe Lamps.

On Monday the 3d of *December*, Inst. the Revd. JOHN LEWIS MAYOR, begun to teach French, Latin and Greek. Attendance will be given from two to five o'clock in the afternoon, and from six to eight in the evening, saturday excepted. Mr. *Mayor* is to be spoke with at Mrs. *Faviere's*, near the *Long-Bridge*.

Reading, writing, and arithmetick in all its parts, vulgar and decimal, logarithmetical and instrumental; geometry, trigonometry, plain and spherical; surveying, gauging and dialing, astronomy, the projection of the sphere upon the plan of any circle, with the calculation and projection of the eclipses of the luminaries; Also navigation, as plain, mercator, and great circle sailing, by all the various ways heretofore taught, *viz.* geomatrically, logarithmetically, tabulary, or instrumentally; also by a new and compleat method, without the help of books, tables, scales, or mathematical instruments: Also merchants accounts are carefully taught at the corner house, near the *Quaker Meeting*, in *Crown-Street*, (near *Oswego-Market*) where young men inclin'd to learn, may be boarded, and where gentlemen may have any sort of writing authentically drawn, by *JOHN NATHAN HUTCHINS.*

Advertising for pupils

Fraktur

Among the Pennsylvania Germans the art of penmanship was highly developed, and certificates were decorated with what is known as the fraktur method.

Courtesy, Philadelphia Museum of Art, Philadelphia.

Birth certificate, Pennsylvania. 1784. Fraktur

School House

Nathan Hale School. New London, Co Etching by James H. Fincken
Courtesy, Colonial Society of America.

The Almanack

The most widely read publications in all the colonies next to the Holy Bible were the almanacs. Farmers planted their crops according to the phases of the moon as recorded in the "almanack." Great faith was placed in the prognostications of these cheap publications. Interesting reading matter was placed in many of them, following the example of *Poor Robin*, a facetious English almanac. Court sessions, distances between towns, currency rates, and other facts were also given. In 1752 the New Style calendar was adopted, causing much confusion in dates. Conservatives clung to Old Style.

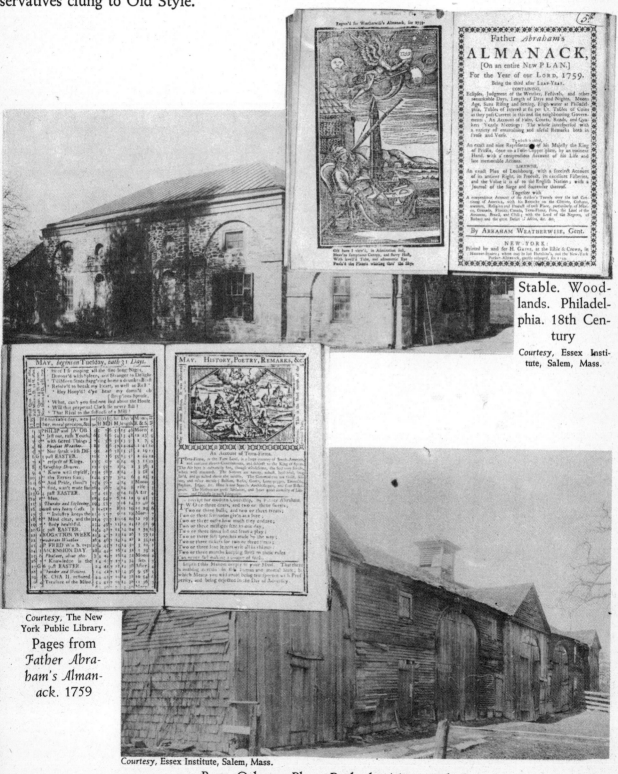

Stable. Woodlands. Philadelphia. 18th Century

Courtesy, Essex Institute, Salem, Mass.

Courtesy, The New York Public Library.

Pages from *Father Abraham's Almanack.* 1759

Courtesy, Essex Institute, Salem, Mass.

Barn. Osborne Place, Peabody, Mass. 18th Century

Conestoga Wagon

The Pennsylvania Germans developed a peculiar type of wagon adapted to transporting heavy loads long distances. They called this freight carrier the Conestoga Wagon.

Courtesy, Baltimore and Ohio Railroad.

Conestoga wagon

Conestoga wagons carried this equipment.

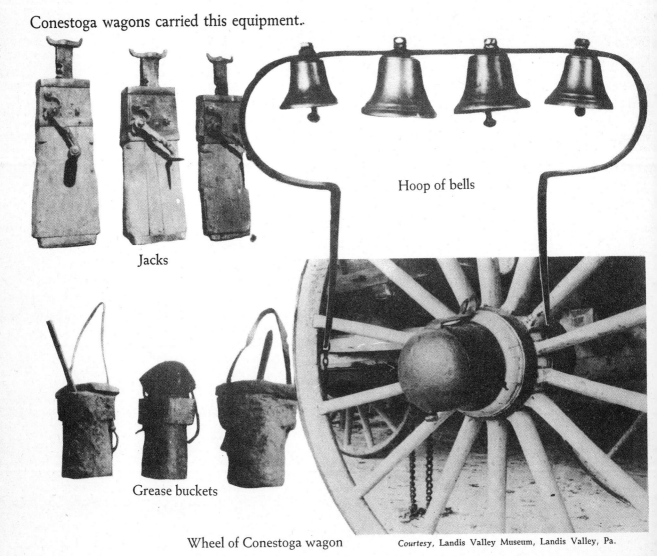

Jacks

Hoop of bells

Grease buckets

Wheel of Conestoga wagon   *Courtesy,* Landis Valley Museum, Landis Valley, Pa.

Other Vehicles

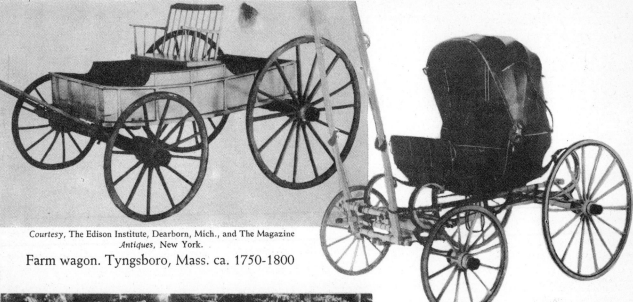

Courtesy, The Edison Institute, Dearborn, Mich., and The Magazine *Antiques*, New York.

Farm wagon. Tyngsboro, Mass. ca. 1750-1800

Courtesy, The Magazine *Antiques*, New York, and The Edison Institute, Dearborn, Mich.

Buggy. New Hampshire. ca. 1780

Left Ox cart. Engraved from an original painting by G. Harvey

Courtesy, Stokes Collection, The New York Public Library.

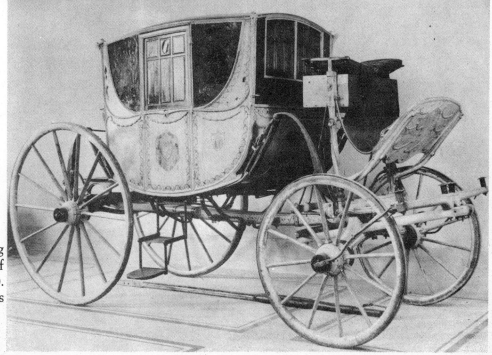

French coach belonging to James Beekman of New York. ca. 1770. Note the coat of arms on the panel

Courtesy, The New-York Historical Society, New York.

Trade Unions

Labor was becoming self-conscious and societies were being organized for protection and improvement.

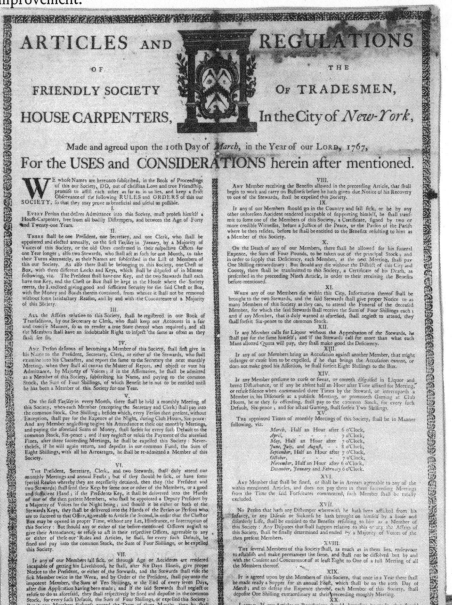

The house carpenters of New York form a society

Carpenters at work

Diderot and D'Alembert *Encyclopedie.*
Recueil des planches. 1762-72.

The Graphic Arts

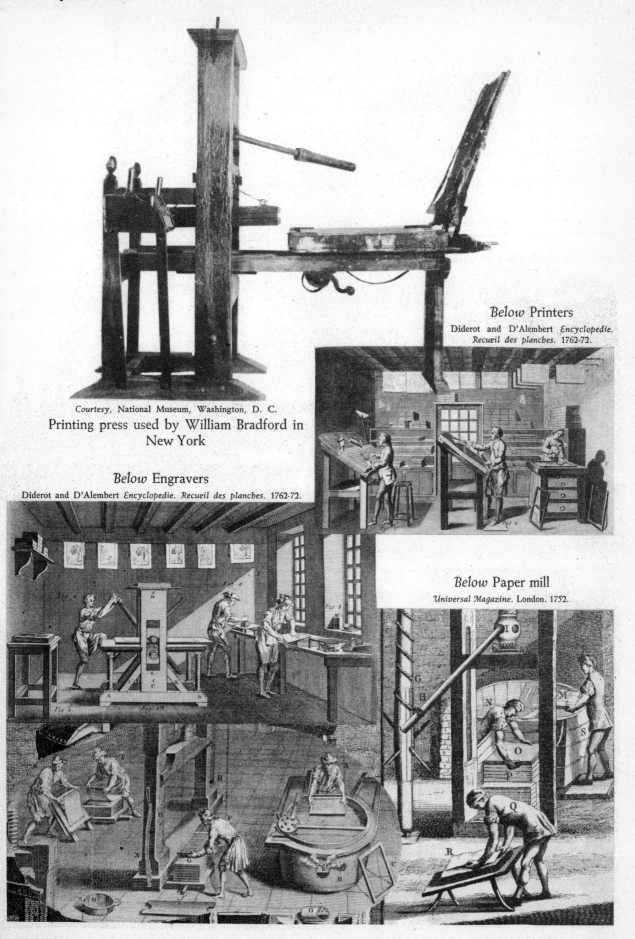

Courtesy, National Museum, Washington, D. C.

Printing press used by William Bradford in New York

Below Engravers

Diderot and D'Alembert *Encyclopedie. Recueil des planches.* 1762-72.

Below Printers

Diderot and D'Alembert *Encyclopedie. Recueil des planches.* 1762-72.

Below Paper mill

Universal Magazine. London. 1752.

Woodcuts

Newspaper illustration was extremely crude. A few small woodcuts were used in the advertising columns. The same ones were repeated over and over.

Courtesy, Tapley Salem Imprints (1927).

Electricity

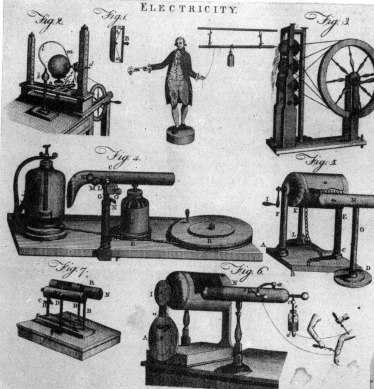

Benjamin Franklin and other scientists were experimenting with the Leyden jar and other electrical apparatus, but the powers of the newly-discovered phenomenon were but dimly recognized.

Left Electrical apparatus
Encyclopedia. Philadelphia. 1798.

Stonecutter's Art

The artists who cut inscriptions on tombstones were kept busy. Some of them became very proficient.

The Bible In Iron

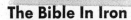

Courtesy, Bucks County Historical Society, Doylestown, Pa.
Stove plate made in Pennsylvania. Biblical subjects were popular

Courtesy, Essex Institute, Salem, Mass.
Gravestone. Charter Street Burying Ground, Salem, Mass.

Left Pennsylvania German tombstone
Courtesy, Landis Valley Museum, Landis Valley, Pa.

Native Born Artists

Many leading American artists went to London to further their art studies—a few, such as Benjamin West and John Singleton Copley, remained there to take their place alongside the leading British painters. West even became the president of the Royal Academy in 1792, holding this distinguished honor until 1820.

Courtesy, Metropolitan Museum of Art, New York.

The American School. Painting by Matthew Pratt. 1765. This shows Benjamin West's studio in London. West is shown standing at the left correcting a drawing held by Matthew Pratt

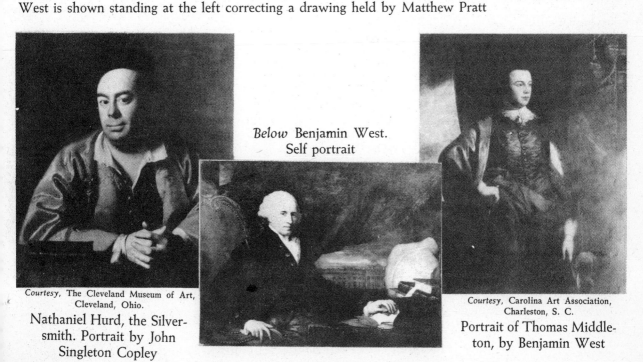

Below Benjamin West. Self portrait

Courtesy, The Cleveland Museum of Art, Cleveland, Ohio.

Nathaniel Hurd, the Silversmith. Portrait by John Singleton Copley

Courtesy, Carolina Art Association, Charleston, S. C.

Portrait of Thomas Middleton, by Benjamin West

Architecture

The first settlers built their houses themselves. As wealth increased professional architects were paid to make designs for mansions and public buildings.

Courtesy, Yale University Art Gallery.

William Buckland, architect. Portrait by Charles Willson Peale

Below Plan of the palace of Gov. William Tryon of N. C., by John Hawks. 1767

From British Public Record Office, London.

Courtesy, Connecticut Magazine.

State House, New Haven, Conn. 1763

Wansey The Journal of an Excursion to the United States of North America. 1796.

State House. Philadelphia. Designed by Andrew Hamilton and John Kearsley

Fort Duquesne

We shall now turn to the military affairs of the American colonies. The final struggle between France and England for possession of America was set off by a clash for control of what is now Pittsburgh. The French had built Fort Duquesne at that strategic site.

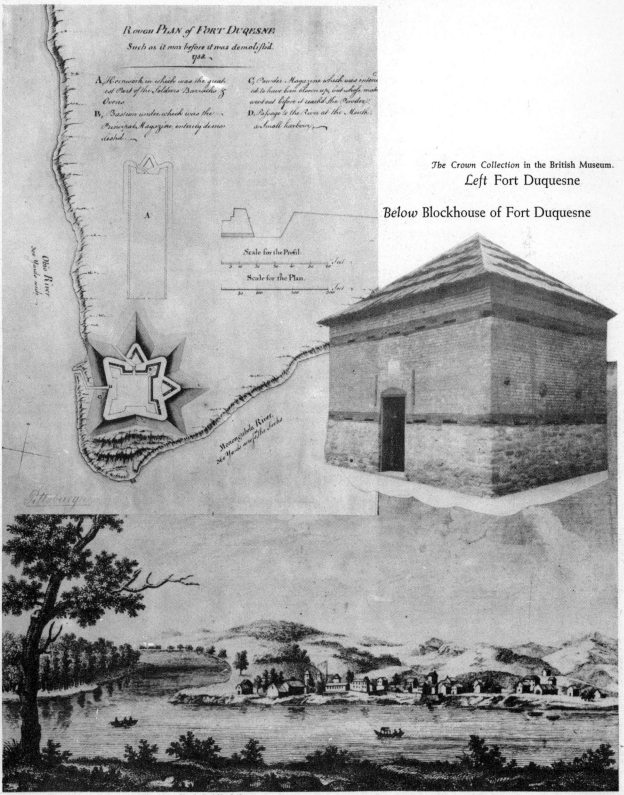

The Crown Collection in the British Museum.

Left Fort Duquesne

Below Blockhouse of Fort Duquesne

Courtesy, The Stokes Collection, The New York Public Library.

View of Pittsburgh. Drawn by V. Collot or his companion Joseph Warin. 1796

Braddock's Expedition

In 1755, General Edward Braddock marched towards Fort Duquesne with a large force of British and provincial troops, but was defeated, and lost his own life in the battle. His insistence on arranging his troops in close formation instead of dispersing them among the trees in Indian fashion, cost him the victory. George Washington, a young Virginia surveyor, who knew Indian tactics as well as the terrain, had pleaded with Braddock to alter his strategy, but to no avail. Washington barely escaped with his own life in the disaster that followed.

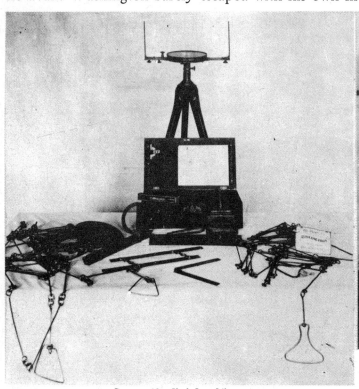

Courtesy, The Valentine Museum, Richmond, Va.

Field desk of Virginia Walnut said to have been used in Braddock's campaign

Courtesy, New York State Library.

Surveying instruments of George Washington. Now owned by the New York State Library, Albany

Birthplace of George Washington, Bridges Creek, Westmoreland County, Va. Currier & Ives lithograph

The Ohio Country

The rich land of the Ohio Valley was the ultimate object of the British penetration. Traders had established posts in this country, but as long as the French were at Fort Duquesne the English settlements were jeopardized. In 1758 Brigadier-General John Forbes, and Colonel Henry Bouquet, who was second in command, captured Fort Duquesne. Forbes had advanced westward from Bedford, Pa., building Forbes Road through the wilderness as he went and studding it with blockhouses.

Fort Loudon

The capture of Fort Duquesne was partly offset by the loss of Fort Loudon on the Little Tennessee River to the disgruntled Cherokee Indians in 1760.

Colonel Bouquet in conference with the Indians. After a painting by Benjamin West

Vignette by F. O. C. Darley

Courtesy, Harvard University Library.

Plan of Fort Loudon by William Gerard De Brahm, the engineer who constructed it

Right Judd's Friend, or Outacite, Creek Indian. Sketch by Sir Joshua Reynolds, made in 1762 when Outacite was taken to London by Lieutenant Henry Timberlake

The Indians were divided in their loyalties, some fighting on the English side and some on the French. Sir William Johnson of New York Province won the lasting friendship of the Six Nations by acting as their agent and benefactor. His marriage to an Indian girl proved that his affection was genuine. He negotiated treaties for them and served as their military leader during the French and Indian wars.

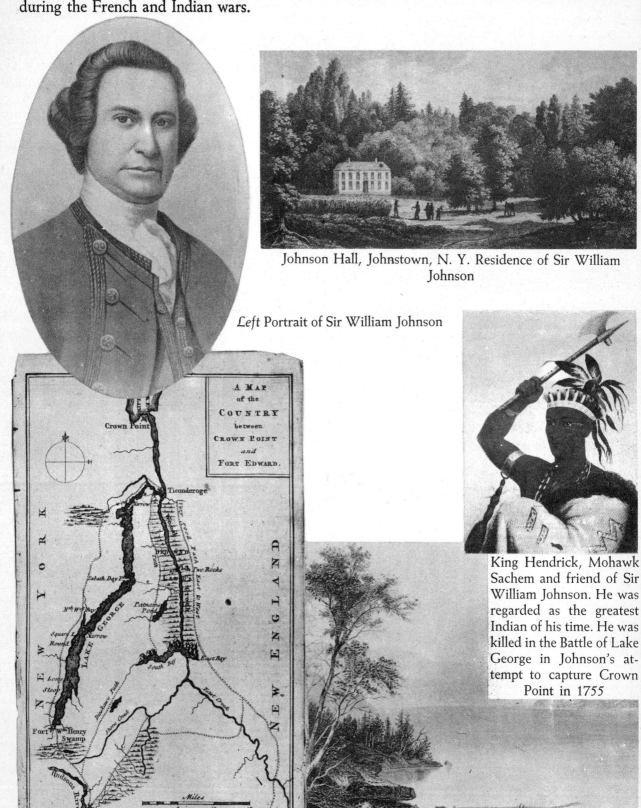

Johnson Hall, Johnstown, N. Y. Residence of Sir William Johnson

Left Portrait of Sir William Johnson

King Hendrick, Mohawk Sachem and friend of Sir William Johnson. He was regarded as the greatest Indian of his time. He was killed in the Battle of Lake George in Johnson's attempt to capture Crown Point in 1755

Gentleman's Magazine. 1759.

Picturesque America. 1872-74.
Lake George in New York

Friends or Foes?

The Mask of the Twisted Face

According to Indian legend an imposter was struck on the side of his face by a moving mountain when he dared to challenge the power of the creator.

Left Mask of the Twisted Face. Mohawk
Courtesy, Museum of the American Indian, Heye Foundation, New York City.

The spirit of the Indian still haunts the hills and valleys of the white man.

Right Doctor mask. Seneca
Courtesy, Museum of the American Indian, Heye Foundation, New York City.

By the Honorable
JOHN PENN, Esquire,

Lieutenant Governor and Commander in Chief of the Province of *Pennsylvania* and Counties of *New-Castle, Kent* and *Suffex* on DELAWARE.

To all to whom these Presents shall come, or may concern ; Greeting :

WHEREAS
               prayed my
    Licence to trade with the Nations or Tribes of Indians, with whom his Majesty is connected, and who live under his protection ; and   given security to observe such Regulations as his Majesty shall at any Time think fit, by himself, or by his Commissaries to be appointed for that Purpose, to order and direct for the Benefit of the Trade with the said Indians ; and not to trade or traffick with ; or vend, sell, or dispose, of any Goods, Wares or Merchandizes of any Kind whatever, to any Indian or Indians within the Country of any the Indian Nations aforesaid, beyond the Settlements of the Inhabitants, except at
the Forts or Posts which are already, or shall hereafter be established by his Majesty, and garrisoned by his Troops. I Do THEREFORE hereby authorize and impower the said
          to trade with the said Nations or Tribes of Indians for the Space of one Year from the date hereof. This Licence to be void, and the Security forfeited in Case the said
          shall refuse or neglect to observe such regulations as aforesaid.

    GIVEN under my Hand, and Seal at Arms, at PHILADELPHIA, *the*
    Day of   176 *In the*   *Year of the Reign of Our Sovereign Lord*
    GEORGE *the Third, by the Grace of* GOD, *of* GREAT-BRITAIN, FRANCE, *and* IRELAND, KING,
    Defender of the Faith, and so forth.

By His HONOUR's *Command,*

Licence to trade with the Indians

Rogers' Rangers

Major Robert Rogers and his Rangers terrified the French and Indians with their daring raids, and their method of attack was based on the Indian tactics of camouflage and ambush rather than on the traditional British open formations which cost so many lives. Rogers married Elizabeth Brown, a Portsmouth, N. H., belle, wrote a play on the Indian chief Pontiac, and, embittered over the government's lack of recognition of his talents, turned traitor during the American Revolution.

Major Robert Rogers

Elizabeth Browne (Mrs. Robert Rogers). Portrait by Joseph Blackburn

Left Powder horn used in the French and Indian wars. It belonged to Michael B. Goldthwaite. Dated Oct. 2, 1756, at Fort William Henry

Courtesy, Maine Historical Society, Portland, Me.

PONTEACH:

OR THE

Savages of America.

A

TRAGEDY.

LONDON:
Printed for the Author; and Sold by J. Millan, opposite the *Admiralty*, *Whitehall*.
M.DCC.LXVI.
[Price 2 s. 6 d.]

Title-page of a play written by
Major Robert Rogers

All Gentlemen Volunteers, and Others.

THAT have a Mind to serve his Majesty King GEORGE the Second, for a limited Time, in the Independant Companies of Rangers now in *Nova-Scotia*, may apply to Lieutenant *Alexander Callender*, at Mr. *Jonas Leonard's*, at the Sign of the *Lamb* at the South End of *Boston*, where they shall be kindly entertained, enter into present Pay, and have good Quarters, and when they join their respective Companies at *Hallifax*, shall be compleatly cloathed in blue Broad-Cloth, receive Arms, Accoutrements, Provisions, and all other Things necessary for a Gentleman Ranger: And for their further Encouragement, his Excellency Governor CORNWALLIS has by Proclamation lately published, promised a Reward of *Five Hundred Pounds*, old Tenor, for every *Indian* Scalp or Prisoner brought in, which Sum will be immediately paid by the Treasurer of the Province, upon the Scalp or Prisoner being produc'd.
N. B. Lieutenant *Callender* has obtained Leave from His Honour the Lieutenant Governor, to beat up for Rangers in any Part of this Province.
Boston, September 8. 1750.

JUST PUBLISHED,
(*And sold opposite the Prison in Queen-Street:*)

TRue RELIGION delineated; Or, EXPERIMENTAL RELIGION as distinguished from FORMALITY on the one Hand, and ENTHUSIASM on the other, set in a Scriptural and Rational Light.

Excerpt from *Boston Weekly News Letter.*
Oct. 4, 1750

Residents of New England villages gathered at the taverns and churches to hear the latest news from soldiers home on furlough.

Hanson *History of the Old Towns of Norridgewock and Canaan.* 1849.

Oosoola, Me. A typical New England village

Whitefield *The Homes of Our Forefathers.* 1880-86.

Blockhouse. Winslow, Me.

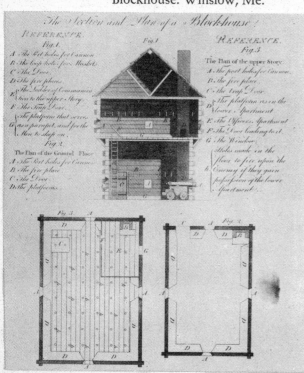

Marion J. Bradshaw *The Maine Land.* 1941.

First Congregational Church, Kennebunkport, Me. Built 1764

Left Plan of an American block house

Anburey *Travels Through America.* 1789.

Fort Oswego on Lake Ontario was the key to the Great Lakes. The British strongly fortified it and built their ships there.

A South View of OSWEGO, on Lake Ontario, in North America.

Explanation
The River Onondago
Lake Ontario

Fort Oswego. Note the shipbuilding going on

London Magazine. May 1760.

Left H. M. Ship *Oswego*, built at Oswego in 1755. Length 43 feet, beam 15 feet, 10 light guns and swivels, crew about 42 men

Courtesy, The Marine Collection, Canada Steamship Lines Limited, Montreal, Canada.

Right H. M. Ships *Huron* and *Michigan*. Built at Navy Island above Niagara Falls in 1763. Pontiac attacked them at the siege of Fort Detroit. They were 80 ton ships, length 60 feet, beam 14 feet, with 10 four-pounders and 2 swivels

Courtesy, The Marine Collection, Canada Steamship Lines Limited, Montreal, Canada.

Courtesy, The Marine Collection, Canada Steamship Lines Limited, Montreal, Canada.

The French fleet, Lake Ontario. 1757. Shows *L'Huron, La Marquise de Vaudreuil*, and other vessels.

Left Whaleboats used in 1758 by Col. Bradstreet's expedition to Fort Frontenac. They were brought up the Mohawk River from the Hudson, portaged over the Great Carrying Place to Lake Oneida, and then down the Onondaga River to Fort Oswego. Note the howitzers and shields. The boats were 35 feet long. Bradstreet used about 200 of them in this expedition

Courtesy, The Marine Collection, Canada Steamship Lines Limited, Montreal, Canada.

Ticonderoga. Note the whaleboat and howitzer

The Crown Collection in the British Museum.

Quebec

The stronghold of the French was at Quebec. It was an almost impregnable fortress. Here we see the French troops being reviewed at Quebec.

Courtesy, William H. Coverdale Collection, and the Canada Steamship Lines Limited, Montreal, Canada.

Reviewing troops at Quebec. Water color by an unknown artist, probably a soldier stationed there around 1750

Account of the military and naval engagements of 1760

The Crown Collection in the British Museum.

Plan of Fort Erie. Built by John Montresor

Stamp Act

In 1765 Great Britain passed the Stamp Act. It amounted to taxation without representation. From one end of the American colonies to the other the issue was hotly debated, and the unpopular measure was repealed in 1766.

Sorrow

Newspaper reaction to the Stamp Act

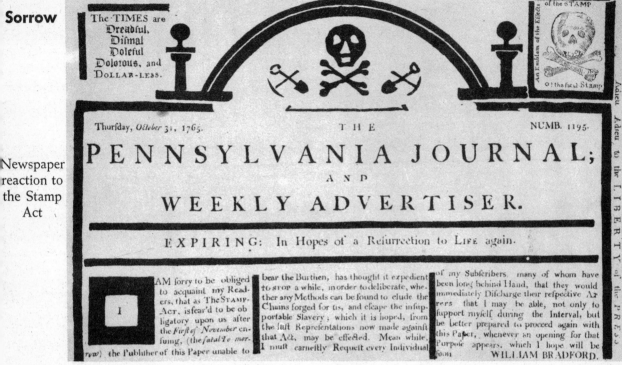

The TIMES are Dreadful, Dismal, Doleful Dolorous, and DOLLAR-LESS.

An Emblem of the Effects of the STAMP. O! the fatal Stamp.

Adieu Adieu to the LIBERTY of the PRESS.

Thursday, October 31, 1765.   THE   NUMB. 1195.

PENNSYLVANIA JOURNAL;
AND
WEEKLY ADVERTISER.

EXPIRING: In Hopes of a Resurrection to Life again.

I AM sorry to be obliged to acquaint my Readers, that as The STAMP-ACT, is fear'd to be obligatory upon us after the *First of November* ensuing, (the *fatal To-morrow*) the Publisher of this Paper unable to bear the Burthen, has thought it expedient to stop a while, in order to deliberate, whether any Methods can be found to elude the Chains forged for us, and escape the insupportable Slavery; which it is hoped, from the last Representations now made against that Act, may be effected. Mean while, I must earnestly Request every Individual of my Subscribers, many of whom have been long behind Hand, that they would immediately Discharge their respective Arrears that I may be able, not only to support myself during the Interval, but be better prepared to proceed again with this Paper, whenever an opening for that Purpose appears, which I hope will be soon.   WILLIAM BRADFORD.

England Take Heed!

Peters *A General History of Connecticut.* 1829.

Unpopular Tories were hanged in effigy at Lebanon, Conn.

Right Announcement of the repeal of the Stamp Act

Courtesy, The New York Public Library.

Joy

Glorious News.

BOSTON, Friday 11 o'Clock, 16th *May* 1766.
THIS Instant arrived here the Brig *Harrison*, belonging to *John Hancock*, Esq; Captain *Shubael Coffin*, in 6 Weeks and 2 Days from LONDON, with important News, as follows.

From the LONDON GAZETTE.

Westminster, March 18th, 1766.

THIS day his Majesty came to the House of Peers, and being in his royal robes seated on the throne with the usual solemnity, Sir Francis Molineux, Gentleman Usher of the Black Rod, was sent with a Message from his Majesty to the House of Commons, commanding their attendance in the House of Peers. The Commons being come thither accordingly, his Majesty was pleased to give his royal assent to

An ACT to REPEAL an Act made in the last Session of Parliament, intituled, an Act for granting and applying certain Stamp-Duties and other Duties in the British Colonies and Plantations in America, towards further defraying the expences of defending, protecting and securing the same, and for amending such parts of the several Acts of Parliament relating to the trade and revenues of the said Colonies and Plantations, as direct the manner of determining and recovering the penalties and forfeitures therein mentioned.

Also ten public bills, and seventeen private ones.

Yesterday there was a meeting of the principal Merchants concerned in the American trade, at the King's Arms tavern in Cornhill, to consider of an Address to his Majesty on the beneficial Repeal of the late Stamp-Act.

Yesterday morning about eleven o'clock a great number of North American Merchants went in their coaches from the King's Arms tavern in Cornhill to the House of Peers, to pay their duty to his Majesty, and to express their satisfaction at his signing the Bill for Repealing the American Stamp-Act, there was upwards of fifty coaches in the procession.

Last night the said gentlemen dispatched an express for Falmouth, with fifteen copies of the Act for repealing the Stamp-Act, to be forwarded immediately for New York.

Orders are given for several merchantmen in the river to proceed to sea immediately on their respective voyages to North America, some of whom have been cleared out since the first of November last.

Yesterday messengers were dispatched to Birmingham, Sheffield, Manchester, and all the great manufacturing towns in England, with an account of the final decision of an august assembly relating to the Stamp-Act.

10

THE AMERICAN REVOLUTION

Courtesy, Essex Institute, Salem, Mass.

Boy's shoe. Period of the American Revolution

The boy who wore this shoe lived in stirring times. Great issues were at stake. He was old enough to listen attentively to his elders who quoted the words of James Otis:

"Taxation without Representation
is Tyranny"

These words would be repeated by generations yet unborn.

James Otis. Portrait after Joseph Blackburn. 1755

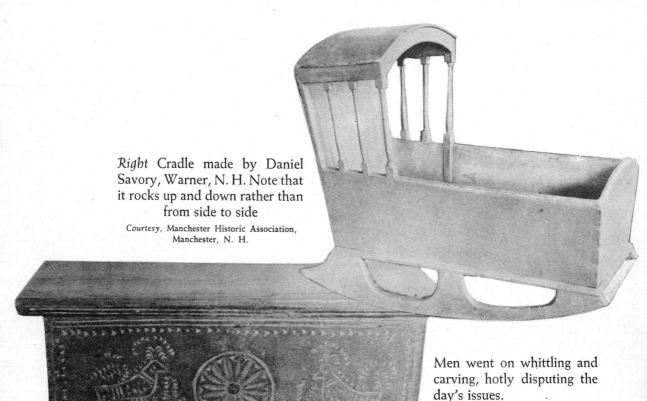

Right Cradle made by Daniel Savory, Warner, N. H. Note that it rocks up and down rather than from side to side

Courtesy, Manchester Historic Association, Manchester, N. H.

Men went on whittling and carving, hotly disputing the day's issues.

Carved oak box.
Connecticut. 18th Century

Courtesy, Old Quinabaug Village, Sturbridge, Mass.

Working—Waiting . . .

Reconstructed blacksmith shop of Elkanah Deane, Williamsburg, Va. 1772 *Courtesy,* Colonial Williamsburg, Inc.

Cocked hat   *Courtesy,* New Hampshire Historical Society, Concord, N. H.

Forged iron balance scale. Connecticut. Made by H. Jackson. 1770 *Courtesy,* Old Quinabaug Village, Sturbridge, Mass.

Danger Signal

Wise statesmen in England, particularly Edmund Burke and William Pitt, foresaw the danger of armed rebellion in America if unjust taxes continued to be imposed.

Pitt's views were so esteemed in America that the people of New York erected a statue to him, which the British soldiers mutilated when they captured the city, during the American Revolution. The Americans had previously melted down the statue of George III, in New York, and made it into bullets.

Courtesy, The New-York Historical Society, New York.

Statue of William Pitt after British soldiers had mutilated it.

Courtesy, The New-York Historical Society, New York.

Americans demolishing the Statue of George III. Woodcut by Alexander Anderson

William Pitt

"Master of the Puppets"

In Boston, Samuel Adams expressed the voice of the patriots. He dared to speak of democracy, even to haughty Thomas Hutchinson, Governor of Massachusetts. Hutchinson referred to Adams as "Master of the Puppets".

Courtesy, Museum of Fine Arts. Boston.

Samuel Adams. Portrait by John Singleton Copley

Freedom of Speech and Assembly

Patriots delivered democratic speeches in Faneuil Hall in Boston, at town meetings, or at the Liberty Tree. Almost every American town had a Liberty Tree, under which patriots gathered to organize and protest.

"BY UNITING WE STAND, BY DIVIDING WE FALL".

Thus wrote John Dickinson of Pennsylvania.

Bowen's Boston News-Letter and City Record. 1826.

Liberty Tree. Boston

Benjamin Franklin was sent to London to safeguard American rights. For exposing damaging correspondence by Gov. Hutchinson of Massachusetts, he was rebuked by the Privy Council and deprived of his post as Post-Master-General.

John Dickinson. Portrait by
Charles Willson Peale

JOIN, or DIE.

Cartoon by Benjamin Franklin. 1754. This was often reprinted in colonial newspapers until 1789

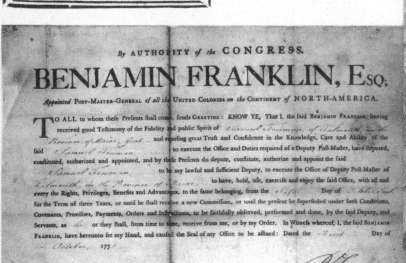

By AUTHORITY of the CONGRESS.

BENJAMIN FRANKLIN, Esq;

Appointed Post-Master-General of all the United Colonies on the Continent of NORTH-AMERICA.

Post-master's appointment signed by Benjamin Franklin

Trumbull *M'Fingal*. 1795 edition. The town meeting caricatured here shows a tense scene between Tories and Patriots

More Troops Arrived In Boston

Engraving by Paul Revere. 1770. Date depicted 1768

British troops quartered on Boston Common. Water color by Christian Remick. 1768. The house at the right is the elegant mansion of the wealthy merchant and patriot, John Hancock

The Boston Massacre

On March 5, 1770, occurred the Boston Massacre. One snowy night a few civilians taunted and assaulted a British sentry. Owing to a misunderstanding of an order, the British troops, hurriedly called out, fired on the small crowd, killing three and wounding eight, two of whom died from their wounds. Feeling ran high, and Paul Revere made his lurid engraving, which fanned the flames of emotion to an even higher pitch. This old print is a classic example of propaganda.

Right The Boston Massacre. Engraved by Paul Revere. 1770. The State House is shown in the background. This incident was celebrated in poems, sermons, and orations, year after year, on the anniversary of the so-called massacre

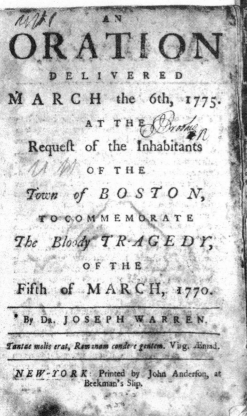

Title-page of an oration by Joseph Warren, commemorating the Boston Massacre

Two leading patriots, Josiah Quincy and John Adams, through a sense of duty, defended the British officers responsible for the incident, and they were acquitted, but the die was cast. Blood had been shed.

Birthplace of John Adams. Braintree, Mass.

Whitefield, *The Homes of Our Forefathers.* 1880-1886.

The Regulators

In North Carolina the extravagances and abuses of Governor Tryon were exasperating the tax-ridden citizens into open revolt. An organization called The Regulators marched into the courtroom at Hillsborough, N. C., and demanded redress for wrongs. Troops were called out to punish The Regulators, and at the Battle of Alamance, May 16, 1771, they were dispersed, but shots had been fired against the representatives of the British Crown.

Scene of the Battle of Alamance. Drawn by Benson J. Lossing

Execution of James Pugh, one of The Regulators. Commemorative tablet

Left Tryon's Palace. New Bern, N. C. Designed by John Hawks

Lossing *Pictorial Field Book of the Revolution.* 1852.

In Williamsburg, Va., the Royal Governor entertained his Tory guests as usual, and the actions of the rabble at Boston and at the Battle of Alamance were strongly censured. Loyal British subjects should stand firm against these upstart agitators and "democrats".

Supper Room. Governor's Palace. Williamsburg, Va.
Courtesy, Colonial Williamsburg, Inc. Photo by Richard Garrison.

The Boston Tea Party

On the night of December 16, 1773, occurred the Boston Tea Party. The British had imposed a tax on this popular commodity, and remembering the Stamp Act, the Americans were in no mood to pay what they regarded as an insolent levy, and meetings were held under the Liberty Trees in Boston, Philadelphia, Charleston, New York and other American cities. British ships were warned not to unload their cargoes of tea. A party of patriots disguised as Indians boarded an English vessel at Griffin's Wharf in Boston and dumped 342 chests of tea into the harbor.

Courtesy, The New-York Historical Society, New York.

The Boston Tea Party. English caricature. 1774

Lettsom's *The Natural History of the Tea-tree.* 1799.

Bohea Tea Plant

Brethren, and Fellow Citizens!

YOU may depend, that those odious Miscreants and detestable Tools to Ministry and Governor, the TEA CONSIGNEES, (those Traitors to their Country, Butchers, who have done, and are doing every Thing to Murder and destroy all that shall stand in the Way of their private Interest,) are determined to come and reside again in the Town of Boston.

I therefore give you this early Notice, that you may hold yourselves in Readiness, on the shortest Notice, to give them such a Reception, as such vile Ingrates deserve.   JOYCE, jun.
(Chairman of the Committee for Tarring and Feathering.)

☞ If any Person should be so hardy as to Tear this down, they may expect my severest Resentment.   Joyce, jun.

Courtesy, The Colonial Society of Massachusetts, Boston.

The Boston Tea Party. A Handbill

Courtesy, Metropolitan Museum of Art, New York.

Silver teapot by Paul Revere

"Give Me Liberty or Give Me Death"

On March 20, 1775, Patrick Henry arose before a body of patriots assembled in St. John's Church in Richmond, Va., and in reply to British acts of tyranny shouted: "Give me liberty or give me death!" The effect was electrical. Virginia stood ready to stand by courageous Massachusetts if armed rebellion should come.

Courtesy, Valentine Museum, Richmond, Va.
St. John's Church. Richmond, Va.

Duyckinck *National Portrait Gallery*. 1862.
Patrick Henry

Right Walnut table belonging to Patrick Henry
Courtesy, The Valentine Museum, Richmond, Va.

Left The churchyard of St. John's Church, Richmond, Va.
Courtesy, Valentine Museum, Richmond, Va., and the Metropolitan Museum of Art, New York.

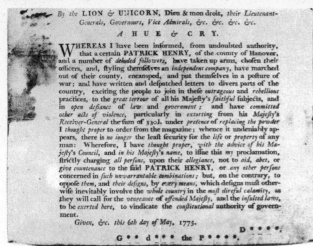

By the LION & UNICORN, Dien & mon droit, their Lieutenant-Generals, Governours, Vice Admirals, &c. &c. &c. &c.

A HUE & CRY.

WHEREAS I have been informed, from undoubted authority, that a certain PATRICK HENRY, of the county of Hanover, and a number of *deluded followers*, have taken up arms, chosen their officers, and, styling themselves an *independent company*, have marched out of their county, encamped, and put themselves in a posture of war; and have written and despatched letters to divers parts of the country, exciting the people to join in these *outrageous* and *rebellious* practices, to the *great terror* of all his Majesty's *faithful* subjects, and in open *defiance* of *law* and *government*; and have *committed* other *acts of violence*, particularly in *extorting* from his Majesty's *Receiver-General* the sum of 330l. under *pretence of replacing the powder* I thought proper to order from the magazine; whence it undeniably appears, there is *no longer* the least security for the *life* or *property* of any man: Wherefore, I have thought proper, *with the advice of his Majesty's Council*, and *in his Majesty's name*, to issue this *my proclamation*, strictly charging *all persons*, upon their *allegiance*, not to aid, abet, or give countenance to the said PATRICK HENRY, or *any other persons* concerned in *such unwarrantable combinations*; but, on the contrary, to oppose *them*, and *their designs*, by *every means*, which designs must otherwise inevitably involve the *whole country* in the *most direful calamity*, as they will call for the *vengeance of offended Majesty*, and the *insulted laws*, to be *exerted here*, to vindicate the *constitutional* authority of government.

Given, &c. this 6th day of May, 1775.

G * * d * * * the P * * * *. D * * * *.

A Hue and Cry for Patrick Henry. 1775. This was a bold parody on the official proclamation issued by Governor Dunmore and reveals the temper of the times

Colonial lanterns

Apollo Room. Raleigh Tavern. Williamsburg, Va. When the Governor of Virginia angrily dissolved the House of Burgesses, the patriots reassembled in the Apollo Room of the Raleigh Tavern and made defiant speeches

"The British Are Coming!"

Committees of Public Safety were organized throughout the colonies. Minute-men were trained for emergencies. In Massachusetts, Paul Revere, William Dawes, Samuel Prescott and others, who were in close touch with Samuel Adams, John Hancock, and Joseph Warren, were instructed to keep their eye on the movements of the British troops in Boston. If they marched out of town for a surprise attack, lanterns should flash signal lights and couriers were to ride to Lexington and Concord to rouse the countryside to arms. The British crept out of Boston on the night of April 18, 1775, and Paul Revere and his aides carried out their well-rehearsed orders. A skirmish was fought at Lexington on the morning of April 19, and the Revolutionary War was on.

An Impartial History of the War in America. 1780.

American Rifleman

The Battle of Lexington

1 *Major Pitcairn at the head of the Regular Granadiers*
2 *The Party who first fired on the Provincials at Lexington*
3 *Part of the Provincial Company of Lexington*
4 *Regular Companies on the road to Concord.   A Doolitle Sculpt*
5 *The Metinghouse at Lexington*
6 *The Public Inn*

Courtesy, The New York Public Library.

The Battle of Lexington. April 19, 1775. Engraving by Amos Doolittle

The British troops overwhelmed the few provincials at Lexington and marched to Concord, where later in the day they were defeated and sent reeling back towards Boston.

The Battle of Concord

1 *Companies of the Regulars marching into Concord*
2 *Companies of Regulars drawn up in order*
3 *A Detachment destroying the Provincial Stores*
4 & 5 *Colonel Smith & Major Pitcairn viewing the Provincials who were mustering on an East Hill in Concord*
6 *The Townhouse* 7 *The Meetinghouse*

Courtesy, The New York Public Library.

British troops entering Concord, Mass. Engraving by Amos Doolittle

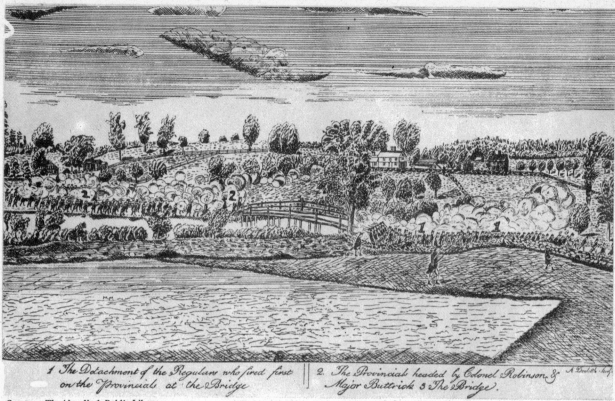

1 The Detachment of the Regulars who fired first on the Provincials at the Bridge   2 The Provincials headed by Colonel Robinson & Major Buttrick 3 The Bridge.   A Doolittle Sculp.

Courtesy, The New York Public Library.

Battle at North Bridge, Concord. April 19, 1775. Engraving by Amos Doolittle

Colonial Uniforms

Sprengel *Allgemeines Historisches Taschenbuch.* 1784.

British sentry. American Revolution. Print published by Rudolph Ackermann, London

Dorchester Heights

Subsequently the British occupied Dorchester Heights, overlooking Boston; and the Americans occupied Breed's Hill, which rose above Charlestown.

"View of Boston Shewing the heights of Dorchester, taken from
Mount Whoredom. 24th Janry 1776. No. 1"

Courtesy, The New York Public Library.

Dorchester Heights. A drawing by Archibald Robertson, Lt. General, Royal Engineers. 1776

"No. 5. Continuation from No. 4 to No. 1, which completes the circle of Boston
from the same Point. In this shewn, Chas. Town in Ruins, Bunker's hill,
Noodles Island & that part of the Town call'd North
End & New Boston. 7th March 1776"

Courtesy, The New York Public Library.

View of Boston. A drawing by Archibald Robertson, Lt. General, Royal Engineers. 1776

Bunker Hill

On June 17, 1775, occurred the battle of Breed's Hill, though Bunker Hill, slightly northward, gave its name to the battle. The British troops marched up the hill in close formation, and the withering fire of the provincials cut them down like blades of grass. It was the worst casualty the British army had suffered, but when the Americans ran out of ammunition the British were able to occupy the hill.

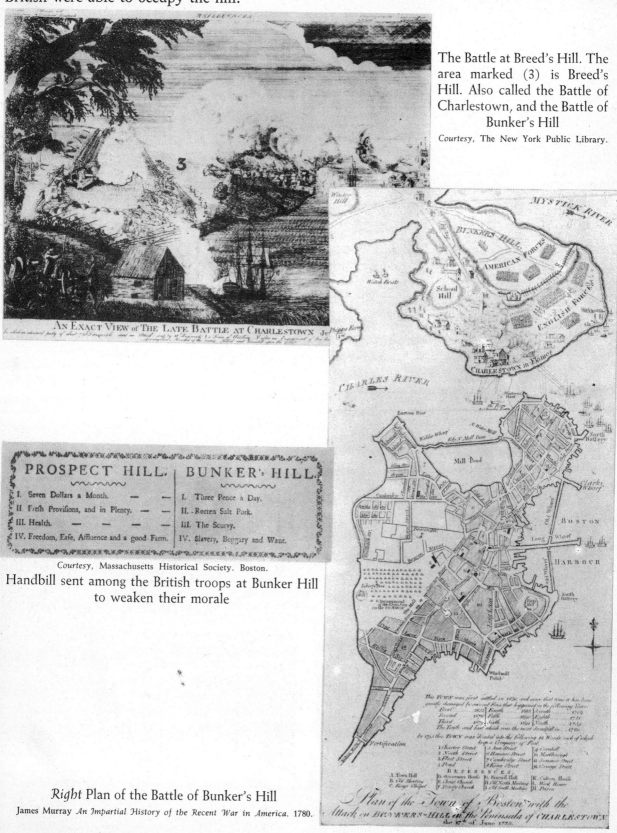

AN EXACT VIEW of THE LATE BATTLE AT CHARLESTOWN Jn.

The Battle at Breed's Hill. The area marked (3) is Breed's Hill. Also called the Battle of Charlestown, and the Battle of Bunker's Hill

Courtesy, The New York Public Library.

PROSPECT HILL. | BUNKER'S HILL.

I. Seven Dollars a Month. — — I. Three Pence a Day.
II. Fresh Provisions, and in Plenty. — II. Rotten Salt Pork.
III. Health. — — — III. The Scurvy.
IV. Freedom, Ease, Affluence and a good Farm. IV. Slavery, Beggary and Want.

Courtesy, Massachusetts Historical Society. Boston.

Handbill sent among the British troops at Bunker Hill to weaken their morale

Right Plan of the Battle of Bunker's Hill

James Murray *An Impartial History of the Recent War in America.* 1780.

George Washington Takes Command

On July 3, 1775, George Washington took command of the Continental Army under an elm tree in Cambridge, Mass., near the campus of Harvard College.

George Washington. Portrait by Charles Willson Peale

Washington Elm. Cambridge, Mass.

View of Harvard College. Engraved by Paul Revere. 1768

Courtesy, The Essex Institute, Salem, Mass.

Holden Chapel. Harvard College

Loubat *The Medallic History of the United States.* v. 2. 1878.

Medal celebrating George Washington and the siege of Boston. Designed by Pierre Simon Duvivier. This was the first medal voted by Congress

"Keep Your Powder Dry"

The army which Washington had at his command was poorly trained, poorly equipped, and poorly paid. He needed cannon, and he needed gunpowder. Ethan Allen and his Green Mountain Boys, in concert with Benedict Arnold and his Connecticut troops, surprised the garrison at Fort Ticonderoga and hauled the captured cannon through the Green Mountains by ox teams, bringing them safely to the outskirts of Boston.

Powder magazine. North Attleboro, Mass. Built 1768

Courtesy, Colonial Williamsburg, Inc. Photo by Richard Garrison.

Powder magazine. Williamsburg, Va. Built ca. 1714

Courtesy, Charleston Museum, Charleston, S. C.

Powder magazine. Charleston, S. C. Built 1703

Courtesy, Essex Institute, Salem, Mass.

Powder house. Marblehead, Mass. Built 1755

Guns and Rifles

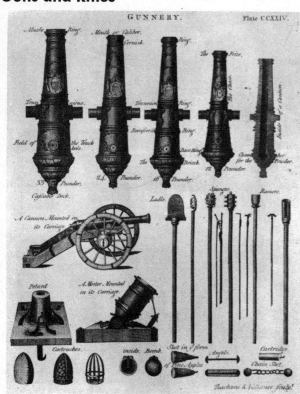

Courtesy, Landis Valley Museum, Landis Valley, Pa.

Bullet moulds

Courtesy, The New York Public Library.

Gunnery. *Encyclopedia*, Philadelphia. 1798

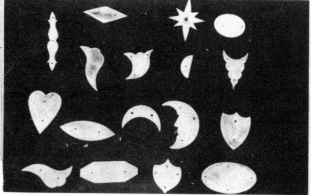

Courtesy, Landis Valley Museum, Landis Valley, Pa.

Silver ornaments for rifle stocks. Made by German gunsmiths in Pennsylvania

Left Revolutionary pistols

Courtesy, Landis Valley Museum, Landis Valley, Pa.

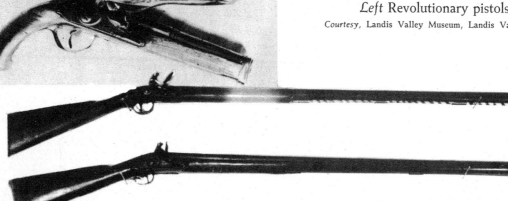

Courtesy, Landis Valley Museum, Landis Valley, Pa.

"Kentucky Rifles"

The Pennsylvania Germans made these long-barreled weapons which helped win the American Revolution. They were adapted to American tactics and terrain. The British could not cope with the deadly accuracy of the "Kentucky Rifles".

Loyalists

British officers found a welcome in the homes of the Loyalists, those men and women in America faithful to the Crown. John Adams always said that at least one-third of the population did not want independence, and that another third did not care one way or the other. This pro-British sentiment threatened at times to sabotage the war efforts of General Washington. Money and goods he needed for his tattered army were carried out of the country by the Loyalists, in connivance with the British fleet.

Courtesy, Harvard University.

Isaac Royall and family of Massachusetts. By Robert Feke. Royall was a Loyalist

Left Gov. John Wentworth of New Hampshire
Courtesy, The New York Public Library. Portrait by John Singleton Copley.

Lady Frances Wentworth. Wife of Governor John Wentworth of New Hampshire. Portrait by John Singleton Copley
Courtesy, The New York Public Library.

Some of the Loyalists, or Tories, were tarred and feathered by excited mobs. Many lesser indignities were perpetrated.

Engravings by E. Tisdale in the first illustrated edition of John Trumbull's *M'Fingal*, a burlesque on the Loyalists

Courtesy, The New-York Historical Society, New York.

Army button worn by the New York volunteers, a Loyalist unit

Courtesy, Essex Institute, Salem, Mass.

Colonel Benjamin Pickman, Loyalist, of Massachusetts

Photographed by Pach Bros.

Cadwallader Colden, Loyalist Governor of New York. Portrait by Matthew Pratt. 1772

TEUCRO DUCE NIL DESPERANDUM.

First Battalion of PENNSYLVANIA LOYALISTS, commanded by His Excellency Sir WILLIAM HOWE, K.B.

ALL INTREPID ABLE-BODIED

HEROES,

WHO are willing to serve HIS MAJESTY KING GEORGE the Third, in Defence of their Country, Laws and Constitution, against the arbitrary Usurpations of a tyrannical Congress, have now not only an Opportunity of manifesting their Spirit, by assisting in reducing to Obedience their too-long deluded Countrymen, but also of acquiring the polite Accomplishments of a Soldier, by serving only two Years, or during the present Rebellion in America.

Such spirited Fellows, who are willing to engage, will be rewarded at the End of the War, besides their Laurels, with 50 Acres of Land, where every gallant Hero may retire, and enjoy his Bottle and Lass.

Each Volunteer will receive, as a Bounty, FIVE DOLLARS, besides Arms, Cloathing and Accoutrements, and every other Requisite proper to accommodate a Gentleman Soldier, by applying to Lieutenant Colonel ALLEN, or at Captain KEARNY's Rendezvous, at PATRICK TONRY's, three Doors above Market-street, in Second-street.

Courtesy, The New York Public Library.

Broadside. Philadelphia. 1777

Left The King appeals to all loyal subjects

By the KING,

A PROCLAMATION,

For suppressing Rebellion and Sedition.

GEORGE R.

Printed by *Char*

"THESE ARE THE TIMES THAT TRY MEN'S SOULS" wrote Thomas Paine, whose fiery appeals to the Patriots offset the Tory satire of Jonathan Odell and Joseph Stansbury.

Left Thomas Paine. Portrait by Charles Willson Peale

Declaration of Independence

In 1776 the Continental Congress assembled in Philadelphia to prosecute the war and to make a public declaration of principles. From this Congress came the memorable document known as *"The Unanimous Declaration of the Thirteen United States of America,"* popularly known as *The Declaration of Independence.*

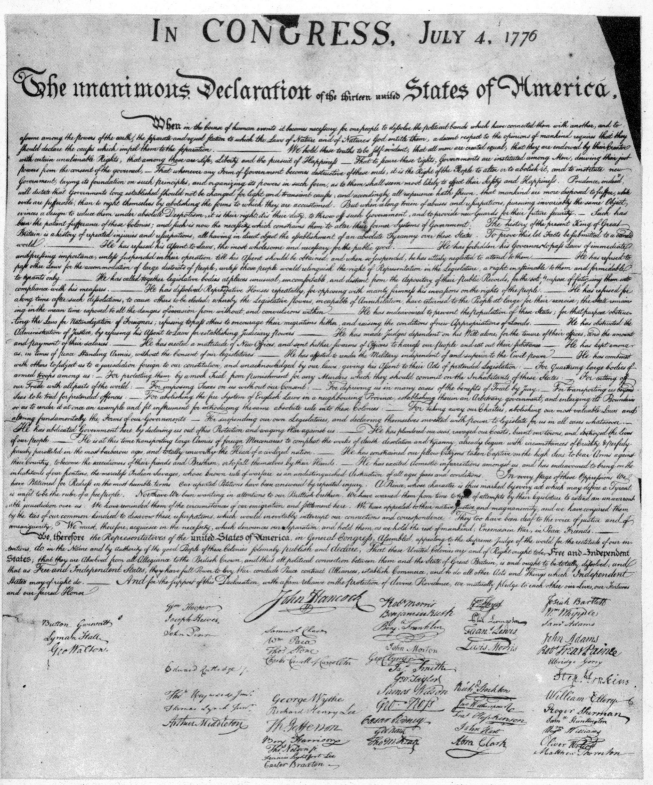

The Declaration of Independence. The original draft was written by Thomas Jefferson

Some of the Signers

These were the men whose faith and foresight created a model of government which was, and is, the hope of mankind.

Benjamin Franklin. Pennsylvania
From Portrait by Charles Willson Peale.

Francis Hopkinson. New Jersey
From Portrait by Robert Edge Pine.

Thomas Jefferson. Virginia
Bust by Houdon.

Charles Carroll of Carrollton.
Maryland
From Portrait by Chester Harding.

John Hancock. Massachusetts
From Portrait by John Singleton Copley.

Philip Livingston. New York

Elbridge Gerry. Massachusetts
Portrait by J. Bogle.

Some of the Signers

George Read. Delaware
From Portrait by Robert Edge Pine.

John Adams. Massachusetts
Portrait by John Singleton Copley.

Richard Henry Lee. Virginia
Portrait by Charles Willson Peale.

William Hooper. North Carolina
From Portrait by John Trumbull.

Stephen Hopkins. Rhode Island.
Hopkins is figure at right with hat
From Portrait by Robert Edge Pine.

Joseph Hewes. North Carolina
From Portrait by L. C. Tiffany.

Oliver Wolcott. Connecticut
From Portrait by John Trumbull.

Some of the Signers

Lyman Hall. Georgia

Josiah Bartlett. New Hampshire
From a drawing in Emmet Collection.

Matthew Thornton. New
Hampshire
From a drawing in Emmet Collection.

Roger Sherman. Connecticut
Portrait by Ralph Earl.
Courtesy, Yale University Art Gallery.

Samuel Chase. Maryland
Portrait by Charles Willson Peale.

John Witherspoon. New Jersey
Portrait by Charles Willson Peale.

Arthur Middleton. South Carolina
From Portrait by Benjamin West.

Independence Hall

In the State House in Philadelphia *The Declaration of Independence* was adopted on July 2, 1776, although July 4 is the traditional date of its annual celebration. On July 8, the document was publicly read, and the Liberty Bell may have pealed forth the good news from the State House, although the steeple was so rickety at that time that the ringing of the bell was considered unsafe.

State House, Philadelphia (Independence Hall). An engraving by J. Rogers

Left South door of Independence Hall
Courtesy, Essex Institute, Salem, Mass.

Another view of the State House. Philadelphia
Columbian Magazine. 1778.

Liberty Bell. Now in Independence Hall. It was cracked and silenced on Washington's Birthday in 1846. Its Biblical inscription reads: "Proclaim Liberty throughout all the land unto the inhabitants thereof." It weighs over 2080 pounds

Wanted: Soldiers and Sailors

As the war dragged on without decisive results many soldiers returned to their farms and shops when their terms of enlistment expired. A few deserted. Proper food, clothing, and medical attention could not be furnished the troops because of the breakdown in the supply system. Bad roads delayed transportation. The Continental Congress was too new to be thoroughly trained in the act of prosecuting a costly war. The manpower problem was acute. Criticism of General Washington's conduct of the war began to be heard.

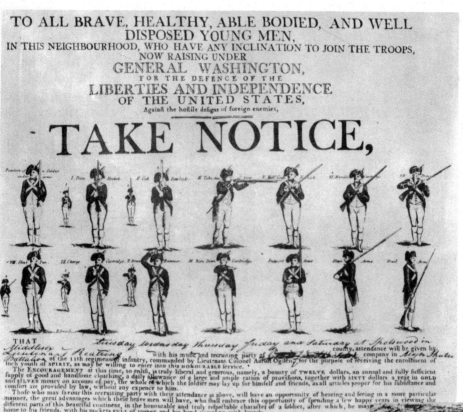

Army recruiting poster.
Pennsylvania

Courtesy, Pennsylvania Historical Society.

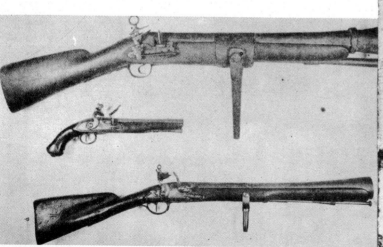

Courtesy, Essex Institute, Salem, Mass.

Naval blunderbus—swivels and pistol. J. B. Cone Collection

Right Navy recruiting poster

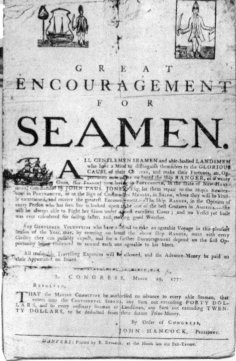

Money Was Scarce

It took money to wage war, and there was little to be had. Coin was almost non-existent, and Congress sanctioned paper money. The colonial currency, and that issued by the separate states, served as models.

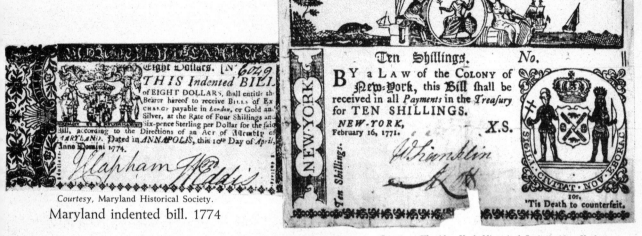

Courtesy, Maryland Historical Society.

Maryland indented bill. 1774

Courtesy, The New-York Historical Society, New York.

Ten shilling note issued by the Colony of New York. Feb. 16, 1771. Note the warning to counterfeiters

Left Rhode Island bill. 1780

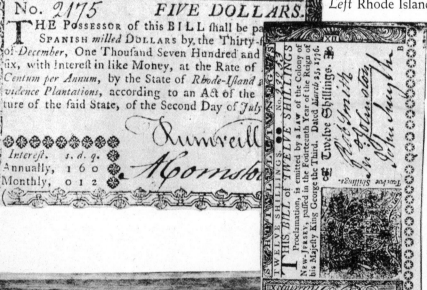

Courtesy, The Collection of George R. D. Schieffelin.

Twelve shilling note. New Jersey. 1776

Left Currency table published in the New York *Pocket Almanac.* 1774

"Not Worth a Continental"

Anburey *Travels Through America*. 1789.

Robert Morris
Financier of the American Revolution
From a portrait by Ed. Savage.

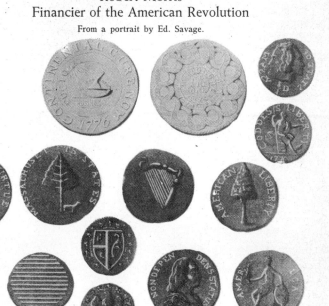

Continental currency. 1779

Dickeson *American Numismatical Manual*. 1859.

Tokens issued in America during the American Revolution

Courtesy, Maryland Historical Society.

Chalmers and Barry Coins minted in Maryland in 1783. Chalmers was an Annapolis goldsmith

The War In New York

When the British troops evacuated Boston, General Washington went to New York to prepare for the attack that was almost sure to come. In July, 1776, the British landed on Staten Island, and within a few weeks had pushed Washington's army out of Long Island, and out of Manhattan Island. On Nov. 16th they captured Fort Washington on the Hudson River. General Washington had no choice but to retire to New Jersey.

The attack on Fort Washington. 1776. Drawn on the spot by Thomas Davies, a Captain of Artillery. The Morris House appears at the top of the hill to the left. Hessian troops made up the bulk of the attacking force

Left Ruins of Trinity Church. New York City. Date depicted ca. 1780. Almost five hundred buildings were burned Sept. 21, 1776, and the patriots blamed the British for it

Courtesy, The New York Public Library.

Right Roger Morris House. New York City. Now called the Jumel Mansion, which served as Washington's headquarters in Sept. 1776

Valentine's Manual. 1854.

Blockade

Simultaneously with the landing in New York, the British fleet struck a blow at Fort Sullivan, at Charleston, S. C. The war was spreading. The British plan was to blockade the American ports.

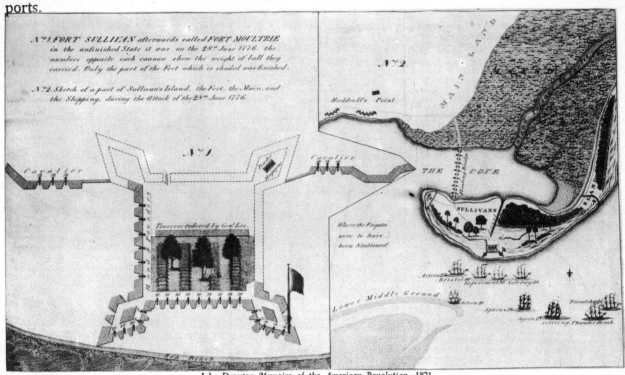

John Drayton *Memoirs of the American Revolution.* 1821.

Plan of Fort Sullivan. 1776

Some of the best early views of American ports were made by the excellent artists accompanying the British fleet in the Revolutionary War.

Courtesy, National Park Service.

View inside ship museum, York-town, Va., showing replica of a gun deck of a British frigate

Atlantic Neptune. 1781.

Portsmouth, New Hampshire. 1777

Hope . . .

Anburey *Travels Through America.* 1789.

View of General Burgoyne's camp on the Hudson River. 1777

And Fate

Anburey *Travels Through America.* 1789.

Remnant of Burgoyne's Army interned at Charlottesville, Va.

Southern Heroes

Courtesy, Carolina Art Association, Charleston, S. C.

The Battle of Eutaw Springs was fought around this tavern. Water color by Charles Fraser. 1800

General Francis Marion, whose bold forays against the British lines of communication earned him the soubriquet of the "Swamp Fox". He participated in the Battle of Eutaw Springs

Above Brigadier-General Daniel Morgan, in buckskin uniform. He was the hero of the Battle of Cowpens (S. C.) Jan. 17, 1781

Left Brigadier-General Lachlan McIntosh, who was in the siege of Savannah, and the defense of Charleston

Portraits from Herring and Longacre *National Portrait Gallery of Distinguished Americans*. 1836.

British army buttons
found on the battle-
grounds of the Amer-
ican Revolution

Courtesy, The New-York
Historical Society, New York.

Right Portrait of Colonel Marinus
Willet, by Ralph Earl, showing the
type of officer's uniform worn by the
Americans

Courtesy, Metropolitan Museum of Art, New York.

J. Milbert *Itineraire Pittoresque du fleuve Hudson.* 1829. v. 3.

Haverstraw, New York. This shows the Hudson River scenery much as it appeared in George Washington's times. He had to transport his army across this river when he evacuated Westchester County

"Yankee Doodle"

The song the American troops sang as they went forth into battle was *Yankee Doodle*. Originally composed by the British to poke fun at the green provincial troops, this lively ballad was adopted by the American patriots during the American Revolution, some years after its first appearance, the exact date of which is a subject of controversy. The American soldier has always marched to humorous ditties.

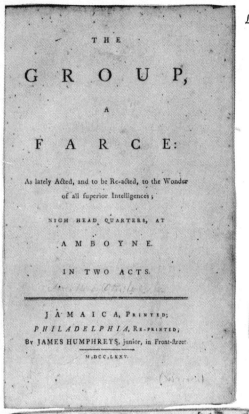

Left Title-page of *The Group*, a patriotic play
by Mercy Warren. 1775

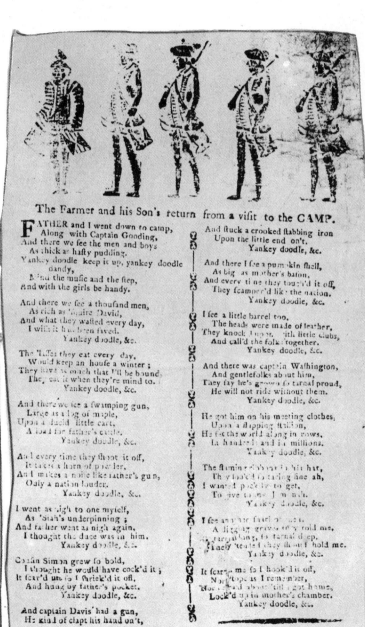

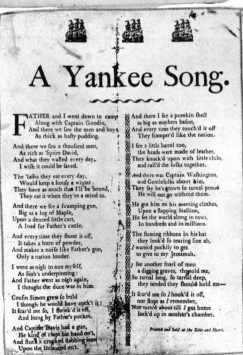

Courtesy, New York Public Library.

Two versions of the ballad *Yankee Doodle*

Out of the American Revolution emerged a school of native playwrights, including Mercy Warren, and the real beginnings of American drama. Mercy Warren's brother, James Otis, was a gifted orator, and her husband, James Warren, was an American general.

At the Delaware

After retiring from New York, General Washington moved his army to New Jersey and then to Pennsylvania. He recrossed the Delaware River to strike two hard blows at Trenton, Dec. 26, 1776, and Princeton, Jan. 3, 1777, before retreating to Philadelphia.

Courtesy, Metropolitan Museum of Art, New York.   Washington Crossing the Delaware. Painting by Emanuel Leutze

While neither contemporary nor authentic, this picture has, through its long popularity, established itself as the symbol of Washington's great exploit.

He conscripted all the ferrymen up and down the Delaware to facilitate the moving of his men and supplies across the river. Here we see a typical ferry with its pontoon approach.

Columbian Magazine. August, 1787.
Gray's Ferry. Schuylkill River. Pa.

Philadelphia

Sir William Howe, who commanded the troops that took New York, entered Philadelphia in triumph, after defeating the Continental Army at the Brandywine, Sept. 11, 1777. This British victory was offset by American victories at Oriskany, New York, and Bennington, Vermont, followed by the capture of Burgoyne's army, but Washington's own army was condemned to face a hard winter at Valley Forge.

An Impartial History of the War in America.
1780.

Sir William Howe

Duyckinck National Portrait Gallery.
1862-67.

General John Stark, Hero of
Battle of Bennington

Left General John Stark's powder horn

Courtesy, Manchester Historic Association, Manchester, N. H.

Rationing

Courtesy, The New York Public Library.

Rationing notice issued by Sir William
Howe. Philadelphia. 1777

From *Godey's Lady's Book*, 1844.

Chew Mansion. Germantown, Pa.

In Enemy Hands

There were many Tory Loyalists in Philadelphia, and the British officers went to assemblies and to the theatre. Wartime Philadelphia was gay and fashionable. Howe and his aides were entertained at country estates in the environs of the city.

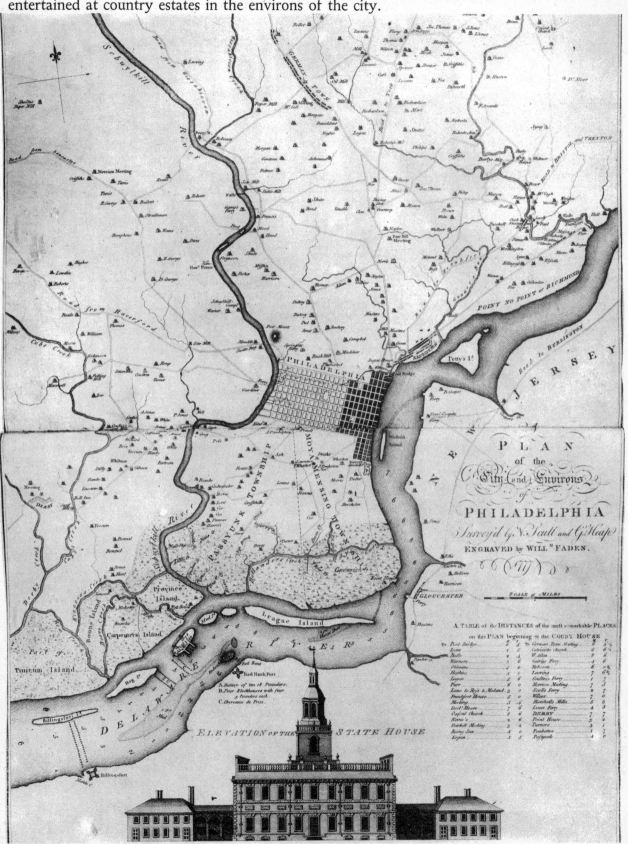

Plan of the City and Environs of Philadelphia. Engraved by William Faden. 1777. Note the fine drawing of the State House

The Mischianza

Major John Andre designed stage settings for a spectacular *fête champêtre* and military pageant at "Walnut Grove", the Wharton family estate, in honor of Sir William Howe, May 18, 1778. One London firm sold £12,000 worth of laces, silks and other finery for the entertainment. Later Andre was captured by the Americans in New York State and hanged, being charged with plotting with Benedict Arnold for the betrayal of West Point.

Ticket and invitation to the Mischianza (or Meschianza)

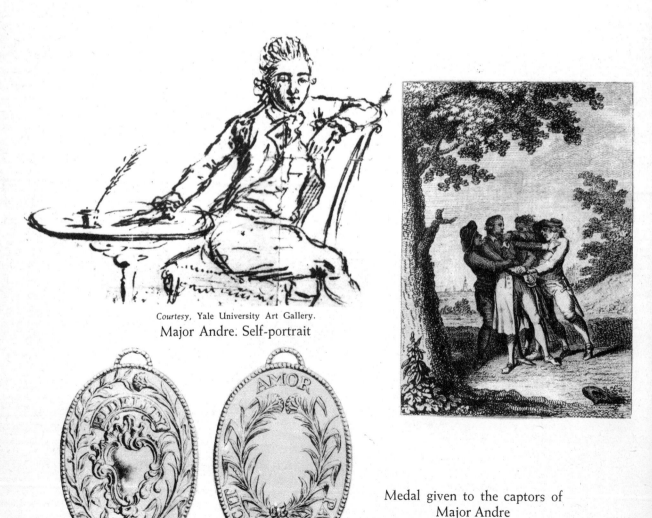

Courtesy, Yale University Art Gallery.

Major Andre. Self-portrait

Medal given to the captors of
Major Andre

Loubat *The Medallic History of the United States.* v. 2.
1878.

Traitor

Benedict Arnold performed brilliant feats, including a classic march to Quebec through the Maine wilderness, and held the respect of his leader George Washington, but Congress was so tardy in its recognition of his valuable services that he became embittered. While in command at Philadelphia he fell in love with Peggy Shippen, the darling of Philadelphia society, and enthroned her at Mt. Pleasant after their marriage. He soon fell into debt, received further rebukes from Congress, and finally turned traitor.

Benedict Arnold

Peggy Shippen (Mrs. Benedict Arnold) and child. Portrait by Daniel Gardner

Courtesy, Pennsylvania Historical Society, Phila.

Courtesy, Philadelphia Museum of Art. Philadelphia.

Room from Mt. Pleasant. Philadelphia

West Point
A. Constitution Island; B. Chain stretched across the Hudson River to prevent the passage of British ships; C. Fort Clinton. After a view in the *New York Magazine*

The Robinson House across the River from West Point. Benedict Arnold established his headquarters here. He was having breakfast with George Washington in this house when news of the capture of Andre reached him

Christ Church In Philadelphia

Both the British and the Americans attended service at Christ Church, begun in 1727 by the architect John Kearsley, one of the designers of Independence Hall. Benjamin Franklin's pew, along with George Washington's, is still pointed out. Franklin lies buried in its churchyard.

Photo by Frank Cousins. *Courtesy*, Essex Institute, Salem, Mass.

Interior of Christ Church. Philadelphia

Photo by Frank Cousins.

Pulpit of Christ Church. Installed 1770

Life Went On

Philadelphians found time to read the latest book on horsemanship, and to attend balls and plays.

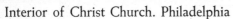

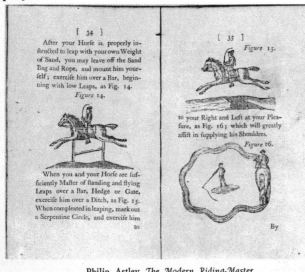

Philip Astley *The Modern Riding-Master*
Philadelphia, 1776

Right Costume of the period of the American
Revolution

Courtesy, Metropolitan Museum of Art, New York.

Valley Forge

While the British were enjoying the comforts and pleasures of Philadelphia, Washington's tattered army was half-starved and half-frozen at bleak Valley Forge. It was America's darkest hour.

Courtesy, Valley Forge Park Commission.

Washington's Headquarters at Valley Forge

Right Washington's food problem
Courtesy, Pennsylvania Historical Society.

By His EXCELLENCY
GEORGE WASHINGTON, Esquire,
GENERAL and COMMANDER in CHIEF of the Forces
of the UNITED STATES OF AMERICA.

BY Virtue of the Power and Direction to Me especially given, I hereby enjoin and require all Persons residing within seventy Miles of my Head Quarters to thresh one Half of their Grain by the 1st Day of February, and the other Half by the 1st Day of March next ensuing, on Pain, in Case of Failure of having all that shall remain in Sheaves after the Period above mentioned, seized by the Commissaries and Quarter-Masters of the Army, and paid for as Straw

GIVEN *under my Hand, at Head Quarters, near the Valley Forge, in Philadelphia County, this 20th Day of December,* 1777.

G. WASHINGTON.

By His Excellency's Command,
ROBERT H. HARRISON, Sec'y.

LANCASTER: Printed by JOHN DUNLAP.

Left Camp bedstead used by George Washington at Valley Forge
Courtesy, The New-York Historical Society, New York.

Right Military kit said to have been used by Colonel Nicholas Fish during the Revolutionary War. The fork and spoon are hinged. No such elegance was found at Valley Forge

Courtesy, The New-York Historical Society, New York.

Help From Abroad

A military genius from Germany, Baron Von Steuben, came to Valley Forge and was appalled at what he saw. He took over the military training of the Continental Army and instructed them in the arts of war. He made disciplined soldiers from raw recruits. The Polish patriot, Thaddeus Kosciusko, and the young French hero, the Marquis de LaFayette, also came to help America win freedom. LaFayette brought troops.

Baron Von Steuben
Portrait by Charles Willson Peale. 1780

Left Thaddeus Kosciusko

LaFayette. Portrait by Charles Willson Peale

French troops landing at Newport, R. I.

Sprengel *Allgemeines Historisches Taschenbuch.*
1784.

French Troops

The sight of these gaily uniformed French troops heartened the weary Americans. It was the beginning of a lasting friendship between the two countries.

Courtesy, Vinkhuizen Collection. The New York Public Library.

French soldier. 1779   French soldier. 1772

Diderot and D'Alembert Encyclopedie. Recueil des Planches. 1762-72.

French soldiers

The American Navy

With the aid of the French fleet, the American Navy more than held its own, and the iron ring of the blockade was broken. The greatest naval hero of the war was John Paul Jones.

Courtesy, The New-York Historical Society, New York.

Commodore Esek Hopkins. Commander in Chief of the American fleet. Mezzotint published in London by Thomas Hart. 1776

John Paul Jones. Engraving by Moreau the Younger. 1780. Jones, in the *Bon Homme Richard*, won an epic naval battle for Captain Richard Pearson, in the *Serapis*, Sept. 23, 1779

Naval Button. American Revolution

Courtesy, The New-York Historical Society, New York.

Courtesy, Essex Institute, Salem, Mass.

A "Cohorn" Used in the main-top

Pine-tree flag of an American cruiser. 1776. It had a green tree on a white bunting. On the reverse was the motto "Appeal to Heaven". Note the liberty cap on the flag pole

What Sailors Had To Know

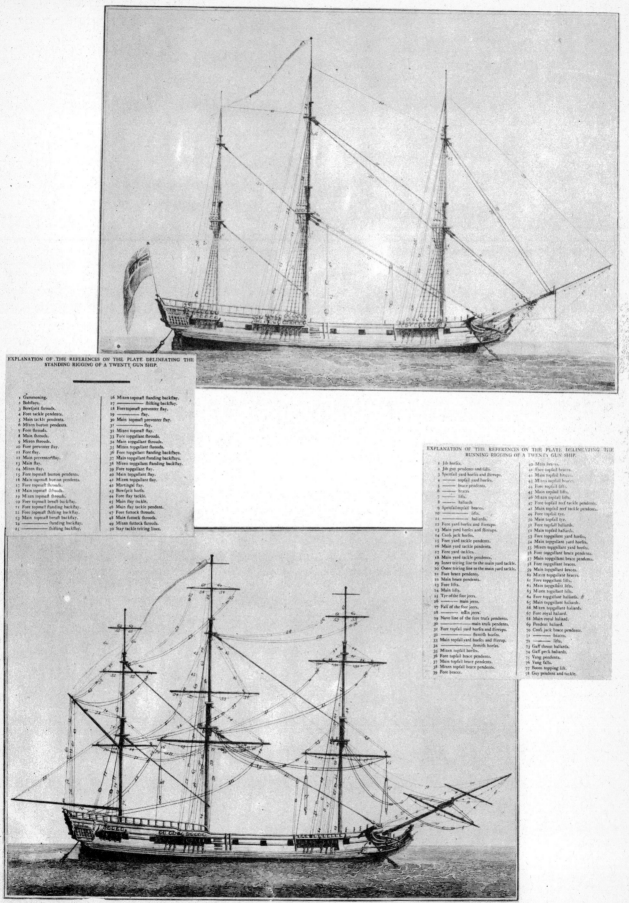

Illustrations from Steel, *The Elements and Practice of Rigging and Seamanship.* 1794

What Sailors Had To Know

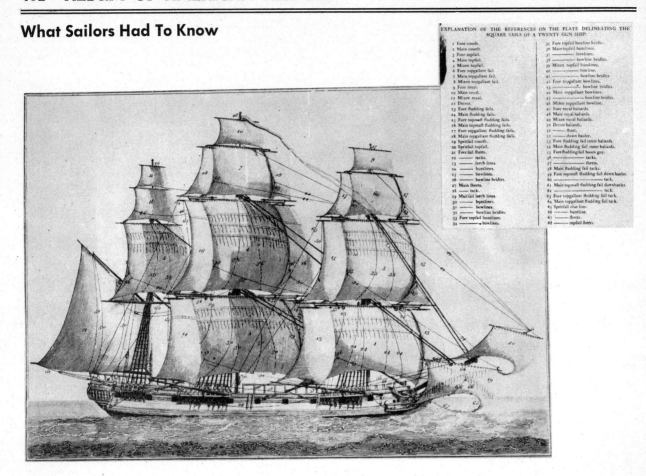

Illustrations from Steel, *The Elements and Practice of Rigging and Seamanship.* 1794

Human Suffering

Many American and British soldiers were kept in filthy prisons, and those who were wounded on the battlefield received very little medical attention owing to the lack of doctors and surgeons. Amputations were crude and painful.

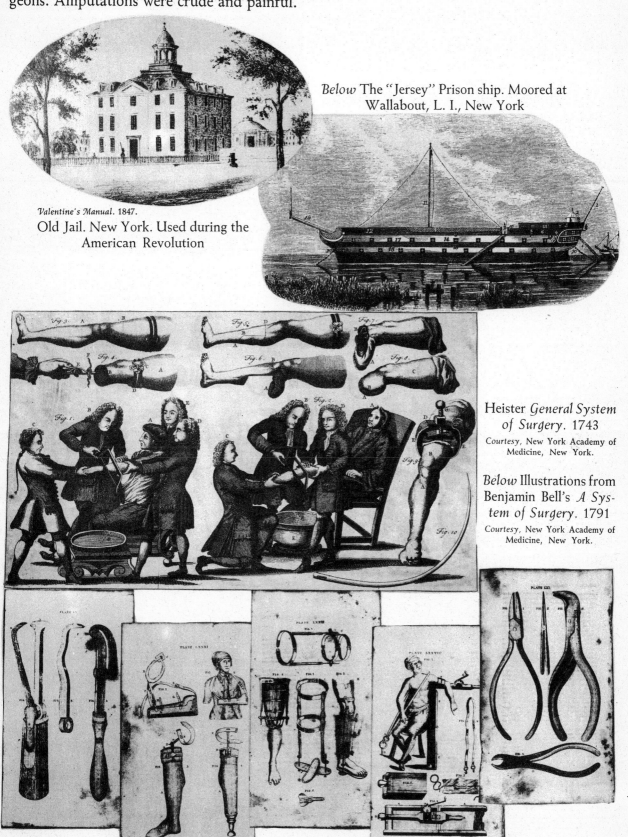

Valentine's Manual. 1847.

Old Jail. New York. Used during the American Revolution

Below The "Jersey" Prison ship. Moored at Wallabout, L. I., New York

Heister *General System of Surgery.* 1743

Courtesy, New York Academy of Medicine, New York.

Below Illustrations from Benjamin Bell's *A System of Surgery.* 1791

Courtesy, New York Academy of Medicine, New York.

Yorktown

The Battle of Yorktown, fought not far from Jamestown, Va., where the first English settlement in America was founded in 1607, practically brought the Revolutionary War to a close. George Washington, the hero of the long struggle, returned to private life at his home in Mount Vernon, after taking leave of his officers at Fraunces Tavern in New York.

Illumination.

COLONEL TILGHMAN, Aid de Camp to his Excellency General WASHINGTON, having brought official acounts of the SURRENDER of Lord Cornwallis, and the Garrifons of York and Gloucefter, thofe Citizens who chufe to ILLUMINATE on the GLORIOUS OCCASION, will do it this evening at Six, and extinguifh their lights at Nine o'clock.

Decorum and harmony are earneftly recommended to every Citizen, and a general difcountenance to the leaft appearance of riot.

October 24, 1781.

Courtesy, Colonial Society of America.
Fraunces Tavern. New York. Etching by Robert Shaw

Mount Vernon

Left View of Mount Vernon, Home of George Washington

Weld *Travels through the States of North America.* 1799.

Right View of Mount Vernon. Engraved by Francis Jukes after a drawing by Alexander Robertson. 1800. Date depicted 1799

Courtesy, Stokes Collection. The New York Public Library.

The Society of the Cincinnati

To perpetuate the friendships made on the field of battle, Washington and his officers formed the Society of the Cincinnati in 1783. Its social traditions have always been maintained.

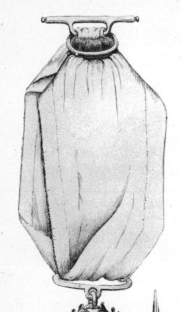

Courtesy, Colonial Society of New York. Etching by James H. Fincken.

Headquarters of Baron Von Steuben, Verplanck House, Fishkill, N. Y. where the Society of the Cincinnati was founded

Flag of the Society of the Cincinnati. The American eagle is a prominent feature

From a drawing by L. F. Grant, in Thomas *The Society of the Cincinnati.*
Published by G. P. Putnam's Sons

The United States Seal

The first United States Seal. 1782. Designed by William Barton and Charles Thomson

The "Stars and Stripes"

The American flag, the "Stars and Stripes", dates officially from June 14, 1777, and was a marine flag in the beginning, being so used by John Paul Jones. The story that Betsy Ross made the first "Stars and Stripes" is only one of many flag myths. There were numerous variations in the design of this flag, and many claimants for the honor of first displaying it.

Courtesy, The Easton Public Library, Easton, Pa.
The Easton Flag. An early version of the "Stars and Stripes"

Sprengel *Allgemeines Taschenbuch.* 1784.

The "Stars and Stripes". The top stripe is red, the next blue, and the next white on a blue field

The American Eagle Was Beginning to Scream

The eagle became the symbol of American independence and began to appear on seals, trade marks, and as a decorative motif in the arts and crafts.

Catesby *The Natural History of Carolina.* 1754.
The American Eagle

Woodcut by Alexander Anderson

Left The eagle motif in furniture

Peace . . .

War-weary patriots emptied their powder horns and went back to field and shop.

Courtesy, New Hampshire Historical Society,
Concord, N. H.
Powder horn of John Calfe

American primitive painting. Artist
unknown. Found near Lancaster,
Pa.
Courtesy, Mr. Harry Stone. New York City.

They put away their uniforms with the new buttons which
bore the letters U.S.A.

Pride . . .

Army button. Amer-
ican Revolution
Courtesy, The New-York Historical Society, New York.

They hung their rifles over the mantel piece.

And Hope

Across a peaceful land the church bells
pealed a message of hope

First Parish meeting house. Portland, Me.
1740. The bell was added in 1758, the
steeple in 1761
Willis, *The History of Portland*. 1833.

Birth of a Nation

The unexploited natural resources of the United States awaited the pioneer. Free men poured from the Eastern seaboard, crossed the mountain barriers and swarmed into the Ohio and Mississippi valleys, poured through the Cumberland Gap and along the Wilderness Road into Tennessee and Kentucky.

Picturesque America. 1872-74.

The Cumberland Gap

Men like Daniel Boone and Simon Kenton were the trail-blazers of empire. They saw great herds of buffalo.

Courtesy, The Filson Club,
Louisville, Ky.

Daniel Boone

Courtesy, The Filson Club,
Louisville, Ky.

Simon Kenton

Catesby *The Natural History
of Carolina.* 1754.

Rivers . . .

Men of Connecticut crossed the Housatonic and the Hudson and pushed towards Ohio.

Picturesque America. 1872-74.

And Roads

The Housatonic River

Christopher Colles published his *The Roads of the United States*, in response to the demands of a travel-minded generation.

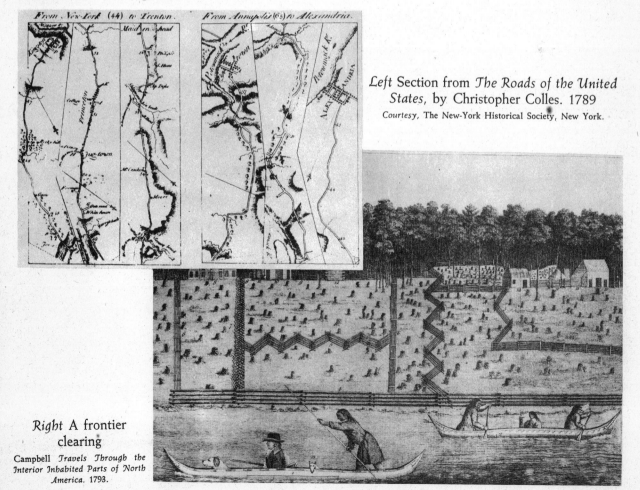

Left Section from *The Roads of the United States*, by Christopher Colles. 1789

Courtesy, The New-York Historical Society, New York.

Right A frontier clearing

Campbell *Travels Through the Interior Inhabited Parts of North America.* 1793.

On the March

Through Pennsylvania lumbered the Conestoga wagons, the freight trains of the era.

Conestoga Wagon. Drawing by F. O. C. Darley

Covered Wagon. A banknote engraving

Courtesy, Maryland Historical Society, Baltimore, Md.

Marylanders headed westward

New towns sprang up on the frontier.

Basil Hall *Forty Sketches made with the Camera Lucida in North America.* 1829.

Wilderness settlement

Mason *The Lure of the Smokies.* 1927.

Courtesy, Houghton Mifflin Co., Boston.

"Howdy, stranger!"

Westward Ho!

From Niagara Falls to far south of the Natural Bridge, America was on the march, pushing ever westward.

Weld Travels Through the United States of North America. 1799.

Niagara Falls

The Natural Bridge, Virginia

Towns of Destiny

Courtesy, The Stokes Collection, The New York Public Library.

Detroit, Michigan. 1794

Courtesy, The Stokes Collection, The New York Public Library.

Baltimore, Md.

Art Past Art Present

FOURTH EDITION

David G. Wilkins
UNIVERSITY OF PITTSBURGH

Bernard Schultz
WEST VIRGINIA UNIVERSITY

Katheryn M. Linduff
UNIVERSITY OF PITTSBURGH

Prentice Hall

Upper Saddle River, New Jersey 07458

Library of Congress Cataloging-in-Publication Data

Wilkins, David G.
    Art past, art present / David G. Wilkins, J. Bernard Schultz,
Katheryn M. Linduff.—4th ed.
        p. cm.
        Includes bibliographical references and index.
        ISBN 0-13-088977-6
        1. Art—History.   I. Schultz, Bernard, (date)   II. Linduff,
Katheryn M.   III. Title
    N5300.64   2000
        709—dc21   00-020899

VP/Editorial Director: *Charlyce Jones Owen*
Publisher: *Bud Therien*
Assistant Editor: *Kimberly Chastain*
Director of Production and
    Manufacturing: *Barbara Kittle*
Production Editor: *Louise Rothman*
Editorial Assistant: *Wendy Yurash*
Prepress and Manufacturing Manager: *Nick Sklitsis*
Marketing Director: *Beth Gillett*
Marketing Manager: *Sheryl Adams*

Creative Design Director: *Leslie Osher*
Interior and Cover Design Director: *Kathryn Foot*
Manager, Production/Formatting
    and Art: *Guy Ruggiero*
Electronic Page Layout: *Joesph Lisa, Scott Garrison,
    and Annette Murphy*
Photo Researcher: *Francelle Carapethyan*
Cover Photo: *Guggenheim Museum, Bilbao, Spain,
    Erik Samper/Liaison Agency*

For permission to use copyrighted material, grateful acknowledgment is made
to the copyright holders listed on pages 621–624,
which is considered an extension of this copyright page.
This book was set in 10.5/12.5 Cantoria MT Light by Prentice-Hall, Inc.,
and printed and bound by RR Donnelley & Sons Company.
The cover was printed by Phoenix Color Corp.

©2001, 1997, 1994, 1990 by Prentice-Hall, Inc.
A Division of Pearson Education
Upper Saddle River, NJ 07458

Printed in the United States of America
10 9 8 7 6 5 4 3 2 1

ISBN 0-13-088977-6

Prentice-Hall International (UK) Limited, *London*
Prentice-Hall of Australia Pty. Limited, *Sydney*
Prentice-Hall Canada, Inc., *Toronto*
Prentice-Hall Hispanoamerica, S.A., *Mexico*
Prentice-Hall of India Private Limited, *New Delhi*
Prentice-Hall of Japan, Inc., *Tokyo*
Simon & Schuster Asia Pte. Ltd., *Singapore*
Editora Prentice-Hall do Brasil, Ltda., *Rio de Janeiro*

Contents

CHAPTER FOUR

Art From 200 to 1400   131

CHAPTER EIGHT

Eighteenth-Century Art   379

CHAPTER NINE

Nineteenth-Century Art   399

CHAPTER TEN

Twentieth-Century Art   471

Getting Started

SULTAN MUHAMMAD

The Feast of Sadeh and the Discovery of Fire by the Persian King Hushang, from the *Tahmasp Shah-nameh*. c. 1520–25. Manuscript illumination, 9½ × 9⅟₁₆″. Metropolitan Museum of Art, New York. The Persian national epic, the *Shah-nameh*, was originally composed by the poet Firdawsi between 975 and 1010. This *Shah-nameh*, which contains 258 miniatures, was created in the royal studios in the Persian capital at Tabriz. Commissioned by Shah Isma'il and his son Tahmasp. For further information see fig. 6-63.

PIETER BRUEGEL THE ELDER

Peasant Wedding Feast. c. 1566. Oil on wood, 3′8⅞″ × 5′4⅛″. Kunsthistorisches Museum, Vienna. The bride is the smug woman seated in front of the suspended cloth with a crown above her head. To either side are the groom and the couple's parents. To the right, a priest is in conversation with a distinguished-looking man who probably represents the landowner for whom these peasants worked. For further information, see fig. 6-62.

Why *Art Past/Art Present?*

Art Past/Art Present is based on the idea that works of art can communicate to us through time and history. On a purely visual level they may engage us, but further study will reveal that they constantly remind us of the diversity and communality of human experience. To understand the visual language of art and to be receptive to its communication, however, requires active participation. How can we begin to establish a dialogue between ourselves and works of art? How can we achieve an understanding of past and present art from other societies, historic and current? And, in an age teeming with information, how do we move from information to knowledge and understanding? *Art Past/Art Present* has been designed to help us begin to answer these questions. The book opens with a section called "Experiencing Art" (pp. 1–7) that establishes some of the language and techniques useful for analyzing art and for understanding art and artists within a historical context.

What is the basic approach of *Art Past/Art Present*?

In creating *Art Past/Art Present*, we accepted the underlying assumptions that art results from the human experience of life and that art is itself fundamentally expressive. We wanted to offer to the interested reader a clear, concise, and integrated treatment of a limited number of works from around the world.

Why is history so important in understanding works of art?

In *Art Past/Art Present*, the works are discussed within a historical framework. This emphasizes the circumstances under which they came into being and helps us to analyze how they were viewed and how they functioned at that time; this approach is known as **contextualism**. Art should be studied in concert with history, politics, religion, geography, society, and culture in general, including music and literature, in order to more fully understand the scope and diversity of our human history. Chapters 2 through 10 of *Art Past/Art Present* each open with an overview of developments in history and art for each particular time period: prehistoric, ancient, 200 to 1400, fifteenth century, sixteenth century, seventeenth century, eighteenth century, nineteenth century, and twentieth century. A special section at the end of each overview discusses the role and status of artists during this period; when possible, self-portraits of artists are illustrated in this section. Following the overviews for each period, there are two- and four-page units that focus on a key work. These key works establish a chronology for *Art Past/Art Present*.

Why such a distinct chronological approach?

If you thumb through *Art Past/Art Present* looking at the top right-hand corner of the pages, you'll see a series of boxes with dates that are chronological in sequence. In our minds there is historical accuracy in this chronology, for it means that the works and events are presented roughly as they happened; it can only be informative to be reminded, for example, that Donatello, Ghiberti, and Van Eyck (pp. 250–259) were all working at about the same time, or that the rock-cut Hindu temple at Ellora (pp. 172-173) was being carved at the same time that the Muslims were erecting the huge mosque in Córdoba (pp. 174-77). This interweaving of European, Asian, and American developments offers important insights into contemporary developments around the globe. At the same time, the organization of *Art Past/Art Present* in two- and four-page units means that the teacher or reader can focus on each unit independently.

1565	Tobacco is introduced into Britain
c. 1566	**Pieter Bruegel the Elder, *Peasant Wedding Feast***
1578	China's population reaches 60 million

What is the point of the boxes in the upper right corner of the pages?

The box lists historical events and cultural developments from the period in order to build context for the works of art being discussed. While there is no direct connection between the fact that the earliest Buddhist architecture in Japan (pp. 168-71) was built in the seventh century, during the same period when Muhammad began preaching openly, or that Shakespeare's *Hamlet* was written at about the same time that Caravaggio's *Entombment of Christ* (fig. 7-14) was painted, such chronological connections help us build a more complex and complete sense of the development of human accomplishment and historical events around the globe.

What kind of important information is found in the captions to the illustrations?

The main point of the captions is to provide some of the basic facts that identify the work of art:

Name of artist if known: While many early works are anonymous, in later periods we know many artists not only by name but also as personalities. An artist's birth and death dates are given when their name is first mentioned in the text; nationality is given in the index.

Title: Titles only became necessary when people began listing works or displaying them, and chroniclers, collectors, and art historians have had to invent titles for many earlier works; you may sometimes notice that the title of a work of art in one book is different from that given in another. Some historic or popular titles are wrong, as is the case with Rembrandt's *Militia Company of Captain Frans Banning Cocq* (fig. 7-27), which is now popularly but incorrectly known as *The Night Watch*.

Date: The date of creation is always a useful piece of information, but many early dates are uncertain or questionable. When a date is uncertain, we have used c. (from "circa," the Latin term for "about") before the date. We don't know the exact date for Leonardo's *Portrait of a Woman* (now known as the *Mona Lisa*, see fig. 6-21), but we think it was painted sometime between 1503 and 1505, hence the date given in the caption is c. 1503–05.

Materials: This is an important category because artists are often restricted in the kinds of materials that are available. Each material offers its own potential and restrictions, and understanding the role of the materials (the medium) in the

MICHELANGELO BUONARROTI

DAVID 1501–04. Marble, height 13'5". Galleria dell' Accademia. Commissioned by the Cathedral Administration to be placed on a buttress below the dome of Florence Cathedral (see fig. 5-42). For further information see fig. 6-18.

artist's creative experience is often helpful.

Size: Size is given in feet and inches, height before width. This is another crucial category, because an understanding of the actual size of a work can help us to better understand the impact of that work when seen in the original. That Michelangelo's *David* is 13'5" tall is crucial for understanding the impact of this figure; by including a human figure in our illustration, we provide visual evidence for the impact of the sculpture's scale and presence.

Original and present location: Many works in the past were created by the artist for a specific setting, but few survive as originally placed. This loss of context means that we often need to try to recreate some sense of the original setting. The survival of Michelangelo's Sistine Ceiling (pp. 300-303) and Soami's Zen Buddhist Dry Garden (fig. 6-79) in their original setting demonstrates how important setting can be in understanding a work of art. Present location tells us where we can go to see a work; below some captions, in small print, is further information about location and copyright.

Patron: In most earlier periods works of art were commissioned from the artist by a patron. The patron could be an individual, a family, a social group, a ruler, a government, and so forth. Knowing who needed and who paid for the work can often add insight into our understanding of the function and context for a work.

What should be read first, the captions or the text?

The factual information in the captions is mainly useful for identification purposes, but longer captions allow us to include additional information and discussion about that specific work. We would recommend that the captions be read first, followed by the text, which generally focuses on the broader cultural and historical ideas that are helpful in understanding the work of art.

Why is it important to list the patron in the captions?

Most of the works of art created in the past were made at the command or request of a patron: a person or group who commissioned the work and subsequently paid for it. This system is so different from current practices, in which artists create what they want to and then hope to find a buyer (the one important exception is architecture), that it seemed important to stress the roles of patrons not only as the persons who provided the money, but also the persons who needed the work and who probably gave specific information, requirements, and restrictions to the artists.

Why are some words in the text printed in boldface?

These boldfaced terms emphasize some of the new and perhaps unfamiliar terms that are helpful in understanding works of art; boldfaced terms are defined in the glossary on pp. 598–605, where each term is defined and where reference will be made to a specific work of art that illustrates or demonstrates the term.

Why are some passages in the text printed in blue?

These highlighted passages are either historical documents that are roughly contemporary with the creation of the work or quotations from artists themselves. We would emphasize that the words of those who lived when these works were created have particular authority and offer important insights for us today. This is contextualism at its best, because it allows us to read what was being said about the work at the time of its creation.

Themes

A new feature of this fourth edition is a series of nine double-page spreads devoted to art historical themes such as

The Nude/The Body, Representing Nature, and *The Artist as a Revolutionary*. Each of these thematic discussions presents a group of works that can be more fully understood when seen in the context of other works representing the same theme. These spreads demonstrate some of the common themes that can be deduced when we look at artistic developments over history and around the globe. As a group, the works demonstrate how a comparison and contrast between works from different periods can illuminate how art has changed over time.

Maps

Twenty-one detailed maps are intended to help you determine the location of works of art and architecture discussed in the book.

Technique Boxes

Technique boxes have been placed in the text chronologically, at the moment when the particular technique originated or when it was most important for artistic developments. Clear diagrams accompany descriptions of, among others, *Chinese Piece-Mold Bronze Casting, Proportions of Gothic Cathedrals*, and *Printmaking*.

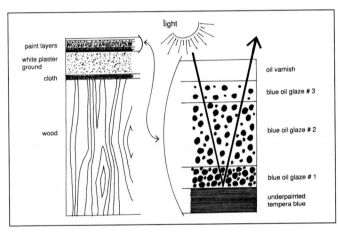

Schematic diagram of a section of a Flemish fifteenth-century oil painting, demonstrating the luminosity of the medium. The arrow suggests how light penetrates translucent oil glazes.

Art Past/Art Present Boxes

These boxes have been added chronologically at points where it seemed appropriate to discuss the relationship between the art of the time and the modern world. Examples include *The Impact of the Ancient Greek Orders* and *Chinese Aesthetic Theory*.

BC or BCE, AD or CE?

The dating system used throughout this book is the Western system, which is based on the year of the birth of Christ as a dividing point. Many other cultures, including China, Israel, and the Muslim world, use a system based on historical events that are important to them; for business purposes, however, these cultures often use the dates common in the West. While the traditional designations used in Western culture for the periods before and after the birth of Christ have been BC "Before Christ" and AD "Anno Domini," "the year of the Lord," in this book we have adapted the new designations for these periods: BCE "Before the Common Era" and CE "Common Era."

Why include a bibliography?

We see *Art Past/Art Present* as only your first introduction to the larger and more complex world of the art that has been created over the centuries and around the world, not to mention the new art that is being created in our own times. The bibliography on pp. 606–608 lists books in English that will lead you further into this world. Happy Reading!

Acknowledgments

Of course we owe thanks to the generous efforts and insights of many people, including the several anonymous readers who have commented on the manuscript in its several editions. We are especially indebted to colleagues and former colleagues at the University of Pittsburgh and West Virginia University who willingly lent their authoritative understanding to different parts of the text:

Robert Anderson
Kahren Arbitman
William Arnett
Vange Beldecos
Laura Crary
Roger Crum
Urban Couch
Ed De Carlso
Robert H. Getscher
Ann Sutherland Harris
Fil Hearn
Hsu Miao-lin
Marcia Menihan

Kristina Olson
Margaret Rajam
Patricia Rice
Matthew Roper
Janet Snyder
John Super
Thomas Tavella C.S.P.
Frank Toker
Mahdu Wangu
H. Anne Weis
John Whitty
John Williams

Among those who offered guidance for this edition, we particularly acknowledge Tyler Jennings, Katherine Wilkins, and Mary Louise Soldo Schultz. The expanded, up-to-date bibliography is the work of Rebecca L. Wilkins.

At Prentice-Hall, Norwell "Bud" Therien, Jr., brought integrity to this project, and Louise Rothman oversaw this publication with a gracious dignity

David G. Wilkins
Bernard Schultz
Katheryn M. Linduff

NAM JUNE PAIK   *Electronic Superhighway,* 1995.   Multiple television monitors, laser disc players, laser discs, neon, and other mixed media, 15 x 32 feet.   COURTESY NAM JUNE PAIK AND THE HOLLY SOLOMON GALLERY.

Experiencing Art

A Brief Insight

NOTHING IS VISUALLY STILL OR QUIET ABOUT THIS
*work. Intense neon lights define state boundaries of the
continental U.S.A., while the monitors within each state offer a
constantly flowing array of images. Within this kaleidoscope, closed-circuit
cameras fed images of those viewing this work into some of the monitors,
forcing viewers to become part of the work of art while simultaneously
standing before it.*

*How is your experience different when you view a painting in a
museum, or watch television, or surf the net? Do you have different physical
and psychological responses in these distinct situations? If we accept that all
these experiences are visual in nature, can we find similarities among them?
Can the media of TV and computers, for example, be brought into the
realm of art?*

*These are some of the questions raised by the multimedia work you are
now viewing. The artist, Nam June Paik, has given over fifty years of
creative thought and activity to examining the relationship between art and
technology, and to expanding the ways through which art and audience can
interrelate. Paik's multimedia creation leads you to consider the complex,
yet satisfying, dialogue between yourself and a work of art.*

Experiencing Art

1–1 NAM JUNE PAIK.

ELECTRONIC SUPERHIGHWAY. 1995. Multiple television monitors, laser disc players, laser discs, neon, and other mixed media, 15 × 32 feet.

I magine—You are walking in New York City. As you pass the large windows of an art gallery, you notice, out of the corner of your eye, a familiar image, a huge map of the United States. When you pause to look more closely, you can see that it fills an entire wall, and that the borders of the states are defined in brilliant neon (fig. 1-1). You see flickering colored lights, barely discernible at this distance, but you can't really make out what they are. The familiarity of the map image puts you at ease while the unusual materials and format simultaneously provoke your interest. Is this map a work of art? You know that a museum's mission is to display and preserve works of art—but a commercial art gallery is here to sell art, so you hesitate to go inside for a closer look at this intriguing map. But it is so compelling that you overcome your hesitation and open the door. The gallery staff acknowledge your visit with a welcome.

As you approach the dazzling wall, you discover that the entire "map" is backed by video monitors of various sizes—this explains the flickering lights you noticed. Clusters of monitors can be seen within each state's borders, and the images of their screens differ from state to state. Viewed as a whole, the work seems overwhelming; the steady glare of the neon contrasts with the patterns of color and movement that, state by state, dance across the video screens. You search the wall to find a place where you can focus your attention on a single sequence of images. This, you believe, just might be a way to open a path of understanding to the complexities of this unexpected work.

As you stare at the monitors within one state's neon borders, you begin to recognize some of the images. In Alabama, you see the Reverend Martin Luther King, Jr., and the early struggles of the civil rights movement, while to your left, scenes from the 1943 Rodgers and Hammerstein musical *Oklahoma!* identify that state; harsh realities and human triumphs are thus juxtaposed to an imaginative Broadway musical. As you look from state to state, you find more conflicting images. American historical traditions are recounted with images of Abraham Lincoln in Illinois and the Alamo in Texas—but the Texas videos also include television footage of the 1993 fire that consumed the Branch Davidian compound near Waco. Gradually, you begin to sort out the visual information on the monitors; you can, more and more, identify images with states. But just as you are becoming more comfortable with the visual and ideological complexity, you are surprised again. When you look at New York, you see *yourself* on the video monitor, viewing this very work at this very moment. Unlike the monitors from other states, whose images primarily depict historical sequences or scenic views, the monitors within the borders of New York State are linked to closed-circuit video cameras pointed at onlookers in the gallery. The immediacy of the present moment is thus inserted into the work; the image of you and your interaction with the "map" instantly becomes an element of the work itself: as you are viewing it, you become part of it.

Your latest discovery about this work is captivating; you have seen works of art before, but they remained still objects before you, allowing time for quiet contemplation. This work challenges the traditional interaction between you and art at the same time as the work is bombarding you with many simultaneous layers of information; the work in its present form could not exist without your participation. The rapid, compressed delivery is familiar to you from watching TV, but the scope of it—and the insertion of *you* as an active participant—leads you to question some of your assumptions about art.

Now is the moment to find out more about this work. You read in the label nearby on the wall that the artist is Korean-born Nam June Paik (b. 1932) and that the work, which is composed of neon, video monitors, and laser disks, is called a video **installation.**• This installation was especially created by Paik for this specific gallery location, the Holly Solomon Gallery. The title, *Electronic Superhighway*, is now a familiar term in our culture. It evokes the promise of new modes of communication, but Paik's video installation also reveals that communication is not merely a matter of crossing distances, but of traversing time as well.

The panorama of diversity and rapidly changing images in *Electronic Superhighway* is, in many ways, a meditation on the meaning of the United States—its past and its present, and even how they may merge to form the future. Before you, perception collides with history, dreams with reality. And *you*, by your presence in New York City at this time, are a participant in this colossal structure of images and meanings.

Nam June Paik's *Electronic Superhighway* is a work of our time, founded on the recognition that electronic communications media are cultural forces in contemporary society. It disturbs our preconceptions about art and introduces real time as an element in our dialogue with the work at the same time that

---

• Terms that are bold-faced in the text are defined in the Glossary at the back of the book.

it questions the construction of history. In the broader view, it could be argued that Paik's demonstration of how communication crosses time, from past to present, touches the heart of our experience of art no matter when it was created.

How to Experience Art

When you encounter an unfamiliar work of art in a gallery or museum—or even when you're walking down the street—one way to open your communication with it is to ask some general questions that can help you to understand that work as a visual expression and as a historical experience. Some questions you might ask are:

» Does the work of art communicate specific emotions and feelings? That is, what is its **expressive content**?

» Does it belong to a clearly recognizable artistic tradition? Is it related to a particular **historical style**?

» Who was the artist (or artists), and did the artist's personality play a role in the creation of the work? Does the work demonstrate **individual style**?

» What can a visual examination and analysis of the work tell us? How can a **formal analysis** be useful?

» How are the various visual elements of the work arranged? What is its **composition**?

» What materials is it made of? What is the **medium**?

» How have the artist or artists used these materials? What **techniques** were employed to make the work?

» Did someone commission the artist or artists to create the work and did they also pay for it? Who were the **patrons**?

» Why was it made? What purpose did it fulfill? What was its **function** when it was first created?

» Was it created for a specific location, and did the artist adjust the composition for that location? Has the artist used **collocation**?

» What is its subject matter and what does it represent? What are its **iconography** and **iconology**?

» What can it tell us about the ideas, beliefs, or attitudes current in the period when it was created? What is its **historical significance** and its **historical context**? Who is or was its audience?

» As a member of the audience, you can also ask what it is that you bring to this work, and how your personal history and experiences might give you a very particular response to the work. What is your personal response?

These questions are not a comprehensive list, nor do all these questions apply to every work. The key concept in each question is restated with highlighted terms (**bold-faced** in the questions and the discussion that follows) that are part of a specialized vocabulary for sharing ideas and information about works of art.

Viewing Art

1-2 *MENKAURE AND HIS WIFE, QUEEN KHAMERERNEBTY II,* found at Menkaure's temple complex, next to his pyramid at Giza, Egypt. Dynasty 4, c. 2515 BCE. Greywacke with faint remains of paint, height 54½". Museum Expedition, Courtesy, Museum of Fine Arts, Boston. Commissioned by King Menkaure.

What is there about a statue of rulers who lived thousands of years ago (fig. 1-2) that attracts our interests? How can even mythological figures, so far removed from our experiences (fig. 1-4), engage our attention? Art's power to communicate to us rests on an analysis of a work's visual qualities and an understanding of the work's **expressive content** and its relationship to its historical period. One central goal of art history, then, is to increase our understanding of sometimes puzzling works from past cultures, and even from our own. This book attempts to provide a global perspective, but we need to recognize from the very beginning that most of us have a greater familiarity with the traditions of relatively recent Western (European and American) art than with those of other cultures and historical periods. This means that we must often make an additional effort to understand works from cultures outside of the Western tradition.

Understanding Style

To construct a framework for analyzing art created in the past, as well as in the present, modern art historians use classifications that rely on the concept of **style**. The word *style* (from the Latin *stylus*) originally referred to a writing instrument, but over time the meaning changed to include the manner—or art—of handwriting. Each of us writes differently, and our handwriting has a personal quality related to whether we are left-handed or right-handed, how we learned to write, and even the period in which we live. Documents from past centuries easily demonstrate how handwriting styles have changed over time. In art history, **historical style** is the term used to describe how the appearance of a work of art is tied to the period during which it was created. Works of art from the same historical period and culture often share similar visual characteristics. In art history, specific periods and cultures tend to be examined within a chronology, or time sequence, and the history of art is often presented as a succession of period styles.

The term *style*, however, can also have a more intimate meaning, referring to the particular manner of visual expression used by an individual artist, which is known as **individual style**. This style can change as the artist develops and matures. Relationships may also be detected between the individual style of an artist and the historical style of the time in which he or she lived. To study style, art history uses a technique called **formal analysis**, which is an examination of the visual aspects of a work and how its integral parts unite to produce a distinctive historical and individual style. The vocabulary of formal analysis, introduced in some of the questions at the end of the previous section, helps us to describe the visual structure of works of art.

Analyzing Two Works

To begin to understand the many ways in which works of art can be approached, we shall consider in some detail examples from different historical and cultural periods.

The sculpture *Menkaure and His Wife, Queen Khamerernebty* (fig. 1-2), carved in ancient Egypt about 4,500 years ago, proclaims stability; the poses of the Egyptian king and his queen are confined within a rectangular **composition**, and there is no suggestion of movement. There is a slight hint of portraiture in their faces, but their bodies are **idealized**, abstracted to conform to a standard of perfection dictated by Egyptian cultural preferences. The value of stability is also proclaimed in the work of the eleventh-century Chinese artist Guo Xi (c. 1020–90), titled *Early Spring* (fig. 1-3). This scroll painting represents a mountainous landscape with parts of the scene "obscured by" dense atmosphere. Waterfalls cascade down the lower portion of the mountain to the right. As with the Egyptian sculpted figures, a rectangular format encloses the composition. The monumentality of the mountain is reinforced by its central and dominant position, it occupies almost the entire painted surface of the scroll. The craggy rocks and skeletal trees suggest that we are also viewing the understructure, the essence of nature.

The perception of *Menkaure and His Wife, Queen Khamerernebty* as both stable and rigid results from several visual elements: The **axis**, an imaginary center line passing through each figure, conforms to a vertical line. Vertical or horizontal components appear to be bal-

1-3 GUO XI *EARLY SPRING.* Northern Song dynasty, 1072. Hanging scroll, ink and slight color on silk, length 5'. National Palace Museum, Taipei, Taiwan, Republic of China. The inscription on the upper right of the picture was executed by Emperor Qianlong (1736–1795) of the Qing Dynasty (1644–1911). Inscriptions are often added to pictures in China long after the paintings are executed. They are sometimes written directly on the painting as in this example, or in a separate space added to the scroll as in "Sailboats in the Rain by Xia Gui (fig. 4-60). An inscription by a noted scholar or emperor was highly valued and added to the prestige of the painting. The poem added to *Early Spring* reads:

> Leaves are twisted on the trees and the stream is melting,
> On the top are dwellings of the immortals.
> We do not need a willow tree to tell the season,
> The mountain is already misted with the coming of spring.

anced and in equilibrium. The vertical axes combine with the rectangular composition to communicate a contained, balanced stability. The vertical axes also contribute to the stiff posture of the figures, producing a rigidity reinforced by the compact outlines of the sculpture, which is a monolithic, rectangular solid.

The enormous mountain in Guo Xi's painting peaks in the center of the composition; this work too has an **axial composition**. Although curvilinear elements and diagonal elements can be seen in the painting—for example, in the bending branches, the flow of water over the tiered falls, and the outcropping of rock at the bottom—the soaring verticality of the central mountain dominates the scene. Set within a rectangular format, the visual authority of this axial mountain establishes stability within the composition.

Comparing Works of Art

Although both works communicate a sense of stability and permanence, each makes a distinct impact on us. The individual expression of each work is related to the **media** (materials) and **technique** that the artist employed. *Menkaure and His Wife, Queen Khamerernebty*, carved by an anonymous artist or workshop of artists, is made of greywacke, a dense, hard, and brittle stone found in Egypt. In contrast, the subtle atmospheric, spatial, and structural effects in *Early Spring* are achieved by Guo Xi's adept handling of brush and ink.

The subject matter of the two works is also distinctive. The art-historical examination of subject matter is expressed on two levels: What is the subject matter? What is its meaning within the work's historical context? **Iconography** (from the Greek *eikon*, "image," and *graphein*, "to describe" or "to write") is the art-historical study of the specific subject matter of the work, while **iconology** (from the Greek for "image discourse") interprets the *meaning* of the subject matter as it can be understood within the historical culture that produced it.

Menkaure and his queen ruled in ancient Egypt, and the iconography of the sculpture is their representation as royal personages. The subject of Guo Xi's painting is the landscape, a visual investigation of the appearance and structure of nature in China. Inquiry into the iconology of these works, however, leads to the realm of **historical significance** and **historical context**, for religious, political, social, economic, scientific, philosophic, and other values can all come to bear on the interpretation of a work's meaning and function.

The portrait of Menkaure and his wife is one of several similar sculptures intended to provide a home for the enduring aspect of the individual personality, called the *ka*, that the Egyptians believed continued after death; this was its **function** when it was created. Its original location was within a funerary precinct, close to the king's pyramidal tomb. The stable, rigid form of the sculpture conveys its expressive content, a majestic and enduring presence. More importantly, this form also protects it from breakage, thus safeguarding the home of the *ka* in the afterlife. This enduring strength is reinforced by the use of greywacke as a medium.

Within the Chinese tradition, landscape paintings were not simply depictions of nature; rather, they were intended to express the continuing essence of the living, natural world. Artists such as Guo Xi were highly educated, and the paintings they created were thought to enrich the human spirit by allowing the individual viewer, through contemplation, to become aware of a universal order that governs natural and human affairs. In the Western tradition, values of stability, permanence, and constancy were often associated with the human figure in art, but in China these qualities were expressed in landscape painting. Possibly, too, the underlying stability of both works bears some relationship to the powerful centralized governments that controlled both Egypt and China during the periods when the works were created.

Viewing Baroque Sculpture

Apollo and Daphne (fig. 1-4), created in Italy by Gianlorenzo Bernini (1598–1680), communicates an expressive content that is markedly different from *Menkaure and His Wife, Queen Khamerernebty* and *Early Spring*. This sculpture, with its emphasis on dramatic movement, is from the Baroque period in Western art; its stylistic qualities of visual, dynamic flux are shared with painting and architecture from that period. The figures, representing the mythological story of Apollo and Daphne, express a transient moment forever caught in time. This Baroque sculpture is also **naturalistic**, for the figures, drapery, landscape, and tree segments all reproduce the appearance of these forms in nature. (The term *realism*, which is sometimes confused with *naturalism*, refers to subject matter drawn from everyday life.)

Unlike the formal qualities of the two earlier works, which emphasized axial stability and stasis, Bernini's sculpture is composed primarily on a diagonal axis. Diagonal components, which break the equilibrium of the vertical and horizontal, communicate movement. If *Menkaure and His Wife, Queen Khamerernebty* appears closed and self-contained in space, *Apollo and Daphne* seems open and expansive. This openness is due to the extension of the figures' limbs and drapery out into the immediate space; here the surrounding space is energized by the sculptural form. The medium, it is important to note, is Italian marble, which is soft and more easily carved than greywacke.

The iconography of Bernini's sculpture is drawn from a specific literary source from ancient Rome, Ovid's *Metamorphoses* (I, 545–59), written in the late first century BCE or the early first century CE◆:

◆ This book uses the abbreviations BCE ("before the common era") and CE ("common era") rather than BC ("before Christ") and AD ("Anno Domini," "year of our Lord").

So ran the god and [Daphne],
one swift in hope,
　　The other in terror, but he
ran more swiftly,
　　Borne on the wings of love,
gave her no rest,
　　Shadowed her shoulder,
breathed on her streaming hair
　　Her strength was gone, worn
out by the long effort
　　Of the long flight; she was
deathly pale, and seeing
　　The river of her father, cried,
"O help me,
　　If there is any power in the
rivers,
　　Change and destroy the body
which has given
　　Too much delight!" And hardly
had she finished,
　　When her limbs grew numb
and heavy, her soft breasts
　　Were closed with delicate
bark, her hair was leaves,
　　Her arms were branches, and
her speedy feet
　　Rooted and held, and her head
became a tree top,
　　Everything gone except her
grace, her shining.

Although the figures of Apollo and Daphne are represented naturalistically, they are legendary figures from Greek mythology. As described in the passage from Ovid, the god Apollo desires the lovely Daphne, daughter of a river god. She prays to her father to be delivered from Apollo's unwanted advances, and when Apollo finally catches her, her father transforms her into a laurel tree. In Bernini's sculpture, Daphne's left side is metamorphosing into a trunk, while her fingers and hair become branches and leaves. The expression Bernini puts on Apollo's face is a complex mixture of joy, at the attainment of his goal, and wonder, as his hand embraces Daphne only to touch not flesh but bark.

　　The iconology of Bernini's sculpture communicates both general and particular aspects of Italian Baroque culture. It demonstrates the popularity in seventeenth-century Italy of literature and art from ancient Greece and Rome—Ovid's writings were popular

1-4 GIANLORENZO BERNINI

APOLLO AND DAPHNE. 1622–25. Marble, height 8′. Galleria Borghese, Rome. Commissioned by Cardinal Scipione Borghese.

BERNINI, *APOLLO AND DAPHNE*, BORGHESE GALLERY, ROME.

sources for learning Latin, so all educated people would have known this tale. Besides delighting visitors, *Apollo and Daphne* also showed off the intellectual and artistic taste of its **patron**, Cardinal Scipione Borghese, an important member of the Roman aristocracy and an official of the Catholic Church.

　　Discerning style, formal analysis, iconography, iconology, function, and historical context are beginning steps to understanding the meaning of a work of art. Works of art themselves are far from being mute—but to hear them speak, we must be open to the expression and content of their language.

Analyzing Art

1-5 Pond and garden of Katsura Imperial Villa, near Kyoto, Japan. 1620–23. Commissioned by Prince Hachijo Toshihito and his son Toshitada. This view looks toward the pond from a narrow veranda and through two rooms of a wing of the villa. The white-based veranda on the left is a corner of the first-built section of the rambling villa (compare figures 7-53 and 7-54).

Your personal approach to works of art may begin with queries about the historical or cultural significance, with an interest in individual style and the biography of the artist, or with an examination of subject matter. But the most fundamental approach is to look carefully at the work as a visual object and to begin to analyze how it communicates to us. This section sets out to help you understand how to do what is called a **formal analysis**.

One element that is common to almost all forms of visual expression is the manipulation of space. We have an immediate relationship with space— we exist and move in it, and during much of our daily lives, we are sheltered by structures that enclose space.

Analyzing Architecture

Three-dimensional space is real space. Artists and architects who work with real space often use space as a positive element in the composition or design. This perception of space, and the merging of interior with exterior space, is, for example, a key feature in understanding the architecture of the Katsura villa near Kyoto, Japan (fig. 1-5). The design of these rooms, inspired by some of the tenets of Zen Buddhism, creates a subtle integration of the building with its environment. The architectural features are restrained and simple; wooden supports reveal their natural beauty, and the translucent paper of the sliding screen walls produces a soft interior light. As the sliding walls are moved, different vistas of the garden appear and the spatial definitions of the rooms change. The emphasis on delicate horizontals and verticals makes the irregularity of nature even more evident; the distinction between the artificial and the natural is emphasized. The design of this Japanese royal retreat reminds us that the boundaries between architectural and real space are not always immutable—an understanding that also guides our experience of Fallingwater, designed by Frank Lloyd Wright (1867–1959).

Both the twentieth-century Fallingwater (fig. 1-6) and the sixteenth-century Villa Rotonda (fig. 1-7) by Palladio (1508–80) were designed as country homes for private patrons: Fallingwater for the Kaufmann family of Pittsburgh, who used the home as a summer retreat, and the Villa Rotonda for a retired official of the Catholic Church, who used the villa for receptions and entertaining. Like the Katsura villa, each structure communicates a particular architectural effect, and each relates to its setting in a different manner.

The most striking feature of Fallingwater is the way the structure responds to the site, a characteristic of many of Wright's designs. The architect once commented:

A good building is one that makes the landscape more beautiful than it was before.

1-6 FRANK LLOYD WRIGHT Fallingwater, Bear Run, in the Allegheny Mountains of southwestern Pennsylvania. 1936. Commissioned by Pittsburgh business executive Edgar Kaufmann.

1-7 PALLADIO Villa Rotonda (also known as the Villa Americo and the Villa Capra), Vicenza, Italy. c 1567–70. Commissioned by Paolo Almerico, Apostolic Referendary of popes Pius IV and Pius V.

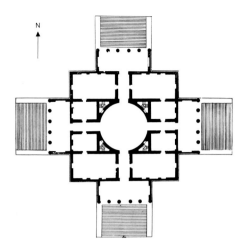

1-8 PALLADIO Plan of Villa Rotonda.

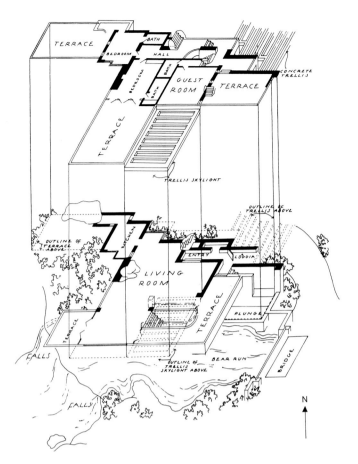

1-9 FRANK LLOYD WRIGHT Plan of Fallingwater drawn in perspective.

In creating Fallingwater, he integrated the design with the natural environment, while at the same time establishing in the landscape a forceful abstract arrangement of rectangular forms. The large terraces allowed the Kaufmanns and their guests to enjoy the sun and views into the surrounding forest.

The ledges of rock that form the falls at the site create a horizontal pattern. This is echoed in the thrusting, horizontal terraces above, which project out from a massive vertical core faced with local stone quarried near the site. Nature's design has been reinterpreted and reinforced by the abstract architectural forms integrated within it.

Situated very differently—on the crest of a hill and backed by a wooded area—the Villa Rotonda is an impressive and commanding structure. Its four porches, set at right angles to each other and extending from a central domed core, dominate the site. These porches serve a practical as well as an aesthetic function, for they afford the guests varied views of the surrounding countryside and, since each is partially enclosed on the sides, they offer the possibility of always being able to find a shady spot away from the hot Italian summer sun.

The exterior design of the Villa Rotonda expresses a stable harmony. Symmetry governs the arrangement of the architectural forms, and vertical and horizontal elements are carefully balanced. The visual equilibrium revealed on the exterior also governs the interior design. The plan (fig. 1-8) is composed of proportional geometric shapes: a central, circular space is circumscribed by a square plan. From the central space, halls radiate to each porch. The cross axes of the halls are aligned with the cardinal points—north, south, east, and west. This desire to orient a building in relation to a perceived order in nature was an aspect of the Renaissance aesthetic that formed the basis of Palladio's architecture.

In contrast, the exterior design of Fallingwater is asymmetrical. A unified composition is achieved, nevertheless, by balancing the horizontal thrust of the terraces against the vertical massing of the central core. Another unifying feature is the adherence to rectangular forms through-out. The asymmetrical balance of Wright's exterior concept also characterizes the plan and interior (figs. 1-9, 1-10). Rooms and hallways repeat the rectangular forms of the exterior. Like the Villa Rotonda, the rooms also correspond to the cardinal points, but Wright's asymmetrical design allows for the largest room, the living room, to have a southwest exposure, which maximized the Kaufmann's enjoyment of the afternoon sun. Following a concept similar to that expressed in the Japanese pavilion (see fig. 1-5), Wright extends the rooms of the house into the space of the environment, while in Palladio's design the distinction between the building and its environment is firmly stated.

The Villa Rotonda was built to accommodate many guests, and its plan provided easy access into and out of the building; the symmetry of the halls and rooms around the central space allowed

1-10 FRANK LLOYD WRIGHT   Interior, Fallingwater. This historic photo shows the living room area of Fallingwater when the house was first completed, in 1936. Note the rows of built-in light bulbs, which is an early, revolutionary use of indirect or ambient lighting in a domestic setting. Later these bulbs were covered with translucent screens to hide the light source.

for clearly understood patterns of circulation. Fallingwater, by contrast, was designed for a family of three, and although the living room and terraces are large, the bedrooms are small, the halls narrow. As a private home for a small family, Fallingwater had no need for expansive patterns of circulation.

The principles of construction used to build the Villa Rotonda have a long tradition in architectural history. They include the use of **walls**, and **post-and-lintel** system (see fig. 3-27), and the **arch** (see fig. 3-118). The design confers a stable dignity on the building that recalls the tradition of ancient Greece and ancient Rome.

In contrast, the manner in which Fallingwater's terraces are thrust out over the waterfall creates a dramatic effect. This adventurous architectural achievement was accomplished by the use of modern construction materials that have a high **tensile strength**— that is, they strongly resist the strain of the architectural load and the pull of gravity. In Fallingwater, the terraces are made of concrete reinforced with steel rods. The availability of these materals gave Wright the possibility of using the **cantilever**, a horizontal projection into space.

Architecture serves both utilitarian and aesthetic purposes. Buildings are

expressions of their time. As we encounter different forms of architecture, we would do well to recall the understanding of John Ruskin, the influential nineteenth-century English art critic, who wrote, "All architecture proposes an effect on the human mind, not merely a service to the human frame."

Analyzing Sculpture

Like architecture, sculpture is an art of real space, and space is an integral element in analyzing sculpture. Depending upon the composition of the sculpture, the surrounding space can play a role in

1-11   DANIEL CHESTER FRENCH

MINUTEMAN. 1874–75. Bronze with granite base, height 7'. Old North Bridge, Concord, Massachusetts. The American writer Ralph Waldo Emerson proposed French for this commission. Commissioned by the Town of Concord.

the effect and communication of the work. *Minuteman* (fig. 1-11), by Daniel Chester French (1850–1931), and *Cubi XIX* (fig. 1-12), by David Smith (1906–65), though very different in appearance, nevertheless share a similar spatial involvement.

The bronze statue of the Minuteman at Concord was commissioned to celebrate the centennial of the famous Revolutionary War battle fought there. The heroically scaled statue depicts the citizen-soldier of the American Revolution poised with a plow in one hand and a musket in the other. The figure stands alert and determined. The sculpture is **representational**, and although the medium is bronze, the artist has finished the surface to create the illusion of different textures: the flesh suggests the anatomical structure beneath, the folds of the clothing respond to the body and to gravity, and these textures contrast with the cold metallic handle of the plow. Such representational qualities help us recognize the forms and realize the sculpture's commemorative, historical purpose.

David Smith's *Cubi XIX* is a **nonrepresentational** work of art, for it does not imitate actual figures or objects. In Smith's sculpture, the medium is stainless steel. Smith has wire-brushed the surface of the steel, giving a textural unity. The brushed steel surfaces reflect, in a diffused way, the atmospheric light around them. The appearance of the sculpture, then, changes in response to atmospheric conditions; it might appear dull gray-blue on an overcast day or reflect a slight golden glow on a sunny day.

Both *Minuteman* and *Cubi XIX* are examples of **sculpture in the round**, that is, sculpture finished on all sides, to be viewed from many different vantage points. And, as already noted, these sculptures share a similar relationship with space. Both have forms that develop from a vertical axis—the arms and right leg of *Minuteman* and the geometric steel forms of *Cubi XIX*. Both sculptures are set on bases. The large granite base of *Minuteman* contributes to our recognition of the statue as a commemorative work; *Cubi XIX*'s base primarily offers support, but its design is in keeping with the nonrepresentative composition. The composition of each work is also animated by a suggested movement. With *Minuteman*, this sense is created by the contrast of the vertical axis of the figure with the diagonals of the right leg and musket. *Cubi XIX* offers an interplay of vertical, horizontal, and diagonal forms.

The compositions of French's *Minuteman* and Smith's *Cubi XIX* urge us to consider the sculptures from different viewpoints. The diagonal of the Minuteman's musket, which is reinforced by the implied movement of the right leg, creates an oblique motion that invites us to walk around the sculpture. In a similar way, diagonal elements break the planarity, or two-dimensional, view of Smith's work, drawing us around the sculpture to consider how the composition changes from varying points of view. Both sculptures make use of the three-dimensional space in which they, like ourselves, exist.

Analyzing Ritual Art

Minuteman and *Cubi XIX* are alike in yet another way; as a sculptural object, each remains stationary. Although movement is implied in each sculpture, movement actually occurs only when the viewer walks around each work. This situation is radically different when we consider the *Bird of the Night (Butterfly)* mask from the Bwa ethnic group in Africa (fig. 1-13). Although we are used to seeing African masks displayed in cases in museums and galleries, such static presentations deny their original use, which can only be understood within the context of village rituals.

In these rituals, the *Bird of the Night* figure appears after the first rains of the season. The mask adorns a dancer whose other garments cover the entire body. The fluttering movements of a butterfly are imitated by the dancer. In these rituals, the mask, created by a carver, is united with the raffia garment, with musicians, and with the movements of the dancer—a combination intended to express the essence,

1-12 DAVID SMITH

CUBI XIX. 1964. Stainless steel, height 9'5⅛". Photographed at Bolton Landing, New York; now in Tate Gallery, London. The abstract title of this sculpture reinforces its nonobjective content. It is number 19 in a series of twenty-eight sculptures by Smith that present variations on compositions of rectangular and cylindrical stainless-steel forms.

1-13   Bwa culture, Africa. Ritual dancer wearing painted wooden *Bird of the Night* (*Butterfly*) mask and raffia body suit. Twentieth century. Wood, paint, and raffia. Burkina Faso, Upper Volta River region.

not an exact visual representation, of the butterfly. The purpose of the mask is thus only fulfilled in the context of the ritual as a whole. To try to understand this Bwa mask as a sculptural form, we must, then, consider it within this dynamic context and within the spiritual context of the village and the participation in the ritual of the onlookers. Although the villagers may remain static, the mask, garment, and dancer constantly energize the space of the village through actual movement. On a more profound level, the ritual is meant not merely to transform the space of the village but also to affect the quality of life.

Sculpture that incorporates the concept of movement is encountered in many works, especially during the twentieth century. As we have seen, our understanding of Paik's *Electronic Superhighway* (see fig. 1-1) was in part based in observing motion on the video screens.

Some aspects of twentieth-century art share another quality with the Bwa mask, garment, and ritual: they are

ephemeral, lasting for only a short time. The creation of the mask, its use, and its eventual disintegration are part of a cyclical continuation of daily life and ritual within many African societies. The concept of permanence, which underlies much Western art, is not a characteristic of this work. In fact, the emphasis on permanence in Western art has been challenged in the twentieth century as such ephemeral art forms as conceptual, performance, and earth art (see Chapter 10) have gained popularity.

Analyzing Installation Art

Installation art, too, denies the western European tradition of the work of art as a singular static object by fashioning an environment, often temporary, within a museum, gallery, or other public space. Although there are almost as many types of installation art as there are examples, many of these works set out to charge and transform the space within which the viewer is moving.

One American installation artist, Judy Pfaff (b. 1946), responded to a literally enormous challenge when

she accepted a commission for a work for the Pennsylvania Convention Center in Philadelphia. *cirque, Cirque* (fig. 1-14), developed over a period of several years, took seven months to execute; the installation itself, when many fragile forms had to be hung from the ceiling of the huge space, was especially difficult. The result, however, is a sequence of colorful forms that flow and surge through what was once just empty space above visitors' heads. But what happens when that "space" does not really exist, as is the case with the two-dimensional medium of painting?

Analyzing Painting

An understanding of space is crucial for understanding the traditional medium of painting. Artists who have worked with two-dimensional surfaces usually have attempted either to create the illusion of three-dimensional space or to accept and emphasize the flatness of that surface. The distinction is apparent in the two paintings illustrated here.

In *Christ Giving the Keys to Saint Peter* (fig. 1-15), Pietro Perugino (1450–1523) painted recognizable figures, landscape, and architecture from the visual world. Perugino's painting is **illusionistic**, for the objects represented seem to be tangible and weighty and appear to exist within actual space. In contrast, the painting by Piet Mondrian (1872–1944) does not have forms that resemble those in the visual world (fig. 1-16). The work is **nonobjective**, or nonrepresentational.

Traditionally, a **painting** can be defined as a two-dimensional surface to which liquid colors or inks have been applied. Flatness, the most distinctive attribute of paintings, is a starting point in their analysis. The flat surface is known as the **picture plane**, and in Mondrian's painting the two-dimensional colors and shapes reinforce the flatness of this plane. In illusionistic

1-14 JUDY PFAFF

CIRQUE, CIRQUE. 1995. Installation with 9 miles of steel and aluminum tubing and with glass orbs that extends across 70,000 square feet of space. Installed at the Pennsylvania Convention Center, Philadelphia. Commissioned by the City of Philadelphia and the State of Pennsylvania, together with the Pennsylvania Convention Center's One Percent for Art Program.

paintings, such as Perugino's, the picture plane seems transparent, like a large window.

Both paintings are made up of shapes. Mondrian's are black lines and squares or rectangles of a single color. Perugino's shapes are naturalistic objects: figures, trees, mountains, a public square, and a building. In both paintings, forms are organized into a composition. Perugino's composition is arranged to emphasize the figures of Christ and Saint Peter in the middle. A row of Christ's disciples on each side frames them, and the Renaissance-style structure in the background helps draw attention to them. The receding lines of the square's pavement converge at a central point. Perugino's composition is balanced, symmetrical, and centralized.

The composition of Mondrian's painting is neither centralized nor symmetrical, but it is balanced. We are drawn to the edges of the composition by the red, yellow, and blue found there. These colors are placed so that they balance each other, with no single color dominating. Mondrian's composition, however, might be described as decentralized, for it leads us to the periphery without concentrating our attention on any single area or element. His painting seems simple, but he has developed such a perfect balance that any change in color or composition would destroy the work's equilibrium.

Mondrian's composition is easier to analyze than Perugino's, for it exists completely in two dimensions. Perugino's composition must be analyzed both in terms of the patterns on the two-dimensional surface and as an illusion of three-dimensional reality. Note, for example, that when we analyze the painting as a two-dimensional object, the lines of the pavement converge toward a central point, but in actual space, these lines would be parallel to each other. This controlled spatial effect is a system of creating depth (**perspective**) known as **scientific perspective**. Other devices used by Perugino to help create his illusion are **atmospheric perspective** (the sky shades from blue toward white at the horizon, and the forms near the horizon are blurry and softened in color), **diminution** (forms in the distance are smaller), and **overlapping** (forms are placed in front of other forms). For a diagram of the painting see fig. 5-27.

1-15 PIETRO PERUGINO

CHRIST GIVING THE KEYS TO SAINT PETER. Fresco in the Sistine Chapel, Vatican, Rome. 1482. 11′5½″ × 18′8½″.
Commissioned by Pope Sixtus IV.

Perugino's medium was the technique of painting directly on a wet plaster wall, known as **fresco**, or *buon fresco*; Mondrian's medium was **oil paint** on canvas. Both artists used a technique of smooth, regular brushstrokes. Because most of the forms in both paintings are sharply defined, with precisely delineated edges, they can be termed **linear** (the opposite effect, in which broad, free brushstrokes are used to define form, is termed **painterly**; for an example see figure 6-52).

Perugino's colors are naturalistic, that is, taken from nature, which enhances his illusionism. Mondrian's selection of **hue** (the property that gives a color its name) is restricted to the **primary colors**: red, blue, and yellow. Perugino changed the **value** (relative darkness or lightness of the color) and **intensity** (the level of richness or saturation of the color) of his colors to suggest the changes in value and intensity that result when light hits a form and creates highlights and shading; these changes are called **modeling**. Mondrian used pure colors, which are colors at their maximum or full intensity (fig. 1-17).

Perugino's painting was created during the Renaissance in Italy; it is one of a series of paintings of the lives of Moses and Christ that decorate the side walls of the Sistine Chapel in Rome (visible in fig. 6-36). *Christ Giving the Keys to Saint Peter* reveals the abilities of a Renaissance artist to reproduce natural effects within a

1-16 PIET MONDRIAN.

COMPOSITION NO. 8. 1939–42. Oil on canvas, 29½″ × 26¾″.

PIET MONDRIAN, DUTCH, 1872–1944. COMPOSITION NO. 8, 1939–1942. OIL ON CANVAS. 29 ½ × 26 ¾ IN. (74.9 × 68.0 CM). SIGNED WITH INITIALS AND DATED 39–42. PHOTOGRAPHED 5/31/94. KIMBALL ART MUSEUM, FORT WORTH, TEXAS. MICHAEL BODYCOMB, MONDRIAN/HOLTZMAN TRUST.

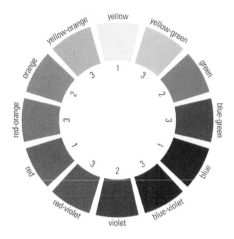

1-17 Color wheel. In the technical terminology used to discuss light and color, black and white are not considered to be colors. When color is understood in terms of light, black is understood as the absence of all color and white as the mixture of all colors. On the color wheel red, yellow, and blue (numbered 1 above) are known as the primary colors because all other colors are made of a combination of these three hues; the secondary colors are orange, green, and purple (numbered 2 above). Complimentary colors, often juxtaposed by artists to achieve vivid coloristic contrasts, are the two colors directly opposite each other on the color wheel, such as blue and orange or red and green.

harmonious and clear composition. Mondrian's painting, on the other hand, is related to his personal philosophy and to the principles of the de Stijl movement. While searching for a truly "universal means of expression," Mondrian wrote that beauty and harmony could only be expressed by "abstraction of form and color, that is to say, in the straight line and the clearly defined primary color." His search for pictorial balance must be related to the search for political balance—peace in the years following World War I. Despite their pronounced differences, these two paintings share a surprisingly similar expressive content: they are orderly, serene, and, ultimately, calming. Both artists achieve visual harmony and balance. The formal analysis we have undertaken for each painting has a clear relationship to the historical and cultural background important for each work.

1-18 A scholar studying a Chinese hand scroll.

In addition, these works also conform to the common expectations that paintings adorn walls or ceilings. In some cultural traditions, however, two-dimensional works can only be seen in more intimate circumstances. A horizontal Chinese hand scroll (fig. 1-18) is meant to be viewed by one person or, at most, a limited group of people, in a quiet, contemplative atmosphere. And unlike the paintings by Perugino and Mondrian, a scroll painting is not seen in its entirety at one time. Usually only one or two feet of a longer scroll can be seen at a time, as you unroll it from right to left. This format is intensely personal, with you controlling the pace of the journey; time thus becomes an important element in the experience of the work. The movement of simultaneously turning the two ends of the scroll to advance it cannot be rushed, which encourages contemplation. Perugino's large-scale illusionism is typical of much of Western art, but the more abstracted vision of nature seen in the typical Chinese hand scroll is consistent with the small-scale intimacy of the scroll format and the emphasis on the surface of the painting that is

apparent when you unroll it. When the viewing is complete, you roll and tie the hand scroll and place it in a box out of sight for safekeeping.

Whether we are considering a work of art as public as an installation in a civic building or as intimate as a hand scroll, the artist's ability to transform our experience—and even our environment—is an important factor in the constantly evolving art at the beginning of the twenty-first century. But the artist's role and impact throughout history have not always been so clearly recognized.

Art and Artists in History

1-19 KÄTHE KOLLWITZ.

SELF-PORTRAIT. 1934. Lithograph, 8¹/₁₆ × 7³/₁₆″. Philadelphia Museum of Art. This German artist was the first woman to be elected to the Prussian Academy of Arts.

1-20 ANCIENT GREEK, "LENINGRAD PAINTER."

GREEK POTTERS AT WORK, detail of Greek vase. c. 450 bce. Private Collection, Milan

The impact of *Self-Portrait* (fig. 1-19) by Käthe Kollwitz (1867– 1945) is direct and penetrating. Her face occupies the entire surface and demands that we confront her expression. Kollwitz published several series of prints depicting the social and political struggles of the poorer classes in Germany in the late nineteenth and early twentieth centuries. These struggles, with which she identified, have left their mark on *Self-Portrait.* The personal revelation of the involvement of the artist that we see here is especially typical of modern works.

Virtually all cultures, ancient or modern, have nurtured specialists who design and/or embellish everyday items or materials used in ritual. Whether Hopi, African, Mesoamerican, European, or Asian, these men and women were highly skilled workers. Sometimes those considered best at such expression were recognized as "artists" and were elevated in their society to a high level of regard; in some cultures they were encouraged to sign their works. Although not all these creators are recognized as artists, the visual arts—grand or modest, public or private, religious or secular—are a regular

feature of human culture, and those who create these works are fundamental to most societies. Individuals in some cultures, for example fifth-century China and fifteenth-century Italy, began to write down their aesthetic aspirations and deeply held values as expressed in the visual arts.

Throughout most of Western history, definitions of art were different from our modern view. The word **art** is derived from the Latin *ars,* meaning either "manual skill" or "professional activity." The term has historically been used broadly, encompassing what we now think of as the sciences, as well as

1-21 JOHANN ZOFFANY

The Life Drawing Class at the Royal Academy. 1772. Oil on canvas, 40 × 58 ″. Collection Her Majesty the Queen, Windsor Castle, Windsor, Berkshire, England. Zoffany's painting shows all the members of the Royal Academy except for Angelica Kauffmann and Mary Moser, women who, within this restrictive academic climate, were not permitted to attend the life drawing class because of the nude male models. Zoffany ingeniously included them by showing their portraits hanging on the side wall. The sculpted figure with a raised right arm, just below the lamp, is an *écorché*, a sculpture of a flayed anatomical figure used to study surface muscles.

many practical handicrafts and occupations. An artist, for example, might practice the art of painting, while a physician practices the art of medicine.

Artists in Ancient Greece and Rome

As early as the classical world of ancient Greece and Rome, the making of art was generally viewed as a manual profession taught in workshops, and it was not related to the more esteemed liberal arts—mathematics, grammar, philosophy, and logic—which were distinguished by intellectual, speculative thinking. This workshop tradition is illustrated in *Greek Potters at Work* (fig. 1-20), Apprentice

vase painters, some female, are working side by side with the head of the shop. Although we know that women were sometimes involved in the workshops, they must have been given lesser positions, for no Greek vase signed by a woman is known.

Artists in the Middle Ages

During the Middle Ages in the West, from about 500 to 1500 CE, art continued to be identified as a manual profession. Artists formed **guilds**—legal organizations rather like trade unions. While guilds assured professional standards, they also reinforced the distinction

that was then drawn between manual arts—including the production of works of art—and the so-called liberal arts.

Artists in the Renaissance and Beyond

The traditional classification of the Western visual arts as manual, or mechanical, arts was transformed in the fourteenth and fifteenth centuries. Both artists and writers began to emphasize the scientific and intellectual aspects of art, often incorporating the liberal arts into the education of artists. It was argued that arithmetic, for example, was necessary for the study of proportion,

1-22 UNKNOWN CHINESE PAINTER

PORTRAIT OF NI ZAN. Yuan dynasty, c. 1340. Scroll, ink on paper, 11⅛ × 24″. National Palace Museum, Taipei, Taiwan, Republic of China. Chinese literati painters worked alone, seated at desks in their studios. Paintings were executed on the flat surface of the table with natural-bristle brushes in watercolor and ink on silk or paper. All necessary brushes, paints, and inks were close at hand. For a painting by Ni Zan, see figure 4-5.

and that geometry figured in the calculation of perspective. The artist was beginning to be seen as an educated professional versed in both the practice and the theory of art. This attitude that the artist had to be a skilled and educated individual was accompanied by a new social status: artists became the companions of intellectuals, princes, popes, and emperors.

This evolution affected the classification of the visual arts in Europe. By the sixteenth century, painting, sculpture, and architecture were grouped together as the arts of *disengo* (an Italian word that refers both to the making of drawings and to the concept of design) and were elevated to a status higher than other utilitarian arts. Discussion of art theory became commonplace among intellectuals, and treatises defined art and discussed its developing history. By the later sixteenth century, academies began to replace the workshop tradition; artists were now educated in both the practical and the theoretical aspects of art, as can be seen in the painting (fig. 1-21) depicting the male members of London's Royal Academy attending a class with live models. Plaster casts of the works of classical sculpture, which were

thought to exemplify the highest ideals of art, line the walls. The members of the academy are involved in discourse on the subject of life drawing.

This association of the arts of *disengo* with the intellectualism of the liberal arts was one of the mainstays of the new academic education given to artists. By the eighteenth century, art academies had proliferated throughout Europe. From this academic wellspring, a definition of the fine arts (*les beaux arts*) developed that included, painting, sculpture, poetry, music, and dance on the basis that these are the arts that delight us. Arts that primarily serve a utilitarian purpose continued to be termed mechanical arts, while architecture, which was considered to combine usefulness with beauty, occupied a third, independent category.

Artists in the Nineteenth and Twentieth Centuries

Although our understanding of art's role within the fine arts is relatively recent, developments in the West since the

nineteenth century have already begun to challenge those academic definitions of art. Early in the nineteenth century, when dramatically changing economic and social conditions were transforming Western cultural values, the concept of the artist as a member of the **avant-garde** (French for "vanguard") was born; as recently as the 1980s and 1990s a group of artists in China began to follow the same principles. Attacking the conservatism of academic training and public taste, many artists assumed roles as prophets, intent on leading society toward a modern, often utopian, vision of life. In our time, the parameters within which visual artists work have changed. **Happenings** and performance art have blurred the distinctions between the traditional media of the visual arts and other art forms, including speech, music, dance, film, and video.

Artists in China

Among cultures outside the Western tradition, China nurtured the oldest continuous painting tradition in the world. Its historical isolation, imperial patronage, art academies (begun as early as the eighth century CE), and a bureaucratic elite of Confucian scholar-officials contributed to a unique tradition in the visual arts. Most Chinese artists were not only painters but also poets, calligraphers, government officials, antiquarians, scholars, collectors, connoisseurs, and mystics. Painters such as Ni Zan (fig. 1-22) were part of the cultured elite who were the main participants in the Chinese classical tradition. Among the Chinese aristocracy, painting and **calligraphy** were revered media for the preservation of social, political, and aesthetic values.

Artists in Africa

In other cultures, the position of artists varies. In early Africa, for example, the artist was traditionally a prominent member of the community not only as the creator of pictures on rock surfaces but also as the one who decorated implements for hunting and other daily activities. In Africa today, artists hold a respected position, although the social status is not the same everywhere. There often continues to be a sharp dividing line between the arts practiced by men and women. In some regions, men are still responsible for house building, tool making, and carving, while women are known for dyeing, spinning, weaving, and pottery making.

In Africa, professional techniques are usually learned and handed down from father to son or mother to daughter, and certain crafts are family enterprises. In some cases, there is also apprenticeship—for instance, if a young male shows talent for **carving**, he might apprentice with a well-known sculptor and his family would be obligated to provide the teacher with gifts. If his skill comes to the attention of the chief, the artist is ordered to help create the attributes of chiefdom: thrones, crowns, scepters, drums, portraits, and articles of personal adornment. Village artists live solely on the patronage of their particular chief, and their talents and ideas usually conform to his wishes. The artists' role nevertheless often has significance to the village as a whole through their creation of ritual objects.

1-23. WODAABE WOMAN DECORATING A CALABASH, NORTHEAST NIGERIA. C. 1981. The woman is probably decorating the calabash for her personal use.

In northeast Nigeria, Wodaabe women carve gourds into objects called calabashes that are important in both daily and ceremonial life (fig. 1-23). Only a few of these utensils are used to hold porridge and milk; a greater number are treasured as ceremonial possessions (newborn babies are traditionally bathed in calabashes) and are a woman's riches and sources of prestige. Calabashes are covered with designs that the artist cuts into the surface after the gourd is dried in the sun. Most of the patterns are geometric: triangles, half moons, suns, and sinuous lines. The designs are passed down from generation to generation and vary only slightly according to individual imagination. The patterns are thought to protect both the receptacle and its contents.

Artists in India

Part of the daily obligation of village women in India is to maintain the exterior walls or plazas of their homes with painted designs or rice-powder patterns (see fig. 10-19). These "painted prayers" are thought to protect their families and locate tremendous spiritual power in the artistic activity of women.

In India, as elsewhere, religion is a major force that stimulates art and architecture. Most systems of Indian thought consider the phenomenal world to be illusory, perceived and interpreted by the senses. These perceptions yield information of a personal rather than a universal nature. The challenge for the Indian artist is, therefore, to express concepts beyond the limits of the phenomenal world. The artist creates symbolic devices, or *murtis* (images, icons, or sculpture), that render the abstract, transcendent realm more approachable and comprehensible. Communication of universal religious ideals, not egoistic expression, is the goal of the Indian artist. As a result, variations on traditional artistic "rules" are limited, and few names of ancient artists are known. However, the task of the artist, whether the creator of Hindu temple sculpture or painter of house designs, is an important one, for a devotee can gain access to spiritual power by viewing an image. Such a belief gives the visual artist an especially important role in Indian culture.

What we call art has assumed many forms and functions in world history, and the role of the creative individuals we call artists has constantly been reformulated, as we shall see.

The so-called "Great Serpent Mound," seen from the air; built around 1070 ce in Adams County, Ohio, by a prehistoric Amerindian tribe (perhaps the culture we now call "Fort Ancient"); for more information see fig. 2-8 and pp. 28-29.

CHAPTER TWO

Prehistoric Art

A Brief Insight

THE FUNCTION OF PREHISTORIC WORKS LIKE THIS large snake-shaped mound in Ohio is uncertain because we have no documentation to help us interpret their meaning. Prehistory is defined as the period before writing, and without written records we have only the works themselves and archaeological evidence to help us interpret them. For many prehistoric cultures, however, even the archaeological evidence is slight. Nevertheless, the importance of the animal world for prehistoric cultures is evident in the works that survive, including mounds like this one, representations of deer carved on bone fragments, and the bulls, deer, bison, and other animals painted and carved on cave walls and cliffs. The tremendous scale and complex pattern of the "Great Serpent Mound" indicate that it almost certainly had a religious purpose for those who built it; it may have functioned as a site for prehistoric ritual, perhaps as part of a celebration of the life cycle (birth, puberty, death) or as a way of defining the tribe's relationship with nature. Whatever its original use, the mound survives as a thought-provoking reminder of our human ancestors.

Prehistoric Art

2-1 *CATTLE, HORSES, BISON, AND DEER*, axial gallery, Lascaux cave, Dordogne, France. Paleolithic in Europe, c. 15,000–13,000 BCE. Cave painting, animals lifesize.

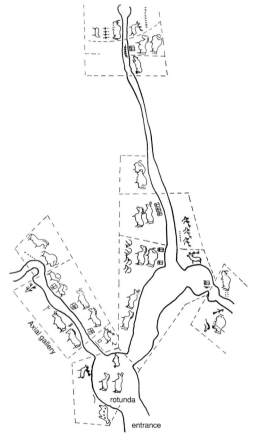

2-2 Plan of the Lascaux cave. Like most cave paintings, those at Lascaux are not all near the entrance and many are rather difficult to reach, supporting the theory that they are ritualistic rather than decorative.

In a cave at Lascaux, France, painted animals—cattle, horses, bison, and deer—roam across walls and ceilings (fig. 2-1; see also fig. 2-3). The **naturalism** of these Paleolithic images is striking, for the animals are represented by means of a lively application of line and color that reveals careful observation and a profound understanding of the animals' anatomy and movement. In some areas, the natural undulation of the cave's surface matches the painted forms to give the animals a subtle three-dimensionality, and their apparent animation would have been enhanced by the quivering flames of the lamps or torches used for illumination when they were painted. These images, created in the period known as prehistory—the time before the development of writing—present many mysteries; their function and meaning are still uncertain.

The Paleolithic Period

The origins of image making go back at least as early as the Paleolithic (c. 35,000–8000 BCE), a period characterized by the use of worked stone tools (the term *Paleolithic*, "Old Stone Age," is derived from the Greek words *palaios*, "old," and *lithos*, "stone"). Most Paleolithic people were migratory

2-3 *BULLS*, rotunda, Lascaux cave.

hunter-gatherers who journeyed in bands with twenty to thirty or even more members. Their contact with other groups may explain similarities in Paleolithic art over vast geographic areas. As they followed the migrations of animal herds, it is presumed that men hunted while women, in addition to bearing and caring for children, gathered mainstay dietary staples—plants, fruits, nuts, and fish.

The Paleolithic period overlapped the last Ice Age, when glacial ice extended to areas in southern Europe. During the warmer months, when temperatures reached 60° Fahrenheit, people probably lived in tents covered with animal skins. As cold weather approached, however, many sought protection in rock shelters, in mammoth-bone shelters, or in mouths of caves. But some caves were sought out for other purposes, which we still do not fully understand; it is in these caves that we find their remarkable paintings.

The Discovery of Paleolithic Painting

During the summer of 1879, a Spanish archaeologist was digging near the entrance of a cave near Altamira, in northern Spain. He was hoping to find artifacts like the prehistoric tools with images of animals that had, beginning in 1840, been unearthed in France. His young daughter wandered into the cave, and soon her cries were heard. When her anxious father entered, he found her excitedly pointing to images of bison—animals that had disappeared from Spain more than 12,000 years earlier—painted on the ceiling. Cave art had been discovered. But the paintings at Altamira were not be accepted as prehistoric until 1902; only after similar discoveries elsewhere would archaeologists accept the fact that such imagery and style could have been achieved by prehistoric people. Lascaux, the most impressive of these sites (see figs. 2-1–2-3), was not discovered until 1940, and new discoveries in the 1990s have continued to expand our knowledge of Paleolithic cave painting.

Paleolithic Art

Near the entrance of the cave at Lascaux, in an area known as the rotunda (fig. 2-3), a grouping of bulls was painted on the cave walls. Look at the two bulls on the right. The smaller one, the first to be painted there, is represented in a quiet pose, as if grazing; its shape is created as a solid area of color. Painted over it at some later date is the outline that defines a large bull ambling to the left. Only a few details, such as the eye and shoulder vein (a target for the hunter?), are drawn within the contour lines. Both images were created by artists sensitive to the anatomy and liveliness of these wild animals.

Sometimes Paleolithic artists drew directly on the wall with chunks of red, yellow, brown, or black minerals or earth, but more often they created **pigments** by grinding minerals and mixing them with animal fat, vegetable oil, or bone marrow. They could apply these paints to the wall using a brush made of animal hair or a frayed stick; dots of color were sometimes pressed onto the wall with their fingers. Broader areas of color could be applied by blowing

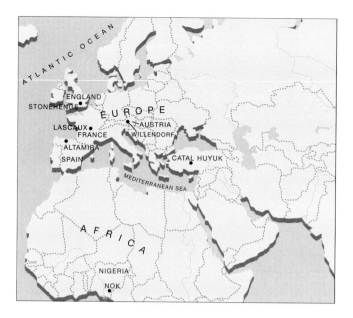

paint through a hollow reed or bone or by spitting the paint mixed with saliva against the wall. Whatever technique was employed, the skill was often remarkable, not only in the fluid execution of the forms, but also in the exacting observation and memory of the artist, who reproduced these naturalistic animal forms—some seemingly in movement—by lamp or torchlight.

In Paleolithic cave art, painted or sculpted images of animals often make use of natural protrusions in the cave wall or floor. The human imagination was evidently inspired by areas of natural relief that suggested the forms of a particular animal; by adding paint or by carving, representational images were created. The theory that art originated in such an "image by chance" was stated in the West by the fifteenth-century artist and theoretician Leon Battista Alberti. In his book *On Sculpture*, Alberti writes about the birth of sculpture:

> I believe that the arts of those who attempt to create images and likenesses . . . originated in the following way. They probably observed in a treetrunk or clod of earth and other similar inanimate objects certain outlines in which, with slight alterations, something very similar to . . . Nature was represented. They began . . . [to] take away or otherwise supply whatever seemed lacking to effect and complete the true likeness.

Alberti had not seen cave art, but recent archaeological discoveries have lent support to his supposition. Alberti's desire to explain the goal of art as representational is related to western European attitudes about the visual arts. Where the attempt to create what might be termed "inner likenesses" dominates, as in China, Japan, Africa, Polynesia, and much of South and Southeast Asia, works are judged not on observational accuracy but on the ability to convey

behavior, expression, or character.

In cave art, some animal images are shown pierced with spears or points, possibly as a practical demonstration to younger hunters. But the location of the paintings and the overpainting of images on successive occasions, perhaps hundreds or even thousands of years apart, suggest that they may have served a ritual purpose. The practice of re-creating the animals through representation may in some cases have been an attempt to capture their life spirits and thus help ensure a successful hunt. Whatever the function of the images, it seems to have been important that they be lively and identifiable by species. The rare occurrence of the human figure in Paleolithic art ranges from the representational to the schematic, but the majority are sticklike figures. Perhaps it was feared that too naturalistic a representation could capture the life spirit of the human being portrayed.

Of the sculptures that survive from the Paleolithic era, one type—involving about 150 sculptures from central Europe and Eurasia—poses unique problems of interpretation. Barely a few inches in height, these figures represent females whose breasts, abdomens, hips, and thighs have been emphasized (fig. 2-4). Traditionally these figures have been viewed as images of fertility, perhaps for use in a ritual dealing with childbearing, and the exaggeration of the parts of the body related to reproduction is sometimes assumed to be a conscious abstraction by the artist. Scholars have also suggested that these figures represented the "ideal" Ice Age woman, with the fat accumulation desirable to conceive and bear healthy children during periods of food scarcity. Other explanations propose that these figures functioned as guardian figures or as dolls. Recent scholarship has demonstrated that as a group, they display various stages in a woman's life, from youth, maturity, and pregnancy to old age. Some archaeological evidence suggests that they were both made and used by women. Our uncertainty about the function of these sculptures is directly related to the limited evidence we have about Paleolithic life and culture.

The Neolithic Period

The Ice Age that had dominated the life of Paleolithic peoples began to give way to a more moderate climate about 10,000 BCE in Europe. This warming trend increased the food supply for the hunter-gatherers. During the Mesolithic (Middle Stone Age), the transitional period that followed the Paleolithic era and lasted varying lengths of time in different parts of the world, techniques of gathering food became more efficient, and the cultivation of plants began. These developments led to the Neolithic era (New Stone Age) in about 8000 BCE in the Middle East, Africa, and Asia and about 5000 BCE in Europe. The Neolithic period is characterized by the domestication of plants and animals and the

2-4 *STATUETTE OF A WOMAN*, found at Willendorf, Austria. Paleolithic in Europe, C. 25,000–20,000 BCE. Stone, height 4⅜″. Museum of Natural History, Vienna. Statuettes such as this one have been traditionally, but improperly, known as Venuses. Other similar figures are carved from mammoth ivory or modeled in clay. The navel of this figure is a natural indentation in the stone. Whether such works were made by particular artisans on demand or by individuals for their own use is unknown.

ERICH LESSING/NALURHISTORISCHES MUSEUM, VIENNA, AUSTRIA/ART RESOURCE

development of a sedentary life-style. The bands of hunter-gatherers settled into larger, kinship-based communities, probably as a result of several factors, including defense (scenes of human conflict are found in Mesolithic rock painting), economy, changing ecology, and religion. Job specialization developed at this time. Architecture of stone, mud bricks, and timber provided more permanent homes, and the development of pottery for storing and protecting food also contributed to a stabilized environment. In western Europe, Eurasia, Korea, Japan, and parts of Southeast Asia, Neolithic peoples raised large stone monuments, as at Stonehenge (see fig. 2-9).

Neolithic Art and Architecture

A modest clay pot is evidence of one of the most consequential transitions in the development of humanity (fig. 2-5). Its design reveals its function as a container for food, and the twisted cord impressions suggest an aesthetic desire to make the object look pleasing. These designs, however, may also be

explained as an aid in firing; they allowed heat to more thoroughly enter the body of the clay. Firing at high temperatures would make the pot water-tight. Pottery was important to the stabilized living environment of the Neolithic period because fired clay vessels were essential for cooking, transporting, and storing food.

The origins of pottery vessels are uncertain, but we now know that pots, first fashioned in the Mesolithic period, became a standardized production in the Neolithic. Early clay pots may have been molded over a round stone or hand-built by coiling (building up the walls of the vessel by successively adding long ropes of clay and then smoothing the joints). The pots were usually fired in open pits over fires of wood or dung, but soon special furnaces called kilns were developed for the firing of clay objects. The patterns on some early vessels may be adapted from weaving patterns. Perhaps wet clay was used to strengthen and waterproof woven baskets, and clay vessels were then made in imitation of the clay-impregnated baskets. By approximately 3000 BCE, the **potter's wheel**, a revolving stand for forming clay vessels, was in use throughout western Asia and in parts of China; it greatly increased productivity and encouraged the development of new modes of decoration. Pottery making also signaled economic changes, for the making of clay vessels apparently became a specialized activity of craftworkers, who could trade their wares for other goods within their own community. Later, pottery was sometimes traded from one community to another.

Çatal Hüyük, a sophisticated settlement of about 10,000 people that prospered from approximately 6700 to 5700 BCE, has provided additional information about developments during the Neolithic period. Besides agriculture and animal breeding, Çatal Hüyük was also an important center for trade. One of the shrines excavated

2-5 *POT*, found in the River Thames near Hedsor, Buckinghamshire, England. Neolithic in Europe, c. 3100–2500 BCE. Terra-cotta, height 5″. The British Museum, London. Whether such works were made by particular artisans on demand or by individuals for their own use is unknown.

there contains a painting of a red bull surrounded by miniature human figures (fig. 2-6). Unlike Paleolithic paintings, which were executed directly on cave walls or ceilings, here a surface of white plaster was prepared first. If a new painting was required, another layer of plaster was laid over the previous painting to avoid the super-imposition seen in some Paleolithic painting. The bull here probably relates to a religious ritual, for it was most likely a symbol of the male deity, embodying strength and fertility; bull skulls and horns were found in some shrines. The bull at Çatal Hüyük lacks the naturalism and vitality of its Paleolithic predecessors; it is less descriptive of a particular animal and more a diagrammatic symbol. This transformation might be the result of a different function for the image of the bull, or it might also reflect an abstraction brought about by sequential repetitions of an earlier painting of a bull. This more schematic rendering of the animal and the increase in the number of human figures portrayed are characteristic of Mesolithic and Neolithic painting. But the treatment of human and animal figures varied considerably in different Neolithic communities.

In Nigeria, on the Jos Plateau, Neolithic finds have confirmed an early figurative sculpture tradition in sub-Saharan Africa. Among the most striking of these **terra-cotta** (fired clay) human and animal figures are the Nok heads (fig. 2-7), so called because of their initial discovery in the tin mines of the village of Nok. Apparently these heads were once joined to fully modeled figures. In a tradition characteristic of much of African art, the features of the heads are both emphatically naturalistic and powerfully abstracted. Whether or not such heads were meant to be an early form of portraiture is unknown. The placement and function of the Nok sculptures also is not known; it has been argued that some of them were finials to decorate

2-7 Nok culture, Africa. *HEAD*. Prehistoric in Africa, C. 600 BCE–250 CE. Fired, burnished terra-cotta, height, 13½″. The Cleveland Museum of Art, Cleveland, Ohio. Notice the decorated cap worn by the figure, and the triangular area of tattooing or scarification on the cheek.

1966, ANDREW R. AND MARTHA HOLDEN JENNINGS FUND, 1995.21

2-6 *ANIMAL HUNT*, restoration of Shrine AIII.1, Çatal Hüyük (Turkey). Neolithic in the Middle East, C. 6000 BCE.

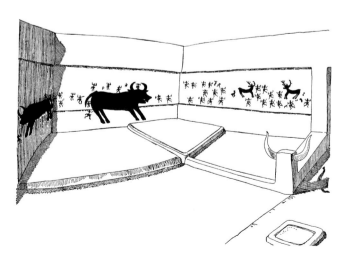

secular, civic, or sacred architecture. Other scholars stress the likelihood that such figures honored ancestors, probably in part to communicate with the spirit world of the deceased. Recent scholarship suggests that these works may have been made by women. As with other prehistoric art, more extensive archaeological investigation is needed in order to begin to interpret their use.

On the North American continent, the most conspicuous remains from the Neolithic period are giant earth mounds, such as the Great Serpent Mound in Ohio (fig. 2-8). One of a number of mounds in the form of animals, the Great Serpent Mound consists of a low embankment, nearly a quarter of a mile long, which depicts a giant ser-

2-8 Fort Ancient culture (?), North America. The Great Serpent Mound, Peebles, Adams County, Ohio. Prehistoric in the Americas, c. 1070 CE, length 1,254', average width 20', height approx. 4–5'. The "patron" would probably be the entire community, and perhaps everyone participated in the construction. The Fort Ancient culture was a Mississippian group that lived in the central Ohio Valley from c. 900 to c. 1600 CE.

pent uncoiling. Although the builders and purpose of this mound remain unknown, the Great Serpent Mound may have been associated with the prehistoric Fort Ancient Amerindian culture.

In other known Mississippi River valley mounds, which were used for the placement of sacred objects or as burial sites, a superstructure was formed over a pit that was dug in what was to be the eventual shape of the mound. Clay or earth was then piled over this super-structure to complete the mound. Most earthworks are oriented toward the east, perhaps invoking a ritual of renewal involving the rising sun.

During the Neolithic in western Europe, orientation toward the sun was also found at Stonehenge in England (fig. 2-9), an extraordinary stone monument erected during this period. Among the common types of stone monuments erected during this era for burials and ritual spaces were stones weighing several tons that were raised upright. A single large block is known as a **megalith** or as a menhir when it is placed upright. When placed in a row, menhirs become a cromlech. Such monuments are not unique to Neolithic Europe but are also found across central Asia and into East and Southeast Asia dating from the Neolithic period.

2-9 Stonehenge, Salisbury Plain, Wiltshire, England. Neolithic in Britain, C. 2750–1300 BCE. Earth markings and megaliths of gray sandstone and igneous bluestone; diameter of outer embankment about 300′, diameter of outer circle of stones 106′; original height of tallest stone approx. 24′. Stonehenge was constructed in four stages between C. 2750 and 1300 BCE. Some of the megaliths were transported as far as 190 miles, probably by being dragged on sleds and floated on rafts. They may have been raised using a series of levers. Earthen ramps were constructed to place the lintel stones. The entire community probably supported and participated in the construction.

The testimony of prehistoric monuments in Europe—remarkably later than elsewhere—is best evoked by the remains of Stonehenge, where an outermost ring of smaller stones set flush to the ground surrounds an inner ring, or cromlech. The innermost group of stones is composed of pairs of stones with lintels (trilithons); they form a horseshoe that defines an axis within the circular plan. The axis at Stonehenge is oriented, through this horseshoe and the heel stone, toward the point on the eastern horizon where the sun rises on the dawn of the summer solstice. Other stones seem to have been aligned in relation to the setting sun on the winter solstice and various phases of the moonrise.

The arrangement of the stones at Stonehenge reveals the importance of celestial events for Neolithic peoples. The emphasis on the summer solstice implies that it was the most important of these events. The scale of the complex and the difficulty of construction suggest that Stonehenge was also a setting for religious rituals, again with the summer solstice as the major festival. This union of religion with celestial events is common in early belief systems. An understanding of the regular cycles of the seasons based on celestial observation is also intimately related to the planting and cultivation of crops, and thus both ritualistic and practical needs may have been served by Stonehenge.

In the Middle Neolithic in Asia in the fourth millennium BCE, sophisticated developments were underway. In China from north to south, several cultures began to produce refined jade artifacts signaling trends toward social inequality, craft specialization, and public architecture; one of these cultures, called the Hongshan, was centered on the Liao River drainage in northeast China. A variety of ritual features were recovered there, and their size and careful spatial organization illustrates an attention to activities far beyond a daily subsistence routine (fig. 2-10).

At Dongshanzui several round and square features were excavated. The enclosing walls and an open area identified by the archaeologists as a "plaza" give this site

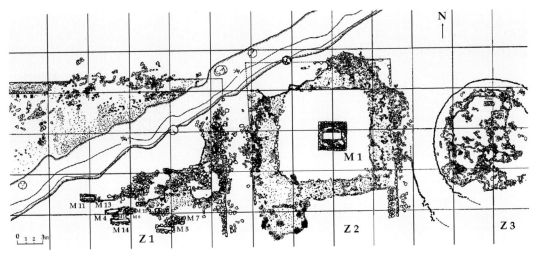

2-10 Hongshan Culture. Ritual Center. Prehistoric in China, C. 3500–3000 BCE, main square area approximately 50′ × 50′. Excavated at Dongshanzui, Lianoing Province, People's Republic of China. The imposition of geometric shapes onto the landscape and their orientation to the cardinal points of the compass, as here, are elements found in many prehistoric sites around the world. Like most prehistoric monuments, the "patron" would most likely have been the entire community.

the illusion of being a compound. While no daily or utilitarian artifacts were identified there, human figurines of clay, jade animal carvings, and painted clay cylinders were found in large numbers. A human burial accompanied one of the circular stone pavements. A large site, it probably served as a communal ritual center for, and was maintained by, surrounding villages.

Prehistoric Art and the Prehistoric Artist

Prehistoric art embraced a variety of forms and media. There were carvings in ivory and other materials, modeled clay figures, an array of tools and functional objects, such as sewing needles and spears, and even musical instruments. The earliest known flute, for example, was carved of bone about 30,000 BCE.

Study reveals that the efficiency of tools and instruments increased as civilization passed from the Paleolithic into the Neolithic era. Many of these tools had geometric designs or outlines of fish or other animals incised or carved into them.

If much prehistoric art was in fact involved with rituals, then the men and/or women who created the images may have been the individuals in the community who functioned as shamans, mediators with the spirit world. The ability to lead rituals and to create images may have been a specialized talent that was perpetuated through one or a few persons in each group. Perhaps they were recognized in their communities as having superhuman powers that would allow them to make efficacious images that could help lead the community to spiritual experience. If so, then it is possi-

ble that the images were produced in rituals observed by most or all of the community; they could thus be understood as public art in the most profound sense.

In settled Neolithic communities, the creation of pots, stone knives, and other objects was most likely bound to the developing division of labor. Artisans were often specialists; they were potters, stone carvers, leather workers, and others whose works are lost to us because their materials were perishable. This early production must have been carried on both by specialists and by families. Pottery probably began as a family activity, but as the demand increased, the most skilled potters became specialists who were allowed to concentrate on the production of pots instead of other tasks.

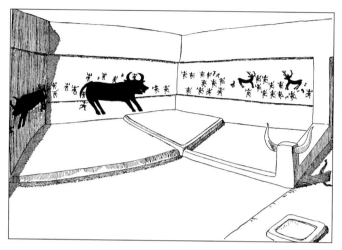

2-11 Animal Hunt, shrine from Çatal Hüyük (Turkey), c. 6000 BCE (see further information, see fig. 2-6 and pp. 27-28).

2-12 African ritual dancer, Bwa culture, 20th century (for further information, see figs. 1-13, 10-32 and 10-33).

The shrine excavated at Çatal Hüyük is abandoned and, to us, mysterious. Although the images painted on the walls clearly represent bulls and human figures and bull horns form part of the decoration, there is little evidence that would explain how these images and this room once functioned. From what we have learned about shrines in other prehistoric and historic societies, however, it seems reasonable to assume that the Çatal Hüyük shrine originally provided the setting for a ritual. Ritual function also seems logical for some other prehistoric sites, including Stonehenge in Great Britain (fig. 2-9). Without the discovery of additional evidence we cannot presume to reconstruct these prehistoric rituals, but our assumption that these sites contained and directed ritual activities is an important factor in helping us understand their original function. If we enliven one of these sites in our imaginations with human figures wearing some kind of distinctive garments and, perhaps, chanting, playing musical instruments and/or dancing, we can begin to sense some of the magic such a site once offered. Even if our imaginative reconstruction is wrong in all its details, it nonetheless can provide us with a generalized notion of how such sites once functioned and how much we lose if we don't indulge in such a re-creation. The African ritual illustrated is likewise incomplete, for our reproduction lacks the movement, the rhythmic drumming, and the location of the ritual within a Bwa village. In this case the site of the ritual is not a special structure, but the village as a whole, and the observers would include the whole community. This photograph serves as a reminder that when we see an African mask in a museum, we must go beyond understanding it as an aesthetic object by picturing it within its role as part of a social and communal ritual. Ritual is common to all human societies; it can be religious, political, civic, social, familial, domestic, or personal—or a combination of these. It is important to remember that many examples of what we today call art were created to play a role in a specific ritual, and our understanding of such works can only be enhanced if we perceive them within their original ritual context.

These paintings seem to document rituals performed by members of a cult that worshipped Bacchus, the ancient Roman god of wine and fertility. Because the cult of Bacchus was secret, these paintings provide insight into important moments in cult behavior and ritual, including flagellation and divination. What is missing are not only the transitional developments between these moments of high drama, but also the sounds and the emotions of the participants as they enacted their roles within a particular, and probably secret, space.

2-13 Ancient Roman frescoes from the Villa of the Mysteries, C. 30 BCE (for further information, see figs. 3-108 and 109 and pp. 112-14)

Although examples similar to the objects depicted here survive in museums and church treasuries, this painting shows such objects in use during the ritual of the mass. Note the rug, the cross and altarpiece on the altar, the cloth that decorates the altar front, and the book from which the priest is reading the service. Candles are commonly used in religious ritual, as seen here. The garments of the priest distinguish him from the other figures and suggest his role in the ritual enactment. What we are seeing, however, is just one moment during the mass; we miss the processions at the beginning and end, the gestures, the sound of readings and bells, and the smell of incense. Hidden behind the priest on the altar would be a chalice for wine (for an example see fig. 4-85) and a tray for bread.

2-14 MASTER OF SAINT GILES. *THE MASS OF SAINT GILES,* C. 1500 (for further information see fig. 4-6)

The many rituals that survive in our modern world include not only religious services, but also Labor Day parades, presidential inaugurations, graduation ceremonies, and, it can be argued, going to the art museum, the opera, the ballet, and other performances. Concerts by popular groups now often include scenery and lights and demand choreographed responses from the audience; the same is true of cult films, such as *The Rocky Horror Picture Show*. In a secular society, cultural rituals come to play an increasingly important role. While many cultural activities can be passive in nature, with spectators viewing a performance, installation art, as seen in this example by Ilya Kabakov, demands participation. Installation art is temporary, lasting only as long as the exhibition in which it is featured; it is then dismantled after being documented by photography. Often we can enter the work, as here, and we may even be asked to change it by moving something or taking something away with us. We thus come to play a role in a ritual designed by an artist.

2-15 ILYA KABAKOV *WE ARE LEAVING HERE FOREVER* (for further information, see fig. 10-149).

QUESTIONS

1. What repeated rituals in life are meaningful to you (a religious service, a concert by a popular group, a family event such as a holiday meal or family reunion)?

2. Do these rituals involve visual objects?

3. How would a photograph of one of your rituals be incomplete in suggesting the richness and complexity of your experience and response?

EXEKIAS *ACHILLES AND AJAX PLAYING DRAUGHTS.*   Ancient Greek container for storing wine, oil, or another liquid, made and painted about 630 BCE by Exekias with a scene of Achilles and Ajax Playing Draughts (for more information see fig. 3-59 and p. 74).   BLACK FIGURED AMPHORA, ATTIC. MUSEO GREGORIANO ETRUSCO, VATICAN MUSEUMS, VATICAN STATE. SCALA/ART RESOURCE, NY.

Ancient Art

A Brief Insight

ART CAN OFTEN BE A REMINDER OF OUR COMMON humanity, of the emotions and activities that we share. This painting, made in ancient Greece more than 2500 years ago, illustrates what is still a common activity: playing a board game. We know by the inscriptions, however, that these men are Achilles and Ajax, soldiers who fought in the Trojan war described by the poet Homer in the Iliad. With the invention of writing at the beginning of the ancient world, increased information is available about the subject and function of the works today visible at museums and archaeological sites. Greek vases such as this one were both functional and decorative. We know that they were also traded internationally during ancient times; some of the most beautiful of these works have been found in Italy, for example, in Etruscan tombs. In its skillful patterning and subtle detail, this painting demonstrates the refinement of execution and complexity of technique that characterizes much ancient art. The Greeks are, of course, only one of the diverse cultures around the globe discussed in this chapter on ancient art.

Ancient Art

The remarkable scene found on the back of this hand mirror (fig. 3-1)—a winged man huddled over an object on an altar—is unexpected, and at first it is enigmatic. But because our knowledge of ancient cultures is much greater than our understanding of prehistoric art, we know that this scene represents a practice that was common among ancient peoples. They believed widely that the interpretation of natural occurrences and objects provided omens that could predict the future. The flight patterns of birds, the position of lightning, the cracks on a bone thrown in a fire, or, as is depicted here, the "reading" of the spots on the liver of a sacrificed animal were important ways in which ancient peoples tried to understand the present and the future. The owner of this mirror would have been reassured by her faith in the power of divination to help determine decisions and choose appropriate behavior.

The increased information that characterizes the ancient world is the result of one of the most important developments in the history of humanity: the invention of writing. This historical beginning of the ancient period took place in different locations at different times. In Western terms, the ancient world is thought to end at the time of the decline of the Roman Empire, but a more positive demarcation for the end of the ancient period might be the beginning of the expansion of the living religions of Judaism, Christianity, and Buddhism, about 200 CE.

This emergence of writing in the ancient period enables us to know much about our mirror. It is the word *Calchas*, written in Etruscan script on the mirror, that identifies the diviner practicing here. The subject and style of the engraved design are drawn from the traditions of Greek mythology, which were popular with the people who created and used the mirror, who are known as Etruscans. Like many surviving ancient objects, Etruscan mirrors are most often excavated from tombs, where they were buried with their owners so that they could be used in the afterlife. And, like many objects that survive from the world's ancient cultures, this Etruscan mirror served both practical and religious purposes.

3-1 Etruscan. *CALCHAS DIVINING THE FUTURE*. c. 400 BCE. Bronze, engraved back of a mirror, diameter 6″. Vatican Museums, Rome. The highly polished bronze surface of the reverse would have functioned as a mirror; the handle is lost.

Beyond being an example of ancient art, the Etruscan mirror is also a reflection of the particular society that created and used it. The Etruscan civilization (see also pages 68–69) was a loosely bound federation of city-states in central Italy that paralleled the ancient Greek culture in time. Because the Etruscans' written language has yet to be translated, our knowledge of their beliefs and practices is largely derived from the archaeological evidence of their complex burial practices. They apparently believed in an afterlife that was a continuation of their earthly existence, and their grave goods, like this mirror, suggest that the deceased were commonly buried with virtually all the goods they used in life. The **naturalism** evident in the figure of the winged Calchas, the surrounding grapevine, the table, and the vase characterizes a style of representation often found in the ancient Western civilizations of Greece, Etruria, and Rome, but it is unlike the more abstracted styles practiced in ancient China and India.

Similar burial practices prevailed in China, where twentieth-century archaeological investigations have revealed a wealth of objects in grave settings. In clear contrast to the naturalism of the Etruscan mirror, ancient Chinese bronze vessels, like this *fang ding* (fig. 3-2), first attract our attention because of the combination of their powerful yet simple shapes with overall geometric designs. Careful examination of the *fang ding* reveals that what at first seems to be nonrepresentational patterning is based on the forms of animals, parts of animals, or combinations of parts of beasts and/or birds. The main motif is the most famous pattern used on early Chinese bronzes, the ***taotie***, or monster mask. The typical *taotie* is symmetrical, with each part repeated across the central axis; eyes, ears, an open jaw, and feet are parts of all *taotie*. Sometimes the ears resemble those of oxen or cows; other times they appear to be closer to deer. Why references to certain animals were made is not known, but the image always suggests power and presumably also shows considerable respect for the animal kingdom.

Vessels such as this one were created to hold offerings of food and wine during ancient Chinese ceremonies dedicated to the veneration of ancestors. Sets of these containers were placed on family altars and were also buried in tombs of members of the ruling and aristocratic classes. These early bronze vessels sometimes had inscribed dedications to the deceased; beginning about 1000 BCE, inscriptions refer to historic events and legal transactions and are an important source of information about ancient Chinese life. The tombs where such vessels have been found also contained bronze weapons, some of which are inlaid with semiprecious stones, as well as ceramic vessels and objects carved from jade and other stones. These luxurious objects were intended to confirm the political, military, and spiritual power of their patrons.

Anyang (see map, page 149), where this *fang ding* was excavated, was the last capital of the Shang dynasty (c. 1766– 1122 BCE); the vessel's decoration also referred to the royal clan that ruled China during this period. The *taotie* on all four sides of the *fang ding*, for example, is thought to be the particular emblem of the Shang dynasty. The animal forms that create the vessel's patterns are believed to represent mediums through which earthly beings could communicate with the spirits of their ancestors. This idea is related to ancient shamanistic religious practices in China and elsewhere in which communication with the spirit world was aided by animals thought to have special powers of transcendence. A priest or holy person, often wearing a mask or ritual dress made up of animal parts (horns, feathers, skins), was understood to change not only appearance but also state of being, to transcend this world to that of the spirits; in some cultures these beliefs and practices have continued into the twentieth century. The interrelationship between the spiritual and physical worlds demonstrated in many ancient objects studied here was an aspect that governed much of everyday life in ancient civilization.

History

As husbandry, communal living, and the other distinguishing characteristics of Neolithic culture continued to emerge, some geographical areas gradually developed a more complex, urban existence. In fertile river valleys where abundant food was available—the Tigris and Euphrates in Mesopotamia, the Nile in Egypt, the Indus and Ganges in India, and the Huang Ho and Yangtze in China—large urban civilizations developed.

The first cities became administrative and/or religious centers for the surrounding territory, and many built monu-

3-2 Chinese. *Fang ding*, from Tomb 1004, Houziazhuang, Anyang, Henan Province, China. Shang dynasty, c. 1150 BCE. Bronze, height 24½". Academia Sinica, Taipei, Taiwan, Republic of China. Commissioned by a member of the Shang imperial family.

mental works of public architecture as symbols of their new central governing authority. As these cities and their territories grew in size and population, production became specialized and a division of labor developed, often reinforcing class distinctions. In some cultures, the administrative authority of the political/military and religious classes, which often existed in a symbiotic relationship, was supported by a system of taxation or tribute.

One key factor in the development of many ancient civilizations was the emergence of systems of writing and mathematics, which evolved in response to the needs of the new urban centers. The promulgation of laws and the keeping of records helped to provide order and continuity within the new complexity of urban life. Writing and mathematics also made possible the advent of literature and science.

These aspects of a more complex and interrelated urban life-style, or civilization, were present in different measures in societies beginning about 4000 BCE, but their development was not uniform. In Mesopatamia and Egypt, they began about 4000 BCE; they date in India to about 2200 BCE and in China to 2000 BCE. In the Americas, settled life was known in the first millennium BCE. In western Europe, civilization emerged noticeably late, as is indicated by the realization that the prehistoric monument of Stonehenge (see fig. 2-9) dates from the same time as historical developments in Sumer and Egypt.

Art of Ancient Societies

What we know about ancient civilizations most frequently comes from analyses of archaeological remains, artifacts produced by skilled artisans, and literature written by ancient authors. Literary remains are virtually nonexistent (or cannot be translated) from some ancient cultures, however, and most of the artifacts from archaeological investigations provide only a limited sample of evidence. Nevertheless, most early peoples produced materials that can help us understand their attitudes about spiritual as well as political, social, and economic matters.

Monumental architecture and public works such as temples, baths, amphitheaters, and granaries reflect societies that cared about issues of public as well as spiritual health. Many large-scale ancient architectural and sculptural monuments were dedicated to a combination of political and spiritual ideas, but in China spiritual and political power were more often expressed in ritual vessels and burial practices than by architecture. Although many ancient sculptures and paintings represented deities or leaders, some examples also recorded everyday activities.

Works of ancient art and architecture were made from a wide variety of enduring media, from common limestone to the most precious metals and gems, but the "perishable" arts, such as literature, dance, and music, are largely lost to us. In many cultures they may have been as significant as their more permanent visual counterparts, and our understanding of each ancient culture is in some way partial and incomplete. Nevertheless, study of the remains that have come to light provides clues to the common as well as the distinctive traits of human behavior worldwide.

The role of the arts is clearly reflected in new types of art objects that began to be produced in China from about the sixth century BCE onward. Sometimes these objects reveal new approaches to representation as well. One, the painted silk banner from the tomb of the so-called Lady from Dai (fig. 3-3), in south China, is an important early example of polychrome painting in China. Banners of this type, which were described in literary accounts, were probably carried in funerary processions before being buried with the deceased, and this one was found draped over the innermost of four coffins. Its iconography is descriptive and its presentation naturalistic in contrast to the geometricized patterns found on earlier ritual bronzes (see fig. 3-2). What is depicted on the banner is the path of souls after death, from the underworld to the earthly realm, and then to what is known as the Land of the Immortals. The underworld, or watery realm, is represented by the fish and deities of that world of darkness. The soul is then called back to earth, where it rejoins other souls and is feasted by the family of the deceased. The detail here portrays Lady Dai as she is feasted on earth. The top of the banner describes the Land of the Immortals, where creation tales are told.

This particular banner reflects two philosophies that arose in ancient China. As in many other ancient cultures, the preoccupation with the attainment of immortality characterizes most funerary art. The native nature philosophy of China, called Daoism, guided the selection of tombs' contents and their placement in the grave. At the same time, the naturalistic depictions of human beings reflect the impact of Confucianism, with its self-reflective attitudes toward human life. In the ancient world, as this banner shows, the arts could be a sensitive barometer of changes in social and intellectual order.

The Ancient Artist

In most ancient civilizations, artists—the men and women who created what we now commonly refer to as works of art—were counted among the ranks of laborers, and their products were seen as the result of manual effort. Most works of art were the product of a group of trained artists working together in a workshop, with various individuals undertaking differing aspects of the process of production. Apprentices in these workshops learned traditional forms and techniques, which ensured a continuity of artistic and iconographic formulas.

During the ancient period most works were commissioned by patrons, but because historical records are scarce, often we do not know their names. This does not mean that we should forget their important role in defining to the artist the kind of work they needed and how they felt it should function; in this period art was still very much a collaboration between the person(s) who commissioned the work and the artist and workshop that produced the finished product.

The role of rulers in ordering works of art to bolster their regime and express their wealth and beneficence was a common one during this period. Although rulers sometimes took pride in employing artists of significant talent, these instances did not contribute greatly to the social or economic prestige of the artist. In Greece, the personality and individual style of a number of artists are documented. Although these artists were personally admired, their profession was nevertheless viewed as lacking the philosophical and educational values of the liberal arts. Later Roman patrons valued Greek works of art as well as Greek artists, but Roman artists usually remained anonymous.

In China and India, embellished objects such as cast bronzes and stone carvings were designed and produced by craftspeople who usually worked together as a team; their specialized knowledge may have given them distinctive status in their communities. The creation and construction of

3-3 Chinese. *LADY DAI WITH ATTENDANTS*, detail of T-shaped banner found in the Dai Tomb, near Changsha, Hunan Province, China. Han dynasty, c. 180 BCE. Painted silk, 6′8¾″ × 3′ at top. The central figure seen here is about 10″ tall. Historical Museum, Beijing. Commissioned by Lady Dai or her family.

the many vast ancient religious and urban complexes required cooperation, specialization, and overall coordination—prerequisites for ancient civilization. Although recognition of the role of the individual is prominent in modern attitudes about art and artistic creation, it was not an important factor in most ancient societies.

As we move into our discussion of the ancient world and later historical eras, we will adhere to a relatively strict chronological development. This means we will move, for example, from Europe to China, Japan, and then India before returning to Europe. Our goal here is to emphasize simultaneous developments around the globe.

Art Past/Art Present *The Concept of the Classical*

The terms *classic* and *classical* are widely used today, yet they have a number of different—and potentially confusing—meanings. In the context of ancient Greek art, for example, the term *Classical period* refers to a particular period within the development of Greek art (see pages 84–89); it received that name because in the nineteenth century it was seen as the high point of Greek art and culture. The term *classical*—with a small *c*—has a broader meaning, referring generally to the principles of order, harmony, balance, and clarity that are evident in much Greek and Roman art and architecture; this usage is based on the importance of these works during the Renaissance and later periods. An even broader usage is evident in the terms *classics* and *Classical World*, which are used today to refer to the study of the literary and other accomplishments of the Greeks and the Romans, and when we speak of something as a "classic," we are suggesting that it has a timeless significance.

3-4 EXEKIAS

ACHILLES AND AJAX PLAYING DRAUGHTS. Black figured amphora, Attic.
(for further information see fig. 3-59 and p. 74).

MUSEO GREGORIANO ETRUSCO, VATICAN MUSEUMS, VATICAN STATE. SCALA/ART RESOURCE, NY.

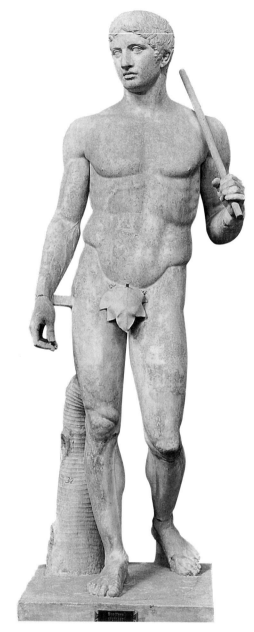

3-5 POLYKLEITOS

Ancient Greek, *DORYPHOROS*.
(for further information see fig. 3-72 and pp. 84-85).

The signature of Exekias on this ancient Greek pot and the name Polykleitos that can be associated with the sculptured figure from the same period reveal an important new attitude about art and artists. When artists sign their works or when artists are discussed as individuals in contemporary writings, both of which happened in ancient Greece, it means that the artist is being recognized in society as a individual, one whose creations are distinct from those of other artists. Polykleitos, who created the original *Doryphoros*, was literate (in some societies artists have been illiterate) and he wrote a book, *The Canon* (now lost), to record his theories about the harmonious proportions of the human body. While we have isolated examples of named artists in other ancient societies—Imhotep, the ancient Egyptian architect (see p. 51), is probably the earliest named artist in world history—the survival of the names of dozens of artists from ancient Greece is a new phenomenon. The notion of individual accomplishment and the fame it can engender is not limited to artists, and among the well-known figures of ancient Greece are Pericles the ruler-patron, Herodotus the historian, Sophocles the playwright, Plato the philosopher, and many others. The fact that artists shared in this development represents the earliest documented moment in human history when artists achieved high status and cultural significance as individual creators.

Although the ideal of the famous artist virtually disappeared from western art during the middle ages, it reappeared with the changes that characterized the Italian Renaissance. Lorenzo Ghiberti completed two sets of bronze doors for the Baptistery in Florence; both are signed and both offer a self-portrait; the portrait from the second set is illustrated here. For the second doors, Ghiberti added a pretentious inscription that praised his "marvelous art." Ghiberti also wrote one of the first autobiographies, in which he recorded his sense of his own importance and listed his works. Ghiberti was clearly concerned with personal fame, an idea that re-entered western culture at the time of the Renaissance.

The number and character of self-portraits in a society indicate attitudes about artistic status. A self-portrait can reveal an artist's personal ideas about his or her role in society. In this example, painted when it was difficult for a woman artist to be successful, Artemesia paints herself *as* painting, taking advantage of the fact that the word for "painting" in Italian is the feminine noun *la pittura*.

3-6 LORENZO GHIBERTI

SELF-PORTRAIT
(for further information see figs. 5-8, 5-32–5-33).

3-7 AREMESIA GENTILESCHI

SELF-PORTRAIT AS THE ALLEGORY OF PAINTING
(for further information on this see fig. 7-7)

In a tradition that goes back to the nineteenth century, Morimura's *Futago* exposes the artist as an individual personality; this manipulated photograph features the artist in two guises. He was the model for both the nude and the maid. His choice of a subject drawn from western art (compare Manet's *Olympia*, fig. 9-53), the depiction of the artist himself (disguised but recognizable), and the manner in which he combines costumed figures with painted backgrounds would hint to any expert that this is by Morimura. In other words, this artist has developed a personal iconography and style that reveal his presence in all his works.

3-8 MORIMURA *PORTRAIT (Futago)*
(for further information see fig. 10-154).

QUESTIONS

Individuals who live in western democratic societies are usually highly conscious of their individuality. One aspect of this is the individualized signature that we are encouraged to develop, which is so personal that it can be used as a legal test on financial documents such as checks and credit card receipts.

1. How are the design and format of your signature distinctive; are these elements intended to tell the viewer something about yourself?

2. How is your sense of individual identity conveyed to others by the manner in which you dress or by the objects with which you surround yourself?

Sumerian Art

3-9   Vessel, found at Uruk (modern Iraq). c. 3200–3000 BCE. Alabaster, height 36″. Iraq Museum, Baghdad. The reliefs celebrate the goddess of fertility through offerings of fruit.

3-10   *WORSHIPPERS AND DEITIES*, found at the Temple of Abu in Tell Asmar (modern Iraq). c. 2750 BCE. Gypsum, height of tallest figure approx. 30″. Iraq Museum, Baghdad, and The Oriental Institute, University of Chicago.

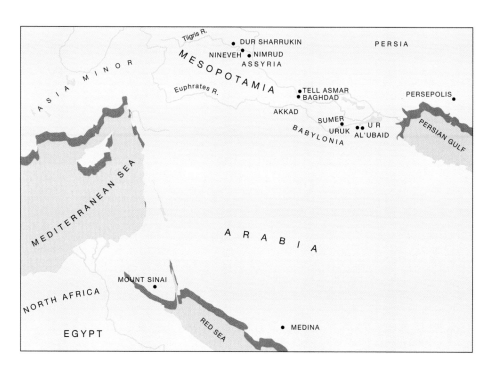

Our study of individual cultures of ancient art opens with an impressive large carved stone vessel more than 5,000 years old (fig. 3-9). Its **reliefs** of processions and offerings reveal the importance of ritual and ritual objects, while the clarity of representation that characterizes the figures and their gestures suggests the rigid repetition and controlled movements typical of a ritual intended to please or placate the god or gods that directed the community's destiny. The vessel is, however, only a reminder of what must have been a public event full of chants, music, movement, and perhaps incense.

In the Middle East, civilization began in Egypt and Mesopotamia at about the same time, between 4000 and 3000 BCE. Sumerian civilization was flourishing by about 3200 BCE, when the Sumerians brought the Tigris and Euphrates rivers under control for irrigation. At its height, the Sumerian civilization included more than a dozen loosely unified city-states fortified with walls, gates, and towers. Each had a population of between 10,000 and 50,000 inhabitants.

The Sumerians developed a flourishing agricultural economy, along with trade, commercial enterprise, and technological innovation, notably the invention of the wheel. The Sumerians also invented writing. One scholar attributes a number of "firsts" to the Sumerians, including the first schools, the first historian, the first love song, and the first library catalogue. Sumerian developments in ethics, education, and written law were influential in later cultures. Sumerian literature too was noteworthy—the epic *Gilgamesh*, which tells how a king's quest for glory and immortality ends when he discovers that even the bravest heroes must face death, has been called the first great poem in the West.

Sumerian religion was polytheistic, with more than 3,000 gods and goddesses. It was also animistic, encompassing virtually all aspects of nature. The divine, which was manifested in nature, was present in every object, and each city had a patron deity. Groups of standing Sumerian figures, found within shrines, are identified by inscriptions as representations of gods, priests, and individuals (fig. 3-10). They would have faced a cult statue of the main god or goddess, which may have had a more abstract form. The worshipers have rigidly clasped hands and large inlaid eyes. The statuettes of individuals would have served to present the life spirit of the donor in an attitude of continuous and vigilant prayer—a permanent and ever-alert substitute for the donor.

The awe-inspiring sculpture shown in figure 3-11 presumably surmounted the entrance of a temple. The central figure—a threatening lioness-headed eagle with wings spread—is Imdugud, the force that exists within a storm cloud. This frontal deity with outstretched wings is framed by symmetri-

3-11   Storm God and Two Stags, lintel from a temple at Al'Ubaid (modern Iraq), c. 2500 BCE. Copper sheets over wooden core (restored), length 7'10". The British Museum, London.

3-12   Ziggurat, UR (modern Iraq). c. 2100 BCE. Fired brick over mud-brick core, original height approx. 70', base 210 × 150'. Commissioned by several Sumerian rulers, including Ur-Nammu.

cal stags, which surely represent other natural forces, to create a composition that is commanding in its simplicity.

The most impressive structure of a Sumerian city was the **ziggurat** (from the Akkadian "pinnacle" or "mountain-top"). The Greek historian Herodotus gave us a verbal picture of a ziggurat: it dominated the city, had spiral ramps, and at its apex, a temple with a large couch and table of gold to be used by the god when he came down to earth. The best-preserved ziggurat is at Ur (fig. 3-12), the city thought to be the childhood home of the Old Testament figure Abraham. The structure was built on the ruins of earlier ziggurats by several Sumerian kings, including Ur-Nammu, who wrote one of the earliest codes of law. This ziggurat's main deity was Ur's patron, the moon god Nanna-Sin. At the New Year festi-

val, processions ascended the three staircases and proceeded through a ceremonial gateway to a temple with a cult statue and sacrificial altar.

The Sumerian mother goddess was Ninhursag, the "Woman of the Mountain," and the mountains were the source of the water that nourished their country. As human-made sacred mountains, ziggurats enabled rulers and priests to ascend to the residence of the gods to ask for divine guidance. An early Mesopotamian text refers to a ziggurat as the "bond between heaven and earth."

Ancient Egyptian Art

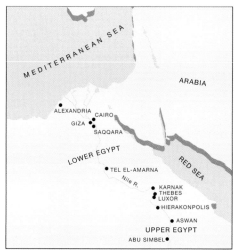

3-13 *KHAFRE*. Old Kingdom, c. 2570–2544 BCE. Diorite, height 5'6". Egyptian Museum, Cairo. This is one of a number of similar sculptures found in King Khafre's Valley Temple at Giza (see fig. 3-27), site of the three Great Pyramids from the Old Kingdom (see fig. 3-22). The temple is located along the causeway that connects Khafre's pyramid with the colossal statue of Khafre as the god Hu, later known as the Great Sphinx (see fig. 3-23). Commissioned by Khafre.

The over-lifesize figure of Khafre, shown majestically seated on his throne (fig. 3-8), expresses the absolute authority of the Egyptian ruler. The idealized body is as architectonically rigid as the throne. There may be a hint of portraiture in the face, but the effect of the figure is grand and intimidating. Khafre's head is embraced by the wings of the Egyptian sky god Horus, represented as a falcon, to symbolize the god's divine protection.

The statue, carved from an extremely hard stone and compactly composed, gives the appearance of being able to last forever. And, indeed, the solid, rigid character of this sculpture was the artist's way of meeting an extraordinary demand—that of creating a sculpture that to serve its purpose had to endure for eternity. The Egyptians believed that the *ka*, the part of the human spirit that defined a person's individuality and that would survive on earth after death, needed a physical dwelling place. The corpse of Khafre was mummified to provide this home, but if this mummy should decay or be destroyed, one or more sculptures of the deceased ruler could provide a home for the *ka*. The need to provide for the *ka*—as well as to accommodate other beliefs about death—underlay the creation of much of the surviving art and architecture from ancient Egypt.

History

The Nile River plays a central role in Egyptian geography, civilization, and art; the Greek historian Herodotus wrote that Egypt was the "gift of the river." The 900 miles of the river sustained life in an otherwise arid desert region, and Neolithic settlements along its banks date from as early as 8000 BCE. The Nile, swollen by torrential rains, flooded its banks every summer and deposited fertile silt to support agricultural development. The flanking desert protected the rich Egyptian civilization from foreign invaders. The economy prospered, and crop production included flax for the making of linen and papyrus for paper and rope.

By the fifth millennium BCE, settlements along the Nile coalesced into distinct cultural areas. The northern area was known as Lower Egypt because of the flow of the Nile from the south to the north; Upper Egypt was to the south. Around 3150 BCE,◆ a legendary king now identified with Narmer (see pages 48–49) united Upper with Lower Egypt, establishing a political state that endured almost continuously for more than 2,000 years.

This vast expanse of Egyptian history is subdivided into three major periods of political stability and cultural and economic growth known as the Old, Middle, and New Kingdoms. The Old Kingdom (c. 2700–2190 BCE) was characterized by an expansion of the central authority of the ruler, who oversaw Egypt's local administrative provinces. Its economic prosperity is evident in the funerary precinct at Giza, which includes the three largest pyramids in Egypt (see fig. 3-22). Politicial unrest led to the end of the Old Kingdom when an economic depression, perhaps caused in part by lavish expenditures, was compounded by a famine, and local governors of the provinces broke the central authority of the ruler.

◆ The dating system used is based on that established by the French Egyptologist Nicolas Grimal.

The Middle Kingdom (c. 2040–1674 BCE) saw a reunified Egypt. Sesostris III strengthened the central government, and new trade routes were established, stimulating the economy. The Middle Kingdom ended when a group of foreign settlers, the Hyksos, took advantage of a weakened government and of a new weapon—the horse-drawn chariot—to establish a separate kingdom.

Within a century, however, the Hyksos were expelled and Egypt entered a final period of cultural and economic prosperity, the New Kingdom (c. 1552–1069 BCE). The architectural remains of the New Kingdom reveal a vigorous economy, political stability, and the assured power of the ruler. This latter quality is reflected in the statue of the female ruler Hatshepsut (fig. 3-14).

There was an important, if short-lived, disruption in Egypt during the New Kingdom. The reign of Akhenaten (ruled 1352–1336 BCE), known as the Amarna period because his capital was located near present-day Tel el-Amarna, witnessed the transformation of many traditional cultural and artistic values. Akhenaten, whose name means "One Who Is Effective on Behalf of Aten," was devoted to the worship of a single god, Aten. Akhenaten mandated the worship of Aten as the official state deity, and during his reign tried to change the complex polytheistic foundation of Egyptian religion to monotheism. Viewing the relief of Akhenaten with Nefertiti and their children (fig. 3-15), we see that some of the usual conventions of Egyptian art have been retained, such as the simultaneous combination of frontal and profile views (see page 49). But the artist has imparted a new naturalism to the figures. Unlike the earlier geometric treatment of the figure, the bodies of Akhenaten and his family are given sensuous curving forms that contribute to the relaxed intimacy of the scene. The fact that Akhenaten's queen is seen on the same scale as the ruler himself reveals the equality that characterized the Amarna period; in other Egyptian

3-14 *HATSHEPSUT*. New Kingdom, c. 1478–1458 BCE. Limestone, height 6'6". The Metropolitan Museum of Art, New York. Hatshepsut, Western history's first recorded female monarch, governed Egypt from about 1478 to 1458 BCE. Commissioned by Hatshepsut.

3-15 *AKHENATEN WITH NEFERTITI AND THEIR CHILDREN*. New Kingdom, c. 1348–1336/5 BCE. Limestone, 13 × 15". Stele, Altar at Amarna, Nefertiti and Ahknaten. Staatliche Museen zu Berlin, Preussischer Kulturbesitz, 'gyptisches Museum. Commissioned by Akhenaten and/or Nefertiti.

3-16 Temple of Ramesses II, Abu Simbel. New Kingdom, c. 1279–1212 BCE. Height of sculpture approx. 67'. In 1968, these gigantic figures of sandstone, which had been cut directly into the cliff side, were disassembled and raised more than 200 feet to save them from being flooded by the lake created when the Aswan Dam was built. Originally commissioned by King Ramesses II, who dedicated the temple to himself as a god; the moving of the statutes was commissioned by the United Nations.

periods, women are usually shown as smaller in scale. The god Aten, represented as the disc of the sun with rays terminating in human hands, presides over this domestic scene. Akhenaten was neglectful of foreign affairs, and his rule weakened Egypt. After the Amarna period, the rigid conventions of older ways returned. Many of the images of Akhenaten were destroyed, and an attempt was made to, quite literally, erase him from history. Subsequent rulers established an authoritative continuity with their predecessors. The statues of Ramesses II (ruled 1279–1212 BCE) that flank the entrance to his mortuary temple at Abu Simbel (fig. 3-16) recall the formal rigidity of the Old Kingdom statue of Khafre. But the colossal size of these sculptures reveals the grandeur typical of the New Kingdom. The Ramesses dynasty, which lasted until 1085 BCE, was the last significant dynastic family of the New Kingdom. During the following centuries, the power and splendor of the empire abated, and in 332 BCE Egypt was conquered by Alexander the Great.

Religion

Egyptian religion was a complex faith that included polytheism, magic, politics, and a steadfast belief in an afterlife. Wonder at the forces of nature and the spirit of animals led to the development of polytheism, with local gods or goddesses being affirmed in different communities. Early depictions of these deities include representations as animals, such as Horus (the sky god as a falcon), or as animal-headed humans, such as Anubis (a jackal-headed god associated with mummification).

For the Egyptians, whom Herodotus described as "religious to excess," magic was an important part of their religion. Believing that the spiritual world governed all aspects of life, the Egyptians even accompanied the commonplace practice of taking medicine with ritualistic incantations. Religion was also bound to politics. The ruler was viewed as a god who had absolute authority in secular and religious matters. During some reigns the god or goddess worshiped by the ruler would become the center of the

state religion and be imposed over local religious practices.

Extensive religious ritual accompanied the belief in an afterlife, and the most important entity of the human soul to be served in the afterlife was the *ka*. The Egyptians believed that after death the *ka* would require an earthly abode. Thus, the body of the deceased should be preserved through mummification (the word *mummy* is from the Arabic *mumiya*, meaning "bitumen"—a petroleum substance mistakenly believed to have been used in mummification), and statues of the deceased should also be provided in case of the accidental loss of the mummy. The process of mummification, strictly governed by religious ritual, took seventy days. The lungs, stomach, liver, and intestines were removed to separate containers called canopic jars, while the body was treated with chemical solutions to draw out moisture before being wrapped in as many as twenty layers of linen. The world of the afterlife was associated with the sunset and, therefore, the west; a song inscribed on an early tomb reveals the reward for the *ka*:

> The span of earthly things is a dream, but a fair welcome is given him who has reached the West.

Art of Ancient Egypt

Providing service to the *ka* was a mainstay of artistic production in Egypt. Tomb walls were sculpted and/or painted with everyday scenes (see figs. 3-33, 3-34) to recreate a pleasant environment, and small servant figures were provided to perform common duties. Woodworkers constructed and artists decorated a series of coffins, which fit inside each other. A stone coffin is called a **sarcophagus** from the Greek *sarkophagos*, "flesh-eating stone").

In addition to the artistic preparations made especially for the use of the *ka* in the afterlife, jewelry and items of

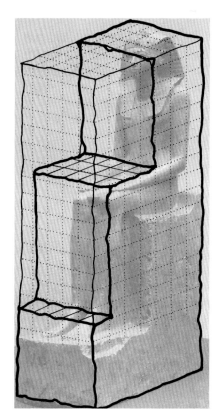

3-17 Throne of King Tutankhamen. New Kingdom, c. 1336/5–1327 BCE. Gold, silver, colored glass paste, glazed ceramic, and inlaid calcite, height 45″. Egyptian Museum, Cairo. The top of the throne's footstool, a portion of which is glimpsed in the foreground, has a representation of defeated enemies. Tutankhamen, whom we popularly know as King Tut, was a ruler of relatively minor importance in Egyptian history. He followed Akhenaten's son and died at an early age, perhaps violently. Tutankhamen's fame is primarily due to the fact that his tomb furnishings were largely intact when discovered by the British archaeologist Howard Carter in 1922. Commissioned by Tutankhamen.

3-18 Diagram of the ancient Egyptian proportional system as reconstructed for the statue of *HATSHEPSUT* (see fig. 3-14). Egyptian workshops used a strict proportional scheme that allowed the efficient execution of painted and sculpted figures. A squared grid, drawn on the wall or on three sides of a block of stone, was used to demarcate the height and width of each figure's shoulders, waist, feet, and other body parts, following a standard formula. When applied to a block of stone, this system allowed unnecessary areas of the block to be chiseled away by unskilled assistants.

personal use were placed in the tomb. The throne of King Tutankhamen (fig. 3-17) displays the conspicuous wealth of the New Kingdom, while the relaxed figurative poses demonstrate influence from the Amarna period.

Although much of preserved Egyptian art relates to funerary practices, the desire to provide the *ka* with the means for enjoying life as it was experienced before death meant that this art also is an important record of everyday experience. Tomb paintings, for example, document the labor of the lower classes as well as festive occasions for the nobility, but even commonplace scenes adhere to time-honored conventions of artistic practice. The strict grid of proportions followed (fig. 3-18) and the combination of frontal with profile views (see fig. 3-20) create a static figure typical of Egyptian art.

The relatively unchanging nature of Egyptian artistic practices reveals the stability of its civilization, yet artists were not slaves to formulas. Akhenaten caused a religious, political, and artistic revolution, but even before him, other currents brought degrees of diversity and vitality to Egyptian art, as is seen in the portrait bust of Ankhaf (fig. 3-19). The bust of Ankhaf displays a subtle and individualized surface anatomy and reveals an attentive sense of life.

The Egyptian Artist

In ancient Egypt, as in most early civilizations, no distinction was drawn between the artists who designed sculptures and paintings and the skilled laborers in workshops who brought their concepts into being. Artists labored as members of the lower classes. The exception was the architect, who enjoyed the status of a court official. Imhotep, the first recorded artist of Western history, designed the Old Kingdom funerary complex at Saqqara (see fig. 3-26). His fame was so great that by the New Kingdom he was deified as the god of learning and medicine.

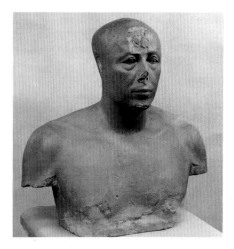

3-19 *ANKHAF*. Old Kingdom, c. 2570–2544 BCE. Painted limestone, partially molded in plaster, height 22″. Harvard–MFA Expedition, Courtesy, Museum of Fine Arts, Boston. This bust of Ankhaf, an official under Khafre buried at Giza, was found in his tomb. Commissioned by Ankhaf.

Ancient Egyptian Art:
The Palette of Narmer

3-20 *VOTIVE PALETTE OF KING NARMER* (SIDE A). Old Kingdom, c. 3150–3125 BCE. Slate, height 25″. Egyptian Museum, Cairo. The shieldlike shape and shallow indentation reveal that this is an enlarged, ceremonial version of an everyday object, a palette used for the grinding of pigments for eye shadow. This palette was found at Hierakonpolis, a sacred city of prehistoric Egypt. Probably commissioned by Narmer.

3-21 *VOTIVE PALETTE OF KING NARMER* (SIDE B).

In the past, important historical developments often led to the creation of objects that commemorated or interpreted the event. One of the earliest surviving works of Egyptian art, the *Votive Palette of King Narmer*, was apparently created to mark the unification of Egypt. Narmer, who has been identified with Menes, the first king of the first Egyptian dynasty, appears three times. As the largest figure on side A (fig. 3-20), he wears the crown of Upper Egypt and brings under his control a figure who probably represents Lower Egypt. At the bottom of side A are two more defeated antagonists and small symbols of a fortified city and a gazelle trap that suggest victories in the city and countryside.

The nearby human-headed figure with six papyrus blossoms, being held captive by the god Horus (shown as a falcon), almost certainly refers to the submission of Lower Egypt to Upper Egypt. The use of symbols to represent complex ideas is an innovation that points to the later development of Egyptian hieroglyphs, in which figures or pictures signify words or sounds.

At the bottom of side B (fig. 3-21), Narmer himself appears as a symbol—a horned bull, victorious over an enemy and the enemy's fortified city. Near the top of side B, Narmer, wearing the crown of Lower Egypt and accompanied by a processional retinue, views the decapitated corpses of enemies, their heads between their legs. The central symbol at the top of both sides represents Narmer's name and his palace. It is flanked by horned animals representing the sky mother, Hathor, to whose shrine the palette was probably offered. In addition to Narmer's assumption of the two crowns, the union of Egypt is also suggested by the joining of two fantastic, long-necked lionesses on side B, their serpentine necks intertwined to form the shallow indentation that refers to the function of the object as a palette.

A number of the most important surviving works of art from predynastic Egypt are similar palettes or fragments of palettes. The decoration is usually about political subjects. Apparently the larger versions of

these palettes were displayed as **votives** (gifts made to a god or goddess), and they may also have been used to grind and mix the pigments that adorned the eyes of the cult statue of the deity. The *Votive Palette of King Narmer* probably had several functions: as an object to be used in a religious ritual; as a votive offering to the god or goddess (most likely Hathor); and as a commemoration of the military and territorial victories of Narmer. Such a union of political statement with religious ritual is typical of Egyptian art and culture.

Narmer is, in every case, represented as unnaturally larger than his subordinates and enemies through the use of hierarchical scale, which is common in Egyptian religious and political art. Narmer's large scale and the lucid design make the meaning of the palette more easily comprehensible. The human figures are presented in a design that clarifies the parts and their interrelationships—legs, head, and arms are seen in strict profile, while the torso and the eye are seen directly from the front. These renderings demonstrate the same clarity seen in the three-dimensional figure of Khafre (see fig. 3-13), but here they are united and suppressed into what is essentially a two-dimensional medium: **low relief** (see box). As unrealistic as this representation is, it is easily read and it emphasizes strength. This style of representing the figure would continue in Egyptian art for more than 3,000 years.

Technique *Relief Sculpture*

The technique of sculpting figures or forms that are part of (or, less commonly, attached to) a background is known as **relief sculpture**. Because the figures are very flattened, the style of carving in the *Narmer* palette is known as **low relief**, or **bas-relief**. There is no differentiation in color, but light hitting the delicately varied levels of relief allows us to read the forms. This technique, difficult to perfect, was also practiced by later artists. The Egyptians also excelled at an unusual type of low relief known as **sunken relief**, in which the figures are recessed into the surface (see fig. 3-15). **High relief** is relief sculpture with forms that project substantially from their background (see fig. 3-87). In Egypt, as well as in later cultures, relief sculpture often has color added to support its design (see fig. 3-33).

The Egyptian Pyramids

3-22 Great Pyramids at Giza. Old Kingdom, c. 2601–2515 BCE. Limestone and granite, original height of pyramid of Khufu 480′, length of each side at base 755′. The three pyramids, from the left, were built by the Egyptian kings Menkaure (see fig. 1-2), Khafre (see fig. 3-13), and Khufu. The Great Pyramids were viewed as architectural wonders even in the ancient world; they are, in fact, the only surviving work from the list of "Seven Wonders of the World" compiled in antiquity. Constructed as royal tombs, they are the best known of more than eighty pyramids built in ancient Egypt. The pyramid of Khafre is the only one that preserves any of its outer dressed stone exterior. Many stones were taken from the site to build medieval and modern Cairo. Commissioned by Kings Menkaure, Khafre, and Khufu.

3-23 King Khafre as the god Hu, later known as the "Great Sphinx," Giza. Old Kingdom, c. 2570– 2544 BCE. Sandstone, height approx. 65′. Carved from sandstone on this site, the sphinx, with the pyramid of Khafre in the background, is part of the funerary precinct of Khafre, and its face bears his features, probably as Hu, the reincarnation of the sun god Re. The name *sphinx*, meaning stranger or mysterious person, was first used by the ancient Greeks; we do not know what name the Egyptians gave this monument. Commissioned by Khafre.

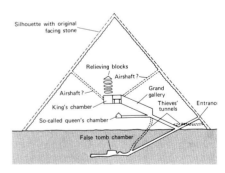

3-24 Section of the Great Pyramid of Khufu, Giza.

Associating the transition to the afterlife with the sunset, the pyramids—the burial places of the rulers—were located on the western side of the Nile River (figs. 3-22,

3-23, 3-24). Today the desert area around the pyramids reveals little of the complex of funerary temples (see fig. 3-27) and other grave sites that once formed a huge necropolis ("city of the dead").

Graves in predynastic Egypt were usually shallow pits marked with mounds of sand near the edge of the desert. By about 2900 BCE, nobles were buried in underground chambers marked by mud-brick structures called **mastabas** (from the Arabic *mastabah*, "bench") with **battered** (sloped) **walls** (fig. 3-25). Mastabas contained offerings to the *ka* and chambers for a statue of the deceased.

About 2681 BCE, during the Old Kingdom, King Zoser commissioned Imhotep to design and construct a funerary complex at Saqqara (fig. 3-26). The architectural climax was a large step pyramid, a solid structure that suggests the superimposition of progressively smaller mastabas.

It is not completely clear why the pyramidal form was used in this funer-

ary context. One theory suggests that it is derived from the cult image of the sun god Re, a pyramidal stone that represented the rays of the sun descending to earth. A widely accepted view is that the pyramid fulfilled both practical and spiritual needs by offering a secure abode for the *ka* and by assisting the ruler's spirit in its ascent to heaven. A text found inside a pyramid states:

I have trodden these rays as ramps under my feet where I mount up to my mother Uraeus on the brow of Re.

The later complex at Giza was constructed between 2601 and 2515 BCE, and each pyramid took more than twenty years to build. Surveyors began the laborious and exacting process by observing a star in the northern sky, then orienting the square base so that each edge faced a cardinal direction—north, south, east, or west. Labor was supplied not by slaves but by the Egyptian people themselves, who gave their time during the three months of the summer flood, when their farmland was under water; records reveal that they were paid with food and drink. The high waters of the Nile facilitated the transport of granite from quarries miles away from Giza, but much of the limestone used was quarried at the site, perhaps around the statue of the Great Sphinx. The stone blocks were transported, probably on a type of sled, up inclined ramps, and the capstone was polished or gilded to catch the first and last of the sun's rays. False passages were constructed to discourage grave robbers, but almost all Egyptian royal tombs were plundered in ancient times.

3-25 Reconstruction with section of mastabas. Old Kingdom.

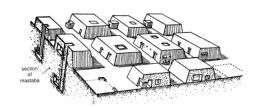

3-26 Model of the funerary district of Zoser, Saqqara. Old Kingdom, c. 2681–2662 BCE. Height of original stepped pyramid approx. 200'. The complex at Saqqara represents the earliest-known use of cut stone for architecture, and its architect, Imhotep, is the earliest-known named artist in world history. Commissioned by King Zoser.

The Egyptian Temple

3-27 Valley Temple of Khafre, Giza. Old Kingdom, c. 2570–2544 BCE. Limestone and red granite. Post-and-lintel construction is exemplified in this temple, and it was here that twenty-three portrait statues of Khafre, including figure 3-13, were originally housed. The roof structure has collapsed. A causeway led from the temple to the pyramid of Khafre (see fig. 3-22), some 600 yards farther from the Nile. Commissioned by Khafre.

This Old Kingdom temple (fig. 3-27), composed of spaces defined by large, square columns, is quite simple, but over time the Egyptian temple evolved in response to the rituals enacted there (see figs. 3-27–3-32). Beginning with a long row of sphinxes flanking the avenue to the entrance, the organization of a New Kingdom temple is strictly axial, relating to the progress of the king's procession, and is characterized by **bilateral symmetry** (the forms are identical on both sides of the central axis). As the procession advanced, the king passed through a clear sequence of architectural spaces, beginning with the open road flanked by sphinxes, then moving into the sacred precinct through the pylon, whose broad sloping towers and flag-poles flank the central doorway. He then proceeded into one or more **colonnaded** courtyards open to the sky and framed on two or three sides by rows of **columns**. Next he entered a large room filled with columns known as the **hypostyle** hall (see fig. 3-30). The only light here filtered down from the **clerestory**, the raised area along the central axis, where there are long vertical openings (for later examples of clerestories, see figures 4-18, 4-92). The final sequence of rooms, all fully enclosed, became progressively smaller, lower, and darker until the priest and/or the king entered the most sacred chamber which contained the cult statue. The Temple at Luxor (see fig. 3-28) was exceptional, for there were two sacred chambers; the one at the very back, which was entered directly from the exterior wall, was where the sacred boat of Amun was placed after carrying the king across the Nile from Karnak.

The enormous New Kingdom temples at Karnak and Luxor (see figs. 3-28, 3-30) are among the largest religious structures ever built. They played an important role in Egyptian religion and politics, especially the annual festival of Opet, a twenty-four-day celebration of the New Year, when the Nile was at full flood. At this time, the king and his family came to Karnak to participate in the procession that accompanied the golden statue of Amun, the chief Egyptian deity, to the shrine of his wife (the goddess Mut) and son (Khonsu, the moon god) at Luxor. The king, who was traditionally identified with Amun, emerged from the **pylon**, or entrance gate, at dawn, so that he

3-28 Courtyard built by Amenhotep III, Great Temple of Amun-Mut-Khonsu, Luxor. New Kingdom, c. 1390–1352 BCE. View of hypostyle hall from courtyard. The temple is dedicated to Amun, the sun god; his consort, Mut; and Khonsu, the moon god. Commissioned by Amenhotep III.

was framed by the pylon's flanking towers while the sun rose behind him (fig. 3-29). Such ritual reinforced his identification with the sun god.

The hierarchical and exclusive quality of Egyptian society is expressed in these temples, for only a select few could follow the king into the courtyard, and fewer yet into the hypostyle hall. The enormous walls that enclose the sacred enclosure (more than a mile long at Karnak) excluded the multitudes and reminded them of their inferior social, political, and religious status, as did the overwhelming scale of the structures themselves.

Temple architecture stressed stability, weight, monumentality, and durability. These temples were meant to endure, and Amenhotep III (ruled 1390–1352 BCE) described a temple he had built at Thebes as

. . . an eternal, everlasting fortress of fine white sandstone, wrought with gold throughout; it is made very wide and large, and established forever.

The massive stone walls of Egyptian temples were solid, without windows; weight and stability were further expressed by the heavy cornices and battered walls of the pylon. Virtually all surfaces were covered with low or sunken relief carvings that emphasize the mass and weight of the stone. The hypostyle hall was a veritable forest of huge fat columns (at Karnak, the largest were 69 feet tall and 12 feet in diameter, with a circumference of almost 33 feet; see fig. 3-30), and the effect was claustrophobic and intimidating. The solidity and austerity of these Egyptian temples directly reflect the stable and controlled civilization that created them.

3-29 Reconstruction drawing of a typical pylon gate, showing the rising sun emerging above the central doorway at dawn.

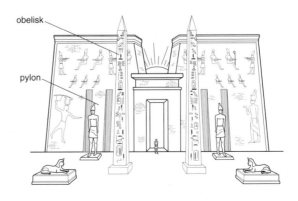

3-30 Model of central section, hypostyle hall, Temple of Amun, Karnak. New Kingdom, c. 1294–1212 BCE. The Metropolitan Museum of Art, New York. The columns and capitals of this hypostyle are so large that dozens of people could stand on top of one of the capitals, and it takes at least eight people, holding hands, to span the circumference of a column near the base.

THE METROPOLITAN MUSEUM OF ART, LEVI HALE WILLARD, BEQUEST, PURCHASE 1890

The type of construction used for Egyptian colonnaded court-yards and hypostyle halls (see figs. 3-28, 3-30) is known as **post and lintel**, the post being the vertical supporting member, usually a cylindrical column, and the lintel being the horizontal member, often known as the **entablature** (see fig. 3-27). The only simpler types of construction are the wall and the mound. The engineering dynamics of post and lintel are straightforward—the weight of the lintel presses downward on the post, which must be strong enough to support the lintel's weight. If the lintel is too long or lacks sufficient **tensile strength** (longitudinal strength sufficient to support itself without breaking), it may collapse in the middle or shear and break where it meets the post. When columns are used, they are usually decorated, espe-cially at the top, or **capital**. In Egypt, the column and capital may resemble greatly enlarged papyrus, date palms, or bundled reeds (see figs. 3-28, 3-30)—forms that may derive from the use of bundled natural elements in early Egyptian architecture. Although the post-and-lintel system is simple, the rhythmic placement of the columns and the relationship of vertical to horizontal allow many architectural and aesthetic variations.

Egyptian builders were restricted by the available materials, which included vast amounts of stone but virtually no wood. The dense and brittle nature of the local stone kept the lintels short and the posts heavy and close together. The hypostyle hall was virtually the only large enclosed space that could be constructed.

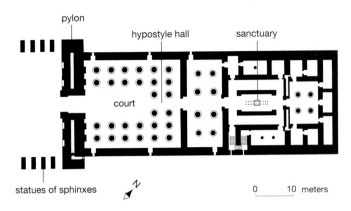

pylon

hypostyle hall   sanctuary

court

statues of sphinxes

0   10 meters

3-31 Plan of the Temple of Khonsu, Karnak. New Kingdom, c. 1186–1154 BCE. Statistics for a much larger temple precinct at Karnak reveal the tremendous scale of some of these projects; The nearby Temple of Amun, for example, is 1,220 feet long and its sacred enclosure encompasses 62,000 acres.

The drawings of architecture in this book are meant to aid in your understanding of principles of design and construction. Some of these diagrams reveal how a building would look if it were sliced through, as in a **plan** (or **ground plan**; figs. 1-8, 3-31), which shows the building as if cut off approximately one foot above the floor level. In the plan, solid lines are structure, with open-ings indicating doors and windows; lighter lines indicate floor patterns; dotted or light lines are used to indicate the patterns of the ceiling (see fig. 4-90). A **cross section** shows the build-ing sliced through from side to side (see figs. 3-42, 4-21), while a **longitudinal section** slices the building from front to back (fig. 3-32). An **elevation** shows the exterior surfaces and their decoration diagrammatically, not as the human eye would see them (see figs. 3-89, 6-34). A relatively recent kind of diagram is the **isometric projection**, which offers a view of the exterior and/or interior from a specific point of view in (figs. 3-32 and 3-94) the projection is cutaway and combined with a ground plan and longitudinal section. Because of the artificial and two-dimensional nature of most of these dia-grams, an understanding of any building usually requires an examination of several diagrams.

Today, buildings are erected using architect's diagrams simi-lar to those discussed, but we still do not know much about the use of drawings by architects, engineers, and construction crews in the past. The earliest surviving examples date from the Gothic period, in the thirteenth century. In some earlier periods, archi-tects and engineers apparently laid out the plan of the building full scale on the ground, and then used pegs and string or vines in order to mark the outline of the structure.

3-32 Isometric projection with plan and longitudinal section of the Temple of Khonsu. Originally commissioned by Ramesses III and Ramesses IV, with later additions.

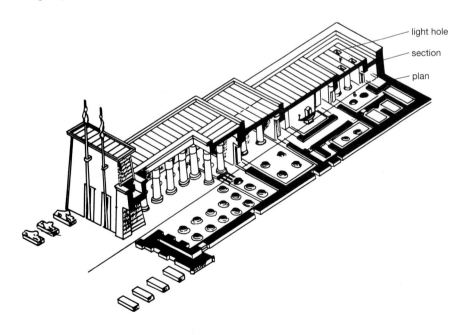

light hole

section

plan

Egyptian Tomb Paintings and Painted Reliefs

3-33 *TI WATCHING A HIPPOPOTAMUS HUNT*, in the Tomb of Ti, Saqqara. Old Kingdom, c. 2510–2460 BCE. Painted limestone, height approx. 46″. On the wall opposite this painted relief are three small openings intended to allow three lifesize statues of Ti to gaze permanently at this hunting scene. Commissioned by Ti, overseer of the Sun Temples of Kings Neferikare and Nyuserre.

The walls of Egyptian tombs were decorated with painted, low-relief sculptures or with paintings on plaster applied over the walls. The requirement that tomb decoration preserve pleasant everyday life for the delight of the *ka* throughout eternity means that these paintings tell us a great deal about ancient Egyptian life and customs and have a broad human interest and appeal.

The largest single scene among the hundreds of painted reliefs in the Old Kingdom tomb of a government official named Ti depicts a hippopotamus hunt, with Ti standing in the boat (fig. 3-33). The emphasis on this particular scene suggests that it has a deep significance, and the hunt here probably refers not only to the general concept of victory but also specifically to Ti's victory over death. Ti is represented in the typical Egyptian style, and the composition emphasizes clarity and repeated patterns. The Egyptian artist had to work within the strict limitations imposed by the function of the work; invention was not prized, and a new viewpoint or treatment might render the object or experience unavailable to the *ka* in the afterlife. This approach, which is not naturalistic, uses only frontal and profile viewpoints, the characteristic points of view in Egyptian art.

The zigzag pattern that represents the water of the Nile is based on the hieroglyph for water, which is also the hieroglyph for the Nile itself; in Egypt the Nile was water, and water was the Nile. The parallel lines that create a foil for the organic shapes of the figures and animals indicate a setting deep in the marshes, for these are the stems of the same reeds that burst into leaf and blossom near the top of the relief. In this upper area, predators stalk birds, creating striking patterns against the geometric stalks as well as a metaphor for the hunt taking place below.

Pond in a Garden (fig. 3-34) from a New Kingdom tomb, with its rectangular pool with ducks, fish, and lotus blossoms surrounded on all sides by flowering and fruit-bearing trees, provides a demonstration of the Egyptian approach to representation. Completeness and clarity were demanded of the Egyptian painter, for anything not clearly included in the tomb painting would not be available to the *ka* in the afterlife. This explains why each object has to be shown in its most easily recognized view—the pond is represented as if seen from above, while everything else is in profile. The relationships among the objects in

3-34 Pond in a Garden, fragment from the Tomb of Nebamun, Thebes. New Kingdom, c. 1400 BCE. Paint on plaster wall, 24 × 28″. The British Museum, London. Commissioned by Nebamun, "scribe and counter of grain."

reality are also made clear in the representation: fish, ducks, and lotus are seen as within the pool, while the trees surround it. The trees are seen right side up and sideways, but not upside down—those at the bottom side of the pool are upright. Despite the lack of a consistent viewpoint for the scene and the flatness with which each object is rendered, we can still easily recognize that this is, indeed, a pond in a garden.

Technique *Figure-Ground Relationships*

The distinct contrast that can be noted between forms and background in most works of art is called the **figure-ground relationship**. In *Ti Watching a Hippopotamus Hunt*, for example, we read the humans and the cat, birds, fish, foliage, and boat as "positive" elements—figures—isolated against "negative" backgrounds—the ground—behind them. A similar effect can be noted when works of sculpture and architecture are isolated and stand out against or within their surroundings. In analyses of works of art, the positive-negative, figure-ground relationship is always an important component. In some modern works, artists have achieved visual ambiguity by allowing the positive and negative forms to assume virtually equal importance in the composition.

The Indus Valley Civilization

3-35 Reconstruction of the Great Bath, granary, and houses, Mohenjo-Daro, Indus Valley (modern Pakistan). c. 2100–1750 BCE. Of the buildings excavated at Mohenjo-Daro, the most spectacular is the Great Bath, used for ritual bathing, which measures 40 by 30 feet and was sunk about 8 feet below the surface of the surrounding pavement. It was built from meticulously laid bricks set in gypsum plaster over a waterproof bitumen layer. A nearby well provided the water, which could be emptied through a massive drain. Excavation of Mohenjo-Daro, which is located northeast of present-day Karachi, Pakistan, was begun on a grand scale between 1922 and 1927 under John Marshall of the Archaeological Survey of India; since 1931, a number of other teams have worked at the site. Evidence suggests that Mohenjo-Daro, like other Indus Valley sites, was occupied from about 2700 to 1500 BCE; the stratified settlement debris investigated by archaeologists was 100 feet deep. The ancient center rises 40 feet above the surrounding plain; the highest point is formed by an artificial platform of mud and mud bricks.

At about the same time as the Old Kingdom in Egypt and Neolithic building activity at Stonehenge, the first civilization in South Asia arose at a group of sites in the Indus River Valley, in modern-day Pakistan and India (see map, page 149). Many of these Indus Valley civilization sites are divided into two major areas—a lower, usually eastern, section of domestic buildings, craft workshops, and private shrines and an elevated section in the west containing public ritual buildings. A number of similarities among these sites—consis-

tent use of a writing system, modular sizes of baked brick for houses and public buildings, settlement layouts, pottery styles, systems of weights and measures—suggest that a central administration controlled production and distribution of goods and services. Such a body probably controlled trade within the Indus Valley and outside at least as far as Mesopotamia. There is evidence that they imported raw materials, exotic stones, gold, copper, and tin, but few manufactured or prestige goods from outside have been found.

What is surprising is that the Indus Valley sites lack royal burials, great funerary structures, monumental art, and other symbols of prestige and authority. The absence of larger, more ornate houses and exotic luxury goods suggests that there was no wealthy class. So it would seem that the usual model of a kingdom or empire, headed by a priest-king and supported by a royal clan holding authority through dynastic succession, did not apply here, as it did in the ancient palace-temple societies of Egypt, Mesopotamia, China, and Mesoamerica. In addition, there is little evidence of the military influence consistently found in other ancient empires. The raised platforms seem to define social and functional space and were not intended to provide an area to defend citizens from external enemies.

Mohenjo-Daro (fig. 3-35) is an important Indus Valley site because of the age, scale, and richness of the finds, including numerous stone seals, the majority of which are engraved with an animal and a short inscription. That the most frequently represented animal is a profile view of a bull, the beast of burden revered in later Hindu India, suggests that there may be some connection between these early finds and later Indian religious developments. A similar conclusion is suggested by our example, with its depiction of a frontal male figure wearing buffalo horns and surrounded by animals (fig. 3-36). He is depicted ithyphallic (he is shown with an erect phallus) and is seated in the position of yogic meditation. The writing on the seal still defies translation, although nearly 4,000 other inscriptions have been identified. This exceptional figure may be an early rendering of the Hindu god **Siva**, the "Lord of the Animals," thought to have procreative powers, or it may be a representation of a chief with concerns for appeasing the wild kingdom. We do know that seals were used for administrative purposes, such as sealing bales of merchandise or marking storage boxes, and most inscriptions seem to record the names and administrative titles of their users.

Excavators have also found, inside many houses, a large number of small, elaborately dressed terra-cotta figures of women. These statuettes are thought to be part of private devotion to the powers of fertility, and, in fact, emphasis on the female procreative powers continues today in both Hindu and Buddhist iconography in Asia.

The lower, eastern part of Mohenjo-Daro had a grid of streets and lanes roughly oriented north-south and east-west, with blocks of houses entered

| c. 2100–1750 BCE | **Great Bath, granary, and houses, Mohenjo-Daro** |
| c. 2000 BCE | Systematic astronomy in Egypt, Babylon, India, and China |

3-36   Seal with Ithyphallic Figure, found at Mohenjo-Daro, Indus Valley (modern Pakistan). c. 2100–1750 BCE. White steatite, height 1⅜". National Museum, New Delhi, India. The seals found at Mohenjo-Daro are rectangular or square, unlike the cylindrical seals found in ancient Mesopotamian centers.

through narrow lanes. Although the houses varied in size, they all had rooms arranged around a central courtyard, usually with a well in a small room off the court and a bath and latrine draining through the wall into either a soak pit or a covered drain under the street surface. Some two-story houses had brick stairs and tubular drainpipes extending from the upper story. Plumbing installations for the provision of water, bathrooms with polished brick floors, and the exterior drains found here are without parallel in other early historic societies.

Although there are public buildings on the raised platform that forms the highest part of the site, including a large granary and the Great Bath, no large community temple has so far

been located at Mohenjo-Daro. The entire raised platform may have served as a ritual center, for at related sites, fire altars have been identified in the raised platform areas, as well as in private houses. The speculation about fire and water in ritual activity in the Indus Valley civilization is linked to their central role in the two major religions that emerged later in that region: Vedic Hinduism and Zoroastrianism.

The reason for the collapse of the Indus Valley civilization is not fully known, but it is often explained as a result of natural events such as earthquakes, which changed the course of the rivers, causing the population to desert its settlements.

Aegean Art:
Minoan and Mycenaean

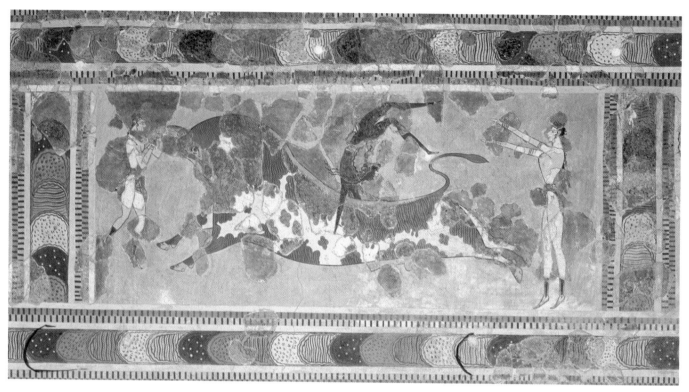

3-37   Minoan. *BULL LEAPING*, from the palace at Knossos, Crete. c. 1750–1450 BCE. Fresco, height approx. 32″ including borders. Archaeological Museum, Heraklion, Crete. The Greek myth of Theseus and the Minotaur may have been based on the bull-leaping ritual demonstrated here and the labyrinthine structure of the palace at Knossos (see fig. 3-39). This fresco was not complete when it was found, and the fragments have been pieced together and the missing areas painted in; this gives the impression that the painting is better preserved than it is. There is no guarantee that the restored areas are completely accurate.

BULL-LEAPING (TOREADOR FRESCO), FROM THE PALACE AT KNOSSOS. MINOAN, CA. 1450–1400 BCE. ARCHAEOLOGICAL MUSEUM, HERAKLION, CRETE, GREECE. SCALA/ART RESOURCE, NY

During the second millennium BCE, two distinct cultures flourished in the Aegean area (see map, page 71). As in many other early civilizations, the animal was an important motif in both cultures, as evidenced by the *Bull Leaping* fresco from Knossos (fig. 3-37) and the Lion Gate at Mycenae (see fig. 3-41). The contrast between the fluid movement of the jumping bull and the severe rigidity of the guardian lions, however, reflects the differences between these cultures.

The ancient Minoan civilization, named in modern times after King Minos from Greek mythology, flourished on the island of Crete. The ori-

gins of the Minoan civilization, which was based on agriculture and a wide seafaring trade, are unclear. Archaeological evidence has long been interpreted as showing that an early culture, Minoan I, developed about 2000 BCE to 1700 BCE and was followed by Minoan II, which declined relatively

3-38   Minoan. *SNAKE GODDESS* OR *PRIESTESS*, found at the palace at Knossos, Crete. c. 1800–1550 BCE. Faience, height 11⅝″. Archaeological Museum, Heraklion, Crete. The medium, faience, is a type of earthenware decorated with glazes that was used as early as the predynastic period in Egypt.

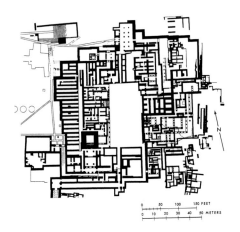

3-39 Minoan. Plan of palace at Knossos. c. 1800–1300 BCE. It may have been the complex plan of this palace that gave rise to the ancient myth of the Minotaur and the labyrinth at the Palace of Minos. Commissioned by a series of Minoan kings.

c. 1750–1450 BCE	**Minoan *Bull Leaping* fresco**
c. 1700 BCE	Judaism is founded by Abraham
c. 1500 BCE	Silk is woven by the Chinese
c. 1300 BCE	Alphabetic script is developed in Mesopotamia
c. 1190 BCE	Troy is destroyed
c. 1122 BCE	Zhou dynasty founded in China

abruptly after about 1450 BCE. Recent findings, however, indicate that a volcanic eruption, which is probably the cause of the rapid decline, occurred about 1620 BCE, thus throwing off previously accepted dating by several hundred years. Because the date question is still unresolved, we shall use broad dates for works of art for the Minoan culture. Natural catastrophes, perhaps volcanic eruptions with related earthquakes and tidal waves, may have caused the end of Minoan culture—and may, in fact, be the historical explanation for the legend of the city of Atlantis, which is said to have disappeared beneath the sea.

The earliest Minoan artifacts exhibit a preference for abstract curvilinear designs that in the Minoan

3-40 Minoan. c. 1700–1400 BCE. Like the Bull Leaping fresco from the palace seen in fig. 3-37, the scattered fragments of decoration that survived from this room have been reconstituted and restored in an attempt to give an indication of the original decorative program. Commissioned by a Minoan king or queen.

3-41 Mycenaean. Lion Gate, Mycenae, Greece. c. 1300–1200 BCE Limestone, height of carved slab 9'6". This historic photograph shows Heinrich Schliemann, the director of the excavation, standing to the left of the gate. The woman seated to the right is his Greek wife, Sophia. The huge slab on which the lions are carved fills a triangular opening in the construction, which helps to relieve weight on the lintel. The missing heads were originally attached with dowels. It is possible that they were carved or cast from a different material, and they may have represented human heads.

Excavations of the palace at Knossos have also brought to light statuettes related to Minoan religion. Although the Minoans' belief system remains mysterious, figures such as this small, snake-brandishing woman (fig. 3-38) may represent a goddess, perhaps the earth mother, or a devotee.

The remains of palaces indicate that the royal residences were combined with administrative offices, servants' quarters, and ceremonial and storage rooms. At Knossos, these rooms are grouped around a central courtyard in a rambling, labyrinthine design that seems to have developed over time without a predetermined plan, rooms being added as they were needed (fig. 3-39).

The interior decorations of the palace exhibit the lively, rhythmic qualities common in Minoan art; brightly colored fresco paintings depict scenes of ceremony, ritual, and animal and marine life (fig. 3-40).

As the Minoan culture began to decline, the Mycenaean rose to supremacy in the Aegean area. This Bronze Age culture, which flourished about 1400–1100 BCE, was named for the walled city of Mycenae on the Greek mainland, which was known for its fortifications. It was the military force from this culture that, as the ancient Greek poet Homer wrote, "launched a thousand ships" to attack Troy.

The only entrance into Mycenae was through the monumental architectural gateway now known as the Lion Gate (fig. 3-41). Atop the lintel, a relief sculpture displays symmetrical bodies of lions flanking a column that rests on altars. The scale of the relief and the stylized yet subtle animation of the lions' bodies proclaim the heraldry of royal power.

Homer's *Iliad*, the epic poem that tells of the war between the Trojans and the "Greeks" or Hellenes—a group that included the Mycenaeans—was long considered to be a product of human imagination, but its vividness

II culture were joined to representational forms to create dynamic and lively images, as in the *Bull Leaping* **fresco** (fig. 3-37). This fresco depicts a ritual or ceremonial event held in the central court of the palace at Knossos, in which trained athletes grasped the horns of a charging bull

and vaulted over its back. An undulating rhythm defines the bull's forward motion; the line of its neck is continued in its elongated, curving body, lending grace to what must have been a strenuous and dangerous activity. Bright, contrasting colors add to the vitality of the scene.

intrigued Heinrich Schliemann, a German business executive and amateur archaeologist. In 1870, he began to excavate sites in Asia Minor, a peninsula between the Black Sea and the Mediterranean Sea, where he found the archaeological remains of Homer's Troy, and in Greece, where he excavated Mycenae. The investigations spurred by Schliemann's discoveries gave credence to the legends of ancient Greece and brought to light the robust activity of the ancient Aegean area.

The Mycenaeans were the descendants of Greek-speaking peoples who invaded the peninsula of Greece between about 2000 and 1700 BCE. They were active traders, especially with the Minoans, and Mycenaean goods have been excavated in Italy and Syria. Mycenae was only one of a number of fortified towns that shared a common culture and language, although each was ruled by an independent monarch. Mycenaean kings were buried in large round tholos tombs accompanied by their personal treasures, including weapons. The tomb shown here (fig. 3-42) is remarkable for its size and the precision of its cut stone blocks, some of which weigh several tons.

Two styles are found in Mycenaean art. One was inspired by the vivacity of Minoan art, but a second style, perhaps native to the Mycenaeans, offers a more abstract mode of representation. The gold funeral mask from a royal tomb excavated at Mycenae was once probably placed over the face of a deceased king (fig. 3-43). While offering some individual characteristics, such as the mustache and beard, the arched eyebrows and treatment of the ears display a more abstracted approach.

The Mycenaean culture ended when the Dorians entered the peninsula from the north about 1100 BCE and conquered the Mycenaeans, but their legacy and that of the Minoans nourished the evolution of later Greek culture.

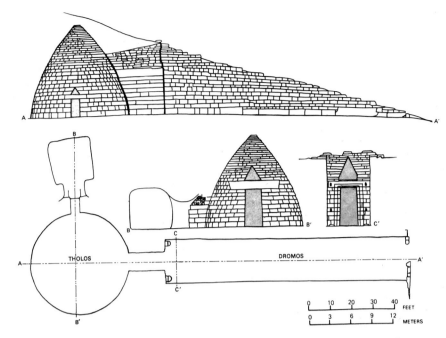

3-42 Mycenaean. Plan and sections of the tholos tomb popularly known as the Treasury of Atreus, Mycenae (after A. W. Lawrence). c. 1300–1200 BCE. Stone, height approx. 45″. Because of their shape, such tholos ("round") tombs are also known as beehive tombs.

3-43 Mycenaean. Funerary mask, found at Mycenae. c. 1550–1500 BCE. Gold, height approx. 12″. National Archaeological Museum, Athens.

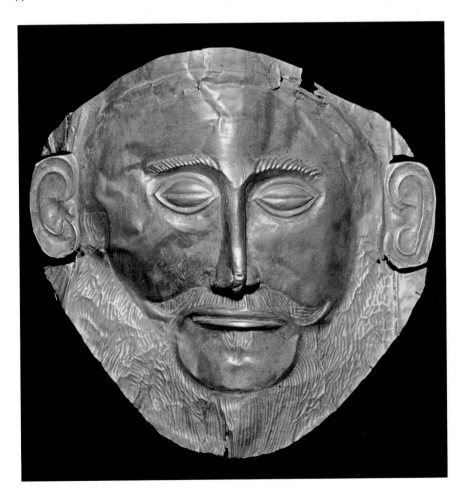

Ancient China: The Shang Dynasty

3-44 *FANG DING*, from the Tomb of Lady Hao, Anyang, Henan Province, China. Shang dynasty, c. 1200 BCE. Bronze, height 16¾". Cultural Relics Bureau, Beijing. Our knowledge of ancient China has been greatly enriched by archaeological findings in the tombs of the Shang, the first documented historical Chinese dynasty (c. 1766–1122 BCE). The richest finds have been near modern Anyang, a ceremonial center for the Shang that included the royal burial grounds as well as official temples and palaces built on pounded-earth platforms. Commissioned by Lady Hao or her family.

3-45 Pendant in the shape of a hawk, from the Tomb of Lady Hao, Anyang, Henan Province, China. Shang dynasty, c. 1200 BCE. Jade, height 2⅜". Cultural Relics Bureau, Beijing. Commissioned by Lady Hao or her family.

The *fang ding* shown here (fig. 3-44) is from the Tomb of Lady Hao at Anyang, which was of modest scale compared to the royal tombs opened there in the late 1920s and 1930s. Its undisturbed chamber yielded a tremendous amount of magnificent tomb furniture, making it the best-preserved tomb ever excavated at Anyang, the last capital of the Shang dynasty, which was occupied c. 1300–1050 BCE. The tomb was an oblong shaft approximately 13' × 18'6". Along the eastern and western walls, at a depth of about 20 feet, were elongated niches with sacrifices: sixteen human beings and six dogs. Tomb furniture was placed in eight layers both above and on the chamber top, in the chamber between its walls and the coffin, and inside the coffin itself. Of the total of 1,900 pieces, about 460 were sacred bronze vessels, tools, and weapons; almost 750 were jade; and about 560 were bone objects. There were also some sculptures and ivory carvings and 5 pottery vessels. In addition to the 1,900 pieces, there were nearly 6,900 cowrie shells, presumably used as currency. The immense wealth of this tomb and others at Anyang (see map, page 149) indicates that the Shang had control of and created great resources.

Some of the earliest examples of Chinese writing are Shang inscriptions on bronze vessels and on animal bones or turtle shells, used as oracles, that were excavated there.

More than 190 bronze vessels from the tomb bear inscriptions that refer to Lady Hao and suggest her status and death date. A foreigner, she was a general who became the consort of King Wu Ting. The materials found in her tomb confirm her acceptance into the Shang elite because she was allowed to use the clan emblem, the *taotie*. At the same time, she also seems to have retained cultural affiliation with her non-Shang parent culture, as evidenced by the jade hawk (fig. 3-45) and frontier-style bronze knives, horse gear, and mirrors also found in her tomb.

The Shang faith was **shamanistic**, which required offerings of food for the ancestors. The shamans, or *wu*, and their associates, diviners who predicted the future, served as mediums between the supernatural and human worlds. These ritual leaders, who could write and keep accounts, also served as archivists and historians.

c. 1766–1122 BCE	Shang dynasty in China
c. 1360 BCE	Population of Thebes, Egypt, is 100,000
c. 1200 BCE	***Fang ding* from the Tomb of Lady Hao**
c. 1200 BCE	Women are professional musicians in Egypt, Assyria, and Babylon
c. 1100 BCE	Dorians enter Greek peninsula

Shamanism was reflected in the rituals and burial at Anyang, which paid homage to ancestors and to the spirits of the natural world. Many of the materials used at these ceremonies were decorated with the *taotie* mask that was the emblem of the ruling clan (see page 37). By claiming that communication with the spirit world, including ancestors, was only possible through the use of such vessels, the rulers and the elite may have been creating and maintaining their status separate from the masses. Because they controlled the production of bronze as well as the ceremonies that made use of bronze vessels and weapons, they demonstrated their dual power—access to the spirit world and military domination.

Technique *Chinese Piece-Mold Bronze Casting*

In ancient China, the industries involved in making sacred vessels and ritual implements were located in Anyang. The production of bronze, an alloy of copper, tin, and sometimes other minerals, was a sophisticated activity. It required a team of specialists—miners, refiners of ores for the alloy, designers, metallurgists to determine appropriate alloy makeup for the shapes and designs involved—all coordinated by a central authority. The process used was a sophisticated **piece-mold casting** method, which depended on knowledge of the properties of different clays. The designer produced an exact model of the desired final product in fine clay, complete with the incised designs on the surface. Heavy clay was packed around the model to create the mold. Once the model was removed, the distance between the model and mold was kept uniform by bronze spacers. The entire assemblage was packed in sand (not shown here) and heated, then molten bronze was poured into the opening to form the sacral vessel (fig. 3-46). After the casting cooled, details on the surface of the bronze were filed and polished to produce a sharp design and shiny surface.

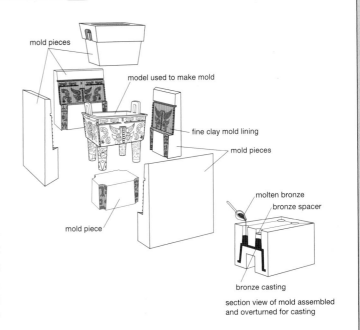

mold pieces

model used to make mold

fine clay mold lining

mold pieces

mold piece

molten bronze

bronze spacer

bronze casting

section view of mold assembled and overturned for casting

3-46   The technique of bronze casting in ancient China as shown for the fang-ding in fig. 3-2.

Assyrian and Early Persian Art

The Assyrians and Persians successively controlled Mesopotamia. The Assyrians established a powerful kingdom in northern Mesopotamia from the ninth through the seventh centuries BCE, while the early, or Achaemenid, Persians were centered in southern Mesopotamia during the sixth and fifth centuries BCE (see map, page 42). Both cultures were known for their powerful kings, who tried to conquer and control vast territories. The Assyrians in particular were feared for their atrocities during war, but the Persians, who for a brief period even conquered Egypt, tried to establish a reputation for benevolent rule and had greater success in creating a huge empire.

Assyrian and early Persian palaces were similarly decorated, with low reliefs lining the palace rooms and passages. In Assyrian palaces, the themes were ritualistic, honorific, militaristic, or any subject that would impress the visitor with the unquestionable power and undeniable majesty of the royal personage. This sense of commanding omnipotence can also be seen in other palace sculptures, such as the *Lamassu* (fig. 3-47), which seems to have been intended to intimidate visitors—especially foreign ambassadors—before they entered into the presence of the Assyrian king. The threatening content is supported by the treatment of the stone; its high polish emphasizes its density, while the patterns and fine detail of the beard and wings stress the massive scale and powerful forms. The figure is given five legs to present a convincing stance from both the front view, on approach, and the side, in passing.

The Assyrian palace at Dur Sharrukin, where the *Lamassu* stood, covered more than 25 acres and had more than 200 courtyards and rooms. Here and at the ancient sites of Nimrud and Nineveh, continuous low reliefs depicted Assyrian military victories and the subsequent pillage and carnage. The reliefs emphasized the

3-47 Assyrian. *HUMAN-HEADED WINGED BULL (LAMASSU)*, from the gateway of the Palace of Sargon II, Dur Sharrukin (modern Khorsabad, Iraq). c. 720 BCE. Limestone, height 14'. The Louvre, Paris. Commissioned by King Sargon II.

3-48 Assyrian. *DYING LIONESS*, from the North Palace of Ashurbanipal, Nineveh (modern Kuyunjik, Iraq). c. 645–635 BCE. Limestone, height of figure approx. 14″. The British Museum, London. Commissioned by King Ashurbanipal.

3-49 Early Persian. Royal audience hall (Apadana) and stairway of the Palace of Darius, Persepolis (modern Iran). c. 500 BCE. Commissioned by King Darius.

Assyrian king's strength in battle or in sport. In one series, he is shown engaged in a hunt in which lions were released from cages. The king is represented victorious in his chariot, surrounded by dead and dying animals. In the detail pictured (fig. 3-48), a lioness is shown in her death throes, dragging her paralyzed legs behind her and uttering a cry or moan of death.

The early Persian Palace of Darius at Persepolis (fig. 3-49) had grand staircases decorated with reliefs. The reliefs depict seemingly endless processions and scenes in which, following an old Middle Eastern tradition, a fierce beast is represented attacking a domesticated animal. Such scenes are open to a number of levels of interpretation. On one level, they probably symbolize Persian power and victory, but they may also refer to political and even to cosmic conflict.

These imposing staircases led to a sequence of magnificent square throne rooms and ceremonial chambers filled with large columns. The largest was 250 feet square, with columns at least 40 feet high. The capitals—the decorated elements at the tops of the columns—are unusual and uniquely Persian, with gigantic figures of paired bulls (fig. 3-50). Stylistically, the debt of the Persians to Assyrian art is evident in the contrast between bold, simple masses and fine, abstract detail, but the Persian compositions have an increased refinement and elegance.

3-50 Early Persian. Bull capital, from the Apadana, Palace of Darius, Persepolis (modern Iran). c. 500 BCE. Width 12′3″. The Louvre, Paris. Commissioned by King Darius.

Etruscan Art

3-51 Ash urn, found at Castiglione del Lago, Italy. c. 650–600 BCE. Terra-cotta, approx. 18½" high. Archeological Museum, Florence, Italy. Etruscan burial practices, which varied widely from city to city, included cremation, as here, and inhumation. Probably commissioned by the family of the deceased.

3-52 Etruscan Sarcophagus with reclining couple, from Cerveteri, Tuscany, Italy. c. 525–500 BCE. Terra-cotta, length 6'7"; the figures are lifesize. Museo Nazionale de Villa Giulia, Rome, Italy. A simlar sarcophagus in the Louvre in Paris has many traces of color, suggesting that this one may also have been naturalistically painted. Probably commissioned by the family of the deceased.

The breasts, arms, hands, and head that personalize this abstracted container (fig. 3-51) may have been enhanced by a wig made of real hair and by pieces of jewelry. As a container for the ashes of the deceased, it would have been placed in her tomb and surrounded by other possessions, which probably would have included a hand mirror (see fig. 3-1). The wig would most likely have been made from the hair of the deceased, and other personal details may have been added to the urn in paint. This type of ash urn is only one of the ways in which the Etruscans honored the dead.

The origin of the people we know as the Etruscans is debated, but by the eighth century BCE they had established themselves in a group of cities in Etruria (present-day Tuscany, in central Italy) and were the most important power on the Italian peninsula (see map, page 100). These cities were fiercely independent and often had distinctive burial practices. During the seventh and sixth centuries BCE, Etruscans ruled as kings of Rome, and by the fifth century they controlled most of central Italy. They were active traders, and their works in bronze, especially armor, were exported throughout the ancient world. During the fourth and third centuries BCE, the Etruscan cities were defeated and annexed by the Romans, and the Etruscan culture was absorbed into the Roman sphere.

Etruscan inscriptions have been translated, but there is no surviving body of Etruscan literature, so like many other, earlier prehistoric civilizations, Etruscan civilization is studied primarily from archaeological remains. Like other early Mediterranean cultures, including Egypt, the Etruscans believed that the body or ashes of the deceased should be accompanied by household and other everyday objects to guarantee a satisfying afterlife. Thus, much of our knowledge of the Etruscans is based on their tombs, carved in rock and/or frescoed, and on the tomb furnishings, which included gold and bronze objects of superb artistry (see fig. 3-1) and fine imported goods, such as Greek vases. Needless to say, most of the evidence we have concerns the life-styles of the upper class.

On one Etruscan sacrophagus, a couple reclining on a banqueting couch engages us with beguiling smiles (fig. 3-52). The construction of a terra-cotta group of this scale and complexity is an impressive technical accomplishment, but equally remarkable is the representation of their relaxed positions and their inner

3-53   Tomb of Hunting and Fishing, Tarquinia, Italy. c. 510–500 BCE. Fresco.
Probably commissioned by the family of the deceased.

delight. That this work's original function was as a sarcophagus suggests the Etruscans' relatively content and reconciled outlook on death. Reclining in this manner is a Greek tradition, but the representation of a man and a woman reclining together is typically Etruscan. It suggests a respect for women that was unknown in Greece and rare in other early cultures.

Many Etruscan works were inspired by Greek examples, but the Etruscans' style is generally bolder and simpler and displays little interest in the symmetry so favored by the Greeks. Much Etruscan iconography emphasizes everyday activities, but there are also frequent references to Greek myths, and it is clear that divination (see fig. 3-1) was an important Etruscan activity. Especially in such large-scale pieces as the sarcophagus and in figures and decoration used on architecture, Etruscans made important technical innovations in the use of terra-cotta, a fired clay. Most Etruscan artists did not sign their works; there seems to have been no cult of the artist, as there was in Greece.

Simple bright colors, bold geometric and natural patterns, and clearly drawn figures combine in Etruscan tomb paintings to create a lively and vigorous effect. Typical Etruscan themes include banqueting figures—referring to the banquets that were part of the Etruscan funeral ritual—complete with the dancers and musicians that provided entertainment, as well as scenes of pleasurable daily life to be enjoyed by the deceased. In the Tomb of Hunting and Fishing (fig. 3-53), a profusion of wildlife guarantees success in the hunt; above, the deceased (and perhaps the living) are shown banqueting.

Ancient Greek Art

3-54 Severe style. *APOLLO AND THE BATTLE OF THE LAPITHS AND THE CENTAURS*, detail from the west pediment, Temple of Zeus, Olympia. 470–456 BCE. Marble, over-lifesize. Pausanias attributes the pediments at Olympia to the artists Alkamenes and Paionios. Archaeological Museum, Olympia.

In the midst of a chaotic combat (fig. 3-54), the over-lifesize figure of the Greek god Apollo majestically restores order. He occupies the axis of the composition, and his calm yet commanding presence contrasts with the outburst of surrounding activity. His idealized human physique and dignified bearing make him an appropriate introduction to the study of ancient Greek art.

This Apollo is part of a group of figures that originally decorated the triangular end (or **pediment**; see figs. 3-77, 3-78) of the **gable** (pitched) **roof** of the Temple of Zeus at Olympia. The composition is clear, the movement is bold and direct, and the details of anatomy and drapery are easily read by the viewer standing 50 or more feet below. The sculptures illustrate a mythological subject. Among the guests at a wedding feast are drunken centaurs (creatures who are half-human, half-horse), who attempt to abduct the Greek women; after a fierce battle they are subdued. This theme had an immediate significance for the Greeks of that time: their victory over the Persians in 479 BCE was symbolically expressed in the victory over the centaurs. On a more profound level, the calm presence of Apollo represents the mastery of reasoned order over brute force. The scene had a special meaning because of its location at Olympia, for during the Olympian Games, a truce was observed among the Greek city-states.

History

About 1100 BCE, a people called the Dorians entered the Greek peninsula from the north and overwhelmed the Mycenaeans. Gradually a new culture evolved. By the eighth century BCE, the two great Homeric poems, the *Iliad* and the *Odyssey*, had been composed, and Greece had evolved into a grouping of independent city-states. Each city-state (*polis*) commanded the loyalty of its citizens in local religious, military, and economic matters, and their fierce independence prevented the political unification of Greece. In 776 BCE, the first Olympian Games were held. Called once every four years, they were held in honor of Zeus, ruler of the gods. Winners gained personal fame and were often honored in art. The winners of the footrace at similar games held in Athens, for example, were celebrated in such works of art as a victory vase, the **Panathenaic amphora** (fig. 3-56).

During the eighth century BCE, developing commerce among the city-states led to a prosperous economy. One of the major products was pottery, and a Geometric-style vase (fig. 3-55), with its bands of simple repeated patterns, demonstrates the artistic beginnings of the Greeks. The animals on the neck of the vase are arranged in a repeated rhythm. In the largest, central band are rather abstracted figures representing female mourners pulling

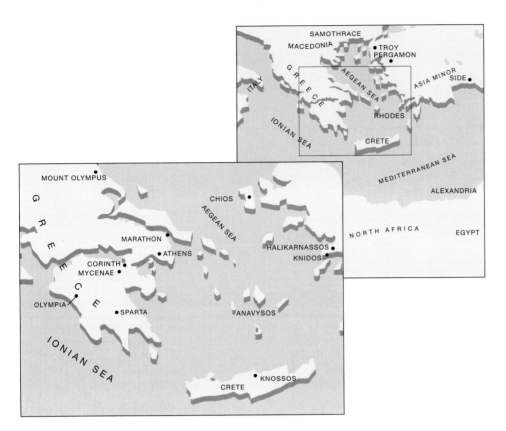

3-56 Archaic style. *PANATHENAIC AMPHORA WITH RUNNERS*. c. 520 BCE. Painted terra-cotta, height 24½″. The Metropolitan Museum of Art, New York. The Panathenaic amphora was a large, specially decorated vessel given as a prize in the Panathenaic Games held in Athens, which were similar to the Olympian Games. It was filled with oil made from olives grown on special trees. Commissioned by the Panathenaic organizing committee.

their hair at a funeral; the deceased lies on his bier. The scene is related to the purpose of such vases, which was to mark a grave site and thus play an important role in honoring the dead. Oil, poured into the vases to commemorate the deceased, flowed through the open bottom and into the ground.

During what is known in art as the Archaic period, from the seventh to the early fifth century BCE, trade routes expanded, and the Greeks began to colonize areas of southern Italy and Asia Minor. At this time, the Greeks began to produce lifesize figurative sculpture and to construct marble temples.

The early fifth century BCE was a time of significant artistic and political changes. In both sculpture and painting, a more naturalistic rendering of the human figure emerged. In architecture, the forms of the Greek temple underwent a process of visual refinement that gave them a new sense of elegance.

In 490 BCE, the Persians invaded Greece. The city-states formed a defensive alliance and defeated the invasion force at Marathon, about 26 miles northeast of Athens. After the battle, a courier ran to Athens bringing

3-55 Geometric style. *MOURNERS AROUND A BIER*. c. 750 BCE. Terra-cotta, height 5′1″. National Archaeological Museum, Athens. The decorated pottery vessels of the Greeks, regardless of use, are traditionally known as vases. Vases such as this one are sometimes referred to as Dipylon vases because they were found at the Dipylon Cemetery in Athens. Probably commissioned by the family of the deceased.

news of the victory; he fell dead of exhaustion after exclaiming, "Rejoice, we conquer." His run is commemorated in today's 26-mile marathon races. Ten years later, the Persians captured and sacked Athens, but in 479 BCE the Greeks again defeated the Persians, this time at the naval battle of Salamis. During the thirty years following the second Persian defeat, Athens, which had agreed to supply the navy for the Greek military alliance, continued to collect taxes from the other city-states. During this period, Athens became the preeminent political and economic center, but only at the cost of jealousy from the other city-states.

Although beset by internal political conflicts, the Greeks, who called them-

3-57 Reconstruction model of the Acropolis, Athens. c. 400 bce. Royal Ontario Museum, Toronto, and J. Walter Graham. The pedimented building in the right foreground is the Propylaea; the name means gateway to a sacred or secular precinct. It was the only entrance to the Acropolis, and the building to its left is the earliest known example of a building built for the display of works of art; because art is inspired by the Muses, it was called a museum. For the Parthenon, see pp. 86–89.

selves Hellenes, shared a common language and culture. They divided the world into two types of people: those whose native language was Greek, and others, who were called *barbaroi* ("barbarians"). As a result of the Persian wars, the self-aware Greeks continued to define how their culture was distinct from that of the barbarians.

The mid-fifth century BCE in Greece is known as the Classical period of art and culture. Its center was Athens, where a politician named Pericles was chief general of the city from 460 to 430 BCE. The Athenian government is often cited as the first democracy in the Western world, although only free men were allowed to vote.

Pericles used the wealth of Athens and the taxes collected from other city-states for an ambitious campaign of renewal, including rebuilding the temples destroyed by the Persians on the Acropolis (from the Greek *akros*, "highest," and *polis*, "city"), an outcropping of rock that dominates the center of Athens (fig. 3-57). To the Greeks, it was the sacred location where Poseidon, god of the sea, and Athena, goddess of wisdom, had contested for control of the city. Poseidon caused salt water to flow from a spring, but Athena's gift of an olive tree was deemed more benefi-

cial and the city was thus dedicated to her. As late as the second century CE, a saltwater spring and an olive tree could still be found on the Acropolis.

Pericles seems to have recognized the value of providing an intellectual, physically healthy, and aesthetically pleasing environment for the citizens of Athens. Later, when war had broken out in Greece, he offered a funeral oration for Athenian soldiers:

Our constitution is called a democracy because power is not in the hands of a few, but of the people. Our laws secure equal justice for all in their private disputes, and our public opinion welcomes and honors talent in every brace of achievement; what counts is not membership in a particular class, but the actual ability a man possesses.

Yet ours is no mere work-a-day city. No other provides so much recreation for the spirit—contests and sacrifices all the year round, and beauty in our public buildings to cheer the heart and delight the eye day by day.

We are lovers of the beautiful without being extravagant, and

lovers of wisdom without being soft. We regard wealth as something to be used properly, rather than as something to boast about. . . . We decide and debate, carefully, and in person, all matters of policy, for we do not think there is an incompatibility between words and deeds.

Our city is an education to Greece.

As the political dominance of Athens grew, so did the resentment of the other city-states. The Peloponnesian War, which erupted in 431 BCE, plunged Greece into turmoil. When the war ended in 404 BCE, the power of Athens was broken, and Sparta and Corinth assumed a more prominent role in the political affairs of Greece. By the later fourth century BCE, however, a new force from the north commanded attention, and the next chapter of ancient Greek history was written by two Macedonian kings, Philip and Alexander (see pages 92–95).

Intellectual and Scientific Activities

The love of wisdom Pericles described found expression in philosophy and science as well as in art. From the mid-fifth through the fourth centuries BCE, philosophy developed from the speculative questioning of Socrates and the ideal forms of Plato to the natural observations by Aristotle. The Greek admiration for the human mind and for our ability to reason is a new development in western culture and this, in concert with the Greek admiration for the beauty of the human body, has important implications for art. The philosophical questioning of the Greeks, in fact, helps to explain why their artistic forms were constantly evolving.

At the heart of the Greeks' world view was the belief that human reason—and especially mathematics—could understand and define the rational order inherent in the universe. In the sixth century BCE, Pythagoras wrote of the relationship between mathematics and musical harmony, noting that a stretched string, when plucked, produces a certain note by its vibration. When the string is measured and plucked at points that correspond to exact divisions by whole numbers—½, ⅓, etc.—the vibrations produce a harmonious chord. If the string is plucked at any other interval, the sound seems discordant. To the Greeks, this discovery had a powerful impact. If the sounds of nature were governed by the order of mathematics, then the universe itself must obey the harmony of mathematical concurrences. This notion of a universal harmony that could be perceived by human reason came to govern the rules of art and architecture during the Classical period.

Religion

The Greeks worshiped numerous gods and goddesses, who ruled over all aspects of life and death. Leader among the gods was Zeus (see fig. 3-69); Hera, wife of Zeus, was queen of the gods and protector of women. Apollo was the Greek god of rational thought and also of music, while his counterpart, the popular and hypnotic Dionysos, represents the irrational aspects of human life, fertility, and the powerful energy of the life force. Although some Egyptian gods had been represented in human form, it was the Greeks who fully anthropomorphized their deities, giving them both human form and human attributes.

Sacrifices to the gods were joined with great festivals that might include athletic games, such as the Olympian and other games, and theatrical productions. Greek theater developed from the rituals honoring Dionysos, a popular god and patron of drama and song. The Greek playwrights Æschylus, Sophocles, Euripides, and Aristophanes wrote plays to be performed during an annual Athenian festival honoring Dionysos. These plays are characterized by their profound and subtle expression of human motivation and behavior.

Greek Art

The philosophical questioning that pervaded Greek intellectual life helps to explain why Greek art underwent a dramatic evolution of successive styles over a relatively short, 500-year period. The beginnings are represented in the Geometric phase (see fig. 3-55). The abstract features of Archaic period sculptures (see figs. 3-62, 3-63) were transformed into the Severe style (see figs. 3-54, 3-64, 3-69, 3-70) and then into the idealized representations of the Classical period (see figs. 3-72, 3-78–3-80), which sought to equate the perfection of art with the harmonies of the natural order. By the time of Alexander the Great (ruled 336–323 BCE), the realistic and emotionally dramatic representations of what is known as the Hellenistic style were common (see figs. 3-83, 3-86, 3-87). In painting, flat shapes (see fig. 3-55) gave way to elements of illusionism (see figs. 3-58 and 3-85); see page 91 for a discussion of a Greek painting competition), while in architecture proportions and decorative elements underwent a progressive transformation toward a more refined ideal (compare figs. 3-66 and 3-73, 3-74). The continuous process of revision characteristic of Greek art is only one manifestation of the questioning and philosophical Greek mind. Greek art and architecture has had a profound impact on many later cultures, including our own. The Romans copied famous Greek illusionistic paintings and mosaics—for example, the *Unswept Floor* by Sosos (fig. 3-58). And the Greek architectural orders, so popular in the Renaissance and later periods, have been revived recently in the postmodern style.

The Greek Artist

The Greeks valued both intellectual and physical achievements, so it is not surprising that they would begin to praise the artist as an individual with unique talents. An exceptional development in the seventh century BCE, with virtually

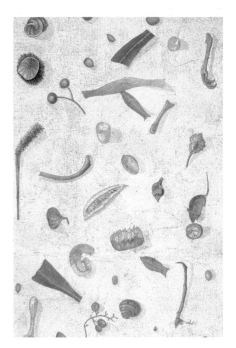

3-58 HERACLEITUS

THE UNSWEPT FLOOR. Mosaic variant of a second-century BCE painting by Sosos of Pergamon. Second century CE. Musei Vaticani, Museo Gregoriano Profano, ex Lateranense, Rome.

STUDIO CANALI, MILANO, ITALY.

no precedent in earlier cultures, occurred when artists began with regularity to sign their works. Such signatures are an indication of personal pride; they might also be an early form of advertising. Literary sources from both ancient Greece and ancient Rome offer descriptions and criticisms of works of art that were considered famous. By the fourth century BCE, such references begin to include comments on the personalities of specific artists and anecdotes about their lives. An ancient discussion of the fourth-century BCE painter Apelles, recorded by the Roman author Pliny, reveals the respect enjoyed by a successful artist:

Nevertheless the painter who surpassed all those who were born before him and all those who came later was Apelles. . . . He produced volumes, which contain his doctrine. . . . He . . . was also gifted with a courteous nature and . . . was on quite good terms with Alexander the Great.

Greek Vase Painting

3-59 EXEKIAS

ACHILLES AND AJAX PLAYING DRAUGHTS, detail of black-figure decoration on an amphora. c. 530 BCE. Painted terra-cotta, height 24″. The stories represented on Archaic vases, which usually told of Greek mythological or historical events, were at first illustrated with black figures on a red background. Works in this style are known as black-figure vases. Exekias was both painter and potter of this vase.

During the Archaic period, the decorative bands prevalent on earlier Geometric vases (see fig. 3-55) were relegated to the base and neck, and increased surface area was given to figurative narration. This vase (fig. 3-59) depicts the Greek warriors Achilles and Ajax playing draughts (an ancient game related to checkers) during a lull in the Trojan War, which Greece waged against Troy after the Trojan Paris abducted Helen, wife of the king of the Greek city-state Sparta. The signature "Exekias painted me and made me" indicates an artist talented in both pottery and painting—a rarity in ancient Greece, where a division of labor was usually practiced in the production of vases (see fig. 1-20). The composition, with its strong symmetry and the manner in which scene and decoration are related to the shape of the vase, reveals the Greek search for balance and harmony.

The various shapes of Greek vases developed according to both purpose and the Greek interest in aesthetic forms. By the Archaic period, specialized forms had become associated with specific functions (fig. 3-60).

After a vase was formed but before it was fired, the painter, using **slip** (a mixture of clay particles in water, sometimes combined with wood ash), painted black figures in silhouette. Details of the decoration and of the figures' anatomy, drapery, and armor were made by incising lines into the surface before firing. Working with a sharp pointed tool known to modern artists as a **burin**, the artist engraved lines through the slip, exposing the terra-cotta color beneath. As the vase was being fired, the air vents in the kiln were closed, causing the entire vase to turn black for a period as the red iron oxide of the terra-cotta was converted into black and magnetic iron oxides. When the air vents were again opened, the iron in the clay body returned to its red-orange color except in those areas covered by slip. In the firing, the slip had formed a glazed surface coating, sealing these areas from the air. They remained black, creating the black figures and decoration on the vase. On black-figure vases, the artist delighted in decorative geometric patterns that asserted the two-dimensional quality of the figures.

Around 530 BCE, a new technique that reversed the figure-ground colors was introduced, perhaps by a student of Exekias known as the Andokides Painter. This technique, the **red-figure style**, presents figures and objects silhouetted against the painted black background. Details of anatomy and costume are painted on, rather than incised into, the surface of the vase.

The vase with the *Death of Sarpedon*, signed by Euxitheos and Euphronios, was created shortly after the introduction of this new technique (fig. 3-61). The scene, described in Homer's *Iliad* (XVI, 426 ff.), depicts the body of Sarpedon, a fallen Trojan hero, being carried from the battlefield by personifications of Sleep and Death. The god Hermes, who will lead Sarpedon's soul to Hades, stands behind. The figures convey a physical and emotional presence that is new to Greek vase painting. Somber facial expressions betray the tragic loss. We sense the physical strain required to lift the body, while diagonal patterns of limbs and flowing blood pull the composition downward. Details of anatomy and drapery are more naturalistically rendered than in the black-figure style. Also, the rendering of some parts of the body as if seen in sharp recession is an early example of **foreshortening**. The greater naturalism is made possible by use of the brush, in contrast to

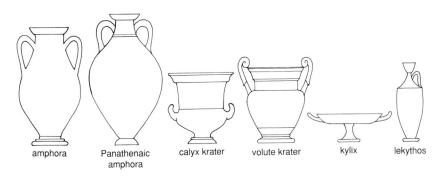

3-60 Typical Greek vase shapes. The amphora and Panathenaic amphora are containers to store wine, olive oil, honey, or water. The calyx krater and volute krater are bowls for mixing wine with water, which was the Greek custom. They kylix is a drinking cup, and the lekythos is a container for olive oil.

3-61 EUPHRONIOS (painter) AND EUXITHEOS (potter)

DEATH OF SARPEDON DURING THE TROJAN WAR, red-figure decoration on a calyx krater. c. 515 BCE. Painted terra-cotta, height 18″. The Metropolitan Museum of Art, New York. Red-figure vases feature red figures against a black ground. For another example see fig. 1-20

BEQUEST OF JOSEPH H. DURKEE, GIFT OF DARIUS OGDEN MILLS, AND GIFT OF C. RUXTON LOVE, BY EXCHANGE, 1972 (1972.11.10)

the incising tool employed by the black-figure painter.

The level of artistry reached in these vases testifies to a refined understanding of both functional and visual values. The black-figure **amphora** has two handles for carrying and an opening large enough to admit a ladle. The broad opening of the red-figured **calyx krater** made possible the mixing of water and wine. In each of our examples, the painter has adapted the composition to the form of the vase. The arched backs of Achilles and Ajax echo the inward curvature of the amphora, while the composition on the calyx krater, with the horizontal body of Sarpedon balanced by the vertical pose of the attendants and the parenthetical effect of Sleep and Death, emphasizes the inverted trapezoidal form of the vase. It was this ability to join form, function, and decoration that made Greek vases so highly valued throughout the ancient world.

Greek Sculpture:
Archaic Style and Severe Style

3-62 Archaic style. Kouros, from the Tomb of Kroisos, Anavysos, Greece. c. 520 BCE. Marble with red paint on the hair, headband, and pupils of the eyes, height 6'4". National Archaeological Museum, Athens. The inscription on the base reads: "Stop and grieve at the tomb of the dead Kroisos, slain by wild Ares in the front rank of battle." Commissioned by the family of Kroisos or his military comrades.

The earliest large-scale Greek sculptures (c. 600 BCE) are indebted to Egyptian prototypes that were certainly known to the Greeks, who had a trading station in Egypt as early as the mid-seventh century BCE. But by about 520 BCE, when the kouros (youth) from Anavysos was created (fig. 3-62), the new direction Greek art would take was already evident. The Greek figure represents an athletic ideal and a new understanding of the organic nature of the human body. And although the Greek figure maintains a stance derived from Egyptian models (see fig. 1-2), with one leg advanced and hands clenched at the sides, the stone passages (which in Egyptian figures connect the forward to the rear leg and the arms to the torso) have been carved away. The Greek figure seems tense and prepared to take action, not frozen for all eternity. In contrast to Egyptian sculptures, most Greek male figures are nude. Greek athletes competed nude at the games held during religious festivals, but the nudity also demonstrates new Greek attitudes concerning the beauty and integrity of the human body. The slight smile, which suggests a confident assurance consistent with the buoyant energy of the body, recognizes the psychological and emotional aspect of human life in a manner foreign to most Egyptian art. These Greek nude male sculptures were set up as votive offerings at shrines and were used as grave monuments. The youthful figures sometimes marked the tombs of older men, which suggests that they represented a philosophical and aesthetic ideal, not specific individuals.

The Archaic female figure seen in fig. 3-63 is known as a kore (plural korai); the early examples are always shown dressed. Their function seems to vary; some were found in cemeteries and probably were viewed as dedications to the deceased, while others may repre-

3-63 Archaic style. Kore, from Chios (?). c. 510 BCE. Marble fragment with red, blue, and violet paint, height approx. 22". Acropolis Museum, Athens. Such Archaic sculptures of female figures are much rarer than their male counterparts.

sent the goddesses Hera or Athena. The female nude did not become common in Greek art until the fourth century BCE (see fig. 3-82). The gentle swelling of the body beneath the draper suggests an interest in the organic and sensuous qualities of the human figure, while rich visual patterns are offered by the subtle and varied textures of pleated drapery and plaited hair. This particular example preserves much of the color that was painted on the marble to enhance both its beauty and the lifelikeness of the sculpted figure.

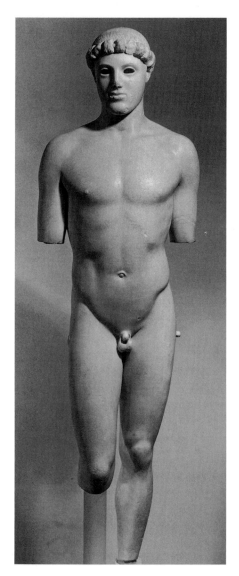

The style of Greek sculpture from about 650 to 480 BCE is usually referred to as Archaic. Figures from the first half of the fifth century BCE, which are now seen as moving toward the Classical style of the second half of the century, are usually designated Severe style (or Early Classical style or Transitional style, c. 480–450 BCE). These changes in style are the result of the constant questioning with which the Greeks examined many aspects of their culture.

The kouros known as the *Kritian Boy*, because it is similar to works attributed to the Greek sculptor Kritios, represents the figure in a position that combines flexed and relaxed muscles (fig. 3-64). Although the kouros's feet are lost, enough of the figure survives to reveal that it was represented in the relaxed and realistic position known since the Renaissance as **contrapposto** (see p. 85). The weight of the body is borne on one leg, while the other is relaxed. Contrapposto (from the Latin *contrapositio*, "counterpositioning") is related to a natural, relaxed stance; it has its basis in real life. Contrapposto affects the entire body, for the counterpositioning juxtaposes the forward, relaxed leg to the opposite shoulder, which also moves forward. The resulting figure seems to stand freely. Imaginary horizontal lines drawn through knees, pelvis, and shoulders will be seen to rotate around the figure's axis. More importantly, contrapposto suggests the potential for movement, making possible a figure that offers a new momentary quality. In addition, a sculpted figure standing in contrapposto becomes freestanding, a **sculpture in the round**, intended to be seen from multiple viewpoints. Contrapposto creates a unified figure standing in space, banishing the static Egyptian views (frontal, left profile, right profile) that had conditioned Greek sculpture at its origins.

To understand the revolutionary quality of this kouros, we must try to view it as would a Greek of the period. The pose, which must have seemed startlingly new and amazingly naturalistic, is enhanced by a softness and organic unity in the articulation of the muscles. The sculptor appears to have breathed life into the stone itself. Western European culture would never be the same.

3-64   Severe style. Kouros, also known as the *Kritian Boy*. c. 480 BCE. Marble fragment, originally with inlaid eyes, height 36".

Art Past/Art Present   *The Impact of the Ancient Greek Orders*

The ancient world may be remote from us in time, but it still has an impact on our lives in many ways. One of the most obvious is the importance of the ancient Greek architectural orders on modern architecture and design. The Greeks developed a system of architectural decoration and proportion for columns in their structures (see pages 78–79) that was adapted, with very little change, by other ancient cultures—especially by the Romans (see figs. 3-93, 3-114, 3-116, 3-117). Many Christian churches during the medieval period, particularly in areas that had been colonized by the Greeks or the Romans, used variations on these orders (see figs. 4-63, 4-68, 4-71, 4-83, 4-89). During the Italian Renaissance, when many forms and subjects from antiquity were revived, the Greek orders became the dominant architectural decorative device. The orders continued to have an impact in subsequent centers, and in the postmodern style (see Chapter 10), when all historical architectural forms became open to revival, the Greek orders and other Greek forms became of major significance once again.

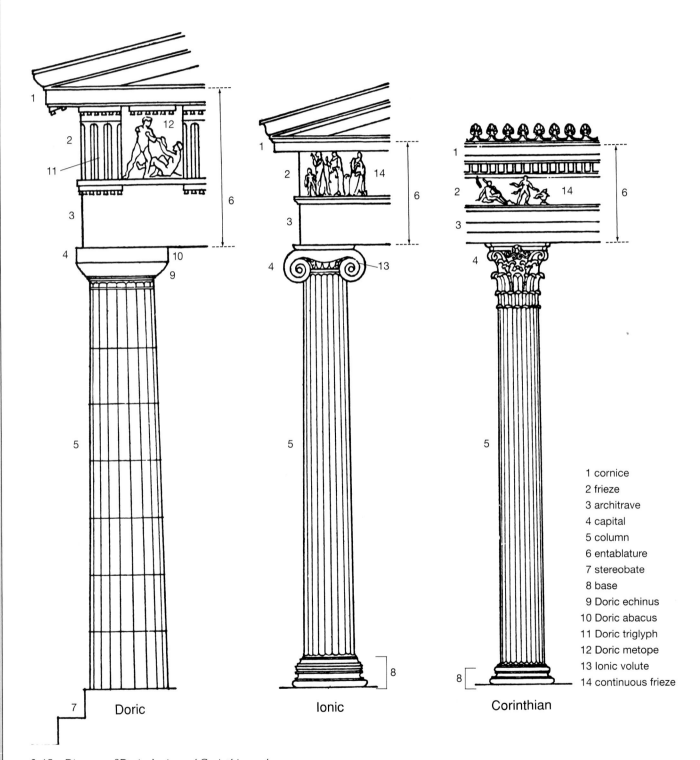

3-65   Diagram of Doric, Ionic, and Corinthian orders.

Doric

Ionic

Corinthian

1 cornice
2 frieze
3 architrave
4 capital
5 column
6 entablature
7 stereobate
8 base
9 Doric echinus
10 Doric abacus
11 Doric triglyph
12 Doric metope
13 Ionic volute
14 continuous frieze

An **order** gives aesthetic definition and decoration to the post-and-lintel system (see page 54). Between the seventh and fifth centuries BCE, the Greeks developed three architectural orders—the Doric, Ionic, and Corinthian—which have been in virtually continuous use up to the present day. The Greeks' invention and development of these orders (fig. 3-65) reveal a philosophical and analytical approach to architecture. An order is composed of a group of specific architectural elements that are designed to integrate with each other and with the building as a whole. An order also dictates the proportional scheme governing the interrelationships of the parts. The elements of an order include the **column**, with its **capital**, and the **entablature**, composed of **architrave**, **frieze**, and **cornice**. A column can be decorated with vertical lines or raised areas, known as **flutes**, which accentuate its cylindrical and vertical quality.

The classical orders became the most basic design element for architecture. They were used not only as supports but also as decoration on buildings that were not post-and-lintel construction (for example, the Flavian Amphitheater known as the "Colosseum"; see fig. 3-113). Half-round decorative columns were often attached to a supporting or enclosing wall. These are known as **half columns** or **engaged columns**. When they are flattened, they are called **pilasters**.

An order, however, offers more than mere articulation and decoration, for it also carries the cultural significance of its origins in ancient Greece, and it can be used to impart to a building the dignity, harmony, and sense of philosophical reason that are part of the Western heritage from Greece. The orders are generally regular and predictable, and when the harmonious relationships and proportions are ignored, there is a strong sense of violation.

The **Doric order**, well established by 600 BCE, is vigorous and austere: its fluted columns are strong in appearance and stand directly on the **stereobate** (stepped platform), without a decorated base. The Doric **echinus** appears to be a resilient cushion tucked between the column and the square **abacus**, suggesting in a clear, visual manner the nature and even the idea of support. Together, echinus and abacus provide a simple and muscular transition from the vertical column to the horizontal superstructure. The Doric architrave is broad and simple, and the frieze area is decorated with **triglyphs**, which alternate with **metopes** (originally metopes seem to have been painted panels of terracotta; later they were sculpted). The first-century BCE Roman architect Vitruvius argued that the Doric order was originally derived from wooden architecture and that the tapering of the column was based on the use of tree trunks for early columns.

The **Ionic order**, which was first used in the sixth century BCE, is lighter in proportion and more elegant in detail than the Doric. Columns have richly decorated bases, and the Ionic capital is characterized by a scroll-like motif called a **volute**. Ionic temples often feature a continuous frieze in place of the triglyphs and metopes. The planar, frontal Ionic volutes created a problem at corners, which was solved by the development, during the fifth century BCE, of the **Corinthian order**, which employs a cylindrical capital decorated with acanthus leaves. The increasing elegance of the Greek orders is revealed by the constantly changing proportions of the column. In the Doric, the relationship of height to diameter is usually 4:1 to 6:1 or even 7:1. For Ionic, it is 7:1 to 8:1; Corinthian can be 8:1 to 9:1.

Greek Doric Architecture

3-66 Second Temple of Hera, Paestum, Italy. c. 460 BCE. Southern Italy and Sicily were colonized by the Greeks beginning in the seventh century BCE (see map, page 100). The earliest Greek temples were small shrines containing a cult statue. During the eighth and early seventh centuries BCE, large wood temples with peristyles were built. By the later seventh century BCE, stone construction began to replace wood, partially as a practical response to the problem of supporting the heavy terra-cotta roof tiles. Stone construction, which coincides with the advent of monumental stone sculpture, reflects a confident new spirit, a spirit of permanence and achievement. The temples constructed in these colonies during the sixth and fifth centuries BCE are among the best-preserved examples of Greek architecture.

A Greek Doric temple (see figs. 3-66, 3-73, 3-75) is an imposing structure, an autonomous object that is complete within itself. The architectural forms are vigorous and assertive. The vertical fluting of the columns, reinforced by the triglyphs in the frieze above, produces an upward thrust that is held in balance by the horizontal articulation of the entablature and gable roof. The visual forces are in equilibrium, yet the temple is not visually static. Its massive forms communicate an almost muscular vitality.

The walled inner sanctuary, or **naos** (from the Greek "to dwell"), contained the cult statue (see fig. 3-76). On the exterior, the perimeter of the temple is surrounded by a **colonnade**, or continuous row of columns, called a **peri-style** (from *peri*, "around," and *style*, "column"); such temples are termed **peripteral** (see fig. 3-74). It seems that only priests or priestesses and their attendants were allowed inside the temple. Most rituals occurred outside, at an altar in front of the temple. The temple might thus be thought of as a sculptural background for the ritual.

A post-and-lintel system forms the peristyle, while walls enclose the naos. Columns support the entablature and roof. The pediments at each end of the gable roof are in some temples filled with sculpted figures. The roof was originally made of wood rafters covered with terracotta tiles.

3-67 Diagram of the evolution of Doric proportions to scale. For further discussion of the importance of proportional relationships in Greek art and architecture, see pp. 78–79, 84–85.

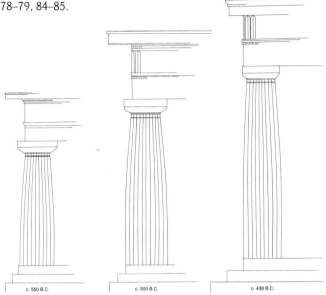

c. 550 B.C.   c. 500 B.C.   c. 438 B.C.

3-68 Scythian, *STAG*. Seventh-sixth century BCE, from Kostromskaya in the Kuban, Commonwealth of Russia. Gold, height 12". Hermitage Museum, St. Petersburg.

Technique   *Greek Temple Construction*

Once the design for a temple was determined, stonecutters began to cut marble at quarries. The blocks of stone, formed to specifications to reduce transportation weight, were moved to the construction site in specially designed carts pulled by teams of animals. After the temple's foundation had been built, the peristyle was set up. Columns were constructed of unfluted cylindrical units called **drums**, held in place by wood centering pins. The drums for the columns and the blocks of stone for the walls of the naos were lifted into place with pulleys and cranes. No mortar was used to hold the stones in place. The blocks of the naos walls were secured by iron clamps encased in lead to prevent rusting. The roof was constructed of wood beams and rafters. A beam supported the apex of the gable roof, while additional support for the roof was provided by columns inside the naos. Finally, as the temple neared completion, the columns were fluted. The fluting disguised the joints of the drums and, by creating patterns of shadows, reinforced the three-dimensionality of the columns.

The changing proportions of the Doric order seen in the evolution of the proportion of and relationship among column, capital, and entablature (fig. 3-67) reflect the search for an aesthetic harmony that was integral to Greek art. The diagram also reveals the increasing scale of the Doric temple over time.

While the bold stone architecture erected by Greek settlers on the Italian peninsula reveals a settled population, in other parts of the world there were flourishing nomadic societies. The Scyths, for example, were a Western Asian nomadic group who lived on the Central Asian steppes. Beginning in the eighteenth century, archaeologists began to excavate great burial mounds in the Kuban River Basin near the Caucasus Mountains; as early as the fifth century BCE these peoples had been identified as the Scyths by the Greek author Herodotus. The Scyths were horse-riding people and, as inhabitants of the vast steppes where wild animals were a daily threat to their herds and their livelihood, they respected these wild creatures and took them as an important part of their symbol system. The gold stag (fig. 3-68), with its exaggerated rack of horns and drawn-up legs, is depicted with a physical power much greater than its small size. It was buried with its royal owner in a tomb that was filled with sacrificed horses and riders and with the belongings of the deceased: gold plaques and belt hooks representing animals either singly or in combat, horse trappings, leather quivers, bronze arrowheads, shields of iron, and other items typical of their nomadic lifeways.

Greek Bronze Sculpture: Severe Style

3-69 Zeus. c. 460 bce. Bronze with inlaid eyes, teeth, lips, and nipples, height 6'10". National Archaeological Museum, Athens. Lost in an ancient shipwreck at about the time of Christ, this sculpture was found in the sea near Cape Artemision in 1926. It is sometimes identified as representing Poseidon, god of the sea.

This larger-than-lifesize figure of Zeus originally held a lightning bolt, the god's symbol, in his right hand (fig. 3-69). His energetic movement is communicated by the tensed muscles of torso and abdomen, the distended veins, the buoyant position of the feet, and the arms, which are outstretched for balance and to help the god focus on his victim. The left foot is supported only on the heel and outside edge; the right touches only with the ball and toes. Three prongs in the soles held the figure in position on its base. Zeus's pose expresses the perfect physical development of the god and his complete physical control, while his severe facial expression complements the aggressive action.

Such a position would be impossible in marble, for marble's lack of tensile strength would not allow the outstretched arms, while the pose of feet and legs would not support the weight of the upper body. Because of its greater possibilities for both naturalistic effects and convincing movement, bronze was the favored sculptural medium of the Greeks after the Archaic period. But few ancient Greek bronzes have survived because they could so easily be melted down and the bronze reused for weapons or other purposes. In this figure, the color of the

3-70 Charioteer, from the monument dedicated by Polyzalus of Gela in the Sanctuary of Apollo, Delphi. c. 477 BCE. Bronze with inlaid stone and glass eyes, height 5'11". Archaeological Museum, Delphi. This figure and its quadriga were buried after they were damaged, perhaps in an earthquake. Only fragments of the horses and chariot survive. Commissioned by Polyzalos, Tyrant of Gela, to celebrate the victory of his quadriga in the Delphic Games.

PHOTOGRAPHER: ALISON FRANTZ.

bronze suggests a naturally suntanned, oiled body (the Greeks oiled their bodies when exercising), and the inlaid eyes and teeth, fringed sheet bronze eyelashes, and inlaid colored lips and nipples reinforce the naturalistic impact.

The *Charioteer* (fig. 3-70) was originally part of a large votive monument that included a chariot and four horses, a grouping called a **quadriga**. The patron, a tyrant from Sicily, commissioned the work as an offering to Apollo and a commemoration of the victory of his team and charioteer in the Delphic Games. The subtle and delicate pose evolves from a slight twist of the upper body. The figure wears the appropriate racing garment, and the artist has emphasized the subtle patterns of the delicate material as it is caught and pleated by a belt and ribbons or straps. The head represents the ideal Greek type, with a strong nose that continues the line of the forehead, large eyes and ears, full jawline, broad cheeks, and prominent lips. The expression is alert and self-confident, with a hint of the pride that is appropriate to a winner in the games.

Technique *Greek Lost-Wax Bronze Casting*

The earliest-known bronze monumental sculptures in Greece date from the late sixth century BCE, but they were preceded by the casting of bronze body armor, which may have suggested and supported the development of bronze sculpture. Ancient Greek bronzes are hollow-cast of an alloy of copper and tin by what is known as the **lost-wax method** (fig. 3-71). A sculptor begins by forming a mass of clay (or some other malleable material) into the rough shape of the planned sculpture, but slightly smaller. This is covered with a layer of wax of the thickness desired for the finished bronze and modeled to approximate the surface finish of the planned sculpture. This wax coating is then encased in another layer of damp clay. When it has dried, the wax is melted away, leaving a hollow mold between core and exterior (supports hold the two in place). Molten bronze is poured into the mold. After it cools and hardens, the mold is broken or cut away, leaving bronze that has assumed the form first created in wax.

It is difficult to cast large figures in bronze, for the bronze can cool before it has reached the full extent of the mold. The ancient Greek bronzes discussed here were therefore cast in several sections. The *Charioteer*, for example, is composed of seven pieces and, as is common, pieces of different textures were cast individually—the figure's right arm, for example, was cast separately and is fitted into the opening left in the sleeve when the drapery was cast. Actual cloth, impregnated with wax, may have been used to help form the draped patterns of the costume, and it has also been suggested that the ancient Greek sculptors may have created body parts using clay molds made from living human figures.

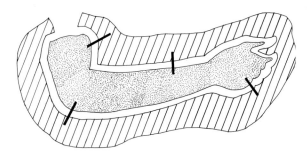

inner core of clay

wax, later replaced with bronze

outer mold of clay

metal pins that hold inner core in place when wax is melted out

3-71   Lost-wax bronze casting. Conjectural reconstruction of technique for right arm of figure 3-70. To compare Chinese piece-mold bronze casting c. 1200 BCE, see pp. 64-65.

After casting, the bronze was tooled and polished (worked with tools and an abrasive) to achieve the finished surface. Lips, nipples, and eyebrows were sometimes highlighted and given a realistic reddish cast by being overlaid with copper or with bronze of a high copper content. Fringed sheet-bronze eyelashes, inlaid stone and glass eyes, and teeth of silver, marble, or ivory were applied after the polishing of the bronze was complete. These additional colors and materials enhanced the beauty of the work, impressed the observer with the skill of the artists, and, most importantly, played a vital role in achieving the verisimilitude desired by the Greeks. They made these beautiful and ideal figures seem even more real.

Greek Classical-Style Sculpture

3-72 POLYKLEITOS

DORYPHOROS (SPEAR CARRIER), Roman copy after a lost bronze original of c. 450 BCE. Marble, height 7′. National Archaeological Museum, Naples, Italy. This copy is generally considered to be the best version of Polykleitos's lost figure, but the spear that it once carried is missing, and the bronze original would not have had the tree trunk behind the right leg or the marble bar supporting the right arm.

Beauty . . . arises . . . in the commensurability [proportion] of the parts, such as that of finger to finger, and all of the forearm to the upper arm, and . . . of everything to everything else, just as it is written in the *Canon* of Polykleitos. For having taught us in that book all the proportions of the body, Polykleitos supported his treatise with a work; he made a statue according to the tenets of his treatise, and called the statue, like his book, the *Canon*.

Unfortunately, both Polykleitos's written text and the original bronze version of his demonstration piece—described here by Galen, a Greek physician, writing in the second century CE on Greek aesthetic theory—are lost. Nevertheless, the numerous surviving, more-or-less-complete marble copies of the original statue, which was made about 450 BCE, verify its significance in the classical world. Although Polykleitos called his example *The Canon* after the principles of proportion it was intended to demonstrate, the popular name, which we have inherited from antiquity, is the *Doryphoros (Spear Carrier)*.

The specific subject of the *Doryphoros* (fig. 3-72) is probably an ideal Olympic athlete, but the statue was more importantly a demonstration of the system of perfect proportions that Polykleitos had perceived in the human body and established in his lost text. The *Doryphoros* was considered to be an ideal figure because its proportions adhered to common fractions (exact divisions by whole numbers) of the figure's height. Because Polykleitos's original figure and text are lost, the precise measurements of his canon remain undetermined, but the later Roman writer Vitruvius advocated a rule whereby the head (from the crown of the hair to the chin) was one-eighth of the total height, the width of the shoulders one-quarter the height, and so on, until every anatomical feature and the proportions among them were woven into a system of mathematical measurements. The Doryphoros can be understood as a visual example of the often-quoted statement by the ancient Greek philosopher Protagoras that "man is the measure of all things." Such a demonstration of mathematical relationships could lead to a dull sculpture, but the *Doryphoros* exhibits a firm muscular structure that is enlivened by the contrapposto stance.

A century before the *Doryphoros* was created, the Greek philosopher and mathematician Pythagoras had presented mathematical proportion as the basis of musical harmony. Polykleitos's proportional system was, however, more than a set of abstract principles, for it bears an important relationship to the Greek belief in the agreement between natural and mathematical harmony, a belief that brought a new vitality to the human figure in sculpture and to the visual arts in general.

Vitruvius reported that the proportions governing the human figure in art also determined the proportions of Greek temples: "Further, it was from the members of the body that [the Greeks] derived the fundamental ideas of measures." Vitruvius defines proportion, in a manner similar to our understanding of the Polykleitian canon, as "a correspondence among the measure of an entire work, and of the whole to a certain part selected as a standard." Just as the Greeks gave human characteristics to their gods, they also humanized their architecture. The relative proportions, the capital as the head of the column, and the slight muscular swelling of a Doric column, or **entasis** (see page 87), all contribute to an empathetic understanding between us and the temple. This empathy was an extension of the Greeks' rational definition of their world.

Technique *Contrapposto in Sculpture*

The relaxed stance seen in the *Spear Carrier* was a recent development in Greek sculpture, but it had a powerful and long-lasting influence on later works. In the Italian Renaissance, when this stance was one of many features of ancient art that were revived, it became known by the term **contrapposto**. In ancient Greek art, contrapposto emerged tentatively during the period that art historians have named the Severe or Transitional period. One of the earliest surviving examples is the kouros known as the *Kritian Boy* (see fig. 3-64), but in that case the twisting of the figure in space—the natural outcome of balancing the body over one supporting leg—is only delicately suggested. With the *Spear Carrier*, the twisting of the body and the tilting of the pelvis are more evident.

The origin of this pose in ancient Greek sculpture can be understood as an outcome of the Greeks' interest in the ideal nude human body, in athletic achievement, and in understanding how the parts of the body work together organically. The development of contrapposto is also related to the development of **sculpture in the round**; the twisting of the body encourages us to view it from different viewpoints to fully understand the pose.

The ancient Romans adopted contrapposto along with many other Greek artistic ideas; the impact of the pose is evident in the *Augustus* (see fig. 3-97). But the interest in contrapposto did not last long after the rise of Christianity. Although contrapposto can still be seen in the Early Christian figure of the *Good Shepherd* (see fig. 4-15), the otherworldly ideals of Christianity eventually rendered the relaxation and informality of the contrapposto pose inappropriate (see, for example, the pose of the Gothic *Beau Dieu* from Amiens, figure 4-97).

Contrapposto reappears in the Italian Renaissance as a result of the joint interests in naturalism and ancient art. In *Saint Mark* (see fig. 5-14), the sculptor Donatello manipulates the drapery to emphasize the contrapposto, using fine, flutelike lines of material to emphasize the supporting leg and broader, draped patterns to accentuate the relaxation of the other leg. Notice how Saint Mark's right shoulder drops back in contrast to the forward position of his left knee. (For other Renaissance examples of contrapposto, see figures 5-15, 5-47, and 6-18.) Michelangelo sometimes exaggerated the twist of the contrapposto pose to achieve a dramatic, emotional effect, as in his *Saint Matthew* (see fig. 6-19); in the Renaissance, this more twisted pose was known as the *figura serpentinata*.

Greek Architecture:
The Parthenon, Athens

3-73 KALLIKRATES AND IKTINOS

Parthenon, Acropolis, Athens. 447–438 BCE; sculpture completed by 432 BCE. Pentelic marble, 111 × 237' at base. The temple to Athena, goddess of wisdom and fierce protector of Athens, was built after the Persian wars, when Athens was controlled by Pericles, who insisted that the Athenians rebuild the temples the Persians had destroyed. The name *Parthenon* means "maiden," and the temple was dedicated to Athena, the maiden (*parthenon* was the name given to the room in a home where unmarried, virginal daughters lived). The Parthenon was the preeminent religious structure in Athens. It later served as a Christian church dedicated to Mary and, in the later Middle Ages, as the cathedral of Athens. After the conquest of Athens by the Turks, it served as a mosque. It was severely damaged in 1687, during a war between the Venetians and the Turks. Commissioned by Pericles, ruler of Athens.

In the history of human accomplishment, the Parthenon on the Acropolis in Athens is one of the most famous monuments (see figs. 3-73–3-80). Its significance is not due to its basic form, which continues the Doric temple type developed more than a century earlier (see pp. 80-81). Rather, it is the harmony and grace of its proportions that make the Parthenon great. Its fame derives from its beauty.

The Parthenon's grandeur made it a monument to the wealth, power, taste, and piety of Athens. It was entirely surfaced in white Pentelic marble, including even the roof. The interior has two chambers—a smaller

3-74 Plan of the Parthenon.

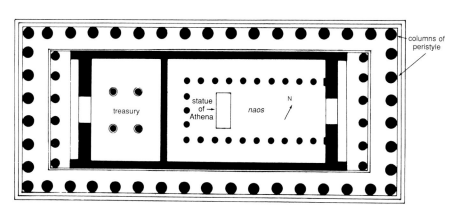

one where city's treasures were stored, and the naos, where an ivory-and-gold statue of Athena in military dress was enshrined (fig. 3-76). Although all people could look in from the door, it seems that only a few were allowed to enter these chambers. The rituals in honor of Athena were held outside, at a sacrificial altar to which the Parthenon was the backdrop. The Parthenon was enlivened by many sculptures (see figs. 3-76 to 3-80).

The grace and beauty of the Parthenon are the culmination of a long Greek search for the ideal temple. The simple dynamics of the post-and-lintel system became a vehicle that encouraged Greek architects to attempt to achieve the most satisfying equipose. Compared to the Second Temple of Hera at Paestum (see fig. 3-66), the Parthenon offers a new grace and elegance.

There are a number of remarkable visual refinements in the Parthenon. All the horizontal lines—steps, stylobate, stereobate, entablature—are raised slightly in the middle, ostensibly to correct the sag that the human eye imparts to a long horizontal (and also to add the practical advantage of helping rainwater to run off). Like the other optical refinements of the Parthenon, the lifting of the middle of the horizontals gives the building elasticity and a sense of life. Such adjustments made the structure more difficult to engineer and construct, for each block of marble had to be cut to fit its exact place. Other refinements include the tilting inward of the columns to enhance the effect of stability and compactness, and the placement of the three corner columns closer together to compensate for the dissolving effect of light at the corners; for the same reason, the corner columns were made slightly thicker than the others. The entire stylobate is tilted upward at the southwest corner to make the building more impressive both from the city below and from the entrance to the Acropolis.

Perhaps the single most revealing refinement is the **entasis** of the columns,

447–438 BCE   **Kallikrates and Iktinos, Parthenon, Athens**
440 BCE   Sophocles, *Antigone*

3-75   Reconstruction model of the Parthenon. The Metropolitan Museum of Art, New York.

LEVI HALE WILLARD BEQUEST. PURCHASE, 1890 (90.35.2)

which do not taper in a straight line but bulge outward about one-third of the way up from the base. The entasis creates an effect of muscular elasticity that helps give the Parthenon a human, organic quality. Later copies and variations often seem rigid and cold because they lack these refinements. The Parthenon is a monument that reveals the analytical quality of the human mind and the Greek search for the harmonious, the ideal, and the beautiful.

3-76   View of the naos of the Parthenon copy in Nashville, Tennessee, with its reproduction of the lost 40-foot statue of Athena by Phidias that once adorned the naos of the ancient Greek Parthenon. The modern version, which sets out to be as accurate as possible given the limited evidence available, was created by sculptor Alan Laquire. Laquire's sculpture copies the colors of the original, but in Phidias's version the flesh was composed of carved pieces of ivory while the dress and armor were made of thin sheets of gold; the figure was supported by a ship's mast. Phidias's equally gigantic ivory-and-gold statue of the enthroned Zeus, once in the god's temple at Olympia, was called one of the seven wonders of the ancient world. Only the great Egyptian pyramids (fig. 3-22) survive from this list; the other five were the Lighthouse at Alexandria, the Mausoleum at Hallicarnassus, the Hanging Gardens of Babylon, the Colossus of Rhodes, and the Temple of Diana at Ephesus.

Greek Sculpture: The Parthenon

3-77 Diagram of the Parthenon sculptures in their original positions. The sculpture is attributed to Phidias and his workshop.

The Parthenon's architectural beauty and richness were enhanced by the sculpture that was integrated into the Doric design (figs. 3-73–3-80). The pediments at both ends were filled with over-lifesize figures, there were ninety-two metopes sculpted in high relief, and a continuous low-relief frieze, 550 feet long, encircled the outside of the naos wall. Like the edifice they adorn,

these sculptures display an impressive mastery of form and technique. They were all completed in about twelve years, indicating that there must have been a large workshop of sculptors and assistants, but their general consistency of design suggests that a single sculptor was in charge. This sculptor most probably was Phidias (c. 490–430 BCE), who also designed the ivory-and-gold statue of Athena that stood in the naos (see fig. 3-76). The consistency of the sculptural conception suggests that Phidias provided drawings—perhaps on the stone itself—to guide the sculptors.

The iconographic themes are related to the dedication of the Parthenon to Athena, to the victories of the Greeks over the barbarians, and to Athens's political leadership among the city-states in Greece. The east pediment presented the *Birth of Athena* (fig. 3-78), the west the *Contest between Athena and Poseidon*. The metopes featured a series of battle scenes, including a battle between centaurs and men. Until recently, the continuous frieze had been thought to represent the procession of the Great Panathenaea, a celebration held every four years in honor of Athena, with musicians, elders, horse-

men, chariots, and sacrificial cattle and sheep. A new interpretation—still controversial—relates the procession to an episode from the mythological history of Athens in which a daughter of the king offers to die to save the city; she is joined in a death pact by her two sisters. Whatever the actual subject, the frieze presents a vivid depiction of the participants in an ancient ritual procession.

On the east pediment the dramatic birth of Athena—who sprang full grown, wearing armor, from the head of her father, Zeus—is conveyed by figures who move outward from the central episode. There is a coherent unity of time and place similar to that which developed in contemporary Greek drama. The magnificent group of seated and reclining goddesses, for example (fig. 3-79), turn as they become aware of the birth. To compose within the sloping pedimental shape was a challenge for the Greek artist, but these goddesses, shown in graceful, natural poses and beautifully unified as a group, do not seem forced into the increasingly constricted space of the pediment. Their voluptuous bodies are clothed in clinging drapery that is gathered and folded into patterns emphasizing

3-78 Reconstruction of the east pediment of the Parthenon, showing the BIRTH OF ATHENA by Phidias and his workshop. The darkened figures show the original location of the *Three Goddesses* (see fig. 3-79). The darkened sections in the pediment indicate surviving fragments; the light lines are conjectural figures. The scenes in the metopes are extant.

3-79 PHIDIAS AND WORKSHOP

THREE GODDESSES ON MOUNT OLYMPUS, from the east pediment of the Parthenon, Athens. c. 438–432 BCE. Marble, height of center figure 5'; the figures are slightly over-lifesize. The British Museum, London. These three figures have been identified as Hestia, Dione, and Aphrodite. The Parthenon pediments were more than 90 feet long, and at the center they rose to a height of more than 11 feet. The platform on which the figures were placed was about 3 feet deep.

3-80 PHIDIAS AND WORKSHOP.

HORSEMEN, from the frieze of the Parthenon. Marble, height approx. 43". The British Museum, London.

The Parthenon frieze is a tour de force of low-relief carving that offers the illusion of as many as six figures and horses overlapping within a low relief that is no more than three inches deep (fig. 3-80). The relief is carved more deeply near the top as a concession to the placement of the frieze, high above the spectator's head. By thus giving the work greater readability, the Greek sculptor makes it clear that this frieze is for the enjoyment and enlightenment of the human spectator and is not merely a decoration added to the temple in honor of the goddess.

The Parthenon's sculptures had additions made of metal, some perhaps gilded, for the armor, straps, and other refinements. Many of the details of the figures were heightened by paint, although there is still controversy over the actual colors used. A bright blue has been proposed as the background for the pedimental figures, a red background for metopes and frieze. The hair of the figures may have been gilded; the drapery hems probably had painted patterns taken from actual Greek garments. Color would have enhanced the beauty of the marble figures and clarified the compositions for the Athenians, who saw the Parthenon as a monument to their success as well as to the generosity of their patron goddess.

the sculptural presence of the figures. The clarity of the poses is remarkable, as is the graceful and flowing role they play within the triangular composition. Filling the outermost corners of the pediment are, on the left, the sun god's rising chariot to signify dawn and, on the right, the horses of the moon's chariot. These forms are cut off by the pediment, perhaps to suggest that the realm of the gods continues beyond any artificial restrictions.

CHAPTER 3   Ancient Art

Greek Sculpture and Painting: Fourth Century BCE

3-81 PRAXITELES

HERMES AND DIONYSOS. (c. 400–300 BCE) National Archeological Museum, Athens, Greece. Scala/Art Resource, NY.

Despite political instability in Greece after the Peloponnesian War ended in 404 BCE, the fourth century was a time of creativity and stylistic experimentation. We can see beginnings of stylistic change in *Hermes with the Child Dionysos* (fig. 3-81). As Hermes, messenger of the gods, holds him, the infant Dionysos, a god and patron of drama and song, reaches forward, probably to grasp a bunch of grapes that Hermes may have held in his right hand. The articulation of muscles contrasts with that of the *Doryphoros* (see fig. 3-72). While the spear carrier's muscles were clearly defined, those of Hermes have a softer, more natural appearance. Hermes' stance reinforces this new organic unity, and the axis of the figure follows a shallow **S** curve, which adds to the sense of relaxation. What we can determine from this copy after Praxiteles (370–330 BCE), who was one of the dominant artists of the fourth century, indicates a continued evolution toward naturalism in Greek sculpture and a new, refined elegance.

Praxiteles also sculpted a statue of Aphrodite (Venus), the goddess of love and beauty, that was purchased by the city of Knidos, in Asia Minor, and installed in a shrine there that was open on all sides, so that her beauty would be visible from all directions (fig. 3-82). This *Aphrodite* is the first monumental figure in Greek art to depict the female nude in three dimensions. Her nudity is explained by the vase and drapery under her left hand: she is represented either entering or leaving her bath. Lucian, a second-century BCE Greek rhetorician who saw the statue, observed:

> So strongly has the artists' art prevailed, that the recalcitrant and solid nature of the stone has been transformed in each limb. . . . [As we viewed the figure from behind], unforeseen amazement at the goddess' beauty seized us.

The *Aphrodite*, like the *Hermes*, is freestanding and is composed as sculpture in the round. The diagonal movement of the right arm and hand and the slightly lifted left leg create an impelling motion across and, by implication, around the body. Unlike earlier Greek sculpture, which primarily has a frontal orientation, these works invite us to admire the sculptor's ability to create a complex, multifaceted composition in space.

We know from literary sources that the sense of drama and spatial involvement that characterized fourth-century sculpture was paralleled by advances in painting, but unfortunately no certain examples of fourth-century painting survive. Nevertheless, ancient literary sources offer accounts of accomplishments in perspective and illusionism that already astonished viewers by the beginning of this period. The first-century CE writer Pliny the Elder reported, for example, on a contest between two late-fifth-century BCE artists:

> [Parrhasios] entered a contest with Zeuxis, and when the latter depicted some grapes with such success that birds flew up to the [painting], Parrhasios then depicted a linen curtain with such verisimilitude that Zeuxis, puffed up with pride by the verdict of the birds, eventually requested that the curtain be removed and Parrhasios' picture shown . . . when Zeuxis understood his error, [he] conceded defeat . . . because he himself had only deceived birds, but Parrhasios had deceived him, an artist. It is said that afterward Zeuxis painted a picture of a boy carrying grapes, and when the birds flew up to them, he approached the work and, in irritation with it, said, "I have painted the grapes better than the boy, for if I had rendered him perfectly, the birds would have been afraid." (Pliny, *Natural History*, XXV)

The ability of painters to render the naturalism of appearance paralleled the subtle anatomical features, spontaneous attitudes, and increased spatial involvement of contemporary sculpture. These trends would develop as the influence of Greek culture spread throughout the eastern Mediterranean region.

4th century BCE	**Praxiteles,** *Hermes*
399 BCE	Socrates is condemned to death
331 BCE	Alexander defeats Darius
323 BCE	Death of Alexander the Great

3-82 PRAXITELES

APHRODITE OF KNIDOS, Roman copy after lost original. c. 360– 330 BCE by Praxiteles. Marble, height 6′8″. Vatican Museum, Rome. The first-century CE Roman writer Pliny tells us that Praxiteles made two similar statues, one clothed and one nude, and that the Knidians daringly bought the nude example. Pliny tells us that a stain on the back of the figure was "an indication of lust" left by a man who had hidden himself in the shrine during the nighttime in order to embrace the statue.

Hellenistic Art

3-83 *WINGED VICTORY OF SAMOTHRACE*, from the Sanctuary of the Great Gods, Samothrace. c. 190 BCE. Marble, height 8'. The Louvre, Paris. This figure celebrates a naval victory, perhaps a victory of the navy of Rhodes at Side in 190 BCE. At Samothrace, the statue was erected on a darker gray marble base in the form of the prow of a ship, and to give the effect of a ship coming into harbor, statue and base were set in two pools, one with a rippled marble bottom and a second with huge boulders. Most likely commissioned by the victorious admiral or the ruler he represented.

Despite the loss of head and arms, the *Winged Victory of Samothrace* expresses heroic triumph (fig. 3-83). The diagonal forward thrust of the body creates a dynamic effect of forward movement. The posture is strengthened by the complex and subtle patterns of drapery that envelop the figure, as well as by the contrasting position of the unfurled wings. Effects of wind are felt as the drapery both presses against the body's surface and unfurls in vigorous forms that billow into space, echoing the movement of the wings. The dramatic spatial involvement and dynamic movement displayed by the *Winged Victory* are typical of the art of the Hellenistic period (c. 400–100 BCE).

History

In the late fourth century BCE, while the Greek city-states maintained a tenuous political stability, the hereditary kings of Macedonia, a kingdom to the north of Greece, strengthened their political power. Philip II, king of Macedonia, proposed a plan for the unification of Greece under his rule. In 338 BCE, while the Greeks debated his proposal, Philip defeated them. Philip's union of Greece with Macedonia was the initial step in a grand design to establish an empire that would include Persia. After Philip II was killed by an assassin in 336 BCE, his son Alexander, nineteen years old, ascended the throne. Following the vision of his father, he led a military campaign against Persia and defeated King Darius in 331 BCE (see figs. 3-85, 6-60). Later conquests extended the boundaries of his vast Hellenistic empire south through Egypt and east to the borders of India before Alexander died in 323 BCE.

Alexander had been educated by Greek standards, and his tutor was Aristotle, the philosopher and natural scientist. The young conqueror envisioned a unity between the Greeks and the Persians based on the cultural values of Hellenism, the ideas and ideals of Classical Greece. After his death, Alexander's dream of unity was fractured by the reality of political conflict among his own generals. Soon his empire was divided into smaller independent powers. Common to these diverse regions, however, was the unifying influence of Greek culture.

Alexandria, founded by Alexander in Egypt in 332 BCE, became a famous center of learning. The great library there may have contained as many as 500,000 volumes, representing the accumulated wealth of knowledge of the ancient world. The library was part of a complex known as the museum (from the Greek *mouseios*, "of the Muses," referring to the ancient Greek goddesses of art and music). The major centers of Hellenistic art production, which were founded outside the Greek mainland, included Alexandria, the island of Rhodes, and Pergamon in Asia Minor (see map, page 71).

Art of the Hellenistic Period

The developing naturalism that characterized Greek fourth-century sculpture and painting deepened in the Hellenistic period and united with an interest in realism in subject matter. The appreciation of art was no longer restricted to the educated citizens of the city-states, however; the new empathetic and dramatic art appealed to a wider audience. These displays of human emotion and drama in art paralleled the melodramatic staging of contemporary Greek theater.

Many portrait busts of Alexander were created to distribute throughout the empire and even beyond, images of the young man as a dynamic conqueror. They emphasize his mental and physical alertness through a combination of deeply set eyes, a furrowed brow, a naturalistically open mouth,

225 BCE	Romans defeat the Celts
221 BCE	1st Chinese empire (Qin) established
215 BCE	Romans defeat Hannibal at Nola
c. 190 BCE	*Winged Victory of Samothrace*

and a strong twisting of the head on the neck. A similar emotional, inspired quality is evident in coins of Alexander that were created by his successors (fig. 3-84).

The Hellenistic emphasis on dramatic and emotional naturalism can be related to a changed philosophical outlook epitomized in the teachings of Aristotle (384–322 BCE). Aristotle's teacher, Plato, had viewed material objects as mere imperfect reflections of ideal forms. Aristotle, in contrast, stressed the roles of natural observation and experience in understanding reality. He sought to comprehend nature by perceiving its manifestations in the biological and earth sciences. The direction of Aristotle's philosophy, based on a penetrating observation of nature, parallels the dramatic naturalism of fourth-century and Hellenistic art.

Hellenistic Painting

As with Hellenistic sculpture, much of our knowledge of specific paintings is based on literary sources and/or Roman copies in fresco or in **mosaic**—designs composed of a number of small pieces (in various periods pebbles, stone, tile, and glass have been used for mosaics). The *Battle of Alexander the Great and King Darius* (fig. 3-85), for example, is thought to preserve the composition of a Hellenistic painting mentioned in literary sources. The successful representation of vivid and energetic activity demonstrated in the mosaic testifies to the continuing advances in illusionism in Hellenistic painting. Alexander rides into the battle from the left, raising his spear; Darius anxiously looks back toward his pursuer. The foreshortening of the cen-

3-84 *ALEXANDER THE GREAT WITH AMUN HORNS*, 4-drachma coin, issued by Lysimachus. c. 300 BCE. Silver, diameter 1⅛". Alexander was one of the earliest rulers to appear on coins; this example shows him with the horns of the Egyptian god Amun. Commissioned by the Hellenistic ruler Lysimachus, king of Lysimachia.

tral horse, seen from the rear, and the frantic activity of the team pulling Darius's chariot add complexity to the tumult of the battle. Within the turbulent scene, the Hellenistic painter added a detail to demonstrate virtuosity: reflected in a Greek shield below Darius's chariot is the anguished face of a young Persian about to be crushed by the wheels of the chariot. The representation of suffering and death was a challenge to the Hellenistic artist (see figs. 3-86, 3-87), and here the horror reflected on the Persian's face dramatically communicates the personal reality of battle.

Hellenistic Sculpture in Pergamon

The *Dying Trumpeter* (fig. 3-86), one of a group depicting defeated Gauls from a large monument at Pergamon, displays the psychological and physical naturalism

3-85 *BATTLE OF ALEXANDER THE GREAT AND KING DARIUS OF PERSIA*, Roman mosaic copy of a lost Hellenistic painting of c. 300 BCE. Stone and glass mosaic, height 10′6″. National Museum, Naples. Found in the House of the Dancing Faun at Pompeii, this impressive mosaic uses more than a million small pieces of stone and glass to create the illusion of the battle. The lost Hellenistic original may have been by Philoxenos or Helena of Alexandria, an early example of a documented woman artist. Commissioned by the owner of the House of the Dancing Faun.

that characterizes Hellenistic art. Distinguished as one of the invaders from the north known as Gauls by his matted hair, his mustache, and the metal collar, or torque, around his neck, this soldier is shown pierced in the side; his blood spews from the wound. His face mirrors defeat, and we experience his last moments of life. Even in the marble copy, a keen observation of surface anatomy complements the psychological drama of impending death; both body and soul are rendered with unsparing reality.

During the mid-third century BCE, the Hellenistic kingdom of Pergamon became a major political power and art center. In 230 BCE, King Attalus I of Pergamon defeated an invasion by the Gauls, who had entered Asia Minor following their invasion of Greece in 279 BCE. In defeating the foreign invaders, Attalus I was able to establish his kingdom as the principal political force in the Middle East. By commissioning works that represent the noble deaths of the enemy, Attalus made his own victory seem even more impressive.

During the Hellenistic period, art no longer exclusively served the worship of the gods or the embellishment of the city-states; it could extol the exploits of a political leader and so act to capture public support. This motive underlay construction of the great Altar of Zeus and Athena at Pergamon (fig. 3-87). The balance between theme and form demonstrated in the earlier *Dying Trumpeter*, however, gives way by the second century to an emphasis on drama that approaches the melodramatic.

The altar was raised on a platform about 20 feet high. Approaching the steps that lead to the altar, viewers encountered a dramatic frieze in such high relief that the sculpted figures seem to kneel and fall out onto the steps. The frieze depicts the Gigantomachy—a mythological battle between the giants and the Greek gods. At Pergamon, the overt display of emotion and the convulsive interlacing diagonals of the figural composition combine to create an overwhelmingly dramatic presentation and, thereby, a new level of expression in Western art.

3-86 *DYING TRUMPETER*, Roman copy after a lost bronze original of c. 230–220 BCE from Pergamon. Marble, lifesize. Capitoline Museum, Rome. Commissioned by King Attalus I of Pergamon.

3-87 Reconstructed Altar of Zeus and Athena, from Pergamon. c. 181–159 BCE. Marble, 120 × 113' at base; height of frieze 7'6"; the figures are well over lifesize. Staatliche Museen zu Berlin, Preussischer Kulturbesitz. Commissioned by King Eumenes II of Pergamon to commemorate the victory of King Attalus I over the Gauls.

Early Buddhist Art

3-88 The Great Stupa and the West Torana, Sanchi, India. Begun third century BCE, with later additions and enlargement. Brick and rubble originally faced with painted and gilded stucco, rails and gateways of yellow limestone; height of dome 54′. Stupas were the first sacred Buddhist buildings, and the Great Stupa at Sanchi is the oldest surviving example. The core of the structure probably originated in the third century BCE. Here, as in many Indian stupas, the original building was encased in a mass of earth and stone before it was enlarged, for it was considered a sacrilege to destroy any of the original monument. Originally commissioned by the Indian ruler Asoka; later supported by the lay Buddhist community.

The Great Stupa at Sanchi, on a hill rising out of the plain not far from modern Bhopal in central India (fig. 3-88), is a monumental burial mound known as a **stupa**, whose form dates back to prehistoric times. The stupa, as used for the burial of princes, had the shape of a large hemisphere. At an early date, this kind of tomb developed into a commemorative monument and was adopted by Buddhists as one of their main symbols and as the center of their religious compounds. The stupa could be a tomb, placed over remains of the Buddha or other holy Buddhist individuals, or it could act as a symbol to commemorate a sacred place, such as a site where an important event took place in the Buddha's life. The stupa played an important role in Buddhist beliefs, for it became the symbol of nirvana, or final enlightenment, the goal of Buddhism.

All such monuments follow a similar plan (fig. 3-89). They are solid mounds of rubble and brick, faced with stone; the upper parts are covered with white stucco that was originally decorated and partly gilded. The stupa is surmounted by a three- (or more) part "umbrella" symbolizing the three most basic aspects of Buddhism—the Buddha himself, the Buddha's law, and the monastic community. The rail around the umbrella shaft is thought to reflect the ancient concept of marking off the precinct around a sacred tree. The symbolic meaning of the stupa and its various elements are complex and multifaceted. The mound can refer to the World Mountain and also to the universe, while the umbrella shaft is sometimes interpreted as the axis of the universe.

On the base around the hemispherical dome is a narrow path along which processions move. A second path is at ground level, where pilgrims can circumambulate clockwise, symbolic of walking the Path of Life around the World Mountain, following an ancient Indian rite of retracing the path of the sun while making offerings and ritual performances. The path is enclosed within a tall stone railing, which isolates the sanctuary from the outside world. Access to it is gained through four monumental gateways (torana) 32 feet high, oriented to the cardinal directions. The uprights and crossbars are lavishly carved with stories from the life of the Buddha; with jataka tales, edifying legends in which the Buddha is shown as compassionate and wise in previous lives; and with guardian figures called yakshas and yakshis (fig. 3-90), ancient gods and goddesses of fertility. These lively sculptures are a dramatic contrast to the massive character of the stupa and railing.

It is significant that the Buddha himself is not represented in figural form—a kind of symbolism called **aniconic**, or "without image." His presence is suggested by symbols such as a wheel, footprints, a throne, or the Boh tree (pipal) where he received enlightenment (fig. 3-91), all important emblems of his life. At that time, it was thought to be impossible to represent the Buddha in human form because he had already passed into nirvana, an otherworldly state of being.

A richly decorated structure such as the Great Stupa took decades to complete. In its former splendor, it had smooth white or gaily colored plastered exteriors and sculpted decoration highlighted with polychrome painting. The sculpture depicted stories similar to folk tales that brought the life of the Buddha to visitors in familiar terms. The incorporation of

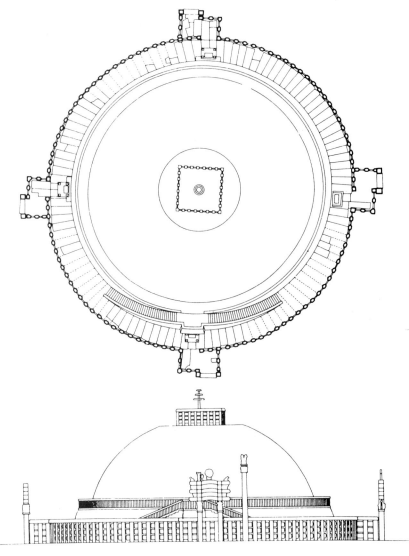

3-89 Plan and elevation of the Great Stupa. The stone railings that create the enclosure are probably based on wooden prototypes. Why the gates are not on axis with the openings in the enclosuring fence is uncertain, but the enforced right angles that this placement requires for the worshiper may also be based on earlier prototypes. Perhaps these changes in direction allude to the swastika design that appears in other earlier Indian contexts, or perhaps they are derived from farmers' gates, designed to keep cattle out of the fields.

the yakshas and yakshis was also a way to relate the monument to the people, for these sensuous deities had been worshiped as bearers of human and natural fertility long before Buddhism. The complicated but rhythmic pose of the voluptuous yakshi (see fig. 3-90) reveals the early importance of dance in Indian worship; it also refers to the legend that a yakshi could, with one touch of her heel, instantly bring a tree into full fruition.

3-90　Yakshi, from the East Torana, Great Stupa. c. 10–30 CE.

The massive domes of stupas frequently incorporate within their mass a system of concentric or radial supporting walls arranged by symbolic, rather than technical, considerations. They face the points of the compass and represent rays leading out from the center, a plan in the form of a **mandala**, or diagram of the cosmos (see fig. 5-3). This pattern is in no way perceptible from the exterior but was of crucial importance for the sacred substance of the monument. The importance of the mandala in Buddhist belief and practice is attested by its survival into the present day.

These early constructions celebrate the life of the historic Buddha (Sanskrit for "the Enlightened One"), a man called Siddhartha Gautama. Born about 563 BCE of a noble family living in the foothills of the Himalayas, he gave up his princely life to seek out

the cause of the suffering that he discovered around him. India of the sixth century BCE was undergoing rapid and violent political and social change. Like many of his contemporaries, Prince Gautama renounced his former life and, as an ascetic, contemplated and discussed the sorrows of the world with other learned recluses on the outskirts of villages. At age thirty-five, he sat under a large pipal tree in the town of Gaya and resolved not to leave his seat until the riddle of suffering was solved.

After hosts of temptations, he sank deeper and deeper into meditation, and at dawn on the forty-ninth day he knew the truth, the secret of suffering and how to overcome it—by releasing the mortal soul from the cycle of rebirth. He had reached nirvana. He remained seated under the Tree of Wisdom (the Boh tree), meditating on the truths he had found. He

then journeyed to Deer Park (modern Sarnath) and preached his first sermon—in Buddhist phraseology, he "set the Wheel of the Law in motion." Soon he had a band of sixty ascetics who became his followers as he preached the Buddhist dharma (doctrine). For eight months of each year they wandered from place to place, but in the rainy season they stopped to live in huts at one of the parks given by wealthy lay followers. These were the first of the many Buddhist monasteries of later times.

The Buddha's quest was a personal one. He sought nirvana, a refined stage of enlightenment accepted by adherents of various religions of the time. Nirvana marked an end to the cycle of rebirth and was thought to be a state of enduring permanent bliss called the Supreme Truth or Reality. Buddhist dharma claims that there is no existence without suffering, that the cause of suffering is egocentric desire, and that the elimination of desire will end suffering.

After the Buddha's death at age eighty, in about 483 BCE, the religion grew and changed along with the political institutions of India. The third leader of the first great Indian empire, called the Mauryan dynasty (322–183 BCE), was Asoka (ruled c. 273–232 BCE). He expanded Mauryan political influence over much of the Indian subcontinent. According to tradition, Asoka was moved to remorse and pity by the horrors of war and came to the conclusion that true power was realized through religion, not force. He became an active patron of Buddhism and supported the communities of monks. The political might of the Mauryans, as well as their patronage, brought the full institutionalization of Buddhism. A set of Buddhist religious offices (services) was created; monks occupied monasteries that acquired property; the canon of Buddhist texts was expanded, diversified, and refined. Asoka himself is said to have erected 84,000 stupas over the relics

3-91 *BOH TREE*, detail of the East Torana, Great Stupa. c. 10–30 CE.

of the Buddha throughout the empire. Thus, the search for personal enlightenment by one man, the Buddha, became an institution involving millions of people supported by one of the great ancient empires.

Stupas became the center of life in the monasteries, which included buildings used as lecture halls, kitchens, and hostels. Their locations and the lifeways of the monks were guided by recollections of the Buddha's life. These **chaityas** (sacred locations) were to a remarkable degree coincident with trade routes of the day, as the initial spread of religion under the state patronage of Asoka was linked to commerce. Because Buddhists enjoyed the protection of the state, traders associating with them came under the same protective umbrella. Monasteries were safe havens that received the financial support of their visitors. The symbiosis between monks and traders ultimately took this religion out of India and into China, Korea, Japan, and Southeast Asia.

The Art of the Roman Republic

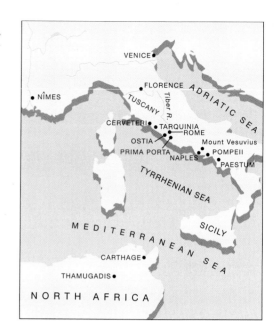

3-92 *HUSBAND AND WIFE*, grave relief from the Via Statilia, Rome. First century BCE. Marble, height 6'. Capitoline Museum, Rome. Probably commissioned by the couple themselves or their family.

This grave marker (fig. 3-92) exhibits the Roman continuation of the old Mediterranean practice of marking graves with images of the deceased, but the stern man and his dignified wife communicate the austere values and virtues of the Romans of the Republican period (c. 510–31 BCE), as they were defined by ancient writers: he seems sober and determined, demanding and uncompromising, while his wife appears dutiful and obedient, consistent with the prescribed role of women during the Republic. The Romans of the early Republic were self-disciplined, devout, conservative, and supporters of traditional values. They admired military valor and prized family, heritage, and the state. They respected law and legal obligations. Their language, Latin, is remarkable for its lucid order and rigid rules.

The Romans of the Republican period showed little interest in art, and even later, during the Roman Empire, Romans seldom indulged in the philosophical debates about the nature of art that had been so important for the Greeks. But a Roman strength that persisted into the Empire was the ability to absorb whatever was useful or good from other traditions. In art, the Romans owed a rich debt to the Etruscans and the Greeks. Only in a few areas did the Romans of the Republic make significant new contributions—most notably in architecture and engineering, especially in the use of concrete, the arch, and the vault (see pages 116–25).

The Romans' interest in and devotion to the family explains their interest in individual portraiture. It was traditional for patrician families to preserve wax, terra-cotta, or marble portrait heads of their ancestors. These portraits were kept in

3-93 Temple of Portunus (formerly called Temple of Fortuna Virilis), Rome. Late second century BCE.

The most conspicuous position in the house, enclosed in a wooden shrine

and

When any distinguished member of the family dies they take [the busts] to the funeral,

according to the first-century BCE historian Polybius. Roman portraits often emphasize the peculiarities of an individual (moles, wrinkles, large ears) in order to capture the uniqueness of the specific person. This respect for the individual—although usually limited, as in most early cultures, to the male—can

be related to Roman republicanism, for a system of government that encourages individual responsibility seems to lead to the development of naturalistic portraiture in art (for later examples, see seventeenth-century Holland, page 354, and early America, page 392).

History

In the eighth century BCE, the Romans were only one of several groups of people living in villages along the Tiber River. But by the third century BCE, they governed a state that encompassed the Italian peninsula. In the subsequent two centuries they

defeated Carthage in North Africa and annexed Greece, Spain, Asia Minor, and the south of France. The government developed as a republic, with rule by two consuls, a hierarchy of public officials, and a senate.

The early Romans had no defined policy of expansion, but their interest in commerce led them into contact with many of their neighbors. Eventually, the Romans were forced to protect their borders and guarantee their peace after attacks from the outside. In about 390 BCE, the Gauls sacked Rome, and later Carthage led Rome into war. The rapid growth of the city of Rome, which by 250 BCE had almost 100,000

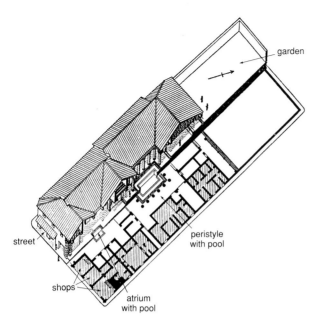

3-94 Isometric projection with plan and longitudinal section of the House of Pansa, Pompeii, Italy. Second century BCE. There are shops on each side of the entrance. The women who died in this house during the Vesuvius disaster were wearing gold ear pendants, necklaces, and rings. When the eruption began, a sculpture of Bacchus was placed for safety in a copper kettle in the garden.

residents, required an increasingly large territory to support it. The Romans were generally benevolent conquerors who absorbed rather than suppressed, offering citizenship to the conquered and acknowledging the significance of local traditions. Personal ambitions and the difficulties of governing vast territories and the huge city of Rome, however, led to administrative difficulties and eventually to civil wars and attempts by military figures to seize control. The Republic came to an end in 31 BCE, when Octavian, who later became the emperor Augustus (see fig. 3-97), assumed power and established the Empire, which lasted from 31 BCE to about 400 CE.

3-95 Atrium, House of Menander, Pompeii. c. 70 CE. The atrium is a feature well suited to the Mediterranean climate. The outer walls of the house were usually windowless, and the atrium allowed light and fresh air to enter, as well as rainwater, which was gathered in a central pool to flow into a cistern. The atrium functioned as a sitting room and usually contained the shrine for the household gods; on each side were small chambers for dining and sleeping. House built by Quintus Poppaeius, a relative of Poppeia, the wife of the Roman emperor Nero.

Republican Architectural Developments

The Temple of Portunus in Rome (fig. 3-93) demonstrates the derivative nature of Republican religious architecture. The high podium, restriction of steps to the front, and deep porch are related to temples created by the Etruscans, while the suggestion of a peripteral colonnade is Greek. Note, however, that only the porch columns are freestanding; those of the sides and back are merely sculpted portions of the wall structure—engaged or half columns. The temple is, therefore, not peripteral but **pseudo-peripteral**. This design emphasizes the enclosed interior space, in contrast to the importance of the exterior in the Greek tradition. The columns provide a graceful rhythm and announce that this structure is a temple, but the pseudo-peripteral design reveals the Romans' lack of interest in the aesthetic unity and logic characteristic of their Greek source.

Architectural innovation during the Roman Republic appeared primarily in great public buildings and engineering projects. The Roman Forum (see figs. 3-100, 3-125) well illustrates several of these characteristics. Here, the arch and vault were combined with the

new use of concrete (see pages 118–21) to make possible the relatively rapid construction of large, impressive complexes. Also, the **forum** design is a clear sequence of public and sacred spaces along an axis through which visitors moved. This molding of space and control of the observer's experience would be important features of Roman imperial architecture.

The Roman House and Villa

Most of our knowledge of Roman life is the result of materials preserved by the eruption of the volcano Vesuvius in 79 CE. Volcanic ash buried the seaside town of Pompeii, preserving shops, temples, houses, drainage and sewage systems, furnishings, food, and even the anguished positions of a number of victims. Although this event occurred during the period of the Roman Empire, the houses that were preserved there were little changed from their Republican antecedents. A letter by Pliny the Younger described the disaster:

> The buildings were now shaking with violent shocks. . . . Outside . . . there was the danger of falling pumice-stones. . . . As a protection against falling objects [the people] put pillows on their heads . . . they were still in darkness, blacker and denser than any ordinary night. . . . We also saw the sea sucked away and apparently forced back by the earthquake . . . a fearful black cloud was rent by forked and quivering bursts of flame, and parted to reveal great tongues of fire, like flashes of lightning magnified in size. . . . People bewailed their own fate or that of their relatives, and there were some who prayed for death in their terror of dying. Many besought the aid of the gods, but still more imagined there were no gods left, and that

3-96 Frescoed room from the House of the Vettii, Pompeii. 63–79 CE. Commissioned by the Vettius brothers, Conviva and Restitutus.

the universe was plunged into eternal darkness for evermore.

The houses and villas of middle- and upper-class Romans followed a regular plan, with rooms arranged along a longitudinal axis from entrance to garden (fig. 3-94). The plan is dominated by the **atrium**, an open courtyard (fig. 3-95). Rooms were decorated with richly patterned ceilings and wall paintings (fig. 3-96), but actual furnishings were minimal. Couches, used for resting, sleeping, studying, and dining while reclining in the Greek fashion, were usually the most elaborate pieces of furniture. Virtually all houses in Pompeii had water pipes with taps, as well as pipes leading out to a sewer or trench.

The main rooms had mosaic floors, and the decoratively patterned floors of marble and stone in the richest homes copied famous Hellenistic paintings or patterns. One reproduction of a Hellenistic design featured the *Unswept Floor* (see fig. 3-58), a realistic depiction of the debris one might find underfoot after a banquet, complete with shadows to make it more realistic—pity the poor servant who had to clean such a design after a night of Roman revelry. Another mosaic was a copy of a famous Hellenistic painting, the *Battle of Alexander the Great and King Darius of Persia* (see fig. 3-85). Vestibule mosaics feature images of a chained dog and the words "Beware of the Dog" or a human skeleton and "Enjoy life while you have it."

The variation in design of the wall paintings at Pompeii reveals how fashions of decorating changed. Executed in a durable **fresco secco** technique (see page 114), these works were intended to transform the rooms into an elegant ambience for living and entertaining. The simplest appear to be walls paneled in fine marbles, but in some the wall is "painted away" by an image that suggests continuous space. The subjects include realistic or fantastic views of architecture, landscapes, still lifes, portraits, and themes from Greek and Roman mythology theater.

The Art of the Roman Empire

3-97 *EMPEROR AUGUSTUS*. 15 CE. Marble, with traces of paint and perhaps also gilding, height 7'. Vatican Museums, Rome. This work, discovered at the villa of Augustus's wife, Livia, at Prima Porta (see fig. 3-110), 9 miles south of Rome, is sometimes known as the *Augustus Prima Porta*. The back is not complete, so the statue must have been intended for a niche. It may have been a cult statue, for after his death Livia was made the priestess in charge of the cult of the defied Augustus. Fragments of paint, such as reddish circles for the irises of the eyes, reveal that details were once painted. Perhaps commissioned by Augustus's wife, Livia.

the Earth Mother with a cornucopia—symbolic of abundance—and of a Parthian, a Roman enemy, surrendering a battle standard in the presence of divinities, an act which refers to a major diplomatic coup. These triumphs were also celebrated in poetry by the first-century BCE Roman poet Horace:

> Your age, Augustus, permitted the fields to bear rich harvests once more, and returned to the skies the battle standards, wrenched from the proud barbarians.
>
> (Horace, *Carmina*, IV, 15, 4–7)

The sculpture probably dates after Augustus's death, for it represents the emperor without boots, suggesting that he has been deified. The winged baby boy and dolphin by Augustus's right foot helps support the marble figure. The boy probably represents Cupid, the son of Venus, and thus refers to Augustus's divine lineage as a descendant of Aeneas, son of Venus. The facial features identify the figure as Augustus, but they also represent an ideal, for Augustus was always shown in his early maturity, as here, although he was seventy-six when he died. In pose, the model was the Greek *Spear Carrier* (see fig. 3-72), which the Romans thought was a representation of another Trojan War hero, Achilles; a complimentary comparison between Augustus and Achilles was almost certainly intended. This sculpture, then, is an idealized portrait of a specific emperor; although it is based on classical Greek prototypes, its iconography and scale are specifically Roman, for they exalt the emperor and the Empire.

History

In 31 BCE, Octavian, grand-nephew and adopted son of Julius Caesar, became the sole ruler of Rome and all its territories; in 27 BCE, the Roman Senate named him *Augustus* ("noble, honored, consecrated one"), and after

Remember thou, O Roman, to rule the nations with thy sway—these shall be thine arts—to crown peace with law, to spare the humbled, and to tame the proud in war.

(Virgil, *Aeneid*, VI, 851–53)

The emperor Augustus, who commands our attention with his declamatory gesture in this over-lifesize statue

(fig. 3-97), claimed descent from Aeneas, whose deeds are recounted in Virgil's epic poem *Aeneid*. Aeneas was the legendary founder of the city of Rome, and Augustus was the founder of the Roman Empire, which lasted from 31 BCE to about 400 CE. Both statue and poem were intended to legitimize Augustus's rule and assert his imperial authority. Augustus wears parade armor decorated with reliefs of

3-98 Reconstruction of the Altar of Peace (Ara Pacis), Rome. 13–9 BCE. Marble, approx. 34′5″ × 38′ × 23′. Commissioned by the Roman Senate to mark Augustus's victorious return from Gaul and Spain in 13 BCE.

his death they declared him a god. Brilliant and resourceful, Augustus— who wrote that he "found Rome a city of brick and left it a city of marble"— became the first emperor and ruled the Empire longer than any who followed him. He continued the expansion of the Roman state, as did his successors, and by the death of Trajan in 117 CE, Rome's population was about 750,000 and the Mediterranean had become a "Roman lake." The difficulties of governing this enormous area and its diverse population made the Romans experts at efficiency and organization. They had little time for or interest in the philosophical speculations that had formed Greek art and culture. Their most significant contributions are in world government and order, encompassing such diverse issues as legal codes and city planning.

The Romans had a strong sense of their historical importance and their contributions to world history. Julius Caesar wrote an account of the Gallic Wars. The emperor Claudius wrote two historical works now lost and Augustus made a list of his accomplishments known as the *Res Gestae*. Roman attitudes toward history and art are expressed in the Altar of Peace, or Ara Pacis (fig. 3-98), in Rome. This monument commemorated the *Pax Romana* ("Roman Peace"), which had been declared by the Roman Senate in 13 BCE to express and celebrate the peace brought by Augustus to Italy and to the Roman state. Although they were aware of the significance of the *Pax Romana*, they could not know that never again would peace prevail for so many years over so vast an area. The Senate's declaration and the richly decorated altar were intended to bring recognition to this historic fact and to establish it as a Roman accomplishment and ideal. Augustus, accompanied by his family and friends, appears in the procession representing the altar's dedication. Although the stylis-

tic sources for the reliefs lie in such Greek models as the Parthenon frieze (see fig. 3-80), Greek idealism is ignored in favor of documenting a specific historic moment and distinctive individuals. The presence of Augustus and other members of the imperial family at this sacrifice reveals piety and concord; the more important figures are in higher relief for emphasis and focus. Even the decorative motifs glorify the Empire and allude to its peace-giving role, for the garlands below refer to the abundance made possible by peace.

The City of Rome

Rome, which at its largest had a population of nearly a million, was in many ways similar to a modern city. It had impressive public spaces with state buildings and religious structures, as well as shopping areas, apartment buildings of five or six stories, and rooming houses. Most of the population lived in

3-99 Apartment house, Ostia. Second century CE.

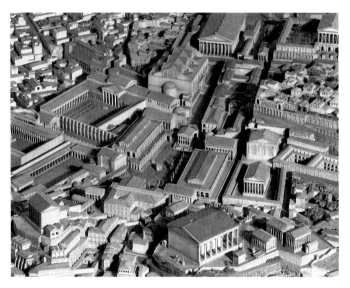

3-100 Reconstruction model of the Roman and Imperial Forums in Rome. Early fourth century CE. Museum of Roman Civilization, Rome. See figure 3-125 for plan. Originally commissioned by the Republican government of Rome; expanded by various Roman emperors.

3-101 *MARCUS AURELIUS*. 161–80 CE. Bronze, over-lifesize. Now in the Capitoline Museum, Rome. Marcus Aurelius, who wrote the *Meditations*, has the longish hair and full beard that characterized the "poetic" emperor. The "military" emperor was clean-shaven and had short hair. The bronze statue is an impressive technical accomplishment, but it survived being melted down only because during the Middle Ages it was thought to represent Constantine, the fourth-century emperor who accepted Christianity. Commissioned by Marcus Aurelius.

rental housing; a fourth-century CE document lists 46,602 apartment and rooming houses in the city and only 1,797 private homes. The apartment houses at Ostia (fig. 3-99), the port of Rome, were three or four stories high with an inner garden court and balconies, similar to late-twentieth-century apartment blocks.

The emperors kept the urban populace happy by providing food, facilities, and entertainment. Elaborate programs of building in the imperial forums (fig. 3-100) impressed the public with the power and magnificence of a specific emperor and of the state. Theaters and **amphitheaters** provided places of entertainment for tens of thousands, and the public baths (see figs. 3-123, 3-124) offered facilities for communal bathing and exercise, as well as for social and intellectual gatherings.

Roman Imperial Art

The size and diversity of the peoples within the Roman Empire meant that Roman imperial art encompassed a variety of types and styles, especially as local traditions were incorporated into works of art. Here we have chosen to limit our discussion almost exclusively to works of art created within the city of Rome and for its inhabitants. The majority of the artists employed by the Romans were of Greek ancestry. Greek artists were imported as early as 500 BCE, during the Republic, and works of art were also ordered from artists active in Greece. The demand for Greek works,

new and old, accelerated after the Romans sacked Corinth in 146 BCE and brought a number of impressive Greek works to Italy.

Among the most characteristic monuments of Roman art are those that honor the Empire and emperor. They are often built on an enormous scale to communicate the size, power, and authority of the Empire and the specific ruler. Huge buildings and interrelated groups of buildings that express the grandiose aspirations of the Empire were made possible by the new techniques of construction that had been developed during the Roman Republic. The Empire's use of the arch, the vault, and concrete—devices that made feasible not only the large and magnificent monuments of ancient Rome, but also the powerful molding of space so important in Roman architecture—is among the most significant of all Roman accomplishments (see pages 118–21).

The creation of works of art honoring and commemorating an emperor's

3-102 Arch of Titus, Rome. 81 CE. Marble over concrete core. Commissioned by Titus.

3-103 *SPOILS OF THE TEMPLE AT JERUSALEM EXHIBITED IN ROME*, relief from the Arch of Titus (see fig. 3-102). Marble, height 6'7". Commissioned by Titus.

3-104 Column of Trajan, Rome. 113 CE. Marble, height originally 128'. If the reliefs on the column could be stretched out, they would be more than 650 feet long. Commissioned by Trajan as part of the Forum of Trajan.

deeds and victories was a constant challenge to artists in the service of the Empire. One type of monument honoring emperors and generals was the equestrian monument, but the only surviving example is the *Marcus Aurelius* (fig. 3-101). This figure has the same commanding gesture as the *Augustus* (see fig. 3-97), but here his power is emphasized by his control over his lively and rather nervous horse. Originally, a figure of a defeated enemy was probably shown crouching under the horse's upraised hoof.

Another commemorative monument is the triumphal arch. Although its origins can be traced to the Republican period, the first to be called *arcus triumphalis* were the large and permanent triumphal arches erected during the reign of Augustus. Eventually there were more than fifty in Rome. The Arch

of Titus (figs. 3-102, 3-103) memorializes Titus's suppression of a Jewish revolt and his capture of Jerusalem in 70–71 CE. The arch itself is simple and handsome, with a compact and tightly knit composition of horizontal and vertical members enframing the tunnel vault. The simple basic form, an arch enclosed within a rectangle, is enlivened by architectural details, and originally the whole was surmounted by a huge bronze quadriga with the emperor. The reliefs under the arch represent, on one side, the triumph of Titus, who is shown riding in a chariot led by a personification of the goddess Roma. On the other side is the parading of the treasures of the Temple in Jerusalem—including the seven-branched menorah, the ceremonial candleholder—through the streets of Rome, where the procession is about to pass under a triumphal arch (see fig.

3-103). The deified Titus, who died shortly before the monument was completed, is shown in the center of the vault, being carried to heaven on the back of an eagle.

Commemorating the emperor Trajan's early-second-century victories over the Dacians in eastern Europe is a huge freestanding column (fig. 3-104), as tall as a twelve-story building. It was originally topped with a monumental gilded bronze statue of the emperor, which has been replaced with a statue of Saint Peter. The column itself has a spiraling relief, carved in a lively and direct style, that tells in detail the episodes of Trajan's campaigns and victories. Although every detail of every scene is not visible to the viewer, the scale of the column and the length of the relief convey the extent and complexity of Trajan's exploits. Some of the upper scenes could have been read by people on the balconies of the courtyard of Trajan's library, which surrounded the column (see fig. 3-125). The column and library were only part of Trajan's contributions to the imperial forums, which he, like other emperors, embellished as a way of asserting his presence and impressing the people with his magnificence.

Technology, Organization, and Engineering

To run a large empire, to communicate and move supplies, and to feed the masses gathered in growing cities demanded important new developments in technology and organization. Innovations such as the arch, the vault, and concrete helped solve engineering and construction problems on a large scale; they ultimately affected the production and style of works of art. The celebrated Roman roads, bridges, and aqueducts were engineered to solve the particular problems of a specific area or terrain, and some are still in use today.

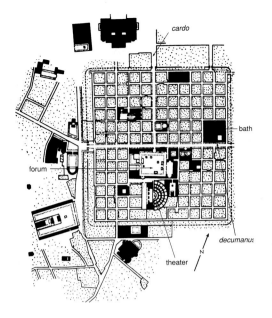

3-105 Plan of Thamugadis (Timgad), Algeria. Although most Roman town plans were laid out with main axes that were north-south and east-west, Thamugadis, founded c. 100 CE under the emperor Trajan, is slightly off-axis.

The Roman interest in order, efficiency, and organization is revealed by the Roman town plan (fig. 3-105), which was developed following Egyptian, Greek, and Hellenistic prototypes and which spread throughout the Roman world, from London to North Africa. Streets are laid out in a grid pattern within fortified walls, and the center of the town is marked by the intersection of the two main thoroughfares—the *cardo*, running north-south, and the *decumanus*, running east-west. Nearby is the forum—the social, political, and commercial heart of the city. The intersecting *cardo* and *decumanus* divided the city into quarters, each of which is further subdivided by streets meeting at right angles; only irregular or large buildings such as theaters or public baths disrupted this regular plan. This Roman solution to urban design is evident in major cities of the Western world, where avenues cross streets in grid patterns.

Roman Religion and the Mystery Religions

The more important official Roman deities were derived from the gods and goddesses of the Greeks, but their names were changed: Zeus became Jupiter, Aphrodite became Venus, and the elusive Dionysos was transformed into Bacchus, for example. But the number of Roman deities gradually expanded, for when the Romans conquered and annexed a new area, the local deities were usually added to the Roman hierarchy of gods. At the Pantheon in Rome (see fig. 3-122), there was even an altar dedicated to those gods whom the Romans had yet to discover.

During the later Empire, the religious life of many Romans was dominated by participation in mystery religions, cults that centered on a savior who promised some kind of life after death. Their widespread popularity and the ultimate acceptance of Christianity as the official Roman religion have been seen as a reaction to the materialism and spiritual emptiness of ancient Roman life. Other mystery religions centered around the worship of Isis, an Egyptian goddess whose temple at Pompeii included a shrine with a reservoir of holy water from the Nile, and Cybele, the Great Mother (*Magna Mater*). An ancient Roman temple of Mithras, a militant god-hero who represented the victorious forces of light over darkness, was discovered in the remains of ancient Roman London during reconstruction after the bombings of World War II.

Mithraism, an especially important late Roman cult, was widespread throughout the Empire as a result of its popularity with members of the army.

The End of Rome's Empire

Political, religious, and spiritual turmoil and threats from Northern barbarians characterize the later Empire. Diocletian (ruled 284–305) consolidated imperial rule, but he also banned and persecuted the Christians. Constantine lifted the ban on Christianity in 313 and later may have converted to the religion himself. But Rome lost much of its importance when Constantine shifted the imperial capital to Constantinople, which he had founded at a site on the Bosphorus named Byzantium (present-day Istanbul. In 395, at the time of the death of the emperor Theodosius I, the Empire was divided in half. But while the Eastern Empire, centered around Constantinople, enjoyed political stability, the Western Empire was beset with uprisings from Germanic peoples, including the Visigoths, who captured and sacked Rome in 410.

Late Roman Sculpture

Constantine's sculpted head (fig. 3-106) has a dramatic and intimidating impact, not just because of its enormous size, but also as a result of the powerfully abstracted facial features. Portraiture has moved away from the highly realistic busts of Republican and early imperial Roman art. Although Constantine's head retains certain specific physical traits, such as the thick, muscular neck and the Roman nose known from his other portraits, these realistic features are joined with abstract patterns in the treatment of the hair over the forehead and the huge, staring eyes. The treatment of the eyes suggests Constantine's authoritarian power, his deified presence, and his ability to penetrate the

3-106 *CONSTANTINE*, from the Basilica of Maxentius and Constantine, Rome. Early fourth century CE. Marble, height of head 8'6". Palazzo dei Conservatori, Rome. These arm and head fragments are part of a colossal statue, originally about 30 feet tall, of the enthroned emperor Constantine initially placed in the apse of his basilica (see fig. 3-117). The head and limbs were carved from marble; the torso was fashioned of a brick core covered with wood and overlaid with bronze. The head once had a metal diadem. Commissioned by Constantine.

world of the divine. There are indications from contemporary literary sources that the late Roman emperors, who were viewed as gods while they were living, were adorned like statues of gods and behaved in a manner that encouraged belief in their deified status.

It is difficult to determine why the new abstracted patterning occurs during the late Roman Empire, a period sometimes referred to as late antiquity. This innovation cannot be dismissed as a lack of technical ability on the part of the artist, for it seems to be used intentionally to promote such abstract concepts as imperial authority or divine power.

New spiritual attitudes are evident in late antiquity with the mystery cults and early Christianity. The most eloquent spokesperson for these values was Plotinus, a third-century philosopher. One of his pupils, Porphyry, wrote a biography of Plotinus in which he noted the difficulty of artists who wanted to create a portrait of the philosopher:

Plotinus . . . gave the impression of being ashamed that he dwelt in a body [and] he deemed it so degrading to submit himself to being a subject for a painter or sculptor that he said to Amelius, who asked him to permit his portrait to be made, "It is not sufficient just to carry around that image which nature has imposed on us, without making concessions to it by deciding to leave behind a more lasting image of the image, as if it were one of those things which is particularly worth seeing."

The antiphysical attitude of Plotinus is in sharp contrast to the historical and naturalistic values that had been so prized in Roman figurative art. As in the colossal head of Constantine, inner spiritual life is deemed more significant than an exact portrait representation. We shall see in our examination of subsequent transformations that such an approach is consistent with the development of Early Christian art.

The Roman Artist

In ancient Greece, artists had been famous and respected, but during both the Republic and the Empire, artists in the service of the Roman state became anonymous laborers once again. Few artists are known by name; not a single painting bears

3-107 HAGESANDROS, ATHENODOROS, AND POLYDOROS

LAOCOÖN AND HIS SONS. Early first century BCE(?). Marble, height 8'. Vatican Museums, Rome. This sculptural group was carved by three Greek sculptors from the island of Rhodes. Although they were Greek, they were probably working for a Roman patron who commissioned a work reminiscent of earlier Hellenistic art. The group was excavated in Rome in 1506, and its representation of heroic struggle and powerful muscular anatomy had an immediate impact on Italian Renaissance artists, including Michelangelo.

a signature, and only a few are documented as the work of a particular artist. In most cases, the large and elaborate programs of Roman art seem to have been accomplished by groups of artists working together, probably in well-organized workshops, and submerg-ing their individuality in the concept of a unified project.

Most of the few names of artists that are recorded are Greek, and these are names of sculptors. Even during the Republic, it was recognized that Greek sculptors repre-sented a long-standing tradition of excellence. The famous *Laocoön and His Sons* (fig. 3-107), once thought to be a work of the Greek Hellenistic period imported to Rome, is now believed to be a Roman work created by Greek sculptors working in a revival of the Hellenistic style for a Roman patron.

Roman Frescoes and Illusionism

3-108 *BACCHIC MYSTERIES*, painting in the Villa of the Mysteries, Pompeii, Italy. c. 30 BCE. Fresco, room approx. 29 × 19'; height of figures approx. 5'. Whether these paintings, which are superb in quality, are original Roman works or copies of a lost Hellenistic painting from Pergamon is still debated by experts.

3-109 *BACCHIC MYSTERIES*, detail of painting in the corner of the room in the Villa of the Mysteries, with a flagellation scene. Whipping in this context may be a ritual meant to ensure fertility.

3-110 *GARDEN*, painting from the villa of Livia, wife of the emperor Augustus, at Prima Porta, near Rome. Late first century BCE. Fresco, height of wall 10'. Museo delle Terme, Rome. The statue of Augustus in fig. 3-97 was also discovered at Livia's villa. Commissioned by Livia.

This room of frescoes (fig. 3-108) representing Bacchic (or Dionysiac) mysteries is exceptional in quality and subject, as well as in scale, for nearly lifesize figures such as these are rare in Roman painting. In addition, these frescoes are one of the first examples of **mural painting**—painted wall decoration that is integrated with the physical space and architecture of its setting.

The secret rites depicted here have not yet been fully explained, but this painting reveals the importance of the cult of Bacchus, god of wine and fertility, in Roman life. It has been proposed that the sequence of scenes, which seems to read from left to right,

represents either the initiation of a new member into the cult or the transitions in the life of a young woman when she marries and becomes a Roman matron.

The central figures, badly damaged, represent the enthroned Ariadne, with Bacchus reclining on her chest. The initiate, or bride (not visible here), enters on the far left. She is enthroned as a matron on the far right (not visible in this view). In the interim, she encounters various trials and experiences. Among the dramatic episodes is the imminent unveiling of a large phallus to the right of the central figures of Ariadne and Bacchus. The regular, architectural rhythm of the

paneling behind the figures sets off their poses, while the strong red background adds an element of drama appropriate for the subject.

The most dramatic episodes are represented at the two corners, where the artist took advantage of the walls meeting at 90-degree angles to represent interacting figures. At one corner, a fierce half-man, half-beast woods deity known as a silenus, who may be reading the young woman's fortune in the residue left in a wine cup, looks back at her as she flees in terror. At the other corner, a winged figure in a spiraling movement flogs the initiate or bride, who reclines on the lap of another woman (fig. 3-109). The large scale

Fresco painting (*fresco* is Italian for "fresh"), which involves painting directly on a plaster wall, was used by the Egyptians, Greeks, Romans, and later civilizations as well. When properly executed, it is durable, and when it is subtly related to its particular architectural setting, as in the cycle at the Villa of the Mysteries at Pompeii, (figs. 3-108–109), it can be both decorative and dramatic. Generally, fresco painters have to cover large expanses of wall, and they often work quickly; the sketchy and suggestive quality of most Roman and later frescoes creates a lively and vivacious effect. (For a discussion of the somewhat more complex fresco technique that developed in Italy during the later Middle Ages and the Renaissance, see page 247.)

The Roman fresco painter began by applying two or three layers of fine plaster to the wall surface to be decorated. The background was painted on the top layer of plaster—sometimes while it was still moist—and left to dry. Each plaster patch (fig. 3-111) reveals one day's work. The natural pigments, which were made from earth, minerals, and animal or vegetable sources, were mixed with limewater. Glue and wax were sometimes added to create a hard and shiny surface. Painting onto wet plaster is called **buon fresco** (*buon* is Italian for "good" or "true") and painting on the already hardened dry plaster is known as **fresco secco** (in Italian *secco* means "dry").

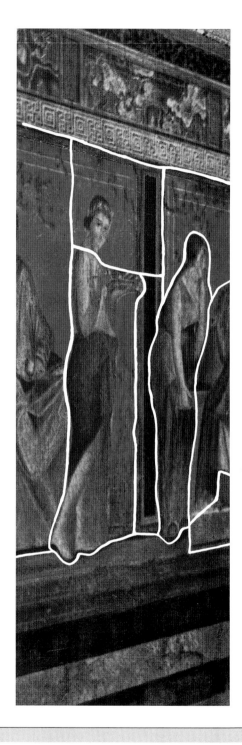

3-111 Diagram of fresco patches at the Villa of the Mysteries. An examination of the surface of the frescoes reveals that they were painted in patches that follow the outlines of the figures. In later Italian fresco technique, each of these patches would be known as a *giornata* (Italian for "day").

and otherwise undocumented subject of this fresco cycle make it one of the most important works preserved by the eruption of Mt. Vesuvius.

One of the most enchanting of all Roman fresco decorations is the illusionistic painting that covered all four walls of a room in the Villa of Livia at Prima Porta (fig. 3-110). It represents a garden with fruit trees, flowers, and songbirds set off by a background of sky. The fresco has all the freshness of nature's colors: the rich greens of the garden; the varied shades of fruit, flowers, and plumage; and a wonderful blue sky. All are executed with a light touch of the brush, as if the wind were just beginning to stir this idyllic environment.

3-112 *STILL LIFE WITH EGGS AND THRUSHES*, painting from the House (or Villa) of Julia Felix, Pompeii. Before 79 CE. Fresco, 35 × 48". National Museum, Naples. The house where this fresco was found during excavations in 1755–57 is the largest yet discovered at Pompeii. The fresco shown here is one of a sequence of still-life paintings of food. Commissioned by the original owner of the house.

Livia's garden room (fig. 3-110) is more delightful and seductive than a framed painting of a garden, for it creates the illusion that we are in a natural setting. Such illusionism also played a role in *Still Life with Eggs and Thrushes* (fig. 3-112), for in both works the artists want to fool us into believing, albeit momentarily, that we are looking out into a real garden or at a real dish of eggs. This type of **illusionism**, which is also known by the French phrase *trompe l'oeil* ("fool the eye"), is a pleasant bit of trickery. Such paintings are meant to amuse and delight us, as was recognized by the Roman author Philostratus the Younger, writing about 300 CE:

> To confront objects which do not exist as though they existed and . . . to believe that they do exist, is not this, since no harm can come of it, a suitable and irreproachable means of providing entertainment?

The illusionism of Roman paintings is inherited from an earlier tradition that developed in Greece (see the discussion of a Greek painting contest on page 91). The sense of pleasure in experiencing illusionism is not unique to the Greeks and Romans, as is revealed by the popularity of *trompe l'oeil* in later societies and even today.

There are several criteria for a successful illusionistic or *trompe l'oeil* painting. The objects in the painting should be represented in their natural scale in a clearly structured space, as is the case with both Livia's *Garden* and the *Still Life*. In the *Garden*, the artist has carefully developed the depicted space in overlapping levels within the painted illusion. **Cast shadows** define the placement of each object within the illusionistic space, as is especially evident in the *Still Life*, and the objects are naturalistically modeled with transitions from light to dark that indicate both the three-dimensionality of the objects and the source of the light (later, at the time of the Italian Renaissance, this treatment of shading will become known as *chiaroscuro*, from the Italian words for "light" and "dark"). Naturalistic lighting effects suggest the textures of the objects: note the different textures of the eggs and the metal vessels in the *Still Life*. Often, painters introduce an object in the immediate foreground that establishes the frontal plane of the illusionistic space; this form, known as a *repoussoir* (French, meaning "to push back"), can be noted in the low, openwork fence in the foreground of Livia's *Garden*.

The use of the *repoussoir* in the *Still Life* is especially interesting, for the illusionism is heightened by painting the bowl of eggs as if it extends *over* the frontal plane of the base—the *repoussoir*—to jut out into our space. To make the illusion convincing, the subject matter is usually everyday objects that need no explanation. The goals of such art are obvious, for the purpose, beyond Philostratus's "entertainment," is to impress us with the technical skill of the artist.

Roman Architecture:
The Flavian Amphitheater

3-113 Flavian Amphitheater (Colosseum), Rome. Begun 72 CE; dedicated 80 CE; construction completed 96 CE. Approx. 615 × 510'. The building was damaged in later centuries, when much of the dressed stone of the outer surface was taken away to be used in the construction of other buildings. Commissioned by Vespasian; completed by his sons Domitian and Titus.

3-114 Reconstruction model of the Flavian Amphitheater. Museum of Roman Civilization, Rome.

Through the ages, the Flavian Amphitheater has conveyed the scale and strength of the Roman Empire (figs. 3-113, 3-114). Begun by Vespasian, an honored military leader and first emperor of the Flavian dynasty, it was built in part to reassure the Roman citizenry that the cruelty and self-indulgence of the reign of Nero, the last Julio-Claudian emperor, had ended; to establish a site for the amphitheater, Vespasian destroyed the lake and ostentatious pleasure gardens of Nero's house. The amphitheater was dedicated by Vespasian's son Titus with gladiatorial games that lasted more than a hundred days and featured a thousand gladiators and the deaths of thousands of animals.

The Roman **amphitheater**, or arena, was so well conceived that it has become the prototype for the modern sports stadium. The oval plan

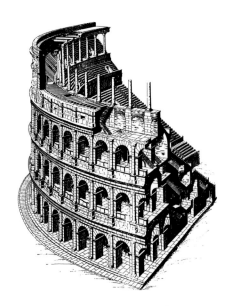

3-115 Isometric projection, with section, of the Flavian Amphitheater.

seems to have developed from the idea of facing and enclosing two theaters (*amphitheather* derives from the Greek *amphi*, "around," and *theatron*, "theater"). The Flavian Amphitheater, the largest amphitheater of the ancient Roman world, could hold about 50,000 spectators. They were sheltered from sun and rain by an awning rigged by sailors and supported by horizontal poles anchored in the top level. Eighty arched passageways on the ground floor provided entrance to a double row of **annular tunnel vaults** (fig. 3-115) encircling the arena, which led to interior stairs to vaulted passages on the upper levels. Such a plan permitted easy access and exit by the huge crowd of spectators.

Construction materials included travertine, brick, concrete, and tufa (see page 121). When finished, the exterior was faced with blocks of local travertine stone, held in place by iron clamps. The exterior design was unified by the repetition of arches flanked by half columns. The capitals on the three arched stories change from Doric below to Ionic and Corinthian for the second and third floors; Corinthian pilasters articulate the fourth level.

The amphitheater was an arena for displays of combat: gladiators battled both other gladiators and animals, while animals, especially lions and tigers brought from Africa, were pitted against one another. Women gladiators participated until 200 CE. The fight was usually to the death, a practice that may have evolved from an earlier Etruscan ritual in which a deceased relative was honored by a fight to the death between slaves. The floor of the Flavian Amphitheater was landscaped with trees and large rocks. Animals were raised by lifts from underground chambers, now visible after excavations. Reportedly the amphitheater could be artificially flooded for contests mimicking naval battles. Although a few Romans denounced these games as bloody spectacles, most viewed them as displays of courage and virtue.

To the ruling families of Rome, the games also served a political purpose. At times, the unemployment rate reached approximately 15 percent, and, in addition to religious festivals, approximately 150 days each year were celebrated as holidays. Providing spectacular games became a political scheme to keep an often idle population entertained and content.

During the Early Christian era, some martyrdoms may have occurred here, but most public persecutions were held in the Roman circuses (arenas especially designed for chariot races). After Christianity was legally recognized by the emperor Constantine in 313 CE, growing numbers of Christians argued against the brutality of the games. Gladiatorial contests were banned in the early fifth century, but the animal games continued into the sixth century.

Until at least the mid-fourth century, a colossal (almost 100 feet tall) bronze statue of Nero as the sun god stood next to the Flavian Amphitheater. In the eighth century, a guidebook to Rome applied the term *Colosseum*, taken from the colossal sculpture, to the amphitheater itself, and ever since it has been known popularly by this name.

3-116 Reconstruction drawing of the interior of the Basilica Ulpia, Forum of Trajan, Rome (after Canina). c. 98–117 CE. For a plan of the Basilica Ulpia and its location within the Imperial Forums, see figure 3-125. Commissioned by the emperor Trajan as part of the Forum of Trajan.

The dramatic contrast between the two ancient Roman interiors seen here is directly related to the materials and engineering used in their construction. The huge Basilica Ulpia from the Forum of Trajan (fig. 3-116) was based on post-and-lintel construction; the even larger and grander Basilica of Maxentius and Constantine (fig. 3-117), begun more than 200 years later, is built with rubble, brick, and concrete using a vaulting system based on the arch. When concrete hardens, it becomes monolithic, and today some of the huge vaults of the Basilica of Maxentius and Constantine are still standing in Rome. Not a column of the Basilica Ulpia is in place, in part because its great columns were reused in new construction during later centuries. Both the Basilica Ulpia and the Basilica of Maxentius and Constantine functioned as law courts when originally constructed.

The arch was known to the peoples of the Middle East, as well as to the Egyptians, the Greeks, and the Etruscans, but it was the Romans, beginning in the Republic, who recognized its utility for engineering projects and its potential for spanning large spaces to create huge public buildings. Post-and-lintel construction spans an opening with a flat beam of wood or stone, but an **arch** (fig. 3-118) is a means of construction by which an opening—usually semicircular—is spanned by a number of elements (stone or bricks) that are smaller than the opening itself; these elements are most often wedge-shaped blocks known as **voussoirs**. The central voussoir is called the **keystone**. All the vaults discussed here are based on the arch.

Arches and vaults are constructed upon a wooden support known as **centering**, which can be removed and reused. The point at which the arch or vault begins to curve inward and upward is known as the **springing**; the blocks immediately below the springing may jut out to support the centering (for an example of such blocks still in place, see fig. 3-119). The dynamics of the post-and-lintel systems are relatively simple, with the **thrust** of the weight of the lintel pressing downward on the supporting

3-117 Reconstruction view of the interior of the Basilica of Maxentius and Constantine, Rome, as planned by Maxentius. c. 306–313 CE. This basilica was begun by Maxentius and taken over by his rival Constantine, who completed it. The colossal head and arm of Constantine in fig. 3-106 were found here. Originally commissioned by Maxentius, completed by Constantine.

posts. The dynamics of an arch or vault, however, create outward diagonal thrusts that must be counteracted by **buttressing**, providing a masonry support that counteracts the thrust (as indicated by the arrows in fig. 3-118; for a later example, see fig. 4-92).

A **vault** is a structural system for a ceiling and/or roof that is based on the arch. The simplest type of vault is a **tunnel** (or **barrel) vault**, a deep, continuous arch that can cover a large area. Although light can enter at either end, the buttressing prohibits large openings along the sides. For a bridge and aqueduct such as the Pont du Gard (fig. 3-119), however, short tunnel vaults provide a solution. The lowest row is made up of tunnel vaults that are deep enough to support the road and protect the foundation against the force of the river during spring floods. An identically proportioned row of arches provides the extra height needed for the aqueduct at the top, which is raised on much smaller arches, four over the wider central arch and three over those to the sides. When tunnel

vaults and arches are placed in rows, each neutralizes the outward thrust of the adjacent member, but those on the ends must be well buttressed, a function here performed by the riverbanks to either side. The Pont du Gard is, however, more than a remarkable surviving example of Roman engineering skill; its simple design, handsome proportions, and rhythmic subtlety make it an impressive work of art. (For other structures that utilize the tunnel vault, see figs. 3-102, 4-68, 4-106, and 7-3.)

The three great square vaults that spanned the central area of the Basilica of Maxentius and Constantine (see fig. 3-117) were each formed by the intersection at right angles of two tunnel vaults; these are called **cross** (or **groin) vaults**. The outward thrusts of a cross vault are concentrated at the corners, and buttressing is only required at these points. When placed in a row, as here, or in groups, cross vaults can span vast areas and still permit large windows. (For other

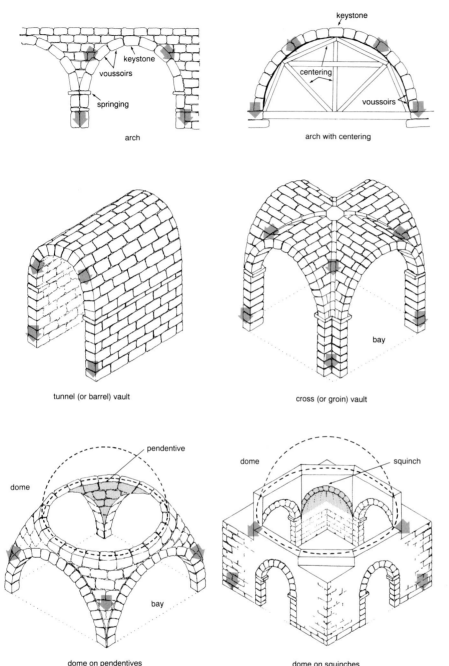

3-118. Diagrams of a round arch, an arch with centering, a tunnel (or barrel) vault, a cross (or groin) vault, a dome on pendentives, and a dome on squinches. The arrows suggest the general direction of the outward thrusts that must be buttressed, but only the drawing of the arch includes the buttressing that is essential in all vaulted systems.

buildings with cross vaults, see figs. 3-113, 3-114, 3-115, 3-123; 4-31, and 4-83) The vertical members that support a cross vault are known as **piers**. The area between each group of piers is known as a **bay**.

Series of vaults are usually arranged in straight lines, but sometimes the architectural needs demand another arrangement. When a tunnel vault is arranged in a curving or circular configuration, it is known as an **annular tunnel vault**; a series of cross vaults in a curving configuration are known as **annular cross vaults** (see figs. 4-70, 4-84, and 4-90).

A **dome** is a hemispherical structural system that can be understood as an arch rotated 180 degrees on its axis. It must, therefore, be buttressed on all sides. The problem of light can be solved by opening the top of the dome with an

3-119 Pont du Gard (bridge and aqueduct), near Nîmes, France. Late first century BCE. Length 900′; height 162′. The total length of the acqueduct system of which this was a crucial part was 30 miles. Commissioned by one of the Roman emperors, perhaps Augustus, to provide water to encourage the settlement of Nîmes.

oculus, as in the Pantheon (see fig. 3-122), by piercing the edges of the dome with small windows (see fig. 4-28) that are framed by heavy buttresses, or by raising dome on arches or tunnel vaults (see fig. 6-33). To attain greater height, a dome may be raised upon a **drum**, a cylindrical or polygonal wall that provides continuous support (see fig. 5-42).

When a dome is placed at the juncture of tunnel or barrel vaults, as occurs often in Christian church architecture (see figs. 5-40, 5-41), it must be located over a square base. The transition from the circular base of the dome to the piers or walls below has traditionally been handled in two ways. One method is the use of four **pendentives**; these are curving triangular segments of a larger dome that help create a visual and supportive transition from the four supporting piers to the dome above (see figs. 4-28, 4-76). The second system uses **squinches**: arches, lintels, or corbels that jut across the corners to create an octagonal base for the dome (fig. 4-51).

In many of the finest Roman buildings and engineering projects, such as the Pont du Guard, the material used was **dressed stone**: each piece was cut for its specific position and no mortar was employed. Repeated arches, such as those of the Pont du Gard, meant that a certain number of stones of regularized shape could be cut, and the structure could be fabricated at the site from stones cut and marked at the quarry to indicate their specific placement.

The most revolutionary Roman innovations in arches and vaulting occur in combination with the development of *opus caementicium*—cement (fast-drying, hardening volcanic sand) used to produce **concrete**. Roman construction methods were transformed when the Romans began to quarry large amounts of *pozzolana*, a silicate that functioned as a natural cement, near Naples in the second century BCE. The *pozzolana* was combined with broken pieces of stone and/or brick and water to provide a building material that hardened into a solid mass. Concrete was cheap, readily available, flexible, and fire-resistant. A lightweight stone was mixed with the cement for vaults, to lighten the weight and reduce the amount of buttressing needed. Cut stone and concrete were to remain the two most basic building materials of Western culture until the introduction of metal—iron and then steel—during the nineteenth century.

Other materials used by the Romans include brick, mud brick, and various stones that could be quarried nearby. Near Rome two kinds of stone were common—**travertine**, a kind of marble, and **tufa**, a soft volcanic rock that hardens on exposure to air. For the finished surface of their buildings, the Romans were not satisfied with concrete, which they usually covered with painted stucco, marble, or *opus incertum*, a facing of irregularly shaped small blocks of travertine or other stone.

The arch, vaults, and concrete were developed by the Romans precisely because they solved the Roman demands for enormous scale, for efficiency and economy, and for flexibility. They helped to create and to convey the power and majesty of the Roman Empire.

Roman Architecture: The Pantheon, Rome

3-120   Model/conjectural reconstruction of the Pantheon and its forecourt in ancient Roman times. Museum of Roman Civilization, Rome. The Roman Pantheon was dedicated to all the gods of the Roman religion; its name derives from the Greek *pan* ("every") and *theos* ("god"). An inscription on the exterior pediment ("Marcus Agrippa . . . built this") is misleading, for it refers to an earlier temple built on this site in 27 BCE. The gilding of the exterior dome further enhanced the references to the sun that are so important in this building. The current structure was erected by the emperor Hadrian, who, with characteristic modesty, copied the inscription from the earlier temple.

The Pantheon was regarded in ancient times as one of Rome's most important temples. It joins two disparate architectural designs, a Corinthian portico and a domed rotunda (figs. 3-120–3-122). Viewing the building from today's significantly raised street levels, the modern visitor is immediately aware of the cylindrical walls and dome, but they were not so visible in antiquity. A colonnaded forecourt and the portico, which was raised atop a flight of steps, masked these elements. The impressive entrance, with towering monolithic marble columns and huge bronze doors, gave no hint of the cylindrical walls of the rotunda; an ancient visitor who entered the structure must have been awestruck at the unexpected interior. The concrete dome, the largest built in Europe prior to the twentieth century, is perfectly hemispherical, and the distance from the floor to the top of the dome is the same as the diameter of the rotunda. The interior proportions, then, are governed by the geometrical purity of a sphere.

A series of transverse barrel vaults hidden within the more than 20-foot-thick walls concentrates the weight of the dome on eight massive supports. The concrete of the dome must have been poured in sections over a huge mold supported by a centering structure so complex it would have made the interior look

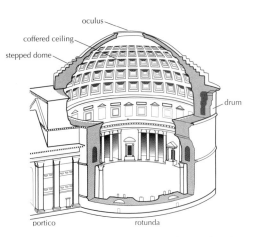

3-121 Cutaway of the Pantheon, showing the stepped buttressing that helps to contain the outward thrust of the dome. 117–25 CE. Height of interior 144'. Commissioned by the emperor Hadrian.

like a dense forest of hewn lumber. The weight of the dome is relieved by a series of **coffers** (the recessed panels—here square—that decorate the interior surface of a vault), which also add geometrical articulation to the hemisphere. The thickness of the dome decreases from 20 feet at the springing, where it is reinforced with stepped buttressing, to only 6 feet at the **oculus**, the circular opening 30 feet in diameter at the apex of the dome. The oculus allows adequate light, and the rain that enters is drained off by small, inconspicuous openings in the floor, which slopes slightly toward the center of the building.

In the Pantheon, Roman gods were represented by sculptures along the walls, while the dome assumed the symbolic significance of the heavens. Perhaps the most dramatic effect of the Pantheon is the harmony it demonstrates with the natural world. As the sun passes through the sky, a natural spotlight is cast into the rotunda, progressively illuminating the interior. To the Romans, the sun symbolized the eye of Jupiter, and its penetrating presence inside the temple seemed to make the deity manifest.

The Pantheon expresses the vision of the Roman Empire. It is a technological wonder of construc-

3-122 Interior of the Pantheon, as seen in an eighteenth-century painting of that name by Giovanni Panini.

GIOVANNI PAOLO PANINI (ROMAN, 1691–1765), *INTERIOR OF THE PANTHEON*, ROME C. 1734. OIL ON CANVAS. 1.283 × .991 (50½ × 39); FRAMED 1.441 × 1.143 (56¾ × 45). (C)1995 BOARD OF TRUSTEES, NATIONAL GALLERY OF ART, WASHINGTON. SAMUEL H. KRESS COLLECTION. PHOTO BY RICHARD CARAFELLI.

tion—like the vast network of highways, some still in use today, that were built to communicate with the corners of the Empire. The materials used in its construction and decoration, which were transported from lands as distant as Tunisia and Egypt, expressed the extent of Roman domination. The Pantheon relates the order of Roman rule to the Romans' reverence for a universal order.

Roman Public Architecture

3-123 Central hall, Baths of Caracalla, Rome, as recreated in a rather imaginative nineteenth-century drawing by G. Abel Blonet. 211–17 CE. Commissioned by the emperor Caracalla.

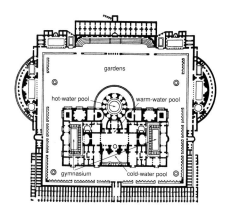

3-124 Plan of the Baths of Caracalla.

The Roman taste for grand architecture found expression in two secular building types, the bath and the basilica. Visiting the bath, which was built at state expense and could be entered for a nominal fee, was a ritual of daily life for the Roman citizen, for the baths fostered both intellectual and social life. There were many baths throughout the Empire, but the most elaborate were those in Rome, built by the emperor Caracalla (ruled 211–17).

The Baths of Caracalla complex (figs. 3-123, 3-124) covered 50 acres and accommodated approximately 1,600 people at one time. Initially, mixed bathing was permitted, but later the sexes were segregated, with women and men bathing at different times. The plan was organized along a central axis; the tepidarium (warm-water pool), calidarium (hot-water pool, usually circular in shape), and frigidarium (cold-water pool) were all located on the axis. Gymnasia flanked the pools; and gardens, barber and hairdresser shops, libraries, and meeting rooms completed the complex. Water, transported by aqueducts from

outside the city and heated by fires in basements, was passed to the pools in clay or lead pipes.

A visit to the bath usually began with physical exercise, followed by a stay in the steam room. In the calidarium, oil was used to cleanse the body. After cooling down in the tepidarium and frigidarium, a visitor received a massage, which completed the bath. The visitor might then take a walk in the gardens, study in the library, or attend lectures.

Lavish marble, stucco, and painted decoration embellished the interior surfaces. By the first century CE, the Roman political leader and author

Seneca, recalling the austere values of the Roman Republic in his *Moral Epistles*, complained that new bath structures were too ornate:

> We think ourselves poor and mean if our walls are not resplendent with large and costly mirrors; if our marbles from Alexandria are not set off by mosaics . . . if our vaulted ceilings are not buried in glass; if our swimming pools are not lined with Thasian marble, once a rare and wonderful sight in any temple. . . . What a vast number of statues, of columns that support nothing, but are built for decoration, merely in order to spend money!

Most Romans would not have agreed with Seneca, for they viewed the ritual of bathing and socializing within an opulent architectural environment as one of the joys of civilized life.

Another dramatic public space created by the Romans was the basilica (from the Greek *basilike*, "royal court"), a large building, often with an interior colonnade. Derived from earlier Greek buildings with colonnades, the basilica was entered on its longitudinal side. The interior was divided into three areas: two side areas known as **aisles** or **side aisles**, which flanked a large central axial hall called the **nave** (from the Latin *navis*, "ship," due to its resemblance to the upturned hold of a ship). Sometimes both ends of the nave terminated with an **apse**, a large niche composed of a half cylinder surmounted by a half dome (see fig. 3-117).

The basilica served a variety of secular purposes for the Romans; business and administrative offices were located there, and law courts met there. Often, too, the apses contained shrines to deities. Basili-

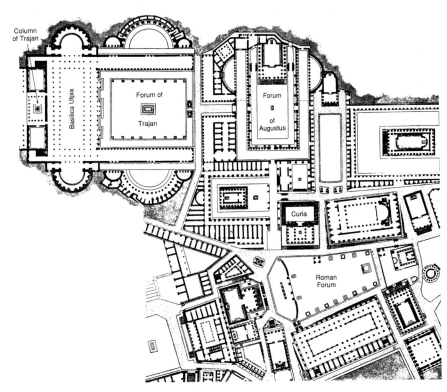

3-125   Plan of the Roman and Imperial Forums, Rome, with the Basilica Ulpia. Compare to the reconstruction in figure 3-100 and the reconstruction of the Basilica Ulpia in figure 3-116. Originally commissioned by the Republican government of Rome; expanded by various Roman emperors.

cas usually adjoined a forum, the public square that was the center of commercial and social activity. The Roman Forum was developed beginning in the sixth century BCE. Later, imperial forums, built by different emperors, are unified along a longitudinal axis (see figs. 3-100, 3-125). At the northwestern end of this axis is the Forum of Trajan, with the Basilica Ulpia (see fig. 3-116, Ulpius was Trajan's family name). The Basilica Ulpia adjoined libraries that flanked the Column of Trajan (see fig. 3-104). Given the Basilica's size—it is more than 400 feet long—the Roman architect was confronted with the problem of how to light the vast interior space. To solve this problem, the wooden gable roof of the

nave was raised above the aisles to permit clerestory windows.

Roman baths, forums, and basilicas gave the Western world a heritage of architecture and ideas. Our spas and community centers reflect the public baths on a more modest scale, while the forum survives in Italian piazzas and in our own public squares. The basilica served as the prototype for Christian churches in western Europe.

Mesoamerican Art: Teotihuacán

3-126 Ceremonial plaza at Teotihuacán, Mexico. c. 100 BCE–750 CE. The complex covers 13 square miles. Photo taken from the top of the Pyramid of the Moon, facing south along the 3-mile-long Avenue of the Dead. The Pyramid on the Sun, in the upper left, faces west.

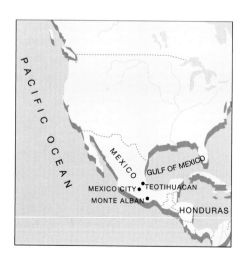

After 1,200 years, Teotihuacán stands today as mute testimony to the genius of unknown creators. Begun around 100 BCE on a dusty tableland north of modern Mexico City, it was both the first metropolis in the Americas and a remarkable example of city planning. At its height, Teotihuacán encompassed about 2,600 major structures, including markets and multifamily apartment compounds set along spacious esplanades. A city of temples, it was dominated by two majestic altars, each set atop a pyramid (see fig. 3-126). Its population was greater than that of the Athens of Pericles, and its area was larger than that of Rome during the Empire. It exercised dominion over central Mexico and Honduras in the region known as Mesoamerica. In the middle of the eighth century, the people of Teotihuacán abandoned their capital. This site was so historically rich and impressive to the Aztecs that they named it Teotihuacán, or the "birthplace of the gods," when they built their capital there in the twelfth century. It is the Aztec names for this place and its gods that we use today.

Monumental architecture such as that of the huge complex at Teotihuacán was not common in earlier Mesoamerican cultures. In the much earlier Olmec tradition, for example, free-standing sculpture was important. Stelae of many sizes served as historical commemorations and customarily included representations of historical leaders and written glyphs that refer to them. Images of gods, such as the figurines found in a cache at the Olmec ceremonial site called La Venta (fig. 3-127), were abundant. These sixteen jade and serpentine figurines are grouped in front of a row of six slender jade celts as though they were taking part in a ritual. These figures, common in this region and period, represent curiously sexless figures with baby faces that have been given the name *were-jaguars*. The figures must have been used in rituals.

It is commonly held by archaeologists that the Olmec civilization was a theocracy. Peasants supported the rulers with their agricultural surplus and their labor in return for assurance that the rituals carried out by the priests in the centers would help bring some degree of security to their lives and their agricultural livelihood. With the Olmec religion emerged priests, large ceremonial centers, and a complex iconography that illustrated the religious beliefs. A number of gods were portrayed; the most notable was the jaguar god seen here, who was prevalent at La Venta and other Olmec ceremonial sites.

Monumental architecture appeared at Teotihuacán in the first century CE with one of the most ambitious undertakings in all of Mesoamerica—the Pyramid of the Sun (fig. 3-126). Built over a cave held sacred since even earlier times, the Pyramid of the Sun (c. first century CE) retains the stepped outline of earlier pyramids in Mesoamerica, but here the scale is gigantic. The ground plan reveals a square base 738 feet across. The total height, including a temple that once stood on the upper platform, would have been about 246 feet.

Built in Teotihuacán somewhat later during the same period is the

c. 100 BCE–750 CE	Teotihuacán, Mexico
320 CE	Gupta dynasty begins to unify India
325 CE	Council at Nicea, first ecumenical council of the Christian Church
410 CE	City of Rome is sacked

3-127 Olmec, Ceremonial Group of Sixteen Figurines, in course of excavation in 1942. c. 1000 BCE. Serpentine, jade, and conglomerate figures, celts are jade; height of figurines between 6⅝″ and 7⅜″. Offering 4 at La Venta, Tabasco, Mexico.

Pyramid of the Moon (c. 150–225 CE), whose structure is more sharply delineated on its surface and is of more modest size than its counterpart. The placement of the smaller pyramid in the northern part of the valley, on gradually rising terrain, brings the upper platform to roughly the same altitude as that of the Pyramid of the Sun. These two edifices, with their severe contours set against the mountainous landscape on the horizon, dictated the features of the city's growth. For example, the Pyramid of the Sun is oriented precisely at the point on the

horizon where the sun sets over Teotihuacán the day it reaches its zenith at the summer solstice. Furthermore, the slightly later Avenue of the Dead, the city's main thoroughfare, runs strictly parallel to the main facade of the Pyramid of the Sun and is perfectly aligned with the axes of the Plaza of the Moon and the Pyramid of the Moon. With these pyramids completed, a gigantic urban plan began to emerge that reflected current ideas about astronomy and the desire to identify with the semiarid, serene landscape of this central Mexican plateau.

3-128 Facade of the Temple of the Feathered Serpent, Teotihuacán, Mexico. c. 150 CE. Each serpent head weighs 4 tons.

The fundamentals of these urban complexes were set in Mesoamerica by earlier peoples. The use of truncated pyramids as a temple base, the careful placement of terraces, platforms, and temples to form plazas, and the skill at handling open spaces using fixed axes (probably set according to symbolic considerations) were constant from earlier periods. Such monuments as these pyramids are not strictly architectural since they do not function as enclosures of space; rather, they work as sculpture, with exterior space acting as a constructed, environmental art form.

Teotihuacán was the civic, religious, political, and economic center for the surrounding valleys. Also in the city were foreign enclaves, thousands of artisans in the market places, and a ritual center of monumental proportions. During religious festivals the city population would swell even more with pilgrims. At its peak in the second and third centuries CE, Teotihuacán attained a maximum population of about 200,000. At this time, a second stage of building reflected the abrupt spurt in urban growth. The Avenue of the Dead was laid out, and around it rose a number of ceremonial complexes. Residential sectors that were once mainly to the

northwest of the two great pyramids began to grow in all directions—outward from the Avenue of the Dead and from the broad east and west avenues perpendicular to it.

During this period an important architectural refinement was initiated, the **tablero**, a heavy, projected, rectangular molding outlined by a thick frame. This detail appeared on all religious structures, whether a simple altar, ceremonial platform, small temple, or majestic pyramid. Perhaps the most splendid example of the tablero is on the Temple of the Feathered Serpent (fig. 3-128). The meaning of feathered serpents is not clear, but they probably carried a double message—political and cosmic. They have been interpreted as symbols of rule, fertility, the calendar, and the beginning of time. The images were later given Aztec names, Quetzalcoatl (plumed serpent) and Tlaloc (deity associated with water). Aside from the symbolic and aesthetic appeal of the Temple of the Feathered Serpent, its structure reflects technological advances. The entire nucleus of the temple is reinforced with a skeleton of limestone. The colossal heads are deeply anchored into the core of the tableros and show great sophistication in the joining of stone, since use of hard metal tools was not known to these builders.

The plan of the entire city is noteworthy for the regularity of the city blocks and the density of residential sectors. The layout of the city was based on a module of 187 feet, which formed the standard blocks in residential areas. Multiples of the module apparently formed other compounds in the city as well and divided it into a grid, which suggests the existence of rigorous city planning as well as a centralized ruling group, both spiritual and temporal. Rivers were rechanneled, and the city at its height included large reservoirs, steam baths, specialized workshops, open-air markets, administrative buildings, theaters, and areas set aside for ball games and other public functions.

The Palace of Zacuala—an excellent example of what must have been the luxurious residence of a rich Teotihuacán merchant or high functionary—included a chapel decorated with brightly colored mural paintings depicting the storm god (fig. 3-129). In this painting, the storm god is casting seeds to the earth as if planting. A speech scroll issues from his mouth, ending in a sign symbolizing water and precious things. The deity is surrounded by a fringe of volutes representing waves and clouds. The composition refers to the water god in the guise of a patron of fertility and abundance. The opulence and spaciousness of the palace attest to the existence of a powerful upper class and

3-129   Representation of Tlaloc (god of rain) c. 400–650 CE. Drawing from a fresco, palace wall of Zacuala, Teotihuacán.

to the importance of spiritual devotion in connection with that wealth.

Teotihuacán was apparently the most highly urbanized center of its time in the New World. The period of its life span, roughly from 100 BCE to 750 CE, was a spectacular one in Mesoamerica, with high points reached at Teotihuacán, at Monte Albán in Oaxaca, and in the Maya region. Each had a planned urban center with astronomical orientation for streets and buildings, monumental architecture, and intellectual achievements such as the perfection of the calendar, mathematics, writing, and astronomy (the latter especially among the Maya). This was a splendid age of the arts and architecture, which was reflected in the pyramid-temples at Teotihuacán and Tikal, and in mural painting, ceramics, and mosaics. Professional people and artisans were organized into guilds. Traders were also well organized, and large and efficient markets offered goods from many regions. Merchants brought feathers from exotic tropical birds, cotton, cacao,

jade, and turquoise into Teotihuacán for sale. The society was sharply stratified, militaristic, and theocratic. The predominance of religious representations in Teotihuacán as well as the presence of altars in the central courtyards of each house testify to the importance of religion in this community. Religious, civic, and secular activities were joined in the centers, which supported priest-chieftains, nobles, merchants, poets, musicians, actors (who were highly respected and took part in religious and secular ceremonies), artists, laborers, farmers, servants, and slaves.

After a period of increased internal conflict, the city was attacked. Its palaces were burned and its temples were reduced to rubble. This was a process of ritual destruction and desacralization that was unprecedented in scope and scale in Mesoamerica. Temple and state were one; to destroy Teotihuacán politically was to destroy it ritually. The artistic legacy of its people, however, endured and was adapted in other times and places in Mesoamerica.

View of one portion of the interior of the Islamic Mosque in the Spanish city of Córdoba. Construction was begun in 786, and the building was gradually enlarged over the next 200 years (for more information see figs. 4-49–4-51 and pp. 174–77).

Art from 200 to 1400

A Brief Insight

THE SCALE OF THIS ENORMOUS MOSQUE BUILT FOR Islamic worship reveals the religious fervor that characterizes much of the art and architecture produced in the period from 200 to 1400. The rows and rows of columns and arches were intended to focus the attention of the devout toward Mecca (today in Saudi Arabia), the direction in which Muslims face when praying five times a day.

The mosque's location at Córdoba in Spain, hundreds of miles from the Near East where Islam was founded, is only one of many examples that demonstrate the expansion of Buddhism, Judaism, Christianity, and Islam beyond the locality where each was founded. Here the reuse of columns and capitals from ancient Roman and Christian buildings in Córdoba was intended to demonstrate that a new religion was replacing older practices; when the city was later reconquered by the Christians, however, a church (not visible here) was built in the middle of the mosque in an attempt to reclaim the whole structure for Christianity. Around the world, religion was an inspiration for many works of art and architecture during this period.

Art from 200 to 1400

4-1 German Romanesque. Reliquary in the shape of a church, from the convent of Hochelten in the Lower Rhine region of Germany. c. 1170. Gilt cast bronze, enamel, and walrus ivory reliefs on a wooden core, height 21½″. Victoria and Albert Museum, London. This reliquary was probably made by a workshop in Cologne, Germany.

The similarities and differences between a small Christian object shaped like a domed church (fig. 4-1) and a huge Hindu relief carved into the living rock (fig. 4-2) remind us that religious art and architecture can take many different forms. We can use these two works to begin to reveal some of the issues addressed by art during the complex period from 200 to 1400.

During this period, religions that continue to be important in today's world—Hinduism, Shintoism, Buddhism, Judaism, Christianity, and Islam—expanded beyond their places of origin and in several cases greatly increased their numbers of followers. New centers with monuments were dedicated to serve the needs of religious practitioners that included priests, other members of religious hierarchies, and the common people. Art and architecture played important roles in supporting these developments. Although the function of religious art may at first seem self-evident, a study of objects and buildings created at different times and in different places for distinctive religions reveals a wide variety of uses: to explain dogma, to confirm believers in the faith, to convert nonbelievers, and to connect religious beliefs to political leaders and institutions—these are only a few of the ways in which religious art and architecture were used during this period.

The miniature Christian church, for example, functioned as a **reliquary**—a container for the bones of a holy person or for objects associated with one or more such persons (see also fig. 4-65). Reliquaries were displayed to the faithful, who hoped to benefit from their proximity to such holy things. The specifically Christian content of this object is evident in the **iconography** of the **reliefs**, which feature Old Testament prophets, Christ, the apostles, and scenes from the life of Jesus, including the crucifixion.

To understand this work better, the spiritual content of Christianity, which played a crucial role in forming the life and culture of the Middle Ages in Europe, must be examined. This is difficult to summarize, in part because of the many different interpretations of Christian belief that eventually developed. Christianity, a religion of salvation, emphasizes the inner, spiritual life, offering the promise of life after death for the soul in Paradise. Medieval Christianity emphasized belief in a single God understood as a Trinity,

---

4-2 Indian. *DESCENT OF THE GANGES*. Mahamallapuram, India. Middle Pallava period, C. 625–74. Carved on a natural granite cliff, height 20′. Commissioned by the Pallava king Mahendra-Varman I or his son King Mamalla.

an indivisible unity of three persons: God the Father, the creator; Jesus Christ, his son, who assumed human form in what is known as the Incarnation; and the Holy Spirit, who is believed to be continuously active in the world. Jesus Christ is held to be the son of God, born to a pious woman known as the Virgin Mary. He died after being nailed to a cross and left to die by suffocation in an event known as the crucifixion, as seen on the lower part of the reliquary, after being charged with blasphemy. Medieval Christian art also often depicted the Last Judgment (see figs. 4-72, 4-73, 4-107), when Christ would come at the end of time to judge humanity and thereby determine who would enter Paradise. The richly colored enamels and carved panels of the reliquary may be an explicit reference to the gold-studded walls of the City of God, the Heavenly Jerusalem mentioned in the Bible. This object was useful in confirming faith and in expressing the spiritual goals of Christianity; because important relics brought pilgrims to a church and, therefore, wealth to the local community, there may also have been a commercial and political function.

In the Hindu relief at Mahamallapuram, it is again both form and iconography that express religious content. The site, in South India on the shores of the Indian Ocean (see map, page 149), was an important pilgrimage center for Hindu believers; it may have become identified with the holy because of the unusual rock formations found along the sandy beaches. On some outcroppings of granite, sculptors carved shrines and reliefs of immense proportions. The *Descent of the Ganges* is carved on the face of a cliff; above the relief is a natural pool. During the rainy season, the overflow cascades down the natural cleft to be collected in what was once a natural pool at the base. Over millennia, this cleft had been smoothed by the flowing action of the water. This natural phenomenon may well have inspired carving the cliff with the story of the gift of holy water from the gods in heaven.

The Hindu religion developed a complex set of stories to explain the workings of nature, especially the fertility of crops and procreation. The traditions emphasize a single godhead that is capable of an infinite number of manifestations—assuming male, female, animal, and mixed animal and human forms—which helps to explain the great number of figures and animals in the relief. In personal terms, the most important aspect of Hinduism is the belief in reincarnation—every individual will return to life as another

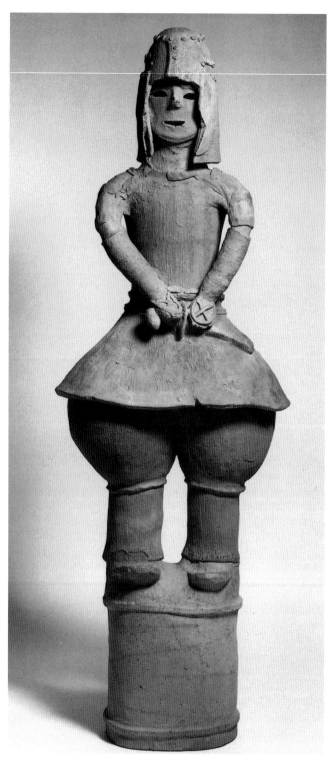

4-3 Proto-Historic Japan. *HANIWA OF A WARRIOR*. Kofun (Old Tomb) period, 3rd–6th century. Earthenware, height 47⅜″. Asian Art Museum of San Francisco, The Avery Brundage Collection, San Francisco, California. Hundreds of these earthenware figures of warriors, women, and animals—all known as *haniwa*—once encircled the huge mound tombs of the Japanese Yamato rulers, which were shaped like keyholes and surrounded by moats. For a work by a contemporary Japanese artist that uses the Haniwa figure, see fig. 10-155. Commissioned by a Yamato ruler.

living creature, and good behavior in one life will lead to a higher state of existence in the next. The religion is thought to have combined ancient beliefs about fertility with ideas derived from such social customs as hierarchy and caste. The highest order of gods is a trinity: Brahmin the creator, Vishnu the preserver, and Siva the destroyer. Images of these deities and many others and their multitudinous activities were thought of as aids in contemplation and as a focus for identification. The southern Hindu tradition, as at Mahamallapuram, and its art forms were passed along the trade routes across the seas to Cambodia and Indonesia.

Although the iconography of some of the details in the *Descent of the Ganges* is still debated, the composition focuses attention on the cleft near the center. This water is usually identified with the Ganges, one of the three sacred rivers of India, and is thought to have life-giving powers. Representatives of the multitudinous living beings of the world—deities of the river, elephants, lions, gods, human beings, and even a cat and mice—are assembled here as the holy river is seen being given from heaven to earth. The god Siva, one of the major manifestations of the godhead in the Hindu religion, appears several times to express the destructive and creative aspects of nature. Because this monument was commissioned by the local rulers as they were establishing their kingdom, its large and impressive scale and choice of subject may have been related to political needs as well.

History

The growth of powerful proselytizing religions was only one manifestation of worldwide change during this long period. A number of important political entities flourished at this time, including the Gupta rule in India; the successive Han, Sui, Tang, and Song dynasties in China; the Maya and Aztec cultures in the Americas; and the Carolingian, Ottonian, and French Gothic cultures in Europe. The establishment of a national identity, the writing of history, and the creation of art forms that were peculiar to that culture were important factors in many cultures. This was the period, for example, when the Japanese state defined itself as a political institution—the name it gave itself was Yamato—and the *Haniwa of a Warrior* (fig. 4-3) is an example of the kind of art that was established within this culture during the period of self-definition.

There was commercial, intellectual, cultural, scientific, and religious exchange on a large scale over great distances. Many Buddhists undertook pilgrimages from East Asia back to India, and the pilgrimage roads in Europe led the devout from northern Europe down to Spain and Italy. The Gupta period (4th–7th century) was described by a Chinese pilgrim-monk after his travels to India between 405 and 411. He was immensely impressed with the generous and efficient government of the Guptas, which had established magnificent cities and fine hospitals and seats of learning. He wrote of the general prosperity and said that "the surprising influence of religion cannot be described." It was a time of cultural expansion and colonization into Central Asia, China, Southeast Asia, and Indonesia. Indian visual arts, especially sculpture and painting produced for Hindu and Buddhist patrons, became an international standard in Asia (see fig. 4–4). The Crusades, which were preached as "Holy Wars" against the Muslims, led to increased contact between the Christian West and Islam. This period saw the commercial silk routes flourish between East and West. The Venetian Marco Polo's travels from Baghdad to the China Sea between 1271 and 1295 are known through his book *The Description of the World*, which was spread through dozens of translations and hundreds of manuscripts. Polo studied not only China's natural environment but also its economy (which already used paper money), its architecture, its urban planning, and especially its industries, many of which were more advanced than those in Europe at the time. On his return home, he described additional observations and recorded stories he had heard about Java, India, and areas of Africa. His observations influenced Western perceptions of the East for centuries, while the success of his travels encouraged others interested in the trade in exotic goods to undertake similar explorations in hopes of commercial success. Ni Zan's painting of the *Rongxi Studio* (fig. 4-5) is the kind of style of Chinese painting that Marco Polo might well have seen at the home of the Chinese literati. In Japan in the sixth century, the Yamato rulers and the Shinto religion were already being challenged by the new religion of Buddhism, imported into Japan through Korea. The commercial, political, and religious travel meant that works of art, foreign styles, scientific inventions, and other intellectual developments were shared across the continents of Europe and Asia.

Islamic writers preserved much of ancient Greek and Roman literature and philosophy, making it possible for these traditions to be reintroduced into European culture. Islamic science, mathematics, and medicine became well known in Europe at the same time. Scientific advances included astronomical investigations in India and Mesoamerica and the invention of gunpowder in China. Other inventions were the wheelbarrow, the compass, paper, and the spinning wheel. Practical, labor-saving inventions meant that there was less need for the slave labor that had characterized much of the ancient world. As large and powerful cultures and religious traditions developed, there was also contact through wars, including the religious and commercial wars in the eleventh, twelfth, and thirteenth centuries known as the Crusades. An increased awareness of diverse cultures was a hallmark during much of this period.

4-4 Indian. *THE FIRST SERMON*. Gupta period, c. 475 CE. Stela made of Chunar sandstone, height 63". Sarnath, Uttar Pradesh, India. Sarnath, Museum of Archaeology. A standard Gupta period image of Buddha represents him seated in a cross-legged, yogic pose, with the soles of his feet up and his hands held in the symbolic gesture of teaching, which is referred to as "turning the Wheel of the Law." Buddha's noble past is referred to by placing him on a throne decorated with lions, the symbol of royalty. Behind his head is a halo, which indicates the universal nature of this deity, who is viewed as clothed in the sun. The subject and position were standardized, but the elegant, refined style of presentation seen in this version was a contribution of the Gupta sculptors.

Art and the Christian Church

In much of Europe, the dominant medieval institution—culturally, educationally, spiritually, and often politically—was the Christian Church. In both East and West,

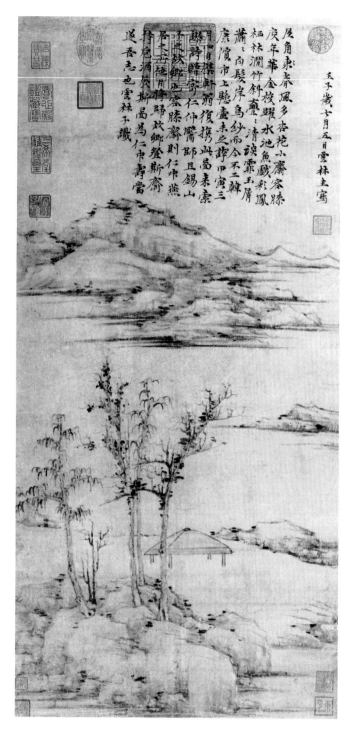

4-5 NI ZAN

RONGXI STUDIO. 1372. Hanging scroll, ink on paper, height 29⅜". National Palace Museum, Taiwan, Republic of China. For a portrait of Ni Zan, see figure 1-22.

monasteries and nunneries. The expanding institutions and hierarchy of the Church created a great demand for works of art.

Christianity developed a series of rites and services known as the liturgy. The central Christian rite was the Mass, or Eucharist, a service at which the Last Supper was reenacted and salvation for repentant believers was promised. By the early fourth century, this service was usually held in a church at an altar, which became the focus for the ritual and for works of Christian art. The painting shown in figure 4-6 demonstrates the rich decoration at a medieval altar. A priest, dressed in elaborately decorated vestments, stands at an altar with a bejeweled cross, a gold altarpiece, and a brocaded altar frontal. He raises the host, a consecrated piece of bread that stands for the body of Christ. (Missing from this representation is a chalice, the vessel that holds the wine standing for Christ's blood; see fig. 4-85).

Although a unified style cannot be defined for all European medieval art, many works from this period, including Islamic works, offer a stylistic treatment that emphasizes spiritual values through an intentional denial of the ancient classical traditions of **naturalism** and **illusionism**. This broad generalization offers some unity to the art produced in the diverse styles of the medieval period in Europe. Islamic motifs were sometimes borrowed from models known from Spain, Africa, and western Asia. In addition, the majority of surviving European medieval works of art are directly related to and created for the rituals and practices of the Christian Church. The notion of the Church as an institution is suggested in the form taken by the reliquary (see fig. 4-1).

The Scroll and Book

In the painting depicting the Christian Mass, the open book that is prominent on the altar suggests the importance of written texts during this period. Judaism, Christianity, and Islam are all religions with a holy book— a text that is at least in part believed to have been dictated to humanity by God. As a result, these texts are often decorated and enclosed in a rich, bejeweled container. Lettering and decorating such texts were often considered to be acts of religious devotion.

The hand-lettered, decorated book or scroll played an important role in the artistic developments in all three of these religions. The Bible, for example, was held to be a compendium of divine proclamations and a record of God's actions in history. It has two sections: the Old Testament, which encompasses the books of the Jewish faith, and the New Testament, composed of four versions of the life of Jesus (the Gospels, written by the Evangelists—Matthew, Mark, Luke, and John) and other writings. Throughout the Middle Ages, Jewish Torah scrolls, Christian Bibles, Islamic

some Christians withdrew from the world into monasteries and nunneries to follow a life of work and prayer. The Church developed a ruling hierarchy headed by the pope (the bishop of Rome, the first of whom had been Saint Peter) and local bishops that included the heads of

4-6 MASTER OF SAINT GILES

THE MASS OF SAINT GILES c. 1500. Oil on wood, 24¼ × 18". The National Gallery, London. A late-fifteenth-century painter here represents a ninth-century miracle taking place at an altar at the Royal Abbey Church of St.-Denis, near Paris. The combination of setting, costume, objects, and gestures preserved in this painting could be taken as a reminder that ritual in many religions probably included many of these same qualities, as well as additional ones. This representation of ritualistic religious behavior in action should be compared with other examples of ritual behavior, such as the African tribal rituals seen in figs. 1-13 and 10-32 and 10-33 and the American tribal ritual seen in fig. 10-35. As a group they remind us that setting, special clothing, choreographed gestures and movements, and objects are important characteristics of the ritual experience.

Korans, service books, and private prayer books were written by hand—usually on treated animal skins (**vellum** or **parchment**). Because they represented the word of God, they were often adorned with fine materials, and many Christian books were also illustrated. Islamic culture avoided the representation of the human figure (see pages 174–77), but copies of the Koran were decorated with calligraphic decorative patterns (for a later example, see fig. 6-59).

Handwritten, illustrated, and decorated manuscripts were also an important part of religious and secular tra-ditions in other parts of the world. In the Far East, novels and religious tracts were printed in books or written on hand scrolls, which unrolled from right to left (see fig. 1-18). Readers held the scrolls in both hands, and only a small portion was visible at any one time. Vertical scrolls like the *Rongxi Studio* were usually stored in boxes, but they could be hung on the wall for purposes of contemplation.

The Artist

In Europe, there are few signed works of art during the medieval period before the fourteenth century. The identity of the artist was not relevant during a period in which individuality generally was seen as unimportant; many medieval works were, in fact, produced by groups of artists and artisans working together. The artists of the Middle Ages included an important new class of artist: monks and nuns who, living within monastic communities, joined artistic productivity with the religious life. In Europe, the crafting of **manuscripts** and other liturgical objects was such an important activity that abbots of monasteries and even bishops continued to be active as artists after they had risen in the ecclesiastical hierarchy. But there were also "lay" artists, who lived in cities and were not connected to any religious order. There is evidence that by the tenth century these lay artists were organizing themselves into professional organizations, rather like trade unions, called **guilds**.

In most other cultures during this period, artists worked in groups, and the large endeavors required by religious practices were produced by workshops of artists and laborers. There are isolated instances of signed works, but these are not common. The main exception to this attitude toward the artist is in China, where the status of the artist as a scholar-intellectual, often working within the court, means that the majority of works are signed (see pages 5–6, 21).

4-7 Synagogue excavated at Dura-Europos, 244/245 CE
(for more information see fig. 4-12 and pp. 140–141)

4-8 Cathédrale de Chartres, 1194–1220
(for more information see figs. 4-88 to 4-93 and pp. 208–12)

The years between 200 to 1400 are a period of exploration and expansion, and it was during this period that four world religions that are still important today—Buddhism, Judaism, Christianity, and Islam—expanded beyond the locales where they were founded. The Jewish Synagogue discovered in Dura-Europos was a surprise to archaeologists, but its unexpected painted program of scenes from the Old Testament was perhaps created in response to the painted decorations found in the shrines of the other religions that were flourishing in this small frontier town. More than any other architectural type, religious monuments most often incorporate sculpture, painting, or other media to illustrate the stories and/or tenets of the religion, as is the case here. While this synagogue is on a small scale, the French Gothic cathedral at Chartres is by far the largest structure in the small market town where it was built. The high vaults and glowing stained-glass windows are meant to be a metaphor for the Heavenly Jerusalem, the paradise longed for by Christians, while the numerous sculptures that decorate the exterior create an environment of holy figures to inspire the faithful. The whole structure, with its decoration, is intended as a religious metaphor, while the emotional impact of the effect of weightlessness created by complex Gothic engineering hints at the denial of earthbound existence offered by paradise.

Islam is a monotheistic religion (one of the main tenets of Islam is "There is no God but God alone"), and when the Ottoman Turks conquered Constantinople in 1453, they converted all the Byzantine churches, including the sixth-century Hagia Sophia (see figs. 4–28 to 4–30), into mosques. In the Suleimaniye Mosque, built almost a millennium later, the Byzantine domed model has been appropriated by the Muslims; apparently the manner in which the interior space was unified by the high, floating dome at Hagia Sophia was considered appropriate to express the monotheistic basis of Islam and also the communal nature of Muslim worship.

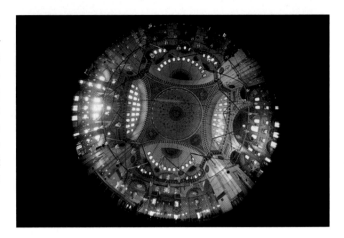

4-9 Suleimaniye Mosque in Istanbul, 1551–58 (for more information see figs. 6-66 to 6-68)

The great temple at Ellora is not architecture per se because it is not constructed but sculpted. The "buildings" and interiors are carved directly out of a rock cliff, emphasizing the intimate connection with nature that is so much a part of Hindu belief. The multitudinous sculpted figures are related to the infinite number of deities in the Hindu pantheon.

4-10 The Kailasantha Temple at Ellora, India, c. 760–800 (for more information see figs. 4-47 and 4-48)

4-11 TADEO ANDO

JAPANESE BUDDHIST WATER TEMPLE, 1992 (for more information see fig. 10–139)

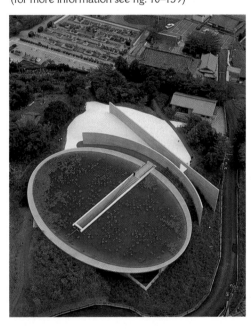

The emphasis on inner knowledge and self-understanding in Buddhist belief seems to explain this modern Buddhist temple. Walking down the steps "into" the lotus pond becomes a metaphor for the inward search of Buddhist meditation.

QUESTIONS

1. Visit an example of religious architecture in your neighborhood during a service or "event."

2. Discuss how people are "using" the structure, and ask yourself how the structure and its decoration refer to the beliefs and ideals of the particular religion.

Jewish Art:
The Synagogue at Dura Europos

4-12 Reconstruction of the west wall, with the Torah niche, of the synagogue, Dura Europos (modern Syria). 244/45. Tempera on plaster, length of wall approx. 40′. National Museum, Damascus. The Roman frontier city of Dura Europos, located in Mesopotamia, was a crossroads and minor trading center. It has provided rich archaeological information, especially in its several places of worship, which included a synagogue, a Christian site with a baptistery with frescoes, temples to Bel, Zeus, and Mithras. The Torah niche in the synagogue is decorated with a shell, a motif taken from Roman art, where the shell is often used to signify a holy place. In this niche were placed scrolls that contain the first five books of the Bible, the sacred writings of Judaism. Attributed to Moses, these books contain the basic rules of the Jewish faith, including the Ten Commandments, which tradition holds were given to Moses by God on Mount Sinai.

Discovered in 1932, the synagogue at Dura Europos, in modern Syria (fig. 4-12), astonished archaeologists and scholars. Quite unexpectedly, its capacious house of assembly had figurative decoration: a complicated sequence of paintings of Old Testament scenes in bands around all four walls. Both scripture (the second of the Ten Commandments: "You shall not make for yourself a graven image [idol], or any likeness of anything that is in heaven above, or that is in the earth below, or that is in the water under the earth") and historical writings seem to imply that it is unlawful for

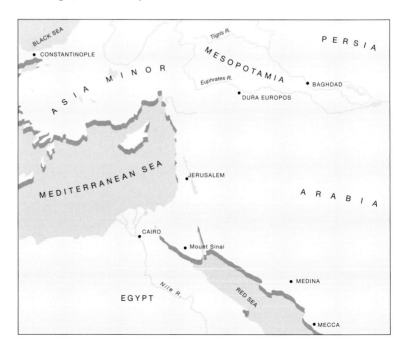

Jews to make or have images. That this prohibition was not followed by all Jews is revealed by archaeological discoveries at Dura and elsewhere. The cycle at the Dura synagogue includes such scenes as Moses receiving the Law, Moses leading the chosen people out of Egypt, Exodus and the Crossing of the Red Sea, and even a cityscape with a representation of Jerusalem and the Temple of Solomon.

The Jewish religion is monotheistic and is based on the worship of Yahweh, or God. The origins of Judaism are traced to a covenant made between God and Abraham, in which God promised Abraham that he would give him a mighty race of descendants and a Promised Land if his followers would stop worshiping idols. The emphasis in the services held in the synagogue and at home is on the telling of Jewish history, the reading of the laws, and the interpretation of those laws. Judaism has a strong scholarly tradition, and it is possible that the extensive narrative cycle in the synagogue at Dura Europos was used in part as an educational tool, to illustrate and teach the history and laws of the religion. The large number of competing religions practiced in Dura, each with its own sanctuary, may have encouraged the Jews there to decorate their synagogue.

In terms of art, Dura Europos was an unimportant provincial city, and the conventions of the figures and the use here of iconographic stereotypes and compositions known from other sites suggest that the Dura cycle was derived from a **pattern book**—a book of images, prepared as an artist's tool, that preserved a tradition of illustrated scenes, in this case from the Old Testament. In *Moses Giving Water to the Tribes* (fig. 4-13), Moses stands in a relaxed **contrapposto** position derived from ancient Greek and Roman art, but both the schematic nature of the composition—with smaller figures representing the tribes of Israel placed evenly around the edge of the scene—and the unrealistic way streams of water reach out

4-13 *MOSES GIVING WATER TO THE TRIBES AND ELIJAH REVIVES THE WIDOW'S CHILD*, detail of figure 4-7. The figures are smaller than lifesize. *Moses Giving Water to the Tribes* depicts Numbers 21:16–18, when a well was dug after God told Moses to "gather the people together, and I will give them water." In a continuous narrative that represents the widow twice and the child three times, *Elijah Revives the Widow's Child* shows the widow of Zarephath presenting her dead child to Elijah, Elijah resuscitating it, and the widow holding the revived child (I Kings 17:8–24).

to each tent are consistent with other developments at this time. The Jews, a small minority at Dura, cre-ated an impressively decorated synagogue that expresses their piety and the dignity of their traditions.

Early Christian Art

4-14 *THE THREE HEBREW YOUTHS IN THE FIERY FURNACE*, fresco in the Christian Catacomb of Priscilla, Rome, Italy. Early 3rd century. Approx. 20 × 30″.

*T*he *Three Hebrew Youths in the Fiery Furnace*, from a Christian cemetery (fig. 4-14), represents the Christian use of the Old Testament story of three righteous Hebrew youths who were saved by God after being thrown into a furnace for refusing to worship idols. Three frontal figures, their arms raised in a position of prayer, stand amid flames. Their pleas for deliverance are answered, and a dove, symbolic of the Holy Spirit, descends bearing a branch symbolizing victory and/or peace. The message of the painting is direct: faith brings salvation.

Catacombs, underground burial complexes used by Jews and Christians, were originally known by the Greek term *coemeteria* ("places of rest," from which we derive our word *cemetery*).

Later, the term *catacomba*, which initially referred to a specific cemetery in Rome, came into general use. The walls of the narrow, labyrinthine passages in the catacombs, cut from soft rock, had horizontal niches to hold the bodies of the deceased. Larger chambers, also underground, were used for funerary rites. Catacombs were not secret burial places, as legend has it, although they may have been used as hiding places during times of Christian persecution.

The painting of *The Three Hebrew Youths* expresses the faith of the early Christians by promising salvation in time of need and suffering. The Old Testament story was perceived as a precedent or what is known as a pre-figuration for New Testament teachings. Christians understood Christ as

the Messiah who fulfilled the prophecies of the Old Testament, and theologians and artists often associated the two religious traditions. The style of the painting is animated, continuing a Roman manner of painting using fluid paint and flowing brushstrokes. Some modeling is used, but the strong outlines flatten and dematerialize the figures, and the emphasis on their enlarged eyes enhances the spiritual intent.

History

A few years after Christ's death and resurrection, Paul (originally named Saul), a Jew who had persecuted Christians, was converted to the new faith (see fig. 7-16). He zealously preached the message of Christ and converted many to Christianity. By about 40 CE, the term *Christian* was first used to designate these followers of Christ's teachings, and about 70–80 CE, when the Gospels of the New Testament were being written, Christianity broke decisively with Judaism.

By the early second century, an internal structure and hierarchy were being formed within the Church, and liturgical rites for worship were developed. Although subject to periodic and often vicious persecution, the new religion, with its emphasis on spiritual values, spread rapidly. In a letter written to the Roman emperor Trajan in 110, Pliny the Younger warned of this

> extreme superstition. . . . Many of all ages, of all ranks, of both sexes, are being brought into danger, and will continue to be brought. The blight of this superstition has not been confined to towns and villages; it has even spread to the country.

Art

Early Christian art (c. 150–400 CE) developed gradually, in part because of intermittent persecution. Stylistically the new art was initially dependent on Roman and Hellenistic sources. In many cases, only the Christian subject matter indicates its religious function. Early Christian artists worked in a diverse range of media. Painters not only decorated church and catacomb walls but also created book illustrations. Sculptors made marble **sarcophagi** and ivory carvings. A favored medium for church decoration was **mosaic** (see pp. 156–159).

One house at Dura Europos was converted for Christian services in 231. It included a baptistery with an image of the Good Shepherd (from the parable in Luke 15:3–7) above a scene of Adam and Eve in the garden. Here Old and New Testaments are intellectually related—the Good

4-15 *GOOD SHEPHERD*. Late 3rd century. Marble (restored), height 39″. Vatican Museums, Rome. The composition of the standing figure with an animal across his shoulders, as in this Good Shepherd sculpture, is derived from ancient Greek representations of Hermes the shepherd or Orpheus with the animals.

Shepherd becomes a reference to Christian redemption, overcoming the sin of Adam and Eve. The Good Shepherd image appears often on Early Christian sarcophagi and reliefs, and even as single figures (fig. 4-15), but it is uncertain whether these beardless youths represent Christ as the Good Shepherd or the more general concept of God caring for his flock. In any case, the humble modesty of the figure is consistent with the spirit of early Christianity.

Early Christian artists were challenged to express the promises and mysteries of their new faith. As in ancient Roman art and in most later medieval art, artists were laborers who worked in a communal situation, and their works are anonymous. They created the means to communicate the ideals of Christianity as it changed and became more public. These anonymous artists, at once conventional and innovative, helped effect a transition from the ancient to the medieval world.

4-16   *PASSION SARCOPHAGUS.*   Second half of 4th century. Catacomb of Domitilla, Rome.

From Judaism, Christianity inherited a disposition against representing the divinity, an **aniconic** attitude that was also supported by the Christian criticism of the earlier practice of worshiping idols. As questions arose about the appropriateness of figurative art in the early Church, a vocabulary of symbols was developed to express abstractly the tenets of the new faith. One common Early Christian symbol is the so called Chi-Rho, the combination of the first two letters of the Greek word for *Christ*, *X*, and *P*, to form a monogram for Christ ☧, as seen at the top center of the sarcophagus (fig. 4-16); this symbol is related to the story of the dream of the Roman emperor Constantine, who had a vision that he would be victorious under this sign.

The Early Christian repertory of symbols was varied (fig. 4-17), but it seems unlikely that any were used as "secret" symbols for communication between members of this new and sometimes-persecuted religious group. Other Early Christian symbols include the anchor, referred to in Paul's letter to the Hebrews (6:19), which became a symbol of resolution and hope; and the fish, which became a symbol for Christ because the first letter of each word in the phrase "Jesus Christ, Son of

God, Savior" forms the Greek word *ichthus*, "fish." Because ancient legend held that the flesh of the peacock was immune to decay and its feathers contained the complete spectrum of colors, the bird itself came to symbolize eternity. The A, alpha, and Ω, omega—first and last letters of the Greek alphabet—were adapted because the Bible reports that Christ had said, "I am Alpha and Omega, the beginning and the end" (Revelation 1:8). A curving vine and grapes refer both to God's relationship with his people ("I am the vine, you are the branches"; John 15:5) and to the wine used in the Mass.

With time, the use of symbols was gradually combined with that of narrative representation, as is seen in the so-called *Passion Sarcophagus* (fig. 4-16). The narrative sequence is not the expected left-to-right development, and the culminating scenes of the sequence, Jesus' crucifixion and resurrection, are reserved for the central area, where they are given a highly symbolic treatment. In the earliest scene of the narrative sequence, to the right of center, we see the arrest of Jesus; this is then followed on the far right with the scene of Pilate washing his hands. The next scene, the mocking of Jesus, with a soldier crowning him with a crown of thorns, is

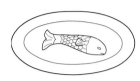

The fish, as it appears in a number of Early Christian catacomb paintings.

Peacocks, grapes and grape vines, and a form of the Chi-Rho monogram on a fourth-century sarcophagus made for a Christian.

A plaque bearing the alpha and omega letters, a Chi-Rho, and a lamb—"the Lamb of God, which taketh away the sin of the world!" (John 1:19)

4-17   Early Christian symbols.

to the immediate left of the center, while on the far left we see the fourth scene, Simon helping Jesus carry his cross. In the center, the crucifixion is referred to by the cross, while the subsequent resurrection, on Easter Sunday morning, is indicated by the elevated placement of the Chi-Rho enclosed in a triumphal wreath. The enclosing of the Chi-Rho within the wreath, an ancient Greek and Roman symbol that refers to victory, suggests the soul's desire to triumph over physical death. The sleeping soldiers below represent the Roman soldiers who fell asleep while guarding the tomb and who therefore did not witness the resurrection symbolized above, but they also refer to those who deny Christ's resurrection. The doves perched on the cross are symbols of Christian souls and also of peace and purity.

Early Christian Architecture

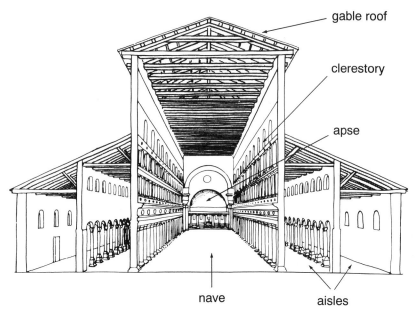

gable roof

clerestory

apse

nave

aisles

4-18 Cross section and reconstruction of the interior, Old St. Peter's Basilica, Rome. C. 333–90. Interior length approx. 368′. This basilica was demolished in the sixteenth century, when today's imposing edifice (see figs. 6-30–6-34) was begun. The earlier church then became known as Old St. Peter's. Commissioned by the Roman emperor Constantine.

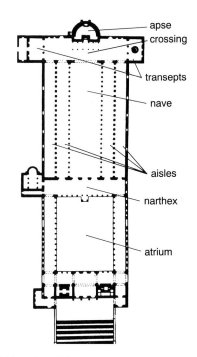

apse

crossing

transepts

nave

aisles

narthex

atrium

4-19 Plan of Old St. Peter's Basilica.

Old St. Peter's Basilica was a prototype for developments in Christian architecture (figs. 4-18, 4-19). The plan was initially adapted from the Roman **basilica** (see fig. 3-116), which was usually entered on its long side, but the Christian church was entered through an **atrium** and **narthex** (entrance hall) on its short side. This narthex was usually on the west, and the altar was toward the east, an orientation followed in most later medieval churches.

The interior division of space, with a **nave** flanked by side **aisles**, is similar to certain Roman basilicas. Old St. Peter's has **transepts** (from the Middle Latin *transseptum*, "transverse enclosure"), a feature that would become traditional in Christian Churches. These architectural spaces, extensions to the north and south, meet the nave at the **crossing**. Transepts create a cross shape; the term *cruciform* (cross-like) *basilica* designates Early Christian churches

with transepts. At St. Peter's, as in many Roman basilicas, wooden beams supported a **gable roof**, and **clerestory** windows allowed light to illuminate the nave. Many of the **columns** used in building Old St. Peter's were taken from earlier Roman buildings; materials thus reused are known as *spolia* (Latin, "spoils"). The group of spiral columns that decorated the altar area at Old St. Peter's had a special significance, for they were thought to have been taken from the Temple of Solomon in Jerusalem.

The size of Old St. Peter's mirrors the triumphant attitude of Christianity following the Edict of Milan in 313, which granted religious freedom to the Christians. Constantine realized the unifying strength that the newly recognized religion could bring to his reign. Many privileges, including tax exemptions and donations of land and money, were granted the Church. Constantine personally contributed to

the construction of St. John Lateran in Rome (begun 313), which marks the first use of the basilica plan for Christian architecture. Constantine's support was further evidenced by his decision to build Old St. Peter's, which was both a martyrium (built over the grave site of Saint Peter, it marked and commemorated his martyrdom) and a basilica used for worship. It is believed that the development of the transept at St. Peter's derived from the need for additional space for worshipers and pilgrims around the shrine and a desire to separate Peter's grave from other tombs in the nave.

Old St. Peter's had a rather plain brick exterior, but the interior was adorned with precious materials, including marble Roman columns, mosaics, and frescoes. The decorated interior contrasted with the plain exterior, subtly reminding the visitor that the beauty of the inner spirit was more important than external, physical adornment. From the entrance, one's attention was focused on the high altar, set below an enormous arch on which a mosaic depicted Christ, Saint Peter, and the emperor Constantine with the inscription:

> Because under Your guidance the world rose triumphant to the skies, Constantine, himself a victor, built You this hall.

In the apse, where in a Roman basilica a statue of the emperor might be located (see fig. 3-106), another mosaic displayed an enthroned Christ flanked by Saints Peter and Paul. A reference to Christ as the supreme judge is thus found at a point where, in a Roman basilica, law had been dispensed. (In some churches, the cathedra, or throne, of the bishop was set in the apse. These churches, where bishops preside, are called **cathedrals**.) With the support of Constantine, who probably converted to Christianity near the time of his death, the flourishing Christian faith transformed the architectural forms and imperial symbolism of ancient Rome.

Another type of ancient Roman design adapted by the early Christians was the **centrally planned** structure, in which the main parts of a building radiate from a central point. It was used for baptisteries and mausoleums. Santa Costanza exemplifies the centrally planned structure (figs. 4-20 and 4-21). Built about 354 as a mausoleum for Constantine's family, it features a central altar within a ring of paired columns that support the **dome** and clerestory. Between the columns and the outer wall is a circular corridor that at Santa Costanza is **barrel-vaulted** and decorated with mosaics; it is called the **ambulatory** (*ambulare*, "to walk"). Four large niches in the walls define the shape of a Greek cross (a cross with four equal arms). The cross circumscribed by the circular plan symbolized salvation and eternal life for the Christian and was thus an appropriate design for a Christian tomb.

312	Constantine, after having a vision of the cross, defeats Maxentius
c. 333–90	**Old St. Peter's Basilica, Rome**
410	Visigoths sack Rome

4-20   Interior, Santa Costanza, Rome. c. 354. Commissioned by the Roman emperor Constantine for the members of his family.

4-21   Plan and longitudinal section of Santa Costanza.

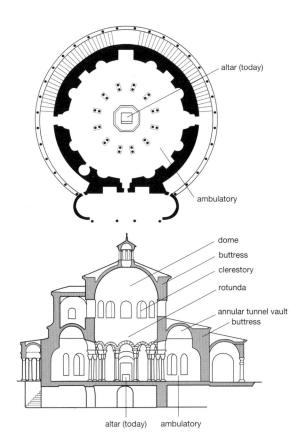

altar (today)

ambulatory

dome
buttress
clerestory
rotunda
annular tunnel vault
buttress

altar (today)   ambulatory

The Shinto Shrine at Ise, Japan

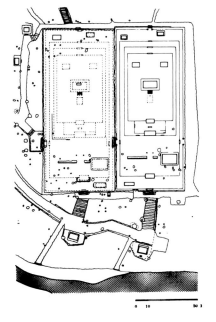

4-22 Naiku (Inner) Shrine complex, Shinto shrine, Ise, Japan. Late 5th–early 6th century. *Ise*, the name of the city in central Japan where the shrine is located, is used to refer to all the shrines collectively, as well as to the land on which they are situated. The original patron is unknown; the patron for rebuilding every twenty years is the Japanese ruling family and the nation of Japan.

4-23 Plan of the Naiku Shrine buildings and the old shrine compound.

Shinto, the indigenous religion of the Japanese people, has its origins in animism. The focus of Shinto is reverence for *kami*, the deities and supernatural qualities perceived in such natural objects as trees, rocks, waters, and mountains. The spirits of deceased emperors, heroes, and other famous persons are also revered as *kami*. *Kami* receive tribute at shrines in the form of offerings of food, music, dance, and the performance of such traditional skills as archery and sumo wrestling.

The Ise complex includes the Naiku (Inner, western) Shrine (figs. 4-22, 4-23), which houses the sun goddess Amateratsu Omikami, the divine ancestor of the Japanese emperors, and the Geku (Outer, eastern) Shrine, which is dedicated to a local god. From prehistoric times, this area has been a sacred place and pilgrimage site. It is the recognized seat of the ancestral deities of the imperial house, and in modern times, under State Shinto, it

has become the shrine of the entire Japanese nation.

The initial construction of the Inner Shrine is thought to date from the late fifth to the mid-sixth century. Because only members of the imperial family worshiped there, Ise became the center for imperial rites. In the elaborate annual ritual calendar, the most important ceremonies were the Niiname-sai (first-fruits festival) and the Daijo-sai (enthronement ceremony), during both of which the emperor offered pure food to the deities and consumed a ceremonial meal that the deities were thought to share.

The *shoden* (fig. 4-24)—or main sanctuary of the Naiku complex—and other shrine buildings are erected in an ancient style of architecture using undecorated wooden members and a simple, thatched roof. They are raised above the ground on wooden piles, a custom associated with the humid climate of Oceania, from which this style may have been derived. The natural, unadorned materials of the build-

ing are believed to represent a sympathetic association between nature and architecture. According to a tradition originating with the emperor Temmu (ruled 673–86), the shrines are rebuilt every twenty years in order to approximate the cycle of growth and decay in nature. Although the custom fell into disuse in the Middle Ages, the latest rebuilding at Ise took place in 1993 and repeats precisely the plan of the earliest documented structure of the *shoden*, dating from 690–97.

The Shinto complex at Ise has roots in prehistoric practices. The seasonal changes that had special significance for early cultivators greatly affected daily life. Farmers depended on *kami* to help them. They propitiated the *kami* to ensure the success of their seasonal activities: sowing, planting, harvesting. A sacred annual cycle was observed, and the rituals of *kami* worship were the mainstay of everyday activity.

The earliest Shinto sanctuaries were simple piles of boulders or stones that marked the sacred dwelling places

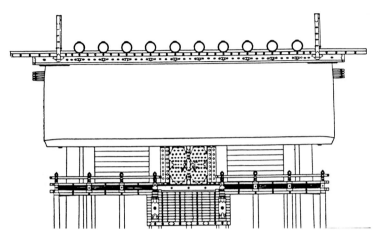

4-24 Front elevation of the *shoden* (main sanctuary). Earliest documented structure 690–97; rebuilt 1993).

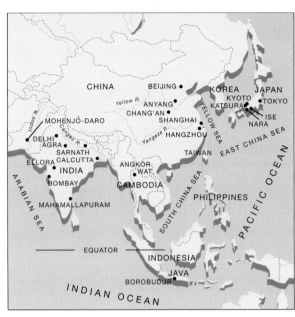

of the *kami*. In early Japan, the *kami* were regarded with awe and were segregated from the secular world. Their sanctuaries became hallowed ground, and access was forbidden except on ritual occasions. Priests could approach the *kami*, but only during special rites in which they acted as mediators between human beings and the *kami* world.

In order to make the domain sacred, the physical bounds of the sacred and profane had to be demonstrated. The stone monument in which *kami* were thought to dwell was first enclosed by a ring of rocks. This "heart pillar" (*shin no mihashira*) lies buried deep in the ground at Ise and is dressed in the evergreen boughs sacred to Shintoism. These *sakaki* branches symbolize the tree where the divine mirror (the "literal" body of Amateratsu Omikami) was hung and where the sun goddess was enshrined. A later period saw the development of the **torii arch**, which marks the entrance to a Shinto sacred area.

Two occurrences led to the establishment of these sanctuaries as Shinto shrines. First, the introduction of Buddhism from China via Korea in the sixth century led the Japanese emperor to welcome Buddha as a great *kami* whose visible representation was housed in an impressive Buddhist temple. This had a profound influence on the development of Shinto shrines and on the emergence of permanent shrine sanctuaries in particular. Second, the gradual deification of the emperor led to the establishment of an official Shinto shrine. At least as early as the late third and fourth centuries CE, Yamato rulers unified the competing clan lineages in the Yamato Plain under the aegis of their lineage, the sun line. The emperor came to be regarded as a living *kami*, with his divinity surpassing that of other *kami*. With this new status for the emperor, political and religious authority were joined. The union was sanctified at the Inner Shrine at Ise. The symbol of succession from the sun goddess to the sun line, the sacred necklace of *magatama* (jewels representing

the soul spirit, which can enter the body of the possessor), is still the emblem of enthronement for the emperors of Japan and is kept at Ise, where Shinto doctrines were first systematically expounded. Today, the site is venerated, and pilgrimages there are, in part, an expression of patriotic sentiment.

Byzantine Art

4-25 *TRANSFIGURATION OF CHRIST*, apse mosaic, Monastery of St. Catherine, Mount Sinai, Egypt. c. 560. The Monastery of St. Catherine is at the foot of Mount Sinai (see map, page 140), where, according to the Old Testament, God gave the Ten Commandments to Moses. Isolated in the Sinai Desert, the monastery, which has been in continuous use since the sixth century, is a repository of early manuscripts and other works of art (see fig. 4-27). Original patron of the monastery complex was the Byzantine emperor Justinian.

In Christian tradition, the Transfiguration occurred when three apostles accompanied Christ to the top of a mountain. While they prayed, Christ was lifted up into the sky, surrounded by an aura of heavenly light, and appeared flanked by the Old Testament prophets Moses and Elijah (Matthew 17:1–13). The voice of God the Father was heard from a cloud: "This is my beloved Son: hear him." In the mosaic of the *Transfiguration of Christ* at the monastery at the base of Mount Sinai, Christ is represented on the axis surrounded by a **mandorla** (almond-shaped **halo**) of blue light, which emphasizes his resplendent white robes (fig. 4-25). Moses and Elijah symmetrically flank Christ, while the apostles below gesture with wondrous exclamation. The divinity of Christ is demonstrated in a scene with a spiritual emphasis that removes it from our physical world. No geographic details are given, and the event is bathed in a golden light symbolic of spiritual enlightenment. Although modeling is used, the linear patterns of the shadowed areas and the complete absence of cast shadows denies the figures any illusion of weight or mass.

History

In 323, Constantine decided to move the capital of the Roman Empire from Rome to the eastern part of the Empire, to an historic trading center on the Bosphorus called Byzantium (from which we derive the name for the Byzantine civilization). The eastern provinces of the Empire, already strongly

God (fig. 4-26). The figures on each side of Isaiah are classical personifications: Night is a female contrapposto figure wearing a Greek costume and with a veil of stars over her head, while Dawn is a boy with a lighted torch. The gold background is still dominant, as it was four centuries earlier in the *Transfiguration* at Mount Sinai, but elements of landscape recalling Hellenistic and early Roman painting have been revived. The classicizing influence is more strongly stated here than in comparable manuscript **illuminations** from western Europe.

The Icon and Iconoclasm

One unique form of painting that developed in Orthodox Christianity was the **icon** (Greek for "image"). Used during religious services and to decorate churches, an icon is a consecrated religious painting that displays a holy person or event and is viewed as a vehicle to communicate with the spiritual world. Some icons were believed to date from the time of Jesus, and the most famous were thought to be of divine origin. The *Madonna and Child Enthroned with Saints Theodore and George and Angels* (fig. 4-27) is a rare surviving example of a sixth-century icon. The drapery patterns tend to flatten the figures, but the modeling and the slight contrapposto positions seen in the saints continue the classical interest in naturalism. Above the Virgin, two angels look sharply upward to God, whose hand descends into the pictorial space, emitting a strong ray of light. The static composition of the Virgin and saints, with their intense staring eyes, is characterisic of icon paintings. The medium is **encaustic** (from the Greek *enkaiein*, "to burn in"). It involves mixing dry pigments with hot wax, a technique that creates an effect that is both translucent and brilliant.

By the later sixth century, the faithful attributed miraculous powers to certain icons. Conservative

Christianized, had become increasingly more important, and the new capital was far from the political instability of Rome and the threats of barbarian invaders. The new capital, dedicated in 330, was named Constantinople.

Constantine's decision was a wise one. A port located at the center of regional trade routes and surrounded by rich timbered forests and agricultural fields, Constantinople developed rapidly as an economic and cultural center. This growth lead to an increased military capability, and, during the reign of the emperor Justinian (ruled 527–565), areas of the Empire that had been lost—Italy, southern Spain, and North Africa—were again brought under imperial rule. Under Justinian, an intelligent and efficient emperor, Byzantine civilization prospered. His wife, Theodora, a former circus performer, gave resolute counsel in assisting to govern the Empire. Justinian and Theodora shared a vision of reviving the grandeur of the Roman Empire while advancing the Christian faith (see figs. 4-32–4-35).

But Justinian's military gains proved costly and short-lived. Later, the Empire was reduced through uprisings in western Europe and, beginning in the seventh century, through the rapid advance of the Islamic religion, which with zeal spread the ideals of the prophet Muhammad to Arabia, Persia, North Africa, and Spain. The location of Constantinople meant that the influence of Roman culture was gradually supplanted by Greek taste and values, and Greek replaced Latin as the official language at court. Disagreements within the Church led to an official split in 1054 between the Western, or Roman, Church and the Byzantine, or Orthodox, Church, with its center in Constantinople. This split helps explain why the Christian Crusaders, on their way to fight the Muslims in 1204, diverted their campaign and captured and sacked Constantinople. They ruled the area for about fifty years. Byzantine cultural and political stability was later restored, but in 1453 Constantinople fell to the Ottoman Turks and was later renamed Istanbul.

Art

Many aspects of ancient Greek art and culture were preserved or revived during the long history of the Eastern, Byzantine Empire. The revival of antiquity that occurred in the tenth century, for example, can be seen in a manuscript painting from the *Paris Psalter* (a book of Psalms) in which Isaiah's prayers are met by a ray of light that extends from the hand of

4-26 *PRAYER OF ISAIAH*, from the *PARIS PSALTER*. c. 900. Manuscript painting on vellum, 14 × 10¼".
Bibliothèque Nationale, Paris.

factions, called iconoclasts (image destroyers), feared that the icons themselves had become objects of worship, which would be heretical; the divine nature of Christ, they argued, should not be represented, and to do so would encourage idolatry. They were countered by the iconodules (image venerators), who argued that because Christ had become human (the doctrine of the Incarnation), it was permissible to depict him in this human form. The dispute erupted into open and at times bloody conflict between 726 and 843, a period in Byzantine history known as the iconoclastic controversy. During this period, icons and other religious images were damaged or destroyed, accounting for many losses of works of Early Christian and Byzantine art. A final victory for the iconodules occurred in 843; even today, one Sunday in the Orthodox

Christian Church calendar celebrates the restoration of images.

The Byzantine Artist

Byzantine artists, like their Roman predecessors, were trained and practiced in a workshop system. While they constructed and decorated public buildings and churches, the collective efforts of these artists in different media were coordinated by an official overseer. As is true of much of the Middle Ages, artists worked in anonymity.

Specialized workshops produced a variety of media, including mosaics, mural and icon paintings, manuscript illustrations, and small sculpture. Large-scale figurative sculpture, one of the cornerstones of Greek and Roman art, was seldom produced during the Byzantine era, perhaps out of fear that such works would have the connotations of earlier idols. Byzantine carvers produced sarcophagi reliefs and small, exquisitely refined ivories to adorn religious and secular objects.

4-27 *MADONNA AND CHILD ENTHRONED WITH SAINTS THEODORE AND GEORGE AND ANGELS.* 6th century. Encaustic on wood, 27 × 19⅜″. Monastery of St. Catherine, Mount Sinai.

Byzantine Architecture: Hagia Sophia

4-28 Anthemius of Tralles and Isidorus of Miletus, architects. Interior, Hagia Sophia (Holy Wisdom), Istanbul (Constantinople), Turkey. 532–37. Hagia Sophia, 270′ in length, covers almost 1.5 acres, and the great central dome, 108′ in diameter, crowns at a height of more than 185′. Hagia Sophia had important political functions, for it served as the palace chapel for the Byzantine emperors and it was the site of their coronations. After the Ottoman Turks captured Constantinople in 1453, Hagia Sophia was converted to an Islamic mosque. Towering minarets, from which the faithful were called to prayer, were added to the exterior, while on the interior the Christian mosaics were covered and eight huge discs with sayings from the Koran and names of Muslim prophets were added. Hagia Sophia influenced later developments in Islamic mosque architecture (see figs. 6-67–6-69). Today, the former imperial church and mosque is a state museum. Commissioned by the Byzantine emperor Justinian.

The interior of Hagia Sophia (fig. 4-28) offers a dramatic interplay of two crucial architectural elements: space and light. On entering, the visitor is astonished by the enormous interior space. Flanked by semi-domes on two sides, the central dome rests like a colossal canopy on four gigantic but largely hidden piers. The windows at the base of the dome create rays of light that dematerialize these supports. The high dome appears suspended, hovering in space above us.

Just as the drama of light at the Pantheon in Rome (see fig. 3-122) represents a metaphysical joining of the physical and spiritual worlds, so too was the amplitude of light within Hagia Sophia bound to the religious purpose of the building. Originally, the light was even more intense, for the windows around the dome were successively decreased when the dome was rebuilt due to structural damage from earthquakes in 558, 989, and 1346. Light was an integral part of Hagia Sophia's effect, for when combined with the immense interior space and mosaics, the building created a powerful physical and spiritual experience, as recorded by Procopius, the court historian to Justinian, writing shortly after the church was decorated:

> The sun's light and its shining rays fill the church. One would say that the space is not lit by the sun without, but that the source of light is to be found within, such is the abundance of light. . . . So light is the construction, the dome seems not to rest on a solid structure, but to cover the space with a sphere of gold suspended in the sky. . . . The scintillations of the light forbid the spectator's gaze to linger on the details; each one attracts the eye and leads it on to the next. The circular motion of one's gaze reproduces

4-29   Exterior, Hagia Sophia, with later Islamic minarets.

itself to infinity. . . . The spirit rises toward God and floats in the air, certain that He is not far away, but loves to stay close to those whom He has chosen.

This remarkable synthesis of light and architectural form was conceived by Anthemius of Tralles, an artist and scientist, and Isidorus of Miletus, an architect and engineer. During a brief, six-week period, they evolved a new architectural plan that combined the longitudinal orientation of the basilica with the central plan (figs. 4-29, 4-30). Unlike Roman architects, who preferred to support a dome on a **drum**, Anthemius and Isidorus raised the central dome on

pendentives, curving triangular segments that provide the transition from the square plan of the piers to the circular base of the dome (see fig. 3-118), and flanked it with semi- or **half-domes**. The huge piers reduced the load-bearing function of the walls, allowing for large amounts of window space (such nonsupporting walls are known as **screen walls**). That Hagia Sophia was completed in just five years demonstrates the importance of the building in Justinian's plans. It is reported that at its dedication in 537, the emperor compared his accomplishment to that of Solomon, builder of the Temple in Jerusalem, when he proclaimed, "Solomon, I have outdone thee!"

4-30   Plan of Hagia Sophia.

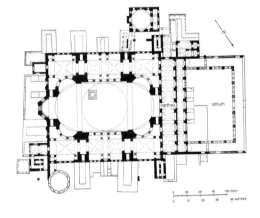

Byzantine Art: San Vitale, Ravenna

4-31 Interior, San Vitale, Ravenna, Italy. 526–47. Ravenna had been the capital city of the Ostrogoths, a Germanic people who conquered Italy by 493. In 540, the city was taken by Justinian's army and became a regional Italian capital and the local religious center of the Byzantine Empire. Commissioned by the Byzantine emperor Justinian and the local bishop, Maximianus.

a complex ideological program that joins Old and New Testament scenes, symbols, decorative patterns, and imperial portraiture. The unity of the mosaic program is defined by the axial placement of a number of images and symbols of Christ on, for example, the apex of the arch and at the center of the **groin vault**, where a lamb symbolizes Christ and his sacrifice. The monogram *Chi-Rho* ☧ leads to the most important of these references, the youthful Christ seated in the apse. These align with the altar, where Christ's sacrifice is reenacted during the Mass.

The offering of bread and wine at the altar is prefigured by scenes from the Old Testament. In the semicircular area enclosed by the arch (**lunette**) to the left of the altar, Abraham is depicted offering hospitality to three angels symbolic of the Trinity (see fig. 4-32). To the right, Abraham is shown about to sacrifice his son Isaac, a narrative prophetic of Christ's sacrifice.

On the left wall of the apse, a rectangular mosaic depicts Justinian with ecclesiastical personnel on his left, civil and military personnel on his right (fig. 4-33). Justinian carries the vessel that held the bread for the Mass; on the soldier's shield at the left border, a Chi-Rho monogram indicates the political importance Christianity had assumed within the Empire.

Justinian's placement communicates his position as head of both Church and State (in the Byzantine Empire, the emperor appointed the patriarch of Constantinople, the leader of the Eastern [Orthodox] Church). Individualized portraits are restricted to Justinian and his close associates. Although the figures overlap and some modeling is suggested, the gold background denies the illusion of real space. It is as if the earthly court of Justinian has been transfigured into a spiritual realm. As emperor, Justinian wears a jeweled crown, while as the

4-32 Mosaics, San Vitale. c. 547. In the lunette, *ABRAHAM FEEDING THE THREE ANGELS* is represented. Between the columns is a glimpse of *Justinian, Bishop Maximianus, and Attendants* and the inlaid marble decoration below the mosaics.

T he centrally planned church of San Vitale has the plain brick exterior that characterized much Early Christian and Byzantine architecture, but inside a comprehensive mosaic program synthesizes Christian iconography with imperial Byzantine politics (figs. 4-31, 4-32). It is

4-33 *Justianian, Archbishop Maximianus of Ravenna, and Attendants*, apse mosaic, San Vitale, c. 547.

4-34 *Theodora and Attendants*, apse mosaic, San Vitale. c. 547.

earthly representative of God, he is shown with a halo. A rainbowlike mosaic band rises above his head to descend to the opposite mosaic of the empress Theodora, shown bringing the chalice of wine to the altar (fig. 4-34). The open passageway represented on the left of the mosaic is a subtle indication of the fact that women are expected to observe the religious ceremonies at San Vitale from the galleries on the second floor.

4-35 *JUSTINIAN,* detail of figure 4-32. c. 547.

The technique of mosaic seems to have developed from an earlier technique of pressing pebbles into plaster to form a durable and decorative floor covering. By the late fifth century BCE, Greek artists began arranging the pebbles into abstract and figurative designs. Soon, natural stones were replaced by cut pieces of colored stone, especially marble, called **tesserae** (singular: tessera, from the Greek *tesseres*, a square). The term *tesserae* is also used for the pieces of stone and glass in wall mosaics, as at Ravenna (fig. 4-35). At first, Roman mosaic was used primarily on the floors of private homes (see fig. 3-58), but occasionally it also decorated walls. Roman wall mosaics began to use glass tesserae in many colors, as well as gold tesserae, formed by sandwiching gold leaf between two layers of glass. The early Christians used mosaics to embellish the walls of their churches, but it was during the Byzantine era that the most splendid effects were achieved, as walls and vaults were covered with glass and marble mosaics enhanced by the predominant gold background.

In creating a mosaic, the image is first outlined on the floor, wall, or vault. Successive areas of this surface are then covered with fresh cement or plaster and tesserae are placed into it, following the established design. As the cement or plaster hardens, the tesserae will be held firmly in place. When tesserae were set into walls and vaults, care was taken to adjust each so that its surface was at a slight angle to that of the neighboring tesserae. As the changing light from the windows strikes the polished or glass tesserae, the changing angles of refraction create a shimmering and ethereal effect, a vision particularly suited to the mystical values of Christianity.

The figure of the *Pantocrator* at Daphni, Greece (see fig. 4-75), is an example of fully mature Byzantine mosaic technique. The tesserae are arranged to reinforce the definition of an edge or surface; note, for example, how the curved patterns on Christ's forehead create a sense of three-dimensional form while strengthening the vigorous facial expression. Except for the gold background, large areas of a single color are avoided. At Daphni, the highlighted area of Christ's brown robe contains gold and red tesserae to make it seem not merely lit, but radiant and, therefore, suffused with spiritual energy.

Anglo-Saxon Metalwork

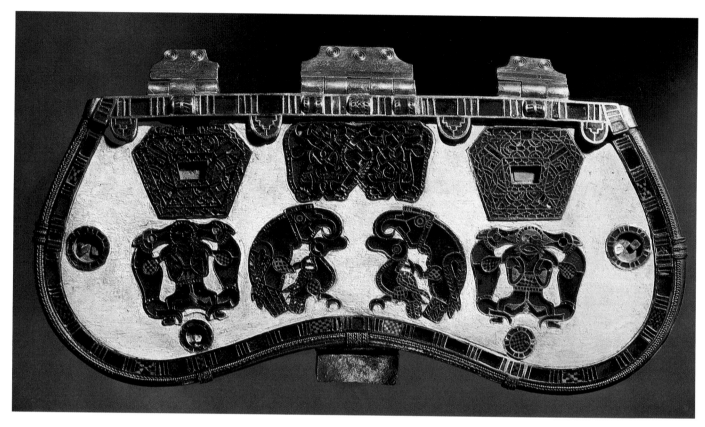

4-36 Sutton Hoo purse cover. c. 620. Gold with Indian garnets and cloisonné enamels, originally on an ivory or bone background (now lost), length 8″. The British Museum, London. Found in 1939 in a ship-burial mound at Sutton Hoo, England, as part of the treasure of a king who probably died between 625 and 640, this purse lid of precious materials and exceptional technical proficiency once adorned a cloth or leather pouch. It would have been attached to the owner's belt by hinges. When placed in the burial mound, it contained gold coins and ingots. The huge ship, approximately 89 feet long, in which the treasure was buried would have required thirty-eight rowers. The richness of the treasure, which included a helmet, shield, spears and a sword, bowls, drinking horns, remains of a musical instrument, and twenty-six pieces of gold jewelry, reveals the status of the deceased, who is still not identified with certainty. With the spread of Christianity, the old tradition of ship burial, which provided the soul with a vehicle in which to travel to the next world, gradually declined, but some of the objects found suggest that the Sutton Hoo king may have been a convert to Christianity.

The heavily patterned style of the Sutton Hoo purse cover is distinctive (fig. 4-36). In its use of valuable materials and in its emphasis on fine craft, it continues the interest—typical of earlier pastoral people who lived in central and western Europe—in art that is valuable, portable, and a part of personal adornment. The most characteristic motif of Anglo-Saxon and Irish metalwork is the **interlace**, a complex pattern composed of a single line that intertwines and overlaps, filing completely the available space. This common motif can be found in small works made in pre-Roman Gaul (France) and in ancient Roman and Early Christian works as patterns of intertwining vines and plants. Here it has a strongly two-dimensional effect. In Anglo-Saxon art, the interlaced line is often given an animal head, the mouth of which bites down on its own tail.

The discoveries at the Sutton Hoo mound confirmed the reports of rich possessions and similar burial practices found in the somewhat later Anglo-Saxon poem *Beowulf*:

> And there they brought the beloved body
> Of their ring-giving lord, and laid him near
> The mast. Next to that noble corpse
> They heaped up treasures, jeweled helmets,
> Hooked swords and coats of mail, armor

Carried from the ends of the
earth; no ship

Had ever sailed so brightly
fitted,

No king sent forth more
deeply mourned. . . .

Take these treasures, earth,
now that no one

Living can enjoy them.

The Sutton Hoo treasury offers valuable evidence for a civilization about which we have little information. There are few written records and only limited monuments and archaeological remains. Many documented works were melted down, destroyed by fire, or lost during attacks and invasions. We do know that the Anglo-Saxons descended from Germanic peoples who emigrated to England in the fifth century. Christianity, which had flourished in Roman Britain in the fourth century but then had waned, was strengthened in 597, when Pope Gregory the Great dispatched Augustine, later bishop of Canterbury, and forty missionaries to convert Ethelbert, king of Kent, and his court. Christianity and pre-Christian rituals existed side by side for a period; as late as the seventh century, an Anglo-Saxon king dedicated one altar to earlier gods and another to Christ.

The few fragments of Anglo-Saxon poetry and documentation that have survived reveal an aesthetic that delighted in luminous materials (especially gold) and in the color red. The interest in filling every available space with pattern or design seems to be related to the Anglo-Saxons' Germanic origin and traditions. The artists included monks, nuns, and laypeople. By the end of the Anglo-Saxon period, there is some evidence that craft guilds—medieval organizations of lay artists—were beginning to develop in England. When artists are mentioned, special attention is always given to the worker in precious metals, and it is on pieces of fine metalwork that we find the few artists' signature of this period.

Hiberno-Saxon Manuscript Illumination

4-37 BISHOP EADFRITH

Carpet page, from the LINDISFARNE GOSPELS. c. 698. Manuscript painting on vellum, 13½ × 9¾″. The British Library, London. The Lindisfarne Gospels contains a dedication to God and local saints that also identifies the artists involved: "Eadfrith, bishop of the church at Lindisfarne, originally wrote [lettered] this book for God and St. Cuthbert and—jointly—for all the saints whose relics are in the island. And Ethelwald, bishop of the Lindisfarne islanders . . . covered [bound] it . . . and Billfrith, the anchorite, . . . adorned it with gold and with gems . . . and Aldred, unworthy and most miserable priest, glossed [translated] it in English between the lines. . . . [They] made or, as the case may be, embellished this Gospel Book for God and Cuthbert." Eadfrith (Bishop from 698 until his death, in 721) was both scribe and decorator. Another inscription reveals a typical medieval rationale for artistic creation: "Thou living God, be thou mindful of Eadfrith, Ethelwald, Billfrith, and Aldred a sinner; these four have, with God's help, been engaged upon this book."

The interleaf motif found in Anglo-Saxon metalwork (see fig. 4-36) was dramatically integrated into a Christian context in a series of manuscripts produced in Anglo-Saxon (English) and Irish monasteries between 600 and 800. Similarities in style and other interrelationships make it difficult to distinguish English from Irish production, which is perhaps best called Hiberno-Saxon (Hibernia was the ancient Latin name for Ireland). In some of these manuscripts, whole pages are devoted to abstract designs—these are now called **carpet pages** because of their resemblance to the complex patterns found in Turkish and other Islamic carpets. In this example, from the *Lindisfarne Gospels* (fig. 4-37), geometric panels are set within a surging sea of blue and red interlace. In the middle of each side are the confronted heads of two dogs or of two birds of prey. If we follow the patterns, we discover that the lines forming the outer borders of the decoration are their much-elongated bodies; at the corners, these lines are attached to a leg that is intertwined with the leg of a beast from the adjacent side.

The techniques used by the Hiberno-Saxon monks who made these manuscripts are difficult to reconstruct, and exactly how they accomplished such minuscule patterns without the aid of a magnifying glass is unknown. In one of the *Lindisfarne* carpet pages, the geometric pattern was first drawn on the back of the page using a ruler and compass, and the most important points of the design were then pricked through the vellum to provide a guide for the painter. The isolation of different types of decoration into geometric areas sets up maximum contrast between the widely varied patterns: fine and broad interlace, with and without animal-form additions, and swelling, swirling shapes. As a result, the interrelationship of the patterns as positive and negative forms and their placement in depth (which patterns seem to be in front of or behind others) are tantalizingly difficult to decipher. The intensive and time-consuming nature of the design and execution is probably related to the austere and isolated nature of life in a Hiberno-Saxon monastery.

Monasticism flourished in Ireland earlier than in England, and Irish monastic **scriptoria** (halls where manuscripts were written and decorated) were producing important volumes by the middle of the sixth century. In England, the monastic tradition was established in the early seventh century, when King Oswald founded the monastery at Lindisfarne.

The earliest surviving Hiberno-Saxon religious manuscripts reveal an interest in decorating the letters themselves, a not surprising development when we remember that the words are believed to be proclamations of God. This tendency reaches its peak in the *Book of Kells* (fig. 4-38). When the text in the Gospel of Saint Matthew (1:22) reaches the crucial point where the Incarnation of Christ is mentioned, the letters burst out in joyful, exuberant patterns. A whole page is devoted to the three words *Christi autem generatio* ("the

4-38   *INCARNATION* page, from the *Book of Kells.* c. 800. Manuscript painting on vellum, 13 × 9½". Trinity College Library, Dublin.

birth of Christ"), with most of the page devoted to the first three letters of *Christi* (*XPI*). The *X* is the dominant form, and it surges outward in bold and varied curves to embrace Hiberno-Saxon whorl patterns. Free-form interlace fills other areas, and simple colored frames set off the large initials amid the consuming excitement. The human head that forms the end of the *P* also dots the *I*. Near the lower left base of the *X*, a small vignette shows cats watching while two mice fight over a round wafer similar to those used in the Mass—a scene surely of symbolic intent, even if the exact meaning is lost to us today.

The pulsating vitality of the word of God and the exciting news of the impending birth of his son, Jesus Christ, are thus visually demonstrated. A twelfth-century writer who was shown a precious manuscript in Ireland—perhaps the *Book of Kells* itself—wrote:

> Look more keenly at it and you will penetrate to the very shrine of art. You will make out intricacies so delicate and subtle, so exact and compact, so full of knots and links, with colors so fresh and vivid, that you might say that all this was the work of an angel and not of a man.

The Chinese Imperial City of Chang'An

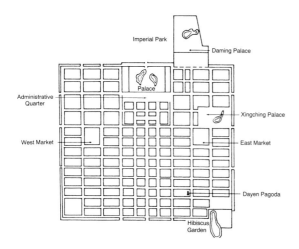

4-39 Plan of Chang'an (see map, page 149). Tang dynasty, 7th–8th century. The wall surrounding the city was almost 26 miles long, enclosing an area of almost 42 square miles. Chang'an, an ancient city in the Wei River valley, served as the capital of China during the powerful Han (206 BCE–220 CE) and Tang (618–907 CE) dynasties. It was the eastern terminus of the silk road, which joined China with the markets of western Asia and, as early as the second century, with Europe. Chang'an played an important role as a center for the transmission of the ideas and art forms that poured into China during the Tang dynasty. Commissioned by the imperial government.

4-40 ZHANG XUAN

COURT LADIES PREPARING NEWLY WOVEN SILK, detail of 12th-century copy, after an 8th-century hand scroll. Color on silk, 14½ × 57¼". Chinese and Japanese Special Fund. Courtesy, Museum of Fine Arts, Boston. The copy shown here has been attributed to the twelfth-century emperor Hui Zong. Rich, glowing colors describe the scene, while a detailed precision embellishes the treatment of the fabric of the dresses worn by the women. Commissioned by the imperial academy.

During the Tang dynasty (618–907), Chang'an became the cultural capital of East Asia (fig. 4-39). Laid out on a huge scale following important traditional practices, it was held in such esteem that it became a model for contemporary capitals in Korea and Japan. It was by far the largest city in the world at

4-41 *BACTRIAN CAMEL WITH PACK SADDLE.* Tang dynasty, 1st half of 8th century. Earthenware with polychrome lead glaze, height 37". The Nelson-Atkins Museum of Art, Kansas City, Missouri. The Tang dynasty is notable in the history of Chinese ceramics for the dynamic energy of its shapes, the development of colored glazes, and the perfection of porcelain. Fine white earthenware is often clothed in a polychrome glaze made by mixing copper, iron, or cobalt with a colorless lead silicate to produce a rich range of colors, from blue and green to yellow and brown. Both form and glaze convey a vigor that is true to most historians' view of life at the Tang court in the eighth century. This camel would have been placed in a tomb chamber.

PURCHASE: ACQUIRED THROUGH THE GENEROSITY OF NUMEROUS DONORS

that time; the present city on the site, Xi'an, occupies only about one-seventh the area of the Tang capital.

Production of different kinds of art in Chang'an reflects the city's importance as a Chinese capital as well as its position as an international center for trade. *Court Ladies Preparing Newly Woven Silk* (fig. 4-40) gives us an intimate view of aristocratic women; the ceramic *Camel* (fig. 4-41) represents the position of Chang'an as the terminus for the caravans across the silk route toward the west.

The city that was to become Chang'an began to take shape in the later sixth century, when a man rose to power in northwest China who reunified the traditional Chinese lands after nearly four centuries of political instability and invasions from outside. In 581, he became Emperor Wen, the first ruler of the Sui dynasty, and he and his advisers were determined to build a capital city on a new and unprecedented scale at the site of the earlier Han dynasty (206 BCE–220 CE) capital. Their project for this "City of the Great Ascendancy" covered thirty-one square miles, but it was merely a skeleton when Wen took up residence in 583. With the founding of the Tang dynasty in 618, the city was expanded and renamed Chang'an—"City of Enduring Peace." At the height of the Tang, in the late seventh and eighth centuries, the city's population reached more than one million inside the walls, with probably another million in nearby satellite towns. Based on the principles of symmetry and axiality, Chang'an was the first totally planned Chinese city. The Tang leaders who conceived Chang'an intended to do more than create a city that would meet their practical needs. Such a city would dramatize their social order, express their hierarchy of values, and convey their view of the cosmos and their place in it.

First, to choose an auspicious site they turned to the ancient Chinese divination practice of *feng-shui*, which is still used today. Chang'an's location had been venerated for two millennia. Already, in the first century CE, a poet named Pan Gu had summed up its advantages in "Rhapsody on the Western Capital," a poem included in a collection known as the Wen Xuan:

In abundance of flowering plants and fruits
it is the most fertile of the Nine Provinces

In natural barriers for protection and defense
it is the most impregnable refuge in heaven and earth

This is why its influence has extended in six directions
This is why it has thrice become the seat of imperial power.

As a perennial fulcrum of power—strong, fertile, and well populated—the site was practical as well as symbolic.

Second, the beginning of construction on the new Tang capital had to be properly timed. The most auspicious time and place to build were determined by centuries-old oracle-divination procedures similar to the divinatory and ritual-symbolic rites carried out by Greek, Etruscan, and Roman builders before embarking on the construction of new cities. Great importance was attached to the orientation of the city to ensure that it would be fully consonant with the natural order. Early descriptions of city planning (from the *Zhou li*, or *History of the Zhou Dynasty*, from the first millennium BCE) report that special officers took the shadow of the sun at noon and made observations of the North Star by night on successive days until they came to an accurate calculation of the four cardinal directions that would determine the city's orientation. No doubt astronomers were also employed to assure that the orientation was attuned to the cosmic order.

4-42 Reconstruction of the Linde Hall of the Daming Palace, Chang'an. Tang dynasty, 7th century. The roof was made of ceramic tiles, and the tiles on the ridges and eave ends were glazed. Green and black tiles were excavated at the site, and we assume, based on textual evidence, that the exterior wall colors were primarily red and white with gold details, a striking combination with the black and green roofs. Commissioned by the imperial government.

Once properly sited and oriented, the city was surrounded by a rectangular wall of pounded earth (see fig. 4-39). There were gates in the outer walls except on the north, and broad north/south avenues led to each of the gates on the south wall. The city was subdivided into major zones. To the extreme north was the inner city, where the emperor held court, performed rituals of office, and resided with his harem. To the east and west of the avenue leading to the central southern gate were the imperial ancestral hall and the Altar of Earth.

In 634, the second Tang emperor, Taizong, expanded the city to the northeast of the inner city, beyond the city walls, where he built a complex of palaces and other buildings that come to be known as the Daming Palace. Tang texts record that Hanyuan Hall, which has been excavated, was the site of ceremonies for the New Year and the winter solstice and that it was used for the investiture of new emperors, the changing of reign titles, and the inspection of troops and presentation of captives. Nearby was the Linde Hall (fig. 4-42), the other excavated Tang-period building of the Daming Palace, which was used by

the emperor for feasting high officials. Both the Linde Hall and the Hanyuan Hall have similar architectural components, including covered **arcades** (or "flying galleries") that enclosed each building complex, side pavilions, and platforms that raised the entire building above ground level. Linde was a triple hall complex with a two-storied roof over the central building. The three halls lead directly from one to the next, without connecting arcades.

Beginning in the Han dynasty, ritual halls had weight-bearing walls at the sides and pillars that supported the main beams at the center. Reinforcing vertical struts that rested on the floor beams were fitted into the wall, while horizontal wooden pieces connected the struts. A wall beam was placed on top of the walls for added support. According to building regulations of the Tang, only the most important halls could have the **hipped roofs**, with their triangular, angled ends, as seen in figure 4-42.

The remaining part of the city, known as the outer city, included 110 wards, most of which were predominantly residential; two were given over to marketplaces built and controlled by the government. The east

market connected with the roads leading to the second Tang capital of Louyang, and the west market was the center of foreign trade and foreign residence. The ancient system of walled blocks was used for the whole outer city; the ward gates opened at sunup and closed at dusk, and it was a crime to be found on the streets after curfew. The residential wards were laid out on a grid pattern. The sides of these streets were lined with drainage ditches and planted with shade trees. The mansions of the aristocrats and officials were concentrated in wards near the Daming Palace and the east market, while those of commoners were found in the more densely populated area around the west market. Near the city parks at the extreme southeast corner of the outer city were a number of government-controlled entertainment districts. An elevated, covered roadway connected the parks so that the emperor could enjoy outings without being seen by his subjects.

Chang'an was an international capital, and the diplomatic envoys, religious missionaries, merchants, and students from many parts of the world who congregated there brought with them foreign religions, including Zoroastrianism, Manichaeanism, Judaism, Islam, and Nestorian Christianity. The most grand and numerous of the religious complexes in Chang'an were those of Buddhism and Daoism; some even occupied whole wards. The foreign goods brought by the city's exotic visitors were much sought after by the aristocracy, as well as the middle class.

The building of Chang'an was accomplished by able leadership in an era of peace and prosperity at home and enormous prestige abroad. In the early eighth century, Ming Huang, a brilliant leader, took the throne. He cherished and upheld the Confucian order, and in 745 he founded the Imperial Academy of Letters (Han-lin Academy). Talent and wealth were concentrated in his court. His favorite scholars, poets, and painters, his schools of drama and music, his orchestras (two of which came from Central Asia), and his famous mistress, the beautiful Yang Guifei, were in attendance. Court painters and poets were kept busy by the emperor recording portraits and cultural and social events of court life.

During the reign of Ming Huang, the court painter Zhang Xuan was celebrated for his paintings of "young nobles, saddle horses, and women of rank." None of his work survives in the original, but one copy, *Court Ladies Preparing Newly Woven Silk*, is generally thought to illustrate the eighth-century Tang court tradition of scroll painting (see fig. 4-40). In the section reproduced here, court women of different ages are stretching and ironing a piece of newly woven silk. The dignified, realistic, and vigorous presentation is surely comparable to court life itself at that moment, even though only the barest essentials of the scene are recorded. The relationship of the women in space is clear, but we are not told where they are, only what their relationship is to each other. Each woman refers to and is intimately connected to another through participation in the task itself and by gesture and location in space. This section of the scroll records an actual activity, but it may also refer to the broader theme of the maturation of court women from childhood (the small figure playing under the stretched silk), to adolescence, to the coming of age, to adulthood. Each step is distinguished by position, dress style, coiffure, size, and shape of figure.

The same realism that marks high court painting also characterizes the tomb figurines made during the Tang period. The presence of a ceramic camel in one's tomb must surely have referred to the importance of trade in the life of the deceased. The restrained energy and solidity of modeling found in the glazed ceramic camel illustrated here (see fig. 4-41) are typical of the best of this type of sculpture, which was made for the burials of both the aristocracy and the gentry.

Late in the ninth century, Chang'an fell victim to the ravages of a rebellion; in 904 many of its buildings were razed, and the royal court activities were transported to the second capital at Louyang. Although its political importance declined, it remained a bustling trading center.

Buddhist Art at Horyuji

4-43 Horyuji complex, near Nara, Japan. Asuka period, 7th century. Stone, wood, plaster, and tile. Commissioned by Imperial Prince Shotoku.

Horyuji is the oldest Buddhist temple in East Asia whose main parts have survived (figs. 4-43, 4-44); no earlier examples of Buddhist temples in China or Korea survive. Founded in 607, it is a treasure house of immense value for this phase of Buddhist development. One enters the temple-monastery complex through the **chumon**, the gate on the south face of the encircling **cloister**, and finds to the left (west) a **pagoda** and to the right (east) the main hall, or **kondo**, known as the Golden Hall. The *pagoda* and the *kondo* are equidistant from the *chumon* and are simultaneously visible as the worshiper enters. Instead of proceeding into the depths of the compound through a succession of buildings, as was the custom in China, the pilgrim makes a lateral turn. Lateral movement rather than linear penetration is repeatedly favored in Japanese spatial conceptions through history. Nevertheless, the individual buildings of Horyuji are typically continental—that is, Chinese or Korean—in style. They stand on raised stone bases and are built on a **bay** system, with post-and-lintel construction, tile roofs, and elaborate **tou-kung bracketing** (see fig. 4-45) designed to transmit the thrust and weight of the heavy tile roof down through the wooden members to the principal columns that support the structure.

The *kondo* is oriented to the four cardinal directions with a stairway on

7th century	Horyugi, Nara
7th century	Rise of the Japanese feudal nobility
612	Monastary of St. Gall is founded in Switzerland

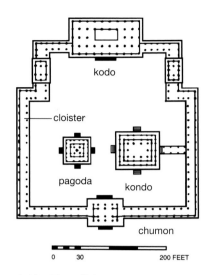

4-44   Plan of Horyuji.

each side leading to a double door. Its interior is almost completely taken up by a platform and numerous statues. The main function of the *kondo* is to enclose them; it is a shrine rather than an assembly hall for a community (the *kodo*, on the north end outside the cloister, was set aside for sermons and disputations). In the *kondo* are the images of the main statue of the Buddha in a triad (see fig. 4-46). This group is the spiritual center of the temple complex and is therefore lavishly embellished: the posts and beams are painted and **gilded**; the ceiling, a canopy, represents Paradise or heaven. On each wall are paintings (damaged by fire in 1949) that represent the Buddha and the paradises of the cardinal directions. This program of statues and paintings in the *kondo* makes the temple a terrestrial representation of the Buddha's blissful realm. The sight of gilded statues radiating the light of Buddha's wisdom and mercy is intended to inspire the believer. All the figures combine in a **mandala**, the center of which—the center and axis of the cosmos—is occupied by Buddha seated on his lotus throne (for a later example of a mandala see fig. 5-3). In that way, the temple is similar to a **stupa** (see pages 96–99).

The Spread of Buddhism to Japan

Buddhism was the first world religion known to history. From its main center of origin in north-eastern India, it spread across vast areas of Asia, radiating outward in all directions—except toward the west—bringing its universal doctrine of salvation for all

---

Technique   *Tou-Kung Bracketing*

At least as early as 1100 BCE in China, wooden blocks were added at the point where columns supported beams. They served as a type of cushioning that increased the surface of contact and thus reduced the span. Later, as in this Japanese example, cantilevered beams were projected outward from the top of eave columns to form a bracket arm. These structural innovations allowed the deep eaves characteristic of this style of architecture. Eventually the blocks and the brackets were carved and painted, and elaborate *tou-kung* bracketing became an important part of the Japanese aesthetic.

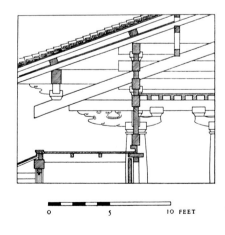

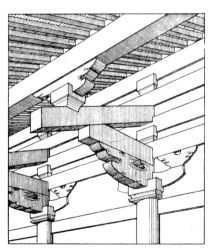

4-45   Tou-kung eaves at the Horyuji *kondo*.

4-46 TORI BUSSHI (MASTER CRAFTWORKER TORI)

SHAKA TRIAD, Golden Hall (*kondo*), Horyuji. Asuka period, 623. Bronze with gilt, height of central figure 5'9¼". The Buddha's hand gesture is in the *abhaya* mudra, the gesture of reassurance that suggests "fear not." Commissioned by Imperial Prince Shotoku.

human and other living creatures, its philosophy and ethics, its learning and art. It bridged the differences among the rich and creative cultures of India, China, Japan, and Southeast Asia. In the course of the first millennium CE, Buddhism led to the rise of a great spiritual and cultural community with far-ranging and profound inner unity of spiritual consciousness, manifest in remarkable similarity in patterns of life and thought, and not the least in art.

The faith grew to a national religion in India under King Asoka (ruled c. 273–232 BCE), and by the second century CE, missionaries had carried the tradition to northwest India and the provincial Greco-Roman world in Gandhara (Afghanistan). There new schools developed, called Mahayana, which taught that salvation was open to all people through faith and good works. The Buddha, in their view, ceased to be primarily an earthly teacher and was thought of as pure

abstraction, as the "universal principle," the godhead, from whom truth radiates with a blinding light across the universe. The Buddha reached far beyond the grasp of mortal beings, but there were approachable deities in this newer Buddhism: bodhisattvas, ones destined for enlightenment who had earned the right to enter Nirvana but postponed it in order to help others.

Buddhism reached Japan in the middle of the sixth century from Korea after centuries of development in China. The introduction of Buddhism had a far-reaching effect on many aspects of Japanese life. The *kami* (spirits) of the nature religion of Japan (Shinto) were important but had no specified forms or attributes. In contrast, principles of the Buddhist faith were expounded in Chinese texts and by a clergy and communities of nuns and monks who performed minutely prescribed religious functions inside halls filled with the pungent smell of incense and with statues of the holy in human form. Buddhism channeled silent and spontaneous interaction with the spirits into an organized program of ritual observance and explained the mysteries of life in a set of laws.

The rise of Buddhism in Japan was accelerated during the life of Prince Umayado, better known by his Buddhist name of Prince Shotoku ("Wise and Virtuous," ruled 593–622). He was an avid scholar and learned leader whose cultural activities affected Japanese civilization substantively. Born into a court that had been receiving Buddhist images from Korea for twenty-one years and that was coming to terms with the new faith, Shotoku grew up in an atmosphere of cultural ferment. The pro-Buddhist Soga clan was actively upholding its beliefs, but not without opposition by adherents to the native religion, Shinto (see pages 148–49). Buddhist chapels were burned and statues damaged. Soga no Umako (died 626), head of the powerful family, placed his niece on the throne as Empress Suiko (ruled 592–628) and ordered Prince Shotoku, then only nineteen years old, to act as regent. Prince Shotoku attempted to centralize power and to unify the clan chiefs, whose rivalries had previously dominated Japanese life. He used as a model the Chinese court and thereby played a leading role in the absorption of Chinese aristocratic culture in Japan. Shotoku built his palace at Ikaruga and next to it erected a Buddhist temple modeled after Korean buildings. By 614, or fifty years after the presentation of the first Buddhist statue to Japan, there were 46 temples and 1,385 ordained Japanese monks and nuns. After Shotoku's death and during the struggle for power, both his palace and his temple were destroyed. Shotoku's legacy, the primacy of learning and moral values, was so firmly implanted among the aristocracy and clergy, however, that the ruined temple was soon rebuilt and was called Horyuji.

Buddhist sculpture preceded Buddhist architecture outside of India, for images were brought in the luggage of missionaries, travelers, and pilgrims across the great trade routes of Central Asia. Such icons were set up in shrines built in the traditional Chinese style, and the shrine complexes grew until the monastery or temple became a kind of palace with courtyards, pavilions, galleries, and gardens. No attempt was made to imitate Indian temples, and the stupa was transformed into the pagoda, the multitiered tower that serves as a relic hall.

The main image in the *kondo* at Horyuji bears the date 623 and is the work of a caster of statues named Tori, a descendant of Chinese immigrants. The Mahayana Buddhists believe that there will be an infinite number of Buddhas, all of them manifestations of the One Absolute Buddha. Although he was thought to be beyond the limits of human vision, practitioners began to believe that one manifestation was revealed to the living and could therefore be represented. These images were used to help the beholder to understand existence beyond form and substance. The Buddha is represented with a serene and remote aspect, larger than life (fig. 4-46). He wears a monk's robe and is seated in the position of meditation. His elongated ears, the mark on his forehead, and his hair recall his noble birth. His attendants, the smaller bodhisattvas, are dressed in worldly clothing with crowns and jewels indicating their dedication to assisting earthly beings in their suffering. Buddha's frontal, seated pose, his dress, and his hand gestures (**mudras**) are all prescribed by tradition. This manner of presentation—so similar to prototypes from Korea, China, and even India—speaks of an ecumenical tradition fueled both by the assimilative nature of Mahayana Buddhism and by the economic and political aspirations of the leaders who embraced the religion.

Hindu Art at Ellora

4-47 Kailasantha Temple, Ellora, India. Rashtrakuta dynasty, c. 760–800, with later additions. Height *96'*. The site at Ellora (see map, page 149) has thirty-four Hindu, Buddhist, and Jain rock-cut temples that date from the mid-sixth to the tenth century. The earliest temples are dedicated to the worship of the Hindu god Siva. They include elaborate pillared halls leading to shrines in the rear wall, which house *lingams* (stylized phallic symbols of Siva's procreative energies). By 600, the caves became a center for Buddhist worship, with Buddhist images carved both in the shrines of pillared halls and in the apsidal *chaitya* worship hall, where the Buddha is carved on the front of a monolithic stupa. Later, about 675 to 720, three-storied Buddhist caves focused worship on multiple Buddhas and other deities. A second wave of Siva worship in the eighth century included the building of this Hindu temple under the patronage of the Rashtrakutan monarch Krishna II (ruled 757–83).

The Kailasantha Temple (the name given to the entire eighth-century complex) is carved from a cliff to resemble a free-standing temple complex behind a high screen wall (figs. 4-47, 4-48). Although some sections are dedicated to different Hindu gods, the monument is literally a "magic mountain" in living rock where the theme of Mount Kailasa, the sacred mountain abode of Siva and his consort Parvati, is repeated several times. The artists, who wanted to rep-resent the universe in this massive carving, oriented the structure to correspond to the four cardinal directions—the world compass. At the core of the temple is the place intended for individual worship in the Hindu faith; here was buried a box containing earth, stones, gems, herbs, roots, metals, and soils that was intended to tie the temple to ancient fertility beliefs and to emphasize the vitality of the religion.

The temple is an achievement of sculpture rather than architecture. It is composed of a court 276 feet long and 154 feet wide and a central tower 96 feet tall. The sheer physical problem of carving this tremendous temple from the living rock is awesome. Since the sculptors began working at a height above the tower, the total depth of the cut was about 120 feet—as high as a twelve-story building.

Upon entering this massive complex, one is aware of the contrast of the strong sunlight and the deep blue shadows cast by the surrounding

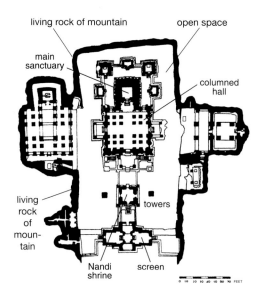

living rock of mountain open space

main sanctuary

columned hall

living rock of moun- tain

towers

Nandi shrine   screen

0 10 20 30 40 50 60 70 FEET

4-48   Plan of the Kailasantha Temple. The plan reveals the layout more clearly than any view. At the entrance, a large stone screen demarcates secular from religious space. Next is the Nandi shrine, flanked by the two towers. That small shrine is followed by three porches leading to a columned hall, which functioned as a gathering place, and to the main sanctuary. Five subsidiary shrines on a second-story terrace outside the main sanctuary are dedicated to various deities associated with Siva. The sides of the tremendous pit created by the carving of the temple have secondary shrines in the vertical walls: the Shrine of Absolutions (or the Shrine of the Three Rivers), with representations of the three sacred rivers; a long series of sculptures at the rear; a second-story temple carved in the rock with a set of reliefs relating to Siva; a series of reliefs of avatars (incarnations) of Vishnu and aspects of Siva on the ground floor, surrounding the sides and completely enclosing the back wall; and a two-story complex on the right, once connected by a bridge to a porch, with representations of the Great Goddess (Devi) and the Seven Mothers. The large frieze sculptures that narrate the stories of the *Mahabharata* and the *Ramayana* on the south wall illustrate sacred literature. Numerous smaller shrines complete the group. Although the building of this great complex took place over a long period of time, it nevertheless represents a single architectural and sculptural conception.

mountainside, which dramatizes the movement of space along the pathways and across the sculptural reliefs. The sculptural figures gesture wildly to enhance an overall sense of drama and exaltation for the believer. The boldness of conception and the skill in execution suggest centuries of tradition in which carving techniques and an understanding of the rock medium were developed, enabling craftworkers to push this southern Indian type of rock-cut temple to its limits.

Hinduism encompassed a broad variety of beliefs and practices; not all were shared by all Hindus, and some even contradicted each other.

In fact, the religion is unusual in its tolerance of diversity. Completely decentralized, it has no hierarchy of clergy and no supreme authority— unlike Christianity, Islam, and Buddhism. The roots of the religion can be found 4,000 years ago in India, and as it developed it absorbed and reinterpreted the beliefs and practices of diverse groups of people. Assimilation occurred differently in various parts of India, and today, as in the past, the subcontinent is a repository of heterogeneous beliefs. That the worship of deities is a highly personal activity is reflected in the plan of Hindu temples, as well as in their sculptural reliefs.

For instance, several of the shrines at the Kailasantha Temple do not have an interior sanctuary at all. (The Nandi shrine and the main shrine are open only on the second level.) Even when they are entered, the interior space is so small that an individual approach to the sacred images is required. Hinduism's personal approach to the gods is indicated in the thousands of different manifestations of the deity. Today this religion is vital to more than 750 million adherents in India, Sri Lanka, Pakistan, and East and South Africa, as well as on a number of islands in the Caribbean and Southeast Asian oceans.

Islamic Art at Córdoba

4-49 Interior, Mosque, Córdoba, Spain (see map, page 151). Begun 786. This is a view across the hypostyle hall, looking west. Originally commissioned by Caliph Abd ar-Rahman I ad-Dakhil ("the immigrant"); the later expansions were commissioned by Caliphs Abd ar-Rahman II and III, Al-Hakam II, and Al-Mansur.

In its present form, the interior of the Mosque at Córdoba is a vast column-filled space, 584 feet on the north-south axis and 410 feet on the east-west axis (fig. 4-49). It covers an area of 240,000 square feet, a space larger than any known church, including St. Peter's in Rome. This interior is viewed neither as a home of the gods nor as a place for liturgical worship. It is a place for the faithful to gather for prayer, all facing toward Mecca together to emphasize the unity of the faith.

Today, Islam is the religion of more than a billion believers throughout the world, with largest populations in Asia, Africa, and parts of Europe. *Islam* is a term that refers to the religion, to the whole body of believers ("Muslims"), and to the countries in which they live. The youngest of the world's major religions, Islam developed in Arabia in the seventh century CE (see map, page 140). The area had been a frontier of the Roman Empire and was a land of independent nomadic peoples, a few trade outposts, and conflicting religious traditions.

The founder of Islam was Muhammad, who was born in Mecca in about 570 and believed himself to be a prophet of divine revelation. He was forced to flee in 622 but established himself in the rival city of Medina, where he gathered converts. The Muslim calendar dates from this flight, or hegira. In 630, he returned in triumph to Mecca. After his death in 632, the religion gained momentum and began to spread in Arabia and the Middle East.

Muhammad himself set up no priesthood and no organized church. However, the Koran, in which were collected the sayings of God as they were revealed to Muhammad in Arabic, became the guide for all life's endeavors. The "Five Pillars" of Islam set out duties for all believers. First, one must recite the creed "There is no god but God: Muhammad is the Messenger of God." Second, there is the duty of worship and prayer after ritual washing and while facing the direction of Mecca, five times a day and in the mosque on Fridays. Third, one must completely abstain from food, drink, and sexual activity in the daylight hours during Ramadan, the ninth lunar month, when Muhammad first received revelations from God. Fourth is the duty of almsgiving. Fifth is the duty of hadj, a pilgrimage to Mecca, which every Muslim should undertake before death. The jihad (crusade) is not one of the pillars of Islam.

Islam developed later than Judaism, Christianity, and Buddhism, and it acknowledges these religions and believes itself to be their fulfillment. Indeed, Muslims believe that Abraham, Moses, and Christ all preached Islam but that their followers changed their teaching into the religions of today. In the Muslim view, only the Koran and Muhammad's preaching preserved unchanged the message of God. Characteristic of Islam is the blending of ethnic and universal elements. It opens its ranks to all, stressing the unity of the faithful before Allah (God), regardless of race or culture. It was, however, a

national religion, firmly centered in Arabia and its political aspirations. As Islam expanded its political control, the purpose was not to convert unbelievers. Those who wanted to share the privileged status could join Islam but had to become Arabs by adoption; they had to learn the Koran in Arabic and to adopt the social, legal, and political framework of the Muslim community. Unlike the spread of Buddhism, Islam absorbed and adapted the conquered and their cultural heritage.

Early in the history of Islam, no demands were made on the visual arts. Muhammad condemned idolatry, and the Koran considered statues among the handiwork of Satan. Painting and representation were not specifically mentioned, but they were also generally avoided. During the fifty years following the death of the prophet, a Muslim place of prayer could be a Christian church or Persian columned hall taken over for the purpose, or even a rectangular field surrounded by a fence or ditch. These were the first **mosques**, or places for prayer.

Mosques of all periods have one element in common: the marking of the **qibla**, a wall in the direction to which Muslims must turn in prayer. That wall faces the direction toward Mecca and was often marked by a colonnade. By the end of the seventh century, Muslim rulers of conquered domains began to erect mosques and palaces on a large scale as visible symbols of power; they were intended to outdo all pre-Islamic structures in size and splendor. The conquerors drew on craftworkers gathered from Egypt, Syria, Persia, and even Byzantium, whose designs and decoration echo their west Asian background and expansive spirit.

By the eighth century, within a hundred years of the death of Muhammad, the Muslims had conquered and converted most of the Middle East and the African provinces of Byzantium as well as Spain, where they captured Toledo in 711. The Muslims entered Spain as a military force and lacked women, so nearly all took Spanish wives. Furthermore, during this time many Christians converted to Islam and retained their Romance language, giving Islamic culture in Spain a unique flavor soon reflected in architecture as well.

The greatest monument of the reign of the first Muslim ruler of Spain, the caliph Abd ar-Rahman I (ruled 756–88), was the Mosque at Córdoba, which he built in one year, 786–87. The building was necessitated by the increased numbers of Muslims who needed a place of worship. Abd ar-Rahman I purchased part of the site from the Christians, saving the rather short Roman and Visigothic marble columns and capitals that had been taken by the Christians from earlier buildings. These columns and the arches above were incorporated into a new mosque that became famous for the placement of double rows of arches above columns. The super-imposition of two tiers of arches gave added height and spaciousness, while the long rows of columns and arches helped direct the worshipers' attention toward the qibla and, thus, the road to Mecca. The superimposed arches over columns were repeated by a succession of rulers as they enlarged the mosque in 832–48, 961, and 987. The first expansions enlarged the mosque in the original direction, but eventually the river that passes through Córdoba required an expansion to the side.

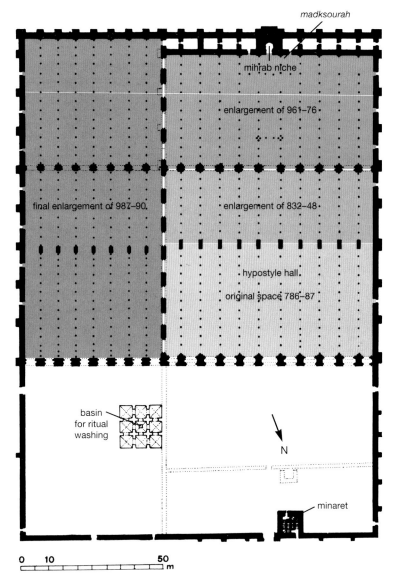

madksourah

mihrab niche

· enlargement of 961–76 ·

final enlargement of 987–90.

· enlargement of 832–48 ·

·hypostyle hall.

·original space 786–87

basin for ritual washing

N

minaret

0   10   50
                m

4-50   Plan of the Mosque, Córdoba, 786–990. This plan shows the enlargements of 832–48, 961–76, and 987–90, the final expansion. The qibla and its mihrab at Córdoba do not literally face Mecca, but they do point in the same direction as the road that leaves Córdoba for that city. The structure was converted back to Christian use after the reconquest of Córdoba in 1236.

The interior "forest of columns" in the mosque emphasizes the democratic nature of Islam and the fact that Muslim worship stresses personal contact with Allah. Individual worshipers who entered the mosque for service would begin praying at their own rate and not in concert with a leader or with other worshipers, as is the case in most other religions. Red-and-white horseshoe-shaped arches seem to extend endlessly to either side, but the view ahead, the direction toward Mecca, is open and direct. The overall plan is a traditional Muslim one (fig. 4-50). It has a crenelated, rectangular perimeter enclosing a forecourt with a basin for ritual ablution (washing). At one point, the qibla is hollowed out to form the sacred niche, or **mihrab**. Overlooking

the courtyard is the **minaret**, the tower from which the muezzin ("crier") calls the faithful to prayer five times a day.

In 961–76, the caliph Al-Hakam II, mindful of his capitals' prestige, built a superb, gleaming mihrab, preceded by a triple *madksourah*, or enclosure reserved only for the caliph. The enclosure is roofed by three ribbed domes, which rest on an unusual series of interwoven multi-layered arches (fig. 4-51). All these interior areas are faced with mosaics against a background in gold.

Unlike Christianity or later Buddhism, the Islamic faith did not permit figurative representations of God or his prophets, and these mosaics, like most Islamic art, are stylized. No liv-

ing creature is represented on Islamic religious structures, and the Koran is embellished with a luxurious, calligraphic version of Arabic lettering called **Kufic** (mistakenly named after the belief that the script originated in Kufa, in Iraq). Kufic script, complemented by abstract ornamental designs, became the main decoration in the form of inscriptions on mosques, secular buildings, and even utilitarian objects in metal, clay, and weavings in wool (for carpets, see fig. 6-64). This Islamic preference for linear surface decoration was used in the interior decoration of mosques. At Córdoba, the dome before the mihrab is typical, for it includes a stylized gold inscription in Kufic script at its base and a web of ornament above and

4-51 Central dome of the *MADKSOURAH*, the area in front of the mihrab, Mosque, Córdoba. 961–76. Colored stucco, tile, and glass mosaic. From the chain in the center of this dome was once suspended a silver lamp with 1,000 glass-cupped oil lamps. The ceiling of the small mihrab behind this is covered with a single large piece of stone, carved in the shape of a shell. Commissioned by Caliph Al-Hakam II.

below, made up a variety of designs disciplined by symmetry, repetition, and rhythmic order.

Mosques serve both religious and secular functions. Following prayer in the mosque, the man who led the worship or his representative might speak on secular matters. This Arabic respect for learning contributed to advances in astronomy, mathematics, medicine, and optics through centuries of support of its scholars. Such tradi-tions continue in the modern world and predominate in Egypt and Syria, Saudi Arabia, Turkey, Albania, Iraq, Pakistan, Afghanistan, Iran, Yemen, Indonesia, Malaysia, Morocco, Tunisia, and Libya.

Carolingian Art

4-52 *Saint Matthew*, from the *Gospel Book of Archbishop Ebbo of Reims*, produced in Reims, France. 816–23. Manuscript painting on vellum, 10¼ × 8¾". Bibliothèque Municipale, Épernay, France. Commissioned for Archbishop Ebbo under the direction of Peter, abbot of the monastery of Hautvillers.

During the reign of Charlemagne (also called Carolus Magnus, ruled 768–814), there was an interest in reviving the political unity and cultural ideals of the Roman world. This attraction can be seen in the image of Saint Matthew (fig. 4-52), which demonstrates how the art of this era— known as Carolingian art—could revive aspects of ancient classical style and yet remain true to medieval principles. Matthew wears a toga, and the modeling of the head, hands, and feet creates a sense of three-dimensional illusionism; the anonymous artist has clearly been inspired in part by a source imbued with the spirit of Hellenistic illusionism. In addition, the work shows the inspiration of Roman models in the

seemingly spontaneous technique, but here the fluid strokes of the brush— developed in Roman art to suggest movement—express a frenzy of divine inspiration that threatens to subsume both figure and landscape. Shimmering gold highlights on the toga, hair, and landscape heighten the liveliness, for they appear and disappear with changes in the reflected light.

The term *Carolingian* refers to the reigns of Charlemagne and his immediate successors, although in terms of art the particular qualities of Carolingian art did not endure long after his empire was divided by three grandsons in 843. Charlemagne, whose seal read *Renovatio Romani imperii* ("the revival of the Roman Empire"), intended to create a

Holy (that is, Christian) Roman Empire. He greatly expanded the Frankish kingdom he inherited, establishing a buffer between his kingdom and the Islamic threat in Spain and the East. On Christmas Day 800, Pope Leo III crowned Charlemagne emperor of Rome at St. Peter's Basilica.

Charlemagne's renewal included an interest in reform and education and a demand for order and efficiency. He codified law, issuing legal decrees from his capital at Aachen. He established a stable currency, ordered the creation of schools throughout his empire, reformed monastic life, corrected the calendar, established a large library, and encouraged the production of corrected copies of manuscripts, including the Bible. He required the use of a new, more easily readable style of lettering that is the basis of the typeface still used in most books. Literacy was a major goal, in part because it would enable people better to understand Christian doctrine and to participate in Church services. Charlemagne could read, but Einhard, his biographer, tells that he also wanted to learn to write and that he kept notebooks under his pillow, so that "he could try his hand at forming letters during his leisure moments."

Charlemagne's Palace at Aachen included a chapel (fig. 4-53), a centrally planned structure based on the most important church in the last Roman capital in the West, San Vitale in Ravenna (see fig. 4-31). Charlemagne received permission from the pope to remove columns and capitals from structures in Rome and Ravenna to incorporate into his palace complex. The large scale and simple forms of the building are an effort to relate it explicitly to the imperial style of ancient Rome and to confirm Charlemagne's importance as the "Holy Roman Emperor." To emphasize the Christian nature of his rule, Charlemagne modeled his throne on that of Solomon, described in the Old Testament, and placed it in the Palace Chapel opposite the altar.

4-53 ODO OF METZ

Interior, Palace Chapel of Charlemagne, Aachen, Germany. 792–805. Commissioned by Charlemagne.

The Carolingian ideal of a world that would combine the greatness of the ancient past with the Christian vision is revealed in a letter that was sent to Charlemagne in 799:

If many people became imbued with your ideas a new Athens would be established in France— nay, an Athens fairer than the Athens of old, for it would be ennobled by the teachings of Christ, and ours would surpass all the wisdom of the ancient academy. For this had only for its instruction the disciples of Plato; yet, molded by the seven liberal arts, it shone with constant splendor. But ours would be endowed with the sevenfold fullness of the Holy Spirit, and would surpass all secular wisdom in dignity.

The Monastery in the West

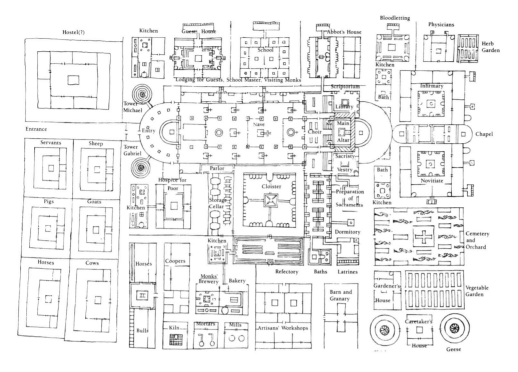

4-54 Plan of St. Gall Monastery. c. 819. Traced and drawn on five pieces of parchment sewn together, 44 × 30". Monastery Library, St. Gall, Switzerland. The St. Gall plan, traced from another plan now lost, represents an ideal formula to be adjusted for each particular site and needs. It even suggests the appropriate location of furnishings. Its orderly design may be related to the reforms of the monastic system within the Carolingian empire, discussed at meetings in Aachen, Germany, in 816 and 817. Not a document that normally would have been saved, it may have survived only because a life of Saint Martin was written on the back.

The monastery was perhaps the single most important institution in Europe during the medieval period. The St. Gall plan reveals the complex and varied needs of a monastic community (fig. 4-54). The central structure is the church itself, which has a basilical form following Early Christian models; the nave and side aisles provide additional altars needed because each priest was required to say Mass daily. At the western end of the church plan is a smaller apse with two towers forming an entrance facade known as a **westwork**. A Carolingian innovation in church design, the westwork helped to create an impressive entrance and was the source from which the traditional two-towered church **facade** would develop.

The subsidiary structures include a separate house for the abbot who ruled the monastery and, for the monks, a complex attached to the church that included a dormitory, latrine, bathhouse, and **refectory** (dining hall), as well as a cloister for walking and meditation. Outbuildings housed kitchen, mill, bakery, drying house, brew house, storerooms, barns, workrooms for artisans, and other facilities necessary for a self-sufficient community of approximately one hundred. There were also, set apart, a chapel and housing for those who were studying to become monks. A separate house, with its own kitchen, served special visitors. The services that the monastery provided the public included an infirmary, complete with herb garden, and a hospital for the poor. Usually there was a lodge for travelers. In an area adjacent to the main altar were the library and the scriptorium, where manuscripts were copied and illustrated. The orchard served as the monastic cemetery. The complex seen here would have been surrounded by vast fields worked by the monks and hired laborers.

Monasticism has its roots in the early days of Christianity in the Middle East and Egypt, when many Christians retreated into the desert or lived in caves in order to spend their lives praying, remote from the distractions and temptations of the world. Many chose to live a life of complete isolation, but some banded into communities that mark the beginnings of the monastic tradition. During the sixth century, Benedict of Nursia (later Saint Benedict) gathered so many followers that he wrote a rule (c. 535–40) for their behavior. This became the basis for later medieval monastic organization, in part because Charlemagne imposed it on all monasteries in his empire; by the seventh century, a variant of the Benedictine rule was in use for women. Benedict required that the monks remain within the monastery for life and that they observe poverty, chastity, and obedience. A simple, humble garment and hairstyle were specified. The monks swore obedience to an elected abbot; daily life was a well-organized regimen of work, study, and prayer. There were at least eight

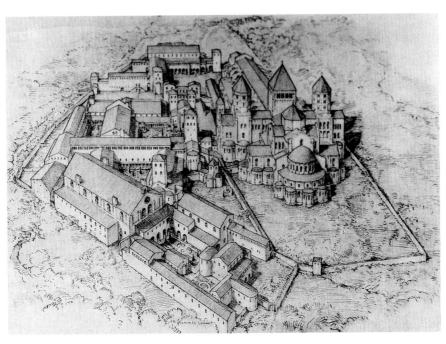

4-55   Reconstruction of the Romanesque monastery and third church, Cluny, France. c. 1157. The huge Romanesque church seen here, the largest in Europe at the time of its completion, was begun in 1088 under the aegis of the abbot, Hugh de Semur. At the time of this reconstruction, the monastery probably housed about 300 monks and priests. The church and monastery were largely destroyed by Napoleonic edict in 1810.

daily services of psalms, hymns, and prayers. Work included all aspects of labor. Many monks and nuns became skilled in the arts, but Benedict's rule warns against the pride that could accompany artistic achievement:

> Let such craftsmen as be in the monastery ply their trade in all lowliness of mind if the abbot allow it. But if any be puffed up by his skill in his craft . . . such a one shall be shifted from his handicraft, and not attempt it again until such time as he has learnt a low opinion of himself, and the abbot bids him resume.

Through an emphasis on literacy and education, which were required to participate fully in the Christian life, the monasteries played a vital role in continuing and preserving the Western heritage. A number of ancient works of literature, science, and philosophy survive only in copies handwritten by monks and nuns.

In the course of the Middle Ages, there was a proliferation of monastic orders, but their rules were similar. Most were located in the country, away from the temptations of city life and far from other human beings. In the thirteenth century, two new orders, the Franciscans and the Dominicans, were approved by the pope. They emphasized public service and education in the urban environment, and their monasteries were established within the cities to serve the sick and the poor (see page 207).

No monastery was built that exactly followed the design of the St. Gall plan, in part because any complex of such scale would evolve slowly over time and in relationship to the peculiarities of the particular setting. The Romanesque monastery at Cluny, however, can be studied as an example of a fully developed medieval monastery (fig. 4-55).

Cluny, the mother church of a reformed Benedictine order that played an important role in monastic renewal during the eleventh and twelfth centuries, became one of the most important centers for learning and patronage of art in Europe. It was famous for the splendor and beauty of its services, and its third church, begun about 1085 and consecrated in 1131–32, was, with a length of 555 feet, the largest church in all Europe. The monastic complex at Cluny has virtually all the same facilities as the St. Gall plan; especially impressive is the amount of space given over to the huge infirmary.

Buddhist Art in Indonesia

4-56 Buddhist Temple of Borobudur, Java, Indonesia. Sailendra dynasty, 835–60. Lava stone; perimeter of lowest gallery 1,180′; diameter of crowning stupa 52′. Borobudur was rediscovered by Europeans in 1814, but few could understand it because of their inability to read Asian languages and the scripts in which Buddhist texts were written. Although the Javanese are predominantly Muslims today, they prize this monument and rescued it from neglect and severe water and atmospheric conditions through a ten-year restoration, which concluded in 1985. Now the structure is secure and its many reliefs can be properly seen again. Borobudur was built by a family of kings known as the Sailendras, or "Lords of the Mountains." The Buddhist ruler who started work on Borobudur was named Indra, after the god who lives on top of Mount Sumeru and who appears in several sculpted reliefs of the lower galleries.

The Buddhist temple called Borobudur (fig. 4-56) is situated on a hill above the fertile Kedu Plain in central Java (see map, page 149). The plain, covered with rice fields and coconut groves, is surrounded by high-peaked mountains. According to legend, Borobudur was designed by a divine architect named Gunadharma, whose profile is said to be visible in the outline of nearby mountains. Far from having been the work of a single designer, however, Borobudur was remodeled four times within its first century. Originally the site was recognized as sacred by the Hindus, who around 780 began to erect a structure on the hill. Workers cut terraces into the sides of the hills and erected a massive stone structure with three levels that correspond to the first three levels of the current monument. Such large human-made terraces have been found in other locations on Java and are thought to have been the sites of historical equivalents of the modern *punden*, rituals performed to obtain power from ancestors in order to purge evil influences.

The current stepped shape was built by the Buddhists partly to accommodate the earlier foundation. The lowest part of what we see today is an undecorated base measuring 370 feet on each side. Originally, 160 relief panels illustrating Buddhist writings about heaven and hell adorned the base just above the ground. That base proved to be too narrow to support the monument and had to be rebuilt with the broader, unadorned base seen today.

From this base rise five square terraces with **balustraded** galleries. The inner and outer walls at each level are covered with carved panels illustrating the path toward enlightenment.

The three circular terraces hold seventy-two stone **stupas**, each about 12 feet high. The diamond-shaped perforations carved into the stupas on the two lower terraces express the idea of change and movement. On the top terrace, the openings are square and are thought to express calm and stillness. Each stupa contains a sculpted figure of the Buddha that is visible only as the monument is ascended. The entire monument is crowned with an enormous stupa containing an unfinished figure of the Buddha.

Borobudur is thought to have served many purposes, and it has been interpreted in many ways—as a visualization of the doctrine for the initiate; as a **mandala** for meditation (see fig. 5-3); as a symbolic mountain; and as a stupa that was a center of ritual activity in the ordered Buddhist world. Borobudur's design is most commonly compared to the Diamond World mandala, a type associated with the esoteric Tantric Buddhism practiced in Tibet and Nepal. Borobudur's form and hilltop location recall the setting of the jewel tower on Mount Sumeru (the World Mountain), where the Diamond World mandala was first described as being located in Tantric cosmology. We have no proof, however, that Borobudur was actually used as a mandala.

Borobudur's most convincing interpretation is as a stupa and/or symbolic mountain, an interpretation that combines both Javanese and Buddhist concepts. Some scholars argue that the main stupa on top of the monument originally contained a Buddhist relic. It seems that Javanese Buddhists came to Borobudur as pilgrims—to climb this holy, human-made mountain and thus to attain spiritual merit. This stepped pyramid provided a place where Buddhists could physically and

4-57 *Prince Sudhana's Search for Enlightenment*, upper terrace of the Temple of Borobudur. 835–60. Lava stone, height 20".

spiritually pass through the ten stages of development that could transform them into bodhisattvas, enlightened disciples of the Buddha.

As a symbolic mountain, this human-made holy monument can be understood as a continuation of the hill on which it sits. Mountains were important religious symbols in both pre-Buddhist Java and in the imagery of Mahayana Buddhism. The Javanese tradition of building terraced sanctuaries on high places, which continues today, began in prehistoric times; the upper stories are often built to evoke a holy mountain.

Mountains were equated with powerful spiritual forces, and as the pilgrims approached Borobudur all they could see were hundreds of statues gazing over the surrounding plain. In addition, the statues in niches suggest Javanese ascetics meditating in mountain caves as well as the gods who live in the caves on Mount Sumeru. The statues suggest that the pilgrim may have to endure self-denial and overcome physical discom-

fort in order to gain the highest stage of development when reaching the stupa at the summit.

In order to follow the complete narrative sculpted in the reliefs, the pilgrim had to make ten circuits—four times around the first gallery and twice around each of the next three. While moving slowly upward, the pilgrim was symbolically retracing the steps of the bodhisattvas who attained enlightenment by successfully passing through all ten stages of existence. The 1,460 narrative panels on the monument were created to illustrate Buddhist scriptures: the *Vision of Worldly Desire*; the *Jataka Tales*, or the *Previous Lives of the Buddhas*; the *Life of the Guatama Buddha*. As the pilgrim circumambulated, the reliefs illustrated stories from these tales. Figure 4-57 illustrates a scene describing the young Prince Sudhana's search for enlightenment from the epic *Travels of a Young Man in Search of Wisdom*. The figure of the prince is sheltered by a royal umbrella, and his elaborate headdress sets him apart from the other figures.

Chinese Art: Landscape Painting

4-58 LI CHENG (ATTRIBUTED)

BUDDHIST TEMPLE IN THE HILLS AFTER RAIN. Five Dynasties/Northern Song Dynasty, c. 950. Hanging scroll, ink and slight color on silk, height 42". The Nelson-Atkins Museum of Art, Kansas City, Missouri. The red ink markings seen in the lower right were stamped using carved stone stamps and were made by later owners of the painting to record their possession. The silk on which this scene was painted has darkened significantly, changing the tonal relationships. The authorship of few tenth-century landscape paintings is known with certainty. Descriptions of the work of these artists by critics of their own time make attributions such as this possible, however. Commissioned by the imperial court.

In this landscape attributed to Li Cheng (active from about 940 to 967), the autumn skies are clearing, leaving only mist in the low valleys and above the mountain pathways (fig. 4-58). In the immediate foreground are a group of huts and two pavilions built over water. The buildings and figures are painted with such detail that we can distinguish peasants and courtiers at their meals in the rustic inn and scholars at the wine shops gazing off into the landscape from the pavilions. The temple that occupies the center of the painting is parallel to the peaks that dominate the distance. Such axially symmetrical monumental configurations of mountains and water came to be associated with the Chinese empire in the tenth century—grand, ordered, and powerful.

Li Cheng as a person was thought to represent the ideal Chinese painter—an artist who claimed descent from the imperial clan of the Tang dynasty (618–907), was educated in the humanities through study of the *Classic Books* (ancient texts on history, philosophy, and literature), and was occupied with painting for his own delight without ambition for honors or advancement. A scholar and a gentleman, he enjoyed a quiet life devoted to the philosophic study of Nature as opposed to merely copying forms in the out-of-doors (nature). **Monochrome** ink paintings of landscape were the preferred type of art produced by Li Cheng and his colleagues.

Like many other landscape painters of the tenth century, Li Cheng had a preference for autumnal or wintry scenes full of bleak, stony crags, gnarled trees with leafless crab-claw-shaped branches, and looming distant peaks. He shares with other landscapists of the period a preference for monochrome ink, laid on the silk in broad and jagged strokes, to describe the essential outlines of the rocks, trees, and buildings. These shapes are then broken up and modeled with **washes** of ink. On top of the washes are placed **cun**, small brushstrokes dabbed on quickly to create the sense of texture (fig. 4-59). Such paintings were then mounted on a vertical hanging or horizontal hand scroll. Closely associated with calligraphy, the brush paintings of China were produced for and by the intelligentsia, who painted as an avocation.

The Chinese doctrine of realism seen here aims for truth to natural appearance but not at the expense of a pictorial examination of how Nature operates. In Li Cheng's painting, the bent and twisted trees, for example, are organically constructed to expose their full skeletons—roots, trunk, branches, and even the dormant buds ready for spring awakening. This approach to realism also explains the attitude behind **shifting perspective** in Chinese painting. In *Buddhist Temple* we are invited to "enter" the picture on the lower left and to explore as we move through the landscape. We can wander across the bridge, look down at rooftops, up at pavilions and the temple, and across to the towering peaks, but we cannot take a panoramic view from a single position outside (or inside) the painting, and the artist does not intend that we do so. Rather, little by little, nature is revealed as if we were actually walking in the out-of-doors. In this sense, the Chinese landscape painter combines the element of time in much the same way as it is experienced in music. Shifting perspective allows for a journey and for a powerful personal impact on the individual participant. These paintings were meant to be visual exercises that allowed for examination of both the structure of nature or the universe and the contemplation of minute details. The power of these paintings is to take us out of ourselves and to provide spiritual solace and refreshment.

c. 900   Vikings discovered Greenland
c. 950   **Li Cheng (attributed),** *Buddhist Temple in the Hills after Rain*
988   Christianity introduced into Russia

4-59   *Buddhist Temple in the Hills after Rain*, detail.

Guo Xi, a pupil of Li Cheng, declared in an essay that

> The virtuous man above all delights in landscapes.

The virtuous (or Confucian) man during this period accepted his civil responsibilities to society and to the state, which tied him to an urban life as an official, but he could nourish his spirit by taking imaginary trips into nature through viewing a landscape painting such as Guo Xi's *Early Spring* (see fig. 1-3).

There was important support for landscape painters during the Five Dynasties (907–60) and the Northern Song dynasty (960–1126). An important occurrence of the period was the initial printing of the *Classical Texts* in 953; for the first time, books became inexpensive and abundant. Scholars multiplied, and the knowledge of ancient literature was more widespread. The political consequences of the expansion of the literate class was manifest in the Song, the third centralized empire in Chinese history. The unification of the empire was the work of policy rather than conquest, a powerful submission of an aristocracy weary of disunion and aware of its own cultural identity. The traditional civil service examination system returned civilians to positions of prestige and power in government that had been lost under previous military dictatorships. The prevailing pacifist policies and a series of enlightened sovereigns who were tolerant, humane, artistic, and intellectual provided substantial and consistent patronage for the arts. The collection of the Song emperor Hui Zong (ruled 1100–26; see fig. 4-40), for example, was said to include 159 paintings by Li Cheng. The Song period produced the first important academy of painting in the Far East; among the early members were the landscapists.

The Song dynasty was an age of many-sided intellectual activity—poetry, history, and especially, philosophy. Characteristic of Song thought was the return to older Chinese sources, a conscious archaism and cultural introspection. The renaissance of

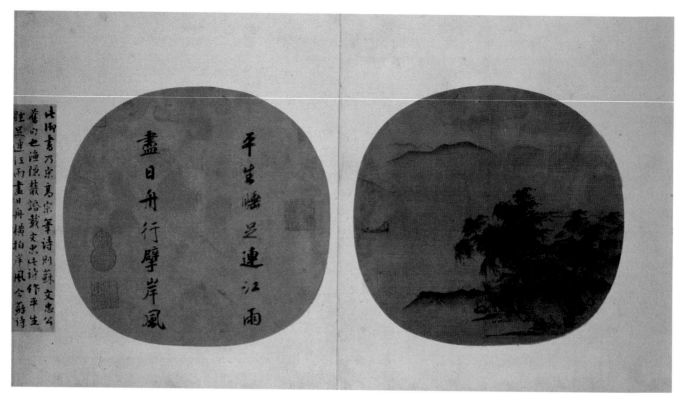

4-60 XIA GUI (ATTRIBUTED) *SAILBOAT IN THE RAIN*. Song Dynasty, c. 1180. Fan-shaped album leaf, ink and light color on silk, 9⅜ × 9⅞″. Chinese and Japanese Special Fund. Courtesy, Museum of Fine Arts, Boston. Commissioned by the imperial court. The inscription in the album leaf to the left of the painting is written by the Emperor Gaozong (1127–1162) of the Southern Song Dynasty, and is based on a poem written by Su Shi (1036–1101), a Northern Song poet. The Emperor changed some of the words in the original to suit his own mood:

> While sailing through endless rain,
> I enjoyed a good sleep.
> While boating all day long,
> we cut through the wind from the shore.

classical literature branched off into the formation of a new system of philosophy called neo-Confucianism, which enveloped traditional moral and ethical teachings with Daoist thinking about nature and the cosmos, especially as presented in the *I-jing (Book of Changes)*. No distinction was made between the law of nature and moral law. The world was thought to be inspired by the "Supreme Ultimate" (or what the Daoists called the *dao*, or the Way); the neo-Confucianists referred to this as *li* (law), a moral law that was identical to the ethical code upon which human conduct should be modeled. These Song thinkers were also interested in correspondences in nature. The manifestation of *li* in painting included faithfulness to nature as well as conventionalized symbols for representation of rocks,

foliage, bark, water, and so forth. *Li* also governed the way a picture was put together.

Under pressure from the Jin Tartars on the northern borders of China, the Song court fled south in 1127. In 1135, a new capital was founded at Hangzhou (see map, page 149), where the academy of painting was reestablished under imperial patronage and every effort was made to assemble an imperial art collection equal to that of the Northern Song emperors. The Southern Song rulers were even more concerned with internal affairs than their predecessors, and a new mode of painting evolved that focused on depiction of what was nearby and up close.

Later Southern Song landscape painters such as Xia Gui (active 1180–1230) concentrated on rivers, lakes,

and mists of south China (fig. 4-60). Xia Gui developed a shorthand manner in which forms are suggested rather than depicted, as they had been in the earlier style of Li Cheng and Guo Xi. His softer and less literal expression is organized asymmetrically, in a style called a "one-corner" composition by the Chinese. There is more mist than ink, and the subjective expression omits large sections of the landscape to concentrate on closer components. Xia Gui evokes a mood; he does not describe a particular place. He and other painters at court were associated with the politically weak and ineffectual court of the Southern Song in subsequent periods. For later Chinese critics, who commingled aesthetic and moral judgment, the Southern Song paintings were less highly valued than they were in Japan and the West.

Chinese painting is derived from the art of writing and is, therefore, a linear art. Its brushwork is imbued with calligraphic formulas. The highest aesthetic aim of the literati painters was to capture the spirit of what was depicted, rather than merely its appearance (see fig. 1-22). For these literati painters, the creative process embodied the *dao*, or Way of Nature, with its holistic vision of organic and metaphysical properties. In many Chinese paintings, idea and technique are one; the act of painting and the picture itself both carry meaning. Interestingly, these literati artists did not create sculpture or architecture, which were the work of highly skilled artisans.

Among the Chinese aristocracy, painting and calligraphy were revered media for examination and for the preservation of social, political, and aesthetic values. The earliest-known treatise on aesthetics was written in the second quarter of the sixth century by a man named Xie He (c. 500–c. 535). Called the *Gu hua pin lu (Classified Record of Ancient Painters)*, it graded earlier painters into six classes. What made the treatise so influential was its Preface, known as the Six Canons of Painting, which were used to judge painters and paintings. Because its language is filled with abstract philosophic thinking and presents generalized and theoretical prescriptions for painting, the canons have been translated and interpreted many times. An approximate translation of the Six Canons is:

1. A painting must have spirit or breath of life (*qi yun*).
2. The brushwork must be structurally sound.
3. The painting must faithfully portray forms.
4. A painting must have fidelity of color.
5. A painting must also be a properly planned composition.
6. A painting must transmit knowledge of past painting traditions.

The first canon, animation through spirit consonance, emphasizes the need for painting to have *qi yun*. **Qi** was thought to be the cosmic spirit that vitalized all things; to capture its essence was fundamental for "good" painting. Canons 2–5 clearly concentrate on technical matters, and canon 6 emphasizes the transmission of and reverence for tradition. Each generation of artists established a sense of external and internal reality in painting that could be challenged and reconsidered during the following period. Xie He's treatise remained the backbone of aesthetic criticism until the modern period in China, when its imperial, elitist roots were challenged by new socialist policies.

The ideals of painting of the tenth century were written down by a contemporary of Li Cheng named Ching Hao. In his essay *Record of Brush Methods*, or *Essay on Landscape Painting*, Ching Hao recorded his thoughts through a narrator, an old man whom he pretended to meet while wandering in the mountains. This wise man told him the six essentials of painting:

spirit, rhythm, thought, scenery, brush, and ink.

This logical system, based on Xie He, first lays down the concept of painting and then its expression. It distinguishes further between resemblance, which reproduces the formal, outward aspects of what is depicted, and truth (or spirit), which involves knowing and representing inner reality. Correct balance between representing visible forms of nature and their deeper significance was the goal of these Chinese painters.

Ottonian Art

4-61 *CHRIST WASHING THE FEET OF SAINT PETER*, from the *Gospel Book of Otto III*. c. 1000. Manuscript painting on vellum, 8 × 6". Bavarian State Library, Munich, Germany. This Gospel Book, created for the Ottonian emperor Otto III, is lavishly decorated with twenty-nine full-page illustrations of the life of Jesus Christ and a double-page portrait of the patron. Commissioned by Otto III.

The bold exaggeration of the arm and hand of Christ in this manuscript painting (fig. 4-61) reveals the Ottonian artist's determination to create a representation that is simultaneously clear and dramatic. The emphasis is on Christ's divinity, as seen in the gesture of blessing, rather than on the mundane theme of the washing of feet. The placement of Christ's haloed head in the center of the composition, against an empty gold field, emphasizes his majesty. The complicated architectural forms, inconsistent in perspective and out of scale with the figures, inform the viewer that this is an indoor scene. The busy patterns of the drapery add energy, and the emphatic, staring eyes of the participants suggest that something significant is taking place.

4-62 Doors with scenes from the Old and New Testaments. c. 1015. Bronze, height approx. 15'. St. Michael's, Hildesheim, Lower Saxony, Germany. These doors and a huge bronze candlestick, 12'6" tall (not shown), were commissioned by Bishop Bernward (later Saint Bernward). The candlestick, decorated with scenes from the life of Jesus, is a Christianized version of ancient Roman imperial triumphal columns (see fig. 3-104). Commissioned by Bishop Bernward.

That Christ is clean-shaven reveals the influence of Early Christian or Byzantine models.

Like Charlemagne, the Saxon prince Otto I (ruled 936–73) wanted to revive the ancient Roman Empire, and he brought Germany and most of northern Italy, including Rome, under his control before being crowned emperor by the pope in 962. Otto established a centralized government, and his lineage—his son Otto II, who married a Byzantine princess, and his grandson Otto III—ruled until 1002. Their reforms in education and monasticism were similar to those of Charlemagne, and Ottonian art flourished until at least the middle of the eleventh century.

Ottonian patrons and artists continued elements of iconography and style from the Carolingian tradition, as well as from the ancient Roman, Early Christian, and Byzantine periods. There were some large-scale architectural projects and several active centers for manuscript illustration, ivory carving, and work in gold and bronze.

The imperial connotations of Ottonian rule are clear in the bronze candlestick and doors at St. Michael's, Hildesheim. The bronze doors (fig. 4-62), the first cast in Europe in centuries, have sources in both ancient Roman and Byzantine art. The figures have a lively intensity expressing strong emotions and psychological interaction; in the most famous of these scenes, fourth from the top on the left side of the door, an accusing God confronts Adam. Adam in turn points to Eve, who tries to put the blame on the dragon-like serpent on the ground.

The **choir** area of St. Michael's is raised so the monks can conduct their services while pilgrims continue to have access to the relics in a crypt below. The alternation of paired columns with **piers** in the **nave arcade** is new (fig. 4-63) and may be an attempt to divide the nave into

4-63 Interior, St. Michael's, Hildesheim. 1001–31. Badly damaged by bombing during World War II, St. Michael's has been restored. Commissioned by Bishop Bernward.

more clearly defined units. The nave is higher and narrower than in earlier churches, creating a pronounced vertical emphasis. On the exterior, turrets at the **transepts** and two **crossing** towers create a fortresslike massing of monumental forms, pierced by small windows, that predicts the later developments of Romanesque art (see fig. 4-69). The Ottonian revival, as short-lived as Charlemagne's, demonstrates the importance of political and economic stability for the production of works of art and architecture.

Romanesque Art

4-64 *CHRIST IN MAJESTY WITH ANGELS, SYMBOLS OF THE EVANGELISTS, AND SAINTS,* from San Clemente, Tahull, Spain. c. 1123. Apse fresco, diameter of apse approx. 13′. Museo de Arte de Cataluña, Barcelona.

4-65 Sainte Foy reliquary. Later 10th century. Gold with filigree and precious stones over wooden core, height 33½″. Cathedral Treasury, Conques, Rouergue, France. The masklike face of this reliquary, which enshrines the bones of the saint, is made from an ancient Roman gold face guard and parade helmet to which inlaid enameled eyes have been added. The forearms and hands date from a post-Romanesque restoration. For the church at Conques that enshrined Sainte Foy's remains, see figures 4-68–4-70.

The term *Romanesque* ("Roman-like") was first applied in the nineteenth century to designate medieval art of the tenth to the mid-twelfth century, which is distinguished by a Europe-wide revival of monumental architecture, sculpture, and mural painting. In the Tahull apse painting, the enthroned Christ in Majesty, surrounded by a mandorla, is symmetrically flanked by angels and the symbols of the Evangelists: the angel for St. Matthew, the lion for St. Mark, the ox for St. Luke, and the eagle for St. John (fig. 4-64). A row of standing saints below includes the Virgin Mary. The hierarchical presentation and the iconlike stare of the figures associate the painting with the Byzantine tradition (see fig. 4-34). But here the abstraction of earlier medieval art is intensified and the drapery folds have a life of their own; instead of being used to reveal the body beneath the drapery, they flutter and fold in abstract patterns. Each body part is treated independently, with heads and hands exaggerated in scale. **Foreshortening** is avoided, as in the unnaturalistic rendering of Christ's book, which bears the inscription "I am the light of the world." The simple and direct presentation, harsh modeling, unnatural but bold colors, and frontal stiffness combine to create the commanding composition representative of much Romanesque art.

History

During the tenth century, Europe stirred with revived economic, social, and cultural life. The attacks of migrating peoples, a source of conflict and political unrest for centuries, abated, in part because of their conversion to Christianity. The 1054 split between the Western, or Roman, and the Byzantine, or Orthodox, branches of Christianity would never be resolved, despite efforts at reunion in later centuries. After the split, the Roman Church under the papacy consolidated its religious and political power in western Europe. England was united with much of France after the duke of Normandy's conquest in 1066 (see fig. 4-67), and Norman victories in southern Italy and Sicily freed those areas from Byzantine control. The new political stability fostered an expanded economy.

The Church gradually increased its influence in secular affairs, coming into conflict with the feudal nobility. The power and energy of the Church were manifested in the enormous undertaking of the Crusades, which began in the 1090s as an attempt to capture the "Holy Lands" from the Muslims and to establish commercial activity on a broader scale. The Reconquest, the war against the Muslims in Spain, led to the capture of Córdoba by Christian forces in 1236.

Art and the Pilgrim

The mainstays of earlier medieval workshop production—manuscript illumination, ivory carving, and metalwork—continued throughout the Romanesque period. More significant is the widespread revival of monumental architecture and art that distinguishes the eleventh century.

The pilgrimage, which earlier in the Middle Ages had been prescribed for the atonement of sin, became a regular feature of Christian life during the Romanesque period. Pilgrims traveled over defined routes, known as the pilgrimage roads, either to Rome or to

4-66 *SAINT MARK*, from a Gospel Book produced at Cambrai, Nord, France. Second half of the 11th century. Manuscript painting on vellum, 10¾ × 7⅞". Bibliothèque Municipale, Amiens.

Santiago de Compostela in western Spain. At St. Peter's in Rome or the Church of St. James in Santiago, pilgrims invoked God's intercession. To prepare spiritually for their destination at Santiago or Rome, pilgrims visited churches and monasteries along their routes, where they could pray before the relics of saints. These relics were usually encased in precious reliquaries such as that of Sainte Foy at Conques (fig. 4-65); many of the jewels that adorn her golden cloak were gifts from pilgrims. Pilgrims were sheltered in monasteries, which since the earlier medieval period had functioned as centers of learning and hospitality. During this period, developments in Church architecture responded to the needs of both clergy and pilgrims.

Manuscript Illumination

The **illumination** (illustration and decoration) of manuscripts continued to be a significant medium of painting during the Romanesque period. The figure of Saint Mark in the Gospel Book (fig. 4-66), which displays the same intense color and bold outlines as the monumental apse painting from Tahull, is enlivened by an abstract curvilinear design. The saint, seated in his study, turns to grasp a scroll from his symbol, the lion. Framed within an arch, the scene is animated by the twisted body of the lion, whose contorted movement is echoed in the drapery around the arch and the diagonals of Mark's robe. The contrast between the stable framing of the scene and these lively patterns creates a dynamic interpretation of divine inspiration.

The Bayeux Tapestry

The unique embroidered narrative of the *Bayeux "Tapestry"* (fig. 4-67) depicts the events that led to the Norman invasion of England and their victory at Hastings in 1066.

ISTI MIRANT STELLA

HARO

Our detail shows the English king, Harold, enthroned in his castle. A messenger informs the king that his rival, William, duke of Normandy, has ordered a fleet of ships to be built in order to cross the English Channel. In the sky to the left of the castle is Halley's Comet,

which was visible in England in late April 1066; at the time, it was interpreted as a signal of impending disaster for Harold. The inscription reads: *Isti mirant[ur]stella* ("These men marvel at the star").

The sequence of historical events is narrated in a lively, engaging man-

ner. The curving axes of the figures of King Harold and the messenger animate the scene, while the abstract tree to the right, with its undulating rhythm, demonstrates the continuation of Anglo-Saxon **interlace** motifs (see pp. 160–61)

4-67 *KING HAROLD RECEIVING A MESSENGER*, detail from the *BAYEUX TAPESTRY*. c. 1070–80. Embroidered wool on linen, height 20"; total length 231'. Centre Guillaume Le Conquérant, Bayeux, Normandy, France. Despite the fact that the technique is embroidery, this work is traditionally known as the *Bayeux Tapestry*. It was probably executed by a group of women artists, who specialized in the needle arts. In more than seventy-five scenes accompanied by Latin inscriptions, the work tells the story of the victory of William the Conqueror over King Harold during the Norman conquest of England, in 1066. The embroidery, probably commissioned by Bishop Odo of Bayeux, half-brother of William, was intended for display in a great secular hall.

and asserts a vitality drawn from nature that permeates much of the work. The limited colors are used decoratively rather than descriptively, and the abstract rhythms of the composition enliven the historic narrative.

The Romanesque Artist

Artists, benefiting from the economic growth of the period, organized **guilds** to ensure quality and control in the production of art and the training of apprentices. Guilds offered protection for the artists as a group, encouraged a greater amount of self-regulation, and promoted an increased social prestige. Still, however, few works are signed and dated.

Romanesque Architecture at Conques

4-68 Nave, Abbey Church of Ste.-Foy, Conques, Rouergue, France. c. 1080–1120. The monastic church of Ste.-Foy was located along one of the pilgrimage roads to Santiago de Compostela, Spain. The present Romanesque structure was built around an older church probably begun during the Carolingian period. Although located along pilgrimage routes, Conques later remained isolated from the urban development that affected many other medieval towns, and with the exception of two nineteenth-century towers, the church has been spared the restoration activity that so often transformed medieval architecture. The church is dedicated to a third-century virgin martyr, Sainte Foy (known in English as Saint Faith), whose relics were brought to Conques about 870 (for the reliquary preserved here, see figure 4-65). Originally commissioned by Abbot Odolric c. 1052; the cloister was begun by Abbot Begon.

4-69 Abbey Church of Ste.-Foy, Conques. For the tympanum over the central doorway, see figure 4-72.

4-70 Plan of the Abbey Church of Ste.-Foy, Conques.

Viewing the **crossing** and the **apse** of the Abbey Church of Ste.-Foy from the **nave** (fig. 4-68), we can immediately see why nineteenth-century historians coined the term *Romanesque* to describe this style of architecture. The use of round arches and stone vaults is reminiscent of ancient Roman building practice, and, like Roman architecture, the monumental scale establishes an austere, massive presence. The wooden truss roof common in Early Christian and Carolingian architecture has now given way to the favored construction feature of Roman architecture, the vault. At Ste.-Foy, the **barrel vault** of the nave is reinforced with **transverse arches** (arches that traverse the nave). On the exterior, vertical

buttresses make the interior rhythm of the **bays** readable from outside (fig. 4-69). On exterior and interior, then, the articulation of the individual bays creates an order and unity characteristic of Romanesque architecture. The transverse arches also make it possible to construct a thinner barrel vault, allowing for slightly larger windows. Romanesque stone vaulting also served other purposes, for it helped prevent the spread of fire, a prevalent threat with wooden truss-roof buildings, and it acoustically enhanced the liturgical chants of the monks.

Another feature of the Romanesque pilgrimage church was the use of a semicircular **ambulatory** (fig. 4-70). Adapted from ancient Roman and Early Christian centrally planned build-

ings, it is here used to solve a specific problem. At churches with monastic foundations, it was necessary that the monks occupy the area around the high altar for numerous services. The ambulatory connecting the side aisles in one continuous passageway allowed large numbers of pilgrims to move through the church, stopping to pray and venerate relics in the apsidal chapels without disturbing the monks.

Romanesque Sculpture

4-71 *Pentecost, the Peoples of the Earth, and Saint John the Baptist,* tympanum and lintel, central portal, Abbey Church of La Madeleine, Vézelay, Burgundy, France. 1120–32. Stone. Probably commissioned by Abbot Pontius.

In the central **tympanum (lunette** above the door) at Vézelay, Christ is on the axis, enthroned in a mandorla with his arms outstretched (fig. 4-71). Axiality and hierarchical scale convey Christ's significance, while the angularity of his legs and the swirling drapery, similar to those in contemporary manuscript illumination (see fig. 4-66), animate his presence. Rays of illumination and inspiration, the gift of the Holy Spirit, flow from his hands (his left hand has been broken off) to the head of each apostle. Eight **archivolts** (arches of decorative and narrative motifs that enframe the tympanum) show the apostles preaching the Gospel and healing spiritual and physical ailments. In the outer archivolts, the zodiac symbols and representations of monthly labors signify that Christ is lord of all time and of everything in the world. On the sides of the doors (**jambs**) and on the central post

(**trumeau**) are sculpted figures of saints and prophets.

The complex iconography of the Vézelay tympanum reveals the inspired spirituality of the later Middle Ages. Representations of the human race from all over the world—some based on medieval legends of exotic peoples and therefore fantastically conceived—are shown in the compartments to the sides, while laborers and pilgrims appear in the **lintel**. John the Baptist, who predicted the coming of Christ, is placed on the trumeau in a position that visually and symbolically expresses his support of Christ. The tympanum, then, is both direct and complex in its iconography and would thus function to illuminate the Christian content for more than one level of society. Such sculptures were important in teaching church doctrine.

Tympanum sculpture often spoke to the emotions of the people. The

Last Judgment scenes at Conques and Autun emphasize the alternatives of eternal reward or everlasting punishment (figs. 4-72, 4-73). At Conques, Christ's judgment is reinforced by literary inscriptions. Axially positioned on the throne of justice, Christ announces to the saved:

Come, the blessed of my Father, take possession of the kingdom that has been readied for you.

To the damned he proclaims:

Away from me, accursed ones.

At Autun, the events of the Last Judgment are dramatically portrayed. Across the lintel, humanity waits to be judged; the scales represent the weighing of souls to determine whether the evil a person has done outweighs the good. To Christ's right (our left), the blessed

4-72 *LAST JUDGMENT*, tympanum and lintel, west portal, Abbey Church of Ste.-Foy, Conques, Rouergue, France. c. 1120. Stone, approx. 12 × 22'. Traces of paint remain on this tympanum, reminding us that color once played an important role in the total effect. Commissioned by the abbot of Conques.

4-73 GISLEBERTUS (?)

LAST JUDGMENT, tympanum and lintel, west portal, Cathedral of St.-Lazare, Autun, Burgundy, France. c. 1125–35. Stone, approx. 12'6" × 22'. An inscription on the tympanum that mentions the name Gislebertus has been interpreted as revealing the name of the master of the sculptural workshop at Autun, but a recent interpretation suggests that this might be the name of the patron.

enjoy their reward in heaven; to his left, the damned begin an eternity of punishment at the hands of fantastic, demonic creatures. These horrific devils served as visual demonstrations of the punishment for sin, reinforcing the sermons preached inside the cathedral.

Later Byzantine Art

4-74 *VIRGIN OF VLADIMIR.* 12th century. Tempera on wood, 31 × 21". Tretyakov Gallery, Moscow. This icon, which was probably created in Constantinople, was taken to the Russian city of Vladimir and then to Moscow, where Russians hoped it would ward off an attack by the Tartars. Only the faces date to the twelfth century, for, like many icons, the drapery has been repainted in a style similar to that of the original, but stiffer and more abstract.

4-75 *PANTOCRATOR*, mosaic in central dome, Church of the Dormition, Daphni, Greece. c. 1100.

Only a few types of Madonna and Child compositions were permitted in Byzantine art, and each was dependent on an old and venerated tradition. Invention and variation were discouraged, and the figures gradually became more stylized and remote from visual reality; perhaps as a result of the powerful control of the emperor, Byzantine art in general is conservative and less open to innovation than is art in western Europe. The *Virgin of Vladimir* (fig. 4-74) is the type known as the *Glykophilousa* or *Eleousa* (the "affectionate, loving one"), which features the Christ Child pressing his cheek to his mother's. Mary looks out at us with a solemn expression and large eyes that seem to convey an intense melancholy. Her delicate features—long thin nose, tiny mouth, and sharply defined eye sockets—remove her from the realm of the physical and sensuous. The shape of her veiled head, which is clearly drawn with a compass, is geometric and two-dimensional. Despite the stylized formulas that controlled

4-76 CANALETTO

VENICE: THE INTERIOR OF S. MARCO BY DAY. The Royal Collection, Copyright Her Majesty Queen Elizabeth II.

4-77 *ASCENSION*, mosaic in dome, San Marco. Late 12th century. Grouped below in a circular arrangement are the apostles, two angels, and the Virgin Mary, with palm trees to suggest a landscape setting. Between the windows are figures of Virtues. In the pendentives are the Evangelists, with settings of cities and rivers to suggest the worldwide influence of their works. Commissioned by the Venetian doges.

Byzantine production and curtailed artistic invention, the anonymous artist of the *Virgin of Vladimir* so beautifully expresses Christ's love for Mary and her somber compassion for the devout that it is easy to understand why this became one of the most popular of icons in Russian culture.

Mosaics continue to be the primary medium of decoration in church architecture. The *Pantocrator* (from the Greek, "omnipotent") is an image of the triumphant Christ that was the usual theme for the dome or apse of a church (fig. 4-75).

Close trade and diplomatic relations between the Republic of Venice in Italy and the Byzantine Empire also led to cultural and artistic influences. San Marco was rebuilt beginning in the eleventh century (fig. 4-76) on the model of a five-domed church built by Justinian that combined the domed **central plan** with the **Greek cross plan**. The splendid decoration of San Marco's interior—patterned marble floors and lower walls covered with slabs of veined marble, culminating in barrel vaults and domes covered with thousands of square feet of Byzantine-style gold mosaics—was so large a project that it was not fully completed until the seventeenth century. In the central dome, the story of Christ's ascension into heaven is represented (fig. 4-77), with Christ placed at the apex of the dome—it is clear that the composition evolved in relationship to the shape and space of the dome.

The exterior domes of San Marco are elevated high above the interior domes to create a festive and impressive design against the sky. Such picturesqueness, ultimately Byzantine in origin, is also seen in the later churches of eastern Europe, Greece, and Russia (see fig. 6-4), as well as in the onion domes of Eastern-rite churches all over the United States.

Angkor Wat:
Cult of the God-King

4-78 Temple complex, Angkor Wat, Kampuchea (Cambodia). First half of 12th century. The inner wall of the temple measures 3,363 × 2,625'; the entrance building is 1,148' long. The site was rediscovered in the nineteenth century, and in the twentieth century modern archaeology and physical science retrieved it from the jungle and preserved it until it was ravaged again by neglect and the perils of war in the 1970s. At this time, there is yet another international effort to save this unique monument. Commissioned by Khmer rulers.

The word *Angkor* (from *nokor*, Sanskrit for "city") means "the city," or "the capital," in the Khmer language of ancient Cambodia. Geographically, the term denotes about 75 square miles of fertile plain between the Kulen Hills and the lake of Tonle Sap where, between the ninth and thirteenth centuries, Khmer kings constructed capitals (see map, page 149). These centers encompassed a sophisticated irrigation system that controlled the vagaries of monsoon rains and drought so that enough rice could be grown to support about a million inhabitants. They also included major building complexes in brick, stone, and a reddish-pink stone called

laterite. The temple that later became known as Angkor Wat is the largest and most artistically accomplished complex in this area (fig. 4-78).

Altogether, these creations of conquerors and artisans embodied an integrated concept of the universe that was rooted in myth and deep religious belief. They express a combination of physical and spiritual grandeur similar to those found in Egypt and Greece, among the Maya and Aztecs in Mexico, and in the Gothic cathedrals of Europe.

The monuments built at Angkor testify to the creative ability of the Khmer civilization. Established to the north and west of the floodplain of Kampuchea, the Khmer kingdom en-

dured a sequence of rapid changes in religious faith. Greatly influenced by Indian culture, the Khmer kingdom began in the sixth century. Although there were more than thirty rulers in quick succession, Yasovarman I (ruled 889–900), Suryavarman II (ruled 1113–50), and Jayavarman VII (ruled 1181–1219) are outstanding. They were devotees of Siva, Vishnu, and the Buddha, respectively, but their faith was eclectic and was not so much a devotion as a source of power. Through the newly designed cult of the *devaraja* (*deva*, "god," and *raja*, "ruler"), or god-king, the ruler derived both sanctity and power.

The emperors concentrated their building activity at Angkor, and each

First half of 12th century	Temple complex, Angkor Wat
1100	Earliest recorded English mystery play
1122	Persian poet Omar Khayyam dies
1150	University of Paris has its beginnings

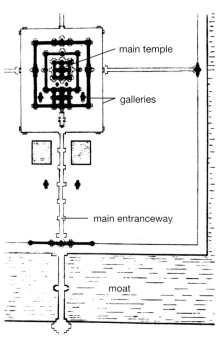

4-80   Plan of Angkor Wat.

4-79   *CHURNING OF THE SEA OF MILK*, sculptural relief, interior gallery wall, Angkor Wat. First half of 12th century. Stone. Almost the entire surface of the temple is chiseled with a variety of decorations, including bas-reliefs of Vaishaivite Indian myths and epics, historical triumphs, and dancing figures. More than 1,600 *apsaras* (celestial nymphs) in different moods and expressions are found at the corners and along the walls of the temple. In *Churning of the Sea of Milk*, Vishnu, the Hindu deity who is known as the Preserver, saves the universe from catastrophe by appearing in his avatar—a saving manifestation—as a tortoise. Hoping to obtain the Dew of Immortality, the gods and demons (*asuras*) made a truce so they could churn the Sea of Milk using a serpent wound around the World Mountain. When the mountain began to sink into the sea, Vishnu, in the guise of a tortoise, sat beneath it to support it. The sea gave forth delights, including the dew, which Vishnu obtained for the gods by assuming the form of a desirable woman, Mohini, who seduced the *asuras* into abandoning the elixirs. The gods defeated the demons, and Vishnu was credited with reconstituting the balance of good and evil. Carved in a style that is formal and that expresses a ranked order among the participants, the silhouetted and repeated forms resemble the rhythmic and measured ritual dances performed by the court dancers of ancient Cambodia. Commissioned by Khmer rulers.

competed to outdo his predecessor. Suryavarman II constructed the temple at Angkor Wat in the first half of the twelfth century to house his mausoleum. He dedicated it to Vishnu, whose exploits are portrayed in virtually every sector of the temple (fig. 4-79), but Siva and the Buddha also appear at the site. The complex symbolically represents Mount Meru (Sumeru), the World Mountain and, traditionally, Vishnu's adobe.

The simple plan approximates the World Mountain and embodies the ancient Khmer concept of the axis of the universe (fig. 4-80). The three galleries that rise toward the center are separated by paved courtyards. The highest, at the center, is capped by a large central tower. The area of the temple is surrounded by moats 623 feet wide.

The temple at Angkor Wat shows that the artists possessed a sound knowledge of three-dimensional geometry, which was necessary to create a perfect step pyramid. The rise of the terraces is so well calculated that all appear to be of equal height, without obscuring the view of the other terraces.

These monuments of Khmer art were considered the embodiments, or continuations after death, of the kings and their world. The state cult of *devaraja* gave religious and secular power to the god-kings. Authority was concentrated in these leaders, and the architecture erected by them echoes their dominance over the land. After the thirteenth century and the demise of the Khmer kingdom, these buildings fell into neglect and were gradually repossessed by nature until they were discovered in modern times.

The Japanese Narrative Scroll

4-81 TAKAYOSHI (attributed)

Third illustration of the "Kashiwagi" chapter of *THE TALE OF GENJI*. Late Heian period, c. 1120–30. Hand scroll, ink and color on paper, height 8½". Tokugawa Museum of Art, Nagoya, Japan. *Genji monogatari (The Tale of Genji)* is a long work of prose fiction written, probably in the early eleventh century, by Murasaki Shikibu (978?–1031?), a lady-in-waiting at the court of Emperor Ichijo (ruled 986–1011). Often called the world's first novel, *The Tale of Genji* was an immediate and lasting success, revolutionizing the art of prose fiction in Japan. Nothing like it had been written before, and both the content and the romantic mood of *Genji* inspired generations of poets. Well-known themes and episodes from *Genji* also appear in No plays from the fourteenth century through the Edo-period (1615–1868), in puppet and Kabuki theater presentations, and in modern plays and film. Over the centuries, chapter titles and memorable episodes from the novel became popularized as the subjects of parlor games, depictions on folding screens, and in illustrated scrolls, books, and woodblock prints. The palace architecture described in the text became an inspiration for later imperial structures (see figs. 1-5, 7-47, 7-48).

The "Kashiwagi" scene from *The Tale of Genji* illustrates one of the major concerns of the story (fig. 4-81). Prince Genji is playing out a theme that is closely linked to Buddhist concepts current in Japan in the eleventh and later centuries—that all acts have consequences. Good works will be rewarded by good fortune, sins will bring calamity, and there may be retribution for past deeds even in one's future life. Here he is declaring that the child in his arms in his, although the baby is actually the son of another.

The Tale of Genji survives in fifty-four chapters, although there may have been more. The story covers about seventy-five years, beginning with the birth of the hero, Genji, and concluding after his death. The principal setting for the novel is Kyoto (see map, page 149), then the capital of Japan, and much action occurs in the urban mansions and gardens of the aristocracy and royal family.

Genji, an imperial prince, was born to the favorite wife of the emperor, a woman too low in rank for him to inherit the throne. A handsome, cultured, and sensitive man, he had many romances. His intrigues and affairs take up two-thirds of the novel, leaving the last third to tell of the loves and lives of two young men, Genji's heirs in Kyoto. The scene in figure 4-81 explores the effect on Genji of committing a great sin against his father. In his youth, Genji fell in love with his father's youngest wife, Fujitsubo, a woman whom he was encouraged to see because she looked so much like his birth mother, who died when he was an infant. This liaison produced a son, a child who was passed off as the emperor's own and who eventually succeeded to the throne. Fujitsubo, the beloved consort of the emperor, was so tormented by guilt that she became a nun to expiate her sin. The full consequence of this past deed came to Genji, however, only in middle age, when his youngest wife had an extramarital affair that resulted in a son whom Genji had to publicly avow as his own, just as his father had done with Genji's son.

The ceremony acknowledging this son, illustrated here, is depicted in the first known illustrated version of the novel. As the scroll is unrolled and read from right to left, the brown surface of the courtyard—originally silver—and a verandah placed at a sharp angle come into view. The roof and interior walls of the building have been removed and replaced by bamboo blinds and curtains of state—white cloth curtains with loose black ties hang from horizontal poles. At the base of the curtain appears the bottom of a twelve-layered robe, the garment of a lady-in-waiting. Above, red and black lacquered plates are heaped with food. The colors of the garments and the careful placement of the food dishes indicate that a ceremony is in progress. Two-thirds of the way across the scene, figures appear: Genji at the top with the baby in his arms, ladies-in-waiting below. In the extreme upper left of the illustration, the child's mother is indicated by a mound of fabric.

The text accompanying this scene describes Genji's thoughts as he goes through the painful ritual. He knows that the attendants realize that he is not the father. The artist suggests his emotional discomfort by the physical awkwardness of his placement at the top of the sharply slanting floor, where the space is so cramped that he cannot even raise his head. Architecture plays an important role in the telling of this episode—it interrupts the leftward motion of the illustration and shields the figures from view, thus playing out the theme of retribution.

Despite the title of her novel and the centrality of the hero, Genji, Murasaki Shikibu took interest in exploring the lives and characters of many noblewomen. Genji's greatest love, Murasaki, is introduced in the novel as a child, and the reader can follow her as she matures and finally dies. Few women enjoy thoroughly happy lives in this novel, for the point is made over and over that in a polygamous society delicate distinctions of status often dictate behavior. Murasaki, for instance, is beautiful, talented, and witty, and she is perceived by Genji and her readers alike as the focus of Genji's life. Even so, she is constantly afraid of losing his affection. She suffers two humiliations. First, she is unable to provide him with a child and is therefore charged with raising his daughter by another woman. Second, because of her relatively low status and lack of powerful relatives, she is disqualified as his principal wife, an honor given instead to a woman described as a vapid and childish princess.

Another of the main themes of the novel for both male and female characters is the transient quality of experience and the resulting emotional intensity. The scattered placement of the women in figure 4-82 and the slightly opened door give ample indication of the potential of the past and future moment in that scene. This picture depicts a group of women and their maids as heads and hands emerging from masses of drapery. Naka no Kimi is having her hair combed after washing. Her half-sister, Ukifune, faces her and looks at a picture scroll while a maid reads from a text. The tension and dismay that Ukifune felt because of an attempted seduction only hours before is described in the text and is subtly indicated here by the tension between her half-hidden figure and the mundane setting of the scene.

4-82 TAKAYOSHI (attributed)

First illustration of the "Azumaya" chapter of THE TALE OF GENJI by Murasaki Shikibu. Late Heian period, c. 1120–30. Hand scroll, ink and color on paper, height 8½". Tokugawa Museum of Art, Nagoya, Japan. The creation of the *Genji* scrolls must have been a monumental project. The novel in English translation is nearly 1,000 pages long. Only twenty pictures from this early illustrated version survive, but it must have originally included one or more illustrations for each of the fifty-four chapters. Most estimate that there were ten scrolls in all. Scholars trying to determine how the scrolls were made conclude that there were five teams who worked on the project. Each team included a nobleman noted for his calligraphy and his cultural sophistication, a group of painters, including a principal artist (the *sumigaki*, or painter who draws in black ink), and specialists in the application of traditional pigments. Once a particular episode was chosen, the *sumigaki* planned the composition and sketched it on the scroll in fine black lines. Then the pigment specialists applied layer upon layer of paint within the lines. The *sumigaki* returned to paint in the details of the faces—tiny red mouths, narrow eyes, noses of a single hooked line, thin mustaches, short beards. The painting technique used in the *Genji* pictures, the application of layers of paint over an underdrawing, is called *tsukuri-e* ("constructed" or "built up"). The technique and style of the *Genji* and other illustrated narrative scrolls dating from this period came to be known as the *yamato-e* style, or "Japanese pictures." *The Tale of Genji* lent itself well to the horizontal illustrated scroll, the *emakimono*, a uniquely East Asian format. Both Chinese and Japanese languages were traditionally written in vertical lines from right to left, so the horizontal format of the *emakimono*, laid out and unrolled from right to left, provided a familiar way to relate text and image. The juxtaposition of textual passages of varying lengths with pictorial images was a potent format for many centuries and was translated in modern times into the medium of film with ease, for instance. The preference for highly formalized compositions and stylized depictions of figures carries over with little variation into single frames of twentieth-century films directed by Ozu (see figs. 10-94 & 95) and Kurosawa, among others.

Gothic Art

4-83 Interior, the Royal Abbey Church of St.-Denis, near Paris, Île-de-France, France. 1140–44. This view shows the ambulatory and radiating chapels. Here, where Gothic architecture was invented, we see some of the distinctive attributes of the style in the union of pointed arches, ribbed groin vaults, and large stained-glass windows. Commissioned by Abbot Suger.

The Gothic style, the preeminent style in Europe from about 1140 to 1400, was first defined in architecture, and architectural motifs appear throughout Gothic painting, sculpture, and decorative arts. Gothic is easily identifiable because of its unique vocabulary: pointed arches, ribbed cross vaults, flying buttresses, cluster piers, and glowing stained-glass windows. The development of Gothic architecture seems to have been inspired by Abbot Suger (1081–1151), friend and adviser to the French kings

Louis VI and VII, when he had the facade, ambulatory, and radiating chapels of the Royal Abbey Church of St.-Denis rebuilt (figs. 4-83, 4-84). The beauty of the Gothic style and the importance of St.-Denis, the French church where the coronation regalia were stored and kings and queens were buried, helped to popularize the new style throughout France. The brilliant colors of the large stained-glass windows of chapels and ambulatory were designed to lead the sensitive observer to imagine the glories of the Heavenly

Jerusalem, the holy "City of God" in Paradise. In other words, the architecture was intended to help the worshiper rise from the physical, material world to an immaterial, spiritual realm. Suger wrote about how his new architecture created a "crown of light"—a frequent metaphor for the divine:

> For bright is that which is brightly coupled with the bright,
> And bright is the noble edifice which is pervaded by the new light;

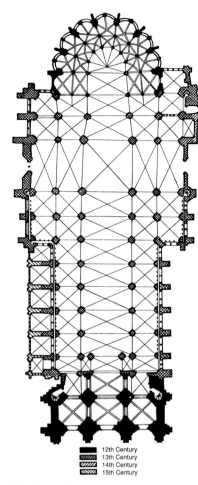

4-84 Plan of the Royal Abbey Church of St.-Denis as it exists today, showing the various building campaigns. Abbot Suger rebuilt the facade (consecrated 1140) and the chapels and ambulatory (1140–44); from 1231 to 1281, the old Carolingian nave and upper choir were rebuilt in the mature Gothic style.

Which stands enlarged in our time,

I, who was Suger, being the leader while it was being accomplished.

Abbot Suger

In an inscription over the west portal of the facade, Abbot Suger gives himself credit for the rebuilding of St.-Denis; no artists' or architects' names are mentioned. His new vision of architecture is based on his belief that the material beauty and splendor of the church would lead worshipers to a new understanding of God and the spiritual realm, as is further clarified in an inscription once on the golden doors of the west facade of the church:

Marvel not at the gold and the expense but at the craftsmanship of the work.

Bright is the noble work; but, being nobly bright, the work

Should brighten the minds, so that they may travel, through the true lights,

To the True Light where Christ is the true door.

Suger specifically compared the church at St.-Denis to the Holy Jerusalem, the City of God: St.-Denis and other, later Gothic cathedrals, then, are intended to suggest the Paradise that awaits the pious Christian.

History

Growth during the Gothic period and financial and social developments meant that life changed dramatically for much of the population. The development of international banking was centered in rapidly growing cities. Paris was the mercantile hub of Europe, and its popular annual trade fairs brought together Europeans of many cultures. Among the merchandise bought and sold were works of art. The complex life in the cities led to better-educated administrators and bureaucrats.

That France was preeminent in the arts in Europe during the later Middle Ages is not unexpected, for in the twelfth and thirteenth centuries Paris was the leading intellectual center in Europe and the capital of a strong monarchy (the Capetian line of French kings ruled from 987 to 1328). The University of Paris, the model for late-medieval universities, including Oxford, Cambridge, and Padua, became the focus for a new rational approach to philosophy and theology known as Scholasticism, which examined, questioned, clarified, and codified Christian dogma and practice. Thomas Aquinas, a professor at the University of Paris, wrote the *Summa Theologica* (1267–73), an encyclopedia that set out to systematize and encompass all knowledge on theology and the world.

The Crusades, which had begun in the late eleventh century, continued into the Gothic era, but with little political or military success. They were a significant financial and human drain on western Europe, but they encouraged the development of banking, new methods of taxation, and a more complex money economy. In western Europe, many scientific and philosophical developments resulted from contact with the Islamic culture.

Art

The term *Gothic* originally had a pejorative connotation. It was coined during the Italian Renaissance to refer to the whole of medieval art, which, from the perspective of the Renaissance, seemed crude and without reason. Judged to be the work of barbarians, medieval art was called Gothic after the Visigoths, an early Germanic people who sacked Rome in 410. During the Gothic period itself, the new architecture was known as *opus modernum* ("modern architecture"), *opere francigena* ("French architecture"), or pointed architecture.

Gothic art is elegant, highly decorated, and characterized by the use of sumptuous, colorful materials. Architecture included churches, urban monastic complexes, and castles. Sculpture was focused on church portals and on elaborate tombs with architectural frames. Painting was largely limited to manuscript illuminations. The decorative arts—secular and liturgical—encompassed works in gold and other fine materials (fig. 4-85), including ivory and precious gems. Increasing personal wealth meant that secular works—personal jewelry, tapestries, ivory boxes, and mirror backs—became more common.

The figural pose that characterizes Gothic art is revealed in the *Madonna of Jeanne d'Evreux* (fig. 4-86). The Madonna stands in the Gothic "hip-shot" position, in which one hip juts

4-85 *ABBOT SUGER'S CHALICE*. c. 1140; reworked later. Silver gilt and agate, with jewels, height 8″. National Gallery of Art, Washington, D.C. The beauty of Suger's architecture is reflected in the costly vessels he had made for liturgical use. This chalice was created by adding a rim, foot, and handles to an ancient agate cup made in Alexandria in the second century BCE. It was originally inscribed *Suger Abbas* ("Abbot Suger"). For a view of equally rich objects on an altar at the church of St.-Denis, see figure 4-6. Commissioned by Abbot Suger.

4-86. *MADONNA OF JEANNE D'EVREUX*. 1339. Silver gilt with enamel, height 27″. The Louvre, Paris. This work was presented to the abbey of St.-Denis in 1339 by the French queen Jeanne d'Evreux. The stylized iris held by the Madonna is the fleur-de-lis, the symbol of French royalty. Commissioned by Jean d'Evreux.

out to support the Christ Child; the effect is less naturalistic than elegant, giving the body a flowing S-curve shape. The small head of the Madonna is also a Late Gothic mannerism. In typical Gothic fashion, the body is completely covered by heavy drapery. The small scale of this statuette, its precious materials, and its delicate figure type and flowing drapery patterns reveal the sophistication and elegance of the fully developed Gothic style.

The *Annunciation* page from a Parisian **book of hours** (fig. 4-87)

reveals the elaboration of decoration common in Gothic art. The *Annunciation* was traditionally one of the most ornate of all pages, for it is the moment of the Incarnation, when the seed of God was placed in the womb of the Virgin Mary and Christ was conceived and became flesh. In prayer books, it is represented before the texts for matins, the first service of the day, and therefore serves as a frontispiece not only to that important service but also to the whole of the book. Here the artist sets the scene in an

elaborate churchlike structure, complete with altar and **altarpiece**; all the architectural motifs are Gothic. Although Gabriel holds a scroll bearing his message, Mary looks upward toward God, and it is from his figure that the dove of the Holy Spirit emerges. Old Testament prophets, whose writings were believed to predict the virgin birth and the coming of Christ, appear in the upper stories of the Gothic structure, while baby angels playing musical instruments populate the elaborate floral motifs of the borders. Typical of the growing interest in symbolism is the use of a number of complex symbols that elaborate on the content of the narrative. The caged bird behind Mary, for example, which at first seems to be merely a household decoration, is a symbol for Christ's Incarnation, when his soul was "caged" within a physical body, while the mating birds in the border nearby refer by contrast to the nonsexual manner by which God's seed found its way to Mary's womb. The spider and ladybug may refer to the devil, who was understood as ever-present.

The Franciscans

The urbanization of Europe was accompanied by significant developments in monasticism that shifted the emphasis from rural retreats of work, prayer, and meditation to large complexes within cities, where the monks could serve the poor and sick and preach the word of God in the language of the people. In the early thirteenth century, Francis of Assisi founded a popular new mendicant (begging) order, the Franciscans, which emphasized poverty and humility. The sermons and writings of his followers reveal a new emphasis on human emotion in interpreting the lives of Jesus and the saints. Legend tells us that Francis developed the tradition of the Christmas pageant to make Christianity more immediate and meaningful for the populace. This innovation is related to the rapid and widespread development of religious drama—mystery plays—during this period. A Franciscan monk, writing in the late thirteenth century about the birth of Jesus, urges a special kind of imaginary participation. He speaks directly to the reader, advising:

> You too . . . kneel and adore your Lord God and then His Mother, and reverently greet the saintly old Joseph . . . beg His mother to offer to let you hold [the baby Jesus] a while. Pick

4-87 *ANNUNICATION*, from the *LONDON HOURS*, created in Paris by an Italian artist. c. 1400–10. Manuscript painting on vellum, 9 × 6″. The British Library, London. This book of hours was made for the Parisian market, for it features the particular devotions and saints common in Paris. The coat of arms at the bottom of each page was left blank in order to be painted later with the arms of the purchaser, revealing that this book was a commercial production made for the art market and was not commissioned by a specific patron. This late phase of Gothic is sometimes called the International Gothic style because it was pervasive throughout Europe during the period c. 1400–25.

> Him up and hold Him in your arms. Gaze on His face with devotion and reverently kiss Him and delight in Him.
>
> (*Meditations on the Life of Christ*)

The Gothic Artist

During the Gothic period, the vast majority of works of art were not signed, but we begin to find references to specific artists in a few documents and inventories, where named artists are praised for their skill. A number of the architects/contractors who designed and constructed the cathedrals are known from inscriptions and documents. Some traveled widely: the Frenchman William of Sens was called to England to rebuild Canterbury Cathedral, and Villard de Honnecourt went to Hungary and Switzerland. Several artists are noted as active in more than one medium; André Beauneveu, for example, who was working for Charles V of France in 1364, was a painter, sculptor, designer of tapestries, and consultant to architectural projects. Nevertheless, the majority of Gothic artists were anonymous. Later, during the Italian Renaissance, the art historian Giorgio Vasari would be puzzled by the Gothic artist's "indifference to fame."

The Gothic Cathedral: Chartres

4-88 Nave, Cathedral of Nôtre-Dame, Chartres, Île-de-France, France. 1194–1200. Chartres Cathedral is the most memorable of French Gothic cathedrals, not only for the superb quality of its architecture and sculpture but also because it alone preserves virtually all its original stained-glass windows. Begun again after a fire in 1194 destroyed the earlier cathedral (except for the west facade, with its sculpture [see fig. 4-99], the crypt, and some of the stained glass, including *"Nôtre Dame de la Belle Verrière,"* fig. 4-101), the new construction was largely completed by 1220. Commissioned by the bishops of Chartres.

Entering a great Gothic cathedral is a thrilling, emotional, and—many would say—spiritual experience. The emphatic verticality of a Gothic **nave** urges upward, and it is easy to experience a sense of weightlessness and immateriality, a physical condition that can be related to spiritual enlightenment (figs. 4-88, 4-89). Space seems to expand not only upward but also outward to the sides as we look both upward and through the nave **arcade** into the side aisles. Space is also a dominant experience in such earlier architecture as the ancient Roman Pantheon (see fig. 3-122), but the simple, monumental union of dome and cylinder of the Pantheon is in sharp contrast to the complex interrelationships and forms of varied sizes of the Chartres interior. In the Gothic structure, the experience of space is less lucid, and the ultimate effect, a combination of height, dark corners, and glowing **stained-glass windows**, is mystical and other-worldly.

From its foundations, sunk 25 feet or more into the earth, to the height of its vaults and roof (at Beauvais, the tallest of all cathedrals, the vaults peak at 157 feet over the floor and the peak of the roof reaches 223 feet above the street), the Gothic cathedral is a monument to the determination, engineering daring, and physical energies of patrons, architects, and builders. Despite construction campaigns that lasted over decades and even centuries, not one of the great French Gothic cathedrals was ever fully completed; the vision of patrons and architects was too ambitious— too glorious—to be realized.

The high, narrow nave of the Gothic cathedral is the climax of a long tradition in Christian art in which architects tried to create a physical space that would express the spiritual goals of the Christian religion. The Gothic interest in ever-increasing height, lightness, and slenderness of proportion is evidenced by the statistics, given on p. 210.

A tall church was thought to please God. In addition, it could fuel the rivalry between neighbors, for during the Middle Ages the local cathedral was the emblem not only of the sanctity of the town's population but also of their wealth, power, and pride.

A unique combination of **pointed arch**, **ribbed groin vault**, and **flying buttress** (see page 212) defines Gothic architecture. Although each of these elements had been used earlier

4-89   View of the nave wall, Chartres Cathedral.

	Approx. Height of the Nave Vaults	Approx. Width of the Nave	Proportion of Nave Height to Width
Laon, Cathedral 1160–1205	80′	37′6″	2.13:1
Paris, Nôtre-Dame 1163–96	115′	40′	2.88:1
Chartres, Nôtre-Dame 1194–1220	120′	45′6″	2.64:1
Bourges, St.-Étienne 1195–c. 1270/80	117′	44′	2.66:1
Reims, Nôtre-Dame designed 1210	125′	46′	2.72:1
Amiens, Nôtre-Dame designed 1220	144′	48′	3:1
Beauvais, Cathedral (vaults before apse) designed 1230s	157′	47′	3.36:1

elsewhere, it is their combination into a coherent and rational system that is new in the Gothic period. The pointed arch, seen everywhere in Chartres' interior (see fig. 4-89), continuously directs our attention upward. The ribs of the vaults help define the parts of the architectural structure and also create a series of lines that keep the eye moving. The ground plan of Chartres (fig. 4-90) is not remarkably different from earlier Christian traditions; the new statement is in the construction and decoration. The rational basis of Gothic architecture demands that each element be explicable and interrelated (as in the Gothic philosophical system known as Scholasticism), and each vault is related to and visually supported by a **colonnette** (a thin column) that begins at floor level. Groups of colonnettes turn the supporting **piers** into **cluster piers**. The interior elevation (see fig. 4-92) is composed of a nave arcade, a **triforium** (a narrow gallery that opens the structure where normally there would be an expanse of wall), and an enormous, window-filled **clerestory**.

In most structures, we are aware of a continuous and relatively dense wall surface punctured and punctuated by doors and windows, but in the Gothic cathedral there is so little wall—and what remains is so dissolved or disguised by the linear patterns of ribs and colonnettes—that windows and wall are no longer alternatives. They are unified into an energetic skeleton with huge openings filled with vibrantly colored stained-glass windows. The flying buttresses—hidden from an interior view by the stained-glass windows—are clearly visible on the exterior and add lightness and visual energy to the exterior (see fig. 4-94).

The ideal Gothic church would have had seven spired towers—a twin-towered western facade (a development from the Carolingian westwork; fig. 4-91), a tower at the **crossing**, and twin towers at both north and south **transepts**. Such a massing of vertical forms pointing upward suggests the dissolution of the mass of the structure and a denial of gravity consistent with the motivations and aspirations of the cathedral builders.

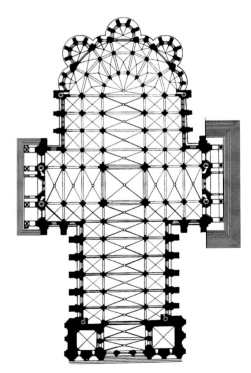

4-90   Plan of Chartres Cathedral.

4-91　West facade, Chartres Cathedral. The mismatched towers of the Chartres facade give it a distinctive personality and reveal the changing nature of the Gothic style. The shorter, transitional Romanesque-Gothic tower was completed before the fire of 1194; the elaborately decorated, fully Gothic example was not begun until 1507. For sculptures from the facade, see figure 4-99.

The Gothic cathedral is based on complex engineering principles (fig. 4-92). It is founded on the dynamic interaction/equilibrium between the outward **thrust** of the high cross vaults and the flying buttresses that contain this thrust. The desire for both height and maximum window openings led to the creation of a structure aptly described as "skeletal"; every element is manipulated to help meet these goals.

The Gothic cathedral is the result of the union of three distinct constructional elements:

Pointed arch: its design achieves a vertical emphasis, and the angle at which the sides meet at the apex focuses attention at the point of its greatest height. The pointed arch makes possible the unity of space characteristic of a Gothic structure. Since a pointed arch can rise to any height (fig. 4-93) despite its width (unlike a round arch), it can vault a **bay** of virtually any shape—such as those of Abbot Suger's ambulatory (see fig. 4-83). In addition, the outward thrust of a pointed arch is reduced, because it is more vertical than that of a rounded arch. Thus, lighter buttresses are required and larger areas of wall can be replaced with stained-glass windows.

Ribs of the vault: these not only make the vaults appear lighter, they allow for a physically lighter structure. The ribs were constructed first and because of their weight-bearing potential, the surfaces of the vault can be composed of lighter materials. These surfaces, sometimes called the **web**, or infilling, seem stretched, like a fabric or skin, between the linear, skeletal supports of the ribs.

Flying buttress: this development, by transferring the thrust and weight to an exterior support some distance from the wall, permits a lighter structure and a greater expanse of windows. In earlier architecture, heavy buttresses created by thickening parts of the wall surface cut down on the amount of light that reached the windows and gave the structure a ponderous exterior appearance.

The structural dynamics of the Gothic cathedral—which today we can analyze with computers and study through models—were explored by Gothic architects by building three-dimensional models of arches and buttresses. At times, the Gothic desire for height and lightened structure led to difficulties. At Beauvais Cathedral, the choir vaults peak at 157 feet above the floor, making the interior of the church as tall as a fifteen-story building; they collapsed due to inadequate foundations, piers, and buttressing and were rebuilt with additional supports and buttresses. A huge crossing tower—perhaps 500 feet tall—was then built, but when it collapsed, work stopped, and Beauvais today consists of little more than an apse.

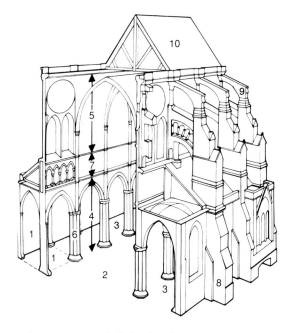

1. bay
2. nave
3. aisle
4. nave arcade
5. clerestory
6. cluster pier with colonnettes
7. triforium
8. buttress
9. flying buttress
10. wooden roof

4-92 Isometric projection and cross section showing the structure and parts of Chartres Cathedral.

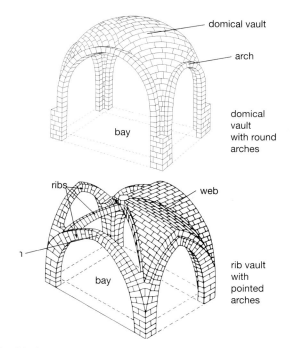

domical vault

arch

domical vault with round arches

ribs

web

bay

rib vault with pointed arches

bay

4-93 Vaults constructed using round and pointed arches. The pointed arches enable the openings on each side and the center to reach a unified height over a rectangular bay.

The French Gothic style spread rapidly, and by the mid-thirteenth century, buildings all across Europe demonstrated Gothic qualities. But local traditions, native artistic practices, and regional cultural factors often meant that these buildings also had individual characteristics. The ability of Gothic architecture to express late-medieval attitudes is revealed by its pervasive popularity as an architectural style. This is especially remarkable in light of the political connotations expressed by the Gothic style because of its origins at the French Royal Abbey Church of St.-Denis.

In England, the emphasis in religious architecture is on length rather than height, and at Salisbury (fig. 4-94) the nave, which is only 81 feet tall, is 449 feet long; on the interior a strong cornice enhances the effect of horizontality. Salisbury's nave is crossed by two transepts, a typical English development, and the climax behind the high altar is not the French polygonal apse with radiating chapels but a flat wall surface pierced by Gothic pointed windows. On the exterior, the facade, known as a screen facade because it hides the configuration of nave and side aisles, is lower and broader than French examples, and the emphasis is on the central crossing tower rather than on the two-towered western facade seen in France (see fig. 4-91).

In Italy, the Gothic arch was used for doors and windows, and the pointed, ribbed cross vault was common, but at San Francesco (fig. 4-95) the small windows and the emphasis on a continuous wall surface seem diametrically opposed to the diaphanous window walls of the French examples. In this Italian example, the wall is visually "painted away" with frescoes, rather than being physically pierced, as elsewhere. Rather than the shallow rectangular bays of the French Gothic, Italian churches often feature square or nearly square bays, and the triforium is often eliminated. Clarity replaces complexity, and there is a feeling of solid physical presence and massive bulk.

Typical of Late Gothic developments in Germany is the hall church (fig. 4-96). The aisles often reach the same height as the nave, and the piers can seem thin and insubstantial in the midst of the open and airy surrounding spaces.

None of the developments of Gothic architecture outside France has the same emphasis on engineering and structural complexity seen in the French sources; in fact, most Gothic churches outside France lack flying buttresses, and seldom do their patrons and architects desire to attain either the height or the narrowness of proportion of the French examples.

4-94 English Gothic. Exterior, Salisbury Cathedral, Salisbury, Wiltshire, England. 1220–70. The high crossing tower and the flying buttresses were added in the fourteenth century. Commissioned by the bishops of Salisbury.

4-95 Italian Gothic. Nave, San Francesco, Assisi, Umbria, Italy. 1228–53. The Church of San Francesco was begun in 1228, as soon as Saint Francis, who had died in 1226, was canonized. The walls are covered with fresco cycles of the Old and New Testaments and, on the lowest level, the life of Saint Francis. Commissioned by the Franciscan friars of Assisi.

4-96 German Gothic. Nave and choir, St. Sebald, Nuremberg, Franconia, Germany. 1361–72.

Gothic Sculpture

4-97 *BEAU DIEU*, trumeau, central portal, west facade, Cathedral of Nôtre-Dame, Amiens, Île-de-France, France. c. 1225–35. Stone. The popular name for this rather severe figure of the blessing Christ is the *Beau Dieu*, the "Beautiful Lord." Like most Romanesque and Gothic portal sculpture, this figure was original polychromed. Commissioned by the bishops of Amiens.

As in Romanesque church facades, sculpted figures populate the exterior of Gothic churches, not only on the three western portals but also on as many as six transept entrances, three on the north and three on the south, as well. The west facade at Amiens reveals how the number of figurative sculptures and the extent of applied decoration have increased (fig. 4-98). The deep porches contain rows of **jamb** and **archivolt** figures; narrative reliefs decorate many other areas. The sculptures represent figures and scenes from the Bible, including both Old and New Testaments, as well as more secular themes, such as the signs of the zodiac and the labors that the Middle Ages thought were characteristic of each month of the year. The facade as a whole is intended to represent all God's creation. Its order, as commanded by the axial figure of Christ on the trumeau, reflects the divine order of the Christian world.

The earliest Gothic portal sculptures, the *Ancestors of Christ* at Chartres (fig. 4-99), already display significant differences from their Romanesque predecessors. The elongated figures are columnar, for their restricted poses reflect the vertical columns behind them. Drapery folds fall in abstract, linear patterns unrelated to underlying anatomical structure. But these drapery patterns are unlike those of Romanesque figures, which are lively and expressive; at Chartres the drapery quietly reinforces the figures' verticality. The faces of the Chartres jamb figures, while still somewhat stylized, convey a softer and more naturalistic quality than, for example, the severe face of Christ in the tympanum at Vézelay (see fig. 4-71).

As portal sculpture developed through the Gothic period, especially during the early thirteenth century, the figures began to be sculpted in higher and higher relief and began to lose their columnar emphasis. The Amiens Christ exemplifies the increasing naturalism of

As they approached the main, western door of Amiens Cathedral, the faithful were greeted by the **trumeau** sculpture of Christ holding a book and making a gesture of blessing (fig. 4-97). The book, probably the Gospels, symbolizes Christ's words and deeds, but this image of the teaching Christ is also combined with the victorious Christ, as represented in the lion and the dragon trampled under his feet. In Christian tradi-

tion, the dragon symbolized the Devil, and in this context the lion was understood as a symbol of the Antichrist. Unlike Romanesque trumeau figures, with their lively abstract patterns, the Amiens Christ is not only naturalistic but also has a quiet and stately presence. The simple verticality of the figure echoes the inherent architectonic role of the trumeau, the drapery falls in a naturalistic manner, and Christ's face has been given a human, solemn dignity.

4-98   West facade, Amiens Cathedral. c. 1225–35. Commissioned by the bishops of Amiens.

4-99   *ANCESTORS OF CHRIST*, column figures, right jamb, central door (royal portal), west facade, Cathedral of Nôtre-Dame, Chartres, Île-de-France, France. c. 1145–55. Stone. Commissioned by the bishops of Chartres.

4-100   *VIERGE DORÉE*, trumeau figure, south portal, Amiens Cathedral. c. 1250. Stone. This sculpture is popularly known as the *Vierge Dorée* ("Gilded Virgin") because parts of the figure were originally decorated with applied gold leaf. Commissioned by the bishops of Amiens.

early-thirteenth-century Gothic sculpture, while retaining the serious dignity that characterized the jamb figures at Chartres from about eighty years earlier.

The *Vierge Dorée* at Amiens (fig. 4-100) dates about twenty years later than the Amiens Christ. Now a new, relaxed elegance characterizes the sculpture. The figural proportions are elongated, and Mary's body follows an exaggerated curve created by the tilt of the hip to support the arm holding the Christ Child. The drapery, falling in broad folds, contributes to the statue's elegance and emphasizes her sophisticated pose. A warm, affectionate smile plays across Mary's delicate face as she gazes at the child. The reverent dignity of the *Beau Dieu* and the human charm of the *Vierge Dorée* express the diverse vitality that occurs in the development of Gothic sculpture. The figures that decorate Gothic portals reintroduced monumental figural sculpture to western Europe.

4-101 *"NÔTRE DAME DE LA BELLE VERRIÈRE,"* Cathedral of Nôtre-Dame, Chartres, Île-de-France, France. 12th century (central portion); 13th century (surrounding angels). Stained glass, approx. 16′ × 7′6″. This venerated window is known as *"Nôtre Dame de la Belle Verrière"* ("Our Lady of the Beautiful Window"). The *Enthroned Virgin and Child* section that forms the central portion survived when Chartres Cathedral burned in 1194. As the cathedral was being rebuilt in the new Gothic style of the thirteenth century, the earlier window was flanked by panels with angels in a more fully Gothic style.

The brilliant contrast between the blues and reds of *"La Belle Verrière"* establishes a dynamic equilibrium, and the other colors and the black paint used to define faces, drapery, and other details enrich and dramatize the window (fig. 4-101). The glowing, gemlike windows that decorate a Gothic structure help create the ideal of the church as a metaphor for the Heavenly Jerusalem, which was described in the Bible as having foundations composed of precious stones (Revelation 21:19).

"La Belle Verrière" exemplifies two styles—the transitional style between Romanesque and Gothic and the fully mature Gothic style. The rigid axiality of Mary and the Christ Child (whose faces have been restored) is eased only slightly by the tilt of Mary's head. In contrast, the angels in the side panels are more animated, and the pieces of colored glass used to form the image have bolder, more varied colors.

Like the exterior sculptural program of a Gothic church, the figurative imagery of a stained-glass window instructed the people through symbolic imagery and narratives from the Old and New Testaments. But with stained glass, this instructive purpose was joined with a spiritual, almost mystical,

4-102 A craftsperson, making a stained-glass window, is fitting the lead strips, which in section are shaped like a sideways **H** around the glass. The original design, used to determine the shapes of the glass pieces, is visible in the foreground.

effect. On an average day, the light level outside has been measured as approximately 9,000 lumens, but the reading for the interior space of Chartres is only a few lumens; in other words, there is 1,000 times more light outside than inside. As our eyes adjust to the dark, cavernous space, a radiance of light seems to burst from the windows, where images executed in stained glass appear suspended in an aura of colored light. As light passes through these windows, it causes them to glow with a radiant richness and to cast beams and spots of color throughout the interior.

Abbot Suger wrote about how the sumptuous quality of Gothic objects brought him into the mystical presence of the divine:

> Thus, when—out of my delight in the beauty of the house of God—the loveliness of the many-colored gems has called me away from external cares, and worthy meditation has induced me to reflect, transferring that which is material to that which is immaterial, on the diversity of the sacred virtues: then it seems to me that I see myself dwelling, as it were, in some strange region of the universe which neither exists entirely in the slime of the earth nor entirely in the purity of Heaven; and that, by the grace of God, I can be transported from this inferior to that higher world in an anagogical manner.

Stained-Glass Technique

The origins of stained-glass windows, which are composed of pieces of colored glass joined by lead strips (fig. 4-102), are uncertain. Colored-glass windows and windows made of thin stone through which light could filter were already in use in Early Christian and Byzantine churches, and although stained-glass windows became more common during the Romanesque period, it was only during the Gothic period that they became a crucial and integral part of the architecture and a major means of artistic expression.

The colored glass is produced by adding metallic oxides to the molten glass (pot metal glass) or by fusing a layer of colored glass onto clear glass (flashed glass). During the late Middle Ages, the design for a window would be drawn in chalk on a flat table, then pieces of glass were cut to fit each small shape or area of the design. The details of faces and drapery were added by painting in black enamel, which was then fused to the glass by firing. The fragments of glass were assembled, with lead strips bonding them in place, over the design. Because these glass-and-lead designs were heavy, armatures of iron bands were used to strengthen and support the windows when they were installed in the church. Stained glass is one of the most radiant and vibrant media in the history of human expression.

Early Italian Painting

4-103 GIOTTO

Madonna Enthroned with Angels and Saints, from the church of Ognissanti, Florence, Tuscany, Italy. c. 1300. Tempera on wood, 10'8" × 6'8¼". Galleria degli Uffizi, Florence, Italy. Originally commissioned by an unknown patron for the Church of Ognissanti (All Saints) in Florence, this panel is sometimes called the *Ognissanti Madonna*.

GIOTTO DI BONDONE. ITALIAN, (C. 1267–1337) SCALA/ART RESOURCE

Once Cimabue thought that in painting
He commanded the field, and now Giotto has the acclaim.

As this quotation from Dante's *Divine Comedy* reveals, Cimabue (c. 1251–1302) was once the most important painter in Florence. His style represented a final statement of the Byzantine influence in Italy. Dante wrote that it was soon superseded by the revolutionary style of Giotto (1266/7– or 1276–1337), an assessment that we share with Giotto's contemporaries. A comparison between their compositions of the Madonna and Child reveals the significance of Giotto's innovations (figs. 4-103, 4-104). The scale and simple composition of Cimabue's painting create an impressive and severe effect consistent with the expressions of the faces. In contrast, Giotto reestablishes the connection between the art of painting and the nature of objective reality, an attitude not evident in painting since ancient Roman illusionism. Giotto's figures are represented as massive, weighty forms that seem to exist within a spatial continuum in which gravity is an inescapable factor. These large, bulky figures have strongly modeled, naturalistic drapery, as seen in the flowing folds of the angels kneeling in the foreground (unfortunately, the darkening of the blue of the Madonna's robe and the repainting of her knees and lap have deprived the central figure of some of its original sense of weight and presence).

The heavy marble throne of Giottos' *Madonna* seems solidly fixed in space; Cimabue's wooden throne is lighter and less rational (there are no back legs). In both Cimabue's and Giotto's panels, the figures to the sides overlap, but in Giotto's they seem to stand solidly on the ground; Cimabue's angels seem to be floating in an abstract decorative pattern.

The placement of Giotto's figures in space is clearly structured: the kneeling angels overlap the standing angels, who in turn overlap the throne; in the grouping of saints, Giotto lets some of the haloes overlap shoulders and even faces. Giotto surrounds the Madonna and Child with figures placed to create a natural, believable effect, with no loss of dignity or emphasis.

Equally important for Giotto's revolution is the new responsiveness of the figures, which even in this traditional subject is of such intensity that a dramatic effect is created. The angels respond to the impressive presence of the Madonna and Child with spontaneous expressions of awe. The Madonna and Child have neither the remoteness nor the insubstantiality seen in Byzantine art, and their parted lips and direct gazes convey a significant human presence.

Giotto's painting, with its recognition of both the physical and the psychological natures of human activity, is in direct contrast to the schematic composition and expressionless figures of Cimabue's panel. Giotto transformed the art of painting; by emphasizing the concept of the "painting as a window," he established an approach that would endure until the revolutionary experiments of Cézanne and the Cubists in the late nineteenth and early twentieth centuries (see figs. 9-79, 9-80, 10-46, 10-49).

4-104   CIMABUE

MADONNA ENTHRONED WITH ANGELS AND PROPHETS, from the high altar of Santa Trinita, Florence. c. 1285. Tempera on wood, 11'7" × 7'4". Uffizi Gallery, Florence. Tradition has it that Cimabue was the teacher of Giotto. The two Florentine painters are used by Dante to elucidate the fleeting nature of fame.

Giotto, The Arena Chapel Frescoes

4-105 GIOTTO *LAMENTATION*, fresco in the Arena Chapel, Padua, Italy. c. 1303–05. Approx. 6′ × 6′6″. The Arena Chapel was built and decorated for Enrico Scrovegni, a wealthy Paduan businessperson. It was attached to the Scrovegni Palace, which had been built on the site of the ancient Roman arena of Padua, hence the name Arena Chapel. Commissioned by Enrico Scrovegni.

4-106 GIOTTO Frescoes, Arena Chapel. The Arena Chapel has windows on only the right-hand wall, as seen in this view; the left is completely filled with the bands of narratives. Below are figures of the Virtues and Vices. High on the triumphal arch is a fresco of God sending Gabriel to earth; below, to either side, are the kneeling figures of Gabriel and the Virgin at the moment of the Annunciation and Incarnation. The vault above is decorated with blue sky, gold stars, and holy figures appearing in circular, windowlike frames. The virtues and vices appear as figures in **grisaille** (gray and white, simulating sculpture), which alternate with illusionistic marble panels on the lowest level.

As in his *Madonna* (see fig. 4-103), the figures in Giotto's *Lamentation* (fig. 4-105) offer an illusion of weight and mass not seen in painting since antiquity. At the same time, they convey a convincing drama and expression of emotion. Through gesture and placement, the composition, with its simple friezelike arrangement and sloping hillside setting, focuses attention on the dramatic core of the narrative, the heads of the Virgin and Jesus in the lower left corner. Two heavy figures seen from the back enframe this tender and private moment and communicate the tragic loss and mute pain appropriate to the agonized farewell of a mother to her son. The simple landscape of barren hill and dead tree both directs our attention to the narrative focus and expresses the sense of loss communicated by the figures. The Lamentation and the related theme of the **Pietà**, which are not mentioned in the Bible, are subjects that emerged with the demand for a more emotional religious art in the late-medieval period.

Giotto's *Lamentation* must be examined in relation to its context. In the Arena Chapel (fig. 4-106), Giotto painted a continuous cycle of scenes from the lives of the Virgin and Jesus that starts near the top and, reading left to right, spirals around to culminate in six final scenes on the left wall. The cycle as a whole has a continuous left-to-right development, and this last section begins with an exceptionally strong left-to-right movement in a representation of Jesus carrying the cross. This movement is halted by the centralized composition of the *Crucifixion*, but in the subsequent *Lamentation*, Giotto forces our attention backward and downward to the conjunction of the heads of the Virgin and Jesus. Giotto demands that we stop and concentrate on the *Lamentation*. The impact of the event is conveyed to us not only by the variety of human emotions expressed by Jesus' followers as they gather around his body but also

4-107 GIOTTO *LAST JUDGMENT*, fresco in the Arena Chapel. c. 1303–05. Approx. 33′ × 27′6″. Filling the inside of the entrance wall, and therefore the last thing viewers see as they leave, is a panoramic representation of the Last Judgment. It was intended as a visual reminder to the faithful of the divergent destinies of the blessed and the sinful.

by the reflection of these emotions in the angels who flood the sky with grief. Such a strong emphasis on experience and empathy is surely related to the preachings and writings of the followers of Saint Francis (see p. 207).

In the *Last Judgment*, Christ appears in the center, flanked by saints and angels; below, on his right side, are the blessed, while to our right are the damned (fig. 4-107). Near the center, to the left of the cross that marks the dividing line between Paradise and eternal damnation, is a representation of Enrico Scrovegni offering his chapel, represented as a model held by a monk, to the Virgin. Scrovegni's purpose in having the chapel erected and painted is thus clarified, for in making this offering he hoped to cleanse his money and that of his father; both had accumulated for-

tunes by charging exorbitant rates of interest, a sin called usury that the Church condemned. Dante chose Enrico's father as the arch-usurer, and placed him in the seventh circle of hell in his *Divine Comedy*.

There are references to virtues and vices in other areas of the chapel. They appear as figures in **grisaille** (gray and white, simulating sculpture), which alternate with illusionistic marble panels on the lowest level.

The Renaissance artist Lorenzo Ghiberti said the Arena Chapel was "one of the glories of the earth," and the modern artist Henri Matisse announced that, on looking at a scene in the Arena Chapel, "I understood at once the feeling which radiates from it, and which is instinct in the line, the composition, the color."

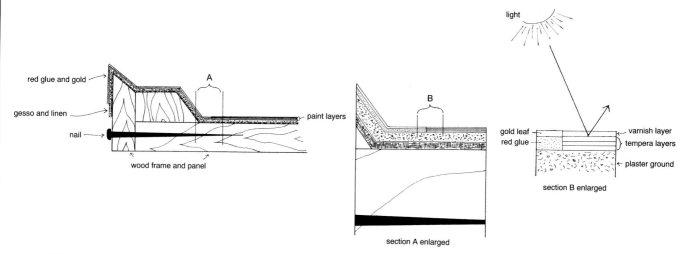

4-108 Schematic diagrams of a section of a typical late-medieval tempera painting. Tempera is opaque, and the arrow (right) suggests that light penetrates only the translucent varnish layer on the surface of the tempera (section B enlarged, far right). Notice how the frame is integral to the initial construction and not something that is added later (above). The layers of paint in these diagrams are consistently shown as regular for the purposes of clarity, but in reality layers of paint vary in thickness, as has been demonstrated by electronic microscopy examinations of slivers of paint removed from paintings.

During the fourteenth and fifteenth centuries, Giotto, Masaccio, Piero della Francesca, Mantegna, Botticelli, and other Italian artists created paintings in **tempera** and in **fresco**, two techniques that were as distinctive in appearance as they were in execution. Fresco (see pages 112–14) and tempera both have their origins in antiquity; in fourteenth-century Europe, they were well established as alternative techniques understood and used by the same artist but often for different settings and purposes.

The use of tempera paint dates back to the Egyptians. The support for tempera paint is usually wood (fig. 4-108), and large panels such as those of Giotto and Cimabue (see figs. 4-103, 4-104) are composed of planks glued together, with an integral frame constructed at the same time. To provide an appropriate surface for the paint, the wood panel was covered with linen or canvas and several layers of gesso, a fine plaster made of glue and gypsum and/or chalk. Onto this surface the painter drew preliminary designs, probably with charcoal. The final design was scratched into the plaster surface, following the outlines of the forms to be painted. Thin sheets of gold leaf were applied, using red glue, to the background areas. The paint used was composed of ground pigments combined with egg and perhaps a little vinegar. The paint, which dried quickly, was applied methodically in numerous thin coats to prevent flaking.

The finished paintings are characterized by rich colors against a luminous gold ground. Many later painters enhanced their work by elaborately decorating the gold background. Using delicate carving tools, they impressed floral and Gothic decorative patterns into the surface of the gold to create borders and halo designs that caught the light and shimmered on the reflective surface.

As in tempera painting, the creation of a fresco demanded a number of sequential steps (fig. 4-109). The work would be commissioned and a legal contract drawn up. At this point, the painter probably was advanced money to pay for the purchase of necessary materials. Small drawings might be prepared to show to the patron for approval before the contract was signed. After the contract was signed, scaffolding was erected, and a layer of rough plaster (*arriccio*) was applied over the brick or stone wall surface. To mark the subdivisions, a string soaked in red color was held up to the surface and then snapped to create horizontal and vertical guidelines. The artist then made preliminary charcoal drawings on the *arriccio*. These drawings were reinforced with pale ocher paint and the charcoal erased. The ocher painting was reinforced in *sinopia* (red paint); such full-scale compositional drawings are called *sinopie*. At this point the *sinopie* could be viewed and approved by the patron. The final layer of fine plaster (*intonaco*) was then applied.

In the true fresco technique (**buon fresco**), a patch of plaster large enough to be completed the next day is applied at the end of a day's work. Each daily patch is known as a **giornata** (Italian for "day"). The patches are usually applied in sequence, beginning with the upper left area of the wall, then moving across the top, and ending with the lower right (see fig. 5-22).

The wetness of the plaster, which changes over the course of the day, has to be taken into account by the painter. When the

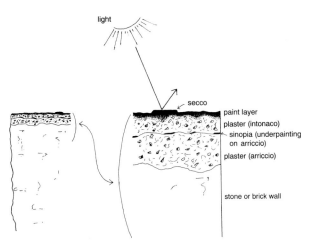

4-109 Schematic diagram of sections of a typical late-medieval fresco painting. The arrow suggests how light does not penetrate the surface of a fresco painting.

plaster is quite wet, the paint sinks into the plaster surface (up to ¼ inch) and bleaches slightly. If the artist is painting a large passage of drapery beginning in the morning and ending in the afternoon, during the later part of the day a little water must be added to the paint so that the last areas to be painted will not be darker in hue. As the plaster dries, a chemical reaction takes place: the carbon dioxide of the air combines with the calcium hydrate in the plaster, producing calcium carbonate. After all the *giornate* are painted, haloes are gilded. **Fresco secco** (color with glue in the **vehicle**—egg white or lime) is used for some details. Blue is usually applied in this fashion.

The process and the end results of fresco and tempera are different. Fresco, for example, is faster than tempera. No wooden frame has to be built and covered with fine layers of plaster, and the artist works on a large scale with a bigger brush and with a relatively thin paint that applies easily. This technique is also much cheaper than tempera, partly because of the speed involved in its execution and the fact that the materials with which the painter works are less expensive. Tempera is slower because it is a finer technique, meant to be seen close up. Because the colors dry rapidly, only one thin coat can be applied at a time, and each color must be built up in layers. Tempera works were painted in the *bottega* (shop), but frescoes had to be painted directly on the wall, where both the artist and the patron assumed they would be forever. This concept of painting in place meant that the painter frequently took into consideration the architecture and lighting of the setting.

Tempera paintings are usually brilliant in color, with deeply saturated hues, while frescoes tend to be slightly washed out, of **higher value**, and less deeply saturated because the pigment sinks into the plaster. Brighter colors are used for tempera paintings because finer pigments are employed in this medium and they are meant to be seen close up; in fresco, cheaper, more earthy pigments are used, partly because large quantities are necessary.

Tempera is more conservative; it discourages experimentation because the entire conception must be worked out before the carpenter begins to construct the panel. Fresco encourages experimentation because it is easily corrected if the artist's first effort is not acceptable: the still-damp plaster can be scraped off and the artist can start again the next day. While fresco invites spontaneity, tempera is so methodical that the artist is encouraged to be very precise. Fine detail can be emphasized, whereas frescoes are frequently high on the wall and forms are therefore suggested rather than spelled out in detail (see fig. 5-23). The fresco technique favors a broad style of painting, which is more exciting than the accuracy and precision of the tempera technique. The distance between the viewer and the painted wall also allows fresco painters to be more dramatic and to use a few prominent gestures to communicate ideas and expression. Frescoes are generally larger, the figures are usually about lifesize, and the style is often illusionistic.

Both media are durable, partly because of the care with which they are executed. Both represent careful refinements of experiments over many years, and they are technically sound. However, frescoes deteriorate if moisture seeps through from behind, and the wood support of the tempera panel can warp, crack, or rot. Another common difficulty with frescoes is that fine details painted in the *fresco secco* technique can flake away.

One motivation for an artist to work in both media is the fact that fresco painting is not feasible in the winter, when the increased humidity in Italian churches meant that the plaster did not dry quickly enough (documents survive that tell us about frescoes that grew moldy rather than drying). During the winter the painter could be busy in the *bottega*, making tempera paintings.

The Royal Art of African Kingdoms

4-110   Ife culture. *HEAD OF QUEEN OLOKUN*, from the Ife kingdom, Nigeria. 11th–15th century. Brass, height to top of ornament approx. 36″. The British Museum, London. The metal used to cast the heads found at Ife is often called bronze, but as an alloy of copper and zinc, it is more properly classified as brass. Commissioned by an Ife ruler.

4-111   Edo culture. Altar head, from the Benin kingdom, Nigeria. 17th century. Cast alloy of copper and iron, height 8¾″. National Museum of African Art, Smithsonian Institution, Washington, D.C. This head once supported a decorated tusk, as in figure 4-112. Commissioned by a Benin ruler.

4-112   Benin culture. Royal Ancestral Shrine, Benin kingdom, Nigeria. Ancestral shrines for Benin kings in the present-day palace compound display brass commemorative heads that support elaborately carved ivory tusks. Ivory was precious, its whiteness symbolizing purity and peace. The monarch, or *oba*, received one tusk from every elephant killed in the kingdom. Carved tusks, some as long as 6 feet, were also a symbol of longevity. Numerous other ritual objects rested on the altars, including cast brass bells and figurative sculpture. Commissioned by various Benin rulers.

The main subject of Ife art is the human head, rendered naturalistically but with the regularized features of an idealized portrait (fig. 4-110). The *Head of Queen Olokun* is presented with a serene and regal countenance that comes from a sculptural tradition known first in clay and then in metal. The more than 15 million Yoruba-speaking people who now live in Nigeria and the Popular Republic of Benin are the descendants of the makers of this head. They have a long history in West Africa. They were, and continue to be, one of the largest and most prolific art-producing groups of Africa.

Their urbanism is ancient and legendary, probably dating from as early as 800–1000 CE, according to excavations at two sites, Owo and Ife. These were only two of numerous city-states headed by sacred rulers (both men and women) and councils of

elders and chiefs. The city-states best known for their sculpture and cultural life were Ife, Benin, and Owo. Ife is regarded by the Yoruba as the place of origin of life itself and of human civilization, and the dynasty of kings there remains unbroken to the present day. It is probably the oldest continuous kingship in the world.

Ife, situated in the southwest of what is now Nigeria, is the oldest of these city-states. Its first settlement dates from the eighth century, but little is known about its rise to power. By 1100, artists at Ife had already developed a refined and highly naturalistic sculptural tradition in terra-cotta and stone, which was soon followed by works in copper, brass, and bronze. The terra-cotta heads and works cast in brass found at Ife are known to date between the eleventh and sixteenth centuries.

South of Ife was the kingdom of Benin, which built its capital at Benin

11th–15th century	*Head of Queen Olokun*
1167	Founding of Oxford University
1220	First giraffe is shown in Europe
1364	Aztecs build Tenochtitlán in Mexico

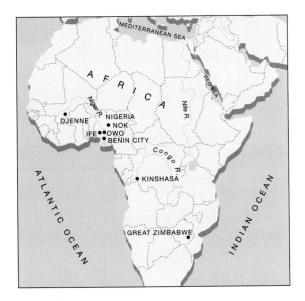

4-113 Yoruba culture. *Head of a Woman*, from Ugba' Laja site, Owo, Nigeria. 15th century. Terra-cotta, height 6⅞". Nigeria National Museum, Ile-Ifer.

City. When the Portuguese arrived there in 1485, the highly organized Benin society was headed by a wealthy and military powerful monarch called the *oba*. He lived in a large city with a regular grid pattern of tree-lined avenues. The *oba* was supported by a large aristocracy and an efficient group of bureaucrats. Artists and craftsworkers, including metal casters and ivory carvers, were organized into guilds, worked exclusively for the king, and lived in special compounds in the city. The system was maintained until 1897, when a British expedition sacked and destroyed the city. The British soldiers went to Benin City to avenge the death of an English consul who was killed when he entered the city in violation of the orders of the *oba*. The Benin leader had forbidden the visit of foreigners because he was absorbed in rituals in honor of his ancestors. The thousands of works of art taken as booty were sold in London to cover the cost of the expedition and are now in the major museums of Europe.

The art of Benin is court art, the principal aim of which was the glorifi-

cation of the ruler. Each newly enthroned *oba* ordered brass memorial heads to be cast in honor of his father (fig. 4-111). These heads are not individualized portraits intended to portray a particular monarch, but rather their function is to memorialize both one *oba* and all *obas*. They are testimonies to royal descent and were one of the six essential items (the others include wooden heads, the royal sword, brass bells, sculpted leopards, and carved ivories) to sit on the ancestral altar of the palace to emphasize the king's prestige and power (fig. 4-112). As commemorative images, they represented the enduring power of inherited leadership.

The *obas* were believed to have both divine and Edo (the local ethnic group) lineage, and all beings, whether living or spiritual, were thought to possess life force, or *ase*. Priests, initiates, diviners, rulers, and elders could learn to use *ase* for the benefit of themselves and those around them. The tangible world of the living (*aye*) interacted with the invisible realm of

the spiritual forces (*orun*), which included gods, ancestors, and spirits. The tangible and spiritual aspects of all *obas* were meant to be realized in the brass heads.

Another kingdom, Owo, maintained close ties to Ife and also experienced the powerful artistic and cultural influences of Benin City. Excavations at Ugba' Laja uncovered the ruins of a thatched-roof mudhouse, thought to be a shrine, that contained objects associated with rites of sacrifice—terra-cotta heads (fig. 4-113), incomplete small figures, fragments of larger figures and groups, ceramic pots, iron implements, and polished stone axes. In technical execution and style, the head from Ugba' Laja falls within the naturalistic tradition also characteristic of the art of their neighbors, the Ife. The vertical striations that line the face represent the scarification that was performed to signify the rite of passage to adult life. The heirs of this sculptural tradition remain active and influential as artists in West Africa today.

Bronze statue of the mythological hero Hercules defeating his enemy Antaeus, made by Antonio Pollaiuolo of Florence, probably for the Medici family, in the 1470s (for more information see figs. 5-46 and pp. 262-63).

Fifteenth-Century Art

A Brief Insight

HOW CAN A STATUE SO SMALL PACK SUCH A CULTURAL *wallop? At about a foot and a half in height, Antonio Pollaiuolo's Hercules and Antaeus is much smaller than many of the figural sculptures we have studied so far. Yet, in content and form, it speaks volumes about the Italian Renaissance.*

Two Greek mythological figures are locked in mortal combat. Hercules is lifting Antaeus off the ground, depriving him of contact with Mother Earth, his mother and the source of his strength. The strain of this struggle is evident in their anguished faces, taut muscles, and the momentary effect of the composition.

Such a naturalistic representation of human figures, caught in a physical and emotional drama, was introduced to Western art in the Hellenistic and ancient Roman periods. These attitudes toward the figure in art, reintroduced in fifteenth-century Italy, helped to establish the foundation for the cultural epoch known as the Renaissance. In addition, both the theme of the work, from Classical mythology, and the intent to imitate bronze statuettes found in ancient tombs, contribute even further to its character as a Renaissance work. Clearly, a work of art need not be grand in size to have a monumental effect. ⌒

Fifteenth-Century Art

5-1   PIERO DELLA FRANCESCA

RESURRECTION. c. 1460. Fresco approx. 8′ × 6′6″; the figures are approx. lifesize. Pinacoteca, Sansepolcro, Italy.
Commissioned by the chief magistrates of Sansepolcro for their state chamber.

Many of the artistic developments in European art that occurred in the fifteenth century in Italy and Flanders can be seen in *Resurrection* (fig. 5-1) by Piero della Francesca (c. 1420–92) and *Deposition* (fig. 5-2) by Rogier van der Weyden (1399?–1449). Both are large, with lifesize figures, and offer a **naturalism** not seen in painting since the time of the ancient Romans. The figures are realistically proportioned, seem to have weight and to occupy illusionistic space, and suggest the potential for movement. In addition, they are charged with emotional and psychological tensions that demand a response from the viewer. Piero's resurrected Christ fixes us with a com-

5-2 ROGIER VAN DER WEYDEN

DEPOSITION. c. 1435–38. Oil on wood, 7'2⅝" × 8'7⅛". Prado, Madrid. The symbol of the commissioning guild, the crossbow, is used for a decoration in the side spandrels. Commissioned by the Crossbowmen's Guild of Louvain for the Church of Nôtre-Dame hors-les-murs.

pelling gaze, while in Rogier's painting waves of emotion sweep through the followers as they receive the body lowered from the cross. They weep, convulse, and faint.

Nevertheless, significant differences between the two works suggest the artistic and cultural distinctions between Italy and Flanders at this time: it is during the fifteenth century that we begin to find the development of sharply different traditions within Europe. Piero's Christ is like a Greek god—his handsome musculature and dignified bearing can be compared to the Apollo from Olympia (see fig. 3-54). Such an interest in classical motifs and types is seldom found in Flemish painting. Piero's forceful triangular composition, with Christ's head at the apex and the sleeping soldiers grouped below, reveals the Italian concern with harmony and order. Rogier's composition is much more visually complex, and its flowing forms weave a pattern of pathos and despair. This concentration is reinforced by Rogier's Flemish attention to precise detail, made possible by new developments in oil painting (see pages 258–59).

Fifteenth-Century Developments

In fifteenth-century Europe, the foundations were being laid for many of the developments that help explain later Western attitudes. In fact, the fifteenth through seventeenth centuries have been called the "Early Modern" period in the study of Western history. Because so much of the Western world view has its origins then, European artistic developments of this time must be discussed in some detail.

There were continuing developments in—and increasingly important contacts among—all parts of the world in the fifteenth century. The explosion of publications in the West (the first printed edition of Marco Polo's *Description of the World* was published in Germany in 1477) inspired interest in the other cultures, and Columbus's explorations in 1492 were to lead to extensive contacts between Europe and the Americas in the sixteenth century.

While western Europe was undergoing rapid developments and changes in the form and content of its art, Asian art was characterized by the continuation of earlier forms,

5-3   Tibet, School of the Ngor Monastery. *MANDALA OF JNANADAKINI*. Late 15th century. Opaque watercolor on cloth, 33¼ × 28⅞″. The Metropolitan Museum of Art, New York.

especially within the Buddhist tradition that had, by this time, spread from its origins in India throughout most of Asia. The form of the fifteenth-century *Mandala of Jnanadakini* from Tibet (fig. 5-3), for example, follows that of centuries-old examples, but the use of brilliant color is typical of Tibetan art in the fifteenth century. *Mandala* means "circle," and this Buddhist symbol for the structure

of the universe was used for meditation and to introduce devotees to a higher spiritual order. A mandala can be painted, as here, or made in colored sand, or used as the basis for the Buddhist temple design, as in the substructure of the stupa at Sanchi (see fig. 3-88) or as at Borobudur, in Java (see fig. 4-56). In this Tibetan example, the center is controlled by a *dakini*, a female demigod who represents the

CHAPTER 5   Fifteenth-Century Art

absolute principle in Buddhist cosmology. The four quadrants represent the four directions; four cosmic Buddhas, each a different color, preside over the four quadrants. The geometric harmony of this Tibetan mandala has formal similarities with the design of many Italian works of the fifteenth century, creating an unexpected aesthetic parallel between works created in two diverse, unrelated cultures.

In East Asia during this period, China under the Ming dynasty (1368–1644) was the most stable political entity. The arts were used to revive and reassert the stability of Chinese traditions. Early in the century, architects designed much of the layout of Beijing, including the Temples of Heaven and Earth and the palace known as the Forbidden City. The symmetry and balance of these plans reveal the stability and power of the Chinese imperial authority at this time, while the design also communicates a cosmological order traditional in China. In Japan, the fifteenth century was a period of constant warfare and absence of central authority, although the trades and arts continued to flourish during these troubled times. It was during this period that Zen Buddhism became dominant in Japanese religious and intellectual life. There was a renewed interest by the Japanese in Chinese culture, perhaps because of the stability that China represented in Asia.

The Idea of a Renaissance

Our use of the term *Renaissance* (French for "rebirth") is drawn from a conception of history found in the writings of the sixteenth-century Italian painter, architect, and writer Giorgio Vasari, whose historical fame rests primarily on his *Lives of the Most Eminent Painters, Sculptors, and Architects* (1550, 1568), a history of Italian art and artists. Vasari champions the work of ancient Greece and Rome, describing medieval art as a "disastrous decline," and argues that in Italy during the fifteenth and sixteenth centuries

> art has been reborn and reached perfection in our own times.

Vasari's concept influenced the French historian Jules Michelet, who in 1855 gave the title *La Renaissance* to a volume of his *Histoire de France* and thereby extended the idea of the Renaissance to embrace a cultural phenomenon that included northern Europe. Michelet's Renaissance was characterized by "the discovery of the world and the discovery of man." The reasons behind the appeal of antiquity in this period are not easy to simplify, but the richness and splendor of antique monuments, even in ruins, had had an impact throughout the Middle Ages, and as society and economic life blossomed at the end of the medieval period, such monuments provided appropriate models for new construction. The new self-confidence expressed in politics, business, and learning in the fifteenth century found important models and inspiration not only in ancient texts but also

in ancient sculpture, especially the Greek emphasis on the dignity and beauty of the human figure and the Roman ability to capture the individual in portraiture.

For Italian Renaissance artists, the models of classical antiquity provided an impetus for artistic transformation, but it would be a mistake to view these artists as merely copying ancient works of art. They adapted the classical aesthetic to the attitudes of their own times, creating works of art distinctly different from those of antiquity. This "rebirth" of the antique encompassed not only works of art, but also the recovery of ancient texts and classical literary style. Leonardo Bruni, a diplomat and scholar versed in Latin and Greek (see fig. 5-4), is characteristic of the new scholarship in his careful reading of antique texts and his application of ancient civic values to his own time, which led to a new historical consciousness fundamental to the growth of Renaissance humanism (see pages 232–33).

Naming the Styles

The transition from the late Middle Ages to the Renaissance in the cosmopolitan European centers of Flanders and Italy was a gradual one, and many aspects of Renaissance society and art evolved slowly from medieval traditions. Historians still debate if fifteenth-century Flemish painting is best understood as a late manifestation of the Gothic or as a Northern version of the Renaissance. Because neither *Gothic* nor *Renaissance* is a completely appropriate term for these Flemish works, they are here identified under an independent designation: fifteenth-century Flemish painting. In Italy, and especially in Florence, new Renaissance ideas dominate the production of art during most of the fifteenth century. This period is generally known as the Early Renaissance, to distinguish it from the late fifteenth and early sixteenth centuries, when the culmination of earlier ideas resulted in the period called the High Renaissance (see page 286).

History

As our introductory paintings reveal, much of the artistic activity of western Europe during the fifteenth century was centered in Florence and Flanders. Scholar Leonardo Bruni praised Florence as

> the new Athens on the Arno.

He likened the civic values of his time to those fostered in democratic Athens and in Rome during the Republic. Although Bruni praised Florentine republicanism, contrasting it to the despotic rule in other Italian city-states, in actuality Florence was led by an oligarchy of commercial interests. The Florentine government was eventually dominated by the Medici family, whose wealth was derived from banking and commerce. Beginning with Cosimo de' Medici, the family consolidated the reins of power behind a facade of republicanism.

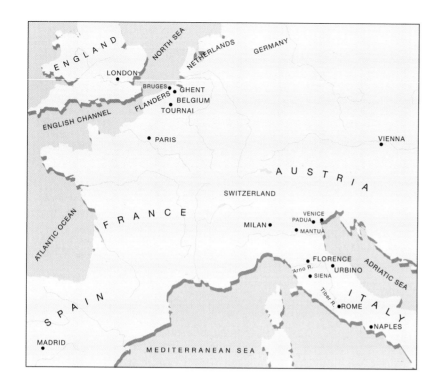

5-4 BERNARDO ROSSELLINO

TOMB OF LEONARDO BRUNI, c. 1445. Marble with traces of paint and gilding, height to top of arch 20′. Santa Croce, Florence, Italy. Commissioned by the Signoria of Florence or the College and Council of Arezzo.

His descendants firmly tightened their political control, and Lorenzo ("Lorenzo the Magnificent") ultimately ruled as a benevolent tyrant. Toward the end of the century, the domination of the Medici and the conspicuous wealth and humanist interests of the Florentine citizenry were challenged by the fiery sermons of the Dominican Friar Girolamo Savonarola. Following the exile of the Medici in 1494, Savonarola assisted in restoring a more representative form of government. But as Savonarola continued to act as the harsh conscience of Florence, the Church and some of the citizenry turned against him, and he was executed for heresy in 1498. Florence maintained her republic until 1512, when the Medici again regained control.

In Flanders, an area roughly equivalent to present-day Belgium, a prosperous new merchant society based on the wool trade and banking was established during the fourteenth and fifteenth centuries. The flourishing city of Bruges was the most important center, and the presence of foreign bankers, such as the Medici from Florence, made it the banking capital of northern Europe. Other important centers included Ghent and Tournai. As in Italy, trade guilds controlled manufacturing, as well as the production of works of art.

Flanders was distinguished by a rich and diverse culture, which included a revolutionary school of composers that dominated European musical developments throughout the century. Northern intellectuals, however, were not very interested in the revival of the forms and subject matter of ancient Greece and Rome that were so important to the Italians, and in Flanders some arts, especially architecture and the decorative arts, remained Gothic well into the sixteenth century.

Italian Renaissance Humanism

The Renaissance concept of humanism (as distinct from the modern concepts of humanitarianism and secular humanism) had a profound philosophical foundation. The title *humanist* was originally applied to a teacher of humanistic studies, a curriculum that included rhetoric, grammar, poetry, history, and moral philosophy; at the base of many of these disciplines was the study of ancient texts on these topics in Latin and, eventually, in Greek as well. Already in the fourteenth century, scholars and writers had been inspired by the ideas they found in ancient Greek and Roman texts, which confirmed their new intellectual and scientific interest in understanding the world. The praise for the deeds of great figures from antiquity that the humanists found in the Greek and Roman texts supported the notions of pride and fame that were becoming important in a society whose major figures were successful business entrepreneurs and bankers. During this period, humanism was, with some effort, integrated with

Christianity; it sought to supplement faith by insisting on the dignity of the individual and the human potential for achievement. Although the development of humanism was centered in Florence, by mid-century most of the important courts in northern Italy had been significantly influenced by humanism.

Humanist values are visually exemplified on the Tomb of Leonardo Bruni (fig. 5-4), the Florentine diplomat and champion of humanist education. An effigy of the deceased Bruni rests atop a bier supported by two eagles, standards of ancient Rome. Crowned with laurel, the ancient symbol of honor and victory, and with his hands embracing the book he wrote, *History of the Florentine People*, Bruni lies eternally in state. On the sarcophagus below is a Latin inscription in classical lettering:

> At Leonardo's passing, history grieves, eloquence is mute, and it is said that the Muses, Greek and Latin alike, cannot hold back their tears.

These antique literary references are reinforced by the classicizing architecture of the tomb. The Corinthian pilasters and round arch may refer to the ancient Roman triumphal arch (see fig. 3-102). Over the arch, two putti hold aloft Bruni's coat of arms. The relief of the Virgin and Child within the arch is the only reference to Christianity. Such a union of ancient traditions and Christian theology was one of the primary goals of humanism. It had an influence on many works of art, including Botticelli's *Birth of Venus* (see fig. 5-60)

Italian Renaissance Art Theory

Humanism played an important role in the development of art theory. Leon Battista Alberti, well educated in humanistic studies, was attracted to the new work of such Florentine artists as Filippo Brunelleschi, Donatello, and Masaccio. He noted that these artists revived classical art, and using a literary approach that joined his knowledge of the principles of classical poetry and rhetoric, he wrote about the new art in *De pictura (On Painting)* in 1435. This cornerstone of Western art theory discusses the noble purpose of painting, the painter as an educated professional, and the use of mathematical principles, including scientific perspective (see pages 248–49), in painting. *On Painting* gave art and artists a new dignity and opened the way for a new level of literary discussions on art.

The Union of the Classical and the Natural

Natural observation, an important feature of fifteenth-century art, was addressed by the late medieval artist Cennino Cennini in his practical manual for painters, *The Craftsman's Handbook*, written c. 1400. He recommended learning to draw from works of recognized masters:

5-5 DONATELLO

Equestrian monument of Erasmo da Narni (*GATTAMELATA*). c. 1445–53. Bronze, originally with gilded details, height 12′2″. Piazza del Santo, Padua. Erasmo da Narni was a famous mercenary general who was employed by the Venetian government to raise and lead its armies; his nickname, Gattamelata, means "honeyed cat." Commissioned by the Venetian Senate.

> Now you must forge ahead again, so that you may pursue the course of this theory. . . . Having first practiced drawing for a while . . . take pains and pleasure in constantly copying the best things which you can find done by the hand of the great masters.

Having established the importance of studying great works, Cennini turned to nature:

> Mind you, the most perfect steersman that you can have, and the best helm, lie in . . . copying from nature. And this outdoes all other models; and always rely on this with a stout heart, especially as you begin to gain some judgment in draftsmanship.

To the Renaissance artist, copying from nature led not only to the heightened perception gained from meticulous observation but also to an attempt to understand the principles that govern the order and processes of nature.

5-6 PEIRO DELLA FRANCESCA

BATTISTA SFORZA AND FEDERIGO DA MONTEFELTRO. 1474. Oil and tempera on wood, each 18½ × 13". Galleria degli Uffizi, Florence. Federigo da Montefeltro ruled Urbino from 1444 until 1482. His wife, Battista Sforza, bore him eight daughters and one son. Federigo was a soldier and a prolific patron of artists and architects. Probably commissioned by Federigo da Montefeltro.

This sympathy with the natural word was a decisive aspect of Renaissance art.

The equestrian monument *Gattamelata* (fig. 5-5), by Donatello (c. 1386/90–1466), combines naturalistic observation with a well-known antique type, as exemplified by the *Marcus Aurelius* (see fig. 3-101). An ambitious feat of bronze casting, it was the largest sculpture cast in bronze since antiquity. With the bronze *David* (see fig. 5-47), probably commissioned for the Medici Palace courtyard (see fig. 5-43), Donatello revived the lifesize, freestanding, nude figure. The acceptance of nudity in art is related to the humanist insistence on the dignity of the individual and the view that the human figure is a microcosm of the macrocosm, a smaller, symbolic reflection of the larger universe.

European Intellectual Activity

The Gutenberg Bible—the first complete book to be printed using independent, movable type—was made between 1450 and 1456. By 1460, woodcuts were being used for illustrations in books; as an inexpensive method of producing illustrated books in large quantity, they contributed to the development of sciences. Knowledge was more easily shared when a printed illustration could offer an exactly repeatable image, unchanged by the hand of a copyist. Through the medium of printing, knowledge reached a level of circulation only recently surpassed by modern media, with the computer and the internet.

Changing Patterns of Patronage in Europe

During the fifteenth century, artists and workshops received a variety of secular and religious commissions. Rulers continued to employ works of art for the traditional purposes of exalting and consolidating their power, but now their imagery more often had an ancient basis and/or was inspired by models from antiquity. A relatively new development is patronage by city governments in the Italian communes and patronage by the mercantile class in Flanders and Italy; based on the writings of the humanists, patronage was now viewed as an important activity of the responsible and enlightened citizen. While devotional images were produced in increasing numbers to adorn the rooms of the expanding middle class, new types of art—portraits, mythological subjects, and secular decorations—were commissioned by individuals to adorn their private palaces, town houses, or country villas. In many instances, patrons and family members were represented in the wings or at the sides of works they commissioned (see fig. 5-18).

In Florence, Cosimo de' Medici was generous in his support of libraries. He took an avid interest in the art of Donatello, and his patronage of scholars helped support the formulation of Neoplatonism, a complex humanist philosophy that sought to fuse Plato's ideals with Christian thinking by emphasizing how the spiritual aspects of life can overcome physical limitations. Cosimo's grandson Lorenzo the Magnificent collected antique works of art and encouraged commissions for Florentine artists; he was also a good friend and supporter of the young Michelangelo. Such involvement with the arts was not solely altruistic, for support of humanist scholarship and the arts demonstrated benevolence and was useful in forming public opinion and securing fame.

Rulers often commissioned portraits. Piero della Francesca gave his patrons, the rulers of Urbino (fig. 5-6), an almost omnipotent presence. They seem elevated above everyday affairs, and the broad landscape backgrounds suggest the extent to ducal power. On the reverse, they are shown on triumphal carts surrounded by allegorical figures that represent Virtues.

The Fifteenth-Century Artist in Europe

The dignity of the individual and the new self-consciousness promoted by the humanists had an important influence on attitudes about artists. In contrast to the prevalent medieval attitude that the artist was a humble craftsperson serving God, some Renaissance artists were viewed as trained intellectuals, versed in the classics and geometry. Artists became famous; in 1481, for example, an author named Cristoforo Landino made a list of Italian and Flemish artists and praised them for their skill and innovations; he even suggested that Donatello could be "counted among" the ancient masters—the highest praise possible at the time. Artists began to sign their works with more frequency, and one artist, Lorenzo Ghiberti, wrote his autobiography. The modern ideal of the artist as a genius has its origins in these developments in the fifteenth century.

During the first half of the fifteenth century, Flemish and Italian artists began to create self-portraits, a sure indication of their new status. In 1433 Jan van Eyck depicted a man wearing a fantastic turban—a tour de force of painting—and looking out at us with an especially penetrating gaze (fig. 5-7). On the frame are van Eyck's motto ("The best I

5-7 JAN VAN EYCK

SELF PORTRAIT? 1433. Oil on wood, 10¼ × 7½". The National Gallery, London. Because of the acute gaze and the motto on the frame, this painting often has been identified as the artist's self-portrait.

5-8 LORENZO GHIBERTI

SELF-PORTRAIT, from the East Doors of the Baptistery (see fig. 5-33), Florence. 1425–52. Gilded bronze, approx. height 3'. Museo dell' Opera dell Duomo, Florence. Commissioned by the Opera of the Baptistery and the Arte di Calimala.

can do") and the date. Artists even began to include self-portraits within their works. Lorenzo Ghiberti's "Gates of Paradise" (see fig. 5-33) have both a self-portrait (fig. 5-8) and a self-promoting inscription that praises the "marvelous art" with which Ghiberti made the work.

5-9 BALDOVINETTI

PORTRAIT OF A YOUNG WOMAN, C. 1465
(for more information see fig. 5-48).

5-10 MINO DA FIESOLE

PORTRAIT OF PIERO DE' MEDICI, 1453 (for more information see fig. 5-51).

These two portraits of fifteenth-century individuals are just two of hundreds of such portraits produced during the century in Italy and Northern Europe. This phenomenon reveals a new social development—an interest in an individual who is living and working in the world—that is characteristic of the Renaissance and helps mark this period as the beginning of the modern world. While both portraits reveal individualized features, the woman remains anonymous and her treatment is basically decorative, while the bust of the man is identified with the sitter's name and age, the year of the portrait, and the signature of the artist. Portraiture as an art offers the sitter and/or the artist the possibility of "improving" the actual appearance of the sitter; whether this has been done is, however, after time difficult to determine. Of greater interest to the historian is what a sculpted or painted portrait tells us about the attitude toward the individual in society at the time when it was made.

5-11 *PORTRAIT OF QUEEN HATSHEPSUT,*
Ancient Egyptian, C. 1478–1458 BCE
(for more information see fig 3-14 and p. 45).

In most early cultures, portraiture was limited to rulers, such as this image of an Egyptian Queen, or to aristocrats. Like many ruler portraits, there is a greater emphasis on indications of Hatshepsut's rank than there is on the queen as a specific individual.

5-12   JULIA CAMERON
ALFRED LORD TENNYSON, 1865
(for more information see fig. 9-57).

The invention and development of photography in the nineteenth century caused a disruption for the many artists who expected to continue to earn a reasonable living producing portraits of the wealthy and members of the emerging middle class. Julia Cameron is already using photography as a creative medium, and rather than merely snapping the famous British poet, she sets up a composition that seems to emphasize the inward nature of his inspiration.

5-13   JACOB LAWRENCE   *SELF-PORTRAIT,* 1977
(for more information see fig. 10-22).

Like many twentieth-century works, Jacob Lawrence's *Self-Portrait* sets out to establish an immediate communication with the viewer. The painter is close to us and looks out toward us as he rubs his chin in a traditional gesture of thoughtfulness. It's almost as if he's wondering how he might paint *our* portrait.

QUESTIONS

1. Study a painted or photographic portrait of a living individual in a magazine or newspaper; is the portrait composed or treated in such a way that it emphasizes certain characteristics of the individual?

2. How might your own portrait—photographed, painted, or sculpted—be contrived to emphasize specific qualities about yourself that you would like to communicate?

3. Would this portrait be intended for your contemporaries, or for the future?

Early Renaissance Sculpture in Florence

5-14 DONATELLO

SAINT MARK, from Orsanmichele, Florence. c. 1411–14. Marble, originally with some polychromy and metal details, height 7'10". This statue of the Evangelist is shown in its original Gothic setting in the Guild of Linen Weavers and Peddlers' niche—one of fourteen niches assigned to Florentine trade guilds—on the civic granary and shrine of Orsanmichele. Instead of the usual geometric base traditionally used for figures sculpted in stone (see fig. 3-72), here Donatello suggests that St. Mark is standing on a pillow, a device that increases the illusion that the figure could step out of his niche and into our world. Notice the symbol of the winged lion on the niche itself; this is a symbol of St. Mark. Commissioned by the Guild of Linen Weavers and Peddlers.

onatello's *Saint Mark* (fig. 5-14) overlooks a Florentine street, surveying the urban scene with an expression that conveys a questioning intelligence. It is reported that when Michelangelo saw the work he proclaimed

> that he had never seen a figure which had more the air of a good man than this one, and that if Saint Mark were such a man, one could believe what he had written.

In other words, for Michelangelo the *Saint Mark* expressed integrity. In medieval art, the evangelists had been depicted as figures receiving divine inspiration (see fig. 4-52). Donatello's Renaissance interpretation emphasizes the more human attributes of wisdom and reason. In addition, Donatello's *Saint Mark* attains the dignity we accord an individual, for in physiognomy and body type he suggests a specific, compelling personality. The revival of antiquity, so important for the Italian Renaissance, is readily apparent, for *Saint Mark* is closer to ancient Greek and Roman figures than any figure created during the long interval of the Middle Ages. The emphatic **contrapposto** of the saint, which helps establish his naturalism, was influenced by ancient examples (see fig. 3-72).

The *Four Saints* (see fig. 5-15), on the same civic structure as *Saint Mark*, represents Christian stone carvers who, during the late Roman Empire, were put to death when they refused to make an a idol of Roman god. Their serious demeanor and the open mouth and oratorical gesture of the figure on the right suggest their sculptor, Nanni di Banco (c. 1385–1421), has depicted the moment in their legend when they debate whether to compromise their religious beliefs by making the idol or submit to death. Nanni's inspiration from ancient Roman models is obvious in the heads, one of which has a stubbly beard carved in a Roman manner, and in the drapery folds of the togas. Although such an interest is consistent with Renaissance attitudes, Nanni's antique references could also be viewed as part of his effort to establish historical veracity. What could be more appropriate than to emulate ancient Roman models when creating representations of figures who had lived in the late antique period? The new Renaissance respect for historical accuracy may thus have played a role in the conception of this sculptural group.

5-15 NANNI DI BANCO

FOUR SAINTS. c. 1410s. Marble, height 6'. Orsanmichele Florence. Commissioned by the Guild of Sculptors and Stone Masons for its niche at Orsanmichele. The four figures on the base seem to represent the activities of the various members of the commissioning guild, including laying stone, carving architectural details, and sculpting figures, in this case a nude putto or baby angel. Recent cleaning has revealed that the stone on which the large figures seem to be standing is a veined grey stone and not the white marble used for the figures; this supports the suggestion that the figures could step out of their niche, as is also indicated by the manner in which feet and drapery project forward over the edge, into the spectator's space.

Flemish Painting:
The Limbourg Brothers

5-16 THE LIMBOURG BROTHERS

FEBRUARY, calendar page from the
*TRÈS RICHES HEURES DU DUC DE
BERRY*. Before 1416. Manuscript
painting on vellum, 11⅜" × 8¼". Musée
Condé, Chantilly, France. This
manuscript is listed in an early
inventory as "The Very Rich Hours of
the Duke of Berry." The patron was
John, duke of Berry (and brother of
Charles V of France), whose library
included more than 300 manuscripts.
The artists were three brothers—Pol,
Herman, and Jean Limbourg. The
calendar pages, which traditionally
accompany the listing of saints' feast
days, included the labors of the month
and zodiac signs with various
astrological calculations.
Commissioned by John, duke of
Berry. GIRAUDON/ART RESOURCE, NY

The puff of frosty breath from the mouth of the figure hurrying across the farmyard and the smoke curling from the chimney are the kinds of subtle details that characterize the comprehensive realism developing in Flemish painting at the beginning of the fifteenth century (fig. 5-16). The traditional calendar page for February showed people sitting by a fire, but the Limbourg brothers' representation encompasses a modest farm, complete with dovecote, beehives, and sheepfold, set within a vast snowy landscape with a distant village. Several figures reveal the peasants' restricted winter activities. The sky is no longer merely a flat blue background, but offers atmospheric midwinter effects that reveal the Limbourgs' study of natural phenomena.

The Limbourgs' attention to the naturalistic effects also extends to biblical stories. Taking inspiration from the passage in Matthew's Gospel that, at the time of the crucifixion, "there was darkness over all the land" (27:45), they created a panoramic crucifixion scene in tones of gray that suggest the naturalistic effects of an eclipse (fig. 5-17). In a blaze of gold, blue, and red, God the Father appears to bless his dying son. In the top right roundel, an astronomer surveys the heavens, searching for an explanation for this unexpected phenomenon.

The *Très Riches Heures* marks a final phase in the development of manuscript painting in the North (for earlier examples of medieval manuscripts, see figs. 4-26, 4-37, 4-38, 4-52, 4-61). This sumptuous manuscript, with 130 illustrations, includes devotions for different periods of the day in a format that is called a book of hours, thus the book's name. The heightened interest in representing naturalistic lighting effects, panoramic landscapes, and precise details explains why this manuscript has been so admired and its compositions so often copied by later artists.

| Before 1416 | Limbourg Brothers, *Très Riches Heures* |
| 1417 | Movable type is used by printers at Antwerp |

5-17 THE LIMBOURG BROTHERS.

CRUCIFIXION IN THE DARKNESS OF THE ECLIPSE, from the *TRÈS RICHES HEURES DU DUC DE BERRY*. Before 1416. Manuscript painting on vellum, 11⅜ × 8¼". Musée Condé, Chantilly, France.

Flemish Painting: Robert Campin

5-18 ROBERT CAMPIN

ANNUNCIATION WITH PATRONS AND SAINT JOSEPH IN HIS WORKSHOP c. 1425–30. Oil on wood, 25¼ × 24⅞″ (center); 25¼ × 10¾″ (each wing). The Metropolitan Museum of Art, New York The Cloisters Collection, 1956. The patron who commissioned this work is represented kneeling in the left wing; his wife, beside him, has been painted over the green grass, suggesting that she was added after the picture was finished, probably at the time of their marriage. It was perhaps at this same time that Campin made the work even more realistic by painting over the gold leaf that had originally filled the central windows, substituting sky, clouds, and coats of arms in the stained-glass windows indicating that the patron was a member of the Ingelbrechts family. This work is often referred to as the *Mérode Altarpiece* because it was owned by the Mérode family during the nineteenth century. Robert Campin is sometimes known as the Master of Flémalle. Commissioned by a member of the Ingelbrechts family.

ROBERT CAMPIN (ACTIVE BY 1406-DIED 1444), *THE ANNUNCIATION*. TRIPTYCH. OIL ON WOOD. CENTRAL PANEL: H. 25¼ IN. × W. 24 ⅞ IN (64.1 × 63.2 CM). EACH WING: H. 25⅜ IN. × W. 10⅞ IN. (64.5 × 27.3 CM). THE METROPOLITAN MUSEUM OF ART, THE CLOISTERS COLLECTION, 1956. (56.70) PHOTOGRAPH (C) 1996 THE METROPOLITAN MUSEUM OF ART.

This folding **triptych**, or three-part devotional picture (fig. 5-18), represents a further development of the revolutionary new qualities evident in Flemish manuscript painting at the beginning of the fifteenth century (see figs. 5-16, 5-17). Perhaps most startling is the precision with which its artist, Robert Campin (documented from 1406, died 1444), rendered objects and figures. Naturally lit, they are modeled with subtle transitions from light to shadow that make them seem three-dimensional and weighty. This naturalism results from the union of

the fine detail of oil paint with a revolutionary precision of observation on the part of the artist (see pages 258–59). It almost seems as if no artist had ever seen shadows with such clarity before—certainly no artist had ever rendered them so precisely. Such naturalism demands intense concentration in both vision and technique.

Accompanying this naturalism of representation is the realistic depiction of the subject, for a biblical event from the distant past is represented as if it had taken place in a fifteenth-century Flemish house.

Gabriel enters to announce to a distinctly Flemish Mary that she will be the mother of the son of God, while Mary's husband Joseph, a carpenter, is shown in a fifteenth-century workshop in the right wing. Campin's depiction of this setting offers valuable evidence about woodworkers' shops and tools, including a folding shelf on which Joseph offers a mousetrap for sale directly from his shop. As secular as this may seem, locating the Annunciation within a contemporary setting is intended to make the sacred events more comprehensible and meaningful. Such an

c. 1422	England resumes war with France
c. 1425–30	Campin, *Annunciation*
1427	Thomas à Kempis, *The Imitation of Christ*

approach to religious **iconography** is paralleled in popular devotional literature and is probably also related to the representation of such subjects in contemporary religious theater.

To understand Campin's interpretation, we must look beyond the dazzling surface realism, since pervasive symbolism (sometimes called "disguised symbolism") gives a religious content to virtually every object in the painting. The three lily blossoms on a single stalk that decorate the Virgin's table, for example, refer to the Christian Trinity; the bud is Christ. An especially intriguing symbol is Joseph's mousetrap, for it expresses the late-medieval notion that God married the Virgin to a devout older man to prevent the Devil from discovering that her child was the Son of God; in such an explanation Joseph became a "mousetrap" set by God.

The candle on the Virgin's table (fig. 5-19), just extinguished, releases a puff of smoke that suggests that the painting represents a precise moment in time. Light is a common metaphor for divinity, and the light of the Virgin's candle is extinguished because of the entry into the room (and into the world) of divine light in the person of Christ, who appears as a minuscule baby entering on rays of light through a round window on the left. The candle might also refer to the late-medieval custom of the bridal candle, which was extinguished when the marriage was consummated, or to the symbolism of the extinguished candle as an indication that a vow has been fulfilled. The blowing out of the candle and the presence of Christ within the Virgin's chamber would then express the moment of the Incarnation. Notice that this religious content is expressed by everyday objects and that, in keeping with his naturalistic

5-19 ROBERT CAMPIN

ANNUNCIATON, detail.

ROBERT CAMPIN (ACTIVE BY 1406–DIED 1444), *THE ANNUNCIATION.* TRIPTYCH. OIL ON WOOD. CENTRAL PANEL: H. 25¼ IN. × W. 24⅞ IN (64.1 × 63.2 CM), EACH WING: H. 25⅜ IN. × W. 10¾ IN. (64.5 × 27.3 CM). THE METROPOLITAN MUSEUM OF ART, THE CLOISTERS COLLECTION, 1956. (56.70) PHOTOGRAPH (C) 1996 THE METROPOLITAN MUSEUM OF ART.

bias, Campin has not used haloes for his figures.

Robert Campin's style is known from a small number of paintings, all of which are similar in their use of ordinary people as models, their depiction of drapery with sharp, rather abstracted folds, and their crowded compositions, which avoid empty spaces (*horror vacui*). The use of ordinary people and an everyday setting can be related to a revolution in 1423 in Tournai, where

Campin lived. A new democratic government, led by representatives of the craft guilds, was established. This democratic, mercantile culture helps to explain the middle-class setting and virtues of Campin's Annunciation triptych, with its delight in a typical household and the inclusion of Joseph as a hardworking husband and father.

Italian Renaissance Painting: Masaccio

5-20 MASACCIO

THE TRINITY WITH THE VIRGIN MARY, SAINT JOHN, AND TWO DONORS, fresco in Santa Maria Novella, Florence. c. 1425–28. 21'10½" × 10'5"; the figures are approximately lifesize. On the vertical axis, God the Father holds the cross, presenting his crucified son to us. A flying dove, symbol of the Holy Spirit, hovers between their heads. At the foot of the cross stand Mary and John the Evangelist; Mary's gesture and outward glance engage our attention. The kneeling profile figures are the donors who commissioned the painting. Their identity remains uncertain, although he wears the red robe of a Florentine official. The bottom portion of the painting contains a skeleton resting on a ledge. Above the skeleton, an inscription in classical lettering reads: "I was once what you are; what I am, you will be." The inclusion of the skeleton and the inscription add a *memento mori* (a reminder that all must die) context to the theme. Such references to human mortality were popular in the fourteenth and fifteenth centuries, when plagues often ravaged the populace.

The triangle, symbol of the Trinity, becomes the unifying compositional form in *The Trinity with the Virgin Mary, Saint John, and Two Donors* (fig. 5-20) by Masaccio (1401–28). With the head of God the Father forming the apex and the donors comprising the base, the triangular composition, popular in the Early Renaissance, is visually clear and easy to read. This clarity is supported by the illusionary space created by the use of **scientific perspective** (see pages 248–49). To the viewer positioned in front of the painting, the effect is of an actual chapel with real figures. The architectural forms are closely related to the Renaissance architecture being developed by Filippo Brunelleschi at this time (see figs. 5-40, 5-41). He may well have assisted Masaccio with this aspect of painting. The clarity of the composition is combined with boldly three-dimensional figures recalling those painted by Giotto. Masaccio here has advanced the innovations of Giotto by combining them with the coherent illusory space that distinguishes Renaissance painting.

A short time before he was commissioned to paint *The Trinity*, Masaccio was employed with another artist, Masolino (c. 1400–40/47), in decorating the Brancacci Chapel with scenes primarily from the life of Saint Peter. In the *Tribute Money* (based on Matthew 17:24–27), Jesus and his apostles are confronted by a tax collector who requests that a temple tax be paid (fig. 5-21). Jesus instructs Peter to go to the edge of the sea, to our left, where he finds the necessary coin of tribute in the mouth of a fish. To the right, Peter pays the tax collector, an act prophetic of Jesus' words "Pay to the emperor what belongs to him, and pay to God what belongs to God" (Matthew 22:15–22). Because three different episodes take place within the

5-21   Left wall and portion of altar walls of Brancacci Chapel, Santa Maria del Carmine, Florence, with frescoes by Masaccio (c. 1425–28), Masolino (c. 1425–28), and Filippino Lippi (1484). Height of each register 8'. Scenes shown here include *The Expulsion of Adam and Eve* and *The Tribute Money* by Masaccio (top register, left wall); *Preaching of Saint Peter* by Masolino (top register, altar wall); *Saint Peter in Prison* by Filippino Lippi (lower register, left scene on left wall); *Resurrection of the Son of Theophilus and the Chairing of Saint Peter* by Masaccio and Filippino Lippi (lower register, main scene on left wall); and *Saint Peter Healing with His Shadow* by Masaccio and Masolino (lower register, altar wall). Commissioned by a member of the Brancacci family.

unified space of the composition, *The Tribute Money* exemplifies continuous narration, a thematic device that had been used in ancient Roman painting and sculpture (see fig. 3-104).

The coherent perspective of *The Tribute Money* unifies the space, while boldly modeled figures reveal a light source that corresponds to the real light that falls into the chapel from a single window on the altar wall. The building at the right, which obeys the laws of scientific perspec-tive, draws our attention to the head of Jesus, while **atmospheric per-spective** envelops the trees and hills of the background. Within this spatial illusionism, Masaccio's figures act out the story with simple, direct, and dignified movements.

Masaccio's sculpturesque modeling and bold narrative presentation are especially evident in *The Expulsion of Adam and Eve* on the same wall. Hav-ing disobeyed God, Adam and Eve are driven out of Paradise by their own guilt and shame. In Masaccio's interpreta-tion, Adam hides his face in his hands, leaving his genitals uncovered. Masac-cio thus emphasizes the psychological rather than the physical nature of Adam's shame. The figure of Eve, which was inspired by an ancient sculp-ture of the Modest Venus, conceals her nakedness but throws her head back in a moan as she bewails their fate.

Masaccio's figures, instilled with psychological presence, recall the human gravity of Donatello's sculpture,

First day

Second day

Third day

Figure of Eve was completed in final, fourth day

5-22 *Giornata* diagram for *The Expulsion of Adam and Eve.*

while the classicizing architecture and use of the scientific perspective reveal his relationship with Brunelleschi. Although he died in his twenties, Masaccio translated into paint the Renaissance innovations of Donatello and Brunelleschi, and he influenced later generations of Renaissance artists, including Michelangelo. An epitaph, composed in the sixteenth century, recognized Masaccio's contribution:

> I painted, and my picture was lifelike, I gave my figures movement, passion, soul: they breathed.
>
> (Annibale Caro, as cited in Vasari's *Life of Masaccio*)

The speed of Masaccio's execution is indicated in the **giornata** diagram for *The Expulsion of Adam and Eve* (fig. 5-22), which indicates that it was completed in only four days. The breadth and simplicity of Masaccio's painting technique are also revealed in the classically inspired head of an apostle from *The Tribute Money* (see fig. 5-23).

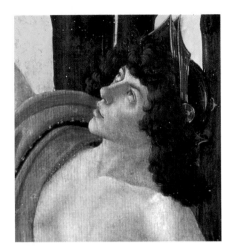

5-23 Head of apostle, detail from Masaccio's *THE TRIBUTE MONEY* (see fig. 5-21). Fresco.

5-24 Head of Adam, detail from Jan van Eyck's *THE ALTARPIECE OF THE LAMB* (see fig. 5-30). Oil on panel.

5-25 Head of Mercury, detail from Botticelli's *REALM OF VENUS* (see fig. 5-59). Tempera on panel with oil glazes.

To understand the three different painting techniques—**fresco**, **oil**, and **tempera**—available to fifteenth-century European painters, we can compare Masaccio's fresco head (fig. 5-23) with the head of Adam, painted in oil by Jan van Eyck (fig. 5-24), and the head of Mercury, painted in tempera with oil glazes, by Botticelli (fig. 5-25). Although each head offers its own distinctive reality, the bold masses of Masaccio's head contrast with the finer detail that characterizes the other two heads. Masaccio's apostle, rendered in fresco, is broadly and quickly painted with strong contrasts of light and dark to create a powerfully modeled form.

Van Eyck's head of Adam, painted in oils, shows the artist's interest in representing surface texture: notice the cracked lips, the wrinkles of the forehead, and the masses of curls that make up the mustache, beard, and hair and that seem to be composed of individually painted hairs. Botticelli's Mercury is painted with tempera with some use of oil glazes; here the artist is less interested than Masaccio or van Eyck in modeling to create an effect of mass, but his drawing of the head, tilted back into space and slightly foreshortened, is very convincing. Using oil glazes, Botticelli captures the translucency of the human eye when it is struck by light.

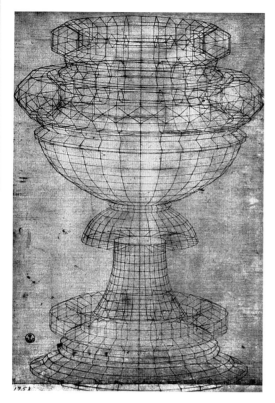

5-26   PAOLO UCCELLO

Perspective drawing. c. 1430–40. Pen and ink on paper, 13⅜ × 9½″. Gabinetto dei Disegni, Galleria degli Uffizi, Florence. Vasari tells us that Uccello delighted in making such complex studies and that he often worked late into the night, "seeking to solve the problems of perspective." When called to bed by his wife, Uccello would reply, "Oh, what a sweet thing is this perspective!"

5-27   Diagram of Perugino's *CHRIST GIVING THE KEYS TO SAINT PETER* (see fig. 1-15) showing the orthogonals and transversals of the scientific perspective scheme. The gradually shaded areas in the background indicate the blurring and color modulations characteristic of atmospheric perspective.

The perspective drawing by Paolo Uccello (1397–1475) is a virtuoso rendering of a geometricized chalice combined with other objects that are at least partially transparent (fig. 5-26). The geometricized rings at the top and base are derived from Uccello's studies of a wire- or wicker-frame construction (*mazzocchio*) that was wrapped with cloth to create a type of male headgear popular in the fifteenth century. Perhaps it was the faceting of the skeletal structure of this headdress that led Uccello to study the chalice with a similar geometric, linear emphasis.

The study of perspective, the rendering of figures or objects in illusory space, was an important innovation in Renaissance art. Perspective had been a conscious development in ancient Greek painting, and many examples of Roman art attest to the accomplished use of perspective in antiquity. During the Middle Ages, however, pictorial reproduction of the physical world became less significant within a culture that emphasized spiritual and otherworldly values. Perspective gradually became valued in the later Middle Ages, but a coherent system allowing artists to determine the relative diminution of size of figures and objects was lacking.

That problem was solved by Filippo Brunelleschi (1377–1446), the Early Renaissance architect (see pages 260-61). Around 1415, Brunelleschi demonstrated a **scientific perspective** system (also called **linear** and **vanishing-point perspective**) in two lost paintings. His new perspective system was incorporated in works by other artists, including Masaccio in *The Trinity* and *The Tribute Money* (see figs. 5-20 and 5-21); Perugino in *Christ Giving the Keys to Saint Peter* (see figs. 1-15, 5-27); Donatello in *Feast of Herod* (figs. 5-28, 5-29); as well as Ghiberti and Leonardo (see figs. 5-32 and 5-64).

5-28 DONATELLO

Feast of Herod, from the Siena baptismal font. c. 1425. Gilded bronze, 23½″ square. Baptistery, Siena, Tuscany, Italy. Donatello uses continuous narration to depict the story of the beheading of John the Baptist. Within the distant arch in the left background, the just-severed head is given to a servant; in the left foreground, it is presented to Herod, who recoils in horror. In the right foreground, Salome still seems to sway with the rhythms of her dance. Commissioned by the Cathedral Administration of Siena

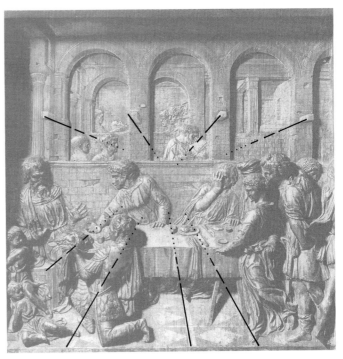

5-29 Diagram of the orthogonals of the perspective scheme of Donatello's *Feast of Herod*.

Within the complex architectural structure of the *Feast of Herod*, Donatello narrates the dramatic events surrounding the beheading of Saint John the Baptist. His use of scientific perspective assists in visually unifying these events. The diagonal lines created by the recession of architectural elements parallel to each other, such as those of the floor in the foreground, converge at a vanishing point. The convergence of these diagonal lines, which are called **orthogonals**, helps Donatello determine the accurate diminution of figures and architecture.

Scientific perspective is based on the assumption that parallel lines receding from us seem to converge at a point on the horizon. This is the basis for the meeting of the orthogonals at the vanishing point. Scientific perspective also assumes that the diminution in size of objects is in direct proportion to their distance from us and that space is, therefore, quantifiably measurable.

What Brunelleschi arrived at through empirical study, Alberti stated with theoretical reasoning in his book *On Painting*. By constructing orthogonal lines crossed by **transversals** (lines that recede parallel to the **picture plane**) on the planar surface of a painting or relief, a receding modular grid pattern is created. This pattern establishes a coherent, mathematically measurable illusory space within which the artist can determine the proportional diminution of objects distant from the viewer. In a fully developed example of Renaissance illusionistic painting, such as Perugino's *Christ Giving the Keys to Saint Peter* (see figs. 1-15, 5-27), scientific perspective is combined with **atmospheric perspective** for a unified effect that encompasses vast spaces, correctly proportioned figures, and the subtle qualities of the sky and distant landscape as they appear to the eye.

Flemish Painting:
Hubert and Jan Van Eyck

5-30 HUBERT AND JAN VAN EYCK

THE ALTARPIECE OF THE LAMB (interior). Completed 1432. Oil on wood, 11′5¾″ × 15′1½″. Cathedral of St. Bavo, Ghent, Belgium. This work is also known as *The Ghent Altarpiece*. An inscription of the frame identifies the patron as Jodocus Vijd, the date of completion as 1432, and the painters as Hubert and Jan van Eyck. Hubert died before September 18, 1426, and the role each brother played in the conception and execution of the many panels has been much debated. Scholars today generally agree that the altarpiece includes a number of works by Hubert, some of which may have been left unfinished at his death, which Jan combined into a totality, adding works conceived by Jan (in particular, the figures of Adam and Eve) to complete the altarpiece. This may explain the juxtapositions in figural scale between the parts of the altarpiece. The luminous technique and fine detail that unify the painting are considered to be the work of Jan, who by the sixteenth century had been credited with the invention of oil painting.

The iconography is complex. The lower panels represent the Triumph of the Lamb of God, with crowds of saints pressing inward to worship the symbolic lamb on the altar. The upper panels include God the Father in the center flanked by the Virgin Mary and Saint John the Baptist, musical angels, and Adam and Eve. Above Adam and Eve are small grisaille scenes of the story of Cain and Abel.

Adam and Eve were among the few subjects that permitted Northern artists to represent the nude, but Jan's virtually lifesize figures are unprecedented. Jan's commitment to naturalism here confronts traditional restrictions, for although the figure of Adam is clearly based on a nude model (notice the sunburned face, neck, and hands; see fig. 5-24), Eve is an imaginative re-creation based on contemporary ideals rather than on observation of a live model. The small, high breasts and bulbous abdomen are Gothic stylizations. The emphasis on the large abdomen stresses the role of childbearer assigned to women in the fifteenth century. Commissioned by Jodocus Vijd, a wealthy landowner and member of the Ghent city government, and his wife, Isabel Borluut.

In scale and wealth of detail, *The Altarpiece of the Lamb (The Ghent Altarpiece)*, a large, hinged **polyptych** (multipaneled **altarpiece**), is an overwhelming accomplishment—the most impressive of all early Flemish paintings (figs. 5-30, 5-31). The diverse scale and size of the panels and the variety of subjects represented allowed Hubert van Eyck (1370–1426) and Jan van Eyck (before 1390–1441) to paint Flemish interiors, vast landscapes, illusionistic sculpture, portraits of living donors, the male and female nude, elaborate brocades, bejeweled and gold-embroidered borders, and musical instruments. Jan van Eyck's ability to re-create the visual world in oil paint is staggering, but among the wealth of details offered by *The Ghent Altarpiece*, the most unforgettable may be the artist's difused self-portrait in the studio, which is reflected in one of the pearls in the papal crown worn by God the Father, the central figure of the interior. This tour de force of painting is one of several "reflected" self-portraits found in the work of Jan van Eyck (see also fig. 5-37).

Jan van Eyck's ability to represent textures as if they were real is based on his acute examination of light and how it reacts differently when it strikes and reflects from various surfaces. He composed his paintings to emphasize this phenomenon, juxtaposing materials to contrast textures and heighten his illusion. Jan's figures seldom express strong or dramatic emotions. The wonder that his paintings generate comes from his ability to observe reality and to convey in oil paints the excitement of vision.

5-31 HUBERT AND JAN VAN EYCK

THE ALTARPIECE OF THE LAMB (exterior). Oil on wood, 11'5¾" × 7'6¾". The donors of the altarpiece, Jodocus Vijd and Isabel Borluut, are shown in the lower panels, kneeling before Saints John the Baptist and John the Evangelist, patrons of the city of Ghent. In the upper register is a scene of the Annunciation; the top-most panels show representations of the Old Testament prophets Zachariah and Micah and two sibyls.

Italian Renaissance Sculpture: Lorenzo Ghiberti

5-32 LORENZO GHIBERTI

STORY OF JACOB AND ESAU, from the East Doors of the Baptistery, Florence. c. 1429–37. Gilded bronze, 31¼" square. Museo dell' Opera del Duomo, Florence. The story of Jacob and Esau, from the Old Testament book of Genesis (25:19–28:5), tells how Jacob and his mother, Rebecca, conspired to steal the birthright of Jacob's twin but slightly older brother, Esau, by deceiving the boys' father, the old and nearly blind Isaac, into giving his blessing to Jacob instead of Esau. In Ghiberti's representation, the scene of the arranged blessing of Isaac is shown at the right, with Rebecca looking on, while the central figures represent the moment when Isaac and Esau discover the deception. Commissioned by the Opera of the Baptistery and the Arte di Calimala.

Lorenzo Ghiberti (1378–1455) represents the *Story of Jacob and Esau* with grand, classicizing architecture and graceful figures gathered into beautiful groupings (fig. 5-32). His ideal and orderly Renaissance world makes no reference to the treachery and emotional trauma inherent in the Old Testament narrative. Ghiberti chose to subordinate these unpleasant realities to his Renaissance interest in harmony. The fifteenth-century concern for fine detail and exquisite finish is obvious in every area of the relief, from the delicate Corinthian **capitals** of the architecture to the shaggy fur of Esau's hunting dogs in the foreground. The regular recession of the Brunelleschian scientific perspective (see pages 248–49) and the subtle diminution in the height of the relief, from the virtually three-dimensional figures of the left foreground to the low-relief figure of Rebecca praying in the upper right corner, create a convincing, controlled illusion. The four female figures in the left foreground, who pose with such exquisite grace, play no role in advancing the narrative and have been added by Ghiberti to enhance the beauty of the work of art.

In his autobiography, Ghiberti states that when he was offered the commission for the doors (fig. 5-33),

> I was given a free hand to execute it in whatever way I thought would turn out most perfect and most ornate and richest.

In this he seems to be following the precepts of the theorist Leon Battista Alberti, who, in *On Painting*, had defined the qualities of the perfect narrative painting (*istoria* or *historia*) in the following manner:

> The first thing that gives pleasure in a "historia" is a plentiful variety. Just as with food and music, novel and extraordinary things delight us for various reasons but especially because they are different from the old ones we are used to, so with everything the mind takes great pleasure in variety and abundance. . . . I would say a picture was richly varied if it contained a properly arranged mixture of old men, youths, boys, matrons, maidens, children, domestic animals, dogs, birds, horses, sheep, buildings and provinces.

5-33 LORENZO GHIBERTI

East Doors of the Baptistery (also known as the Gates of Paradise). 1425–52. Bronze and gilded bronze, 18′6″ × 12′. Museo dell' Opera del Duomo, Florence. Ghiberti's doors are the last of three sets of doors made for the portals of the Florentine Baptistery. His themes are drawn from the Old Testament. The doors were commissioned in 1425 and erected in 1452. The creation of wax models for the ten narratives has been dated 1429 to 1437, and the finishing of the details consumed most of the 1440s. Ghiberti employed a large workshop of assistants and apprentices to help him with the doors, which were by far the most expensive sculptural work produced in Florence during the fifteenth century. Most of the individual panels represent several scenes of a continuous narrative within a single architectural or landscape setting. For Ghiberti's self-portrait on the doors and a reference to the Latin inscription, see page 235. The area between a baptistery and a cathedral was known as the *paradiso*, which helps to explain the name attributed to Michelangelo, who supposedly said that Ghiberti's doors were worthy to serve as the Gates of Paradise.

The technique of wood carving is what is known as a **subtractive technique**, in which the artist or artists start with a solid piece of material and create the work by gradually removing areas and pieces (for marble carving, also subtractive, see page 291). This is a technique that does not tolerate mistakes; once a piece is removed, it can be reattached only with difficulty.

The traditional techniques of working in wood pose special problems for the sculptor. A variety of metal gouges, chisels, and knives are employed, but particular care is a constant requirement lest the wood fiber split. Some gouges are struck with a wooden mallet; others, in a more delicate but firm manner, can be pushed by hand. Restrictions are imposed by the size of a log; large wooden sculptures often have to be composed of a number of pieces joined together. Because wood expands and contracts during changes in temperature and humidity, care must be taken during the carving process to prevent the wood from cracking later.

Donatello's *Penitent Magdalene* (see figs. 5-34, 5-35) was carved from a single piece of wood, and its technique represents a distinctive break from earlier figurative wood carving. Previous to Donatello, sculpted wood figures usually had a broad expanse of drapery across the front to hide the large hollow space that had to be carved from the rear of the statue to prevent splitting as the wood dried. This limited the sculpture to a frontal viewpoint but ensured minimal surface cracking because most of the expansion and contraction of the wood was contained by the hollow area in the back. The *Penitent Magdalene*, with its subtle contrapposto pose, is more nearly a sculpture in the round. The hollowed gap between the legs allows for the expansion and contraction of the wood while visually contributing to the naturalism of the figure.

Virtually all medieval and Renaissance wood figures are polychromed to increase their naturalism, and many have gilded details. A thin coat of fine plaster, called **gesso**, was applied over the wood to provide a neutral base for the paint, and a range of naturalistic color would be painted on the figure. In this case, gold tint was added to the brown of the hair to refer to the traditional red hair of the Magdalene.

Donatello's lifesize, naturalistically **polychromed** wood sculpture of *Penitent Magdalene* (figs. 5-34, 5-35) is an example of a type of sculpture commonly used for popular devotion during the Middle Ages and Renaissance. Such sculptures, sometimes

5-34 DONATELLO

PENITENT MAGDALENE. Late 1430s–1450s? Wood with polychromy and gilding, height 6'2". Museo dell' Opera del Duomo, Florence.

5-35 DONATELLO
Penitent Magdalene, detail.

wearing real clothing, still adorn altars or are carried in religious processions in some areas of Europe; for an earlier example, see the polychromed wood German Gothic *Pietà* (see fig. 5-67).

By Donatello's day, the legend of Saint Mary Magdalene identified her as a beautiful prostitute who repented when she was forgiven by Jesus; she became one of his most devout followers. Because she was thought to be the woman who used her hair to anoint Jesus' feet, long hair became one of her attributes. She was present at the Crucifixion, where she is often identifiable because of her beauty and her long flowing red hair, and it was to the Magdalene that Christ first appeared on Easter morning, after his Resurrection. After the Crucifixion, she lived a life of penance in the wilderness, eating little (one legend has it that she was fed by angels) and clothed only in her own long hair. Because of her history, the Magdalene became the patron saint for fallen women and widows.

Donatello's patrons apparently requested that he represent her at the end of a long period of penance, when fasting and living in the desert have reduced her to an old, virtually starving woman. There is still a memory of her former beauty in her refined bone structure and her elegant, **contrapposto** stance, while intense devotion is conveyed by the upward tilt of her head and the trembling manner in which her hands are raised in prayer.

Flemish Painting: Jan Van Eyck

5-36   *(opposite)* JAN VAN EYCK

PORTRAIT OF GIOVANNI ARNOLFINI AND GIOVANNA CENAMI (?). 1434. Oil on wood, 32¼ × 23½". The National Gallery, London. The identification of the figures is not certain but is based on an early inventory that names them as "Hernoul le Sin with his wife"; a later inventory states that the panel had wooden shutters, painted to resemble jasper, and that the gilded frame had verses from the writings of the Roman poet Ovid. Giovanni Arnolfini was a successful Italian cloth merchant and money lender from Lucca who lived in Flanders; Giovanna Cenami, who was Giovanni's widow when he died in 1472, also came from a wealthy Lucchese family active in Paris and Flanders. Probably commissioned by Giovanni Arnolfini and Giovanna Cenami, if these are indeed the two figures represented in the painting.

This tantalizing and unparalleled image (fig. 5-36) is one of the enigmas of art history. With its compelling characters, its puzzlelike combination of objects, and the truly breathtaking detail of its execution, it demands an explanation. But extensive research, numerous articles, and several books examining betrothal and marriage practices and other social behavior have failed to provide an identification for the couple and what it is, exactly, that they are doing in the image; the motivation behind the commissioning of this painting thus remains uncertain. For the purposes of clarity here, we will examine the picture in some detail and include some of the questions and theories about it in parentheses.

The couple is shown standing in elegant dress in a bedchamber (Is this a portrait of a real room?). The positions of their hands seem to indicate that an oath is being taken, suggesting that the painting might have functioned as a kind of legal document (Does the picture represent their engagement or their marriage?). The function of the painting as a document is supported by the wording above the mirror: "Jan van Eyck was here, 1434." Two figures standing in the doorway of the room are reflected in the mirror (Is one the painter? Were both required as witnesses?).

The man's huge hat and fur-trimmed cape suggest his wealth and status, as do the many yards of material in the woman's train, which she holds up in a pose that emphasizes her abdomen (to stress the idea that she is ready to bear children?). Her hair is forced into nets to create the fashionable "horns" of the period, and her head covering is trimmed with elaborate ruffles. The fact that both have covered their heads seems important. Both have removed the sandals that they would have worn in the dirty streets outside (Is this an example of their cleanliness, or might it refer to the sacramental nature of marriage, based on the fact that Moses removed his sandals when he met God in the burning bush on Mount Sinai; Exodus 3:1–10?).

Wealth and a high standard of living seem evident. The elaborate chandelier is polished, but its single burning candle seems unnecessary. (Could the candle represent the presence of Christ,—or could it even be an erotic symbol?). The large, expensive mirror is decorated with scenes of Christ's passion; next to it hangs a glass rosary (Is this another indication of piety, or perhaps, because light can pass through glass without changing it, a symbol of the bride's virginity?). The oranges, imported from Spain, would have been rare in northern Europe at this time (Are they another symbol of virginity?). The alert dog in the foreground stands between us and them (Is the dog a symbol of fidelity—Fides, the origin for the popular nickname "Fido"—or of erotic desire?). That the dog might be symbolic is suggested by the fact that he is not reflected in the mirror, surely not an accidental omission on the part of this precision-minded artist. The bed might be a dowry present from the groom, and the chair beside it has a statuette of Saint Margaret emerging triumphant from the dragon; Margaret is one of the patron saints of women in childbirth. Jan van Eyck's symmetrical composition stresses the individuality of the figures although the woman is shown, as is traditional, as more passive.

Because there is no similar portrait in all of Italian or Flemish fifteenth-century painting, it seems unlikely that the purpose of this work was simply to record their betrothal or marriage. There must have been something special about the relationship between these two individuals that demanded this representation. A recent theory proposed that Giovanna's dowry might have been paid to Giovanni when she was too young to be given over to him; the painting might thus have been for her, still living in her father's house, a promise of her future role and prosperity. A related lost painting by van Eyck that represented a nude woman in this same room (Giovanna?) does not seem to be of much help in interpreting this painting. Whatever the function of this portrait, the desire of this couple to record their relationship has given them immortality.

5-37 JAN VAN EYCK

ARNOLFINI (?) portrait, detail of fig. 5-36.

JAN VAN EYCK, *THE PORTRAIT OF GIOVANNI* (?) *ARNOLFINI AND GIOVANNA CENAMI* (?) (THE ARNOLFINI MARRIAGE), 1434. OIL ON OAK PANEL, 32½ × 23½ IN. NATIONAL GALLERY, LONDON, UK/BRIDGEMAN ART LIBRARY/NEW YORK.

5-38 JAN VAN EYCK.

ARNOLFINI (?) portrait, detail of fig. 5-36.

JAN VAN EYCK, *THE PORTRAIT OF GIOVANNI* (?) *ARNOLFINI AND GIOVANNA CENAMI* (?) (THE ARNOLFINI MARRIAGE), 1434. OIL ON OAK PANEL, 32½ × 23½ IN. NATIONAL GALLERY, LONDON, UK/BRIDGEMAN ART LIBRARY/NEW YORK.

The details from Jan van Eyck's *Arnolfini* (?) portrait display impressive virtuosity (figs. 5-37, 5-38). The contrasting textures of the various materials are convincingly illusionistic. Such precise detail is made possible not only by the artist's acute perception but also by the development of oil paint as a primary vehicle, a step that revolutionized Flemish painting in the early years of the fifteenth century.

None of the materials used here (fig. 5-39) is new. The support was similar to that used for tempera painting (see fig. 4-108), a wooden panel covered with a layer of fine white plaster (gesso), sometimes with a layer of canvas or linen between the wood and the plaster. Van Eyck probably explored compositional ideas by drawing on the plaster with charcoal and "erasing" unsuccessful

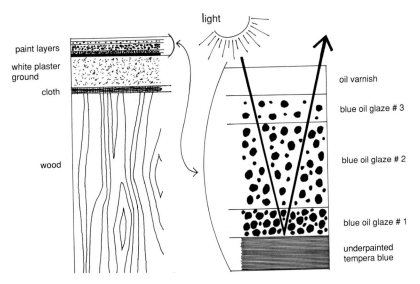

paint layers
white plaster ground
cloth
wood

light
oil varnish
blue oil glaze # 3
blue oil glaze # 2
blue oil glaze # 1
underpainted tempera blue

5-39　Schematic diagram of a section of a Flemish fifteenth-century oil painting, demonstrating the luminosity of the medium. The arrow suggests how light penetrates translucent oil glazes.

designs with a feather. He would then have reinforced a satisfactory composition with fine lines created with a brush dipped into tempera paint. The pigments used to create the color are the same powdered materials used by artists working in tempera (see pages 222–23). Oil as a drying vehicle had been known and used since ancient times. During the medieval period, oil was the final layer given a tempera painting to create a luminous surface finish. Here it is used as the primary vehicle.

Oil is a translucent vehicle; in making oil paint, particles of powdered pigment are suspended in this translucent vehicle, as shown in the diagram of a section of a Flemish panel painting. When it is applied in many thin layers (**glazes**), light will penetrate the layers and will be reflected, creating a gemlike brilliance of color. This new resonant richness makes Flemish oil paintings such as those of van Eyck and Campin distinctly different in appearance from their tempera antecedents.

Oil dries more slowly than tempera, and its speed of drying can be further slowed by adding turpentine, permitting the artist to blend colors to create the subtle tonal modulations that help suggest light falling on an object. Van Eyck's fine detail is accomplished by using oil and soft, fine brushes, and the resulting transitions from color to color and the smooth surface finish offer virtually no hint of the artist's brushstrokes.

The greater resonance of color and the new realism of Flemish paintings are also due to the changed **color palette**. In tempera painting, a particular **hue**, such as red, would be mixed with white to achieve the transitions from shadow (red at its maximum intensity) to highlight (white). In the oil technique, the same red would usually be mixed with black to accomplish the change from highlight (red near its maximum intensity) to shadow (black). In tempera paintings, then, colors are modeled upward toward white, while in oil paintings most colors are modeled downward toward black. The greatest intensity of a hue in tempera painting is in the shadows, while in oil it occurs between shadow and highlight. Most importantly, the scheme used in oil paintings is closer to what we observe in reality. Flemish painters learned this laborious craft as apprentices. Only years of watching and practice could prepare a young artist for a career working in such a painstaking and methodical technique. The results of their patient work are evident in the superb condition of many of these paintings today.

To learn how to paint like Campin and van Eyck took more than technical skill, however, for the artist had to learn how to see—how to distinguish the distinct patterns of light and shadow observable on the surface of, for example, velvet, wood, brass, and glass in various lighting conditions. In the work of these two artists, the precision of depiction is intimately related to the fact that all these objects are mirrors of religious truths. A candle is not just a candle and a triple lily is more than a floral oddity. Like other techniques, the development of the fine oil technique of the Flemish painters was a response to a distinct need: they created a technique that would allow them to endow objects with a magical potency—a dazzling realism—that could suggest the deeper meanings that lie behind observation. Their new style is rooted in the complexities of medieval symbolism and theology, but it contains a seed of the new Renaissance concern with the individual and the world. It is no surprise that the motto of Jan van Eyck (see fig. 5-7) is *Als ich can* ("The best I can do").

Italian Renaissance Architecture: Brunelleschi

5-40 FILIPPO BRUNELLESCHI

Nave, Church of Santo Spirito, Florence. Begun 1436. In this view, we are looking toward the crossing and high altar; the elaborate canopy over the altar is a later, obtrusive addition. Commissioned by the abbot of the Monastery of Santo Spirito.

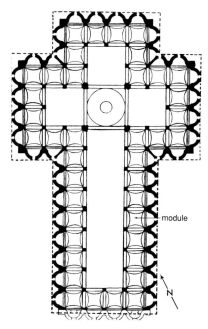

5-41 FILIPPO BRUNELLESCHI

Plan of the Church of Santo Spirito.

The interior of the Church of Santo Spirito (fig. 5-40) provides a conspicuous contrast to Gothic architecture, which overwhelms us with its towering vertical emphasis (see fig. 4-88). In Brunelleschi's light-filled Renaissance church, on the other hand, we perceive a measured order and harmony. Here the human reason of the architect and faith in a rational God and universe create architecture that is an alternative to the spiritual striving of the Gothic.

The satisfying regularity of Santo Spirito is derived from the use of simple proportional schemes similar to those used in ancient Greek and Roman architecture. The plan (fig. 5-41) makes it clear that each of the square **bays** of the **aisle** or the **ambulatory** can be understood as a basic module (another interpretation proposes that the basic module is the area of the dome; for the purposes of our explanation here, we have chosen the smallest unit that functions in this system). With this in mind, it can be demonstrated that the relationships that govern the interior design of Santo Spirito are few and simple: 1:1, 1:2, 1:4, and 1:8. The square **crossing**, under the **dome**, is four times as large in plan as the basic module, as are the **altar** and **transept** areas that surround it (1:4). The nave is twice as wide as the module (1:2). An elevation or a view inside the church reveals how this proportional system continues in the three-dimensional structure. The bays of the aisles and ambulatory are four times as tall as they are wide (1:4), and the nave is twice as tall as the aisles and ambulatory (4:8). The nave is composed of an **arcade** (a series of arches supported by **columns** or **piers**) and of the **clerestory** above it. The arcade and clerestory are each as high as the nave is wide. This proportional approach is combined with the use of **round arches** and **capitals** based on ancient models. The result is an architecture that revives both the principles and the forms of classical antiquity. The regular placement of windows and the avoidance of both the stained-glass windows of French Gothic and the frescoes of Italian Gothic mean that Brunelleschi's church is well illuminated and free of shadows.

Brunelleschi secured his fame as an architect and engineer by designing the enormous dome for the cathedral in Florence and engineering its construction (fig. 5-42). The Florence Cathedral, begun in 1296 to replace an earlier church, is a Gothic structure, but from its inception a dome over the crossing was intended. The difficulties of constructing such an immense dome—the largest in Europe since antiquity—were solved by Brunelleschi in the early fifteenth century with a design that was responsive to and harmonious with the original Gothic

5-42 FILIPPO BRUNELLESCHI

DOME, Florence Cathedral. 1420–36. Commissioned by the Wood Guild and the Cathedral Administration.

design. The pointed profile, with eight external **ribs**, is more Gothic than Renaissance, yet the eloquence of its grand scale and simple harmony express the clarity characteristic of the new Renaissance architecture. The cathedral dome was an architectural, engineering, and psychological feat. That so large a dome could be constructed without **cen-** tering (see fig. 3-118; Brunelleschi designed a self-supporting system) was a technological achievement. In this joining of scale, design, and technology, the Florentine people found a source of civic as well as religious pride. Brunelleschi's dome continues to dominate the skyline of Florence, a visual expression of a domineering spirit in the arts.

The Italian Renaissance Palace

5-43 MICHELOZZO

COURTYARD, Medici Palace, Florence. 1445–59. The Medici, who were bankers, were among the richest families in Florence. In the course of the fifteenth century, they gradually assumed control of the Florentine government. Commissioned by Cosimo de' Medici.

5-44 Exterior, Medici Palace. This early print shows the palace before later extensions and changes. Unlike medieval castles, the Renaissance palazzo is found within the city, and its owner was as likely to be a merchant or a banker as a noble. Such palaces housed the entire family, including married children and grandchildren.

The Medici Palace presents a departure in domestic architecture (figs. 5-43, 5-44). The centralized courtyard is decorated with a classical-style arcade reminiscent of the **atrium** or garden **peristyle** of an ancient Roman house (see fig. 3-95). In his references to antiquity and lucid regularity in the courtyard, Michelozzo (1396–1472) reveals the new attitudes of the Renaissance. As a composition, the palace is a three-story masonry block, with regularly spaced windows and a large **cornice**, which projects out from the roof. The **rustication** (use of roughly carved blocks) of the street-level story is gradually reduced on the upper two floors, and the heights of the floors are equally decreased. Lucid regularity is also demonstrated in the plan. It has been suggested that the regularity of the Medici Palace was inspired by the description of ancient Roman houses given by Vitruvius, the first century BCE Roman architect and

theorist. The decoration of the palace included portrait busts of the Medici (see fig. 5-51), likewise based on ancient sculptural models.

Many of the paintings and sculptures in the Medici Palace had distinctive secular themes. The bedroom of Lorenzo de' Medici was decorated with panels by Uccello representing the Battle of San Romano, a victory credited to Niccolò da Tolentino, a friend and supporter of Cosimo de' Medici (fig. 5-45). Tolentino died later in an accident, perhaps arranged by Cosimo's enemies, and his victory at San Romano may have been commemorated at the palace in order to suggest that he was a Medici martyr.

Small bronze sculptures could be found throughout the palace. Antonio Pallaiuolo (1429?–98) exemplifies an episode from the adventures of Hercules in a powerful bronze statuette (fig. 5-46). Hercules was the mythological founder of Florence, and

the use of the Hercules theme at the Medici Palace may have been a way of identifying the Medici with the city and its traditional founders and heroes. This also explains the presence of a statue of Donatello's *David* (fig. 5-47) in the Medici courtyard, for the youthful David was also a symbol of the city.

1441	Africans are sold as slaves in the markets of Lisbon
1445–59	**Michelozzo, Medici Palace**
1453	Fall of the Byzantine Empire

5-45 PAOLO UCCELLO

NICCOLÒ DA TOLENTINO DIRECTING THE ATTACK, from a series of three paintings illustrating the Battle of San Romano. c. 1450s. Tempera and silver foil on wood, 5'11½" × 10'6". The National Gallery, London. Originally the three panels decorated the bedroom of Lorenzo the Magnificent. Their combined length was more than 34 feet. Commissioned by a member of the Medici family, perhaps Cosimo de' Medici.

5-46 ANTONIO PALLAIUOLO

HERCULES AND ANTAEUS. c. 1470s. Bronze, height 18". Museo Nazionale del Bargello, Florence. Antaeus was the son of Mother Earth, and to defeat him, Hercules had to lift him up and crush him while he was separated from his maternal source of power. Probably commissioned by a member of the Medici family.

5-47 DONATELLO

DAVID. 1440s? Bronze with gilded details, height 5'2¼". Museo Nazionale del Bargello, Florence. David is documented in the courtyard of the Medici Palace (fig. 5-38). Donatello's representation of the Old Testament hero is consistent with the biblical story (I Samuel 17:38–51). The broad shepherd's hat would have cast David's face into shadow, leaving his expression enigmatic. This is the first lifesize nude sculpture in the round since antiquity. Probably commissioned by Cosimo de' Medici.

The Beginnings of Portraiture in Europe

5-48 ALESSO BALDOVINETTI

PORTRAIT OF A YOUNG WOMAN. c. 1465. Tempera on wood, 25 × 16″. The National Gallery, London. The elaborate hairstyle and high, plucked forehead are typical of Renaissance fashion. Among the most expensive and elaborate parts of a Renaissance woman's costume were her detachable sleeves; here, the decoration on the sleeves may be a reference to her name or family.

5-49 DOMENICO GHIRLANDAIO

PORTRAIT OF A MAN AND A BOY. c. 1480. Tempera and oil on wood, 24⅜ × 18⅛″. The Louvre, Paris. The artist has used the man's disfiguring disease (rhinophyma) as an aesthetic device, repeating similarly rounded forms for the boy's curls and the trees.

5-50 DOMENICO GHIRLANDAIO

PORTRAIT OF A MAN ON HIS DEATHBED. c. 1480. Silverpoint and point of the brush, heightened with white on pink prepared paper, 11⅝ × 12⅝″. Nationalmuseum, Stockholm. This is a preparatory drawing for figure 5-49. The beautiful drawing that creates a Mannerist style frame for Ghirlandaio's portrait was drawn by the sixteenth-century artist Vasari, who decorated this drawing when it was in his personal collection.

The silhouette or profile portrait (fig. 5-48) immediately reveals variations in individual physiognomy. Portraiture was revived in the fifteenth century, and Alesso Baldovinetti (c. 1425–99) used the profile formula of the earliest Renaissance portraits. It was quickly superseded by three-quarter or full-view portraits and sculpted portraits. By the time of Leonardo da Vinci's *"Mona Lisa"* (see fig. 6-21), portraiture was a well-established subject, and it continued to provide an important means of support for artists until the advent of photography in the nineteenth century.

1457	"Futeball" and "golfe" are forbidden by Scotland's Parliament
1464	Royal postal service is established in France
c. 1465	**Baldovinetti,** *Portrait of a Young Woman*

5-51 MINO DA FIESOLE

PORTRAIT OF PIERO DE' MEDICI. 1453.
Marble, height 18". Museo Nazionale del
Bargello, Florence. An inscription on the
work identifies the artist, sitter, and date, as
is common in male busts of this type.
Probably commissioned by Piero de' Medici.

5-52 HANS MEMLING

MADONNA AND CHILD WITH MARTIN VAN NIEUWENHOVE. 1487. Oil on wood, each 17⅜ × 13".
Hospital of St. John, Bruges, Flanders (Belgium). The inscriptions across the bottom date the
work, identify the patron, and state that he was twenty-three years old. A merchant, Martin
van Nieuwenhove later served as mayor of Bruges. These two wooden panels are hinged,
and they normally would have been displayed not flat, as is suggested here, but angled, a
position that would have enhanced the intimacy between the two figures. Commissioned by
Martin van Nieuwenhove.

The precise function of the earliest portraits is not certain, and it is possible that Baldovinetti's sitter died young and the portrait was commissioned as a remembrance after her death. Such is certainly the case with the *Portrait of a Man and a Boy*, for the drawing Domenico Ghirlandaio (1449–94) made from the man's corpse survives (figs. 5-49, 5-50). The delicate and beautiful face of the child, unmarked by time, looks up with respect and love toward the old man.

The bust-length portrait sculpture became popular in the mid-fifteenth century in Florence, partly in response to ancient Roman sculptural precedents. These portraits were sometimes placed over the doorways of Renaissance palaces. The earliest surviving marble bust (fig. 5-51) represents a member of the Medici family, the richest and most politically important family in the city.

The simultaneous evolution of painted portraits in Flanders during the fifteenth century included a devotional type that represented an individual in an attitude of prayer with an image of the Madonna and Child (fig. 5-52). These **diptychs**, which served as private devotional images, were hinged so they could travel easily and be self-supporting when opened. In the example by Hans Memling (c. 1430–94), the donor's natural three-quarter view contrasts with the frontal placement of the Madonna; the architectural setting suggests a Flemish room. The realistically depicted stained-glass window behind the donor represents Saint Martin, the patron's name saint, and the donor's place in heaven seems assured by the inclusion of his coat of arms in the window behind the Madonna. The convex mirror behind the Virgin Mary's right shoulder is a symbol of virginity. It reflects the foreground figures, confirming an intimate relationship between the real and sacred worlds.

Italian Renaissance Painting: Andrea Mantegna

The Camera Picta ("Painted Room") is a dazzling and witty tour de force of illusionism that proves the brilliance of both the artist, Andrea Mantegna (1431–1506), and his patron, Lodovico Gonzaga, duke of Mantua (fig. 5-53). The magnificence of a Renaissance prince or princess was in part determined by the abilities of the artists at their court. The painted illusion created by Mantegna and his workshop at the Ducal Palace in Mantua completely covers the vaulted ceiling and two walls. Most of the vault is painted with **grisaille** and gold decorative patterns in a classical style that simulate stucco relief decoration. This design emphasizes the ceiling's flat surface and serves as a foil for the central area, with its unexpected illusion of a circular opening with a balcony and a view up to the sky and clouds. The painted figures around the **balustrade** seem to interact with us and with each other, and a huge pot of plants, precariously supported on a pole, threatens to fall into the room. This fictive space is populated with imaginary figures, baby angels derived from ancient Roman precedents and known in Italian art as putti. One is struggling, for he has caught his head in one of the round openings of the balustrade.

5-53 ANDREA MANTEGNA

Camera Picta, Ducal Palace, Mantua, Lombardy, Italy. 1465–74. Frescoes, wall with fireplace 19′6″ × 26′6″; diameter of illusionistic balcony in the middle of the ceiling, 5′. The room is approximately 26′6″ square. The figures over the fireplace represent Mantegna's patron, Lodovico Gonzaga, duke of Mantua, with his family and followers, and the scene to the left depicts a meeting between Cardinal Francesco Gonzaga and his father, Lodovico. The ceiling decoration has illusionistic relief portraits of ancient Roman rulers. The side walls are defined by painted balustrades and pilasters. This room is now popularly known by a later name, the Camera degli Sposi ("Room of the Married Couple"), in reference to the patron and his wife, who are shown seated in the fresco over the fireplace. Commissioned by Duke Lodovico Gonzaga.

Technique *Foreshortening*

Mantegna's putti in the Camera Picta, represented as if seen from below, are rendered in a technique known as **foreshortening**. This technique involves representing a figure or object as if seen in sharp recession.

Mantegna's *Christ*, however, demonstrates how easily we accept an unrealistic representation (fig. 5-54). If we were to look at a corpse from this sharp angle, we would not see it as Mantegna painted it but with much larger feet and a somewhat smaller head. Mantegna's treatment, however, serves to pull us into his composition and to fix our attention on the wounds of Christ.

Dürer's woodcut (fig. 5-55) is less a demonstration of an actual technique used by artists than an illustration of the principles of foreshortening and how the technique can be studied (and illustrated in a book). The line of sight of the observer is represented by the cord fastened to the wall on the right. A piece of paper that can be swung aside has been placed in an upright frame. After the end of the cord is held on a place on the lute, the point where the cord passes through the frame is marked by the intersection of two movable threads. The paper is then swung back into place and the point transferred to the paper. The connect-the-dots diagram that results provides an accurate image of a lute seen in sharp foreshortening, as is evident in the illustration.

For other examples of sharp foreshortening, see the Virgin's left arm in Leonardo's *Madonna of the Rocks* (fig. 5-61), the artist's arm in Parmigianino's *Self-Portrait in a Convex Mirror* (fig. 6-10), Adam's right arm in Michelangelo's *Creation of Adam* (fig. 6-36), the Christ Child's left leg in Titian's *Madonna of the Pesaro Family* (fig. 6-50), Europa's left thigh in Titian's *Rape of Europa* (fig. 6-53), Venus's legs in Bronzino's *Allegory of Time and Lust* (fig. 6-56), and the figure of the horse and the body of the recumbent St. Paul in Caravaggio's *Conversion of St. Paul* (fig. 7-16).

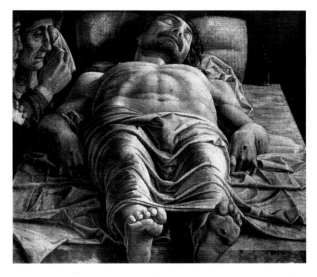

5-54 ANDREA MANTEGNA

A Foreshortened Christ. c. 1466. Tempera on canvas, 26¾ × 31⅞". Bera Gallery, Milan, Italy. This painting, sometimes called *Lamentation over the Dead Christ*, is almost certainly identical with the painting listed in an inventory of Mantegna's house as *A Foreshortened Christ*. It may have been painted by the artist for his personal devotion.

5-55 ALBRECHT DÜRER

Artist Drawing a Lute with the Help of a Mechanical Device. 1525. Woodcut, 5⅛ × 7¼". This woodcut was designed as an illustration for Dürer's treatise. *A Course in the Art of Measurement with Compass and Ruler*, published in Germany in 1525.

5-56   LEONARDO DA VINCI

MADONNA AND CHILD WITH CAT. c. 1478–80. Pen and ink, 5⅛ × 3¾″. The British Museum, London.

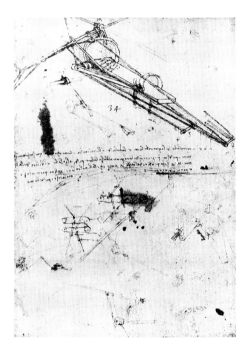

5-57   LEONARDO DA VINCI

DRAWING OF A FLYING MACHINE, from the *Codex Atlanticus*. c. 1490. Pen and ink. Biblioteca Ambrosiana, Milan.

Leonardo's pen-and-ink study of the *Madonna and Child* is a spontaneous, animated drawing in which Mary greets the Christ Child's attempt to embrace a struggling cat with tender approval (fig. 5-56). Quick and repetitive lines impart a pulsating energy to the theme. This rapidly executed design represents a revolutionary approach to the use of preliminary compositional studies.

Previous to Leonardo (1452–1519), drawings by artists were often characterized by meticulous execution, not only because

such precision was part of the Early Renaissance aesthetic but also because they were done on an expensive surface such as vellum. By the mid-fifteenth century, the availability of cheap paper (a development in response to the demands of the new publishing industry) meant that drawing could become more common and more spontaneous. Leonardo was a decisive influence in developing the quick artist's sketch, which is so much a part of artists' work even today. He wrote:

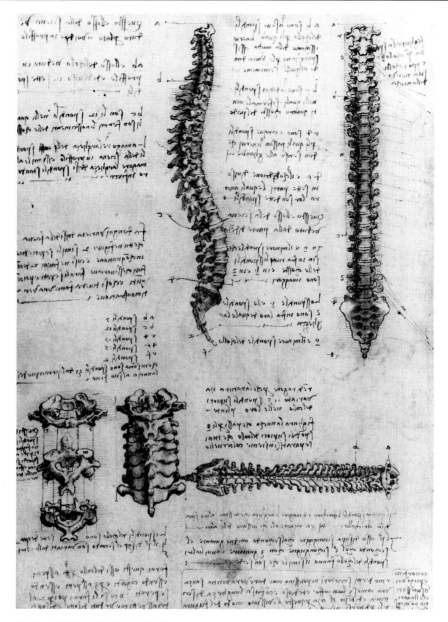

5-58 LEONARDO DA VINCI

STUDY OF THE SPINE. c. 1510. Pen, brown ink, and wash over traces of black chalk, 11¼ × 7⅞". Royal Library, Windsor Castle, Berkshire, England.

You will first attempt in a drawing to give to the eye an indication of the intention and the invention which you first made in your imagination, then proceed to take away and add until you are satisfied.

After determining a basic composition, a Renaissance artist would make drawings studying the various elements within the composition. Leonardo's *Study for the Head of Judas* (see fig. 5-65) reveals the exacting interplay between his observing eye and talented hand. All these studies were then joined in a final, full-scale preparatory drawing known as a **cartoon** (from the Italian *cartone*, which refers to the thick paper used for this purpose).

For Leonardo, drawing was not restricted to studies for works of art. "Art," he wrote, "truly is a science," and his remarkable examination of subjects ranging from engineering to the earth sciences found expression in more than 3,500 surviving pages of his notebooks. Numerous drawings, such as his projected flying machine (fig. 5-57), make visible Leonardo's powers of observation and imagination. Other investigations probed the physical sciences, including anatomy. His drawing of a spine from front, side, and back views—a didactic device still used in modern anatomy textbooks—demonstrates a knowledge of anatomical structures far in advance of that available to the medical profession at that time (fig. 5-58).

Italian Renaissance Painting: Sandro Botticelli

5-59 SANDRO BOTTICELLI

REALM OF VENUS (OR PRIMAVERA). c. 1482. Tempera on wood with oil glazes, 6′8″ × 10′4″. Galleria degli Uffizi, Florence. This painting is first documented in 1498 in the Florentine palace of Lorenzo di Pierfrancesco de' Medici and Giovanni di Pierfrancesco de' Medici. The former, a cousin of Lorenzo the Magnificent who married in May 1482, was most likely the patron.

The *Realm of Venus* and the *Birth of Venus*, by Sandro Botticelli (1445–1510), are among the first large-scale paintings to be devoted to mythological themes since antiquity. Botticelli's figures are other-worldly deities who do not belong to the realm of the real. Their exquisite beauty asserts their divine nature.

The *Realm of Venus* (fig. 5-59) represents Venus reigning in a garden where it is always spring. The citrus fruit shown here was sacred to her. On the left, Mercury drives away the clouds seen in the upper left corner. Venus reigns as goddess of love and marriage, and Botticelli's painting may be a decoration made to celebrate a marriage. The unpredictable nature of love is suggested by the blindfolded Cupid, son of Venus, who shoots an arrow at her attendants. The physical nature of love is suggested by Zephyr, on the far right, who has the nymph Chloris in his arms. After seducing and marrying her, he returns her to the garden, where we witness her transmogrification into the goddess Flora, who strews flowers. Flora is the goddess of spring (*primavera* in Italian). Her festival, Floralia, was celebrated in April and May, months ruled by the astrological deities Venus and Mercury.

Botticelli's *Birth of Venus* (fig. 5-60) celebrates the ancient myth that Venus was born full grown. Here she is blown ashore in a storm of roses by Zephyr and Chloris, to be received by one of her attendants. Her pose is based on ancient sculptures, but she is hardly sculptural. The elegance of the

5-60   SANDRO BOTTICELLI

BIRTH OF VENUS. c. 1484–86. Tempera on canvas, 5′9″ × 9′2″. Galleria degli Uffizi, Florence. Who commissioned this secular, mythological painting is unknown, but most likely the patron chose the subject and suggested the particular interpretation. The most popular previous secular decorations for Florentine palaces had been Flemish tapestries, and the patterns, colors, and gold highlights of Botticelli's painting may be an attempt to relate to and even rival tapestries. The unusual fact that this is painted on canvas suggests that it may originally have functioned as a processional banner. Most likely commissioned by a member of the Medici family.

figure is set off by the intertwining patterns of Venus's hair. The enframing figures enhance her unexpectedly introspective quality. The *Birth of Venus* is strongly reminiscent of a passage in Alberti's *On Painting*:

> Let [hair] wind itself into a coil as if desiring to knot itself and let it wave in the air like unto flames. . . . Let no part of the drapery be free from movement. . . . It will be well to put into the painting the face of the

wind Zephyr or Auster blowing among the clouds, showing why the drapery flutters.

Humanist philosophy in Florence during the later fifteenth century was dominated by Neoplatonism, and in Neoplatonic terms, Venus personified beauty, and beauty equaled truth. The Neoplatonic philosopher Marsilio Ficino wrote in a letter:

> Venus [is] Humanitas. . . . Her soul and mind are Love and

Charity, her eyes Dignity and Magnanimity. . . . The whole, then, is Temperance and Honesty, Charm and Splendor. . . . How beautiful to behold!

The Neoplatonists went even further and equated Venus, source of divine love, with the Virgin Mary. Such an approach to ancient themes may explain why, in the final analysis, Botticelli's figures of Venus both seem to be so meditative.

Italian Renaissance Painting:
Leonardo Da Vinci

5-61 LEONARDO DA VINCI

MADONNA OF THE ROCKS. 1483–85. Oil on wood, transferred to canvas, 6'2½" × 48". The Louvre, Paris. A second version of this painting is in the National Gallery, London. The exact meaning of Leonardo's painting remains mysterious and elusive, with the holy group set within a darkened cave. Detailed foreground naturalism is combined with a background that seems to belong to a primitive world, where the forces of nature are still carving the mountainous landscape. Commissioned by the Confraternity of the Immaculate Conception for their chapel in San Francesco Grande, Milan.

LEONARDO DA VINCI, FLORENTINE, 1452–1519. *VIRGIN OF THE ROCKS*, 1483–85. LOUVRE, PARIS

In his *Lives of the Artists*, Vasari viewed the High Renaissance of the late fifteenth and early six-teenth centuries as the perfection and culmination of all the investigation and experimentation that had character-ized Early Renaissance art, and he rightly argued that the transition to the High Renaissance occurred with the art of Leonardo da Vinci. One aspect of this transition took place when Leonardo developed a new unified composition in which he grouped figures to suggest a solid geometric form, such as a pyramid or cone. In Leonardo's *Madonna of the Rocks*, the figures are related to each other to form a pyramid (fig. 5-61). Mary's head forms the apex; her right arm extends to grasp the infant Saint John the Baptist, who is worshiping the Christ Child. To our right, the angel's head and billowing red cloak define another side of the triangle, while the Christ Child, who blesses the Baptist, extends the triangle forward, anchoring the pyramid. In a splendid example of foreshortening, Mary extends her left hand over the Christ Child, as if to offer protection and blessing. For Leonardo, the achievement of a unified composition did not mean a static presentation—the language of gesture in the *Madonna of the Rocks*, for example, is varied and complex.

Leonardo's use of the pyramidal composition has multiple meanings. As a compositional scheme, the pyramidal grouping offers visual unity and stability, while it also carries the religious association of the Christian Trinity. As a geometric form, the pyramid relates to the Renaissance macrocosmic/microcosmic tradition, based in antiquity, which held that everything in the universe is governed by the order and precision of geometry. This tradition equated the human figure, or microcosm (small world), to the universe, the macrocosm. This complex philosophical notion found expression in a number of drawings known as the *Vitruvian Man*, the most familiar of which is by Leonardo (fig. 5-62). The image of a human figure with arms and legs outstretched to touch both a circle and a square is based on a passage from the ancient Roman writer Vitruvius, who suggested that there is a consonance

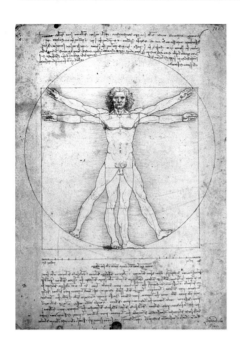

5-62 LEONARDO DA VINCI

Florentine, 1452–1519. *Vitruvian Man: Study of the Human Body [Le proporzioni del corpo umano]*, c. 1492. Pen and ink, 13½ × 9⅝″. Gallerie dell'Accademia, Venice, Italy.

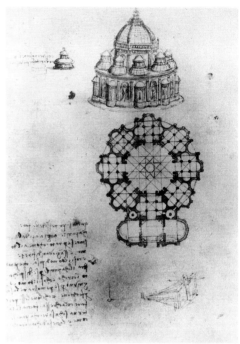

5-63 LEONARDO DA VINCI

View and plan of a centrally planned church. c. 1489. Pen and ink, 9¹⁄₁₆ × 6⁵⁄₁₆″. Institute de France, Paris. No patron, but perhaps related to churches commissioned for Milan by Duke Lodovico Sforza.

between the human body and the perfection of geometry that related the body to the mathematical systems inherent in the universe. This fundamental belief in macrocosmic/microcosmic analogy influenced Italian artists to compose figures in geometric configurations, thus creating a visual harmony alluding to the ideal harmony of the universe. Leonardo experimented with the unified composition in many studies, always seeking to incorporate a variety of poses to reflect the vitality of life.

In the 1480s. Leonardo began to design a series of **centrally planned churches** (fig. 5-63). These drawings, which evolve from simple to more complex structures, were probably intended for a treatise on architecture. Not one of Leonardo's designs was built. His involvement with centrally planned

structures may have been in part inspired by Alberti's book *On Architecture*, which dates from about 1450. Alberti, citing the common appearance of the circle in bird nests and other forms in nature, recommended the central plan as an ideal one for church architecture. Theologically, the circle, without beginning or end, was considered symbolic of the perfection of God. Leonardo's conceptions of centrally planned churches as embodied in his drawings often combined exterior views with sections and/or plans. Drawn while Leonardo was working in Milan, they influenced Donato Bramante, who would later develop the centrally planned structure for St. Peter's in Rome (see figs. 6-30–6-34).

Italian Renaissance Painting: Leonardo's *The Last Supper*

5-64 LEONARDO DA VINCI

LAST SUPPER, wall painting in the Refectory, Santa Maria dell Grazie, Milan. c. 1495–98. Oil, tempera, and varnish, 14′ × 28′10½″; the figures are over-lifesize. The Dominican monastery of Santa Maria delle Grazie was supported by Lodovico Sforza, duke and ruler of Milan, who commissioned Leonardo to paint *The Last Supper*. This view shows the painting in the course of the recent restoration, which has brought to light subtle details of facial expressions and radiant colors that had been covered by earlier restorers, who repainted rather than cleaned the surface.

According to Leonardo da Vinci,

Painted figures ought to be done in such a way that those who see them will be able to easily recognize from their attitudes the thoughts of their minds.

Leonardo's *Last Supper*, painted in the dining hall of a monastery, exemplifies his maxim that figures should express emotional and psychological realism (fig. 5-64). The stable and calm figure of Jesus, who is both on the axis and at the focal point of the scientific perspective construction, forms a triangle that, while symbolic of the Trinity, also gives visual stability to the composition and contrasts with the activity of the apostles who flank him.

The agitated movement of the apostles reveals their psychological turmoil in reaction to Jesus' declaration, "I say unto you, that one of you shall betray me" (Matthew 26:21). The impact of these words on the apostles is understandable when we realize that they had left their families, friends, and professions to follow him. Now, when celebrating a Passover meal, Jesus announces that one of them will be a betrayer. The apostles' reactions are shown in different physical attitudes that reveal such psychological responses as surprise, piety, uncertainty, and faithfulness.

The powerful emotional drama that we perceive in the *Last Supper* is but one level of meaning in Leonardo's complex painting. In earlier Last Supper paintings, Judas had been shown on our side of the table, removed from the space occupied by Jesus and his apostles. Leonardo, however, kept Judas with his fellow apostles. The fourth figure from the left, he is shown recoiling from Jesus. Judas is the only figure whose face is lost in shadow, a subtle indication that he is lost from the light of Jesus.

Leonardo has joined the depiction of these two episodes with a third. The hands of Jesus are directed toward the bread and wine on the table, suggesting the institution of the Eucharist.

The activity of these dramas is contained within an impressive organization. Light from the upper left (following the placement of windows in the refectory) defines the figures. The grouping of the apostles on each side of Christ provides symmetry, while the positioning of the apostles in four groups of three discloses the numerical symbolism of the spiritual (3 is the number of the Trinity) and material (4 is the number of the elements) components of creation. This expression of universality, is also apparent in the number 12: in keeping Judas with the eleven faithful apostles, Leonardo retains the integrity of the number 12, which refers not only to the apostles but also to the months of the year and the hours of day and of night, extending the numerical symbolism to include the cycles of time.

It is now difficult to discern the subtle details that Leonardo intended, for in an attempt to achieve a new subtlety in mural painting, Leonardo, always the inventor, mixed his pigments with a combination of oil, tempera, and varnish, producing a paint that proved disastrous almost from the start. However, we can glean some sense of its intended effect from surviving preliminary drawings. The study for the head of Judas exhibits an acute understanding of anatomy and physiognomy (fig. 5-65). Such detailed, descriptive observation, found in numerous studies, was joined to a unified, yet complex narrative interpretation.

1492	Christopher Columbus lands at San Salvador and Cuba
1492	Death of Lorenzo the Magnificent
1492	First known reference to smoking tobacco
c. 1495–98	Leonardo, *Last Supper*

5-65 LEONARDO DA VINCI

STUDY FOR THE HEAD OF JUDAS, preparatory drawing for the *Last Supper*. 1495–97. Red chalk on red prepared paper, 7⅛ × 5⅛". Royal Library, Windsor Castle, Berkshire, England. Leonardo draws attention to the figure's neck in order to refer to Judas' suicide by hanging after his betrayal. No patron, but related to Leonardo's work for Duke Lodovico Sforza.

Art Past/Art Present *Leonardo's Last Supper Restored*

On Friday, May 28, 1999, Leonardo's restored *Last Supper* was unveiled after more than twenty years of painstaking work by Pinin Bambilla Barcilon, who, in her own words, restored the painting "centimeter by centimeter," at a total cost of $7.7 million. Leonardo's work had been in extremely bad repair. Ever the inventor, Leonardo disavowed the traditional fresco technique (see pp. 222-23, and painted with an oil and egg medium on dry plaster, an experiment that led to an early deterioration of the surface. Successive repaintings, humidity, pollution, and the abuse of the refectory (the room was used as a stable by French invaders and suffered from bomb damage in World War II) led to an ever-worsening condition. Various art experts have estimated that only between 20 percent and 50 percent of Leonardo's painting has survived.

As with most significant art restorations, the *Last Supper* opened to mixed reviews. While new details of the painting were brought to light in the process, such as items of food, finger bowls, wine glasses, and the decoration on the tablecloth, many questions were raised. Some experts were shocked by the intensity of the colors. Had the restorer gone too far, perhaps removing parts of Leonardo's original painting? Is this a restoration or yet another repainting? Were not the repaintings themselves part of the history of the work? Such questions feed the continuing debate and controversy. Some critics have called the restoration "catastrophic," saying that the painting now looks like a "postcard," while others have hailed it as an eminent achievement.

Italian Renaissance Sculpture: Michelangelo's St. Peter's *Pietà*

5-66 MICHELANGELO BUONARROTI

PIETÀ. 1498–99. Marble, height 5'8½"; the figures are over-lifesize. St. Peter's Basilica, Vatican, Rome, Italy. On August 27, 1498, a twenty-three-year-old sculptor from Florence, Michelangelo Buonarroti, signed a contract in Rome for a Pietà, intended as a tomb sculpture. The contract was repeating tradition when it stated that the completed group should be the "most beautiful work of marble in Rome," but the work Michelangelo created within about a year and a half fulfilled the terms of the contract in a new and unparalleled way. Commissioned by the French Cardinal Jean de Bilhères Lagraulas for the chapel where he planned to be buried at Old St. Peter's in Rome.

1497   Vasco da Gama lands in India
1498–99   Michelangelo, St. Peter's *Pietà*
1498   Savonarola is burned at the stake in Florence

The Rome *Pietà* by Michelangelo Buonarroti (1475–1564) demonstrates a command of concept and tragic expression, drawn with consummate skill from an inert block of marble (fig. 5-66). The Virgin Mary, seated on a rock, cradles the lifeless body of her son, which has just been taken down from the cross. With the open gesture of her left hand, she presents her son's sacrifice to us. The design of the sculpture, with its sweeping passages of drapery, is coherently resolved into a pyramidal composition.

The theme that we call the Pietà (Italian for "pity" or "piety") is not found in the Bible. The image first appears in northern European Gothic sculptures in which anatomical details are exaggerated to emphasize Jesus' suffering and death. The German Gothic *Pietà* illustrated here demands an immediate and powerful devotional response from the viewer (fig. 5-67).

Michelangelo's biographer Ascanio Condivi, writing in 1553, recorded that with the St. Peter's *Pietà* the sculptor wanted to show "that the Son of God truly assumed human form," so that his physical suffering could be easily understood. But Michelangelo's conception of humanity is also rooted in the idealism of the Italian Renaissance, and he avoided the distortions of earlier Northern Pietà images in favor of an interpretation that conveyed his views on the integrity and beauty of the body. While still a young man in Florence, Michelangelo had studied human anatomy, and from early dissection practice he learned the structure of the human body. His authority over anatomy is displayed here in the figure

of Jesus. In a more subtle way than with earlier Pietàs, we can identify with Jesus' humanity and better understand his suffering and death. Unlike the wailing mother of the Gothic *Pietà*, Michelangelo's beautiful figure of Mary bears her sorrowful burden with quiet, meditative resignation. Michelangelo here suggests an inner suffering restrained by dignity.

In describing the St. Peter's *Pietà*, Vasari, in his book *Lives of the Artists*, observed the beauty and technical achievement of the sculpture:

> Among the lovely things to be seen in the work, to say nothing of the divinely beautiful draperies, is the body of Christ; nor let anyone think to see a greater beauty of members or more mastery of art in any body, or a nude with more detail in the muscles, veins and nerves over the framework of the bones, nor yet a corpse more similar than this to a real corpse. Here is perfect sweetness in the expression of the head, harmony in the joints and attachments of the arms, legs, and trunk, and the pulses and veins so wrought, that in truth Wonder herself must marvel that the hand of a craftsman should have been able to execute so divinely and so perfectly, in so short a time, a work so admirable; and it is certainly a miracle that a stone without any shape at the beginning should ever have been reduced to such perfection as Nature is scarcely able to create in the flesh.

5-67   GERMAN GOTHIC

PIETÀ. Early 14th century. Polychromed wood, height 34½″. Provinzialmuseum, Bonn, Germany.

The sculpture was an astounding success in Rome. Vasari goes on to report, however, that when the *Pietà* was newly finished, questions arose as to the identity of the artist. To end any doubts, Michelangelo carved his signature on the ribbon that crosses Mary's torso. The Rome *Pietà* is the only work Michelangelo ever signed.

View of a portion of the ceiling frescoes in the Sistine Chapel in the Vatican, Rome, painted by Michelangelo, 1508–1512, by order of Pope Julius II (for more information see fig. 6-35—6-37 and pp. 300-303).

Sixteenth-Century Art

A Brief Insight

EVEN BEFORE ITS COMPLETION IN 1512, MICHELANGELO'S Sistine Chapel ceiling was acknowledged to be a masterpiece. Writing a few decades later, one art historian recorded the almost breathless excitement of the unveiling: "When the work was thrown open, the whole world came running to see what Michelangelo had done; and certainly it was such as to make everyone speechless with astonishment." (Giorgio Vasari)

The term masterpiece initially was applied to an exemplary work crafted by a person who, having completed years of study, known as an apprenticeship, sought to attain the rank of "Master" in the rigidly controlled artists' guild. Our concept of the masterpiece has been expanded to include an outstanding work of art representing one of the most impressive attainments of an artist or cultural period.

The Sistine Chapel ceiling ranks as one of several masterpieces created during the sixteenth century. The heroic scale and powerful presence of the figures are characteristic of the High Renaissance. But the sixteenth century was a time of great change, and the faith and optimism displayed by the figures here eventually gave way to other insights into the human condition.

Sixteenth-Century Art

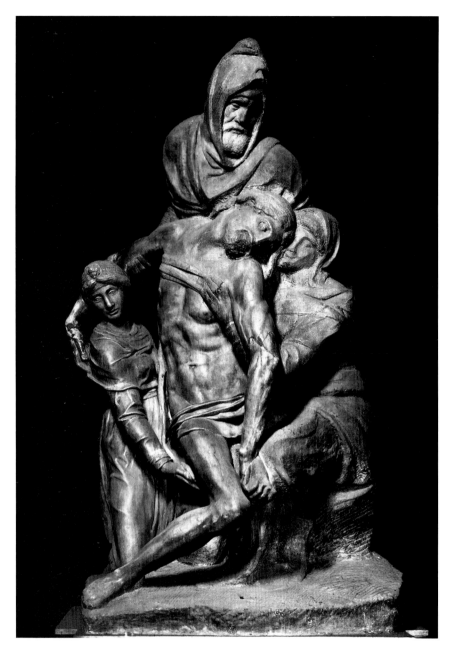

6-1 MICHELANGELO BUONARROTI

PIETÀ. c. 1547–55. Marble, height 7'8". Museo dell' Opera del Duomo, Florence, Tuscany, Italy. After working on this sculpture for almost a decade, Michelangelo smashed it in anger, leaving it seriously damaged. He presented the damaged work to a pupil, who repaired it and laboriously finished the figure of Mary Magdalene on our left. Although based on Michelangelo's design, she is now too small for the composition and no longer seems to be supporting Jesus' right arm. Jesus' left leg, which was once positioned over Mary's, is completely lost. Theories have been advanced as to why Michelangelo attacked the work. Giorgio Vasari, writing in 1568, stated that the artist discovered that the marble was flawed.

By the middle of the sixteenth century, when Michelangelo's Florence *Pietà* was created, the optimism that had characterized so much of fifteenth- and early-sixteenth-century Italian Renaissance art had evaporated. This new pessimistic mood is conveyed by Michelangelo's *Pietà* (fig. 6-1). We sense the dead weight of Jesus' body in the angular arrangement of limbs, the head collapsed to one side, and the efforts needed to support the body. To our right, the Virgin tenderly presses her face against her son's head. Behind, the towering figure of Nicodemus, a follower of Jesus, compassionately helps support his dead master.

Although the legacy of the High Renaissance is evident in the musculature of the body of the central figure, the elongated figures and unstable composition break the norm of Renaissance harmony. Grief has seized the participants, and this emotional impact is reinforced when we realize that Nicodemus is a self-portrait of the artist. Michelangelo (1475–1564), who was about seventy-two years old when he began carving the Florence *Pietà*, intended it to be placed over his own tomb. Its unsettling emotional content reflects his personal psychological condition and may also be related to the tumultuous conflicts of sixteenth-century Europe.

6-2   Chinese. Porcelain dish decorated with chrysanthemum patterns. Ming dynasty, Hung Wu period, 1369–98. Underglaze blue on porcelain, diameter 18″. Östasiatiska Museet, Stockholm, Sweden.

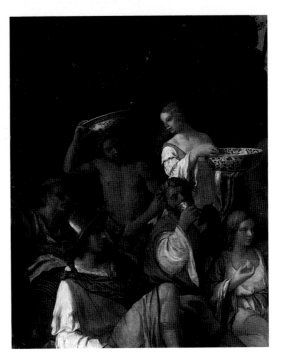

6-3   GIOVANNI BELLINI

FEAST OF THE GODS, detail showing Chinese Ming porcelains. 1514. Oil on canvas, 5′7″ × 7′2″. National Gallery of Art, Washington, D.C. Commissioned by Alfonso d'Este for his Studiolo in the Castle of Ferrara.

WIDENER COLLECTION

History

The extent and importance of contacts between widespread and highly diverse cultures that had so long been a feature of global history were expanded in the sixteenth century, especially through the dramatic increase in traffic on the high seas, new explorations, and new interest in mapping the globe. The precious objects and fine goods (such as spices) of one culture were exchanged for the luxury goods of another culture. The high-quality porcelains

of the Ming dynasty (fig. 6-2), for example, found their way to the West, where they were greatly prized. Only after centuries of experimentation could the West begin to approximate the fine quality of these Chinese wares, and it is no accident that we still refer to our finest dishes as "china." One of the earliest representations of such china

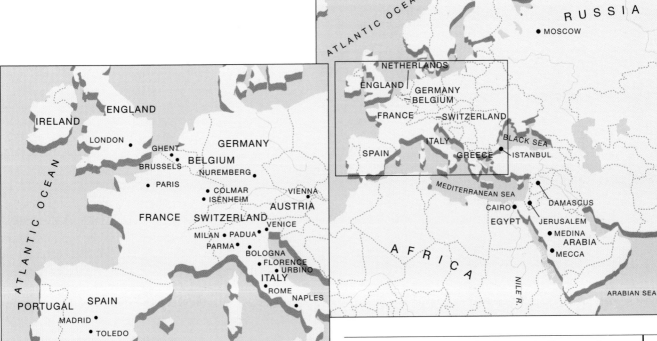

6-4 POSTNIK AND BARMA (?)

Cathedral of St. Basil the Blessed, Moscow, Russia. 1554–60 and later. No other work of architecture by either of these men is known; the names may be legendary or Barma ("mumble") may be Postnik's nickname. The structure was initially dedicated to the Virgin Mary, but it became known as St. Basil's when a holy man of that name was buried there in the 1550s. Commissioned by Tsar Ivan IV, the Terrible.

in European painting is in the *Feast of the Gods* (fig. 6-3) by Giovanni Bellini (1430–1516); the context makes it clear that such dishes were thought to be the appropriate vessels for deities. One of the great surviving collections of Chinese and Japanese porcelains was ordered by the Turkish sultans and is now on display in Istanbul.

Other contacts were less commercial. In 1582, a Jesuit priest named Matteo Ricci arrived in China and established a sinicized Jesuit Order in Guangzhou (Canton). He presented the emperor with a mechanical clock, the first in China, and guaranteed his continuing presence there as the only person who could keep it in working order. The underlying purpose of his mission was to establish a long-standing Christian base in one of the world's most populous, non-Christian nations.

In 1526, the Mughal empire, which would last until 1756, was established in India. The Muslim emperor Akbar (ruled 1556–1605) attempted to reconcile Muslim, Hindu, and Christian thought. In this philosophy of reconciliation, Mughal artists incorporated European elements, such as scientific perspective and atmospheric effects, into their paintings. Akbar and the two emperors who succeeded him were avid patrons of the arts.

The main political protagonists of the European sixteenth century—a period convulsed by shifting alliances—were the popes in Rome and the rulers of northern Europe. Pope Julius II succeeded in establishing the papacy as a major political power early in the century, but the newly strengthened Church conflicted with the expansive plans of secular rulers in the North, where the strife between Emperor Charles V of the Hapsburg line and Francis I, king of France, affected many aspects of sixteenth-century life. In 1520, Charles V was crowned Holy Roman Emperor, a position that Francis I had also sought. The territories ruled by Charles V were vast; they encompassed Spain, the Netherlands, and parts of northern Italy, Germany, and central and northern Europe. France was effectively isolated, but even a brief imprisonment did not deter Francis from his conflict with the emperor. Charles was usually aligned with the pope, but a significant break in this alliance occurred in 1527, after Pope Clement VII backed Francis I in an attempt to check the increasing power of the emperor. Charles V's troops entered and pillaged Rome that year and even imprisoned the pope. But the attention of Charles V was also directed toward the East, where he attempted to counter the expansion of the Ottoman Turks under Suleiman the Magnificent, who had extended his empire into eastern Europe and North Africa.

In areas that remained isolated, the local traditions sometimes became gradually more extreme and individualized. Russia, Christianized in 988, had adapted Byzantine forms—especially the multidomed, centrally planned church. Over time in Russia, however, the drums that supported the domes were heightened and the domes themselves took on a helmet shape, with a point at the top, and eventually they became "onion" domes, with heightened curves dominating the shape. The most extreme example of this trend came in the sixteenth century, when Ivan the Terrible commissioned a nine-domed church to commemorate his victory over the Tartars at Kazan. St. Basil's, next to the Kremlin on Red Square in Moscow, has become a symbol of Russia precisely because its forms are unparalleled in other cultures (fig. 6-4). The exotic quality of the structure may have been intentional on Ivan's part, for he might well have wanted a structure that was based on Russian traditions but which would, at the same time, give a new and distinct identity to his capital in Moscow. The later, seventeenth-century decoration of the domes with the forms and colors of Russian folk traditions has given the monument an even more distinct Russian flavor.

Throughout the century, expansion across the Atlantic continued. The Spanish were particularly active in colonizing. In 1513, Vasco Múñez de Balboa crossed Panama to reach and name the Pacific Ocean, and Juan Ponce de León established a settlement in Florida. In the late fifteenth and early sixteenth centuries, a Florentine merchant and seafarer, Amerigo Vespucci, charted eastern coastline areas of South America. In 1507, the mapmaker Martin Waldseemüller, drawing on Vespucci's information, demonstrated that Vespucci had reached land masses separate from Asia and suggested that they be named after Vespucci; hence they came to be called the Americas.

Intellectual and Scientific Developments in Europe

Although the vast majority of Europeans still felt bound to the scientific beliefs and superstitions that had guided life for centuries, important discoveries in the sixteenth century laid the foundation for the modern development of science. These discoveries were aided, in part, by the tremendously expanded publication of books. By 1600, about 2,000 books per year were being produced, a rate double that of a century earlier.

In 1543, two publications appeared that began to overturn many incorrect beliefs about human anatomy and the universe that had been based on the writings of ancient authors. De humani corporis fabrica (On the Fabric of the Human Body), written by Andreas Vesalius, began to clear away traditional misconceptions about anatomy and provide a base for later advances in medicine. Also in 1543, the Polish astronomer Nicolaus Copernicus, in De revolutionibus orbium coelestium (On the Revolution of the Celestial Spheres), asserted his theory of a heliocentric universe in which the planets revolve around the sun. This "modern" view of the universe, which had been held by a minority of philosophers since antiquity, was later popularized by Galileo Galilei, whose teachings, challenged by the Catholic Church, demonstrated the conflict between the new scientific reason and traditional religious authority.

The Protestant Reformation

The most significant religious event of the sixteenth century—one that would forever change the history of Christianity—was the Reformation. Over the centuries, the Catholic Church had become increasingly materialistic. The rebuilding of St. Peter's in Rome (see pages 298–99) and the construction of a new papal palace there led to the expansion of such unscrupulous practices as the selling of indulgences. According to Catholic belief, before gaining access to heaven, souls had to enter purgatory to suffer for their earthly sins. An indulgence allowed a person to "buy" a soul out of purgatory by the payment of a "donation." The proceeds of this expedient were shared by the local Catholic hierarchy and the papacy. Indulgences were especially solicited in Germany, leading to disillusionment within the local clergy.

A German Augustinian monk, Martin Luther (fig. 6-5), publicly questioned these practices, arguing that faith alone could "buy" salvation, in opposition to the Church's position that faith needed to be combined with good works. Aiming at reform from within, Luther drafted ninety-five theses, which he nailed to the doors of Wittenberg Cathedral on October 31, 1517. Among his theses, he argued:

6-5 LUCAS CRANACH THE ELDER

PORTRAIT OF MARTIN LUTHER. 1533. Oil on wood, 8¼ × 5⅞". German National Museum, Nuremberg, Germany. This is one of some fifty portraits of Luther painted by Cranach and his workshop.

> 27. There is no divine authority for preaching that the soul flies out of purgatory as soon as the money clinks in the bottom of the chest. . . .
> 50. Christians should be taught that, if the pope knew the exactions of the indulgence-preachers, he would rather the church of Saint Peter were reduced to ashes than be built with the skin, flesh, and bones of his sheep.

Luther called on German rulers to assist in promoting reform within the Church, but when he repudiated papal supremacy, Church authorities ruled that he was no longer a member—they excommunicated him.

The Reformation was soon bound to political realities. Most of the German princes were glad to restrict the power of the Church, which was draining their territories of wealth. Luther was given protection by Northern rulers, who were grasping the opportunity to counter Church authority and seize Church property. In 1529, Charles V ordered that measures be taken against those who dissented from the Catholic faith. The Lutheran princes who protested the emperor's order became known as Protestants. The open conflict that erupted in 1546 ended in 1555 with an agreement known as the Peace of Augsburg, which declared that the religion of a ruler determined the religion of that area. It was a victory for the Protestants.

Protestantism spread, with different groups developing in different areas of Europe. In England, Henry VIII requested that Pope Clement VII annul his marriage. Papal refusal led to the 1534 Act of Supremacy, which made the English sover-

6-6 RAPHAEL

MADONNA AND CHILD WITH SAINT JOHN THE BAPTIST (also known as *LA BELLE JARDINIÈRE*). 1508. Oil on wood, 48 × 31½". The Louvre, Paris. The infant John the Baptist, kneeling in the foreground, holds a cross and wears an animal skin to refer to the time he will spend in the wilderness. Commissioned by Filippo Sergardi.

eign the head of the English (Anglican) Church. In Switzerland, another Protestant movement flourished under John Calvin. Calvinism stressed the supremacy of the Bible as a guide for moral conduct. By the end of the century, approximately one-fourth of western Europe's population was Protestant. The ramifications of these developments for art became obvious in the course of the seventeenth century and later.

The Counter-Reformation

The response of the Roman Catholic Church to the Reformation is usually known as the Counter-Reformation. Voices calling for reform had been heard within the Catholic Church even before the Lutheran challenge, but the rapid growth of Protestantism led the Church to call a major council at Trent, in north Italy. Between 1545 and 1563, the Council of Trent established policies for internal reform and planned a strategy to combat the spread of Protestantism,

6-7 PARMIGIANINO

MADONNA AND CHILD WITH ANGELS AND A PROPHET (known as the
MADONNA WITH THE LONG NECK). 1534–40 (unfinished). Oil on wood,
7'1" × 4'4". Galleria degli Uffizi, Florence. Commissioned by Elena
Baiardi for the Church of the Servites, Parma, Italy.

6-8 LUDOVICO CARRACCI

MADONNA AND CHILD WITH SAINTS JEROME AND FRANCIS (or *MADONNA
DEGLI SCALZI*). 1590–93. Oil on canvas, 7 × 5'. Pinacoteca Nazionale,
Bologna, Italy. Commissioned by a member of the Bentivoglio family
for their chapel in the Chiesa della Madonna degli Scalzi, Bologna.

which was viewed as a heresy. Enforcement of the
Church's beliefs and policies was given to the Inquisition, an
ecclesiastical court established in the late Middle Ages to
punish heretics.

Calls for an educated priesthood were met by a new order
of priests founded by Ignatius of Loyola in 1534. Loyola, from
Spain, had been a soldier in the armies of Charles V. While
recovering from a leg wound, he read the lives of Christ and
the saints and determined to devote his life to Christ and the
defense of the Church. He founded the Society of Jesus,
commonly referred to as the Jesuits, which was distinguished
by its missionary zeal, preaching, and scholarly interests. As
teachers, Jesuits founded many influential schools and were
counted among the intellectual leaders of the time. Their
achievements contributed to a restored respect for the
Catholic Church.

At the final session of the Council of Trent, the Church
reaffirmed the value of art in promoting religious education.
According to the council, religious art should appeal to the
emotions, be morally acceptable, and use clear compositions. Accuracy in theology was required; failure to meet
these requirements made the artist answerable to the
Inquisition. The impact of this policy contributed to new
directions in art and was of significance for artistic and
iconographic developments in the seventeenth century.

European Sixteenth-Century Art

During the sixteenth century in Italy, three successive styles
can be deduced: High Renaissance, Mannerism, and early
Baroque; because of the importance of Italy as an artistic
center, these styles would have an important impact on the

rest of Europe in the sixteenth century and into the seventeenth. Three paintings with a similar theme demonstrate the visual characteristics of each style.

Madonna and Child with Saint John the Baptist by Raphael (1483–1520) exemplifies the union of ideality and naturalism that characterizes the High Renaissance (fig. 6-6). Bathed in soft gold light, the seated Madonna tenderly embraces the Christ Child. The relaxed pose of the child lends a note of informality. The flowers and plants are painted with precise observation, and naturalism is also evident in the modeling of the figures and in the atmospheric perspective of the distant landscape. Such naturalistic details, however, are part of an idealized composition seen in the pyramidal grouping. In Raphael's painting, the world as it is seen is joined to ideals of perfection. A divergent branch of High Renaissance art would develop in Venice, with greater experimentation with colors, broader brushstrokes, and more dynamic compositions.

Madonna and Child with Angels and a Prophet (fig. 6-7) by Parmigianino (1503–40) was painted about thirty years after Raphael's *Madonna*. This Mannerist painting exhibits an aristocratic elegance: elongated figural proportions are evident (note especially the fingers of Mary's right hand), while the languid body of the Christ Child, the prominent leg of the angel, and the drapery clinging to Mary's torso create a distinctly sensual effect. The illusion of space is consciously disjointed, with columns (unfinished) in the background that rise to gigantic proportions. Derived from the Italian term *maniera*—meaning "style" in the sense of sophistication, elegance, and poise—Mannerist art moved away from the classical values of the High Renaissance. Mannerist artists sought to create an artificial and complex construction to demonstrate their intellectual and technical virtuosity and the sophistication of their patrons.

The *Madonna degli Scalzi* (fig. 6-8) by Ludovico Carracci (1555–1619) might be seen as a reaction against the visual complexity of Mannerist painting. Dating from late in the century, it can be considered an early Baroque work since the painting displays many of those features that will characterize Baroque art as it develops in the seventeenth century. The figures are rendered with an easily understood naturalism. Mary, raised on the axis on a crescent moon, holds a lively Christ Child. Christ extends his hand to Saint Francis, on our right, while Saint Jerome, with his symbolic lion, looks attentively from the left. A halo of golden light surrounds Mary's head. The light reflects on a host of angels joyously playing musical instruments. Carracci's emphasis on religious expression, visualized in a simple yet forceful composition, has an emotional appeal well suited to communicate the aims of the Counter-Reformation Church.

In northern Europe, the ideality of the Italian High Renaissance art affected many artists, especially Albrecht Dürer (1471–1528). Much of Northern painting, however, continued an adherence to a strict naturalism that can be related to the developments of Flemish painting during the

6-9 ALBRECHT DÜRER

PRAYING HANDS. 1508–09. Brush, heightened with white, on blue-grounded paper, 11½ × 7¾". Albertina, Vienna, Austria. This is among a number of surviving drawings for one of Dürer's most famous works, the *Heller Altarpiece*, which was commissioned by Jacob Heller, a merchant of Frankfurt.

fifteenth century (see pages 242–43, 250–51, 256–59). Dürer's drawing of *Praying Hands* (fig. 6-9), for example, demonstrates the continuing commitment to naturalistic observation and fine detail by Northern artists.

The Sixteenth-Century Artist in Europe

The new respect for the artist as an intellectual, which had developed in the fifteenth century (see page 235), made impressive gains during the sixteenth century. In Italy, both Michelangelo and Raphael earned the nickname *il divino* ("the divine one"), a sign that the artist was now being viewed as an almost godlike creator. Artists continued to make self-portraits throughout the century. Parmigianino's unusual *Self-Portrait in a Convex Mirror* (fig. 6-10) reflects the intellectual and aesthetic conceits associated with Mannerist art.

Art theory continued to evolve within an intellectual climate that nourished it, and other types of writings contributed to the elevated social status of the artist. Baldassare

6-10 PARMIGIANINO

Self-Portrait in a Convex Mirror. 1524. Oil on wood, diameter 9⅝".
Kunsthistorisches Museum, Vienna. Parmigianino's *Self-Portrait* is
actually painted on a convex wooden panel to heighten the illusionism.

6-11 SOPHONISBA ANGUISSOLA

Portrait of the Artist's Three Sisters with Their Governess. 1555.
Oil on canvas, 27³⁄₁₆ × 37". Narodowe Museum, Potsdam, Germany.
Sophonisba Anguissola, who was also trained in music, languages,
and literature, is the first nationally recognized woman artist of
whom we have any certain knowledge. She is credited with inventing
a new type of group portraiture in which the sitters are shown in
lively activity and psychological interaction rather than being merely
aligned and accompanied by conventional props. Here she shows her
sisters during a game of chess, an intellectual activity usually
restricted to men at this time. The picture thus makes an important
point about the capabilities of young women during this period, in
which so many restrictions on female behavior were accepted. At
the same time, it demonstrates the artist's interest in capturing
complex personal interrelationships through gesture and expression.

Castiglione, an Italian diplomat and literary figure, included
witticisms and more serious discussions on art in his *Book of
the Courtier*. Benvenuto Cellini's fame as an artist was
buttressed by his theoretical writings and a roguish *Autobiography* that still enjoys great popularity.

Giorgio Vasari, an artist active at the Medici court in
Florence, published his *Lives of the Most Eminent Painters,
Sculptors, and Architects* in 1550 and revised it for a second
edition in 1568. Vasari viewed Renaissance art as an evolu-
tionary progression (see page 231). Beginning with Giotto in
the fourteenth century, he argued, Italian art had been rescued from the "dark ages" to be restored in the light of classical eloquence. Each generation of artists built upon the
foundation set by the previous generation until perfection
was reached with the High Renaissance. Throughout the
Lives, Vasari noted the regard in which great rulers held
artists, enjoying their friendship and advice.

When Vasari wrote the *Lives*, he had more in mind than
just art history. He was promoting the establishment of an
art academy. His efforts assisted in founding the Florentine
Accademia del Disengo (Academy of Design) in 1563. In
this academy, and in many other academies that followed,
artists were educated within a broad liberal-arts context.
This enhanced education made it more possible for at least
some artists to mingle with the higher social ranks. The
artistic, intellectual, and social gains made by artists during
the sixteenth century gave us a new concept of the artist,
that of an inspired genius.

One benefit of these social changes for the artist was
that the profession began to open its ranks, however slowly
at first, to women. During the Middle Ages, women artists
had been active primarily as embroiderers and manuscript
illuminators. By the sixteenth century, women were
becoming established as painters as well. In Italy, both
Sophonisba Anguissola (fig. 6-11) and Lavinia Fontana (fig.
6-12) developed high reputations.

6-12 LAVINIA FONTANA

Self-Portrait. c. 1577. Oil on copper, diameter 6". Galleria degli
Uffizi, Florence. This self-portrait, which shows the artist in her
studio, captures the confident elegance of Mannerist portraiture.
Lavinia Fontana, from Bologna, was the daughter of a painter. She
married a fellow student in her father's studio on the condition that
she be free to follow her career. Her husband apparently assisted her
by painting frames or by painting the clothing in some of her
portraits. A portrait medal of 1611 shows her painting in an attitude
that suggests that she, like Michelangelo, was divinely inspired.

6-13 TITIAN

"Venus" of Urbino (for more information see fig. 6-41).

6-14 MICHELANGELO

David (for more information see fig. 6-18).

While the nude human figure is now widely accepted as an appropriate subject for art, this was not always the case. The nude was an uncommon subject during the period 200–1400, for example, but it was reintroduced into European art during the Italian Renaissance, the period when these two works were created. Although both Michelangelo's *David* and Titian's reclining nude are idealized representations of the nude body, the role they performed in society was distinct. It is not certain whether Titian's figure was a stereotypically ideal female or was intended to be a portrait, perhaps somewhat idealized, of a real woman, but documents tell us that the work was ordered by a male patron, and it was most likely intended for his personal pleasure and perhaps also for him to show to his male friends.

This, then, was a private erotic work. Michelangelo's colossal idealized male nude, on the other hand, was commissioned to be placed in a public setting and its purpose was political. The muscular quality and heroic scale of the nude was meant to express to both the Florentines and their enemies the potential power of the Florentine state. Florence might be small like David, the Old Testament boy who defeated the giant Goliath, but it was a city to be feared. The re-emergence of the idealized nude as a subject in the Renaissance is an important indication of new attitudes about the validity of life in this world in European thought. The idealism seen here is, of course, only one of the many uses to which artists have put the nude human figure.

The choice of the nude female body for representation in the prehistoric era is most likely related to the presumed function of this work in a fertility ritual. Notice the exaggeration of the breasts, abdomen, and thighs: all parts of the body related to childbearing. In this functional object, the ideal of the human body as a beautiful thing is not an issue.

6-15 Prehistoric Statuette of a Woman (for more information see fig. 2-4 and p. 26).

ERICH LESSING/NATURHISTORISCHES MUSEUM, VIENNA, AUSTRIA/ART RESOURCE.

While to western eyes the voluptuousness of this figure, with its large breasts and dance-like stance, seems to offer the promise of sexual pleasure, the purpose of this figure on the gate at the Buddhist stupa at Sanchi reminds us that in many cultures sexuality is in part a metaphor for the fertility of the broader natural world. This *Yakshi* refers not so much to the sexual act as to the continuation of the family, group, or tribe, and the fecundity necessary for the good harvest needed for survival.

6-16 Buddhist, *YAKSHI* from Sanchi (for more information see figs. 3-88 and 3-90 and pp. 96–99).

6-17 REMBRANDT *BATHSHEBA WITH KING DAVID'S LETTER* (for more information see fig. 7-36).

Rembrandt's use of the nude female body in this painting may be the result of a challenge that the artist posed himself: could he de-emphasize or even deny the sexual qualities of the nude female figure by emphasizing her psychological/emotional state? If you know the story (see p. 362), you know that it was Bathsheba's body that led her into a dangerous predicament, one that would eventually lead to the murder of her husband. By choosing to represent Bathsheba as a mature nude woman, weighty and naturalistic, Rembrandt makes her seem all the more vulnerable.

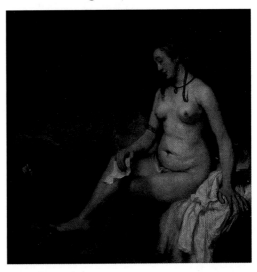

QUESTIONS

1. Find an example of an advertisement, a billboard, or a television commercial that uses the nude (or almost nude) body and examine how the body is being used to help sell a product. Is the use of the body related to the product, or is the body irrelevant in this case?

2. How do you think individuals or governments in other cultures would respond to this advertisement?

Italian Renaissance Sculpture: Michelangelo

6-18 MICHELANGELO BUONARROTI

DAVID. 1501–04. Marble, height 13′ 5″. Galleria dell' Accademia, Florence. In 1873, the statue was moved from its original location, at the entrance of the Palazzo della Signoria, to the Accademia, where a special setting had been constructed for it. The medium is white marble from Carrara, near Pisa. These quarries still yield vast quantities of fine-quality marble for artistic and architectural use. On a sheet of paper with drawings for the right arm of *David* and for a bronze statue of the same subject, Michelangelo wrote a couplet: "David with his sling / and I with my bow / Michelangelo." These lines have been interpreted with reference to Michelangelo's psychological state as he was about to carve the *David*. Just as David had the most meager of weapons, a sling, with which to battle Goliath, Michelangelo had only a simple sculptor's bow with which to attack the huge block of marble already misshapen by earlier attempts to carve it. For Michelangelo, the bow was a sculptor's drill, used for boring into the marble. It was one of the limited number of traditional sculptor's tools used by his predecessors. The drill is still an important tool in certain kinds of sculpture. Commissioned by the Cathedral Administration to be placed on a buttress below the dome of Florence Cathedral (see fig. 5-42).

Michelangelo's huge sculpture of the Old Testament hero David is a stirring embodiment of physical and psychological strength (fig. 6-18). Michelangelo chose an unusual moment to represent, for he shows David before his battle with the enemy Goliath. The sling is over his shoulder and the stone rests in his right hand, but his muscles are taut and a defiant scowl seizes his face. The figure pulls powerfully to the left, away from the implied enemy, and David's apprehension is further indicated in the swelling veins in his hand and the sucking in of his breath revealed in the tensed muscles of his abdomen. In Michelangelo's interpretation, David has become human. In his *Lives*, Vasari, referring to the huge block of white marble from which Michelangelo carved the *David*, said that the sculptor had brought

to life a thing that was dead.

In saying that Michelangelo had given life to the stone, Vasari alluded not only to his artistic accomplishment but also to the history of the block of marble from which the *David* was carved. Quarried in 1464, before Michelangelo's birth, the enormous block was brought to Florence to be carved, perhaps under the supervision of the aging Donatello, as a *David*, one of a series of Old Testament prophets to be placed high above street level on the buttresses of the cathedral. The stone, partially carved, languished in the courtyard of the cathedral workshop for decades.

We do not know to what extent the stone had been carved before Michelangelo received the commission to finish the statue in 1501 and cannot, therefore, judge the difficulties he had to overcome. We do know that it was decided not to hoist the completed sculpture into position on the cathedral buttress. Perhaps there was fear that the sculpture might be damaged, or the work may have been too impressive to be removed from close public attention. A committee that included Leonardo da Vinci and Botticelli decided to place the *David* at the entrance to the Palazzo della Signoria, the center of Florence's civic government. That decision was significant, for the meaning of the *David* gained an enhanced political impact.

Michelangelo's *David* was carved after the expulsion of the Medici, when the republican traditions of Florence had been reasserted. The Medici would again rule the city in 1512, but at the time of the *David*, the democracy and liberty of the old Florentine republic reigned, and Michelangelo's sculpture was seen as a manifestation of those civic virtues. Just as the biblical David had triumphed against the physical power of Goliath, so too had the Florentine people courageously restored their republic. The *David* symbolized the Florentines' defiance of tyranny.

Fulfilling its new role as a political symbol, the *David* partook of the Renaissance in yet another way. While conforming to the designation *statua*, as public sculpture had been explained by the ancient Roman writer Pliny the Elder, Michelangelo's *David* also elevated *statua* to a grand and heroic scale. With the *David*, Vasari proclaimed that even the cherished art of ancient Greece and Rome had been surpassed:

Without any doubt this figure has put in the shade every other statue, ancient or modern, Greek or Roman . . . such were the satisfying proportions and the beauty of the finished work. . . . To be sure, anyone who has seen Michelangelo's *David* has no need to see anything else by any other sculptor, living or dead.

Technique *Stone Sculpture*

6-19 MICHELANGELO BUONARROTI

Saint Matthew. 1504–08. Marble, height 8'10". Galleria dell' Accademia, Florence. This unfinished sculpture is the only figure begun by Michelangelo for a series of twelve apostles originally commissioned for Florence Cathedral. The project was abandoned when Michelangelo was called to Rome to work for Pope Julius II. Commissioned by the Cathedral Administration.

6-20 MICHELANGELO BUONARROTI
Saint Matthew, detail.

Like carving in wood (see pp. 254-55), working in marble is a **subtractive** technique. Benvenuto Cellini's sixteenth-century *Treatise on Sculpture* prescribes that, after the clay model for a sculpture is completed,

> you draw the principal views of your statue onto the stone . . . The best method I ever saw was the one that Michelangelo used; when you have drawn on your principal view you begin to chisel it round as if you wanted to work a half relief, and thus gradually it comes to be cut out.

This half-relief effect is evident in the *Saint Matthew* (fig. 6-19), which is carved back from one face of the block, with the result that large areas of marble still fill the background. Cellini also describes the chisels used. Excess stone was removed with a pointed chisel, while toothed or clawed chisels were employed as the sculptor neared the surface of the figure. Marks from the toothed chisel are visible in the detail of the *Saint Matthew* (fig. 6-20). Work with a flat chisel would then remove the ridges left by the toothed chisels, and a series of files would be used to finish the surface. Drills were utilized for areas of deep undercuts, and polishing was achieved with a close-grained pumice stone. Even today, centuries later, sculptors continue to work with traditional chisels like those used by Michelangelo. Only the electric drill has eased the physically demanding process of carving a figure in stone.

Italian High Renaissance Portraiture

6-21 LEONARDO DA VINCI

Portrait of a Woman (known as the *Mona Lisa*). c. 1503–05. Oil on wood, 30¼ × 21″ (cut down). The Louvre, Paris. The sitter is unknown, despite the traditional title. Vasari said that she was the wife of Francesco del Gioconda, which led to the popular name *La Gioconda* for the painting. Vasari also tells that Leonardo employed musicians or jesters during the sittings for the portrait to keep her full of merriment and to chase away any trace of melancholy that might arise from the boredom of sitting quietly posed, repeatedly, for long hours. Leonardo, who seems to have worked on the painting over a number of years, took it with him when he went to France, where he died in 1519. After Leonardo's death, the painting was owned by Francis I of France. In the early nineteenth century, Napoleon kept the portrait in his bedroom. The painting has been cut down; it was once wider, and the figure was shown enframed by columns on each side. Today, only the column bases survive. Commissioned by her husband, Francesco del Gioconda?

The *Mona Lisa*, probably the best-known painting in the history of art, is difficult to appreciate today (fig. 6-21). Covered by layers of yellowing varnish and a sheet of thick glass, the painting seems to have none of the naturalistic effects reported by Vasari:

> The nose, with its beautiful nostrils, rosy and tender, seemed to be alive. The opening of the mouth, united by the red of the lips to the flesh tones of the face, seemed not to be colored but to be living flesh.

Leonardo became famous for his ability to represent subtle shadows and to create a sense of mystery by gently modeling forms through a careful blending of tones, and while these effects survive in the *Mona Lisa*, the freshness of his color and observation is obscured. What remains clear is Leonardo's composition, which became a model for later Renaissance portraits. As in his earlier works (see figs. 5-61, 5-64), the basic form is a pyramid. Leonardo naturally integrates the hands into his portrait, adding another vehicle for the expression of personality into the tradition of portraiture.

Even in the Renaissance, the mystery of the sitter must have excited the imagination of the viewer. The androgynous quality—neither fully female nor fully male—and the self-satisfied expression, created by the blurring of the corners of the mouth and eyes, are tantalizing. Our uneasiness is in part created by the unexpected plucked eyebrows and forehead fashionable in the Renaissance. Also disturbing is the fantastic landscape setting. Note that the horizon lines are clearly on different levels. Perhaps the most remarkable single aspect of the painting is the manner in which this woman looks directly into the viewer's eyes; for a Renaissance man this would have been unsettling, for Renaissance etiquette books warned women that they should never look directly at a man. Whoever she is, the *Mona Lisa* continues to project and protect her mysterious secret.

In Raphael's *Donna Velata (Veiled Woman)*, the natural beauty of the woman and the High Renaissance style are mutually compatible (fig. 6-22). The High Renaissance demand for unity is evident in the sweep of her veil, which unites complex forms into the favored High Renaissance conical composition. The rounded forms of her head and eyes are repeated in the necklace, as well as in the curves of the neckline and bodice; the pearl set against her dark hair becomes a microcosm of the whole composition. The costume is a coloristic symphony in shades of gold and white, a scheme that emphasizes the flesh tones and draws attention to the dark eyes and hair. The elaborate sleeve, a painter's triumph, confirms Raphael's technical skill.

c. 1503–05	Leonardo, *Portrait of a Woman* (*Mona Lisa*)
1506	Machiavelli establishes a citizen militia in Florence
1511	Pocket watch is first mentioned

6-22 RAPHAEL

PORTRAIT OF A WOMAN (now known as *DONNA VELATA*). c. 1513. Oil on canvas, 33½ × 23½". Pitti Gallery, Florence. It is suspected that the beautiful sitter for this portrait was Raphael's beloved, the baker's daughter (*la fornarina*) mentioned by Vasari.

Art Past/Art Present *Fame, Time, and the Mona Lisa*

Writing at the close of the nineteenth century, an art historian described Leonardo's *Mona Lisa* as an "indecipherable and fascinating enigma" that has been affecting admirers for "nearly four centuries." Actually, this particular interpretation of the painting was a more recent development. For almost three and one-half centuries following the painting's creation, the *Mona Lisa* had been respected as a fine portrait, which demonstrated, in the words of Vasari,

> how faithfully art can imitate nature.

This view began to change within the context of various philosophical and art movements of the nineteenth century, including the aesthetic doctrine of "art for art's sake." In 1873, the English critic Walter Pater wrote of the painting as follows:

> The presence that rose thus so strangely beside the waters, is expressive of what in the ways of a thousand years men had come to desire. . . . She is older than the rocks among which she sits; like the vampire, she has been dead many times, and learned the secrets of the grave. . . . The fancy of perpetual life . . . is an old one. . . . Certainly Lady Lisa

might stand as the embodiment of the old fancy, the symbol of the modern idea.

This interpretation helped to create the foundation for a new range of critical thought concerning the *Mona Lisa*, and, in the process, brought a new level of fame to the work. In 1916, Sigmund Freud, the founder of psychoanalysis, concluded through psychosexual analysis that the painting was important to understanding Leonardo's homosexuality. Concerning the famous mysterious smile, Freud wrote, "When in the prime of his life Leonardo re-encountered that blissful and ecstatic smile as it had once encircled his mother's mouth in caressing, he had long been under the ban of an inhibition, forbidding him ever again to desire such tenderness from women's lips." Given the increased notoriety of the *Mona Lisa*, is it any wonder that Marcel Duchamp utilized a reproduction of it in a nihilistic Dada work?

Our views of works of art are often conditioned by critical issues that both challenge and transform our perception of the work through time. The fourteenth-century Italian humanist poet, Petrarch, was right when he wrote that "time alters fame."

German Printmaking: Albrecht Dürer

6-23 ALBRECHT DÜRER

ADAM AND EVE. 1504. Engraving, 9⅞ × 7⅝″ (for a detail, see figure 6-26). Dürer, one of the first artists to sign and date his works, may have done so because of the lively business in forgeries of his prints. No patron; made as part of a commercial endeavor.

ALBRECHT DÜRER, GERMAN, 1471–1528. *ADAM AND EVE*, 1504. ENGRAVING, 4TH STATE, 9.875″ × 7.625″. THE METROPOLITAN MUSEUM OF ART, FLETCHER FUND, 1919.

The increasing contact between Italian and Northern artistic traditions is demonstrated in Dürer's *Adam and Eve* (fig. 6-23). The precise detail of the heavily wooded background reflects Northern tradition, while the use of antique models for the figures reveals Dürer's contact with Italian Renaissance art. Dürer's difficulty in blending these two styles is evident, for the figures resemble sculptures rather than living beings and seem out of place in this forest setting. Nevertheless, they are striking in their elegance—which is not surprising, for Dürer studied proportional systems for the human body from nature and from classical and Italian Renaissance sources, and he completed two volumes of a proposed four-volume *Treatise on Human Proportions*. The animals in the background bear an important relationship to the figures, for they symbolize the various "humors," fluids within the body that were believed to control personality. The rabbit stands for the lechery of humanity, which will become active as soon as Adam takes a bite of the apple held by Eve.

This blending of Northern and Renaissance is also seen in Dürer's *Knight, Death, and the Devil* (fig. 6-24). The central figure, dressed as a Renaissance knight, is an allegorical representation of the Christian soul. He is every human being, riding through life, which is shown as a landscape filled with terrors. The Devil is a hideous horned monster, and Death, his crown entwined with serpents, brandishes an hourglass as a reminder of the inevitability of death. These imaginative creations belong to a Northern tradition, but the knight and his sturdy mount are inspired by classical and Renaissance works Dürer had seen in Italy.

Dürer's prints brought him international fame. During his lifetime, he was internationally recognized as the leading German artist. When Dürer was in Venice, the Senate offered him a regular salary if he would become a citizen there, and he was also employed by Maximilian I, the Holy Roman Emperor. Dürer loved to travel, and in 1520–21, in the Netherlands, he saw a room full of Aztec gold treasures sent back by Hernán Cortés. He praised these exotic objects, writing,

> I have seen nothing that rejoiced my heart so much as these

6-24   ALBRECHT DÜRER

KNIGHT, DEATH, AND THE DEVIL. 1513. Engraving, 9⅝ × 7½″. Dürer called this print *The Rider*, but scholars have related the symbolism to Erasmus's handbook, *Instructions for the Christian Soldier*, published in 1504. The initials, with the *A* encompassing the *D*, create a unique monogram, an indication of Dürer's pride in his work. No patron; made as part of a commercial endeavor.

ALBRECHT DÜRER, 1471–1528, *THE KNIGHT, DEATH, AND THE DEVIL*. ENGRAVING, 1513, 9⅜ × 7⅜ INCHES. THE METROPOLITAN MUSEUM OF ART, HARRIS BRISBANE DICK FUND, 1943. (43.106.2)

6-25   ALBRECHT DÜRER

FOUR HORSEMEN OF THE APOCALYPSE. c. 1497–98. Woodcut, 15½ × 11″ (for a detail, see figure 6-27). The *Apocalypse* series, of which this is a part, was based on the Book of Revelation in the Bible. It consisted of fifteen prints with relevant texts on the back in German or Latin. No patron; made as part of a commercial endeavor.

things, for . . . I marveled at the subtle ingenuity of men in foreign lands.

Dürer's engravings were intended for a sophisticated audience of wealthy print collectors, but he also produced more reasonably priced and easily understood prints in series for a popular audience. These works, executed in the bolder and more direct medium of woodcut, were printed in large quantities to be sold at fairs and carnivals. The subject matter is both more traditional and more direct, as in the *Four Horsemen of the Apocalypse* (fig. 6-25), drawn from Revelation 6:1–8. Death ("on a pale horse") in the foreground and the other riders follow Revelations' description: Famine has a pair of scales, War a sword, and "the conqueror" (Pestilence, or the Plague) carries a bow. Dürer's patterns reinforce the relentless motion of the horsemen as they ravage humanity. The Apocalypse and Last Judgment were popular themes just before 1500, when it was feared time would end and Christ would appear to judge humanity.

Dürer had sympathies with the Protestant movement, and when he heard a rumor that Luther had been murdered, he wrote,

If Luther is dead, who will explain the Gospel to us now?

6-26 ALBRECHT DÜRER

ADAM AND EVE, enlarged detail of figure 6-23. Engraving.

Enlarged details from an **engraving** and a **woodcut** by Dürer reveal his acute vision and the technical accomplishment and expression he achieved in these two media (figs. 6-28, 6-29). They are especially impressive given the distinctive technique of these two major types of printmaking. In the engraved head, multiple fine lines, often placed parallel (**hatching**) and perpendicular (**cross-hatching**) to each other, create highlights, modeling, and subtle pockets of shadow. In addition, these lines suggest the illusion of specific textures. In the woodcut head, the effect is more linear, and the sharp distinctions between light and dark patterns add drama and movement to the work. In woodcuts, the defining lines either follow the naturalistic shapes or are grouped parallel to each other.

The **printmaking** processes involve pressing a piece of paper (or, rarely, some other absorbent material, such as **vellum** or silk) against a surface to which ink has been applied (technically known as the **print form**). When the paper is removed, a reversed impression adheres to it; this is known as a **print**. In most print media, the surface of the print form can be re-inked and a number of additional prints (an **edition**) produced. The development of this relatively cheap means of mass-producing an image, which was related to improvements in the quality of paper and a tremendous decrease in its price, had a dramatic impact on western European culture. Now avidly bought by museums and collectors, most of the earliest prints were simple book illustrations or modest, inexpensive religious images intended for popular consumption. In the hands of such skilled artists as Dürer, however, the techniques became sophisticated, their expression more subtle, and the iconography more complex.

6-27 ALBRECHT DÜRER

FOUR HORSEMEN OF THE APOCALYPSE, enlarged detail of figure 6-25). Woodcut.

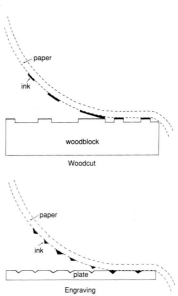

6-28, 6-29 These diagrams of the woodcut and engraving techniques show schematically in section the moment when the paper is being lifted from the woodblock or the plate at the completion of the printing process. Note how the ink is transferred from the print form to the print.

The woodcut was first developed in China in the late ninth century; the earliest European examples date from the late fourteenth century. Woodcut is called a **relief process** because the lines and surfaces to which the ink adheres are higher than the parts that are not to be printed. To create a woodcut, the artist draws the design on a piece of wood sawed lengthwise along the grain (fig. 6-28). Using a knife or chisel, he or she then cuts away the background areas, leaving the raised design. When the woodblock is inked, the ink adheres to the raised surfaces. Dampened paper is applied, and the print can be made by hand or in a printing press. Approximately a thousand good prints can be made before the prints reveal that the block is showing signs of wear. Our understanding of the woodcut technique makes Dürer's accomplishment even more impressive, for, unlike earlier harsh and simple images, his designs suggest the illusion of three-dimensional forms with light playing over them.

Engraving is known as an **intaglio process** (from the Italian *intagliare*, "to carve" or "to cut") because the areas that print are incised into the surface of the print form. In engraving, the print form is a thin metallic plate, usually of copper. With a sharply pointed steel instrument called a **burin**, the artist incises grooves in the surface of the plate (fig. 6-29). The plate is then inked with a heavy, viscous ink and wiped with a rag (or the palm of the hand), leaving the ink in the grooves. The paper used for printing an engraving is slightly moistened before being applied to the inked plate. Plate and paper are then run through a printing press, which can apply the sufficient pressure (more than is needed to print a woodcut) to force the paper to pick up the ink in the grooves. The printed lines that result are sharply defined and slightly raised. Several hundred high-quality prints can be made before weak lines on the print reveal that the copper plate is wearing down.

New St. Peter's, Rome

6-30 DONATO BRAMANTE

Medal showing Bramante's design for the new St. Peter's, Rome. 1506. The British Museum, London, England. Bramante's design was commissioned by Pope Julius II. Twelve impressions of this commemorative medal by Caradossa were enclosed in the cornerstone of the new St. Peter's. Commissioned by Pope Julius II.

On April 18, 1506, Pope Julius II, who was aggressive in both religious and political matters, laid the foundation stone for a new St. Peter's. As part of a campaign to restore Rome so that it would be worthy of its status as the capital of Christendom, he commissioned Donato Bramante (1444–1514) to rebuild the structure, an event commemorated in a medal issued that year (fig. 6-30). Since the late fourteenth century, St. Peter's and the Vatican had been home to the popes, and although Old St. Peter's (see figs. 4-18 and 4-19) was one of the most revered churches in Christendom, it had fallen into disrepair and no longer seemed grand enough to serve as the church that marked the burial spot of the first pope and, now, the religious center for the papacy.

Bramante's design (fig. 6-31), never completed, would have replaced the Early Christian **basilica** with a **centrally planned** church, a plan appropriate to St. Peter's function as a martyrium and consistent with Renaissance philosophical ideals (see p. 273 and fig. 5-63 for a discussion of the intellectual basis for the centrally planned church in the Renaissance. Four equal arms, terminating in **apses**, radiate from a central **crossing** crowned with an immense dome surrounded by smaller domes. The underlying geometry of the design is simple, producing a monumental effect not unlike the unified compositions offered in painting and sculpture by Leonardo, Raphael, and Michelangelo.

The boldest aspect of Bramante's conception is its colossal scale. Bramante set out to surpass the monumental architectural remains of ancient Rome, creating a structure that would dominate all Rome. Bramante is reported to have stated that he was inspired to

> place the Pantheon (figs. 3-120 to 3-122) on top of the Basilica of Constantine (fig. 3-117)

(the diameter of the dome of St. Peter's is 138 feet, only about 6 feet smaller than that of the Pantheon).

Before journeying to Rome, Bramante had known Leonardo in Milan in the 1480s and 1490s and had experimented with centrally planned church designs. For St. Peter's, Bramante joined the central plan, thought to be symbolic of God's perfection, with a Greek cross pattern. The spaces between the cross arms enclose this central plan within a square. Unlike the **cruciform basilica** plan of Old St. Peter's, where the cross shape emphasized salvation, Bramante's central plan was intended to express the universal harmony of God's created world.

The new St. Peter's was not consecrated until November 18, 1626, more than 120 years after Bramante's reconstruction was begun. The work encompassed the reigns of twenty popes and the efforts of fourteen architects, including Raphael, Michelangelo, and Bernini. Each succeeding architect had to contend with Bramante's original plan, as well as the advancing construction of the building under successive architects. Michelangelo took charge of construction in 1546, noting that

> every architect who has departed from Bramante's plan . . . has departed from the right way.

1506 Bramante, new St. Peter's basilica
1513 Late Gothic tower of Chartres Cathedral is finished
1513 Machiavelli, *The Prince*

6-31 DONATO BRAMANTE

Plan of new St. Peter's, Rome. 1506.
Commissioned by Pope Julius II.

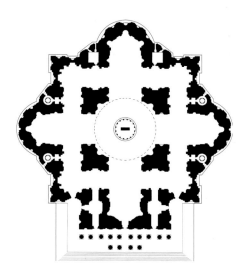

6-32 MICHELANGELO BUONARROTI

Plan of new St. Peter's, Rome. 1546–64. Pope Paul III appointed Michelangelo chief architect of St. Peter's. The artist, burdened by his advancing age and numerous other artistic projects, took charge of the construction of St. Peter's without pay and for the "salvation of his soul," as he expressed it. Late in the sixteenth century, an argument developed over whether the design of St. Peter's should be limited to Michelangelo's central plan or whether a nave should be added to create the more traditional axial composition that dates back to Old St. Peter's (see fig. 4-19). In the early seventeenth century, a nave was added by Carlo Maderno that, from both the outside and the inside, obscures the view of the great dome that Bramante and Michelangelo planned would be the central and unifying feature of the church. Commissioned by Pope Paul III.

Michelangelo's plan (fig. 6-32) retains the integrity of Bramante's central plan, but it achieves a more cohesive unity by simplifying it, giving a new lucidity to the exterior form and the interior spaces. This unity is further expressed in the use of the **giant order** (**pilasters** or **columns** that span more than one story of the structure) on both the exterior and the interior. On the exterior,

Michelangelo's wall design is more varied than Bramante's, sheathing the building like muscle and flesh over bone and creating an external vitality enveloping the inner, structural core (figs. 6-33, 6-34).

The commanding dome of St. Peter's (see fig. 7-25), also based on a design by Michelangelo, was erected by Giacomo della Porta (c. 1540–1602) between 1588 and 1591. Struc-

tural reasons dictated that it be slightly more pointed, to exert less thrust, than Michelangelo's original design. The dome retains Michelangelo's grand scale and articulation and is a worthy climax to Bramante's earlier vision.

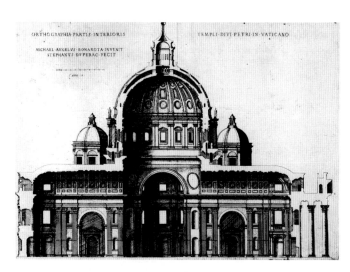

6-33 MICHELANGELO BUONARROTI

Longitudinal section of St. Peter's (engraving by Dupérac, 1569).

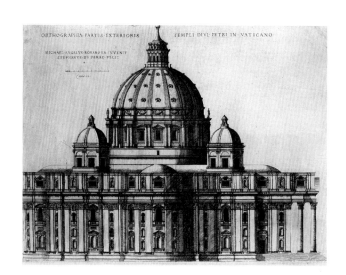

6-34 MICHELANGELO BUONARROTI

Longitudinal elevation of St. Peter's (engraving by Dupérac, 1569).

Michelangelo, Sistine Chapel Ceiling

6-35   MICHELANGELO BUONARROTI

CREATION OF ADAM, detail of frescoes (after completion of cleaning in 1990) on the Sistine Chapel ceiling, Vatican, Rome. 1508–12. Commissioned by Pope Julius II.

He who made everything, made every part,

And then chose what was most beautiful,

To reveal on earth the excellence of His creation,

And the divine art with which He made it.

(Michelangelo, "Sonnet," c. 1510)

In the gap between Adam's listless hand and God's commanding gesture, the energy of creation is concentrated (fig. 6-35). Seldom in the history of art has such a small space been endowed with such powerful meaning. God the Father, his thrusting, forward movement intensified by his billowing cloak, sweeps dramatically toward Adam. A host of putti accompanies God, who with his left arm embraces a female figure who may represent Eve or the Virgin Mary. Adam reclines in a barren landscape, his arm supported by his upraised knee. His figure is so powerfully muscled that even in repose we sense the energy that will be released once God touches him and endows him with a soul, with life.

Following his triumph in Florence with the colossal *David* (see fig. 6-18), Michelangelo was called to Rome in 1506 by Pope Julius II, nephew of Sixtus IV. It was in this same year that the heroically muscled Laocoön group (see fig. 3-107) was excavated in Rome. At first Julius asked Michelangelo to design and execute a grand papal tomb for himself, but by 1508 he had commissioned him to paint the ceiling of the Sistine Chapel, where fifteenth-century artists had decorated the walls with frescoes (fig. 6-36). Michelangelo accepted the task grudgingly; as he describes in a sonnet (fig. 6-37), painting the ceiling was a demanding physical labor:

6-36   *(right)* MICHELANGELO BUONARROTI

Sistine Chapel ceiling frescoes and *Last Judgment* (after completion of cleaning in 1990), Vatican, Rome. The Sistine Chapel, named after its builder, Pope Sixtus IV, was constructed in the late 1470s. The walls were decorated by such leading artists as Perugino (see fig. 1-15), Botticelli, and Ghirlandaio with scenes from the lives of Moses and Christ. Originally the vault was simply decorated with gold stars on a blue ground. The chapel's floor uses an inlaid marble floor in patterns that were centuries old. The concentric circles that establish the main patterns have been used in floor design in Rome for many centuries; their centers are slabs of beautifully colored and/or patterned marble that are slices of broken columns, here recycled for use in the floor.

6-37 MICHELANGELO BUONARROTI

Sonnet with a caricature of the artist standing, painting a figure on the ceiling over his head. c. 1510. Pen and ink, 11 × 7″. Casa Buonarroti, Florence. In the sonnet, Michelangelo complains of the physical difficulties of painting the Sistine Chapel ceiling in terms that reveal he worked standing, not lying down.

I've got myself a goiter from this strain . . .

My beard toward Heaven, I feel the back of my brain

Upon my neck, I grow the breast of a Harpy;

My brush, above my face continually,

Makes it a splendid floor by dripping down. . . .

Pointless the unseeing steps I go.

In front of me, my skin is being stretched

While it folds up behind and forms a knot,

And I am bending like a Syrian bow. . . .

Although the scheme is often discussed as if Michelangelo were his own iconographer, the complexity of the cycle suggests that the ceiling's intricate iconography was developed in consultation with his patron and one or more theologians. Our first impression of the ceiling is of a maze of complexly posed human figures that have to be seen from different viewpoints (see fig. 6-36). Order, however, is created by the painted architectural framework. The central spine of the ceiling has a sequence of nine scenes, alternating in size from small to large, from passages in Genesis (1:1–9:27).

To see the figures along the side walls, the viewer must turn 90 degrees to the left or right. The largest figures are the Old Testament prophets and ancient Sibyls, who, possessed by the spirit of God, foretold the coming of Christ. In the window **lunettes** and **spandrels**, Michelangelo portrayed the ancestors of Christ.

Another level of figures, nude males called *ignudi* ("nudes"), are seated in poses that vary from the decorative to the energetic. They support painted bronze medallions decorated with scenes from the Old Testament that refer to wise and just rule. Garlands of oak leaves and acorns, emblems of Julius II's family, are held by some of the *ignudi*, but their primary role is to embellish Michelangelo's cycle.

As our eyes ascend from the first level of ancestral figures toward the histories, the figures in each horizontal level are distinguished by an increasing freedom of movement. In Neoplatonic philosophy (see page 235), unrestricted figural movement was symbolic of the freedom of the human soul to ascend to the divine, for as the soul ascended, it was believed to be less and less restricted by the bonds of earthly matter: the eloquent movement displayed by the *ignudi* is a metaphor for the freedom of the soul.

The symbolism of our aspiration to join God is conveyed by the central histories, which relate God's love in the acts of creation and in the story of Noah. The cycle runs backward in time, but it has an internal logic. Michelangelo begins over the entrance door with the sin and disobedience of Noah, the most righteous man God could find on earth, to stress the sin-fulness of all humanity. What redeems this human sin is the love of God, with which the cycle concludes in the first moment of the Creation. God's initial act of love, dividing Light from Darkness, is painted directly over the altar.

Art Past/Art Present   *Vasari and Modern Scholarship*

There is no other work to compare with this excellence, nor could there be; and it is scarcely possible even to imitate what Michelangelo accomplished. The ceiling has provided a veritable beacon to our art, of inestimable benefit to all painters, restoring light to a world that for centuries had been plunged into darkness.

With these words, Giorgio Vasari summarizes Michelangelo's achievement in painting the Sistine Chapel ceiling. This quotation, taken from Vasari's *Lives of the Most Eminent Painters, Sculptors, and Architects* (see p. 231), also betrays the prejudice he held toward the art of the Middle Ages. Vasari perceived the history of art as an organic entity that moved from birth to maturity and then on to perfection and decline, and he advanced the concept of the Italian Renaissance as a "rebirth" that led to perfection in art. Since the publication of the first edition of the *Lives* in 1550, they have remained popular, ensuring the continuation of an attitude that exalted the Renaissance at the expense of the previous period. This, along with what seems to be a careless treatment of the facts at some points, has placed Vasari and his work at the center of debate and controversy.

Vasari, however, is at his best when he shares with us the critical thought and language of his time. When he writes of the Renaissance sculptor Donatello, for example, Vasari concludes that the artist

possessed invention, design, skill, judgement, and all the other qualities that one may reasonably expect to find in an inspired genius. Donatello was very determined and quick, and he executed his works with the utmost facility. . . .

This list of critical values cited by Vasari gives us insight, from a distance of centuries, into how the culture of the Italian Renaissance viewed the art of its own time.

Raphael, Stanza Della Segnatura

6-38 RAPHAEL

PHILOSOPHY (popularly known as *THE SCHOOL OF ATHENS*), fresco in the Stanza della Segnatura, Vatican, Rome. 1509–11. 19 × 27'. Commissioned by Pope Julius II.

Raphael's *Philosophy* has long been viewed as the ideal of High Renaissance painting (fig. 6-38). Figures that represent ancient philosophers in a variety of postures are composed within a classicizing architectural setting. The use of **scientific perspective** directs our attention to the two figures in the center. The vaults and niches with sculpture remind us of the decoration of the baths of ancient Rome (see fig. 3-123) and of Bramante's church of St. Peter's

(see fig. 6-33), being erected nearby by the same patron.

The philosophers in the center are the gray-haired Plato, holding his *Timaeus*, a book on the origin of the universe, and Aristotle, who holds his *Nicomachean Ethics*. Plato points heavenward to indicate his philosophical approach to the world of ideas, while Aristotle gestures over the earth to suggest that the universe can only be understood through examining the natural world. Other philosophers can be

identified by their attributes. Euclid, the geometrician, seen bending over a compass in the right foreground, has the features of Bramante, a friend of Raphael who secured this commission for the painter from Julius II. Plato bears a resemblance to Leonardo, who was in Rome at this time. Raphael's self-portrait near the right border looks out at us. By portraying the historical personalities from antiquity with the visages of contemporary people, Raphael gave personal meaning to the ideal of the Renais-

1509–11	Raphael, frescoes, Stanza della Segnatura
1514	Papal proclamation against slavery and the slave trade
1515	Thomas More, *Utopia*

6-39 RAPHAEL

Stanza della Segnatura. 1509–11. *Theology*, known as the *Disputà*, is on the wall opposite *Philosophy*, and in the lunette over the window are three Virtues. The room originally functioned as Julius II's study and personal library; only later did it receive the name by which it is known today. The themes chosen for the walls—Philosophy, Theology, Justice, and Poetry—relate to its use as a library. The ability of the High Renaissance to simplify and clarify is evident in this program, which encompasses the four basic realms of scholarship and literature. It has also been suggested that the four themes refer to the pope's interest in Truth (Philosophy and Theology), Goodness (Justice), and Beauty (Poetry). Early sources reveal that Pope Julius II himself designed this impressive iconographic program.

sance as a revival of classical values.

Another portrait is the brooding figure in the left central foreground, who appears self-absorbed. His inclusion was an afterthought, for he was painted on a fresh patch of plaster. The figure represents the philosopher Heraclitus, who expressed the solitary, nature of the creative temperament. In pose, the figure recalls the prophets from the Sistine ceiling, while the face

suggests that it is a portrait of Michelangelo. Raphael added the figure in homage to the older master, probably after the partially completed Sistine ceiling was unveiled in August 1511.

Theology presents groupings of saints in heaven and theologians on earth, all gathered around a central axis which descends from God the Father, Jesus Christ, and the Holy

Spirit to the Eucharist displayed on the altar (fig. 6-39). Raphael's composition suggests an apse, and the fresco visually embodies the concept that it is persons—in heaven and on earth— who make up the Church. *Philosophy* and *Theology* in the Stanza della Segnatura express the union the Renaissance forged between Christian theological values and the classical philosophical tradition.

High Renaissance Painting in Venice

6-40 GIORGIONE (completed by TITIAN)

SLEEPING VENUS. c. 1510. Oil on canvas, 3′6¾″ × 5′9″; the figure is lifesize. Staatliche Gemäldegalerie, Dresden, Germany. The painting was apparently damaged at an early date and a kneeling cupid near the feet of the figure, which is the attribute that identified the main figure as Venus, was painted over. An early source suggests that Titian completed both the cupid and the landscape. Giorgione, who died in the great plague of 1510, may have left the work unfinished. The face of Venus has been repainted, probably in the nineteenth century.

6-41 TITIAN

VENUS OF URBINO. 1538. Oil on canvas, 3′11″ × 5′5″. Galleria degli Uffizi, Florence. The work was painted for Guidobaldo II della Rovere of Urbino. Although a letter from Guidobaldo to his agent refers to the painting not as Venus, but as *la donna nuda* ("the nude woman"), the roses in her hand and the myrtle, a symbol of Venus, growing in the pot in the background, support an identification with Venus. The dog at her feet has been recognized as an emblem of marital fidelity. Commissioned by Duke Guidobaldo II della Rovere of Urbino.

Giorgione's *Sleeping Venus* helped establish the reclining female nude as a standard type in the history of European art (fig. 6-40, for a later example, see fig. 9-53). This subject is obviously erotic, and Giorgione's composition accentuates the sensuous quality of the female body by contrasting the swelling forms of the upper contour—head, breast, abdomen, and wrist—with the long curve of the bottom edge of the figure. The elegant slenderness of Venus's body is emphasized by her pose, with the right arm raised and the right ankle and foot hidden behind the left. The shimmering white drapery and deep red pillow accentuate and enhance the warm flesh tones of the body, isolating the figure in a verdant green landscape with a luminous Venetian sky and clouds. Giorgione established a new oil-painting technique in which the forms are rendered without detail (see pages 314-15). In *Sleeping Venus*, the technique emphasizes the delicacy and softness of the body. The landscape setting removes the figure from the more erotic setting of a bed, and by representing Venus with her eyes closed, as if asleep, Giorgione encouraged the male patron and his friends to observe her beauty without embarrassment. At the same time, such a pose establishes a certain distance and restraint, and the kneeling cupid may have served as a guardian figure. The ultimate effect is of a slender figure dreaming in a warm Italian landscape.

It is not surprising that one of the first paintings of the sensuous nude was created in Renaissance Venice. The "Queen of the Adriatic," Venice had for centuries been the major trading center between Europe and Asia, and it cultivated its reputation as the most cosmopolitan city in Europe with exotic buildings, fine food, and beautiful courtesans.

Titian's painting (fig. 6-41) was modeled on Giorgione's, perhaps at the request of the patron. The same red, white, and green tones enhance the flesh of the painted figure, but now the setting is an interior, complete with a bed with rumpled sheets and bed curtains. Now the nude is awake: she looks directly at us, posing without embarrassment. Titian's ability to suggest texture is especially evident in the locks of wavy red hair that flow onto her shoulders. The maids in the background are gathering her garments from a Renaissance chest.

Giorgione's *Tempestuous Landscape with a Gypsy and a Soldier* is a difficult work, and scholars have long debated its specific iconographic meaning (fig. 6-42). A young man and a nude woman nursing a child occupy the foreground; their relationship is inexplicable, but the "soldier" seems to be watching over the "gypsy." The landscape that dominates the composition offers both ruins and contemporary buildings. A lightning bolt crosses the background, and the trees are dramatically silhouetted against the eerie light of the stormy sky. The main purpose of this painting may be to set a mood rather than to tell a story, and perhaps we appreciate it best by surrendering

6-42 GIORGIONE

Tempestuous Landscape with a Gypsy and a Soldier (traditionally known as *The Tempest*). c. 1505–10. Oil on canvas. 30¼ × 28¾". Galleria dell' Accademia, Venice. A reference to the painting in 1530 calls it "the little landscape on canvas with the tempest [and] gypsy and soldier."

GIORGIONE (DA CASTELFRANCO), ITALIAN, (C. 1477–1510). *TEMPESTA* (THE TEMPEST), OIL ON CANVAS. GALLERY DELL' ACCADEMIA, VENICE, ITALY. SCALA/ART RESOURCE.

logic to feeling. That an emotional sensation should be the main purpose of a work of art is a new idea in the history of art, but one that seems consistent with the Venetian interest in the suggestive and poetic.

Hieronymus Bosch,
"Garden of Earthly Delights" Triptych

6-43 HIERONYMUS BOSCH

CREATION OF EVE IN THE GARDEN OF EDEN; "GARDEN OF EARTHLY DELIGHTS"; HELL (interior of the *"GARDEN OF EARTHLY DELIGHTS"* triptych). c. 1510–15. Oil on wood, 7'2⅝" × 6'4¾" (center); 7'2⅝" × 38¼" (each wing); the figures in the foreground of the central panel are approximately 10–14 inches tall. Prado, Madrid, Spain. The iconography of the work has been much debated, and there is no general agreement as to its meaning or exact purpose; one suggested interpretation relates it to the contemporary interest in alchemy, a subject investigated in some of Bosch's other works. The work may have been commissioned by Hendrik III of Nassau for the palace of the House of Nassau in Brussels, where it was hanging in 1517. In this setting, the painting must have been a novel secular decoration and a focus for intellectual discussions. Perhaps commissioned by Hendrik III.

The left and right wings of the interior of Bosch's **triptych** represent traditional Christian subjects (figs. 6-43—6-44). The left wing shows the Garden of Eden, with God the Father creating Eve as Adam looks on, while the right wing presents a vision of hell after the Last Judgment. Placed between these views of humanity's past and future is the central panel, which has been interpreted as representing the present, when humanity indulges the sins, begun in the Garden of Eden, that can lead to hell. Bosch's moral stance seems evident, and few of the hundreds of naked figures cavorting in the expansive garden of the central panel express even momentary delight. In the central section a man looks up guiltily as he embraces a woman, while nearby figures greedily gather around a giant floating berry. A pearl seeps from between the legs of a couple lying within a giant shell carried by another man. Hundreds of unexpected episodes and surprising details capture our admiration for the painter's imagination in expressing humanity's determined perversity. In the landscape are real and imaginary birds and beasts, including the owl, symbol of perverted wisdom (it can see only in the dark), and huge raspberries, strawberries, and other fruits whose multiple seeds hint at rampant promiscuity. It has been suggested that the theme here is humanity before the great flood, when God, grieving "that he had made man on the earth," destroyed all but Noah and his family (Genesis 6:5–6; 6:11–13). Whatever the exact theme, seldom in the history of humanity has the role of evil in the world been more astonishing and unexpectedly depicted.

6-44 HIERONYMUS BOSCH

"GARDEN OF EARTHLY DELIGHTS," detail of central panel.

HIERONYMUS BOSCH (C. 1450–1516). *GARDEN OF EARTHLY DELIGHTS* (DETAIL). CENTER: ALLEGORY OF LUXURIA. MUSEO DEL PRADO, MADRID, SPAIN. GIRAUDON/ART RESOURCE.

In light of the iconography of the main panel, a reexamination of the wings reveals unusual details. The birds, beasts, and plants that inhabit the Garden of Eden include composite creatures that suggest that even in Eden unnatural cross-fertilization has taken place. Life in God's creation is violent: the animals and birds of Paradise already stalk and devour each other. The expression on Adam's face as he ogles the newly created Eve suggests that, in Bosch's interpretation, sexual pleasure is the first thought of the first man.

The devils that populate Bosch's *Hell* provide further evidence that he is the first great artist of the fantastic. The ponds in the left and center panels give way in *Hell* to a wasteland, above which rises an edifice created by a combination of a dead tree and a man that represents the "tavern of lost souls." The Devil is enthroned as a frog with a bird's head who endlessly devours sinners. They are excreted only to face further torment. Although the triptych as a whole is related to Last Judgment paintings, it offers no view of souls in Paradise. In this world, it seems, there is no redemption.

Details about Bosch's life help little in clarifying his art. His grandfather and father were both painters. Bosch himself seems to have had a successful life. He was a member of the Brotherhood of Our Lady, a pious religious group, and through his wife he owned a large estate. Internationally known, he received commissions from the archduke of Austria, and his works were collected by important connoisseurs. It has been suggested that the tree-man in the center of *Hell* is a self-portrait. The face, which is in sharp contrast to the other, generalized figures, looks askance at the suffering around him. Bosch has been claimed by the twentieth-century Surrealists as their true ancestor.

German Painting: Matthias Grünewald, *Isenheim Altarpiece*

6-45 MATTHIAS GRÜNEWALD

SAINT SEBASTIAN; CRUCIFIXION; SAINT ANTHONY; with the *LAMENTATION* below, exterior of the *ISENHEIM ALTARPIECE*. c. 1512–15. Oil on wood, 9′9½″ × 10′9″ (center); 8′2½″ × 3′½″ (each wing); 2′5½″ × 11′2″ (base). Musée d'Unterlinden, Colmar, France. The altarpiece was painted for the chapel of the monastic Hospital of St. Anthony at Isenheim, near Colmar. The hospital specialized in treating patients with skin diseases, including leprosy and syphilis, and the monastery chapel was a pilgrimage shrine for those suffering from such diseases. Given the mission of the hospital, the scars and sores on Jesus' body are poignant and appropriate. In the late medieval period, it was believed that all physical illness was a manifestation of spiritual illness, and the first step in treating patients at the Hospital of St. Anthony was to bring them before this *Crucifixion* to pray. Grünewald's representation of Jesus was created so that patients could identify with his sufferings. Probably commissioned by the abbot of the monastery.

The monumental *Crucifixion* by Matthias Grünewald (1455–1528) depicts all the gruesome details with unsparing realism (fig. 6-45). Jesus is dead: his head falls dramatically to the side, the blood pouring from the wound in his side begins to congeal, and his body is covered with wounds from the flagellation. The weight of his body pulls down on the crossbar, and the torture wrought by the nails in his hands and feet is painful to see. The lower abdomen is violently compressed, while the rib cage almost bursts through the skin as a result of the anguished death by suffocation brought about by crucifixion. As the Bible relates, darkness envelopes the scene. The painting also emphasizes the suffering of the Virgin Mary, Saint John the Evangelist, and Mary

c. 1512–15	Grünewald, *Isenheim Altarpiece*
1513	Ponce de León plants orange and lemon trees in Florida
1513	Balboa discovers the Pacific Ocean
1513	First European ship lands in China
1519	Leonardo da Vinci dies in France
1520	Raphael dies in Rome

Magdalene. Saint John the Baptist points to the figure on the cross, stating, "He must become more important, while I must become less important" (John 3:30). The dark sky and red garments add drama.

The choice of subjects and their interpretation can be directly related to the position and role of Grünewald's altarpiece within the monastic and hospital complex at Isenheim. Usually the wings were kept closed to emphasize the Crucifixion and Saint Sebastian, invoked by sufferers of the plague and other diseases, and Saint Anthony, patron saint of the monastery. When the *Crucifixion* panel was opened (notice that Grünewald has painted Jesus' body to the right of the opening), the joyful scenes of the *Annunciation, Mystical Nativity*, and *Resurrection*, painted with vivid, luminous colors, became visible (fig. 6-46). Certainly these inner panels would have been shown on the feast days of the subjects celebrated here—the Annunciation, Christmas, and Easter. And since Christ's resurrection is celebrated every Sunday, they would most likely have been visible on a weekly basis as well. The innermost decoration, with sculpted figures and two scenes from the life of Anthony, would have been shown on Saint Anthony's feast day.

The contrasts between the various layers of the altarpiece are explicit. In the *Resurrection*, an immediate contrast to the grisly *Crucifixion*, Christ's body is healed and his wounds have become glowing, ruby-like jewels. He rises weightless and triumphant while the soldiers guarding the grave fall helplessly in confusion below. The restored beauty of Christ's body would have encouraged hope on the part of the hospital's patients. Even in the joyful scenes, however, a sense of the crucifixion as Christ's destiny is found, for the cloth in which Mary holds the Christ Child in the *Mystical Nativity* (for a detail, see fig. 6-51) is the same tattered fabric that serves as his loincloth when he is crucified.

Titian's Altarpieces

6-47 TITIAN

MADONNA OF THE PESARO FAMILY. 1519–26. Oil on canvas, 16' × 18'10";
the figures are approximately lifesize. Santa Maria Gloriosa dei Frari,
Venice, Italy. The main patron was Jacopo Pesaro, who led papal
troops to victory over the Turks in 1502. The armored figure with the
banner and the turbaned Turkish prisoner allude to Pesaro's victory.
Commissioned by Jacopo Pesaro.

6-48 TITIAN

MADONNA OF THE PESARO FAMILY as seen in situ in its original frame
in the Church of Santa Maria Gloriosa dei Frari, Venice. Titian's
painting was created to be placed here, in the left side aisle, and his
asymmetrical composition is in part inspired by the viewpoint from
which one approaches the altar. Titian's huge columns are related
to those of the nave of the Gothic structure. X-rays have revealed
that Titian tried several solutions to the painting's architectural
setting, including one that continued the architectural forms of the
painting's frame, before deciding to use dramatic columns to relate
his painting to its largest architectural context.

Titian's *Pesaro Madonna* pioneered a dynamic new compositional mode that was championed by Venetian painters during the
sixteenth century (figs. 6-47, 6-48).
Nothing in earlier Renaissance art prepares us for this asymmetrical composition, with the Madonna set off to one
side before grandiose columns seen in

diagonal recession. The six male members of the Pesaro family who gather
below, the patron Jacopo on the left
and five others to the right, are introduced to the Madonna and Child by
Saints Peter and Francis. The movement inherent in Titian's composition is
also found in the twisting figure of Saint
Peter at the center and in the Madonna

and Child, who direct their attention in
opposing directions. The chubby Christ
Child kicks his foot and plays with his
mother's veil with a liveliness unusual in
religious art (see fig. 6-50).

Titian's *Assumption of the Virgin*
maintains the symmetrical, triangular
Renaissance composition, but it accom-
plishes an effect of dynamic spontaneity

through movement, strong color, and painterly brushstrokes (fig. 6-49). The composition is like a target, with the standing figure of the Virgin Mary placed within a circle created by the semicircular frame and a ring of clouds and flying putti below. Above, God the Father sweeps in with open arms to welcome and crown her. The main figures of God the Father and the Virgin wear garments of a brilliant red, and the Virgin's dominance is enhanced by the strong blue cloak that enfolds her. Titian's triad of primary colors is consistent with High Renaissance practices in Rome. Before a realistic blue sky below, two apostles stand out in the group due to their red garments and eloquent gestures. They create the base of Titian's compositional triangle. The combination of rich color with a simple composition is perfect for the altarpiece's position, which demands that it be legible from the main entrance of the church. The ultimate effect is of grandeur and visual richness.

6-49 TITIAN

ASSUMPTION OF THE VIRGIN. c. 1516–18. Oil on wood, 22′6″ × 11′10″; the figures are over-lifesize. Santa Maria Gloriosa dei Frari, Venice. This huge altarpiece is still in situ in its original Renaissance frame on the main altar of the Frari in Venice. Despite the rivalry of the light that flows in from the Gothic apse windows, the painting's composition is even discernible from the entrance to the church, some 300 feet away. Commissioned by Germano da Caiole, the abbot of the Monastery of the Frari.

6-50 Venetian. TITIAN

Madonna of the Pesaro Family, detail of figure 6-47.

6-51 German. MATTHIAS GRÜNEWALD

Mystical Nativity with Musical Angels, detail of figure 6-46.

This detail from Titian's *Pesaro Madonna*, although substantially reduced in size, reveals the new style of painting pioneered in Venice during the first years of the sixteenth century (fig. 6-50). The traditional techniques of Renaissance painting—tempera on wooden panel and fresco—had proved unsatisfactory in the humid Venetian climate, and by about 1500 oil painting on canvas was becoming the accepted medium. The development of a new technique for painting in oils began with Giorgione (see figs. 6-40, 6-42), who softened his forms and blurred their edges, partly as a result of the influence of Leonardo da Vinci, who visited Venice in 1500. Titian, Giorgione's pupil and friend, went further to develop a style using bold, large strokes that had a profound impact not only on later Venetian painters but also on many other artists in later centuries, including Rubens and Velázquez. Titian's lively, broad brushstrokes have what is known as a **painterly** quality because the motion of his hand is so evident; these painterly brushstrokes are consistent with his interest in movement and asymmetrical compositions.

In creating a large painting such as the Pesaro *Madonna*, Titian would first paint or stain the canvas a medium brownish-red. He would then boldly outline his forms in dark paint and reinforce them by modeling them in monochrome, from white to black. After this underpainting dried, Titian would add layers and layers of colored translucent oil **glazes** (varnish, often with a small amount of color), building up a rich, sonorous color through their superimposition. Tradition has it that Titian once exclaimed that he used

glazes, thirty or forty!

to achieve this rich effect.

Titian's looser painting technique, as seen in the detail from the *Madonna of the Pesaro Family* gives pictorial unity because of the continuous texture of brushstrokes. In contrast, the detail from the painting by Grünewald (fig. 6-51) demonstrates hidden brushstrokes, an emphasis on precise detail, and the creation of the illusion of varying textures. Grünewald's style represents a continuation of the oil technique first developed by Robert Campin and Jan van Eyck (see pages 242–43, 250–51, 256–59).

Later in Titian's life, his brushstrokes became even more bold, and he used large, thick strokes (**impasto**), often of pure color, to define form. In the *Rape of Europa*, (figs. 6-52, 6-53), impasto is evident in the scales of the fish in the foreground, the feathers of the cupids flying at the top, the mountains, and the quickly sketched figures of Europa's abandoned friends, waving from the distant shore. The shape and direction of the brush-

6-52 TITIAN

RAPE OF EUROPA. c. 1559–62. Oil on canvas, 6′1″ × 6′9″. Isabella Stewart Gardner Museum, Boston, Massachusetts. One of a series of *poesie* (poetic mythological themes) painted for Philip II of Spain, this picture depicts the moment when Zeus, having disguised himself as a bull, abducts a beautiful princess. Titian was inspired by the story as it is told in Ovid's *Metamorphoses* (II, 870–75). The unexpected nature of the abduction is expressed in the awkward position of Europa, who seems about to slip off the back of the bull/Zeus. Commissioned by Philip II of Spain.

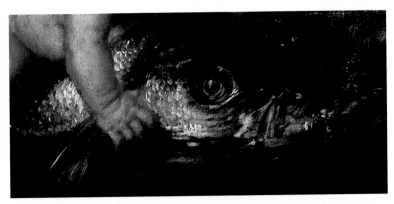

6-53. TITIAN. *RAPE OF EUROPA*, (detail). Isabella Stewart Gardner Museum, Boston.

strokes reinforce the movement of the figures and the directional patterns of the composition. While Titian's rich strokes and bold color accentuate the painting's surface, the diminution of the distant figures and the solidly depicted Europa produce a dramatic effect of space enhanced by the apricot and purple sky in the distance.

Later Michelangelo and the Development of Mannerism

6-54 MICHELANGELO BUONARROTI

Medici Chapel, including the Tomb of Giuliano de' Medici and the altar wall. 1524–34. Marble, length of reclining figures approx. 7'. New Sacristy, San Lorenzo, Florence. The Giuliano de' Medici commemorated here was the son of Lorenzo the Magnificent and brother of Pope Leo X, who in part sponsored Michelangelo's work at San Lorenzo, the Medici family church in Florence. Michelangelo's plan was never fully completed, and the artist never saw the Medici Chapel sculptural and architectural ensemble as we see it today; it was assembled by assistants following his designs and instructions. On the wall opposite the Tomb of Giuliano, Michelangelo designed a similar tomb for Lorenzo, the grandson of Lorenzo the Magnificent. Lorenzo is depicted as Contemplative Life, with allegories of Dusk and Dawn beneath his idealized portrait. Commissioned by Cardinal Giulio de' Medici, who later became Pope Clement VII.

Michelangelo's Medici Chapel introduces a new vitality and complexity to the interrelationship between sculpture and architecture in sixteenth-century art (fig. 6-54). In the Tomb of Giuliano de' Medici, an idealized portrait of Giuliano as Active Life is seated, clad in ancient Roman armor. Resting atop the sarcophagus are allegories, the female Night and the male Day. Michelangelo's plan called for two allegories of rivers to be placed on a platform below.

The allegories of the times of day symbolize the passage of time as it consumes mortal life, while the river allegories were perhaps intended to represent the Arno and Tiber to refer to Medici power in Florence and Rome. In his position above, Giuliano transcends both time and matter, fulfilling the spiritual ascent emphasized by the Neoplatonic philosophers (see page 235) and the resurrection to eternal life celebrated in Masses for the dead (a fresco of Christ's resurrection was intended for the altar wall).

The figures of Night and Day are twisted in a manner related to contrapposto, but with a more extreme twisting of the body parts. This type of posture became known later in the century as the *figura serpentinata* ("serpentine figure"). This pose became a hallmark of Mannerist art.

In the Medici Chapel, the poses are further enlivened by the walls, which give way to planes that articulate different levels of surfaces. The **cornice** extends forward into the space of the chapel. The "movement" of these architectural forms establishes an interplay between the architecture, the sculpture, and the space of the chapel. The visual energy and artistic license exhibited here characterize Mannerism (see pages 318–19), a style that followed and countered the classical idealism of the

High Renaissance. Michelangelo's freedom of expression was viewed by younger artists as a force of liberation: Vasari wrote,

> Thus all artists are under a great and permanent obligation to Michelangelo, seeing that he broke the bonds and chains that had previously confined them to the creation of traditional forms.

In 1534, Michelangelo left Florence for Rome, never to return. Rome at midcentury was a changed city. The sack of Rome in 1527 by the imperial troops under Charles V had been brutal. The impact felt from the Reformation caused further turmoil. The psychological climate was leaden.

Michelangelo was commissioned to paint *The Last Judgment* in the Sistine Chapel, where he had painted the ceiling earlier. Although the ceiling expressed God's love and the promise of salvation (see fig. 6-36), now pessimism broods (fig. 6-55). Christ, on the axis and surrounded by an aura of light, looks toward hell and raises his right hand against the wicked. Mary recoils next to him,

> slightly timid in appearance and almost as if uncertain of the wrath and mystery of God,

wrote the artist's biographer Condivi, in 1553. Angels blow trumpets to awaken the dead.

In the bottom register, to our left, the dead rise. To our right, the damned are being dragged down to eternal torment. Above, figures ascend to heaven. In the semicircular lunettes at the top, angels wrestle with the instruments of Christ's passion. Around Christ, martyrs brandish the weapons used to torture and kill them.

To the right of Christ, Saint Bartholomew, who was flayed, looks to Christ. He holds a knife in his right hand, while his flayed skin hangs from his left hand. The face on the skin was identified as Michelangelo's self-portrait only in 1925. The anguished facial

6-55 MICHELANGELO BUONARROTI

THE LAST JUDGMENT. 1534–41. Fresco, 48 × 44'. Sistine Chapel, Vatican, Rome. Originally, many of the figures in *The Last Judgment* were nude, but in the climate of the Counter-Reformation, some observers found nudity offensive in a papal chapel. Between 1559 and 1565, drapery was added to many of the figures and most of these were not removed during the recent restoration. Commissioned by Pope Paul III.

MICHELANGELO, *GIUDIZIO UNIVERSALE THE LAST JUDGMENT* (DETAIL), SISTINE CHAPEL. FRESCO, ON ALTAR WALL OF SISTINE CHAPEL. PHOTO: A. BRACCHETTI/P. ZIGROSSI, FEBRUARY 1995. THE VATICAN MUSEUMS, ROME. © NIPPON TELEVISION NETWORK CORPORATION TOKYO; 1996.

features add a highly personal message to the painting.

Of Michelangelo's *Last Judgment*, Condivi wrote:

> In this work Michelangelo expressed all that the art of painting can do with the human figure, leaving out no attitude or gesture.

Mannerism

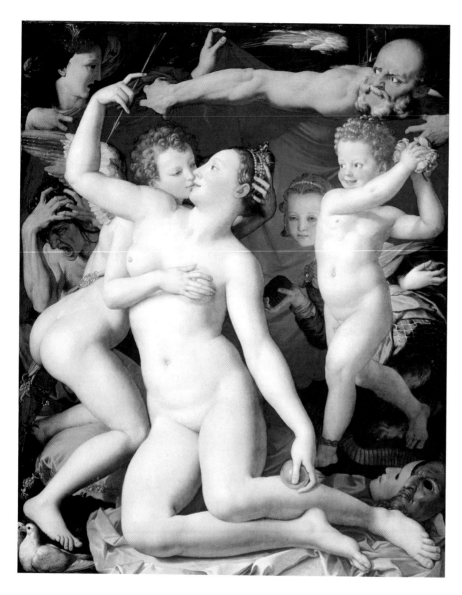

6-56 BRONZINO

The Allegory of Time and Lust. c. 1545. Oil on wood, 5'1" × 4'8¾". The National Gallery, London. Much about this painting remains a mystery to us. Although the circumstances of its commission are unknown, it may have been made for the Medici to give to Francis I of France. Probably commissioned by Duke Cosimo de' Medici.

Il BRONZINO, *VENUS, CUPID, FOLLY, AND TIME (THE EXPOSURE OF LUXURY)*, C. 1546. OIL ON WOOD, APPROX. 61 × 56 ¾ IN. NATIONAL GALLERY, LONDON.

The *Allegory of Time and Lust* by Bronzino (1503–72) is a visually and iconographically complex painting (fig. 6-56). At the top, allegories of Time and Fraud pull back a blue curtain, revealing the central figure of Venus, who, exposed by a cool, harsh light, is being caressed by her son, Cupid. Additional allegorical figures, including Deceit, to the right, behind the putto, and Jealously (recently interpreted as representing Syphilis), demonstrate the results of lust. The iconography of the work is still debated; this difficulty reveals the complex intellectual themes of

Mannerist art. The crowded figures and varied poses address a new style of highly artificial composition and unusual spatial effects. For another example of Mannerist painting, see Parmigianino's *Madonna with the Long Neck* (fig. 6-7).

Mannerism often invited the knowledgeable viewer to appreciate the subtle and hidden conceits of the work. Mannerist art was not intended to appeal to a mass audience. The works of Michelangelo and Raphael provided a starting point for the Mannerists, who developed selected ideas and forms to achieve a stylized, artificial elegance.

These traits are evident in Cellini's *Saltcellar of Francis I*, which reveals the artist's delight in demonstrating both technical accomplishment and artistic invention (fig. 6-57). In its graceful refinement, the *Saltcellar* reflects the conspicuous wealth and manner of sixteenth-century European courts. In its decorative treatment of counterbalanced nude figures and complex iconographic details, it demonstrates the visual and thematic complexities that occur in Mannerist art. The work was created to delight both the eye and the mind.

6-57 BENVENUTO CELLINI

SALTCELLAR OF FRANCIS I. 1543. Gold and enamel, 10¼ × 13⅛". Kunsthistorisches Museum, Vienna. Cellini's saltcellar (a receptacle for table salt) was commissioned by the French king Francis I.

BENVENUTO CELLINI (1500–1571), "SALIERA (SALTCELLAR), NEPTUNE (SEA) AND TELLUS (EARTH)," 1540–1543. GOLD, NIELLO WORK, AND EBONY BASE. HEIGHT: 26 CM. KUNSTHISTORISCHES MUSEUM, VIENNA, AUSTRIA. ERICH LESSING/ART RESOURCE, NY

6-58 GIAMBOLOGNA

RAPE OF THE SABINE WOMAN. Completed 1583. Marble, height 13'6". Loggia dei Lanzi, Florence. The theme is drawn from an event that occurred in the early years of ancient Rome, when the Romans abducted Sabine women as wives. No patron, but purchased by Duke Cosimo de' Medici.

Rape of the Sabine Woman, by Giambologna (1524–1608), with its twisting, spiraling, upward movement, was titled only after its completion (fig. 6-58). Contemporary sources reveal that the artist was initially inspired by the challenge to compose a group of multiple interlocking figures in dynamic movement. Giambologna's solution, based on a use of the *figura serpentinata*, offers varied visual expressions when viewed from different positions. The interplay of the figurative forms, emphatically stressed along diagonals, contributes to the work's dynamism, while the spiraling movement compels us to walk around the sculpture. This complex and energetic spatial involvement is a characteristic of late-sixteenth-century sculpture; it continues the course set earlier by Michelangelo's figural style. But whether the sculpture is monumental or more intimate, the dazzling display of the artist as virtuoso performer is apparent.

Early Landscape Painting

6-59 PIETER BRUEGEL THE ELDER

DECEMBER LANDSCAPE (commonly known as *HUNTERS IN THE SNOW*). 1565. Oil and tempera on wood, 3'10⅛" × 5'3¾". Kunsthistorisches Museum, Vienna. This landscape is part of a series of six that represented different times of the year; five survive today. They probably were originally displayed in the home of a wealthy Antwerp banker.

December Landscape (fig. 6-59), by Pieter Bruegel the Elder (1525/30–69), emphasizes nature not only by the vast sweep of the terrain but also by the manner in which the season—as expressed by the landscape—dominates and controls the activities of the peasants. Trudging peasants with a pack of motley dogs lead us into a village scene with skaters in the middle ground. The landscape culminates with distant, atmospheric peaks reminiscent of the Alps, which Bruegel crossed on a trip to Italy. The leaden gray-green of the sky and its subtle transformation in the colors of the frozen ponds, in combination with the stark, silhouetted trees and birds, evoke the time of year, the kind of day, and even the temperature of the moment.

In earlier periods, landscape was often viewed as an adversary, a frightening and unpredictable element populated with thieves and the unknown. With the exception of some ancient Roman frescoes and mosaics, landscape as a theme developed only late in the history of art. These examples from the sixteenth century are some of the first paintings to convey appreciation for landscape.

One of the first artists to show an interest in the expression power of landscape was the German painter Albrecht Altdorfer (1480–1538). His *Battle of Alexander and Darius* is both landscape and history painting (fig. 6-60; for an earlier representation of the same subject, see figure 3-85). The global scope of the landscape is tied to Altdorfer's historical narrative, for

6-60 ALBRECHT ALTDORFER

Battle of Alexander and Darius. 1529. Oil on wood, 5′2¼″ × 3′11¼″. Alte Pinakothek, Munich, Germany. Altdorfer's panoramic landscape combines observation with historical fantasy. Its ostensible subject is the ancient battle at Issus, where Alexander the Great defeated the Persian king Darius in 331 BCE. This historical theme almost certainly refers to the sixteenth-century hope that German troops would be able to stop the advance of the Ottoman Turks into Europe. Commissioned by the city of Regensburg at the request of Duke Wilhelm of Bavaria.

ALBRECHT ALTDORFER, GERMAN, (C. 1480–1538). *THE BATTLE OF ISSUS*, 1529. OIL ON PANEL, 62 × 47 IN. PINAKOTHEK, MUNICH. ARTOTHEK.

6-61 EL GRECO

Toledo. c. 1600–10. Oil on canvas, 47¾ × 42¾″. The Metropolitan Museum of Art, New York. The artist we now know as El Greco ("the Greek") was born Domenikos Theotokopoulos on the island of Crete. He studied in Venice (where he received his nickname) and lived in Toledo, Spain, from about 1575 until his death in 1614.

H. O. HAVEMEYER COLLECTION. BEQUEST OF MRS. H. O. HAVEMEYER, 1929 (29.100.16)

he wants to suggest that the battle at Issus was a struggle for control of the known world. This earthly conflict even seems to take on a cosmic significance, for Altdorfer presents a struggle between the setting sun and the rising moon as they vie for superiority in the background.

Dramatic landscape also marks the work of El Greco (1541–1614). The configuration of hills, valleys, and monuments in this painting identifies the city as Toledo (fig. 6-61), but both the natural forms and the city's structures have been stretched and verticalized to create a nervous effect that is height-ened by the somber colors and stormy sky. Along the banks of the river and on the hillsides are tiny human figures, who are dominated and threatened by the landscape. El Greco's vision of the city where he lived is less a portrait than a vehicle to convey a mood of drama and, perhaps, religious ecstasy.

Sixteenth-Century Painting

6-62   PIETER BRUEGEL THE ELDER

PEASANT WEDDING FEAST. c. 1566. Oil on wood, 3′8⅛″ × 5′4⅛″. Kunsthistorisches Museum, Vienna. The bride is the smug woman seated in front of the suspended cloth with a crown above her head. To either side are the groom and the couple's parents. To the right, a priest is in conversation with a distinguished-looking man who probably represents the landowner for whom these peasants worked.

In his *Peasant Wedding Feast,* Bruegel emphasizes the rustic nature of peasant life (fig. 6-62). The grain-filled barn of a prosperous landowner is the site where a wedding feast is being celebrated. In the right foreground, two men carry food on a huge makeshift tray composed of a door balanced on sticks. A guest reaches eagerly to pass the plates. The composition is based on the strong right-to-left diagonal recession of the table, which is opposed by the movement of the figures carrying the food. The lower right corner offers a glimpse of a chair; the left has a figure pouring beer into a miscellany of jugs and a child licking his fingers. Bruegel's palette, with simple browns set off by white, red, and the abundant gold of the grain, suggests the rich simplicity of peasant life.

For the twentieth-century observer, Bruegel's paintings of peasant life provide a fascinating source of knowledge about lower-class life, but the function of these paintings for Bruegel and his contemporaries is uncertain. Details of the present picture suggest some criticism of peasant life: the smugness of the bride, the gluttony of the participants, the fact that the priest and the landowner have withdrawn from the rest of the crowd. In the absence of evidence to the contrary, however, it is reasonable to suggest that Bruegel was recording, not condescending.

Bruegel was a friend of intellectuals, and his works were collected by connoisseurs. During Bruegel's lifetime, the Netherlands was engaged in a long battle for independence against foreign overlords. Some of his paintings representing war refer to this conflict, and in some, details convey

1565	Tobacco is introduced into Britain
c. 1566	**Pieter Bruegel the Elder, *Peasant Wedding Feast***
1578	China's population reaches 60 million

6-63   SULTAN MUHAMMAD

The Feast of Sadeh and the Discovery of Fire by the Persian King Hushang, from the *Tahmasp Shah-nameh*. c. 1520–25. Manuscript illumination, 9½ × 9¹⁄₁₆". Metropolitan Museum of Art, New York. The Persian national epic, the *Shah-nameh*, was originally composed by the poet Firdawsi between 975 and 1010. This *Shah-nameh*, which contains 258 miniatures, was created in the royal studios in the Persian capital at Tabriz. Commissioned by Shah Isma'il and his son Tahmasp.

GIFT OF ARTHUR A. HOUGHTON, JR., 1970. (1970, 301.2) PHOTOGRAPH © 1992 THE METROPOLITAN MUSEUM OF ART.

the dignity of the local populace. In this light, it is tempting to question whether Bruegel's emphasis on local traditions could also have a patriotic connotation. The peasant pictures represent the vitality of Northern life, but without obvious reference to the Spanish overlords who governed the subservient nation.

In sharp contrast to the earthy naturalism of Bruegel's *Peasant Wedding Feast* is the elegant richness of color and pattern in Sultan Muhammad's Persian miniature of the *Feast of Sadeh* (fig. 6-63). The lack of perspective and the emphasis on repeated decorative patterns, typical of much Islamic art, can surely be related to the prohibition on the representation of figures and animals in the Islamic religious tradition. Because the *Shah-nameh* was a secular, historical text, it was exempt from these restrictions. The vivid contrasts that evolve when one vivid pattern is contrasted with another has, by the sixteenth century, become a standard quality in Islamic architecture and art. Note here that the figures share the same basic head type and that the repeated poses of the bodies show little interest in the anatomical investigations and the complex positions typical of western art in the sixteenth century; in other words, the heads and figures serve as additional patterns within the composition, creating an aesthetic unity. Islamic legend tells that fire, here seen in a central position, was accidentally discovered by King Hushang when he threw a rock that hit a stone and caused sparks to fly. The manner in which rocks and plants defy the frame to jut out onto the page is a typical Persian device that continues the vitality of the patterning beyond normal boundaries and adds a sense of life and energy to the scene.

Islamic Art of the Ottomans

6-64 Prayer rug Second half of 16th century. Silk warp and weft with cotton and wool pile, 5'8" × 4'2". The Metropolitan Museum of Art, New York. The composition symbolizes the gardens of Paradise. In the central compartment hangs a mosque lamp designating a mihrab. The four tiny hexagonal buildings above the central niche represent heavenly pavilions, perhaps the domiciles of the souls of the righteous.

THE JAMES F. BALLARD COLLECTION, GIFT OF JAMES F. BALLARD, 1922 (22.100.51)

6-65 Illuminated frontispiece of a Koran. Transcribed by Ahmed Karahisari in 953; illuminated edition for Suleiman I, 1546–47. Gold marginal drawings, watercolors on folios, each 11⁷⁄₁₆″ × 7⁵⁄₁₆″. Topkopi Sarayi Museum, Istanbul, Turkey. The Ottomans, like other Islamic societies, regarded calligraphy as the noblest of the arts. To copy the holy book, the Koran, was considered an act of piety and devotion. Commissioned by Sultan Suleiman I the Magnificent.

6-66 SINAN

Suleimaniye Mosque, Istanbul. 1551–58. Commissioned by Sultan Suleiman I the Magnificent.

During the mid-sixteenth century, the Ottoman Empire (1299–1922) under the leadership of Sultan Suleiman I (1520–66) extended in the west to Greece, Albania, and Yugoslavia; into central Europe; across North Africa; to the central, historic Islamic lands of Saudi Arabia and the regions along the Arabian Gulf and the Red Sea. The Ottoman sultan—the central political leader, chief military officer, and protector of Islam—was also guardian of Mecca, Medina, and Jerusalem, the holy cities of the Islamic world, and ruled over the cultural centers of Damascus and Cairo.

The centralized administrative structure of the Ottoman state was also applied to artistic production. Societies of artists—including calligraphers, painters, bookbinders, jewelers, metalsmiths, woodworkers, tailors, hatmakers, and bootmakers—were created to respond to the needs of the palace. Each society had a chief, a deputy chief, master workers, and apprentices. All were paid daily wages by the state. The most influential of these groups was the *nakkashane* (imperial painting studio), which formulated decorative themes and designs employed in manuscripts, such as the pages of the Koran illustrated here (fig. 6-65). The *nakkashane* was the creative source for the Ottoman court style. Its influence could be felt in all parts of the empire.

The most conspicuous feature of Ottoman court art of this period is the representation of nature in depictions of flora in perpetual growth. This theme, executed in styles that reflected both mystical and naturalistic approaches, was meant to highlight the essence of nature: beauty and perpetuity. Objects produced in the imperial workshops re-created an enchanted forest inhabited by mythical creatures and naturalistic flora.

Suleiman's court architect, Sinan (c. 1491–1588), was responsible for all construction throughout the empire, including roads, bridges, and waterworks. On top of the highest hill in the imperial Ottoman capital of Istanbul, Sinan designed a huge mosque complex (*kullïye*) for Suleiman (figs. 6-66–6-68), which included four colleges, a Koranic school, baths, a hospital, a market street, an inn for travelers, a soup kitchen, and, in the adjoining cemeteries, tombs for Suleiman and his wife Roxelana. The purpose of such a complex was to fulfill Islam's requirement that all Muslims practice charity; the design of the mosque had its roots in Byzantine architecture. When the Ottoman Turks captured Constantinople in 1453, one of Mehmet the Conqueror's first acts was to declare that Hagia Sophia (see figs. 4-28–4-30), the Byzantine palace chapel and coronation church, should become a mosque. The enormous scale of this domed building and its connection to the Byzantine palace meant that it had a political content that Mehmet intended to neutralize. At the same time, Hagia Sophia's grand but ethereal unified space also meant that it would be appropriate for the worship of the single god, Allah, of Islam. Later Ottoman mosques were inspired by Hagia Sophia, and Suleiman apparently gave Sinan the challenge of creating a rival to the older structure in the

6-67   Dome, Suleimaniye complex.

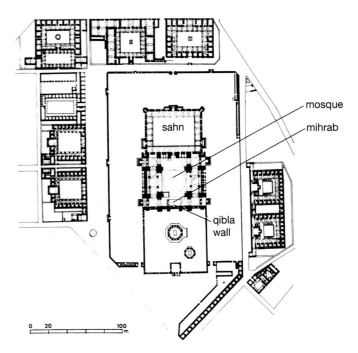

6-68   Plan of Suleimaniye complex.

Suleimaniye. Sinan followed the basic design of the Byzantine church, but his space is even more centralized and simplified. He indicates the **qibla** and the **mihrab** by a sophisticated use of marble, stained glass with calligraphic designs, and wood, ivory, and mother-of-pearl–decorated doors and shutters.

Originally the mosque at the Suleimaniye was filled with prayer rugs, or *seccades*. Each *seccade* includes a depiction of a mihrab. The niche oriented the *seccade*—and the worshiper—toward Mecca.

CHAPTER 6   Sixteenth-Century Art   325

Late-Sixteenth-Century Architecture

6-69 PALLADIO

San Giorgio Maggiore, Venice. Begun 1566. Andrea di Pietro della Gondola was given the nickname "Palladio," an allusion to Pallas Athena, the Greek goddess of wisdom. Commissioned by the monastery's abbot, Andrea Pampuro da Asolo.

6-70 Interior, San Giorgio Maggiore, Venice.

The church of San Giorgio Maggiore, with its white marble **facade** radiant against the blue sky and water, is built on an island just across the lagoon from the main public square of Venice (fig. 6-69). Renaissance architects had long wrestled with one major problem of facade design for **basilica** churches: how to reconcile the different roof heights of the **nave** and side **aisles** within a visually coherent design. Palladio's novel solution was to superimpose a classical temple facade, complete with pediment and tall engaged columns that reach the height of the nave, over a second, broader temple facade, indicated by fragments of a pediment and short pilasters that cover the side aisles. The use of the **giant order** unifies the double-tiered arrangement, while the **pediments** create a dynamic, axial accent. The facade is vigorous and simple. Its commanding scale and Renaissance harmony carry especially well from the public square near San Marco.

The articulation of the facade design is carried through the interior (fig. 6-70), where the short pilasters of the side aisles again confront the giant order of engaged columns as on the facade.

Palladio's designs, whether for ecclesiastical or secular architecture, such as the Villa Rotonda (see fig. 1-7), express visual harmony. Palladio's proportional systems were derived from musical scales, and they governed the interrelationship of all of the parts of a building as a totality.

Palladio had an incalculable influence on later developments in Western architecture because his ideas were published in editions illustrated with ground plans, sections, and elevations of his buildings. Palladio's *Four Books on Architecture*, first published in 1570, found their way into many great European and American libraries, including those of Robert Adam (see fig. 8-3) and Thomas Jefferson (see figs. 8-25–8-26).

The concerns of the Counter-Reformation and the Council of Trent found an important architectural expression in Il Gesù, the main church of the Jesuit Order in Rome (figs. 6-71–6-73). The design, by Giacomo da Vignola (1507–73), emphasizes the importance of having a unified congregation during services. The side aisles are transformed into chapels that open off the nave, and the **transepts** have been shortened, creating a monumental interior space that is both compact and unified.

The classical vocabulary of columns, **entablatures**, and pediments on the facade (see figs. 6-73) has its roots in Renaissance designs, but della Porta's combination offers a new sense of drama. The pilasters and engaged columns create a sequence that builds, visually and literally, toward a climax at the central door, which is framed by both a rounded and a triangular pediment and is emphasized by a cornice that, instead of being flat, is thickened at certain points to emphasize the architectural rhythms of the pilasters and columns below; this is called a **broken cornice**. On the upper story, a temple facade has a similar effect. The design, created by the dynamic interplay of architectural elements, will be further developed by Baroque architects in the seventeenth century.

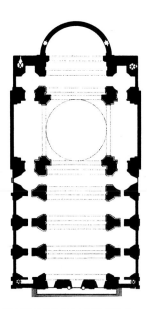

6-71   GIACOMO DA VIGNOLA

Plan of Il Gesù, Rome. 1568. Commissioned by the Jesuit Order.

6-72   GIACOMO DA VIGNOLA

Interior, Il Gesù, as represented in a 1639–41 painting by Andrea Sacchi and Jan Miel, which shows a visit to the church by Pope Urban VIII. The painting is now in the Galleria Nazionale d'Arte Antica, Rome. Between 1672 and 1685, Gaulli and Bernini decorated the nave ceiling with the *TRIUMPH OF THE NAME OF JESUS* (see fig. 7-5).

6-73   GIACOMO DELLA PORTA

Facade, Il Gesù, Rome. c. 1575–84. Although the church's original architect, Vignola, had submitted a design for the facade, the Jesuit who was in charge of the church's construction, Father Giovanni Tristano, chose della Porta's design instead. Commissioned by the Jesuit Order and Father Giovanni Tristano.

Veronese and the Impact of the Counter-Reformation

6-74 PAOLO VERONESE

LAST SUPPER/FEAST IN THE HOUSE OF LEVI. 1573. Oil on canvas, 18'3" × 42'. Galleria dell' Accademia, Venice. Veronese continued to paint in the Venetian High Renaissance style. Probably commissioned by Andrea Buono, a friar in the monastery at Santi Giovanni e Paolo.

At first glance, this huge and sumptuous painting by Paolo Veronese (1528–88) seems to represent a secular banquet (fig. 6-74). The setting is a palatial loggia, and the figures at the table are surrounded by richly costumed servants. However, Veronese created this work in response to a commission to paint a Last Supper for the refectory of the monastery of Santi Giovanni e Paolo in Venice. His interpretation of the Last Supper was questioned by the patron, at which point Veronese was called before one of the Inquisition tribunals established by the Catholic Church (see page 285). The transcript from his trial survives, giving us rare insight into a confrontation between the needs of the Counter-Reformation Church and the nature of artistic freedom in Italy during the Renaissance:

INQUISITIONER: What is the significance of those armed men dressed as Germans, each with a halberd [battle weapon] in his hand?

VERONESE: We painters take the same license the poets and jesters take. . . . They are placed here so that they might be of service because it seemed to me fitting that the master of the house, who was great and rich, should have such servants.

INQUISITIONER: And that man dressed as a buffoon with a parrot on his wrist, for what purpose did you paint him on that canvas?

VERONESE: For ornament, as is customary. . . .

INQUISITIONER: Did anyone commission you to paint Germans, buffoons, and similar things in that picture?

VERONESE: No, milords, but I received the commission to decorate the picture as I saw fit. It is large and, it seemed to me, it could hold many figures.

INQUISITIONER: Are not the decorations which you painters are accustomed to add to paintings or pictures supposed to be suitable and proper to the subject . . . ? Does it seem fitting at the Last Supper of the Lord to paint buffoons, drunkards, Germans, dwarfs and similar vulgarities?

VERONESE: No, milords.

INQUISITIONER: Do you not know that in Germany and in other places infected with heresy [Protestanism] it is customary with various pictures . . . to mock . . . and scorn the things of the Holy Catholic Church in order to teach bad doctrines to foolish and ignorant people? . . .

VERONESE: Illustrious Lords, I

6-75 JACOPO TINTORETTO

Last Supper. 1592–94. Oil on canvas, 12′ x 18′8″. San Giorgio Maggiore, Venice (see page 326) for a discussion of San Giorgio Maggiore). Tintoretto's painting is stylistically related to Mannerist developments. Probably commissioned by Michele Alabardi, prior of San Giorgio Maggiore.

do not want to defend it, but I thought I was doing right. I did not consider so many things and I did not intend to confuse anyone.

The tribunal contended that Veronese's *Last Supper* lacked decorum because the inclusion of so many extra figures was inappropriate to the subject. It was suggested that the secular elements could be viewed as an attempt to confuse and belittle the Church's authority. Veronese's additional figures, however, should be understood as a reflection of the extravagances of Venetian society rather than the ideas of the Reformation, and the artist based his defense on artistic license. He argued that artists should have the right to adorn and decorate their work as they saw fit. Ultimately he satisfied the tri-

bunal by changing the name of the painting to suggest that it represented another New Testament story, the feast in the house of Levi (Luke 5:29–39), in which Jesus dined with tax collectors.

The *Last Supper* (fig. 6-75) by Jacopo Tintoretto (1518–94) shares elements with Veronese's painting, such as the inclusion of servant figures and animals, but it offers an emphasis on the mystical content of this subject that is in keeping with the attitudes of the Counter-Reformation Church. The strong diagonal of the table is a departure from the traditional Last Supper format, in which the table was placed parallel to the picture plane (see fig. 5-64). The powerful thrust of the table into space creates a visual tension that comple-

ments Tintoretto's dynamic treatment of the theme. Jesus rises, his head surrounded by an intense glowing halo, to offer the bread, predicting the Eucharist, to the apostles. The space of the room is energized and spiritualized by ethereal angels, whose transparent, swirling forms emphasize the spirituality of this moment. The visual drama of the painting demands an emotional response from the viewer, while its didactic role promotes the Counter-Reformation ideal of the Church as the path to salvation.

The Art of Zen Buddhism in Japan

6-76. Teahouse, Japan. Momoyama period, c. 1573–1615. Hara Collection, Yokohama, Japan. The teahouse, usually small and humble in appearance, was designed out of natural materials in order to blend with its setting. The interior, where the tea ceremony took place, was entered through an entrance that was usually so small that guests had to bend low or even crawl through its opening. This gesture was presumably symbolic of shedding one's status. In the soft interior light, guests were to admire the painting or calligraphy hanging before them and eat the sweets and sip the tea prepared for them by the host and tea master.

6-77 Cold water jar (*mizusashi*). Momoyama period, late 16th century. Shino ware, stoneware with feldspathic glaze over painted iron-oxide decoration, height 7″. Seattle Art Museum, Seattle, Washington.

6-78 SESSHU

WINTER LANDSCAPE. Ashikaga period, c. 1500. Hanging scroll, ink and slight color on paper, height 18¼″. Tokyo National Museum, Tokyo, Japan. In 1431, at age eleven, Sesshu entered a Zen monastery and was ordained early as a priest. He became a student of Zen priest-painters, and in 1468 he went to China for a year, where he studied Chinese landscape painting and was honored as a Zen priest. From 1481 to 1484, he made pilgrimages all over Japan to study landscape. His paintings, which gained him a wide reputation in Japan, were intentionally different in temperament and effect from the Chinese paintings that he knew so well (compare fig. 4-58). Sesshu's paintings, spontaneous and natural, deemphasize complexity; *Winter Landscape* is both direct and simple. His brushstrokes, firm and bold, are thought to be animated with the spirit of transience because they are executed rapidly and spontaneously. These qualities are essential to the Zen conception of the transience of the spirit and of life. Probably commissioned by the Ouchi family, rulers of Yamaguchi, Honshu's westernmost province.

During the fifteenth and sixteenth centuries, a period of civil disorder in Japan, islands of response and tranquillity could be found in many bustling urban centers. The gate into the precinct of a temple or teahouse (fig. 6-76) led from the ordinary world into a realm devoted to repose and beauty. At the teahouse, the host invited friends of like artistic tastes not only to share tea but also to enjoy an inspired choice of art objects. The ceramic (fig. 6-77) and **lacquer** wares used for serving the tea, the particular scroll painting chosen for that day (fig. 6-78), and the garden (fig. 6-79) all contributed to the har-

mony of the experience. With the changing seasons and moods, this experience could never be recaptured in quite the same way again.

The animating spirit of the age was Zen, a meditative sect of Buddhism (see page 171). It was the religion of the samurai, who were the patrons of the arts associated with *cha no yu*—the art of tea. The Zen sensibility is primarily concerned with inner rather than outer form. Thus, each object was intended to speak directly to the heart or fulfill the spirit. Recognition of inward form required mental discipline that was based on the ephemeral, the transience of life. Zen taught that there was no

Buddha except the Buddha in your own nature and that only through meditation could you realize your own Buddha nature. You achieved enlightenment—an intuitive identification of spirit and object—when you realized unity with yourself and with all things. Zen doctrine, simple and direct, had an immediate appeal to the pragmatic, military samurai. The arts were inspired by the Zen apprehension of the spiritual identity of all things, by an appreciation of direct, intuitive perception, and by aesthetic standards that stressed subtlety, allusiveness, and restraint.

Tea was brought to prominence by monks who went to China to study Zen Buddhism in the twelfth century. Tea functioned as a stimulant to aid their study and meditation and was considered a medicinal beverage. Tea made its way into the society through the teachings of Zen to become the focus of gatherings of the nobility and the samurai and, eventually, the common people.

The most famous and revered Zen tea master, Sen no Rikyu, lived in the sixteenth century. He developed a set of aesthetic ideals that became the basis for Japanese etiquette and taste as part of the tea ceremony. The ceremony had four requirements: harmony, respect, purity, and tranquillity. Two all-important tea ceremony qualities were *sabi* (studied nonchalance) and *wabi* (quiet simplicity). The choice of unadorned, unpretentious tea utensils represented a pursuit of these qualities in material form. The goal was to recognize and appreciate (or create) with discriminating taste the inherent characteristics of all things associated with tea.

Japanese gardens, which were attached to private homes as well as monasteries, were planned to correspond to the essentials of Zen beliefs. Because they were a means for Zen self-examination, spiritual refinement, and ultimate enlightenment, they were not created for idle viewing or simple pleasure. Zen qualities are unmistakable in the dry gar-

6-79 SOAMI (attributed)

Dry garden of the Daisenin of Daitokuji, Kyoto, Japan. Ashikaga period, early 16th century. The garden is sited on a small space on the east side of the building. Its depth from the edge of the veranda, where one would mediate upon it, to the wall opposite is no more than 10 feet.

den at Daisenin (fig. 6-79), a temple at Daitokuji in Kyoto, attributed to Soami—a painter, poet, and practitioner of broad aesthetic knowledge and talent. Here, stones and gravel represent a course of water falling over a waterfall, racing along a mountain riverbed, and finally flowing into a broad river (at the bottom). It was thought to preserve an individual, spontaneous expression and could, therefore, never be copied or even approximated. It was an object of meditation.

The gardens associated with homes and areas surrounding the teahouses are usually "wet" gardens. Guests could wander through them, appreciating the qualities of nature emphasized in the design before eventually arriving at the rustic, intimate house where tea would be served.

Zen objects and practices required an expression of restraint, vitality, and intimacy that was intended to capture the "inner form" of life's spirit so essential to the core of Zen thought.

View of the Dutch countryside, with the town of Haarlem in the background and the bleaching of linen in the foreground, painted by the Dutch painter Jacob van Ruisdael about 1670 (for more information see fig. 7-56 and pp. 376–77).

Seventeenth-Century Art

A Brief Insight

THIS SUNLIT VIEW OF A DUTCH PANORAMA WITH A church in the distance is for us a pleasing reminder of the ever-changing beauty of nature. During the seventeenth century when it was created, however, the painting of landscape in Europe was a relatively new art. That landscape painting should first flourish in the Netherlands is not a surprise, for the Dutch at this time were intensely proud of their country. Although their new nation was small, the land had been won only after a fierce struggle against foreign overlords. That is why it was important for Ruisdael to represent the Dutch land not as an idealized vision but as it really is, a flat plain below a sky full of clouds, with the sun breaking through only in patches. The bleaching of cloth, in the foreground, was an important local industry, and the windmills we see in the background, used to help drain the marshy soil, were typical only in the Netherlands at this time. To have such an image hanging in their home would inspire a Dutch merchant and his family with feelings of patriotism. The new mercantile, bourgeois, and democratic society of the Netherlands at this time led to new developments in art, and the art thus becomes a kind of historical record that helps us understand the culture in more detail. Nations with other priorities and traditions during the seventeenth century produced art that is distinctly different from the Dutch example seen here.

Seventeenth-Century Art

7-1 GIANLORENZO BERNINI

DAVID. 1623. Marble, height 5'5". Galleria Borghese, Rome, Italy. Commissioned by Cardinal Scipione Borghese.

In their exuberant representation of vivacious movement and in the ways they engage our attention, Bernini's *David* and Hals's *Merry Drinker* (figs. 7-1, 7-2) are characteristic of much of the art produced during the seventeenth century in Europe. In his depiction of the Old Testament hero David, Bernini (1598–1680) has caught the figure coiled in space like a taut spring, about to sling the stone at the giant Goliath. His bursting energy urges us to move out of the line of fire. In the painting by Frans Hals (c. 1581–1666), a man invites us to join him in a drink: we impulsively want to reach out

and grab the glass he holds so precariously. The loose brushstrokes and warm, golden color enhance the movement and naturalism of the painting.

In creating his tour de force, Bernini, an Italian, was certainly aware that his work would be compared to the sculptures of David by his two great predecessors, Donatello and Michelangelo (see figs. 5-47, 6-18). He rivals their accomplishments by representing a new moment in the David narrative. His choice of the instant of greatest action is consistent with much of European seventeenth-century art. Hals's painting is a work virtually without precedent, in

7-2 FRANS HALS

MERRY DRINKER. 1628–30. Oil on canvas, 31⅞ × 26¼″. Rjksmuseum, Amsterdam, Netherlands.

part because it is the product of a new kind of society—the mercantile, bourgeois, Protestant nation established in the Netherlands in the seventeenth century. Despite significant differences in medium, size, and function, these works are similar in the artists' determination to involve us in the action they represent and in their emphasis on depicting arrested motion.

The art of the seventeenth century, however, is not this simple. The two qualities cited above, which are part of a movement within the century known as the European Baroque (see pp. 337–39), are not shared by all seventeenth-century European works, in part because of increasingly complex and diverse developments in history.

History

Europe had become steadily more prosperous in the course of the sixteenth century, partly as a result of the influx of wealth from the Americas and the development of new

markets there. European wealth continued to increase in the seventeenth century, especially in areas with stable governments and strong commercial and trading interests. The centers of European financial power gradually shifted northward, to the rapidly growing cities of Amsterdam, Paris, and London.

Much of the pluralism of seventeenth-century art can be related to historical developments, for it is during this century that many of the national identities recognized today were consolidated as the map of Europe assumed territorial divisions similar to those of the present day. New, or newly powerful, national entities had a profound influence on artistic developments.

The establishment of the new republic of the Netherlands was perhaps the most dramatic historical development of the seventeenth century in Europe. By 1609, the rebels from the northern Netherlands won their independence after a decades-long war against Spanish Catholic overlords. The new nation was unlike any other in Europe, for it was a true republic, with no traditional hereditary aristocracy. It was governed by merchants, who quickly developed a sound commercial basis for the economy. By providing goods at more reasonable prices, they developed markets all over Europe and the Americas. Although the Netherlands became largely middle class, a number of successful business entrepreneurs achieved great wealth. Amsterdam became the fastest-growing city in Europe, and the Netherlands soon had a more highly urbanized population than any other European country. In addition, it became Europe's leading maritime power, establishing the East and West India Companies and taking control of much of international commerce, including a monopoly on the spice and slave trades. The Dutch were both Protestant and tolerant, and Jews who fled Poland, Spain, and Portugal during this period largely settled in the Netherlands. Amsterdam also became a lively intellectual community and the most important book-publishing center in Europe. It was in the Netherlands that the new theories of the French philosopher René Descartes, which were founded on the principle of universal doubt, were published. It should be no surprise that important new developments in art occurred here.

By the end of the seventeenth century, France, with a population of approximately 19 million, was the largest nation in Europe and the strongest and wealthiest. Reunited by Henry IV at the beginning of the century, the monarchy consolidated its power under a series of energetic and able administrators—Richelieu, Mazarin, and Colbert—during the reigns of Louis XIII and Louis XIV. Under Louis XIV, the Sun King, who ruled until 1715, the centralization of power and wealth under the monarchy was completed. The power of the traditional nobility in France was broken, and the king governed as a supreme and autocratic ruler. By the end of the century, France had an army of 150,000 that was feared throughout Europe.

The decline of Spain as a European power, which had begun in the sixteenth century, continued. Spain's economy was stagnant, despite its important territories. It still controlled the southern Netherlands (or Flanders, roughly equivalent to today's Belgium) and all of Italy south of Rome, including the huge shipping port of Naples. But the conservative rigidity of the Spanish court restricted growth. The Spanish Netherlands remained Catholic and under the control of a traditional aristocracy, but it had been substantially weakened by its foreign overlords, and the country's outstanding Baroque artist, Peter Paul Rubens, found his most important commissions outside his homeland.

The central and northern portions of the Italian peninsula were still controlled by local city-states, the largest of which were Milan and Venice. Here, too, the economy stagnated, with Venice gradually losing its traditional maritime supremacy in the Mediterranean to English and Dutch shippers, whose prices were substantially lower. The most powerful political force in Italy was the papacy in Rome, which, during the seventeenth century, flourished under dynamic and ambitious popes. They rebuilt Rome with glorious Baroque monuments, fought Protestantism, and reasserted the authority of the Catholic Church.

Germany was devastated by the Thirty Years' War (1618–48), which destroyed the power of the Holy Roman Empire and killed at least one-third of its population. Political turmoil consumed energies in England, where King Charles I, an important collector and art patron, was overthrown and beheaded in 1649.

In 1644, the Ming dynasty in China, which had ruled since 1368, fell as a result of an economic depression, governmental incompetence and corruption, and factionalism. It was succeeded by the Qing (Manchu) dynasty, a group of outsiders who would rule until 1912. The Manchu emperors quickly adopted Chinese ways, supporting literature and the arts by collecting earlier Chinese art and commissioning works in a traditional Chinese style.

Edo (Tokyo) continued to be the capital of Japan during this period. The elegance of the Momoyama period (1573–1615) was replaced by the so-called Edo period (1615–1868), a time of military dictatorship. Samurai—warrior aristocrats—and an expanded mercantile class were important patrons of the arts, and following their interests, the developing arts were sometimes secular in tone and content. European traders and missionaries were expelled in 1638, and Japan remained almost totally isolated until the nineteenth century.

In India, the Mughals continued to extend their authority—and Islam—over North India, which was largely unified as the Mughal empire under Shah Jahan. It was this Mughal ruler who brought in international craftspeople, including stonecutters from Italy, to design and build one of the most famous of Mughal monuments, the Taj Mahal in Agra, India (c. 1632–48), as a tomb and shrine for his beloved wife, Mumtaz-i-Mahal.

Intellectual and Scientific Activity in Europe

The explosion of printed information that followed the invention of movable type in the fifteenth century led to greatly increasing levels of literacy. By the end of the seventeenth century, almost half of the adult male population of Europe was literate. In addition, scientific questioning, which had been made more possible after the Reformation, led to important advances in medicine and the other sciences by such major figures in scientific theory and invention as Bacon, Galileo, Newton, Harvey, Hobbes, Kepler, Locke, Leeuwenhoek, Descartes, and Pascal. Many of the European capitals developed academies and learned institutions in science and in other areas, which began publishing scholarly periodicals to promote the advancement of knowledge. In literature, poetry and drama found a new, more vivid and emotional expressiveness in the works of Milton, Corneille, Molière, Racine, and Shakespeare. The caricature, a humorous or critical portrait based on exaggeration, had been invented earlier, but in the seventeenth century it was popularized and developed by Bernini and Annibale Carracci. At the end of the century in Florence, a group interested in reviving ancient Greek drama offered musical presentations that led directly to the development of opera. One of the first of these compositions was Jacopo Peri's *Euridice*, which was performed at the marriage by proxy of Marie de' Medici to Henry IV of France in 1600 (see page 350). One of the guests was the artist Rubens.

The Styles of Seventeenth-Century European Art

Given the complexity of the historical and intellectual developments of this period, it should not be a surprise to learn that seventeenth-century art encompasses a number of different styles. The most typical style is known as the Baroque, a term sometimes confusingly applied to all art produced in the seventeenth century. In painting, this style is characterized by asymmetrical compositions, powerful effects of movement, and strong lighting in combination with dramatic interpretations of subject matter. Similar effects in sculpture are accomplished, often with rich materials and surprising light sources from hidden windows. In

7-3 ANNIBALE CARRACCI

Ceiling fresco, Farnese Gallery, Farnese Palace, Rome. c. 1597–1604. 67 × 20'. Commissioned by Cardinal Odoardo Farnese.

Baroque architecture, the classical orders continue to be used as vocabulary, but they are arranged in new patterns that are dynamic and energetic. The Baroque is a style that was especially suited to the goals of autocratic rulers of the Counter-Reformation Catholic Church. The origins of the word *baroque* are uncertain, although some have traced it to the Portuguese word *barroco*, meaning an irregularly shaped pearl; in any case, the term *baroque* seems to have first been used to describe works of art in the eighteenth century, when it became a derogatory term for works that were considered strange, irregular, and irrational.

During the seventeenth century, there was also interest in continuing the classicism of the High Renaissance, although with a greater complexity of composition and in a grander and more highly decorative manner. These stylistic qualities were usually reserved for subjects drawn from classical mythology or history. This style can be called Baroque Classicism. A

7-4 GIANLORENZO BERNINI

FOUNTAIN OF THE FOUR RIVERS. 1648–51. Marble and travertine, with Egyptian-style obelisk. Piazza Navona, Rome. The obelisk recycled here, long thought to be an ancient Egyptian original, is in reality an ancient Roman imitation commissioned by the emperor Domitian in the first century CE for the circus (a racetrack and site for other games) that he built in Rome at this location. Commissioned by Pope Innocent X Pamphili. The church in the background, designed by the Italian Baroque architect Francesco Borromini (see pp. 356–357), is Sant'Agnese in Agone.

typical example is Annibale Carracci's ceiling fresco decoration for the Farnese Palace in Rome (fig. 7-3). The theme is mythological (the loves of the ancient gods) and his sources of inspiration include Michelangelo, Raphael, and classical sculpture; compared to these earlier works, however, the ceiling decoration is more complex and ornate. In painting, the main example is the French artist Nicolas Poussin (see pp. 768–69). Examples of Baroque Classicism in architecture are Versailles (see fig. 7-49) and Christopher Wren's St. Paul's Cathedral in London.

A third style, the Dutch Baroque, is limited to painting. This style is represented by thousands of Dutch paintings of Dutch subjects, characterized by their realism and naturalism. Although some of these paintings can be shown to have certain elements in common with Baroque works elsewhere (as was demonstrated with Hals's *Merry Drinker*). Dutch Baroque paintings are noted for their relatively small scale and their emphasis on Dutch subjects. Mythological and religious subjects were usually avoided. The exception is the work of Rembrandt (1606–69), who cannot be characterized as a Dutch Baroque artist (as the style has been defined above) and whose style at different times in his life has affinities both with the Baroque and with Baroque Classicism.

Some seventeenth-century works overlap categories, and some fall outside the three that have been defined here (as do those of the Spanish painter Velázquez). The stylistic distinctions drawn here are merely an aid in understanding the complex art of this century. These distinctions will be refined and expanded in subsequent discussions of individual works, but in the final analysis it must be admitted that seventeenth-century works of art cannot be easily categorized.

Seventeenth-Century European Art

In Italy, Flanders, and Spain—countries that remained Catholic—the Counter-Reformation (see pp. 284–86) led to the production of dramatic Baroque religious images, especially of subjects that fostered and supported Catholic beliefs: the lives of Jesus and the Virgin Mary, the miracles and martyrdoms of saints, and the lives of monks, nuns, and priests. Elaborate cycles of paintings of religious subjects and dramatic sculptural groupings were produced for churches throughout the Catholic world. Architecture in these areas generally followed the same enthusiastic Baroque style.

In the Netherlands, the prevailing religion of Calvinism, which forbade the representation of God or Christ, led to a virtual moratorium on the production of religious subjects (again, Rembrandt stands as a distinct exception). At the same time, the absence of aristocratic or royal patronage meant a decline in interest in mythological subjects. The lively artistic production in the Netherlands specialized in naturalistic paintings of Dutch subjects—landscapes, **genre** themes (the representation of scenes of everyday life), still lifes, portraits—for the home. There was little interest in grand architectural or sculptural projects.

In the countries that had a strong court and aristocracy—France, Flanders, Spain—and in the Italian cities of Florence, Naples, Rome, and Venice, the production of portraits and history paintings continued to provide an important livelihood for painters. Royalty, such as Charles I of England or Marie de' Medici, queen of France, the noble families of Rome, and members of the clergy, not to mention the papacy, provided lucrative commissions for artists. France offered the most extensive development of art and architecture in the service of autocracy since the ancient Roman Empire.

Although fountains had played a role in urban planning and garden decoration since ancient Roman times, new possibilities in fountain design were explored by that inventive Baroque genius Bernini. His most triumphal fountain, in the Piazza Navona in Rome (fig. 7-4), has an Egyptian-style obelisk raised over a rocky landscape with four monumental figures—each as big as Michelangelo's *David*. They symbolize what at the time were considered to be the four main rivers of the world: the Danube, Nile, Rio della Plata, and Ganges. The theme of the fountain, a

7-5 GIOVANNI BATTISTA GAULLI (assisted by GIANLORENZO BERNINI)

TRIUMPH OF THE NAME OF JESUS. Ceiling fresco, with gilded stucco surround and white stucco angels by Antonio Raggi, Il Gesù, Rome. 1672–85. Gaulli is also known by the nickname "Baciccio." This decoration fills the blank ceiling seen in figure 6-72. Commissioned by Father Oliva, Father General of the Society of Jesus.

papal commission, is consistent with the Counter-Reformation, which suggests that all the peoples of the world will be converted to Catholicism through the efforts of an energetic papacy and the revived Church of the Counter-Reformation. Bernini forces the water of the fountain to cascade in sheets to create the maximum noise and splash. The water, integral to his conception, is incorporated into both design and theme. He even incorporates the drain into this design, for a smiling, cavorting fish "swallows" the water, adding yet another sound to this lively complex. The fountain has a new excitement and energetic dynamism consistent with Baroque attitudes.

One of the most dramatic expressions of the Baroque aesthetic and Counter-Reformation ideals is Baroque ceiling painting. The figures in Gaulli and Bernini's *Triumph of the Name of Jesus* (fig. 7-5), which is set off by a wide gilded frame held by angels in relief, seem to come to life. Struggling, suffering figures appear to fall down toward us, into the space of the church, while at a vast distance high in the sky, the monogram of Christ (*IHS*) glows with an unearthly intensity. The painting offers a view of heaven, with angels and ranks of the faithful adoring Christ's name, while the rays of light that flow downward force disbelievers away from this mystic vision, into a realm of shadowy darkness. With a touch of wit, Gaulli here heightens his illusion by interrelating the painted figures with the three-dimensional stucco forms: the foot of one of the stucco angels who surround the frame gives an extra push to one of the sinful figures being cast out of Paradise. A great deal of the success of the illusion painted on the vault of the church of Il Gesù is due to the gilded stucco frame and ceiling **coffering**, which establish a point of reference for the spatial development. The progressive diminution of the figures is joined with gradually intensifying light to lead us past the frame, beyond the limits of the architecture, while the clouds and figures that overlap the frame seem to be emerging into our space. Their position within the church seems confirmed by the shadows they cast on the coffering. This ensemble seems to fulfill the tenets of the Council of Trent of more than a century earlier. With vigor and enthusiasm, it seduces and overwhelms us in an attempt to convince us of the truth of what we see.

The Seventeenth-Century Artist

Seventeenth-century European artists were willing to undertake huge projects, and the most successful were entrepreneurs like Bernini and Peter Paul Rubens (1577–1640), who managed large workshops of assistants and apprentices. Only with such help could they have carried out gargantuan projects like Rubens's Marie de' Medici cycle and Bernini's sequence of works for St. Peter's (see pages 352 and 353). The Baroque is also the period of the virtuoso, in art no less than in drama and music. Artists enjoyed demonstrating their creative powers to enthusiastic patrons, and a typical Baroque work was an incredible tour de force. In Bernini's *Apollo and Daphne* (see fig. 1-4), marble has been transformed to suggest textures that convey the mythological miracle: hair becomes leaves and toes take root as bark encompasses the instantaneously frozen figure of Daphne.

Another important development, new in the history of art, took place in the Netherlands in the seventeenth century, where there was such a demand for paintings that a free market in works of art developed. Rather than waiting for a commission to work on a specific project for a specific patron, Dutch artists made more general works for a wide

7-6 PETER PAUL RUBENS

SELF-PORTRAIT WITH ISABELLA BRANDT. 1609–10. Oil on canvas, 5'9" × 4'5½". Alte Pinakothek, Munich, Germany. This double portrait was painted at the time of the couple's marriage, apparently for Rubens's own collection. The studied informality of the pose is unexpected, but the elegance of the costumes reveals Rubens's aristocratic aspirations.

and popular audience. These works were bought not only by citizens but also by art dealers, who established shops selling art. For the first time, the relationship between the artist and the public began to approach the situation we know today. Speculation in works of art became a part of the commercial activity of the Netherlands. In fact, there was so much activity that artists could support themselves working as specialists in a single category, such as marine painting, flower painting, or genre painting.

In France, where the king and his ministers controlled all aspects of culture, artists were less free than elsewhere. An academy determined production and through lectures and publications enforced the state-favored style of Baroque Classicism. In most of Europe, the Renaissance tradition of the artist as a respected intellectual continued to develop in the seventeenth century, aided by the explosion in art criticism and in writing about art that was a part of the enormous increase in publishing during the century.

With the exception of the Netherlands, patronage in Europe during this period was still quite traditional. Rulers and popes continued to commission grand projects, and the aristocracy built and decorated palaces and commissioned paintings from well-known artists that would enhance their reputation as sophisticated and knowledgeable individuals. Because of the growing respect for artists, patrons often allowed them more freedom in selecting subject matter and

7-7 ARTEMISIA GENTILESCHI

SELF-PORTRAIT AS THE ALLEGORY OF PAINTING. 1630. Oil on canvas, 38 × 29″. The Royal Collection, Great Britain. In this unusual allegorical portrait, Artemisia Gentileschi reveals a special identification with her profession. Her unruly hair suggests the divine frenzy that was held to be an important indication of genius during this period.

7-8 JUDITH LEYSTER

SELF-PORTRAIT AT THE EASEL. c. 1635. Oil on canvas, 29⅜ × 25⅝″. National Gallery of Art, Washington, D.C.

determining its interpretation; in other words, the concept of artistic "genius" led not only to greater respect for the artist, but also to greater independence. As previously mentioned, in the Netherlands the growing art market meant that most artists painted general works for the market and did not work on commission; it is this exceptional circumstance that helps explain Rembrandt's remarkable career and his selection, in later years, of themes that he found psychologically and artistically challenging (see figs. 7-36–7-38, 7-41). The relative cheapness of canvas meant that artists could take a chance on a little-known subject or could even produce paintings for their own collections, as is the case with Rubens's painting of his country house (see fig. 7-56). Where patrons are known for the works in this section, they are listed in the captions; where no patron is listed, this means that either the patron is unknown, the work was created for the market, or the work was produced for the artist's own satisfaction. The latter case is true only for a very few works during the seventeenth century, but by the nineteenth century, it is perhaps fair to say that most of the works that we consider to be of exceptional interest were created to satisfy the personal needs of the artist.

The public's interest in the artist and the artist's new self-confidence are expressed in the increasing number of self-portraits. In the two preceding centuries, the self-portrait was exceptional, but a much larger percentage of seventeenth-century artists made commanding and impressive representations of themselves, and it was during this period that the Medici of Florence began a collection of self-portraits. Among the most impressive examples is Rubens's charming *Self-Portrait with Isabella Brandt* (fig. 7-6).

The interest in self-portraits by women artists that we noted in the sixteenth century continued in the seventeenth. Perhaps the most remarkable is Artemisia Gentileschi's *Self-Portrait as the Allegory of Painting* (fig. 7-7), a representation in which the painter says, in essence, "I am painting." The Dutch artist Judith Leyster represents herself informally at the easel, smiling out at us with ease and a typical Dutch familiarity (fig. 7-8).

How a society represents nature in paintings and how it manipulates it in gardens reveals important attitudes about the relationship between humanity and nature in that society. Ruisdael's *Dutch Landscape*, for example, is profoundly naturalistic, and this simple fact reveals that the Dutch were comfortable with their land; by the very fact of representation and display they also reveal their pride. The Dutch had just won this countryside after a long war against Spanish overlords, and they prized representations of their country—flat, with a sky full of clouds, and with Dutch industry flourishing in the foreground—in their homes. Notice that the painting has no central focal point and that the view seems uncontrived and natural. In contrast, the almost contemporary design for the garden at the French royal palace at Versailles reveals how ordering and correcting nature was used by the French king to demonstrate his power and authority. Nature is controlled here, and the vastness of the endeavor (from the palace's terraces, the gardens seem almost infinite) suggests a different attitude toward nature than we see in the casual panorama offered by Ruisdael. In the French garden, straight pathways, great bodies of geometrically ordered water with fountains as focal points, and rows of carefully planted trees dominate the experience of the visitor and testify to the ability of the king to bring even nature under his control.

7-9   JACOB VAN RUISDAEL

Dutch Landscape from the Dunes at Overveen
(for more information see fig. 7-55).

7-10   *Versailles Garden*
(for more information see figs. 7-49–7-51).

In prehistoric societies, nature was a life-giver, and understanding how nature worked could mean life or death for the tribal society. Stonehenge, set in the middle of the Salisbury Plain so that the horizon is visible in all directions, allowed early humanity to plot out the movements of the sun on the horizon. Establishing the timing of the summer and winter solstices allowed these early peoples to determine best when early spring planting might take place. But Stonehenge is clearly more than just a useful agrarian calendar. The monumental scale of the complex and the labor needed for its construction suggests that it must also have been a center for a religious ritual that honored life-giving natural forces.

7-11 STONEHENGE
(for more information see fig. 2-9 and p. 30).

The idea that nature is a gift from the gods to humanity is common in many cultures, and this concept is vividly expressed in this large scene, which has been sculptured directly into a giant boulder found at the Holy Hindu site of Mahamallapuram. Over centuries a natural crevice had been created on the surface of this boulder by the dramatic fall of water during rain, and this natural phenomenon became connected to the Hindu belief that the Ganges River had flowed down from heaven, a gift from the gods in the distant past. By carving figures of gods, water spirits, humanity, and animals on the rock, the legend was made explicit, and a natural phenomenon came to serve religious belief.

7-12 Hindu. *DESCENT OF THE GANGES* Relief
(for more information see fig. 4-2).

Turrell's monumental work, perhaps the largest single work of art in the world, is created of the landscape itself, like the Hindu relief at Mahamallapuram. The pathways and rock-cut chambers that will eventually be created here, however, are not related to any particular religious viewpoint. Rather they are intended to draw the viewer's attention to the overarching sky and the patterns of movement and of light created by the sun, the moon, and the stars. In this way, Turrell's work becomes a modern parallel to the prehistoric site at Stonehenge.

7-13 JAMES TURRELL Roden Crater
(for more information see fig. 10-159).

■ QUESTIONS

1. What is your own relationship with nature and how has it been formed? Did art or nature photography play a role?

2. What work of art from the past best expresses how you feel about nature?

Caravaggio and His Influence

7-14 CARAVAGGIO

ENTOMBMENT OF CHRIST. 1603–04. Oil on canvas, 9′10¼″ × 6′8″; the figures are over-lifesize. Vatican Museums, Rome. In 1642, this painting was listed as being Caravaggio's greatest work. Commissioned with funds left by Pietro Vittrice for his chapel at Santa Maria in Vallicella in Rome.

E ntombment of Christ, by Caravaggio (1573–1610), is an arresting painting (fig. 7-14), for it seems as if we are really there—the figures are naturalistic, the strong light gives them a sharp physical presence, and their actions and emotions are convincing. The figures stand on a great tomb slab that seems to jut out of the picture into our space. This intrusion into our space commands that we participate in the experience, as does the gaze of Nicodemus, the old man who looks out at us with a troubled, weary expression. We seem to be below, in a dark and empty space. Caravaggio may be suggesting that we are standing in the tomb of Jesus. The figural composition flows downward from the upper right, beginning with the dramatic gesture of one of the Marys, who raises her hands in supplication, and concludes with the descending dead weight of the body of Jesus. The painting is clear, direct, and moving.

Two particular qualities characterize this powerful painting as the work of Caravaggio: the strong lighting and the inclusion of lower-class figure types. The light enters in a bold flash, creating strong highlights and deep pockets of shadow. It seems like a sudden illumination in a world full of darkness. The figures, modestly dressed, range in age from the youthful women to the old, tired figure of the Virgin Mary. Their wrinkles and bare feet are only two of the obvious means by which Caravaggio gives his figures a striking actuality.

Our participation in a dramatic religious event is demanded by *Christ with the Doubting Thomas* (fig. 7-15). The lifesize figures are half-length, and our presence as spectators, standing before the picture, fulfills the semicircular grouping of Christ and the apostles. The composition seems to need us to be complete. In the biblical

7-15 CARAVAGGIO

CHRIST WITH THE DOUBTING THOMAS. c. 1602–03. Oil on canvas, 42⅛″ 57½″. Neues Palast, Potsdam, Germany. Commissioned by Vincenzo Giustiniani, an important collector of Caravaggio's work.

story, Thomas doubts that the figure appearing to the apostles is Christ. Christ tells him that for proof he should stick his finger in the wound in his side. The text implies that Thomas did not do this, but Caravaggio has chosen to represent Christ forcing Thomas's finger into the wound. Such a shocking, physical emphasis is not uncommon in Caravaggio's works. Although the Bible stresses the humble origins of the apostles, Caravaggio is one of the few artists who gives them a compelling reality and dignity.

Not everyone appreciated Caravaggio's vigorous realism. A seventeenth-century critic said that one of his paintings lacked "proper decorum, grace, and devotion." But Caravaggio's art was revolutionary precisely because it was not ennobled by a concept of beauty and because he did not adhere to the idealistic theories of art that had evolved during the Renaissance.

Caravaggio's mastery at depicting internal emotion is evident in his representation of the conversion of Saint Paul (fig. 7-16). In the biblical story (Acts 9:1–9), the Roman Saul was traveling toward Damascus to persecute Christians when "suddenly a light flashed from the sky all around him," and he fell to the ground. He heard a voice saying, "Saul, Saul, why do you persecute me?" When Saul asked, "Tell me, Lord, who you are," the reply was, "I am Jesus, whom you are persecuting."

7-16 CARAVAGGIO

CONVERSION OF SAINT PAUL. c. 1601. Oil on canvas, 7′6½″ × 5′10″. Santa Maria del Popolo, Rome. Commissioned by Tiberio Cerasi, general papal treasurer under Pope Clement VIII.

7-17 ARTEMISIA GENTILESCHI

JUDITH AND HER MAIDSERVANT WITH THE HEAD OF HOLOFERNES. c. 1625. Oil on canvas, 6'½" × 4'7¾"; the figures are over-lifesize. The Detroit Institute of Arts. The story of Judith and Holofernes is told in the biblical Old Testament Apocrypha. Judith was a virtuous Jewish widow who saved her people during a siege. Entering the Assyrian camp, she captured the attention of the enemy general Holofernes and, after he became intoxicated at a banquet, beheaded him. She became a symbol of Fortitude and, because she played a role in saving her people, is often seen as a prototype for the Virgin Mary.

Saul, who was blinded by the "brilliance of the light" for three days, was converted to Christianity and baptized with the new name of Paul.

Divine revelations and mystical conversions were common themes in the art of the Counter-Reformation. In Caravaggio's painting, the powerful light comes from almost directly overhead, and Caravaggio suggests that the force of the light has thrust Paul to the ground. Paul reaches out to embrace the light in a natural gesture that is both supplicating and receptive.

Although Caravaggio seems to have had no direct pupils, his art had a potent impact on Italian art and on the many foreigners studying and working in Rome. His close followers are known as Caravaggisti. The Caravaggesque movement became international when French, German, Spanish, Flemish, and Dutch artists returned home from Italy to teach and work. Prints copying

7-18 JUDITH LEYSTER

GAY CAVALIERS (also known as *THE LAST DROP*). c. 1628–29. Oil on canvas, 35⅛″ × 29″. Philadelphia Museum of Art. Leyster was a teacher (in 1635 she had three male students) and a successful, independent artist who painted genre pictures, portraits, and still lifes. Her production diminished after she married a fellow artist and had three children.

paintings by Caravaggio and his followers also had an impact on these developments, and artists who never visited Rome and probably never saw an original painting by Caravaggio knew and were inspired by the great Italian painter's innovations.

In the monumental *Judith and Her Maidservant*, by Artemisia Gentileschi (c. 1597–after 1651), we are intruders—walking in on an episode charged with excitement and fear (fig. 7-17). The Caravaggesque qualities are evident in the dramatic tension, powerful light, and realistic figures. Holofernes has been decapitated and the head is being wrapped for their escape when Judith hears an unexpected sound. The momentary effect achieved as the nervous women look up is dramatized by

the light. The painting communicates a mood of tension and emotional drama that few of Caravaggio's followers could match. Artemisia, daughter of the painter Orazio Gentileschi, specialized in large-scale paintings of biblical or mythological subjects, often choosing themes that featured female heroes. She was proud of her accomplishments, and after finishing a painting for one patron declared: "This will show your Lordship what a woman can do."

Caravaggio never included a source for the strong light that illuminated his subjects, realizing the mystery and drama that an unknown light source can convey. But his followers often chose to introduce the light source into the painting, as is the case with Artemisia Gentileschi's *Judith*. The

addition of the light source opens up new possibilities of expression, as seen in Artemisia's painting: when Judith holds up her hand to shield her vision from the candle's glare, the strong shadow cast on her face adds an additional element of suspense.

In Judith Leyster's *Gay Cavaliers* (fig. 7-18), the illumination once again emanates from a candle. The figures are posed to catch the light from different angles, enhancing the composition's lively, momentary effect. Their abandoned gestures of delight in the intoxication of alcohol and tobacco (a new vice in the seventeenth century) are naturalistic, but we are uncertain whether or not Leyster intended any critical comment.

Baroque Genre Painting

7-19 DIEGO VELÁZQUEZ

WATER CARRIER. c. 1619. Oil on canvas, 41½ × 31½ ″. Wellington Museum, London. This is an early work by Velázquez, painted when he was only about twenty. He created this genre painting to be presented to the king of Spain as a demonstration of his skill.

In the *Water Carrier*, by Diego Velázquez (1599–1660), the simple act of offering, accepting, and consuming a glass of water gains dignity and import (fig. 7-19). The old water seller, who has brought a jug of fresh spring water from the mountains to the city, offers a youth a goblet of water sweetened with a fresh fig. In the shadowy background, a man is drinking. Both the heat of the day and the coolness of the water are revealed in the rivulets of condensation that run down the earthenware jug in the immediate foreground.

The influence of Caravaggio is evident in the half-length, lifesize figures, dark background, and strong light, as well as in the impressive dignity with which these individuals are represented. The composition is simple and pyramidal, focusing attention on the expressions: the downcast eyes of the old man, who is seen in profile; the hesitation in the three-quarter face of the boy; the meditation of the central figure, shown frontally. The somber mood suggests that this scene of everyday life has a deeper significance. The old man seems to be passing on the gift of life to the shy boy. The mood has been described as "sacramental."

Velázquez's profound interpretation of a genre subject is not unique in the seventeenth century, for there are many genre paintings by other European painters that communicate the dignity and seriousness of everyday life. At the same time that Caravaggio gave a new profundity to his religious subjects by infusing them with reality (see fig. 7-15), genre themes were being given a new seriousness as patrons and painters found the sacred and the holy in the everyday.

An equally serious quality is found in *Peasant Family* (fig. 7-20), by Louis Le Nain (1593?–1648). The somewhat awkward composition lends reality to this quiet gathering, while the figures display an impressive dignity. When seen in color, the generally drab colors of their home and clothing are relieved by the warm tones of the fire and by the deep ruby red of the glass of wine, which is held as if in preparation for a visitor. While this and similar paintings by Louis Le Nain and his brothers are impressive, their function within the elegant, court-oriented culture of seventeenth-century France is not easily understood.

Genre had its greatest popularity in the Netherlands, where straightforward representations of Dutch home and tavern life were especially popular. In contrast to the works of Velázquez and Le Nain discussed here, most Dutch genre paintings emphasize a pleasing and homey domesticity. The greatest of the Dutch genre painters was Jan Vermeer (1632–75), who produced only about forty paintings in his lifetime. *A Maidservant Pouring Milk* (fig. 7-21) is typical in its subject: a single woman is shown in the corner of a room, with light coming from a window in the left wall. The setting offers typical objects from a Dutch kitchen, including a footwarmer on the floor and a border of Dutch blue-and-white tiles. It is Vermeer's depiction of light that elevates this humble subject to the status of a masterpiece. Dots of paint make the objects sparkle and glow. It is as if we sense for the first time the beauty inherent in everyday things. Evidence in this and other paintings suggests that Vermeer studied his subjects through a **camera obscura**, an apparatus for projecting an image onto an interior screen of a darkened box, lit only by a small hole, so that the image could be traced (see also page 442). Vermeer's use of the camera obscura explains the slight abstraction in the treatment of light in his work, which heightens its impact. Like other Baroque painters, Vermeer owes a debt to Caravaggio, whose interest in and emphasis on light sensitized the artists of the entire century.

Vermeer most often used models in elegant contemporary clothing, and his focus on a humble subject here may have a specific iconographic meaning. The bread and milk provide the basic nourishment necessary for human life, and by portraying the clean kitchen and humble, hardworking maid, Vermeer may be making a statement about the virtues of domestic life.

7-20   LOUIS LE NAIN
PEASANT FAMILY. c. 1640. Oil on canvas, 44½″ × 62½″. The Louvre, Paris.

7-21   JAN VERMEER
A MAIDSERVANT POURING MILK. c. 1660. Oil on canvas, 17⅞″ × 16⅛″. Rijksmuseum, Amsterdam.

Peter Paul Rubens

7-22   PETER PAUL RUBENS and workshop

ARRIVAL AND RECEPTION OF MARIE DE' MEDICI AT MARSEILLES. 1621–25. Oil on canvas, 13′ × 10′. The Louvre, Paris. This is one of a series of twenty-one huge paintings celebrating Marie de' Medici's life that she commissioned from Rubens for the newly completed Luxembourg Palace in Paris.

In Rubens's painting of Marie de' Medici (fig. 7-22), we are thrust into a world of fantasy, where jubilant mermaids and a bare-breasted allegorical flying figure celebrate the arrival on French soil of the new wife of the king. The scene represents a historical event, but it has been transformed to express what the patron felt was the underlying meaning of the event. Marie, who had been married by proxy to Henry IV of France, was not met by her husband, who, history reveals, was at a hunting lodge with his favorite mistress. Rubens has painted Marie being welcomed by the personification of France. Above, Fame trumpets Marie's arrival. Marie's crossing had been rough, and Neptune, mythological god of the seas, and his mermaids jubilantly celebrate her safe arrival. By allegory, vivid colors, and lively movement, Rubens has created a pageant to satisfy the aspirations of his royal client.

Rubens was one of the best-educated and most intellectual artists of the seventeenth century. He was certainly the only artist of the period to receive an honorary degree from Cambridge University. He served as court painter and ambassador for the rulers of the Spanish Netherlands and was as active as a diplomat as he was an artist. He counted many members of the royalty and nobility among his friends. He was widely traveled, and his influence helped to make the Baroque an international style.

As a diplomat, Rubens worked tirelessly to promote peace in Europe. One of his most profound allegorical paintings conveys his opinions on the meaning of war for humanity (fig. 7-23). Rubens himself explained the content in a letter:

> The principal figure is Mars, who has left the Temple of Janus open (which according to Roman custom remained closed in time of peace) and struts with his shield and his bloodstained sword, threatening all peoples with disaster; he pays little attention to Venus, his lady, who, surrounded by her little love-gods, tries in vain to hold him back with caresses and embraces. On the opposite side, Mars is pulled forward by the Fury Alecto with a torch in her hand. There are also monsters signifying plague and famine, the inseparable companions of war. Thrown to the ground is a woman with a broken lute, as a symbol that har-

7-23   PETER PAUL RUBENS and workshop

ALLEGORY OF THE OUTBREAK OF WAR. 1638. Oil on canvas, 6'9" × 11'3⅞". Pitti Gallery, Florence, Italy. Commissioned by Ferdinando II, Grand Duke of Tuscany.

mony cannot exist beside the discord of war; likewise a mother with a child in her arms indicates that fertility, procreation, and tenderness are opposed by war, which breaks into and destroys everything. There is furthermore an architect fallen backwards, with his tools in his hands, to express the idea that what is built in peace for the benefit and ornament of cities is laid in ruin and razed by the forces of arms . . . you will also find on the ground, beneath the feet of Mars, a book and a drawing on paper, to indicate that he tramples on literature and other refinements. . . . The sorrowing woman . . . clothed in black with a torn veil, and deprived of all her jewels and ornaments is unhappy Europe, which for so many years has suffered pillage, degradation, and misery affecting all of us so deeply that it is useless to say more about them.

This passage reveals the intellect of Rubens and his knowledge of traditional subject matter and history.

Bernini's Works for St. Peter's

7-24 GIANLORENZO BERNINI

BALDACCHINO. 1624–33. Bronze with gilding, height 93'6". *CATHEDRA PETRI.* 1656–66. Marble, bronze with gilding, stucco, alabaster, and stained glass. St. Peter's Basilica, Vatican, Rome. Bernini's use of twisted columns was inspired by a series of ancient twisted columns, once in Old St. Peter's, which were thought to have decorated the great Temple of Solomon in Jerusalem. Commissioned by Popes Urban VIII Barberini and Alexander VII Chigi.

As a glowing dove of the Holy Spirit descends, angels and golden rays fill the apse of St. Peter's, and the columns of the **baldacchino** (canopy) over the high altar appear to writhe with excitement (fig. 7-24). We seem to be witnessing a miracle.

Bernini's *Baldacchino* solved some important problems. It provided a focal point for the vast interior by marking the burial spot of Saint Peter and the high altar of the **basilica**, without blocking the view to the **apse** or overwhelming the interior. The dark bronze and gilded highlights stand out against the white marble of the basilica's architecture, as do the dynamic spiral columns and the beautiful angels, curving **volutes**, and the flaps decorated with tassels—all emulating temporary cloth baldacchinos—on the top. Later, Bernini's *Baldacchino* became a frame for the *Cathedra Petri*, a multimedia climax at the end of St. Peter's that enshrines, like a huge reliquary, a wooden and ivory chair thought to be the papal throne used by Saint Peter. Four figures of early theologians—Saints Ambrose, Athanasius, John Chrysostom, and Augustine—support the reliquary just as they had approved the primacy of Saint Peter and the Roman Church in their writings. One of Michelangelo's windows has been changed by the addition of a stained-glass, alabaster, and gilded stucco representation of the Holy Spirit surrounded by golden rays and radiant putti, which sweep out with Baroque splendor to dominate Michelangelo's Renaissance apse.

Bernini's **colonnade**, which shapes the piazza in front of St. Peter's, is more than just an impressive entrance to the basilica, for it also serves to define the space where the faithful gather to receive the papal blessing (fig. 7-25). Bernini's design is based on an oval with a width of almost 800 feet. As we enter this huge and richly decorated space, the broad axis creates a dynamic effect, and space seems to expand to either side. When Bernini built the piazza, the area was surrounded by medieval houses and narrow, winding streets, an approach that would have rendered the spatial explosion of the piazza even more impressive. Huge travertine columns—284 placed in rows of 4—define the piazza without closing it off from the surrounding areas. As a result, it can be

1624–33	**Bernini,** *Baldacchino*
1626	Purchase of Manhattan island
1628	Harvey publishes on the circulation of the blood

7-25 GIANLORENZO BERNINI

Colonnade, St. Peter's, Rome. Begun 1656. Travertine, longitudinal axis approx. 800'. A drawing reveals that Bernini conceived of the sides of the colonnade as a representation of the embracing arms of the pope and, therefore, of the Catholic Church as an institution. Commissioned by Pope Alexander VII Chigi.

quickly emptied when a crowd wants to disperse.

Bernini, who was appointed main architect for St. Peter's in 1637, worked on the building and its decoration for forty-two years, until his death. Among his other works are two papal tombs, another tomb, the altar decoration of the Chapel of the Holy Sacrament, and the nave decorations. From the ancient Roman bridge that was the ceremonial entrance to the Vatican, which Bernini and his assistants adorned with statues of angels in the 1660s, to the dramatic *Cathedra Petri*, works by Bernini transformed St. Peter's from a Renaissance structure into a Baroque experience.

The Dutch Baroque Group Portrait

7-26 FRANS HALS

BANQUET OF THE OFFICERS OF THE CIVIC GUARD OF ST. GEORGE. 1627. Oil on canvas, 5'10½" × 8'5½". Frans Halsmuseum, Haarlem, Netherlands. The Dutch civic militia groups of the first half of the seventeenth century descended from groups that played a crucial role in gaining the independence of the Netherlands. They continued to have important functions, including guarding the cities and keeping order, and it became traditional that they have their portraits painted. Often, as here, they are shown at the annual banquet given them by the city. Commissioned by the Civic Guard of St. George.

The boisterous members of Frans Hals's militia seem to be inviting us to join their celebration in the *Banquet of the Officers of the Civic Guard of St. George* (fig. 7-26). Just to the right of center, a man holds his glass upside down; he was a brewer, and the artist suggests that he is more than slightly inebriated. The vivacious activity of Hals's lifesize figures as they turn, converse, and gesture seems completely spontaneous. Hands are raised, mouths are open, and figures glance in various directions. The suggestion of movement is enhanced by the diagonals in the composition, by repeated strokes of strong color, and by the use of bold diagonal brushstrokes.

The group portrait had its first important development in the democratic, bourgeois Netherlands, and its first great artist was Frans Hals, who overcame the inherent repetitiveness of this subject, in which a painter had to represent a group of individuals, all about the same age and all of whom were similarly dressed. The democratic traditions of the Netherlands demanded that the individuals be shown as equals, and usually each paid the painter an identical amount to be included. Hals is able to capture the individuality of each member, as well as the exuberant union that joins the group into a whole.

Rembrandt's *"Night Watch"* is surely the most famous painting known by a completely misleading name. The scene is not represented taking place at night, and the correct title is *Militia Company of Captain Frans Banning Cocq* (fig. 7-27). Rembrandt's dramatically composed and lit portrait of the members of this Amsterdam militia company offers a radical solution to the problems of the militia portrait. Rembrandt subordinates the democratic ideal to pictorial drama and focus, creating a sense of unified action. The moment chosen is not the indulgent banquet, but the captain and lieutenant ordering the militia to march. The other members of the company, as well as certain additional figures—a young woman with a dressed bird hanging from her belt (the bird's claws were the emblem of the militia guild), a boy firing a rifle, and others—are gathered in seemingly spontaneous groupings. Bold light and lightly colored costumes emphasize the main figures and give focus to the composition. A number of subordinate figures are virtually lost in shadow. They were added by

1627	Hals, *Banquet of the Officers of the Civic Guard of St. George*
1630	Bubonic plague kills 500,000 Venetians
1633	The Inquisition forces Galileo to retract his defense of the Copernican system
1636	"Haarlem" is founded by Dutch settlers on Manhattan island

Rembrandt to create variety; they were not militia members who had paid to be included for posterity. The composition, rich and complex, is truly Baroque. The figural composition is set off by the off-center gateway—a reference to an ancient triumphal arch—in the background.

No sound evidence supports the often repeated story that the members of the company themselves were unhappy with Rembrandt's brilliant and unexpected solution to the problem of the group portrait. The painting was praised in the seventeenth century; one of Rembrandt's pupils wrote:

> It will outlast all its competitors, being so artistic in conception, so ingenious in the varied placement of figures, and so powerful that, according to some, it makes all the other pieces there look like decks of playing cards.

Rembrandt was the most famous Dutch artist of the seventeenth century and virtually the only one with an international reputation. As a young man, he had hoped to be a history painter, but his earliest success came as a painter of group and individual portraits. In 1642, the year of this group portrait, his wife Saskia died, leaving him with an infant son to raise. His art had already shown signs of change, and after 1642 he sought subjects and techniques that would satisfy a personal need for profundity and emotional depth (see figs. 7-36, 7-38, 7-41).

7-27 REMBRANDT

MILITIA COMPANY OF CAPTAIN FRANS BANNING COCQ. 1642. Oil on canvas, 12'2" × 14'7". Rijksmuseum, Amsterdam. This group portrait, Rembrandt's largest surviving work, is usually known, inaccurately, as *"The Night Watch"* because layers of dirty varnish once made it seem like a night scene. The painting was part of a series of group portraits of militia companies that decorated a great hall in the headquarters of the Amsterdam civic guard. The patrons were members of Cocq's company, each of whom paid a sum consistent with his prominence in the painting. In the eighteenth century, the painting was cut down, and as a result, the composition was transformed. Rembrandt's group portrait was commissioned for a specific position. To reconstruct the angled view that a spectator would have had when approaching the work from the only doorway in the room, hold this book at an angle so that the painting is to your right and sharply receding. This clarifies a number of elements in Rembrandt's composition, including the glance and gesture of Captain Cocq, who, it can now be understood, was looking toward the spectator. Rembrandt adjusted his composition to gain maximum effectiveness, given the intended location of his painting. The other civic militia portraits in the same hall included the artist's self-portrait, and Rembrandt, with wit, represented himself in the back of the crowd. All we see is an eye, part of his nose and forehead, and a painter's beret. Commissioned by Captain Frans Banning Cocq and the members of his militia company.

Baroque Architecture: Francesco Borromini

7-28 FRANCESCO BORROMINI

Dome, San Carlo alle Quattro Fontane, Rome. 1638–41. Dedicated to a recently canonized saint, Carlo Borromeo, this church is also named after its location at an intersection with four fountains (*quattro fontane*) representing the four seasons, one on each corner. Commissioned by the Spanish Discalced Trinitarians.

This dome by Francesco Borromini (1599–1677) almost appears to be a hallucination (fig. 7-28). The hovering oval form, with its elastic **coffers**, seems to bear no relation to the heavy, solid stuff of architecture. If we blink, will it disappear, descend, or snap back into a circular shape with regular coffering? Startling and unbelievable architecture is typical of the works of Borromini. His Baroque monuments tantalize us with their energy, complexity, and tension. The oval form used here is one that has an inherent dynamism, for an oval establishes an axial direction and presents a variation in curvature, but Borromini also exaggerates the diminution of the coffering to suggest that the dome is larger than reality, and by adding hidden windows at the base of the dome, he creates a floating, levitating sensation. The excitement generated by the dome at San Carlo is resolved by the circle in the middle of the lantern, which is decorated with a triangle, symbol of the Trinity and emblem of the Trinitarian Order, which commissioned the church.

The demand that we be involved, the effect of captured movement, and the dramatic lighting of this architecture are consistent with the Baroque innovations examined in the paintings of Caravaggio and his followers. This small church is only one example of Borromini's brilliant inventiveness in creating new and exciting experiences within the classical vocabulary of architecture.

The complexity that characterizes the interior of San Carlo (fig. 7-29) rivets our attention as we try to discern the logic and order we expect in a building based on the classical orders. The **entablature** is composed of contrasting flat and concave sections that surge around the small interior, while the patterns of columns and of triangular and semicircular **pediments** create two overlapping and interlocked systems. The design is both logical and brilliantly complex. Architectural historians have analyzed the mathematical formulas on which Borromini based his structures. In this case, he evolved his design from the triangle, symbolic of the Trinitarian Order. At its most basic level, then, the shape of San Carlo alle Quattro Fontane has a form and an iconographic content that can be related to both a particular religious order and the Christian religion in general.

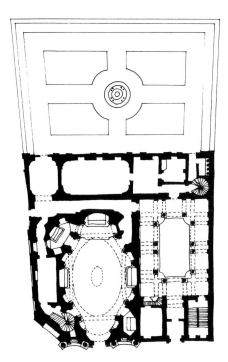

7-29 FRANCESCO BORROMINI

Plan of San Carlo alle Quattro Fontane. 1638–41. Note how Borromini has located his church within the irregular space available to him.

The facade predicts the interior in the grouping of four evenly spaced columns, in the undulation of the surging entablature, and in the scale of the lower story of columns (fig. 7-30). When one is standing in the narrow street before the church, however, the complex energies of contrasting concave and convex forms over-whelm any sense of logic. The upper row of columns completely masks the dome, making it a total surprise for the unsuspecting observer entering the church.

7-30 FRANCESCO BORROMINI

Facade, San Carlo alle Quattro Fontane. 1665–67. Although the facade was completed long after the rest of the church, it is probably based on plans that Borromini had drawn earlier. For another Roman Baroque church by Borromini, Sant'Agnese in Agone, see fig. 7-4.

Bernini, *Ecstasy of Saint Teresa*

7-31 GIANLORENZO BERNINI and workshop

ECSTASY OF SAINT TERESA. 1645–52. Marble and bronze, height approx. 11'6"; the figures are over-lifesize. Cornaro Chapel, Santa Maria della Vittoria, Rome. Teresa, a sixteenth-century nun and a leading personality in the Counter-Reformation Church in Spain, founded a new, stricter reformed group of Carmelite nuns known as the barefoot Carmelites. For this reason, she is represented as barefoot in Bernini's sculpture. She wrote a number of works about the mystical life, including a popular and widely read *Autobiography* in which she detailed the visions and ecstasies she experienced. Commissioned by the Venetian Cardinal Federigo Cornaro as part of a burial chapel for his family.

GIANLORENZO BERNINI, *THE ECSTASY OF ST. TERESA.* (1645–52). MARBLE. HEIGHT OF GROUP: C. 11'6". CORNARO CHAPEL, STA. MARIA DELLA VITTORIA, ROME. SCALA/ART RESOURCE.

It pleased the Lord that I should sometimes see the following vision. I would see beside me . . . an angel in bodily form. . . . He was . . . short and very beautiful, his face so aflame that he appeared to be . . . all afire. . . . In his hands I saw a long golden spear and at the end of the iron tip I seemed to see a point of fire. With this he seemed to pierce my heart several times . . . he left me completely afire with a great love for God. The pain was so sharp that it made me utter several moans; and so excessive was the sweetness caused me by this intense pain that one can never wish to lose it, nor will one's soul be content with anything less than God. It is not bodily pain, but spiritual, though the body has a share in it— indeed a great share.

(Teresa of Ávila, *Autobiography*)

Bernini has visualized Teresa's words and experience in his sculpted altarpiece (fig. 7-31), capturing in the saint's pose and facial expression the combination of "sweetness" and pain she describes so vividly and physically. Her figure seems to convulse, her arm is limp, and her head slumps back, her mouth open and her eyes half-closed. The figure of the angel smiles radiantly, and its drapery ripples with flamelike folds that evoke Teresa's words.

Bernini's interpretation, however, encompassed more than just Teresa's description of this single ecstasy. It relates this experience to other aspects and events of her life and to contemporary attitudes about ecstasies and saints. Teresa's miraculous death, as described by those who witnessed it, is evident here in the beauty Bernini gives the saint. Although her homeliness is documented, at the moment of her death, when she was in her sixties, witnesses testified that she became youthful and beautiful and that she died while in a state of ecstatic love for God. The relationship between ecstasy, death, and fervent love of God and the ideal of the marriage of the soul with the divine are revered parts of the mystical tradition that has its roots in the Old Testament love poetry of the Song of Songs. Teresa herself had written a commentary on the Song of Songs, in which she related Christian death and ecstasy to the soul's desire to expire in the anguish of divine love. Bernini shows the saint levitating, transported off the ground by heavenly clouds. Levitation is described by Teresa in the context of other ecstasies she experienced after attending Mass. By levitating the figure, Bernini makes his sculptural group more impressive and its effect more momentary, while in the context of Teresa's life he also refers to her devotion to the Eucharist, an appropriate emphasis in an altarpiece.

Bernini's representation of the ecstasy of Teresa is itself a miraculous apparition, for the large white figures of the angel and the saint float above the altar. Originally they must have glowed in a gentle, mysterious light that flowed dimly down on golden rays from a window filled with stained glass. Today, electric lights have been added, which make the lighting more dramatic than Bernini intended.

The vision of the miraculous ecstasy is enhanced by the enshrinement of the altarpiece group in a pedimented tabernacle. This niche, made of brilliant multicolored marble, is the centerpiece of a visually sumptuous chapel complex, every detail of which was designed by Bernini (fig. 7-32). The back wall is covered with marble paneling that is broken by the surging pediment above the niche, which undulates outward and upward. The ceiling is frescoed with a burst of heavenly light, and angels seem to pour down into the chapel, accompanying the angel in Teresa's ecstasy. The front of the altar is decorated with a gilded bronze and lapis lazuli relief of the Last Supper, while the floor tombs are decorated with inlaid figures of gesticulating skeletons in foreshortening, as if those buried below were being resurrected by the saint's ecstasy.

Bernini unites painting, sculpture, and architecture in a beautiful totality, one that breaks down the barriers between the world in which we live and the work of art. The tabernacle and figures invade our space, demanding that we become involved. A text on a banner held by angels on the entrance arch offers words that, Teresa

7-32 The Cornaro Chapel as seen in a seventeenth-century painting. Staatliches Museum, Schwerin, Germany.

wrote, were spoken to her by Christ during one of her visions: "If I had not already created heaven I would create it for you alone."

7-33 REMBRANDT

A Man Rowing a Boat on the Bullewyk. c. 1650. Quill pen and brown wash heightened with white, 5¼ × 7⅞". Devonshire Collection, Chatsworth, Derbyshire, England. The location is a tributary of the Amstel River, near Amsterdam, with the spire of the Ouderkerk (Old Church) in the background. The white used here is an opaque paint that allowed Rembrandt to suggest white highlights.

The freshness of nature is captured in Rembrandt's spontaneous drawing of a still tributary near Amsterdam (fig. 7-33). A few quick pen strokes capture the wind as it riffles the leaves of the trees around the cottage. Rembrandt applied **wash** (ink thinned with water) with a brush to achieve the darker shadows that give weight to the mass of the cottage and create the reflection of the trees and cottage on the surface of the water. A thin wash at the top suggests the sky, and a bold, dark mass in the lower left corner establishes the *repoussoir*. Rembrandt's economy of means captures the flux of nature.

Throughout the centuries, artists have made and used drawings for a great variety of purposes (see pp. 268-69). We normally think of drawings as being preparatory—studies made in the process of creating a larger, more finished work in another medium—and such is often the case. Although almost all drawings created before the Renaissance are lost, this does not mean that artists in earlier periods did not use preparatory drawings. Egyptian and Greek stonecarvers, for example, probably drew guidelines on the four sides of their blocks of stone before they began carving, and their contemporaries surely made some kind of sketch or drawing prior to beginning to paint or to construct a building. Many later paintings are based on drawings on the plaster or canvas surface (known as **underdrawings** because of their position under the finished work). Artists have also made drawings as records of completed works, often as a means of documenting their production. Finely finished drawings were sometimes made to be presented to collectors and friends. These are known as **presentation drawings**. Drawings were first systematically collected during the Renaissance, when the artist was recognized as a genius whose every creative effort was worth preserving.

There are many media in which drawings have been executed: charcoal, lead pencil, pen and ink, chalk in various colors, **pastel**, and points made of silver, gold, or other metals. Wash, **watercolor**, and **gouache** (see page 457) are also considered drawing techniques, even though they are liquid media applied with a brush. Although paper is the most widely accepted support for drawings, artists have also used **vellum**, **parchment**, and other materials.

Hundreds of drawings were executed by Rembrandt in virtually every drawing medium that was available to him. Although some can be identified as studies for paintings or **etchings**, the majority are sketches of **genre** scenes, landscapes, and animals. All the evidence suggests that Rembrandt made his drawing of *A*

7-34 REMBRANDT

Saskia in a Straw Hat. 1633.
Silverpoint drawing on white prepared
vellum, 7⅛ × 4⅛". Staatliche Museen zu
Berlin, Preussischer Kulturbesitz,
Kupferstichkabinett. The drawing is
inscribed: "This is drawn after my wife,
when she was 21 years old, the third
day after we were engaged—8 June
1633." Rembrandt and Saskia were
married in 1634.

7-35 REMBRANDT

Two Women Teaching a Child to Walk. c. 1637. Red chalk drawing on rough grayish
paper, 4⅛ × 5". The British Museum, London.

Man Rowing for his own pleasure, for none of his landscape
paintings are endowed with this kind of naturalism. We know
from an inventory of his possessions that Rembrandt sorted his
drawings and stored them by subject. The implication is that
when he began a new painting or etching, he could look
through his drawings for inspiration drawn from life.

When Rembrandt made a drawing of his fiancée, Saskia,
shortly after they became engaged, he chose the difficult technique of **silverpoint** on specially prepared vellum (fig. 7-34).
During the fifteenth and sixteenth centuries, drawing with
sharpened points of silver (or gold) on specially prepared paper
or vellum had been common, but by the seventeenth century,
this medium was rare. The virtue of this particular technique is
that it creates a very fine line. It was especially favored by artists

interested in precision, such as van Eyck, Dürer, and da Vinci.
Silverpoint and goldpoint demand a special proficiency, for the
drawn lines cannot be erased or changed. Before the silver oxidizes and darkens, the shimmering lines have a sumptuous
effect. Rembrandt has chosen the perfect medium to capture
forever the face of his fiancée.

In a drawing executed with soft red chalk, Rembrandt has,
with incredible economy, captured a hesitant child, wearing a
padded hat for protection, in the process of learning to walk
(fig. 7-35). The child is encouraged by two women, one of
whom, on our right, betrays her age by her stiffness. There is no
setting, nor is there a single extraneous detail. It is a tiny drawing of the utmost simplicity, but the moment of life that it captures is precious.

Rembrandt: Late Paintings

7-36 REMBRANDT

BATHSHEBA WITH KING DAVID'S LETTER. 1654. Oil on canvas, 55⅞ × 55⅞". The Louvre, Paris. A repeated motif in the Old and New Testaments is the sinfulness of humanity; the Old Testament king David, slayer of Goliath and the author of the Psalms, is no exception. After David had forced a married woman, Bathsheba, into his bed, he connived to have her husband, Uriah, killed in battle so he could marry her. In Rembrandt's painting, Bathsheba holds the message from David, who has summoned her to the palace, while her maid prepares her for this first meeting with the king.

Rembrandt's later works are characterized by subjects of universal human significance, as in this example of the story of Bathsheba (fig. 7-36). The main subject here is the female nude, but the interpretation emphasizes her inner emotions and meditation. Rembrandt has overturned tradition by painting a nude figure that is more emotional than physical, more thoughtful than sensuous. In keeping with the Dutch interest in naturalism, his model is a mature and dignified woman, one who is capable of understanding the profound implications of the king's demands. Despite the secondary figure at her feet, Bathsheba is alone in her predicament.

Dutch artists in general avoided emotionally complex themes, but the restriction on religious subjects and the general disinterest in historical and mythological themes in the Netherlands were irrelevant to Rembrandt. Perhaps in reaction to the unemotional art being created by other Dutch artists, Rembrandt chose to probe deeply into human life for subject matter and to paint religious subjects if their emotional content interested him. Rembrandt's works often have a direct and sympathetic correlation with the events of his life and the people whom he loved. The model for Bathsheba is probably Hendrickje Stoffels, Rembrandt's second, common-law wife, whom he was unable to marry because of financial restrictions in the will of his deceased wife, Saskia. In 1654, the same year that Rembrandt painted

1650   World population is about 500 million
1652   War is declared between England and Holland
1654   Rembrandt, *Bathsheba with King David's Letter*

Bathsheba, Hendrickje was called before the council of the Reformed Church and barred from receiving communion because she was living with a man to whom she was not married. The connection between Hendrickje's difficulties and the Bathsheba story is indirect, but the human predicament is related.

The *Return of the Prodigal Son* is Rembrandt's largest history painting (fig. 7-37). The impressive figures are over-lifesize. The son, in rags and worn-out shoes, has thrown himself to his knees to indicate his repentance. The aged father bends over him, pulling the young man toward him with stiff hands. The son gently lays his head on his father's chest and closes his eyes. Time seems to stop. The richness of their inner experience is in part expressed abstractly by the textures of the **impasto** (raised brushstrokes of thick paint) with which Rembrandt paints their garments and by the warm, sonorous colors. Jesus' parable used the human story to illustrate a moral: God will forgive sinners who repent. Rembrandt uses the same story to emphasize a human experience—the forgiving love of a parent for a child.

7-37   REMBRANDT

RETURN OF THE PRODIGAL SON. c. 1662–68. Oil on canvas. 8′8″ × 6′8″. Hermitage Museum, St. Petersburg, Russia. Jesus' parable of the prodigal son (Luke 15:11–32) was popular with the followers of Caravaggio, and especially with the Dutch Caravaggisti. Here Rembrandt represents the most profound moment in the story: the son, reduced to poverty, returns home to discover that his father, who still loves him, will forgive him.

7-38   REMBRANDT

CHRIST PREACHING. c. 1652. Etching with drypoint and burin, 6⅛ × 8⅛″. Rembrandt was internationally famous as a printmaker during his own lifetime, and his prints regularly sold for high prices. Less than twenty years after Rembrandt's death, the Florentine art historian Filippo Baldinucci would write: "This artist truly distinguished himself . . . in a certain most bizarre manner which he invented for etching on copper plates. This manner too was entirely his own, neither used by others nor seen again; with certain scratches of varying strength and irregular and isolated strokes, he produced a deep chiaroscuro of great strength."

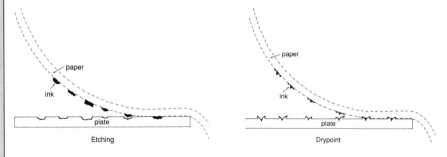

7-39, 40   Diagrams of the etching and drypoint techniques. The more blurred lines of the drypoint technique are the result of the burr of the drypoint line.

Rembrandt presents us not with a specific biblical subject but with an interpretation of Jesus as a humble and gentle teacher who stands within the crowd in a city street to preach (fig. 7-38). He is surrounded by people of all ages, rich and poor, and in Rembrandt's representation they react as individuals to Jesus' words. Some ponder his meaning, but others seem uninterested. A child busies himself drawing in the dust in the foreground.

Rembrandt's technique is **etching**, and this is one of a number of prints produced from the same plate for collectors of prints. It is the etching technique that permits the creation of blurred lines and a soft, atmospheric quality not possible in **woodcut** or **engraving**. Etching is not a new technique—Dürer and other printmakers had experimented with its possibilities—but it was Rembrandt who first realized its potential for expression.

Etching is an **intaglio** technique (see page 297), and the same thin copper plate used for engraving functions as the **print form** (fig. 7-39). To create an etching, one must cover the plate with an

etching ground, an acid-resistant, resinous mixture. The artist scratches through this ground with a steel **etching needle**, creating lines that expose the copper. When the design is completed (or when the artist wants to test the progress of the composition), diluted acid (nitric, iron chloride, or hydrochloric) is poured over the plate, or the plate is dipped into an acid bath. The acid eats into the copper, creating grooves where the needle has scratched through the ground. The ground is then cleaned off and the plate is inked and printed, as in the process for printing and engraving. If the results are unsatisfactory or incomplete, the ground can be reapplied, the design can be strengthened or completed with the needle, and the acid bath can be used again. Another alternative is to strengthen the lines by using the **burin** (as in engraving) and/or drypoint (see page 365). Only about 50 excellent and 200 reasonably good prints can be made from an etched plate.

An eighteenth-century development in the etching process was the soft-ground etching, which uses a greater percentage of

7-41 REMBRANDT

THREE CROSSES. 1653. Drypoint and burin (first state), 15¼ × 17¾". Rembrandt made successive changes to the plate in producing later states of this print.

tallow or wax in the ground. A thin sheet of paper is laid over the ground, and a drawing is made on the paper. When the paper is lifted, a soft, grainy impression is left on the plate. The plate is then etched, using a weak acid bath.

The etching technique encouraged freedom and spontaneity, for the etching needle moves easily through the ground to scratch the plate (unlike the concentrated pressure needed to push the burin through the resistant copper to create an engraving). Although an etched line lacks the sharp and precise quality of an engraved line, its blurriness creates the atmospheric effect that we admire in Rembrandt's work. Rembrandt's earliest printed works were pure etchings, sometimes with the use of the burin for strengthening. Later, to achieve an even greater effect of atmosphere, he began to add lines in drypoint, as is the case in *Christ Preaching*.

Drypoint is the technique of scratching directly into the copper plate with the etching needle (fig. 7-40). This method creates grooves that have tiny raised ridges of copper, known as the **burr**, to either side, where the expelled material is forced by the needle. These drypoint ridges catch the ink and create rich areas of deep, soft shadow. The necessary pressure applied by the press during printing will wear down the burr rather quickly, and only about ten good and twenty reasonably good impressions can be made. In *Christ Preaching*, drypoint lines

are visible in the beard and hair of Jesus and in the deep shadows of his drapery.

A few of Rembrandt's last prints are executed entirely in drypoint, with an additional use of the burin for certain sharp details. Rembrandt's last print was probably the large *Three Crosses* (fig. 7-41), which he worked on over a period of years. He created three successive stages, known as **states**, in 1653 by reworking the plate and a final, almost completely reworked fourth state in the early 1660s. It is a profoundly moving personal interpretation of the Crucifixion based on the text in Luke 23:44–47:

> And it was about the sixth hour, and there was a darkness over all the earth until the ninth hour. And the sun was darkened, and the veil of the temple was rent in the midst. And when Jesus had cried with a loud voice, he said, Father, into thy hands I commend my spirit: and having said thus, he gave up the ghost. Now when the centurion saw what was done, he glorified God, saying, "Certainly this was a righteous man."

The centurion is kneeling, to suggest that Rembrandt is representing the very moment of the death of Jesus. The powerful shaft of light is a momentary blaze, a heavenly response to Jesus' words and his death. In this late work, Rembrandt avoids painstaking detail to emphasize powerful emotional experiences.

Spanish Painting: Diego Velázquez

7-42 DIEGO VELÁZQUEZ

LAS MENINAS (THE MAIDS OF HONOR). 1656. Oil on canvas. 10'5" × 9'; the figures are lifesize. Prado, Madrid. The cross on Velázquez's chest indicates that he has been made a Knight of the Order of Santiago. As Velázquez did not receive this honor until 1659, three years after the painting was dated, the cross must have been added later. Probably commissioned by Philip IV of Spain.

7-43 DIEGO VELÁZQUEZ

LAS MENINAS, detail of Princess Margarita.

For just a moment, Velázquez's painting convinces us that the little princess and her attendants—including dwarfs and a large dog—are posing just for us (fig. 7-42). Although *Las Meninas* is a large picture, its subject seems intimate and even casual. We glimpse a large dark room in the palace, where the painter is at work on a huge canvas. He looks out and leans back, raising his brush as he prepares to apply a stroke of paint. In the foreground is the five-year-old Margarita, daughter of Philip IV, surrounded by her maids (*las meninas*) and the dwarfs and developmentally disabled people who were a traditional part of life at the Spanish court. With the exception of the princess, all these figures are represented in the midst of movement, as is Velázquez. Note especially the figure to the right who, one hand raised, awakens the dog, which slowly raises its head. Velázquez's illusionism, which is supported by his loose brushstroke and the blurred edges of the

1656   Velázquez, *Las Meninas*
1656   Pendulum clock is invented
1657   London's first chocolate shop opens

forms (fig. 7-43), attempts to convince us that we are seeing reality.

But is the princess posing for us? The shimmering surface on the back wall is a mirror that reflects the figures of King Philip and Queen Mariana. A real mirror would have reflected the whole room, but Velázquez, with artistic license, includes this reference to his royal patrons as the sole element that reminds us that what we are looking at is indeed a painting.

In Velázquez's *Portrait of Juan de Pareja* (fig. 7-44), the sitter looks out with calm and assured dignity. Velázquez's loose brushstroke and subtle light create an effect of immediacy and, again, reality. The painting is a coloristic triumph, for within a restricted palette of white, black, grays, and beiges, Velázquez creates an impressive variety of tones. The restriction of color is no accident, for this portrait of one of Velázquez's assistants was a practice piece. Velázquez was in Rome, buying paintings and ancient sculptures for King Philip, when he received the commission to paint a portrait of Pope Innocent X. This particular portrait was a difficult task, for the pope, who had a ruddy complexion, had to be painted wearing red papal garments, seated in a red chair in a setting dominated by red hangings.

To prepare himself for this challenge, Velázquez posed a similar problem by painting Juan de Pareja, who was of Moorish descent, using a restricted color palette based on his flesh tones. The picture was a sensational success. After it was exhibited at the Pantheon, Velázquez was elected to the Rome Academy. One contemporary remarked that although all the other paintings in the exhibition were art,

this alone was truth.

7-44   DIEGO VELÁZQUEZ

PORTRAIT OF JUAN DE PAREJA. 1650. Oil on canvas, 32 × 27½″. The Metropolitan Museum of Art, New York.

FLETCHER FUND, ROGERS FUND, AND BEQUEST OF MISS ADELAIDE MILTON DE GROOT (1876–1967), BY EXCHANGE, SUPPLEMENTED BY GIFTS FROM FRIENDS OF THE MUSEUM, 1971 (1971.86).

Baroque Classicism: Nicolas Poussin

7-45 NICOLAS POUSSIN

ARCADIAN SHEPHERDS. c. 1660. Oil on canvas, 34¼ × 47¼″. The Louvre, Paris. The inscription on the tomb is *Et in Arcadia Ego* ("Even in Arcadia I [Death] am to be found"). Painted for Cardinal Rospigliosi and bought by Louis XIV in 1685.

The idealized painting of Nicolas Poussin (1594–1665) transports us to remote antiquity, where we stand with shepherds and a shepherdess by a monumental tomb (fig. 7-45). Arcadia is an idyllic region in Greece where, during the ancient golden age, it was believed that humanity had lived peacefully and harmoniously with nature. To the shepherds who lived there, life seemed perfect until they discovered a tomb and realized that death is a reality that they will someday have to confront. Despite the dramatic implications of the subject, the mood of the painting is calm and contemplative. In Poussin's approach, even death becomes philosophical.

Poussin's style is consistent with his intellectual interpretation of the subject. The composition is lucid and the poses of the figures are clearly articulated and interrelated. To assure satisfying compositions, Poussin worked them out by arranging miniature wax figures on a stage in a small box until he was pleased with their disposition. The colors are cool and simple, the light regular and undramatic, and the brushstroke controlled. The influence of the High Renaissance style of Raphael is evident, and the costumes and facial types reveal Poussin's careful study of ancient art. Poussin's paintings are among the finest examples of Baroque Classicism. The landscape is based on the area around Rome, which Poussin knew well.

Nicolas Poussin was probably the most classical, intellectual, and philosophical painter of the seventeenth century. Although born in France, he spent most of his mature life in Rome.

7-46 NICOLAS POUSSIN

LANDSCAPE WITH THE BODY OF PHOCION CARRIED OUT OF ATHENS. 1648. Oil on canvas. 47 × 70½″. Phocion was a loyal Athenian general whose character was in many ways like that of Poussin: he was stern, prized economy, and was dedicated to truth. His austerity and moral rectitude, however, made him hated by the popular faction in Athens, which, when it gained power, had Phocion executed on a false charge of treason and decreed that his body had to be carried outside the city for burial. This is the event shown in Poussin's painting. Later, Phocion was given an honorable burial in Athens. Commissioned by Serisier, a Lyons silk merchant. National Museum and Gallery, Cardiff, Wales, on loan from the Earl of Plymouth.

A close circle of similarly minded French friends in Rome and Paris were the patrons for his well-studied, thoughtful compositions. They preferred heroic or stoic themes from antiquity.

Poussin's landscapes always include a narrative subject, usually one drawn from antiquity. In *Landscape with the Body of Phocion Carried out of Athens*, the landscape setting is clearly not taken from nature (fig. 7-46). Poussin has rearranged nature to provide the properly sober, clear, and balanced setting for his profound theme.

Dutch Still-Life Painting

7-47 MARIA VAN OOSTERWYCK

STILL LIFE WITH A VANITAS THEME. 1668. Oil on canvas, 29 × 35″. Kunsthistorisches Museum, Vienna. Maria van Oosterwyck did not come from an artistic family, but tradition tells us that she was determined to become a still-life painter. She developed an international reputation and produced works for Louis XIV of France and the members of other European royal houses.

Realistic still-life painting is a democratic art—one needs no background in aesthetics or art theory to appreciate the ability of Maria van Oosterwyck (1630–93) to render the butterfly that lights on the book or the mouse nibbling at the grain, not to mention the fresh flowers, skull, and globe (fig. 7-47). There is even a fly on a book to the right and a self-portrait of the artist reflected in the flask to the left. It was in the democratic Netherlands that such still lifes were most fully appreciated, and the market for pictures such as this one was so large that artists could become specialists in still-life painting and hone their skills so as to produce increasingly more brilliant depictions of objects in ever more elaborate profusion.

Sixteenth- and seventeenth-century art theorists, however, largely ignored still-life painting, as they also neglected the painting of landscape, genre, and portraits. These types of art were considered unimportant because they were merely copies from nature. A painter's most significant accomplishment, they argued, was a history painting, the conception, design, and execution of which demanded intellectual prowess and academic training. The painter of histories also needed an understanding of anatomy and experience in drawing the male nude. Still-life, landscape, portrait, and genre paintings were considered to be much less valuable than history paintings and generally sold at much lower prices.

During the seventeenth century, a number of women artists excelled at still-life painting, in part, perhaps, because this was a category of art in which they could succeed without threatening the long-established dominance of male artists. Because at this time women were not admitted to the academies, they hardly had the option of receiving training in creating history paintings. The two artists examined here were both products of the more liberal Dutch culture, but during the sixteenth and seventeenth centuries there are documented French, Flemish, and Italian women still-life artists as well.

The theorists underestimated still-life painting. To select the forms of a still-life painting and arrange them into a satisfying composition, with coordinating and contrasting patterns of textures and colors, demand different skills from those required of the history painter. And still-life paintings are not always purely decorative displays, devoid of any deeper meaning. The title of Van Oosterwyck's painting reveals that it forms part of a distinguished tradition of seventeenth-century paintings on the theme of Vanity, one of the minor vices, that expressed the transience of the things of the world and the inevitability of death. Such paintings were especially popular in the Netherlands, where the tradition of complex symbolism goes back to Van Eyck (see page 257). In the most impressive of these compositions, of which Van Oosterwyck's is an example, each element contributes its own special content to the meaning of the whole. The hourglass, for example, refers to the inexorable passage of time. The fly is a symbol of sin, ever present in the world, and the mouse symbolizes evil. The large book is labeled "Reckoning. We Live in Order to Die. We Die in Order to Live."

An early source tells us that Van Oosterwyck was pious, and the underlying Christian hope of her still-life painting is expressed in these words and in the butterfly, symbol of the resurrection of Christ and the salvation of humanity. Although the skull is an obvious reference to death, when it is wreathed in ivy, as here, it refers to life after death. All these objects and symbols are united in a skillful composition that takes maximum advantage of contrasting forms, colors, and textures.

Flower Still Life by Rachel Ruysch (1663–1750) is arranged along a prominent diagonal that is enhanced by the curving stems of the blossoms at the upper right and lower left (fig. 7-48). The simple centrality of the vase and niche is enlivened by the diagonal recession of the table and by the contrast in light to either side. On the right, a light area silhouettes the forms and emphasizes their irregularity, while on the left, a completely different effect is accomplished by setting off the complexity of many small blossoms against the dark background. Ruysch's father was a professor of anatomy and

7-48   RACHEL RUYSCH

FLOWER STILL LIFE. After 1700. Oil on canvas, 30 × 24″. The Toledo Museum of Art, Toledo, Ohio. Rachel Ruysch is ranked among the greatest still-life painters in the Netherlands, and her international reputation continued after her death. She was apprenticed to an important still-life painter at the age of fifteen and by eighteen was active as a painter in the same genre. From 1708 to 1716, she was court painter to the elector Palatine in Düsseldorf, Germany.

botany, and his collection of scientific specimens may have inspired her inclusion of the insects found so often in her paintings. She depicts them with impressive accuracy, a technical precision that reveals her participation in the new scientific interests and investigations of the seventeenth century.

The Palace at Versailles

7-49 LOUIS LE VAU and JULES HARDOUIN MANSART

Garden facade, Palace of Versailles, France. 1669–85. Begun by Louis XIV, who decided to enlarge a royal hunting lodge eleven miles southwest of Paris, Versailles officially became not only the main royal residence in 1682 but also the governmental seat. The administrator J.-B. Colbert, who also advised Louis on political, economic, and religious matters, and the painter Charles Lebrun were in charge of the artists and workers—sometimes as many as 30,000 at one time—who created the buildings and grounds. At its height, the palace served a court that totaled almost 20,000 people, including 9,000 soldiers quartered in the town and about 4,000 servants who lived within the palace itself. Commissioned by Louis XIV.

The palace of the French kings at Versailles is the largest and most emulated royal residence in the world (fig. 7-49); as it stands today, it is largely the work of two architects, Louis Le Vau (1612–70) and Jules Hardouin Mansart (1646–1708).

The palace has hundreds of rooms, and its facade is almost a half mile long; the garden encompasses 250 acres. Its impressive scale actually made a political statement, for it was intended to assert for the French populace and nobility, as well as for foreigners, the power of the French monarch. In some ways, the very creation of Versailles may have played a role in establishing and perpetuating that power.

The expansive length of the garden facade itself makes a powerful architectural statement, but the architects faced the problem of how to articulate such a long structure. They decided not to break the mass in any dramatic way and chose to emphasize the horizontal sweep by articulating the second floor with **pilasters**. They created punctuation points with columned pavilions that jut out only slightly from the mass of the structure, with sculpture decorating their **cornices**. The design and ornament are completely classical, in keeping with the French interest in drawing a relationship between the principles of order and control and the rule of the French monarchy.

The Salon de la Guerre offers a rich scheme of multimedia Baroque decoration (fig. 7-50). A huge oval stucco relief over the fireplace with a monumental equestrian figure of Louis XIV immediately draws our attention. Below, dark bronze reliefs represent prisoners in chains, while above, gilt stucco angels trumpet his fame and offer him the hero's crown. The relief in the fireplace shows the muse of history, Clio, recording Louis's triumphs. The combination of materials—stucco, bronze, gilded stucco, and marble—and the parquet floors, mirrors, paintings on the ceiling, and a crystal-and-gold chandelier testify to the wealth of the king, while the iconography emphasizes his imperialis-

1669	**Le Vau and Hardouin Mansart, Versailles begun**
1669	Antonio Stradivari makes violins in Cremona, Italy
1670	Molière, *Le Bourgeois Gentilhomme*

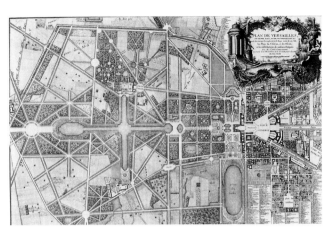

7-51 ANDRÉ LE NÔTRE

Plan of the gardens and park, Versailles (17th-century engraving). Designed 1661–68; executed 1662–90. Note that the main streets of the town of Versailles, at the bottom of the map, converge on the palace to emphasize its significance. André Le Nôtre, son of a royal gardener, became the greatest designer of formal gardens and parks in seventeenth-century Europe. The layout of the garden uses radiating diagonals and dramatic long vistas. Commissioned by Louis XIV.

7-50 JULES HARDOUIN MANSART, CHARLES LEBRUN, and ANTOINE COYSEVOX

Salon de la Guerre (Room of War), Palace of Versailles. Begun 1678. This room, at one end of the Hall of Mirrors, is a pendant to the Rome of Peace at the opposite end; the decoration of these rooms celebrated recent French victories. The sculptor Coysevox is responsible for the huge stucco relief of *Louis XIV on Horseback* over the fireplace. The painted ceiling, the theme of which is France at war, is by Lebrun. The Hall of Mirrors was named for the large mirrors opposite the arched garden windows. As decoration, this room had bejeweled trees and gold and silver furniture, but these were melted down in 1689 and 1709 to help pay for French wars. Commissioned by Louis XIV.

tic ambitions. Such a room was primarily a setting for court rituals and would be in use especially on those occasions when its particular iconography would be most effective.

In the great park, ponds and pathways seem infinite, and at each cross-road there are several choices of direction in which to proceed (fig. 7-51). The vistas and paths offer surprises: fountains, basins, terraces, flights of steps, sculptural groups, flowerbeds, hedges, and even small architectural monuments. Nature on a vast scale has been tamed and ordered, to provide a place of pleasure for the king and his court. Although the most basic purpose of the park is the same as that of the palace—to reflect the glory of the French monarchy and the king's centralized authority—André Le Nôtre (1613–1700) has also been sensitive to the delights of nature that such a park can offer to the observer. The plan informs us of the general layout; however, Le Nôtre's park was not designed to be seen from above, but by the human spectator, walking, choosing pathways and vistas.

Japanese Art

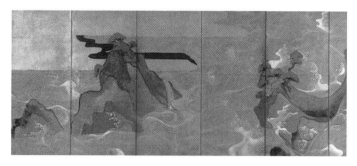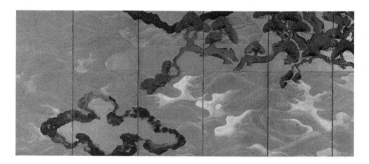

7-52a and 7-52b   SOTATSU

Pair of six-panel *byobu*, known as the *MATSUSHIMA SCREENS*. 17th century. Ink, color, and gold leaf on paper; each screen is 4'9⅞" × 11' 8½".

The highly decorative mode of painting that flourished in the seventeenth century in Japan characterizes native Japanese taste. Painting was executed on large-scale surfaces: sliding door panels (*fusuma*) or folding screens (*byobu*), usually executed in pairs. The style is characterized by the use of bold colors with gold leaf and by the use of stylized motifs for the houses of royalty, the aristocracy, and commoners. The most popular themes demonstrate a revival of the basic Japanese concerns with the natural world and with people and their activities, including such genre themes as horse races, theatrical performances, bathhouse prostitutes, and even Westerners. One pair of *byobu* (fig. 7-52a and 7-52b) by Sotatsu (active 1600–40) are called the *Matsushima Screens* because they are thought by some scholars to depict Matsushima, one of the *sankai*, or three most beautiful landscapes in Japan. This bay near Sendai, far to the north of Kyoto, is dotted with small pine-capped islands. Other scholars argue that these *byobu* are not specific and only represent exceptionally beautiful passages of landscape. Still others argue that because the islands in the pictures resemble rocky configurations along the shore near Ise, these *byobu* illustrate a poem from *The Tales of Ise* that

deals with the feelings of a man who, banished from the capital, gazes at the surf and white-capped water as he crosses a beach; because the twelfth-century illustrators of *The Tale of Genji* used natural elements to reflect human emotions, there is historical precedent for this interpretation. Whatever the subject, there is no question that the artist's vision has distorted reality, as is evident in the passage in which gold clouds turn into rocky shores where pine trees cling and grow.

One of the favorite books of Imperial Prince Toshihito (1579–1629) was *The Tale of Genji* (see pp. 202–03), and many of the details of the Imperial Villa he commissioned at Katsura (see figs. 1-5, 7-53, 7-54), southwest of Kyoto, were inspired by this tenth-century novel. The last palace built by the novel's main character, Genji, was called Katsura, and it too was located along the Katsura River. As described in the novel, it was subdued and relatively unostentatious. It contained a large lake with several artificial islands, a rustic fishing pavilion, and a lodge next to the racetrack for the games that were held there in conjunction with festivals at the Kamo shrine in Kyoto. Toshihito's new royal seventeenth-century residence consisted of a main *shoin* (a large residence) with a bam-

boo-floored moon-viewing platform, a smaller *shoin*, and a music room placed in a garden, all set out in accordance with descriptions in *The Tale of Genji*. For a discussion of the villa see also page 8.

One of the imperial family's important symbolic roles was to maintain traditional Japanese culture, which was accomplished at Katsura Villa by retaining native choices in design and in decorative styles. Traditional Japanese aesthetic expression is recalled in all elements of the house—the use of natural wood structural members (fig. 7-53), irregular and asymmetrical planning of room sizes and their positions (fig. 7-54), sliding paper doors, as illustrated in *Genji* manuscripts (see fig. 4-81), and the abrupt contrasts of textures in the rocks, plants, water, and dry areas of the gardens.

At other villas of the period, the rank of individuals, so important in the samurai culture of this period, were emphasized through different floor levels or by the placement of connotative images in the *tokonoma*, a shallow, recessed platform where paintings and flower arrangements or objects of value were placed. Because Katsura Villa was designed for the imperial family as a place where they could put aside issues of class in a relaxed atmosphere, there are no such provisions for emphasizing rank. This less

17th century	Sotatsu, *Matsushima Screens*
1670	Minute hands are first used on watches
1670	André Le Nôtre lays out the Champs-Elysées in Paris

7-53 General view of *SHOIN*, Katsura Imperial Villa, Kyoto, Japan. 1620–63. For an interior view, see figure 1-5. Commissioned by Prince Hachijo Toshihito and his son Toshitada.

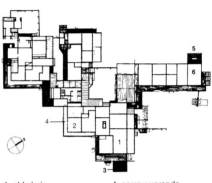

1 old *shoin*   4 narrow veranda
2 middle *shoin*   5 visitors carriage rest
3 moon-viewing platform 6 vestibule

7-54 Plan of *SHOIN*, Katsura Imperial Villa.

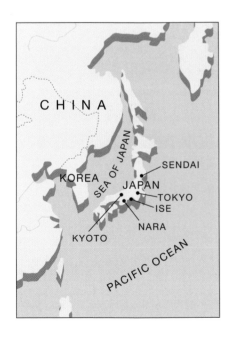

formal character is consistent with *The Tale of Genji*.

Seventeenth-century art in Japan was dominated by a spirit of reflection and a return to established traditions. The standard set by the nobility focused on the art of tea and on such classics of Japanese literatures as *The Tale of Genji* and *The Tales of Ise*. Japanese aristocrats were expected to know *The Tales of Ise* by heart. The Katsura Villa and the screens by Sotatsu are characterized by the self-assuredness and return to historical precedent so important in this period of political stability and economic prosperity.

Landscape Painting

7-55 JACOB VAN RUISDAEL

DUTCH LANDSCAPE FROM THE DUNES AT OVERVEEN. c. 1670. Oil on canvas, 21⅞″ × 24⅜″. Mauritshuis, The Hague, The Netherlands.

During the seventeenth century, the flat expanses of the Netherlands, reclaimed from the sea and wrested from Spanish domination, were painted thousands of times by Dutch painters. These paintings were avidly collected by the proud and patriotic citizens of the new nation. Although there had been a sporadic interest in landscape among Northern painters during the sixteenth century, now, for the first time in the history of Western art, landscape became a truly popular theme. In the seventeenth century, the Netherlands was more highly urbanized than any other European nation, and the nostalgia felt by city dwellers for open countryside may have been an additional factor in explaining the popularity of landscape painting.

Despite its relatively small size, *Dutch Landscape from the Dunes at Overveen*, by Jacob van Ruisdael (1628/29–82), captures the salient features of the Dutch countryside: land, sky, and a changing relationship between light and shade (fig. 7-55). More than two-thirds of the canvas is given over to the clouded sky, which is the dominant feature of the Dutch countryside. The

c. 1670   **Van Ruisdael, *Dutch Landscape***
1675   Native American population drops to about 20,000
1675   Antonie van Leeuwenhoek invents the microscope

7-56   PETER PAUL RUBENS

LANDSCAPE WITH HET STEEN. c. 1636. Oil on panel, 51⅝″ × 7′6¼″. The National Gallery, London. This view of Het Steen, the country estate Rubens bought in 1635, remained in his possession during his lifetime.

sky becomes the mediator by which we perceive the land as well. As the clouds rush by, the earth is intermittently revealed by patches of bright light.

Ruisdael's landscape is precisely identifiable, for the Gothic church that rises among red tile roofs in the background is St. Bavo in Haarlem. The ubiquitous Dutch windmills, so necessary to keep the land drained of excess water, dot the countryside; in the foreground, small figures stretch linen to be bleached, a proud reference to the prosperous Haarlem linen industry. The function of this realistic image is clear: to represent and exalt the local countryside and its livelihood.

Although other seventeenth-century painters occasionally demonstrate an interest in landscape—Poussin with his classical landscapes (see fig. 7-46) and Rubens with his view of the Flemish countryside—these are exceptions, and only in the Netherlands did a truly national school of landscape painters develop.

Although the Dutch seem to have preferred realistic views of local scenery, Dutch painters also produced a variety of other types of landscape painting, including seascapes with Dutch vessels and rather fantastic views of wild scenery. A number of Dutch artists settled in Rome, where they painted views of the sun-drenched Italian countryside that were popular back home.

The sixteenth-century Flemish interest in landscape found a successor in Rubens, whose landscapes have the same tumultuous vitality and visual excitement as his religious, mythological, and allegorical pictures. In his landscapes, Rubens puts us in contact with the growth and energies of the world of nature. In his *Landscape with Het Steen* (fig. 7-56), the rising sun is a shimmering silver-yellow disk near the right edge of the painting. A hunter and his dog in the foreground draw our eyes to a stump, which in turn leads us to an undulating row of trees that surge into the landscape toward the fresh, glowing morning sky. Simultaneously, a peasant family in the shadowy left foreground draws our attention to the opposite direction. Rubens's personal energies and his understanding of the dynamic and ever-changing nature of landscape are here united.

CHAPTER 7   Seventeenth-Century Art   377

Cornelia, the Mother of the Gracchi, was painted by the Swiss artist Angelica Kauffmann in 1785 (for more information see figs. 8-29 and p. 397).

Eighteenth-Century Art

A Brief Insight

DURING THE SECOND HALF OF THE EIGHTEENTH century in Europe, culture was transformed by a renewed interest in the civilizations of ancient Greece and Rome. Politicians, writers, architects, and artists were inspired by Classical Antiquity, and they promoted lessons from ancient literature and history as models for contemporary behavior. Works in the ancient "manner" with moralizing subjects drawn from antiquity, like the one shown here, are said to be a style which today we term "Neoclassical."

Due to the continuing lack of educational opportunities for women in the rigidly controlled art academies, it was still difficult for women to develop the skills necessary to create works in what the academies considered the most exalted area of artistic endeavor, history painting. Angelica Kauffmann, the artist who painted this work, achieved success in this area and as a result was chosen to be a founding member of the Royal Academy in London; this was an important early breakthrough for women artists. This painting, which is meant to reproduce the historical style of ancient Rome, depicts a Roman woman, Cornelia, who was asked by a friend to display her jewels; the friend was surprised when Cornelia presented her children. The theme clearly is maternal and moralistic; feminist art historians have held that such insight would be particularly relevant to a woman artist. Kauffmann's painting, like much of Neoclassical art, is meant to instruct her contemporaries in what were thought at the time to be the enduring values of life. ⤚

379

Eighteenth-Century Art

8-1 GERMAIN BOFFRAND

Salon de la Princesse, Hôtel de Soubise, Paris. 1736–39. The term *hôtel* in this context refers to the lavishly adorned town houses of the French aristocracy. Commissioned by François de Rohan, Prince de Soubise.

GERMAIN BOFFRAND (FRENCH, 1667–1754) AND CHARLES-JOSEPH NATOIRE (FRENCH, 1700–1777). THE PRINCESS SALON, HOTEL DE SOUBISE, PARIS, 1732. WAYNE ANDREWS

This interior design for the Princess's Salon (fig. 8-1), by Germain Boffrand (1667–1754), exemplifies the decorative exuberance of the Rococo style, which in the eighteenth century succeeded the Baroque. The decoration of the oval room is animated with carved and painted woodwork, stucco, and a series of integral paintings depicting the tale of the mythological lovers Cupid and Psyche. The web of gold woodwork and stucco ornament suggests that the white walls seem to be thin screens, while the undulating movement of the curving **cornice** joins the rhythm of the delicate arches to further enliven the interior. The effect is elegant and ebullient.

Some similar aesthetic qualities are apparent in the beautiful wooden synagogue of Wolpa, Poland (fig. 8-2), but here the effect is dependent solely on architectural form and definition of space rather than on richness of materials and refinement of decorative patterns. This and other wooden synagogues of this period in Poland, all destroyed in the Holocaust, provide an important example of how a period style—in this case the Rococo—could be combined with local folk art traditions to serve a particular need. Here the local eastern European tradition of wooden architecture has been transformed to produce a large religious structure of great sophistication in design. The unknown architects have simultaneously combined a series of balconies, intended for use by the women of the congregation, with elegant curving forms that pull our eyes upward. The four great columns—here timber **piers**—that support the structure were traditional in synagogue design and are a reference to the destroyed Temple of Solomon in Jerusalem.

Just slightly more than twenty years after the Rococo elegance of the Princess's Salon, the English architect Robert Adam (1728–92) began remodeling Osterley Park House. The fireplace niche in the entrance hall (fig. 8-3) demonstrates Adam's use of an alternate eighteenth-century style, Neoclassicism, in which the ornamentation is based on antique prototypes, from the **pilasters** and **coffered half dome** to the wall moldings. The axis is visually reinforced by the Neoclassical relief set over the fireplace, while flanking niches with their antique sculptures balance the composition and add further

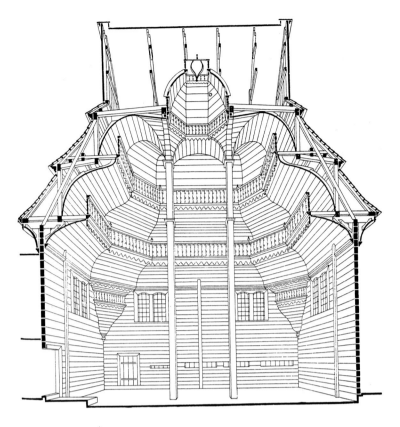

8-2 Synagogue, Wolpa, Poland (now destroyed). 18th century. Wood. The wooden synagogues in Poland were systematically destroyed during the Holocaust, but fortunately they had been well documented in photographs and drawings.

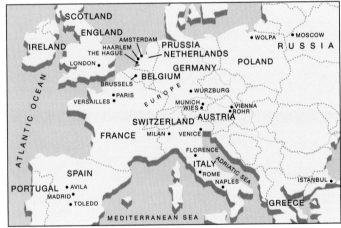

8-3 ROBERT ADAM

Fireplace niche, Entrance Hall, Osterly Park House, Middlesex (London), England. Begun 1761. Adam's adaptation of classical architectural forms was so successful that one phase of the English Neoclassical style is known as the Adamesque. Commissioned by Francis Child.

references to the cultures of classical antiquity. In contrast to Boffrand's Rococo interior and the Wolpa synagogue's exuberant spatial effects, Adam's Neoclassical design is disciplined and controlled. The antithesis between these designs reflects the enormous artistic contrasts of the eighteenth century.

History

The eighteenth century was a period when the difference between the West and the rest of the world became even more pronounced. During this period, traditional values dominated most of the countries of Asia. Both Japan during the Edo period (1615–1868) and China during the Qing dynasty (1644–1912) continued to be almost exclusively concerned with internal affairs. Both demonstrated a concern with understanding and continuing their own traditions and excluding Western influence. Japan remained closed to the West during this period. In northern India, the Mughal empire was in decline, but in art there was a con-

8-4 HYACINTHE RIGAUD

PORTRAIT OF KING LOUIS XIV OF FRANCE. 1701. Oil on canvas, 9 × 6'.
The Louvre, Paris. Commissioned by Louis XIV.

tinuation of traditional values and ideas. During the eighteenth century, Russia and Austria made important gains
against the Ottoman Turks, although the Ottoman empire
would last until 1918. It was in the West in the eighteenth
century, however, that the revolutionary currents of
democracy began to rewrite the face of politics, of social
structure, and of art.

The memorable opening lines from Dickens's novel
about the French Revolution can describe the European
eighteenth century as a whole:

> It was the best of times, it was the worst of times, it
> was the age of wisdom, it was the age of foolishness,
> it was the epoch of belief, it was the epoch of
> incredulity, it was the season of Light, it was the sea-
> son of Darkness.

(Charles Dickens, *A Tale of Two Cities*, first published 1859)

It was a century of social, cultural, and artistic contrasts;
prodigious scientific and technological advances; and
sweeping political changes. Historians often refer to the
close of this century as the period that marks the beginning
of the modern Western world.

Politically, the century opened with the dominance of
France under Louis XIV. The Baroque portrait by Hyacinthe
Rigaud (1659–1743) conveys the solemn majesty of his
authority and the opulence with which the French monarchs were surrounded (fig. 8-4). After Louis XIV's death in
1715, however, France's military and political influence
began to abate. Frederick the Great, who came to the
throne in Prussia in 1740, seized the opportunity to expand

and establish the German states as the premier military force
on the Continent. To check Prussia's growing political and
military strength, France and Austria entered an alliance. In
the resulting conflict, known as the Seven Years' War
(1756–63), Prussia was victorious. France's holdings and
influence in the Americas were diminished when Quebec
surrendered to the English in 1759 (see fig. 8-29), effectively
ending the French and Indian War in North America.
Austria was defeated in the Seven Years' War but prospered
in the latter part of the century under Maria Theresa and her
son, Joseph II, to become one of Europe's most distinguished cultural centers.

England's economic stability and political importance grew
steadily through the century. By the 1750s, England was
established as an important maritime power, and the victory
over the French in North America gave the English command
of much of that continent. By the close of the century, England
enjoyed the highest per capita income in western Europe as
the new industrial economy took root. London's population
grew to more than 1 million, the first modern city to reach that
size. At the same time, George III, who ruled from 1760 to
1820, saw the power of the monarchy wrested away by Parliament. Increased taxation led the American colonies to declare
independence in 1776; and, with French assistance, the
colonies defeated the British at Yorktown in 1781. A peace
treaty was signed between England and the new American
nation in 1783.

The growing desire for self-rule, one of the features of
the philosophy of the Enlightenment (see the next section) in
response to the authoritarian rule of Europe's traditional
absolute monarchs, also affected developments in France.
During the reign of Louis XVI and his wife, Marie
Antoinette, lavish government expenditures led to economic
depression. As relations between the French aristocracy
and the people deteriorated, the National Assembly was
formed in 1789 to compose a written constitution for
France. During the French Revolution, a constitutional
monarchy was established, but internal political factions and
outside military pressure threatened the new government.
Within France, hostility against the aristocracy rose to a
fever pitch by 1792, and in the bloody executions that
followed, even Louis XVI and his queen were guillotined.
Within this context of domestic uncertainty and foreign
wars, a young military commander, Napoleon Bonaparte,
rose in power and, at the age of thirty in 1799, was made the
first consul of the French Republic.

Intellectual and Scientific Activity in Europe

The eighteenth century has been called the Age of
Enlightenment. The influence of the Catholic Church
declined, and philosophical investigations were directed less

8-5 ELIZABETH VIGÉE-LEBRUN

PORTRAIT OF MARIE GABRIELLE DE GRAMONT, DUCHESSE DE CADEROUSSE. 1784. Oil on wood, 41⅜ × 29⅞". The Nelson-Atkins Museum of Art, Kansas City, Missouri. Elizabeth Vigée-Lebrun wrote: . . . "I could not endure powder. I persuaded the handsome Duchess De Gramont-Caderousse to put none on for her sitting. Her hair was ebony black, and I divided it in the forehead, disposing it in irregular curls. After the sitting, which ended at the dinner hour, the Duchess would not change her headdress but go to the theatre as she was. A woman of such good looks would, of course, set a fashion: indeed, this mode of doing the hair soon found imitators, and then gradually became general. This reminds me that in 1786, when I was painting the Queen, I begged her to use no powder, and to part her hair on the forehead. 'I should be the last to follow that fashion,' said the Queen, laughing; 'I do not want people to say that I adopted it to hide my large forehead.'"

PURCHASE: ACQUIRED THROUGH THE GENEROSITY OF NUMEROUS DONORS.

8-6 THOMAS CHIPPENDALE (probably)

Bed. 1750–54. Wood, japanned in red and gilt. Victoria and Albert Museum, London.

to theological than to secular and scientific issues. Descartes's belief in the supremacy of human reason and the centrality of natural sciences, which dates from the seventeenth century, was inherited and advanced by eighteenth-century philosophers. The Enlightenment was marked by faith in human reason, natural human rights, science, and progress toward a utopian society. This joining of the natural sciences with philosophical questioning strengthened the belief in empiricism, a view that human knowledge was pragmatically gained from experience and sensation. The foremost proponent of empiricism from the late seventeenth century was the English writer John Locke. Locke's treaties on government, based on his experience with the rise of parliamentary government in England, avowed that a nation's power derived from its people. The people entered into a social contract with their government and retained the right to dissent and withdraw support if their government proved no longer responsive to their will and needs. Locke's political

philosophy guided the American Revolution and the drafting of the U. S. Constitution and, through Voltaire, assisted in fomenting the French Revolution.

Empiricism also fertilized the growth of the natural sciences. Building on Isaac Newton's observations and discoveries, advances continued in physics, mathematics, and astronomy. In 1759, Edmund Halley's name was given to the comet that returns every seventy-six years. Zoology, botany, and mineralogy were established as scientific disciplines. The chemist Antoine Lavoisier was the first to demonstrate correctly the process of combustion; he later named the reactive element that is essential for life, oxygen. Constant improvements in such devices as the telescope, microscope, barometer, and thermometer allowed for greater accuracy in scientific observation.

Technology benefited from this increasing scientific knowledge. New processes in metallurgy contributed to the use of iron as a building material, and the perfection of the steam engine by James Watt in 1769 brought Europe closer to the momentous and far-reaching economic and social changes of the Industrial Revolution.

Eighteenth-Century Art In Europe

The Rococo and Neoclassical styles dominated the visual arts in Europe during the eighteenth century. The term *Rococo*, derived from the French *rocaille* (literally "rockwork" or "rubble"), was first used to designate a style of French art associated with the reign of Louis XV. In early eighteenth-century France, charm and finesse were the hallmarks of an artificial code of social behavior. The Rococo's light ornamental elegance, as exemplified in the portrait (fig. 8-5) by Elizabeth Vigée-Lebrun (1755–1842), completed the artificiality of aristocratic values and tastes.

The contact with other cultures that brought new styles and aesthetic ideas into European art reveals not only an interest in new and exotic ideas but also a typical European superficiality in response to outside cultures and influences. The bed illustrated here (fig. 8-6), probably by the famous English furniture maker Thomas Chippendale (1718–79), was inspired by the elegant forms of Chinese architecture, especially the pagoda roof. In Europe, this style, known as *chinoiserie*, was popular for chairs, tables, wallpaper, porcelain, clocks, and other decorative arts. Pieces of Chinese porcelain of elegant simplicity were enshrined in elaborate Rococo mounts. Although Europeans in general made little attempt to understand the Chinese civilization, there were few European eighteenth-century palaces that did not have a room decorated in this style. This approach to foreign cultures—borrowing without understanding—reveals the attitudes typical of Westerners during much of the early modern period.

The Neoclassical style, first named in the mid-nineteenth century, developed as an alternative to the Rococo in the eighteenth. Fueling the Neoclassical style at mid-century was a reawakened interest in classical antiquity spurred by the rediscovery of two Roman cities that had been buried by the first-century eruption of Mount Vesuvius: Herculaneum was found in 1738 and Pompeii in 1748. The revival movement of Neoclassicism is the first in a series of revivals—some nostalgic, some ideological—that would flourish in the nineteenth century, and because of this, Neoclassicism is sometimes understood as the first step in the development to the broader movement known as Romanticism (see pages 408, 418-19).

The most eloquent spokesperson for Neoclassical taste was the German art historian Johann Winckelmann, who had his portrait painted by Angelica Kauffmann (1741–1807), one of the most famous artists of the period. He viewed the rationality and ideality of classical art as the summit of artistic achievement. In his influential *Thoughts on the Imitation of Greek Art in Painting and Sculpture* of 1755, Winckelmann wrote:

> Good taste, which is spreading more and more throughout the world, had its beginning under a Greek sky. . . . To take ancients for models is our only way to become great, yes, unsurpassable if we can. As someone has said of Homer: he who learns to admire him, learns to understand him; the same is true of the art works of the ancients, especially the Greeks.

Neoclassical art was well suited to the changing political realities of the late eighteenth century. Compared to the light-hearted and aristocratic elegance of Rococo art, the Neoclassical style offered a restrained design that was intended to convey a moral dignity. As ancient classical edifices first bore witness to the representative governments of Athens and Rome, what better style was there to emulate during the new age, which asserted that each individual had natural rights—or, in the words of the Declaration of Independence, "inalienable rights"—and that among these was a voice in government? To the Neoclassicists, the art and history of the classical world offered models to be used as guides for human behavior and achievement.

The Eighteenth-Century Artist in Europe

The education of artists in academies was now firmly established in Europe. The Royal Academy of Painting and Sculpture in Paris, founded in 1648, flourished, sending promising students to Rome to study classical art. Its primacy was gradually challenged by the Royal Academy of Arts, founded in London in 1768, which also championed Neoclassicism. The guiding spirit of England's Royal Academy was Joshua Reynolds (1723–92), a painter who had spent two years in Italy studying both ancient and Renaissance art (see fig. 8-22). As the Royal Academy's first president, Reynolds delivered fifteen *Discourses*, which expressed his views on learning the "grand style" of art and outlined an education based on imitating the perfection of nature as revealed through classical and High Renaissance art:

> The moderns are not less convinced than the ancients of [the] superior power existing in art; nor less sensible of its effects. . . . The *gusto grande* of the Italians, the *beau ideal* of the French, and the great style, genius, and taste among the English, are but different appellations of the same thing. It is this intellectual dignity . . . that ennobles the painter's art . . . we must have recourse to the ancients as instructors . . . they will suggest many observations, which would probably escape you, if your study were confined to nature alone.

Reynolds also recommended the study of the "great masters" of the Italian Renaissance:

> I would chiefly recommend, that an implicit obedience to the Rulers of Art, as established by the practice of the great masters, should be exacted from young students. That those models, which have passed through the approbation of ages, should be considered by them as perfect and infallible guides; as subjects for their imitation, not their criticism.

Although the Royal Academy was founded to raise the status of both the arts and the artists, its conservative dogmatism, as revealed by Reynolds's preemptory language, began

8-7 ADÉLAIDE LABILLE-GUIARD

SELF-PORTRAIT WITH TWO PUPILS. 1785. Oil on canvas, 6'10¾" × 4'11⅞". The Metropolitan Museum of Art, New York. Labille-Guiard was instrumental in convincing the French Academy to lift its quota on women members, who had been limited to four, and to allow women professors.

to be viewed by some as a constrictive environment. The tradition of the academy, which in the later sixteenth century had begun as part of a liberating ambiance for the artist, was now becoming a conservative cloak, dictating priority to history painting, which was promoted as the most noble of artistic expressions. History painting drew its iconography from the classical past and, less often, the more recent past. Themes were selected that could be interpreted on several levels. Academic history painters most often picked themes that exemplified an elevated code of human behavior. Such themes were considered appropriate for the "grand style" or the "grand manner" in art.

To truly understand the "grand style," every artist who aspired to gain professional fame felt compelled to make a tour of the antiquities of Italy. We can understand the importance of viewing the actual artistic remains of the classical and Renaissance past from the letters of Benjamin West (see pp. 396-97), an American painter who, en route to London, traveled from 1760 to 1763 through Italy. West later wrote to another American artist, John Singleton Copley, advising him on what to see in Italy:

8-8 ANGELICA KAUFFMANN

SELF-PORTRAIT HESITATING BETWEEN THE ARTS OF MUSIC AND PAINTING. 1791. Oil on canvas, 4'10" × 7'2". Nostell Priory, Yorkshire, England.

In regard to your studies in Italy my advice is as follows: That you pursue the higher Excellences in the Art, and for the obtaining of which I recommend to your attention the works of Ancient Sculptors, Raphael, Michelangelo, Correggio, and Titian, as the Source from which true taste in the arts have flowed.

In terms of patronage, little changed in the eighteenth century. The grandest projects were those commissioned by royalty, nobility, and the church, but in a democratic society like America the state also began to become an important patron, as revealed in Thomas Jefferson's Capitol for the State of Virginia (see fig. 8-24). Portraits were staple product for both painters and sculptors. The growing importance of academies and their exhibitions and competitions (such as the Prize of Rome) meant, however, that artists were encouraged to develop large display pieces with a subject of their own choosing. Some artists, such as Hogarth (see fig. 8-16) and David (see fig. 8-27), created works that make a powerful personal statement intended for the public; their belief that art can change or reform society led to some of the most idealistic art of this period and has had an impact on our belief in the power of art to the present day.

Eighteenth-century artists' self-portraits reflect the vitality of the different art styles that characterized the Age of Enlightenment. Adélaide Labille-Guiard (1749–1803) continued the Rococo style into the latter years of the century. Noted for her abilities as both an artist and a teacher, she depicted herself, in elegant dress, at her easel with two attentive students (fig. 8-7). An early self-portrait by Angelica Kauffmann (fig. 8-8) shows the young artist between figures representing the classical allegories of Music and Painting. Kauffmann, who was an accomplished musician, here adapted the Neoclassical style to demonstrate her dilemma at having to choose between music and painting as a career.

8-9 ANGELICA KAUFFMANN

Self-Portrait Hesitating between the Arts of Music and Painting
(for more information see fig. 8-8).

The meanings and messages that underlie representations of women in visual culture can only be assessed after a comparison with evidence about the role and status of women within the relevant society. Many of the images of "beautiful ladies" found in museums, for example, may have been created not to celebrate women but to define and control their appearance and behavior through visual example. These two representations of eighteenth-century women, however, demonstrate that during this period women were gradually claiming new roles in Western culture, especially in the arts. Angelica Kauffmann's self-portrait suggests that she had skills in both music and art and represents publicly her ability as an individual to choose between them. While in Shakespeare's time the roles of women in plays were taken by men, by the eighteenth century these roles were being played by women, some of whom, like Sarah Siddons, became the media stars of their generation. Thomas Gainsborough's portrait shows an elegantly dressed woman, but the strongly naturalistic quality in the face and pose emphasizes that this woman is an individual.

8-10 THOMAS GAINSBOROUGH

Portrait of Mrs. Sarah Siddons
(for more information see fig. 8-23).

Heroic women are not uncommon in literature, mythology, and religion; one of the most impressive of these is the Hebrew woman Judith, who defeated the enemy by cutting off their general's head, as seen in this image by a woman artist. Artemisia Gentileschi exalts Judith and her maid by their large scale (in the original painting the women are larger than life-size), and the danger and suspense of their mission is clear in the moment that is depicted. Artemisia Gentileschi represented this subject several times, and she surely intended that the brave Judith be understood as a model for female behavior.

8-11 ARTEMISIA GENTILESCHI *JUDITH AND THE HEAD OF HOLOFERNES* (for more information see fig. 7-17).

ARTEMISIA GENTILESCHI, ITALIAN, (1593–C. 1652). *JUDITH AND MAIDSERVANT WITH THE HEAD OF HOLOFERNES.* THE DETROIT INSTITUTE OF THE ARTS, DETROIT, MICHIGAN

As is the case with many representations of aristocratic women, the artist here has emphasized the elegant costumes, elaborate hair-styles, and refined poses of the women. While many portraits and representations of women from earlier periods suggest that women should be elegant but inactive, in this Chinese scroll painting the women are shown working to prepare one of China's traditional luxury goods, silk.

8-12 ZHANG XUAN (after) *COURT LADIES PREPARING NEWLY WOVEN SILK* (for more information see fig. 4-40).

In this riveting self-portrait, Alice Neel defies the western tradition that the female should be beautiful, seductive, and intended for the male viewer. She paints herself as she is, looking in a mirror, at the age of 80; perhaps this portrait was inspired by that milestone birthday. By representing herself holding a brush, she alerts the viewer that this is a self-portrait, a fact strengthened by the way in which she stares toward the mirror crucial for self-portraiture.

8-13 ALICE NEEL *SELF PORTRAIT* (for more information see fig. 10-24).

QUESTIONS

1. Select a representation of a woman from a contemporary magazine or an advertisement that features a woman. What does this representation tell you about attitudes toward women at this time in history?

2. Is this representation typical of broader attitudes, or is it exceptional?

Eighteenth-Century Painting in Europe

8-14 ANTOINE WATTEAU

A PILGRIMAGE TO THE ISLAND OF CYTHERA. 1717. Oil on canvas, 4'3" × 6'4½". The Louvre, Paris. As Watteau's reception piece for the French Royal Academy, this painting was listed as *"une fête galante,"* a new category of painting in which elegant aristocratic men and women are represented partying in a landscape setting.

8-15 JEAN-HONORÉ FRAGONARD

HAPPY ACCIDENTS OF THE SWING. 1767. Oil on canvas, 31⅞ × 25⅜". Wallace Collection, London. Commissioned by Baron de Saint-Julien, Receveur général des biens du clergé.

A *Pilgrimage to the Island of Cythera*, by Antoine Watteau (1684–1721), combines reality and fantasy to express the transitory nature of romantic love (fig. 8-14). Delicately scaled couples in the eighteenth-century dress move slowly toward a fanciful ship that will return them from the island of Cythera, mythical home of Venus, goddess of love. The statue of Venus at the right has been adorned with garlands by these pensive lovers, who came to worship at her shrine and engage in the rituals of her cult. Their reluctance to leave pleasure behind is expressed in their gestures and poses, while muted colors and light brushstrokes express the transience of love. The composition moves from the statue of Venus to the vessel of departure, reversing our normal reading direction and heightening the bittersweet nature of the departure. Watteau simultaneously conveyed the poetry of love and

suggested how remote it is from everyday reality. Romantic love survives only in the world of imagination.

Fragonard's painting, on the other hand, reaffirms the pleasures of lovers' games (fig. 8-15). Jean-Honoré Fragonard (1732–1806) received the commission for the painting from Baron de Saint-Julien, who specified the details of the subject. His mistress is in a swing pushed by a bishop

so high that her slipper falls off the tip of her foot and her skirt shoots upward for the delight of the indiscreet eyes of a charming youth reclining among the flowers beneath her; happily there hovers above him a cupid whose gesture enjoins him to keep the secret of what he has seen.

The theme incorporates an obvious pun, for the baron served as the government representative who collected the taxes paid by the church. His title

was *Receveur général des biens du clergé* ("Receiver general of the 'goods' offered by the clergy"). Fragonard's pastel palette, which centers around the pink dress and blue-green trees, and the delicate lightness of his brushstroke help to underline the frivolity of the subject.

The qualities seen in these two works help define Rococo painting. The colors are usually light, and the thin paint is delicately brushed onto the surface. The figures are generally small and delicate in proportion, and the composition creates a flowing, idyllic movement. Common themes are superficial scenes from court life, especially romance.

A series of paintings done by William Hogarth (1697–1764), *Marriage à la Mode*, presents a satirical view of modern life and exposes the difficulties of a loveless "city" marriage of convenience (fig. 8-16). The serious nature of both the nouveau riche and the nobility is evi-

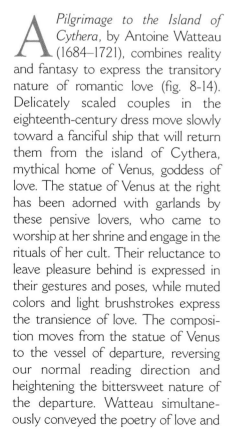

8-16   WILLIAM HOGARTH

MARRIAGE À LA MODE, SCENE II. 1743. Oil on canvas, 27½ × 35¾″. The National Gallery, London. This is the second scene in a series of six. To Hogarth's contemporaries, *"à la mode"* implied something fashionable but cheap and short-lived. The series was subtitled *Modern Occurrences in High Life*. Hogarth's painted series on moral subjects was reproduced as popular engravings. The artist compared himself to dramatists and novelists, saying that he "considered subjects as writers do," adding, "My picture was my stage and men and women my actors. The inspiration of contemporary English theater (Gay) and literature (Fielding, Defoe) on Hogarth is well documented. In two earlier series, Hogarth chronicled *A Harlot's Progress* (1728–30), which follows an attractive young girl from her arrival in London, where she is discovered by a procuress, to her death, and *A Rake's Progress* (1735), in which a weak young man wastes his father's fortune, ending up in an asylum, probably the infamous English Bedlam.

dent throughout the series, which begins with the signing of the marriage contract between the daughter of a rich, social-climbing merchant and an impoverished nobleman (Count Squanderfield). In a sequence of six scenes, their marriage progresses through adultery, the murder of the husband by the wife's lover (Silvertongue), and her death by suicide, leaving their only child an orphan. Our scene shows the husband returning at 1:20 P.M. with a hangover after a night on the town. The dog sniffs at a woman's cap hanging from his pocket. His pose is meant to suggest

sexual exhaustion. This wife's pose and the overturned chair and scattered music suggest that her lover is the music teacher, who seems to have departed quickly. Extravagance is evident in the ugly mantelpiece, with its ostentatious display of a bric-a-brac, and the stack of bills held by the clerk. The painting over the mantel features a figure of Cupid, Venus's son and assistant, blowing a bagpipe—an inharmonious phallic symbol—amid ruins. The venereal disease that will ultimately infect the couple's child is already evident in the black spot on the husband's neck. In style, the

looseness of Hogarth's brushstrokes is indebted to the example of contemporary French painting.

Romantic love—its dream and disappointments, pleasures and pains, realities and fantasies—becomes a central theme in Rococo art. The variety of interpretation, demonstrated in these three examples, and the probing character of the representations reveal the important changes that are taking place as the themes of art are broadened, revealing an expanded interest in the psychological and emotional states that affect people in their everyday lives.

Rococo Architecture and Sculpture

8-17 JOHANN BALTHASAR NEUMANN, GIAMBATTIST TIEPOLO, and ANTONIO BOSSI

KAISERSAAL (IMPERIAL HALL), EPISCOPAL PALACE, WÜRZBURG, GERMANY. 1735–44. The 1751–52 frescoes by Tiepolo represent scenes glorifying the twelfth-century German emperor Frederick Barbarossa and the bishop of Würzburg. The stucco work is by Antonio Bossi. The Italian painter Tiepolo spent three years in Würzburg decorating this official residence of the prince-bishops of Würzburg. Commissioned by the Prince-Bishop of Würzburg.

The Kaisersaal documents the life of the aristocracy in the eighteenth century (fig. 8-17). One must imagine it filled with elaborate furniture of the period, its crystal chandeliers lit with flickering candles. The shape of this elegant salon is too complicated to be either an oval or an octagon, but it is surmounted by a high oval dome pierced by windows. The columns seem to be a beautiful pink marble, but like most such columns in Rococo buildings they are stucco painted and polished to give the illusion of marble. The lightness of the architecture is enhanced by the large irregular frescoed oval and by two scenes enframed by elaborate, gilded curtains. Painted figures and animals by Giambattist Tiepolo (1696–1770) wander out onto the entablature to chat, sit, and look down at us.

The Rococo style in architecture developed in France at Versailles about 1700 and flourished in southern Germany in part because of political connections. The palace at Würzburg was built by a family of local hereditary prince-bishops who set out to surpass Versailles (see fig. 7-49). The Rococo style is perhaps at its most exuberant here, where all restraint seems to evaporate in gilded decoration, fake marble columns, and an indissoluble union of painting and architecture. Although it owes its origins to the classical vocabulary of the Renaissance, the Rococo offers a new lightness of color and of movement and a new delicate scale of ornament, which are in contrast to the more ponderous forms and colors of Baroque architecture.

Equally exuberant is the church nicknamed Die Wies near Munich (fig. 8-18). Here Rococo architecture and decoration become a visionary premonition of the heavenly Jerusalem. Die Wies is a pilgrimage center where devout Catholics of all classes worship at the shrine of a miraculous statue of Christ. Virtually every surface is decorated—this is architecture that does not let the eye rest—and like the French Gothic style (see fig. 4-88), its celestial metaphor is in part

8-18 DOMINIKUS ZIMMERMAN

Interior, Die Wies, Germany. 1745–54. The frescoed vault and stucco decoration are probably by Johann Baptist Zimmerman, the architect's brother. The exterior of this structure is rather plain, and the contrast between exterior and interior is an important part of the architectural experience. Commissioned by the local bishop.

8-19. EGID QUIRIN ASAM. *ASSUMPTION OF THE VIRGIN*, detail. 1721–23. Painted and gilded stucco and stained glass. Monastery Church, Rohr, Germany

accomplished by an attempt to deny visually the weight of architectural forms. The white gilded stucco **capitals** have a flamelike movement, and irregularly shaped windows pierce the walls. The openness and lightness of the oval "nave" area contrast with the colors of the architectural climax at the altar, where the statue is enclosed within a shrine of red and white columns. The vault is pierced with curving, Rococo openings that let light in from the windows in the outer wall. This denial of the principles of vaulted architecture makes Die Wies seem like an apparition not dependent on normal structural systems. Nor does it seem to be subject to the force of gravity. The exuberance of Catholic Rococo architecture may be in part a reaction to the severity characteristic of contemporary Protestant architecture.

At the Monastery Church of Rohr, a light-filled white and gold nave directs attention to the richer colors of the columns behind the high altar that enframe a monumental sculpture group (fig. 8-19). While gesticulating apostles surround a Rococo sarcophagus, we gasp as we seem to witness the Virgin being carried to heaven by angels. The architecture seems to open and a golden stained-glass window offers a portal to heaven. Since the Renaissance, religious drama had used special effects of lighting (candles, torches, fireworks) and theatrical machinery to make transcendent miraculous events seem more realistic and more dramatic, and one of the most successful Counter-Reformation tools employed by the Jesuits in southern Germany was the use of sacred theater as a teaching device. This *Assumption*, by Egid Quirin Asam (1692–1750), is a permanent version of one of these theatrical representations.

Eighteenth-Century Portraiture

8-20 JOHN SINGLETON COPLEY

PORTRAIT OF PAUL REVERE. c. 1768–70. Oil on canvas, 34⅞ × 28½″. Courtesy, Museum of Fine Arts, Boston. Paul Revere was a political activist in Boston. His famous night ride to warn Bostonians of the advance of the British army occurred on April 18, 1775. Copley's family was sympathetic to the British, and the artist left the colonies forever on the eve of the Revolution. Commissioned by Paul Revere.

PAUL REVERE. CA. 1768–70. COPLEY, JOHN SINGLETON, U.S., 1738–1815. OIL ON CANVAS, 35 × 28⅛ IN. (88.9 × 72.3 CM.) GIFT OF JOSEPH W., WILLIAM B., AND EDWARD H.R. REVERE. COURTESY, MUSEUM OF FINE ARTS, BOSTON

8-21 ROSALBA CARRIERA

PORTRAIT OF LOUIS XV AS A YOUNG MAN. 1720–21. Pastel on paper, 18½ × 14″. Museum of Fine Arts, Boston. Most likely commissioned by Louis XIV or Louis XV.

ROSALBA CARRIERA, *LOUIS XV AS A BOY*. 1720. PASTEL ON PAPER, 19 × 14 IN. COURTESY, MUSEUM OF FINE ARTS, BOSTON; FORSYTH WICKES COLLECTION

The honest and informal portrait of the Boston silversmith and engraver Paul Revere by John Singleton Copley (1738–1815) represents both the New England work ethic and Copley's artistic joy in rendering exact visual detail (fig. 8-20). The darkened background focuses our attention on Revere and the tools and products of his trade in the foreground. He wears the simple work clothes of an artisan. Such a straightforward approach, which dignifies labor and craft, was in keeping with Puritan values. Copley convincingly portrays a sense of immediacy between Revere and ourselves. It is as though we have discovered Revere deep in thought, almost as if he has for-

gotten the engraving of the teapot and is now engrossed in the contemplation of more difficult issues. Revere's eyes meet ours, and his raised right eyebrow seems to signify acknowledgment of our presence. It is clear that Copley delighted in the naturalistic representation of figures and objects. Note how the sharp, detailed reflection of Revere's fingers in the silver teapot contrasts with the diffused reflection of his shirt on the polished wooden worktop.

Copley and Benjamin West (see fig. 8-29) are acknowledged as American's first significant artists. Copley's fame in the colonies was established primarily by his ability as a portraitist. His sensitive observation and carefully devel-

oped talent earned him a distinguished reputation and a significant financial income, both in the colonies and in his later career in Britain. Although portrait painting ranked behind history and religious painting in the classification of subject matter, it was an economic mainstay for many artists.

Rosalba Carriera (1675–1757), in her painting of France's young king Louis XV (fig. 8-21), demonstrates the elegant grace of Rococo portraiture. The soft, delicate effect is achieved not only by the blending of high-value colors but also by the use of **pastel** as a medium. Carriera, a Venetian artist, became famous for her ability to render portraits in pastel. Her influence in France and Italy popularized the medium in the eighteenth century.

In England, two competing artists excelled in portraiture: Joshua Reynolds, president of London's Royal Academy, and Thomas Gainsborough (1727–88). Our two portraits, which display the abilities and different approaches of these two artists, both represent Sarah Kemble Siddons, a popular actress of the period (figs. 8-22, 8-23).

True to his philosophy that painting should aspire to the "grand style," Reynolds chose to depict Siddons as a classical allegorical figure, the muse of tragic drama. She sits on a throne, head and eyes raised as if in response to divine, creative inspiration. Behind her are figures symbolizing Pity and Terror, the attributes of tragic drama. Reynolds's composition directly recalls Michelangelo's figures of prophets and Sibyls on the Sistine Chapel ceiling (see fig. 6-36) in order to demonstrate his ability to adapt and update the Renaissance style.

When Gainsborough painted the same celebrated actress, he chose to portray her as an elegantly dressed, confident woman. The painting, which recalls the traditions of Venetian and Baroque portraiture, is a sumptuous treat for our eyes. The blues and whites of her dress enhance the warm, golden tones of her shawl and muff, while the magnificent black hat is silhouetted against a deep red curtain. Gainsborough's painterly technique and luxurious colors create an impressive portrait of a dynamic woman.

1750	World populations is about 750 million
1760	Population of American colonies is about 1.6 million
1762	Catherine the Great becomes Tzarina of Russia
1762	Jean-Jacques Rousseau's *Social Contract* published
1764	Mozart, age eight, writes his first symphony
c. 1768–70	**Copley, *Portrait of Paul Revere***
1770	Boston Massacre
1772	Joseph Priestley and Daniel Rutherford separately discover nitrogen
1773	Boston Tea Party

8-22 JOSHUA REYNOLDS

ALLEGORICAL PORTRAIT OF SARAH SIDDONS AS THE TRAGIC MUSE. 1784. Oil on canvas, 7'9" × 4'9½". Henry E. Huntington Library and Art Gallery, San Marino, California. Reynolds painted two versions of this portrait; the second, painted in 1789, was intended for his agent, Desensans.

8-23 THOMAS GAINSBOROUGH

PORTRAIT OF SARAH SIDDONS. 1783-85. Oil on canvas, 49¾ × 39¼". The National Gallery, London.

Thomas Jefferson and Neoclassical Architecture in the United States

8-24 THOMAS JEFFERSON

State Capitol, Richmond, Virginia. 1785–89.
Commissioned by the State of Virginia.

8-25 THOMAS JEFFERSON

University of Virginia, Charlottesville. 1817–26.

You see I am an enthusiast in the subject of the arts. But it is an enthusiasm of which I am not ashamed, as its object is to improve the taste of my countrymen, to increase their reputation, to reconcile them to the respect of the world, and procure them its praise.
(Thomas Jefferson, in a letter to James Madison, 1785)

Jefferson's Virginia State Capitol (fig. 8-24) must have surprised many Richmond residents (see map, page 426), for it was the first public building in the youthful American republic to be modeled on the classical temple form. Thomas Jefferson (1743–1826) designed the building while he was serving as U.S. minister to France, where he was inspired by both French architects already working in the Neoclassical style and the ruins of the ancient

Roman civilization in Gaul. He was especially influenced by a Roman temple at Nîmes, in southern France, which is similar to the Temple of Portunus in Rome (see fig. 3-93). Jefferson wrote in a letter that he had gazed at the temple for hours, "like a lover at his mistress." While maintaining its basic design, he greatly enlarged it for the Virginia State Capitol. The resulting structure, with its Ionic portico, pediment, and classical proportions, confers a solemn, dignified appearance—appropriate, as Jefferson himself believed, to the ideals of a young democratic nation.

Although the Neoclassical architectural style flourished throughout the Western world, it was particularly meaningful in the United States, as the nation adopted a democratic form of government following the Revolution. The emula-

tion of Roman buildings was viewed as an appropriate vehicle to express architectural dignity and command public respect. For Jefferson, public architecture demanded a moral content. The nobility of the Neoclassical edifice would serve as a guide to the behavior and aspirations of the young republic. The Neoclassical architectural style in the United States is also known as the Federal style because of its prominent use for government buildings.

In 1817, Jefferson, now a former president, began planning the first state university in the United States. His design for the University of Virginia, in Charlottesville, harmonizes the stateliness of the Federal style with the practical needs of an educational community (fig. 8-25). The mall is dominated by the Rotunda, an adaptation of the ancient Pantheon in Rome (see

8-26 THOMAS JEFFERSON

Monticello, Charlottesville, Virginia. 1768–82; remodeled 1796–1809. The Italian name *Monticello* ("Little Mountain") was adopted by Jefferson because of the hilltop setting of his home.

fig. 3-120). The Rotunda contained the library; the individual pavilions along the mall each housed a different academic discipline, including living quarters for the faculty and classrooms.

Jefferson's design for his country home, Monticello, demonstrates the adaptability of Neoclassical architec-tural features to domestic buildings (fig. 8-26). The use of antique architectural elements is evident, but Jefferson's sources for the composition here are also drawn from the Renaissance, particularly the villas of Palladio. The Villa Rotonda (see fig. 1-7) and others inspired the main block, with its domed ballroom, while other Palladian villas in the countryside around Venice were the source for wings that reach out to embrace the landscape and unify the house with the farms and countryside that support the estate. Soon houses throughout the United States would sport Doric, Ionic, and Corinthian porticoes as an indication of American democratic ideals.

Neoclassical Painting

8-27 JACQUES-LOUIS DAVID

DEATH OF SOCRATES. 1787. Oil on canvas, 4′3″ × 6′6″. The Metropolitan Museum of Art, New York, New York. The liberal philosophy of Socrates, the fifth-century BCE Athenian philosopher, stressed the worth of the individual over that of the state in a manner that upset Athenian officials. Because he could not be brought to trial for his philosophical beliefs, he was tried for "impiety," found guilty, and ultimately sentenced to death. It was clear that he could have gone free had he renounced his teachings, but Socrates himself pointed out that death had been the verdict of a legitimate court. Following Athenian practice, he drank hemlock. Commissioned by Charles-Michel Trudaine, a lawyer at the French Parliament.

THE METROPOLITAN MUSEUM OF ART, CATHERINE LORILLARD WOLFE COLLECTION, WOLFE FUND, 1931 (31.45)

Heroic suicide may seem to be a contradiction in terms, but the purpose of David's theme (fig. 8-27), painted in the unsettled years in France before the Revolution, was to demonstrate the need to live by principles and the heroism of the stoic virtue of absolute self-sacrifice. Jacques-Louis David (1748–1825) depicted a heroic, muscular Socrates reaching for the cup of poisonous hemlock held by a distraught disciple. With an exclamatory gesture, Socrates points upward, insisting on the truth of his ideals. On viewing the painting, one contemporary observer remarked,

This is the triumph of virtue which is raised higher than all other things by a heroic courage and an inspired soul.

Although the theme of the death of Socrates is taken from the classical past, David's choice and interpretation of the subject are strictly contemporary, and within the cultural context of late-eighteenth-century France, they would have been easily understood. In 1758, the philosopher and writer Denis Diderot had detailed a proposed drama on Socrates' death that popularized the theme with artists and writers. Socrates' unwavering devotion to his ideals provides the theme for this history painting. Both the lesson and David's representation were acclaimed by critics and the public. The work offered a guide for moral behavior in the troubled social climate of France. David became a supporter of the French Revolution and the *Death of Socrates* illustrates his belief that paintings "of heroism and civic virtue offered the eyes of the people [will] electrify its soul, and plant the seed of glory and devotion to the fatherland." The crisp modeling of the figures creates precise, linear, sculptural forms, revealing David's academic training and approach, while the planar space of the painting suggests that ancient relief sculpture may have been one of David's inspirations.

The Swiss painter Angelica Kauffmann (see fig. 8-8) also championed the virtues of history painting. The theme of Kauffmann's *Cornelia* (fig. 8-28) is drawn from Roman antiquity. Cornelia was renowned as a devoted mother. When a friend who had displayed her own jewelry asked to see Cornelia's gems, Cornelia presented her two sons. The personal and emotional implications of the theme are clear, and it should perhaps be pointed out that Kauffmann selected and successfully represented a subject that would be recognized as revealing a particular feminine insight. Kauffmann's elegant yet disciplined Neoclassical compositions gained her an international reputation.

In his *Death of General Wolfe* (fig. 8-29), Benjamin West (1738–1820) popularized a new concept within the category of history painting, for West represented the figures in contemporary costume, avoiding the antique clothing and setting that, according to traditional academic rules, could elevate a subject to its universal significance. West's earliest biographer recounted that Joshua Reynolds, president of the Royal Academy, had advised West to

8-28 ANGELICA KAUFFMANN

Cornelia, Mother of the Gracchi. 1785. Oil on canvas, 40 × 50″.
Virginia Museum of Fine Arts, Richmond. Purchased by George
Bowles of Wanstead, Essex, who was an important collector of
Kauffmann's works.

ANGELICA KAUFFMANN (BORN SWISS, 1741–1807), *CORNELIA POINTING TO HER CHILDREN
AS HER TREASURES*, CA. 1785. OIL ON CANVAS 101.6 × 127 CM. VIRGINIA MUSEUM OF FINE
ARTS, RICHMOND. THE ADOLPH D. WILKINS. C. WILLIAMS FUND, PHOTO: KATHERINE
WETZEL. (C) VIRGINIA MUSEUM OF FINE ARTS

8-29. BENJAMIN WEST. *Death of General Wolfe*. 1770. Oil on
canvas, 4′11½″ × 7′. The National Gallery of Canada, Ottawa. The
story of the death of the British commander James Wolfe on the
battlefield at Quebec in 1759 was inspirational. After three months
of stalemate, Wolfe led his troops to victory over a much larger
French force but, mortally wounded, he died in the arms of his
officers at the moment of victory. George III commissioned a replica
of this painting from West

BENJAMIN WEST (1738–1820), *THE DEATH OF GENERAL WOLFE*, 1770, OIL ON CANVAS, 152.6
× 214.5 CM. TRANSFER FROM THE CANADIAN WAR MEMORIALS, 1921 (GIFT OF THE 2ND
DUKE OF WESTMINSTER, EATON HALL, CHESHIRE, 1918). NATIONAL GALLERY OF
CANADA, OTTAWA, ONTARIO..

adopt the classic costume of antiquity, as much more becoming the inherent greatness of . . . [the] subject than the modern garb of war, and that West had replied: The event intended to be commemorated took place on the 13th of September, 175[9], in a region of the world unknown to the Greeks and Romans, and at a period of time when no such nations, nor heroes in their costume, any longer existed. The subject I have to represent is the conquest of a great province of America by the British troops . . . If, instead of the facts of the transaction, I represent classical fictions, how shall I be understood by posterity! . . . . I want to mark the date, the place, and the parties engaged in the event; and if I am not able to dispose of the circumstances in a picturesque manner, no academical distribution of Greek or Roman costume will enable me to do justice to the subject.

West's composition was stimulated by a serious study of classical sculpture and of the works of Renaissance and Baroque artists, and his painting, a popular success, pioneered an important change in the representation of contemporary history. Although he avoided classical costume, West did refer to the tradition by including the Native American as a personification of America. The painting successfully communicates the tragedy of the death of Wolfe, an event that inherently demonstrated the universal values of self-sacrifice, courage, and patriotism. King George III commissioned a copy of West's painting and made him the official history painter at the British court.

The Eiffel Tower, named for its architect-engineer Gustave Eiffel, was erected in Paris between 1887 and 1889 (for more information see fig. 9-46 and pp. 435–36).

Nineteenth-Century Art

A Brief Insight

THE EIFFEL TOWER, A WELL-KNOWN SYMBOL OF THE city of Paris, was designed in 1887 as a temporary structure for an 1889 World's Fair celebrating the centennial of the French Revolution. As the tallest structure in the world at its time, it became a potent symbol for the fair, and from its various levels fair-goers had panoramic views over the city; after the fair was over, the decision was made to keep the tower as a tourist attraction.

A structure such as this would have been impossible before the development of the metal structural system and the invention of the elevator. Such technological innovation is one of the hallmarks of the nineteenth century, the century famous for the Industrial Revolution.

While today the Eiffel Tower is a symbol of Paris known around the world, many late-nineteenth-century Parisians were dismayed by the tower, lamenting the revolutionary manner in which Eiffel boldly exposed the metal structure. Critics were also appalled because his design made no reference to earlier architecture, as was expected at the time. The controversy around the Eiffel Tower is only one of many raised by the revolutionary art that was produced and widely debated during the nineteenth century.

There are several factors that help define the Eiffel Tower as a modern work: the frank exposure of materials, the avoidance of any reference to earlier cultures, and the emphasis on the abstract design of bold lines that unifies the construction of steel beams into a soaring whole.

Nineteenth-Century Art

9-1 EUGÈNE DELACROIX

LIBERTY LEADING THE PEOPLE. 1830. Oil on canvas, 8′6⅜″ × 10′8″. The Louvre, Paris.

The ideal of revolution so important for the development of the modern world and so central to the history, ideology, and art of the European nineteenth century is expressed in two paintings by Eugène Delacroix (1798–1863) and Claude Monet (1846–1926). Delacroix's subject (fig. 9-1) celebrates the July Revolution of 1830, when an uprising of Parisians mounted a revolutionary red, white, and blue flag—the tricolor—on the spires of Nôtre-Dame Cathedral and forced the abdication of Charles X, as well as the adoption of a new charter that doubled the number of citizens who elected the legislative chamber. This was a modest but important triumph for the liberals, lower bourgeoisie, and skilled workers who had led the revolt. In Delacroix's painting, the personification of Liberty, holding the tricolor, leads an army of Parisian rebels over the bodies of their dead comrades

toward victory. Delacroix's technique, too, is revolutionary, for in reaction to the sharp linearity of the prevailing Neoclassical style (see pp. 396–97, 414–15), he introduces blurred edges, strong colors, and loose brushstrokes in an active style appropriate to his modern subject. Of Delacroix's significance, the later painter Paul Cézanne would say,

"We all paint differently because of him."

From later in the century, Monet's revolutionary painting (fig. 9-2) expresses Impressionist ideals. In defiance of the criteria that had been taught in European art academies since the Renaissance, the Impressionists challenged the emphasis given to traditional subject matter and exalted the importance of the momentary glimpse of a real scene. Monet chose this particular cityscape not in response to

9-2 CLAUDE MONET

RUE ST.-DENIS FESTIVITIES ON JUNE 30, 1878. 1878. Oil on canvas, 29⅞ × 20½″. Musée des Beaux-Arts, Rouen, France.

patriotic fervor, for example, but because he was challenged by the problem of how to represent the visual effect of the brilliant colors and the ever-changing movement offered by the flags. Monet's goal was to capture a visual "impression" of what the eye sees, regardless of subject. Traditional critics were as upset by this attitude about subject matter as they were by his loose brushstrokes.

History

Economic, technological, and political revolutions dominate the history of the nineteenth century in Europe and the United States. The Industrial Revolution, with its mechanization of production in factories, transformed life for a large percentage of the population in Europe and America. The rapidly expanding lower and middle classes, concentrated in the cities near their factory jobs, organized to demand democracy and more humane treatment. The spirit of reform that began in the nineteenth century led eventually to universal suffrage in much of the world. The institutions, life-styles, and class structures that resulted had an important impact on art.

During the nineteenth century, the world seemed to become a smaller place as steam-powered trains and ships led to increased world trade. The expansion of communications with the establishment of inexpensive newspapers

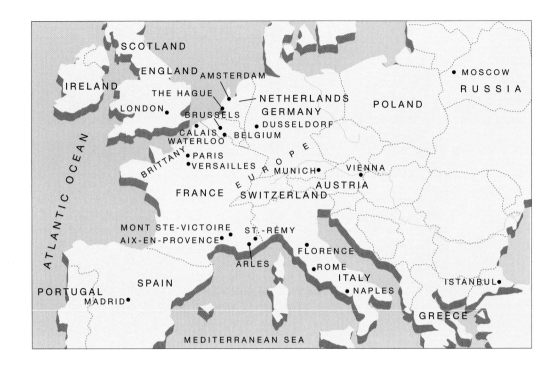

and periodicals, printed on high-speed printing presses, and the development of the telegraph and telephone led to greater international awareness. An interconnected world gradually evolved, prompted by world trade and centered around the great international fairs held in the second half of the century. The establishment of European colonies in Africa, Asia, and Australia brought Western culture into contact and conflict with local traditions and beliefs. More and more artists traveled from America, China, Japan, and elsewhere to study in France and Germany, and soon even painters from Pittsburgh were submitting works to the Salon in Paris and the Royal Academy exhibitions in London. Inexpensive reproductions of works of art were widely distributed.

Napoleon dominated European history in the first decade of the nineteenth century, leading French armies to victory until he controlled all of Europe. Only Britain, which defeated Napoleon's navy at Trafalgar, was able to repel the French. Napoleon was proclaimed emperor of France in 1804 and king of Italy in 1805. Determined to break the traditional and historic power of the Catholic Church and its clergy, Napoleon closed monasteries and destroyed symbols of ecclesiastical and monastic power. To enlarge his own private collections and those of the French state, he appropriated many works of art. He attacked Russia in 1812 and took Moscow, but in retreat his army was virtually annihilated. Napoleon abdicated in 1814, returned briefly to power in 1815, and was defeated by the English at Waterloo. The new European borders set at the Congress of Vienna in 1815, after Napoleon's defeat, established a balance of power that endured until World War I.

The French Revolution and later revolutionary uprisings in France in 1830 and 1848, as well as the success of the new democracy in the United States, gave impetus to other revolutionary movements. Throughout Europe there was an increased demand for "liberty, equality, and fraternity [nationalism]"—there were eleven revolutionary uprisings in major European cities in 1848–49. The nineteenth-century demands for revolution, however, would reach their most profound outcome with the Russian Revolution of 1917. Great Britain remained stable, and the British Empire underwent tremendous expansion accompanied by an astonishing economic development—the result of peace, industrialization, and the world market provided by the empire. The power of the British naval and merchant marine was unrivaled. In the United States, rapid expansion and industrialization led to prosperity and optimism, but this mood was dissipated by the divisive Civil War (1861–65), and after the war American culture became increasingly dependent on conservative European models. By the end of the nineteenth century, nationalistic desires for unification in Italy and in Germany had succeeded.

The British Empire brought the English language and the British bureaucratic system to many different regions of the world; the largest and most dramatic of these was India. India had played an important role in trade since the seventeenth century, when British, Dutch, French, and other European traders had arrived there in search of luxury goods in demand in Europe: spices, fine cottons, silk, opium, and indigo, among others. India prospered from this trade, which was conducted by trading companies that held monopolies; the most important of these was the British East India Company, which also acted as a political and mil-

9-3 KUNISADA

A Woman Frightened by Thunder. 1849–53. Woodblock print, 14½ × 10⅛". This print was part of a large collection of more than 200 Japanese prints owned by the Post-Impressionist painter Vincent van Gogh; the artist owned 165 prints by Kunisada alone. Japanese prints were a formative influence on many French nineteenth-century painters, especially Manet, Monet, Degas, Toulouse-Lautrec, and Van Gogh. The choice of subjects from everyday life, the bold silhouetting and complex patterning of their designs (especially evident here in the pattern of the mosquito netting over the designs of the woman's costume), the truncation of the forms (note the flying reed shade in the upper right corner and the lightning bolt that flashes into the room), the high viewpoint, and the diagonal recession of the architectural settings were all characteristic of Japanese art, and all had an effect on the development of modern French painting.

itary force, helping to secure British rule in India by the mid-nineteenth century. British officials were in charge of virtually all of India, but there was no single central authority. By the end of the century, India had become a part of the world economy, and, based on the British example, a modern bureaucratic system had been established. Interest among Indian artists in European painting and architecture was another result of the British colonization of India.

During the nineteenth century, Japan was gradually opened to the West. In 1804, a representative of the czar of Russia arrived, and in 1846 and 1853, respectively, Commodores Biddle and Perry of the United States were received. The treaties that were negotiated between Japan and the Western powers led to increased communication, and the delegates who left Japan to take up posts in the Western world returned with the news of Western industrial progress. Japanese students began to go to Europe to study. By 1889, the new Meiji Constitution was in place,

and in the next twenty years Japan waged wars against China and Russia; by the end of the nineteenth century, Japan also had become an "imperial" power.

Asian works of art were imported into Europe and collected by individuals and museums, and by the end of the century, the collecting of works from Africa was well under way, aided by European colonization of that continent and the attempt to suppress its local traditions. Although Asian works had a significant impact on the development of art (for example, Impressionism; see pp. 446–51) and on popular taste and collecting (see fig. 9-3) during the nineteenth century, the impact of the African works was not felt until the twentieth century. European-style painting was known in Asia, primarily through the works of Japanese artists returning from Europe and from reproductions in Chinese and Japanese journals, and by the end of the nineteenth century there was a widespread interest in western European art.

It would be oversimplifying to draw direct relationships between each of the global historical events we have summarized and the developments in art with which this chapter deals, but our study of earlier art has often demonstrated the intimate connection between historical events that affected the lives and attitudes of large groups of people and the art that was produced at the same time. As both the world and art have become more complicated and interrelated, we must continue to try to grasp the role of historical change in new developments in art. We also must not neglect the role that art may have played in defining and transforming history.

The Industrial Revolution

By the mid-nineteenth century, Britain led the world in the mechanized production of inexpensive goods for mass public consumption. Such production became the financial base for England's expansion during the century. Simultaneously, the Industrial Revolution spread through much of Europe and into America, and there was fierce competition for the global markets for mass-produced goods. When power-driven machinery revolutionized the production of textiles, entrepreneurs established huge mills in which hundreds of workers manufactured vast amounts of cheap fabric. Factory-made nails and milled lumber, produced by the power-driven sawmill, revolutionized the housing industry in America. The rapid spread of the railroads transformed transportation, the delivery of merchandise, and communications.

The new industrial production was celebrated in a series of international exhibitions, beginning with the Great Exhibition of the Works of Industry of All Nations at the Crystal Palace in London in 1851 (see fig. 9-44). This exhibition was intended to emphasize England's role as the world's greatest manufacturing center, but it also became a challenge to other countries to compete with England's commercial successes.

9-4 ÉDOUARD MANET

A BAR AT THE FOLIES-BERGÈRE. 1881–82. Oil on canvas, 37½ × 51". Courtauld Institute Galleries, Home House Trustees, London. Many of the barmaids who worked at the Folies-Bergère were also prostitutes. Manet's presentation of this woman is as a commodity that is as readily available as the goods on the bar. At the same time, however, her expression creates a strong sense of the woman as an individual with a personal emotional life. In Manet's oil sketch for the painting, the background is more easily read as a mirror reflection; in the final version, the reflection of the woman and her customer is changed to emphasize the flatness of the pictorial surface and the unreal aspect of the painting. In describing the painting while it was in the studio, Georges Jeanniot, one of Manet's friends, noted that "he did not copy nature at all closely; I noted his masterly simplification. . . . Everything was abbreviated." This painting was exhibited at the Paris Salon in 1882.

By bringing together handicrafts and manufactured goods from all over the world, the exhibition introduced new styles and techniques into the prevailing Victorian taste.

The Industrial Revolution raised standards of living for large groups of people, but it also created unsafe working conditions and led to unemployment. The difficulties of urban life were documented in contemporary novels by Charles Dickens (*Oliver Twist*, 1838) and Victor Hugo (*Les Misérables*, 1862). The issue of the isolation and alienation of the individual in a modern, urban society is expressed by Édouard Manet (1832–83) in his depiction of the barmaid, who probably also worked as a prostitute, in *A Bar at the Folies-Bergère* (fig. 9-4). The Industrial Revolution also transformed art, for the mass production of cheap prints developed a new audience for art. Reproductions of paintings were available virtually everywhere. Illustration flourished, led by such entrepreneurs as Currier & Ives in the United States. The mass production of furniture and other household goods led to a reaction in the second half of the century, when the finely finished works of the individual craftsperson were exalted in the Arts and Crafts and the Art Nouveau (see fig. 10-8) movements.

European Intellectual and Scientific Activities

In Europe, the social and financial inequities that were amplified by industrialism led to a number of responses—socialism, anarchism, utopian movements, and revolutionary communism. The latter was explicitly defined by Karl Marx and Friedrich Engels in the *Communist Manifesto*, published in 1848. Similar sentiments about inequity led to revolutions in China, Russia, and India in the twentieth century.

Intimately connected with industrialization were advances in science, engineering, and technology. Science replaced philosophy as the most influential university discipline. New scientific theories, especially Charles Darwin's *The Origin of Species* (1859), with its message of the "sur-

9-5 HENRI DE TOULOUSE-LAUTREC

AT THE MOULIN ROUGE. 1892. Oil on canvas, 48⅜ × 55¼″. The Art Institute of Chicago. The dramatic lighting of the face in the foreground, which reflects the strong color of the cabaret's gas lighting, reveals the Impressionists' interest in representing the effect of light on their subjects.

THE ART INSTITUTE OF CHICAGO, HELEN BIRCH BARTLETT MEMORIAL COLLECTION

vival of the fittest," deeply affected attitudes about religion and the meaning of life.

The explosion of activity in the fields of literature and music makes it impossible to mention all the important figures at work during the nineteenth century. Some of the artistic movements had parallel developments in literature and music. Romanticism, for example, was expressed in literature in poetry, historical novels, fantasy and horror tales, and romance and adventure stories by such figures as Lord Byron in England, Johann Goethe in Germany, Victor Hugo in France, and Aleksander Pushkin in Russia. Romanticism and Realism are united in the works of Dickens. The Romantic movement in music includes Frédéric Chopin (who even wrote a piece called "Revolutionary Étude"), Johannes Brahms, Richard Wagner, and Pëtr Tchaikovsky. Impressionism is paralleled in music in the compositions of Claude Debussy. Art criticism flourished, and partisans of both conservative and "modern" art developed.

Art

Communication and interrelationships between parts of the world increased rapidly and dramatically in the course of the nineteenth century, and the chronological structure of this book becomes both more revealing and more logical as we examine the art of this period. In earlier centuries, the chronological organization allowed us to demonstrate the simultaneity of distinctly different developments in art in various parts of the globe and to study broader trends, such as the spread of world religions, in their widest historical context without isolating, for example, Christianity, Islam, and Buddhism. In the nineteenth century, the chronological structure emphasizes the interrelationships that evolved as the world shrank. We can, for example, see how art in Asia began to have an important effect on art in Europe and understand the impact of European developments on art in the United States and Asia. During this period, Japanese prints responded to Western ideas about illusionism and perspective, for example, while at the same time some Japanese aesthetic qualities seen in the prints helped to transform European and, subsequently, American painting. Thomas Eakins certainly knew the paintings of the Realist Courbet and of the Impressionists, although the Impressionists seem to have had less impact than Courbet; Eakins's student Tanner, however, felt more strongly the influence of the Impressionists.

No brief survey of global art can encompass or even refer to every development in every nation. In surveying

9-6 FRÉDÉRIC-AUGUSTE BARTHOLDI

LIBERTY ENLIGHTENING THE WORLD (now known as the *STATUE OF LIBERTY*). 1870–86. Hammered copper over wrought-iron pylon designed by Gustave Eiffel; height from base to top of torch 111′6″. New York Harbor. Commissioned by the French American Union.

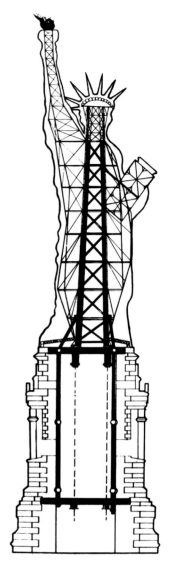

9-7 GUSTAVE EIFFEL

Diagram of the construction of the *Statue of Liberty*.

the nineteenth century, we shall focus on French developments because they had such a potent impact on art and on attitudes about art and the artist in the nineteenth and also in the twentieth century. Many of our current popular attitudes about art have their sources in French nineteenth-century developments. We also shall explore extensively American art and architecture during this century because they provide an excellent example of both the dependence of American art on European innovations and a certain independence that leads into American twentieth-century developments.

The subjects of nineteenth-century European and American painters ranged from historical, mythological, and religious themes to scenes of the everyday life of the working classes. By the end of the century, even the vulgar characters and activities of a popular dance hall had become acceptable as a theme for art (fig. 9-5). The development of exhibitions, such as those at the Parisian Salon and London's Royal Academy, and of art galleries in every major city in Europe and the United States meant that

more and more painters and sculptors were producing works for exhibition and for the general art market. As the percentage of commissioned works declined, there was a growing division between artist and public, and the gulf between conservative and revolutionary artists, who assumed the title of **avant-garde**, gradually became wider. Although the development of photography robbed painters of a traditional means of support, the elite continued to commission painted portraits. Landscape became a particularly popular subject, perhaps because it was such a good vehicle for expressing aesthetic theories. Despite the significance of the Industrial Revolution, scenes of industry were relatively rare.

The popular print developed with the growth of newspapers and periodicals to become a prominent vehicle for social protest (see pp. 424–25). The photograph, invented in the nineteenth century, was used both as a journalistic and

9-8   Malanggan. Tableau, New Ireland. 19th–20th century. Bamboo, palm and croton leaves, painted wood, approx. 8′ high. Museum für Völkerkund, Basel, Switzerland.

as a documentary tool. In sculpture, the heroic monument dominated the century and was considered to be the primary challenge of the sculptor (see figs. 9-6, 9-7, 9-12), but the diversity of the century is seen in examples of traditional architectural sculpture and in works that demonstrate revolutionary attitudes about sculpture (see fig. 9-60). In architecture, new forms were demanded by the dramatically increasing pressure of population and business crowded in great urban centers. Impressive technological and engineering advances made possible the skyscraper, the railroad station, and the great bridges (see fig. 9-45) and monuments, such as the Statue of Liberty, of the later nineteenth century.

In other parts of the world during the nineteenth century, the idea of modernism, so important in the West, was seldom an important issue. In India, China, Japan, the continent of Africa, and elsewhere, local traditions in art continued with little transformation. In the Melanesian island nation known as New Ireland, for example, the masks used in traditional island rituals (fig. 9-8) were not changed by contact with European culture. Similar to the ritual practices in Africa and elsewhere, dancers wore these intricate masks for rituals that commemorated ancestors and initiated youths into adulthood in villages throughout the South Pacific islands. Most of these masks were carved from a single piece of wood; the generous use of openwork, sliverlike projections, and overpainting subdivides the objects into minute geometric patterns that create an elaborate, fragmented appearance.

When they were not in ritual use, the pieces were set up in a tableau at a special house, where they could be seen by Western visitors. Only in the twentieth century did such objects command the attention of Western artists for their brilliant and complicated abstracted designs.

Global communication and contracts, however, meant that there was an increasing awareness of developments everywhere, and some art students from Asia studied in Paris and other Western centers and quickly introduced into their own cultures an interest in the latest Western styles. When Impressionism was introduced into Japan it was equated with modernism, and it thereby won approval from some industrialized and political leaders who were seeking economic parity with the West. In general, however, Western styles had little impact on the well-established local traditions, which were closely attached to notions of Japanese cultural identity. Like the importation of Japanese style into the West, in most cases the Japanese interest in Western style was purely aesthetic. The democratic principles that underlay Impressionism, for example, were not brought into Japan by Japanese artists who had worked in Paris.

The Primacy of France in World Art

Not all the great works of art produced during the nineteenth century were made by French artists, but it was developments in France that gave names to the revolutionary

9-9 HENRI ROUSSEAU

The Sleeping Gypsy. 1897. Oil on canvas, 4'3" × 6'7". The Museum of Modern Art, New York.

GIFT OF MRS. SIMON GUGGENHEIM

nineteenth-century movements in modern art, and much of the new art created in Europe and the United States reflected the latest French styles. The sequence of movements in France was watched with interest, enthusiasm, and, occasionally, dismay, and in the rest of the world it was the French styles that were considered to be "modern." The annual art exhibitions of the French Salon were world-famous and were the ones in which virtually all serious European and American artists desired to be included. To be represented in a Salon could make one's reputation.

Conservative interests dominated the Salon exhibitions, however, and when the Salon jury of 1863 rejected a number of works that we would consider modern (for example, see figure 9-52), there was such an outcry that a special exhibition of the rejected works, known as the Salon des Refusés, was established:

> Numerous complaints have reached the Emperor on the subject of works of art which have been refused by the jury of the exhibition. His Majesty, wishing to let the public judge the legitimacy of these complaints, has decided that the rejected works of art are to be exhibited in another part of the Palace of Industry. This exhibition will be voluntary, and artists who may not wish to participate need only inform the administration, which will hasten to return their works to them. This exhibition will open on May 15. Artists have until May 7 to withdraw their works. After this date their pictures will be considered not withdrawn and will be placed in the galleries.

(Proclamation of the Salon des Refusés, 1863)

The Styles of Nineteenth-Century Art in the West

The basic styles defined in this century receive their names from terms applied to paintings—to French paintings in particular. The new style at the end of the eighteenth century, Neoclassicism, continued in popularity well into the nineteenth century, especially in the arts of architecture and sculpture (see pp. 414–15). It received a special impetus from Napoleon's enthusiastic support for a variation of Neoclassicism known as Empire, which supported his new status as emperor. Soon, however, the rational and lucid order of the Neoclassical style and its belief that art should express universal truths were challenged by a style that might be considered its antithesis, Romanticism. This style, with its expression of spontaneous, strong, and even violent individual feelings, is in part based on a new distrust of rationalism. In architecture, Romanticism, in combination with a new interest in history and historical precedent, helps explain the interest in reviving earlier styles, especially the Gothic Revival (see pp. 426–27), so important in American and European architecture. Some critics have included the Neoclassical style within the general category of Romanticism because of the nostalgic manner in which Neoclassical artists looked back to the past.

In France, Romanticism was challenged by two styles: Academic Art and Realism. Academic Art is the term applied to the conservative and even reactionary art—heroic, moral themes rendered in exact verisimilitude—that prevailed in the French Salon exhibitions and in the French academies. Realism encompasses everyday subjects rendered with emphatic boldness. By denying to art the exalted mission preached in the academies, Realism was considered to be revolutionary. Realist attitudes about subject matter and technique influenced the Impressionists, who set out to represent a momentary impression of light, color, and atmosphere in paintings of contemporary subjects. A number of painters who went through an Impressionist phase but later moved on to other styles are known as Post-Impressionists. The end of the century saw the beginnings of new qualities that would lead to the development of expressionist trends in the twentieth-century. In addition, there were styles in architecture and the decorative arts that can be subsumed in the general category of Victorian, which implies a heavy, elaborately decorated style of sumptuous materials, complex silhouettes, and varied textures and colors. In reaction to the Victorian style and to the industrialization of the arts were the utopian style of the Arts and Crafts Movement as developed by William Morris and the effulgent Art Nouveau style (see fig. 10-8).

Amid the eclecticism and variety of late-nineteenth-century art, some uniquely personal styles emerged that would deeply affect the course of early modern art, including those of the Post-Impressionists and of the self-taught artist Henri Rousseau (1844–1910). Rousseau was working as a toll collector (hence his nickname, "Le Douanier," or "customs officer") when, in his early forties, he retired to devote himself to painting. Such works as *The Sleeping Gypsy* (fig. 9-9) are a synthesis of artistic naïveté, innocent vision, and serious intent. Although *The Sleeping Gypsy* recalls the exoticism of Romantic artists, the direct rendering of the forms, the sparse landscape, and the naive foreshortening create an almost hallucinatory scene. Rousseau insisted that he painted images "from life," but his fantastic scenes appealed to Picasso and the avant-garde of Paris, who befriended Rousseau in 1908. The author Guillaume Apollinaire expressed the modernist attitude toward Rousseau when he observed:

> His paintings were made without method, system, or mannerisms. From this comes the variety of his work. He did not distrust his imagination any more than he did his head. From this came the grace and richness of his decorative compositions.

The Nineteenth-Century Artist

During the nineteenth century in Europe and America, the individuality of the artist as a creative and expressive personality took on an even greater importance. One logical outcome of this inclination was more personalized and revealing self-portraits, as in the portrait Francisco Goya (1746–1828) painted of himself on the verge of death (fig. 9-10). By the end of the century, the revealing personal drama evident in the self-portraits of Vincent van Gogh

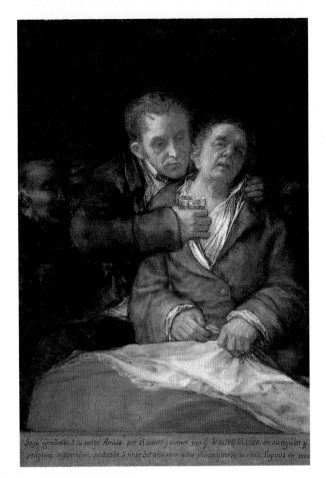

9-10 FRANCISCO GOYA

SELF-PORTRAIT BEING ATTENDED BY DR. ARRIETA. 1820. Oil on canvas, 45½ × 31⅛". The Minneapolis Institute of Arts. The inscription at the bottom of this painting reads: "Goya, in gratitude, to his friend Arrieta, for the skill and care with which he saved his life in his acute and dangerous illness, suffered at the end of 1819 at the age of 73. Painted in 1820."

THE ETHEL M. VAN DERLIP FUND, 1952

9-11. VINCENT VAN GOGH. *SELF-PORTRAIT WITH BANDAGED EAR AND PIPE.* 1889. Oil on canvas, 20⅛ × 17¾". Private collection

9-12 Photograph of Harriet Hosmer in Rome, at work on the clay model for her statue of *Senator Thomas Hart Benton*, c. 1862. The completed work in bronze was the first public sculpture in the state of Missouri. It was placed in Lafayette Park, St. Louis, Missouri, and dedicated in the spring of 1868. Commissioned by a committee appointed by the Missouri Legislature.

9-13 EDMONIA LEWIS

Forever Free. 1867. Marble, height 41¼″. The Howard University Gallery of Art; Washington, D.C.

(1853–1890) is not unexpected, although his particularly dramatic evolution from Impressionism could not have been predicted (fig. 9-11). The modern Western conception of the artist as a political and social liberal and a revolutionary is largely a product of such nineteenth-century personalities as Théodore Géricault, Gustave Courbet, and James McNeill Whistler. In the Renaissance, artists had worked hard to convince their upper-class and noble patrons that they were individuals worthy of recognition and status. In the nineteenth century, artists began to emphasize their bonds to the middle and lower classes. Georges Seurat planned to write a book about his principles and techniques that would enable anyone to paint a masterpiece.

The change in the status and attitude of the artist is also related to the change in the relationship between the artist and the patron. By the beginning of the nineteenth century, there were probably as many artists painting works for their personal satisfaction and for exhibition as there were artists painting particular works on commission from influential and demanding patrons. The one exception to this generalization might be portraiture, but during the second half of this century the development of the photo-

graphic portrait (and the portrait painted *over* a photograph) meant that only a few artists could hope to earn their living painting portraits. The new democratic ideals so important for nineteenth-century developments encouraged a broader clientele in Europe, America, and Japan to begin collecting art, and artists responded to this climate by an increasing interest in everyday subject matter. Consequently, most of the works listed in Chapter 9 will not have any indication of patronage in the caption.

Throughout the nineteenth century, the educational and professional opportunities that were opening for women, however slowly, increased the ranks of women artists. The number of women whose works were exhibited in the annual French Salon swelled from fewer than 30 early in the century to almost 800 in just over seventy-five years. As was true of the eighteenth century (see page 385), many American artists studied and worked in Europe. Among them was a group of women sculptors whom the writer Henry James collectively named "the white marmorean flock." James identified the leader of this group as Harriet Hosmer (1830–1908). A friend of Hosmer's described the artist as a woman who, at the very outset of her life, refused to have her feet cramped by the little Chinese shoes, which society places on us all, then misnames our feeble tottering, feminine grace.

Hosmer, known for her vigorous and independent personality, journeyed to Rome in 1852 to study the revered arts of antiquity and the Renaissance and to be part of an international community of artists. By the end of the decade, her studio was an established part of the European art scene, and she enjoyed a range of patrons from Europe, England, and America.

As a sculptor, Hosmer struggled to cast aside stereotypical and sexist attitudes toward women artists. Her Neoclassical sculptures of women offered nineteenth-century audiences representations of feminine strength, and when she received the commission from the state of Missouri for a colossal statue of Thomas Hart Benton (fig. 9-12), Hosmer wrote,

> Your kindness will now afford me an ample opportunity of proving to what rank I am really entitled as an artist unsheltered by the broad wings of compassion for the sex.

Hosmer's statue of Senator Benton exemplifies the Neoclassical ideal of joining the values of antiquity—here demonstrated by the pose, drapery, and scroll—to subjects of the contemporary world.

Hosmer welcomed another American sculptor, Edmonia Lewis (1845–90), to Italy in the 1860s. Lewis's mother was a Native American from the Chippewa nation, and her father was an African American who worked, in Lewis's words, as a "gentleman's servant." Nicknamed "Wildfire," Lewis spent much of her youth with the Chippewas, but at the insistence of her brother she became a student at Oberlin College. Following an incident of racial violence directed toward her, Lewis traveled to Boston in 1863. There she developed her talent as a sculptor and her views as an abolitionist. *Forever Free* (fig. 9-13) was created shortly after Lewis arrived in Italy; it depicts the moment of the triumph of freedom for African American slaves, whose chains of bondage have just been broken. As a sculptor, Lewis was engaged not only by the theme of her works, which later would be expanded to reflect her Native American heritage, but also by the compositional challenge of creating multifigured groups.

Art Past/Art Present *Looking Beyond the Art: Romanticism*

To understand a culture more fully, comparisons between the visual arts and other cultural manifestations, such as literature or music, can often be helpful. In some periods there may be only tangential connections, but in other instances a revealing consistency in the arts can be discerned: such is the case with Romanticism. The Romantic movement in Europe and America, which flourished in the late eighteenth and the nineteenth centuries, emphasized the importance of the individual and of each individual's personal and imaginative response to the world. Emotion and intuition were held to be as important as (or more important than) reason, which had dominated the previous period and which can be related to Neo-Classical art and the earlier movement known as the Enlightenment. Mysticism or spiritualism also became important, and there was a broad interest in the mysterious, the irrational, and the visionary. It should be clear from this summary that Romanticism in art, music, and literature is an attitude of mind and not a coherent style. Among the artists represented in this book, those who have been identified as Romantic painters are Bingham, Cole,

Constable, Delacroix, Friedrich, Géricault, Goya, and Turner. In architecture, Romanticism is characterized by the return to earlier styles, and especially those of the Middle Ages, such as the Gothic. The picturesque, irregular garden was a Romantic ideal, and the power and sublimity of nature played a role in both Romantic art and literature.

Some of the greatest names in British literature, such as Lord Byron, Coleridge, Keats, Shelley, and Wordsworth, are thought of as Romantics; in other countries the Romantic writers include Balzac, Goethe, Hugo, and Schiller, and, in America, Emerson, Hawthorne, Longfellow, Melville, Poe, and Thoreau. Romantic composers include Beethoven, Berlioz, Brahms, Chopin, Liszt, Mendelssohn, Schubert, Schumann, Tchaikovsky, Verdi, Wagner, and many others. The most obvious trait of Romantic music is the long and expressive melody, and many Romantic composers were inspired in their opera plots and song cycles by Romantic literature. By 1850 Romanticism in art and literature was being challenged by Realism, but in music Romanticism continued until almost the end of the century.

9-14 DAUMIER

FREEDOM OF THE PRESS: DON'T MEDDLE WITH IT (for further information, see fig. 9-33).

The idea that art might be shocking and that many artists are revolutionaries is a modern one; you'll notice that all the works discussed in this section have been drawn from the nineteenth and twentieth centuries. While it could be argued that the majority of earlier works of art and architecture were created explicitly to express the status quo and perhaps even to help institutionalize those who were in power, in the course of the nineteenth century this traditional function for art came into question. Daumier's print, for example, champions the public's right to question and challenge those in power. Degas's colored wax sculpture, with its real fabric and applied hair, is a narrower revolution, for it was an attack on the centuries-old tradition that the best sculpture is carved of marble or cast in bronze.

9-15 DEGAS

LITTLE FOURTEEN-YEAR-OLD DANCER (for further information, see fig. 9-60).

9-16 XU BING *CELESTIAL BOOK*
(for further information, see fig. 10-144).

Xu Bing's Celestial Book, with its invented (but Chinese-like) characters, was exhibited in Beijing during the rather relaxed period before the Tiananmen Square Massacre; after that episode it would not have been allowed because of the manner in which it criticized traditional values by mocking Chinese writings. The idea that the artist is a revolutionary is so widespread in modern society that challenges by artists to the status quo can, in tightly controlled societies such as Communist China, be perceived by the authorities as being as provocative as outright political defiance.

9-17 CÉZANNE *MONT-STE.-VICTOIRE*
(for further information see fig. 9-80).

While some artists, such as Daumier and Xu Bing, seem to be most interested in encouraging political reform, other artists, like Degas, set out to challenge conservative artistic agendas. Cézanne, for example, questioned the traditional western notion of the painting as a window. While we can still recognize the sky, the mountain, the buildings, the road, and the trees, Cézanne's blocky brushstrokes and vivid, repeated colors (notice the purple repeated in the foreground, the green in the sky) unify the pictorial surface, emphasizing that a painting is first and foremost a flat object. Even more important for the future is the way in which Cézanne incorporated more than one viewpoint into his view, an introduction of the idea of time that was important for the later development of Cubism.

9-18 JACKSON POLLOCK *CONVERGENCE*
(for further information, see fig. 10-97).

Jackson Pollock carried Cézanne's revolution even further, for he eliminated all representation from his works, and challenged the idea that the painter should work on a stretched canvas with brushes. By dribbling house paint from sticks onto a length of canvas stretched on the floor, Pollock introduced the idea of the accidental and the automatic into Western art.

▮ QUESTIONS

1. Study the newest art you can find by either visiting local galleries and museums or by studying a recent edition of an art magazine that features contemporary art. What new developments do you find?

2. How are they evidence of the continuing revolutionary nature of art today?

The Continuation of Neoclassicism

9-19 ANTONIO CANOVA

NAPOLEON AS MARS THE PEACEKEEPER. 1803–6. Marble with gilded bronze staff and figure of victory, height 11'. Wellington Museum, London. This work was commissioned by Napoleon, who wanted to be immortalized by Canova, then considered by many to be Europe's greatest artist. The sculpture was bought by the British government and presented to the Duke of Wellington, who had defeated Napoleon at Waterloo.

9-20 JEAN-FRANÇOIS THÉRÈSE CHALGRIN AND OTHERS. ARC DE TRIOMPHE, PARIS. 1806–36. Height 164'. Inspired by ancient Roman triumphal arches, Napoleon decided to commemorate his military victories with this commission, the largest arch ever built. It was not completed until long after his downfall. For one of the sculptures on the arch, see figure 9-26.

How well sculpture conveys political concepts and how quickly the political situation changes are revealed in the monumental representation of Napoleon by Antonio Canova (1757–1822), commissioned by the emperor himself in 1802 (fig. 9-19). Napoleon is represented nude in the guise of Mars, ancient Roman god of war. By the time the sculpture was delivered, in 1811, Napoleon's position had become less secure. The heroic concept no longer seemed completely relevant, and Napoleon decided not to put the work on public display. After Wellington defeated Napoleon, he was given the statue as a trophy of victory, as well as a reminder of how quickly the powerful can fall. It is still displayed in Wellington's home in London.

Throughout the nineteenth century, Neoclassical architecture was popular, especially for public buildings and monuments. The Arc de Triomphe (fig. 9-20) is Napoleon's inflated and grandiose version of ancient Roman triumphal arches, which honored victorious emperors, and its original function was exactly the same. Unfinished at his death, the sculptures added after it was completed honor instead the heroic people of the French Revolution.

The style of Jean-Auguste-Dominique Ingres (1780–1867) in *Jupiter and Thetis* demonstrates the continuing impact of the Neoclassical mode in painting (fig. 9-21). The sculpturesque modeling of the heroically posed Jupiter and the crisp drapery folds of Thetis's garment reveal Ingres's academic training. Painted while Ingres was working at the French Academy in Rome, *Jupiter and Thetis* was sent back to the Academy in Paris. The references to antiquity go beyond the theme, for the pose of Jupiter, the Roman equivalent of the Greek Zeus, king of the gods, was derived from the lost ancient cult statue of Zeus from his temple at Olympia.

9-21 JEAN-AUGUSTE-DOMINIQUE INGRES

JUPITER AND THETIS. 1811. Oil on canvas, 11'4⅝" × 8'5¼". Musée Granet, Aix-en-Provence, France. This painting, based on an episode from the Trojan War delineated in the *Iliad* (I, 493–542), depicts Thetis, a sea nymph and mother of Achilles, pleading with Jupiter to look favorably upon a request she has delivered from Achilles.

9-22 HORATIO GREENOUGH

GEORGE WASHINGTON. 1832–41. Marble, height 12'. National Museum of American History, Smithsonian Institution, Washington, D.C. Commissioned by Congress in 1832, this colossal work was intended for the Capitol Rotunda. Greenough, America's first famous sculptor, was an expatriate who worked in Italy, where his designs were carved by local stone carvers. The *George Washington* was completed and delivered in 1841, by which time the enthusiasm for Neoclassical sculpture in the United States had passed, and the sculpture was poorly received.

HORATIO GREENOUGH, *GEORGE WASHINGTON*, 1840. MARBLE, 345.4 × 259.1 × 209.6 CM. NATIONAL MUSEUM OF AMERICAN ART, SMITHSONIAN INSTITUTION

Created by Phidias, this magnificent sculpture of ivory and gold was considered one of the finest artistic accomplishments of classical civilization.

This lost statue of Zeus was also the inspiration for the monumental sculpture of George Washington (fig. 9-22) by Horatio Greenough (1805–52). In a typical Neoclassical effort to aggrandize and immortalize Washington—to clarify his significance for later generations—Greenough posed the great founder as the most powerful Olympian god. With rhetorical gestures, Washington offers us a sword and points upward in a declaratory manner, much like David's determined Socrates (see fig. 8-27). Most nineteenth-century Americans would not have known Greenough's source, and without this reference, the statue seemed at best ridiculous. The abrupt juxtaposition of Washington's portrait set on an idealized seminude body led to a disappointed reaction from the statue's patrons and the public. Blaming the harsh interior light of the Rotunda of the U.S. Capitol, Greenough had the sculpture moved outdoors, where it proved to be even less appreciated. The history of Greenough's *George Washington* reveals the increasingly rapid manner in which style and attitude can change—an important feature of the modern world. This impressive sculpture, with its monumental scale and commanding composition, continues to convey the heroic and even godlike characteristics often ascribed to Washington during the period of the early republic.

Francisco Goya

9-23 FRANCISCO GOYA

THE EXECUTION OF MADRILEÑOS ON THE THIRD OF MAY, 1808. 1814–15. Oil on canvas, 8′9″ × 13′4″; the figures are life-size. Prado, Madrid. *Madrileños* is the name given to the residents of Madrid. Napoleonic troops occupied Spain from 1808 to 1814, and this painting is one of a pair by Goya that represents an uprising against the French in Madrid on May 2, 1808, and the execution of rebels and a number of innocent victims during the night of May 2–3. This was a decisive act in the consolidation of French power in Spain, and the French commander, Napoleon's brother-in-law Murat, announced that "yesterday's events have given Spain to the emperor." But the riots of May 2 also marked the beginning of Spanish resistance to the French occupation throughout the country (underground warfare is still called guerrilla warfare, from the Spanish term for "little war"). In 1814, after Napoleon was defeated, Goya petitioned the new Spanish government for support to "perpetuate with his brush the most notable and heroic actions or events of our glorious insurrection against the tyrant of Europe." The two paintings were commissioned by the government that same year.

Despite Goya's commission to perpetuate the

most . . . heroic actions . . . of our glorious insurrection,

The Execution of Madrileños on the Third of May, 1808, is a brutal and unsettling painting (fig. 9-23). It emphasizes a confrontation between helpless individuals and the inhuman power of an anonymous authority. The universality of Goya's interpretation overwhelms the specific event of the title. These Spaniards are not heroes but victims—perhaps even

9-24 FRANCISCO GOYA

Great Courage! Against Corpses! c. 1810–15. Etching, 4 × 6" (No. 39 from *The Disasters of War* series). Goya's title for this series was *The Fatal Consequences of Spain's Bloody War with Bonaparte and Other Striking Caprichos*. The titles of the etchings in this series evoke Goya's intent: *With Reason or without It; One Cannot Bear to See This; No One Can Know Why; They Cry in Vain; And There Is No Remedy; This Is Worse, Even Worse, Barbarians!; Cartloads to the Cemetery; Bury and Shut Up; I Saw This; Why?*

innocent victims—rounded up to be murdered by French troops. Goya represents the terror and helplessness they feel as they confront death from a faceless firing squad. More victims are marching slowly up the hill, testifying to the extent of the French brutality. Goya commemorates history while simultaneously condemning war and its effect on the individual.

The simple composition and focused light concentrate our attention on the terror and desperate helplessness of the central figure. The night setting, dramatic chiaroscuro contrast, and right-to-left composition heighten the drama, and Goya's

loose brushstroke emphasizes the writhing movement of the victims. The color scheme is dull, with the exception of the red for blood splashed on the left foreground.

Goya published several series of prints, including a large group now known as *The Disasters of War*. Begun during the Napoleonic occupation and continued in the repressive political period after the French withdrawal, they were not published until 1863, after Goya's death. In some of these prints, the nationalities of the French and Spanish soldiers are clear, but which are the torturers and which the tortured alternates. Other scenes, like

the one reproduced here (fig. 9-24), are less specific; they provide Goya's comments on the terrible inhumanity created by war. Even the title condemns the futility and cruelty of this act. Many of the prints represent atrocities Goya witnessed during the occupation, and his cry of "Enough!" resonates across the centuries. The creation of these prints may have helped the artist deal with his emotions of helplessness, frustration, and sorrow, but the demons he expelled remain to haunt us. The **etching** medium, with its rough, scratchy lines, here serves as an appropriate vehicle for Goya's expression.

Romanticism

9-25 THÉODORE GÉRICAULT

THE RAFT OF THE MEDUSA. 1818–19. Oil on canvas. 16'1" × 23'6". The Louvre, Paris. In preparing for this enormous painting, Géricault read published accounts of the event, interviewed survivors, and visited hospitals and morgues to study dying and dead people.

The momentous *Raft of the Medusa*, by Théodore Géricault (1791–1824), signals a departure in the development of history painting, for its subject is not a heroic event but a needless modern tragedy (fig. 9-25). When the French frigate *Medusa* sank off the African coast, the captain and senior officers commandeered the lifeboats, abandoning 150 other survivors to a makeshift raft. After floating for thirteen days, the fifteen who were still alive were rescued. Géricault represents the moment when they first sight the ship that will rescue them on the horizon. The inexperienced captain of the *Medusa* owed his position to his noble birth and his connections with the French government. Géricault's painting is intended both as a dramatic record of the event and as a condemnation of a government that would allow such a thing to happen. Whereas in the past most works of art that made a political statement were designed to sustain the government in power, Géricault's social and political consciousness demanded that he create a work that was critical.

The precise modeling of the figures and their dramatic gestures and varied poses reflect Géricault's study of the art of Michelangelo and Rubens, while the strong chiaroscuro, diagonal composition, and agitated figurative poses remind us of Baroque painting. But here these visual devices have been adapted to a theme of continuing and uncertain conflict. As the survivors excitedly catch sight of a ship on the horizon, they are in constant danger of

1818–19	Géricault, *The Raft of the Medusa*
1818	Byron, *Don Juan*
1819	Children under nine are forbidden to labor in mills in England

being engulfed by the turbulent sea. Géricault's painting re-creates a frightful, emotional drama.

The Raft of the Medusa introduces us to Romanticism, a new style that challenged the dominance of Neoclassicism in the early nineteenth century. Émile Zola, the French novelist and critic, would help define Romanticism when he wrote,

> A work of art is part of the universe as seen through a temperament.

Romanticism stressed the subjective view of the artist, which meant that it was not dominated by a single, unified style. Romantic artists freely looked to a variety of past art styles, as well as to nature around them, to express their temperament. Opposing the rational and restrained aesthetic of Neoclassicism, Romanticism championed the unbridled spirit of the human imagination. The expression of the artist's feelings and convictions became paramount.

The powerful and contagious emotional surge of Romanticism is evident in the enormous high-relief sculpture, by François Rude (1784–1855), that decorates one of the piers of the Arc de Triomphe (fig. 9-26). An angry and determined figure representing the Genius of Liberty urges the people forward with a vigorous right-to-left movement. Despite the specific title, Rude depicts the soldiers in classical nudity or wearing ancient armor to express a universal theme—humanity's fight for liberty.

9-26 FRANÇOIS RUDE

The Departure of the Volunteers of 1792 (popularly known as *"La Marseillaise"*). 1833–36. Limestone, height about 42'. Arc de Triomphe, Paris (see fig. 9-20). So stirring was Rude's sculpture that it soon received the nickname *"La Marseillaise,"* after the French national anthem, which was written in 1792 and first gained popularity when it was sung in the streets of Paris by troops from Marseilles. Commissioned by the French Government of King Louis Philippe.

Romantic Landscape Painting

9-27 JOHN CONSTABLE

THE HAY WAIN. 1821. Oil on canvas, 51¼″ 73″. The National Gallery, London. Constable's naturalism was in part inspired by his study of the innovations in landscape by Dutch seventeenth-century painters; see Ruisdael's *Dutch Landscape* (fig. 7-55).

This interpretation of English scenery by John Constable (1776–1837) is affectionate, with its simple cart, humble cottage, and a dog standing at the river's edge (fig. 9-27). The composition is unaffected and natural, as if we have accidentally come upon this quintessential English scene. But Constable's painting is unified by the cloudy English atmosphere and by flecks of light and color—surprisingly loosely applied—that re-create the sparkling luminosity of the English countryside after the rain. Despite its naturalistic basis, the work can also be termed Romantic. Constable said that

> painting is for me but another word for feeling.

Here the rush of feeling lies in Constable's love for and exaltation of his native countryside.

In the nineteenth century, landscape painting became a vehicle by which Romantic artists expressed their personal thoughts and emotions. One of the earliest was the German painter Caspar David Friedrich (1774–1840), who wrote:

The painter should depict not only what he sees before him, but also what he sees inside himself. . . . Close your physical eyes so that you see your picture first with your spiritual eye. Then bring forth what you saw inside you so that it works on others from the exterior to their spirit.

Friedrich often encourages a quiet meditation before nature, as in his *Abbey in an Oak Forest* (fig. 9-28), in which a funeral procession of monks is moving slowly past the ruins of a

Gothic structure. The barren, skeletal branches of the towering oak trees, their linear patterns echoing the window tracery of the Gothic ruins, are set against the somber, leaden sky, suggesting the void of death. Friedrich has captured one of the moods of nature, filling it with melancholy by the addition of the procession. Winter and time have blanketed nature and the product of human endeavors. Friedrich and other nineteenth-century landscape artists (see fig. 9-38) sought to communicate the grandeur of nature and to thus inspire an almost religious reverence.

The concept of struggle was also an important theme of Romanticism. The human struggle against the seemingly overwhelming forces of nature is expressed in *The Slave Ship* (fig. 9-29), by Joseph M. W. Turner (1775–1851). This painting, ablaze with a fiery red sunset that almost consumes the activity of the theme, depicts a slave ship heading into a typhoon. Turner's evocative use of color and broad brushstrokes create an urgent, anxious feeling. To lighten the ship's load, the captain inhumanely has thrown overboard his cargo—the slaves. Although we witness their death struggle in the water, the final outcome of the brutal slavers and their ship will be determined by nature, as the ship itself faces the fury of the impending storm.

9-28   CASPAR DAVID FRIEDRICH

ABBEY IN THE OAK FOREST. 1809–10. Oil on canvas, 3′8″ × 5′8½″. Schloss Charlottenburg, Berlin.

9-29   JOSEPH MALLORD WILLIAM TURNER

THE SLAVE SHIP. 1840. Oil on canvas, 35¾ × 48¼″. 99.22. Museum of Fine Arts, Boston.

Japanese Woodblock Prints

9-30 KATSUSHIKA HOKUSAI

THE GREAT WAVE, from *THIRTY-SIX VIEWS OF MOUNT FUJI*. c. 1823–29. Woodblock print, 9½ × 14¾″. Courtesy, Museum of Fine Arts, Boston. The initial impetus behind a *ukiyo-e* woodblock print came from the publisher, who often dictated the subject matter and style. Its creation was the result of close and complex collaboration among a number of individuals. The design, created by the artist-designer, was carved into blocks of wood by a carver, who had to modify the artist's line from the original brush drawing; then it was printed by other specialists. Cooperation was essential, and compromise for aesthetic reasons or to enhance marketing must have been common. The earliest prints were black and white, with color applied by hand. With the development of color printing about 1741, each color was printed from a separately carved block; the coordination of printing so that each color was properly placed was a difficult technical procedure. Commissioned by the publisher.

The particular combination of subject matter and style seen in these two prints is called *ukiyo-e* ("pictures of the floating world"). The term *floating* is here used in the Buddhist sense of something that is transient or evanescent, as experienced in everyday life and especially in the world of pleasure: theater, dancing, love, festivals, and the like. In both examples, we see the fleeting nature of *ukiyo-e*: in one, the rising of a huge wave that enframes a view of Mount Fuji; in the other, the humble but distinctive aspect of the cotton merchants' lane in Tokyo at one moment in time.

The term *ukiyo-e* is especially associated with Japanese woodblock prints. In Japan it is also used more broadly to describe a style that originated in painting and incorporated influences from a number of sources. These sources include the narrative picture scrolls (*emaki*) of the twelfth century, the decorative style brought to its peak by such painters as Sotatsu (see his *byobu*, fig. 7-52b), bold Chinese compositions and brushwork incorporated into the tradition of Japanese Kano painting, and aspects of naturalism drawn from both Japanese traditions and the West. These elements came together in *ukiyo-e*, a new art that satisfied the demands and interests of the merchant and plebeian classes of urban Japan. *Ukiyo-e* prints, which were relatively inexpensive, were readily available for purchase by these new classes of collectors, and their bold colors and familiar subject matter gave them wide appeal.

The printing of single sheets and books had been known in East Asia since the eighth century, but this woodblock technique, traditionally used to produce cheap Buddhist icons, painting manuals, and textbooks, did not fully exploit the medium either technically or aesthetically. During the eighteenth century, however, the new interest in the urban, everyday world and the new market among the moderately well-to-do motivated the swift development of woodblock prints. The prints were mass-produced and responded quickly to changing urban fads and fashions.

During the eighteenth century, most *ukiyo-e* prints were dedicated to the representation of the figure, but as the popular taste for figure prints became more garish in the nineteenth century, some innovative artists-designers turned to urban and landscape subjects. Some of these were produced in series of prints around a central subject, such as *Thirty-six Views of Mount Fuji* by Hokusai (1760–1849) or *Fifty-three Stages of the Tokaido* (a travel guide) and *One Hundred Famous Views of Edo* (Tokyo) by Hiroshige (1797–1858).

Hokusai's *Thirty-six Views of Mount Fuji* holds the viewer's interest by the inventiveness in which Fuji, the sacred Japanese mountain, is in each print incorporated into the Japanese landscape or scenes of everyday life. Often, there are unusual and dramatic juxtapositions, as in *The Great Wave* (fig. 9-30), where the men in the skiff are dwarfed by the huge, clawing wave. The sense of imminent danger contrasts with the calm and majestic shape of the ever-present mountain in the background.

c. 1823–29	**Hokusai, *The Great Wave***
1826	Fenimore Cooper, *The Last of the Mohicans*
1829	Greece wins its independence from Turkey
1830	Berlioz, *Symphonie fantastique*
1830	U.S. population reaches 12.9 million, including 3.5 million African American slaves

9-31 ANDO HIROSHIGE

COTTON GOODS LANE, ODENMA-CHO MOMEN DANA, from *ONE HUNDRED VIEWS OF EDO*. 1858. Edo is an earlier name for Tokyo. Woodblock print, 14⅜ × 10″. Art Institute of Chicago. The pristinely uniform architecture seen here was a particular feature of the *Odenma-cho* ("the cotton-goods merchants' quarter") and was unusual for wealthy Edo merchants. The enclosure of a row of several shops under a single roof is a house form usually reserved for backstreet tenements. The alternating crests and names identify three separate establishments, which are further defined by the low projecting ridges running down the roof face. According to the authorities, the cotton merchants were entitled to use the boxlike structure running along the entire roof as a distinguishing mark. The enclosures on top of the ridge held buckets that trapped rain water to be used in case of fire. Commissioned by the publisher.

CLARENCE BUCKINGHAM COLLECTION 1928.301

Cotton Goods Lane (fig. 9-31) by Hiroshige represents a street in the heart of Tokyo. The care taken with architectural details in the scene is matched in the handling of human activity. Hiroshige has shortened one of the cloth *noren* so that we can peer inside a shop, where the merchants sit among piles of cloth, presumably tallying the day's profits. The subtle disarray of the dress of the two geisha suggests that they are returning from providing entertainment and perhaps sharing drinks with patrons.

Although these artists were contemporaries and were both interested in depicting the transitory, Hokusai's subjects were less varied and particular than Hiroshige's. Hokusai's style is characterized by willful inventiveness and daring organization, while Hiroshige's focus is on the subtleties of a particular place and mood. Most of these print designers were also painters, but interest in their paintings has been eclipsed in the West by the popularity and availability of their prints.

Honoré Daumier and the Political Print

9-32 HONORÉ DAUMIER

RUE TRANSNONAIN, April 15, 1834. 1834. Lithograph, 11½ × 17⅝". This print was published in *L'Association mensuelle*, July 1834. Probably commissioned by the publisher of the periodical.

The dying baby lying under its dead father (fig. 9-32) is the most moving detail provided by Honoré Daumier (1808–79) in his condemnation of the brutality of French governmental policy in dealing with the working classes. The specificity of the title was chosen so that there could be no doubt about the subject. In April 1834, workers in Lyon and Paris, led by the secret Society of the Rights of Man, rioted to demonstrate against harsh working conditions and the passage of a new law forbidding unionization. On the night of April 14–15, a sniper in Paris killed an officer. In retaliation, a number of innocent residents of the sniper's building were killed by the police, including a woman and a child. Daumier's printer, Charles Philipon, wrote of this print:

> This is not caricature . . . it is a blood-stained page in the history of our days, traced by a vigorous hand and inspired by noble indignation . . . he has created a picture which will never lose its worth or duration, even if it consists of only black lines on a sheet of paper

Daumier's print was publicly displayed and was sold in mass quantities in a journal in which Daumier's other political and humorous prints often appeared. Already in 1832, at the age of twenty-four, Daumier had served five months in prison because he had caricatured King Louis Philippe as Gargantua, but this experience did not weaken his determination to make statements through his prints about the moral and political problems and issues of his day.

Daumier made thousands of prints in a long career, and no one was safe from his attacks: radical artists, bored and quarrelsome married couples, naughty children, amateur artists, arrogant connoisseurs, corrupt politicians, and even figures from classical antiquity and mythology were lampooned. One of the popular political periodicals that published Daumier's work was called *La Caricature*. Its name helped popularize the term we use today for exaggerated and humorous representations.

Daumier's heroes most often came from the working classes. In *Freedom of the Press* (fig. 9-33), a youthful typographer, fists clenched, stands ready to defend free speech and the liberty of writers, artists, and publishers to comment on contemporary affairs. The vignette in the right background shows the defeated French king Charles X, who had been driven from power in 1830 in part as a result of criticism leveled by the press. Other European monarchs come to his aid as he is exiled. The sturdy hero looks toward the arrival of the current king, Louis, and his stance indicates that he is again ready to do battle to protect his rights.

The opinions and criticism revealed in popular prints by Daumier and others, however, eventually became too much for the government to bear. In 1835, laws were passed that proclaimed that "Frenchmen have the right to circulate their opinions in published form," but that "drawings" were such an "incitement to action" that complete liberty in this realm was no longer permitted. After this point, Daumier's prints became more humorous and less political.

9-33 HONORÉ DAUMIER

FREEDOM OF THE PRESS: DON'T MEDDLE WITH IT. 1834. Lithograph, 11½ × 17⅝". This print appeared in *La Caricature*, March 1834. Probably commissioned by the publisher of the periodical.

Technique *Lithography*

Lithography ("stone drawing"), invented in Germany in 1798, became the most popular print medium of the nineteenth century, as lithographs came into use to illustrate newspapers and books (fig. 9-34). Lithography is based on the affinity of grease for grease and the antipathy of water to grease. The **print form** is usually a very smooth slab of limestone on which the artist creates a composition using either a greasy crayon or lithographic ink applied with a pen or a brush. The resulting design adheres chemically to the surface of the stone. When the stone is moistened, the water stays only in the nongreasy areas and the greasy ink that is subsequently applied with a roller adheres only to the composition. A dampened paper is applied, stone and paper are put through a press, and a lithograph is created. The technique, spontaneous and relatively cheap, was especially appropriate for the mass media of the nineteenth and early twentieth century because the design can be mechanically transferred from the original print form to additional stones, allowing a large and rapid print edition.

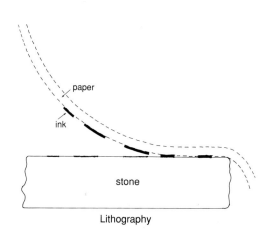

9-34 Diagram of the lithography technique.

Romantic Revival Architecture

9-35 CHARLES BARRY AND AUGUSTUS W. N. PUGIN

HOUSES OF PARLIAMENT, LONDON. Begun 1836; opened 1852; completed 1870. Barry, who won the 1835–36 competition to design the new Houses of Parliament, hired Pugin to help with the detailing. The resulting Gothic Revival complex even has Gothic Revival inkwells and coatracks. Commissioned by Parliament and King William IV.

The decision to rebuild the Houses of Parliament in the Gothic Revival style (fig. 9-35) was not based solely on aesthetic grounds. A more profound cultural and moral basis declared that the Gothic style was historically appropriate, for it had flourished in England during the late medieval period. And, more important for the nineteenth century, the Gothic was perceived as a style that expressed spiritual goodness, truth, and the properly reverent relationship between humanity and God: it thus became the quintessential Christian style. One critic in 1836 described it as

> a style of architecture which belongs peculiarly to Christianity . . . whose very ornaments

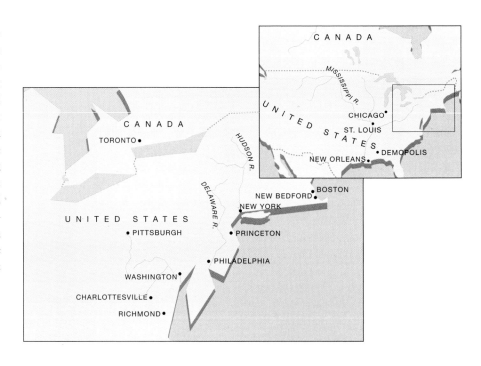

remind one of the joys of life beyond the grave; whose lofty vaults and arches are crowded with the forms of prophets and martyrs and beatified spirits, and seem to resound with the choral hymns of angels and archangels . . . the architecture of Christianity, the sublime, the glorious Gothic.

The Romantic architects of the nineteenth century revived a multitude of historical styles, but each was understood within a specific cultural, moral, and historical context that encompassed both the nineteenth century and the period when the style originated. The Greek Revival in the United States, for example, as witnessed in a house in Demopolis ("City of the People"), Alabama (fig. 9-36), and in hundreds of banks, courthouses, churches, and homes throughout the country, was a response to a movement to find an architectural style appropriate for the political ideals of the young nation. Thomas Jefferson had championed the Neoclassical style (see pages 394–95), but the early nineteenth century turned more directly to the monuments of ancient Athens, history's first documented democracy, for inspiration.

In the United States, the Greek style was gradually supplanted in popularity by the Gothic Revival style. The house by A. J. Davis in New Bedford, Massachusetts (fig. 9-37), is decorated with the architectural vocabulary invented for the great French Gothic cathedrals. The scalloped decoration (cusping) in the eaves and the lacy patterns of the porch posts—cut from wood—are an American version of the gilded ornamentation on a medieval Gothic reliquary. The widespread popularity of this "carpenter" Gothic movement and other revival styles can be explained in part by the cheap pattern books produced by architects and publishers that brought such fantasy within the range of every pioneer with a saw.

1836	**Barry and Pugin, Houses of Parliament begun**
1836	Ralph Waldo Emerson, *Nature*
1837–1901	Reign of Queen Victoria

9-36   Gaineswood, Demopolis, Alabama. 1842–c. 1860. Wood. The heritage of the early-nineteenth-century American enthusiasm for things Greek survives in structures, often by unknown or purely local architects, in the Greek Revival style in stone, wood, and stucco, in coordinating furniture and decorative arts, and in such place names as Demopolis; Troy, New York; Olympia, Washington; and Sparta and Athens, Michigan.

9-37   ALEXANDER JACKSON DAVIS

House for William Rotch, New Bedford, Massachusetts. 1845. Commissioned by William J. Rotch.

American Romantic Painting

9-38 THOMAS COLE

SCHROON MOUNTAIN, ADIRONDACKS. 1838. Oil on canvas, 39⅜ × 63″. Cleveland Museum of Art. Philip Hone, who had served as mayor of New York City, in 1838 wrote, "I think every American is proud to prove his love of country by admiring Cole." Although the landscape seems wild and uninhabited, Cole includes two Native Americans wearing red-feathered headdresses in the foreground.

HINMAN B. HURLBUT COLLECTION

> A landscape is great in its proportion as it declares the glory of God, not the works of man.
>
> (Asher B. Durand, *Letters on Landscape Painting,* 1855)

Enthusiasm for the God-given beauty and richness of the American landscape is the subject of this painting (fig. 9-38) by Thomas Cole (1801–48). A dramatic natural confrontation is emphasized as the sweeping peak seems to soar victorious above the clouds. The season is autumn, when the American landscape offers a special coloristic splendor not found in the landscapes of Europe. Schroon Mountain is located near the source of the Hudson River in the Adirondack Mountains, in New York State, and after visiting there in 1837, Cole wrote:

> The scenery . . . has a wild sort of beauty . . . quietness—solitude—the world untamed . . . an aspect which the scene has worn thousands of years. . . . I do not remember to have seen in Italy a composition of mountains so beautiful or pictorial as this.

Cole's emphasis on the uniqueness of American scenery is significant, for in his paintings, nationalistic spirit was joined to the ideal of the American landscape as a new Garden of Eden—a God-given paradise that would guarantee the nation's future greatness. Cole himself was to write:

> Those scenes of solitude from which the hand of nature has never been lifted affect the mind with more deep-toned emotion than aught which the hand of man has touched. Amid them the consequent associations are of God, the Creator. They are his undefiled works, and the mind is cast into the contemplation of eternal things.

9-39 GEORGE CALEB BINGHAM

FUR TRADERS DESCENDING THE MISSOURI. 1845. Oil on canvas, 29 × 36″. The Metropolitan Museum of Art, New York. Bingham's original title for this work was *French Trader and Half-Breed Son.* There is still debate about the identification of the tethered animal. In a later version of this same theme, however, it is clearly a bear cub.

MORRIS K. JESSUP FUND, 1933 (33.61)

Later, the landscape painter Asher B. Durand wrote that every American family should own a painting of the American landscape, counseling that it should hang in the parlor, over the table where the family Bible was kept.

Earlier American painters had concentrated on portrait painting (see page 392), an art that flourishes in democratic, mercantile societies. In the late-eighteenth and early-nineteenth centuries, however, a number of painters went to Europe to study, returning home full of enthusiasm for Neoclassical history painting (see pp. 396–97). They soon discovered that the intellectual subjects of history painting held little appeal for the American public or patrons. Beginning in the 1820s, American scenery was identified as the ideal subject for American artists, and it was Thomas Cole who was recognized by his contemporaries as the first great painter of the American landscape. Landscape seemed an especially democratic art, for its meaning was immediately accessible to the public, without scholarly reference.

In the painting by George Caleb Bingham (1811–79), our romantic, atmospheric view of the wide American river is momentarily disrupted as a dugout canoe moves downstream, close to us and in sharp focus (fig. 9-39). The trailing smoke from the trader's pipe reveals the speed of the current. The old trader and his son look at us with contrasting expressions—the boy seems bemused, the father serious.

Bingham's composition places the canoe parallel to the **picture plane** to emphasize both the horizontal vastness of the mighty river and its right-to-left movement. A surprising percentage of the painting is given over to the sky, where the sudden luminosity of dawn highlights the wispy clouds. The subdued colors and blurred forms of the atmospheric setting give emphasis to the foreground forms, which are richer in color and pattern and more precisely executed. These forms are in turn blurred in the splendidly painted reflection. Bingham's painting of life on the frontier, an evocation and exaltation of the American West, was intended for an audience in the urbanized cities of the East.

French Realism: Gustave Courbet

9-40 GUSTAVE COURBET

THE STONE BREAKERS. 1849. Oil on canvas, 5′3″ × 8′6″. Formerly Gemäldegalerie, Dresden (destroyed in 1945).

COURBET, GUSTAVE (1819–1877) *DIE STEINKLOPFER*, 1851. OL/LW. EHEM. DRESDEN, GEMÄLDEGALERIE (KRIEGSVERLUST)

The art of painting can consist only in the representation of objects visible and tangible to the painter. An epoch can be reproduced only by its own artists. I mean by the artists who have lived in it. I hold that the artists of one century are fundamentally incompetent to represent the things of a past or future century. . . . It is in this sense that I deny the existence of an historical art applied to the past.

(Gustave Courbet, 1861)

To our eyes, there is nothing offensive about *The Stone Breakers* (fig. 9-40), by Gustave Courbet (1819–77), for the scene of a youth assisting an older man in breaking stones for a roadbed is a **genre** subject, an objective view of life in the mid-nineteenth century. When it was first exhibited, however, *The Stone Breakers* shocked and angered critics and public alike. During the Neoclassical and Romantic eras, the significance of a painting was judged by the didactic virtue of its theme and by the painter's adherence to academic rules of composition and execution. Courbet broke these rules, insisting that the only goal of the artist was to reproduce "objects visible and tangible to the painter." To those schooled in traditional attitudes about art, however, commonplace figures and subjects seemed trite, even vulgar.

Courbet's words were given an even fuller expression in *A Burial at Ornans* (fig. 9-41). We stand at the side of a grave during a funeral in Courbet's hometown, outside Paris. Virtually without comment, Courbet records the visual facts: a priest and attendants reciting prayers, the mourners and a gravedigger, a dog, and a hole in the ground in the immediate foreground. No spiritual promises of an "eternal reward" are apparent here. The emotional pulse of Romantic painting has given way to simple, direct observation.

When Courbet's *Burial at Ornans* and another large painting were rejected by the jury of the Universal Exposition of 1855, an infuriated Courbet withdrew the eleven pictures

1846	Potato famine in Ireland
1848	First convention of women's rights, New York
1848–49	Revolutions in France and elsewhere
1849	**Courbet, *The Stone Breakers***

9-41 GUSTAVE COURBET

A Burial at Ornans. 1849. Oil on canvas, 10'3½" × 21'9". Musée d'Orsay, Paris.

COURBET, *BURIAL*, 1959. REUNION DES MUSEES NATIONAUX RMN

they had accepted and had his own exhibition building constructed, where, with customary bravado, he held a solo show in competition with the official exhibition. The so-called *Realist Manifesto*, which may have been written in part by the Realist writer and critic Champfleury, was actually the introduction to the catalog of Courbet's private exhibition:

The title of "realist" has been imposed upon me, as the men of 1830 had imposed upon them the title of "romantics." Titles have never given a just idea of things; were it otherwise, the work would be superfluous. Without trying to clear up the degree of correctness of a qualification which no one, one must hope, will be asked to understand exactly, I will limit myself to a few words of explanation to cut short any misunderstanding.

I have studied the art of the masters and the art of the moderns, avoiding any preconceived system and without prejudice. I have no more wanted to imitate the former than to copy the latter; nor have I thought of achieving the idle aim of art for art's sake. No! I have simply wanted to draw from a thorough knowledge of tradition the reasoned and free sense of my own individuality.

To know in order to do: such has been my thought. To be able to translate the customs, ideas, and appearance of my time as I see them—in a word, to create a living art—this has been my aim.

In a letter, Courbet wrote to a patron that Realism was

a holy and sacred cause, which is the cause of Liberty and Independence.

Throughout the 1850s, Courbet's paintings gained greater public acceptance, although critics also became more vociferous, accusing him of being a propagandist for leftist or socialist causes. Courbet's redirection of subject matter toward the realism of the commonplace was an important influence on younger French artists, especially Édouard Manet and the Impressionists (see pages 440–41 and 446–51).

Academic Art

9-42 EMANUEL LEUTZE

WASHINGTON CROSSING THE DELAWARE. 1851. Oil on canvas, 12'5" × 21'3". The Metropolitan Museum of Art, New York. When this painting was exhibited in New York in 1852, some 50,000 people paid to see it, and the wide sale of a reproductive engraving made it one of the most famous images in the United States. Leutze worked hard to make his painting authentic, but history buffs will note a number of errors.

Washington Crossing the Delaware (fig. 9-42) exemplifies the Academic approach to history painting, with its blend of a serious subject, historical fact (or what passes for historical fact), artistic manipulation, precise detail, and a carefully digested blend of elements from the High Renaissance and Baroque. Although he had grown up in the United States, Emanuel Leutze (1816–68) returned to his native Germany to spend many years teaching and studying at the influential Academy at Düsseldorf. Many American painters studied there, returning to the United States to advocate the

strict and precisely painted realistic style for which the Düsseldorf Academy and Leutze were famous.

The highest goal of Academic painters was to create history paintings of significant moral import, paintings that would document the past and provide inspiration and guidance for the future. In his painting, Leutze set out to express the significance of Washington's crossing of the Delaware. His success can be judged by the manner in which his treatment continues to capture the public's enthusiasm. It is through this painting that generations of schoolchildren have come to understand a famous national event; rather than represent-

ing history, Leutze's painting has played a role in forming it.

The success of the picture is based on its precise and studied realism, a style that makes its historical theme convincing, and on its striking composition, with a valiant Washington shown standing heroically against the wind.

The Horse Fair (fig. 9-43), by Rosa Bonheur (1822–99), was one of the most famous paintings of the nineteenth century. After creating a sensation at the Salon of 1853, it toured to crowds in the United States for three years. The painting's success can be attributed to its academic realism, which extends from an expert

1850	London becomes the world's largest city (2,320,000)
1850–59	U.S. receives 2.5 million immigrants
1851	**Leutze, *Washington Crossing the Delaware***
1851	First submarine cable, under the English Channel

9-43 ROSA BONHEUR

THE HORSE FAIR. 1853; retouched 1855. Oil on canvas, 8′ × 16′7½″. The Metropolitan Museum of Art, New York. Like many European women artists in the period before 1900, Rosa Bonheur was the daughter of an artist. She and her sister and two brothers all began receiving art lessons while young; Rosa, the eldest and most successful, began to study at the Louvre at the age of fourteen and by nineteen was exhibiting in the Paris Salons. Her works enjoyed great critical and popular success. In 1865, the empress of France awarded her the Cross of the French Legion of Honor, declaring "genius has no sex." The youthful horse trainer in the center, wearing a black cap, may be a self-portrait.

GIFT OF CORNELIUS VANDERBILT, 1887 (87.25)

understanding of animal anatomy (Bonheur went often to horse fairs, disguised as a boy, to draw from the living animals) to the precise rendition of the pebbles in the foreground. The effective composition is the result of numerous studies of details and of the whole design. Most impressive is the powerful movement of the horses and men that surges, almost uncontrolled, across the breadth of this huge painting. Bonheur here modified her usually fine brushstroke for a bolder stroke to enhance the effect of rippling energy, and the natural colors of the horses are heightened by contrast with the brilliant colors worn by the grooms.

Paintings and sculptures of animals were popular during the nineteenth century, in part because they functioned as metaphors for the human content that painters were reluctant to represent. The combination of grace and power in Bonheur's handsome horses communicates an ideal of energy and vitality.

New Materials and Engineering in Architecture

9-44 JOSEPH PAXTON

Detail of the interior, the Crystal Palace, London. 1850–51 (destroyed). Cast iron, wrought iron, and glass, length 1,848'; width 408'. Engraving by R. P. Cuff after W. B. Brounger. Drawings Collection, Royal Institute of British Architects, London. The Crystal Palace was an enormous structure erected to house the Great Exhibition of the Works of Industry of All Nations—the first in a series of nineteenth-century international exhibitions that presaged the world's fairs of our own day. The largest single enclosed volume erected up to that date, it covered almost one million square feet of floor space. It was later disassembled and rebuilt on another site. Commissioned by the Building Committee of the Commissioners of the Great Exhibition of the Works of Industry of All Nations.

The Crystal Palace (fig. 9-44) demonstrates two developments that transformed architecture during the second half of the nineteenth century: the importance of new, artificial materials and the advantages of prefabrication. This huge structure of prefabricated cast-iron membering and glass was made and erected in nine months, proving the speed and economy of such a procedure. The basic module used in the design of the building was not based on aesthetic principles but on a practical fact: the maximum width of the glass that could be manufactured was approximately 4 feet. The cast-iron components were based on the larger module of 24 feet, and no single prefabricated part was allowed to weigh more than a ton. Because it was

9-45 JOHN A. AND WASHINGTON A. ROEBLING

Brooklyn Bridge, New York. 1869–83. Stone piers with steel cables, maximum span 1,595′. John Roebling died in 1869, just as construction on the bridge was beginning, and his son brought his plans for the bridge to completion. Commissioned by the New York Bridge Company, under an act passed by the New York State Legislature.

intended to be a temporary, utilitarian structure (the exhibits of machinery and other works of art and industry were the focus), the references to earlier architectural styles demanded in nineteenth-century buildings were not required. One perceptive critic pointed out that

> here the standards by which architecture had hitherto been judged no longer held good,

but the fact remains that the Crystal Palace was not considered to be architecture with a capital *A*. There was no reevaluation here, as there was with virtually all other nineteenth-century structures of significance, which were endowed with references to traditional architectural styles (see pp. 426–27).

The new technological investigations and accomplishments of the nineteenth century were widely published in books and technical journals, and thus their impact could be immediate and universal. Metal and glass were at first held to be fireproof, but iron proved to be susceptible to melting and collapse in a conflagration. Ironically, the Crystal Palace itself was ultimately destroyed by fire, but only in 1936.

New York City's Brooklyn Bridge, by John A. Roebling (1806–69) and his son Washington A. Roebling (1837–1926), pioneered another new material—steel (fig. 9-45). The advantages of using metal for bridges were first realized in a cast-iron bridge erected in England in 1779. In bridge building, cast iron (an iron alloy that is easily cast but of low tensile strength) was subsequently replaced by wrought iron (a much purer, malleable iron), and then wrought iron was replaced by steel (a malleable iron alloy with very high tensile strength). The Brooklyn Bridge is more than half again as long as any earlier bridge, and its

9-46 GUSTAVE EIFFEL

Eiffel Tower, Paris. 1887–89. Wrought-iron superstructure on a reinforced concrete base, original height 984'; current height 1,052'. Eiffel's design was the winning entry from 700 submissions in a competition to design a temporary structure for the Paris Universal Exposition of 1889, which celebrated the 100th anniversary of the French Revolution. Until the erection of the Empire State Building in 1930–32, the Eiffel Tower was the tallest structure in the world. Commissioned by Monsieur Lockroy, Minister for Trade and the General Commissioner for the Exhibition of 1889.

four huge cables are formed from parallel galvanized drawn-steel wires that were spun in place to create an ultimate strength of 71.5 tons per square inch. But despite the modern technology that made this huge span possible, the dramatic masonry supporting piers were given Gothic arches.

Before he won the competition to build a temporary structure for the Universal Exposition of 1889, Gustave Eiffel (1832–1923) had established an international reputation as an engineer and designer of bridges, locks, and the skeleton for the *Statue of Liberty* (see fig. 9-7). The purpose of his tower (fig. 9-46) was to provide a dramatic and unforgettable symbol for the exposition and, by elevators, to make it possible for fairgoers to have fabulous views of Paris. But Eiffel also set out to design a pleasing structure, and he disguised the underlying modern grid frame on which the work is engineered with sweeping curves and dramatic proportions. Even so, the design was criticized as a monstrosity, and the architect Charles Garnier (see page 438) circulated a petition demanding that it be demolished.

But the most significant development in the later nineteenth century was the invention of the skyscraper (see page 466). As business and population were concentrated in rapidly growing cities, the need for expansion upward became evident. Louis Sullivan, in his *Autobiography of an Idea*, wrote:

> The tall commercial building arose from the pressure of land prices, the land prices from pressure of population, the pressure of population from external pressure.

In 1852, Elisha G. Otis invented the Otis safety elevator, which he demonstrated at a New York industrial fair in 1854. By 1857, the first commercial passenger elevator had been installed in a New York building, and in 1861 Otis made a significant improvement by patenting a steam-powered elevator. Before Otis's invention, the height of a building had been limited by how many flights of steps the owner was willing to make his clients climb. With an elevator, the height was limited only by the potentials of the material available and the economics of tall construction.

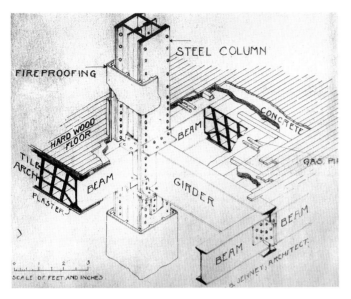

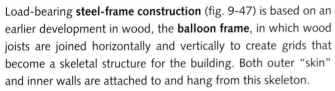

9-47 WILLIAM LE BARON JENNEY

Detail of steel-frame construction, as used in the Fair Store, Chicago. 1890–91.

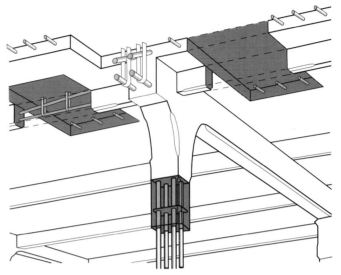

9-48 FRANÇOIS HENNEBIQUE

Diagram of monolithic reinforced-concrete joint; patented 1892.

Load-bearing **steel-frame construction** (fig. 9-47) is based on an earlier development in wood, the **balloon frame**, in which wood joists are joined horizontally and vertically to create grids that become a skeletal structure for the building. Both outer "skin" and inner walls are attached to and hang from this skeleton.

Load-bearing steel-frame construction employs the same method, but the load-bearing members are prefabricated steel I beams. In tall buildings, the steel frame offers several significant advantages. The high tensile strength of steel, for example, makes possible a substantial reduction in both the amount of material needed and the thickness of the walls. In a brick- or stone-walled structure, each story that is added to the height means a significant increase in the thickness of the walls at the base:

It was inherent in the nature of masonry construction to fix a new limit of height; as its ever-thickening walls ate up

ground and floor space of ever-increasing price, as the pressure of population rapidly increased.

(Louis Sullivan, *The Autobiography of an Idea*, 1926)

Steel is much stronger than masonry, and its tensile strength means that the finished building will have the elasticity necessary to allow it to move and respond to the pressure from high winds, a problem in a masonry building, which will topple because it cannot sway.

Reinforced concrete (fig. 9-48), in which concrete is strengthened by embedded wire rods or mesh, was developed in France in the second half of the nineteenth century. The steel gives the concrete an impressive tensile strength. It is a remarkably flexible material and can be formed at the site, during construction, or prefabricated. As is typical of the nineteenth century, this economical new construction method was first used only for utilitarian structures such as mills.

Most urban structures were of heavy masonry (that is, stone or brick) construction, and the taller the building, the heavier the lower stories had to be to support the tremendous weight of the increased height. All this changed with the development of the load-bearing steel cage, based on the new lower price of steel due to the invention of the Bessemer process (1855), and of reinforced concrete.

Late-Nineteenth-Century Revival Architecture

9-49 CHARLES GARNIER

The Opéra, Paris. 1861–75. Commissioned by Emperor Napoleon II as one of the focal points for his rebuilding of the center of Paris. For a model for one of the sculptures chosen to decorate the façade, *The Dance* by Carpeaux, see fig. 9-58; for Marcello's *Pythia*, chosen for the interior, see fig. 9-59.

Many mid- to late-nineteenth-century buildings impress us by their scale, richness of materials, and inventive abundance of historical references. The style of the design for the Paris Opéra (fig. 9-49), by Charles Garnier (1825–98), has been called Second Empire Italianate Neo-Renaissance/Baroque, revealing the eclecticism of this building. More sumptuous than any Baroque structure, it established a standard of extravagant decoration for cultural institutions that would have a wide impact, affecting even the development of the motion picture "palace" in twentieth-century America. The opulence of the exterior, with its sculptures (see fig. 9-58), mosaics, and gilded details, is continued in the interior with a magnificent grand staircase, foyer, and auditorium. Garnier stated his philosophy in pointing out that a

> staircase crowded with people was a spectacle of pomp and elegance

and that

> by arranging fabrics and wall hangings, candelabra . . . and chandeliers, as well as marble and flowers, color everywhere, one makes of this ensemble a brilliant and sumptuous composition.

This is the kind of architecture that is popularly termed Victorian, whether it was built within the empire of Queen Victoria or not.

The courthouse and jail (fig. 9-50) erected in Pittsburgh by Henry Hobson Richardson (1838–86) for one of the world's great industrial centers use a modern version of the Romanesque style that avoids decoration to emphasize mass, weight, and solidity. The heavily **rusticated** walls, corner pavilions, and tall, centralized tower of the courthouse express the enduring authority of law and government. In contrast, the jail offers irregular masses, a lively silhouette, and the unexpected placement of openings, effects that may refer to lawlessness and a lack of order. This "iconography" is not accidental, for the building specifications from the Allegheny County commissioners indicated that

> the buildings should suggest the purpose for which they were intended.

A low bridge, inspired by examples in Venice, allows a secure transfer of the accused to trial in the courthouse. Richardson's particular, personal use of the Romanesque style had a widespread popularity in the

1859	Darwin, *The Origin of Species*
1860	Nine U.S. cities have populations over 100,000
1861	Most of Italy is united as one kingdom
1861–75	**Garnier, the Opéra, Paris**

1880s. Perhaps its sheer weight and architectural presence were reassuring after the disruptive trauma of the Civil War. Richardson's first biographer wrote of the courthouse:

> It is as new as the needs it meets, as American as the community for which it was built. Yet it might stand without loss of prestige in any city in the world.

Richardson himself was most pleased with its massive scale:

> If they honor me for the pigmy things I have already done, what will they say when they see Pittsburgh finished?

In the closing decades of the nineteenth century, a monumental classical style was re-created in the works of America's most popular architectural firm, McKim, Mead, & White. Their white granite Boston Public Library (fig. 9-51) seems like a grandiose Renaissance palace. A row of impressive round arched windows emphasizes the second floor. The inspiration from Renaissance palaces is perhaps not purely aesthetic, for the trustees' commission was for a "palace for the people." A dignified inscription across the facade states the building's public purpose and patrons:

> The Public Library of the City of Boston, Built by the People and Dedicated to the Advancement of Learning.

This is the most important building of a movement sometimes known as the American Renaissance.

9-50 HENRY HOBSON RICHARDSON

Allegheny County Courthouse and Jail, Pittsburgh, Pennsylvania. 1884–88. Richardson died without seeing these buildings completed; when he realized that he was seriously ill, he wrote: "Let me have time to finish Pittsburgh and I shall be content without another day." This illustration reproduces a print of the design Richardson submitted to win the competition for the project. It preserves the original appearance of the entrance portals and the steps, which are today modified. Commissioned by the Allegheny County Commissioners.

9-51 MCKIM, MEAD, & WHITE

Public Library, Boston. 1887–95. Commissioned by the Trustees of the Library.

Édouard Manet

9-52 ÉDOUARD MANET

LE DÉJEUNER SUR L'HERBE (THE PICNIC). 1863. Oil on canvas, 7′ × 8′10″. Musée d'Orsay, Paris.

A commonplace woman of the demimonde, as naked as can be, shamelessly lolls between two dandies dressed to the teeth. These latter look like schoolboys on a holiday, perpetrating an outrage to play the man, and I search in vain for the meaning of this unbecoming rebus. . . . This is a young man's practical joke, a shameful open sore not worth exhibiting this way. . . . The landscape is well handled . . . but the figures are slipshod.

(A critique of *Le Déjeuner sur l'herbe,* 1863)

In *Le Déjeuner sur l'herbe* of 1863 (fig. 9-52), Édouard Manet (1832–83) created a scandal, even at the Salon des Refusés (see page 408). Its iconography is perplexing. We are unashamedly confronted by a female nude, her dress and undergarments thrown down near a basket of luscious fruit in the foreground. She is accompanied by two fully clothed men, while in the middle ground a second woman bathes in a small lake. The visual impact of Manet's style is equally powerful and unexpected, for the startling lack of modeling in the female nude and the large strokes of thick, rich paint had not been seen in earlier French painting. The bold, luscious passages of paint that create the fruit are especially beautiful. In iconography, Manet based his *Le Déjeuner sur l'herbe* on the combination of dressed men and nude women seen in a well-known Renaissance painting in the Louvre, the *Concert Champêtre (Pastoral Concert),* which at the time was thought to be by Giorgione (scholars today attribute it to Titian), while he took the figural composition intentionally from a print after the much-revered

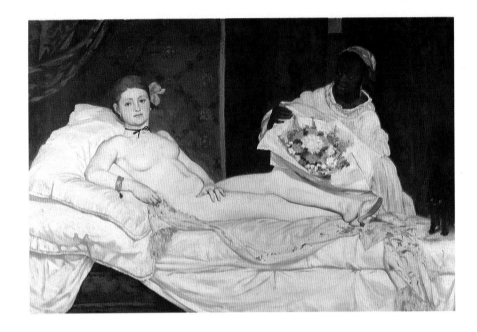

9-53 ÉDOUARD MANET

OLYMPIA. 1863. Oil on canvas, 4'3" × 6'2¾". Musée d'Orsay, Paris. Of Manet's *Olympia*, the later painter Cézanne would say, "Our Renaissance dates from it."

Raphael. Manet's updating of earlier artistic sources may have a deeper social meaning, representing the polarity of French society, with the natural world confronting the artificial, or the painting may simply represent artists picnicking with their models. We shall probably never know the exact meaning or meanings, but we do know that from Manet onward, a new course was set for avant-garde painting of the late nineteenth century, as artists would begin to turn further and further away from prescribed academic rules in painting.

Two years after the French critics and public were shocked by *Le Déjeuner*, they were sent reeling by Manet's entry in the 1865 Salon (fig. 9-53). The scandal revolved around both Manet's methods of painting, with loose brushstrokes and flat areas of color, and his disrespect for proper subject matter. One of Manet's sources was Titian's *Venus of Urbino* (see fig. 6-41), a painting that had helped establish the theme of the reclining nude female figure as a subject for art. But now, in the pose usually reserved for an idealized female

nude, Manet has realistically painted Victorine, a model. In addition, Manet has changed Titian's sleeping dog, a symbol of fidelity, into a lively black cat, a traditional symbol of lust in European art. Titian's servants attend to their work, but Olympia's maid brings flowers—a gift, it would seem, from a grateful or prospective client. Even the title (*Olympia* was a generic term for a lower-class prostitute at the time) suggests the shocking subject of Manet's painting.

Manet did have his champions, however, and one was the noted author and critic Émile Zola. In writing a defense of Manet, Zola pointed out that Manet's paintings are responsive to life, rather than to academic traditions of art:

M. Manet's temperament is dry, trenchant. He catches his figures vividly, is not afraid of the brusqueness of nature and renders in all their vigour the different objects which stand out against each other. His whole being causes him to see

things in splotches, in simple and forceful pieces. . . . Don't bother looking at the neighboring pictures. Look at the living persons in the room. Study the way their bodies look against the floors and walls. Then look at M. Manet's paintings: you will see that there lies truth and strength.

Manet's devotion to painting form as he saw it, irrespective of its meaning, is summarized in Zola's comments as one of Manet's subjects:

I remember posing for hours on end. . . . Now and again, half dozing as I sat there, I looked at the artist standing at his easel, his features taut, his eyes bright, absorbed in his work. He had forgotten me; he no longer realized that I was there.

When Manet died in 1883, Zola, Degas, and Monet all served as pallbearers. Renoir and Pissarro paid their respects, and even the reclusive Cézanne came to Paris from Provence.

Early Photography and Photographic Technique

9-54   NADAR (GASPARD-FÉLIX TOURNACHON)

GEORGE SAND. 1864. Albumen print, 7⅞ × 6¼". George Eastman House, Rochester, New York. "George Sand" was the pen name of Aurore Dupin, a French novelist and feminist.

Nadar's portrait of George Sand (fig. 9-54), with its controlled lighting and careful attention to pose and detail, was part of a series that included the major French literary and artistic figures of the mid-nineteenth century. That such a series should be produced is not novel, but that it was produced using the relatively new photographic medium greatly assisted the legitimization of photography. Nadar (1820–1910) pioneered the use of interior studio lighting in portraits that communicated the dignity of his sitters.

One of the components of photography (from the Greek *photo*, "light," and *graphis*, "to write" or "to describe") dates back centuries. The **camera obscura** (from the Latin, meaning "dark room") was an enclosed box with an opening at one end. Rays of light passing through the opening projected an inverted image on the opposite wall. The camera obscura had

been in use since the Renaissance, primarily as an aid in understanding perspective. Artists traced the projected image inside the "camera." What was lacking, however, was a method to "fix" that image, a process whereby it could be made permanent. In the early eighteenth century, it was discovered that silver salts were light sensitive, and, building on this and other, more recent advances, Joseph-Nicéphore Niépce in 1826 created the first photograph using a camera obscura and a pewter plate coated with bitumen, a light-sensitive substance. Niépce's first photograph required an eight-hour exposure time.

In 1829, the elderly Niépce formed a partnership with Louis Daguerre, who, in 1837, successfully produced the first **daguerreotype**, which used a chemically treated silver-plated sheet of copper to retain the image. The result was a far clearer image than Niépce's, with a greatly reduced exposure time. Improvements in the next decade made the daguerreotype practical, with an exposure time of 30–60 seconds. Daguerre's excited claim,

> I have seized the light, I have arrested its flight,

announced the beginning of modern photography.

Developments in photography quickened. In 1839, William Henry Fox Talbot, a British scientist, invented the photographic negative, allowing multiple prints to be made from the same exposed plate, and by midcentury glass-plate negatives were being used to produce remarkable sharp images. Our illustration (fig. 9-55) shows a modern version of a camera.

The early relationship between photography and art was, at best, a difficult one. Some photographers, such as Oscar Rejlander (1813–75), sought to make photography an art by copying the traditional themes found

9-56   OSCAR REJLANDER

THE TWO PATHS OF LIFE. 1857. Combination albumen print, 16 × 31″. George Eastman House, Rochester, New York. To achieve this tableaulike effect, Rejlander photographed the background and each of the figures separately. These thirty negatives were then printed on one photographic paper.

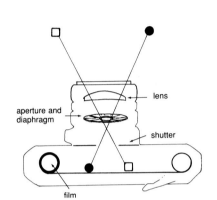

9-55   Diagram of a modern camera.

in contemporary Academic Art. *The Two Paths of Life* (fig. 9-56) represents an allegorical subject. As a photograph, it is impressive for its size and technical achievement, for it is a combination of thirty negatives individually printed on a single sheet of paper. The young men on each side of the elderly father must choose between a life of virtue or of vice. Such an overtly theatrical subject was related to the publicly accepted values of Academic Art (see pp. 432–33). Here photography was trying to "copy" painting to win public acceptance.

It was, however, in portraiture that photography found its most immediate and popular use. The reduced exposure time and affordable price made photographic portraits available to almost everyone. Julia Margaret Cameron (1815–79) developed a distinctive style that emphasized the face of the sitter (fig. 9-57). Cameron was fully aware that photography is not just a medium that reproduces reality. Speaking of her portraits, she wrote:

9-57   JULIA MARGARET CAMERON

ALFRED LORD TENNYSON. 1865. Silver print, 10 × 8″. Royal Photographic Society, London. Cameron, who began photography only in her late forties, after she received a camera as a gift, was primarily self-taught. The poet Tennyson was a friend and neighbor.

When I have such men before my camera, my whole soul has endeavoured to do its duty toward them in recording faithfully the greatness of the inner man as well as the features of the outer man. The photograph thus taken has been almost the embodiment of a prayer.

Late-Nineteenth-Century Sculpture

9-58. JEAN-BAPTISTE CARPEAUX.

The Dance. 1867–68. Plaster model, height 15′. Musée de l'Opéra, Paris. Commissioned by Charles Garnier, the architect of the Opéra.

9-59 MARCELLO (ADÈLE D'AFFRY, DUCHESS CASTIGLIONE-COLONNA)

Pythia. 1870. Bronze, height 9′6″. The Opéra, Paris. "Marcello" was the pseudonym used by a talented and successful female sculptor who exhibited at the Paris Salons beginning in 1863. This work was shown at the 1870 Salon, where it was purchased by Charles Garnier to decorate the Grand Foyer of the Paris Opéra (see fig. 9-49).

As architectural sculpture, *The Dance* (fig. 9-58), by Jean-Baptiste Carpeaux (1827–75), is part of a tradition that includes the Parthenon and Gothic cathedrals (see figs. 3-77, 4-97). Charles Garnier designed the Opéra (see fig. 9-49) with large reliefs by the main entrances representing the various arts. Carpeaux, however, went beyond Garnier's intention, making his figures virtually freestanding, an effect further enhanced by their energetic movement. The exuberant, winged male allegory of Dance leaps upward and outward, while the smiling female nudes encircle him, moving outward into our space in a dance. Carpeaux's allegory communicates the joy of dancing, but originally its nudity shocked contemporary Parisians, who demanded its removal.

Movement conveys a different emotional state in Marcello's *Pythia*, who was the oracle at the sanctuary of

9-60 EDGAR DEGAS

LITTLE FOURTEEN-YEAR-OLD DANCER. c. 1881.
Wax, silk, satin ribbon, and hair, height 39″.
Mellon Collection. Degas's model was a
Belgian girl studying at the Opéra in Paris.

Apollo at Delphi and, therefore, the most important prophetess of the ancient Greek world (fig. 9-59). After breathing fumes emanating from the earth, the Pythia, who was believed to be possessed by Apollo, would answer queries and predict future events, employing dramatic gestures and language that were often incomprehensible. Marcello (1836–79) gives the beautiful young woman a pose that conveys her convulsed state. As she jerks forward, her breasts swing out to either side. The smoothness of the flesh is sharply contrasted with the multiple drapery folds and the unruly, flying hair. The snakes hidden in her hair, attributes of Apollo, startle the viewer. *Pythia* is a convincing representation of Greek religious ecstasy as it was understood during the nineteenth century.

Little Fourteen-Year-Old Dancer (fig. 9-60), the only sculpture Edgar Degas (1834–1917) ever exhibited, is now one of his most popular works, and a number of bronze casts, with real cloth tutus and satin ribbons, were produced after his death and are visible in museums. Degas's original is of wax, a material used for popular sculptures that were meant to be intensely realistic, combined with real fabric and hair (this is the same technique still in use for the naturalistic figures seen in wax museums around the world). Degas followed the popular tradition by coloring the wax to resemble flesh, and he heightened the illusionistic reality of the figure by using a silk faille bodice, a tutu of tulle and gauze, fabric ballet slippers, and a satin ribbon to tie back a wig of real hair partially covered with wax. Degas's appropriation of a multimedia technique that mimics the world of reality is consistent with the attitudes of the French Realist and Impressionist painters. By creating a sculpture that had the colors and textures of reality, he, like the Impressionists, was questioning the relationship between vision and art.

When Degas's sculpture was shown at the Sixth Independent Exhibition in 1881, the critics recognized its novelty but received it with hostility because the model was not attractive:

> He chooses her from among the most odiously ugly; . . . she is sturdy and carefully studied, but what is the use of these things in the art of sculpture? Put them in a museum of zoology, anthropology, or physiology, fine; but, in a museum of art, forget it!
>
> (Nina de Villars, 1881)

> I do not always ask that art be graceful, but I do not believe that its role is to represent only ugliness.
>
> (Elie de Mont, 1881)

> . . . a dancer in wax of a strangely attractive, disturbing, and unique Naturalism . . . . The vicious muzzle of this young, scarcely adolescent girl, this little flower of the gutter, is unforgettable.
>
> (Jules Claretie, 1881)

The modernity of Degas's work did not go unnoticed, however, as Joris-Karl Huysmans wrote in 1883:

> The terrible realism of this statuette makes the public distinctly uneasy, all its ideas about sculpture, about cold, lifeless whiteness [compare fig. 9-22], about those memorable formulas copied again and again for centuries, are demolished. The fact is that on the first blow, M. Degas has knocked over the traditions of sculpture, just as he has for a long time been shaking up the conventions of painting.

Impressionism

9-61   CLAUDE MONET

IMPRESSION-SUNRISE. 1872. Oil on canvas, 19½ × 25½". Musée Marmottan, Paris. When their paintings were rejected for the Salon exhibitions, a group of painters, some of whom we today classify as Impressionists, decided to hold independent exhibitions. The first of a series of eight such exhibitions was held in Paris in 1874; it included this painting. The exhibition was sponsored by a group that called itself the Anonymous Society of Painters, Sculptors, Engravers, Etc., a title that indicates the diverse nature of the group's members, who had banded together to create independent exhibitions and not because of any notion of stylistic unity. Monet's painting *Rue St.-Denis Festivities on June 30, 1878* (see fig. 9-2) was included in the Fourth Independent Exhibition, in 1879.

Impressionist paintings such as Monet's *Impression-Sunrise* engage us immediately by their subtle depictions of nature (fig. 9-61). Here Monet's representation of the interaction of light, atmosphere, and color heightens our awareness of the beauty in the seascape at dawn. But it is important to realize that Monet did not set out to paint a beautiful picture.

His goal was to create a painting that recorded reality as he saw it. As an Impressionist, he wanted to capture in paint the visual effect of reality as it appeared to him at that moment. Monet was especially sensitive to transitory effects of color—how color changes in response to shifting light and varying atmospheric conditions. In *Impression-Sunrise*, the combination of

the moving surface of the water and the red/orange rays of the sun provides a perfect vehicle for his demonstration.

Impressionism had a strong scientific basis, although this is not immediately obvious in looking at Impressionist paintings. A critic of the First Independent Exhibition said that Monet, Renoir, Degas, and Morisot should be called by the

9-62   CLAUDE MONET

GARE ST.-LAZARE, PARIS. 1877. Oil on canvas, 32½ × 39¾". Fogg Art Museum, Harvard University, Cambridge, Massachusetts. This painting was exhibited at the Third Independent Exhibition, in 1877.

MAURICE WERTHEIM COLLECTION

new term *impressionists*. They are impressionists in the sense that they render not the landscape, but the sensation produced by the landscape.

The use of the term *Impression* by Monet in his title and the painters' subsequent adoption of the term *Impressionism* suggest the influence of new theories about the physiology of perception. The new color theory emphasized the presence of color within shadows and, in asserting that there was no black in nature, inspired the Impressionists to ban black from their palette. In addition, Impressionism was based on an understanding of the inter-

9-63 AUGUSTE RENOIR

A LUNCHEON AT BOUGIVAL (now known as THE LUNCHEON OF THE BOATING PARTY). 1881. This work was included in the Seventh Independent Exhibition, in 1882. There have been many attempts to identify the figures in this painting. All authorities agree that the woman on the left is Aline Charigot, who in 1890 would become Renoir's wife; their son Jean Renoir, the film director, was born in 1893. The man behind her is probably Alphonse Fournaise, who built the restaurant along the Seine where the luncheon is taking place and whom Renoir often paid in paintings because the artist was frequently short of cash. The man in top hat at the rear is probably Charles Ephrussi, editor of the art journal *Gazette des Beaux-Arts* and an early admirer and collector of the Impressionists. The woman in black with her hands raised has been identified as Jeanne Samary, an actress with the Comédie-Française and a frequent model for Renoir; Ellen Andrée, another actress, has been identified as the woman in the right foreground. The man in the straw hat in the right foreground is the Impressionist painter Gustave Caillebotte. Independently wealthy, Caillebotte collected the works of his fellow Impressionists, and when he died prematurely at the age of 46 in 1894, he left his collection to the French State. The Impressionists were still so controversial, however, that many conservative painters argued against the bequest, and in the end the state agreed to take only about half the paintings; today Caillebotte's bequest forms the foundation for the splendid Impressionist collection at the Musée d'Orsay in Paris.

PIERRE AUGUSTE RENOIR (1841–1919), *LUNCHEON OF THE BOATING PARTY*, 1881. OIL ON CANVAS, 51 × 68 IN. (129.5 × 172.7). SIGNED AND DATED. ACQUIRED 1923. THE PHILLIPS COLLECTION, WASHINGTON, D.C.

related mechanisms of the camera and the eye: just as a photograph is created by light as it passes through a lens to make an impression on light-sensitive paper, so is our vision the result of the light and color that create an "impression" on the back surface of the eyeball. By embracing the principle that subject matter is less important than depicting what is perceived and by determining

that painting should represent as closely as possible what the eye sees, the Impressionist painters are clearly related to the earlier Realism of Courbet and the innovations of Manet (see pp. 430–31 and 440–41). Their works look very different from Courbet's and Manet's because of their scientific interest in how the eye sees and because of their determination to capture quickly

the richness of color that exists in nature, whether in light or in shadow.

Monet's emphasis on painting visual reality means that his subjects are scenes or views of the world around him, but it is not accidental that he was one of the first painters of the modern urban cityscape. By painting the city streets and the railroad station, as the *Gare St.-Lazare* (fig. 9-62),

Monet emphasized the actuality of modern life. In the railroad station, the open air in the background interacts with the light that filters down through the glass roof and the billowing smoke of the engines to provide another appropriate vehicle for Monet's investigation of the ever-changing patterns of light, color, and atmosphere. An Academic painter would never have chosen such a subject but, if required to paint it, would have rendered the clouds of smoke in tonalities of gray. Monet sees not merely gray but shades of blue and lavender as well.

Although Auguste Renoir (1841–1919) embraced the ideas and employed the techniques of the Impressionists, he was interested in human life and relationships, which led him to favor compositions with human figures rather than landscapes. One of his most popular works is certainly *A Luncheon at Bougival*, with its everyday subject, casual composition, strong strokes of arbitrary color, and bold **impasto**—the latter is especially evident in the beautiful shimmering glasses and bottles of wine on the table (figs. 9-63, 9-64).

A Luncheon at Bougival was singled out for praise by critics when it was exhibited in the Seventh Independent Exhibition in 1882, and one critic captured the contemporary, momentary quality of Renoir's subject in writing that the painting is:

9-64 AUGUSTE RENOIR
A Luncheon at Bougival, detail.

a charming work, full of gaiety and spirit, its wild youth caught in the act, radiant and lively, frolicking at high noon in the sun, laughing at everything, seeing only today and mocking tomorrow. For them eternity is in their glass, in their boat, and in their songs.

It was this emphasis on the momentary and the everyday that made paintings such as this one unacceptable to the Salon juries, who favored history paintings of literary subjects that had been executed with controlled academic technique.

Technique *Impressionism*

To capture the subtle effects of ever-changing light, Monet and the other Impressionists painted outside, on the spot, working quickly with loose, bold strokes of color to catch the impression of color in nature before the light changed. The increased brightness of Impressionist paintings (one critic even complained that they made his eyes hurt) was in part made possible by the use of a canvas covered with white underpainting rather than the beige, tan-reddish, or even darker ground that had been traditional since the Renaissance. In addition, an invention of the Industrial Revolution—the collapsible, sealable tube for paint—

made it practical for the Impressionists to work outside, while the development of synthetic pigments meant that the intense colors they needed were no longer prohibitively expensive. Monet applied paint in rich, thick strokes of virtually pure color, without black. The bold physical presence of these strokes and the heightened color emphasize the surface of the painting. Monet also used a painting stroke that maximized accidental effects of color. By dipping a relatively wide brush into two or more pigments, he allowed the colors to blur and blend as the brush stroked the canvas.

Edgar Degas, Berthe Morisot, and Mary Cassatt

9-65   EDGAR DEGAS

The Rehearsal. c. 1873–74. Oil on canvas, 18 × 24 ″. Fogg Art Museum, Harvard University, Cambridge, Massachusetts.

Edgar Degas disliked being referred to as an Impressionist and preferred to call himself a realist or an independent. His work nevertheless demonstrates many similarities to Impressionist works, and he exhibited in several of the Independent Exhibitions. Degas's realism is in part revealed by his subject matter, for, no matter how romantic we may find his representations of ballerinas today, they were considered neither an appropriate nor a beautiful theme for art in his own day. He was often criticized for picking unattractive dancers by critics who did not realize that, like the other Impressionists, he was emphasizing the realities of modern life. He also shared with the Impressionists a

taste for strong and even arbitrary color, despite the fact that most of his work represents figures in rather subdued interiors. The subtlety of natural light in an interior space provided him with a distinct challenge.

In addition to his concern with light and color, Degas had a special interest in the interaction between movement and composition. One contemporary critic wrote that

> Degas continues to be passionately devoted to movement, pursuing it even in violent and awkwardly contorted forms.

He found that movement, especially the repeated, choreographed movement of dancers onstage or in rehearsal, had a greater intensity

when seen from an unexpected viewpoint. In *The Rehearsal* (fig. 9-65), the strong diagonal recession of the dancers' parallel arms and legs and of the windows in the room creates a thrusting perspective; this in turn is balanced by the empty space in the right foreground. The broad brushstrokes reemphasize the pictorial surface. The influence of Japanese prototypes (see fig. 9-3) for Degas's work is evident in the diagonal recession and in the cutting off of the forms by the edges. Degas's peculiarly realistic viewpoint was discussed by one of his friends, Edmund Duranty, who published a pamphlet, *The New Painting*, in 1876. Duranty pointed out how our visual field is limited by

> the frame that endlessly accompanies us . . . cutting off the external view in the most unexpected ways, achieving that endless variety and surprise that is one of reality's greatest pleasures.

We can see the same unusual viewpoint and the compositional motif of the strong diagonal thrust cut off by the edges in *Marine* (fig. 9-66), by Berthe Morisot (1841–95). When this work was shown in the First Independent Exhibition, a critic remarked,

> What a lovely vagueness [there is] in the distance at sea where the tiny points of masts tilt!

Morisot, who once wrote,

> My ambition is limited to the desire to capture something transient,

remains true to Impressionist principles in striving to capture the strong visual qualities of an actual view. The parasol shields the face of the woman—Morisot's sister Edma, also a painter—and as a result her features are left a blur; her identity is less important her function as a colored form within the composition. Light reflects from the warm brown of the stone railing to create a pink shadow on her white dress.

Mary Cassatt (1845–1926), an American who trained in France and spent most of her life working there, exhibited in several of the Independent Exhibitions. In writing about works by Cassatt at the Sixth Independent Exhibition in 1881, a critic defined Impressionist practice:

> Like her brothers in independence, Manet and Degas, Cassatt works relentlessly to bring her eyes to a state of sensitivity, nervous excitement, even irritation, so she can seize the smallest flicker of light, the smallest atom of color, and the slightest tint of shadow.

Another critic, however, voiced the frequent complaint that Impressionist paintings were unfinished, lamenting that Cassatt had changed her style and was now

> aspiring to the partially completed image.

Cassatt's *The Boating Party* (fig. 9-67) reveals the inspiration both of Degas and of Japanese prints in the realistic but unexpected viewpoint it enforces. We are behind the rower, and his dark, bold silhouetted form sets off the pastels of the rest of the composition. Cassatt maximizes realism in the partial profile of the rower and the foreshortening of the child's head. Neither is an attractive view, but both are realistic and skillfully executed. Large areas of unmodeled color and the potent compositional shapes of the green interior of the boat and the partial view of the sail emphasize the two-dimensional quality of her composition. In the greater solidity with which she endows her figures, Cassatt reveals her independence within the Impressionist movement.

c. 1873–74	**Degas, *The Rehearsal***
1873	Jules Verne, *Around the World in Eighty Days*
1874	Women's Christian Temperance Union is founded

9-66 BERTHE MORISOT

MARINE (THE HARBOR AT LORIENT). 1869. Oil on canvas, 17⅛ × 28¾". National Gallery of Art, Washington, D.C. Berthe Morisot, one of the founders of the Impressionist movement, exhibited in seven of the eight Independent Exhibitions, and her works were also accepted at many of the Salon exhibitions. The artist presented this work to Manet after he admired it. After her death in 1895, a large exhibition of her work was arranged by Monet, Renoir, Degas, and the poet Stéphane Mallarmé.

AILSA MELLON BRUCE COLLECTION

9-67 MARY CASSATT

THE BOATING PARTY. 1893–94. Oil on canvas, 35½ × 46⅛". National Gallery of Art, Washington, D.C.

American Realism: Thomas Eakins and Henry Tanner

9-68 THOMAS EAKINS

Portrait of Dr. Samuel Gross. 1875. Oil on canvas, 8′ × 6′6″. Jefferson Medical College of Thomas Jefferson University, Philadelphia. Eakins's realistic portrayal of surgery at Jefferson Medical College reveals how medical practice has changed. In Eakins's day, surgeons operated in their street clothes, and operations were scheduled between 11:00 A.M. and 3:00 P.M. to take advantage of the daylight in the college's amphitheater.

To Thomas Eakins (1844–1916), the Philadelphia physician Samuel Gross was a heroic figure. Gross was a respected surgeon and professor at Jefferson Medical College and a physician with an international reputation. A pioneer in using new techniques in surgery, he was an inspiring educator, teaching medical students both surgical procedures and the human purpose that stood behind the medical profession.

Gross specifically emphasized the significance of clinical instruction, and Eakins represented him in the operating amphitheater at work (fig. 9-68). He is performing an operation in which he specialized, a new, lifesaving treatment for osteomyelitis (infection of the bone), when the diseased bone is cut away. At the same time, he is also teaching, and Gross looks up from the incision in the thigh of the patient, an expression of intense concentration on his face as he searches for words to convey to aspiring doctors the significance of his life's work. He holds a bloody scalpel, the sudden sight of which makes the elderly woman to the left, most likely the patient's mother, cringe.

Eakins's light is focused and concentrated, and the powerful chiaroscuro contrast makes Gross, teacher and surgeon, a dramatic figure. The sharp overhead light directs our attention to Gross's head, silhouetting it against the dark background. The craggy features of the face are emphatically three-dimensional, stressing the serious line of the mouth and throwing the eyes into meditative shadow. Eakins emphasizes the light as it catches Gross's bushy hair and vigorous sideburns. This visually electrifying effect suggests that Eakins is searching for a concrete metaphor for the intensity of Gross's thoughts. The original painting has an overall warm harmony, the result of red underpainting, which unifies and heightens the limited palette, with its strong blacks, flesh tones, and areas of white. Punctuation marks of red draw our attention to the pen of the clinical recorder, the incision, and the bloody hand and scalpel of the surgeon. In contrast to the abstract treatment of Gross's head, his hand and scalpel jump out because they seem to be exactly in focus. Eakins, himself a photographer, seems to have thrown the other parts of his composition out of focus (note especially the loose painting of the instruments in the immediate foreground) to draw attention to the skilled hand and its tool, making them the focal point in his composition. The contrast in treatment between the head and hand is not accidental: while the physical aspect of Gross's accomplishment is completely comprehensible, the workings of his intellect cannot be discerned.

Eakins painted *Portrait of Dr. Samuel Gross* specifically to submit to the arts section at the Centennial Exposition, to be held in Philadelphia in 1876. It was rejected, apparently because the subject was not considered appropriate; other, less significant works by Eakins were accepted. Through the influence of Gross, the painting was exhibited in the medical department of the exposition.

The African American painter Henry O. Tanner (1859–1937) studied with Eakins at the Pennsylvania Academy from 1880 to 1884, but his mature style merged Eakins's realism with stylistic effects learned from the French Impressionists. Tanner moved permanently to Paris in 1891; in 1896, he received an honorable mention at the Salon; and in 1897, his work was awarded a gold medal. In *The Banjo Lesson* (fig. 9-69), the choice and interpretation of the theme grow from Eakins's example, but the lighter palette, softer light, and more delicate brushstroke reveal the influence of the new French style of Impressionism.

9-69 HENRY O. TANNER

THE BANJO LESSON. c. 1893. Oil on canvas, 48 × 35". Hampton University Museum, Hampton, Virginia. Tanner was the first African American artist to achieve an international reputation.

Auguste Rodin

9-70   AUGUSTE RODIN

THE BURGHERS OF CALAIS. 1884–86. Bronze, height 6′10½″. Hirshhorn Museum and Sculpture Garden, Smithsonian Institution, Washington, D.C. In 1884, the city of Calais in northern France commissioned Rodin to fashion a public monument that would honor six leading citizens (burghers) who, in 1347, had offered themselves as hostages to the English king Edward III, who had laid siege to the city. The burghers were ready to sacrifice their lives if their city would be spared. Edward III was so impressed with their courage that he spared both the burghers and Calais.

Auguste Rodin (1840–1917) was commissioned to create *The Burghers of Calais* (fig. 9-70) as a public monument that would display the courage and civic virtue of the Calais burghers. But the work disappointed many at first because it lacked the overtly heroic antique references that then dominated public sculpture. Rodin's re-creation of the six hostages, with its realism and psychological honesty, however, played an important role in bringing a fresh vision of the human figure to late-nineteenth-century sculpture. From his study of the works of such sculptors as Donatello and Michelangelo, Rodin understood how gesture and expression could reveal an inner psychological state. Here the individual burghers betray philosophical questioning, acceptance, defiance, and sorrow. Through Rodin's sculpture, the burghers are revealed to us as human beings like ourselves, not idealized superheroes.

To understand better the impact of Rodin's work, we must keep in mind that Neoclassical and Romantic attitudes still dominated public sculpture. Rodin's physical and psychological naturalism seemed to run counter to critical and public taste, and the psychological depth of Rodin's work was missed by many critics.

Rodin's *Monument to Balzac* (fig. 9-71) is an audacious sculpture in both theme and execution. The novelist is shown wrapped in the heavy robe in which he worked late at night. His dramatic posture and penetrating facial features vividly communicate the fury of creative inspiration. Balzac's face and massive robe seem to be emerging from the plaster, from the raw material from which the sculpture was first formed. This unfinished quality contributes to our perception of a transformation; Rodin, in displaying the process of bringing form from the raw material, has visually expressed the creative energy that has seized Balzac.

Stating his philosophy on the relationship of art and the artist to nature, Rodin wrote:

I grant you that the artist does not see Nature as she appears to the vulgar, because his emotion reveals to him the hidden truths beneath appearances. But, after all, the only principle in art is to copy what you see. . . . There is no recipe for improving nature. The only thing is to see. Oh, doubtless a mediocre man copying nature will never produce a work of art, because he really looks without seeing, and though he may have noted each detail minutely, the result will be flat and without character. . . . The artist, on the contrary, sees; that is to say, his eye, grafted on his heart, reads deeply into the bosom of nature.

9-71 AUGUSTE RODIN

MONUMENT TO BALZAC. 1893–97. Plaster, height 9'10⅛". This historic 1908 photograph of the plaster model is by Edward Steichen, one of America's foremost photographers. Steichen so successfully captured the creative ambiance of Balzac that, on seeing Steichen's photographs, Rodin remarked, "You will make the world understand my Balzac through these pictures. They are like Christ walking in the desert." The sculpture was commissioned by the Société des Gens de Lettres in honor of Balzac, who had been the group's second president. Unhappy with Rodin's interpretation, they rejected the monument.

Winslow Homer

9-72   WINSLOW HOMER

THE FOG WARNING. 1885. Oil on canvas, 30 × 48″. Courtesy, Museum of Fine Arts, Boston.

OTIS NORCROSS FUND

The unusual cloud bank rolling from the background of *The Fog Warning*, by Winslow Homer (1836–1910), warns the fisherman that he is suddenly in mortal danger, for it signals the arrival of a particularly fast-moving and dangerous fog (fig. 9-72). The hunter, preying on nature, suddenly becomes the hunted. Homer's composition heightens the mood of instability and uncertainty by representing the small rowboat being heaved upward by a large swell. The right-to-left thrust of the rowboat is counter to the movement of the fisherman's home vessel in the background, which seems about to sail out of the range of vision. The realistic colors—yellowish-white for the sky, green for the sea, and shades of brown for the boat and the fisherman—are somber and appropriate for this theme.

The bold composition, the diagonal thrust of the boat, and the truncated oar reveal the influence of Japanese woodcuts. Homer's brushstrokes are broad and simple; note especially the rough strokes in the foreground that represent the foamy waves.

The power of natural forces and their challenge to humanity are themes that recur in Homer's most significant works. A New England individualist, Homer spent many winters living in isolation along a particularly dramatic and treacherous stretch of the Maine coastline, where he had many opportunities to observe the power of a turbulent sea.

Technique *Watercolor and Gouache*

9-73   WINSLOW HOMER

THE BLUE BOAT. 1892. Watercolor over graphite, 15⅛ × 21½". Courtesy, Museum of Fine Arts, Boston.

BEQUEST OF WILLIAM STURGIS BIGELOW

Watercolor is aptly named, for it is a medium in which ground pigments are mixed with water and, as an adhesive binder, a little gum arabic. It is usually applied to white paper. The brilliant light effects possible in watercolor are evident in *The Blue Boat*, by Homer (fig. 9-73). The liquidity of the medium is apparent in the broad strokes that convincingly render sky and water. Watercolor is transparent, and in some areas Homer has laid one color over another, creating veils of color. The strong white of the paper shows through in the clouds and water in *The Blue Boat*. Homer commonly added a few touches of **gouache** (an opaque water-color) to strengthen certain areas.

As early as the 1780s, English artists had begun to work seri-ously with watercolor. Homer was one of the founders of the American Watercolor Society, an organization that helped popular-ize the medium among professional artists in the United States. Pre-viously, watercolor had been used for the most part by amateurs.

Post-Impressionism: Gauguin and Seurat

9-74 PAUL GAUGUIN

THE VISION AFTER THE SERMON. 1888. Oil on canvas, 28¾ × 36½″. National Gallery of Scotland, Edinburgh.

9-75 PAUL GAUGUIN

WHERE DO WE COME FROM? WHAT ARE WE? WHERE ARE WE GOING? 1897. Oil on burlap, 4′6¾″ × 12′3½″.

PAUL GAUGUIN, FRENCH (1848–1903). *WHERE DO WE COME FROM? WHAT ARE WE? WHERE ARE WE GOING?*, 1897, OIL ON CANVAS, 54¾ × 147½″. MUSEUM OF FINE ARTS, BOSTON, MASSACHUSETTS. ARTHUR GORDON TOMPKINS RESIDUARY FUND COLLECTION

Parisian Paul Gauguin (1848–1903) painted *The Vision after the Sermon* in the rural area of Brittany, in northern France, which he visited in 1888 to divert his mind and art from what he felt were the restrictive artistic and social pressures of Paris (fig. 9-74). The painting depicts Breton women, deep in prayer, experiencing a vision. We seem to be standing behind the group of women in native dress and a priest in the right foreground. A tree limb creates a strong diagonal across the composition, separating the left middle ground from the "vision" to the right, which represents the Old Testament figure Jacob wrestling with an angel, a story in which God tested Jacob's enduring love. Visual tension results from the conflict between the flat red ground, which creates a strong planarity, and the perspective suggested by the diminution of size. The heavy outlines of the figures combine with the patternlike configuration of the Breton headdresses to create a simple yet forceful composition. Although the red ground may have been inspired by a reli-gious festival that included the blessing of horned animals and bonfires that cast a red glow over the fields at night, Gauguin's choice of color also carries a symbolic content. The red ground symbolizes the theme of struggle, and in choosing it, Gauguin has freed himself from the traditional use of color to describe nature. Here it is used in an abstract, expressive way.

Gauguin left his wife and family, as well as a successful brokerage career in Paris, to seek a more natural, unindustrialized environment, first in

Martinique, then in Brittany and later Arles in southern France, and finally in Tahiti, in the South Seas. In attempting to remove himself from Western centers of civilization, Gauguin sought an unbridled artistic and psychological response to nature.

During his second Tahitian period, Gauguin, in poor health, nearly broke, severely depressed, and planning suicide, painted what he envisioned as a summation of his art and life (fig. 9-75). His suicide attempt failed, and he later detailed the meaning of the painting in a letter. The woman, child, and dog in the right foreground symbolize birth and the innocence of life. The figure near the center tries to pick a fruit from the tree of knowledge in an attempt to understand the meaning of life, while in the left foreground

> an old woman approaching death . . . reconciled and resigned to her thoughts

is joined by

> a strange white bird [that] represents the futility of life.

In the right middle ground, two standing clothed figures betray the sorrow that life's knowledge can bring; the idol to our left expresses the forces that rule our primitive passions. The abstraction of Gauguin's colors and forms plays an important role in communicating his content and demonstrates how far he has moved away from Impressionism.

By the time of the last Independent Exhibition in 1886, Impressionism, which a decade earlier had been considered revolutionary, was gaining increasing critical and public acceptance. New avant-garde styles were now being explored by artists such as Gauguin, who had moved from

9-76   GEORGES SEURAT

A Sunday Afternoon on the Island of La Grande Jatte. 1884–86. Oil on canvas, 6'9½" × 10'1¼".

Impressionism to more individualized styles. *Post-Impressionism* is the generic term now used to embrace the diversity of these individual styles—styles that laid the foundation for modern art.

Georges Seurat (1859–91) was the youngest of the Post-Impressionist painters. His monumental painting *A Sunday Afternoon on the Island of La Grande Jatte* (fig. 9-76), which was two years in preparation and execution, exemplifies his theories of Divisionism, which was also called Neo-Impressionism. The still, transfixed quality of the scene reminds us of the works of the Renaissance painter Piero della Francesca (see fig. 5-1), whose work Seurat admired. But the classicism of Renaissance art has been updated, joined with the modern perception of light and color begun by the Impressionists. Seurat systematized contemporary scientific advances in color theory to create what he terms "optical" painting. Colored paint is methodically applied in a series of small dots (now popularly known as Pointillism, a term not used by Seurat), usually in complementary colors. The resulting surface, covered with thousands of controlled spots of color, is both vibrant and luminous, at once relating to the surface of the picture plane and to forms in an illusory depth bathed in natural light.

Post-Impressionism: Van Gogh

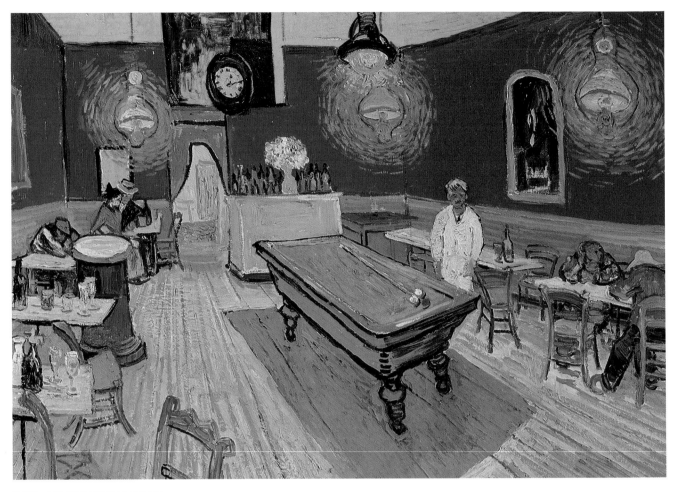

9-77 VINCENT VAN GOGH

THE NIGHT CAFE. September 1888. Oil on canvas, 27½ × 35″. Yale University Art Gallery, New Haven, Connecticut. Van Gogh painted *The Night Cafe* in Arles, in the south of France, where he lived in 1888–89. Vincent wrote that when he painted this picture he stayed up three consecutive nights, sleeping only during the day. On September 17, 1888, he wrote to his brother Theo that "the problem of painting night scenes and effects on the spot and actually by night, interests me enormously."

BEQUEST OF STEPHEN C. CLARK

Today I am probably going to begin the interior of the Cafe where I eat, by gas light, in the evening.

It is what they call here a Cafe de Nuit (they are fairly frequent here), staying open all night. "Night prowlers" can take refuge there when they have no money to pay for a lodging, or are too tight to be taken in. All those things—family, native land—are perhaps more attractive in the imaginations of such people as us . . . than they are in reality. I always feel I am a traveller, going somewhere and to some destination.

If I tell myself that the somewhere and the destination do not exist, that seems to me very reasonable and likely enough. . . .

The room is blood red and dark yellow with a green billiard table in the middle; there are four citron-yellow lamps with a glow of orange and green. Everywhere there is a clash and contrast of the most disparate reds and greens in the figures of little sleeping hooligans, in the empty, dreary room, in violet and blue. The blood-red and the yellow-green of the billiard table, for instance, contrast with the soft tender . . . green of the counter, on which there is a pink nosegay. The white coat of the landlord, awake in a corner of that furnace, turns citron-yellow, or pale luminous green.

(Vincent van Gogh, letter to his brother Theo from Arles, September 8, 1888)

The Night Cafe is only one of the powerfully emotional paintings in a series of works created during Van Gogh's stay in Arles (fig. 9-77). Van Gogh later referred to Arles as the place where

I attain[ed] the high yellow note,

suggesting that this was a particularly strong point in his career. Here he adopted the Japanese belief that the color yellow is symbolic of hope. However, Arles was also a place of despair for Van Gogh, which may help explain the intensity of the Arles works. He said that this painting, given to his landlord in exchange for rent, was

one of the ugliest pictures I have done.

The ugliness of which he writes is intentional, for in this painting color is used arbitrarily, allowing him to express personal meanings and emotions through the "clash and contrast" of glaring yellow, bright green, and "blood" red. In a letter to his brother Theo, who was living in Paris, he explained the psychological impact that he wanted the painting to have:

I have tried to express the terrible passions of humanity by means of red and green . . . the cafe is a place where one can ruin oneself, run mad, or commit a crime.

Van Gogh's goal is in part conveyed to us by the claustrophobia of the tense and threatening atmosphere. Drunks slump over tables within a tilted and close perspective space that is unnerving for the viewer. Van Gogh was here experimenting with the relationship between color, space, theme, and emotions. His efforts make him one of the forerunners of the expressionist trends that become important in the twentieth century. He wanted to express the mood he senses at the cafe, and in doing so, he reveals some of his feelings about his own alienation.

In the early 1880s, Van Gogh was involved briefly in the rapidly changing styles of French painting. Like many other artists, he began to collect Japanese prints (see fig. 9-3), and in *The Night Cafe* we sense their influence in the bold delineation of the forms, the intricate patterning of horizontal and vertical lines, the unusual viewpoint, and the vivid, arbitrary colors. The oddly exaggerated perspective of the painting may also be attributed to other influences, for evidence suggests that Van Gogh may have suffered from temporal-lobe epilepsy; some aspects of his art may have been influenced by the visions he experienced during the beginning of a seizure. We also know that Van Gogh often spent his limited money on alcohol, rather than food, and absinthe,

one of the artist's common indulgences, is known to affect the occipital lobe, which controls vision.

In *The Starry Night* (fig. 9-78), painted in 1889, Van Gogh displays his fascination with the earth and sky, and his philosophies of life and death and their connection to nature:

For my own part, I declare I know nothing whatever about it, but to look at the stars always makes me dream, as simply as I dream over the black dots of a map representing towns and villages. Why, I ask myself, should the shining dots of the sky not be as accessible as the black dots on the map of France? If we take the train to get to Tarascon or Rouen, we take death to reach a star. One thing undoubtedly true in this reasoning is this, that while we are alive we cannot get to a star, any more than when we are dead we can take the train.

(Vincent van Gogh, letter to his brother Theo, mid-July 1888)

This depiction of night "in situ," as Van Gogh described it, reveals his continuing interest in a favorite subject, the flamelike cypress tree used in France and Italy to mark graves. Almost black, the tree dominates the foreground. The night sky overwhelms the little town of St.-Rémy, but the expansiveness of space and the solidity of the earth are formally linked: the tip of the cypress tree crosses the nebula, and the steeple of the church enters the area of the sky.

In a letter to his brother, Van Gogh

9-78 VINCENT VAN GOGH

THE STARRY NIGHT. June 1889. Oil on canvas, 29 × 36¼". Collection, The Museum of Modern Art, New York. Van Gogh can be classified as a Post- or Counter-Impressionist because after painting in the Impressionist style (he saw the Eighth, last Independent Exhibition in 1886 in Paris), he developed his own personal style. Van Gogh eloquently revealed his understanding of his own intense personality and his loneliness by writing, "One may have a blazing hearth in one's soul and yet no one ever comes to sit by it. Passersby see only a wisp of smoke rising from the chimney and continue on their way."

VINCENT VAN GOGH, *THE STARRY NIGHT*. (1889). OIL ON CANVAS, 29 × 36¼" (73.7 × 92.1 CM). THE MUSEUM OF MODERN ART. ACQUIRED THROUGH THE LILLIE P. BLISS BEQUEST

wrote that he felt that nighttime was more colorful than the day—as is suggested here by the vividness and luminosity of the celestial bodies. Deeply saturated colors—purple and violent green—clash, and a thickly painted "glow" surrounds each star, planet, and the moon. These qualities seem to express Van Gogh's testament that there are lives and colors on other planets, and perhaps even better conditions. Here the artist projects his own destiny: death represents not an ending but a metamorphosis.

The significance of nature for Van Gogh is apparent in the following quotation, from a letter he wrote to Theo in September 1889, right after Theo was married:

> Well, do you know what I hope for, once I let myself begin to hope? It is that a family will be for you what nature, the clods of earth, the grass, the yellow corn, the peasant, are for me,

that is to say, that you may find in your love for people something not only to work for, but to comfort and restore you, when there is need for it.

The *Self-Portrait* of 1889 (see fig. 9-11) was probably painted shortly after Van Gogh left the hospital in St.-Rémy in early January 1889. His ear is still bandaged from the self-mutilation he had inflicted in December, when he cut off part of his ear, probably to punish himself because of a quarrel he had had with Paul Gauguin. Van Gogh sent this painting to his family in the Netherlands, probably to reassure them of his health. The very fact that he could paint again revealed his ability to control his feelings, and although he does not deny that he damaged his ear, he shows himself as somber and meditative, smoking his pipe. The placement of the green coat against the red background and the blue cap against orange demonstrates his understanding of how to use complementary colors to achieve rich coloristic and dramatic effects. The violent juxtaposition of the red and orange draws attention to Van Gogh's solemn eyes. As he wrote,

[I find myself filled with] a certain undercurrent of vague sadness, difficult to define. . . . My God, those anxieties—who can live in the modern world without catching his share of them?

Art Past/Art Present — *The Value of Art: Van Gogh*

How is value assigned to art? Certainly personal value—the worth of a work of art to you personally, based on the importance of that work to you and, perhaps, your perception of the value of this work to humanity as a whole—is important. But it is not quantifiable unless you are establishing your own collection or a museum for the public at large.

The financial or market value of a work of art is, as with other luxury items, based on market factors. How much a particular painting by a certain artist will bring at auction is dependent on many factors, including the availability of at least two enthusiastic bidders, the artist's reputation, the historical importance of the work, the availability of similar works by the same artist in the future, and the promotion of the work by the auction house. Important works will sometimes be showcased in an impressive book meant to inform prospective bidders about the significance of the particular work.

In a list compiled in 1999 of the ten most expensive paintings sold at auction, three were by Van Gogh (the first, fourth, and eighth) and five by Picasso; the other artists on this list, each represented by a single work, were Renoir and the Italian sixteenth-century painter Pontormo. At least forty-four paintings by Van Gogh have been sold with a price tag of more than one million dollars each.

This was not, of course, always the case. During his lifetime Van Gogh gave away and traded some of his works, but it seems that he sold only one painting (*The Red Vineyard*, now in the collection of the Hermitage in St. Petersburg, Russia). After the deaths of Vincent in 1890 and his brother in 1891, his brother's widow, Johanna van Gogh-Bonger, began to organize exhibitions of Vincent's works; later she also edited and published Vincent's letters to her husband. Eventually there were sales to museums and important collectors, but much of Van Gogh's work stayed in the family collection until it was purchased by a foundation with funds provided by the Dutch State in 1962. In 1973 the Van Gogh Museum in Amsterdam was opened to display the collection; designed to accommodate 80,000 visitors a year, in recent years the annual attendance has regularly exceeded one million. Now, a little more than a century after his death at the age of 37, Van Gogh has become one of the best known and highly prized of artists. The international demand for his works on the part of museums and collectors and the decreasing supply of available paintings and drawings have led to higher and higher prices for his works.

Post-Impressionism: Cézanne

9-79 PAUL CÉZANNE

STILL LIFE WITH BASKET OF APPLES. 1890–94. Oil on canvas, 24⅜ × 31″. The Art Institute of Chicago.

HELEN BIRCH BARTLETT MEMORIAL COLLECTION

I want to make of Impressionism something solid and durable, like the art of the museums,

wrote Paul Cézanne (1839–1906). In his paintings, Cézanne set himself an impossible task: he wanted to establish an equilibrium between the vivacious color and solid form of three-dimensional objects and the two-dimensional surface of the picture plane. He sought to achieve both illusionistic solidity and a strong compositional structure in two dimensions. His frustration with Impressionism was twofold: Impressionist painters did not create paintings that were compositionally strong, and they were not interested in endowing painted objects with three-dimensional solidity. Cézanne wrote: .

In art, everything is theory, developed and applied in contact with nature.

It is the union of nature with the philosophical truth of the flatness of a painting's surface that absorbed Cézanne's attention.

Cézanne's *Still Life with Basket of Apples* (fig. 9-79) demonstrates his ability to render objects with solidity—note the white napkin, with its deep angular folds and pockets of shadow. The pieces of fruit have a physical presence that is in part the result of an unexpected richness of color, exemplifying Cézanne's dictum that

when color is richest, form is fullest.

He modeled the fruit with pure, unmixed colors, juxtaposing, for example, yellow with green and red. He thereby created a richer effect than that produced by the typical academic practice which rendered modeling by reducing coloristic intensity by adding white or black. Cézanne does not outline his forms to distinguish them from each other. They have rather loosely painted edges, and it is the internal color that creates their solidity. Cézanne once said,

The secret of drawing and modeling resides in the contrasts and relationships of tone.

If we analyze Cézanne's *Still Life with Basket of Apples* as an illusion or as an exercise in accurate drawing, it is a failure: neither the front nor the back edges of the table, for example, are aligned; the wine bottle, itself tilted, offers a distinctive contour on each side; and the pastries stacked on the plate are tilted upward. But our observations are based on the wrong questions. In Cézanne's work, these pictorial "inaccuracies" reveal the moving viewpoint of the artist relative to the objects being painted. Renaissance scientific perspective insisted that the artist's (and therefore the viewer's) eye be at a fixed point. Cézanne, on the other hand, expresses a basic fact of vision: our understanding of an object or space is based on our movement relative to that object or space. The difference in the edges of the table, for example, results because the table edge is seen from lower or higher, closer or farther viewpoints. The issues Cézanne has selected to investigate are difficult ones to resolve. Later, Picasso would praise Cézanne for his

restless striving.

The structured pictorial surface Cézanne accomplished is best expressed in his later works (fig. 9-80).

1890–94	Cézanne, *Still Life with Basket of Apples*
1890	Emily Dickinson poems are published
1890	Oscar Wilde, *The Picture of Dorian Gray*

9-80 PAUL CÉZANNE

MONT STE.-VICTOIRE. 1904–6. Oil on canvas, 25⅝ × 31⅞″. Private collection. Mont Ste.-Victoire in Provence, a symbol of Cézanne's local area, is one of his favorite subjects. In 1901–02, he built a studio in the countryside with a large window facing the mountain.

Although the most significant monument in the landscape is the powerful, thrusting mountain, Cézanne has constructed his painting out of blocks of color, and no one area or object is less strong than another. Cézanne urged painters to

> see in nature the cylinder, the sphere, the cone,

and this painting demonstrates his approach. Surface strength is also accomplished by intermingling blocks of limited color—in this case violet, green, ocher, and blue; the violet of the atmospheric perspective reappears in the foreground, and the green of the middle ground is also found in the sky. When this work is compared to an Impressionist painting, such as *Impression-Sunrise* (see fig. 9-61), two completely different effects can be noted. Cézanne has sacrificed the ravishing, momentary subtlety of color that forms the foundation of Monet's accomplishment in his attempt to create a landscape that has an enduring strength and power. In ancient times, Mont Ste.-Victoire was believed to be a holy mountain, a home of the gods, and in Cézanne's painting it is once again endowed with a mysterious presence. Cézanne's paintings had an important impact on developments in the twentieth century: Matisse called him the

> father of us all.

The Beginnings of the Skyscraper

9-81 LOUIS SULLIVAN

Wainwright Building, St. Louis, Missouri. 1890–91. Commissioned by Catherine Wainwright and her son, Ellis Wainwright, a brewing magnate and commercial leader.

W hat is the chief characteristic of the tall office building? And at once we answer, it is lofty. . . . The force and power of altitude must be in it. . . . It must be every inch a proud and soaring thing, rising in sheer exultation that from bottom to top it is a unit without a single dissenting line.

(Louis Sullivan, The Tall Office Building Artistically Considered, 1896)

To accomplish his lofty exaltation, Louis Sullivan (1856–1924) based his Wainwright Building on a design con-

cept analogous to that of a column (fig. 9-81). The first two stories act as a base that supports the unimpeded vertical members, which rise like flutes on a column to support a cornice, decorated with foliage ornament, that crowns the structure like a capital. This intelligible design hides the load-bearing steel-frame construction, which other early skyscraper architects had emphasized by creating a grid of balanced horizontals and verticals (see page 437). Sullivan chose instead to stress the vertical articulation. Only every second vertical element corresponds to the interior steel cage. In addition, the vertical elements dominate because the windows are recessed between them, and the horizontal membering, obscured behind recessed panels of decorated terra-cotta, is reduced in importance.

The integrity of the design depends on the proportional relationships between the parts and the whole, which Sullivan has carefully calibrated. The wide corners balance and set off the elegant, narrow verticals between the windows, while the effulgent decorative terra-cotta at the cornice level, a full story high, unites with the narrow upper-most cornice to provide an elegant final closure that defines the mass of the structure. The decorated panels below each window provide a typically Sullivanesque touch, offering a pleasant decoration for office workers in adjacent buildings. The total effect is of a finely articulated mass, elegant and substantial at the same time.

The most impressive developments in skyscraper architecture occurred in Chicago, where a devastating fire in 1871 leveled much of the city. During the closing decades of the century, the city's rapidly increasing population spurred a building boom. Sullivan's last major commission was the design for the Schlesinger and Meyer Department Store (fig. 9-82). The idea of a huge urban store carrying luxury items for middle- and upper-class patrons was novel, and Sullivan emphasized elegant public entrances and huge plate-glass windows on the lower floor by fantastic cast-iron ornamentation of his own design. The upper floors, with their huge "Chicago" windows and very plain terra-cotta decoration, refer in a streamlined fashion to the concealed steel cage, but note that the horizontal members are emphatically wider and therefore dominant. Sullivan's sensitivity to the shape and placement of the building as a whole is evident in the cylindrical tower at the corner, an unexpected element adding a vertical punctuation mark that makes the horizontal sides even more forceful. Here Sullivan completely avoids any historical references, creating a building that is one of the first works of modern architecture.

9-82 LOUIS SULLIVAN

Carson-Pirie-Scott Store (formerly Schlesinger and Meyer Department Store), Chicago. 1899; enlarged 1903–4 and 1906. Commissioned by Leopold S. and Daniel Meyer.

Edvard Munch

9-83 EDVARD MUNCH

The Scream. 1893. Oil, pastel, and casein on cardboard, 35¾ × 29″. National Gallery, Oslo. Munch originally titled this work *Despair.*

EDVARD MUNCH, *THE SCREAM*, 1893. CASEIN ON PAPER, 91 × 73 CM. NASJONALGALLERIET, OSLO. © 1998 ARTISTS RIGHTS SOCIETY (ARS), NEW YORK/ADAGP, PARIS. SCALA/ART RESOURCE, NY.

I was walking along the road with two friends. The sun set. I felt a tinge of melancholy. Suddenly the sky became a bloody red.

I stopped, leaned against the railing, dead tired, and I looked at the flaming clouds that hung like blood and a sword over the blue-black fjord of the city.

My friends walked on. I stood there, trembling with fright. And I felt a loud, unending scream piercing nature.

(Edvard Munch, *Diary,* 1892)

The composition of *The Scream* (fig. 9-83) expresses the personal anxiety of Edvard Munich (1863–1944) by creating a formal tension that reinforces the psychological tension that is the theme. As in Munch's description, the sky is a blood red. Its undulating rhythms melt into the blue-black waters of the fjord. The perspective of the bridge is unnatural. Its sharp angle creates a visual tension, for it is caught between the flatness of the picture plane, which is emphasized by the shapes of clouds and water, and the illusory space established by the diminution of Munch's companions and the ships of the fjord. The curving rhythm of Munch's body, transformed into an existential symbol, incorporates itself into the rhythms of the environment. He is becoming one with nature, realizing his worst agoraphobic nightmare. As the figure screams, its face is distorted to resemble a skull, with the iconographic association of death. These visual manipulations communicate an emotional impact not as a representational image, but as a symbol of a schizophrenic psychological state.

The terrifying tension Munch felt that evening was in part the result of his alcoholism and a dread of open spaces. In this condition, Munch experienced himself being pulled into his environment, losing his identity. He heard a scream within him, the scream of nature "dying" in flaming bursts at sunset. The inner scream became so intense that Munch, looking at us, screams to relieve the pain within.

The Scream was one of a series of twenty-two paintings and prints that Munch exhibited as a coordinated group in the opening years of the twentieth century. The exhibition was titled *Motifs from the Life of a Modern Soul,* yet it more often carried the simpler title *The Frieze of Life* (fig. 9-84), which better suggests Munch's intent to represent the flowering and passing of love, life's anxieties, and death. As a young person growing up in Norway, Munch had led a bohemian life, and

9-84 EDVARD MUNCH

THE FRIEZE OF LIFE exhibition. Photograph of the installation at Leipzig, Germany, 1903. Munch divided the exhibition into four sections: Seeds of Love, Flowering and Passing of Love, Life Anxiety, and Death. *The Scream* was exhibited in the Life Anxiety section. The paintings along the wall seen here are, from left to right, *The Red Vine*, *The Scream*, *Angst*, *Evening on Karl Johan Street*, *Death in the Sickroom*, *By the Deathbed*, and *Death and the Child*.

the ideas for the paintings began with his personal, subjective experiences, which were then transformed into broader symbolic themes.

For Munch, the emotionally expressive abstraction of forms was a way of creating art that possessed what he termed a "deeper meaning," one that conveyed the content of the human soul. The impact of his art had a profound effect on the development of early modern painting.

Pablo Picasso painted his *Three Musicians* in a Cubist style in 1921 (for more information see fig. 10-49 and p. 507).

CHAPTER TEN

Twentieth-Century Art

A Brief Insight

HOW DO WE KNOW INSTANTLY WHEN WE FIRST VIEW *Pablo Picasso's* Three Musicians *that it is a modern work? One clue is the abstracted treatment of the figures; another is the way in which the shapes and composition emphasize flatness, forcing us to recognize that this is a work of art, not an illusion of nature or reality. Although European painting had for 500 years been defined by artists' depictions of illusory space, here we are forced to look at the painting's surface, not through it.*

This changed relationship between ourselves and the work of art is part of our modern experience. During the twentieth century many artists moved away from depicting the appearance of natural forms in an attempt to express another approach to the world. Picasso has been quoted as saying "Nature and art, being two different things, cannot be the same thing. Through art we express our conception of what nature is not." In its emphasis on the flat surface, Picasso's painting affirms the reality of painting itself.

Twentieth-Century Art

10-1   GIACOMO BALLA

SPEEDING AUTOMOBILE—STUDY OF VELOCITY. 1913. Oil on cardboard, 26 × 37⅞″. Municipal Gallery of Modern Art, Milan, Italy.

A roaring motorcar which seems to run on machine-gun fire is more beautiful than the *Victory of Samothrace* (see fig. 3-83), wrote Filippo Marinetti, an Italian poet of the Futurist movement, in 1908–09. The works chosen to introduce the twentieth century relate the dynamism of modern art to the vigor of modern life reflected in Marinetti's words. *Speeding Automobile—Study of Velocity* (fig. 10-1), by the Futurist artist Giacomo Balla (1871–1958), is an abstract representation that can be related to a 1910 *Futurist Manifesto*, which declared:

> [T]he gesture . . . we would reproduce on canvas shall no longer be a fixed moment in universal dynamism. It shall simply be the dynamic sensation itself.

Balla's painting represents the propulsive energy of a speeding car; the sequential placement of diagonal lines communicates dynamic force. Balla, an associate of Marinetti's, has visualized the poet's remarks on the new aesthetic of beauty as exemplified by a "roaring motorcar."

The sleek, aerodynamic design of Pininfarina's Cisitalia "202" GT car (fig. 10-2) is both superbly functional—it cuts the wind resistance—and aesthetically elegant. Even stand-

10-2 PININFARINA (designer)

"Cistalia 202 GT" car. 1946. Aluminum body, 49' × 57⅝" × 12'5". Manufacturer: S.p.A. Carrozzeria Pininfarina,
Turin, Italy. The Museum of Modern Art, New York

ing still, the car gives the impression of movement. In function and appearance, both Balla's painting and Pininfarina's automobile are works characteristic of the twentieth century.

History

The decades that opened the twentieth century were characterized by a population boom, unprecedented improvements in living conditions in the Western world, and technological revolution that had the kind of impact on the arts that the poet Marinetti and the painter Balla glorified. By the 1890s, electric lighting and motors were common, and the radio, invented by Guglielmo Marconi in 1895, greatly facilitated communication over vast geographic areas. Television was introduced in the 1920s, computers in the 1940s. One dramatic example of the astounding pace of modern technology was air and space flight. In the United States, the 1903 flight of the Wright brothers at Kitty Hawk, North Carolina, was followed by rapid advances; Charles Lindbergh soloed across the Atlantic in 1927, and in 1969 Neil Armstrong became the first human to set foot on the moon. During the late '90s, two former Cold-War adversaries, the United States and Russia, conducted joint ventures in space.

   Advances in technology were often set against a backdrop of political conflict, war, and violent revolution. By the end of the first decade of the twentieth century,

10-3 VLADIMIR TATLIN

Historic photograph of the model of the Monument to the Third International Communist Conference. 1919–20. The model, 16 feet tall, was of wood and netting; the final building, which was to be of iron painted red and glass, would have been more than 1,300 feet tall.

VLADIMIR TATLIN, *THE FINISHED MODEL*, 1920/THE NATIONAL SWEDISH ART MUSEUMS

10-4 MAX BECKMANN

DEPARTURE. 1932–33. Oil on canvas, 7′3¾″ × 3′9⅜″ (center); 7′3¾″ × 3′3¼″ (each wing). The Museum of Modern Art, New York.

the European nations and Great Britain had built up enormous armed forces. Germany, Austria-Hungary, and Italy were allied against Great Britain, France, and Russia. War became inevitable after Archduke Ferdinand, heir to the throne of Austria-Hungary, was assassinated in 1914. The "Great War," now known as World War I, erupted within months. Although all parties hoped it would be of short duration, it lasted, stagnated in trench warfare, until 1918. The United States committed its armies in 1917. The 1919 Treaty of Versailles ended World War I, but the harsh restrictions imposed on Germany helped set the foundation for yet another conflict. Before World War I ended, events in Russia had brought a new political force to the world scene. A populist revolution of 1917 overthrew Czar Nicholas II, and a "dictatorship of the proletariat" was established by a well-organized party of Bolshevik Communists headed by Vladimir Lenin. Lenin withdrew Russia from World War I in 1918, but internal civil war ended only in 1921. In 1923, the Union of Soviet Socialist Republics (USSR) was formed. Communist parties outside of the USSR had been federated with Soviet communism in 1919 to form the Third International. In proposing a structure that would provide a center for world communism, Vladimir Tatlin (1885–1953), a Russian artist who had visited the **avant-garde** art centers of Berlin and Paris in 1913, offered an ambitious spiraling architectural form (fig. 10-3). The dynamic energy of the Communist party was to be expressed by glass-enclosed meeting rooms that would revolve around the building's axis. The lowest level—a cube—would turn once per year, the pyramid in the center once per month,

and the upper, cylindrical chamber once per day. This ambitious structure, designed to convey the modernity of communism to the world, was never built, and later Soviet structures abandoned the modern style for a severe version of classicism.

Following World War I, economic instability arose as nations returned to peacetime industrial production. Prosperity seemed assured by the late 1920s, but an economic collapse in 1929 plunged the world into a great depression, which in the United States would leave about one in four workers without a job. Compounding the American economic ruin, a drought in the Southwest devastated farming.

During the 1930s, as the West struggled to regain economic stability, the Nazi government of Adolf Hitler took control in Germany, and the Fascist dictators Benito Mussolini in Italy and Francisco Franco in Spain seized power. In 1939, another world war broke out in Europe. World War II reached global involvement following Japan's attack on the American naval base at Pearl Harbor, Hawaii, in 1941. This war ended with the defeat of Germany and Japan, but the explosion of the atomic bomb over Hiroshima, Japan, on August 6, 1945, ushered in the nuclear era, with its constant threat of atomic and nuclear weapons.

Departure (fig. 10-4), by Max Beckman (1884–1950), is a potent image of frustration and inhumanity born of the scars left on Europe from World War I and the growing totalitarian regime of Nazi Germany. The two wings represent scenes of torture and mutilation, while in the center panel the precious realization of freedom is symbolically rendered with the departing queen holding a child. The fig-

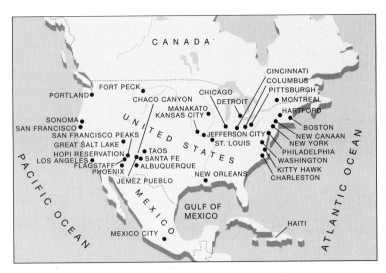

10-5 MAYA LIN

VIETNAM VETERANS MEMORIAL. 1982. Black granite, length 500'. The Mall, Washington, D.C. The jury that selected this winning entry in the competition affirmed that two criteria, stated in the program for the competition, were uppermost in their minds—that the monument should "make no political statement regarding the war or its conduct" and that it should be "reflective and contemplative in nature." Commenting on her conception for the memorial, Lin wrote, "I didn't want a static object that people would just look at, but something they could relate to as on a journey, or passage, that would bring each to his own conclusion." Lin's monument is designed so that the walls point toward the Washington Monument and the Lincoln Memorial. Chosen by the competition jury appointed by the Vietnam Veterans Memorial Fund.

urative exaggerations, harsh brushstrokes, and severe colors contribute to the expression of brutality. Beckmman wrote of the painting:

> On the right wing you can see yourself trying to find your way in the darkness, lighting the hall and staircase with a miserable lamp dragging along tied to you as part of yourself, the corpse of your memories, of your wrongs, of your failures, the murder everyone commits at some time of his life—you can never free yourself of your past, you have to carry the corpse while Life plays the drum. The Queen carries the greatest treasure—Freedom—as a child in her lap. Freedom is the one thing that matters—it is the departure, the new start.

The economic depression of the 1930s and World War II had a profound impact on the world. Increasing industrialization in the United States and the prosperity and development that this industrialization made possible in America, Europe, and Japan led gradually, after the war, to an even greater distance between the developed nations and other countries. The struggle to be free from foreign domination led to the dissolution of the British Empire and

Independence for many countries, but in many cases independence did not lead to broad well-being for the citizens or to the establishment of democratic governments. Tension between the industrialized nations and third-world countries and the struggle for decreasing resources have grown almost continuously during the second half of the twentieth century, and they promise to be increasingly disruptive factors in the future.

In the United States, both foreign and domestic conflicts have marked the years since 1945. Between 1950 and 1953, the United States sent a large contingent of troops to the United Nations force that fought in Korea to stop the aggression of Communist North Korea. The 1950s also witnessed an intensification of the civil rights movement. Led by Martin Luther King, Jr., a Baptist minister who would receive the Nobel Peace Prize in 1964, African Americans were in the forefront of the struggle to achieve equality and dignity in human legal rights. By the early 1960s, American combat troops were becoming deeply involved in a war between North and South Vietnam. In America, efforts to sustain this military involvement were met with bitter domestic divisiveness. By 1973, U.S. forces were withdrawn. In Washington, the *Vietnam Veterans Memorial* (fig. 10-5), designed by Maya Lin (b. 1960), lists the names of the more than 58,000 Americans who lost their lives in that conflict. It is an unprecedented public monument. Simple and direct in design, it creates a solemn environment. The polished surface of the granite on which the names are etched reflects the transient life before it, while the names impose themselves, constantly reminding us of the human suffering and loss that are the ultimate costs of conflict.

Politically, the pulse of change has ever quickened. Throughout the world, there have been challenges to autocratic and tyrannical rule. After a military coup in Burma (Myanmar) in 1988, opposition demonstrators were shot down in Rangoon. Daw Aung San Suu Kyi, an opposition

10-6 THE NAMES PROJECT, San Francisco

AIDS MEMORIAL QUILT, as displayed on the Ellipse facing the White House in October 1996.

leader who later, in 1991, was awarded the Nobel Peace Prize, reacted by asserting that

> you can't solve political problems by massacring people.

In 1989, Chinese troops killed antigovernment demonstrators—mostly workers and students—in Beijing. Yet during the same year, the Berlin Wall, one of the most poignant realities of the Cold War, was torn down, and Germany was reunited after forty-five years. On January 1, 1992, the Soviet Union, a center for world communism for more than seventy years, was formally disbanded. In 1990, Nelson Mandela was released from a South African prison to confront apartheid ever more forcefully; in 1994 he was elected president of South Africa.

At the same time, nationalism became an increasingly serious problem. The 1990s produced regional ethnic violence in Bosnia-Herzegovina and Kosovo in the former Yugoslavia, in Chechnya in the former Soviet Union, and in Rwanda in Africa. In these and other conflicts, hundreds of thousands of individuals died, were murdered, or were forced to become homeless refugees. Attempts to broker peace failed in most cases. Nationalism has probably been a factor in art since prehistoric times, but beginning in the Renaissance in Italy, it became an increasingly important factor; art was a means by which the singularity of a culture, a location, a population could be defined and promoted. In the twentieth century, art continued to be a force of national identity on many levels.

In 1991, a coalition of forces defeated Iraq in the Persian Gulf war after Kuwait was invaded. In subsequent years, terrorist bombs killed six people at the World Trade Center in New York City in 1993 and 160 people at the Federal Building in Oklahoma City in 1995. In 1996, a new constitution granted democracy to South Africa, but that same year saw citizens in Indonesia and South Korea riot in an effort to secure greater self-rule. Amid peace negotiations in various part of the world, terrorism and political oppression continued in the closing years of the twentieth century. The words of Daw Aung San Suu Kyi have yet to be heeded.

On the medical front another struggle arose—AIDS. As a memorial to those who had lost their lives to this pandemic, the American-based Names Project began the creation of an enormous quilt. Each 3-by-6-foot panel contains the name, the image, and sometimes even some of the clothing or possessions of a person who has died from AIDS. Although there is no particular limitation, most of the people commemorated were Americans. The panels were created not by a particular artist or group of artists but by friends or relatives of the deceased; artistic training has here been judged less important than personal knowledge and commitment. During the fall of 1996, when the *AIDS Memorial Quit* had expanded to more than 37,000 panels, it was displayed in its entirety in Washington, D.C. for a few days (fig. 10-6). Like the *Vietnam Veterans Memorial*, the quilt commemorates individuals. In its vast size and communal spirit, the *AIDS Quit* acknowledges the scope of this modern disease and becomes both a memorial and cogent social commentary.

Intellectual and Scientific Activity

Scientific advancements during the twentieth century were revolutionary in many areas. In physics, Albert Einstein's general theory of relativity demonstrated the relationship of geometry to gravity and radically modified our concept of space and time. Our understanding of the very essence of matter has been altered, as the atom has been reduced to its subatomic components.

Throughout the twentieth century, major philosophical movements influenced visual expression. The Existentialist writings of Jean-Paul Sartre and Simone de Beauvoir, for example, emphasized the singularity and isolation of the individual in modern society. Meaning, they argued, is not conferred on us by external forces; it is actualized by indi-

10-7 ALBERTO GIACOMETTI

CITY SQUARE. 1948. Bronze, 8½ × 25⅛ × 17¼″. The Museum of Modern Art, New York.

vidual choices, the consequences of which are solely our responsibility. Existentialism also emphasized the importance of the moment and the fact that we really live only in the present. Their philosophical arguments can be related to the distinctive elongated figures in the sculptures of Alberto Giacometti (1901–66). His standing or walking figures, as in *City Square* (fig. 10-7), are recognizably human, upright, and dignified but lack the particular features that would give them individuality. Their rough contours make them seem nervous or agitated, and they are placed so that there seems to be no physical or psychological interaction. Even the spaces that separate them become poignant barriers to communication. Although the title of the work suggests a space that would normally be bustling with abundant human activity, here the figures seem to exist in solitude and only within themselves. In *City Square*, Giacometti has given visual form to the Existential concepts that were so strongly felt in post-World War II Europe.

Twentieth-century developments in psychology greatly influenced the course of art, especially in the movements of Surrealism and Abstract Expressionism (see pages 530–533, 546–49). Using therapeutic approaches that included free association and the interpretation of dreams in treating his patients, Sigmund Freud established the active and even dynamic role of the human unconscious in guiding behavior. To Freud, unmasking the subconscious was the key to understanding the human mind. Carl Jung extended, modified, and at times countered Freud's theories to develop additional psychological insights into human behavior. Jung advanced the notion of a "collective unconscious," a layer of unconscious that underlies the personal unconscious and that carries the inherited disposition of

our species. The collective unconscious was revealed by the common use of archetypal images, such as the circle, across diverse cultural traditions.

Radical changes were introduced in twentieth-century music. Igor Stravinsky's ballet music for *The Rite of Spring* (1913), with its driving, primal rhythms and fragmented melodies, nearly caused the audience to riot at its first performance. In Germany, the composer Arnold Schönberg devised a new system of musical tonality; Schönberg's pantonality (which is commonly referred to as being atonal) is a free but not unstructured use of musical tones without traditional chord progressions or resolutions. At mid-century, the American composer John Cage began to incorporate elements of chance into his work. One composition from 1952, titled *4′–33*, has a performer come on stage and sit at a piano for 4 minutes and 33 seconds. During this time, the unpredictable sounds from the audience and other accidental noises "create" the musical experience. Cage's avant-garde concept of music has been influential for contemporary poets, painters, and performance artists (see page 562).

Art of the Twentieth Century

Twentieth-century art is often referred to as modern art, although the terms are not exactly synonymous. The concept of modernism is relative within the context of history and until recently was virtually limited to Western art. It expresses an attitude that distinguishes a current time from the immediate past. Renaissance artists, for example, felt themselves to be working in a "modern style." In the history of art, developments in the nineteenth century

10-8 LEON BAKST

FAUN, ballet costume design for Nijinsky for *L'Après-midi d'un Faune*. 1912. Gouache, watercolor, and gold on paper mounted on cardboard, 11¾ × 10½". Wadsworth Atheneum, Hartford, Connecticut. For this costume, Bakst has been inspired by the Art Nouveau style, which flourished in Europe and the United States between about 1880 and 1920. Art Nouveau's emphasis on sinuous line and the natural forms of leaves and flowers and on the hand-crafted object, often made of the finest materials, is in part a reaction to the Industrial Revolution. Art Nouveau subject matter is often sensuous, a development related to the freer morality that was beginning to become common during these years. Commissioned by Sergey Diaghilev for the Ballets Russes production of the ballet.

THE ELLA GALLUP SUMNER AND MARY CATLIN SUMNER COLLECTION FUND

countered well-established traditions in art, laying the foundation for radical and rapid changes. These changes in twentieth-century art have been so distinctive that the term *modern* is applied in both a chronological and a descriptive sense to the works of avant-garde art that challenged earlier traditions. Modernism was a Western construct that only became common elsewhere when artists wanted to challenge the status quo or when they wanted to promote Western values and ideas.

The present century has brought a variety of artistic experiences unparalleled in the history of art. Throughout the century, the avant-garde has rapidly expanded the traditional limits of art by developing new styles, by working in new materials, and by questioning accepted artistic practice. One area in which avant-garde artists made an important contribution was in the theater, designing stage sets and costumes. Picasso, Matisse, Malevich, De Chirico, and Bakst, for example, all designed sets and/or costumes for the ballets presented in Paris and elsewhere by the Ballets Russes under the direction of the group's founder, Sergey Diaghilev. Their decor accompanied modern music commissioned by Diaghilev from Stravinsky, Prokofiev, Ravel, Poulenc, Satie, and others. Diaghilev's original choreographer, Michel Fokine, transformed the very nature of ballet by insisting on dramatic expression in gesture and movement and demanding that dancers use their whole body to convey the emotional message of the music and

the subject; other choreographers who worked with Diaghilev included the dancers Vaslav Nijinsky and George Balanchine. Nijinsky choreographed and danced the lead in the Ballets Russes's *L'Après-midi d'un Faune* (*The Afternoon of a Faun*), set to music written in 1894 by Claude Debussy. The theme, from antiquity, inspired Leon Bakst (1866–1924) to base the women's costumes on the attire seen in ancient Greek art, but his design for Nijinsky in his role of the Faun (fig. 10-8) responded both to the popular Art Nouveau style and to the need for a costume that would heighten the erotic and sinuous movements that Nijinsky choreographed for the Faun, a creature of nature, half animal and half man, who in the ballet experienced his first sexual awakening. Although it was said that the ballet shocked *"le tout Paris"* ("all Paris"), its revolutionary qualities were championed by the sculptor Rodin, among others. In the context of the ballet, Bakst's costume became kinetic art within a collaboration among artists at a moment when freedom of expression was being explored in all the arts.

More traditional currents in art, including realism and illusionism, have also been sustained throughout the century, although critics at the time often ignored the work of artists who worked outside the more "modern" mainstream. Edward Hopper (1882–1967) developed a personal style and iconography devoted to the theme of the loneliness and isolation of the individual. Hopper's settings could

10-9 EDWARD HOPPER

NIGHTHAWKS. 1942. Oil on canvas. The Art Institute of Chicago.

be anywhere in America, and his people are ordinary, nameless figures from the middle class. We have to be careful not to infuse these images with the nostalgia that their settings and costumes now evoke, for Hopper intended his paintings to represent the here and now. In *Nighthawks* (fig. 10-9), painted in 1942, we are cut off from the quiet individuals inside the diner, and the harsh interior light exposes the lack of communication that Hopper so often emphasizes in his images of modern urban life. Like Hopper, other artists fed the stream of realism that flowed, especially in America, throughout the twentieth century. In the '20s and '30s, works by Charles Sheeler (p. 535, fig. 10-83), Grant Wood (p. 535, fig. 10-84,), and Thomas Hart Benton (p. 537, fig. 10-86) celebrated various aspects of American life in a style meant to be open and democratically accessible to all viewers. Realism, however, was found to be responsive to other values. Andy Warhol's *Green Coca-Cola Bottles* (fig. 10-10) focused our attention on the consumer commercialism that has been such a driving force of the American economy since World War II. In the hands of Warhol and other Pop artists (see p. 480), representational art achieved avant-garde status. And, in recent decades, artists like Audrey Flack (p. 570, fig. 10-126) and the late Duane Hanson (p. 569, fig. 10-124) have delighted us with their creative and technical skills as they lead us to consider the complex relationship between art and life.

It is, however, abstraction and nonobjectivity that have become the hallmarks of twentieth-century art. Continuing formal developments advanced by the Post-Impressionist artists, twentieth-century artists expanded the vocabulary of visual expression. Georgia O'Keeffe's *Evening Star III* (fig. 10-11) is from a series of watercolors inspired by viewing the evening star at sunset, but representational associations have here been abstracted to express the rhythmic pulsations of the star over the landscape. O'Keeffe's painting communicates a sensation rather than the appearance of a scene. *The Kiss* (fig. 10-12), by Constantin Brancusi (1876–1957), with its compact, rectangular masses joining two abstract figures, conveys the essence of unity. For Brancusi, the expression of a concept, which in this sculpture is the wholeness of two individuals as symbolized by the kiss, overrode concerns of naturalism. Some artists denied any representational aspects in their work. Helen Frankenthaler's *Tobacco Landscape* (fig. 10-14) is a nonobjective painting belonging to a 1960s style called Post-Painterly Abstraction.

Abstraction held a particularly powerful hold on artists whose concern was the communication of the emotional forces of life. Early in the century, Ernst Ludwig Kirchner (p. 514, fig. 10-59) utilized expressive distortions of form to share his observations on the quickened pulse and anxiety of modern life. But abstraction also served artists like Picasso (p. 505, fig. 10-47), whose aim was the more formal manipulation of the visual elements of art.

In the 1930s, André Kertész (1894–1985), a Hungarian photojournalist working in France, achieved a unique form of figurative abstraction through "straight" photography (fig. 10-13). Kertész achieved these effects of distortion by

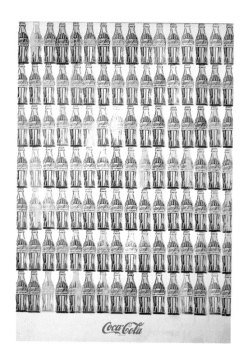

10-10 ANDY WARHOL

Green Coca-Cola Bottles. 1962. Oil on canvas, 6'10¼" × 4'9". Whitney Museum of American Art, New York.

10-11 GEORGIA O'KEEFFE

Evening Star III. 1917. Watercolor on paper, 9 × 11⅞". The Museum of Modern Art, New York.

photographing models reflected in "fun house" mirrors with varied surfaces. The resulting series of photographs are reminiscent of expressionist tendencies and Surrealism in painting.

Other twentieth-century painters have chosen more geometric, angular shapes as their expression of nonobjectivity in painting. Beginning around 1913, Russian avant-garde artists sought to express a purity of emotion through visual statements of geometric shapes (pp. 512-513). With different purposes, "Hard-Edge" and "Op" artists later in the century (figs. 10-108 and 10-110) continued the strong tradition of geometric nonobjectivity.

In viewing twentieth-century art, we witness a tremendous expansion of the materials used by artists. Traditional mediums, such as marble, bronze, and wood for sculpture, will be joined by commonplace, found objects, and even discarded junk in creating **assemblage** works. Even the raw earth has become a significant medium of artistic expression (see fig. 10-122). In composing *Sky Cathedral* (fig. 10-15),

10-12 CONSTANTIN BRANCUSI

The Kiss. 1909. Limestone, height 23". Philadelphia Museum of Art.

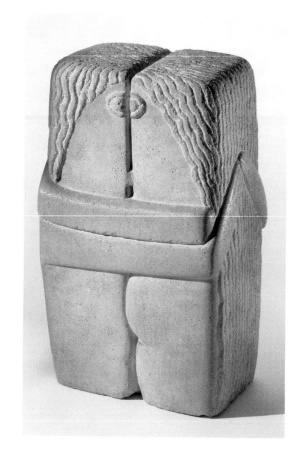

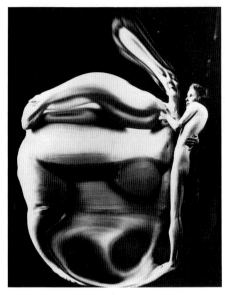

10-13 ANDRÉ KERTÉSZ

Distortion No. 4. 1933, Gelatin silver print. Estate of Kertész. Kertész's *Distortion* photographs, commissioned by a French magazine in 1933, were not published until 1976.

10-14 HELEN FRANKENTHALER

Tobacco Landscape. 1964. Acrylic on canvas, 5′9½″ × 7′5¼″. Private Collection.

Louise Nevelson (1900–88) assembled cut and scrap pieces of wood—parts of furniture, architectural decoration, and the like—in each box. The individual boxes were then arranged to form a wall-like construction. The overall black paint unites the piece, integrating the multiple, diverse forms. Shadows within and among the boxes increase a sense of mystery. In Nevelson's assemblage sculptures, the commonplace has been transfigured.

After mid-century, the fashioning of an art object became less important to some artists. In the **happenings** of the 1950s and 1960s, artists, usually without a preconceived script, performed and directed the activity of the audience during a quasi-theatrical event, often outside the confines of a museum or gallery. *Household* (fig. 10-16), by Allan Kaprow (b. 1927), for example, was commissioned by Yale University. Happenings and performance art have countered traditional definitions of the work of art as a tangible object. Another thrust of artists late in this century has been to break down the distinctions between "high" and "low" art. In the early 1980s, Keith Haring (1958–90) was inspired by the vigor and simplicity of street graffiti, and he began to draw bold chalk compositions onto the black paper that was pasted over ads whose rental time had expired in New York City subway stations. This series of more than 5,000 drawings became known as *Art in Transit* (fig. 10-17); the title refers not only to the location of these chalk drawings but also to their continual removal by the authorities and to the manner in which they boldly challenged the traditional notion of art. Haring's linear, energetic figures are, in the artist's words,

open to everyone,

and in a typical democratic, twentieth-century manner, he often kept the meaning of each composition somewhat vague in order to allow for personal interpretation.

Installation art, which also denies the tradition of a work of art as a unique, singular object, fashions a temporary environment within a gallery space (see figs. 10-144. 10-148, 10-149, 10-150) or, as in the case of Judy Pfaff's *cirque, Cirque*, a permanent object within a large, usually public space (see fig. 1-14). *The Sleep of Reason* (fig. 10-18) by Bill Viola (b. 1951) is a video and sound installation; upon entering a room, we are confronted by a simple arrangement of commonplace objects, including a rather everyday chest with a lamp, a vase of flowers, a clock, and a television set on top. The video shown on the television represents a man sleeping. Suddenly, however, the room goes dark, and huge images of attacking birds, lunging Dobermans, crashing waves, and other disturbing images are projected on the walls, accompanied by thunderous, even terrifying noises. We are jolted from a comfortable perception of reality and, it seems, trapped in a small space surrounded by nightmarish visions. The title of Viola's installation makes reference to a late-eighteenth-century print by the Spanish artist Francisco Goya titled *The Sleep of Reason Produces Monsters*. In Goya's print, a sleeping artist, his head resting on a desk, is beset by winged monsters; Goya clarified the meaning of the image in the accompanying text:

Imagination abandoned by reason produces impossible monsters; united with her, she is the mother of the

10-15 LOUISE NEVELSON

SKY CATHEDRAL. 1958. Wood painted black, 9'7" × 11'3". Albright-Knox Art Gallery, Buffalo, New York.

10-16 ALLAN KAPROW.

From *HOUSEHOLD*, a happening commissioned by Yale University, 1964.

10-17 KEITH HARING

ART IN TRANSIT. 1982. Graffiti in New York City subway station.

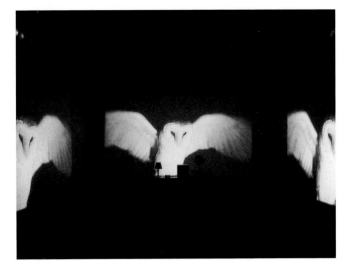

10-18   BILL VIOLA

THE SLEEP OF REASON. 1988. Video and sound installation: 3 videotape projectors, 1 monitor, ¾″ videotape, 2 channels, sound, color and black and white, 14′1″ × 19′3″ × 22′. Carnegie Museum of Art, Pittsburgh.

arts and the source of all their wonders.

For both Goya and Viola, creativity is examined within the interrelationship between reason and imagination. Viola's installation, however, removes us from being observers and forces us to enter a dialogue within this interrelationship.

Western artists have often identified modernism with a search for newness. This search also has led architects to the creation of a more purely formal aesthetic that countered the eclecticism and abundant decoration of the late nineteenth century. At times, this aesthetic was imbued with philosophical meaning, as with the Bauhaus, although in this case an inspiration was found at the Japanese Katsura Villa, outside the Western tradition (see figs. 1-5, 7-53, 7-54). In recent decades, the formalist approach has been challenged by architects who have sought to rehumanize our architectural environments and to question those concepts that have defined Western architectural tradition.

In many rural areas of today's world, however, the quest for newness is not a dominant feature in either art or architecture. Often, the creation of intentionally repetitive art is part of an effort to link generations of individuals. For important occasions, such as a marriage, the birth of a child, or a festival, for example, women in the villages in Rajasthan, in India, paint *mandanas*, or floor designs, at the threshold, on the walls, or in the inner rooms of their houses (fig. 10-19). Each design is produced by following hereditary prescription; women learn from their mothers the precise drawings and techniques required for each *mandana*. Most often the purpose of the *mandana* is spiritual; it acts as a visual prayer to secure blessings on the household. *Man-*

10-19.   Indian village women creating a *mandana*, Rajasthan, India. 1994. Rice paste on floor resurfaced with red ocher and cow dung wash.

danas are but one example of a host of temporary art forms that are regularly created around the globe to reinforce the continuity of ethnic or regional cultural values. In the cultures in which these works are created, they are probably not thought of as "art" in the traditional Western sense, and the women who create them are not thought of as "artists."

10-20 SERGEY EISENSTEIN

POTEMKIN, detail of film stills. 1925.
Eisenstein's film dealt with the 1905 mutiny
aboard the Russian ship *Potemkin* and the
failed anti-czarist uprising.

10-21. QUENTIN TARANTINO, *PULP FICTION*, detail of film stills. 1994.

But the works they create, albeit ephemeral, have a serious purpose that is similar to many of the works that are considered to be art in the West. As communication makes our global community smaller and more accessible, we can more easily understand the integrity to be found in these distinct and meaningful traditions.

One modern international medium of artistic expression is cinema. In the late nineteenth century, experimental photographers succeeded in presenting a "moving picture" by projecting a sequential series of photographs taken at exposures as quick as 1/2000 of a second. The forerunner of our motion-picture projector, however, was the Vitascope, invented by Thomas Armat and manufactured by Thomas Edison in 1895. The projector achieved the illusion of movement by rapidly projecting a series of still photographic images in sequence. The persistence of our vision, from the image retained on the retina of the eye, lets our minds interpret the rapidly shown still frames as continuous movement. By 1895, the Lumière brothers had opened the first public movie theater in France, and soon their *cinématographie* was being shown throughout Europe.

Like other art forms, cinema is primarily a visual experience. Techniques of shooting can effectively manipulate our perspective as we remain stationary. But special to film is the depiction of movement over a course of time. The expression of a continued time has been an important element in many works of art, but with cinema, not only is time actual but our perception of it may be altered by various methods of editing—the "cutting and pasting" of sequences of film together. Sergey Eisenstein's editing in *Potemkin*, rapidly shifting us from scenes of Cossacks firing into a crowd to scenes expressing the anguish of the people, conveys the tragedy of the event (fig. 10-20). The efficacy of the modern medium of cinema was vividly expressed by the Swedish director Ingmar Bergman when he stated:

> I can transport my audience from a given feeling to the feeling that is diametrically opposed to it, as if each spectator were on a pendulum. I can make an audience laugh, scream with terror, smile, believe in legends, become indignant, take offense, become enthusiastic, lower itself, or yawn with boredom. . . . I am able to mystify, and I have at my disposal the most astounding device [the motion-picture camera] that has ever, since history began, been put into the hands of the juggler.

In 1994, the iconoclastic film *Pulp Fiction*, directed by Quentin Tarantino, signaled a radically different aesthetic for the medium. The critic Roger Ebert communicated not only the substance of the film, but also its galvanizing energy when he wrote:

> Tarantino is . . . in love with every shot—intoxicated with the very act of making a movie. It's that very lack of caution and introspection that makes *Pulp Fiction* crackle like an ozone generator. . . . [The film tells] several interlocking stories about characters who inhabit a world of crime and intrigue, triple-crosses, and loud desperation . . . [creating] a world where there are no normal people and no ordinary days— where breathless prose clatters down fire escapes and leaps into the dumpster of doom.

10-22 JACOB LAWRENCE

SELF-PORTRAIT. 1977. Gouache on paper, 23 × 31". National Academy of Design, New York.

Pulp Fiction is a film on the edge, both in style and content (fig. 10-21). Most of the action builds from a consistent theme of crisis control. That theme, however, unfolds with a variety of responses, the structure of which shares much with Postmodernism (see pp. 571–72). Episodes in the film double back upon themselves; we witness the same events from different, highly personal, points of view. This nonsequential construction recalls the plurality of Postmodernism, while the Postmodern dialogue between past and present is felt in the film's inspiration, which lies less in real life than in the parody of older movies. In its essence, *Pulp Fiction* reminds us that truth often is relative to perception.

Finally, the twentieth century has transformed art to such an extent that the artist may become the work of art, in performance art, and the work of art as an object may be deemed less important than the concept or idea to create it. Joseph Kosuth's *One and Three Chairs* (see fig. 10-117), for example, seems to refer to the potential of an art object rather than being one in itself.

The Twentieth-Century Artist

The thing that interests me today is that painters do not have to go to a subject matter outside themselves. Modern painters work in a different way. They work from within.

(Jackson Pollock, 1951)

Pollock's statement, made at mid-century, summarizes the experience of the artist in this century. The rapidity of social change, the impact of technology, and new artistic freedoms have altered many traditional notions of the role and identity of the artist. The twentieth-century artist has forged a new independence with diverse materials, and often works of art are imbued with a highly introspective content. This aspect of self-gratification in art leads us to experience many works as a revelation of the artist's inner self (see Pollock's work, fig. 10-97). It is almost as if this disclosure of the inner self, which in the past was usually restricted to self-portraits, is the main content of many twentieth-century works of art. But the diversity and subjectivity of this new freedom have also posed problems in the critical evaluation of art and even in the identity of the artist. Having broadened the definition of art, customary notions concerning the education of artists and the parameters of a work of art have been opened to a flood of conjectural questions concerning quality, value, and meaning.

The three self-portraits shown here demonstrate how several twentieth-century artists have used the self-portrait as a means of self-examination. Jacob Lawrence, a contemporary African American artist (b. 1917; see also page 537), painted his *Self-Portrait* when he was elected to membership in the National Academy of Design (fig. 10-22); it joined hundreds of portraits and self-portraits of other members in the Academy's collection. Lawrence's direct and compelling painting alludes to both the physical and the intellectual processes of creativity. He is surrounded by the

10-23 FRIDA KAHLO

THE TWO FRIDAS. 1939. Oil on canvas, 5'9" × 5'9". Museo de Arte Moderno, Mexico City.

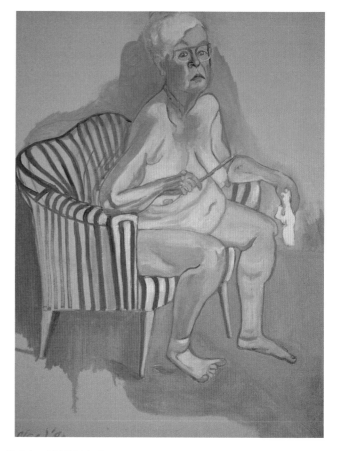

10-24 ALICE NEEL

NUDE SELF-PORTRAIT. 1980. Oil on canvas, 54 × 40". National Portrait Gallery, Washington, D.C.

tools and products of his profession, including, in the upper left background, a work from his *Harriet Tubman* series, which narrated the life of the former slave who, before the Civil War, was responsible for freeing more than 300 slaves. The laborer below the Harriet Tubman painting and the tools and paintings on the shelf refer to Lawrence's *Builders* theme, which had its roots in the artist's youth in Harlem, where he associated with cabinetmakers and carpenters. For Lawrence, this theme symbolized human aspiration, which, in the artist's words,

> came from my own observation of the human condition.

The Two Fridas, a double self-portrait by the Mexican artist Frida Kahlo (1910–54), is a complex image filled with symbolism (fig. 10-23). Although the two figures hold hands and are joined by a common blood system, the duality Kahlo felt is revealed by the contrasting costumes, Mexican and European. Her dual heritage is likewise expressed in the two hearts, for the figure in the European dress has her chest ripped open in a reference to Aztec sacrificial practices, while the other figure's heart resembles Catholic representations of the Sacred

Heart of Jesus. This revealing, if enigmatic, work was painted as Kahlo was being divorced, and the open artery on her lap may refer to her suffering at this time. Such redundant self-revelation is not unusual in twentieth-century art.

From later in the century, the *Nude Self-Portrait* of Alice Neel (1900–84) is a bold statement of the new honesty of the artist (fig. 10-24). The stern modeling and rather austere pose portray a psychological presence that coexists with the probing, unashamed honesty of the nude figure. Such introspective and deliberate honesty, revealed within a wide variety of visual means, can be one of the keys to understanding the modern artist.

The role of the patron, so important in most art before the nineteenth century, was reduced even further in the course of the twentieth century. As Jackson Pollock's quote reveals, the attitude held by artists and the public alike is that artists work "from within." Although most twentieth-century works are created by the artist independently, without a patron or any controlling dictates from outside, there are still exceptions. Most architects, for example, cannot afford to construct a building just to see if someone will buy it. Architects are the most likely of all twentieth-century artists to work on commission, although the mindset of the period is such that some architects, once they understand the function of the building and the particular needs of the client, refuse advice about anything that might concern design. Other examples of patronage might be large public monuments, where clients request a work, informing the artist of the price they are willing to pay, the particular location, and the needs (for example, commemoration or decoration) that the work is intended to fulfill, but here again the artist usually remains free to create a personal solution to these problems.

Artists of the twentieth century have had to respond to a different world from that of their predecessors. Technology and the immediacy of communication have brought us into an era in which isolation is increasingly rare and where the developments in ecology, economics, political change, and even local conflict can have a strong impact on a large part of the world. Artists, like the rest of us, are caught up in global tension, uncertainty, promise, and the search for individual identity.

10-25 PHILIP JOHNSON

Glass House, 1949
(for further information, see fig. 10-95 and p. 545).

These two images of homes are examples of the extremes that can be found in twentieth century art: The aesthetic purity and simplicity of modern abstract art seen in the Glass House is in sharp contrast to the vigor and multiplicity of popular culture suggested by Richard Hamilton's collage representation of a living room. The home that Philip Johnson designed for himself exemplifies a modern aesthetic that asserts that the ideal environment for living imposes geometry on life's irregularities; the Pop art collage draws attention to the manner in which modern life has been dominated by advertising, with its logos, its use of sex to sell products, and its slogans (as in the title of the work, which was probably taken from a magazine article). It is hard to imagine a greater contrast than the one seen here, between the elitism of the artistic and critical community and the actuality of everyday life (although it also has to be recognized that the Pop art collage is an artistic creation intended, on at least one level, to satirize and criticize the commercialism that it at first seems to glorify). Throughout human history, the home—cave, hut, tent, palace, farmhouse, row house, ranch house, apartment, condominium—and its furnishings have been a revealing indicator of the attitudes and aspirations of the people who built and/or used it.

10-26 RICHARD HAMILTON

Just What Is It That Makes Today's Home So Different, So Appealing?, 1956
(for further information, see fig. 10-111 and p. 559).

JUST WHAT IS IT THAT MAKES TODAY'S HOMES SO DIFFERENT, SO APPEALING? BY RICHARD HAMILTON. KUNSTHALLE TUBINGEN, COLLECTION OF Z. F. ZUNDELL, GERMANY

Materials can limit and condition the character of the home. In this Native American village there was a limited availability of wood, and as a result most construction is made of mud brick covered with adobe. The construction that resulted is in harmony with the surrounding landscape in color and substance, and, as is apparent in this view, the forms of these adobe constructions reflect the natural forms in the surrounding area. The manner in which the homes are joined to create a total complex is an indication of tribal unity, as is the lack of any hierarchy of construction.

10-27   Native American, Walpi Village,
Hopi Reservation, twentieth century
(for further information, see fig. 10-36 and pp. 496–97).

If we look beyond the Christian events of the Annunciation and Incarnation, we realize that Campin has provided us with a rare view into a Flemish fifteenth-century living room, complete with furnishings. His goal, of course, was to make the holy events as palpable as possible for his contemporaries, and perhaps also to suggest that Mary and Joseph were similar to the ordinary working people of his village. Campin's determination to provide a setting with which his peers could identify bears the unexpected side effect of welcoming us into their fifteenth-century world.

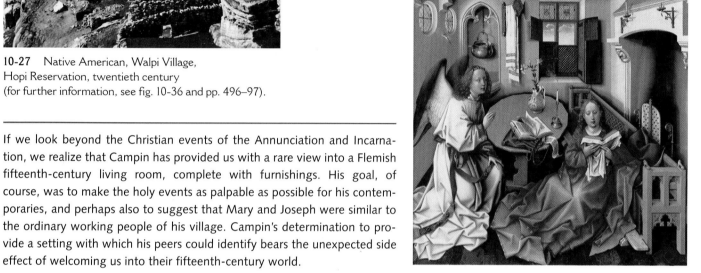

10-28   ROBERT CAMPIN   *ANNUNCIATION*, c. 1425–30
(for further information, see figs. 5-18, 5-19,
and pp. 242–43).

ROBERT CAMPIN (ACTIVE BY 1406–DIED 1444), *THE ANNUNCIATION*.
TRIPTYCH. OIL ON WOOD. CENTRAL PANEL: H. 25¼ IN. × W. 24⅞ IN (64.1 ×
63.2 CM). EACH WING: H. 25⅜ IN. × W. 10¾ IN. (64.5 × 27.3 CM). THE
METROPOLITAN MUSEUM OF ART, THE CLOISTERS COLLECTION, 1956.
(56.70) PHOTOGRAPH (C) 1996 THE METROPOLITAN MUSEUM OF ART

Your Home Here!

10-29   "Insert photo of your home here."

The home or room where you currently live is an expression of you as a person even if you've done little to change or modify it. Your choice of your family, a friend, or a group of friends with whom to live, of a location, of a particular house or apartment, of even a few furnishings, such as a poster or print: These all indicate something about you and your needs and aspirations.

■   **QUESTIONS**

1. What form would your ideal home take, and what would it and its furnishings express about you as an individual living in the twenty-first century?

2. For what audience would this home be intended: you alone? other members of your family? your friends? the "public"? the future?

3. Would you be more concerned with expressing the "real" you, or in projecting an "ideal" version of yourself?

Fauvism

10-30 HENRI MATISSE

THE JOY OF LIFE. 1905–06. Oil on canvas, 5′8½″ × 7′9¾″. The Barnes Foundation, Merion, Pennsylvania. When it was exhibited in 1906, *The Joy of Life* was singled out for criticism. The painter Paul Signac complained that Matisse had "gone to the dogs."

I cannot copy nature in a servile way, I must interpret nature and submit it to the spirit of the picture—when I have found the relationship of all the tones the result must be a living harmony of tones, a harmony not unlike that of a musical composition. . . .

The chief aim of color should be to serve expression as well as possible. . . . What I dream of is an art of balance, of purity and serenity devoid of troubling or depressing subject-matter, an art . . . like an appeasing influence, like a mental soother, something like a good armchair in which to rest from physical fatigue.

(Henri Matisse, *Notes of a Painter*, 1908)

In Matisse's representation of the mythical land of Arcadia (fig. 10-30), lovers embrace and dance to music. The sinuous nudes who inhabit this verdant pasture are defined by the same curving, rhythmic lines that describe trees and foliage, suggesting a harmony between humanity and the natural order. The colors are intense and vibrant. Matisse's monumental painting descends from a tradition of pastoral images that began in antiquity. In this twentieth-century interpretation the broad areas of unmodulated bold color and the powerful flowing linear rhythms create a patterned, flat composition that adheres to the picture plane.

In the opening years of the present century, Matisse, began to make paint-

10-31 HENRI MATISSE

THE DANCE. 1909–10. Oil on canvas, 8′5″ × 12′8″. Hermitage, St. Petersburg. Commissioned by Sergey Shchukin, a wealthy Russian businessperson and important patron of both Matisse and Picasso. Matisse had shown Shchukin a preliminary design in Paris, and Shchukin wrote back to Matisse from Moscow: "I find 'The Dance' of such nobility that I have decided to defy Russian bourgeois attitudes and to place on my staircase a subject with NUDES. It will be necessary to have a second painting, of which the subject might well be music. . . . In my house we have a great deal of music. Each winter there are some ten classical concerts (Bach, Beethoven, Mozart). The panel 'Music' should indicate in some way the character of the house." Shchukin brought Matisse to Moscow for a visit in 1911.

ings in which color, independent of descriptive reality, was exalted for its expressive and sensuous self. Matisse worked in Paris with a group of painters who were exploring this liberation of color, and at a Parisian exhibition in 1905, their works were displayed in a room with a classicizing sculpture, causing the critic Louis Vauxcelles to remark:

Donatello au milieu des fauves! ("Donatello among the wild beasts!").

This witty denunciation gave the name *Fauvism* to this new style.

Within a few years, Matisse was experimenting with further simplifying his style. His boldest experiments were undertaken in a pair of paintings dedicated to Dance and Music, created for Sergey Shchukin, a Russian patron. Shchukin's interest in the art of Matisse and Picasso paralleled the Russian interest in revolutionary statements in music, ballet, literature, and politics. He purchased many of their works when he visited their studios in Paris. In *The Dance* (fig. 10-31), Matisse took the dancers from the center of *The Joy of Life* and expanded them so that they seem ready to burst out of the boundaries of the huge canvas. The figures are almost lifesize, and the powerful curves of their shapes make their movement seem impulsive and unstoppable. The figures are organic and full of life, and yet Matisse avoided using traditional modeling to suggest three-dimensionality. Matisse limited the colors to four, setting the warm orangish hue of the figures and their outlines against two hues from the opposite side of the color wheel: blue and green. The drama and impulsive movement of the dance are conveyed here with limited means and careful control by the artist.

African Art and Ritual

10-32 Bwa culture. Ritual dancers wearing painted wooden plank masks and related raffia body suits at annual purification rites. Twentieth century. Plank masks of wood, paint, and raffia. Burkina Faso, Upper Volta River Region.

For the Bwa, that environment is the savannah just below the desert, which stretches across the continent. They live in small kin-based communities surrounded by the land that they farm.

The visual arts of sub-Saharan Africa are sets of objects, acts, and performance that express and affirm beliefs. The human expression that we call African art is found in masks and costumes, figurative sculpture, body decoration, clothing, decorative arts, instrumental and vocal musical composition and performance, dance, oral performance, and the ways in which all or some of these are brought together in ritual life. Each detail carries or expresses meaning, sometimes multiple meanings depending on the audience and the performer. For example, a chevron in contrasting colors may represent the feathers of a particular bird and the opposition of dark and light. While the artist is recognized for the fullness and effectiveness of her expression, art is seen as the presentation of recurring themes, unchanging elements in daily life. Repetition, affirmation, and continuity are the messages of the arts in Africa.

Outside the major political centers, the village is the dominant political unit. Although the villages are not isolated from each other, distinct and localized patterns of culture, including language and arts, have been maintained. All these groups, however, share a concept about the relationship of human life to nature and perform a series of ritual activities that are outfitted with ritual dress, dance, and music.

In this region agriculture is the predominant source of wealth. The fear of drought or of a delay in the arrival of the rainy season is a source of mental stress that the farmers ease through

These people wearing painted wooden masks and fiber body suits (fig. 10-32) are participants in rites that the Bwa perform to sustain social balance in their communities and to mark the cycle of seasonal renewal and rebirth. These wooden masks are constructed of planks that extend laterally or above a face with ringed eyes. Decoration is geometric (lozenges, checks, triangles, and chevrons) and has been interpreted both in terms of animals that are represented and in terms of the forces or principles with which those

animals are associated. The fiber suits and masks use and portray the fruits of the seasonal cycle that is essential to their agricultural economy. The masks and costumes appear according to that cycle: with the coming of rain and the drying of the terrain after the harvest, as well as when social conditions merit attention and community action.

The Bwa, like other traditional societies across Africa, have a highly articulated spiritual/ritual life that blends the concerns and conduct of daily life with the rhythms of the natural environment.

highly developed institutions and rites intended to preserve the relationship between nature, the source of all life, and survival. The Bwa see nature as essentially benevolent, but the needs, mistakes, and offenses of people upset it. The function of the ritual performance is to chase away the evil that is bound to occur in human communities. This purification role of the dances is indispensable to the cycle of renewal and is directly linked to the creation myth. Such rites are necessary at times of transition—birth, entering adult life, death, planting, and harvest.

The Bwa hold that Wuro, the Supreme Being, installed harmonious order among the sun, rain, and earth at creation. Human beings threaten that equilibrium. The techniques of agriculture involve violation of the soil and that outrages Soxo, the divinity of the bush, and through him, Wuro the Creator. Moreover, if one transgresses the taboos (laws) of society, a sequence of calamities will occur: drought leads to starvation, sickness, sterility, and sometimes even death. Wuro gave some of his bounty to Dwo, who acts as mediator between God and human life to restore balance. Dwo is incarnated in the leaf masks of the Bwa.

Leaf masks and body suits cover the entire body of the dancer (fig. 10-33) and are made in the bush after the millet crop is safely stored. The leaves are from a local tree, the karité (a type of mahogany), and are tied together with vegetable fiber. Feathers or a straw crest indicate that the mask is male. The leaf masks enter the village at dusk and roam the alleys, lightly brushing against storehouses, huts, and the people of the village. The rustling leaves collect all the dust particles, which represent the offenses of human beings. They cleanse what they touch of all their impurities and thus absorb the evil that has accumulated throughout the year. They purify the village. The masks and body suits are perishable and their potency is spent in this activity. They, too, are part of the life cycle and must be regenerated at the end of the next agricultural season.

20th century	**Bwa ritual dancers**
1906	All-Indian Muslim League founded by Aga Khan
1908	Congo Free State becomes the Belgian Congo
1909	First women admitted to German universities

10-33 Bwa culture. Ritual dancer wearing leaf mask and related body suit. Twentieth century. Leaves of the karité tree ("bastard mahogany"), fiber, straw, and colored string. Burkina Faso, Upper Volta River region.

The human community also is regenerated by participation in renewal rites of nature that take place at the end of the dry season, before the first rain falls and planting begins. These rites signify the end of the period of mourning, are a rite of purification, and appeal to the spirits of the underworld. They require the presence of leaf, fiber, and sculpted masks.

Fiber masks are decorated with clan emblems linked to veneration of human lineage. The wooden, sculpted masks are usually rendered in animal form and represent the protective spirits of the village. They include the male flat-horned buffalo, the female buffalo with circularly sectioned horns, the warthog, the cock with its crest, the toucan, the fish, the antelope, and the serpent, which can be as much as 10 feet long. The *Bird of the Night*, or butterfly mask and body suit (see fig. 1-13), appears after the first rains of the season. As the fluttering movements of the butterfly are imitated by the dancer, the essence of the animal is invoked.

As with many African arts, the masks were collected by Western artists, anthropologists, and collectors in the late nineteenth century because they were moved by the masks' direct and powerful formal expression; usually, however, only the carved and painted wooden masks were preserved and exhibited, while the related body suits, constructed of more perishable materials, and the leaf mask and body suit were not included. Only recently have these masks begun to be understood in their own context by outsiders.

Native American Art

10-34 Hopi culture, Arizona. Kachina figures. Twentieth century. Cottonwood roots adorned with mineral paints and other natural materials. The Heard Museum, Phoenix, Arizona.

20th century	Hopi kachina figurines
1906	San Francisco earthquake
1907	Oklahoma is admitted as forty-sixth state

10-35   Hopi culture, New Mexico. Hemis Kachina. Twentieth century. Feathers, yarn, buckskin, and grass.
The design of the headress, with stepped designs called *tablitas*, refers to clouds. The figure holds cattails.

These wooden figurines (fig. 10-34), called *kachin-tihus* (or kachina "dolls"), were carved by Hopi, a people living in northeastern Arizona. The elaborate headdresses, some of them fitted with birds' feathers, are thought to assist in transmitting messages to and from the spirits. Another kind of kachina—a supernatural being who acts as an intermediary between the gods and human beings—is a human figure (fig. 10-35) wearing a ritual outfit and headdress that are not unlike those on the small wooden figurines. As with most Native American art, these examples must be seen as functional—that is, they were not produced solely for their own sake as decorative objects but were meant to serve social and religious purposes. Each example is invested with sacred symbolism.

The spirits with whom these kachinas are intended to communicate are thought to live in the San Francisco Peaks and are believed to visit the Hopi at their current home in Arizona during the first half of the year, when the planting of new crops is being prepared. Among their many powers, these important spirits are thought to exercise control over weather. The Hopi were and still are

10-36 Hopi culture. First Mesa, Walpi Village is the foreground, Hopi Reservation, Arizona. Twentieth century. Seaver Center for Western History Research, Los Angeles County Museum of Natural History.

farmers who grow corn, beans, and squash. Because of their dependence on agriculture in this arid region, they have developed a complex religious life centered around rainmaking and crop fertility.

In the Hopi religion, there are three manifestations of kachinas: the spirit, a human acting as a spirit, and a carved figurine. The spirit, which cannot be seen, is impersonated in rituals by members of the Hopi community. By placing masks over their heads and wearing elaborate ritual dress and headdresses, these men and women are regarded as having taken on the supernatural character of the kachina spirit. Through special masks, costumes, paint, and actions of the impersonators, the otherworldly spirits are

given power, substance, and personality. Kachina figurines are miniature representations (8–10 inches tall) of the masked impersonators.

There are about 250 kachina personalities, though a limited number are favored. They personify a variety of natural elements, including clouds, rain, crops, animals, and even such abstract concepts as growth. Archaeological evidence shows that kachina dolls have been in use since the Hopi first inhabited the southwestern United States, between 1350 and 1400.

The Hopi culture was not much disturbed by European influence until the late nineteenth century, and the Hopi claim that they, more than any other North American people, live "in the old way." Since 1882, the Hopi have

been officially confined to government reservations in northeastern Arizona (page 475). This is the traditional homeland of the Navajo and the Zuni as well as is typified by steep-walled canyons and isolated mesas formed by the steady down-cutting of rivers. Hopi communities are based on cooperation, as their survival in such a difficult environment depends on shared responsibility. They count on ceremonies to give them unity and cohesiveness. Group rituals depend on cooperation and are important models for the whole community to witness.

Hopi villages seem to grow directly out of the mesa top, and their building materials and shapes give them continuity with the living rock on which they are built (fig. 10-36). This is often called an organic mode of building, for there is little conscious separation between what is made by human hands and what is natural environment. Recent research suggests that while the men construct the buildings in the villages, using mud brick, it is the women who, as the figures in charge of the home, are responsible for finishing the structures with adobe and maintaining the fragile adobe surfaces. After the women put the adobe on a new kiva, they sometimes "sign" the structures with their handprints on the roofbeams.

Hopi village life is organized around the plaza, a central space left open for the performance of ritual dances. Preparation for such rituals takes place in an underground chamber called a *kiva*, which represents the underworld from which the Hopi believe their peo-ple emerged in primordial times and also the womb of Mother Earth. Among other beliefs, the *kiva* is where the ritual of growing new food plants for the coming season takes place. This ritual is performed by men, whose upward movement from the dark *kiva* to the open daylight symbolically reenacts the Hopi "origin myth," in which the Hopi emerged from the chaos of the underworld to begin settled agricultural life on the mesas.

Ceremonies in the *kivas* and plaza take place over a seven-month period beginning in December. In the winter, when the earth's vegetation is dormant and covered with snow, the kachina rituals are held at night in the *kivas*. These dances, which include figures dressed as warriors and hunters, emphasize combat and death. Spring and summer rituals take place in the outdoor plaza in daylight and are associated with fertility, themes of growth, and regeneration. They are happy, boisterous occasions involving both men and women in ritual dress who sing and dance in an ordered and stately fashion. Some kachina dancers, however, represent ogres, whose role is to admonish everyone, especially children, to obey the rules of Hopi society. In a society based on cooperation rather than authoritarian control, such kachinas are important for assuring social stability. The kachina figurines serve a didactic purpose: to remind Hopi children of religious and social mores. They are not toys; these art forms are clearly an integral part of life and are thought to ensure Hopi survival.

Art Past/Art Present *Women in Pueblo Society*

In traditional Western Pueblo society, which encompasses both the Hopi culture in New Mexico and the Zuni culture in Arizona, women are central to the ideology. Because the goals of these cultures is the continuity of life, the role of women as childbearers and as feeders is central to their ideology. While men may more commonly play the more public roles in rituals, such as that of the kachina, women's rituals are more often private. While men's role in planting and tending the crops is crucial for the continuation of the village, it is recognized that these crops come from the womb of Mother Earth, which is symbolized in the *kiva*, the underground structure where many rituals take place.

Many of the kachinas represented in the rituals are women, with men taking these roles and becoming the particular female spirits for the duration of the ritual. Among the female kachina spirits are the Mother of the Gods, the Goddess of Hard Substances (turquoise in particular and wealth in general), the Salt Old Woman, and the Seven Corn Maidens.

Because of the centrality of women in Pueblo society, women own the houses and all the household possessions, and the society is matrilineal, with inheritance passing through the female line rather than the male.

Photography

10-37 ALFRED STIEGLITZ

THE STEERAGE. Photogravure, 1907.
George Eastman House, Rochester,
New York

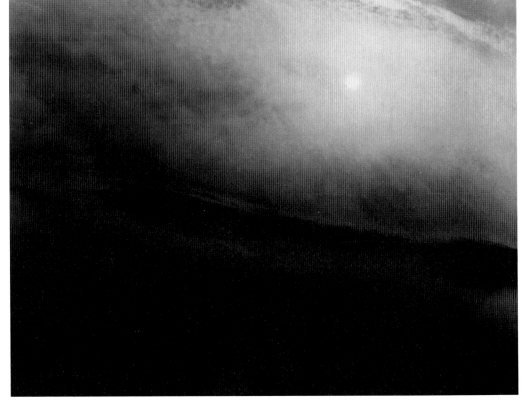

10-38 ALFRED STIEGLITZ

EQUIVALENT. 1930. Chloride print. The Art Institute of Chicago.

The whole scene fascinated me. . . . I saw shapes related to each other. I saw a picture of shapes and underlying that of the feeling I had about life. And, as I was deciding, should I try to put down this seemingly new vision that held me—people, the common people, the feeling of ship and ocean and sky and the feeling of release that I was away from the mob called the rich—Rembrandt came into my mind and I wondered—would he have felt as I was feeling? . . . I had but one plate holder with one exposure plate. Would I get what I saw, what I felt? Finally I released the shutter. My heart thumping . . .

Had I gotten my picture? I knew that if I had, another milestone in photography would have been reached. Here would be a picture based on related shapes and on the deepest human feeling.

These insightful words were shared by the photographer Alfred Stieglitz (1864–1946) as he revealed his psychological understanding of the creative perception that led to his photograph titled *The Steerage* (fig. 10-37). Stieglitz's photograph from 1907 balances the relationship between form and content, and the photograph may be viewed as a work of art in itself, not as an imitation of art.

In 1902, Stieglitz had broken away from the conservative posture of traditional photography to form the Photo-Secession Group. One year later, he founded *Camera Work*, a quarterly publication that stressed, with numerous illustrations, an ever-widening range of photographic innovation. Edward Steichen, a close friend and associate of Stieglitz, collaborated in this creative exploration of photography. His photograph of Rodin's *Monument to Balzac* (fig. 9-71), is an inventive interpretation that transforms a documentary photograph of the sculpture into an evocative visual and psychological experience.

In 1905, Stieglitz founded an art gallery at 291 Fifth Avenue in New York City. "291," as the gallery was known, brought the art of the European avant-garde to the United States. Exhibitions

10-39   MARGARET BOURKE-WHITE

FORT PECK DAM, photograph for the cover of the first issue of *Life* magazine, November 23, 1936. Bourke-White was one of the original staff photographers for *Life* magazine. During World War II, she became the first woman photographer to work with the U.S. armed forces. Commissioned by the editors of *Life* magazine.

10-40   HENRI CARTIER-BRESSON

SUNDAY ON THE BANKS OF THE MARNE. 1938. Gelatin silver print.

included works by Cézanne, Brancusi, Picasso, and such American artists as Charles Demuth and Georgia O'Keeffe. In 1917, Stieglitz began to decrease his gallery and publication involvements to devote fuller attention to photography. *Equivalent*, by Alfred Stieglitz, is an evocative image; the moon and its light are diffused through clouds in the upper right, while below, separated by the diagonal thrust of a cloud, an impenetrable darkness enters the composition (fig. 10-38). The photograph was produced without staging or significant darkroom manipulation, but the emphasis is less on the representational quality of the image than on abstract patterns of light and dark to create a somber, pensive mood. The *Equivalent* series, as well as Stieglitz's earlier work, was guided by a vision that helped establish photography as an independent artistic medium.

An important advance in photography in the 1920s was the development of the hand-held, lightweight, 35-mm roll-film camera. No longer burdened by bulky equipment, the photographer now had a new freedom of mobility. One artist, André Kertész (1894–1985), created a series of photographs with figurative distortion (fig. 10-13).

The cover story for the first issue of *Life* magazine was a photo essay by Margaret Bourke-White (1904–71) about a dam being constructed at Fort Peck, Montana (fig. 10-39). Her photographs revealed both the strength and the promise of industrial development, as is evident in her powerfully abstract compositions of the steel-and-concrete structure and in the dynamics of the lives of the men and women who were bringing the dam into existence.

The French photographer Henri Cartier-Bresson (b. 1908) has sought to communicate in his work what he termed "the decisive moment" in an image where overt activity uncovered a deeper psychological understanding. In *Sunday on the Banks of the Marne* (fig. 10-40), Cartier-Bresson has captured, in a summary manner, the activity of a picnic—wine is being poured and food eaten. From our viewpoint, we have joined the picnickers for lunch, but we can also observe, with some wit, how their corpulent bodies contrast with the sleek design of the boat. Cartier-Bresson believed that a photograph should seize both the scene in front of the eye and what the eye sees when it looks inward, into the self of the photographer.

The Origins of Cubism

10-41 PABLO PICASSO

LES DEMOISELLES D'AVIGNON. 1907. Oil on canvas, 8′ × 7′8″. The Museum of Modern Art, New York. The Avignon to which the title refers is a street in Barcelona's red-light district.

Les Demoiselles d'Avignon, by Pablo Picasso (1881–1973), is a harsh and aggressive painting (fig. 10-41). Inside a brothel, we confront five naked prostitutes with abstracted anatomies. Three figures conceal their faces behind vividly painted African masks that both hide their identity and communicate a frightening ferocity. Picasso considered these masks "magic things" that added a mysterious potency to the work. Compounding the psychological anxiety communicated by these masked figures is a composition that sets formal elements in violent visual combat: warm flesh tones and shades of pink and rust are set against icy blues, while spatial illusionism seems denied by the flat, abstract shapes, despite the manner in which the nude entering from behind parted drapes and the ***repoussoir*** table and still life suggest perspectival recession. The

1907   Picasso, *Les Demoiselles d'Avignon*
1908   Ford Motor Company produces the first Model T
1908   Founding of the Boy Scouts of America

nude figures are discordantly composed of geometric, angular facets and organic, curving passages. *Les Demoiselles d'Avignon*, a paradox of formal and psychological tensions, threatened the tradition of illusionism that had characterized painting since the Renaissance.

The painting began, however, in a less-anguished, more-traditional spirit. In the spring of 1907, Picasso, a young Spanish artist working in Paris, took up the challenge of painting a monumental modern composition of female nudes. After seeing a 1906 Paris retrospective of Cézanne's paintings, Picasso began to apply the planar, geometric simplifications of Cézanne's forms to the study of the human figure. In a preliminary study for the painting, two clothed male figures were surrounded by five female prostitutes. This confrontation, as well as the still-life arrangement on the table, suggests a traditional *memento mori* theme to express the idea that all physical pleasure is passing.

Les Demoiselles d'Avignon seemed a brutal and ugly painting to many of Picasso's friends, including the French painter Georges Braque (1882–1963), but Braque was inspired by the manner in which Picasso was wrestling with the question of pictorial structure and the issues raised by Cézanne. In the summer of 1908, Braque was in southern France, the landscape that had earlier been transformed by Cézanne (see fig. 9-80). Braque's *Houses at L'Estaque* (fig. 10-42) develops the planar simplification and faceted surface structure of Cézanne's paintings, but in contrast to Cézanne's intention, now the houses seem to lack solidity and weight. Braque's eccentric use of modeling highlights different areas of the landscape simultaneously and reinforces the planarity of the pictorial surface.

Reviewing a 1908 exhibition of

10-42   GEORGES BRAQUE

HOUSES AT L'ESTAQUE. 1908. Oil on canvas, 28¾ × 23⅝". Herman and Margit Rupf Foundation, Kunstmuseum, Bern, Switzerland.

Braque's paintings in Paris, which included *Houses at L'Estaque*, the French art critic Louis Vauxcelles (who had earlier given us the name *Fauvism*) wrote that Braque

> despises form, reduces everything .. to cubes. Let us not make fun of him, since he is honest. And let us wait.

Cubism, the style that would result from these experiments by Picasso and Braque, would become one of the most influential movements of early-twentieth-century art.

Frank Lloyd Wright, Robie House

10-43 FRANK LLOYD WRIGHT

EXTERIOR, ROBIE HOUSE, CHICAGO. 1909. Wright's Prairie-style designs, including this house, were published in Europe in 1910. They influenced later developments in modern European architecture, including de Stijl and the Bauhaus. Commissioned by Frederick C. Robie, a relatively young and successful manufacturer of bicycles.

Wright's Robie House (fig. 10-43) is distinguished by an emphatic horizontal design, with rooms and porches extending out from a central core defined by the chimney mass. The structure is so severe and modern in appearance that it is a surprise to realize that the Robie House, with its contemporary appearance, was designed and constructed in the first decade of the twentieth century. Frank Lloyd Wright (1867–1959) had worked as an assistant to Louis Sullivan from 1888 to 1893, but by 1900, Wright had developed a new and personal style. In the opening years of this century, he designed a series of private homes in the Chicago area that shared similar compositional qualities, including an emphasis on the horizontal features of the design. Wright's style at this time,

10-44 Dining room, Robie House, with original furniture designed by Wright. The patron wrote later that he selected Wright as his architect in part because he did not want his house to have "a lot of junk—a lot of fabrics, draperies, and what not, or old-fashioned roller shades with the brass fittings on the ends—in my line of vision, gathering dust and interfering with window washing. No sir. . . ." Wright's sleekly modern furniture and his windows, with their integral, stained-glass decoration, fit the client's expectations.

1909   **Wright, Robie House**

1909   Sigmund Freud lectures in the United States

1910   Japan annexes Korea

which was inspired by the flatness of the terrain where the homes were built, is known as the Prairie style.

In the Prairie style, Wright developed what he termed his organic theory of architecture. The organic concept governs both the design of the structure and its relationship to the site. The cantilevered projections (see below) from the core of the house help to blur the distinction between inside and outside, while the abstract, geometric massing of the architectural forms creates a distinctly modern effect.

The interior design of the rooms continues the geometric emphasis apparent from the outside. Wright's use of furniture, much of which he created specifically for each house, is distinctive for its severely geometric design and its hand-crafted elegance (fig. 10-44). It reiterates and complements the architectural forms and, in its rich use of wood and modern decorative elements, enhances the intimate scale of the rooms.

Viewing the plan, one becomes aware of another feature of Wright's organic theory (fig. 10-45). The spatial flow from room to room, around the central core of the fireplace and stairway, is free and unobstructed; rooms

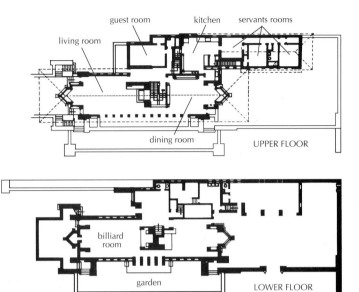

10-45   FRANK LLOYD WRIGHT

Plan of Robie House.

are not boxed off. Interior spaces merge with each other. A new continuity of interior spatial design is established.

The decorative features of the house's exterior are minimal. Instead of applied ornamentation, Wright utilized the color and texture of the materials themselves. On the exterior, red brick contrasts with powerful horizontal accents in stone. The unadorned planarity of the exterior

walls would become one of the distinguishing features of modern architecture.

Certain features of Wright's organic theory are antithetical. For example, the desire to merge the house with the environment is countered by the severely geometric and planar design, but it is precisely the balancing of contrasting design features that distinguishes Wright's achievements.

Technique *The Cantilever*

The **cantilever**, an architectural support system utilized by Wright in both the Robie House and Fallingwater (see fig. 1-6), projects a horizontal architectural member out into space without external support. It is counterbalanced by a weight on the interior end. The materials used in the construction of a large cantilever must possess a high tensile strength; usually steel beams and reinforced concrete are used. For this reason, the cantilever as a method of construction has reached its fullest expression in modern architecture.

Analytical Cubism

The theme of Geroges Braque's *Violin and Palette* (fig. 10-46) is traditional: a still-life arrangement of a violin, a music stand with sheet music, a painter's palette hung on a **trompe l'oeil** nail at the top, and green folds of drapery as a backdrop. Each of these common elements, however, is broken up into disengaged fragments. The violin, for example, is composed of a series of planes or facets that represent parts of the violin as seen from different points of view. They have been reassembled to form a highly abstract composition on the picture plane of the painting.

Braque's fragmented violin is in part the result of influences stemming from Cézanne, who introduced planar modeling and multiple viewpoints in his paintings from the late nineteenth century (see figures 9-80 and 9-81). From 1907 onward, Picasso and Braque, working together in Paris, experimented with this analytical abstraction, applying it to figural and landscape representations. By the fall and winter of 1909–10, they had developed Cubism.

Since the Renaissance, naturalistic illusionism had been a primary concern of painting. Cubism confronted that tradition by asserting a new independence for the painted image. Given the visual clues that Braque offers us in *Violin and Palette*, we conceptually understand, for example, that one of the images refers to a violin. The image does not represent a particular violin as seen from a specific viewpoint. Rather, the simultaneous viewpoints suggest the essence of a vio-

10-46 GEORGES BRAQUE

VIOLIN AND PALETTE. 1909–10. Oil on canvas, 36⅛ × 16⅞". Solomon R. Guggenheim Museum, New York.

lin—those shapes, forms, and colors that define a violin as a distinct object, different from the music stand, sheet music, palette, or drapery. In this process of analysis, seeing becomes both visual and conceptual; we perceive time and space as a total experience, unlike the illusionistic tradition of painting, which fixes a viewpoint at a moment in time.

The initial phase of Cubism, which analyzes objects from different viewpoints to re-create them as planar facets lying near or on the picture plane, is known as Analytical Cubism. The process of abstraction inherent in this visual and conceptual analysis led to ambiguities of interpretation, but Cubism never became nonobjective.

In 1911, a new element was introduced into Analytical Cubist paintings that further emphasized the surface: letters and musical symbols. Picasso's *"Ma Jolie"* (fig. 10-47) contains words, a treble clef sign, and a hint of the five lines of the musical staff. While the shapes of the letters reinforce the planarity of the painting's surface, they also act as a clue, for they were taken from a current popular song. The words also become a reference for the viewer, for above them we can glimpse shapes that suggest a figure holding a stringed instrument. The color has been reduced because Picasso's primary interest is in examining form; color, which depends on light, is deemed extraneous to form. However abstract, the painting offers the persistent observer a representation of a posed model. The network of planar shapes has given a new aesthetic to painting, one that asserts the surface as a two-dimensional field for assembling references to the world.

10-47 PABLO PICASSO

"MA JOLIE" (WOMAN WITH A ZITHER OR A GUITAR). 1911–12. Oil on canvas, 39⅜ × 25¾". The Museum of Modern Art, New York. *Ma Jolie* (French for "My Pretty One") has a double meaning here. It refers both to the words in a popular song and to the name Picasso used for his new lover, Eva, who probably posed for this painting.

Synthetic Cubism

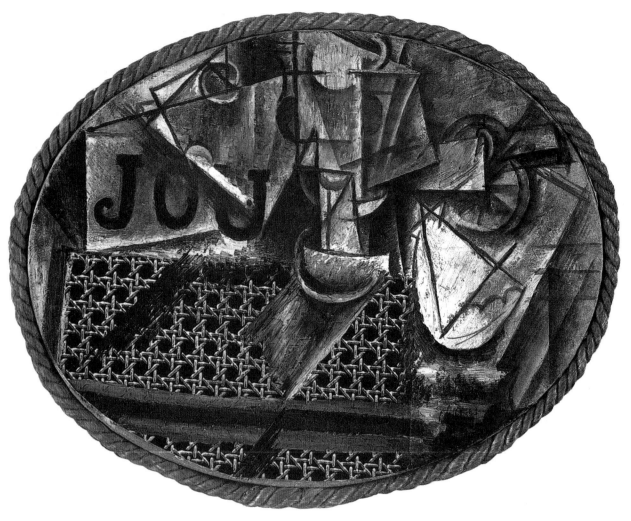

10-48 PABLO PICASSO

Still Life with Chair Caning. 1911–12. Collage of oil and pasted oilcloth, simulating chair caning, on canvas, oval 10⅝ × 13¾″. Musée Picasso, Paris.

© 1996 ESTATE OF PABLO PICASSO/ARTISTS RIGHTS SOCIETY (ARS), NEW YORK

The upper portion of Picasso's *Still Life with Chair Caning* (fig. 10-48) bears the familiar fragmentation of Analytical Cubism. This arrangement of objects includes an oyster shell, lemon slices, a knife, a pipe, and a wineglass, while the *JOU*—the beginning of the French word *journal* ("newspaper")—indicates the presence of a newspaper. These objects have been painted over chair caning. But this chair caning, which seems to be the most realistic aspect of the work, is itself an illusion, for it is in actuality cheap printed oilcloth pasted onto the canvas. Even the frame dares us to consider new expectations of painting, for it is common, ordinary rope instead of a traditional frame.

Picasso's use of the collage medium (see facing page) is an extension of the questions first posed by Analytical Cubism. Now the issues are compounded, for the reality of the painted, conceptualized Cubist still life is joined to printed oilcloth that looks like yet another reality: chair caning. With Picasso's Cubist collage, we are exposed to the paradoxical realities of life and art; although we can recognize the artificial and artful composition of still-life objects, the oilcloth disguises its reality behind the illusion of chair caning.

Still Life with Chair Caning ushers in a new phase of Cubism in which painted elements are combined with commonplace materials. The resulting works join traditional artistic mediums with materials previously considered outside the realm of art. This second phase of Cubism is known as Synthetic Cubism.

Soon the effects of the Synthetic Cubist collage were translated wholly into painting, as seen in Picasso's *Three Musicians* (fig. 10-49). Although some of the patterned areas of this work appear to be collage materials, all in actuality are painted. The abstracted figures retain an objectivity that is clearly recognizable, while the reality of the picture plane is simultaneously emphasized. The tradition of the picture plane as an element through which we view an illusion of space has been overturned. Painting now asserts itself as a completely flat surface.

10-49 PABLO PICASSO

THREE MUSICIANS. 1921. Oil on canvas, 6'7" × 7'3¾". The Museum of Modern Art, New York.

Technique *Collage and Assemblage*

The term **collage**, from the French word *coller* ("to glue"), is used to designate works of art that incorporate such materials as pieces of newspaper, cloth, colored paper, and the like. With their Synthetic Cubist collages and **assemblage** sculptures, Picasso and Barque extended the range of materials accepted in art and influenced later avant-garde movements, including Futurism, Dada, and Surrealism.

The term *assemblage* has broader connotations than *collage*, although historically the word has been used to include collage. Assemblage usually involves a combination of actual three-dimensional objects, some of which are "found" objects from the household or the junkyard, into a coherent composition. Examples of assemblage include Duchamp's "ready-mades" (see fig. 10-66) and the works of Louise Nevelson (see fig. 10-15).

The Influence of Cubism

10-50 MARCEL DUCHAMP

NUDE DESCENDING A STAIRCASE, NO. 2. 1912. Oil on canvas, 58 × 35". Philadelphia Museum of Art. When Duchamp's *Nude* was shown in the Armory Show in the United States, it became the butt of many jokes and cartoons, including one entitled *The Rude Descending a Staircase (Rush Hour at the Subway)*, published in the *New York Evening Sun* on March 20, 1913.

Cubism was tremendously influential on developments in early-twentieth-century art, from Paris to New York, Tokyo, and Moscow (also see pp. 511–515, 521–522). The techniques of planar fragmentation, used in Cubism to portray a conceptual vision, were adapted to express different artistic philosophies. Marcel Duchamp (1887–1968), for example, used a complex sequence of fragmented planes to describe the dynamic movement of a figure descending a staircase (fig. 10-50).

In Italy, the portrayal of the dynamism of modern life was the aim of a group of avant-garde artists who called themselves Futurists. Their task, as expressed in the 1910 *Futurist Manifesto*, was to free Italy from its past artistic traditions and thrust it forward into the twentieth century. The Futurist artists also embraced political anarchy. Among other defiant statements, the manifesto declared:

> that all subjects previously used must be swept aside in order to express our whirling life of steel, of pride, of fever and of speed.
>
> that the name of "madman" with which it is attempted to gag all innovators should be looked upon as a title of honor.
>
> that universal dynamism must be rendered in painting as a dynamic sensation.

Futurist works in painting and sculpture were a response to the challenge established in their manifesto. The intensity of speed suggested in Balla's *Speeding Automobile* (see fig. 10-1) meets the demand for "dynamic sensation," as does the implied stride by Umberto Boccioni (1882–1916) in his *Unique Forms of Continuity in Space* (fig. 10-51). Forms that suggest both working, moving muscles and sweeping drapery folds are thrust outward into space in order to convey the energy of a quickly striding figure. The sculpture is dramatically different when seen from varied viewpoints. Boccioni wrote:

10-51 UMBERTO BOCCIONI

Unique Forms of Continuity in Space. 1913 (cast 1931). Bronze, height 43⅞". The Museum Modern Art, New York.

BOCCIONI, UMBERTO. *UNIQUE FORMS OF CONTINUITY IN SPACE.* (1913), 43¾ × 34⅞". COLLECTION, THE MUSEUM OF MODERN ART, NEW YORK. ACQUIRED THROUGH THE LILLIE P. BLISS BEQUEST

No one can any longer believe that an object ends where another begins. . . . We therefore . . . proclaim . . . the complete abolition of definite lines and closed sculpture. We break open the figure and enclose it in the environment.

Abstraction in Sculpture

10-52 ALEXANDER ARCHIPENKO
WALKING WOMAN. 1912. Bronze, height
26⅜″. Collection Frances Archipenko-Gray.

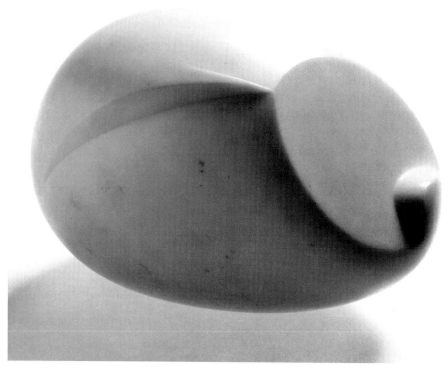

10-53 CONSTANTIN BRANCUSI
THE NEWBORN. 1915. Marble, height 5⅝″. Philadelphia Museum of Art.

The influence of Cubism led to further experimentations in sculpture as well as in painting. In *Walking Woman* (fig. 10-52), Alexander Archipenko (1887–1964) displays the impact of the simplified planar abstraction that we associate with Cubism. Note how the dissected lower left leg resembles the forms of Duchamp's *Nude Descending a Staircase*

(see fig. 10-50). What is novel, however, is Archipenko's transformation of the interpretation of mass in space. He has opened voids in the head and torso areas, where previous figural sculptures had always asserted the strongest concentrations of mass.

Parallel to these Cubist-inspired developments in abstract sculpture, another evolution in sculpture was occurring. In 1904, Brancusi, a Romanian artist, took up residence in Paris. Working in a variety of traditional sculptural mediums and often guided by a subjective synthesis of diverse traditions—including the simplified, abstract features of African and Romanian folk sculpture—Brancusi reduced representational images to elemental forms. Evolving a style based on organic abstraction, Brancusi noted:

They are imbeciles who call my work abstract; that which they call abstract is the most realist, because what is real is not the exterior form but the idea, the essence of things.

Brancusi's concern with portraying the "essence of things," an artistic philosophy that he shared with other members of the European avant-garde, led to the abstraction evident in *The Newborn* (fig. 10-53). The particulars of a baby's head and facial features have been reduced to a primordial egg form with sweeping arcs uniting the forehead with the nose and gaping mouth; the abstracted forms communicate the essence of the cry of a new life.

Brancusi had started in a more traditional mode. *Sleep,* from 1908 (fig.

10-54   CONSTANTIN BRANCUSI

Sleep. 1908. Marble, height 10". National Gallery, Bucharest.

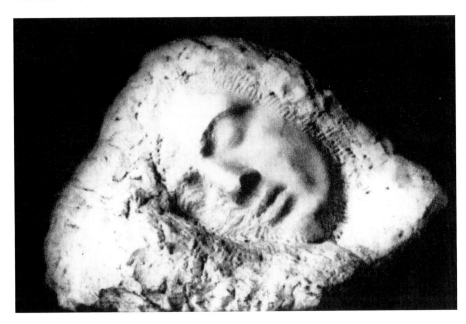

10-54), displays representational facial features, and Rodin's influence is felt in the consciously unfinished forms of the work and in the manner in which the form of the head seems to evolve from the enveloping marble. Seven years later, in *The Newborn*, Brancusi's transformation of form was complete.

One of Brancusi's aphorisms was

simplicity is not an end in art, but one arrives at simplicity in spite of oneself in drawing near to the reality of things.

With *Bird in Space* (fig. 10-55), Brancusi draws us close not to the essence of a natural form, as we have seen above and met earlier with *The Kiss* (see fig. 10-12), but to the essence of a dynamic sensation. The soaring vertically of the gently swelling bronze form and its mirrorlike surface, which further denies its minimal mass, communicate a propulsive yet graceful energy. Here Brancusi proclaims the essence of light.

10-55   CONSTANTIN BRANCUSI

Bird in Space. c. 1924. Polished bronze, height 49¾". Philadelphia Museum of Art.

Malevich and the Russian Avant-Garde

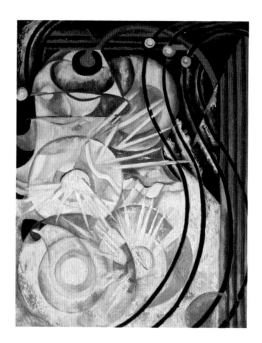

10-56 NATALYA GONCHAROVA

ELECTRIC LIGHT. 1913. Oil on canvas. 41½ × 32″. Musée National d'Art Moderne, Centre National d'Art et de Culture Georges Pompidou, Paris.

Early in this century, the electric light bulb became one of the symbols of modern technological advancement. *Electric Light* (fig. 10-56), by Natalya Goncharova (1883–1962), renders an electric lamp not as a static form but as pure radiant energy. The painting pulsates with light; widening, concentric circles of intense colors emit piercing diagonal rays. And just as intense light can seem to dematerialize its immediate surroundings, in the painting the brilliance of the light seems to float in an indeterminate space. In both concept and presentation, Goncharova's painting clearly states its modernity.

The planar fragmentation of forms seen here is derived from Analytical Cubism, while the iconographic interpretation and dynamic linearity owe a debt to Italian Futurism. In the opening decades of the twentieth century, the works of avant-garde artists were known to Russian artists through periodicals, exhibitions, and private collections in Moscow and St. Petersburg. Goncharova's earlier paintings celebrated traditional Russian themes, but under the influence of Cubism and Futurism, she became one of the leaders of the avant-garde in Russia. Beginning in 1911, Goncharova and her husband, Mikhail Larionov (1881–1964), created a new artistic movement that they called Rayonism. This abstract movement, which sought to give visual expression to dynamic forces, was short-lived, but its impact was felt by other artists, including Kasimir Malevich (1878–1935).

Malevich knew and exhibited with Goncharova and Larionov. By about 1913, however, his Cubist-inspired paintings gave way to geometric abstraction in an attempt, as he would later write,

10-57 KASIMIR MALEVICH

SUPREMATIST COMPOSITION: WHITE ON WHITE. 1918. Oil on canvas, 31¼ × 31¼″. The Museum of Modern Art, New York.

to free art from the burden of the object.

The resulting series of paintings consisted of nonrepresentational compositions dominated by simple geometric shapes. One painting, *Suprematist Composition: White on White* (fig. 10-57), reduces the formal elements of the painting to two squares of white that are separated only by the slightest value contrast. Using geometric and coloristic purity, Malevich intended to communicate pure uncorrupted emotion. He titled this new style Suprematism, writing,

> The Suprematists have deliberately given up the objective representation of their surroundings in order to reach the summit of the true "unmasked" art and from this vantage point to view life through the prism of pure artistic feeling.
>
> (Malevich. *The Non-Objective World*, 1927)

Within the innovative spirit of early-twentieth-century art, traditional interpretations of mass and space in sculpture were constantly and vigorously questioned. The Russian sculptor Naum Gabo (1890–1977) was among the artists who challenged that tradition. Through Cubism, Picasso had introduced construction as a method of sculpture. It was the Russian avant-garde artists of Constructivism, however, who legitimized the approach to modern sculpture. Gabo was a medical and science student in Munich from 1909 to 1914. While there, he was inspired by an interest in the history of art and in the artists' group Der Blaue Reiter (see page 516). Working in Norway during World War I, Gabo, through his brother Anton Pevsner, became aware of the revolutionary spatial implications and geometric shapes of Cubism. Late in 1915, Gabo began to create a series of heads constructed from cardboard, plywood,

1913   Goncharova, *Electric Light*
1913   Suffragists march in Washington, D.C.
1913   First multimotored aircraft

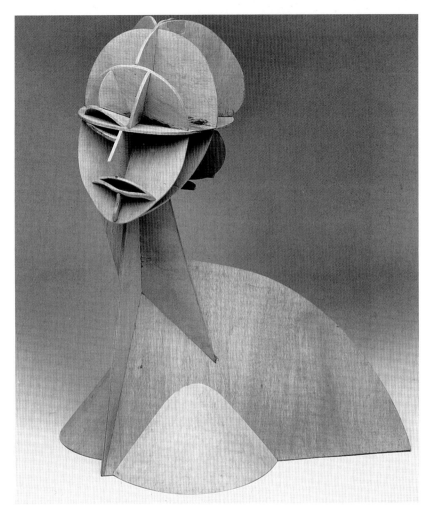

10-58   NAUM GABO

Constructed Head No. 1. 1915 (reassembled 1985). Triple-layered plywood, height 21¼". Collection Städelsches Kunstinstitut und Städlische Gallerie, Frankfurt. To retain an identity distinct from his brother, Anton Pevsner, who was equally influential in the spread of Constructivism, Naum Pevsner changed his surname to Gabo.

or thin metal sheets (fig. 10-58). In these works, the geometric configuration of the constructed planes, whose edges define surface boundaries, also creates internal voids, or pockets, of space. These voids now become a positive element in our perception of the head.

Understanding the impact of this approach, as it defied the traditional mass/space relationship of sculpture, Gabo wrote:

We consider space from an entirely different point of view. We consider it as an absolute sculptural element, released from any closed volume, and we represent it from inside with its own specific properties. . . . In our sculpture space has ceased to be for us a logical abstraction or a transcendental idea and has become a malleable material element.

German Expressionism: Die Brücke

10-59 ERNST LUDWIG KIRCHNER

Steet, Berlin. 1913. Oil on canvas, 47½ × 35⅞″. The Museum of Modern Art, New York. This painting was later included in a 1937 exhibition of "degenerate art" organized by Germany's Nazi government. The exhibition was meant to demonstrate to the public that many works of modern German art were created by artists who were insane and deviant. The show toured Germany until 1941, and Nazi propaganda records state that it was viewed by 3,200,000 persons.

PURCHASE

The modern light of the cities, the movement in the streets—there are my stimuli. . . . Observing movement excites my pulse of life, the source of creation.

For Ernst Ludwig Kirchner (1880–1938), who wrote these words, the dynamic interaction of color and movement on a city street was the paragon of modernity. In *Street, Berlin* (fig. 10-59), arbitrary, intense colors are joined with sharply stylized figures and a distorted perspective to communicate not only the animation of twentieth-century urban life but also the decadence of wealthy Germans on the brink of World War I.

The seeds of the modern movement known as German Expressionism were planted in the late nineteenth and early twentieth centuries by Van Gogh, Munch, Matisse, and the Fauves. Expressionist tendencies, such as distortion of form and intensification of color, had surfaced earlier in the history of German art in the work of artists such as Dürer and Grünewald (see figs. 6-24 to 6-28, 6-45, and 6-46). In the opening years of the twentieth century, artists looked to these artistic precedents to find forms that would express the intensity of feeling that they believed was part of the Northern cultural tradition.

In 1905, a group of young architectural students in Dresden formed an association that they called Küntsler-Gruppe Brücke ("Artists Group of the Bridge"). As an association, Die Brücke was based on the medieval guilds, and the artists lived and worked together as a community. The symbol of the bridge, adopted from Nietzsche's writings, indicated that they conceived their role as a transitionary force by which "all the revolutionary and surging elements" of modernism could bring German art to a new and fulfilling future. The artists of Die Brücke turned away from academicism, looking instead for inspiration to the stylizations and spirituality that they perceived in medieval, African, and Oceanic art, Die Brücke held its first exhibition in 1906.

But while the artists of Die Brücke searched for artistic sources outside of the Western Classical tradition, they also looked into themselves, deeply probing the psychological relationship between the artist and the world. Kirchner examined the complexity of this relationship when, in 1917, he wrote,

. . . with insight into the limits of human interaction, I undertook the withdrawal of the self from itself and its dissolution within the other person's psyche for the sake of a more intense expression. The less I was physically involved, something which quickly occurred as a result of my mood, the more easily and completely I entered into and depicted my subject.

Although not directly related to Die Brücke, the graphic art of Käthe Kollwitz (see fig. 1-19) may be considered within this expressionist context.

Die Brücke's cultural kinship with earlier German traditions led to an interest in the prints of Dürer, and one aspect of the movement was a revival of the woodcut medium. Emil Nolde's *Prophet* (fig. 10-60) is a traditional religious subject, but unlike earlier heroic treatments of this theme, such as the prophets on the Sistine Chapel ceiling (see fig. 6-36), the intentionally rough features and stark black-and-white contrasts communicate an immediate and intensely personal religious experience. In his autobiography, Nolde wrote,

10-60   EMIL NOLDE
PROPHET. 1912. Woodcut, 13 × 9".

A work becomes a work of art when one re-evaluates the values of nature and adds one's own spirituality.

German Expressionism: Der Blaue Reiter

10-61 WASSILY KANDINSKY

FIRST ABSTRACT WATERCOLOR. c. 1913. Watercolor and ink, 19¼ × 25″. Musée National d'Art Moderne, Centre National d'Art et de Culture Georges Pompidou, Paris. Kandinsky identified this as his first nonobjective watercolor, dating this experiment to 1910, but later scholars have suggested that the work more probably dates to about 1913.

Vibrant passages of color and line burst on the surface of this abstract watercolor (fig. 10-61) by Wassily Kandinsky (1866–1944). This ebullient composition of colored shapes and lines does not correspond to any reality in nature; the painting can therefore be termed nonobjective. This important breakthrough, which led to many later developments in twentieth-century art, was accomplished by a number of artists during the second decade of the century.

Kandinsky had begun a career as a law professor when, in 1896, he left Russia to study painting in Germany. His education had included studies in art and music, but the decision to become a professional artist was made in 1895, when he viewed a Moscow exhibition of Impressionist paintings. Particularly impressed by the intense color of one of Monet's *Haystack* paintings, Kandinsky wrote:

> I had the impression that here painting itself comes into the foreground; I wondered if it would not be possible to go further in this direction.

As Kandinsky traveled throughout Europe, he studied German Expressionism and Fauvism, and, returning to Munich in 1908, he painted a series of landscapes that pulsate with color.

A chance occurrence assisted in clarifying Kandinsky's thoughts about nonobjective painting:

> It was the hour of approaching dusk. I was coming home with my box of paints after sketching, still dreaming and caught up in my thoughts about the work I

c. 1913   **Kandinsky, *First Abstract Watercolor***

1913   Thomas Mann, *Death in Venice*

1913   Prentice-Hall, Inc., founded

had done, when suddenly I found myself face to face with an indescribably beautiful picture drenched with an inner glow. At first I hesitated, then I rushed toward this mysterious picture in which I could discern no visible subject, but which appeared to be completely made up of bright patches of color. Only then did I discover the key to the puzzle. It was one of my own paintings, standing on its side against the wall. . . . I knew for certain now that the depiction of objects in my paintings was not only unnecessary but indeed harmful.

The realization that painting could communicate an emotional content without recognizable subject matter was a catalyst in Kandinsky's thoughts about art and the expressive values of color. These issues occupied not just his paintings but also his writings. In late 1911, Kandinsky published *Concerning the Spiritual in Art*, in which he asserted that the function of art was to release us from a

> nightmare of materialism

by revealing an

> internal truth

that awakens the human spirit. The key to this awakening was the

> psychic effect

that colors could evoke:

> Color is a power which directly influences the soul. Color is the keyboard, the eyes are the hammers, the soul is the piano with many strings. The artist is the hand which plays, touching one key or another, to cause vibrations in the soul.

10-62   FRANZ MARC

THE LARGE BLUE HORSES. 1911. Oil on canvas, 3′5⁵⁄₁₆″ × 5′11¼″. Walker Art Center, Minneapolis.

GIFT OF THE T.B. WALKER FOUNDATION, GILBERT M. WALKER FUND, 1942

In writing *Concerning the Spiritual in Art*, Kandinsky drew from many varied and rich sources, including Expressionism, Fauvism, and African and Oceanic art. Expressing a kinship with non-Western artists, Kandinsky wrote,

> Like ourselves, these artists sought to express in their work only internal truths, renouncing in consequence all consideration of external form.

The musical innovations of Arnold Schönberg added further inspiration.

> [Schönberg's] music leads us into a realm where musical experience is a matter not of the ear but of the soul alone—and from this point begins the music of the future.

Kandinsky believed that the emotional power of music could be paralleled by abstraction in painting.

In 1911, Kandinsky, Marc, and other Expressionist artists working in Munich formed an artists' group, which they called Der Blaue Reiter ("The Blue Rider"); the title was derived from a work by Kandinsky that depicted an abstract rider and horse unified by a single value of blue. Der Blaue Reiter was an association of artists who sought to communicate the spiritual values that lie behind the facade of appearances.

In *The Large Blue Horses* (fig. 10-62), by Franz Marc (1880–1916), the curving, swelling contours of the landscape intentionally echo the forms of the horses' backs, expressing the artist's belief in the harmony of animal life within nature. For Marc, the blue of the horses communicated a spiritual principle and the ideal of hope, while the red of the landscape symbolized what the artist called

> brutal and heavy

matter. Marc's paintings wed line, form, and color in an attempt to express the essential concord in the environment.

Fantasy

10-63 GIORGIO DE CHIRICO

THE MELANCHOLY AND MYSTERY OF A STREET. 1914. Oil on canvas, 34¼ × 28½". Private collection.

10-64 MARC CHAGALL

BIRTHDAY. 1915. Oil on cardboard, 31¾ × 39¼". The Museum Modern Art, New York.

Formerly we used to represent things visible on earth, things we either liked to look at or would have liked to see. Today we reveal the reality that is behind visible things, thus expressing the belief that the visible world is merely an isolated case in relation to the universe and that there are many more other, latent realities.

(Paul Klee, 1920)

The attempt to express visually a reality that supersedes that of the objective, physical world distinguishes the early-twentieth-century avant-garde movements of Fauvism, German Expressionism, and Cubism. Another approach to this challenge is found in the works of the artists of fantasy, painters who, questioning rationalist views, explored the expression of their personal, inner visions.

As its title hints, *The Melancholy and Mystery of a Street*, by Giorgio De Chirico (1888–1978), opens to us a world that is disturbing and possibly even forbidding (fig. 10-63). The forms are representational. The arcaded buildings, the wagon, and even the intense light are features that can be found in many Italian piazzas. In De Chirico's painting, however, stark **chiaroscuro** is joined with an exaggerated perspective to create an unexpectedly dramatic spatial illusion. The anxiety created by the convergence of diagonals is heightened by the iconography. The setting is void of life except for a young girl, who innocently plays with a hoop. Her path will take her into the menacing emptiness of the piazza, where the shadow of a large statue falls, almost threateningly, across her path. De Chirico's manipulation of representational forms opens the world of the subconscious and the frightening exaggeration we often sense in dreams. De Chirico considered his paintings to be metaphysical—that is, they offered encounters with mysterious truths beyond our understanding.

In 1912, De Chirico expressed in words the process of his creative invention. He wrote:

I believe that as from a certain point of view the sight of someone in a dream is a proof of his metaphysical reality, so, from the same point of view, the revelation of a work of art is the proof of the metaphysical reality of certain chance occurrences that we sometimes experience in the way and manner that *something* appears to us and provokes in us the image of a work of art, an image, which in our souls awakens surprise—sometimes, meditation—often, and always, the joy of creation.

The juxtaposition of dissociated objects in De Chirico is intended to beckon the unconscious within us.

Marc Chagall (1887–1985) journeyed to Paris from his native Russia in 1910. In *Birthday* of 1915 (fig. 10-64), he shares with us his celebration of love with his new wife, the ecstasy of which elevates the artist off the ground to surprise his bride with a kiss. Although he never forgot his Jewish heritage and the decorative, colorful qualities of Russian folk-art traditions, Chagall was deeply inspired by the avant-garde styles that were invigorating the Parisian art scene. *Birthday* weds the joyful colors of Fauvism and Russian folk art with the multiple viewpoints and simplified planar structure of Cubism. The emphasis on emotion seen here is typical of Chagall's commitment to representing familial and societal relationships. Here, all these elements are combined into a liberated and highly personal aesthetic. Later, Chagall disdained the literary associations of "anecdote" and "fairy tales" that critics saw in his paintings, stating that his works

are only pictorial arrangements of images that obsess me.

This emphasis on the "art" evident in his paintings is an attempt to stress their modernity, but the importance of subject and emotion in his works is evident.

The Swiss artist Paul Klee (1879–1940) usually worked on a small scale, but *Ad Parnassum* is one of his larger

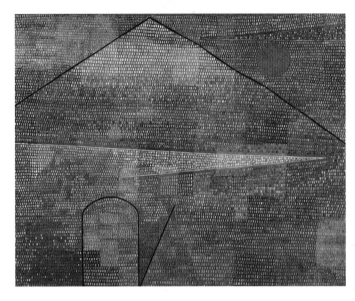

10-65 PAUL KLEE

AD PARNASSUM. 1932. Oil on canvas, 39 × 42". Kunstmuseum, Bern, Switzerland. Klee's wife was a piano teacher, and the title of this work may derive from *Gradus ad Parnassum* (*Steps to Parnassus*), a series of piano exercise based on scales for the beginning piano pupil.

and most ambitious works (fig. 10-65). Klee set out to discover elemental symbols: here the pyramid suggests not only the mysteries of ancient Egypt but also, because of the title, Mount Parnassus near Delphi, which was sacred to the ancient Greeks as the home of the Muses, who inspired creative activities. The red circle that suggests the sun may refer to the role of the sun in world religions, as well as to the concept of gradual enlightenment. The division of the surface into tiny squares of pure color creates a precious and beautiful effect that evokes the shimmering nature of light as it illuminates a form. From a multitude of smaller forms, monumental constructions can be created; from stone blocks come pyramids; from scales, symphonies. But ultimately the full expressive content of Klee's work becomes a matter of individual perception and understanding. Klee believed that there were visual

equivalents for spiritual states, and as so often in his work, the few simple forms of *Ad Parnassum* suggest deep and elemental mysteries.

Like Henri Rousseau, whose naïvely direct yet purposeful paintings were championed by young avant-garde artists in Paris (see fig. 9-9), these painters of fantasy often did not view themselves as depicting the bizarre or fanciful. They equated reality with an inner vision. Questioned about this, Chagall responded,

I am against the terms "fantasy" and "symbolism" in themselves. All our interior world is a reality—and that perhaps more so than our apparent world.

In the visual communication of this "interior world," these artists opened a path of artistic exploration that would lead to Dada (see pp. 520–523) and Surrealism (see pp. 530–533).

Dada

10-66 MARCEL DUCHAMP

Bottle Rack, Fountain, and other works; reproductions of works originally created between 1914 and 1919.
Installation, Moderna Museet, Stockholm.

Marcel Duchamp was an artist of unprecedented and unsettling works that still seem shocking to us today, although some were done more than eighty years ago (fig. 10-66). On the pedestals in the gallery, where we expect to find sculpture, Duchamp has placed a manufactured *Bottle Rack*, a common object used at the time for drying bottles. In 1914, Duchamp felt that he could confer an artistic dignity on a bottle rack by designating it a work of art. Another pedestal supports an upended porcelain urinal, officially titled *Fountain*. Duchamp signed the urinal "R. Mutt," a pun on the name of the company that manufactured it, the Mott Works Company. On the wall behind is a reproduction of Leonardo's

"Mona Lisa" (see fig. 6-21), which Duchamp defaced by adding a mustache, goatee, and, at the bottom, the letters *L.H.O.O.Q.*, which suggest the French phrase for "She has a hot ass." If all of this appears absurd to you— and it certainly did to critics and the public in the early twentieth century— then you are beginning to understand the function of these objects as works of art. Duchamp, a Parisian avant-garde artist who came to New York in 1915, asserted that "found objects" or "ready-mades" could be works of art. This art, however, attempted to counter traditional conventions of form and content by introducing an aesthetic neutrality to the viewer. Looking back at his "ready-mades," Duchamp later commented,

A point which I very much want to establish is that the choice of these "ready-mades" was never dictated by aesthetic delectation. This choice was based on a reaction of visual indifference with at the same time a total absence of good or bad taste . . . in fact a complete anaesthesia. . . . Another aspect of the "readymade" is its lack of uniqueness.

Although they were mass-produced objects intended for a functional use, Duchamp felt that by his saying they were art and by exhibiting them within a gallery, "ready-mades" had entered into the realm of art.

Duchamp never officially declared himself a Dadaist, but his works from

10-67 KURT SCHWITTERS

MERZBILD. 1920. Mixed media collage. Kunstmuseum, Dusseldorf, Germany. *Merz* was a word invented by Schwitters to designate a "mode of artistic creation." Derived, by chance, from the word *Kommerz,* meaning commerce, Schwitters, in 1921, wrote: "The word 'Merz' had no meaning when I formed it. Now it has the meaning which I gave it. The meaning of the concept 'Merz' changes with the change in the insight of those who continue to work with it. Merz stands for freedom from all fetters, for the sake of artistic creation. Freedom is not lack of restraint, but the product of strict artistic discipline. Merz also means tolerance towards any artistically motivated limitation."

KURT SCHWITTERS, GERMAN, (1887–1948), *MERZBILD*, 1920. MIXED MEDIA COLLAGE. KUNSTMUSEUM, DUSSELDORF, GERMANY. PHOTO BY PETER WILLI. THE BRIDGEMAN ART LIBRARY INTERNATIONAL LTD.

1913 onward, especially the "ready-mades," are formally and spiritually akin to those produced by Dada artists. As an artistic, musical, and literary movement, Dada was officially consecrated in 1916 at the Cabaret Voltaire in Zurich. Dada intentionally bred confusion, and even the origin of the title remains, appropriately, a matter of uncertainty: two of Dada's founders—writers Richard Huelsenbeck and Hugo Ball—state that the word, which is French for "hobbyhorse," was discovered by chance in a German–French dictionary, but another founder—the German painter Hans Richter—holds that it was simply

10-68 HANNA HÖCH

CUT WITH THE KITCHEN KNIFE. 1919. Collage of pasted papers, 44⅞ × 35½". Nationalgalerie, Staatliche Museen, Berlin.

HANNAH HÖCH, *CUT WITH A KITCHEN KNIFE*, 1919. COLLAGE, 114 × 90 CM. STAATLICHE MUSEEN ZU BERLIN. PHOTO: JORG R. ANDERS. PREUSSISCHER KULTURBESITZ, NATIONALGALERIE/NG 57/61. © 2000 ARTISTS RIGHTS SOCIETY (ARS), NEW YORK/VG BILD-KUNST, BONN

ditionalism in art and society is found in this total lack of reverence toward artistic media. In 1921, he wrote,

> The medium is as unimportant as I myself. Because the medium is unimportant, I take any material whatsover if the picture demands it. . . . I have taken a step in advance of mere oil painting . . . I play off material against material. . . . The reproduction of natural elements is not essential to a work of art.

Hannah Höch, working in Berlin, introduced a vast array of photographic images to her collages. The prominent ball bearing and gear photos in *Cut with the Kitchen Knife* (fig. 10-68) bring to our attention, within the purposeful yet seemingly nonsensical context of Dada, an early-twentieth-century perspective on the complex interrelationships between machines and humans. Addressing this issue, Höch stated:

> Our whole purpose was to integrate objects from the world of machines and industry in the world of art. . . . we used to bring together elements borrowed from books, newspapers, posters or leaflets in arrangements that no machine could yet compose.

In yet another way of exploring the irrational in art, Swiss artist Jean Arp (1887–1966), created collages by dropping torn pieces of paper randomly onto a paper surface and then gluing them into place (fig. 10-69). These works were composed according to chance. In the words of Arp:

> Dada aimed to destroy the reasonable deceptions of man and recover the natural and unreasonable order. Dada wanted to replace the logical nonsense of men of today by the illogically senseless. That is why we pounded with all our might on the big drum of Dada and trumpeted

the Slavonic word for "yes," and that *da, da* meant only "yes, yes."

Other theories as to the origin of the term have been advanced, but what defined Dada was a nihilistic mocking of traditional values in the arts and, by extension, Western society as a whole. This artistic anarchy grew from a profound psychological disgust. Dada glorified the irrational.

In Germany, Dada nihilism was joined to a political stance which

embraced the ideals of Communism while ridiculing both German militarism and Western capitalism. Kurt Schwitters' trash pictures (fig. 10-67) owe a visual allegiance to Synthetic Cubism (see pp. 506–507), but the collage elements are common trash materials, literally, at times, retrieved from the gutter. Here, content confronts form, as the discarded waste of society is used to compose a work of art. Schwitters's indictment of tra-

the praises of unreason. . . . Dada is senseless like nature.

The senselessness and nihilism of Dada, however absurd, were born from an even greater absurdity, World War I. Dada was an art of social protest, a protest against the senseless slaughter and destruction of life and meaning that, at the time, was continuing without an end in sight:

> We searched for an elementary art that would, we thought, save mankind from the furious madness of these times.

> (Jean Arp).

In this profound search, however, Duchamp's "ready-mades" and works by Dada artists exulted in a liberation of form, content, and artistic processes. In later decades, the mounting supremacy of the creative idea, so nurtured by Duchamp, would reach a fruition in Conceptual Art (see p. 563), while the innovations of artists at mid-century, such as Joseph Cornell (see fig. 10-94) and Robert Rauschenberg (see fig. 10-107) were firmly rooted in the Dada experience. Duchamp, himself understood this. Viewing the art world of the 1960's, he wrote:

> This Neo-Dada, which they call new Realism, Pop Art, assemblage etc., is an easy way out and lives on what Dada did. When I discovered ready-mades I thought to discourage aesthetics. In Neo-Dada they have taken my ready-mades and found aesthetic beauty in them.

10-69   JEAN (HANS) ARP

COLLAGE ARRANGED ACCORDING TO THE LAWS OF CHANCE. 1916–17. Torn and pasted paper, 19⅛ × 13⅝". The Museum of Modern Art, New York.

De Stijl and the Bauhaus

10-70 GERRIT RIETVELD

Schröder House, Utrecht, The Netherlands. 1923–24. One of the radical aspects of this house is the placement of a large, flexible living space with moving and removable partitions on the upper floor; Rietveld, sensitive to the conservative attitudes of the local authorities, labeled the upper floor as the attic when he submitted his plans for their permission. The patron was Truus Schröder-Schräder, a widowed interior designer with three children who wanted a functional, easy-to-maintain house. Her studio was located on the lower floor, as was the kitchen. She took an active part in the planning of the house.

Schröder House, designed by Gerrit Rietveld (1888–1964), is without historical reference. Its simplicity and severity of form make it seem new even today: it offers a timeless modernity (figs. 10-70 to 10-72). At the same time, it is neither simple nor simplistic. The contrasts between wall and opening, solid and void, horizontal and vertical, aggressive and recessive forms establish complex interrelationships, and

the composition, which is determinedly asymmetric in both two and three dimensions, is enhanced by the precision with which the forms are defined. On both exterior and interior, openness integrates the forms of the house with the surrounding space. The Schröder House is a powerful and convincing example of the "equilibrium of equivalent relationships" that was one of the aesthetic goals of the de Stijl movement.

De Stijl ("The Style") was founded in 1917 in Amsterdam by several Dutch artists who felt a mission to carry abstraction to what they termed "its ultimate goal." The group was motivated in part by the tragic events of World War I and was inspired by such modern philosophical movements as Theosophical Mysticism and Neopositivism. Their utopian aspirations are revealed in the name, which suggests that this is the ultimate style, the perfect style that, mass-produced, could satisfy all humanity for the rest of the world's history. This search to find a visual equivalent for spiritual and philosophical purity led to the development of a completely new and abstract style in architecture, painting, sculpture, and the decorative arts. Their motivation was ethical, for they felt that a perfectly balanced and serene art could carry the qualities of harmony and purity into the very soul and being of the viewer. Their ultimate goal was to bring about world understanding, unity, and peace. They avoided individualism and subjectivity, arguing that these concepts had led the world into war:

> The old tends to the individual. The new tends to the universal. The struggle between the individual and the universal is revealed in both the world war and contemporary art.

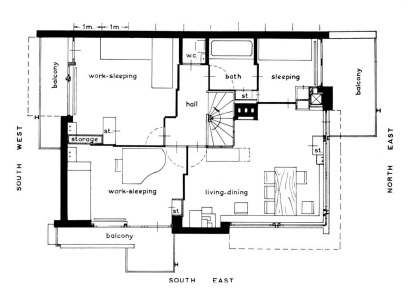

10-71 GERRIT RIETVELD
Plan of Schröder House.

They wanted to create an art that was universal and comprehensible to all humanity, regardless of nationality or creed. "Man adheres only to what is universal," wrote Piet Mondrian, one of the movement's founders, in 1919.

These profound goals reached fulfillment in a series of works produced

10-72 GERRIT RIETVELD

Interior, Schröder House. Visible in this interior view are the movable sliding walls and some of the built-in furniture that Rietveld designed for the Schröder House. The goal was a completely unified formal and aesthetic expression—what the *De Stijl Manifesto* called a structural affinity between object and environment. Also visible here is his famous "red and blue" chair, designed about 1918. The forms of the chair are completely geometric: only the need to make some concession to the requirements of the human body explains the two diagonal forms. A durable formal solution, the chair was designed to be mass-produced at a reasonable price for mass consumption. The colors are carefully controlled, with the structure composed of black bars with yellow ends, and the seat and back given over to one blue and one red plane. The restriction to primary colors is typical of the de Stijl philosophy.

10-73   WALTER GROPIUS

Workshop wing, Bauhaus, Dessau, Germany. 1925–26. The Bauhaus was an influential modern school of architecture and design.

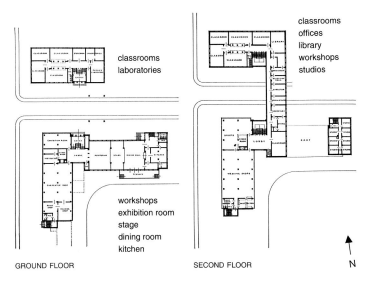

classrooms
laboratories

classrooms
offices
library
workshops
studios

workshops
exhibition room
stage
dining room
kitchen

GROUND FLOOR

SECOND FLOOR

N

10-74   WALTER GROPIUS

Plan of Bauhaus.

by Mondrian between the two world wars (see fig. 1-16). In these abstractions, which are characterized by a studied balance between forms and colors, Mondrian hoped to accomplish, in his words, an "equilibrium of opposites." The universality of this goal, with its search for worldwide peace, is related to the philosophical statements made by other modern

thinkers and artists, as well as to the contemporary founding of the World Court and the League of Nations, which led eventually to the establishment of the first worldwide governmental body, the United Nations, after World War II.

Walter Gropius's philosophy on the unity of the arts guided his design for the new home for the Bauhaus at

Dessau (figs. 10-73 to 10-75). The structure at Dessau exemplified the modernist aesthetic. A complex of classrooms, library, and offices is externally unified by planes of reinforced concrete walls and vast expanses of windows. A rectilinear design, with verticals and horizontals meeting at right angles, governs the plan and determines the exterior articulation.

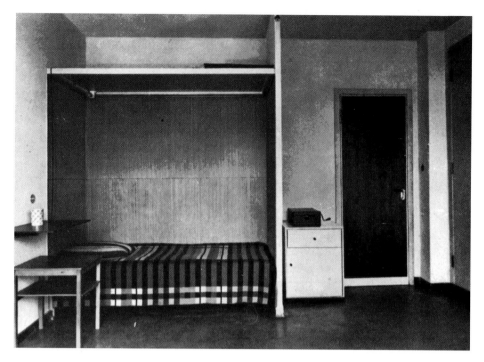

10-75 WALTER GROPIUS

Student dormitory room, Bauhaus.

The plain, unornamented surfaces used throughout the building contribute to its modern, clean appearance. The interior design of the classrooms and even the desks and chairs respond to the design aesthetic that governs the entire structure. Gropius's own office had furniture of his design and a rug, wall hanging, and lighting created in the Bauhaus workshops. The student dormitory room illustrated here reveals how strictly the Bauhaus aesthetic could govern an environment (fig. 10-75). This is what Gropius meant by the "complete building" when, in 1919, he wrote:

> The ultimate aim of all visual arts is the complete building! . . . Today the arts exist in isolation, from which they can be rescued only through the conscious, co-operative effort of all craftsmen. . . . Architects, sculptors, painters, we must all return to the crafts! For art is not a "profession." There is no essential difference between the artist and the craftsman.

Gropius, a German architect and industrial designer, had played a leading role in founding the Bauhaus in 1919 at Weimar. The name *Bauhaus*, chosen by Gropius, is derived from the *Bauhütte*, the medieval German builders' lodge, which housed the masters and craftspeople who built the great cathedrals of the late Middle Ages. The recent Arts and Crafts Movement and Art Nouveau's unity of design had reinforced Gropius's belief in the total integration of the arts. Unlike those late-nineteenth-century movements, however, the Bauhaus philosophy of design was guided by the technology and materials of industrial production.

The design of the building at Dessau, where the Bauhaus relocated in 1924, was itself inspired by the rectilinear massing of Frank Lloyd Wright's Prairie-style designs (see pages 502–503) and by the geometric planarity of de Stijl architecture. The resulting building, with its clean, precise, and almost mechanistically tuned appearance, does not display a regional or national identity. The Bauhaus style has reduced the essence of design to a visual common denominator. It promised, with the assistance of modern technology, a future in which a total design aesthetic would not be restricted by cultural or national boundaries. Reacting to the horror of World War I, the Bauhaus offered a utopian vision where art and architecture would assist in the realization of our common human heritage.

In 1933, Adolf Hitler, then chancellor of Germany, manifesting the intolerance that totalitarian regimes commonly share toward the avant-garde, ordered the Bauhaus closed. Like apostles to foreign lands, those who had worked at the Bauhaus carried its philosophy throughout Europe and to the United States.

Diego Rivera and Mexican Mural Painting

10-76 DIEGO RIVERA

NIGHT OF THE RICH. 1923–28. Fresco, Ministry of Education, Mexico City. Commissioned by José Vasconcelos and Puig Casauranc, ministers of public education.

DIEGO RIVERA *ORGY–NIGHT OF THE RICH* (LA ORGIA–LA NOCHE DE LOS RICOS), 1926. MURAL, 2.05 × 1.54 M. COURT OF FIESTAS, LEVEL 3, NORTH WALL. SECRETARIA DE EDUCACION PUBLICA, MEXICO CITY, MEXICO. SCHALWIJK/ART RESOURCE, NY. (C) BANCO DE MEXICO DIEGO RIVERA MUSEUM TRUST

Only the work of art itself can raise the standard of taste. Art has always been employed by the different social classes who hold the balance of power as one instrument of domination—hence, as a political instrument. One can analyze epoch after epoch—from the stone age to our own day—and see that there is no form of art which does not also play an essential political role. . . . What is it then that we really need? An art extremely pure, precise, profoundly human, and clarified as to its purpose.

(Diego Rivera, 1929)

These mural paintings by Diego Rivera (1886–1957) are on the third floor of an open courtyard in the Ministry of Education building in Mexico City (figs. 10-76, 10-77). They are but 2 of 124 murals that the artist painted during the decade of the 1920s. The scenes present a direct and didactic contrast between the debauchery of the rich, which includes excessive drinking and hoarding money, and the quiet, peaceful sleep of the poor peasants after an honest day's work. A few of the peasants remain awake into the night, educating themselves by lamplight. In the left background of *Night of the Poor*, the Marxist content of the mural is reinforced as bourgeois onlookers disdainfully watch; in *Night of the Rich,* revolutionary soldiers observe the decadent behavior of the wealthy ruling class.

These scenes, and indeed the entire cycle of paintings, are unyielding expressions of class struggle. They communicate the purposes and promises of the Mexican Revolution, which began in 1910 with a dramatic demand for economic and social reform. A decade of internal civil strife and bloodshed followed, and only during the 1920s and 1930s would some of the aims of the revolution be realized. Rivera's paintings propagandize the causes and goals of the continuing revolution.

The impact of Rivera's murals is direct and immediately comprehensible, for here the artist has eschewed modernist abstraction in favor of an easily understood representational form and content. Rivera, who had traveled in Europe, returned home in 1921 to join with other Mexican artists in creating a unique and forceful style that, while borrowing elements from Expression and Cubism, was also rooted in the bold, severe forms of much Central and South American native art. In the hands of the Mexican muralists, art became a vehicle to promote social awareness; in Rivera's words:

> Mural painting must help in man's struggle to become a human being, and for that purpose it must live wherever it can; no place is bad for it, so long as it is permitted to fulfill its primary functions of nutrition and enlightenment.

10-77 DIEGO RIVERA

NIGHT OF THE POOR. 1923–28. Fresco, Ministry of Education, Mexico City. These frescoes are from the final cycle of paintings, begun by Rivera in 1927, for the Ministry of Education. The images in this cycle are loosely related to the words of two revolutionary songs (*corridos*), which appear on the painted festoons. In part, one of the *corridos* reads: "The clock strikes one, two, and the rich keep awake thinking what to do with their money so that it keeps multiplying. It's only seven o'clock at night and the poor have gone to rest. They sleep very peacefully because they are tired. Blessed the tree that yields fruit, but very ripe fruit. Yes, gentlemen, it is worth more than all the hard dollars."

Surrealism

10-78 MAX ERNST

TWO CHILDREN ARE THREATENED BY A NIGHTINGALE. 1924. Oil on wood, with wood construction; 27½ × 22½ × 4½″. Museum of Modern Art, New York. Purchase.

In 1924, Max Ernst's (1891–1976) nightmarish work, *Two Children Are Threatened by a Nightingale* (fig. 10-78), stood at a three-way intersection. The integration of the small gate and house with the large, almost oppressive, frame continues the constructivism of Dada (see pp. 520–23), while the perspective and barren architectural landscape recall the metaphysical paintings of the artist Giorgio De Chirico (see fig. 10-63). The scene represented, along with the title below, offers a frightful and bizarre juxtaposition of elements. A nightingale hardly is a menacing bird, yet here it elicits a response of primordial fear and a hallucinatory horror of abduction. This revelation of anxiety and contradiction, displacement and random association, represents a path of exploration of the subconscious—the path of Surrealism—leading from that intersection.

Twelve years after this work, in 1936, Ernst recalled the process by

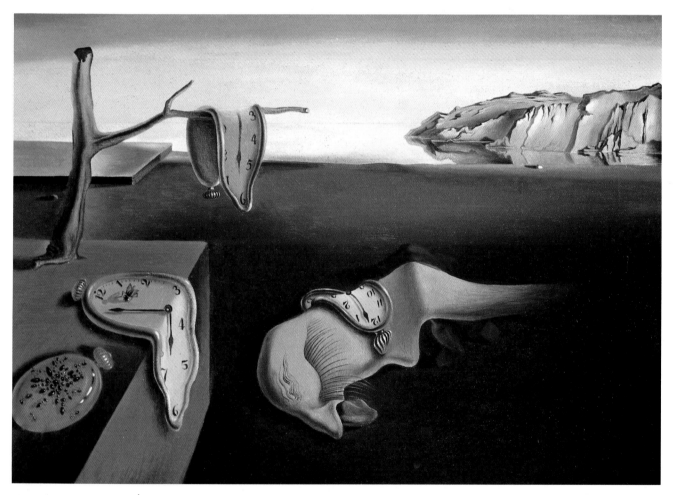

10-79   SALVADOR DALÍ

THE PERSISTENCE OF MEMORY. 1931. Oil on canvas, 9½ × 13″. The Museum of Modern Art, New York.

which the vision and juxtaposition of representational objects led to an awakening of the artist's subconscious:

One rainy day, in 1919 . . . I was struck by the obsession which held under my gaze the pages of an illustrated catalogue showing objects designed for anthropologic, microscopic, psychologic, mineralogic, and paleontologic demonstration. There I found brought together elements of figuration so remote that the sheer absurdity of that collection provoked a sudden intensification of the visionary faculties in me

10-80 ANDRÉ MASSON

BATTLE OF FISHES. 1927. Chalk, charcoal, conté crayon, and oil on canvas, 14¼ × 28¾".
The Museum of Modern Art, New York.

and brought forth an illusive succession of contradictory images . . . piling up on each other with the persistence and rapidity which are peculiar to love memories and visions of half-sleep. . . . It was enough at that time to embellish these catalogue pages, in painting or drawing, and thereby in gently reproducing only that which saw itself in me . . . thus I obtained a faithful fixed image of my hallucination and transformed into revealing dramas my most secret desires . . .

In the hallucinatory world of Salvador Dalí's *Persistence of Memory* (fig. 10-79), watches—sturdy, metallic timekeepers—grow limp and decay like organic refuse; one attracts a fly; ants converge on another. One watch has melted over a biomorphic form that bears a fantastically conceived profile portrait of the artist. A smooth, satiny beach gives onto a limitless

expanse of mirror-smooth water abutted by cliffs. Within this landscape of stillness, the limp watches suggest the inevitable decay of the passing of time.

This painting, by Dalí (1904–89), succeeds in conveying its subconscious, dreamlike vision by the uncanny juxtaposition and fantastic manipulation of representational objects. Dalí's fantasy conveys a frightening psychological oppression in part because its combination of unexpected elements eludes any obvious interpretation.

Surrealism, a literary and artistic avant-garde movement that began in Europe in the early 1920's, was inexorably bound with the psychoanalytic theories of Sigmund Freud; we know, for example, that Dalí read Freud's writings while he was still a student in Madrid. André Breton, the French writer who authored the first *Surrealist Manifesto* in 1924, acknowledged Freud's revolutionary discoveries when, in defining *Surrealism*, he wrote:

SURREALISM, n. Pure psychic automatism, by which it is intended to express verbally, in writing, or by any other means the real process of thought. Thought's dictation, in the absence of all control exercised by the reason and outside all aesthetic or moral preoccupations.

The Surrealist translation of the unconscious into visual form was realized in the figurative works of Dalí and René Magritte, where representational or fantastically conceived forms are juxtaposed within a spatial illusion.

The abstraction of *Battle of Fishes* (fig. 10-80), by André Masson (1896–1987), is the result of automatism, a concept related to Freud's use of "free association" to divulge the subconscious. Breton used the word *automatism* in his definition of Surrealism, and in describing the process for writing an automatist Surrealist composition, Breton suggested that you should

10-81 MERET OPPENHEIM

Object (Le Déjeuner en fourrure). 1936. Fur-covered cup, saucer, and spoon; cup 4¾″ diameter, saucer 9⅜″ diameter, spoon 8″ long, overall 2⅞″ high. Museum of Modern Art, New York.

write quickly without any previously chosen subject, quickly enough not to dwell on, and not to be tempted to read over, what you have written.

This process of "automatic" writing was viewed as a revelation of the subconscious. In art, lines or colors were quickly set down on a surface, without reference to a preconceived theme. The conscious mind would then associate these nonobjective marks with objective forms. In Masson's work, the ferocious battle among fishes that has evolved exhibits his intense anxieties about the brutality of nature, feelings that were born of the physical and mental wounds he received in World War I.

One of the guiding concepts of Surrealism, central to the works we have discussed, is displacement. Here, displacement means a disorientation, which often is achieved by a shocking juxtaposition of elements. Such a juxtaposition awakens new psychological associations for us, associations that may feed from the subconscious. Meret Oppenheim's *Fur-Covered Cup, Saucer, and Spoon* (fig. 10-81), first displayed with an exhibition of Surrealist objects in 1936 in Paris, exemplifies this con-cept. Our tactile associations of the texture and purpose of these objects are jarred by the projected sensations evoked by the fur coverings. In Oppenheim's sculpture, our sense of displacement is derived simultaneously from the recognition of these objects, their altered state, and anthropomorphic associations.

Like Dada (pp. 520–23), Surrealism opened new avenues of creative investigation for artists. In the late 1940s, the impact of this movement was keenly felt by a group of American artists who brought a new identity to the avant-garde (see pp. 547–550).

Modernism in American Painting

Among the rain
and lights
I saw the figure 5
in gold
on a red
fire truck
moving
tense
unheeded
to gong clangs
siren howls
and wheels rumbling
through the dark city.

(William Carlos Williams, "The Great
Figure," 1921)

Charles Demuth (1883–1935), inspired by this poem by the distinguished American poet William Carlos Williams, intended this painting as a modern portrait of the poet; *W.C.W., Carlos,* and the nickname *Bill* appear in the painting (fig. 10-82). This is one of Demuth's "poster portraits," a series inspired by the stark forms and lettering of advertising billboards. The vibrant *5* is repeated, just as the accompanying "gong clangs" and "siren howls" would have echoed off the hard surfaces of the city streets. The blocky red forms refer to the fire truck, the white circles suggest the streetlights, and the quickly pulsating forms of the compositions as a whole visually suggest the jerky rhythm of the poem. The style, with its sharp edges and flat, unmodeled forms, developed in the 1920s in the United States and is known as Precisionism.

In the first four decades of the twentieth century, the influence of modern European art played a significant role in the development of modernism in the United States, aided by exhibitions organized by Alfred Stieglitz at Gallery "291" (see pages 498–99). At the same time, however, the Americans maintained an independent stance and were less willing to give up subject matter than were

10-82 CHARLES DEMUTH

I SAW THE FIGURES 5 IN GOLD. Oil on composition board, 36 × 29¾". The Metropolitan Museum of Art, New York.

CHARLES HENRY DEMUTH *THE FIGURE 5 IN GOLD.* 1928, OIL ON COMPOSITION BOARD, H. 36 IN. W. 29¾ IN. (91.4 × 75.6 CM) SIGNED (LOWER LEFT): C.D. INSCRIBED (BOTTOM CENTER): W.C.W. (WILLIAM CARLOS WILLIAMS). THE METROPOLITAN MUSEUM ART, ALFRED STIEGLITZ COLLECTION, 1949. (49.59.1) PHOTOGRAPH (C) 1996 THE METROPOLITAN MUSEUM OF ART.

their European counterparts. Instead, they searched for contemporary American subjects and evolved styles adapted from one or more twentieth-century European styles. Until 1940, American modernism was conservative by European standards, especially when compared with the avant-garde movements of Dada and Surrealism.

Precisionist style is evident in *American Landscape* (fig. 10-83), by Charles Sheeler (1883–1965), but here the tradition of illusionism continues to dominate. The precise linear rendering of the machinery and the industrial buildings is more than a stylistic device, for it also suggests the role of efficiency in successful

10-83   CHARLES SHEELER

AMERICAN LANDSCAPE. 1930. Oil on canvas, 24 × 31″. The Museum Modern Art, New York. While he was a young art student, Sheeler also worked as an architectural photographer, and this industrial landscape was painted after he was commissioned to document in photographs the Ford Company's River Rouge plant. Sheeler wrote: "Photography is nature seen from the eyes outward, painting from the eyes inward. . . . Photography records inalterably the single image, while painting records a plurality of images willfully directed by the artist."

GIFT OF ABBY ALDRICH ROCKEFELLER

10-84   GRANT WOOD

AMERICAN GOTHIC. 1930. Oil on composition board, 29⅞ × 24⅞″. The Art Institute of Chicago. The *Gothic* in the title refers to the Gothic revival window in the modest Iowa farmhouse behind the figures. When *American Gothic* was shown at an exhibition in Chicago in 1930, it won a prize and was purchased for the museum by the Friends of American Art for $300. It was Grant Wood's first prize and his first purchase by a museum.

GRANT WOOD, (1891–1942), *AMERICAN GOTHIC* 1930, OIL ON BEAVER BOARD, 29⅞ × 24⅞ IN. (74.3 × 62.4 CM). FRIENDS OF AMERICAN ART COLLECTION, ALL RIGHTS RESERVED BY THE ART INSTITUTE OF CHICAGO AND VAGA, NEW YORK, NY, 1930.934

10-85 GEORGIA O'KEEFFE *THE LAWRENCE TREE*. 1929. Oil on canvas, 31¹/₁₆ × 39¹/₁₆″. Wadsworth Atheneum, Hartford, Connecticut. The novelist D. H. Lawrence and his wife, Frieda, were friends of O'Keeffe when she spent the summer of 1929 in New Mexico. O'Keeffe wrote: "I spent several weeks up at the Lawrence ranch that summer. There was a long weathered carpenter's bench under the tall tree in front of the little old house that Lawrence had lived in there. I often lay on the bench looking up into the tree—past the trunk and up into the branches. It was particularly fine at night with the stars above the tree." Lawrence described this tree as "a great pillar of pale, flaky-ribbed copper," and wrote about the wind "hissing in the needles like a nest of serpents."

GEORGIA O'KEEFFE, *THE LAWRENCE TREE*. OIL ON CANVAS. WADSWORTH ATHENEUM, HARTFORD. THE ELLA GALLUP SUMNER AND MARY CATLIN SUMNER COLLECTION FUND. ACCESSION#: 1981.23

industry. Only smoke, sky, and water—now channeled to serve an industrial function—show transient movement. In the nineteenth century, the quintessential American landscape had been a wilderness scene that resonated with the painter's wonder before sublime nature (see fig. 9-39). Following World War I, the machine and industry emerged as heroes. The satisfying nature of Sheeler's composition lies in his carefully calibrated composition, which reveals his idea "that pictures realistically conceived might have an underlying abstract structure."

A similarly precise treatment of forms is evident in the well-known and much-caricatured *American Gothic* (fig. 10-84) by Grant Wood (1892–1942). Wood grew up in the American Midwest, and his intent in the painting was to capture the qualities of hard work and determination that he saw in his family and in many of the citizens of the small towns of Iowa. Wood intended that his figures, whom he identified as a man and his daughter (note the family resemblance and the difference in ages), suggest how the val-

ues of the pioneers were being perpetuated into the modern period by later generations. When painting was exhibited in 1930, it became clear that it could mean different things to different people; while one critic suggested that the painting "has a touch of humor and a heart of gold," another said that it revealed "what is Right and what is Wrong with America."

An art historian has recently pointed out that a sympathetic and supportive interpretation of the characters was more often found in the Midwest, while harsher interpretations came from critics outside the Midwest. In discussing the characters as he represented them, Wood himself said that he had "no intention of holding them up to ridicule" and that although "these people had bad points . . . to me they were basically good and solid people."

O'Keeffe's *The Lawrence Tree* (fig. 10-85) forces us to take an unusual viewpoint—looking directly up—on a starry evening in the American Southwest. O'Keeffe abstracts from nature, using limited colors and forms that are rendered with almost no modeling. But in the subtle organic

shape of the tree, she suggests not only its growth patterns but its arching expansiveness. The poetic, evocative position we assume emphasizes the scope and scale of nature in an almost pantheistic fashion. The appreciation for the majesty of nature that so moved American nineteenth-century artists found a worthy modern successor in O'Keeffe.

The art of Thomas Hart Benton (1889–1975) is a product of Regionalism, an antimodern movement that flourished in the American Midwest in the late 1920s and early 1930s. Regionalist American artists painted local subject matter in a simple, realistic, and comprehensible style. Such an art is determinedly chauvinistic and can perhaps be related to a need during the Great Depression for a reassurance that finds comfort in nostalgia. Benton's large, didactic murals exalted the history and folklore of a specific region: among his ambitious programs is a wall dedicated to *Pioneer Days and Early Settlers* (fig. 10-86) in the Missouri State Capitol. The wall is divided by painted geometric bands that establish an active compositional pattern.

The figures, drawn in Benton's unique and energetic style, reenact local history and legend. The heroism of work, conveyed by the figures to the right—these were inspired by the nudes of Michelangelo (see fig. 6-36)—is a common theme in Benton's art. Such paintings were more than imaginative re-creations of America's past; they were intended to offer criticism, as well as models and inspiration for the future. Benton himself denied the significance of modern art for his work, stating: "I wallowed in every cockeyed 'ism' that came along, and it took me ten years to get all that modernist dirt out of my system."

In summarizing his work, he wrote: "I have a sort of inner conviction that . . . I have come to something that is in the image of America and the American people of my time."

The *Toussaint L'Ouverture Series*, by Jacob Lawrence, joined historical research with intensely personal memories of history lectures the artist had heard during his youth in Harlem (fig. 10-87). Lawrence's work communicates his brutal theme with immediacy: harshly abstract figures, sharp contrast of colors, and even the movement of the tall grass, which is waving like flames, add to the violence of the scene. Like other Social Realist artists in the United States during the 1930s and 1940s, Lawrence uses his work as a vehicle for protest, demonstrating a brutal historical reality. Discussing the purpose of his art in relation to social justice, Lawrence wrote: "Having no Negro history makes the Negro people feel inferior to the rest of the world. I don't see how a history of the United States can be written honestly without including the Negro. . . . We don't have a physical slavery, but an economic slavery. If these people, who were so much worse off than the people today, could conquer their slavery, we certainly can do the same thing."

10-86 THOMAS HART BENTON. *PIONEER DAYS AND EARLY SETTLERS*. 1935–36. Oil and egg tempera on linen mounted on panel, size of wall 25′ × 14′2″. State Capitol, Jefferson City, Missouri. Before receiving this important commission in his home state, Benton had received commissions for mural cycles at the New School for Social Research in New York City, in the library of the Whitney Museum of American Art, and for the State of Indiana's exhibition at the 1933 Chicago World's Fair. The Missouri cycle, which Benton called *A Social History of Missouri*, encompasses three walls; on this wall, Benton depicted early settlers, including a trader giving whiskey to a Native American in exchange for furs, the legend of Huck Finn and Jim with a paddleboat named *Sam Clemens*, and early construction that leads back to a view of later governmental structures. Benton's portrayal is not completely positive, as seen in the smaller scenes below, with a cruel slave driver and the violent expulsion of the Mormons. The public and the Missouri legislature criticized these works for not being more idealistic, and Benton was accused of degrading his state's history and image. Commissioned by the Missouri legislature.

10-87 JACOB LAWRENCE *TOUSSAINT L'OUVERTURE SERIES, NO. 10: THE CRUELTY OF THE PLANTERS LED THE SLAVES TO REVOLT, 1776. THESE REVOLTS KEPT SPRINGING UP FROM TIME TO TIME—FINALLY CAME TO A HEAD IN THE REBELLION*. 1937–38. Gouache on paper, 11 × 17″. Amistad Research Center, Aaron Douglas Collection, Tulane University, New Orleans. The forty-one panels of Lawrence's *Toussaint L'Ouverture Series* tell how the hero, a Haitian slave named Toussaint L'Ouverture, freed his country from French rule during the late-eighteenth and early-nineteenth centuries. The republic of Haiti, founded by L'Ouverture, was the first black republic established in the Western Hemisphere.

Pablo Picasso, *Guernica*

10-88   PABLO PICASSO. *GUERNICA*. May 1–June 4, 1937. Oil on canvas, 11′5½″ × 25′5¾″. Museo Nacional Centro de Arte Reina Sofía, Madrid. Picasso placed the painting on extended loan to the Museum of Modern Art in New York for many years, stipulating that it be given to Spain and her people only when democracy was restored. The painting was returned to Spain in 1981. Commissioned by the Republican Government of Spain

Despite the perplexity of highly abstract shapes, which owe a formal debt to Synthetic Cubism, the *Guernica* mural, inspired by the bombing of an innocent Spanish town during the civil war of 1936–39, achieves an immediate impact (fig. 10-88). An architectonically stable composition underlies the surface tumult, for the verticality of the two side figures, the woman with upraised arms to the right and the woman cradling the dead child on the left, acts to secure the central group, which is resolved in the shape of a triangle. This simplified geometric order imparts an underlying strength to the composition.

The restriction of the color palette to black, white, and values of gray and the newspaperlike lines across the body of the horse remind us of the reporting of disastrous events in newspapers. It was by reading such reports that Picasso learned of the disaster at Guernica (see map, page 472). Writing later, the American painter Ad Reinhardt considered the *Guernica* a "design that diagrams our whole present dark age," and of the limited color range Picasso used, Reinhardt stated, "The dead have no color."

Picasso refused to elaborate on the particular intentions he invested in each figure, preferring to encourage the viewer to understand the work on an emotional, intuitive level. On the right and left sides of the composition, two women, shrieking in anguish with eyes transformed to the shape of tears, look toward the heavens, source of their pain and death. The figure on the left holding a dead child adapts the Pietà theme (see fig. 5-67) to this nightmare, while the woman to the right cries from the flames that have engulfed her house. Below her, another woman drags her mangled leg and, with arms outstretched, seems to be pleading for help. Above, an oil lamp, reminiscent of the light held by allegorical figures of Truth and Liberty, is thrust into the chaos. This light, however, is overwhelmed by the harsh radiance from the bare electric bulb, added to the composition only in the final stages of painting (see fig. 10-89). Previously, this areas had represented the sun or an eye. The change to the electric light is most likely an allusion to technology, which, during the bombing of Guernica, was unleashed as a malevolent and destructive force.

In the central group, a horse has been lanced; its head is twisted back, and the pointed tongue becomes a silent scream of pain and accusation. Although the horse may symbolize the suffering of Spain, it also expresses the totality of a conflict that involves all of nature. The bull suggests brute power, perhaps in reference to Franco and fascism. Below the horse are the dismembered remains of a fallen soldier. His hand, while still clutching a broken sword, also clings to a delicate flower, the only promise of hope in this image of suffering and death.

The brutal Spanish civil war was the result of conflicting political ideologies and of internal tensions that were centuries old. In 1931, the Bourbon monarchy, which had ruled Spain since 1700, was replaced by a republican government that promised social and economic reform, including the redistribution of land and the secularization of certain governmental functions controlled by the Church. Such reforms, which were aimed at countering the political power of wealthy landowners and the clergy, provoked the formation of conservative alliances. During the increasing civil disorder after the elections of 1936 (won by the republicans), General Francisco Franco, claiming allegiance to his nation rather than to any political group, led an insurrection that immersed Spain in civil war. Nazi Germany and Fascist Italy aided Franco, while the USSR assisted the leftist coalition, which included the Communists. The major Western democracies maintained an official position of neutrality, but many individuals supported the republican cause when the cruel reality of Franco's oppression became apparent. After three years and the loss of hundreds of thousands of lives,

10-89 PABLO PICASSO. *GUERNICA*. Photograph of the painting on May 11, 1937, by Dora Maar. This is the first of seven photographs made of the work in progress. Many of the main themes are already established, but virtually all will be dramatically reworked. Note that at this early point defiance on the part of the dead warrior is expressed by his upraised arm and fist.

PABLO PICASSO, *GUERNICA STUDY, SKETCH 15, COMPOSITION STUDY*, 9 MAY 1937. PENCIL 9½ × 17⅞ IN. CASON DEL BUEN RETIRO. MUSEO DEL PRADO, MADRID. © 2000 ARTISTS RIGHTS SOCIETY (ARS), NEW YORK. ARSIU MAS, BARCELONA, SPAIN

Franco established an authoritarian rule that continued until his death in 1975.

In January 1937, in the midst of the civil war, the republican government commissioned Picasso, who was living and working in France, to paint a mural for the Spanish Pavilion at the World's Fair scheduled to open in Paris that year. Picasso had yet to settle upon an exact theme when news of the events of April 26 reached him. On that day, Franco had used his Nazi allies to conduct the first "total" air raid. In what seems to have been an experiment in saturation bombing, the historic city of Guernica, a town of no strategic military significance, was bombarded for more than three hours. When Picasso learned of the bombing, he started to paint a work that would be an invective against both the particular event and the senseless brutality of conflict.

Picasso, whose republican sympathies had already been manifested in satirical etchings that were called the *Dream and Lie of Franco*, wrote:

> In the panel on which I am working which I shall call Guernica, and in all my recent works of art, I clearly express my abhorrence of the military caste which has sunk Spain into an ocean of pain and death.

The story is told that while viewing a photograph of *Guernica*, a Nazi official queried Picasso,

> So it was you who did this?

The reply came sharply,

> No, you did!

Sculpture of the 1930s and 1940s

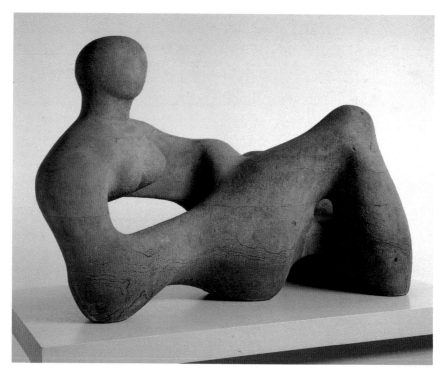

10-90 HENRY MOORE. *RECUMBENT FIGURE*. 1938. Gray-green Hornton stone, length about 54″. Tate Gallery, London. Moore's sources for this style encompass not only modern European sculpture but also the powerfully abstract forms of African and pre-Hispanic art.

Recumbent Figure (fig. 10-90), by Henry Moore (1898–1986), is immediately recognizable as a reclining female figure—one of the traditional themes of Western art. Like many of its antecedents (see figs. 6-40, 6-41), it suggests a voluptuous figure. Although the positions of the head and breasts are evident and the figure is clearly propped up on one elbow, the torso below the breasts is an open cavity, and other forms suggest hips, a knee, and legs, without informing us of the exact pose. Moore's massive, simple forms also suggest the hills and gullies of a landscape. The sculpture interrelates with its environment through the powerful masses and unexpected openings that surround and mold space. Moore has written that

sculpture in air is possible, where the stone contains only the hole, which is the intended and considered form.

The interrelationships of the abstract forms, however, suggest the organic qualities of a living, breathing figure with a potential for movement. Moore never denies the dignity and beauty of the human body, and many of his figures are heroic in scale and in content.

During the 1930s and 1940s, sculptors' interest in abstraction took a number of forms. Henry Moore and Barbara Hepworth (1903–75) guided the development of British abstract art in the 1930s, but Hepworth's sculpture moved further into abstraction. In *Sculpture with Color (Oval Form)*, mass and

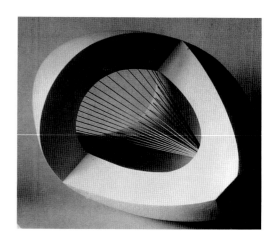

10-91 BARBARA HEPWORTH. *SCULPTURE WITH COLOR (OVAL FORM), PALE BLUE AND RED*. 1943. Painted wood with strings, length 18″. Private collection.

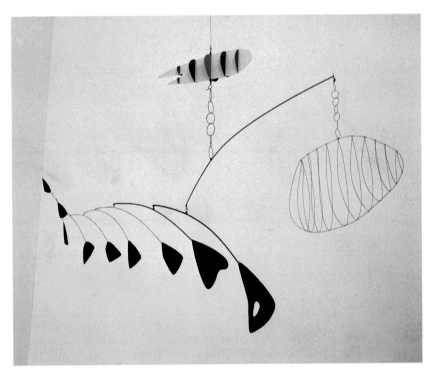

10-92   ALEXANDER CALDER. *LOBSTER TRAP AND FISH TAIL.* 1939. Hanging mobile: painted steel wire and sheet aluminum, 8'6" × 9'6". The Museum of Modern Art, New York. Commissioned by the Advisory Committee for the stairwell of the museum.

space become integral elements in a composition that simultaneously reveals itself as exterior form and interior structure (fig. 10-91). The contrast between exterior and interior is reinforced by color, while the taut strings relate the interior cavity to the exterior surface. Hepworth wrote that this structural relationship of color and string was associated with her perception of nature:

> The colour in the concavities plunged me into the depth of water, caves, or shadows deeper than the carved concavities themselves. The strings were the tension I felt between myself and the sea, the wind or the hills.

In a later comment, she elaborated on the significance of nature:

> In the contemplation of Nature we are perpetually renewed, our sense of mystery and our imagination is kept alive, and rightly understood, it gives us the power to project into a plastic medium some universal or abstract vision of beauty.

A new type of sculpture, named **mobiles** by the artist Marcel Duchamp, was shown at an exhibition in 1932 by the American artist Alexander Calder (1898–1976), who had first been trained as an engineer. Calder's earliest mobiles were moved by hand cranks or motors, but by 1932 they evolved into the lightweight, delicately balanced, suspended sculptures, moved by air currents, that have spawned so many popular variations. Although most of Calder's mobiles are completely abstract, the title of the present example suggests that the graceful movements of the curvilinear forms are a reference to swimming fish (fig. 10-92). In Calder's mobiles, the intimate relationship between form and space attains a new complexity as air currents move the forms slowly through space to create ever-new compositions.

The title that Isamu Noguchi (1904–88) gave his over-lifesize *Kouros* reveals that these abstract

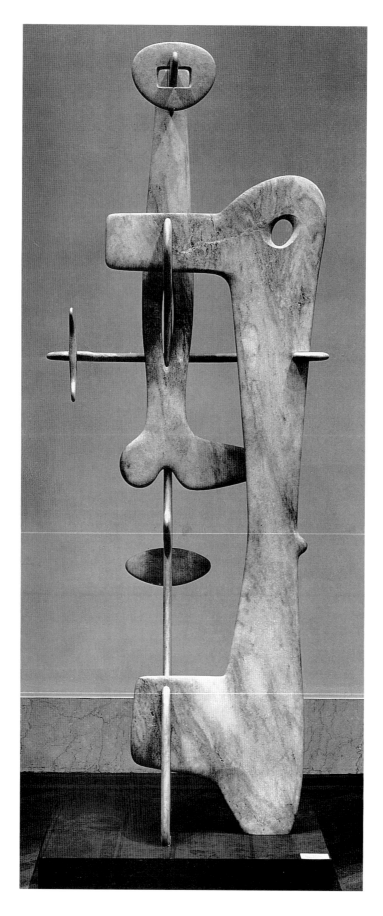

10-93 ISAMU NOGUCHI *KOUROS*. 1944–45. Pink Georgia marble, height 9′9″. The Metropolitan Museum of Art, New York. The slabs of stone are not fastened together, and the sculpture can be disassembled. Noguchi's involvement with Greek themes came in part from his collaboration as a set designer with Martha Graham, the innovative American dancer whose modern ballets were often based on mythic themes.

FLETCHER FUND, 1953

10-94 JOSEPH CORNELL. *MEDICI SLOT MACHINE.* 1942. Construction, 13½ × 12 × 4¼″. Private collection. Cornell intended that his boxes be held in the hands and moved so that the loose elements could rattle and be rearranged.

forms refer to a standing male figure (fig. 10-93), and we are encouraged to compare the sculpture with idealized ancient Greek statues of the sixth and fifth centuries BCE (see figs. 3-62, 3-64). As a modern artist, Noguchi reinvents the human form, substituting thin slabs of stone that interlock at right angles as support for the solid, rounded mass that is central to the body. The individual slabs, however, offer organic shapes and subtly rounded edges that are related to the flowing interpenetration of forms that characterizes a living human form. The frailty of forms and the instability of structure may be intended to convey the emotional anxiety Noguchi sensed in 1944–45, near the end of World War II, when he felt a need for

> constant transfusions of human meaning into the encroaching void.

In his boxes, Joseph Cornell (1903–75) combines three-dimensional objects and two-dimensional charts, photographs, maps, and/or reproductions of works of art, all joined within shallow, glass-fronted enclosures (fig. 10-94). His unexpected juxtapositions of the concrete with the illusory can be poignant, enigmatic, and nostalgic. Each becomes a secluded and private universe intended to stimulate a viewer's imagination and memories. In speaking of a box that made a reference to soap bubbles, Cornell said,

> Shadow boxes become poetic theaters or setting wherein are metamorphosed the elements of a childhood pastime.

In *Medici Slot Machine*, a reproduction of a sixteenth-century painting of a young nobleman is viewed through

a glass with crossed lines, like a gunsight, perhaps to suggest the way that we target the past from a distance. A compass and a watch spring in the circular opening below suggest both space and time. The frame around the boy is covered with old maps of ancient Rome, perhaps a reference to the Renaissance interest in antiquity, while the ball, jacks, and game pieces below refer to the entertainments enjoyed by youth in all periods. These are at best suggestions of Cornell's meanings—the true modernity of Cornell's boxes lies in how they encourage individual, unconscious interpretations. Even the name enhances this quality of personal meaning. Like many modern artists, Cornell avoids reference to specific meaning by selecting names that increase a viewer's sense of wonderment and expectation.

International Style Architecture

10-95 PHILIP JOHNSON. GLASS HOUSE, NEW CANAAN, CONNECTICUT. 1949. The Glass House, the architect's own home, is secluded on a large estate, and privacy is not a problem. A brick cylinder placed asymmetrically provides a fireplace and the enclosure necessary for the bathroom and mechanical equipment. A counter forms the kitchen area, and a freestanding block of closets, not visible in this view, provides storage space.

Glass House, by Philip Johnson (b. 1906), is a satisfying combination of pure geometric form, subtle proportional relationships, and elegant materials (fig. 10-95)—an outstanding example of the modern architectural movement known as the International Style. This style, named by Johnson in 1932 in the context of an architectural exhibition held at the Museum of Modern Art in New York, is based on the refined glass box. It was expressed as early as the 1920s in works by the German architect Ludwig Mies van der Rohe (1886–1969), who later became the director of the Bauhaus (see pp. 526–27). Mies emigrated to the United States in 1937 and became a citizen in 1944. The International Style only came to full fruition after World War II, when Mies was commissioned to create a number of works, including skyscrapers in Chicago and New York and an entire campus for the Illinois Institute of Technology in Chicago. These popularized the style and led to its adaptation throughout the Western world. By the 1960s, virtually every Western capital had many metal and glass skyscrapers.

Even while it was under construction, the Seagram Building was recognized as an especially elegant and impressive modern structure (fig. 10-96). Mies's choice of materials reveals his goals of harmony and elegance, for the exposed structural I beams are composed of bronze that exactly matches the amber-tinted glass. The building is tall and wide when seen from the front, but its relative thinness gives it a soaring refinement. The proportions of the design are based on a simple modular system much like the satisfying Early Renaissance architecture of Brunelleschi (see fig. 5-40). The open lower stories, where there are a bank of elevators and a small glassed lobby, lighten the structure and help establish the proportional integrity of the whole. The building in every way reflects Mies's personal motto,

Less is more.

Because it occupies less than one-half of the site, the building does not have to conform to the restrictions of New York City's set-back law, which explains the staggered rooflines of so many Manhattan buildings. The structure is placed on a large plaza that sets it off as a gigantic sculptural form.

The glass box represents a pure ideological statement without historical precedent or references, but in its materials it is a product of the machine culture. Its origins lie in mass production, prefabrication, and the glorification of the precision of the machine. Even more important, it shares in the utopian ideals that had inspired de Stijl (see pages 524–26), one of its sources; as pure architecture, expressing the Platonic ideal with thoroughly modern materials, it shares in the idealism of much twentieth-century thought.

Despite the purist, reductive beauty of Johnson's Glass House and Mies's Seagram Building, the International Style quickly reached a dead end. The glass box is an impersonal object, and as cities all over the world became crowded with such buildings, many people felt that their environment had become a cold and sterile place in which to live and work. Because the emphasis is on purity of design at the expense of function, such buildings—all of which look similar—demonstrate little interest in the needs of the client or of the people who work in them. In their modern purity, they ignore the subtle relationships to site, climate, or local architectural tradition that were crucial for so many earlier works of architecture.

10-96 MIES VAN DER ROHE. SEAGRAM BUILDING, NEW YORK. 1956–58. The International Style glass-box skyscraper became popular with corporate America because it projected a modern, up-to-date image for the business it housed. Few buildings in this style, however, have the sophisticated elegance of the Seagram Building. Philip Johnson, who assisted Mies in the design of the building, was largely responsible for the creation of the interior spaces. Commissioned by Joseph E. Seagram and Sons Corporation, under the advisement of Phyllis Bronfman Lambert.

Abstract Expressionism
and Post-Painterly Abstraction

10-97 JACKSON POLLOCK.

CONVERGENCE. 1952. Oil on canvas, 8 × 13′. Albright-Knox Art Gallery, Buffalo, New York.

My painting does not come from the easel. I hardly ever stretch my canvas before painting. I prefer to tack the unstretched canvas to the hard wall or the floor. I need the resistance of a hard surface. On the floor I am more at ease. I feel nearer, more a part of the painting, since this way I can walk around it, work from the four sides and literally be in the painting. . . .

I continue to get further away from the usual painter's tools . . . I prefer sticks, trowels, knives and dripping fluid paint or a heavy impasto with sand, broken glass, and other foreign matter added.

When I am in my painting, I'm not aware of what I'm doing. It is only after a sort of "get acquainted" period that I see what I have been about. I have no fears about making changes, destroying the image, etc., because the painting has a life of its own. I try to let it come through. It is only when I lose contact with the painting that the result is a mess. Otherwise there is pure harmony, an easy give and take, and the painting comes out well.

(Jackson Pollock, 1947)

Convergence bursts forth with the dynamism of exuberant colors and interpenetrating layers of undulating paint (fig. 10-97). This weblike mass of colors and rhythms offers a new and provocative approach to painting; it records the process by which the artist's unconscious had been laid bare. Pollock's method of painting is derived from Surrealist automatism, and while creating these innovative works, Pollock, often described as being in a trance-like state and moving with the grace of a dancer, aggressively flung paint onto the canvas, the action of his arm being guided by his unconscious (fig. 10-98). But unlike Surrealist automatism, Pollock did not consciously complete the image to bring it within the realm of objectivity. The painting communicates a raw, expressive energy.

But what are we to make of all this? What does it mean for us to confront this painterly record of an artist's unconscious? Surrealism, one of the roots of Abstract Expressionism (defined below), was bound to the psychoanalytical investigations of Freud, but Carl Jung's concept of a "collective unconscious" is equally significant here. As Pollock has exposed his human unconscious, we should be able to draw meaning intuitively from the painting, as its large scale, abstract rhythms, and intense colors meet an unconscious response in us.

Pollock's drip paintings exemplify one style within Abstract Expressionism, a movement that, beginning in New York after World War II, thrust the United States into the avant-garde of Western art. As we have seen, the roots of Abstract Expressionism were grounded in the psychoanalytical theories of Freud and Jung and in Surrealism. During the 1930s, with the rise of Nazi Germany casting an increasingly foreboding shadow over Europe, many leading European artists came to the United States. The impact of their work and their presence was felt in a major 1936 exhibition of Dada and Surrealism at New York's Museum of Modern Art. European artists, some of whom opened their studios as teachers, found a particularly responsive audience among a younger generation of American artists who, bound with a collective American identity resulting from the common hardships of the Depression, were searching for new avenues of expression. With Sur-

10-98   Photograph of Jackson Pollock painting.

realism illuminating one of the avenues, these American artists assumed control of the avant-garde in the late 1940s.

The term *Abstract Expressionism* had been used earlier in the century to designate the nonobjective paintings of Kandinsky, but it was resurrected in 1946 to describe the works of a group of American painters centered in New York (these artists are also sometimes referred to as the New York School). What joined these artists was not a unified style but a common attitude that stressed the unique individuality of each creative act. These artists were also familiar with the philosophy of Existentialism, with its emphasis on

10-99 MARK ROTHKO

WHITE AND GREENS IN BLUE. 1957. Oil on canvas, 8'6" × 7'. Private collection, New York.

the importance of the experience of the present moment (see pages 476–77); their interest in the actual techniques of creation are an important aspect of the movement.

Within the stylistic differences of the Abstract Expressionist painters, we can discern two fundamental approaches; one, termed Action Painting by the critic Harold Rosenberg in 1952, was a free, gestural expression of paint on the canvas, as demonstrated by the paintings of Jackson Pollock. Another mode, exemplified by the work of Mark Rothko (1903–70), is referred to as Color Field Painting. It displayed limited areas of color within simple and controlled, nonobjective compositions, leaving the shapes and colors to communicate an aesthetic and/or emotional experience.

Rothko, who arrived at this mode of expression after experimenting with the human form and with Surrealist biomorphic compositions, always insisted that paintings must be about

10-100 MORRIS LOUIS. *SARABAND.* 1959. Acrylic resin on canvas, 8′5⅛″ × 12′5″. Solomon R. Guggenheim Museum, New York. The title of the painting is derived from a stately European court dance of the seventeenth and eighteenth centuries. This abstract work would have been titled after it was completed. Perhaps the repeated rhythmic patterns and flowing shapes of the composition suggested this title to the artist.

something, that they must have a strong content:

> It is a widely accepted notion among painters that it does not matter what one paints as long as it is well painted. This is the essence of academicism. There is no such thing as a good painting about nothing. We assert that subject matter is crucial and only that subject matter is valid which is tragic and timeless.

In Rothko's *White and Greens in Blue* (fig. 10-99), horizontal planes stacked vertically carry associations of nature, such as landscape and sky, while also establishing a hierarchical order. The interplay of these elements is joined to an emotive use of color. We draw a melancholic sensation from the sobriety of the colors. The densely darkened green rectangles that weigh down the bottom rectangle of white seem to convey unconsciously the suppression of hope.

Rothko, believing in the evocative nature of his paintings, became increasingly sensitive to charges that his work lacked content, that it was only an exercise in color relationships. An interviewer once posed the question of content to Rothko, who replied:

> I'm interested in expressing only basic human emotions—tragedy, ecstasy, doom, and so on—and the fact that lots of people break down and cry when confronted with my pictures shows that I communicate these basic human emotions. . . . The people who weep before my pictures are having the same religious experience I had when I painted them, and if you, as you say, are moved only by their color relationships, then you miss the point.

The development of Abstract Expressionism provoked the exploration of new techniques. Both Pollock and Rothko experimented by staining raw or unprepared artists' canvas with highly liquid acrylic paint, a technique that produced different effects from the traditional application of brushed paint. Among the artists who adopted the resulting style, which was named Post-Painterly Abstraction by the art critic Clement Greenberg, were Helen Frankenthaler (see fig. 10-14) and Morris Louis (1912–62). In creating *Saraband*, Louis poured acrylic resin onto the canvas and then inclined it at different angles as the paint flowed over and soaked into the canvas (fig. 10-100). The result is a luminous painting composed of rhythmic color veils whose transparency and overlapping forms deny traditional figure/ground distinctions. The staining technique negates the autographic movements of the artist that had been so important in Abstract Expressionism. In *Saraband*, color and canvas are wed in a planarity whose only texture is that of the canvas itself. Even the white color of the canvas becomes an important element of the composition. By questioning the roles of picture plane and illusory space, the artists of this group achieved a reductive purity in abstract painting.

Le Corbusier

10-101 LE CORBUSIER.

Exterior, Nôtre-Dame-du-Haut, Ronchamp, near Belfort, France. 1950–54. Le Corbusier, "the crowlike one," is the nickname of the French architect Charles-Édouard Jeanneret. Nôtre-Dame-du-Haut is built in the foothills of the Alps, on the edge of a high promontory overlooking the town of Ronchamp. It marks the site of an earlier chapel, destroyed in World War II, that had displayed a miracle-working statue of the Madonna now incorporated into the new structure. In ancient times, this area had been sanctified by a pagan shrine. An outside altar and pulpit are used when pilgrimage crowds become too large to be accommodated within the chapel. The building is constructed of reinforced concrete. Commissioned by Canon Lucien Ledeur of Besançon, who hoped the building would help initiate a renaissance in church art and architecture.

In its highly personal, nonrepeating forms, the chapel at Ronchamp by Le Corbusier (1887–1965) offers a dramatic, individualized alternative to the geometric purity of the contemporary International Style in architecture. Like the great French Gothic cathedrals, this structure sets out to astonish and move us by its unexpected and mysterious form and structure (figs. 10-101 to 10-103). The sweeping roof seems thin and billowing, like an air-filled sail. Although the roof is made of natural brown-gray cement, its detachment from the thick, curving walls below gives it a particular lightness. The sail-like roof of Nôtre-Dame-du-Haut creates a relationship with nature, for it seems to respond to the winds that sweep the promontory site. The structural system is based on nature, for Le Corbusier was inspired by a crab shell he picked up on a beach.

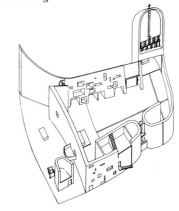

10-102 LE CORBUSIER. Axonometric projection of Nôtre-Dame-du-Haut.

10-103 LE CORBUSIER

Interior, Nôtre-Dame-du-Haut. The interior, approximately 43 × 72′, has pews for only about fifty worshippers.

On the interior (fig. 10-103), the darkness and the thick, roughly textured walls suggest a mysterious cave, while a slit of light between wall and ceiling and the sagging shape of the ceiling itself reinforce the billowing sail effect of the exterior. The thick wall is pierced by irregularly sized and spaced windows filled with stained glass on which traditional religious symbols (a dove, the sun) and phrases ("Marie," "Blessed among Women") have been painted. Like sculpture in the round, the building forces us to move to understand it, and as we explore the structure, three chapels—mysteriously lit by hidden windows in towers—are discovered. The building becomes an adventure and, for some, a journey of personal religious discovery. In discussing the building, Le Corbusier called it totally free architecture,

describing it as

sculpture "of an acoustical nature," that is to say projecting afar the effect of its form and, in return, receiving the pressure of the surrounding spaces. The key is light and light illuminates shapes and shapes have emotional power.

Film in Japan

10-104 YASUJIRO OZU (director). *TOKYO STORY*. 1953. Shukichi (the father) and Tomi (the mother). Script by Kogo Noda and Yasujiro Ozu; photographed by Yuharu Atsuta. The running time of the film is 135 minutes.

Tokyo Story, by the filmmaker Yasujiro Ozu (1903–63), was released on November 3, 1953. Popular in Japan, it was also one of very few Japanese films of this period to be shown abroad. The film focuses on a modern, middle-class Japanese family, the relationships among its members, and how they are affected by events in their everyday lives. Ozu's message concerns how events gradually lead to the dissolution of the traditional family structure that is so important in Japanese life and society. Rather than stressing the cause of domestic turbulence, he emphasized its effect on individual family members. Incidents in everyday life gradually reveal the nature of the characters. These confrontations of family members within the context of daily life are subtle, familiar, and easy for Japanese as well as Western audiences to appreciate. The subject crossed cultural boundaries and allowed viewers in the West a glimpse of Japan not common in the post-war period.

Produced in the context of war weariness and disillusion, this film appeared only one year after the end of the Allied occupation of Japan. The reforms carried out during the post-war period were drastic. Land-reform programs had made owner-farmers out of tenants, the new "peace constitution" had defined the emperor as a "symbol of state" instead of a source of sovereignty, and a long bill of rights gave certain privileges to individuals. The abandonment of war as an "instrument of national policy" meant the renouncement of any buildup of weapons and armies. The civil code was revised in accordance with the sentiments of the new democratic constitution, and as a result the traditional powers of the family head, which were built into the old code, were supposed to disappear. Such reforms had a profound effect on both national policy and everyday life. Made in the midst of these sweeping reforms, *Tokyo Story* reveals the inevitable and unresolved conflict between the demands of life in the modern industrial era and traditional Japanese cultural mores and values, especially those centered around family life. The film examines that conflict thematically and cinematically.

Tokyo Story is integrated around three elements: story, theme, and cinematography. The story is a complex three-part tale that focuses on the parents' relationships with their children. The first section is set in the town of Onomichi, where the old couple lives. The middle section sees the parents at a reunion with their children in Tokyo. Both their son and daughter are busy with their own lives and send the parents off to a hot-springs resort, ostensibly as a treat but actually to get rid of them. The only kindness they experience in Tokyo is found with the widow

10-105. YASUJIRO OZU (director). *TOKYO STORY.* The family at the funeral of the mother.

of their third son, who had been killed in the war. The third section, back in Onomichi, depicts the death and funeral of the mother. The children are called to her deathbed, but she is so ill that she cannot recognize them. The children hurry away after the funeral, but the daughter-in-law stays behind to see the old father settled in. Then she, too, must return to Tokyo, leaving the father in the empty house to contemplate the lonely years that lie ahead.

Ozu's central theme is how one comes to terms with the dissolution of the family and, ultimately, with death. Three alternative solutions are examined, each described in the reactions of the children. Several of the characters are resigned and accept these conditions with sensitivity. Others lack compassion, are indifferent, and regard separation of the family as inevitable. The youngest refuses to accept the dissolu-tion and tries to shore up the family once again. These choices are presented as complementary to one another, and dynamic conflict never arises. Resolu-tion is never reached, and the theme of transience triumphs. The psychological tension created by this thematic and visual structure keeps the viewer aware of the conflicts inherent in modern life.

Given his attachment to daily fam-ily scenes and events, Ozu sets a slow pace that echoes the unfolding of life in the everyday world. The camera is literally fixed at the eye level of some-one seated on the floor on a straw tatami mat in a traditional Japanese house. He uses only three standard shots—long, medium, and close-up—repeating them again and again. The medium shot is the basic unit, and the scenery in each frame is presented with austere formal symmetry (fig. 10-104). Although these standard shots are repeated, they frame the subtle psychological and emotional relation-ships of the moment (fig. 10-105).

Both the framing and the pacing of the film confirm the aesthetic standards that had been held for centuries among Japanese artists and support Ozu's rep-utation as the most traditional of Japan's filmmakers. His visual and the-matic sensibilities—an emphasis on sim-plicity and directness and an interest in the notion of the transience or imper-manence in life—closely resemble those of Zen artists. His black-and-white films have been compared to Zen tem-ple gardens, where simple, unadorned arrangements of dry rocks and raked sand are meant to elicit complex responses (see fig. 6-79). Ozu's tale, told in the modern medium of film and focused on a problem common to the modern world, expresses unmistakably traditional Japanese values.

The Return to the Object:
Jasper Johns and Robert Rauschenberg

10-106 JASPER JOHNS. *Flag*. 1954–55 (dated on reverse 1954). Encaustic, oil, and collage on fabric mounted on plywood, 42¼ × 60⅝". The Museum of Modern Art, New York.

Flag (fig. 10-106), by Jasper Johns (b. 1930), strikes us as a blatantly representational image, even more so when we consider that it was created in the mid-1950s, when various modes of nonobjectivity ruled the avant-garde in painting. The composition is clearly and intentionally recognizable, but in place of the solid colored shapes of red, white, and blue that we expect in a flag, Johns has substituted a painterly texture whose thinness in places reveals collage elements underneath. Johns's painting is not a flag of the United States. The artist has carefully manipulated the surface to emphasize the reality of the painting as a mixed-medium work of paint and collage. This artistic transformation is intended to drain the image of its immediate symbolic content. Johns thus forces us to realize that the painting itself is first and foremost a composition of shapes and colors—an object.

During the early 1950s, a group of artists reacted to the nonobjective aesthetic that had dominated the American avant-garde with Abstract Expression-ism and Hard-Edge painting. Artists such as Johns and Robert Rauschenberg (b. 1925) began to incorporate, in the most literal of ways at times, representational imagery and recognizable objects in their work. This served at least two purposes: it avoided the sometimes uncomfortable defensiveness viewers felt with nonobjective art, while simultaneously offering the image or its combination with actual "found objects," as a given fact of our experience, without reference to symbolic comment. There is no precise name for this artistic activity

10-107 ROBERT RAUSCHENBERG. *MONOGRAM*. 1959. Construction, 3′6″ × 6′ × 6′. Moderna Museet, Stockholm.

of Johns and Rauschenberg in the mid-1950s. It is sometimes referred to as Neo-Dada, but although there is a similarity to Dada in the use of found objects, the artistic transformation of common images and objects and the different philosophical context of the 1950s make these works distinct from earlier Dada.

In *Monogram* (fig. 10-107), Robert Rauschenberg attached a stuffed Angora goat that had a used tire around its midsection to a base that joined collage elements with broad, gestural strokes of paint. Rauschenberg referred to these works as "combines," for they associated elements of life with those of art in a "matter of fact" manner that was inspired by the avant-garde musical compositions of John Case (see page 477). In the words of Rauschenberg:

Any incentive to paint is as good as any other. There is no poor subject.

Painting is always strongest when in spite of composition, color, etc., it appears as a fact, or an inevitability, as opposed to a souvenir or arrangement.

Painting relates to both art and life. Neither can be made. (I try to act in the gap between the two.)

A pair of socks is no less suitable to make a painting with than wood, nails, turpentine, oil, and fabric.

A canvas is never empty.

Amid the abstraction of the American avant-garde, these works of Johns and Rauschenberg emphasized the literal role of the object in the work of art.

Hard-Edge and Op Art

10-108 JOSEF ALBERS. *HOMAGE TO THE SQUARE: AFFECTIONATE*. 1954. Oil on canvas, 31⅞ × 31⅞". Musée National d'Art Moderne, Centre National d'Art et de Culture Georges Pompidou, Paris

The colors in my paintings are juxtaposed for various and changing effects. They are to challenge or to echo each other, to support or oppose one another. The contrasts, respectively boundaries, between them may vary from soft to hard touches, may mean pull and push besides clashes, but also embracing, intersecting, penetrating.

Despite an even and mostly opaque application, the colors will appear above or below each other, in front or behind, or side by side on the same level.
(Josef Albers, c. 1964)

Affectionate (fig. 10-108) is one of a series of paintings of virtually identical composition by Josef Albers (1888–1976). In all these works, square planes of color are set within larger square planes. Differences of color lead to varying perceptions of spatial illusion created without reference to representational forms. In this painting, the red square of the center appears suspended in advance of the darker, burgundy-colored square behind. This spatial configuration, however, is confounded by the lighter colors of the outer two squares, creating a complicated spatial illusion.

Albers, who studied and then taught at the Bauhaus, moved to the United States in 1933. His preference for controlled, geometric compositions derives from the Bauhaus design aesthetic. Early in his career, Albers studied the process of how we perceive and understand illusionism in painting through a series of works that created spatial illusions with nonrepresentational, geometric elements. Albers's studies continued throughout his career, culminating in a series of paintings in the 1950s titled *Homage to the Square*. In the United States, generations of artists were influenced by his teaching and his works.

The term *Hard-Edge Abstraction* was coined in 1958 to indicate a type of abstract painting whose shapes met in clearly defined edges. In the 1950s, Frank Stella (b. 1936) began to work with a series of shaped canvases that broke the rectangular format traditional for paintings. In *Empress of India* (fig. 10-109) the angular outward movement of the lines seems to have determined the boundaries, or shape, of the canvas. To Stella, the destruction of the traditional pictorial format opened to the viewer a greater understanding of the painting as a physical object—a support with colors attached. As Stella said in 1966:

I always get into arguments with people who want to retain the old values in painting—the humanistic values they always find on the canvas. My painting is based on the fact that only what can be seen is there. It is really an object. . . . All I want anyone to get out of my paintings, and all I ever get out of them is the fact that you can see the whole idea without any confusion. What you see is what you see.

Drift 2 (fig. 10-110), by Bridget Riley (b. 1931), exemplifies another movement from the 1960s known as Op art, short for Optical art. It was a descendant of Albers's nonobjective

10-109 FRANK STELLA. *EMPRESS OF INDIA.* 1965. Metallic powder in polymer emulsion paint on canvas, 6′5″ × 18′8″. The Museum of Modern Art, New York.

illusory compositions and Hard-Edge Abstraction. Its medium is **emulsion**, a liquid mixture in which one of the elements does not mix with the others but remains suspended in minute droplets. Although *Drift 2* is a flat canvas, its pattern is composed so that it seems to surge and undulate before our eyes. This illusion of movement, however, is dependent on our perception of the optical effects of pattern. Op art questions the very process by which we see and understand.

10-110 BRIDGET RILEY. *DRIFT 2.* 1966. Emulsion on canvas. 91½″ × 89½″. Albright-Knox Art Gallery, Buffalo, New York

Pop Art

10-111 RICHARD HAMILTON. *Just What Is It That Makes Today's Homes So Different, So Appealing?* 1956. Collage, 10¼ × 9¾". Kunsthalle, Tübingen, Germany. Hamilton's collage was part of a 1956 London exhibition titled "This Is Tomorrow."

JUST WHAT IS IT THAT MAKES TODAY'S HOMES SO DIFFERENT, SO APPEALING? BY RICHARD HAMILTON. KUNSTHALLE TÜBINGEN, GERMANY.

Popular (designed for mass audience); Transient (short-term solution); Expendable (easily forgotten); Low Cost; Mass Produced; Young (aimed at Youth); Witty; Sexy; Gimmicky; Glamorous; Big Business.

These words were used by the British artist Richard Hamilton (b. 1922) to describe Pop art. Hamilton's collage *Just What Is It That Makes Today's Homes So Different, So Appealing?* was both a visual manifesto and a prophetic statement of Pop art (fig. 10-111). The inspiration for Pop art was found in the commercialism that developed, particularly in the United States, and after World War II. Hamilton's work engages us on different levels; the almost-nude figures "update" the tradition of the nude in Western art, yet here they also represent a modern couple and they remind us of one of the rules of advertising—sex sells. They are surrounded by the conveniences and products of modern life, while the "fine arts" include a comic book as a framed picture and a canned ham as a table sculpture. The collage is laced with witticisms, including the use of the word *pop* on the Tootsie Roll wrapper and a portrait of John Ruskin, a conservative nineteenth-century British art critic. Yet within this environment of commercially produced images and intellectual puns, we are greeted with more profound considerations. The ceiling design is actually a photo of the earth taken from space, and the "pattern" of the rug is really a photography of densely packed humanity on a beach.

In the United States, the literal objectivity of artists like Johns and Rauschenberg (see pages 555–56) assisted in the development of Pop art. *As I Opened Fire*, by Roy Lichtenstein (b. 1923), is fashioned after a drawing in an out-of-date adventure comic book that the artist has blown up to an enormous size (fig. 10-112). The expression of the thoughts of the pilot across the top and the emblazoned *BRAT!* are a natural adjunct to the bold and simple style of the planes and blazing guns. The strong areas of flat color, contained by heavy black outlines, are in places created by enlarged patterns of dots inspired by the process used to print color illustrations in comic books and newspapers. Lichtenstein thus draws our attention not only to the overtly melodramatic imagery of the comic book, itself a representative subject of post–World War II culture, but also to the processes by which images are created for mass consumption.

Pop art celebrated objects and ideas that were not only familiar but also banal in their content. Nowhere was the habitual repetition of commercialization felt more fully than in the works of Andy Warhol (see fig. 10-10), who wrote,

> The reason I'm painting this way is that I want to be a machine, and I feel that whatever I do and do machine-like is what I want to do.

Many of Warhol's images were silk-screened by assistants at his workshop, The Factory, suggesting an equation between the processes of art and consumer production. But if Warhol's rows upon rows of Coke bottles, Campbell Soup cans, images of Marilyn Monroe, or accident scenes are born from an aesthetic numbness produced by the commercial environment, they also commu-

10-112   ROY LICHTENSTEIN. *As I Opened Fire.* 1964. Magna on canvas, each panel 5′8″ × 4′8″. Stedelijk Museum, Amsterdam.

© ROY LICHTENSTEIN

nicate how we are in danger of becoming unfeeling "products" within an industrialized environment. American Pop art had an international impact, and even influenced young artists working in China (see pages 585–86).

In the realm of public sculpture, Pop art overturned the traditional values that had been associated with monumental sculpture in public spaces. Claes Oldenburg (b. 1929) and Coosje van Bruggen (b. 1942) have altered the scale or texture of commonplace, manufactured objects (fig. 10-113). The recent installation of groups of scattered shuttlecocks on the lawns on both sides of a museum in Kansas City adds a playful yet thought-provoking contrast to the classically inspired design of the building and its ostensibly serious purposes as a repository for great art. Oldenburg once remarked that

The important thing about humor is that it opens people. They relax their guard and you can get your serious intention across.

10-113   CLAES OLDENBURG AND COOSJE VAN BRUGGEN. *Shuttlecocks* (detail, one of four). 1994. Aluminum and fiberglass-reinforced plastic, painted with polyurethane enamel; each 17′10¼″ high. Each shuttlecock weighs approximately 5,500 pounds. The Nelson-Atkins Museum of Art, Kansas City, Missouri. The artists found many associations between the shuttlecock form and the Western location of this commission, including the visual analogy to Native American feathered headdresses. Commissioned by the Nelson-Atkins Museum of Art and the Morton I. Sosland Family.

PURCHASE: ACQUIRED THROUGH THE GENEROSITY OF THE SOSLAND FAMILY. © CLAES OLDENBURG/COOSJE VAN BRUGGEN

Photography Since 1945

10-114   ROBERT FRANK. *TROLLEY, NEW ORLEANS*, published in *The Americans*. 1958.
Gelatin silver print, 7½ × 8½". The Art Institute of Chicago.

10-115   DIANE ARBUS. *"UNTITLED (6)."* 1970–71. Gelatin silver print.

10-116. JERRY N. UELSMANN. *UNTITLED.* 1984. Photograph

COURTESY OF THE ARTIST

This photograph of a trolley in New Orleans by Robert Frank (b. 1924) has the appearance of a common snapshot (fig. 10-114). The image is at an angle to the picture plane, yet the effect is precisely calculated. The windows create a grid pattern that formally separates the people, who engage our attention. The formal divisions caused by the windows reinforce the apparent psychological separateness of the people; they do not communicate with each other. Frank's photograph is a poignant statement both of human alienation and of segregation in the American South during the 1950s.

Frank, who was born in Switzerland and came to the United States in 1946, traveled thousands of miles throughout the United States, armed with his 35mm camera, in 1955 and 1956. His photographic essay *The Americans*, which demonstrated the vigor of a new photographic aesthetic that revealed the reality often hidden behind the facade of commercial glamour in the postwar United States, had an enormous impact on American photographers. His new "snapshot aesthetic" is one of a number of developments that have distinguished photography since World War II.

We see a similar approach in the work of Diane Arbus (1923–71). Like Frank, she worked in fashion photography. In the late 1950s, she turned toward a more introspective use of the medium. Arbus's photograph, taken at a home for developmentally disabled women, is both disturbing and compelling (fig. 10-115). Arbus takes us into a realm that is too often ignored. She once commented,

I really believe there are things which nobody would see unless I photographed them.

The works of Frank and Arbus are "straight" photographs; the image has not been altered by extensive darkroom manipulation. Artistic and technical creativity in the darkroom, however, has led other artists to unexpected and even surreal results. Jerry Uelsmann (b. 1934), for example, has written that

for me the darkroom functions as a research laboratory.

Uelsmann's photograph (fig. 10-116) was created through the use of multiple enlargers and exposures to a sheet of photographic paper. By masking parts of images on the easels of different enlargers and exposing the same piece of photographic paper on one easel and then another, Uelsmann constructs photographs of composite images. Uelsmann's photographs often reach to our subconscious in a surrealist manner; here, for example, three stoic faces from an ancient Roman grave sculpture and three footprints on a beach remind us of the transitory nature of life. The aesthetic and technical achievements of recent photographers have helped us appreciate a new and far-reaching potential in photography. Much of their work creatively denies the popular axiom that

photographs don't lie.

Conceptual, Performance, Installation, and Video Art

10-117. JOSEPH KOSUTH

ONE AND THREE CHAIRS. 1965. Wooden folding chair, photographic copy of a chair, and photographic enlargement of a dictionary definition of a chair; chair 32⅜ × 14⅞ × 20⅞″ (82 × 37.8 × 53 cm); photo panel, 36 × 24⅛″ (91.5 × 61.1 cm); text panel, 24 × 24⅛″ (61 × 61.3 cm). The Museum of Modern Art, New York.

One and Three Chairs (fig. 10-117), by Joseph Kosuth (b. 1945), informs us of three different realities. First, there is the reality of the folding chair placed between a full-scale photograph of the same chair and a printed definition of "chair" taken from a dictionary. The photograph is a second reality, but it bears an illusory image of the chair. Finally, the definition communicates a verbal description of a chair. The idea that we form from the definition exists in our minds and might therefore be termed a conceptual reality. *One and Three Chairs* presents the actuality, the image, and the idea of a chair, thus demonstrating the relationship between an object and communicative methods of signifying that object.

Kosuth's emphasis on the creative idea and the process of expressing that idea are characteristic of conceptual art. The term *conceptual art* was first used in the early 1960s to designate an artistic philosophy that held the supremacy of the artist's concept and the process intended to achieve it over the actual execution of the work. This modern tradition of stressing the intellectual creative act began with Dada, and especially the "ready-mades" of Marcel Duchamp.

Conceptual art requires that the concept for a work of art be documented, but that documentation need not take the form of a finished, crafted work. It might, for example, be expressed verbally or in another visual medium. In 1967, another conceptual artist, Sol Lewitt, wrote:

> In Conceptual Art the Idea or concept is the most important aspect of the work ... all planning and decision are made beforehand and the execution is a perfunctory affair. The idea becomes the machine that makes the art.

Another contribution from the 1960s that continues to expand the definitions of art is performance art. Historically, such art is related to the happenings of the 1950s. Performance art, which celebrates a temporal experience for an audience, is not geared toward making an object; rather, the artist becomes the work of art, freely acting within a theatrical environment. Performance artists often use a multimedia approach. Joseph Beuys (1921–86), a German artist who was a major practitioner of performance art, incorporated a wide variety of props in his "actions" (as he termed his performances), from found objects to live animals. Beuys, a pilot shot down in a barren frozen area of the Crimea during World War II, used performance art as a means to communicate autobiographical experiences in a symbolic manner, causing us to question the deeper values in our lives. Beuys believed that performance art could reawaken the mind and soul (fig. 10-118).

On the contemporary scene, performance-concerts by Laurie Anderson (b. 1947) synthesize sight and sound. High-tech light displays and projections are synchronized with a pulsating musical background while Anderson's "talking songs" reflect on the issues and realities we face in life. In her 1992 tour (fig. 10-119), her subjects included "War Is the Highest Form of Modern Art," "My Grandmother's Hats," and "The Cardinal Points."

With video art, television becomes a medium of artistic enterprise. Nam

10-118 JOSEPH BEUYS.

Photographic negatives with brown-cross between glass plates in iron frame, 28 × 21 × 2″ (71.1 × 53.3 × 5 cm) with frame. Photos by Ute Klophaus from Beuys's *Iphigenia/Titus Andronicus*. May 1969. This work premiered during an avant-garde theater festival in Frankfurt, Germany. The performance consisted of selected simultaneous readings of Goethe's *Iphigenie* and Shakespeare's *Titus Andronicus* while Beuys, who designed the "set," acted on stage. Beuys's actions included spreading margarine on the stage floor and occasionally clashing cymbals.

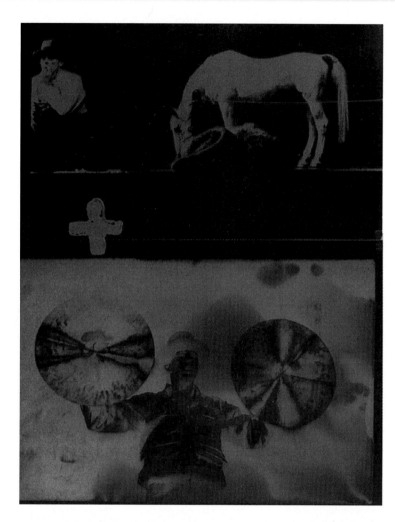

June Paik once remarked,

> As collage technique replaced oil paint the cathode ray tube will replace the canvas.

Viewing *Electronic Superhighway* (see fig. 1-1), we focus simultaneously on multiple association of reality and time. The video montage reminds us of the fast-paced gloss of MTV, offering a plethora of information that is only possible through the advances in electronic communication. For another example of an installation in which video plays a crucial role, see *The Sleep of Reason*, by Bill Viola (fig. 10-18).

Conceptual, performance, and video art have broadened the boundaries of art beyond any traditional definitions, raising intriguing questions about the nature of art as we enter the twenty-first century.

10-119 LAURIE ANDERSON.
Performance-concert of *Stories from the Nerve Bible*. 1992.

The Development of Minimal Art

10-120 DONALD JUDD

UNTITLED. 1968. Eight stainless-steel boxes, each 48" square and placed 12" apart. Private collection.

A series of eight stainless-steel boxes is set directly on the floor, without the pedestals common to the display of sculpture (fig. 10-120). Identical in size and finish, they have been fabricated by metal-workers to the artist's specifications, and the placement of each box and its position in the series have been precisely calibrated. Each box displaces an identical amount of space. Although it might be said that each box retains an individual and objective integrity, the set of eight boxes becomes an indivisible sculptural unit. The highly finished surfaces, the precise manner in which they are related, and the purity of the geometric compositions deny the autographic quality of the hand of the artist in their creation. Such art dissociates itself from those qualities that we usually ascribe to sculpture. These boxes are, simply, visual facts, and they remind us of our own existence in space and the visual nature of our own being.

Donald Judd (1928–94) is the artist of this series of boxes, which exemplifies a style that developed in the 1960s known as Minimalism. The roots of Minimal art extend back in the twentieth century to the structural and spatial considerations of Russian Constructivism, the manufactured ready-mades of Duchamp (see fig. 10-66), and the Hard-Edge Abstraction of such artists as Frank Stella (see fig. 10-109). As an alternative to the emphatic personal emotionalism of Abstract Expressionism, Minimalism presented the work of art as an object of elemental form with the least amount of visual components and divorced from either symbolic or personal expression. Judd, who holds academic degrees in philosophy and art history and was well known as an art critic before the advent of Minimalism, wrote in 1965:

10-121 AGNES MARTIN

NIGHT SEA. 1963. Oil on canvas with gold leaf, 6 × 6′. Private Collection, London. Agnes Martin's work is fundamental for the development of Minimalism, but she does not refer to herself as a Minimal artist.

It isn't necessary for a work to have a lot of things to look at, to compare, to analyze one by one, to contemplate. The thing as a whole, its quality as a whole, is what is interesting. The main things are alone and are more intense, clear, and powerful.

In the late 1950s, Agnes Martin (b. 1912) began a series of paintings based on simple grid patterns. Although her work was influential for later Minimalists, her position within Minimal art is unique. *Night Sea* (fig. 10-121) is composed of a grid of shimmering gold leaf over a soft, almost atmospheric, veil of shaded blue. Her composition is for-mally related to the structured approach of Minimalism; however, the interaction of the radiant geometric lines against the subtle changes of the ground color creates a surface and an effect that are atypical of the objective, planar surfaces of most Minimal painting. Agnes Martin's paintings encourage an intu-itive, almost meditative, response.

Earth and Land Art

10-122 ROBERT SMITHSON

SPIRAL JETTY. 1969–70. Black rock, salt crystals, earth, and red water (algae), diameter 160'; coil length 1,500'; width 15'. Great Salt Lake, Utah. This photograph shows the jetty soon after it was first completed. Smithson died in 1973 in an airplane crash while working on a later project.

Spiral Jetty in the Great Salt Lake (see map, page 475) is an aggressive and dramatic gesture in the natural landscape (fig. 10-122). Robert Smithson (1938–73) used assistants and huge earth-moving equipment to create the work. The top of the jetty functioned as the roadbed as the rock was moved into place in the lake. The jetty was meant to be walked on and to be seen from the shore and the sky. The resulting form, which is both regular and open, transformed the quality and color of the water within the jetty, for the encircled areas of water heated to a higher temperature, changing the amount and color of the local algae. But Smithson's mark on the landscape was not meant to be permanent. He knew it was a temporary structure that would eventually be transformed, if not obliterated, by the forces of nature. Recently it has been hidden by an unexpected rise in the water level of the lake. Although the geometric purity of the spiral form can be related to formalism and Minimalist art, it also has a historical and iconographic content. Smithson learned that early Mormon settlers believed that the Great Salt Lake was bottomless and connected to the Pacific Ocean by an underground canal and that from time to time Pacific currents would cause huge whirlpools to form on the lake's surface. His choice of design was based on this legend.

Beginning in the 1960s, a number of American artists became interested in producing large-scale works of art in the natural environment. This type of art became known as earth art, land art, or environmental art. Some artists moved large amounts of earth, creating a personal statement and transforming the land in a manner offensive to environmentally minded citizens. Others were determined to reassert and even re-create the natural quality of nature. Some projects took advantage of the natural forces in nature: ice, flowing water, wind, even animals and birds. Among the projects designed by the American Walter de Maria was a "lighting field," with tall metal rods that drew lighting to them during a storm, and a kilometer-long brass rod, 2 inches in diameter, which was sunk straight into the earth for 1 kilometer, with only the top showing at ground level. All these projects redirected attention to nature, making us see it with new eyes and a new awareness, and raising the issue of the importance of nature in modern, industrialized society.

Running Fence, by Christo (b. 1935) and Jeanne-Claude (b. 1935), crossed the hills of California north of San Francisco to run into the sea, highlighting by its existence not only the forms of the landscape but also, as it caught the changing effects of light and the shifting winds, the constant movement inherent in nature (fig. 10-123). Perhaps its best vantage point was from an airplane, for only thus could the enormous scope of the project be encompassed in a single view. Part of the creative act for Christo and Jeanne-Claude is not just conceiving and executing a project but raising the funds (through the sale of preparatory drawings and prints), acquiring the legal permis-

10-123 CHRISTO AND JEANNE-CLAUDE

Running Fence, Sonoma and Marin Counties, California. 1972–76 (now removed). 2,050 steel poles set 62′ apart; 65,000 yards of white woven synthetic fabric, height 18′; total length 24½ miles. © Christo 1976. The planning stages of this work began in 1972. The project was completed in four days and remained standing for fourteen. Christo and Jeanne-Claude's determination to create works on such a large scale that they must be executed with the assistance of a large number of workers is related to their interest in involving the broader community; this cooperative and inclusive approach is in direct opposition to the exclusive, individualistic tradition of most modern Western art.

CHRISTO AND JEANNE-CLAUDE, *RUNNING FENCE, SONOMA AND MARIN COUNTIES, CALIFORNIA*, 1972–76. HEIGHT: 5.5 METERS. (18 FT.) LENGTH: 40 KM. (24.5 MILES). COPYRIGHT CHRISTO 1976. PHOTO: JEANNE-CLAUDE

sions required, finding workers who will help with the intensive, large-scale labor and creating a reasonable timetable so that the work can be completed on schedule. Their early works included projects in which objects were stacked (a project to create a great **mastaba** form by stacking 2 million oil barrels has not yet been completed) or the wrapping of objects or buildings in fabric that was then bound with ropes, including the wrapping of more than 1 million square feet of the cliffs of the coast of Australian in 1969. In 1971–72, Christo and Jeanne-Claude closed off a valley in Colorado with an orange nylon curtain 365 feet high and 1,368 feet long (documented in a film, *Valley Curtain*), and in 1983 they surrounded eleven small islands in Biscayne Bay in Miami with 6 million square feet of bright pink polypropylene fabric, exaggerating their natural shapes and turning them into a sequence of enormous pink flowers. Two recent projects involved series of umbrellas on either side of the Pacific, in Japan and California, and wrapping the historic and symbolic Reichstag building in Berlin in silver-colored fabric. This last project, conceived in 1971, was only carried out in 1995.

The New Realism

10-124 DUANE HANSON

TOURISTS. 1970. Fiberglass and polyester, polychromed, 5'4" × 5'5" × 4'3". Scottish National Gallery of Modern Art, Edinburgh. As time passes and clothing styles change, Hanson's figures seem more historic and less naturalistic, but when first created they were meticulous re-creations of individuals whom one might meet on the street. Other figures by Hanson include *Traveler with Sunburn*, *Couple with Shopping Bag*, and *Football Player*.

The interaction between art and life, and our perception of both, take on new meaning with the sculptures of Duane Hanson (1923–1996). The figures seem as real as the actual clothing, camera, and other props. At exhibitions of Hanson's works, viewers commonly speak to the works of art, having mistaken them for living individuals. Hanson casts these fiberglass-reinforced polyester resin figures from molds made from the models and paints the "skin" with meticulous attention to pores, surface blemishes, and other individualistic details. Although the resulting figures share in the visual world of reality, their mute presence and arrested poses create an uncanny gulf between the sculpture and ourselves. Hanson's figures approach, but cannot participate in, life.

Tourists (fig. 10-124) is an example of Hyper-Realist sculpture, itself part of a broader movement known as New Realism that emerged in the late 1960s and early 1970s. Actually, realism in art had never left the twentieth century; Pop art, for example, was first greeted with the label *New Realism*. To many artists, critics, and connoisseurs, realism seemed outmoded when compared to avant-garde abstract and nonobjective art, but given the visual and psychological dearth left by Minimalism, the public and many art dealers embraced this resurgent realism. The meticulous crafting of a work of art again became an element to be enjoyed, even if, on a more profound level, it forced viewers to confront the banality of modern life.

The call to realism was met by painters, many of whom developed techniques that utilized photographs. In viewing *Double Self-Portrait* (fig. 10-125), we seem to be standing on an urban sidewalk, facing the large glass windows and doors of a diner. In these panes of glass, myriad forms—cars, buildings, and street signs—are reflected. It is as if we can "see" in two directions at the same time. Reflected in the lower right area of the central pane of glass is the artist, Richard Estes (b. 1936), with his camera on a tripod. To the left, you can see the second, smaller reflection of the artist that explains the work's title. Estes's camera alerts us that the vivid **trompe l'oeil** realism of the painting is in part based on Estes's photographs of the different elements of the scene. In the final composition, he combined these images with a sharp-focus painted realism, leaving us to explore the conflict between visual reality, photographic information, and the painted surface.

Audrey Flack (b. 1931), who invests her Photo-Realist paintings with psychological and emotional content, begins by arranging a still-life composition that combines objects suggesting both personal and universal meaning. The series of paintings from the mid-1970s that included *Queen* (fig. 10-126) can be related to traditional Vanitas iconography (see fig. 7-47). The watch and the transient beauty of the flower and fruit stress the passage of time, while more personal objects—makeup, photographs, a key chain, a card, and a chess piece—suggest additional layers of meaning. When she is pleased with her arrangement, Flack photographs it with color-slide film. She then projects slides onto a canvas and paints following the guidelines offered by the projected image. Her use of an **airbrush** (a small, high-quality paint sprayer) softens the contours of the objects, giving the finished painting a suggestive and even sensual effect. This soft focus combines with the iconography of the objects to appeal to our emotions in a way that is quite different from the sharp focus and detached objectivity of Estes's urban scene. The fact that Flack's huge, dazzling objects leap out toward us by overlapping the gray border gives them a compelling presence. These modern trompe l'oeil artists delight and intrigue us, just as their ancient Roman counterparts entertained Philostratus the Younger (see page 115).

10-125 RICHARD ESTES. *DOUBLE SELF-PORTRAIT.* 1976. Oil on canvas, 24 × 36″. The Museum of Modern Art, New York.

MR. AND MRS. STUART M. SPEISER FUND. © 1997 RICHARD ESTES/VAGA, NEW YORK, NY/MARLBOROUGH GALLERY, NY

10-126 AUDREY FLACK. *QUEEN.* 1975–76. Oil and acrylic on canvas, 6′8″ × 6′8″. Private collection.

COURTESY LOUIS K. MEISEL GALLERY

Postmodernism

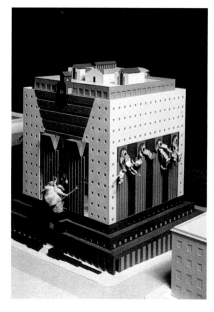

10-127 MICHAEL GRAVES

Portland Public Service Building, Oregon. 1980–82. This model shows one of the architect's designs for the building. When built, the extravagant bows on the side of the structure were flattened and the "acropolis" of structures on the roof, which was originally intended to house the building's mechanical functions, was omitted. The huge figure of Portlandia over the main entrance was designed by the American sculptor Raymond Kaskey. Commissioned by the City Government of Portland.

cept of the building as an anthropomorphic emblem. Graves's building also returns to the use of traditional symbols: the distinct areas of green, terracotta, and blue into which the structure is divided, for example, refer to water, earth, and sky. The huge figure of Portlandia over the main entrance, which is taken from the city's seal, represents a break from the abstract sculpture usually associated with modern public buildings. Here, the symbolism of ornament is wedded to a frolicsome attitude of visual delight.

According to the architectural critic Charles Jencks, the death of "modern" architecture occurred at 3:32 PM on July 15, 1972, in St. Louis, Missouri, when the failed Pruitt-Igoe housing project, which had won a national design award in 1951, was dynamited. With its geometric design, flat roofs, and complete avoidance of ornament, the project had exemplified the purist aesthetic of the International Style (see pages 545–46), but the impersonal nature of its design did not endear it to its residents, and the project eventually fell victim to vandalism and became a site for drug dealing. The destruction of the project by the St. Louis housing authority made it clear that the modern style of architecture was meeting neither individual needs nor social realities in a pluralistic world.

The term *Postmodernism*, first applied to architecture, is also used to refer to developments in other art forms that are characterized by a pluralistic approach to style, medium, and interpretation, as well as a disavowal of the belief in the value of modernism. Postmodernism's emphasis on plurality makes it difficult to offer a succinct definition of the movement, but it is possible to discuss its primary features. Postmodernism, for example, welcomes the artistic past into the

10-128 MARY TANSEY. *PURITY TEST.* 1982. Oil on canvas, 6 × 8'. Collection of the Chase Manhattan Bank, N.A.

COURTESY CURT MARCUS GALLERY, NEW YORK © MARK TANSEY

Portland Public Service Building (fig. 10-127), by Michael Graves (b. 1934), represents the Postmodern style of architecture; by abandoning the "modern" glass box and reintroducing traditional architectural elements and ideas, Postmodernism defines itself as a new style that has moved beyond the modern. Although the Portland Building contains a reference to modernism in its rectangular form, its Postmodern elements include references to historic architectural traditions in its giant **pilasters**, blocklike **Doric capitals**, and enormous **keystone** and the adherence to the con-

present. The process of appropriating, or adapting, traditional art forms into contemporary works allows us to question and examine the role of tradition and context. Postmodernist art celebrates diversity and is unafraid to examine social, political, and historical issues. It is a vehicle that can help us locate and define ourselves within our culture. As the contemporary architect Robert Stern has written:

> The fundamental shift to post-modernism has to do with the reawakening of artists in every field to the public responsibilities of art. Once again art is being regarded as an act of communication.

The development of the Postmodernist aesthetic in art can be related to contemporary developments in French intellectual thought during the 1970s. Critical methods of inquiry based on the writings of Jacques Derrida, Jean Baudrillard, Julia Kristeva, and others offered a new philosophical basis for artistic exploration. The paintings of Mark Tansey (b. 1949) are particularly responsive to this intellectual current. Tansey's compositions are based on his personal response to older images and his thoughtful meditation on history and tradition. In one image, for example, he shows a painter (a self-portrait?) on a ladder with a paint roller, painting out Michelangelo's *Last Judgment*; in another painting, based on a historic photograph of a military surrender, he represented *The Triumph of the New York School*, with the French artists Matisse and Picasso surrendering their preeminence in art to the American Jackson Pollock and the influential modernist

art critic Clement Greenberg. Tansey's paintings are often sepia toned or monochromatic in a reference to old photographs. Although this photographylike quality sets up an expectation of veracity with the viewer, it is challenged by the implausible nature of the image.

In Tansey's *Purity Test* (fig. 10-128), a group of Native Americans on horseback views Robert Smithson's *Spiral Jetty* (see fig. 10-122) from atop a bluff. The juxtaposition poses intriguing questions. The manner in which the Native Americans are represented is a caricature that has a greater resemblance to nineteenth-century paintings of the American West than to historical accuracy. Nevertheless, the work raises the question of how Native Americans might have responded to *Spiral Jetty*, a modern, abstract work in the Great Salt Lake that is based on prehistoric earthworks created by Native Americans and on a legend common among early Mormon settlers. Tansey's naturalistic representation also forces us to wonder what myths Native Americans may have had about the source and meaning of the Great Salt Lake. In the final analysis, we are reminded of the vast differences that can separate cultures and of the difficulties that can be experienced when cultures clash.

Such communication may, at times, include facing the reality of one's cultural past. Sigmar Polke (b. 1941) is one of a group of German Neo-Expressionist artists who have confronted the legacy of their country's past. The dark, looming image of the watchtower in Polke's *Hochstand* (fig. 10-129) calls to mind the concentration camps of world War II and the guarded borders of the

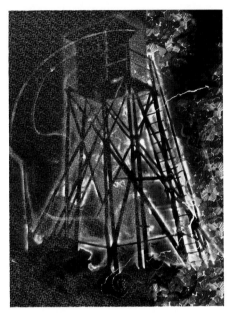

10-129 SIGMAR POLKE. *HOCHSTAND.* 1984. Acrylic, lacquer, and cotton, 10'8" × 7'4". Private collection, New York.

divided Germany. In addition, *Hochstand*, like much Postmodernist work, involves a complex layering of imagery. The watchtower seems to be both emerging from and sinking into a ground of patterned fabric. Besides their historical references, Polke's paintings can also refer formally to stages in modern art. Here the printed fabric pattern alludes to both Pop art and to the P + D (Pattern and Decoration) movement (see pages 577–78), while the overall darkness and dribbling of the paint may refer to the gestural technique used by the Abstract Expressionist painters (see pages 547–50). Polke's complex image can remind us of past political realities at the same time it warns us not to let memory fade behind the numbing onslaught of media culture.

Architecture Since 1970

10-130   PETER EISENMAN. Wexner Center for the Visual Arts, Columbus, Ohio. 1983–88. Commissioned by the Ohio State University and Leslie H. Wexner, Chairman of the Board, The Limited.

Eisenman's architecture speaks to us with words for which there are no substitutes, about the disorder of the modern world, about the weakness of all human action, about the fallibility of our knowledge, about our alienation from our own places. It is a text which speaks. But its speech does not consist in telling any definite tale . . .

These remarks by the contemporary Spanish architect Ignasi de Sola-Morales help to prepare us for a new architectural experience that seemingly is full of contradictions.

In winning the commission to design the Wexner Center for the Visual Arts at the Ohio State University, Columbus, Ohio, in 1983 (fig. 10-130), Peter Eisenman (b. 1932) accepted the challenge to create a building intended to exhibit not only traditional art forms but also whatever new art forms may be created in the future. The result is a building that proclaims its modernity and challenges traditional architectural form. The design of the Wexner Center, set between two existing buildings, is based on a grid that relates it not to the immediate university environment but to the grid patterns of the city of Columbus. Eisenman in this way makes reference to the historical survey grid first established in the early 1800s, when this area was part of the Northwest Territory. Tradition and history are thus affirmed, but through the use of forms that simultaneously assert the modernity of the structure.

The fortresslike towers that make up part of one of the entrances are based on the forms of a towered armory that once stood on this site,

1983–88	Eisenman, Wexner Center
1983	Drought causes widespread famine in Africa
1983	Sally Ride is first U.S. woman astronaut in space

10-131 RENZO PIANO AND RICHARD ROGERS. Georges Pompidou National Arts and Cultural Center, Paris. 1971–78. The center incorporates not only museum spaces for permanent and temporary exhibitions, but a public library and an audiovisual center. Commissioned by Georges Pompidou, president of France, and later named for him.

but a close look reveals that the towers are not complete. Other architectural elements exhibit a similar subversion of architectural form: arches are not complete, the supporting function of some columns is denied, and both form and space assume shapes that defy our visual expectations. At one and the same time, the Wexner Center is related to and discordant with Western architectural traditions.

Critics are still debating whether the Wexner Center is an example of Deconstructivist architecture or not, but some of the concepts that we encounter here introduce us to Deconstructivism, an art theory that is rooted in the literary philosophy of Jacques Derrida and others (see also page 572). In literary deconstruction, where the concept originated, texts are dismantled and freely reassembled without regard to original intent or underlying content. Meaning becomes changeable, it is argued, and depends on the context and the relationship to the reader.

In architecture, Deconstructivism demands that we have a profound understanding of historic architectural forms so that we can understand the manner in which traditions are countered or violated. New possibilities arise as we question the validity of traditions and ponder their role in current developments; the seeming instability of design and form at the Wexner Center embodies complex ideas and suggests that an inherent conceptual instability has pervaded the practice of designing and building structures.

10-132 FRANK GEHRY. Guggenheim Museum Bilbao, Bilbao, Spain. 1997. Commissioned by The Solomon R. Guggenheim Foundation.

Since about 1970, architecture throughout the world has undergone sweeping transformations (see also pages 571–72). At the forefront of many of the newer developments was the Pompidou Center in Paris (fig. 10-131) by Renzo Piano (b. 1937) and Richard Rogers (b. 1933). At first glance, the architecture of the Pompidou Center seems to be completely honest. Not only are the structural elements exposed—without and within—but air-circulation ducting, escalators, and other mechanical equipment are brought into public view and even emphasized. Bright colors are used to designate each different mechanical function, so that we are constantly aware of the operating systems needed to keep the building functioning; in such a program, the mechanical sys-

tems also function as decoration. Inside, all the walls are movable, and each space can be designed as needed. It is not only an adventure in architecture, but also a demonstration in understanding the complex workings of the advanced technology of a huge contemporary building. Leaving the mechanicals on the exterior allows for their easy replacement when they wear out or when new technology becomes available. Rogers has written:

I believe in the rich potential of a modern industrial society. Aesthetically one can do what one likes with technology for it is a tool, not an end in itself, but we ignore it at our peril. To our practice its natural functionalism has an intrinsic beauty.

Architects have also been inspired by the direct bluntness of industrial "architecture," such as oil refineries and grain elevators, where function forms the design.

Frank Gehry's Guggenheim Museum in Bilboa, Spain (fig. 10-132), which almost doubles the size of the Pompidou Center, is a futuristic vision of continuous transformations. Located in a Basque industrial port city, Gehry's innovative museum is part of an extensive renewal campaign meant not only to revitalize Spain's fourth largest city, but also to emphasize a commitment to stability in an area which has known political unrest and terrorism. The concentration of industry in Bilbao inspired the massive forms of the design, while the city's shipbuilding and port activities are reflected in the horizontal expanses of the building, which visually recall ships' hulls.

Yet while traditional industrial architecture acts as a reference point, the Guggenheim Museum transcends the immediacy of its environment. The central imposing organic forms, which interrelate the horizontal and vertical aspects of the design, cluster around an enormous vertical atrium, which the architect refers to as a "metallic flower." The museum is commanding in its grand size and volumetric treatment of space. The titanium shingles, unusual as a building material, offer an interplay of light, environment, and atmosphere, which, combined with the expansive curvilinear forms, cause a continuing and active transformation of the building from different points of view.

Zaha Hadid's winning design for the Contemporary Art Center's new building in Cincinnati, Ohio (fig. 10-133), is, like the architecture we have discussed, both innovative and people-friendly. Faced with the task of creating 20,000 square feet of gallery space on an 11,000-square-foot lot, Hadid designed a vertical series of cantilevered galleries whose placement and angularity exemplify the new and exciting aesthetic of Deconstructivist architecture. The angular forms create a dynamic sensation of geometrically abstract space, countering the repetitive regularity of earlier Modern architectural design. Yet, for all of its new-millennium appearance, Hadid's design offers an open and welcoming accessibility from the street, and interior ramps, by which people access the galleries, allow for changing vistas within the building. Hadid states,

> Multiple perceptions and distant views should create a richer, more perplexing experience, taking your body through a journey of compression, release, and reflection.

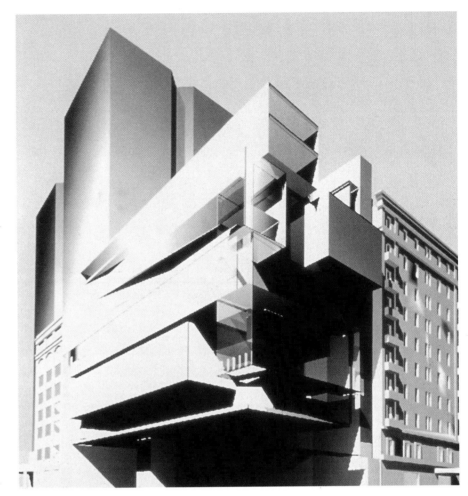

10-133 ZAHA HADID. Computer drawing of Hadid's design for the new Contemporary Arts Center, Cincinnati, Ohio. 2001 completion date. Commissioned by the Contemporary Arts Center, Cincinnati.

The Contemporary Art Center's new building is one of the first major museums designed by a woman architect. In the words of critic Joseph Giovannini,

> The new Contemporary Arts Center is widely anticipated not so much as the beautiful object it will clearly be, but as a building that will conjure a rare and exciting climate of thought.

Both Hadid and Eisenman were featured in the 1988 Deconstructivist architecture exhibition at the Museum of Modern Art in New York City, and they share some of the design aspects and theories of this style. Both, for example, construct buildings in which the most basic elements of traditional design are avoided. While Eisenman's Wexner Center makes a connection with history through a relationship with a previous building on this site and with the history and design of the Ohio city where it is built, Hadid's planned building can be related to the early modern movement of Russian Suprematism (see page 513). By reinterpreting these forms in a huge scale in architecture, Hadid's design engages us in the current dialogue between architectural structures and shifting meaning.

Pattern and Decoration

10-134   MIRIAM SCHAPIRO. *WONDERLAND*. 1983. National Museum of American Art, Smithsonian Institution, Washington, D.C. Acrylic and fabric on canvas, 7'6" × 12'.

The painting is me, torn in two. I present myself as the painter who can organize and master a huge canvas and then there's the other side of me which belongs to all women who were not liberated—all my ancestors who were trapped in a world where they were punished for being women, where nothing they did was good enough. That's what the painting is about.

In these words, Miriam Schapiro (b. 1923) shares with us the meaning of *Wonderland* (fig. 10-134). This large, multimedia work resembles a giant quilt; pieces of needlework, collected during the artist's visit to Australia, are assembled across the surface of the canvas and combined with painted areas. The embroidered detail of a woman and kitchen in the center offers a stereotypical view of women's work, a view that is challenged by Schapiro's artistic creation in the rest of the work.

Schapiro's multimedia *Wonderland* exemplifies what she has termed a "femmage." The term *femmage*, a contraction of *female* and *image*, is also related to the French words *femme* ("woman") and *hommage* ("homage" or "respect"). The iconography of *Wonderland* is specifically feminine; Schapiro writes that her femmages

explore and express a part of my life which I had always dismissed—my homemaking, my nesting. . . . The collagists who came before me were men who lived in cities and often roamed the streets at night scavenging, collecting material, their junk, from urban spaces. My world, my mother's and grandmother's world, was a different one. My "junk," my fabrics allude to a particular universe, which I wish to make real, to represent.

Wonderland complements Schapiro's feminist sensibility in the large scale of the work, its incorporation of fabric, its decorative composition, and the traditional association of the fiber arts with women artists.

Schapiro's vibrant painting belongs to a style often referred to as P + D, an abbreviation for *Pattern and Deco-*

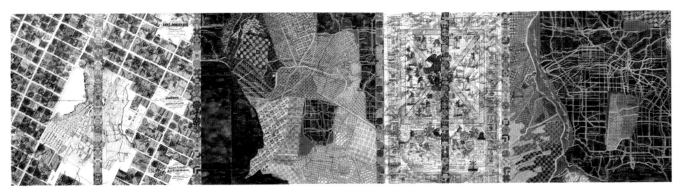

10-135   JOYCE KOZLOFF. *LOS ANGELES BECOMING MEXICO CITY BECOMING LOS ANGELES.* 1992–93. Watercolor, lithographs, and collage on paper, 22' × 87". Private collection.

ration. P + D utilizes repeated nonobjective shapes inherent in decorative motifs, some of which, as here, have been derived from traditional sources. Unlike the severe, impersonal abstraction of Hard-Edge or Minimal art (see pages 557–58 and 565–66), P + D revels in bold colors and less-constrained compositions.

For Schapiro and other artists in this movement, P + D joined a Postmodern concern for content with artistic traditions drawn from all over the world. Over the past centuries, as Western art academies developed a qualitative hierarchy of themes in painting, pattern and decorative work was relegated to an inferior position, outside the realm of fine art. Yet decorative and patterned compositions, with their implied planarity, have been at the core of many artistic traditions, including Anglo- and Hiberno-Saxon art, Islamic art, and Native American art. In addition, P + D

has drawn strength from popular and domestic art forms, such as textiles, that historically have been associated with women.

The rise of P + D in the 1970s coincided with the impact of feminism on art history, contemporary art, and art criticism. One goal of feminist art and criticism is to recover the significant, yet too often neglected, contributions of women in art. Another goal is to explore the issue of a female aesthetic. The principles of feminism influenced the works of Schapiro and many other artists, including Joyce Kozloff (b. 1942).

Kozloff has received a number of commissions for public spaces in which she has demonstrated her personal response to the historical and social traditions of the particular location. *Los Angeles Becoming Mexico City Becoming Los Angeles* (fig. 10-135) is one of a series of map projects that culminated in a large installation for Mankato State Uni-

versity in Mankato, Minnesota, in which Kozloff created tile panels that refer to twelve cities around the world, including Ravenna and Florence, Italy, and Vladivostok, Russia, which lie on the same latitude as Mankato. In the Lost Angeles/Mexico City piece, however, the title and the manner in which the maps and cultural references (including an Aztec map) are combined suggests not a similarity in location, as in the Mankato piece, but an interweaving of cultures that is creating a new and modern synthesis in both cities. These cities, which rank among the largest in the world, are becoming more and more alike. Kozloff writes that she thinks

> of cities as rich, interlocking patterns related to my own earlier decorative work, in which I had always juxtaposed cultural references. I'm struck by the extraordinary geometrics . . .

Neo-Expressionism

10-136 ANSELM KIEFER

MIDGARD. 1980–85. Oil and emulsion on canvas, 11′10″ × 19′9¾″. Carnegie Museum of Art, Pittsburgh. The broken shape in the center that resembles an artist's palette relates to Kiefer's performance art; in one of his performances, he dropped a clay palette and it shattered. As a symbol, this may refer to the Nazi suppression of German artists during the 1930s and also to the difficulty of being an artist in an age dominated by science.

Anselm Kiefer (b. 1945) drew inspiration from Nordic mythology for his panoramic painting (fig. 10-136). Its title, *Midgard,* which is written several times on the surface of the painting, means "Middle Garden," a name traditionally given to the earth by the ancient Norse gods. In Norse mythology, the destruction of the earth comes after three years of winter, when the Midgard serpent and other demons destroy the old gods and all life in a purification that can lead, then, to regeneration. Using enormous scale, a comfortless composition, and barren colors (the artist employed a blowtorch to achieve a scorched effect), Kiefer explores and expands one of the initial and invigo-

rating currents of twentieth-century art, Expressionism. *Midgard* is a dramatic painting of a traditional mythological subject that, in Kiefer's reinterpretation, has the power to grip the contemporary imagination.

Countering the impersonal traits of recent abstraction, Neo-Expressionism reinvests an emotional and empathetic content in painting. *Midgard* seems to express dread and desolation in the vast scorched earth that stretches before us; it is as if our nightmares of nuclear holocaust have become manifest. The only sign of life is the snake in the central foreground, which is moving slowly but inexorably toward a labyrinthine circular area of land that also represents a broken

artist's palette. Kiefer's painting is ultimately ambiguous in its meaning, but the snake and the seashore setting have been seen by some critics as indications of renewal, and the painting may not be as pessimistic as it first seems to be.

Within the pluralistic world of Postmodernism, Neo-Expressionism arose in the early 1980s as a reaction to what some artists perceived to be the emotional aridness of Minimalism and Conceptualism. Neo-Expressionism is an international movement. Nourished in Germany and Italy, it then found adherents in the United States. These artists revived the emotionally laden gestural brushwork and intense colors of Europe's earlier Expressionist

10-137 ROBERT COLESCOTT. *Les Demoiselles d'Alabama: Vestidas*. 1985. Acrylic on canvas, 8′ × 7′8″. New York, Collection of Hanford Yang.

painters. Appropriation of imagery, as we have already seen in the work of Sigmar Polke (see fig. 10-129), became a means of defining contemporary conflict on many levels, from personal through global.

In the United States, the paintings of Robert Colescott (b. 1925) have questioned concepts of identity within a multicultural society. In *Les Demoiselles d'Alabama: Vestidas* (fig. 10-137), the African American artist parodies Picasso's 1907 painting *Les Demoiselles*

d'Avignon (see fig. 10-41), which is regarded as a formative work in the history of modern art. Picasso's abstracted prostitutes are now dressed in garish and revealing clothing, and their racial identities have been expanded to include both black and white women.

Such a direct incorporation of art-historical references opens us to various levels of meaning, as questions of cultural traditions and their transmission are posed. Specifically, the racial

transformation of three of Picasso's figures leads us to realize the glaring omissions of minority artists from Western art surveys, as well as the uninformed appropriation of African art by early modern artists. The issues dealt with by Colescott, from individual identity through the broader context of societal inclusion and noninclusion, are effectively communicated through powerful compositions and an expressive use of content, color, and brushwork.

Japanese Architecture

10-138 ITSUKO HASEGAWA. Shonandai Cultural Center, Fujisawa City, Japan. 1989.

At first sight, the Shonandai Cultural Center (fig. 10-138), designed by Itsuko Hasegawa (b. 1941), seems both futuristic in its vision and overwhelming in its size. The center was built to house a variety of spaces for different purposes, including a theater, community center, and children's pavilion. Fully two-thirds of the enormous Cultural Center is built underground, where rooms and passageways are arranged around a sunken garden. Above ground level, the futuristic-looking structures are set within a garden complex, providing green spaces, a stream, and a pond for quiet contemplation. The gable-roofed buildings are meant to suggest Japanese village architecture, but Hasegawa also views them as reminiscent of mountains when they are seen from the gar-

den. The large spheres symbolically refer to the world, the moon, and the cosmos. The union of nature, village, and universe here is based in the purpose of the center, which is to help the people of Fujisawa City understand their position as citizens of both local and world communities. Writing about the concept for the Shonandai Cultural Center, Hasegawa noted:

> A basic theme of this project was to accept those things that had been rejected by the spirit of rationalism—the translucent world of emotions and the supple and comfortable space woven by nature—and to create a landscape filled with a new form of nature where devices enable one to hear the strange music of the Universe.

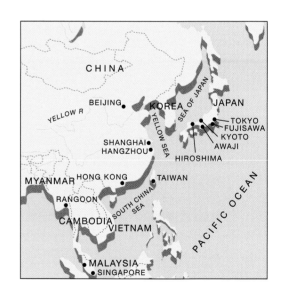

As in the West, architects in Asia are consistently challenging traditions with innovative designs and the use of new techniques and materials.

But whereas the Western theory of Deconstructivism seeks to subvert tradition, avant-garde Asian architects have been concerned with redefining our relationship to architecture and to the natural environment. This relationship is the starting point for many progressive Japanese architects, including Hasegawa and Tadao Ando.

The Water Temple (fig. 10-139), by Tadao Ando (b. 1941), was designed as an addition to an older, traditional Buddhist temple that follows the conventions first laid out for Japanese Buddhist architecture at Horyuji (see figs. 4-43, 4-44). Ando's new temple at the same site, however, breaks decisively with this tradition; the new structure has been described by one critic as

less a building than a series of shaped sensual experiences.

Ando controls our entrance to the temple through a series of concrete walls that guide us and then focus our field of vision on a large, serene pool. This controlled spatial passage suggests that we should undertake a psychological transition as Ando prepares us to enter the spiritual environment of the temple. In the large elliptical pool grow a number of lotus plants, whose blossoms float on and help define the flat and serene surface of the water (in Buddhism, the lotus is a symbol of enlightenment). As paths direct our passage along the edge of the pool, we unexpectedly discover a stairway that descends into the surface of the water. This staircase leads down to the circular shrine that lies underneath; the convex ceiling of the central area of the shrine is the bottom of the pool. The rather narrow form of this staircase as it moves into the water leads us to expect a dark, underwater space, but the red-painted shrine itself is, when reached, unexpectedly lit from windows in a "light room" set where the enveloping hillside drops away. The central circular

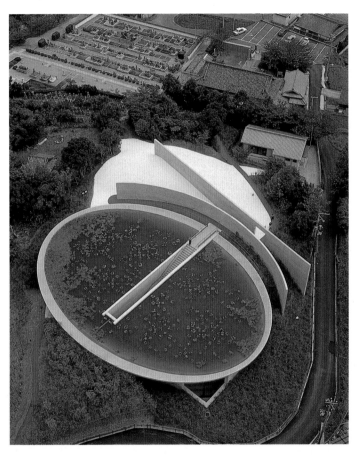

10-139   TADO ANDO. Water Temple, Island of Awaji, Japan. 1992. Honpukuji is affiliated with Old Shingon, a Tantric Buddhist sect that emphasizes meditation based on two mandalas. Commissioned by Honpukuji.

area, with a statue of the Buddha flanked by the two mandalas of the Shingon sect, is surrounded by square rooms to be used for the tea ceremony (see pages 330–31). The progression of spaces, materials, and colors Ando has created for the viewer is intended, obviously, as a metaphor for the sponsoring religion.

Ando himself wrote that his architecture is intended to create a place

for the spirit to rest.

Untraditional in its design, Ando's Lotus Pond Hall uses contemporary innovation to fulfill its centuries-old religious and cultural function.

Appropriation

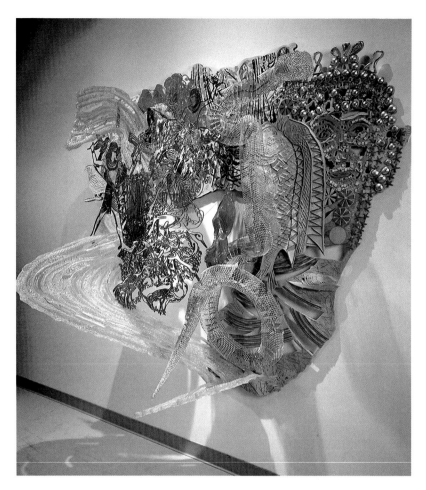

10-140 NANCY GRAVES

CANOPTIC LEGERDEMAIN. 1990. Stainless steel, aluminum mesh, resin, and paper, 7'1" × 7'11" × 3'1". National Gallery of Art, Washington, D.C. The title refers to the representation of Egyptian canopic burial jars in the relief and to the artful trickery with which the artist has hidden references to several past cultures in a single work.

Canoptic Legerdemain by Nancy Graves (1940–95) is a complex three-dimensional interweaving of formal and iconographic elements (fig. 10-140). In many ways, it is an adroit and erudite summation of recent developments in art. Based on the appropriation of art-historical, archaeological, and mythological imagery from the ancient Egyptian, Early Christian, and Byzantine civilizations, some imagery in the work, such as the head of the Empress Theodora (see fig. 4-34), is already familiar to us. The uncoiling snake near the center of the composition has associations with many ancient beliefs, particularly the biblical account of the temptation of Adam and Eve.

Although *Canoptic Legerdemain* is a visual and psychological feast, it is also exemplary of the use of modern technology in art. Laser-cut steel, which was produced from a computer program of Graves's drawings, is joined by a host of materials, from cast and molded resins to more traditional lithographs. Here the mix of painting and sculpture demonstrates the breakdown of barriers between mediums that is typical of Postmodernism. The composition relates art to technology, connects two-dimensional to three-dimensional forms, and unites the past to the present in art. In its expansive vitality, *Canoptic Legerdemain* exemplifies many of the issues that we

shall meet in contemporary art, especially appropriation.

The term *appropriation* designates both a process and an aspect of Postmodernism (see pages 571–72). Although Nancy Graves drew upon art-historical images in the creation of *Canoptic Legerdemain*, other artists have opened themselves to influences from a seemingly endless repertoire of commercial and contemporary cultural images. These images, often including printed texts, are divorced from their original context and are transformed to create new meanings. This recontextualization is a vehicle for some artists to examine social values and to address the inequalities people face in their daily lives. In

10-141 CINDY SHERMAN. *Sèvres Porcelain Soup Tureen: Madame de Pompadour (née Poisson)*. 1990. Silk-screened and hand-painted on Limoges porcelain. Frick Art Museum, Pittsburgh. The inside bottom of the tureen features a silk-screened version of a photograph of dead fish entwined with ropes of pearls. This is surely a play both on the original use for the tureen and on Madame de Pompadour's maiden name, which is the French word for *fish*.

GIFT OF MR. AND MRS. RICHARD M. SCAIFE

10-142 BARBARA KRUGER. *Untitled (You Rule by Pathetic Display)*. 1982. Photograph, 6'1" × 4'1". Krannert Art Museum and Kinkead Pavilion, University of Illinois at Urbana-Champaign.

PURCHASED BY THE ART ACQUISITION FUND

appropriation art, not only has iconography been recast, but also the formats for works have assumed commercial modes, including electronic billboards, posters, T-shirts, and even soup tureens. This commercialization of mediums has assisted the deconstruction of our understanding of art forms, opening us to new possibilities in art.

The earliest photographs of Cindy Sherman (b. 1954) featured the artist herself posed in costumes and settings that re-created the dramatic, posed "stills" that were used to advertise movies in the 1940s and 1950s. The tureen illustrated here (fig. 10-141) is related to a later development, when she photographed herself costumed and in the poses of historical figures or figures in well-known paintings. The shapes, colors, and decorative motifs of the tureen and its platter are appropriated directly from the French eighteenth-century rococo style, but Sherman's modern addition is her silk-screened self-portrait as Madame de Pompadour in a setting that resembles the French royal residence at Versailles (see figs. 7-49 to 7-51). Sherman's low-cut dress and her seductive pose, with her eyes half-closed, refer to the rococo interest in seduction and sexuality. Her contemporary use of images from the past poses many questions concerning the multiple levels of artifice in our society and the multiple personae we may assume to meet this artifice.

Works by Barbara Kruger (b. 1945) are found in a variety of formats, from T-shirts to photomontages (fig. 10-142). Her compositions, inspired by the aesthetics of advertising, are direct. But whereas advertising, most often promotes a stereotypical viewpoint, Kruger's works question and even de-mythologize such attitudes. *Untitled (You Rule by Pathetic Display)* is a feminist critique of male-dominated power structures, in which sexism, cutting like a knife, interrupts and destroys the natural flow of human relations and the advancement sought by women. The prominent knife suggests a further reference to domestic violence, yet the theme of the work, the inanity of power that rules by brute force, may also be interpreted on a more universal level.

Avant-Garde Chinese Art

10-143 YU YOUHAN. *WITH LOVE, WHITNEY.* 1992. Acrylic on canvas, 41 × 57". Courtesy, Hanart T Z Gallery, Hong Kong.

Yu Youhan (b. 1943) painted *With Love, Whitney* (fig. 10-143) using familiar images: the revolutionary leader Mao Zedong and the American popular singer Whitney Houston. Mao is shown applauding one of his own principles; Whitney applauds her own music. The two images were copied in acrylic on canvas from official photographs and were meant to draw attention to the similarity between the manner in which a public image has been created for each well-known personality. Yu has created many paintings with similarly politically charged themes using the impersonal style of presentation made famous by such American Pop artists as Andy Warhol (see fig. 10-10). The Chinese call this style Political Pop, and Yu considers himself to be part of the "Avant-Garde Movement" created by a few young artists who were influenced by ideas about their responsibility to society. Their ideas have had a strong effect on the Chinese art world of the most recent period.

The Avant-Garde Movement, which was possible only after the Cultural Revolution (1977–87), is based on the commitment of certain artists to declare their individuality, which they thought of in a new way in China in the 1970s. These artists used their notion of "humanism" to refer to concepts of human freedom or individualism. The Stars Group, for example, who advocated criticism of society and called for an awakening of human nature, was the most controversial in the early years of the Chinese Avant-Garde Movement. When they were excluded from the National Art Gallery Exhibition in Beijing in 1979, they exhibited their works on a fence outside. The authorities immediately shut down their exhibit, and the response of the Stars Group was to demonstrate for individual human rights in the streets of Beijing. From this time on, Chinese artists played a revolutionary role in Chinese society and politics.

The Chinese Avant-Garde Movement includes artists who have an independent vision of their own work, even though the group's direction has changed over time. These artists are at the edge of society and are part of the intellectual culture, not the official or popular culture. Their goal is to make way for freedom of spirit and expression in a society that, through its official strictures and internal social mechanisms, has not allowed for original thought. From 1979 to 1989, these artists acted on the principle that art could change society and make it free. Their art was politically motivated and critical. By attacking and destroying the traditional order in the art world, they thought that they could lead the way to freedom.

The artists in this movement who take a long view of culture do not limit their thoughts to immediate social concerns or problems, and most of their work is conceptual and philosophical. Some emphasize that life is instinct, others that life is accommodation. All oppose a society that suppresses human nature, and at the same time they praise a pure and simple life. Some have turned to depictions of rural life, of life among the many ethnic minorities in China, or of erotic and sexual encounters.

In *Mirror for Analyzing the World*, Xu Bing (b. 1955) emphasized other concepts (fig. 10-144). Under the influence of Chan Buddhism (Zen Buddhism in Japan), he fabricated 4,000 characters that no one could read, even though they look like traditional Chinese characters. He then used traditional printing techniques to produce long scrolls and books. According to his interpretation of Chan thought, what is important is the laborious artistic process. The work of art is useless in itself. Xu compared his process of creation to the mindless diligence of Chan Buddhist labor, which was thought to empty the mind of useless knowledge and lead to enlightenment. His installations were thought of as extravagant, and critics argued that they expressed nihilist, absurdist, and tragic feelings.

After the Tiananmen Square Massacre on June 4, 1989, and the crushing of the "Democracy Movement" by the Chinese government, avant-garde art in the People's Republic of China changed. At that time, Zhang Peili, an artist working in Hangzhou, said:

> Before the Massacre, there was so much noise, a deafening roar of protest. Then the tanks came and everyone immediately fell silent. That silence was more terrifying than the tanks.

After the massacre, the socially critical aspect of the Avant-Garde Movement could no longer be expressed directly; displays of avant-garde art were banned, and artists could no longer use the visual and performing arts to express criticism of the government and the social order. Artists lost faith in the idea that an individual work could change society, but they began to write that art could function to make the *artist* free—and that to be free was no small matter.

Since 1989 and the government attacks on intellectual culture, the Avant-Garde Movement in China has weakened. With the increasing emphasis on the immediate economic benefits of any activity, both official and popular culture have common priorities that are significantly different from those of the intellectuals. Artists today confront the twin challenges of a commodified society and an entrenched art world. With

10-144 XU BING. *CELESTIAL BOOK: MIRROR FOR ANALYZING THE WORLD*. 1988. Installation with printed paper. Installed February 5, 1989, National Academy of Art, Beijing, People's Republic of China.

the suppression of Chinese critics, critical recognition, and intellectual culture, the artists lost their most important audiences. Many of the most prolific avant-garde artists are now living and working outside of the People's Republic of China, while those working inside have to exhibit and sell their work abroad.

The idealism of the previous period has given way to ironic playfulness of the sort found in Yu's *With Love, Whitney*. This sort of Political Pop is not shown in China but has become very popular outside of the People's Republic in Chinese communities in Taiwan and Singapore, for example, and has many buyers in the West. This particular painting, for instance, is part of the collection of a private club.

Many recent avant-garde paintings and installations transcend the level of psychological and personal feelings of the earlier period to make more universal statements. They have the potential to be dangerous to the traditional artistic culture in China because they seek to create a viable alternative to the older art. Whether they will replace the traditional styles (see pages 184–87) is yet to be seen. Current Chinese art styles rest on three legs: traditional brush painting, realism imported in the beginning of the twentieth century from Europe and the former Soviet Union, and the many streams of international (and largely Western) modern twentieth-century art. The work of the two artists discussed here appropriate from all of these traditions and are part of the global context of our time.

Recent Developments

10-145 YOICHIRO KAWAGUCHI. *COACERVATER.* 1994. CD-ROM, Video.

From the late twentieth century to the early twenty-first century, the tempo of artistic innovation has continued to accelerate while the diversity of forms and purposes of art have, at the same time, widened. The goal of this concluding section is to illuminate, rather than exhaust, the internationalization and multifaceted communication of "art present." This internationalization is expressed, for example, in several works by Japanese artists that are related to global interests while at the same time maintaining certain distinct Japanese qualities.

One increasingly important manner of creating art is through the use of computers, and it also seems clear that the exhibition and distribution of art on CD-ROMs will continue to grow in the years ahead. Although some dealers and museums have been hesitant to exhibit such work, an international exhibition in Helsinki in 1995 devoted to the theme of "Public/Private" included a number of CD-ROM presentations on computer terminals by artists from Australia, England, Finland, Japan, and the United States. The space in which these works were exhibited was often the most crowded area of the museum, and it was clear that children and teenagers were especially interested in this new type of art. Some of the CD-ROMs were interactive, allowing the museum audience to participate in the colorful developments being presented on the screen. One of the Japanese artists, Yoichiro Kawaguchi (b. 1952), offered *Coacervater* (fig. 10-145), in which there was a continuous, flowing change from one abstract form to another in a

sequence of mesmerizing effects. This reproduction shows only one brief view of the continuously developing patterns invented by the artist with the aid of the computer.

On first viewing the six seemingly monolithic sculptures by the British artist Rachel Whiteread (b. 1963), we are reminded of the formal purity of minimalist sculpture. As our attention is engaged by the series (fig. 10-146), we discover that such an association is only a means of entry to a much more complex experience. The compact density of each sculptural form is countered by the use of colored resin as a medium. The resin gives each form a distinctive tonality, while its translucence, in places, denies the initial perception of solidity. Each form is different, not only in size, but also in the varied layers of horizontal projections. And, as we closely examine

10-146 RACHEL WHITEREAD

Six Spaces. 1994. Resin, dimensions variable.

COURTESY KARSTEN SHUBERT

each piece, an array of surface textures becomes apparent.

The subtitle of Whiteread's series, _Six Spaces_, leads us to an identity of the work. The sculpted forms, actually, are casts of negative spaces. Whiteread has cast the voids under chairs, inviting us to consider the interrelationship between everyday functional forms and the spaces which inherently are a part of them. Here, voids become an element of human association.

The shaped canvas paintings of Elizabeth Murray (b. 1940), which traverse the boundaries between painting and sculpture, have their roots in the formalism of the 1960s, particularly the shaped canvases of Frank Stella (see fig. 10-109). Unlike the Hard-Edge, intellectual abstraction of Stella, however, Murray's irregularly shaped canvases and use of strong color create a dramatic and emotional impact. In their complex, vital spatiality and surging, often-aggressive forms, they suggest the tensions that are part of everyday life. _Cracked Question_ engages us both visually and intellectually (fig. 10-147). The intense colors and three-dimensional seething of the canvas create a tension that is reinforced by the fragmentation of a common and easily recognized symbol; the question mark itself becomes the source of questions. We are led away from old bonds or ideas to search for new relationships and

10-147 ELIZABETH MURRAY. *CRACKED QUESTION*. 1987. Oil on six canvases, 13'5¼" × 16'2" × 1'11½". Cordiant Group, Ltd., London.

10-148 LOTHAR BAUMGARTEN. *THE TONGUE OF THE CHEROKEE*, detail. 1985–88. Installation with painted, laminated, and sandblasted glass, 100 × 43'. Permanently installed at the Carnegie Museum of Art, Pittsburgh. Commissioned by the 1988 Carnegie International.

meaning. Murray has asserted a deeper and more personal content of her work, for when she was asked if her paintings are political, she replied,

> I want my work to reflect my feelings about the society we live in; [they're] political in that sense.

Lothar Baumgarten (b. 1944) is a contemporary German artist whose site-specific installation celebrates the achievements of an early-nineteenth-century Native American named Sequoya. Baumgarten's installation (fig. 10-148) is viewed by looking up to a glass ceiling where letter shapes appear on many of the glass panels. These are the eighty-four letters of the Cherokee alphabet as it was invented by Sequoya, who seems to have been the only person in history to develop his own alphabet; he did not understand English, but he used English letters, without a knowledge of their relationship to sound, as a basis, and he added additional letters of his design. In the nineteenth century, Sequoya's alphabet was widely used by the Cherokees, and between 1828 and 1834, the *Cherokee Phoenix* was published in two languages and alphabets—Cherokee and English. The Cherokee language largely died out with the suppression of the Native American population, and Baumgarten's monumental work, which scatters the letters and their accents like random decoration, comments on its demise. This installation informs us both of personal achievements and of the consumption of one culture by another.

We Are Leaving Here Forever (fig. 10-149) is an installation by the Ukrain-ian artist Ilya Kabakov (b. 1933). Entering the darkened rooms with flashlights in hand, the museum visitors became something of archaeological intruders witnessing the remnants of a former collective human presence. In a two-story structure constructed inside the museum, large rectangular openings in the upper-level corridors looked down on a central space. This temporary installation represented an orphanage in the moments just after the children have left, never to return. All that remained were furniture, trash, and pieces of paper, some of which were scattered in corners or posted on the walls. In the large central space, pieces of trash and scraps of paper with phrases in Ukrainian and English were suspended from clotheslines. The words and phrases refer to the anxious voices of the departed occupants or to the faceted network of bureaucratic and personal existence.

Kabakov's installations are haunting and evocative. The suspended bits of paper and trash recall the Stalinist decrees of forced communalization that denied privacy to self and family. But the installation also spoke on a symbolic level of an interval between the immediacy of the remembered past and anxiety about the imminence and uncertainty of the future. Of this anxious time, Kabakov wrote:

> Nothing remains but a sea of useless papers, in which merciless orders, precise timetables, touching letters and notes are all mixed together. Some recall the past and mourn for it. Almost all are full of terror before the imminent uncertainty that awaits them.

On another level, Kabakov's installation reminds us of the insecurity that former Soviets face now that the U.S.S.R. no longer exists.

The installations of Jenny Holzer (b. 1950) employ the high-tech mediums of electronic advertising to present continuous series of short statements that she calls truisms. Prompted by graffiti art in the 1970s, Holzer clandestinely placed posters in public areas near where she lived in New York City; each poster contained a philosophical or popular maxim. Clichés

10-149 ILYA KABAKOV

WE ARE LEAVING HERE FOREVER. Temporary installation with mixed media. Installed at the Carnegie International Exhibition at the Carnegie Museum of Art, Pittsburgh, 1991–92. Commissioned by the 1992 Carnegie International.

10-150 JENNY HOLZER

UNTITLED (SELECTIONS FROM TRUISMS, INFLAMMATORY ESSAYS, THE LIVING SERIES, THE SURVIVAL SERIES, UNDER A ROCK, LAMENTS, AND MOTHER AND CHILD TEXT). Temporary installation with extended helical tricolor LED electronic display signboard, 11″ × 162′ × 4″. Installed at the Solomon R. Guggenheim Museum, New York, 1989–90. Solomon R. Guggenheim Museum, New York. Commissioned by the Guggenheim Museum.

PARTIAL GIFT OF THE ARTIST, 1989

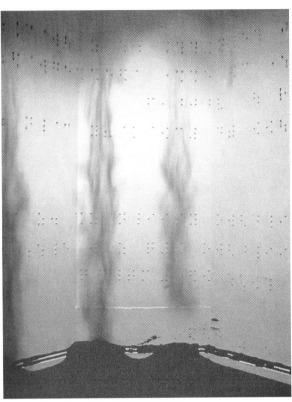

10-151 LOUISE BOURGEOIS. *CELL II*, detail. 1991. Mixed media, 6'11" × 5' × 5'. Carnegie Museum of Art, Pittsburgh.

10-152 ANN HAMILTON. *MYEIN*. Mixed media installation. 1999. Venice Biennale. Commissioned by the United States.

such as "Absolute Submission Can Be a Form of Freedom," "Money Creates Taste," and "Dying for Love Is Beautiful but Stupid" seemed to offer a trenchant commentary on contemporary social issues. Gradually, Holzer developed a conceptual art using computer-controlled light-emitting diode (LED) machines (fig. 10-150). Here, the medium of popular advertising is turned upon itself, revealing how we are manipulated by language, especially the media world's use of it. Holzer gets inside the system, using light bars and short, snappy, visual "sound bites," to critique it and to deconstruct or reveal the mode of manipulation.

Louise Bourgeois (b. 1911) belongs to a generation of earlier modern artists. An accomplished painter and sculptor who was thoroughly schooled in Surrealism, she first achieved prominence in the 1940s and 1950s. In the early 1990s, she created a series of *Cells*; each *Cell* or unit was the size of

a very small room, and each was defined by a grouping of old, hinged doors of various sizes, all painted in various shades of blue. Inside the *Cells*, combinations of found objects and precisely sculpted forms created an almost surrealistic atmosphere. Viewers are not permitted to enter the *Cells*; our vision of the objects in the interiors is confined to peering through windows and narrow openings between the doors.

In *Cell II* (fig. 10-151), old perfume bottles and Bourgeois's white marble sculpture of hands, with fingers tightly intertwined, are arranged on a circular mirror. Bourgeois has revealed that for her the clenched hands symbolize the indestructibility of pain, while the perfume bottles represent the fleeting scents of pleasure. This juxtaposition of opposite, intense sensations gives, in Bourgeois's words,

meaning and shape to frustration and suffering.

By making us voyeurs, Bourgeois reveals not only this private drama of pain but also our inability to mediate or help. Finally, the *Cells* remind us of our ultimate isolation from one another. Drawn from personal experiences and remembrances, Bourgeois's *Cells* communicate the inescapable fact of human pain:

What happens to my body has to be given a formal abstract shape. So you might say, pain is the ransom of formalism.

The Venice Biennale, with a continuous history from 1895, remains one of the most prestigious expositions of contemporary art. Many visitors to the United States Pavilion at the 1999 Biennale were stunned by the installation by Ann Hamilton (b. 1956). A ninety-foot glass and steel wall was constructed in front of the neoclassical-styled pavilion. Inside, a series of rooms, each with white walls, oozed a bright fuchsia-colored powder (fig. 10-152). The powder, released through concealed ceiling vents, flowed slowly down the walls, reminding some observers of toxic waste or blood. Fuchsia powder gathered in irregular pools on the floor. The walls were covered with patterns of large, raised dots, which translated into Braille stories of violence in America. Overlying these associations, a tape of Hamilton's voice recited Lincoln's second Inaugural Address in the international phonetic alphabet.

Hamilton's installation presented a dialogue with history, especially those realities of history which, in the artist's words,

> we cannot look at, that we refuse to see.

The glass and steel wall set before the pavilion also embraced this dialogue, for the distortions of sight that it caused remind us of the subjectivity of historical perception.

The revisualized photograph (fig. 10-154) by Morimura Yasumasa (b. 1951), on the other hand, might at first glance seem to be a simple re-creation of Manet's *Olympia* (see fig. 9-53). But Morimura has not merely reconstructed Manet's setting and photographed models in the positions made famous by Manet; that this is a complex photographic reconstruction becomes obvious when we recognize that the two figures are the same person in different costumes and makeup. This helps explain the term *futago* ("twin") used in the title. The fact that this is a man is apparent from the reclining figure; it is Morimura himself who has assumed the two female roles in the composition. Most of Morimura's work consists of photographs in which the artist takes the roles of figures in famous paintings or of contemporary popular heroes from the entertainment world. At first, we are astonished and amused, but gradually the

10-153 FAITH RINGGOLD

TAR BEACH. 1988. Acrylic on canvas, and tie-dyed and pieced fabric, 6′2″ × 5′9″. Solomon R. Guggenheim Museum, New York.

10-154 MORIMURA YASUMASA.

PORTRAIT (FUTAGO) (after Édouard Manet, *Olympia*, 1863). 1988. Color photographs, four panels, 6′10¹¹⁄₁₆″ × 9′10½″. Carnegie Museum of Art, Pittsburgh. In Japanese, *futago* means "twin."

10-155 YUKINORI YANAGI

HINOMARU ILLUMINATION (AMATERASU AND HANIWA). 1993. Neon and painted steel, with reproductions of ceramic *haniwa* figures; each *haniwa* approx. 39⅜" high. Installation at The Museum of Art, Kochi, Japan, 1993.

serious message of Morimura's work asserts itself. It becomes apparent that his use of computer-generated and photographic imagery is a commentary on the techniques through which cultural information is transmitted today and on how easily falsehood is possible. The photographs may represent Morimura's attempt to make a work that will be as shocking in his day as Manet's was in nineteenth-century Paris. Further, the superimposition of a Japanese artist into a Western work may allude to Japan's twentieth-century appropriation of Western culture and, at the same time, retention of an inherently Japanese integrity. On a more per-

sonal level, Morimura's work raises the issue of what it would be like to change sexes, or what it would be like to be a white prostitute or a black maid in nineteenth-century France, or what it would be like to be Manet's model and to have to pose naked before an artist for many hours. The image should perhaps be understood within the political, economic, and social upheavals that Japan has experienced, especially since the death of Emperor Hirohito in 1989. Morimura's art is more than Postmodern appropriation. It questioned Japan's identity at the close of the twentieth century, raising problems about the role of the artist in

society, and asking us to understand ourselves and our relationship to others and to history in a new light.

Morimura's revisualized photographs are multilevel social and personal commentaries. Our example introduces us to a significant current in contemporary art—Identity Art. The increasing value of self-revelation felt by earlier generations of Modern artists has led numerous contemporary artists to explore issues of personal identity in their work. This identity may be examined in intensely private ways involving, for example, race or sexual orientation, along broader cultural avenues, commenting at times on the complexity of the

10-156 MARIKO MORI

Pure Land, from Esoteric Cosmos, 1997-1998. Glass with photo interlayer, 5 panels: 120″ × 240″ × 8′ 5″.
Courtesy Deitch Projects, NYC.

relationship between the individual and the group, or through fantasy or Pop images. Identity Art often gives a voice to artists who have been formerly excluded from the mainstream; their work, striking the cord of social consciousness, adds immeasurably to the pluralistic reality of art in our time.

Faith Ringgold's work shares with us the realities and dreams of the African American experience in Harlem.

I will always remember when the stars fell down around me and lifted me up above the George Washington Bridge. . . . Sleeping on Tar Beach was magical. Laying on the roof in the night with stars and skyscraper buildings all around me made me feel rich, like I owned all that I could see.

These words form part of the narrative text that Faith Ringgold (b. 1930) used to enframe her multime-dia work *Tar Beach* (fig. 10-153) ("Tar Beach" is the colloquial name given to a rooftop in the inner city at night.) Rich in the complexity of its visual, thematic, and psychological association, *Tar Beach* is composed of acrylic paint on canvas, with tie-dyed and pieced fabric attached to the surface. The quilt reminiscences recall the work of feminist artists in P + D painting (see pages 577–78), while the abrupt but purposeful transitions of perspective communicate the naïveté of children as they stare at buildings and stars from the roof. Ringgold's work visually is simple and direct, yet its human message is multilayered.

The *Hinomaru* series, begun in 1990 by the Japanese artist Yukinori Yanagi (b. circa 1959), aims at deconstructing the myth that the Japanese people are a single "family" ruled by their emperor. Yanagi writes:

The ruling powers of Japan have always resorted to polit-ical myths in order to reinforce the country's unity. . . . As a modern nation state, Japan fabricated a myth of "one people" . . . [arguing] that all Japanese, no matter how diverse, are children of the Emperor.

Yanagi's art champions diversity by satirizing fanatical nationalism. In *Hinomaru Illumination* (fig. 10-155), row after row of repetitive figures based on the prehistoric Japanese *haniwa* type (see fig. 4-3) are grouped in an orderly manner, facing a neon "Rising Sun" flag. Although banned since the end of World War II, this flag has survived as a symbol for ultranationalist groups. *Haniwa* figures were created to surround and protect the tombs of early Japanese emperors; here they symbolically taken on the character of modern company workers, whose individual identity is suppressed in the name of corporate profit. By exposing the myth of "racial

10-157 CHRIS OFILI

SHE, 1997, 8 × 6 feet. Mixed media. Ofili often organizes his exhibitions as installations; each painting rests against the wall and is raised on pieces of varnished elephant dung.

is a meeting of cultures and time. For all of its overtones of Pop Art (see pp. 559–60), Mori's floating self reminds us of images of the Virgin Mary in Renaissance and Baroque Art (see figs. 6-50 and 6-8). She acknowledges a significant influence from Andy Warhol (see p. 480), especially his work that deals with the impact of how communications media transform our understanding. In her installations, Mori evokes multisensory perceptions utilizing the latest of high-tech electronic media, including 3-D video. As one critic wrote of her work:

> (Mori) is aiming to discover the best of the past, present and what can be in the future, to balance the material and the spiritual and to see the way to a future of endless possibilities. . . . Mori and more recent post-Warhol generations . . . are connected to popular culture, not working in reaction to it, and want to be an integral part of it. . . . In the hyperlinked contemporary world, there are no boundaries—television, comics, magazines, new technology, music, fashion, art, and spiritualism meet, mix, and merge.

Differing from the hi-tech approach of Mori, Chris Ofili's dazzling figural paintings utilize more traditional techniques with nontraditional media. The surface of *She* (fig. 10-157) is a multilayered visual delight of color shapes, varnish, bright pastel dots, glitter, and varnished pieces of elephant dung, while the meaning of the work itself penetrates many layers of black cultural experience. Ofili's use of dots of color refers to ancient cave paintings in Zimbabwe. The transformation of elephant dung is rooted in the regenerative nature of that substance. The image, with its rhythmic pulsations of color bands, draws us into our contemporary world, with

purity" perpetuated by ultranationalists, Yanagi attempts to open Japanese culture to the nondiscriminatory acceptance of minorities; his is an art of social meaning.

In a hallucinatory vision recalling a scene from contemporary outer-space films, Mariko Mori (b. 1967), in elegantly flowing Japanese garments, floats over a barren world with primordial pockets of land and

water (fig. 10-156). Mori is accompanied by a host of cartoon-like creatures, yet, for all of its fantasy, the work shares with us a serene, almost mystical quality. It is pageant on a grand scale, attempting to communicate a "sense of spirituality" which, the artist believes, has been lost by us.

Like the revisualized photographs of Morimura Yasumasa, Mori's work

10-158 WILLIAM KENTRIDGE

DRAWING FOR *STEREOSCOPE*, 1999, Video. The title of this film, *Stereoscope*, refers to the optical instrument, invented in the nineteenth century, which made photographs appear three-dimensional.

associations of pop culture and rap music. Ofili's painted figures, occupying much of the picture plane, possess an almost transcendental quality; they act as secular icons of our time.

Stereoscope (fig. 10-158) is a fast-paced, powerfully inventive, and profoundly insightful film concerning the nature of change, violence, and human responsibility. William Kentridge is a South African artist whose films explore the recent history, both convulsive and triumphant, of his country.

Through *Stereoscope*, we follow the quiet deliberations of Soho Eckstein, a fictional businessman who shelters himself from social upheavals. In creating his films, Kentridge employs a unique process of modifying, by

hand, a limited number of charcoal drawings. Each erasure or addition to a drawing is photographed to become one frame of the film. The resulting film is an animation of expressionistic charcoal images whose life interweaves realism and fantasy in communicating an intense social commentary.

The Roden Crater project (fig. 10-159), by American artist James Turrell (b. 1943), is a decades-long work near Flagstaff, Arizona (see map, page 475), that remains to be completed. The goal is to create a natural observatory that is, in many ways, similar to those created by prehistoric peoples at Stonehenge (see fig. 2-9), by the Anasazi at Chaco Canyon, New Mexico, and by other early societies

elsewhere. Using the movements of celestial bodies—the sun, moon, stars, and planets—the crater will track the passage of time. Without damaging the shape and beauty of the crater, Turrell has planned to construct four spaces that will be oriented to the four cardinal directions; each will be designed to catch, reflect, or enclose natural light in a particular, often mysterious manner. Turrell has said,

> in most art and architecture, light is used to illuminate the things. I am very interested in light itself being the thing.

Some of the rooms will function like a larger version of the **camera obscura**

10-159 JAMES TURRELL

Roden Crater project. 1974–present. San Francisco Volcanic Field, near Flagstaff, Arizona. Turrell plans to complete the Roden Crater project sometime between 2000 and 2010.

that was used by the Dutch seventeenth-century painter Vermeer and others; at Roden Crater, the image of the surface of the moon, for example, will be projected onto the wall of one of the chambers every 19.81 years. On a huge scale, Turrell has set out to re-create for modern observers at least a hint of the sensitivity to the rhythms of the sky and the changing seasons that was common among our prehistoric ancestors. That these cycles are still important to us is clarified by Turrell when he says that

> there is a cycle of fertility that comes from the lunar cycle and it's the cycle almost all plants and animals relate to. Humans have the same twenty-nine cycle with fertility.

The Roden Crater project will be accomplished by creating spaces that are intended to be permanent—there is no high technology, and nothing will ever wear out. Like Stonehenge, it will continue its relationship to the heavens even if there is no one there to watch.

During the twelfth and thirteenth centuries in Western Europe, builders sought to reach ever more towering heights in the construction of Gothic cathedrals (see fig. 4-91). Much closer to our time, in the twentieth century, there have been frenzied periods of building activity in which different cities have vied for the title of having the "world's tallest building." Today, we are experiencing another such competition. The reign of the Petronas Towers in Kuala Lumpur, Malaysia, completed in 1997 and the tallest building at the close of the millennium, will be brief, since in 2001, the newest "world's tallest building," the Shanghai World Financial Center in Shanghai, China, (fig. 10-160), is expected to be completed. In the late Middle Ages, Gothic cathedrals had a ratio of nave height to width of approximately 3:1; the ratio of the height of the Shanghai World Financial Center to its width is 8:1.

This current building competition centers around the Pacific rim. In the year 2000, six of the ten tallest skyscrapers are in Asia—illustrating dramatically the changing patterns of world economic development. At the same time, however, it should be recognizing that developments in electronics and computers mean that there is a decreased need for the huge amounts of office space demanded in American cities in the past.

The Shanghai World Financial Center, rising 94 stories to a height

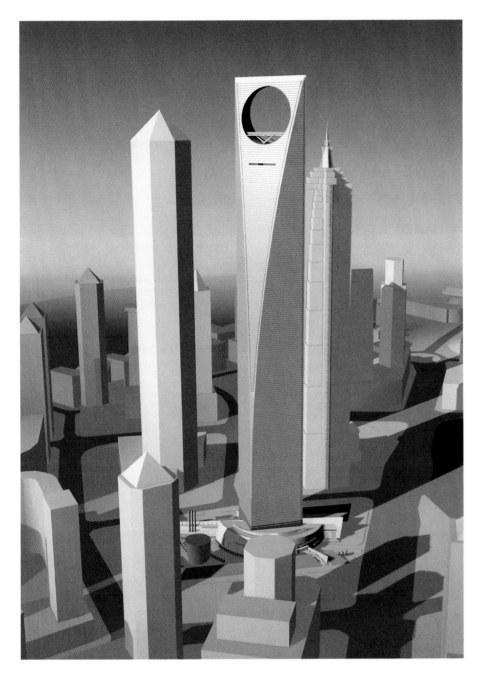

10-160 KOHN PEDERSON FOX

Shanghai World Financial Center, Shanghai, China. 2001 completion date. Previously the world's tallest building had been the Petronas Towers in Kuala Lumpur, Malaysia, which rose to a height of 1,483 feet. Before then, the Sears Tower in Chicago, Illinois, held the record at 1,454 feet.

of 1,509 feet, will house offices, retail shops on the ground floor, a hotel, a gallery, and an observation deck. As architects recently have broken away from the traditional rectilinear style of skyscrapers, often incorporating indigenous designs in their buildings, the architects of the Shanghai World Financial Center have affected a transition from a square base to a horizontal line at the top by combining vertical with long, curving lines on the exterior. At the top, an immense circular opening recalls the form of moongates in traditional Chinese gardens. This aesthetic device, however, also has the practical function of reducing wind stress on the building. The building is sheathed in stainless steel and glass. In reflecting the varied atmospheric colors of the city and sky, the Shanghai World Financial Center participates in the ever active visual life of its urban environment.

The challenge for supremacy in the race for height continues; plans are being laid to construct an even taller building in Melbourne, Australia. Such grand design contests acknowledge the enduring human spirit of competition and achievement.

Glossary

Definitions in the glossary are intentionally short; for further information and illustrations, consult the references listed. Words in CAPITAL LETTERS within an entry are defined in the glossary. An abbreviation used here is e.g., meaning for "example."

A

ABACUS: on a DORIC capital, the flat slab between the rounded ECHINUS and the ENTABLATURE; see fig. 3-65 and p. 78.

ACID BATH: a shallow tray of acid used in the ETCHING technique; see pp. 364–65.

ACROPOLIS: in ancient Greek cities, a fortified citadel and the site of the most important civic and religious buildings. The most famous is in Athens and is now called simply the Acropolis.

ACRYLIC PAINT: a fast-drying synthetic paint MEDIUM developed about 1960; see fig. 10-14.

AERIAL PERSPECTIVE: see ATMOSPHERIC PERSPECTIVE.

AIRBRUSH: a device for spraying paint or other liquid media. The medium is mixed with compressed air and sprayed through a nozzle; see fig. 10-126.

AISLES: corridors flanking a large central area; Old St. Peter's Basilica has two aisles on either side of its central NAVE (figs. 4-18, 4-19). Also known as side aisles.

ALTAR: a raised structure, usually table-like, on which offerings are sacrificed, incense burned, or sacred objects kept. Christian altars usually consist of a consecrated slab—traditionally of stone and called a mensa—on a base.

ALTARPIECE: a painted and/or sculpted work of art that stands as a religious image upon and at the back of an ALTAR; see the Van Eycks' *Altarpiece of the Lamb* (figs. 5-30, 5-31).

AMBULATORY: a circular or semicircular vaulted passage, as a Chartres (fig. 4-90).

AMPHITHEATER: a circular or oval building with tiered seats for sports and entertainment, developed by the ancient Romans; e.g., the Colosseum or Flavian Amphitheater (figs. 3-113, 3-114, 3-115).

AMPHORA: an ancient Greek vase used to store olive oil, honey, or wine; see fig. 3-60.

ANICONIC: the representation of a deity by symbols rather than by figural form, as at Sanchi (fig. 3-91).

ANNULAR VAULT: a structural system composed of a series of vaults arranged in a curving or circular configuration; for examples see the ancient Roman Colosseum (figs. 3-113–3-115) and the AMBULATORY at Chartres (fig. 4-90).

APSE: in architecture, an area composed of a half cylinder or semipolygonal form surmounted by a half dome or VAULTING, as an Old St. Peter's (fig. 4-19) and Chartres (fig. 4-90).

AQUEDUCT: a structure used to transport water in ancient Roman times; e.g., the Pont du Gard (fig. 3-119).

ARCADE: a series of ARCHES with their supporting COLUMNS or PIERS, as in the nave arcades at Chartres (fig. 4-88) and Santo Spirito (fig. 5-40).

ARCH: a means of construction in which an opening, often semicircular, is spanned by a series of wedge-shaped elements (VOUSSOIRS and a KEYSTONE); see fig. 3-118 and p. 120.

ARCHITECTURE: a structure, usually functional, that encloses and defines space.

ARCHITRAVE: in architecture, the lowest part of an ENTABLATURE; see fig. 3-65 and p. 78.

ARCHIVOLTS: the moldings that enframe the TYMPANUM in a Romanesque or Gothic church; often decorated with sculpture, as at Vézelay (fig. 4-71).

ART: traditionally, defined as an object made by a person or persons that communicated a message, concept, or belief. Today art includes so many different kinds of products (including ephemeral performances, for example) that an all-encompassing definition is no longer possible.

ART THEORY: the discussion and establishment of philosophical ideals concerning the goals of art.

ASSEMBLAGE: a work of art that combines actual three-dimensional objects, some of that may be "found" objects from the household or the junkyard; see fig. 10-107.

ATMOSPHERIC PERSPECTIVE: a device, used in painting to suggest PERSPECTIVE, in which forms nearer the horizon are blurred and their color is less intense and higher in VALUE, while the sky gradually shades from blue toward white above the horizon, as in Perugino's *Christ Giving the Keys* (figs. 1-15, 5-27). Also known as aerial perspective.

ATRIUM: an open courtyard, sometimes surrounded by a COLONNADE, found at the entrance to a Roman house (fig. 3-94) or a Christian church (fig. 4-19).

AVANT-GARDE: a French term meaning advanced guard, which, in the nineteenth century, was applied to artists or movements considered to be new, radical, and often revolutionary. For example, the ideas and work of Gustave Courbet were regarded as avant-garde within the context of mid-nineteenth-century French painting; see pp. 430–31.

AVATAR: the descent of a deity into our time and space; an incarnation of a Hindu god; see the *Descent of the Ganges* (fig. 4-2).

AXIAL COMPOSITION or ORGANIZATION: a compositional pattern with a central AXIS and BILATERAL SYMMETRY, giving an impression of balance; see Botticelli's *Birth of Venus* (fig. 5-60).

AXIS: the imaginary straight line that passes through the center of figures or forms, or through an architectural composition. An analysis of the axes of a work helps establish its COMPOSITION.

AXONOMETRIC PROJECTION: a geometrical drawing that depicts a building in three dimensions.

B

BALDACCHINO: a canopy over an altar or throne; e.g., Bernini's at St. Peter's (fig. 7-24).

BALLOON FRAME: an architectural structure in which wooden beams are joined horizontally and vertically to create a gridlike structural system; e.g., Davis's wooden house (fig. 9-37).

BALUSTRADE: a low parapet or barrier formed of uprights, called balusters, topped by a rail.

BARREL VAULT: a deep ARCH that normally requires continuous BUTTRESSING; see fig. 3-118 and pp. 118–21. Also known as a tunnel vault.

BASILICA: to the ancient Romans, a large building used for public administration, as in the Basilica Ulpia in Rome (fig. 3-125). In Christian times, a specific type of structure, with a central NAVE, CLERESTORY, flanking AISLES, and APSE, as at Old St. Peter's (figs. 4-18, 4-19).

BAS-RELIEF: relief sculpture in which flattened figures or forms project only very slightly from the background; e.g., the *Palette of Narmer* (figs. 3-20, 3-21). Also known as low relief.

BATTERED WALL: a wall that slopes or slants inward toward the top, as in ancient Egyptian MASTABAS (fig. 3-25) and PYLONS (fig. 3-29).

BAYS: individual units of space defined by the PIERS and VAULTS in a vaulted structural system; the plan of the Gothic cathedral of Chartres (fig. 4-90), for example, reveals that the NAVE is seven bays long. Bays also refer to the vertical divisions of the exterior or interior surfaces of a building, as marked by such elements as windows, BUTTRESSES, COLUMNS, etc.

BILATERAL SYMMETRY: representations of people and objects in which both halves look essentially identical.

BOOK OF HOURS: a book of private devotions with prayers for the seven canonical hours of the Roman Catholic church. Sometimes contains a calendar and is illustrated with illuminations (figs. 5-16, 5-17).

BUON FRESCO: see FRESCO.

BURIN: a tool with a sharp metal point used in the decoration of Greek vases (fig. 3-59) and in making ETCHINGS (see pp. 364–65).

BURR: the tiny raised fillings of copper on either side of the groove created in the DRYPOINT technique; the burr catches the ink and creates rich areas of deep, soft shadow.

BUTTRESS, BUTTRESSING: the projecting support that counteracts the outward thrust of an ARCH or wall; see figs. 3-118, 4-92, and p. 212.

C

CALLIGRAPHY: fine penmanship or beautiful writing (figs. 4-38, 4-87).

CALYX KRATER: an ancient Greek bowl with handles used for mixing wine with water; see fig. 3-66.

CAMERA OBSCURA: an enclosed box with an opening that allows an image to be projected inside the box; sometimes used by artists, including Vermeer (fig. 7-21), as a tool for understanding PERSPECTIVE recession.

CANTILEVER: a support system in which an architectural member projects horizontally into space, beyond its supports, as in Wright's Fallingwater (fig. 1-6).

CAPITAL: the decorated top of a COLUMN, PIER, or PILASTER; often helps effect an aesthetic transition from the vertical COLUMN to the horizontal ENTABLATURE; for examples from the Greek and Roman ORDERS, see fig. 3-65.

CARITYA: a sacred Buddhist site, complete with a shrine, MONASTERY, lecture hall, and other structures, as at Nara (figs. 4-43, 4-44).

CARPET PAGE: a manuscript page with complex, abstract, decorative patterns, usually Hiberno-Saxon, as in the page from the Lindisfarne Gospels (fig. 4-37).

CARTOON: a full-size drawing for a painting.

CARVING: in sculpture, a subtractive process in which form is created by cutting into a medium, usually stone or wood, thereby releasing, or subtracting, excess parts of the medium (see fig. 5-34). The term also may refer to works of art fashioned by this technique. See also MODELING.

CASEIN: a technique of painting in which PIGMENTS are mixed with a milk protein; see fig. 9-83.

CASTING: a method of producing a copy of a three-dimensional object by pouring a hardening material into a mold; see fig. 3-71 and p. 83.

CAST SHADOWS: the shadows cast by an object onto surrounding surfaces and objects. In a painting, these shadows help increase the ILLUSIONISM, as in the ancient Roman still life (fig. 3-112).

CATACOMB: an underground complex of tunnels and rooms, used in ancient Roman times by Romans, Jews, and Christians for burial purposes; for a painting from a catacomb, see fig. 4-14.

CATHEDRAL: in western Christianity, a church that marks the residence of a bishop; for example, Chartres (figs. 4-88, 4-89, 4-90, 4-91).

CENTERING: the temporary wooden support upon which an ARCH or VAULT is constructed; see fig. 3-118 and p. 120.

CENTRALLY PLANNED: denotes an architectural design in which regularized units radiate, usually at 90° angles, from a central area, often surmounted by a dome, as in the original High Renaissance design for St. Peter's in Rome (fig. 6-31).

CHAITYA HALL: an Indian Buddhist architectural form with a pillared, central nave, two side aisles, an ambulatory, and a high barrel vault; many are carved out of living rock with a STUPA in the apse; see the Great Stupa at Sanchi, pp. 96–99, and the Kailasantha Temple (fig. 4-47).

CHA NO YA: the Japanese tea ceremony; see the art of Zen, pp. 330–31.

CHIAROSCURO: in painting and printmaking, the use of a contrast of VALUES to create effects of MODELING; see the Roman still life (figs. 3-112, 6-51).

CHOIR: in a Christian church, an enclosed area near the altar where the monks or nuns chant the services, as at Chartres (fig. 4-90).

CHUMON: the entrance gate to a Japanese Buddhist temple area, as at Horyu-ji (figs. 4-43, 4-44).

CLERESTORY: in architecture, an area elevated above adjacent rooftops, usually along a central AXIS. Its purpose is to allow light into the interior, and it has windows on the sides, as in the Egyptian HYPOSTYLE hall (fig. 3-30), Old St. Peter's (fig. 4-18), Chartres (figs. 4-88, 4-89), Santo Spirito (fig. 5-40), and elsewhere.

CLOISTER: an open court within a *monastery*, usually with an open ARCADE or COLONNADE; see figs. 4-54, 4-55.

CLUSTER PIER: in the Gothic structural system (fig. 4-92), a pier with groups of COLONNETTES, as at Chartres (fig. 4-89). Also known as a compound pier.

COFFERING, COFFERS: in architecture, recessed geometrical panels—often square—that decorate the interior surface of a VAULT; see the coffers to the DOME of the ancient Roman Pantheon (figs. 3-122) and elsewhere (fig. 7-28).

COLLAGE: a composition in which pieces of materials such as newspapers, cloth, or colored paper are glued to a canvas, paper, or other surface, as in Picasso's *Still Life with Chair Caning* (fig. 10-48).

COLLOCATION: the idea that an artist created a specific work for a specific location and that it is adjusted for that location and the spectator's

viewpoint, as in Caravaggio's *Conversion of St. Paul* (fig. 7-16) and Rembrandt's *Militia Company of Captain Cocq* (fig. 7-27).

COLONNADE: a continuous row of columns supporting an ENTABLATURE or ARCHES; see the Parthenon (figs. 3-73, 3-75).

COLONNETTE: a slender, columnar decorative motif, common in Gothic architecture, as at Chartres (fig. 4-89), where groups of colonnettes create COMPOUND PIERS that support the NAVE ARCADE.

COLOR PALETTE: the selection of colors used by an artist; for an example of a restricted color palette, see Mondrian's *Diamond Painting* (fig. 1-16).

COLOSSAL ORDER: see GIANT ORDER.

COLUMN: a freestanding cylindrical support, often FLUTED and with a CAPITAL, used in PAST-AND-LINTEL construction, as at the Parthenon (fig. 3-73).

COMPLEMENTARY COLORS: colors found opposite each other on the color wheel (see fig. 1-17), which form a neutral gray when mixed but create a vibrant contrast when placed side by side. The complementary color of each of the primary colors (red, yellow, and blue) is obtained by mixing the remaining two primaries; the complementary of red is green (yellow and blue); the complementary of yellow is violet (red and blue); and the complementary of blue is orange (red and yellow).

COMPOSITION: the arrangement or organization of the various elements of a work of art; e.g., the balanced symmetry of Perugino's *Christ Giving the Keys to St. Peter* (fig. 1-15).

COMPOUND PIER: see CLUSTER PIER.

CONCRETE: as developed by the ancient Romans, fast-drying hardening volcanic sand used in architectural construction; see pp. 120–23.

CONTRAPPOSTO: a term describing the position assumed by the human body when the weight is borne on one leg while the other is relaxed; e.g., the *Doryphorus* (fig. 3-72). Contrapposto creates a figure that seems to be relaxed and yet suggests the potential for movement.

CORBEL: an architectural member created as each successive vertical layer of building material, e.g., stone, brick, or wood, projects from the previous layer. It often supports a CORNICE; see pp. 120–23.

CORINTHIAN ORDER: one of the ancient Greek architectural ORDERS; see fig. 3-65 and p. 78.

CORNICE: a projecting MOLDING surmounting and emphasizing a WALL or ARCH. Note the prominent interior cornices of the Pantheon (fig. 3-122) and the heavy cornice capping the Medici Palace (fig. 5-44).

CROSS-HATCHING: in drawings and PRINTS,

superimposed layers of parallel lines (HATCHING) at an angle to one another, used to create shadows and MODELING, as in fig. 6-26.

CROSSING: in a Christian church, the area where the NAVE intersects the TRANSEPTS; for diagrams, see figs. 4-18, 4-92.

CROSS SECTION: an architectural diagram that shows how a building would look from the inside if it were cut by a vertical plane from side to side, for a cross section of the Parthenon, see fig. 3-76. See also LONGITUDINAL SECTION.

CROSS VAULT: a structural system formed by two TUNNEL VAULTS intersecting at right angles; see fig. 3-118 and pp. 120–23.

CRUCIFORM BASILICA: a BASILICA with TRANSEPTS, forming a Latin cross plan, as at Old St. Peter's (fig. 4-19).

CUN: in Chinese painting, small brushstrokes dabbed on quickly to create the sense of a particular texture, as in Li Cheng's painting (fig. 4-59).

D

DAGUERREOTYPE: the earliest practical photographic process; see p. 442.

DEVARAJA: cult of the god-king in the Khmer kingdoms in Cambodia; an amalgam of a state cult and religion. See Angkor Wat, pp. 200–01.

DIMINUTION: a device used in drawing and painting to help suggest PERSPECTIVE. Forms are represented as progressively smaller to suggest their distance from the viewer; see Perugino's *Christ Giving the Keys to St. Peter* (fig. 1-15).

DIPTYCH: two equal-size panels hinged to fold shut or simply hang side-by-side. Most are painted; some are carved in RELIEF.

DOME: an architectural structural system that can be understood as an ARCH rotated 180° around a central axis; see fig. 3-118 and pp. 120–21.

DORIC ORDER: the most vigorous and austere of the ancient Greek architectural ORDERS; see fig. 3-65 and p. 78.

DRESSED STONE: blocks of stone used for construction, each of which is carefully cut and trimmed for its specific place and purpose, as at the ancient Roman Pont du Gard (fig. 3-119).

DRUM: a cylindrical or polygonal wall set atop a building and used to support a DOME; see fig. 5-42.

DRUMS: the individual cylindrical units that are combined to create the SHAFT of a COLUMN; due to the ravages of time, the drums of the columns of the Parthenon are clearly visible today (fig. 3-73).

DRYPOINT: an INTAGLIO printmaking process; see fig. 7-39 and pp. 364–65.

E

ECHINUS: on a DORIC CAPITAL, the rounded, cushion-shaped MOLDING below the ABACUS; see fig. 3-65 and p. 78.

EDITION: a group of prints made from a single PRINT FORM in one of the printmaking processes; see figs. 6-28, 6-29, 9-34. In current practice, artists sign and number each print in an edition.

ELEVATION: an architectural diagram that shows the exterior or interior surfaces of a building and their decoration diagramatically, without the recession and distortion that would result from a single viewpoint; see figs. 6-33, 6-34. Elevation can also refer to one exterior side of a building.

EMULSION TECHNIQUE: a painting technique using a liquid mixture in which one of the elements is suspended as minute droplets, as in fig. 10-110.

ENCAUSTIC: a technique of painting using PIGMENTS dissolved in hot wax; see fig. 4-27.

ENGAGED COLUMN: see HALF COLUMN.

ENGRAVING: an INTAGLIO printmaking process; see fig. 6-29 and pp. 296–97.

ENTABLATURE: the upper part of an architectural ORDER, which usually includes ARCHITRAVE, FRIEZE, and CORNICE; see fig. 3-65.

ENTASIS: the bulging of a DORIC column about one-third of the way up from the base, creating an effect of muscular elasticity; for a subtle example of entasis see the columns of the Parthenon (fig. 3-73).

ETCHING: an INTAGLIO printmaking process; see fig. 7-39 and pp. 364–65.

ETCHING GROUND: the acid-resistance, resinous mixture used to coat the PRINT FORM (a metal plate) in the ETCHING process; see pp. 364–65.

ETCHING NEEDLE: the sharp steel instrument used in the ETCHING technique; see pp. 378–79.

EXPRESSIVE CONTENT: the emotions and feelings communicated by a work of art.

F

FACADE: the front or principal face of a building, as in Palladio's San Giorgio Maggiore (fig. 6-69).

FAIENCE: colorfully glazed earthenware or pottery, whether in the form of sculpture, decorative tiles, or functional vessels; see the Minoan *Snake Goddess* (fig. 3-37).

FERROCONCRETE: see REINFORCED CONCRETE.

FIGURE-GROUND RELATIONSHIP: the contrast between form (or positive elements) and background (or negative ground) in a work of art; see Piero's *Duke of Urbino* (fig. 5-6).

FLUTES, FLUTING: shallow vertical grooves on the SHAFT of a COLUMN that accentuate the column's cylindrical quality; see fig. 3-65.

FLYING BUTTRESS: a structural element in the form of an open half arch that counteracts the outward thrust of an ARCH or VAULT; see fig. 4-92.

FORESHORTENING: the technique used in a painting or RELIEF SCULPTURE to suggest that figures, parts of the body, or other forms are shown in sharp recession, as in Mantegna's *Foreshortened Christ* (fig. 5-54).

FORMAL ANALYSIS: a visual examination and analysis of a work of art that studies how the integral parts of a work of art are united to produce its historical and/or individual style. Introductory formal analyses of works of art are offered for figs. 1-4, 1-6–1-12, 1-15, 1-16.

FORUM: the official center of an ancient Roman town, with temple, marketplace, and governmental buildings; see the forum in Rome (fig. 3-100).

FREESTANDING: see SCULPTURE IN THE ROUND.

FRESCO: a technique of painting directly on a plaster wall or ceiling, usually when the plaster is still wet, as in Giotto's Arena Chapel (fig. 4-106) and Michelangelo's Sistine Chapel ceiling (fig. 6-36); see figs. 3-111, 4-109. Also known as buon fresco. See also FRESCO SECCO.

FRESCO SECCO: a technique of FRESCO painting in which the paint is applied to dry plaster.

FRIEZE: the middle section of the horizontal ENTABLATURE in the ancient Greek and Roman ORDERS; see fig. 3-65 and p. 78.

FUNCTION: the purpose for which a work of art was created; e.g., the function of the Egyptian sculpture of *Menkaure and His Wife, Queen Khamerernebty* (fig. 1-2) was to provide a home for the souls of the pharaoh and his queen throughout eternity.

G

GABLE ROOF: the most common type of roof, formed by two planes that slope downward from a central beam, as on the Parthenon (fig. 3-75). Also known as a pitched roof.

GENRE PAINTING or SCULPTURE: a representation of everyday life, as in Leyster's *Gay Cavaliers* (fig. 7-18).

GESSO: a mixture of glue (size) and gypsum or chalk used to coat a surface that will be gilded or painted, usually with TEMPERA PAINT. Also used to build up BAS-RELIEF sculpture and to mold elaborate picture frames before GILDING.

GIANT ORDER: PILASTERS or COLUMNS that span more than one story of a structure; e.g., the pilasters on the exterior and interior of Michelangelo's design for New St. Peter's in Rome (figs. 6-33, 6-34). Also known as colossal order.

GILDING: the covering of a work of art or part of a work of art with gold leaf or some other gold-colored substance; the background of Giotto's *Madonna* is gilded (fig. 4-103).

GIORNATA: from the Italian word meaning "day." Giornata lines are produced when areas of plaster (intonaco) overlap one another in a FRESCO. In the true fresco technique, these areas of *intonaco* would be painted in one day, before the plaster dried, hence the term *giornata*; see figs. 3-111 and 5-22.

GLAZES: in the art of oil painting, thin layers of

superimposed translucent varnish, often with a small amount of pigment added, to modify color and to build up a rich, sonorous color effect; used by Jan van Eyck (figs. 5-37, 5-38), Titian (figs. 6-47, 6-49), and others. In pottery, the glaze is a thin layer of a colored material that fuses with the surface when heated; the glaze provides the hard and colorful surface of a pottery vessel.

GOUACHE: opaque WATERCOLOR paint.

GREEK CROSS PLAN: a central plan with four arms of equal dimension placed at 90° angles, usually surrounding a DOME, as in Bramante's and Michelangelo's design for New St. Peter's (figs. 6-31, 6-32).

GRISAILLE: the monochromatic painting of objects, often to simulate stone sculpture; see fig. 5-31.

GROIN VAULT: see CROSS VAULT.

GROUND PLAN: an architectural diagram that shows how a building would look from above if it were truncated by a horizontal plane approximately one meter above floor level; see figs. 4-90, 7-29.

GUILDS: legal organizations of merchants, craftspeople, and artists, rather like trade unions, that flourished in the later Middle Ages and the Renaissance. Guilds established standards for training and production and commissioned works of art; see the niches at Orsanmichele in Florence (figs. 5-14, 5-15).

H

HALF COLUMN: a half-round decorative COLUMN attached to a supporting wall. Also known as an engaged column.

HALF-HIPPED ROOF: a type of roof construction in which the ends are vertical and partly HIPPED, or they are hipped using two different angles, as at Nara (fig. 4-43).

HALO: a radiance of light, visually represented as a golden circle or disc, surrounding the head of a holy figure, as in the Byzantine mosaic at Mount Sinai (fig. 4-25).

HAPPENING: a quasi-theatrical event, common in the 1950s and 1960s, in which artists, usually without a preconceived script, performed and encouraged the spontaneous participation of the audience; see fig. 10-16.

HATCHING: in drawings and prints, closely spaced series of parallel lines that create effects of MODELING, as in fig. 6-26. See also CROSS-HATCHING.

HIERARCHICAL SCALE: the representation of figures who are more important politically (or socially) as larger than less important figures, as in *Ti Watching a Hippopotamus Hunt* (fig. 3-33).

HIGHLIGHTS: in painting, areas of HIGH VALUE color which suggest light hitting the form to create MODELING; see the highlights on the metal pitcher in the Roman still life (fig. 3-112).

HIGH RELIEF: RELIEF SCULPTURE in which the forms project substantially from the background;

e.g., the altar at Pergamon (fig. 3-87).

HIGH VALUE: a relatively light color, as in the high value of the yellow trousers in Goya's *Execution of Madrilenos on the Third of May* (fig. 9-23).

HIPPED ROOF: a type of roof construction in which the ends are sloped instead of being vertical.

HISTORICAL CONTEXT: the ideas, beliefs, or attitudes current in the period when a work of art was created. Historical context also encompasses how the work of art was perceived by its audience.

HISTORICAL SIGNIFICANCE: an understanding of how a work of art reveals the ideas, beliefs, or attitudes current in the period when that work of art was created.

HISTORICAL STYLE: a clearly recognizable artistic tradition (see FORMAL ANALYSIS) characteristic of a particular historical or artistic period.

HUE: the property of a color that distinguishes it from others; also the name of a color; see fig. 1-17.

HYPOSTYLE: a type of architectural construction in which the interior space is crowded with continuous rows of COLUMNS or posts, as in the Egyptian hypostyle hall (fig. 3-30) and the Mosque at Córdoba (fig. 4-49).

I

ICON: a special term used in Orthodox Christianity to refer to a painting of a religious subject, as in fig. 4-27.

ICONOGRAPHY: the art-historical study of the subject matter of a work of art, including the investigation of the symbolism and the meaning of the subject in the culture that produced it.

ICONOLOGY: the investigation of how the iconography of a work is related to the HISTORICAL CONTEXT.

IDEALIZATION, IDEALIZED: the improvement and abstraction of forms to conform to contemporary cultural standards of perfection and beauty; e.g., *Menkaure and His Wife, Queen Khamerernebty* (fig. 1-2).

ILLUMINATED MANUSCRIPT: a handwritten book with painted decoration, common in medieval and Renaissance Europe; see figs. 4-26, 4-27, 4-38, 4-52, 4-66, 4-87, 5-16, 5-17.

ILLUSIONISM, ILLUSIONISTIC: when the objects represented in a work of art (usually a painting) seem to be tangible and weighty, existing within actual space; e.g., Perugino's *Christ Giving the Keys* (fig. 1-15); see pp. 248–49.

IMPASTO: raised brushstrokes of thick paint, usually oil, as in Titian's *Rape of Europa* (fig. 6-52).

INCISED RELIEF: see SUNKEN RELIEF.

INDIVIDUAL STYLE: the particular formal qualities (see FORMAL ANALYSIS) used by an individual artist; e.g., the bold colors, thick paint, and heavy brushstrokes characteristic of the works of Van Gogh (figs. 9-11, 9-77, 9-78).

INFILLING: see WEB.

INSTALLATION: a work of art that consists of an ensemble of objects, often three-dimensional, that are especially arranged by the artist for a particular location or site (see fig. 10-150).

INTAGLIO PROCESS: a printmaking process in which the lines to be printed are incised into the surface of the PRINT FORM, such as in the engraving, etching, and drypoint processes; see figs. 6-29, 7-39, 7-40.

INTENSITY: the level of richness or saturation of a color; note the very intense red used in Van Gogh's *Night Cafe* (fig. 9-77).

INTERLACE: common in medieval art and architecture, ornament composed of intertwined lineform elements, such as stylized vines and/or animal forms.

IONIC ORDER: one of the ancient Greek architectural ORDERS; see fig. 3-65 and p. 78.

ISOCEPHALY: a COMPOSITION, usually relatively unnaturalistic, in which the heads of the figures form a horizontal line; see the mosaic of *Theodora and Attendants* at Ravenna (fig. 4-34).

ISOMETRIC PROJECTION: an architectural diagram that includes both a ground plan and a view of the exterior and/or interior from a specific point of view below or above the structure; for an isometric projection of a temple at Karnak, see fig. 3-32.

J

JAMBS: the areas flanking an ARCH, doorway, or window; in Romanesque and Gothic churches, the jambs are often decorated with sculpted figures, as at Amiens (fig. 4-98).

K

KACHIN-TIHU: a small wooden figure or doll (also known as a kachina doll) made by members of the Hopi people (fig. 10-34).

KAMI: in the Shinto religion, Japanese nature spirits thought to endow all things; see the Shinto Shrine at Ise, pp. 148–49.

KEYSTONE: the central VOUSSOIR of an arch, rib, or vault; see fig. 3-118.

KONDO: the main hall at a Japanese Buddhist temple-MONASTERY complex, as at Horyu-ji (figs. 4-43, 4-44).

KUFIC: a style of Arabic CALLIGRAPHY, sometimes used as virtually pure ornament.

KYLIX: an ancient Greek drinking cup; see fig. 3-60.

L

LACQUER: a hard, opaque varnish with a high-polish surface. Originally derived from the sap of a tree native to China, lacquer was used to fashion objects of functional art and religious utensils in East Asia.

LAY ARTIST: during periods when much artistic production was controlled by monks and nuns, a lay artist was one who lived and worked in the city, outside of the MONASTERY, and was often a member of a GUILD.

LEKYTHOS: an ancient Greek container to hold olive oil; see fig. 3-60.

LINEAR: the technique in painting, drawing, or printmaking of creating sharply defined forms of precisely delineated contours, as in Leonardo da Vinci's *Vitruvian Man* (fig. 5-62).

LINEAR PERSPECTIVE: developed in fifteenth-century Europe, a method of representing three-dimensional objects on a two-dimensional plane. Linear perspective has all parallel edges and lines converging as ORTHOGONALS toward one or more VANISHING POINTS on a two-dimensional surface. Also called scientific perspective; see pp. 248–49.

LINGAM: a phallic symbol in the Hindu religion associated with the God Siva; see the Kailasantha Temple, Ellora, India (fig. 4-47).

LINTEL: the horizontal beam spanning opening, as in the POST-AND-LINTEL SYSTEM (fig. 3-27).

LITHOGRAPHY: a printmaking process; see fig. 9-34 and p. 425.

LONGITUDINAL SECTION: an architectural diagram that shows how a building would look from the inside if it were sliced by a vertical plane from front to back; see the Pantheon (fig. 3-121) and New St. Peter's (fig. 6-33).

LOST-WAX BRONZE CASTING: a technique of CASTING bronze and other metals; see figs. 3-71 and p. 83.

LOW RELIEF: relief sculpture in which flattened figures or forms project only very slightly from the background, as in the *Palette of Narmer* (figs. 3-20, 3-21). Also known as BAS-RELIEF.

LOW VALUE: a relatively dark color, as in the low value of the background in Goya's *Execution of Madrilenos on the Third of May* (fig. 9-23).

LUNETTE: a semicircular area enclosed by an ARCH, as at the Byzantine church of San Vitale (fig. 4-31).

M

MADKSOURAH: a special enclosure in a MOSQUE reserved for the calif (ruler), as at Córdoba (fig. 4-49).

MANDALA: a diagram of the Buddhist cosmos, used as a basic design motif in Buddhist art, as at Sanchi (fig. 3-89).

MANDORLA: an oval or almond-shaped HALO that surrounds the body of a holy figure, as in the Byzantine mosaic at Mount Sinai (fig. 4-25).

MANUSCRIPT: a handwritten book produced in medieval and Renaissance Europe. If it has painted decoration, it is known as an ILLUMIANTED MANUSCRIPT; see figs. 4-37, 4-38 and 5-16, 5-17.

MASTABA: a rectangular Egyptian burial monument, with BATTERED WALLS and a flat roof; see fig. 3-25.

MEDIUM/MEDIA: the material or materials of which a work of art is composed, or the technique used to create it; e.g., oil paint on canvas (fig. 9-78), bronze (fig. 5-46), and etching (fig. 7-38).

MEGALITH: a very large stone of irregular shape (not DRESSED) used in prehistoric monuments; see Stonehenge (fig. 2-9).

METALPOINT: a graphic arts technique of drawing with a fine-pointed metal rod, often silver, on paper prepared with a special coating, called a ground. The faint metal line oxidizes to a light brown.

METOPES: the square areas between the TRIGLYPHS in the FRIEZE area of the ENTABLATURE of the DORIC ORDER; sometimes decorated with sculpture, as at the Parthenon (fig. 3-75); see fig. 3-65 and p. 78.

MIHRAB: in a MOSQUE, the ARCH or niche on the QIBLA wall that indicates the direction of Mecca, to which Muslims turn in prayer, as that at Córdoba (figs. 4-49, 4-50, 4-51).

MINARET: the tower in a MOSQUE complex, usually tall and slender, from which the Muslim faithful are called to prayer five times a day; see Hagia Sophia (fig. 4-29).

MIXED-MEDIA: a term used to describe a work composed of a variety of different materials, usually encompassing elements of painting, sculpture, and even architecture (see fig. 10-107).

MOBILE: a sculpture that moves, usually a lightweight, delicately balanced suspended work; see the example by Calder (fig. 10-92).

MODELING/TO MODEL: in painting, drawing, or printmaking, the creation of an effect of weight and mass in an object by the manipulation of VALUE to create HIGHLIGHTS and SHADING, as in fig. 5-61; in sculpture, an additive process in which form is created with a malleable medium such as clay; see CARVING as a subtractive process.

MOLDING: an ornamental band, depressed or projecting, that gives definition to an architectural surface.

MONASTERY: a religious establishment that houses a community of persons who have withdrawn from the world to pursue the religious life; see examples from St. Gall and Cluny (figs. 4-54, 4-55).

MONOCHROMATIC: term used to describe a painting or drawing created by shades of black and white or values of a single color, as in Picasso's *Guernica* (fig. 10-88).

MOSAIC: a pattern made of small pieces (TESSERAE) of stone, tile, or glass, used on floors, walls, or ceilings; see Roman floor mosaics (figs. 3-58, 3-85) and the wall and ceiling mosaics at San Vitale (figs. 4-31–4-35).

MOSQUE: a place of worship in the Islamic religion, as at Córdoba (figs. 4-49, 4-50, 4-51).

MOUND ARCHITECTURE: an early type of architectural construction characterized by the creation of a solid mass, as in the Sumerian ZIGGURAT (fig. 3-12) and the Egyptian pyramids (fig. 3-22).

MUDRA: a hand gesture of Budda, as in fig. 4-46. Each traditional gesture conveys its own meaning.

MURAL PAINTING: large wall decorations; e.g., those at the Villa of the Mysteries (fig. 3-108) and Giotto's Arena Chapel (fig. 4-106).

N

NAOS: the walled inner sanctuary of a Greek temple, where the cult statue is housed (fig. 3-76).

NARTHEX: an entrance hall or vestibule, often found in Christian churches, as at Old St. Peter's Basilica (fig. 4-19).

NATURALISM, NATURALISTIC: when the elements or forms within a work of art closely resemble the appearance of those forms in nature; e.g., Bernini's *Apollo and Daphne* (fig. 1-4).

NAVE: the large central hall, usually AXIAL and often with a CLERESTORY, that characterizes the BASILICA plan (see Old St. Peter's, fig. 4-19, and many Christian churches).

NAVE ARCADE: the series of ARCHES that divide the NAVE from the AISLES; see fig. 4-92.

NONOBJECTIVE: when the forms in a work of art do not resemble forms in the visual world; e.g., Mondrian's *Diamond Painting* (fig. 1-16). Also known as non-representational.

NONREPRESENTATIONAL: see NONOBJECTIVE.

NUNNERY: a religious establishment that houses a community of women who have withdrawn from the world to pursue the religious life.

O

OBA: the name of the monarch in Benin society when the Portuguese arrived there in 1485; see the royal ancestral shrine at Benin (fig. 4-112) and pp. 224–25.

OCULUS: a circular opening in a wall or at the apex of a DOME, as in the ancient Roman Pantheon (fig. 3-122).

OIL PAINT TECHNIQUE: a technique developed in the fifteenth century in which the pigments are mixed with the slow-drying and flexible MEDIUM of oil; see figs. 5-38, 5-39 and pp. 258–59.

ORDERS: a series of Greek and Roman architectural systems that give aesthetic definition and decoration to the POST-AND-LINTEL SYSTEM; see fig. 3-65.

ORTHOGONALS: the converging diagonal lines that meet at the vanishing point in the SCIENTIFIC PERSPECTIVE system, as in Donatello's *Feast of Herod* (fig. 5-28). In reality these lines would be parallel; see fig. 5-29 and pp. 248–49.

OVERLAPPING: a device used in painting and relief sculpture to help suggest perspective.

Forms are placed in front of other forms to suggest their relative placement within the illusion of space.

P

PAGODA: the European name for a tall tower, often with a series of roofs over successive storeys, that marks sacred Buddhist sites in China and Japan, as at the Horyu-ji complex (figs. 4-43, 4-44).

PAINTERLY: in painting, the technique of using large brushstrokes and flecks of paint to define form; see figs. 6-50, 7-26.

PANATHENAIC AMPHORA: an ancient Greek vase awarded as a prize at the Olympic Games; see fig. 3-60.

PARCHMENT: the skin on a calf, sheep, or other animal which is scraped, stretched, and dried to be used as a surface for writing. Used in the medieval period for MANUSCRIPTS.

PASTEL: a drawing medium made of ground pigments mixed with gum water.

PATRON: the person, persons, or organization that asks an artist or artists to create a work of art. Usually they pay for the work.

PATTERN BOOK: a book of images, prepared as an artist's tool, that preserves a tradition of images that can be copied; see fig. 4-12.

PEDIMENT: the triangular end of a GABLE ROOF; in a Greek temple this area is often decorated with sculpture; see figs. 3-54, 3-77, 3-78, 3-79.

PENDENTIVES: in a domed structure, the curved triangular segments that provide a transition from the four supporting piers to the circular base of the dome, as at the Byzantine church of Hagia Sophia (fig. 4-28). For a diagram see fig. 3-118.

PERIPTERAL: a term that describes a building with an exterior PERISTYLE; e.g., the Parthenon (fig. 3-75).

PERISTYLE: a continuous row of COLUMNS that completely surrounds the exterior of a structure, e.g., the ancient Greek Parthenon (fig. 3-75), or an inner courtyard, as in fig. 3-94.

PERSPECTIVE: depth. An illusion of perspective is suggested in many paintings; e.g., Perugino's *Christ Giving the Keys to St. Peter* (fig. 1-15). Devices that help suggest the illusion of perspective include LINEAR PERSPECTIVE ATMOSPHERIC PERSPECTIVE DIMINUTION, and OVERLAPPING.

PICTORIAL RELIEF: relief sculpture that conveys an illusion of depth by using a subtle transition from high to progressively lower relief. See Donatello's *Feast of Herod* (fig. 5-28) and Ghiberti's *Story of Jacob and Esau* (fig. 5-32).

PICTURE PLANE: the flat surface of a picture. The picture plane, denied in such illusionistic work as Perugino's *Christ Giving the Keys to St. Peter* (fig. 1-15), is emphasized as a positive element in many nineteenth- and twentieth-century paintings, such as Mondrian's *Diamond Painting* (fig. 1-16).

PIECE-MOLD CASTING: a method of CASTING metal objects developed in ancient China in which the mold for receiving molten metal is made of a number of sections fitted together and then packed in sand before casting. See fig. 3-46.

PIER: the vertical supports used in an ARCHED or VAULTED structural system; see the supports of the ancient Roman Pont du Gard (fig. 3-119) and the nave piers of the Gothic cathedral at Chartres (figs. 4-88–4-92).

PIETÀ: an iconographic theme in which the dead Christ is shown being held by his mother, as in Michelangelo's *Pietà* (fig. 5-66).

PIGMENT: the substance, usually ground, that is used to give color in the TEMPERA, FRESCO, and early OIL painting techniques.

PILASTER: a shallow, virtually flat version of the columns of the Greek and Roman ORDERS; pilasters are usually decorative, not structural. See fig. 8-3.

PITCHED ROOF: see GABLE ROOF.

PLAN: see GROUND PLAN.

PLATE: the thin metallic plate used as a PRINT FORM in ENGRAVING and ETCHING; see figs. 6-29, 7-39.

POLYCHROME: painted in many colors and often used to describe sculpture.

POLYPTYCH: a work of art composed of four or more leaves or panels.

POESIE: the Venetian name for a theme from mythology treated in a nostalgic and romantic manner; see Titian's *Rape of Europa* (fig. 6-55).

POINTED ARCH: an ARCH in which the sides rise to a point at the apex, as in Gothic architecture (figs. 4-88, 4-92, 4-93).

PORTICO: a sheltered space for walking; usually refers to a COLUMN-lined projection in front of the main entrance to a classical structure.

POST-AND-LINTEL SYSTEM: a simple system of architectural construction in which horizontal architectural members (LINTELS) are supported by vertical supports (posts); see fig. 3-27.

POTTER'S WHEEL: a revolving platform on which clay vessels of regular and often graceful shape are formed. Examples of wheel-produced vessels include the ancient Greek pots shown in fig. 3-55.

PRESENTATION DRAWING: a finely finished drawing made to be given to a collector or friend.

PRIMARY COLORS: red, yellow, and blue. These are HUES that in theory are pure and not the combination of any other hues. On the color wheel (fig. 1-17), all other colors are understood as mixtures of these three hues.

PRINT: a work of art produced by one of the printmaking processes, including WOODCUT, ENGRAVING, ETCHING, DRYPOINT, LITHOGRAPHY, and silkscreen.

PRINT FORM: the surface—wood, copper, steel, glass, stone, etc.—to which ink is applied in any of the PRINTMAKING processes; see figs. 6-28, 6-29, 7-39, 7-40, 9-34.

PRINTMAKING: a series of techniques (WOODCUT, ENGRAVING, ETCHING, DRYPOINT, LITHOGRAPHY, silkscreen, and others) by which prints are produced.

PSALTER: a manuscript of the Psalms of David, as in the *Paris Psalter* (fig. 4-26).

PSEUDO-PERIPTERAL: a building that seems to have a PERISTYLE, but many of the COLUMNS are HALF COLUMNS or PILASTERS; e.g., the Roman Temple of Portunus (fig. 3-93).

PURE COLOR: a color at maximum or full intensity; a HUE without the addition of white, black, or other colors that would reduce the INTENSITY of the color; e.g., the colors used by Mondrian in his *Diamond Painting* (fig. 1-16).

PUTTI: figures of male babies, sometimes male baby angels, popular in Renaissance art, as in Mantegna's frescoes in the Camera Picta (fig. 5-53).

PYLON: the entrance gate to an Egyptian temple complex, with broad BATTERED towers and flagpoles; see fig. 3-29.

Q

QI: Chinese cosmic spirit; used in aesthetics to describe the "life" or spirit of a painting; see Chinese landscape painting, pp. 184–87.

QIBLA: in a MOSQUE, the wall that indicates the direction of Mecca, toward which Muslims turn in prayer; see Córdoba (figs. 4-50, 4-51).

QUADRIGA: a sculptural monument that consists of a figure in a chariot with four horses; the *Charioteer* (fig. 3-70) was part of a quadriga.

R

REALISM, REALISTIC: the use of subject matter drawn from actual life and experience; e.g., fig. 7-16. Not to be confused with the nineteenth-century movement known as Realism (figs. 9-40, 9-41, 9-68).

RED-FIGURE STYLE: style of Greek vase painting from c. 530 BCE to the third century BCE in which the background of a scene is painted with a clay SLIP that turns black in firing, leaving the designs in the natural reddish tones of the clay. Details are also painted with slip and so appear as black lines.

REFECTORY: the dining hall in a MONASTERY or NUNNERY; the location for Leonardo da Vinci's painting of the *Last Supper* (fig. 5-64).

REINFORCED CONCRETE: concrete strengthened with embedded wire rods or mesh; see fig. 9-48. Also known as ferroconcrete.

RELIEF: sculpture in which the design extends from a background surface.

RELIEF PROCESS: a PRINTMAKING process in which the lines and surfaces to which the ink adheres are higher than the parts that are not to be printed; e.g., the WOODCUT process; see fig. 6-28.

RELIEF SCULPTURE: sculpture in which the figures or forms are united with a background; examples of relief sculpture types include LOW or BAS-RELIEF (figs. 3-20, 3-21), HIGH RELIEF (fig. 3-87), SUNKEN RELIEF (fig. 3-15), and PICTORIAL RELIEF (fig. 5-28).

RELIQUARY: a container for a sacred relic, as in fig. 4-1.

REPOUSSOIR: an object in the immediate foreground of a painting that establishes the frontal plane of the illusionistic space; e.g., the low fence in the FRESCOED room known as *Livia's Garden* (fig. 3-110).

REPRESENTATIONAL: when a work of art reproduces the appearance of forms in nature; see Bernini's *Apollo and Daphne* (fig. 1-4).

RIBS: raised structural elements that outline and help support a ribbed VAULT, as at the Gothic cathedral of Chartres (figs. 4-88, 4-89); see fig. 4-93.

ROUND ARCH: also sometimes called a true arch, it is a half-round opening that rises at the SPRINGING from upright supports.

RUSTICATION: the practice of covering building surfaces with massive, rough-cut stones, often with deep-cut grooves at the joints.

S

SARCOPHAGUS: a stone coffin, sometimes decorated with sculpture; see fig. 4-16.

SCIENTIFIC PERSPECTIVE: see LINEAR PERSPECTIVE.

SCREEN WALL: a non-supporting wall, usually with broad expanses of windows, that fills the opening under an ARCH or VAULT, as at the Byzantine church of Hagia Sophia (fig. 4-28). It is screen walls that sheathe the exterior of a modern steel-frame skyscraper.

SCRIPTORIUM: the room or rooms in a MONASTERY where MANUSCRIPTS are copied and illustrated, as in the St. Gall plan (fig. 4-54).

SCULPTURE IN THE ROUND: sculpture that is fully three-dimensional and finished on all sides; e.g., French's *Minuteman* (fig. 1-11). Also known as freestanding.

SECONDARY COLORS: colors created by mixing two or the PRIMARY COLORS; the secondary colors are orange (red and yellow), green (yellow and blue), and violet (red and blue).

SHADING: in painting, drawing, and printmaking, progressive decreases in the VALUE and INTENSITY of colors to suggest the changes that result when light hits a form; note the progressive darkening on the face of the *Mona Lisa* (fig. 6-21). See also MODELING.

SHAFT: in architecture, the vertical cylindrical form that supports the ENTABLATURE; for example, Doric columns are shafts (fig. 3-74).

SHAMANIC: describing a practice in which individuals, called shamans, claim to make contact with and influence gods, spirits, and forces in unseen realms while in ritualized trance states.

SHIFTING PERSPECTIVE: the use of multiple viewpoints in a painting or drawing, as in Li Cheng's and Cézanne's paintings (figs. 4-58, 9-79) or in Cubism (figs. 10-46, 10-47).

SHIN NO MIHASHIRA: a heart pillar buried deep in the ground below the Inner Shinto Shrine at Ise; thought to be the place where the KAMI reside.

SHINTO: indigenous Japanese nature religion with a central focus on reverence for KAMI; see pp. 148–49.

SHODEN: the main shrine building at Ise dedicated to the National Shinto Cult at the Naiku (Inner) Shrine; see pp. 168–71 and fig. 4-24.

SIDE AISLE: see AISLE.

SILVERPOINT: a drawing technique using a sharpened point of silver on specially prepared paper or parchment; e.g., Rembrandt's drawing on his fiancée Saskia (fig. 7-34).

SITE: the specific setting or location for which a work of art or architecture was designed; e.g., the location of Wright's Fallingwater over a waterfall (fig. 1-6).

SIVA: one of the three main Hindu gods, known as the Preserver; see Hindu art at Ellora, pp. 172–73.

SLIP: clay particles and water, sometimes used to decorate a pottery vessel, as in figs. 3-59, 3-61.

SPANDRELS: in architecture, the triangular surfaces to the sides of an ARCH, between the top of the arch and the SPRINGINGS on either side.

SPOLIA: materials taken from an earlier structure and reused, as in the columns and capitals at Old St. Peter's (fig. 4-18) and the Mosque in Córdoba (fig. 4-49).

SPRINGING: the level at which an ARCH or VAULT begins to curve inward and upward; see fig. 3-118 and pp. 120–23.

SQUINCH: ARCHES, LINTELS, and/or CORBELS that just across the corners of a square space to support a dome and to make the transition from the square space to a polygonal or round one; see the squinches that support the dome at Córdoba (fig. 4-51). See also fig. 3-118.

STAINED-GLASS WINDOWS: windows composed of pieces of colored glass joined by lead strips; see fig. 4-102 and pp. 216–17.

STATES: the successive printed stages of a print, especially common in Rembrandt's ETCHINGS and DRYPOINTS (figs. 7-38, 7-41).

STEEL-FRAME CONSTRUCTION: an architectural structure in which steel beams are joined horizontally and vertically to create a gridlike structural system; see fig. 9-47.

STEREOBATE: the stepped platform that forms the base for a Greek temple; the top step is known as the stylobate; see fig. 3-65.

STILL LIFE: a painting of fruit, flowers, game, or ordinary domestic objects. The still life developed as a popular genre in Northern European painting in the seventeenth century.

STUPA: a large hemispherical Buddhist shrine, erected to hold a relic or mark a holy site, as in the Great Stupa at Sanchi (fig. 3-88); the form evolved from earlier burial mounds.

STYLE: a complex concept with several meanings, including HISTORICAL STYLE and INDIVIDUAL STYLE.

SUBJECT MATTER: see ICONOGRAPHY.

SUNKEN RELIEF: an Egyptian style of RELIEF SCULPTURE in which the figures are recessed into the surface (fig. 3-15). Also known as incised relief.

T

TABLERO: in Mesoamerican architecture, a heavy, projecting, rectangular MOLDING outlined by a thick frame, as in the Pyramid of Quetzalcóatl at Teotihuacán (fig. 3-128).

TAOTIE: the stylized monster mask that decorates early Chinese bronzes (figs. 3-1, 3-2).

TECHNIQUE: how an artist or artists uses materials (the MEDIUM or MEDIA) to create a work of art; e.g., the vigorous, heavy OIL brushstrokes of Van Gogh (figs. 9-77, 9-78) or the highly polished finish of Michelangelo's *Pietà* (fig. 5-66).

TEMPERA PAINT TECHNIQUE: a painting technique in which the pigments are combined with egg. The support is usually plaster-coated wood and the background is often decorated with gold leaf, as in Giotto's *Madonna* (fig. 4-103). See also fig. 4-108.

TENEBRISM: a dramatic contrast of light and dark used by Caravaggio and his followers; see pp. 344–47.

TENSILE STRENGTH: the internal longitudinal strength in a stone, steel, or wood beam which enables it to support itself without breaking.

TERRA-COTTA: a hard earthenware, glazed or unglazed.

TESSERAE: the individual cut pieces of stone, glass or other materials used in the MOSAIC technique (see fig. 4-35). One piece is a tessera.

THRUST: the outward force created by an ARCH or VAULT; this must be counter-balanced by BUTTRESSING; see fig. 3-119 and pp. 120–23.

TORII ARCH: two posts capped by two beams—the topmost beam flaring upward—found at the gateway to the sacred precinct of a SHINTO shrine.

TOU-KUNG BRACKET: in Chinese and Japanese architecture, CANTILEVERED brackets, often multiple and complex, that support the beams and roof of a structure, as at Horyu-ji (fig. 4-43).

TRANSEPT: in a cross-shaped Christian church, cross arms placed perpendicular to the NAVE; see fig. 4-19.

TRANSVERSALS: lines that are parallel to each other in reality that recede parallel to the picture frame in the LINEAR PERSPECTIVE system; see fig.

5-29 and pp. 248–49.

TRANSVERSE ARCH: an ARCH that separates one BAY from the next in a series of arched VAULTS.

TRAVERTINE: a limestone, found especially along the Tiber River in Italy, pocked with small spongy holes.

TRIFORIUM: in Gothic construction, an arcaded passageway above the NAVE ARCADE (fig. 4-92) and below the CLERESTORY, as in the cathedral at Chartres (figs. 4-88, 4-89).

TRIGLYPH: in the Doric FRIEZE, the area between the METOPES, decorated with vertical grooves; see fig. 3-65 and p. 78.

TRIPTYCH: a three-part altarpiece or work of art.

TRIUMPHAL ARCH: a kind of free-standing monumental ARCH. They were first erected along routes of victorious returning Roman armies in the second century BCE and later created as non-functional commemorative public monuments.

TROMPE L'OEIL: illusionistic painting that emphasizes realistic effects to convince the viewer that the painted scene or object is actually real and not painted, as in Mantegna's Camera Picta frescoes (fig. 5-53).

TRUMEAU: the central supporting post between the two sides of a double door, which in Renaissance and Gothic churches is often decorated with sculpture, as at Amiens (figs. 4-97, 4-100).

TUFA: a soft, porous rock that hardens with exposure to air; used in construction.

TUNNEL VAULT: see BARREL VAULT.

TYMPANUM: the LUNETTE over the doorway of a church, which is often decorated with sculpture, as in Romanesque (figs. 4-71, 4-72, 4-73) and Gothic (fig. 4-98) structures.

U

UNDERWRITING: a preparatory drawing done directly on the plaster or canvas and over which the artist paints the finished work.

V

VALUE: the relative darkness (LOW VALUE) or lightness (HIGH VALUE) of a HUE.

VANISHING POINT: in a work created using the LINEAR PERSPECTIVE system, the vanishing point is the place where the converging ORTHOGONALS would converge if continued, as in Donatello's *Feast of Herod* (fig. 5-29).

VANITAS: a type of STILL LIFE showing objects that symbolize the impermanence of life, such as skulls, withered flowers, and clocks, and intended as reminders of the futility of amassing knowledge, wealth, and earthly possessions represented by stacks of books, coins, and jewels and fancy garments.

VAULT, VAULTING: a structural system based on the ARCH, including the TUNNEL (or BARREL) VAULT, the CROSS (or GROIN) VAULT, and the DOME; see fig. 3-118 and pp. 120–23.

VEHICLE: the drying liquid in which painting pigments are suspended; as it dries, it adheres the color to the surface.

VELLUM: fine PARCHMENT prepared from calfskin used for the pages in MANUSCRIPTS.

VILLA: a country house, as in the Villa Rotonda by Palladio (fig. 1-7).

VISHNU: one of the three main Hindu gods, known as the Creator; see Hindu art at Ellora, pp. 172–73.

VOLUTE: the spiral scroll motif that characterizes the capital of the IONIC ORDER; see fig. 3-65.

VOLUTE KRATER: an ancient Greek vase used for the mixing of wine with water; see fig. 3-60.

VOUSSOIRS: the individual blocks of stone (or bricks) that compose an ARCH; see fig. 3-118 and pp. 120–23.

W

WASH: ink thinned with water, applied with a brush to add effects of shadow, as in Rembrandt's *A Man Rowing* (fig. 7-33).

WATERCOLOR: pigments mixed with water (and gum arabic as a drying agent); used in Homer's watercolor *The Blue Boat* (fig. 9-73).

WEB: the surfaces of a Gothic RIB VAULT; see fig. 4-93. Also known as infilling.

WESTWORK: a church entrance with a centralized APSE enclosing a chapel on the second story and two flanking towers, typical of Carolingian churches, as in the St. Gall monastery plan (fig. 4-54).

WOODCUT: a relief printmaking process; for a diagram, see fig. 6-28 and pp. 296–97.

Y

YAKSHA, YAKSHI: ancient Indian nature spirits that became gods and goddesses of fertility, as at Sanchi (fig. 3-89).

Z

ZEN: a form of Buddhism (known in China as Chan) that teaches that there is no Buddha except that in one's own nature; only through meditation can one reach one's own Buddha nature; see Zen art, pp. 330–31.

ZIGGURAT: a stepped pyramid of mud brick, used by the Sumerians and the Assyrians as a sacred site; see fig. 3-12.

Bibliography

This is a general, broad bibliography intended to lead the reader to more specific books on individual sites, monuments, artists, and movements. As a rule, it includes only the most important sources, and only those in English.

GENERAL

Addiss, Stephen. *How to Look at Japanese Art*. New York: Abrams, 1996.

Broude, Norma, and Mary D. Garrard. *Feminism and Art History: Questioning the Litany*. New York: Harper & Row, 1982.

Elsen, Albert E. *Purposes of Art*. New York: Holt, Rinehart and Winston, 1981.

Encyclopedia of World Art. 15 vols. New York: McGraw-Hill, 1959–68.

Fernie, Eric (selection and commentary by). *Art History and Its Methods: A Critical Anthology*. San Francisco: Chronicle Books, 1995.

Fleming, John, Hugh Honour, and Nikolaus Pevsner. *The Penguin Dictionary of Architecture*. New York: Viking, 1991.

Goldwater, Robert J., and Marco Treves. *Artists on Art*. New York: Pantheon, 1974.

Gombrich, E. H. *Art and Illusion*. New York: Pantheon, 1972.

———. *The Story of Art*. Oxford: Phaidon, 1995.

Holt, Elizabeth G. *A Documentary History of Art*. 2 vols. Garden City, N.Y.: Doubleday, 1981.

Honour, Hugh, and John Fleming. *The Visual Arts: A History*. Upper Saddle River, N.J.: Prentice Hall, 1995.

Janson, H. W., and Anthony F. Janson. *History of Art*. New York: Abrams, 1997.

Kemal, Salim, and Ivan Gaskell. *The Language of Art History*. Cambridge, Eng.: Cambridge University Press, 1992.

Kemp, Martin. *The Science of Art: Optical Themes in Western Art from Brunelleschi to Seurat*. New Haven, Conn.: Yale University Press, 1989.

Kostof, Spiro. *The Architect: Chapters in the History of the Profession*. New York: Oxford University Press, 1986.

———. *A History of Architecture: Settings and Rituals*. New York: Oxford University Press, 1995.

Lee, Sherman E. *A History of Far Eastern Art*. New York: Abrams, 1994.

Nochlin, Linda. *Women, Art, and Power and Other Essays*. New York: Harper & Row, 1988.

———. and Ann S. Harris. *Women Artists: 1550–1950*. Los Angeles: Los Angeles County Museum of Art; New York: distributed by Random House, 1976.

Sayre, Henry M. *Writing About Art*. Upper Saddle River, N.J.: Prentice Hall, 1995.

Stokstad, Marilyn. *Art History*. New York: Abrams, 1995.

Sullivan, Michael. *The Arts of China*. Berkeley, Calif.: University of California Press, 1984.

Tansey, Richard G. and Fred S. Kleiner. *Gardner's Art Through the Ages*. Fort Worth, Tex.: Harcourt Brace & Company, 1995.

Trachtenberg, Marvin, and Isabelle Hyman. *Architecture, from Prehistory to Post-Modernism*. New York: Abrams, 1986.

Turner, Jane, ed. *The Dictionary of Art*. 34 vols. New York: Grove's Dictionaries, 1996.

Wittkower, Rudolf and Margot. *Born Under Saturn*. New York: Norton, 1969.

PREHISTORY AND ANCIENT

Adam, Robert. *Classical Architecture: A Comprehensive Handbook to the Tradition of Classical Style*. New York: Abrams, 1991.

Adams, Richard E. W. *Prehistoric Mesoamerica*. Norman, O.K.: University of Oklahoma Press, 1996.

Aldred, Cyril. *Egyptian Art in the Days of the Pharaohs 3100–320 B.C.* New York: Thames and Hudson, 1985.

Amiet, Pierra. *The Ancient Art of the Near East*. New York: Abrams, 1980.

Bahn, Paul G. *The Cambridge Illustrated History of Prehistoric Art*. New York: Cambridge University Press, 1998.

Berrin, Kathleen, and Esther Pasztory, eds. *Teotihuacan: Art from the City of the Gods*. New York: Thames and Hudson, 1993.

Boardman, John. *Greek Art*. London: Thames and Hudson, 1996.

———. *The Oxford History of Classical Art*. Oxford/New York: Oxford University Press, 1993.

———. *The Parthenon and Its Sculptures*. Austin, Tex.: University of Texas Press, 1985.

Boëthius, Alexander. *Etruscan and Early Roman Architecture*. New Haven, Conn.: Yale University Press, 1987.

Brendel, Otto. *Etruscan Art*. New Haven, Conn.: Yale University Press, 1995.

Brilliant, Richard. *Arts of the Ancient Greeks*. New York: McGraw-Hill, 1973.

Collon, Dominique. *Ancient Near Eastern Art*. Berkeley, Calif.: University of California Press, 1995.

Henig, Martin. *A Handbook of Roman Art*. Ithaca, N.Y.: Cornell University Press, 1983.

Grand, Paule M. *Prehistoric Art: Paleolithic Painting and Sculpture*. Greenwich, Conn.: New York Graphic Society, 1967.

Groenewegen-Frankfort, H. A., and Bernard Ashmole. *Art of the Ancient World*. Englewood Cliffs, N.J.: Prentice Hall, 1972.

Kubler, George. *Art and Architecture of Ancient America*. Harmondsworth, Eng.: Penguin, 1990.

MacDonald, William L. *The Architecture of the Roman Empire*. 2 vols. New Haven, Conn.: Yale University Press, 1982.

Mason, Penelope. *History of Japanese Art*. New York: Abrams, 1993.

Miller, Mary Ellen. *The Art of Mesoamerica: From Olmec to Aztec*. New York: Thames and Hudson, 1996.

Pollitt, J. J. *The Art of Greece 1400–31 B.C.* (Sources and Documents). Cambridge, Eng.: Cambridge University Press, 1990.

———. *Art and Experience in Classical Greece*. Cambridge, Eng.: Cambridge University Press, 1972.

———. *Ancient View of Greek Art*. New Haven, Conn.: Yale University Press, 1974.

———. *The Art of Rome c. 753 B.C.–A.D. 337* (Sources and Documents). New York: Cambridge University Press, 1983.

———. *Art in the Hellenistic Age*. Cambridge, Eng.: Cambridge University Press, 1986.

Ramage, Nancy. *Roman Art: Romulus to Constantine*. Englewood Cliffs, N.J.: Prentice Hall, 1996.

Smith, William Stevenson. *The Art and Architecture of Ancient Egypt*. New Haven, Conn.: Yale University Press, 1988.

Strong, Donald. *Roman Art*. Harmondsworth, Eng.: Penguin, 1988.

Ward-Perkins, J. B. *Roman Architecture*. New York: Rizzoli, 1988.

———. *Roman Imperial Architecture*. Harmondsworth, Eng.: Penguin, 1981.

ART FROM 200 TO 1400

Conant, Kenneth J. *Carolingian and Romanesque Architecture*. Harmondsworth, Eng.: Penguin, 1978.

Craven, Roy. *Indian Art: A Concise History*. London: Thames and Hudson, 1997.

Davis-Weyer, C. *Early Medieval Art 300–1150* (Sources and Documents). Englewood Cliffs, N.J.: Prentice Hall, 1986.

Dodwell, C. R. *The Pictorial Arts of the West, 800–1200*. New Haven, Conn.: Yale University Press, 1993.

Ettinghausen, Richard, and Oleg Grabar. *The Art and Architecture of Islam, 650–1250*. New Haven, Conn.: Yale University Press, 1992.

Fisher, Robert E. *Buddhist Art and Architecture*. London: Thames and Hudson, 1993.

Frisch, T. G. *Gothic Art 1140–ca. 1450 (Sources and Documents)*. Toronto: University of Toronto Press, 1987.

Grodecki, Louis. *Gothic Architecture*. New York: Rizzoli, 1991.

Hearn, M. F. *Romanesque Sculpture*. Ithaca, N.Y.: Cornell University Press, 1981.

Huntington, Susan. *Art of Ancient India: Buddhist, Hindu, Jain*. New York: Weatherhill, 1985.

Krautheimer, Richard. *Early Christian and Byzantine Architecture*. Harmondsworth, Eng.: Penguin, 1986.

Mango, Cyril. *The Art of the Byzantine Empire 312–1453 (Sources and Documents)*. Cheektowaga, Ont.: University of Toronto Press, 1986.

——. *Byzantium*. London: Weidenfeld and Nicolson, 1980.

——. *Byzantine Architecture*. New York: Rizzoli, 1991.

Os, H. W. van. *The Art of Devotion in the Late Middle Ages in Europe, 1300–1500*. Princeton, N.J.: Princeton University Press, 1994.

Petzold, Andreas. *Romanesque Art*. New York: Abrams, 1995.

Rodley, Lyn. *Byzantine Art and Architecture*. Cambridge, Eng./New York: Cambridge University Press, 1994.

Snyder, James. *Medieval Art: Painting, Sculpture, Architecture 4th–14th Century*. New York: Abrams, 1989.

Swaan, Wim. *The Gothic Cathedral*. New York: Park Lane, 1981.

White, John. *Art and Architecture in Italy, 1250–1400*. New Haven, Conn.: Yale University Press, 1993.

Wilson, David M. *Anglo-Saxon Art from the Seventh Century to the Norman Conquest*. Woodstock, N.Y.: Overlook Press, 1984.

FIFTEENTH AND SIXTEENTH CENTURIES

Blair, Sheila. *The Art and Architecture of Islam 1250–1800*. New Haven, Conn.: Yale University Press, 1994.

Cole, Alison. *Virtue and Magnificence: Art of the Italian Renaissance Courts*. New York: Abrams, 1995.

Cole, Bruce. *The Renaissance Artist at Work*. New York: Harper & Row, 1983.

Gilbert, Creighton. *Italian Art 1400–1500 (Sources and Documents)*. Evanston, Ill.: Northwestern University Press, 1991.

Harbison, Craig. *The Mirror of the Artist: Northern Renaissance Art in Its Historical Context*. New York: Abrams, 1995.

Hartt, Frederick. *History of Italian Renaissance Art*. New York: Abrams, 1994.

Heydenreich, Ludwig, and W. Lotz. *Architecture in Italy 1400–1600*. New Haven, Conn.: Yale University Press, 1996.

Klein, Robert, and Henri Zerner. *Italian Art, 1500–1600 (Sources and Documents)*. Evanston, Ill.: Northwestern University Press, 1989.

Kristeller, Paul O. *Renaissance Thought and the Arts: Collected Essays*. Princeton, N.J.: Princeton University Press, 1990.

Paoletti, John T., and Gary M. Radke. *Art in Renaissance Italy*. New York: Abrams, 1997.

Rosand, David. *Painting in Cinquecento Venice: Titian, Veronese, Tintoretto*. New Haven, Conn.: Yale University Press, 1986.

Snyder, James. *Northern Renaissance Art*. New York: Abrams, 1985.

Stechow, Wolfgang. *Northern Renaissance Art 1400–1600 (Sources and Documents)*. Evanston, Ill.: Northwestern University Press, 1989.

Turner, Jane. *Encyclopedia of Italian Renaissance and Mannerist Art*. New York: Grove's Dictionaries, 2000.

Wittkower, Rudolf. *Architectural Principles in the Age of Humanism*. New York: St. Martin's Press, 1988.

SEVENTEENTH AND EIGHTEENTH CENTURIES

Blunt, Anthony. *Art and Architecture in France 1500–1700*. New Haven, Conn.: Yale University Press, 1988.

Crow, Thomas E. *Painters and Public Life in Eighteenth-Century Paris*. New Haven, Conn.: Yale University Press, 1985.

Enggass, Robert, and Jonathan Brown. *Italy and Spain 1600–1750 (Sources and Documents)*. Evanston, Ill.: Northwestern University Press, 1993.

Gerson, H., and E. H. ter Kuile. *Art and Architecture in Belgium 1600–1800*. Baltimore, Md.: Penguin, 1978.

Guth, Christine. *Art of Edo Japan: The Artist and the City 1615–1868*. New York: Abrams.

Haskell, Francis. *Patrons and Painters: A Study in the Relations Between Italian Art and Society in the Age of the Baroque*. New Haven, Conn.: Yale University Press, 1980.

Held, Julius, and Donald Posner. *Seventeenth and Eighteenth Century Art: Baroque Painting, Sculpture, Architecture*. New York: Abrams, 1971.

Levey, Michael. *Painting and Sculpture in France, 1700–1789*. New Haven, Conn.: Yale University Press, 1993.

Rosenberg, Jakob, Seymour Slive, and E. H. ter Kuile. *Dutch Art and Architecture 1600–1800*. New Haven, Conn.: Yale University Press, 1987.

Schama, Simon. *The Embarrassment of Riches: An Interpretation of Dutch Culture in the Golden Age*. Berkeley, Calif.: University of California Press, 1988.

Varriano, John. *Italian Baroque and Rococo Architecture*. New York: Oxford University Press, 1986.

Wittkower, Rudolf. *Art and Architecture in Italy 1600 to 1750*. New Haven, Conn.: Yale University Press, 1999.

NINETEENTH AND TWENTIETH CENTURIES

Arnason, H. H., and Marla F. Prather. *History of Modern Art*. 4th ed. New York: Abrams, 1998.

Atkins, Robert. *ArtSpeak: A Guide to Contemporary Ideas, Movements and Buzzwords*. New York: Abbeville Press, 1990.

——. *ArtSpoke: A Guide to Modern Ideas, Movements, and Buzzwords 1848–1944*. New York: Abbeville Press, 1993.

Baigell, Matthew. *A Concise History of American Painting and Sculpture*. New York: Harper & Row, 1984.

Boimé, Albert. *A Social History of Modern Art*. Chicago: University of Chicago Press, 1990–93.

Broude, Norma. *Impressionism: A Feminist Reading: The Gendering of Art, Science, and Nature in the Nineteenth Century*. New York: Rizzoli, 1991.

Clark, T. J. *Image of the People: Gustave Courbet and the 1848 Revolution*. Princeton, N.J.: Princeton University Press, 1982.

——. *The Painting of Modern Life: Paris in the Art of Manet and His Followers*. Princeton, N.J.: Princeton University Press, 1989.

Curtis, William J. R. *Modern Architecture Since 1900*. San Francisco: Chronicle Books, 1996.

Daval, Jean-Luc. *Photography: History of an Art*. New York: Rizzoli, 1982.

Eitner, Lorenz. *Neoclassicism and Romanticism 1750–1850 (Sources and Documents)*. New York: Harper & Row, 1989.

——. *An Outline of 19th Century European Painting: From David through Cézanne*. New York: HarperCollins, 1989.

Fry, Edward. *Cubism*. London: Thames and Hudson, 1985.

Gaggi, Silvio. *Modern-Postmodern: A Study in Twentieth-Century Arts and Ideas*. Philadelphia: University of Pennsylvania Press, 1989.

Gates, Henry Louis. *Africa: The Art of a Continent: 100 Works of Power and Beauty*. New York: Abrams, 1996.

Hamilton, George H. *Nineteenth and Twentieth Century Art*. New York: Abrams, 1971.

——. *Painting and Sculpture in Europe 1880–1940*. New Haven, Conn.: Yale University Press, 1993.

Herbert, Robert L. *Modern Artists on Art*. Englewood Cliffs, N.J.: Prentice Hall, 1986.

——. *Impressionism*. New Haven, Conn.: Yale University Press, 1991.

Holt, Elizabeth G. *From the Classicists to the Impressionists*. New Haven, Conn.: Yale University Press, 1986.

Hopi, Kachina, Spirit of Life. The California Academy of Sciences. Seattle: distributed by University of Washington Press, 1980.

Hughes, Robert. *The Shock of the New*. New York: Knopf, 1992.

Hunter, Sam, and John Jacobus. *Modern Art: Painting, Sculpture, Architecture*. New York: Abrams, 1992.

Janson, H. W. *19th-Century Sculpture*. New York: Abrams, 1985.

Levin, Kim. *Beyond Modernism: Essays on Art from the '70s to '80s*. New York: HarperCollins, 1989.

Lucie-Smith, Edward. *American Art Now*. New York: Morrow, 1985.

——. *Art Today*. London: Phaidon, 1995.

——. *Movements in Art Since 1945*. New York: Thames and Hudson, 1995.

McCoubrey, John. *American Art 1700–1960* (Sources and Documents). Englewood Cliffs, N.J.: Prentice Hall, 1965.

Munroe, Alexandra. *Japanese Art After 1945: Scream Against the Sky*. New York: Abrams, 1994.

Newhall, Beaumont. *The History of Photography, from 1839 to the Present Day*. New York: Museum of Modern Art, 1982.

Nochlin, Linda. *Impressionism and Post-Impressionism* (Sources and Documents). Englewood Cliffs, N.J.: Prentice Hall, 1966.

——. *Realism and Tradition in Art 1848–1900* (Sources and Documents). Englewood Cliffs, N.J.: Prentice Hall, 1966.

Noever, Peter, and Regina Haslinger, eds. *Architecture in Transition: Between Deconstruction and New Modernism*. New York: te Neues, 1995.

Phillips, Tom. *Africa: The Art of a Continent*. New York: te Neues, 1995.

Rewald, John. *Post-Impressionism: From Van Gogh to Gauguin*. New York: Abrams, 1990.

——. *The History of Impressionism*. New York: Abrams, 1990.

——. *Studies in Impressionism*. New York: Abrams, 1986.

——. *Studies in Post-Impressionism*. New York: Abrams, 1986.

Rosenblum, Robert, and H. W. Janson. *Nineteenth-Century Art*. New York: Abrams, 1984.

Selz, Peter. *Art in Our Times*. New York: Abrams, 1981.

Smagula, Howard. *Currents, Contemporary Directions in the Visual Arts*. Englewood Cliffs, N.J.: Prentice Hall, 1989.

Thompson, Robert Farris. *African Art in Motion: Icon and Act*. Los Angeles: University of California Press, 1979.

Varnedoe, Kirk. *A Fine Disregard: What Makes Modern Art Modern*. New York: Abrams, 1990.

Wheeler, Daniel. *Art Since Mid-Century*. Englewood Cliffs, N.J. Prentice Hall, 1991.

Wilmerding, John. *American Art*. New York: Viking, 1982.

Index

Mourners around a Bier (Greek), 70-71, *71*
MUHAMMAD (Persian): *Feast of Sadeh*, 323, *323*
MUNCH, EDVARD (Norwegian): *The Frieze of Life*, 469, *469*; *The Scream*, 468, *468*
mural painting: *See also* frescoes. *Guernica*, 538-539, *538, 539*; Mexican, 528-529, *528, 529*
MURRAY, ELIZABETH (American): *Cracked Question*, 587-588, *588*
Mycenaean art, 62-63, *62, 63*
Myein (HAMILTON), 590-591, *590*

N

NADAR (GASPARD-FÉLIX TOURNACHON) (French): *George Sand*, 442, *442*
NAMES PROJECT (American): *Aids Memorial Quilt*, 476, *476*
NANNI DI BANCO (Italian): *Four Saints*, 238-239, *239*
Napoleon as Mars the Peacekeeper (CANOVA), 414, *414*
Napoleon Bonaparte, 414, *414*
Native American art, 489, 495-497, *489, 494, 495, 496*
naturalism, 6, 24, 37, 136, 228-227, *228, 229*
Nature, relating to, 342-343
NEEL, ALICE (American): *Nude Self-Portrait*, 387, 486, *387, 486*
Neoclassical style: architecture, 394-395, 414-415, *394, 395, 414*; painting, 396-397, 414-415, *396, 397, 415*; sculpture, 414-415, *414, 415*
Neo-Dada, 523
Neo-Expressionism, 571, 578-579, *571, 578, 579*
Neolithic art and architecture, 27-31, *27-31*
NEUMANN, JOHANN BALTHASAR (German): Kaiseraal, Würzburg, Germany, 390, *390*
NEVELSON, LOUISE (American): *Sky Cathedral*, 480-481, *482*
Newborn, The (BRANCUSI), 510, *510*
New Canaan, Connecticut, Glass House (JOHNSON), 488, 544, *488, 544*
New Realism, 568-569, *568, 569*
New York City: Brooklyn Bridge, 435, *435*; Seagram Building (MIES VAN DER ROHE), 544-545, *545*
Niccolò da Tolentino Directing the Attack (UCCELLO), *263*
Nigeria, royal art of, 224-225, *224, 225*
Night Cafe (VAN GOGH), 460-461, *460*
Nighthawks (HOPPER), 478-479, *479*
Night of the Poor (RIVERA), 528, 529, *529*
Night of the Rich (RIVERA), 528-529, *528*
Night Sea (MARTIN), 565, *565*
Night Watch (REMBRANDT), 354-355, *355*
Ni Zan, Portrait of (Chinese), 21, *20*
NI ZAN (Chinese): *Rongxi Studio*, 135, 137, *136*
NOGUCHI, ISAMU (American): *Kouros*, 541, 542, *542*
Nok head, 28, *28*
NOLDE, EMIL (German): *Prophet*, 515, *515*
Nôtre-Dame-du-Haut (LE CORBUSIER), 550-551, *550, 551*

Nude Descending a Staircase, No. 2 (DUCHAMP), 509, *508*
Nude Self-Portrait (NEEL), 387, 486, *387, 486*

O

ODO OF METZ, Palace Chapel of Charlemagne, 178, *179*
OFILI, CHRIS: *She*, 594-595, *594*
oil painting techniques, 16, 247, 258-259, *258, 259*
O'KEEFFE, GEORGIA (American): *Evening Star III*, 479, *480*; *Lawrence Tree*, 536, *536*
OLDENBURG, CLAES (American): *Shuttlecocks*, 559, *559*
Olmecs, 126-129
Olympia (MANET), 441, *441*
One and Three Chairs (KOSUTH), 485, 562, *562*
Op Art, 480, 556-557, *557*
Opéra, Paris, 438, 444, *438*
OPPENHEIM, MERET (French): *Fur-Covered Cup, Saucer, and Spoon*, 532-533, *533*
orthogonals, 249
Osterley Park House (ADAM), 380-381, *381*
Ottoman empire, art of, 324-325, *324, 325*
Ottonian art, 188-189, *188, 189*
overlapping, 16
OZU, YASUJIRO (Japanese): *Tokyo Story*, 552-553, *552, 553*

P

PAIK, NAM JUNE (Korean): *Electronic Superhighway*, 1, 2, 3, *xvi, 2*
painting/painting techniques: *See also under specific country*. Academic, 432-433, *432, 433*; Action, 549; analyzing, 14-17; Baroque, 337, 339-351, 354-355, 358-371, 366-377; catacombs, 142, *142*; cave, 24-26, *24, 25*; ceiling, 338, 340, *337, 339*; Color Field, 548-549; Cubism, 500-501, 504-509, *500, 501, 504-509*; Dada, 520-523, *520-523*; eighteenth-century, 388-389, 392-393, 396-397, *388, 389, 392, 393, 396, 397*; Expressionism, abstract, 477, 546-549, *546-549*; Expressionism, German, 514-517, *514-517*; fantasy, 518-519, *518, 519*; fifteenth-century, 228-235, 240-243, 256-257, *240-243, 256*; Flemish, 240-243, 250-251, 256-257, *240-243, 250, 251, 256*; foreshortening technique in, 74, 190, 267, *267*; frescoes, 16, 103, 112-115, 220-221, 247, *112-115, 220, 221*; genre, 348-349, *348, 349*; Hard-Edge, 480, 556, *556*; icon, 6, 132, 151-153; illusionist/*trompe l'oeil*, 14, 112-115, 136, *112-115*; Impressionist, 446-451, *446-451*; landscape (Chinese), 6, 184-186, 184-186; landscape (Romantic), 420-421, 428-429, *420, 421, 428, 429*; landscape (seventeenth-century), 342, 369, 376-377, *332, 342, 369, 376, 377*; landscape (sixteenth-century), 320-321, *320, 321*; manuscript illumination (Ottonian), 188-189, *188*; manuscript illumination (Romanesque), 191-193, *191-193*; modernism, 478, 534-537, *534-537*; mural, 528-529, *528, 529*; naturalism, 6, 24, 37, 136,

228-227, *228, 229*; Neoclassical, 396-397, 414-415, *396, 397, 415*; as object, 554-555, *554, 555*; oil, 16, 247, 258-259, *259, 259*; Op Art, 480, 556-557, *557*; Post-Impressionism, 458-465, *458-465*; Post-Painterly, 477, 550, *550*; Realism, 430-431, 452-453, *430, 431, 452, 453*; Renaissance (early), 232-233, 238-239, 244-249, 252-253, 266-275, *238, 239, 244-249, 252, 253, 266-275*; Renaissance (high), 292-293, 300-315, *292, 293, 300-315*; Romantic, 418-421, 428-429, *418-421, 428, 429*; scientific perspective, 15, 248, 249, 304; scrolls (Chinese), 5, 17, 135, *5, 17, 135*; scrolls (Japanese), 202-203, *202, 203*; seventeenth-century, 337-377; sixteenth-century, 292-293, 300-315; still-life, 370-371, *370, 371*; tempera, 222-223, 247; tombs, 56-57, *56-57*; vase, 19, 74-75, *18, 34, 74, 75*; Venetian technique, 314-315, *314, 315*; watercolor, 456-457, *456, 457*
Paleolithic art, 24-26, *24, 25, 27, 289*
Palace at Aachen, Germany, 178, *179*
Palace of Darius, Persepolis, 67, *67*
PALLADIO, ANDREA (Italian): *Hercules and Antaeus*, 226, 263; San Giorgio Maggiore, 326, *326*; Villa Rotonda, 8, 10-11, *9, 10*
Panathenaic Amphora with Runners (Greek), 70, *71*
Pantheon, Rome, 109, 122-123, *122, 123*
Pantocrator, Daphni, Greece, 159, 199, *198*
Paris: Arc de Triomphe, 414, 419, *414*; Eiffel Tower, 436, *436*; Opéra, 438, 444, *438*; Pompidou National Arts and Cultural Center, 574, *573*; Salon de la Princesse, 380, *380*; Versailles, palace of, 372-373, *372, 373*
Paris Psalter, 151, *152*
PARMIGIANINO (Italian): *Madonna and Child with Angels and a Prophet*, 286, *285*; *Self-Portrait in a Convex Mirror*, 267, 287, *287*
Parthenon, Athens, 86-89, *86, 87, 88, 89*
Passion Sarcophagus, 144-145, *144*
Pattern and Decoration movement, 571, 576-577, *576, 577*
pattern book, 141
PAXTON, JOSEPH (English): Crystal Palace, 434-435, *434*
Peasant Family (LE NAIN), 348, *349*
Peasant Wedding Feast (BRUEGEL THE ELDER), 322-323, *322*
pendant (Chinese), 65, *64*
Penitent Magdalene (DONATELLO), 254-255, *254, 255*
Pentecost, the Peoples of the Earth, and Saint John the Baptist (Romanesque), 196, *196*
performance art, 562-563, *562, 563*
Persepolis, Palace of Darius, 67, *67*
Persian art, early, 66-67, *66, 67*
Persistence of Memory (DALÍ), 530-531, *531*
perspective: atmospheric, 15, 245, 249; drawing, 248-249, *248, 249*; linear or vanishing-point, 248; scientific, 15, 248, 249, 304; shifting, 185
PERUGINO, PIETRO (Italian): *Christ Giving the Keys to Saint Peter*, 14-17, 248, *16, 248*

List of Credits

The authors and publishers wish to thank the museums, galleries, libraries, and churches for permitting the reproduction of works of art in their collections. Photographs have been supplied by the owners or custodians of the works of art, except for the following, whose courtesy is gratefully acknowledged. Figure numbers refer to illustrations.

CHAPTER 1

Chapter opening photo, Nam June Paik, *Electronic Superhighway*, 1995. Multiple television monitors, laser disc players, laser discs, neon, and other mixed media, 15 x 32 feet. Courtesy Nam June Paik and Holly Solomon Gallery, p. xiv; Fig. 1-1, Holly Solomon Gallery, p. 2; Fig. 1-2, Museum of Fine Arts, Boston, p. 4 ; Fig. 1-3, The National Palace Museum, p. 5; Fig. 1-4, Ministero della Pubblica Istruzione, p. 7; Fig. 1-5, Shigeo Okamato, p. 8; Fig. 1-6, Courtesy David G. Wilkins, p. 9; Fig. 1-7, Courtesy David G. Wilkins, p. 9; Fig. 1-9, Marlene Boyle, p. 10; Fig. 1-10, Hedrich Blessing, Chicago, p. 10; Fig. 1-11, Society for the Preservation of New England Antiquities, Boston, p. 12; Fig. 1-12, © 1997 Estate of David Smith/VAGA, New York, NY, p. 13; Fig. 1-13, Liaison Agency, Inc., p. 14; Fig. 1-14, New York Times Pictures, p. 15; Fig. 1-15, Canali Photobank, p. 16; Fig. 1-16, Michael Bodycomb, Kimball Art Museum, p. 16; Fig. 1-17, Pearson Education/PH College, p. 17; Fig. 1-18, Courtesy David G. Wilkins, p. 17; Fig. 1-19, Philadelphia Museum of Art, p. 18; Fig. 1-20, Canali Photobank, p. 18; Fig. 1-22, The National Palace Museum, p. 20; Fig. 1-23, © Carol Beckwith/Estall Photograph, p. 21.

CHAPTER 2

Chapter opening photo, Tony Linck , p. 22; Fig. 2-1, Hans Hinz/ Colorfoto Hinz, p. 24; Fig. 2-3, Colorfoto Hans Hinz, Basel, Switzerland, p. 25; Fig. 2-4, Erich Lessing, Art Resource, N.Y., p. 26; Fig. 2-5, The British Museum, p. 27; Fig. 2-6, James Mellart, *Catal Hüyük*, 1967, p. 28; Fig. 2-7, The Cleveland Museum of Art, p. 28; Fig. 2-8, Tony Linck, p. 29; Fig. 2-9, British Department of the Environment, p. 30; Fig. 2-10, University of Pittsburgh History of Art & Architecture Slide Library, p. 31; Fig. 2-11, James Mellart, *Catal Hüyük*, 1967, p. 32; Fig. 2-12, HOA-QUI, Paris, p. 32; Fig. 2-13, Canali Photobank, p. 33; Fig. 2-15, Richard Stoner, p. 33.

CHAPTER 3

Chapter opening art, Scala, Art Resource, N.Y., p. 34; Fig. 3-1, Archivio Fotografico, monumenti Musei e Galerie Pontificie, The Vatican, p. 36; Fig. 3-2, Chinese, "Fang ding," from Tomb 1004, Houziazhuang, Anyang, Henan Province, China. Shang dynasty, c. 1150 B.C. Bronze, height 24 ½". Academia Sinica, Taipei, Taiwan, Republic of China. Commissioned by a member of the Shang imperial family, Academia Sinica, p. 37; Fig. 3-4, Scala, Art Resource, N.Y., p. 40; Fig. 3-5, Archivi Alinari, Florence, p. 40; Fig. 3-6, Lorenzo Ghiberti, *Self-Portrait*, from the East Doors of the Baptistery, Florence. 1425–52. Gilded bronze, approx. height 3 in. Museo dell'Opra del Duomo, Florence. Commissioned by the Opera of the Baptistery and the Arte de

Calimala. Alinari/Art Resource, NY, p. 41; Fig. 3-7, Rodney Todd-White & Son, The Royal Collection Enterprises Ltd., p. 41; Fig. 3-8, ©Yasumasa Morimura, p. 41; Fig. 3-9, Hirmer Fotoarchiv, p. 42; Fig. 3-10, Victor J. Boswell, The Oriental Institute Museum, p. 42; Fig. 3-11, Hirmer Fotoarchiv, p. 43; Fig. 3-12, Hirmer Fotoarchiv, p. 43; Fig. 3-13, Hirmer Fotoarchiv, p. 44; Fig. 3-14, All Rights Reserved. The Metropolitan Museum of Art, New York, p. 45; Fig. 3-15, M. B'sing, Bildarchiv Preussischer Kulturbesitz, p. 45; Fig. 3-16, Courtesy David G. Wilkins, p. 46; Fig. 3-17, Jean Vertut, courtesy Editions Citadelles & Mazenod, Paris, p. 47; Fig. 3-18, All Rights Reserved. The Metropolitan Museum of Art, New York, p. 47; Fig. 3-20, Hirmer Fotoarchiv, p. 48; Fig. 3-21, Hirmer Fotoarchiv, p. 48; Fig. 3-22, Robert Frerck, Odyssey Productions, p. 50; Fig. 3-23, University of Pittsburgh History of Art & Architecture Slide Library, p. 50; Fig. 3-27, Courtesy David G. Wilkins, p. 52; Fig. 3-28, Hirmer Fotoarchiv, p. 53; Fig. 3-30, The Metropolitan Museum of Art, p. 54; Fig. 3-31, John McKenna, p. 55; Fig. 3-33, Editions Citadelles & Mazenod, Paris, p. 56; Fig. 3-34, The British Museum, p. 57; Fig. 3-35, Alan Sorrell, The Bridgeman Art Library International, p. 58; Fig. 3-36, Four steatite seals, from Mohenjo Daro. National Museum of Pakistan, Karachi, Pakistan, Borromeo, Art Resource, N.Y., p. 59; Fig. 3-37, Scala, Art Resource, N.Y., p. 60; Fig. 3-38, Hirmer Fotoarchiv, p. 60; Fig. 3-39, Kostos Kontos Photostock, p. 61; Fig. 3-40, Kostos Kontos Photostock, p. 61; Fig. 3-41, Deutsches Archaeologisches Institut, Athens, p. 62; Fig. 3-43, Mycenaen. Funerary mask found at Mycenae, c. 1500 BCE. Gold, height approx. 12". National Archaeological Museum, Athens. Hirmer Fotoarchiv, Munich, Germany, p. 63; Fig. 3-44, Courtesy Asian Art Department, The Metropolitan Museum of Art, p. 64; Fig. 3-45, Courtesy Asian Art Department, The Metropolitan Museum of Art, p. 64; Fig. 3-46, Marlene Boyle, p. 65; Fig. 3-47, Agence Photographique de la Réunion des Musées Nationaux, Paris, p. 66; Fig. 3-48, The British Museum, p. 67; Fig. 3-49, The Oriental Institute Museum, Courtesy of the Oriental Institute of the University of Chicago, p. 67; Fig. 3-50, Agence Photographique de la Réunion des Musées Nationaux, Paris, p. 67; Fig. 3-51, Bardazzi Fotografia, Florence, p. 68; Fig. 3-52, Alinari/Scala, Art Resource, N.Y., p. 68; Fig. 3-53, Canali Photobank, p. 69; Fig. 3-54, *Apollo and the Battle of the Lapiths and the Centaurs* detail from the west pediment, Temple of Zeus, Olympia. 470–456 BCE. Marble, over-lifesize. Archaeological Museum, Olympia, Alinari, Art Resource, N.Y., p. 70; Fig. 3-55, Belly handled amphora, Kerameikos, Height 1.55m., National Museum, Athens, Hirmer Fotoarchiv, p. 71; Fig. 3-56, All Rights Reserved. The Metropolitan Museum of Art, p. 71; Fig. 3-57, Royal Ontario Museum, p. 72; Fig. 3-58, Canali Photobank, p. 73; Fig. 3-59, Scala, Art Resource, N.Y., p. 74; Fig. 3-60, Marlene Boyle, p. 75; Fig. 3-61, Copyright © by The Metropolitan Museum of Art, p. 75; Fig. 3-62, Hirmer Fotoarchiv, p. 76; Fig. 3-63, Kostas Kontos, Athens, p. 76; Fig. 3-64, Alison Frantz, Acropolis Museum, p. 77; Fig. 3-66, Cameron, Nigel, Photo Researchers, Inc., p. 80; Fig. 3-67, Marlene Boyle, p. 81; Fig. 3-68, The Bridgeman Art Library International, p. 81; Fig. 3-69, Hirmer Fotoarchiv, p. 82; Fig. 3-70, Alison Frantz, p. 82; Fig. 3-71, Marlene Boyle, p. 83; Fig. 3-72, Alinari, Art Resource, N.Y., Polykleitos. *Doryphoros (Spear Carrier)*, Roman copy after a lost bronze original of c.

450 BCE. Marble, height 7'., National Archaeological Museum, Naples, Italy, p. 84; Fig. 3-73, Courtesy David G. Wilkins, p. 86; Fig. 3-75, The Metropolitan Museum of Art, Greek Architectural Models, 5th C., B.C.: Parthenon in Athens. The Metropolitan Museum of Art, Purchase, 1890, Levi Hale Willard Bequest. (90.35.3), p. 87; Fig. 3-76, © 1977 Gary Layda, Metropolitan Government of Nashville, p. 87; Fig. 3-77, Edmund B. Feldman, *Thinking About Art*, 1985, p. 88; Fig. 3-78, Marlene Boyle, p. 88; Fig. 3-79, The British Museum, p. 89; Fig. 3-80, The British Museum, © Copyright The British Museum, p. 89; Fig. 3-81, Alinari, Art Resource, N.Y., p. 90; Fig. 3-82, Archivio Fotografico, Monumenti Musei e Galerie Pontificie, The Vatican, p. 91; Fig. 3-83, Agence Photographique de la Réunion des Musées Nationaux, Paris, p. 92; Fig. 3-84, The New York Public Library, Picture Collection, The Branch Libraries, p. 93; Fig. 3-85, Scala Art Resource, NY, p. 94. ; Fig. 3-86, Alinari, Art Resource, N.Y., *Dying Trumpeter*, Roman copy after a lost bronze original of c. 230–220 BCE from Pergamon. Marble, life-size, Capitoline Museum, Rome, Commissioned by King Attalus I of Pergamon, p. 95; Fig. 3-87, Bildarchiv Preussischer Kulturbesitz, Altar of Zeus and Athena from Pergamon. c. 181–159 BCE. Marble, 120 x 113' at base; the frieze is 7'6" high. Staatliche Museen zu Berlin, Pergamon Museum, p. 95; Fig. 3-88, Dale Williams, p. 96; Fig. 3-90, Valerie M. Shepherd, p. 98; Fig. 3-91, Canali Photobank, Capriolo, Italy, p. 99; Fig. 3-92, Canali Photobank, p. 100; Fig. 3-93, Fototeca Unione, Rome, p. 101; Fig. 3-95, Deutsches Archäologisches Institut, Rome, p. 102; Fig. 3-96, Gemeinnützige Stiftung Leonard von Matt, Buochs, Switzerland, p. 103; Fig. 3-97, Library of Congress, p. 104; Fig. 3-98, Deutsches Archäologisches Institut, Rome, p. 105; Fig. 3-99, Fototeca Unione, Rome, p. 106; Fig. 3-100, Canali Photobank, p. 106; Fig. 3-101, Robert Frerck/Stone, p. 106; Fig. 3-102, Courtesy David G. Wilkins, p. 107; Fig. 3-103, Alinari, Art Resource, N.Y., p. 107; Fig. 3-104, Courtesy David G. Wilkins, p. 108; Fig. 3-105, Alfred Frazer and Henry A. Millon, *Key Monuments of Architecture*, 1965, p. 109; Fig. 3-106, Robert Frerck/Stone, p. 110; Fig. 3-107, Hirmer Fotoarchiv, p. 111; Fig. 3-108, Canali Photobank, p. 112; Fig. 3-109, Canali Photobank, p. 112; Fig. 3-110, Canali Photobank, p. 113; Fig. 3-111, Marlene Boyle, p. 114; Fig. 3-112, Canali Photobank, p. 115; Fig. 3-113, Italian Government Tourist Board, p. 116; Fig. 3-114, Canali Photobank, p. 116; Fig. 3-115, Cyril M. Harris, *History of Architecture Sourcebook*, 1977, p. 117; Fig. 3-116, The Avery Library, Columbia University, New York, p. 118; Fig. 3-117, A. Boethius and J. B. Ward-Perkins, *Etruscan and Early Roman Architecture*, 1970, p. 119; Fig. 3-118, Marlene Boyle, p. 120; Fig. 3-119, Paolo Koch, Photo Researchers, Inc., p. 121; Fig. 3-120, Courtesy David G. Wilkins, p. 122; Fig. 3-121, John McKenna, p. 122; Fig. 3-122, Richard Carafelli, National Gallery of Art, Washington, D.C., p. 123; Fig. 3-126, Mike Peters, Pearson Education Corporate Digital Archive, p. 126; Fig. 3-127, Kenneth Garrett Photography, p. 127; Fig. 3-128, Library of Congress, p. 128.

CHAPTER 4

Chapter opening art, Adam Lubroth, Art Resource, N.Y., p. 130; Fig. 4-2, Courtesy David G. Wilkins, p. 133; Fig. 4-3, Asian Art Museum Foundation of San

Francisco, all rights reserved, p. 134; Fig. 4-4, Borromeo, Art Resource, N.Y., p. 135; Fig. 4-5, The National Palace Museum, p. 136; Fig. 4-7, Art Resource, N.Y., p. 138; Fig. 4-8, Art Resource, N.Y., p. 138; Fig. 4-9, Courtesy David G. Wilkins, p. 139; Fig. 4-10, Eliot Elisofon, p. 139; Fig. 4-11, Courtesy Tadao Ando, p. 139; Fig. 4-12, Art Resource, NY, p. 140; Fig. 4-13, Erwin R. Goodenough, *Jewish Symbols in the Greco-Roman Period*, Bollingen Series 37, Vol. II: *Symbolism in the Dura Synagogue*, ©1964, Princeton University Press (photographs by Fred Anderegg), reprinted by permission of Princeton University Press, p. 141; Fig. 4-14, Hirmer Fotoarchiv, p. 142; Fig. 4-15, Archivio Fotografico, Monumenti Musei e Galerie Pontificie, The Vatican, p. 143; Fig. 4-16, The Granger Collection, p. 144; Fig. 4-17, John McKenna, p. 145; Fig. 4-18, Lois Fichner Rathus, *Understanding Art*, 1989, p. 146; Fig. 4-19, Lois Fichner Rathus, *Understanding Art*, 1989, p. 146; Fig. 4-20, Deutsches Archäologisches Institut, Rome, p. 147; Fig. 4-21, John McKenna, p. 147; Fig. 4-22, Courtesy of Japan National Tourist Organization, p. 148; Fig. 4-25, Ekdotike Athenon S.A., p. 150; Fig. 4-27, Courtesy of the Michigan-Princeton-Alexandria Expedition to Mt. Sinai, p. 153; Fig. 4-28, Marvin Trachtenberg, New York, p. 154; Fig. 4-29, Turkish Tourism and Information Office, p. 155; Fig. 4-31, Hirmer Fotoarchiv, p. 156; Fig. 4-32, Scala, Art Resource, N.Y., Interior view, San Vitale, Ravenna, Italy, p. 157; Fig. 4-33, The Bridgeman Art Library International, p. 158; Fig. 4-34, Scala, Art Resource, N.Y., *Theodora and Attendants*, The Court of Theodora. Mosaic. San Vitale, Ravenna, Italy, p. 158; Fig. 4-35, Canali Photobank, p. 159; Fig. 4-36, The British Museum, p. 160; Fig. 4-38, Trinity College, Dublin/A.K.G., Berlin/SuperStock, Inc., p. 163; Fig. 4-47, Eliot Elisofon, p. 171; Fig. 4-49, Adam Lubroth, Art Resource, N.Y., p. 174; Fig. 4-51, Raffaello Bencini, Florence, p. 177; Fig. 4-53, Deutscher Kunstverlag, Munich, p. 179; Fig. 4-55, Kenneth J. Conant, Cluny, p. 181; Fig. 4-56, Georg Gerster, Comstock, p. 182; Fig. 4-57, Comstock, p. 183; Fig. 4-61, Bayerische Staatsbibliothek, p. 188; Fig. 4-62, H. Wehmeyer, Hildesheim, Germany, p. 188; Fig. 4-63, Hirmer Fotoarchiv, p. 189; Fig. 4-64, Foto MAS, Barcelona, p. 190; Fig. 4-65, Giraudon, Art Resource, N.Y., p. 190; Fig. 4-66, St. Mark, from a Gospel Book produced at Cambrai, Nord, France. c. 1025–50. Manuscript painting on vellum, 10 ¾ x 7 ⅞". Bibliotheque Municipal, Amiens, p. 191; Fig. 4-67, Bayeus, Musee de l'Eveche. With special authorization of the City of Bayeux. Giraudon/Art Resource, N.Y., p. 193; Fig. 4-68, Caisse Nationale des Monuments Historique, p. 194; Fig. 4-70, Courtesy David G. Wilkins, p. 195; Fig. 4-71, Courtesy David G. Wilkins, p. 196; Fig. 4-72, Caisse Nationale des Monuments Historique, p. 197; Fig. 4-73, courtesy David G. Wilkins, p. 197; Fig. 4-75, Byzantine Visual Resources © 1987, Dumbarton Oaks, Washington, D.C., p. 198; Fig. 4-76, The Royal Collection Enterprises Ltd., p. 199; Fig. 4-77, © Archives, National Gallery of Art, p. 199; Fig. 4-78, Jerry Alexander, Stone, p. 200; Fig. 4-79, B. Arthaud, Grenoble, p. 201; Fig. 4-83, Marvin Trachtenberg, New York, p. 204; Fig. 4-86, Agence Photographique de la Réunion des Musées Nationaux, Paris, p. 206; Fig. 4-88, Art Resource, N.Y., p. 208; Fig. 4-89, Marvin Trachtenberg, New York, p. 209; Fig. 4-91, Courtesy David G. Wilkins, p. 211; Fig. 4-94, British Information Service, p. 213; Fig. 4-95, Marvin Trachtenberg, New York, p. 213; Fig. 4-96, Wim Swann, p. 213; Fig. 4-98, West facade, Amiens Cathedral, c. 1225–35. Commissioned by the bishops of Amiens. Giraudon/Art Resource, NY, p. 215; Fig. 4-99, Courtesy David G. Wilkins, p. 215; Fig. 4-100, Caisse Nationale des Monuments Historique, p. 215; Fig. 4-101, Wim Swaan, p. 216; Fig. 4-102, *Irish Historical Series*, © 1977, p. 217; Fig. 4-103, Scala, Art Resource, N.Y., p. 218; Fig. 4-104, Canali Photobank, p. 219; Fig. 4-105, Canali Photobank, p. 220; Fig. 4-106,

Piero Codato, Cameraphoto, Venice, p. 220; Fig. 4-107, Canali Photobank, p. 221; Fig. 4-108, Marlene Boyle, p. 222; Fig. 4-109, Marlene Boyle, p. 223; Fig. 4-110, The British Museum, p. 224; Fig. 4-111, Bruce Fleischer, p. 224; Fig. 4-112, Eliot Elisofon, p. 224.

CHAPTER 5

Chapter opening art, Antonio Pollaiuolo, Courtesy David G. Wilkins, p. 226; Fig. 5-1, Piero della Francesca *Resurrection*, c. 1460, fresco, approx. 8 ft. x 6 ft. 6 in. Pinacoteca Comunale, Sansepolcro, Italy, Scala, Art Resource, N.Y., p. 228; Fig. 5-2, Toto MAS, Barcelona, p. 229; Fig. 5-3, Copyright © by The Metropolitan Museum of Art (1987), p. 230; Fig. 5-4, Canali Photobank, p. 232; Fig. 5-5, Donatello, Equestrian monument of Erasmo da Nami *Gattamelata*, c. 1445–53. Bronze, originally with gilded details, height 12 ft. 2 in. commissioned by the Venetian Senate. Alinari, Art Resource, N.Y., p. 233; Fig. 5-6, Studio Fotografico Quattrone, Florence, p. 234; Fig. 5-8, Lorenzo Ghiberti, *Self-Portrait*, from the East Doors of the Baptistery, Florence. 1425–52. Gilded bronze, approx. height 3 in. Museo dell'Opera del Duomo, Florence. Commissioned by the Opera of the Baptistery and the Arte di Calimala. Alinari/Art Resource, NY, p. 235; Fig. 5-10, Courtesy David G. Wilkins, p. 236; Fig. 5-11, All Rights Reserved, The Metropolitan Museum of Art, p. 237; Fig. 5-12, Library of Congress, p. 237; Fig. 5-14, Courtesy David G. Wilkins, p. 238; Fig. 5-15, Courtesy David G. Wilkins, p. 239; Fig. 5-16, Giraudon, Art Resource, N.Y., p. 240; Fig. 5-17, The Limbourg Brothers *Crucifixion in the Darkness of the Eclipse*, from the *Très Riches Heures du Duc de Berry*. Before 1416. Manuscript painting on vellum, 11 ⅜ x 8 ¼" in. Musee Conde, Chantilly, France. Giraudon/ Art Resource, NY, p. 241; Fig. 5-18, The Metropolitan Museum of Art, p. 242; Fig. 5-19, The Metropolitan Museum of Art, p. 243; Fig. 5-20, Canali Photobank, p. 244; Fig. 5-21, Studio Fotografico Quattrone, Florence, p. 245; Fig. 5-22, Marlene Boyle, p. 246; Fig. 5-23, Studio Fotografico Quattrone, Florence, p. 247; Fig. 5-25, Sandro Botticelli *La Primavera* detail of Mercury and the Three Graces. Uffizi, Florence, Italy. Scala/Art Resource, NY, p. 247; Fig. 5-26, Gabinetto Fotografico Nazionale, Rome, p. 248; Fig. 5-27, Marlene Boyle, p. 248; Fig. 5-29, Foto Grassi, Siena, p. 249; Fig. 5-32, Lorenzo Ghiberti, *Story of Jacob and Esau*, from the East Doors of the Baptistry, Florence, c. 1429–37. Gilded bronze, 31 ¼ in. square. Museo dell'Opera del Duomo, Florence. Commissioned by the Opera of the Baptistery and the Arte di Calimala. Alinari/Art Resource, NY, p. 252; Fig. 5-33, Eugenio Cassin, Florence, p. 253; Fig. 5-34, Canali Photobank, p. 254; Fig. 5-35, Courtesy David G. Wilkins, p. 255; Fig. 5-39, Marlene Boyle, p. 259; Fig. 5-40, Filippo Brunelleschi, Nave, Church of Santo Spirito, Florence. Begun 1436. Commissioned by the abbott of the Monastery of Santo Spirito. Alinari/Art Resource, NY, p. 260; Fig. 5-42, Andrew Ward, PhotoDisc, Inc, p. 261; Fig. 5-43, Michelozzo, Courtyard, Medici Palace, Florence. 1445–59. Alinari/Art Resource, NY, p. 262; Fig. 5-46, Courtesy David G. Wilkins, p. 263; Fig. 5-47, Donatello (Donato di Bardi) (1386–1466), *Young David*, Bronze (1437) Height 135 cm, Museo Nationale del Bargello, Florence, Italy, p. 263; Fig. 5-49, Agence Photographique de la Réunion des Musés Nationaux, Paris, p. 264; Fig. 5-51, Courtesy David G. Wilkins, p. 265; Fig. 5-53, Michel Desjardins, Agence TOP, Paris, p. 266; Fig. 5-54, Andrea Mantegna *A Foreshortened Christ*, c. 1466, tempera on canvas, 26 ¾ x 31 ⅞ in. Brera Gallery, Milan, Italy. Alinari/Art Resource, NY, p. 267; Fig. 5-56, The British Museum, p. 268; Fig. 5-59, Scala, Art Resource, NY, p. 270; Fig. 5-60, Studio Fotografico Quattrone, Florence, p. 271; Fig. 5-61, Musèe du Louvre, p. 272; Fig. 5-62, Gallerie dell'Accademia, p. 273; Fig. 5-63, Institut de France, p. 273; Fig. 5-64, Canali Photobank, p. 274; Fig. 5-66, Scala, Art

Resource, NY, p. 276; Fig. 5-67, German Gothic. *Pieta*. Early 14th century. Polychromed wood, height 34 ½". Rheinischen Landesmuseum, Bonn, p. 277.

CHAPTER 6

Chapter opening art, Nippon Television Network Corporation, p. 278; Fig. 6-1, Michelangelo Buonarroti *Pieta*, c. 1547–55, marble, height 7 ft. 8 in. Museo dell'Opera del Duomo, Florence, Tuscany, Italy. Alinari/Art Resource, NY, p. 280; Fig. 6-2, Ostasiatiska Museet, p. 281; Fig. 6-3, © 1996 Board of Trustees, National Gallery of Art, Washington, D.C., p. 281; Fig. 6-4, David Toase, PhotoDisc, Inc, p. 282; Fig. 6-5, Germanisches Nationalmuseum, p. 284; Fig. 6-6, Agence Photographique de la Réunion des Musées Nationaux, Paris, p. 284; Fig. 6-7, Studio Fotografico Quattrone, Florence, p. 285; Fig. 6-8, Fotostudio C.N.B., Bologna, p. 285; Fig. 6-9, Albrecht Dürer (1471–1528), German, *Praying Hands*. Drawing. Graphische Sammlung Albertina, Vienna, Austria/ Art Resource, NY, p. 286; Fig. 6-10, Kunsthistorisches Museum Wien, p. 287; Fig. 6-12, Studio Fotografico Quattrone, Florence,, p. 287; Fig. 6-13, Canali Photobank, Capriolo, Italy, p. 288; Fig. 6-14, Michelangelo Buonarroti *David*, 1501–04, marble, height 13' 5" in. Accademia, Florence, Italy. Scala/ Art Resource, NY, p. 288; Fig. 6-15, Erich Lessing, Art Resource, NY, p. 289; Fig. 6-16, © 1997 Valerie M. Shepherd, 289; Fig. 6-17, Agence Photographique de la Réunion des Musées Nationaux, Paris, p. 289; Fig. 6-18, Michelangelo Buonarroti "David", 1501–04, marble, height 13' 5". Accademia, Florence, Italy. Scala/Art Resource, NY, p. 290; Fig. 6-19, Michelangelo Buonarroti *Saint Matthew* 1504–08, marble, height 8 ft. 10 in. Galleria dell'Accademia, Florence. Commissioned by the Cathedral Administration. Alinari/Art Resource, NY, p. 291; Fig. 6-20, Michelangelo Buonarroti *Saint Matthew* 1504–08, marble, height 8 ft. 10 in. Galleria dell'Accademia, Florence. Commissioned by the Cathedral Administration. Alinari/Art Resource, NY, p. 291; Fig. 6-21, Leonardo da Vinci, *Mona Lisa*, Louvre, Paris, France. Scala, Art Resource, NY, p. 292; Fig. 6-23, The Metropolitan Museum of Art, p. 294; Fig. 6-24, The Metropolitan Museum of Art, p. 295; Fig. 6-25, The Metropolitan Museum of Art, New York, p. 295; Fig. 6-26, The Metropolitan Museum of Art, New York, p. 296; Fig. 6-27, The Metropolitan Museum of Art, New York, p. 297; Fig. 6-28, Marlene Boyle, p. 297; Fig. 6-29, Marlene Boyle, p. 297; Fig. 6-30, The British Museum, p. 298; Fig. 6-31, John McKenna, p. 299; Fig. 6-32, John McKenna, p. 299; Fig. 6-34, The Metropolitan Museum of Art, New York, p. 299; Fig. 6-35, Nippon Television Corporation, Tokyo, p. 300; Fig. 6-36, Nippon Television Corporation, Tokyo, p. 301; Fig. 6-37, Gabinetto Fotografico Piazzale, p. 302; Fig. 6-38, Scala, Art Resource, NY, p. 304; Fig. 6-39, Canali Photobank, p. 305; Fig. 6-41, Canali Photobank, Capriolo, Italy, p. 306; Fig. 6-42, Scala, Art Resource, NY, p. 307; Fig. 6-43, Foto MAS, Barcelona, p. 308; Fig. 6-44, Foto MAS, Barcelona, p. 309; Fig. 6-47, Piero Codato, Cameraphoto, Venice, p. 312; Fig. 6-48, Piero Codato, Cameraphoto, Venice, p. 312; Fig. 6-49, Piero Codato, Cameraphoto, Venice, p. 313; Fig. 6-50, Piero Codato, Cameraphoto, Venice , p. 314; Fig. 6-52, Isabella Stewart Gardner Museum, p. 315; Fig. 6-53, Isabella Stewart Gardner Museum, p. 315; Fig. 6-54, Michelangelo Buonarroti *Medici Chapel*, including the Tomb of Giuliano de' Medici and the altar wall, 1524–34, marble, size of entire wall bay 23 x 15 ft; length of reclining figures approx. 7 ft., new Sacristy, San Lorenzo, Florence. Commissioned by Cardinal Giulio de' Medici, who later became Pope Clement VII. Alinari/Art Resource, NY, p. 316; Fig. 6-55, Nippon Television Corporation, Tokyo, p. 317; Fig. 6-56, The National Gallery Company Limited, p. 318; Fig. 6-57, Erich Lessing, Art Resource, NY, p. 319;

The authors and publisher wish to acknowledge the following publications from which quotations were taken: p. 7: Ovid, *Metamorphoses*, trans. by R. Humphries, Bloomington: Indiana University Press, 1969; p. 72: Susan Woodford, *The Parthenon*, Cambridge, England: Cambridge Univesity Press, 1981; p. 165: Arthur F. Wright, "Symbolism and Function: Reflections on Changan and Other Great Cities," *Journal of Asian Studies*, Vol. 24, No. 4, August 1965, p. 669. Reprinted with permission of the Association for Asian Studies, Inc.; p. 277: Giorgio Vasari, *Lives of the Most Eminent Painters, Sculptors and Architects*, trans. by Gaston Du

C. de Vere, New York: Harry N. Abrams, Inc., 1979. All rights reserved; p. 291: Giorgio Vasari, *The Lives of the Artists*, vol. 1., trans. by George Bull, Harmondsworth: Penguin Classics, 1987. © George Bull, 1965; p. 300: Translation by Creighton Gilbert, from *Complete Poems and Selected Letters of Michelangelo*, Princeton: Princeton University Press, 1980; p. 384: Sir Joshua Reynolds, *Fifteen Discourses Delivered in the Royal Academy*, New York: E. P. Dutton, 1911; pp. 396, 430, 431, 455, 490, 528: Robert Goldwater and Marco Treves, *Artists on Art: From the XIV-XX Century*, New York: Pantheon Books. © 1945

by Pantheon Books, Inc. Renewed 1973 by Goldwater and Treves. By permission of Pantheon Books, a division of Random House, Inc.; pp. 445, 449, 450, 451: Translation from Charles S. Moffett et al., *The New Painting: Impressionism 1874-1886*. © 1986 by The Fine Arts Museum of San Francisco. Reprinted with permission.; p. 534: William Carlos Williams, "The Great Figure," from *The Collected Poems of William Carlos Williams: Volume I, 1909-1939*, edited by Christopher MacGowan. © 1938, 1944, 1945 by William Carlos Williams. Reprinted with the permission of New Directions Publishing Corporation.